The **Rough Guic**

D0205428

# The Greek Islands

written and researched by

**Lance Chilton, Marc Dubin, Nick Edwards,
Mark Ellingham, John Fisher, Geoff Garvey and
Natania Jansz**

ROUGH
GUIDES

www.roughguides.com

# Contents

**Beach life** colour
section following p.280

**Greek cuisine** colour
section following p.472

3

◀◀ Yialós, Sými ◀ Farmer in the Amári valley, Crete

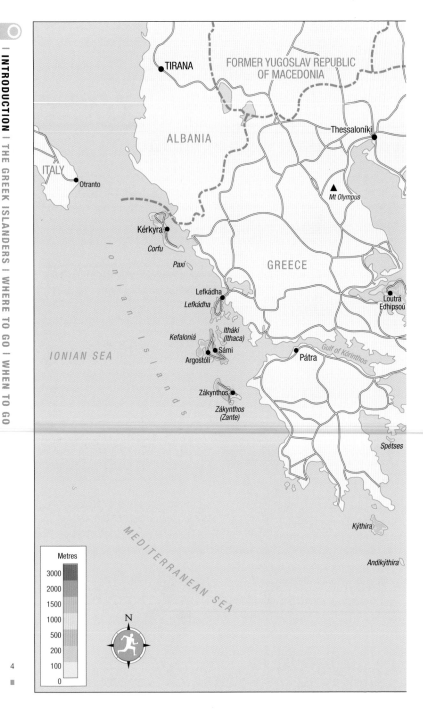

TIRANA

FORMER YUGOSLAV REPUBLIC
OF MACEDONIA

Thessaloníki

ALBANIA

ITALY

Otranto

▲ Mt Olympus

Kérkyra

Corfu

Paxí

GREECE

Loutrá
Edhipsoú

Lefkádha

*Lefkádha*

* Itháki
(Ithaca)*

*Kefaloniá*

Sámi

Argostóli

*Pátra*

Gulf of Kórinthos

IONIAN SEA

Ionian Islands

Zákynthos

*Zákynthos
(Zante)*

Spétses

Kýthira

Andikýthira

MEDITERRANEAN SEA

Metres

3000
2000
1500
1000
500
200
100
0

N

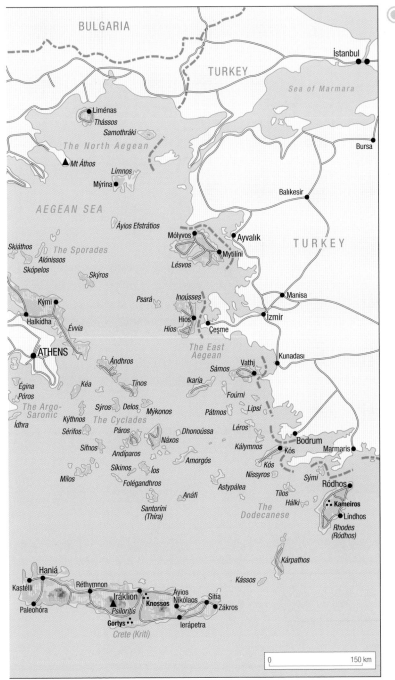

BULGARIA

TURKEY

İstanbul

Sea of Marmara

Liménas
Thássos
Samothráki

The North Aegean

▲ Mt Áthos

Límnos

Mýrina

AEGEAN SEA

Bursa

Balıkesir

Áyios Efstrátios

Skiáthos
The Sporades
Alónissos
Skópelos
Skýros

Mólyvos    Ayvalık
Mytilíni
Lésvos

TURKEY

Manisa

Psará    Inoússes

Kými
Halkídha    Évvia

Hios
Híos    Çeşme

İzmir

ATHENS

Ándhros

The East
Aegean

Égina
Póros
The Argo-
Saronic
Ídhra

Kéa

Tínos

Kýthnos
Sérifos

Sýros    Delos
Mýkonos
The Cyclades

Páros

Sífnos

Andíparos

Milos

Síkinos    Íos
Folégandhros

Sámos

Ikaría

Foúrni

Pátmos    Lipsí

Dhonoússa

Léros

Náxos

Amorgós

Anáfi

Astypálea

Vathí

Kunadası

Bodrum

Kálymnos    Kós    Marmaris

Kós

Nissyros    Sými

Tílos

Ródhos

Santoríni
(Thíra)

The
Dodecanese

Hálki
Kameiros
Lindhos
Rhodes
(Ródhos)

Kárpathos

Haniá
Kastélli
Réthymnon

Paleohóra

Kássos

Iráklion
Psilorítis
Knossos

Áyios
Nikólaos    Sitia
Zákros

Gortys    Ierápetra

Crete (Kriti)

0    150 km

## Introduction to

# The Greek Islands

**It would take a lifetime of island-hopping to fully appreciate the 123 permanently inhabited Greek islands scattered across the Aegean and Ionian seas, but many people make a first visit and are hooked. Remarkably often, the islands do actually match their fantastic travel-poster image; any other country's tourist board would give its eye-teeth for the commonplace vision of purple-shadowed island silhouettes floating on a cobalt-and-rose horizon.**

Closer to hand, island **beaches** come in all shapes, sizes and consistencies, from discrete crescents framed by tree-fringed cliffs straight out of a Japanese screen painting, to deserted, mile-long gifts deposited by small streams, where you could imagine enacting Crusoe-esque scenarios among the dunes. But inland there is always civilization, whether the tiny cubist villages of the remoter outposts or burgeoning resorts as cosmopolitan – and brazen – as any in the Mediterranean.

What amazes most first-time visitors is the islands' relative **lack of pollution**. If you're used to the murky waters of the open Mediterranean as sampled in Spain or much of Italy, the Aegean will come as a revelation, with forty-foot visibility the norm, and all manner of sea creatures visible, from starfish and octopuses on the bottom, to vast schools of fish.

The sea is also a **watersports** paradise: the joys of snorkelling and kayaking are on offer to novices, and some of the best windsurfing areas in the world beckon. Yacht charter, whether bare-boat or skippered, is big business, particularly out of Rhodes, Kálymnos, Kós, Lefkádha, Páros and Pireás; indeed, the Greek islands are rated on a par with the Caribbean for quality sailing itineraries. And during the months when the sea is too cold or the weather too blustery, many islands – not necessarily the largest ones – offer superb **hiking** on surviving mule-trails between hill villages, or up the highest summits.

Although more protected than the Greek mainland from invasions, the various archipelagos have been subject to a staggering variety of **foreign influences**. Romans, Arabs, Byzantines, crusading Knights of Saint John, Genoese, Venetians, French, English, Italians and Ottomans have all controlled different islands since the time of Alexander the Great. The high tide of empire has left behind countless **monuments**: frescoed Byzantine churches, fortified Venetian towns, more conventional castles built by the Genoese and Knights, Ottoman mosques and the Art Deco or Rationalist edifices of the Italian Fascist administration.

▶ Ayía Triádha monastery, Haniá province, Crete

# Fact file

• **Greece** is the southernmost country of the Balkan peninsula, with a surface area of 131,957 square kilometres (50,949 square miles). Few other countries have so many islands – almost 10,000 if you include the smallest – and although they form only about ten percent of Greece's total territory, they provide 48 percent of the country's coastline.

• The **population** is overwhelmingly **Greek-speaking** and 96 percent are **Greek Orthodox**, with noticeable Catholic, Sunni Muslim, Jewish and evangelical Christian minorities, plus pockets of Turkish speakers. Around one million live out on the islands, nearly half of these in towns of over five thousand people.

• Since 1974 Greece has been a **parliamentary republic**, with the president as head of state and a 300-seat, single-chamber parliament led by a prime minister. Forty two of the seats represent islands, with the centre-right Néa Dhimokratía party winning twenty two of these in the 2007 election.

• **Tourism** is the country's main foreign-currency earner, with up to ten million visitors from overseas in a good year. However, although Greece has around fifty percent of the Mediterranean's island hotels, it has less than fifteen percent of the Med's island tourists partly due to the short season on many of the islands. **Shipping** is roughly tied for second place with **agricultural products**, especially olive oil and olives, citrus, wine and raisins.

## Boat people

Seafaring traders are known to have travelled from the islands 12,900 years ago, carrying the cutting stone obsidian from Mílos, and it is likely that they were using boats for fishing too. Maritime transport was essential to the three great early civilizations, Cycladic, Minoan and Mycenaean, while the great religious and trading centre on the tiny, almost entirely resourceless island of Delos developed because of its central position on sea routes. The ship has threaded its way inextricably through subsequent Greek history to the present day, when the majority of islanders still depend on sea transport to bring in their essentials and take them to the mainland. Recent years have seen a dramatic reduction in many sea-crossing times, with fast watercraft bursting with Greek travellers, particularly at Easter, election time and the August summer holidays, but older ferries in their second or third decades still plod along the ancient routes.

Constructions from many of these eras are often juxtaposed with – or superimposed upon – the cities and temples of ancient Greece, which provide the foundation for claims of an enduring Hellenic **cultural identity** down the centuries; local museums amply document the archeological evidence. But it was medieval Greek peasants, fishermen and shepherds, working without an indigenous ruling class or formal Renaissance to impose models of taste or patronize the arts, who contributed most tangibly to our idea of Greekness with their songs, dances, costumes, weaving and vernacular architecture. Much of this has vanished in recent decades, replaced by an avalanche of electric-*bouzoúki*-instrumental CDs, "genuine museum copies" and tacky souvenir shops, but enough remains in isolated pockets for visitors to marvel at Greek popular culture's combination of form and function.

Of course, most Greek-island visits are devoted to more idle pursuits: going lightly dressed, swimming in balmy waters at dusk, talking and drinking under the stars until 3am. Such pleasures amply compensate for certain enduring weaknesses in the Greek **tourism** "product": don't go expecting orthopedic mattresses, state-of-the-art plumbing, Cordon-Bleu cuisine or attentive service. Except at a limited number of upmarket facilities in new or restored buildings, hotel and *pension* rooms can be box-like, wine (unless you're willing to pay dearly for top labels) is pot-luck, and the food at its best is fresh, abundant and simply presented.

# The Greek islanders

To attempt an understanding of the islanders, it's useful to realize how recent and traumatic were the events that created the modern Greek state and **national character** – the latter a blend of extroversion and pessimism which is partly due to Greece's strategic position between the West and the Middle East.

Until the early 1900s, Crete, the east Aegean and the Dodecanese – nearly half the islands described in this book – remained under Ottoman or Italian rule. Meanwhile, many of the present-day inhabitants of these "unredeemed" territories lived in Asia Minor, Egypt, western Europe or the northern Balkans. The Balkan Wars of 1912–13, Greece's 1917–18 World War I involvement fighting Bulgaria, the Greco-Turkish war of 1919–22, and the organized **population exchanges** which followed each of these conflicts had profound, brutal effects. Orthodox refugees from Turkey suddenly made up a noticeable proportion of the population of Crete and the northeast

▶ Gávdhos, off the Cretan coast, is the most southerly landmass in Europe

## Island music

Surrounded but not yet overwhelmed by an ocean of international musical styles and themes, Greek island music remains vibrant and distinctive. With a history much influenced by Byzantine and Ottoman idioms, it can sound very "Eastern" to the Western ear. Island songs, *nisiótika*, often in a pentatonic scale, tell of love, loss and hardship, while popular stringed instruments with a young, upcoming generation of performers include the *lýra* in the south and east, the *violí* in the central Aegean, and Italian-influenced guitars and mandolins in the Ionian. Although somewhat homogenized forms of island music can be the mainstay of tourist-oriented "Greek Nights", more authentic performances are parts of wider cultural festivals in Ámorgos, Folégandros, Itháki, Náxos, Santoríni, Síkinos, Sými, the larger Cretan cities, and elsewhere, although the best sessions can occur when local musicians simply turn up at popular tavernas.

Aegean (especially Límnos, Lésvos and Sámos), and with the forced or voluntary departure of their Levantines, Muslims and (during World War II) Jews, these islands lost their multicultural traits.

Even before the last world war, the Italian occupation of the Dodecanese was characterized by progressively stricter suppression of Greek Orthodox identity, but in general the war years in most other island groups were not quite so dire as on the mainland. Neither was the 1946–49 civil war that followed, nor the 1967–74 dictatorship, so keenly felt out in the Aegean, though benign neglect was about the best many islands could expect until the 1960s. Given the chance to emigrate to Australia, North America or Africa, many entrepreneurial islanders did so, continuing a trend of **depopulation** which had accelerated earlier in the twentieth century, following political union of the northeast Aegean and Dodecanese with the Greek mainland. The uncomfortably close memory of catastrophe, continuing misrule and scarce opportunity at home spurred yet another diaspora.

The advent of **mass tourism** in the 1960s arguably saved a number of islands from complete desolation, though local attitudes towards this deliverance have been decidedly ambivalent. It galls local pride to have become a class of seasonal service personnel, and the encounter between outsiders and villagers has often been corrosive to a deeply conservative rural society. Though younger Greeks are happily adaptable as they rake in the proceeds at resort areas, tourists still need to be sensitive in their behaviour towards the older generation. This is a country where until the 1990s the Orthodox church was – despite its own, ludicrous scandals – an all-but-established faith and self-appointed guardian of national identity, and black-clad elders may be shocked by nude bathing and discomforted by scanty apparel. In the presence of ubiquitous Italian-style espresso bars, internet cafés and ATMs, it's easy to be lulled into thinking that Greece became thoroughly European the moment it joined the EU – until a flock of sheep parades along the main street at high noon, and the 1pm ferry shows up at 3pm, or not at all.

# Where to go

There is no such thing as a "typical" Greek island; each has its distinctive personality, history, architecture, flora – even a unique tourist clientele. Landscapes vary from the lush cypress-and-olive-swathed Ionians to the bare, wind-scoured ridges of the Cyclades and Dodecanese. Setting aside the man-made scars from misjudged developments, it would be difficult to single out an irredeemably ugly island; all have their adherents and individual appeal, described in their account introductions.

Perhaps the best strategy for initial visits is to sample assorted islands from contiguous archipelagos – Crete, the Dodecanese, the Cyclades and the northeast Aegean are all reasonably well connected with each other, though the Sporades, Argo-Saronic and Ionian groups offer limited possibilities for island-hopping, and usually involve a long mainland traipse to get to.

If time and money are short, the best place to visit is well-preserved **Ýdhra** in the Argo-Saronic Gulf,

> The advent of mass tourism in the 1960s arguably saved a number of islands from complete desolation, though local attitudes towards this deliverance have been decidedly ambivalent.

just a short ride from Pireás (the main port of Athens), but an utterly different place once the day-cruises have gone; neighbouring **Spétses** has similar architectural charm and more accessible beaches. Of the Sporades, **Skýros** and **Skópelos** remain the most traditional and aesthetic, with forests, pale-sand beaches and well-preserved capitals. Among the Cyclades,

Fiskárdho's chic harbour, Kefaloniá

cataclysmically volcanic **Santoríni (Thíra)** and **Mýkonos** with its perfectly preserved harbour town rank as must-see spectacles, but fertile, mountainous **Náxos** and gently rolling **Sífnos** have a life independent of cruise-ship tourism and are more amenable to long stays. Dramatically cliff-girt **Amorgós** and **Folégandhros**, rocky **Sýros** with its UNESCO-World-Heritage main town, artistic **Tínos**, secluded **Sérifos** and lonely **Anáfi** with its balmy, south-facing beaches are less obvious but equally satisfying choices. Crete fills an entire Rough Guide itself, but the highlights have to be **Knossos** and the nearby **archeological museum** in Iráklion, the other Minoan palaces at **Phaestos** and **Ayía Triádha**, and the west in general – **Réthymnon** with its intact old town, and the proud city of **Haniá**, whose hinterland extends to the relatively unspoiled southwest coast, reachable via the remarkable **Samariá Gorge**.

**Rhodes**, with its unique Old Town, is capital of the Dodecanese, but picturesque, Neoclassical **Sými** opposite and austere **Pátmos**, the island of the Revelation, are far more manageable. **Kárpathos**, marooned between Rhodes and Crete, has some of the best beaches and walking in the Dodecanese, while **Léros** and **Níssyros** will appeal to those looking for characterful, unspoilt islands that don't necessarily have superb coastlines. From Pátmos or Léros, it's easy to continue north via **Sámos** – still one of the most attractive islands despite recent fires – and **Híos**, with striking medieval architecture, to balmy, olive-cloaked **Lésvos**, perhaps the most traditional of all islands in its way of life.

The Ionian islands are, more than any other region except Crete and Rhodes, package-holiday territory but, especially if you're exiting Greece towards Italy, by all means stop at **Corfu** to savour the Venetian-style main town, which along with neighbouring **Paxí** islet escaped damage from the 1953 earthquake that devastated the southern Ionians. Little **Itháki**, most easily reached from the mainland, is relatively untouristy, given a lack of beaches, though big brother **Kefaloniá** is well and truly in the spotlight owing to spectacular scenery – and (over)exposure in Louis de Bernière's *Captain Corelli's Mandolin*.

# When to go

Most islands and their inhabitants are far more agreeable, and resolutely Greek, outside the **busiest period** of early July to late August, when crowds of foreigners or locals, soaring temperatures and the effects of the infamous **meltémi** can detract considerably from enjoyment. The *meltémi* is a cool, fair-weather wind which originates in high-pressure systems over the far north Aegean, gathering momentum as it travels southwards and assuming near-gale magnitude by the time it reaches Crete. North-facing coasts there, and throughout the Cyclades and Dodecanese, bear the full brunt; its howling is less pronounced in the north or northeast Aegean, where continental landmasses provide some shelter for the islands just offshore. In the Ionian archipelago, an analogous northwest wind off the Adriatic is called the **maïstros**.

You won't miss out on **warm weather** if you come between late May (half-term week in the UK, thus busy) and mid-June – when a wide variety of garden produce and fish is still available – or in September, when the sea is warmest for swimming, though at these times you'll find little activity on the northernmost islands of Thássos, Límnos and Samothráki. During October you'll probably hit a week's stormy spell, but for much of that month the "little summer of Áyios Dhimítrios", the Greek

> In the presence of espresso bars, internet cafés and ATMs, it's easy to be lulled into thinking Greece became thoroughly European the moment it joined the EU – until a flock of sheep parades along the main street at noon, and the 1pm ferry shows up at 3pm, or not at all.

equivalent of **Indian summer**, prevails. While autumn choice in restaurants and nightlife can be limited, the light is softer, and going out at midday becomes a pleasure rather than an ordeal. The only black spot on visits from late August through September are swarms of **flies** and a few aggressive **wasps**, especially in districts with an appreciable grape harvest. The most

Folégandhros's spectacular clifftop Hóra

reliable venues for late-autumn or early-winter breaks are Rhodes and balmy southeastern Crete, where it's possible to swim in relative comfort as late as December.

December to March are the **coldest** and least reliably sunny months, particularly on the Ionian islands, typically the rainiest area from November onwards (though global warming has meant recent wet summers as well). The high peaks of northerly or lofty islands wear a brief mantle of **snow** around the turn of the year, with Crete's mountainous spine staying partly covered well into April. Between January and April the glorious lowland wildflowers start to bloom, beginning in the southeast Aegean. April weather is unreliable, though the air is crystal-clear and the landscape **green** – a photographer's dream. May is often more settled, though the sea is still a bit cool for prolonged dips.

Other factors that affect the timing of a Greek-island visit have to do with the level of tourism and the related **amenities** provided. Service standards, particularly in tavernas, invariably slip under peak-season pressure, and room rates are at their highest from mid-July to August 23. If you can only visit during midsummer, reserve a package well in advance, or plan an itinerary off the beaten track. Between November and April, you have to contend with pared-back ferry and plane schedules (and non-existent hydrofoil or catamaran departures), plus skeletal facilities when you arrive. However, you will find adequate services to the more populated islands, and at least one hotel and taverna open in the port or main town of all but the tiniest isles.

## Average temperatures and rainfall

| | Jan | March | May | July | Sept | Nov |
| | Max \| Min | Max \| Min | Max \| Min | Max \| Min | Max \| Min | Max \| Min |
|---|---|---|---|---|---|---|
| **Crete (Haniá)** | | | | | | |
| Celsius | 16 \| 8 | 18 \| 9 | 24 \| 13 | 30 \| 20 | 28 \| 18 | 21 \| 12 |
| Fahrenheit | 60 \| 46 | 64 \| 48 | 76 \| 56 | 86 \| 68 | 82 \| 64 | 70 \| 54 |
| rainfall (days) | 17 | 11 | 5 | 0 | 3 | 10 |
| **Cyclades (Mýkonos)** | | | | | | |
| Celsius | 14 \| 10 | 17 \| 11 | 22 \| 17 | 28 \| 22 | 26 \| 20 | 19 \| 14 |
| Fahrenheit | 58 \| 50 | 62 \| 52 | 72 \| 62 | 82 \| 72 | 78 \| 68 | 66 \| 58 |
| rainfall (days) | 14 | 8 | 5 | 0.5 | 1 | 9 |
| **Ionian (Corfu)** | | | | | | |
| Celsius | 13 \| 7 | 17 \| 8 | 23 \| 14 | 31 \| 21 | 28 \| 18 | 19 \| 11 |
| Fahrenheit | 56 \| 44 | 62 \| 46 | 74 \| 58 | 88 \| 70 | 82 \| 64 | 66 \| 52 |
| rainfall (days) | 13 | 10 | 6 | 2 | 5 | 12 |
| **Dodecanese (Rhodes)** | | | | | | |
| Celsius | 14 \| 9 | 17 \| 9 | 23 \| 14 | 30 \| 21 | 28 \| 22 | 20 \| 7 |
| Fahrenheit | 58 \| 50 | 62 \| 48 | 74 \| 58 | 86 \| 70 | 82 \| 72 | 68 \| 60 |
| rainfall (days) | 15 | 7 | 2 | 0 | 1 | 7 |
| **Sporades (Skiáthos)** | | | | | | |
| Celsius | 13 \| 7 | 13 \| 8 | 22 \| 14 | 28 \| 22 | 24 \| 18 | 17 \| 12 |
| Fahrenheit | 55 \| 45 | 58 \| 47 | 71 \| 58 | 82 \| 71 | 75 \| 64 | 62 \| 53 |
| rainfall (days) | 12 | 10 | 3 | 0 | 8 | 12 |
| **East Aegean (Lésvos)** | | | | | | |
| Celsius | 12 \| 6 | 16 \| 8 | 24 \| 16 | 31 \| 21 | 28 \| 19 | 18 \| 10 |
| Fahrenheit | 54 \| 42 | 60 \| 46 | 76 \| 60 | 88 \| 70 | 82 \| 66 | 64 \| 50 |
| rainfall (days) | 11 | 7 | 6 | 2 | 2 | 9 |

# 25 things not to miss

*It's not possible to see everything that the Greek islands have to offer in one trip – and we don't suggest you try. What follows is a selective taste of the islands' highlights: outstanding buildings, superb ancient sites and natural wonders. They're arranged in five colour-coded categories, which you can browse through to find the very best things to see and experience. All highlights have a page reference to take you straight into the Guide, where you can find out more.*

**01 Sámos** Page **413** • Despite recent fires, Sámos remains arguably the most verdant and beautiful of the east Aegean islands.

**02 Haniá old town, Crete** Page **286** • Haniá displays haunting vestiges of its Venetian and Ottoman past.

**03 Ýdhra** Page **100** • Ýdhra's perfect horseshoe-shaped harbour is surrounded by grand eighteenth-century mansions.

**04 Windsurfing off Vassilikí, Lefkádha**
Page **562** • Located in a vast, cliff-flanked bay, Vassilikí is one of Europe's biggest windsurf centres.

**05 Váï beach, Crete** Page **267** • A superb beach, fringed by a wild date-palm grove.

**06 Temple of Aphaea, Égina** Page **92** • The beautiful fifth-century-BC Temple of Aphaea is one of the most complete and visually complex ancient buildings in Greece.

## 07 Monastery of Ayíou Ioánnou Theológou,
**Pátmos** Page **398** • Built in honour of St John the Divine, this huge monastery is a warren of interconnecting courtyards, chapels, stairways, arcades, galleries and roof terraces.

## 08 Kérkyra (Corfu) old town
Page **532** • With its elegant Venetian architecture and fine museums, Corfu's capital is the cultural heart of the Ionians.

## 09 Andípaxi
Page **556** • With its aquamarine waters and idyllic beaches, Paxí's satellite islet makes a perfect daytrip destination.

## 10 Hiking in the Samariá Gorge
Page **294** • The magnificent Samariá Gorge is one of Europe's longest.

**11 Chapel of Metamórfosis, Khristós peak, Kós** Page **374** • A hike up 846-metre Khristós peak to the Metamórfosis chapel rewards you with excellent panoramic views.

**12 Harbour, Sými** Page **349** • The mansions of Sými's picturesque harbour, built with wealth from the sponge trade, are part of an architecturally protected area.

**13 Knossos palace, Crete** Page **237** • The most restored, vividly coloured and ultimately the most exciting of Crete's Minoan palaces.

**14** **Lindos acropolis, Rhodes** Page **334** • From the Hellenistic acropolis of Lindos, high above the modern village, you look north along the length of Rhodes island.

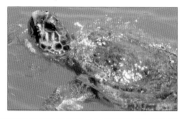

**15** **Loggerhead sea turtle** Page **586** • The Ionian islands harbour one of the Mediterranean's main concentrations of the endangered loggerhead sea turtle.

**16** **Zaharoplastía** Page **58** • Temptation is the essence of these Greek sweet and cake shops.

**17** **Kárpathos: view north from Ólymbos village** Page **317** • The view north from windswept, remote Ólymbos gives a good idea of the rugged coast of unspoilt northern Kárpathos.

**18** **Festivals** Page **63** • Colourful local celebrations seamlessly combine devout belief with popular entertainment.

**20** **Hozoviotíssas monastery, Amorgós**
Page **196** • With its vast walls gleaming white at the base of a sheer orange cliff, the Hozoviotíssas monastery is a dramatic sight.

**19** **Ápella beach, Kárpathos**
Page **316** • One of the most scenic of Kárpathos's east-coast beaches.

**21** **Stéfanos crater floor, Níssyros** Page **364** • No stay on Níssyros would be complete without a visit to the island's dormant volcano.

**22** **Mólyvos, Lésvos** Page **469** • The castle-crowned village of Mólyvos is one of the most beautiful on Lésvos.

**24 Beaches and watersports** Pages **66, 117** & *Beach life* colour section • Greece's expansive coast provides a multitude of opportunities for getting into the water, or just lying next to it.

**23 Kálymnos's cliffs** Page **387** • The island's limestone cliffs and dry weather attract climbers from all over Europe.

**25 Melissáni Cave, Kefaloniá** Page **570** • Take a boat trip through Melissáni Cave, and admire the rock formations and play of light on the cave walls.

# Basics

# Basics

# Getting there

Whatever your starting point, by far the easiest way to get to the Greek Islands is to fly. An increasing number of islands have international airports that see regular charters from Britain, Ireland and the rest of northern Europe, many of which are available on a flight-only basis. Other islands can be reached on domestic flights, connecting with international scheduled arrivals in Athens and Thessaloníki. Even if your starting point is North America, Australia, New Zealand or South Africa, the most cost-effective approach may well be to get to London – or Amsterdam or one of many other northern European cities – and pick up an onward flight from there. Once in Greece, a vast ferry network, connects even the smallest of islands; see Athens and mainland ports, p.35, Getting around, pp.40–42, and details of local ferry services at the end of each chapter.

**Airfares** are highest in July, August and during Easter week, but May, June and September are also popular, and since far fewer flights operate through the winter, bargains are rare at any time.

When buying flights it always pays to **shop around**; check out a few of the general travel websites listed on p.30 (as well as the airlines' own) to get an idea of the going rates, but bear in mind that many such websites don't include charters or budget airlines (such as easyJet) in their searches. Be aware too that a **package deal**, with accommodation included, can sometimes be as cheap as, or even cheaper than, a flight alone, especially for last-minute bookings: there's no rule that says you have to use your accommodation every night, or even at all. If you are under 26, or a full-time student, or over 60, you may well be eligible for special **student/youth or senior fares**, so it's worth asking about these. Remember that all cheap tickets will be restricted in some way – usually with stiff charges if you need to make any changes – so double-check details before buying.

**Overland** alternatives from the UK or northern Europe involve at least two or three days of non-stop travel. If you want to take your time over the journey, then **driving** or travelling **by train** can be enjoyable, although invariably more expensive than flying. We've included only brief details of these routes here.

If you want the organizational work done for you, every mainstream **tour operator** includes the Greek Islands in its portfolio. You'll find far more interesting alternatives, however, through the small **specialist agencies** listed on pp.32–34. As well as traditional village-based accommodation and less-known islands, many also offer **walking** or **nature holidays** and other special interests such as **yoga**, **photography** and above all **sailing**, with options ranging from shore-based clubs with dinghy tuition, through organized yacht flotillas to bareboat charters.

## Flights from the UK and Ireland

The only **direct flights** to the islands are with easyJet or the charter airlines, which increasingly operate like budget airlines, offering seat-only and one-way deals. Don't expect them to be cheap though: unless you book far in advance, there are few bargain **fares** to Greece or its islands. easyJet can in theory fly you from Gatwick or Luton to Athens, **Corfu**, **Crete**, **Mýkonos**, **Rhodes** or **Thessaloníki** and back for as little as £70, but you'll have to move very fast to find fares this cheap. Realistically their prices are little different from those of the scheduled operators, and you can expect to pay £150–200 to get to Athens at most times of the year; more for island flights or if you leave your booking late. Of the full-priced **scheduled** operators, British Airways have several daily flights from Heathrow and Olympic from Heathrow and Manchester (via Heathrow) to Athens and Thessaloníki, while Aegean flies from Stansted to Athens. Olympic and Aegean have the advantage of direct connections to their own domestic flights, though Olympic is notorious for long delays, and is in permanent financial difficulty. From **Dublin**, Aer Lingus have four direct flights a week to Athens from April to October, on which you should hope to find a seat for between €220 and €320. At other times of year, or from any other **regional airport** in the UK or Ireland, you'll have to make at least one stop en route to Greece, in London or elsewhere. It can pay to think laterally here: one of the best routings from Dublin, for example, is on Malev Hungarian airlines via Budapest – with good prices (from around €200) and convenient connections. With any flight to Athens, you can buy a **domestic connecting flight** on Olympic or Aegean to one of almost three dozen Greek mainland and island airports, or there are ferries from Pireás or the nearby ports of Lávrio and Rafína to almost every island.

**Charter flights** offer considerably more possibilities, with direct services from many regional airports to **Thessaloníki** (for the northeast Aegean, the Sporades, Cyclades and Dodecanese), **Kavála** (for Thássos and the northeast Aegean), and **Préveza** (Áktio; for Lefkádha), on the Greek mainland, and to the islands of **Crete**, **Rhodes**, **Kós**, **Corfu**, **Mýkonos**, **Zákynthos**, **Kefaloniá**, **Skiáthos**, **Sámos**, **Santoríni**, **Lésvos** and **Límnos**. On the whole these operate from early May to late October, and again there are few bargains, with prices starting at around £200 return from the London airports, more than that from regional airports (rarely less than €400 from Dublin). Most of the operators now offer flight-only deals, often allowing you to book one way only, either through their own websites or through package and specialist operators; thus you could fly into Athens with one operator and leave from an island with another. Remember that packages may cost little more, and if you're booking at the last minute can even cost less than the flight alone; also that it may cost less to travel via Athens with a connecting flight. Watch out too for **hidden costs**, especially for web bookings – the initial fare quoted may not include taxes, or bags or food.

## Fly less – stay longer! Travel and climate change

Climate change is perhaps the single biggest issue facing our planet. It is caused by a build-up in the atmosphere of carbon dioxide and other greenhouse gases, which are emitted by many sources – including planes. Already, **flights** account for three to four percent of human-induced global warming: that figure may sound small, but it is rising year on year and threatens to counteract the progress made by reducing greenhouse emissions in other areas.

Rough Guides regard travel as a **global benefit**, and feel strongly that the advantages to developing economies are important, as are the opportunities for greater contact and awareness among peoples. But we also believe in travelling responsibly, which includes giving thought to how often we fly and what we can do to redress any harm that our trips may create.

We can travel less or simply reduce the amount we travel by air (taking fewer trips and staying longer, or taking the train if there is one); we can avoid night flights (which are more damaging); and we can make the trips we do take "climate neutral" via a carbon offset scheme. **Offset schemes** run by climatecare.org, carbonneutral.com and others allow you to "neutralize" the greenhouse gases that you are responsible for releasing. Their websites have simple calculators that let you work out the impact of any flight – as does our own. Once that's done, you can pay to fund projects that will reduce future emissions by an equivalent amount. Please take the time to visit our website and make your trip climate neutral, or get a copy of the *Rough Guide to Climate Change* for more detail on the subject.

www.roughguides.com/climatechange

## Flights from the US and Canada

Direct **nonstop** flights from New York to Athens – daily for much of the year – are operated by Olympic Airlines and Delta (both from JFK) and Continental (from Newark). Between May and October, US Airways also flies daily from Philadelphia and Delta from Atlanta. Olympic and its domestic competitor Aegean offer reasonably priced add-on flights within Greece, especially to the Greek Islands. Code-sharing airlines can quote through fares with one of the above, or a European partner, from virtually every major US city, connecting either at New York or a European hub such as London or Frankfurt.

**Fares** vary greatly, so it's worth putting in a little time on the internet, or using a good travel agent; book as far ahead as possible to get the best price. The lowest starting point is around US$600 for a restricted, off-season flight from the east coast, rising to about $1200 for a similar deal in summer; from the west coast, expect to pay ten to twenty percent more. The lower fares are rarely on the most direct flights, so check the routing to avoid lengthy delays or stopovers. Remember too that you may be better off getting a domestic flight to New York or Philadelphia and heading directly to Athens from there, or buying a cheap flight to London (beware of changing airports) or another European city, and onward travel from there.

As with the US, airfares **from Canada** vary depending on where you start your journey, and whether you take a direct service. Olympic flies to Athens out of Toronto, with a stop in Montreal, from one to four times weekly depending on the time of year; they're rarely the cheapest option, though. Air Transat also have seasonal weekly flights from Toronto and Montreal to Athens. Otherwise you'll have to choose among one- or two-stop itineraries on a variety of European carriers, or perhaps Delta via New York; costs run from Can$800 in low season from Toronto to more than double that from Vancouver in high season.

## Flights from Australia and New Zealand

There are no **direct flights** from Australia or New Zealand to Greece; you'll have to change planes in Southeast Asia or Europe.

Tickets purchased direct from the airlines tend to be expensive; travel agents or Australia-based websites generally offer much better deals on fares and have the latest information on limited specials and stopovers. For a simple return fare, you may also have to buy an add-on internal flight to get you to the international departure point.

Fares **from Australia** start from around Aus$2000, rising to well over Aus$3500 depending on season, routing, validity, number of stopovers, etc. The shortest flights and best fares are generally with airlines like Thai, Singapore and Emirates that can fly you directly to Athens from their Asian hubs, though you'll also find offers on Swiss, KLM and other European carriers. **From New Zealand**, the best deals may cost less, but if you miss out, fares are very steep indeed: from as little as NZ$2000, again rising to well over NZ$3500 for a more flexible high-season flight.

If Greece is only one stop on a longer journey, you might consider buying a **Round-the-World** (RTW) fare. With luck you might find something for around Aus$2500/ NZ$2750, although Greece is rarely included in the cheaper deals, which means you might have to stump up around Aus$3400/ NZ$3800 for one of the fully flexible multi-stop fares from One World or the Star Alliance. At that price, you may be better off with a cheaper deal and a separate ticket to Greece once you get to Europe.

## Flights from South Africa

**From South Africa**, Olympic have three direct flights a week between Johannesburg and Athens: the most convenient, though rarely the least expensive option. Alternative routes include EgyptAir via Cairo, Emirates via Dubai, or just about any of the major European airlines through their domestic hub. Prices start at ZAR6000–7000 for a good low-season deal, to easily double that in high season or if the cheaper seats have gone.

## By train

Travelling **by train** from the UK or Ireland takes two-and-a-half to three-and-a-half days and will almost always work out more expensive than flying – and of course the train won't take you to any of the islands. It also takes a fair bit of planning, since there's no through train and tickets have to be bought from several separate operators. However, you do have the chance to stop over on the way, while with an InterRail (for European residents only) or Eurail (for all others) pass you can take in Greece as part of a wider rail trip around Europe. The most practical **route** from Britain crosses France and Italy before taking the ferry from Bari or Brindisi to Pátra (ferries also go direct from Italy to several of the Ionian islands, see box below); the much longer all-overland route goes via Vienna and Budapest. Booking well in advance (essential in summer) and going for the cheapest seats on each leg, you can do this for less than £200, not including incidental expenses along the way. Using rail passes will cost you more, but give far more flexibility. For full details of all the alternatives, check out the Man in Seat 61 website (see p.34).

## By car and ferry

**Driving to Greece** can be worth considering if you want to explore en route or are going to stay for an extended period. The most popular **route** is again down through France and Italy to catch one of the Adriatic ferries (see box below); this is much the best way to get to the Ionian islands, and to Athens for ferries to most other Islands. The much longer alternative through Eastern Europe (Hungary, Romania and Bulgaria) is fraught with visa problems, and only makes sense if you are heading for the northeast Aegean or want to explore northern Greece on the way.

### Online booking

@ **www.charterflights.co.uk** (UK & Ireland). Excellent listings of charter flights from airports throughout the UK and Ireland.

## Italy–Greece ferries

Sailing from **Italy to Greece**, you've a choice of five ports. Regular car and passenger ferries link Ancona, Bari and Brindisi with Corfu, Igoumenítsa (on the mainland opposite Corfu), Kefaloniá, Paxí, Zákynthos and Pátra (at the northwest tip of the Peloponnese). Generally, these ferries run year-round, but services are reduced from December to April. Ferries also sail less frequently from Venice and Trieste to Corfu, Igoumenítsa and Pátra. The longer routes are more expensive, but the extra cost almost exactly matches what you'll pay in Italian motorway tolls and fuel to get to Brindisi. On most ferries you can stop over in the Ionian islands for no extra charge. For direct access to Athens and the Aegean islands head for Pátra, from where you can cut across country to Pireás.

In summer (especially July–Aug) it's essential to book tickets a few weeks ahead. During the winter you can usually just turn up at the main ports (Brindisi and Ancona have the most reliable departures at that time of year), but it's still wise to book a few days in advance if you're taking a car or want a cabin.

The following companies operate ferries; their websites have full route, fare and booking details. Viamare Travel (☎020/8206 3420, @www.viamare.com) is the UK agent for most of these companies, and there are also links and booking for all of them at @www.openseas.gr and @www.ferries.gr.

**Agoudimos** Bari and Brindisi to Corfu, Kefaloniá, Igoumenítsa, Paxí and Pátra: @www.agoudimos-lines.com.

**ANEK** Ancona and Venice to Corfu, Igoumenítsa and Pátra: @www.anek.gr.

**Endeavor** Brindisi to Corfu, Kefaloniá, Igoumenítsa and Pátra: @www.endeavor -lines.com.

**Hellenic Mediterranean** Brindisi to Corfu, Kefaloniá, Igoumenítsa, Paxí and Pátra, plus once or twice weekly to Zákynthos in midsummer: @www.hmlferry.com.

**Minoan** Ancona and Venice to Corfu, Igoumenítsa and Pátra: @www.minoan.gr.

**Superfast** Ancona and Bari to Corfu, Igoumenítsa and Pátra: @www.superfast.com.

**SNAV** Brindisi to Corfu and Paxí: @www.snav.it.

**Ventouris** Bari to Corfu and Igoumenítsa: @www.ventouris.gr.

Ⓦ www.cheapflights.co.uk (UK & Ireland). Ⓦ www.cheapflights.com (US), Ⓦ www .cheapflights.ca (Canada), Ⓦ www .cheapflights.com.au (Australia & New Zealand). No direct booking, but lists flights and offers from dozens of operators, with web links to most.
Ⓦ www.cheaptickets.com (US) Discount flight specialists.
Ⓦ www.ebookers.com (UK), Ⓦ www.ebookers .ie (Ireland). Efficient, easy-to-use flight finder; scheduled flights only.
Ⓦ www.expedia.co.uk (UK & Ireland), Ⓦ www .expedia.com (US), Ⓦ www.expedia.ca (Canada). Discount airfares, all-airline search engine and daily deals.
Ⓦ www.lastminute.com (UK), Ⓦ www .us.lastminute.com (US), Ⓦ www.lastminute .ie (Ireland), Ⓦ www.lastminute.com.au (Australia). Package holiday and flight-only deals available at short notice.
Ⓦ www.opodo.co.uk Owned by, and run in conjunction with, nine major European airlines, a reliable source of scheduled fares anywhere in the world.
Ⓦ www.orbitz.com (US) Comprehensive web travel source, with the usual flight, car rental and hotel deals but also great follow-up customer service.
Ⓦ www.priceline.com (US) Name-your-own-price auction website that has deals at around forty percent off standard fares, as well as a regular flight-finder. Be sure to check the terms before bidding.
Ⓦ www.travelocity.co.uk (UK & Ireland), Ⓦ www .travelocity.com (US), Ⓦ www.travelocity.ca (Canada). Destination guides, hot web fares and deals for car rental, accommodation and lodging.
Ⓦ www.travelonline.co.za (SA) Discount flights and information from South Africa.
Ⓦ www.zuji.com.au (Australia) Now part of Travelocity, with the same destination guides, deals, etc.

## Airlines

**Aegean Airways** Ⓦ www.aegeanair.com.
**Aer Lingus** UK ☏ 0870/876 5000, Republic of Ireland ☏ 0818/365 000; Ⓦ www.aerlingus.com.
**Aeroflot** Australia ☏ 02/9262 2233, Ⓦ www .aeroflot.com.au.
**Air Canada** Canada/US ☏ 1-888/247–2262, Ⓦ www.aircanada.com.
**Air France** US ☏ 1-800/237-2747, Canada ☏ 1-800/667-2747, SA ☏ 0860/340 340; Ⓦ www .airfrance.com.
**Air New Zealand** Australia ☏ 13 24 76, Ⓦ www .airnz.com.au; New Zealand ☏ 0800/737 000, Ⓦ www.airnz.co.nz.
**Air Transat** Canada ☏ 1-888/TRANSAT, Ⓦ www .airtransat.com.

**American Airlines** US ☏ 1-800/433-7300, Ⓦ www.aa.com.
**British Airways** UK ☏ 0844/493 0787, Republic of Ireland ☏ 1890 626 747, US/Canada ☏ 1-800/AIRWAYS, Australia ☏ 1300/767 177, New Zealand ☏ 09/966 9777, SA ☏ 27/11441 8400; Ⓦ www.ba.com.
**Continental Airlines** US domestic ☏ 1-800/523-3273, international ☏ 1-800/231-0856; Ⓦ www .continental.com.
**Delta Air Lines** US domestic ☏ 1-800/221-1212, international ☏ 1-800/241-4141; Ⓦ www.delta.com.
**easyJet** UK ☏ 0905/821 0905, Ⓦ www.easyjet.com.
**EgyptAir** SA ☏ 11/880 4126, Ⓦ www.egyptair .com.eg.
**Emirates** Australia ☏ 03/9940 7807 or 02/9290 9700, New Zealand ☏ 05/0836 4728, SA ☏ 27/0861 364728; Ⓦ www.emirates.com.
**KLM** Australia ☏ 1300/767 310, New Zealand ☏ 09/921 6040; Ⓦ www.klm.com.
**Lufthansa** US ☏ 1-800/399-5838, Canada ☏ 1-800/563-5954, Australia 1-300/655 727, SA ☏ 086127/0861 842538; Ⓦ www.lufthansa.com.
**Malev** Republic of Ireland ☏ 0818/55 55 77, Ⓦ www.malev.hu.
**Northwest/KLM** US ☏ 1-800/225-2525, international ☏ 1-800/447-4747; Ⓦ www.nwa.com, Ⓦ www.klm.com.
**Olympic Airlines** UK ☏ 0871/200 0500, US ☏ 1-800/223-1226, Canada ☏ 514/878 9691 or 416/920 2452, SA ☏ 11/601 7800; Ⓦ www .olympicairlines.com.
**Qantas** Australia ☏ 13 13 13, New Zealand ☏ 0800/808 767; Ⓦ www.qantas.com.
**Singapore Airlines** Australia ☏ 13 10 11, New Zealand ☏ 0800/808 909; Ⓦ www.singaporeair.com.
**South African Airways** ☏ 11/978 1111, Ⓦ www .flysaa.com.
**Swiss** US ☏ 1-877/359 7947, Ⓦ www.swiss.com.
**Thai Airways** Australia ☏ 1300/651 960, New Zealand ☏ 09/377 3886; Ⓦ www.thaiairways.com .au, Ⓦ www.thaiair.com.
**United Airlines** US domestic ☏ 1-800/UNITED-1, international ☏ 1-800/538-2929; Ⓦ www.united.com.
**US Airways** US domestic ☏ 1-800/428-4322, international ☏ 1-800/622-1015; Ⓦ www.usair.com.
**Virgin Atlantic** US ☏ 1-800/821-5438, Australia ☏ 1300/727 340; Ⓦ www.virgin-atlantic.com.

## Charter airlines and package companies

**Avro** UK ☏ 0871/423 8550, Ⓦ www.avro.co.uk. Flights from London and many UK regional airports.
**First Choice** UK ☏ 0871/200 7799, Ⓦ www .firstchoice.co.uk. Package holidays and frequent flights from numerous UK regional airports.

**Thomas Cook** UK ☎0870/750 5711, ⓦwww
.thomascook.com, ⓦwww.flythomascook.com.
Frequent flights and packages from UK regional
airports.
**Thomson** UK ☎0871/231 4691, ⓦwww.thomson
.co.uk, ⓦwww.thomsonfly.com. Part of Tui, the
biggest charter and package operator from the UK,
serving numerous regional airports.

## Flights and travel agents

**Air Brokers International** US ☎1-800/883-
3273, ⓦwww.airbrokers.com. Consolidator and
specialist in RTW tickets.
**Airtech** US ☎212/219-7000, ⓦwww.airtech.com.
Last-minute and standby flight deals.
**Aran Travel International** Republic of Ireland
☎091/562 595. Good-value flights and holidays.
**Argo** UK ☎0870/066 7070, ⓦwww.argo-holidays
.com. Long-established Greek specialist for upmarket
holidays and good flight-only deals.
**BestFlights** Australia ☎1300/767 757, ⓦwww
.bestflights.com.au. Cheap flights and RTW deals
from Australia and New Zealand.
**BootsnAll** US ☎1-888/379-9411, ⓦwww
.bootsnall.com. General agent for independent travel
with flights, hotel reservations and online advice.
**Educational Travel Center** US ☎1-800/747-
5551 or 608/256-5551, ⓦwww.edtrav.com.
Low-cost fares worldwide, student/youth discount
offers, Eurail passes.
**Flight Centre** US ☎1-866/967-5351, ⓦwww
.flightcentre.us; Canada ☎1-877/967-5302,
ⓦwww.flightcentre.ca; Australia ☎133 133,
ⓦwww.flightcentre.com.au; New Zealand
☎0800/243 544, ⓦwww.flightcentre.co.nz; South
Africa ☎0860/400 727, ⓦwww.flightcentre.co.za.
Rock-bottom fares worldwide.
**North South Travel** UK ☎01245/608291,
ⓦwww.northsouthtravel.co.uk. Friendly, competitive
flight agency, offering discounted fares worldwide.
Profits are used to support projects in the developing
world, especially the promotion of sustainable tourism.
**Rosetta Travel** Northern Ireland ☎028/9064
4996, ⓦwww.rosettatravel.com. Flight and holiday
agent, specializing in deals direct from Belfast.
**STA Travel** UK ☎0871/230 0040, ⓦwww
.statravel.co.uk; US ☎1-800/781-4040, ⓦwww
.statravel.com; Australia ☎134 782, ⓦwww
.statravel.com.au; New Zealand ☎0800/474 400,
ⓦwww.statravel.co.nz; South Africa ☎0861/781
781, ⓦwww.statravel.co.za. Worldwide specialists in
low-cost flights and tours for students and under-26s.
**Student Flights** US ☎1-800 255-8000 ⓦwww
.isecard.com/studentflights. Student/youth fares,
plus student IDs and European rail and bus passes.

**Trailfinders** UK ☎0845/058 5858, ⓦwww
.trailfinders.com; Republic of Ireland ☎01/677
7888, ⓦwww.trailfinders.ie; Australia ☎1300/780
212, ⓦwww.trailfinders.com.au. One of the best-
informed and most efficient agents for independent
travellers; branches in all the UK's largest cities, plus
Dublin.
**Travel Cuts** US ☎1-800/592-2887, Canada
☎1-866/246-9762; ⓦwww.travelcuts.com.
Popular, long-established student-travel organization,
with good worldwide offers; not only for students.
**Travelers Advantage** US ☎1-800/835-8747,
ⓦwww.travelersadvantage.com. Discount travel
club, with low airfares, cashback deals and discounted
car rental. Membership required ($1 for two-month trial).
**Travelosophy** US ☎1-800/332-2687, ⓦwww
.itravelosophy.com. Good range of discounted and
student fares worldwide.

## Specialist agents and operators

**Astra** US ☎303/321-5403, ⓦwww.astragreece
.com. Very personal, idiosyncratic two-week tours,
led by veteran Hellenophile Thordis Simonsen, during
spring and autumn, taking in Crete as well as a
number of mainland destinations.
**Cachet Travel** UK ☎020/8847 8700, ⓦwww
.cachet-travel.co.uk. Attractive range of villas and
apartments in the more unspoilt south and west of
Crete, plus Kárpathos and remote corners of Sámos.
**CV Travel** UK ☎0870/606 0013, ⓦwww.cvtravel
.co.uk. Quality villas on Corfu, Kefaloniá, Paxí,
Mýkonos, Lefkádha and Crete.
**Direct Greece** UK ☎0871/664 7731, ⓦwww
.direct-greece.co.uk. Moderately priced villas,
apartments and restored houses on Rhodes, Hálki,
Zákynthos, Kefaloniá, Lésvos, Corfu and Crete.
**easyCruise** UK ☎0871/210 0001, US & Canada
☎1-866/335 4975; ⓦwww.easycruise.com. From
the man who brought you easyJet, short, no-frills
three-to-ten-day cruises around the islands with
prices starting from as low as £180/$350 per person.
**Freedom of Greece** UK ☎01902 324433,
ⓦwww.freedomofgreece.com. Small hotels,
studios and apartments on Crete and smaller islands,
including Angístri, Ándhros, Spetsés and Léros; plenty
of budget options.
**Grecian Tours** Australia ☎03/9663 3711, ⓦwww
.greciantours.com.au. A variety of accommodation
and sightseeing tours, plus flights.
**Greek Islands Club** UK ☎020/8232 9780,
ⓦwww.greekislandsclub.com. Part of Sunvil (see
opposite), specializing in upmarket villas with private
pools, especially in the Ionian islands.
**Greek Sun Holidays** UK ☎01732/740317,
ⓦwww.greeksun.co.uk. Good-value package

holidays, mainly in the Dodecanese, northeast Aegean and Cyclades; also individual island-hopping itineraries.

**Hellenic Adventures** US ☎1-800/851-6349, ⊛www.hellenicadventures.com. Small-group tours led by enthusiastic expert guides, as well as itineraries for independent travellers, cruises and other travel services.

**Hidden Greece** UK ☎020/8758 4707, ⊛www.hidden-greece.co.uk. Specialist agent putting together tailor-made packages to smaller destinations at reasonable prices.

**Homeric Tours** US ☎1-800/223-5570, ⊛www.homerictours.com. Hotel packages, individual tours, escorted group tours and fly/drive deals. Good source of inexpensive flights.

**Inntravel** UK ☎01653/617755, ⊛www.inntravel.co.uk. High-quality packages and tailor-made itineraries and fly-drives to unspoilt areas of the mainland, Crete and smaller islands; also walking and other special-interest holidays.

**Island Wandering** UK ☎0870/777 9944, ⊛www.islandwandering.com. Bespoke island-hopping itineraries between most Greek archipelagos.

**Olympic Holidays** UK ☎0800/093 3322, ⊛www.olympicholidays.com. Huge package holiday company serving a wide variety of islands; all standards from cheap and cheerful to five-star hotel, and often a good source of last-minute bargains.

**Pure Crete** UK ☎0845/070 1571, ⊛www.purecrete.com. Characterful converted cottages and farmhouses in western Crete, plus walking, wildlife and other special-interest trips.

**Simply Travel** UK ☎0871/231 4050, ⊛www.simplytravel.co.uk. Although now part of the vast TUI organisation, Simply still manages a personal touch, and has plenty of excellent, upmarket accommodation in Crete and the Ionian islands.

**Simpson Travel** UK ☎0845/811 6502, ⊛www.simpsontravel.com. Classy villas, upmarket hotels and village hideaways on Crete, Corfu, Paxí and Meganíssi.

**Sun Island Tours** Australia ☎1300/665 673, ⊛www.sunislandtours.com.au. An assortment of island-hopping, fly-drives, cruises and guided land-tour options, as well as upscale accommodation on big-name islands such as Rhodes, Kós and Sámos.

**Sunvil Holidays** UK ☎020/8758 4758, ⊛www.sunvil.co.uk/greece. High-quality outfit specializing in mid- to up-market hotels and villas throughout the islands.

**Tourlite Zeus** US ☎1-800/272-7600, ⊛www.tourlite.com. Specialists in Greek travel, can arrange tailor-made or package vacations.

**Travel à la Carte** UK ☎01635/33800, ⊛www.travelalacarte.co.uk. Established Corfu specialist, now diversified into beach and rural villas on Skiáthos, Skópelos, Alónissos, Hálki, Paxí and Sými as well.

## Walking, nature and special-interest holidays

**ATG Oxford** UK ☎01865/315678, ⊛www.atg-oxford.co.uk. Somewhat pricey but high-standard guided walks on Crete and the Cyclades.

**Classic Adventures** US ☎1-800/777-8090, ⊛www.classicadventures.com. Cycling tours of Crete.

**Exodus** UK ☎0845 863 9600, ⊛www.exodus.co.uk. One-week treks across Évvia or the White Mountains of Crete.

**Explore Worldwide** UK ☎0845/013 1537, ⊛www.explore.co.uk. A variety of tours, many combining hiking with sailing between the islands.

**Free Spirit Travel** UK ☎01273/564230, ⊛www.freespirituk.com. Yoga and meditation in western Crete, plus family and walking holidays.

**Jonathan's Tours** ☎33/561.04.64.47, ⊛www.jonathanstours.com. Family-run walking holidays on Crete, Lésvos, Lefkádha and Zagóri; spring and autumn departures.

**Marengo Guided Walks** UK ☎01485/532710, ⊛www.marengowalks.com. Annually changing programme of easy walks guided by ace botanist (and co-author of this guide) Lance Chilton; typical one-week offerings may include Corfu, Sámos, Sými, Lésvos, Crete and Thássos.

**Naturetrek** UK ☎01962/733051, ⊛www.naturetrek.co.uk. Fairly pricey but expertly led one- or two-week natural history tours; offerings include springtime birds and flora on Sámos or Lésvos, and wildlife of Crete.

**Northwest Passage** US ☎1-800/RECREATE, ⊛www.nwpassage.com. Excellent sea kayaking and hiking "inn-to-inn" tours, plus yoga and art experiences, as well as combinations thereof, mostly in Crete.

**Ramblers Holidays** UK ☎01707/331133, ⊛www.ramblersholidays.co.uk. Spring hiking in Crete, Christmas on Sámos and many more walks, especially in the Dodecanese.

**Sherpa Expeditions** UK ☎020/8577 2717, ⊛www.sherpa-walking-holidays.co.uk. Self-guided and escorted eight-day outings on Crete.

**Skyros Holidays** UK ☎01983/865566, ⊛www.skyros.co.uk. Holistic health, fitness, crafts and "personal growth" holidays on Skýros, as well as well-regarded writers' workshops.

**Swim Trek** UK ☎020/8696 6220, ⊛www.swimtrek.com. Week-long tours of Náxos and the small islands around it, swimming between the islands; the brainchild of Aussie cross-channel swimmer Simon Murie.

**The Travelling Naturalist** UK ☎01305/267994, ⊛www.naturalist.co.uk. Wildlife holiday company that runs excellent bird-watching and wild-flower-spotting trips to Crete, Kós and Lesvós.

**Walking Plus** UK ☎020/8835 8303, ⊛www
.walkingplus.co.uk. Enthusiastic Gilly and Robin
Cameron Cooper offer self-guided off-season walks
in the Cyclades.
**Walks Worldwide** UK ☎01524/242000, ⊛www
.walksworldwide.com. Escorted and self-guided
treks on Corfu, Crete, Ándhros and Evvía.
**Yoga Plus** UK ☎01273/276175, ⊛www.yogaplus
.co.uk. Ashtanga yoga courses in a remote part of
southern Crete.

## Sailing holidays

**Nautilus Yachting** UK ☎01732/867445, ⊛www
.nautilus-yachting.com. Bareboat yacht charter, flotillas
and motor yachts from a wide variety of marinas.
**Neilson** UK ☎0870/333 3356, ⊛www.neilson
.co.uk. Half a dozen excellent beach activity clubs,
plus flotillas and bareboat charter in the Ionians.
**Seafarer Cruising & Sailing** UK ☎0870/442
2447, ⊛www.seafarercruises.com. Ionian,
Sporades and Argo-Saronic flotillas, beach club,
bareboat charter, sailing courses and small-ship
island cruises.
**Setsail Holidays** UK ☎01787/310445, ⊛www
.setsail.co.uk. Bareboat charters across the country,
flotillas and a sail-and-stay programme based on
Skiáthos.
**Sportif** UK ☎01273/844919, ⊛www.sportif
-uk.com. Windsurfing packages and instruction on
Crete, Kós, Rhodes, Sámos and Kárpathos.
**Sunsail** UK ☎023/922 2300, ⊛www.sunsail
.com. Worldwide company with mainland beach club,
plus flotillas and bareboat mainly in the Ionians and
Sporades.
**Templecraft** ☎01732/867445, ⊛www.templecraft
.com. Flotilla holidays in the Ionian archipelago.

**Valef Yachts** US ☎1-800/223-3845, ⊛www
.valefyachts.com. Small-boat cruises around the
islands and luxury crewed yacht or motor boat charter.

## Rail contacts

**BootsnAll** US ☎1-866/549-7614, ⊛www
.bootsnall.com. Eurail passes and other tickets, plus
rail blogs and phone helpline.
**CIT World Travel** Australia ☎1300/361 500,
⊛www.cittravel.com.au. Eurail passes and other
tickets.
**Europrail International** Canada ☎1-888/667-
9734, ⊛www.europrail.net. Eurail passes and other
tickets.
**Eurostar** UK ☎08705/186186, outside UK
☎44/1233 617575; ⊛www.eurostar.com.
**The Man in Seat 61** ⊛www.seat61.com. Named
after British rail buff Mark Smith's favourite seat on
the Eurostar, this brilliant site has full details of all the
possible ways of getting to Greece by train and ferry,
plus links to all the necessary train, ferry and ticket
websites. Also has a rail shop feature, where many
tickets and passes can be purchased.
**Rail Europe** US ☎1-888/382-RAIL, Canada
☎1-800/361-RAIL, UK ☎08448/484064,
Australia ☎03 9642 8644; ⊛www.raileurope
.com, ⊛www.raileurope.co.uk, ⊛www.raileurope
.ca, ⊛www.raileurope.com.au. Official agents for
most tickets including Eurail, InterRail and Eurostar
and discounted rail fares for under-26s on a variety of
European routes.
**Rail Plus** Australia ☎1300/555 003 or 03/9642
8644, New Zealand ☎09/377 5415; ⊛www
.railplus.com.au, ⊛www.railplus.co.nz. Eurail and
other passes.

# Athens and mainland ports

As noted in the "Getting there" section, you may well find yourself travelling to or from the islands via Athens. With its sprawling 1960s and 1970s concrete architecture, Athens may not be the most attractive of cities, but the centre has been transformed since the 2004 Olympics: there's excellent public transportation between the airport and the port (much of it via the centre of town), an unrivalled Classical Greek heritage, great restaurants and a lively street life. A couple of nights' stopover will allow you to take in the Acropolis and the other major ancient sites and museums, wander around the old quarter of Pláka and the bazaar area, and sample some of the country's best food and nightlife. Even in a single day, a morning arrival would give you time for a look at the Acropolis and Pláka before heading down to the port of Pireás (Piraeus) to catch an overnight ferry.

Not all of the islands are accessible from Pireás, so we've also given brief accounts of other useful mainland ports on p.38.

## Athens

Athens' Eleftheríos Venizélos **airport** is at Spáta, 33km southeast of the city. It has comprehensive facilities including several ATMs, bureaux de change and a tourist office. **Public transport** from the airport is excellent. The **metro** (€6 single, €10 return, discounts for multiple tickets) is your best bet, taking you straight into the heart of the city where you can change to the other metro lines at either Monastiráki (for Pireás) or Sýndagma: trains run every half hour from 6.30am to 11.30pm and take around 45 minutes.

**Buses** can be slower, especially at rush hours, but they're also much cheaper, run all night and offer direct links to other parts of the city including Pireás. The most useful are the #X95 to Sýndagma square (at least three an hour, day and night) and #X96 to the port at Pireás via Glyfádha and the beach suburbs (at least two an hour, day and night). **Tickets** cost €3.20 from a booth beside the stops. As on all Athens public transport, you must validate your ticket in a machine at the start of your journey. There are also regional buses from the airport to the nearby ports of **Lávrio** (20 daily, 6.30am–10pm; €4) and **Rafína** (15 daily, 6am–9pm; €3); see p.39.

**Taxis** are subject to the vagaries of traffic and can take anything from forty minutes (at night) to an hour and forty minutes (at rush hour) to reach the centre; the fare should be roughly €18–25 to central Athens or Pireás.

The main **tourist office** is at Amalías 26, just off Sýndagma square (Mon-Fri 9am–7pm, Sat & Sun 10am–4pm).

## Accommodation

Finding **accommodation** in Athens is only likely to be a problem during the midsummer peak – but it's always best to phone ahead or book online. For a quick stay, you want to be right in the centre, and most of those included are in or near Pláka, the oldest quarter of the city, in the shadow of the Acropolis with lots of outdoor restaurants and cafés.

**Acropolis House** Kódhrou 6 ☎210 32 22 344, ⓔhtlacrhs@otenet.gr; Metro Sýndagma. A rambling, slightly dilapidated 150-year-old mansion much loved by its regulars – mostly students and academics, many of whom leave behind books for other guests to read. Furnishings are individual, and some rooms have baths across the hall; not all have a/c, though most are naturally cool. Rates include use of fridge. B&B ❹

**Athens Backpackers** Mákri 12 ☎210 92 24 044, ⓦwww.backpackers.gr; Metro Akrópoli. Very central Athenian-Australian run backpackers with few frills but clean rooms, communal kitchen, internet access, rooftop bar with fabulous views, and great atmosphere. Probably the best spot in town to meet fellow travellers. Dorms €18–25.

**Attalos** Athinás 29 ☎210 32 12 801, ⓦwww .attalos.gr; Metro Monastiráki. Modern from the outside but traditional within, the Attalos has bright, comfortable rooms, well insulated from the noisy street, all with a/c and TV. Some balcony rooms on the upper floors have great views, but rooms facing the internal courtyard at the back are generally larger and quieter. Some triples. ⑤

**Central** Apóllonos 21 ☎210 32 34 357, ⊛www .centralhotel.gr; Metro Sýndagma. Completely refurbished in designer style, with seagrass or wooden floors, marble bathrooms and excellent soundproofing. Family and interconnecting rooms also available; all with a/c, TV and fridge. Large roof terrace with Acropolis views and hot tub. B&B ⑤

**Evropi** Satovriándhou 7 ☎210 52 23 081; Metro Omónia. Very, very basic but great value old-fashioned hotel with spacious rooms occupied only by bed, bedside table and ceiling fan, along with a concrete enclosure for en-suite shower. Reasonably quiet, despite being only a block from Platía Omonías; inexpensive singles available. ②

**Marble House** Cul-de-sac off A. Zínni 35A, Koukáki ☎210 92 34 058, ⊛www.marblehouse .gr; Metro Syngroú-Fix. Family-run, friendly and not far from the action. Simple rooms with and without private bath, some with a/c (for extra charge); also two self-catering studios for longer stays. Often full, so call ahead. ③

**Metropolis** Mitropóleos 46 ☎210 32 17 469, ⊛www.hotelmetropolis.gr; Metro Sýndagma/ Monastiráki. Right by the cathedral, the friendly Metropolis has simple, plainly furnished rooms with vinyl floors, each with a good-size balcony, a/c and TV, some with shared bathroom. Acropolis views from the upper floors. ④

**Ochre and Brown** Leokoríou 7 ☎210 33 12 950, ⊛www.ochreandbrown.com; Metro Thissío. Understated designer hotel with eleven rooms, one of which is a large suite with private terrace and views; all rooms have satellite TV, as well as DVD and CD players. Friendly, comfortable and elegant, with a great location on the fringes of Psyrrí. ⑦

**Phaedra** Herefóndos 16, cnr Adhrianoú ☎210 32 38 461, ⊛www.hotelphaedra.com; Metro Akrópoli. Small, simple rooms with bare tiled floors, TV and a/c, not all en suite (but you get a private bathroom). Polite, welcoming management looks after the place well, and it's quiet at night, thanks to a location at the junction of two pedestrian alleys. One of the best deals in Pláka. ③

**Tempi** Eólou 29 ☎210 32 13 175, ⊛www .travelling.gr/tempihotel; Metro Monastiráki. A long-time favourite with budget travellers: book exchange and shared kitchen, plus handy affiliated travel agency. Rooms are simple and tiny and most have shared facilities, but the view of the flower market at Ayía Iríni across the quiet pedestrian walkway is enchanting. ③

## Eating

Pláka is bursting with touristy **restaurants**, many of them romantically located on the stepped streets beneath the Acropolis. One of the best of this mostly overpriced bunch, with tables outside on a stepped street beneath the Acropolis, is the *Mezedopolio Palio Tetradhio* at Mnisikléous 26, often with live music. For cheaper, more authentic fare head towards Monastiráki or its trendy neighbour Psyrrí: *Baïraktaris* on Platía Monastirakíou serves great Greek classics and kebabs; *Café Abysinia* on nearby Platía Avsinnías offers a more modern (and more expensive) take on traditional Greek cooking and is always busy with a young local crowd; *Taverna tou Psyrrí*, Eskhýlou 12, in the midst of the lively Psyrrí nightlife, is another that's always packed thanks to tasty, excellent-value cuisine.

## The city and sights

The centre of Athens is compact, and anything not in walking distance is well served by the metro, bus or inexpensive taxis. City bus #400 also offers a hop-on/hop-off tour passing all the major sites with basic commentary (€5; buy ticket on the bus; valid for 24hr on this and all other city-centre public transportation).

Even without a tour, finding your bearings is generally pretty easy: the **Acropolis** is visible, around a corner, from almost any part of the city centre. Beneath it to the east lies **Pláka**, with **Monastiráki** curling around to the north. **Sýndagma** (Platía Syndágmatos), the traditional centre of the city and home to the Greek Parliament, lies to the northeast of these two, midway between the Acropolis and the hill of **Lykavitós**. The ritzy **Kolonáki** quarter curls up the hill's slopes above Sýndagma, with a funicular to save you the final climb to the summit and its famous views. Below Kolonáki many of the city's major **museums** can be found along the broad avenue of Leofóros Vassilísis Sofías. On the other side of the avenue, behind the Parliament, lie the jungly **National Gardens**.

To the north, broad avenues lead to **Omónia** (Platía Omonías), the heart of commercial and business Athens. The market and bazaar area lies en route, while beyond to the north are the **National Archeological Museum** and the slightly alternative, studenty neighbourhoods of **Exárhia** and **Neápoli**, with a concentration of lively tavernas and bars. Close to the market you'll find the thriving nightlife of **Psyrrí**, whose modernizing influence spreads to the west in **Keramikós**, **Gázi** and **Metaxouryío**.

The inevitable focus of any visit to Athens, however brief, is the **Acropolis** (daily April–Sept 8am–7pm; Oct–March 8am–4.30pm; €12; Metro Akrópoli). The complex of temples on top, rebuilt by Pericles in the "Golden Age" of the fifth century BC, is focused on the famed **Parthenon**. The extraordinary **New Acropolis Museum**, looking up towards the temples from a site beside Metro Akrópoli, will also be open by the time you read this.

There are other outstanding Classical sites on the south slope of the Acropolis, including the **Theatre of Dionysos** (daily: summer 8am–7pm; winter 8.30am–3pm; €2); the **Ancient Agora** or market area (daily: summer 8am–7pm; winter 8.30am–3pm; €4; Metro Monastiráki) on the opposite side of the Acropolis; the nearby **Roman Forum** (daily: summer 8am–7pm; winter 8.30am–3pm; €2; metro Monastiráki); and the ancient cemetery, the **Kerameikos** (daily summer 8.30am–4pm; winter 8.30am–3pm; €2). Entrance to all of these is included in the Acropolis ticket.

Also unmissable is the refurbished **National Archeological Museum** (Mon 1–7.30pm, Tues–Sun 8am–7.15pm; closes 3pm Tues–Sun in winter; €7; Metro Viktorías or any bus labelled *Mousseio*) at 28 Oktovríou 44. Quite simply the finest collection of Greek antiquities anywhere in the world, its highlights include Homeric-era gold treasures from Mycenae and a vast collection of wonderful sculpture.

## Pireás

The easiest way to get to the ferry port at **Pireás** from Athens is on **metro** line 1; the journey takes around twenty minutes from Omónia or Monastiráki. Alternatively, there are **buses**: #40 (about every 10min 5am–midnight; hourly 1–5am) runs to and from Sýndagma, while #49 from Omónia (roughly every 15min 5am–midnight; hourly 1–5am) will drop you slightly closer to the ferries. Both are very slow, however – allow an hour to be safe. From the **airport**, you can take express bus #X96 (around 1hr 20min). **Taxis** cost about €8 at day tariff from the centre of Athens.

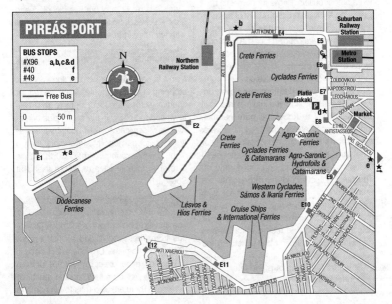

Hundreds of **ferries** leave Pireás daily, so it's perhaps not surprising that a comprehensive list is hard to find: even the tourist office simply look up individual queries on the web (🌐www.openseas.gr). The majority of the ships for the Argo-Saronic and the popular Cyclades leave between 7 and 10am. There is then another burst of activity between noon and 3pm towards the Cyclades and Dodecanese, and a final battery of departures in the evening, bound for a wide variety of ports, but especially night sailings to Crete, the northeast Aegean, the western Cyclades and Dodecanese.

There's no need to buy **tickets** for conventional ferries before you get here, unless you want a berth in a cabin or are taking a car on board; during Greek holidays (Aug and Easter especially) these can be hard to get and it's worth booking in advance – the big companies have internet booking. Flying Dolphin **hydrofoil** reservations are also a good idea at busy times. In general, though, the best plan is simply to get to Pireás early and check with some of the dozens of **shipping agents** around the metro station and along the quayside Platía Karaïskáki (there are plenty of agents in central Athens too). Most of these act only for particular lines, so for a full picture you will need to ask at three or four outlets. Prices for domestic boat journeys vary little, but the quality of the craft and circuitousness of **routes** can be vastly different. If you are heading for Thíra (Santoríni) or Rhodes, for example, try to get a boat that stops at only three or four islands en route; for Crete settle for direct ferries only.

Boats for different **destinations** leave from various points around the main harbour: it can be helpful to know the **gate** number, though these are primarily for drivers. Airport-style buses run from gate E5, near the metro, as far as E1, for the big ferries to Crete, the Dodecanese and the northwest. The main gates and **departure points** are marked on our map, but always check with the ticket agent as on any given day a ferry may dock in an unexpected spot. They all display signs showing their destination and departure time; you can't buy tickets on the

boat, but there's usually a ticket hut on the quayside nearby.

## Other mainland ports

Although Pireás has a wide choice of ferry, catamaran and hydrofoil connections, certain islands can (or must) be reached from **other ports** on the mainland. Below is a quick run-through of the more important and useful.

Note also that there are two islands – Évvia (northeast of Athens) and Lefkádha in the Ionian Islands – that require no ferry and can be reached by bus, and in Évvia's case also by train.

### Alexandhróupoli

The third northern port (6hr by bus from Thessaloníki) has daily ferries and summer-only hydrofoils to Samothráki, plus a weekly departure to Rhodes via Límnos and other northeast Aegean and Dodecanese isles. It's a somewhat unenticing place to stay, though if you get stuck the *Lido* at Paleológou 15 (☎25510 28808) represents by far the best budget-hotel value.

### Astakós

This small port on the western mainland has a daily ferry to Kefaloniá, weekly to Itháki. Astakós is rarely busy but has few places to stay – buses from Athens tend to dovetail with ferry departures, around noon.

### Igoumenítsa

Many ferries from Italy call at Igoumenítsa, stopping at Corfu en route. There are regular shuttles across to Corfu, both to the main town and to Lefkími in the south, plus one or two daily services to Paxí. Hotel vacancies are plentiful as nobody stays more than a night; the *Stavrodhromi* (☎26650 22343) is a reliable, friendly cheapie, 500m inland at Soulíou 14.

### Kavála

The second port of northern Greece (3hr by bus from Thessaloníki, and a charter flight destination from the UK) offers fast access to Thássos, either direct by hydrofoil, or from the nearby roll-on-roll-off shuttle point at Keramotí. There are also links to Límnos and

See p.80 for a map of island ferry connections.

Samothráki, as well as regular service to Lávrio (see below) via other northeast Aegean islands. The city has a line of good tavernas in the old quarter below the castle, but pleasant, affordable hotels are in short supply. In ascending order of comfort and price, try the *Acropolis* (☎2510 223 543) at Venizélou 29, the *Nefeli* at Erythroú Stavroú 50 (☎2510 227 441) or the *Esperia* (☎2510 229 621) at Erythroú Stavroú 42, opposite the archeological museum.

## Kyllíni

This small port, south of Pátra (to which it is connected by bus), is the main departure point for the Ionian island of Zákynthos, and in summer has boats to Póros on Kefaloniá. Little point in staying, if you time things right.

## Kými

This is technically an island port – on Évvia – but is mentioned here as it is the main port for Skýros in the Sporades. Kými can be reached from Athens by bus, which should be timed to dovetail with ferry departures. If you miss the connection, you're limited to two fairly expensive hotels.

## Lávrio

This tiny port, south of Athens (and reachable by bus from there, or direct from the airport) has several daily ferries to Kéa, the closest of the Cyclades, less often to Kýthnos, Kéa's neighbour, as well as two to three weekly departures to Híos, Lésvos, Áyios Efstrátios and Límnos (some continuing to Kaválla or Thessaloníki), and once a week a circular routing around many of the Cycladic Islands.

## Neápoli

A small, undistinguished port at the southern foot of the Peloponnese, with occasional ferry connections to Dhiakoftí on Kýthira, and frequent local boats to the islet of Elafónissos.

## Pátra (Patras)

Pátra is the major port of the Peloponnese, and the main jump-off for Italy and most of the Ionian Islands. The easiest access from Athens is on the train (4hr), since Pátra station is right by the boat terminals. The city

itself is uninteresting, so plan on moving out the same day, if possible. Reasonable hotels handy for the ferries include the *Adonis*, Kapsáli 9 (☎2610 224 213), and the *Atlanta* at Zaïmi 10 (☎2610 220 098).

## Rafína

Another small port near Athens (easily accessible by bus from city or airport). Daily connections to most of the Cyclades or nearby Évvia.

## Thessaloníki

The northern capital is a busy mainland port. There are useful long-haul ferries to Kós and Rhodes via Sámos; to the northeastern Aegean islands; and to Crete via select Sporades and Cyclades. In summer only there are departures to Skíathos, Skópelos and Alónissos in the Sporades. It's worth exploring the Byzantine churches, especially the Áyios Yeóryios Rotónda and tiny Ósios Dhavíd, as well as the Archeological Museum. Hotels are plentiful if mostly uninspiring; worthwhile options include the *Tourist* on Mitropóleos 21 (☎2310 270 501); the *Nea Mitropolis* at Syngroú 22 (☎2310 525 540); the *Pella* at Íonos Dhragoúmi 63 (☎2310 524 222); and the *Orestias Castorias* at Agnóstou Stratiótou 14 (☎2310 276 517).

## Vólos and Áyios Konstandínos

Vólos is the major port of Thessaly, in central Greece. It is most easily reached from Athens by bus (Mavromatéon terminal; 4hr), though there's also a through express train daily, via Lárissa. Ferries and hydrofoils run regularly to the Sporades – Skíathos, Skópelos and Alónissos. Try to complete your journey the same day; failing that, pleasantly situated budget hotels include the *Roussas* (☎24210 21732) at Iatroú Tzánou, 1km east of the dock, or the *Iasson* right by the dock (☎24210 26075). Áyios Konstandínos is an alternative but less active port for the Sporades, again with buses from Athens (Mavromatéon terminal; 2hr 30min).

## Yíthio

This elegant Peloponnese town has daily ferries to the island of Kýthira, plus weekly to Kíssamos in western Crete. It's a four-to five-hour haul by bus from Athens (Kifissoú 100 terminal), changing at Spárti. Budget hotels or pensions in town include the *Grigoris-Matina*, Vassiléos Pávlou 19 (☎27330 22518) and the *Saga* on Tzanetáki, opposite Kranae islet (☎27330 23220).

# Getting around

The extensive network of Aegean ferries, catamarans and hydrofoils will eventually get you to any of the sixty-plus inhabited isles, and between various neighbouring ones. Planes are expensive compared to seagoing transport but can save literally days of travel and, moreover, provide critical links between the smaller islands and Thessaloníki, Rhodes and Crete in particular. On the islands themselves, buses provide skeletal connections, which most tourists supplement by renting a scooter, motorbike or car.

## Sea transport

There are several varieties of sea-going vessels: **roll-on-roll-off** short-haul barges, nicknamed *pondófles* ("slippers"), designed to shuttle vehicles short distances; medium-sized-to-large **ordinary ferries**, which never exceed 17 knots in velocity; the new generation of **high-speed** boats (*tahyplóa*) and catamarans, which usually carry a number of cars, nearly as large as conventional ferries but capable of attaining 27 knots; **hydrofoils**, similarly quick but which carry only passengers; and local *kaïkia*, small boats which do short hops and excursions in season. **Costs** are affordable on longer journeys, though proportionately more expensive for shorter, inter-island connections, and baldly overpriced for monopoly crossings (such as Alexandhroúpoli–Samothráki).

We've indicated most ferry, high-speed, catamaran and hydrofoil **connections**, both on the **map** (see p.80 for a general pattern) and in the "Travel details" at the end of relevant chapters. Don't take our listings as gospel, however, as schedules are notoriously erratic, and must be verified seasonally; details given are for departures between late June and early September (essentially school holidays). **Out-of-season** frequencies are severely reduced, with less populated islands connected only two or three times weekly at most.

The most reliable, up-to-date information is available from the local **port police** (*limenarhío*), which on the Attic peninsula maintains offices at Pireás (☎210 45 50 000), Rafína (☎22940 28888) and Lávrio (☎22920 25249), as well as at the harbours of all fair-sized islands. Busier port police have automated phone-answering services with an English option for schedule information, though frustratingly there's no live human to ask simple questions like will the boat be late/cancelled, etc. Smaller places may only have a *limenikós stathmós* (marine station), often just a single room with a VHF radio. Their officers have complete schedules – and, meteorological report in hand, are the final arbiters of whether a ship will sail or not in stormy weather conditions.

Some companies produce annual **schedule** booklets, which may not be adhered to as the season wears on – check **websites** (if any) for current information. The only attempt at an all-inclusive ferry guide is the Greek travel industry's monthly manual *Greek Travel Pages*, often outdated by the time it's printed; you're better off referring to ⓦ www.gtp.gr.

### Regular ferries

On most **ferry** routes, your main considera-tion will be getting a boat leaving on the day, and for the island, that you want. However, when sailing from **Pireás** to the Cyclades or Dodecanese, you should have a **choice** of at least two, sometimes three, daily departures.

Spanking-new **boats** are unusual, though growing in number as old rust-buckets are retired; you will more frequently encounter a former English Channel or Scandinavian fjord ferry, rechristened and enjoying a new lease of life in the Aegean. The routes and speed of boats can vary enormously and should be checked before ticket purchase; a journey from Pireás to Rhodes, for instance, can take anything from 14 (high-speed boat) to 24 ("milk-run" conventional ferry) hours.

**Tickets** are, in general, best bought a day before departure, unless you need to reserve a cabin berth or space for a car. If a boat fails to sail for mechanical or bad-weather

reasons, your money is refunded; changes to departure date at your own initiative will attract a small penalty charge. During holiday periods – Christmas/New Year, the week before and after Easter, late July to early September (especially the three days before school starts) – and around the dates of elections, ferries need to be booked at least two weeks in advance.

You cannot **buy** your ticket on board; in some cases there may not even be a last-minute sales booth at the quayside, and staff at the gangway will prevent you embarking if you don't have a ticket. The only exceptions are the short-haul, roll-on-roll-off services, for example from Igoumenítsa to Corfu, or the central mainland to Évvia, and small local *kaïkia*, for example the Pátmos–Lipsí–Léros run. All other ticket sales are now **computerized** and have accurate seat/berth allocations to preclude overbookings. Companies with provision for phone or internet booking include Hellenic Seaways,

## The wreck of the Express Samina – and beyond

On September 27, 2000, at 10.20pm in gale conditions, the **Express Samina**, the oldest ship in the domestic fleet, slammed full speed into the Pórtes rocks outside Páros harbour, and sank within minutes. The bridge was unstaffed by most senior officers, who were watching football on television; the junior officer at the helm neglected to override the autopilot while attempting evasive action. The British and Greek navies, exercising in the area, plus Parian fishing boats, together plucked most of the 500-plus aboard from the water, including numerous foreign tourists, but 82 passengers drowned. It was the worst **maritime disaster** in Greece since 1966.

The 34-year-old *Express Samina* was the worst but by no means the only rust-bucket in the Greek domestic fleet. EU regulations normally require ships to be retired after 27 years of service, but Greek shipping interests had wheedled an extension out of their own government to 35 years. With an effective domestic **monopoly** and capped fares limiting revenue, there was little incentive to keep boats up to date. Greek newspapers quickly tallied eighteen ferries 29 years old or older. Newer craft have multiple airtight compartments, so that a single breach in the hull will not be fatal, but the *Express Samina* had just a single compartment and was effectively doomed the moment she hit the rocks and had a gash torn down her entire side.

Since the disaster, various **newly built craft** have taken to the water, in particular catamarans and "high speed" ferries run by more reputable, well-capitalized companies such as Blue Star, NEL, Hellenic Seaways and ANEK, but the fuel-thirsty catamarans in particular only break even financially when three-quarters full and haven't made as much impact as hoped. Moreover, the head of GA ferries went to the European Court in 2007 to successfully overturn the 35-year limit and protect his Methusalan fleet, which will thus be around indefinitely. Meanwhile, many islands are far worse served frequency-wise than before the *Express Samina* wreck, as the transport ministry has failed to make rational schedules a condition of the subsidies for operating unprofitable services.

ANEK, Blue Star, Minoan and NEL, but the actual paper tickets must be picked up at the port offices at least thirty minutes before departure. **Maximum fares** for each route are set by the transport ministry and should not differ among ships of the same type or among agencies, though discounted promotional fares, especially in spring or autumn, are common – ask about offers.

The cheapest **class of ticket**, which you'll automatically be sold unless you specify otherwise, is **deck class**, variously called *tríti* or *ikonomikí thési*. This gives you the run of most boats except for the upper-class restaurant and bar. Conventional ferries, with their glaring overhead lights and plastic bucket seats, seem expressly designed to frustrate summertime travellers attempting to sleep on deck. In such cases it's worth the few extra euros for a **cabin bunk** (second-class cabins are usually quadruple, occasionally triple or double). **First-class** cabins usually cost about the same as a plane flight; the main difference between first and second being the presence of an inside bathroom, just two berths, and a better location. Most cabins are overheated or overchilled, and pretty airless; ask for an *exoterikí* (outer) cabin if you want a porthole (always bolted shut).

**Motorbikes and cars** get issued separate tickets, in the latter case three to four times the passenger deck-class conventional-ferry fare, depending on vehicle size. As with passenger tickets, car fees (spiralling up with fuel costs during 2008) are roughly proportional to distance travelled – though short hops like Rafína–Kárystos are a rip-off. When pondering whether or not to drag your car to an island from the mainland, it's worth doing sums to see if likely rental rates (and availability) at your destination will outweigh the return cost of ferrying your own vehicle.

In 2008, airplane-style per-passenger luggage **weight limits** of twenty kilos were theoretically introduced for all seagoing craft. We've not heard of this being enforced yet, but as fuel gets pricier this undoubtedly will be at some point.

Ferries sell a limited range of overpriced **food on board**; honourable exceptions are the meals served on overnight sailings to Crete. On the short daytime hops between the various islands of the Argo-Saronic, Cyclades and Sporades, stock up beforehand with your own snacks.

## Hydrofoils, catamarans and tahyplóa (high-speed boats)

**Hydrofoils** – commonly known as *dhelfínia* or "Flying Dolphins" – are at least twice as expensive as ordinary ferries, but their network neatly fills gaps in ferry scheduling, often with more convenient departure times. Their main drawback (aside from frequent engine breakdowns) is that they were originally designed for cruising on placid Russian or Polish rivers, and are quite literally out of their depth on the Aegean. Thus they are extremely sensitive to bad weather, and even in moderate seas are not for the seasick-prone. Many don't operate – or are heavily reduced in frequency – from October to June. Hydrofoils aren't allowed to carry scooters or bicycles.

Hydrofoils operate among the **Argo-Saronic** islands close to Athens, (some years) between Alexandhroúpoli and **Samothráki**, between Kavála and **Thássos**, between Vólos and the northern **Sporades**, and in the **Dodecanese** among Rhodes, Sými, Kós, Kálymnos, Léros, Lipsí and Pátmos, with regular forays up to Sámos and occasionally Foúrni. Services in the Argo-Saronic are run by Hellenic Seaways and Vasilopoulos Flying Dolphins, in the Sporades by Hellenic Seaways, and in the northern Dodecanese by Aegean Flying Dolphins. You may see craft with other livery, but they don't appear in "Travel details", as they are chartered by excursion agencies and do not offer scheduled services.

**Catamarans** and **tahyplóa** combine (almost) the speed of hydrofoils with the (relative) reliability and vehicle-carrying capacity of larger ferries. The fact that many are new and sleek, purpose-built in France or Scandinavia, does not preclude frequent breakdowns. **Inside** they are rather soulless: ruthlessly air-conditioned, usually with no deck seating (it's illegal even to go out on deck when the craft is in motion) and with Greek TV blaring at you from numerous screens. Paying extra for *dhiakikriméni thési* (upper class) gets you a better view and less crowding, but there's no escaping the TV. Cabins are nonexistent and food facilities even more unappetizing than on conventional ferries. Car fares are normal, though passenger **tickets** are at least double a comparable ferry journey, ie similar to hydrofoil rates. Their stratospheric fuel costs mean that they haven't become as ubiquitous as anticipated, but they seasonally serve the Pireás–Híos–Lésvos and Pireás-Tínos–Mýkonos–Ikaría–Sámos lines, routes to Crete, the most populated Dodecanese, the Argo-Saronics, the Sporades and the most popular Cyclades.

## Small ferries, kaïkia and taxi boats

In season, *kaïkia* and **small ferries** sail between adjacent islands and to a few of the more obscure satellite islets. These are extremely useful and often very pleasant, but seldom cheaper than mainline services. The more consistent *kaïki* links are summarized in the "Travel details" sections, though the only firm information is to be had on the quayside. *Kaïkia* and small ferries, despite appearances, have good safety records. Swarms of **taxi boats** are a feature of Sými, Rhodes, Hálki, Pátmos, Skiáthos, Alónissos and Itháki, among other spots; these shuttle clients on set routes to remote beaches or ports which can only be reached arduously, if at all, overland. Costs on these can be pretty stiff, usually per person but occasionally per boat.

## Domestic flights

National carrier Olympic Airlines (set to be liquidated and reorganized by early 2009 – this is likely to affect routes and frequencies), Aegean Airlines and Sky Express operate scheduled **domestic flights**. They do usefully link islands with each other, especially from regional hubs like Rhodes, Iráklio and Corfu, though most routes are to and from Athens or Thessaloníki. Aegean often (but not always) undercuts Olympic fare-wise, and surpasses it service-wise, though flight frequencies are sparse; Sky Express is newer (established 2007), pricey and restricted to various routes between Iráklio (Crete) and nearby islands. Aegean publish **schedule booklets** twice yearly (spring and autumn); they are easiest obtained from major airport counters and the odd travel agency. Sky Express schedules can be picked up from their airport offices.

All three airlines are primarily geared to web-based **e-ticket sales**; Olympic has closed all of its town-centre sales offices, except for Athens, Thessaloníki and possibly Iráklion, while Aegean and Sky Express never had many to begin with. Tickets bought through the airline's call centres, airport counters or through travel agencies attract hefty commission. **Fares** to/between the islands, including taxes, cost at least double the deck-class ferry fare to your destination – ticket prices are tiered, with the cheapest economy seats going quickly; those leaving it too late will have only business class at hundreds of euros – one way. On inter-island routes poorly served by boat (Rhodes–Sámos or Corfu–Kefalloniá, for example), consider flights time well bought, and indeed these subsidized peripheral routes cost less than the corresponding hydrofoil journey. The cheapest web fares on both Aegean and Olympic are non-changeable and non-refundable; with more flexible tickets you can **change** your flight date, space permitting, for a fee up to 24 hours before your original departure.

Island flights are almost always full in peak season; if they're an essential part of your plans, make **reservations** at least a month in advance – two wouldn't hurt. If a flight you want is full, **waiting lists** exist – and are worth signing on to; there are almost always one or two no-shows. Olympic flights are prone to **cancellation** especially in very bad weather, since many of their services use small 46- or 74-seat ATR turbo-prop planes or "Dash 8" (De Havilland) 37-seaters, which won't fly in strong winds or (depending on the destination airport) after dark; Aegean uses more robust Avro or Airbus jets, Sky Express BAe Jetstream ones. The 15-kilo baggage **weight limit** can be strictly enforced (on Sky Express's tiny planes it's 12 kilos); if, however, you've just arrived from overseas, you're allowed the standard international limit (20–23 kilos) on Olympic or Aegean.

Additionally, AirSea Lines operate **hydroplanes** between Pátra, Ioánnina, Corfu and all intervening Ionian islands except Zákynthos, as well as between Corfu and Brindisi (Italy). Frequencies are nearly daily, though because of small craft size tickets are expensive.

## Contacts for Greek domestic airlines

**Aegean** Countrywide ☎ 801 11 20 000, ⓦ www
.aegeanair.com.
**Olympic Airlines/Aviation** Countrywide ☎ 801
11 44 444, ⓦ www.olympicairlines.com.
**Sky Express** ☎ 2810 223 500, ⓦ www
.skyexpress.gr.
**AirSea Lines** Countrywide ☎ 801 11 800 600,
ⓦ www.airsealines.com

## Island ground transport

Most islands have some kind of bus service,
but many visitors prefer to rent a two- or
four-wheeler. Even if you just do this for a
day, you can get the measure of a small or
medium-sized island and work out where
you'd like to be based.

### Buses

Bus services on the **major routes** are efficient
and frequent. On **secondary roads** they're
less regular, with long gaps, but even the
remotest villages will be connected a couple
of days weekly by bus to the island (or in
Crete, provincial) capital. These often depart
shortly before dawn, returning to the village
between 1.30 and 3pm. On islands there are
usually, but not always, buses to connect the
port and main town (if different) for ferry
arrivals or departures. The network is nationally run by a single syndicate known as the
**KTEL** (*Kratikó Tamío Ellinikón Leoforíon*).
However, in larger island towns like Mytilíni,
Iráklio and Híos there may be more than one
terminal for services in different directions.

Traditional two-toned cream-and-green
**buses** are slowly being replaced by hi-tech
navy-and-green models. They are amazingly
**prompt** as a rule, so be there in time for
scheduled departures. For major intercity
lines such as Iráklio–Haniá, **ticketing** is
computerized, with assigned seating, and
such buses often get fully booked. On
secondary island routes, it's generally first-
come, first-served, with some standing
allowed, and tickets dispensed on the spot
by an *ispráktoros* or conductor.

### Motorcycles, scooters and bicycles

The cult of the **motorcycle** is highly
developed in Greece, presided over by a
jealous deity apparently requiring regular
human sacrifice; accidents among both
foreign and local bikers are routine occur-
rences, with multiple annual fatalities on the
busier islands. But with caution and common
sense – and an eye to increasingly enforced
regulations – riding a two-wheeler across an
island should be a lot safer than piloting one
through London or New York.

In most cases **accidents** are due to
unskilled manoeuvres on rutted dirt tracks,
attempts to cut corners – in all senses – or
by riding two to an underpowered,
overloaded scooter. Don't be tempted by
this apparent economy – you won't regret
getting two separate automatic scooters, or
one powerful manual bike to share – and
remember that you're likely to be charged
exorbitantly for repairs if you do have a
wipeout. Also, verify that your travel
insurance covers motorcycle accidents.

One worthwhile precaution is a **crash
helmet** (*krános*); many rental outfits will offer
you (an often ill-fitting) one, and some will
make you sign a waiver of liability if you
refuse it. Helmet-wearing is in fact required
by law, with a €185 fine levied for failure to
do so; on some smaller islands the rule is
laxly enforced, on others random police
roadblocks do a brisk commerce in citations,
and foreign riders are most definitely not
exempt.

Reputable establishments demand a full
**motorcycle driving licence** – not a car one
(Class B) for any engine over 80cc (Greek
law actually stipulates "over 50cc"), and you
will usually have to leave your passport as
security. Failure to carry the correct licence
on your person also attracts a stiff fine,
though some agencies demand this rather
than a passport as security.

**Fines** must be paid within ten calendar
days at a post office; proof of payment
should then be taken to the police station to
have the citation cancelled. Non-payment
will mean a court date being set, and the
Greek authorities – so dilatory in other
respects – are amazingly efficient at trans-
lating summons into foreign languages and
serving them at your overseas home
address. No-shows are automatically
convicted, and a conviction will make re-
entry to Greece awkward.

Small **motor scooters** with automatic transmission, known in Greek as *papákia* (little ducks) after their characteristic noise, are good transport for all but the hilliest terrain. They're available for rent on most islands for €10–22 per day. Prices can be bargained down out of peak season, or for a longer period of rental.

Before riding off, be sure to check the bike's **mechanical state**. Bad brakes, non-functioning electrics and worn or oil-fouled spark plugs are the most common defects; dealers often keep the front brakes far too loose, with the commendable intention of preventing you going over the handlebars. If you break down, you're responsible for returning the machine; better outlets offer a free retrieval service.

**Scooters**, generally Honda, Piaggio, Vespa, Kymco or Peugeot brand, are practical enough, but thirsty on fuel; make sure there's a kick-start as a backup, since ignition switches often fail. Bungee cords (a *khtapódi*, or "octopus", in slang) for tying down bundles are supplied on request, while under-seat storage compartments or capacious baskets are often provided. Trendy, low-slung models with fat, small-radius tyres, however, are unstable on anything other than the smoothest, flattest island asphalt. Especially if you intend to go off-road, always choose more traditionally designed bikes with large-radius, nobbly, narrow tyres, if available; the Kymco People model is among the most stable. If you're going to spend your vacation astride a scooter, consider bringing or buying cyclists' or motorcyclists' **gloves**; they may look stupid during summer, but if you lose all the skin off your hands when you go for a spill, the wounds take months to heal, and leave huge scars.

True **motorbikes** with manual transmissions (*mihanákia*) and safer tyres (as described on above) shift gears with an easy-to-learn left-foot pedal action, and can be push-started in second gear if the starting crank fails. For two riders, the least powerful safe models, at nominal extra cost, are the Honda Cub 90 or Yamaha 80 Townmate. Better is the attractive Honda Astrea 100 and its rival-brand clones (eg Kawasaki Kaze, Lifan), very powerful but scarcely bigger than older models. With the proper licence and off-road experience, **dirt bikes** of 125cc and up are available in many resorts. **Quads** – basically modified tractors – are increasingly offered, and while fine for short jaunts off-road, are impractical for road use, seldom have any storage or carrying capacity, and are very unstable on turns (thus helmets supplied). **Mokes** or **dune buggies** – looking like the offspring of a hot-rod and a playground jungle-gym – are also common and equally impractical despite a ramshackle charm.

**Cycling** in the Greek Islands is not as hard going as you might imagine (except in summer), especially on one of the mountain bikes that are now the rule at island rental outfits; they rarely cost more than €9 a day. You do, however, need steady nerves, as roads are generally narrow with no verges or bike lanes (except on Kós and Lefkádha); many Greek drivers consider cyclists a lower form of life, on a par with the snakes regularly found run over.

If you have your own mountain or touring bike (the latter not rentable in Greece), consider taking it along by **plane** (it's free if within your 20–23kg international air allowance, but always arrange it in writing with the airline beforehand to avoid huge charges at check-in). Once in Greece you should be able to take a bike for free on most ferries, and in the luggage bays of buses. Any small spare parts you might need, however, are best brought along, since specialist bike shops are only found in the main island towns.

## Driving and car rental

Automobiles have obvious advantages for reaching the more inaccessible corners of various islands, and the price of **rented vehicles** seems to have dipped slightly in recent seasons. If you intend to **drive your own vehicle** to Greece, remember that insurance contracted in any EU state is valid in any other, but in many cases this is only third-party cover – the legal minimum. Competition in the industry is intense, however, so many UK insurers will throw in full, pan-European cover for free or for a nominal sum, for up to sixty days; shop around if necessary.

EU citizens bringing their own cars are, in theory, free to circulate in the country for six months, or until their home-based road tax or insurance expires, whichever happens first; see remarks on p.70 about keeping a car in Greece for longer. Other nationalities will get a **non-EU car** entered in their passport; the carnet normally allows you to keep a vehicle in Greece for up to six months, exempt from road tax.

## Car rental

High season **car rental** will set you back €220–260 a week at walk-in "rack rates" for the smallest, A-group vehicle from a one-off outlet or local chain, including unlimited mileage, tax and insurance. Outside peak season, at smaller local outfits, you can often get terms of €22–27 per day, all inclusive, with even better rates for three days or more – or prebooked on the web. **Comparison shopping** on the spot (or online) can yield variation in quotes of up to twenty percent for the same conditions over a four-to-seven-day period. Open-top **jeeps** begin at about €50 per day, rising to €80 at busy times and places.

Brochure prices in Greece almost never include VAT at 19 percent, **collision damage waiver** (CDW) and personal insurance. The CDW typically has a deductible of €400–600, some or all of which can be levied for even the tiniest scratch or missing mudguard. To avoid this, it is strongly recommended that you pay the €5–7 extra per day for Super Collision Damage Waiver, Franchise Waiver or Liability Waiver Surcharge, as it is variously called. Even better, frequent travellers should take out **annual excess insurance** through Insurance 4 Car Hire (⊛www .insurance4carhire.com), which will cover all UK- and North America-based drivers – the authors have claimed successfully on various occasions.

Most agencies will require a blank credit card slip as a **deposit** (destroyed when you return the vehicle safely); minimum age requirements vary from 21 to 23. **Driving licences** issued by any EEA state are honoured, but an International Driving Permit (IDP) is required by all other drivers, including Australians, New Zealanders and North Americans. This must be arranged before departure in your home country. Some unscrupulous agencies still rent to these nationals on production of just a home licence, but you can be arrested and charged if caught by the traffic police without an IDP if you require one.

In peak season, you may get a better price through an **overseas booking company** that deals with local firms than if you negotiate for rental in Greece itself. One of the most competitive companies in Britain is Skycars (☎0870 789 7789, ⊛www.skycars .com); a good international online booking agent is ⊛www.rentalcargroup.com. Alternatively, **web searches** (Google "(name of island) car hire") can be very productive. Autorent, Antena, Auto Union, Budget, Payless, Kosmos, National/Alamo, Reliable, Tomaso and Eurodollar are dependable Greek, or smaller international, chains with branches on many islands; most are cheaper than big international operators like Hertz, Sixt or Avis. Specific local recommendations are given in the guide.

In terms of **models**, reputable companies tend to offer the Citroën Saxo, Kia Pikanto, Daewoo Matiz or Fiat Cinquecento/ Seisento/Panda as A-group cars, and Opel (Vauxhall) Corsa 1.2, Fiat Uno/Punto, Peugeot 106, Hyundai Atos/Getz, Renault Clio/Twingo or Nissan Micra in the B group. Any more than two adults, with luggage, will require B category, in which the Atos and the Clio are most robust. In the C or D categories, suitable for two adults and two kids, Renault Mégane or Peugeot 307 are preferable to the Seat Cordoba/Ibiza. The standard four-wheel-drive options are Suzuki open-top jeep (1.3- or 1.6-litre) – great for bashing down steep, rutted tracks to remote beaches.

## Driving in Greece

As in all of continental Europe, you **drive on the right** in Greece. The country has one of the highest (fatal) **accident rates** in Europe, and on the larger tourist islands it's obvious why. Local driving habits can be atrocious; overtaking is erratic, tailgating and jumping stop-signs are preferred pastimes, lane lines go unheeded, turn signals go unused and motorbikes hog the road or weave from side to side. **Drunk driving** is also a major issue; Sunday afternoons in rural areas are particularly bad, and similarly you should be extra vigilant driving late at night at weekends or on holidays. Well-publicized police breathalyzing campaigns are confronting the problem – the legal limit of .025 mcgm blood alcohol is half of that in most countries – with radar guns being deployed against speeders as well.

Matters are made worse by poor **road conditions**: signposting is absent, tree-hidden or badly placed, pavement markings are faded, curves are invariably banked the wrong way and are slick with olive-blossom drop in May, asphalt can turn into a one-lane surface or a dirt track without warning on minor routes, and you're heavily dependent on magnifying mirrors at blind intersections in congested villages. Uphill drivers demand their **right of way**, as do those first to approach a one-lane bridge; **flashed headlights** usually mean the opposite of what they do in the UK or North America, here signifying that the other driver insists on coming through or overtaking. (However, this gesture rapidly repeated from someone approaching means they're warning you of a police control-point ahead.) **Parking** in the biggest island centres is uniformly a nightmare owing to oversubscription. **Pay-and-display** systems (plus residents-only schemes) as in the UK are the rule, and it's not always clear where to obtain tickets (sometimes from a kiosk, sometimes from a machine).

There are a limited number of **express highways** (toll free) on larger islands like Crete, Rhodes and Kós. On Crete especially they're nearly twice as quick as the old roads, and good for novices to Greek conditions. But even here there may be no proper far-right lane for slower traffic, which is expected to straddle the solid white line at the verge and allow speeders to pass.

Seatbelt use is compulsory – you may be fined €175 for non-observance at checkpoints – as is keeping a first-aid kit in the boot (many rental companies skimp on this), and children under the age of 10 are not allowed to sit in the front seats. It's illegal to drive away from any kind of **accident** – or to move the vehicles before the police

appear – and where serious injury has resulted to the other party you can be held at a police station for up to 24 hours. For any substantial property damage, you wait for the police to arrive; they will take down the details of (and probably breathalyze) all drivers, help you (if necessary) fill out the accident report (*filikí dhílosi*, completed by both parties), give a copy to everyone for insurance purposes (or forward one to the rental company if your car is rented), and finally give you permission to leave if the car hasn't been crippled. Though forensics aren't their long suit, they're generally more civil and calm than the Greek drivers actually involved in the accident.

Tourists with proof of AA/RAC/AAA membership are given free road assistance from ELPA, the Greek equivalent, which runs **breakdown services** on several of the larger islands; in an emergency ring ☏10400. Many car rental companies have an agreement with ELPA's equally widespread competitors Hellas Service (☏1057), Interamerican (☏1168) and Express Service (☏1154). However, you will get a faster response if you dial the local number for the province or island you're in (ask for these in advance).

**Fuel** comes as 95-octane unleaded (*amólyvdhi*), 100-octane super or diesel; historically costs have been lower than in France or Italy, but a bit more than in Spain. Lead-replacement fuel for older cars without catalytic converters is called "Super LRP". Most scooters and motorbikes run better on Super LRP, even if they nominally take unleaded.

It's possible to run short of fuel after dark or at weekends anywhere in Greece; most stations close at 7 or 8pm, and nearly as many are shut all day Sunday. This isn't an issue along major highways, but it is a factor everywhere else. One pump per district will always remain open, but interpreting the Greek-only pharmacy-type-rota lists posted at shut stations is another matter. Stations which claim to be open **around the clock** are in fact automated-only at night – you have to use bill-taking machines, which don't give change. If you fill your tank without having exhausted your credit, punch the button for a receipt and get change later during attended hours. Petrol stations run by multinational companies usually take **credit cards**; Greek chains like Aegean, Eko, Elda, Eteka, Jetoil, Revoil and Elinoil tend not to, except in tourist areas or along main highways. Occasionally the cheapest stations may add a two percent surcharge to card transactions.

## Taxis

Greek **taxis** are among the cheapest in the Mediterranean – so long as you get an honest driver who switches the meter on and doesn't use devices to doctor the reading. Many taxis – particularly honest ones – will now generate automated receipts. Use of a meter is mandatory within city or town limits, where Tariff 1 (€0.34/km) applies, while in rural areas or between midnight and 5am the higher Tariff 2 (€0.64) is in effect. On certain islands, set rates apply on specific fixed routes – these taxis might only depart when full. Otherwise, throughout Greece the meter starts at €1, though the minimum **fare** is €2.85 (€2.65 in Athens); baggage in the boot is charged at €0.32 per piece. Additionally, there are surcharges of €2.15 for leaving or entering an airport (€3.20 for Athens, €2.65 for Thessaloníki), and €0.86 for leaving/entering a harbour area. If you summon a taxi by phone on spec, there's a €1.60 fee, while a prearranged rendezvous is €2.65 extra; the meter starts running from the moment the driver begins heading towards you. All such supplemental charges must be set out on a laminated card affixed to the dashboard. For a week or so before and after Orthodox Easter, and Christmas, a *filodhórima* or gratuity of about ten percent is also levied. Any or all of these extras will legitimately bump up the basic rate of €0.64 per rural kilometre.

# Accommodation

There are huge numbers of beds for tourists throughout the Greek islands, so most of the season you can rely on turning up pretty much anywhere and finding a room – if not in a hotel, then in a private house or, more typically, a block of rooms. Only from late July to early September, and around Easter, the country's high season, are you likely to experience problems. At these times, if you don't have accommodation reserved well in advance, you'd be wise to keep well off the main tourist hotspots, turning up at each new place early in the day and taking whatever is available – you may be able to exchange it for something better later on.

**Out of season**, you face a slightly different problem: most private rooms and campsites operate only from late April or early May to October, leaving hotels as your only option. During winter you may have no choice but to stay in the island capital or main port. There will often be very little life outside these places anyway, with all the seasonal beach bars and restaurants closed. On many smaller islands, you will often find just one hotel – and perhaps one taverna – staying open year-round. Be warned also that any resort or harbour hotels which do operate through the winter are likely to have a certain number of **prostitutes** as long-term guests; licensed prostitution is legal in Greece, and the management at many places consider this the most painless way to keep the bills paid.

## Hotels

**Hotels** and self-catering complexes in the larger resorts are often contracted out on a seasonal basis by foreign package-holiday companies, though there are often vacancies available (especially in spring or autumn) for walk-in trade. The tourist police set official **categories** for hotels, which range from L (Luxury), then A down to the rarely encountered E class; all except the top category have to keep within set price limits. The letter system is being slowly replaced with a star grading system; L is five-star, E is no-star, etc. Letter ratings were supposed to correspond to **facilities** available, though in practice there are D-class hotels which are smarter than nearby C-class outfits.

In terms of **food**, C-class hotels are only required to provide the most rudimentary of continental breakfasts – often optional for an extra charge – while B-class and above will usually offer some sort of buffet breakfast including cheese, cold cuts, sausages, eggs and so on. Only the really top places provide full cooked breakfasts.

## Private rooms

The most common island accommodation is **privately let rooms** (*dhomátia*): many newer ones are studios (*garsoniéra*) or apartments (*dhiamérismata*), with at least a rudimentary kitchenette (sink, fridge and heating rings). Like hotels, these are regulated and officially divided into three classes (A to C), according to facilities. The bulk of them are in newer, purpose-built blocks, but a few are still inside people's houses, where you may be treated to disarming hospitality.

Licensed rooms are mostly kept very clean, however limited their other amenities. Many are modern, fully furnished places with en-suite bathroom, TV, air-conditioning (sometimes at an extra charge) and a fridge. There may be a choice of rooms at various prices – owners usually show you the most expensive first. Price and quality are not necessarily directly linked, so always see a room before agreeing to take it.

Areas to **look for rooms**, along with recommendations of the best places, are included in the guide. However, the rooms may find you: owners descend on ferry or bus arrivals to fill any space they have, sometimes waving photos of the premises. Many island municipalities are acting to outlaw this practice, owing to widespread bait-and-switch tactics and the pitching of unlicensed rooms. Rooms can also be a longer journey from the initial meeting than you had expected. In smaller places you'll often see rooms advertised, sometimes in German (*Zimmer*); the Greek signs to look out for are "ENIKIAZÓMENA DHOMÁTIA" or "ENIKIÁZONTEH DHOMÁTIA". In the more developed island resorts, where package holiday-makers predominate, *dhomátia* owners will often require you to stay for at least three days, or even a week.

It has become standard practice for rooms' proprietors, like hotel staff, to ask to keep your **passport** – ostensibly for the tourist police, who require customer particulars – but in reality to prevent you skipping out with an unpaid bill. Some owners may be satisfied with just taking down your details, as is done in most hotels, and they'll almost always return the documents once you get to know them, or if you need them for another purpose.

If you are **stranded**, or arrive very late in a remote village, you may very well find that there is someone with an unlicensed room prepared to earn extra money by putting you up. This should not be counted on, but things work out more often than not.

By law, **prices** and supplements in any establishment should be displayed on the back of the door of your room, or over the reception desk. If you feel you're being overcharged at a place that is officially registered, threaten to report it to the tourist office or police, who will generally take your side in such cases – it's an offence to charge over the permitted price for the **current season**. Small amounts over the posted price may be legitimately explained by municipal tax or out-of-date forms, but usually you will pay less than the maximum. Depending on location, there are often three seasons: typically October to May (low), June to mid-July, and September (mid) and mid-July through August (high). In **winter**, officially from November 1 until early April, private rooms – except in Ródhos Old Town and the biggest towns of Crete – are mostly closed to keep the few open hotels in business.

Even if an establishment has a website and/or email, some proprietors only check their messages at infrequent intervals, if at

## Accommodation price codes

Throughout the book accommodation is categorized according to the following **price codes**, which denote the **cheapest available double room in high season**. Prices are for the room only, except where otherwise indicated. Many hotels, especially those in category ❹ and over, include breakfast in the price; we indicate this by including "B&B" in the listing, but check when booking. During low season, rates can drop by more than fifty percent, especially for stays of three or more nights – exceptions are during the Christmas and Greek Easter weeks. Single rooms, if available, cost around seventy percent of the price of a double.

Old-fashioned rooms in remoter places, sometimes with a shared bathroom, tend to fall into the ❶ price category. Basic en-suite rooms without cooking facilities weigh in at ❷; newer, well-equipped rooms, self-catering studios, and modest C-class hotels occupy the top end of the ❸ niche, the better ones edging into ❹. Category ❺ corresponds to the better-value B-class hotels and the humbler designer inns in trendier centres, while ❻ tallies with most of B-class and the state-of-the-art restoration projects. ❼–❽ means A- and L-class, and the sky's the limit here – €500 is by no means unheard of these days.

| | | | |
|---|---|---|---|
| ❶ €30 and under | ❸ €41–60 | ❺ €86–110 | ❼ €151–200 |
| ❷ €31–40 | ❹ €61–85 | ❻ €111–150 | ❽ €201 and over |

**Youth hostels** typically charge €8–12 for a dorm bed.

all, and **phoning** may be essential for advance booking.

### Villas and long-term rentals

The easiest – and usually most economical – way to arrange **villa rental** is through one of the package-holiday companies detailed on p.32. They represent some superb places, from fairly simple to luxurious and costs can be very reasonable, especially if shared between a few people. Several of the companies will arrange **twin-centre** stays on two islands over two weeks.

On the islands, a few local travel agents arrange villa rentals, though they are often places the overseas companies gave a miss on or could not fill. **Out of season**, you can sometimes get a good deal on villa or apartment rental for a month or more by asking around locally, though in these days of EU convergence and the increasing desirability of the islands as year-round residences, "good deal" means anything under €400 per month for a large studio (*garsoniéra*) or €600 for a small one-bedroom flat.

### Youth hostels

Greece has few **youth hostels**, and they tend, with a few exceptions, to be pretty run-down. Competition from inexpensive rooms and unofficial "student hostels", open to all, means they are simply not as cost-effective as elsewhere in Europe. It's best to have a valid IYHF card, but you can often buy one on the spot, or just pay a little extra for your bed. Extra payment for sheets and towels can bump up the price. Dorms tend to have four to six beds; most hostels have a curfew of 11pm or midnight, and many places only open in spring and summer. The only surviving hostels on the islands are on Thíra, Corfu, Rhodes and Crete. Few of these are officially recognized by the IYHF.

### Camping

**Officially recognized campsites** range from ramshackle compounds to highly organized and rather soulless complexes. Most places cost about €5–7 a night per person, slightly less per tent and €6–8 per camper van, but at the fanciest sites, rates for two people plus a tent can almost equal the price of a basic room. The Panhellenic Camping Association publishes a booklet covering most officially recognized Greek campsites and the facilities they offer; it's available from many EOT offices.

**Freelance camping**, as EOT calls it, was forbidden under a law originally enacted to harass gypsies, but regulations are increasingly enforced against tourists. Another drawback is the increased prevalence of theft in rural areas – we've noted risky places in the text. You'll need at least a light sleeping bag, since even summer nights can get cool; a foam pad is recommended for pitching on harder ground and will also keep you warmer.

If you do camp rough, exercise sensitivity and discretion. Police will crack down on people camping (and especially littering) around popular tourist beaches, particularly when a large community of campers develops. Off the beaten track, however, nobody is very bothered, though it is always best to ask permission locally in the village taverna or café. During high season, when everything – even the authorized campsites – may be full, attitudes are more relaxed, even in the more touristy places. At such times the best strategy is to find a sympathetic taverna, which in exchange for regular patronage will probably guard small valuables and let you use their facilities.

# Food and drink

Despite depressed wages and an economic crunch, most Greeks still socialize outside their homes regularly, sharing a meal with friends or family perhaps once a week. The atmosphere is always relaxed and informal, with pretensions rare outside of certain major resorts. Drinking is traditionally meant to accompany food, though a range of bars and clubs exists.

## Breakfast

Greeks don't generally eat **breakfast**, something reflected in the abysmal quality of most hotel "continental" offerings; the choice of juice tends to be orange and orange, with fresh fruit rare and processed cheese/mortadella the rule at any place below "B" category – make that "A" category in low season, when skimping on ingredients is prevalent. *Méli me voútyro* is syrupy, commercial honey and prepacked pats of butter (or margarine) to slather on bread or *friganiés* (slivers of dry toast). Confusingly, jam is called *marmeládha* in Greek; proper marmalade is rare. Tea means obscure Sri Lankan brands of bag, often left to stew in a metal pot. The only egg-and-bacon kinds of places are in resorts where foreigners congregate, or where there are returned North American- or Australian-Greeks. Such outlets can sometimes be good value (€5.50–8 for the works, including coffee), especially if there's competition.

## Picnics and snacks

**Picnic fare** is easily available at bakeries and *manávika* (fruit-and-veg stalls). **Bread**, alas, is often of minimal nutritional value and inedible within a day of purchase. It's worth paying extra at the bakery (*foúrnos* or *psomádhiko*) for *olikís* (wholemeal), *sikalísio* (rye bread), or *oktásporo* (multi-grain), the latter most commonly baked where large numbers of Germans or Scandinavians are about. When buying **olives**, look out for fat Kalamáta or Ámfissa ones – more expensive, but tastier. However, locally gathered olives – especially the slightly shrivelled *throúmbes* or fully ripened, ground-gathered *hamádhes* – often have a distinctive nutty taste, compensating for large kernels. The best **honey** comes from the less forested islands (such as Límnos, Náxos, Kálymnos, Foúrni and Astypálea) or areas of the mainland. There's no enforced quality control, however, and adulteration scams abound; much that is touted as

51

thyme (*thymarísio*) honey isn't. Always taste if possible – buy a small jar if not.

Honey is the ideal topping for the famous local **yoghurt**. All larger towns have at least one dairy shop where locally produced yoghurts are sold in plastic or (better) clay containers of various sizes. Sheep's-milk yoghurt (*próvio*) is richer and sweeter, scarcely requiring honey; cow's-milk yoghurt is tarter but more widely available. **Feta** cheese is ubiquitous, often with a dozen varieties to choose from, made from goat-, sheep- or cow-milk, or varying proportions thereof. You're allowed to taste before buying; this sampling advice goes for other indigenous cheeses as well, the most palatable of which are the expensive gruyère-type *graviéra*.

Despite EU membership and increasingly exotic tastes, Greece imports very little produce from abroad, aside from bananas, the odd pineapple and a few mangoes. **Fruit** in particular is relatively expensive and usually available only by season, though in more cosmopolitan spots one can find such things as avocados (the light-green Fuerte variety from Crete is excellent) for much of the year. Reliable picnic fruits include several types of cherries (June–July); nectarines and *yiarmádhes*, a giant peach available from August to mid-September (after which they go mealy and should be avoided); *krystália*, small, warty but heavenly green pears that ripen a month or two later; *vaniliés*, orange- or red-fleshed plums (July through early Oct); and the white-fleshed *himoniátiko* melon (called casaba in North America; Sept–Nov), in a yellow, puckered skin with green flecks. Greece also has a burgeoning kiwi industry, and while the first crop in October coincides with the end of the tourist season, availability continues into the following May. Figs are succulent but less portable; there's a crop of larger, relatively bland fruits in May and June, followed by smaller, honey-sweet ones in August and September. Equally delicate are lusciously ripe (often overripe) strawberries from April through June. Salad **vegetables** are more reasonably priced; besides the famous, enormous tomatoes (June to early Oct), there's a bewildering variety of cool-season greens, including rocket, dill, enormous spring onions and lettuces.

Useful expressions for shopping are *éna tétarto* (250g) and *misó kiló* (500g).

Traditional **snacks** can be another culinary delight, though they are being elbowed aside by Western fast food – somewhat less insipid for being home-grown – at nationwide chains such as *Goody's* (burgers, pasta and salad bar), *Everest* and *Grigoris Mikroyevmata* (assorted turnovers, baguette sandwiches), *Theios Vanias* (baked pastries) and *Roma Pizza*. However, independently produced kebabs (*souvlákia*) are widely available, and in most larger centres you'll find *yíros* – doner kebab with garnish in *píta* bread. Other common snacks include *tyrópites* (cheese pies; the best, if available, are the spiral *striftés* or smooth *kouroú*) and *spanokópites* (spinach pies), found at the baker's, as can *voutímata* (dark biscuits with molasses, cinnamon and butter). Pizza can be very good as well, sold *al metro* (by the piece).

## Restaurants

Greek cuisine and **restaurants** are usually simple and straightforward; despite hard times most people still do it regularly, and with care it remains affordable – typically €12–17 per person for a substantial (non-seafood) meal with a measure of house wine. But even if preparation is basic, raw materials should be wholesome – Greeks are fussy about freshness and provenance, shunning pre-fried chips, Moroccan sardines and frozen New Zealand chops. That said, there's a lot of **lazy cooking** in resorts, where menus are dominated by fake pizza, spaghetti bolognese, chops and "tourist moussaká": a dish stuffed with cheap potato slices, and nary a crumb of mince. There are, moreover, growing numbers of **"koultour-iárika"** restaurants, often pretentious attempts at Greek nouvelle cuisine with speciality wine lists, which tend to be long on airs and graces, and (at €25–40 a head) short on value. The exceptions which succeed have been singled out in the text.

In the absence of recommendations, the best strategy is to **go where Greeks go**. And, despite EU regulations increasingly limiting staff hours, they go late: 2–3.30pm for **lunch**, 9.30–11pm (10pm–midnight Fri/Sat) for **supper**. You can eat earlier, but you'll probably get indifferent service and doctored cuisine if you frequent establishments catering to the tourist schedule. One good omen is the waiter bringing a carafe of refrigerated water, unbidden, rather than pushing you to order bottled stuff.

**Waiters** often urge you to order more than you want, then bring things you haven't asked for. Although cash-register receipts are required in all establishments, these are often only for the grand total, and itemized **bills** will be in Greek script. With falling visitor numbers at many popular destinations, bill-padding has become common, as a few unwarranted euros extra per party adds up over time; even without reading Greek, ensure that the number and cost of items tally with what you ordered. Though menu prices are supposedly inclusive of all taxes and service, a small extra **tip** of 5–10 percent directly to the waiter is in order if they've done well.

**Bread** is generally assessed as part of the "cover" charge (€0.50–1.20 per person), so you have to pay for it even if (as so often) it's barely edible; good bread is so remarkable as to warrant mention in the restaurant accounts. **Children** are always welcome, day or night, at family tavernas, and are quickly socialized into the Greek routine of late hours; kids are expected to be kids – playing tag around the tables – but are not allowed to cramp adults' style.

## Estiatória

The two basic types of restaurant are the **estiatório** and the taverna. Distinctions are slight, though *estiatória* (plural) are more commonly found in large towns and tend to have the more complicated, oven-baked casserole dishes termed **mayireftá** (literally, "cooked"). With their long hours, old-fashioned-tradesmen's clientele and tiny profit margins, *estiatória* (sometimes known as *inomayiría*, "wine-and-cook-houses") are, alas, a vanishing breed. An *estiatório* will generally feature a variety of *mayireftá* such as moussakas, macaroni pie, meat or game stews, stuffed tomatoes or peppers, the oily vegetable casseroles called *ladherá*, and oven-baked meat and fish. Usually you point at the desired steam trays to choose these dishes.

Batches are cooked in the morning and then left to stand, which is why *mayireftá*

food is often **lukewarm**. Greeks don't mind this (many actually believe that hot food is bad for you), and most such dishes are enhanced by being allowed to steep in their own juice. **Desserts** (*epidhórpia* in formal Greek) of the pudding-and-pie variety don't exist at *estiatória*, though yoghurt is occasionally served. **Fruit**, however, is always available in season; watermelon (often on the house), melon and grapes are the summer standards. Autumn treats worth asking after include *kydhóni stó foúrno*, or *mílo psitó*, baked quince or apple with honey, cinnamon, or nut topping. Sometimes you may be offered a complementary slice of sweet semolina halva (*simigdhalísios halvás*).

## Tavernas and psistariés

**Tavernas** range from the glitzy and fashionable to rough-and-ready ones with seating under a reed canopy, behind a beach. Really primitive ones have a very limited (often unwritten) menu, but the more elaborate will offer some of the main *mayireftá* dishes mentioned above, as well as standard taverna fare. This essentially means **mezédhes** (hors d'oeuvres) or **orektiká** (appetizers) and **tís óras** (meat and fish, fried or grilled to order). **Psistariés** (grill-houses) serve spit-roasted lamb, pork or goat (generically termed *soúvla* or *tís soúvlas*), chicken or *kokorétsi* (grilled offal roulade). They will usually have a limited selection of *mezédhes* and salads (*salátes*), but no *mayireftá*. In rural areas, *psistariés* are often called *exohiká kéndra*.

Since the idea of **courses** is foreign to Greek cuisine, starters, main dishes and salads often arrive together unless you request otherwise. The best strategy is to order a selection of *mezédhes* and salads to share, in local fashion. Waiters encourage you to take *horiátiki saláta* – the so-called Greek **salad**, including *feta* cheese – because it is usually the most expensive. If you only want tomato and cucumber, ask for *angourodomáta*. *Láhano-karóto* (cabbage-carrot) and *maroúli* (lettuce) are the typical winter and spring salads respectively.

The most common **mezédhes** are *tzatzíki* (yoghurt, garlic and cucumber dip), *melitzanosaláta* (aubergine/eggplant dip), fried courgette/zucchini or aubergine/eggplant slices, *yígandes* (white haricot beans in vinai-grette or hot tomato sauce), *tyropitákia* or *spanakópites* (small cheese and spinach pies), *tyrokafterí* (spicy cheese dip), *revythókeftedhes* or *pittaroúdhia* (chickpea patties similar to falafel), octopus salad, *ambelofásola* (late summer runner beans) and *mavromátika* (black-eyed peas). Greeks are very fond of anything pickled in brine or vinegar, and some of the more "ethnic" tavernas will offer such **marinated delicacies** as *tsitsírava* (terebinth shoots, Sporádhes); *kápari* (wild caper greens; south Dodecanese) or *kritamo* (rock samphire), the latter mentioned in *King Lear* and offered on most of the east Aegean islands. A vitamin- and mineral-rich succulent growing by the sea, it's harvested in June or July and served pickled with fish, or (like *kápari* or *tstsírava*) to jazz up salads.

Among **meats**, *souvláki* and chops are reliable choices, often locally produced. In both cases, pork is usually better and cheaper than veal, especially as *pansétta* (spare ribs). The best *souvláki*, not always available, is lamb; more commonly encountered are rib chops called *païdhákia* (sold by the kilo or by the portion), while roast lamb (*arní psitó*) is considered *estiatório* fare. *Keftédhes* (breadcrumbed meatballs), *biftékia* (similar, but meatier) and the spicy, coarse-grain sausages called *loukánika* are cheap and good. Chicken is widely available but typically battery-farmed in Ípiros or on Évvia. Other dishes worth trying are stewed goat (*gídha vrastí*) or baked goat (*katsíki stó foúrno*) – goat in general is a wonderfully healthy meat, typically free-range and undosed with antibiotics or hormones.

## Fish and seafood

Seaside *psarotavérnes* offer **fish**, reckoned by many to be a quintessential part of a Greek holiday experience. For novices, however, ordering can be fraught with peril; see the box below, and the species list on p.677, for tips.

### Fish story

Fresh, wild **fish** is becoming increasingly rare and expensive as Aegean stocks are depleted and prices climb. Dodges used by unscrupulous taverna proprietors to get around this problem are legion: selling inferior Egyptian or Moroccan products as "local", at full price; swishing frozen specimens around in the sea to make them look more "lifelike"; and complying minimally with the legal requirement to clearly indicate when fish is **frozen** or *katapsygméno* (often only by the abbreviation "kat." "k." or just an asterisk on the Greek-language side of the menu).

Unfortunately from a tourist's point of view, the greatest variety and quantity of fish is on offer outside of summer. **Drag-net trawling** (the *tráta*) occurs between October 1 and May 31, though the season really should end April 30, as most baby fish emerge during May. A modern mechanized trawler or *anemótrata* is extremely destructive to the marine environment, indiscriminately hoovering the sea floor, with one monstrous boat having the impact of a half-dozen old-style wooden craft. During summer, lamp-lure (*pyrofáni*) and trident, stationary drift nets, "doughnut" trap (*kýrtos*) and multi-hook long line (*paragádhi*) are the only permitted methods. Fish caught during these warmer months tend to be relatively scrawny and dry, so are served with a tureen of *ladholémono* (oil and lemon juice) sauce.

Most restaurants use imported and/or frozen fish at this time, or rely on *ikhthyotrofía* (fish farms) for a supply of *tsipoúra* (gilt-head bream) and *lavráki* (sea-bass) in particular. These **fish farms**, heavily subsidized by EU grants, are a Big Thing on the smaller Dodecanese such as Agathoníssi, Sými, Hálki, Astypálea and Kálymnos, as well as on most of the east Aegean islands and certain Ionian islands, often serving as significant local employers. But quality products are not their strong point – farmed fish subsist on a diet of pellet food made from low-grade fish meal or even petroleum by-products, giving them an unmistakable muddy taste. The farms are also something of an environmental disaster, as the parasiticide chemicals used to keep them going are highly toxic.

## Vegetarians

If you are **vegetarian**, you may experience difficulty, and will often have to assemble a meal from various *mezédhes*. Even the staples of yoghurt with honey, *tzatzíki* and Greek salad begin to pall after a while, and many supposed "vegetable" dishes on menus are cooked in stock or have pieces of meat added. Wholly or largely vegetarian restaurants, however, are on the increase in touristy areas and are highlighted throughout the guide where appropriate.

Given these considerations, it's best to set your sights on **humbler**, seasonally migrating or perennially local species. The cheapest consistently available fish are *gópes* (bogue), and *marídhes* (picarel), the latter eaten head and all. In the Dodecanese, *yermanós* (same as Australian leatherback) is a good frying fish which appears in spring; a more widespread, inexpensive May–June treat is fresh, grilled or fried *bakaliáros* (hake), the classic UK fish-and-chip shop species. *Gávros* (anchovy), *atherína* (sand smelts) and *sardhélles* (sardines) are late-summer fixtures, at their best in the northeast Aegean. In the north and east Aegean, *pandelís* or *sykiós* (covina) appears in early summer, highly rated since it's a rock-dweller, not a bottom feeder – and therefore a bit pricier. *Koliós* (mackerel) is excellent either grilled or baked in sauce. Especially in autumn you may find *psaró-soupa* (fish soup) or *kakaviá* (bouillabaisse).

Less esteemed species tend to **cost** €20–38 per kilo; choicer varieties of fish, such as red mullet, *tsipoúra* (gilt-head bream), sea-bass or *fangrí* (common bream), will be expensive if wild – €44–60 per kilo, depending on what the local market will bear. If the price seems too good to be true, it's almost certainly **farmed**. Prices are usually quoted by the kilo (less often by the portion); standard procedure is to go to the glass cooler and pick your specimen, then have it weighed (uncleaned) in your presence. Overcharging, especially where a printed menu is absent, is not uncommon; have weight and price confirmed orally or on a slip of paper at the scales.

Cheaper **seafood** (*thalassiná*), such as fried baby squid (usually frozen) and octopus, is a summer staple of most seaside tavernas, and often mussels, cockles and small prawns will be offered at reasonable sums. Keep an eye out for freshness and season; *kydhónia* and a few other species (see p.677) must in fact be eaten alive for safety. The miniature "Sými" shrimps which are also caught around Rhodes, Hálki and Kastellórizo would anywhere else just be used for bait, but here are devoured avidly; when less than a day old, they're distinctly sweet-flavoured.

As typical species have become overfished, **unusual seafoods**, formerly the province of the poor, are figuring more regularly on menus. Ray or skate (variously known as *platý*, *seláhi*, *trígona* or *vátos*) can be fried or steamed and served with *skord-haliá* (garlic dip), and are even dried for decoration. Sea urchins (*ahiní*) are also a humble (but increasingly scarce) favourite, being split and emptied for the sake of their (reputedly aphrodisiac) roe, eaten raw. Special shears are sold for opening them if you don't fancy a hand full of spines.

Another peculiar delicacy, frequently available on Rhodes, Kálymnos and several nearby islands, are **foúskes** ("blisters"). These marine invertebrates (*figue de mer* in French) live on rocks at depths of 30–40m, and are gathered by sponge-divers for extra income. They're unprepossessing in the extreme – resembling hairy turds – but slice them lengthwise and your opinion will change instantly as you scoop out the liquor and savour the orange-and-yellow innards, which taste much like oysters and cost about the same. Otherwise they're commonly pickled – as *fouskóalo* – in beer-bottles of their own fluids, which tends to overpower their delicate intrinsic taste. The meaty bit of the pinna-shell mollusc – **spiníalo** or **spinióalo** – is similarly harvested, pickled and served as an *ouzomezés*.

## Wines

All eateries will offer you a choice of bottled **wines**, and many still have their own house variety, kept in barrels. This is sold in bulk by the quarter, half or full litre, and served in glass flagons or (more usually) the brightly coloured tin "monkey-cups" called *kantária*. Just ask whether they have wine *varelísio* (barrelled) or *hýma* (in bulk). Per-litre prices depend on locale and quality, ranging from €4–5 (Ikaría, Skýros) to €10–12 (Corfu, Rhodes), with smaller measures (more or less) proportionately. Non-resinated wine is almost always more than decent; if in doubt, order a bottle or can of soda water, which can render even the roughest wine drinkable when added. **Retsina** – pine-resinated wine, a slightly acquired taste – is popular, usually imported in 500ml bottles from the mainland. The brands Yeoryiadhi from Thessaloníki, Liokri from Ahaía, Malamatina from central Greece, Tsantali Asteri and and those prepared by the co-ops on Sámos and Límnos are all quaffable and likely to be more consistent in quality.

Among **bottled wines** available **nation-wide**, Cambas Attikos, Zítsa and Rhodian CAIR products (especially the Moulin and 2400 range) are good, inexpensive whites, while Boutari Naoussa and Kourtakis Apelia are decent, mid-range reds. For a better but still moderately priced red, choose the Merlot of either Boutari and Tsantali, or Averof Katoï from Epirus.

If you're travelling around **wine-producing islands**, however, you may as well sample local bottlings. Almost anything produced on Límnos is decent; Alexandrine muscat is used for whites, the local *límnio* grape for reds and rosés. Sámos is most famous for its fortified (15% alcohol) dessert wines based on the muscat grape, similar to madeira and still exported in large quantities to France for use as communion wine, but the island also has some good premium whites like the organically produced Dhryoussa, and a good **rosé** in Fokianos. Thíra, another volcanic island, has premium **white wines** such as Ktima Arghyrou and Boutari Nykhteri, and the Gentilini Robola white of Kefalloniá is justly esteemed. Páros (Moraïtis), Náxos and Ikaria (Ktima Karimali Ikariotikos or Afames) all have acceptable local vintages, while Crete now has labels superior to the bog-standard Logado, such as Economou (Sitía) and Lyrarakis (Iráklion).

On Rhodes, Alexandhris products from Émbonas are well thought of, as is the Emery label with its Villaré and Athiri Vounoplayias whites, and products of the Triandafyllou winery near Ialyssós, especially their Taxid-heftis white. In the Sporádhes, decent *hýma* or 500ml-bottle white is likely from the Dimitra Co-operative at Anhíalos, while for a step up in quality try products of the Thessalian vintner Apostolakis.

Curiously, island **red wines** are almost uniformly mediocre, except for Methymneos on Lésvos, Karimali on Ikaría and Hatziem-manouil from Kós. Worth a special mention are the *robóla* blended reds of Sámos, combining either local *rítino* or merlot grapes with muscat – a somewhat sweet but very palatable *vin de table* served in the better tavernas.

Usually, though, you're better off choosing **reds from the mainland**. Carras on Halki-dhikí does the excellent Porto Carras, while Ktima Tselepou offers a very palatable Cabernet-Merlot blend. Andonopoulou (Pátra, including an organic line), Ktima Papaïoannou Nemea (Peloponnese), and Tsantali Rapsani (Thessaly) are all superb, velvety reds – and likely to be found only in better tavernas or *káves* (bottle shops). Andonopoulou, Tselepos (Mantinía domaine), Spyropoulos (again Mantinía) and Papaïoannou also do excellent **mainland whites**, especially the Spyropoulos Orino Mantinia, sometimes organically produced.

Other **premium microwineries** on the mainland whose products have long been fashionable, in both red and white, include the vastly overrated Hatzimihali (Atalánti, central Greece), the outstanding Dhiaman-dakou (near Náoussa, red and white), Athanasiadhi (central Greece), Skouras (Argolid) and the two rival Lazaridhi vintners (Dhráma, east Macedonia), especially their superb Merlots. For any of these you can expect to pay €9–16 per bottle in a shop, double that at a taverna. The best current **guide** is Konstantinos Lazarakis' *The Wines of Greece*.

Finally, CAIR on Rhodes makes **"champagne"** ("naturally sparkling wine fermented en bouteille", says the label), in both brut and demi-sec versions. It's not Moët & Chandon quality by any means, but at about €6 retail per bottle, nobody's complaining.

## Cafés, cake shops and bars

A venerable institution, likely to survive the onslaught of mass global culture, the **kafenío** is found in every Greek town, village and hamlet. In addition, you'll come across **ouzerís**, **zaharoplastía** (Greek patisseries), **frappádhika** and **barákia**.

### Kafenía, frappádhika and coffee

The **kafenío** (plural *kafenía*) is the traditional Greek coffee house or café. Although its main business is "Greek" (Middle Eastern) coffee – prepared *skéto* or *pikró* (unsweetened), *métrio* (medium) or (*varý*) *glykó* ([very] sweet) – it also serves instant coffee, spirits such as ouzo, brandy (usually Metaxa or Botrys brand, in three grades), beer, the sage-based tea known as *alisfakiá*, soft drinks and juices. One quality fizzy soft-drink brand to single out is Vólos-based Epsa, with its Orangina-like bottles and high juice content. A refreshing curiosity – confined to Corfu and Paxí – is *tsitsibýra* (ginger beer), a legacy of the nineteenth-century British occupation of the Ionian islands; cloudy, greyish-white and fizzy, it tastes vaguely of lemon and the beginnings of fermentation.

Another refreshing drink is *kafés frappé*, iced instant coffee with or without milk and sugar – uniquely Greek despite its French name. Like Greek coffee, it is always accompanied by a glass of cold water. *Freddoccino* is a newer, cappuccino-based alternative to the traditional cold frappé. Cafés devoted to it, known as *frappádhika*, are ubiquitous in larger towns and resorts, popular with a mostly young crowd, who eke out the expensive drinks for hours and listen to Greek or international music.

"Nes"(café) has become the generic term for all instant **coffee**, regardless of brand; it's pretty vile, and since the 1990s there's been a nationwide reaction against it. Even the smallest island capital or resort will have at least one *frappádhiko* which also does a range of foreign-style coffees – filter, dubbed *fíltros* or *gallikós* (French); cappuccino; and espresso – at overseas prices. Outside of the largest towns, properly made premium coffee is harder to find – and may come from instant packets.

Like tavernas, *kafenía* and *frappádhika* range from designer-chrome and sophisticated to the old-fashioned, spit-on-the-floor or mock-retro variety, with marble or brightly painted metal tables and straw-bottomed chairs. *Kafenía* still form the pivot of life in remoter villages, and many men spend most of their waking hours there, especially in winter. Greek women are rarely seen in more traditional *kafenía*; even in holiday resorts, there is invariably one coffee house that the local men have reserved for themselves.

Some *kafenía* close at siesta time, but many remain open from early in the morning until late at night. The chief summer socializing time is 6–8pm, immediately after the afternoon nap, when one takes a pre-dinner ouzo.

### Ouzo, tsípouro, mezédhes, ouzerís and mezedhopolía

**Ouzo**, *tsípouro* (Thássos and the Sporades) and *tsikoudhiá* (Crete) are simple spirits of up to 48 percent alcohol, distilled from the grape-mash residue of wine-making, and then usually flavoured with anise, cinnamon, pear essence or fennel. There are nearly thirty brands, with the best reckoned to be from Lésvos and Sámos islands, or Zítsa and Týrnavos on the mainland.

You will be served two glasses: one with the ouzo, and one full of water to be tipped into your ouzo just until it turns a milky white. You can drink it straight, but the strong, burning taste is hardly refreshing. It is also usual to add **ice cubes**, a bowl of which will be provided upon request. The next measure up from a glass is a *karafáki* – a deceptively small 200-millilitre vial, and the favourite means of delivery for *tsípouro*. A much smoother, unflavoured variant of ouzo is **soúma**, found chiefly on Rhodes and Sámos. The smoothness is misleading – as with *tsípouro*, two or three glasses of it and you had better not have any other plans for the afternoon.

Formerly every glass of ouzo was accompanied by a small plate of **mezédhes** on the house: bits of cheese, cucumber, tomato, a few olives, sometimes octopus or even a couple of small fish. Nowadays such an "ouzomezés" is a separate, more expensive option. They are often not listed on any formal menu, but if you order a karafáki you will automatically be offered a small selection of snacks.

One kind of establishment, found in the better resorts and select neighbourhoods of the larger islands, specializes in ouzo and mezédhes. These are called **ouzerí** (same in the Greek plural, but we've added 's' through the guide) or **tsipourádhika** (plural) wherever vacationers from the north mainland congregate. In some towns you also come across mezedhopolía, a bigger, more elaborate kind of ouzerí. Ouzerís and mezedhopolía are well worth trying for the marvellous variety of mezédhes they serve (though some mediocre tavernas have counterfeited the name). At the genuine article, several plates of mezédhes plus drinks will effectively substitute for a more involved meal at a taverna (though it works out more expensive if you have a healthy appetite). Faced with an often bewilderingly varied menu, you might opt for a pikilía (medley, assortment) available in several sizes, the largest and most expensive one usually heavy on seafood. At other ouzerís or tsipourádhika the language barrier may be overcome by the waiter wielding an enormous tray laden with all the current cold offerings – you pick the ones you like, then order some hot platters.

## Sweets and desserts

The **zaharoplastío**, a cross between a café and a patisserie, serves coffee, a limited range of alcohol, yoghurt with honey and sticky cakes. The better establishments offer an amazing variety of pastries, cream-and-chocolate confections, honey-soaked Greco–Turkish sweets like baklavás, kataïfi (honey-drenched "shredded wheat"), loukou-mádhes (deep-fried batter puffs dusted with cinnamon and dipped in syrup), galakto-boúreko (custard pie) and so on. If you want a slant towards dairy products and away from the pure sugar, seek out a **galak-topolío**, where you'll often find ryzógalo (rice pudding), kréma (custard) and locally made yiaoúrti (yoghurt). Both zaharoplastía and galaktopolía are more family-oriented places than a kafenío.

**Traditional specialities** include "spoon sweets" or glyká koutalioú (sticky, syrupy preserves of quince, grape, fig, citrus fruit or cherry) and the now-vanishing, ipovrýhio ("submarine"), a piece of mastic submerged in a glass of water.

**Ice cream**, sold principally at the gelaterie which have swept across Greece (Dhodhoni is the posh home-grown chain, Haägen-Dazs the competition), can be very good and almost indistinguishable from Italian proto-types. A scoop (baláki) costs €1.10–1.60; you'll be asked if you want it in a cup (kypelláki) or a cone (konáki), and whether you want toppings like santí (whipped cream) or nuts.

## Bars, beer and mineral water

**Bars** (barákia) are ubiquitous throughout the islands, ranging from clones of Spanish bodegas to seaside cocktail bars, with music or TV running all day. At their most sophisticated, however, they are well-executed theme venues in ex-industrial/craftsmen's premises, or even Neoclassical houses, with both Greek and imported soundtracks. Although we give some recommendations in the guide, most Greek bars have a half-life of about one year; the best way to find current hot spots, especially if they're more club than bar, is to watch for fly-posters in the neighbourhood, advertising bar-hosted events.

**Shots** and **cocktails** are invariably expensive: €5–9. Bars are, however, most likely to stock a range of **beers**, mostly foreign labels made locally under licence at a handful of breweries – almost all owned by the same Athens-based conglomerate – on the central mainland. Amongst mainstream Greek labels (usually 5% alcohol), Alfa, a hoppy lager brewed in Athens, is the best and most consistent; Mythos, a mild lager in a green bottle, was owned by Scottish and Newcastle (which explains their palatable "red" label at 5.5%) before the mass takeover. The only remaining independents are tasty Veryina, brewed in Komotiní and common in the northeastern mainland and isles, and two **microbreweries**, Piraïki Zythopiía, based in Pireás, the other – Craft

– in Athens. The latter produces draught lager in three grades (blonde, "smoked" and black), as well as a red ale; it should become more widely available once bottling of the stuff commences in 2009.

Kronenberg 1664 and Kaiser, a sharp pilsner, are two of the more common **foreign-licence** varieties, the latter available in both light and dark. Most of the market, however, is cornered by bland, inoffensive Amstel – the standard cheapie, also available as a very palatable, strong (7%) **bock** – and by Heineken, still referred to as a "*prássini*" by bar and taverna staff after its green bottle, despite the advent of Mythos. Genuinely imported German beers, such as Bitburger, Fisher, Erdinger and Warsteiner

(plus a few British ones), are found in busier resorts.

**Mineral water**, mostly still, typically comes in half-litre and one-and-a-half-litre plastic bottles. The ubiquitous Loutraki is not esteemed by Greeks, who prefer various brands from Crete and Epirus. In the better tavernas there has been a backlash against plastic bottles – which constitute a tremendous litter problem – and you can now get it in glass bottles. Souroti, Epsa and Ivi are the principal brands of **sparkling** (*aerioúho* in Greek) water, in small bottles; Tuborg club soda is also widespread. Plain **tap water** (*neró tis vrýsis*) is safe to drink almost everywhere.

# Health

Citizens of all European Economic Area (EEA) countries and Swiss nationals are entitled to free medical care in Greece upon presentation of the European Health Insurance Card (EHIC), obtainable in the UK from the post office, by phone or online (℡0845/606 2030, ⊛www.dh.gov.uk/travellers). "Free", however, means admittance only to the lowest grade of state hospital (kratikó nosokomío), and does not include nursing care, special tests or the cost of medication, though the EHIC card should get you discounts on at least some of these. If you need prolonged medical care, you should make use of private treatment, which is slightly less expensive than elsewhere in western Europe – this is where your travel insurance policy (see p.73) comes in handy. The US, Canada, Australia, New Zealand and South Africa have no formal healthcare agreements with Greece (other than allowing for free emergency trauma treatment).

There are no required **inoculations** for Greece, though it's wise to ensure that you are up to date on tetanus and polio. The **drinking water** is safe almost everywhere, though you will come across brackish supplies on many islands, and nitrate levels exceed the advised limits in some agricultural areas. Bottled water is widely available, though you shouldn't be hoodwinked by money-grabbing restaurateurs who claim tap water is unsafe.

## Doctors and hospitals

You'll find English-speaking **doctors** in any of the island capitals and larger resorts. For an **ambulance**, phone ℡166. In **emergencies**, treatment is given free in state **hospitals** (ask for the *epígonda peristatiká* – casualty ward). As an inpatient, you'll get only the most basic care, and food and changes of bedding are not provided (it's assumed your family will do this). Better are the free state-run **outpatient clinics** (*yiatría*) attached to most public hospitals (where there may be a small appointment fee) and also found stand-alone in rural locales. These operate on a first-come, first-served basis, so go early; usual hours are 8am to 1pm, though they're sometimes open in the afternoon too.

## Pharmacies and drugs

A **pharmacy** (*farmakío*) will suffice for most minor complaints. Greek pharmacists dispense medicines which elsewhere could only be prescribed by a doctor; in the larger towns and resorts there'll be one who speaks good English. Pharmacies are usually closed evenings and Saturday mornings but all have a **schedule** (in both English and Greek) on their door showing the complete roster of night and weekend duty pharmacists locally.

Greeks are famously hypochondriac, and pharmacies are veritable Aladdin's caves of arcane drugs and formulas – just about everything available in North America and northern Europe is here, and then some. **Homeopathic** and **herbal remedies** are sold in most of the larger pharmacies alongside more conventional products.

If you use any form of **prescription drug**, bring along a copy of the prescription, together with the drug's generic name; this will help should you need to replace it, and also avoids possible problems with customs officials. For example, in theory all codeine-containing compounds are illegal in Greece, but as long as you have a prescription nobody is going to make trouble for you.

**Hayfever sufferers** should be prepared for the early Greek pollen season from April to June. Pollen from Aleppo and Calabrian pine in April/May can be particularly noxious. Pharmacies do stock appropriate tablets, but it's best to come supplied.

Don't count on getting **contraceptive pills** or spermicidal jelly/foam outside of the largest towns, over-the-counter at the larger pharmacies. **Condoms**, however, are inexpensive and ubiquitous – just ask for *profylaktiká* (less formally, *plastiká* or *kapótes*) at any pharmacy, mini-market or corner *períptero* (kiosk). Sanitary towels are most often sold in supermarkets; **tampons** can be trickier to find in remoter spots.

# Specific health problems

The main visitor health problems relate to **overexposure to the sun**. Don't spend too long out in it, cover up, wear a hat, and drink plenty of fluids in the hot months to avoid any danger of **sunstroke**. By the sea, goggles or a dive mask for swimming and footwear for walking over wet or rough rocks are useful.

## Hazards of the sea

You may meet an armada of **jellyfish** (*tsoúkhtres*), especially in late summer; they come in various colours and sizes ranging from purple "pizzas" – *médhouses* – to invisible, minute creatures. Fenistil ointment is one recommended over-the-counter remedy for jellyfish (and other) stings; welts usually subside of their own accord within a few hours.

Less vicious but more common, black, spiky **sea urchins** (*ahiní*) infest rocky shorelines year-round; if you step on one, a sterilized sewing needle and olive oil are effective for removing spines. If you don't extract them they'll fester, and walking on the wound pushes them in further.

**Stingrays and skates** (Greek names include *platý*, *seláhi*, *vátos* or *trígona*) can injure with their barbed tails: they frequent bays with sandy bottoms where they camouflage themselves, so shuffle your feet getting in. Take care also not to tread on a *dhrákena* (**weever fish**) which also buries itself in shallow-water sand with just its poisonous dorsal and gill spines protruding. If you do, the pain is excruciating, and the exceptionally potent venom can cause permanent paralysis of the affected area. Imperative first aid is immersing your foot in water as hot as you can stand, which degrades the toxin and relieves the swelling and pain, but you should still head straight to the nearest clinic for an antidote injection.

When snorkelling in deeper water, you may spot a brightly coloured **moray eel** (*smérna*) sliding back and forth out of its rocky lair. Keep a respectful distance – their slightly comical air and clown-colours belie an irritable temper and the ability to inflict nasty bites or even sever fingers.

## Sandflies, mosquitoes, wasps and ticks

**Mosquitoes** (*kounóupia*) in Greece carry nothing worse than their bite, but are infuriating. The most widespread solution are small plug-in electrical devices that vaporize a semi-odourless insecticide tablet; many accommodation proprietors supply them routinely. Liquid insect repellents are available from most shops and pharmacies. Small electronic ultrasound generators are a waste of money.

If you're sleeping on a **beach**, use insect repellent, either lotion or wrist/ankle bands, and/or a tent with a screen to deter **sandflies**. Their bites potentially spread two forms of leishmaniasis, difficult-to-diagnose parasitic infections characterized in one form by ulcerating skin lesions, in the other (visceral or kala-azar) by chronic fever, anaemia, weight loss, and death if untreated by long courses of medication.

**Wasps** (*sfigónes, sfíkes*) are ubiquitous during the wine-making season (Aug–Oct) when they're attracted by fermenting grape-mess. Some mind their own business, others are very aggressive, even dive-bombing swimmers out at sea. Domestic **bees** (*mélisses*) can be aggressive near their hives; scrape the embedded sting from your skin with a fingernail to prevent injection of more venom. Alternatively, invest in an Aspivenin suction kit from a big-town pharmacy – lightweight and suitable for removing venom from various stings.

**Ticks** mostly feed on sheep but wait on vegetation for new hosts. Check your legs after walking through long grass near flocks. If it has started to feed, you should detach it carefully by rocking or twisting, rather than pulling it off (which leaves the head embedded); do not use traditional tricks such as solvents or a lighted match. Ticks carry Lyme disease, which is now endemic in Europe.

## Snakes, scorpions and insects

**Adders** (*ohiés*) and **scorpions** (*skorpii*) occur throughout Greece; both creatures are shy – scorpions are nocturnal – but take care when climbing over dry-stone walls where snakes like to sun themselves, and don't put hands or feet in places where you haven't looked first. Wiggly, fast-moving, six-inch **centipedes** (*skolópendres*) which look like a rubber toy should also be avoided, as they bite – hard.

**Snakes**, venomous or not, may bite if threatened; if a snake injects venom, swelling will occur within thirty minutes. If this happens, keep the bitten part still, and all body movements as gentle as possible. If medical attention is not nearby, bind the limb firmly to slow the blood circulation, but not so tightly as to stop the blood flow.

## Plants

If you snap a **wild-fig shoot** while walking, avoid contact with the highly irritant **sap**. The immediate antidote to the active alkaloid is a mild acid – lemon juice or vinegar; left unneutralized, fig "milk" raises welts which take a month to heal. Severe allergic reactions have to be treated with strong steroids, either topical cream (available from pharmacies) or intravenously in hospital casualty wards.

# The media

Although the Greek press and airwaves have ostensibly been free since the end of the colonels' dictatorship in 1974, few would propose the Greek mass media as a paradigm of objective journalism. Many papers are sensational, state-run radio and TV often biased in favour of the ruling party, and private channels imitative of the worst American programming.

**British newspapers** are available at €2–2.75 for dailies, or €4.50 for Sunday editions. You'll find day-old copies (same day by noon in Athens) of *The Times*, *The Daily Telegraph*, *The Independent* and *The Guardian*'s European edition, plus a few of the tabloids, in all resorts as well as in major towns and airports. **American and international alternatives** include *USA Today* and the *International Herald Tribune*, the latter including a free, abridged English translation of the respected Greek daily *Kathimerini* (online at ⓦwww.ekathimerini.com). Among **foreign magazines**, *Time* and *Newsweek* are commonly sold.

There are few surviving **locally produced** English-language magazines or papers. The main English-language newspaper, available in most resorts, is the *Athens News* (weekly every Friday, online at ⓦwww.athensnews .gr; €2.50), in colour with good features and Balkan news, plus entertainment and arts listings.

## Greek publications

Most **newspapers** have an overt political slant, including funding from parliamentary parties. Only a handful of quality dailies have paper-of-record status; these include **centre-right** *Kathimerini* – whose former proprietress Helen Vlahos attained heroic status for defying the junta – and **centre-left** *Eleftherotypia*, especially its weekend editions. *To Vima* (with its excellent *Vimagazino* supplement), *Avriani* and *Ta Nea* stake out pro-PASOK territory, the latter well-regarded for its Saturday magazine, *Takhydhromos*. On the **far left**, *Avyi* is the Syriza forum, while *Rizospastis* acts as the organ of the KKE. On the **right**, *Apoyevmatini* supports Néa Dhimokratía, while *Estia*'s no-photo format

and reactionary politics are both stuck somewhere in the early 1900s.

Among **magazines** not merely translations of overseas titles, *To Pondiki* (*The Mouse*) is a satirical weekly review similar to Britain's *Private Eye*, its spot-on covers accessible to anyone with minimal Greek. *Andi*, an intelligent analytical fortnightly, has reviews, political analysis and cultural critiques, in the mould of Britain's *New Statesman*.

## Radio

Greek **radio** music programmes vary in quality. Since deregulation, every island town has set up its own studio and transmitter, and the airwaves are positively cluttered. The two state-run networks are ER1 (a mix of news, talk and pop music) and ER2 (pop music).

On heavily touristed islands like Rhodes, Corfu and Crete, there will usually be at least one FM station trying its luck at **English programming** by and for foreigners. The Turkish state radio's Third Channel is also widely (if unpatriotically) listened to on east Aegean islands for its classical, jazz and blues programmes. On islands nearer to Athens, check out the world music broadcast, *Odhiki Voithia*, Mondays at 11.59pm, on Sto Kokkino Radio 105.5FM.

## Television

Greece's state-funded **TV stations**, ET1, NET and ET3, lag behind private channels – Antenna, Star, Alpha, Alter and Makedonia TV – in ratings, though not necessarily in quality. Programming is a mix of soaps (both Greek and Latino), game shows, movies and sport, with a leavening of natural history documentaries, costume dramas and today-in-history features. All foreign films and serials are broadcast in their original language, with Greek subtitles. Most private channels operate around the clock; public stations broadcast from around 5.30am until 3am. Numerous **cable and satellite channels** are available, depending on the area (and hotel) you're in.

# Festivals and holidays

Religious ceremonies, mostly celebrations of one or other of a multitude of saints, punctuate the Greek year. With some kind of saint listed literally every day, there are scores of local festivals, or paniyíria, honouring the patron of the local parish church. You're unlikely to travel around Greek islands for long without stumbling on some sort of observance – sometimes spreading right across the town or island, sometimes tiny and local. They are celebrated with gusto and always with respect to local tradition. In addition, a major wedding or baptism will bring out a vast extended family, all of whom expect lavish hospitality. No significant event, in fact, is allowed to go by without some kind of party to mark it – and especially in smaller villages and islands away from the tourist trail, visitors will very likely be invited to join in.

Saints' days are also celebrated as **name days**. If you learn that it's an acquaintance's name day, you wish them "Khrónia Pollá" ("many years", as in "many happy returns").

Some of the more important nationwide festivals and holidays are listed below; **public holidays** are marked with PH. The paramoní, or **eve of the festival**, is often as significant as the day itself, and many of the events are actually celebrated on the night before. If you show up on the morning of the date given you may find that you have missed most of the music, dancing and drinking. Remember too that religious dates will follow the Orthodox calendar – broadly similar to the Catholic year except for **Easter** which, when the dates don't coincide, can fall one to five (more usually one) weeks later than the Western festival. For the precise dates visit ⓦ 5ko.free.fr/en/easter.php.

## Festival and holiday calendar

### JANUARY

**January 1:** New Year's Day (Protokhroniá) in Greece is the feast day of Áyios Vassílios (St Basil). The traditional New Year greeting is "Kalí Khroniá". PH
**January 6:** Epiphany (Theofánia, or Tón Fóton) marks the baptism of Jesus as well as the end of the twelve days of Christmas. Baptismal fonts, lakes, rivers and seas are blessed, especially harbours, where the priest traditionally casts a crucifix into the water, with local youths competing for the privilege of recovering it. PH

### FEBRUARY

**Pre-Lenten carnivals:** These, known in Greek as Apokriátika, span three weeks, climaxing during the seventh weekend before Easter. The Ionian islands, especially Kefalloniá, are also good for Carnival, as is Ayiássos on Lésvos, while the outrageous Goat Dance (see p.514) takes place on Skýros in the Sporades.

### MARCH

**February/March:** Clean Monday (Katharí Dheftéra), the day after Carnival ends and the first day of Lent, 48 days before Easter, marks the start of fasting and is traditionally spent picnicking and flying kites. PH
**March 25:** Independence Day and the feast of the Annunciation (Evangelismós in Greek) is both

a national and a religious holiday, with military parades and dancing to celebrate the beginning of the revolt against Ottoman rule in 1821, and church services to honour the news given to Mary that she was to become the Mother of Christ. There are major festivities on Tínos, Ýdhra (Hydra) and any locality with a monastery or church named Evangelístria or Evangelismós. PH

## APRIL

**March/April:** Easter (April 19, 2009; April 4, 2010; April 24, 2011) is by far the most important festival of the year – infinitely more so than Christmas. The festival is an excellent time to be in Greece, both for its beautiful religious ceremonies and for the days of feasting and celebration that follow, though you'll need to book accommodation months in advance. The mountainous island of Ýdhra, with its alleged 360 churches and monasteries, is the prime Easter resort; other famous celebrations are held at Corfu, Pyrgí on Híos, Ólymbos on Kárpathos and St John's monastery on Pátmos, where on Holy Thursday the abbot washes the feet of twelve monks in the village square, in imitation of Christ doing the same for his disciples. Good Friday and Easter Monday are also public holidays. PH

**April 23:** The feast of Áyios Yeóryios (St George), the patron of shepherds, is a big rural celebration, with much feasting and dancing at associated shrines and towns. At the cattle town of Asigonía in Crete, this is a major event. If it falls during Lent, festivities are postponed until the Mon after Easter.

## MAY

**May 1:** May Day (Protomayiá) is the great urban holiday, when townspeople traditionally make for the countryside to picnic and fly kites, returning with bunches of wild flowers. Wreaths are hung on doorways or balconies until they are burnt in bonfires on St John's eve (June 23). There are also large demonstrations by the Left for Labour Day. PH

**May 21:** The feast of Áyios Konstandínos (St Constantine) and his mother, Ayía Eléni (St Helen): the former championed Christianity in the Byzantine Empire. It's a widely celebrated name day for two of the more popular Christian names in Greece.

**May 20-27:** Battle of Crete (May 20–27). The anniversary of one of the major World War II battles is celebrated in the Haniá province of Crete with veterans' ceremonies, sporting events and folk dancing.

## JUNE

**May/June:** Áyion Pnévma (Whit Monday), fifty

days after Easter, sees services to commemorate the descent of the Holy Spirit to the assembled disciples. Usually, a modest liturgy is celebrated at rural chapels of the Holy Spirit, gaily decked out with pennants; at Pagondas village on Samos, there's a musical festival. Many young Greeks take advantage of the long weekend, marking the start of summer, to head for the islands. PH

**June 29 & 30:** The joint feast of Áyios Pétros and Áyios Pávlos (SS Peter and Paul), two of the more widely celebrated name days, is on June 29. Celebrations often run together with those for the Holy Apostles (Áyii Apóstoli), the following day.

## JULY

**July 17:** The feast of Ayía Marína: a big event in rural areas, as she's an important protector of crops. Ayiá Marina village on Kássos will be *en fête* as will countless other similarly named towns and villages.

**July 20:** The feast of Profítis Ilías (the Prophet Elijah) is widely celebrated at the countless hill- or mountaintop shrines of Profítis Ilías – nowadays on Sámos with a 4WD trip up to the mountain of the same name with sound systems cranked up and barbecue spits turning on arrival.

**July 26:** Ayía Paraskeví is celebrated in parishes or villages bearing that name, especially in Epirus.

**Second half of July:** Réthymnon (Crete) wine festival with a week of wine tasting and traditional dancing.

## AUGUST

**August 6:** Metamórfosis toú Sotíros (Transfiguration of the Saviour) provides another excuse for celebrations, particularly at Khristós Ráhon village on Ikaría, and at Plátanos on Léros. On Hálki the date is marked by messy food fights with flour, eggs and squid ink.

**August 15:** Apokímisis tís Panayías (Assumption of the Blessed Virgin Mary). This is the day people traditionally return to their home village, and the heart of the holiday season, so in many places there will be no accommodation available on any terms. Even some Greeks will resort to sleeping in the streets at the great pilgrimage to Tínos; also major festivities at Páros, at Ayiássos on Lésvos, and at Ólymbos on Kárpathos. PH

**August 29:** Apokefálisis toú Prodhrómou (Beheading of John the Baptist). Popular pilgrimages and celebrations at Vrykoúnda on Kárpathos. On Crete a massive name-day pilgrimage treks to the church of Áyios Ioánnis on the Rodhópou peninsula.

## Cultural festivals

Festivals of music, dance and theatre take place in summer throughout the islands, many at atmospheric outdoor venues. Some are unashamedly aimed at drawing tourists, others more seriously artistic. Some of the more durable include:

**Astypálea Municipal Festival** (July–Aug)
**Itháki Music Festival** (July)
**Ippokrateia Festival** Kós (July–Aug)
**Iráklion Festival** Crete (July-Aug)
**Kornaria Cultural Festival** Sitía, Crete (July–Sept)
**Lató Cultural Festival** Áyios Nikólaos Crete (July–Sept)
**Lefkádha International Folklore Festival** (Aug)
**Manolis Kalomiris Festival** Sámos (July–Sept)
**Ólymbos Festival** Kárpathos (mid-July to early Sept)
**Philippi/Thássos Festival** (early July to early Sept)
**Réthymnon Renaissance Festival** Crete (July)
**Rhodes Eco Film Festival** (June)
**Sými Festival** (late June–early Sept)
**Thíra Music Festival** (Aug–Sept)

## SEPTEMBER

**September 8:** Yénnisis tís Panayías (Birth of the Virgin Mary) sees special services in churches dedicated to the event, and a double cause for rejoicing on Spétses, where they also celebrate the anniversary of 1822 battle of the straits of Spétses with fireworks and feasting. Elsewhere, there's a pilgrimage of childless women to the monastery at Tsambíka, Rhodes.

**September 14:** A last major summer festival, the Ýpsosis toú Stavroú (Exaltation of the Cross), keenly observed on Hálki.

**September 24:** The feast of Áyios Ioánnis Theológos (St John the Divine), observed on Níssyros and Pátmos, where at the saint's monastery there are solemn, beautiful liturgies the night before and early in the morning.

## OCTOBER

**October 26:** The feast of Áyios Dhimítrios (St Demetrios), another popular name day, particularly celebrated in Thessaloníki, of which he is the patron saint. In rural areas the new wine is traditionally broached, a good excuse for general inebriation.

**October 28:** Óhi Day is a national holiday with parades, folk dancing and speeches to commemorate Prime Minister Metaxas' reply to Mussolini's 1940 ultimatum: Ohi! ("No!"). PH

## NOVEMBER

**November 7–9:** The anniversary of the 1866 explosion at Arkádhi monastery in Crete is marked by an enormous gathering at the island's most revered shrine.

**November 8:** Another popular name day, the feast of the Archangels Michael and Gabriel (Mihaïl and Gavríïl, or tón Taxiárhon), marked by rites at the numerous churches named after them, particularly at the rural monastery of Taxiárhis on Sými, and the big monastery of Mandamádhos, Lésvos.

## DECEMBER

**December 6:** The feast of Áyios Nikólaos (St Nicholas), the patron of seafarers, whose many chapels provide the focus for processions and festivities.

**December 25 & 26:** If less all-encompassing than Greek Easter, Christmas (Khristoúyenna) is an important religious feast, and one that increasingly comes with all the usual commercial trappings. PH

**December 31:** New Year's Eve (Paramoní Protohroniá), when, as on the other twelve days of Christmas, a few children still go door-to-door singing the traditional *kálanda* (carols), receiving money in return. Adults tend to sit around playing cards, often for money. A special baked loaf, the *vassilópitta*, in which a coin is concealed to bring its finder good luck throughout the year, is cut at midnight.

# Sports and outdoor pursuits

The Greek seashore offers ample scope for watersports, with windsurfing-boards for rent in most resorts and, less frequently, waterskiing and parasailing facilities. On land, the greatest attraction lies in hiking; often the smaller, less developed islands are better for this than the larger ones criss-crossed by roads. Greeks follow football and basketball avidly and you will see youths playing impromptu games of both everywhere. The only top flight professional teams on the islands during the 2008–09 season, however, were OFI and Ergotelis in Iráklio on Crete (football) and Kolossos in Ródhos Town (basketball).

## Watersports

**Windsurfing** is massively popular around Greece, with Greek gold or silver medalists at the last two Olympics. The country's bays and coves are ideal for beginners, and boards can be rented in literally hundreds of resorts. Particularly good areas, with established schools, include Vassilikí on Lefkádha, Kéfalos on Kós, Zákynthos, western Náxos, Kokkári on Sámos, several spots on Lésvos, Corfu's west coast and numerous locales on Crete. Board rental rates are very reasonable – about €10–15 an hour, with good discounts for longer periods – and instruction is generally also available, typically €50–60 for four hours.

**Waterskiing** is available at most of the larger resorts, and a fair few of the smaller ones too. By the crippling rental standards of the ritzier parts of the Med it's a bargain, with twenty-minutes' instruction often available for €25–40. Jet skiing has become even more popular and is now available in many resorts for around €30 for a ten-minute burst of fuel-guzzling thrills. At many resorts, **parasailing** (*parapént* in Greek) is also possible; rates start at €30 a go. Another burgeoning activity is kitesurfing, which goes for around €20 per hour.

A combination of steady winds, appealing seascapes and numerous natural harbours have long made Greece a tremendous place for **sailing**. Companies offer all sorts of packaged and tailor-made cruises (see p.32). Spring and autumn are the most pleasant seasons; *meltémi* winds make for pretty nauseous sailing between late June and early September, and summer rates can be three times as high as shoulder-season prices. Small boats and motorized dinghies are rented out by the day at many resorts; you'll pay €45–120, depending on season, location and engine size.

Because of the potential for pilfering submerged antiquities, **scuba diving** is still fairly restricted, though the government has relaxed its controls of late and there are now almost one hundred dive centres spread throughout the islands, especially in the Dodecanese, the Ionians, the Cyclades and Crete. Single dives start around €40 and various courses are available. For more information and an update on new, approved sites, contact the Union of Greek Diving Centres (☎210 92 29 532 or 210 41 18 909) or the Hellenic Federation of Underwater Activities (☎210 98 19 961).

## Walking

If you have the time and stamina **walking** is probably the single best way to see the quieter islands. This guide includes descriptions of a number of the more accessible island hikes, such as the well-organised Corfu Trail (see p.552). Other islands with sizeable mountains offering good hiking include Crete and Évvia. For more detail, you may want to buy specific hiking guidebooks; see p.664. See also p.75 for details of hiking maps available, and p.33 for details of companies offering walking holidays on the islands.

# Crime, police and cultural etiquette

Greece is one of Europe's safest countries, with a low crime rate and a deserved reputation for honesty. It is also a deeply traditional country, and it's more likely that you'll (inadvertently or otherwise) give offence than receive it; it pays to be aware of the most common misdemeanours, along with some positive cultural etiquette to observe.

Though undeniably safer than much of Europe – if you leave a bag or wallet at a café, you'll probably find it scrupulously looked after, pending your return – **theft** and **muggings** at archeological sites, in towns, remote villages and resorts have increased recently. With this in mind, it's best to lock rooms and cars securely. There has also been a huge rise in pickpocketing on the old section of the **Athens metro** (not the heavily policed new extension). See p.78 for **emergency phone numbers**.

## Police and potential offences

There is a single, nationwide **police force**, the *Ellinikí Astynomía*, rather than the division into urban corps and rural gendarmerie as in most of Europe. Greek police are prone to be gruff and monolingual, and some have little regard for foreigners. Police practice often falls short of northern European norms, with fit-ups or beatings in custody not unknown. You are required to **carry suitable ID** on you at all times – either a passport, national ID card or a driving licence. Otherwise, the most common causes of a brush with authority are beach nudity, camping outside authorized sites, public inebriation or lewd behaviour, and taking photos in forbidden areas.

**Nude (sun)bathing** is explicitly legal on very few beaches (most famously on Mýkonos) and is deeply offensive to more traditional Greeks. It is, for example, bad etiquette to swim or sunbathe nude within sight of a church, of which there are many along the Greek coast. Generally, if a beach has become fairly well established as naturist, or is secluded, laws go unenforced. Police will only appear if nudity is getting too overt on mainstream stretches. Usually, there

will only be a warning, but you can officially be arrested straight off – facing up to three days in jail and a stiff fine. **Topless (sun)bathing** for women is technically legal nationwide, but specific locales – eg, in front of "family" tavernas – often opt out by posting signs. Similar guidelines apply to **camping rough**; though ostensibly illegal, you're still unlikely to incur anything more than a warning to move on.

The **hours between 3 and 5pm**, the midday *mikró ýpno* (siesta), are sacrosanct; it's not acceptable to make phone calls to strangers – unless you're booking a room – or any sort of noise (especially with motorcycles) at this time. **Quiet** is also legally mandated **between midnight and 8am** in residential areas.

The well-publicized ordeal of twelve British plane-spotters who processed through Greek jails and courts in 2001–02 on espionage charges (they had received warnings on prior occasions) should be ample warning to **take no pictures** at all in and around airports or military installations. The latter are festooned with signs of a bellows camera with a red "X" through it.

Any sort of **disrespect** towards the Greek state or Orthodox Church in general, or Greek civil servants in particular, may be actionable, so best keep your comments to yourself. This is a culture where verbal injuries matter, where libel laws greatly favour plaintiffs, and the alleged public utterance of *malákas* (wanker) can result in a court case.

**Drunkenness** has always been held in contempt in Greece, where the inability to hold one's liquor is considered unmanly and shameful. Inebriation will be viewed as an aggravating factor if you're busted for something else, not an excuse.

**Drug offences** are considered major crimes. Theory is not always practice, but foreigners caught possessing even small amounts of cannabis or harder stuff get long jail sentences if there's evidence that they've been supplying to others. You can be held on remand for up to 18 months without a trial date.

If you get arrested for any offence, you have a right to **contact your consulate**, which will arrange a lawyer for your defence. Beyond this, there is little they can, or in most cases will, do. Details of consulates in Athens and Thessaloníki appear in their respective "Listings" sections. There are honorary British consuls on Rhodes, Crete and Corfu as well.

## Women and lone travellers

Thousands of **women** travel independently in Greece without being **harassed** or feeling intimidated. With the westernization of relationships between unmarried Greek men and women, almost all of the traditional Mediterranean macho impetus for trying one's luck with foreign girls has faded. Any hassle is from the nearly extinct professionally single Greek men, known as *kamákia* (fish harpoons), who haunt beach bars and dance clubs. Foreign women are more at risk of **sexual assault** at certain notorious resorts (Kávos in Corfu, Laganás in Zákynthos, Faliráki in Rhodes and Mália on Crete) by northern European men than by ill-intentioned locals. It is sensible not to bar-crawl alone or to accept late-night rides from strangers (**hitching** at any time is not advisable for lone female travellers). In more remote areas intensely traditional villagers may wonder why women travelling alone are unaccompanied, and may not welcome their presence in exclusively male *kafenía*.

**Lone men** need to be wary of being invited into bars in Athens and a few of the larger ports; these bars are invariably staffed with hostesses (who may also be prostitutes) persuading you to treat them to drinks. At the end of the night you'll be landed with an outrageous bill, some of which goes towards the hostess's commission; physical threats are brought to bear on reluctant payers.

## Cultural hints

**Bargaining** isn't a regular feature of tourist life, though possible with private rooms and some hotels out of season. You may also be able to negotiate better prices for vehicle rental, especially for longer periods. Restaurant bills incorporate a service charge and with the increasing cost of food, drink and services in Greece, generous **tipping** has decreased; if you want to tip, rounding up the bill is usually sufficient. If you receive particular hospitality, avoid reciprocating with excessive cash as this can cause offence.

Most monasteries impose a fairly strict **dress code** for visitors: no shorts, with women expected to cover their arms and wear skirts (though most Greek women visitors will be in trousers); the necessary wraps are sometimes provided on the spot.

# Living in Greece

Many habitual visitors fall in love with Greece to the extent that they take up part- or full-time residence there, more likely buying property than renting it, and probably retired or self-employed rather than working at the prevailing low Greek wage scales. Beyond the first, easy hurdle of obtaining a residence certificate, there are a number of other issues to consider: working, keeping a vehicle, internet connection and animal welfare. For the full scoop on real estate, consult Buying a Property: Greece (Navigator Guides, UK).

## Residence and voting

EU (and EEA) nationals are allowed to stay indefinitely in any EU state, but to ensure avoidance of any problems – eg, in setting up a bank or utilities account – (and to be entitled to vote locally in Euro and municipal elections), you should after the third month of a stay get a **registration certificate** (vevéosi engrafís). This does not need to be renewed and, according to a presidential decree of June 2007, absolutely replaces the previously issued five-year **residence permit** (ádhia dhiamonís). Fill out the required application forms at the local police station or (in the very largest islands) at the aliens' bureau.

EU nationals with a registration certificate become eligible to **vote** in municipal elections (every four years, next in Oct 2010) and Euro elections (in 2009 & 2014), though in the latter case they must choose a country – you can't vote in your previous country of residence and Greece. Bring your passport and certificate to the nearest town hall and you will be entered onto the computerized voter registration rolls in a matter of minutes.

Residence/work permits for **non-EU/non-EEA nationals** can only be obtained on application to a Greek embassy or consulate outside of Greece; you have a much better chance of securing one if you are married to a Greek, are of Greek background by birth (an omoyenís), or have permanent-resident status in another EU state, but even then expect wrangles and delays. Many non-EU nationals working illegally in Greece still resort to the pre-Schengen ploy of heading off to Turkey for a few days every three months and re-entering at a different border post for a new passport stamp; this usually works, but if not, the penalties described on p.73 potentially apply.

## Working

EU membership notwithstanding, **short-term unskilled work** in Greece is usually badly paid and undocumented, with employers notoriously skimping on the requirement to pay IKA (social insurance contributions) for their employees. The influx, since 1990, of well over a million immigrants from various countries – chiefly Albania, south Asia and central Europe – has resulted in a surplus of unskilled labour and severely depressed wages. Undocumented, **non-EU/non-EEA nationals** working in Greece do so surreptitiously, with chronic risk of denunciation to the police and instant deportation. That old foreigners' standby, **teaching English**, is now available only to TEFL certificate-holders – preferably Greeks, non-EU nationals of Greek descent and EU/EEA nationals in that order. If you are a

## Greek-language courses

The longest established outlet is The Athens Centre, Arhimídhous 48, 116 36 Athens (☎210 70 12 268, ⊛www.athenscentre.gr). One to try on Crete is Lexis, 48 Dhaskaloyiánni, 73100 Haniá (☎28210 55673, ⊛www.lexis.edu.gr). There are always adverts in the Athens News for other schools, which come and go.

non-EU/EEA foreign national of Greek descent you are termed *omoyenís* (returned Greek diaspora member) and in fact have tremendous employment, taxation and residence rights.

Others may prefer **tourism-related work**, where your language skills or specialist training garner some advantage. Most women working casually in Greece find waiting jobs in **bars** or **restaurants** around the main resorts; men, unless they are trained chefs, will probably find it harder to secure any position, even washing up. Corfu, with its big British slant, is an obvious choice for bar work; Rhodes, Kós, Crete, Skiáthos, Páros, Íos and Santoríni are also promising. Start looking, if you can, around April or May; you'll get better rates at this time if you're taken on for a season. You might also take staff one of the **windsurfing** schools or **scuba** operations that have sprung up on several islands.

The most common tourism-related work, however, is serving as a **rep for a package holiday company**. All you need is EU nationality and language proficiency compatible with the clientele, though knowledge of Greek is a big plus. English-only speakers are largely restricted to places with a big British package trade, namely Crete, Rhodes, Kós, Skiáthos, Sámos, Lésvos and the Ionian islands. Many such staff are recruited from Britain, but it's also common to be hired through local affiliates in spring. However you're taken on, you're guaranteed five to six months of steady work, often with use of a car thrown in.

## Keeping a car or motorcycle

Both tourist visitors and residents, of any nationality, are only allowed to **keep a vehicle in Greece** with foreign number plates for six months, or until the current road-tax sticker and/or insurance from your home country expires, whichever comes first. After that you face a number of inconvenient choices: re-exporting the car, storing it for six months, or obtaining local registration. Many holiday home-owners long used the six-on, six-off system, storing their EU-plated car off-road under customs seal, but this has become difficult now that most Greek insurers will no longer cover foreign-registered cars. Especially on isolated islands, many foreigners just drive

around for years on foreign plates with no current road tax, but if you're caught – either by ordinary traffic police or plainclothes customs inspectors stationed at busy ferry docks – these personnel are empowered to impound the vehicle immediately, and the "ransom" (basically a fine plus arbitrary import duty) is prohibitive. If circulating with foreign plates, you must always be able to prove that your car has been in Greece for less than six months (the dated ticket for any ferry you may have arrived on from Turkey or Italy is considered sufficient evidence).

Should you decide to import your beloved buggy, **import duties** run anywhere from 30 to 120 percent of the value of the car, depending on its age and engine displacement; the nearest Greek embassy overseas can provide a current table of fees charged. Take your car or motorcycle to the nearest customs compound, where personnel will inspect it and make a written application to headquarters in Pireás; within ten working days you (or rather your designated *ektelonistís* or **customs agent**) will receive an assessment of duty, against which there is no appeal, and which must be paid immediately. For EU-plated cars at least this is blatantly illegal – their owners should get Greek plates at little or no cost on demand – but despite being referred to the European Court several times on this (and always losing), the Greek state shows little sign of stopping this lucrative practice. The only way out is to make a declaration at your nearest Greek embassy or consulate that you intend to take up full-time residence in Greece (ie are not just a holiday-home owner); such an official document should satisfy the most exigent Greek official and get you a pair of Greek plates in a few weeks. In any case, you will immediately begin to save massive amounts of money by paying insurance at local tariffs rather than the inflated rates levied on all foreign-registered cars.

In terms of **maintenance**, the easiest car models to have serviced and buy parts for in Greece are VWs (including old microbuses and Transporter vans), Mercedes, BMWs, Audis, Opels, Ladas, Skodas and virtually all French, Italian, Korean and Japanese makes. British models are trickier, but you should be fine as long as you haven't brought anything too esoteric – the Mini (original or reissue) is, for example, still a cult vehicle in Greece. Fords are represented, and the Opel is the continental brand of Vauxhall.

If this all sounds too much hassle, the **cost of cars and scooters** has plunged in Greece and for many models is much less than Britain – a Korean-made compact runabout starts at around €6500, plus tax, while a nice new scooter can be had for €1500. But remember that there are stiff fines for being caught driving even an 80cc scooter on a car licence (for which the limit is 50cc); budget €450–500 for a licence course, and enough facility in reading Greek to pass the written test.

## Internet connection

Along with most other utilities, Greek telecoms are steadily being deregulated; there are currently two land-line providers (set to grow) and a myriad of internet packages and providers, among which Otenet, Forthnet and HOL are the biggest players. ISP security is poor, however, and Greek email addresses become quickly clogged with spam. About a third of the country geographically still hasn't access to broadband (or **ADSL** as it's universally referred to in Greece); **dial-up** subscriptions cost from €10 per month if you pre-pay for a year, plus modest hourly charges for online time. The Yermanos electronic-widgets chain is one of the most impartial outlets for many providers, though once you're signed on with a particular company it's best to deal direct with them for renewals. ADSL is very overpriced by north European standards – sometimes almost €30 a month for modest speeds – but EU pressure is pushing rates down, maybe to €18 equivalent per month if you pre-pay for a year; specials (ie free connection and router box) also abound.

## Pets and animal welfare

No single issue potentially pits foreign residents (especially British ones) in Greece against their locally born neighbours more than the status of pets and **animal welfare** in general. **Abuse**, especially in the rural areas, is rife: many islands have a remote valley where old donkeys were customarily set loose to starve; hunting dogs are kept chained to outdoor stakes in all weathers, without adequate food or water; surplus kittens are routinely drowned in a weighted sack. Strychnine-bait **poisoning** of "extra" or annoying animals is the rule – so never, ever let your dog run loose. There is also a stubborn resistance at all social levels to neutering, or to spending money on an animal beyond a handful of pet food or a flea collar. Most Greek animal-lovers and pet-owners are urban and/or foreign-educated, as are veterinary practices and pet-supply shops, and they have made little headway against deeply ingrained attitudes. Beasts are seen as part of the rural economy; when their usefulness is over, they are disposed of without sentimentality. It is also deeply offensive to many Greeks for foreigners to feed the under-table cats running in packs, as signs often warn you.

Under both European and Greek law it's an offence to mistreat an animal, but in the countryside you are just wasting your breath. If you feel strongly about the foregoing, support an **animal welfare organization**, found anywhere large numbers of expats are resident – Rhodes, Corfu, Ýdhra and Sámos are prime examples. Two useful UK-run organizations are the Greek Animal Welfare Fund (Wwww.gawf.org.uk) and Greek Animal Rescue (Wwww.greekanimalrescue.com).

# Travel essentials

## Costs

The **cost of living** in Greece has increased astronomically since it joined the EU,

particularly after the adoption of the euro and raising of the VAT rate in early 2005. Prices in shops and cafés now match or exceed those of many other EU member countries (including the UK). However, outside the established resorts, travel remains affordable, with the aggregate cost of restaurant meals, short-term accommodation and public transport falling somewhere in between that of cheaper Spain and pricier Italy or France.

**Prices** depend on where and when you go. Mainland cities, larger tourist resorts and the trendier small islands (such as Sými, Ýdhra, Mýkonos, Paxí and Pátmos) are more expensive, and costs everywhere increase sharply during July–August, Christmas, New Year and Easter.

On most islands a daily per-person **budget** of £35/US$65/€44 will get you basic accommodation and meals, plus a short ferry or bus ride, as one of a couple. Camping would cut costs marginally. On £60/US$112/€76 a day you could be living quite well, plus sharing the cost of renting a large motorbike or small car. See p.50 for accommodation costs. Inter-island **ferry fares**, a mainly unavoidable expense, are subsidized by the government in an effort to preserve remote island communities.

A basic taverna **meal** with bulk wine or a beer costs around €11–15 per person. Add a better bottle of wine, seafood or more careful cooking, and it could be up to €18–30 a head; you'll rarely pay more than that, unless you get tricked into buying overpriced fish. Even in the most developed of resorts, with inflated "international" menus,

there is often a basic but decent taverna where the locals eat.

## Electricity

Voltage is 220 volts AC. Round, two-pin plugs are used; adapters should be purchased beforehand in the UK, as they can be difficult to find locally; standard 5-, 6- or 7.5-amp models permit operation of a hair dryer or travel iron. Unless they're dual voltage, North American appliances will require both a step-down transformer and a plug adapter (the latter easy to find in Greece).

## Entry requirements

UK and all other EU nationals need only a valid **passport** to enter Greece and are not stamped in on arrival or out upon departure. US, Australian, New Zealand, Canadian and most non-EU Europeans receive mandatory entry and exit stamps in their passports and can stay, as tourists, for ninety days (cumulative) in any six-month period – make sure your passport is stamped on arrival, as small ports can be lax in this regard. Your passport must be valid for three months after your arrival date.

Unless of Greek descent, or married to an EU national, visitors from **non-EU** countries are currently not, in practice, being given extensions to tourist visas by the various Aliens' Bureaux in Greece. You must leave not just Greece but the entire Schengen Group – essentially the entire EU as it was

## Discounts

Various official and quasi-official **youth, student and teacher ID cards** soon pay for themselves in savings; they all cost around £10/US$20 (or local equivalent) for a year. Full-time students are eligible for the **International Student ID Card** (ISIC; ⓦwww.isiccard.com), which entitles the bearer to cut-price transport and discounts at museums, theatres and other attractions, though often not accepted as valid proof of age. If you're not a student but aged under 26, you can qualify for the **International Youth Travel Card**, which provides similar benefits to the ISIC. Teachers qualify for the **International Teacher Identity Card** (ITIC), offering insurance benefits but limited travel discounts. Consult the website of the International Student Travel Confederation (ⓦwww.isic.org) for the nearest retail outlet for any of these cards.

**Seniors** are entitled to a discount on bus passes in the major cities; Olympic Airways also offer discounts on full fares on domestic flights. Proof of age is necessary.

before May 2004, minus Britain and Eire, plus Norway and Iceland – and stay out until the maximum 90-days-in-180 rule, as set forth above, is satisfied. If you overstay your time and then leave under your own power – ie are not deported – you'll be hit with a huge fine upon departure, and possibly be banned from re-entering for a period; no excuses will be entertained except (just maybe) a doctor's certificate stating you were immobilized in hospital. It cannot be overemphasized just how vigilant Greek immigration officials have become on this issue.

### Greek embassies abroad

**Australia** 9 Turrana St, Yarralumla, Canberra, ACT 2600 ℡02/6273 3011, ⓦwww .greekembassy-au.org.

**Britain** 1A Holland Park, London W11 3TP ℡020/7221 6467, ⓦwww.greekembassy.org.uk.

**Canada** 80 Maclaren St, Ottawa, ON K2P 0K6 ℡613/238-6271, ⓦwww.greekembassy.ca.

**Ireland** 1 Upper Pembroke St, Dublin 2 ℡01/676 7254, ⓔdubgremb@eircom.net.

**New Zealand** 5–7 Willeston St, Wellington ℡04/473 7775, ⓦwww.greece.org.nz.

**South Africa** 1003 1267 Pretoria St, Hatfield 001, Pretoria ℡012/342-7136, ⓔembgrsaf@global .co.za.

**USA** 2217 Massachusetts Ave NW, Washington, DC 20008 ℡202/939-1300, ⓦwww .greekembassy.org.

## Gay and lesbian travellers

Greece is deeply ambivalent about **homosexuality**: ghettoized as "to be expected" in the arts, theatre and music scenes, but apt to be closeted elsewhere – though the 2004–05 sex scandals amongst the Orthodox clergy blew the door wide open on the prevalent hypocrisy. The age of consent for same-sex acts is 17, although the legal code still contains pejorative references to passive partners. Greek men are terrible flirts, but cruising them is a semiotic minefield and definitely at your own risk – references in (often obsolete) gay guides to "known" male cruising grounds should be treated sceptically. Out gay Greeks are rare, and lesbians rarer still; foreign same-sex couples will be regarded with some bemusement in the provinces but accorded the standard courtesy as foreigners – as long as they refrain from public displays of affection. There are fairly obvious scenes at resorts like Ýdhra, Rhodes and Mýkonos. Skála Eressoü on Lésvos, the birthplace of Sappho, is (appropriately) an international mecca for lesbians.

## Insurance

Even though EU healthcare privileges apply in Greece (see p.59 for details), you should consider taking out an **insurance policy** before travelling to cover against theft, loss, illness or injury. Before paying for a whole new policy, however, it's worth checking whether you are already covered: some all-risks homeowners' or renters' insurance policies may cover your possessions when overseas, and many private medical schemes (such as BUPA or WPA in the UK) offer coverage extensions for abroad.

In Canada, provincial health plans usually provide partial cover for medical mishaps overseas, while holders of official student/ teacher/youth cards in Canada and the US are entitled to meagre accident coverage and hospital inpatient benefits. **Students** will often find that their student health coverage extends during the vacations and for one term beyond the date of last enrolment. Most **credit-card issuers** also offer some sort of basic vacation insurance, if you pay for the holiday with their card – however, it's vital to check what these policies cover.

After exhausting the possibilities above, you might want to contact a **specialist travel insurance** company, or consider the travel insurance deal we offer (see box, p.74). A typical travel insurance policy usually provides cover for the **loss** of baggage, tickets and passport, as well as **cancellation** or curtailment of your journey. Unless an extra premium is paid, most exclude "**dangerous sports**": in the Greek islands this means motorbiking, windsurfing and possibly sailing. Some policies can be chopped and changed to exclude coverage you don't need – for example, sickness and accident benefits can often be excluded or included. They never pay out for medical treatment relating to

## Rough Guides travel insurance

Rough Guides has teamed up with Columbus Direct to offer you **travel insurance** that can be tailored to suit your needs. Products include a low-cost **backpacker** option for long stays, a **short break** option for city getaways, a typical **holiday package** option, and others. There are also annual **multi-trip** policies for those who travel regularly. Different sports and activities (trekking, skiing, etc) can usually be covered, if required.

See our website (ⓦwww.roughguides.com/website/shop) for eligibility and purchasing options. Alternatively, UK residents should call ☏0870/033 9988; Australians should call ☏1300/669 999 and New Zealanders should call ☏0800/55 9911. All other nationalities should call ☏+44 870/890 2843.

injuries incurred whilst under the influence of alcohol or drugs. If you take medical coverage, ascertain whether benefits are paid as treatment proceeds or only after return home, whether there is a **24-hour medical emergency number**, and how much the deductible excess is. With baggage cover, make sure that the **per-article limit** will cover your most valuable possession. UK travel agents and tour operators are likely to **require travel insurance** when you book a package holiday, though it does not have to be their own.

Make any claim as soon as possible, and keep all receipts for medicines and treatment. If you have anything stolen or lost, you must obtain an **official statement** from the police or the airline which lost your bags – with numerous fraudulent claims, most insurers won't even consider one unless you have a police report.

### Internet

Rates at **internet cafés** tend to be about €2–4 per hour, occasionally more. If you are travelling with your own **laptop**, you may well be able to roam in Greece depending on what agreement your home ISP has with any Greek partners. Check with your ISP, and get the local dial-up number, before you leave. Charges tend to be fairly high, but for a few minutes per day still work out less than going to an internet café. Alternatively, you can take out a temporary **internet account** with one of the half-dozen Greek ISPs (minimum one month, cost €10–14 per month). Some hotels and cafés offer wi-fi internet access, usually free to customers.

### Laundries

*Plindíria*, as they're known in Greek, are available in the main resort towns; sometimes an attended service wash is available for little or no extra charge over the basic cost of €8–10 per wash and dry. Self-catering villas will usually be furnished with a drying line and a selection of plastic wash-tubs or a bucket. In hotels, laundering should be done in a more circumspect manner, particularly if the hotel offers laundry as a payable service.

### Mail

**Post offices** are open Monday to Friday from 7.30am to 2pm, though certain main branches are also open evenings and Saturday mornings. **Airmail letters** take 3–7 days to reach the rest of Europe, 5–12 days to North America, a little longer for Australia and New Zealand. Generally, the larger the island (and the busier its airport), the quicker the service. Postal rates for up to 20g are a uniform €0.70 to all overseas destinations. For a modest fee (about €3) you can shave a day or two off delivery time to any destination by using the **express service** (*katepígonda*). **Registered** (*systiméno*) delivery is also available for a similar amount, but proves quite slow unless coupled with express service. For a simple letter or card, a stamp (*grammatósimo*) can also be purchased at authorized postal agencies (usually stationers or postcard shops).

**Parcels** should (and often can) only be handled in the main provincial or county capitals; this way, your bundle will be in Athens, and on an international flight, within a day or so. For non-EU/EEA destinations, always present your box open for inspection, and come prepared with tape and scissors – most post offices will sell cardboard boxes, but nothing to close the package. An array of services is available: air parcel (fast and expensive), surface-air lift (a couple of weeks slower but much cheaper), insured, and proof of delivery among others.

Ordinary **post boxes** are bright yellow, express boxes dark red, but it's best to use those adjacent to an actual post office, since days may pass between collections at boxes elsewhere. If there are two slots, "ESOTERIKÓ" is for domestic mail, "EXOTERIKÓ" for overseas. Often there are more: one box or slot for mail into Athens and suburbs, one for your local province, one for "other" parts of Greece, and one for overseas; if in doubt, ask someone.

The **poste restante** system is reasonably efficient, especially at the post offices of larger towns. Mail should be clearly addressed and marked "poste restante", with your surname underlined, to the main post office of whichever town you choose. It will be held for a month and you'll need your passport to collect it.

## Maps

**Maps** in Greece are an endless source of confusion. Each cartographic company seems to have its own peculiar system of transcribing Greek letters into the Roman alphabet – which, as often as not, do not match the transliterations on road signs.

The most reliable **general touring maps** of Greece are those published by Athens-based Anavasi (Ⓦwww.anavasi.gr), Road Editions (Ⓦwww.road.gr) and newcomer Orama

(Ⓦwww.nakas-maps.gr). Anavasi and Road Editions products are widely available in Greece at selected bookstores, as well as at petrol stations and general tourist shops country-wide. In Britain they are found at Stanfords (Ⓣ020/7836 1321, Ⓦwww .stanfords.co.uk) and the Hellenic Book Service (Ⓣ020/7267 9499, Ⓦwww .hellenicbookservice.com); in the US, they're sold through Omni Resources (Ⓣ910/227-8300, Ⓦwww.omnimap.com). Anavasi is probably the best of the three, for detail of paths and unsurfaced roads: all are based on large-scale military maps, and where they duplicate coverage you may want to buy both.

Touring maps of **individual islands** are more easily available on the spot, although most local ones are wildly inaccurate or obsolete. Reasonably reliable and up-to-date publications include the Anavasi and Road products for **Crete**, plus nearly forty more Road titles for other islands at scales of 1:25000–1:70000, including the Ionians, east Aegean, Sporades and most Cyclades and Dodecanese. Anavasi cover the Cyclades, Sporades, Híos and Kálymnos well at scales of 1:25000–1:60000.

## Money

Greece's currency is the **euro** (€). Up-to-date **exchange rates** can be found on Ⓦwww .oanda.com. Shopkeepers do not bother much with shortfalls of 5 cents or less, especially if they're in their favour.

Euro notes exist in denominations of 5, 10, 20, 50, 100, 200 and 500 euros, and coins in denominations of 1, 2, 5, 10, 20 and 50 cents and 1 and 2 euros. Avoid getting stuck

### Hiking/topographical maps

**Hiking/topographical maps** are gradually improving in quality and availability. **Anavasi** (Ⓣ210 72 93 541, Ⓦwww.mountains.gr/anavasi) publishes a GPS-compatible, CD-ROM-available series covering the White Mountains and Psiloritis on Crete and Mt Dhýrfis on Évvia. Anavasi products use the same sources as Road, but are frequently more accurate. They are sold in the better Athens bookstores, as well as their own shopfront at Stoá Arsakíou 6A in central Athens, but do not have much international distribution.

For hiking in particular areas of Crete, Corfu, Kálymnos, Lésvos, Messinía, Párga, Pílio, Sámos, Sými and Thássos, map-and-guide booklets published by **Marengo Publications** in England also prove very useful. Stanfords (see above) keeps a good stock, or order direct on Ⓣ01485/532710, Ⓦwww.marengowalks.com.

with **counterfeit euro notes** (€100 and €200 ones abound). Genuine notes all have a hologram strip or (if over €50) patch at one end, there's a watermark at the other and a security thread embedded in the middle.

### Banks and exchange

Greek **banks** normally open Monday to Thursday 8.30am–2.30pm and Friday 8.30am–2pm. Always take your passport with you as proof of identity and expect long queues. Large hotels and some travel agencies also provide an exchange service, though with hefty commissions. On small islands with no full-service bank, "authorized" bank agents will charge an additional fee for posting a traveller's cheque to a proper branch.

There are a number of authorized brokers for exchanging foreign cash in Athens and other major tourist centres. When changing small amounts, choose those bureaux that charge a flat percentage commission (usually one percent) rather than a high minimum. There are a small number of 24-hour automatic **foreign-note-changing machines**, but a high minimum commission tends to be deducted. There's no need to **purchase euros** beforehand unless you're arriving at some ungodly hour to one of the remoter frontier posts. All major airports have an ATM or banking booth for incoming international flights.

### Traveller's cheques, credit cards and ATMs

**Traveller's cheques** (ideally in euros) can be cashed at most banks, though rarely elsewhere. Cashing the cheques will incur a minimum charge of €1.20–2.40 depending on the bank; for larger amounts, a set percentage will apply.

**Credit/debit cards** are likely to be your main source of funds while travelling, by withdrawing money (using your usual PIN) from the vast network of Greek **ATMs**. Larger airports have at least one ATM in the arrivals hall, and any town or island with a population larger than a few thousand (or substantial tourist traffic) also has them. Most accept Visa, MasterCard, Visa Electron, Plus and Cirrus cards; American

Express holders are restricted to the ATMs of Alpha and National Bank.

ATM transactions with **debit cards** linked to a current account attract **charges** of at least 2.5 percent on the sterling/dollar transaction value, plus a commission fee of a similar amount; the tourist rate rather than the more favourable interbank rate will be applied. A few banks or building societies (such as Nationwide) waive some or all of these fees. Using **credit cards** at an ATM costs roughly the same, although inflated interest accrues from the moment of use.

Major credit cards are not usually accepted by cheaper tavernas or hotels, but they can be essential for renting cars. Big travel agents may also accept them, though a **three-percent surcharge** is often levied on the purchase of ferry tickets.

In an emergency you can arrange to have **money wired** from your home bank to a bank in Greece. Receiving funds by SWIFT transfer takes anywhere from two to ten working days and your home bank will need the IBAN (international bank account number) for the account to which funds are being sent. Local affiliate offices are thin on the ground, but if you do locate a designated receiving point for Western Union or Amex, you should receive your cash within hours of it being sent.

## Movies

Greek cinemas show the regular major release movies, which in the case of English-language titles will almost always be in English with Greek subtitles. In summer open-air screens operate in all the major towns and some of the resorts, and these are absolutely wonderful. You may not hear much thanks to crackly speakers and locals chatting away throughout, but watching a movie under the stars on a warm night is simply a great experience. There are usually two screenings, at about 9pm and 11pm, with the sound at the latter turned down to avoid complaints of noise from neighbours.

## Opening hours and entrance fees

It's difficult to generalize about Greek **opening hours**, especially museum and site schedules, which change constantly. The traditional timetable starts with shops opening 8.30/9am and closing for a long break at lunchtime. Most places, except banks, reopen in the mid to late afternoon. Tourist areas tend to adopt a more northern European timetable, with shops, travel agencies and offices, as well as key archeological sites and museums, usually open throughout the day.

Private businesses, or anyone providing a service, frequently operate a straight 9am to 5/6pm schedule. If someone is actually selling something, then they are more likely to follow a split shift as detailed below.

**Shopping hours** during the hottest months are theoretically Monday, Wednesday and Saturday from 9am to 2.30pm, and Tuesday, Thursday and Friday from 8.30am to 2pm and 6 to 9pm. During the cooler months the morning schedule shifts slightly earlier, the evening session a half or even a full hour later. In Athens many places keep a continuous schedule (synehés orário) during the winter, but this is not yet universally observed, even with EU pressure, and the threat of its legal enforcement. There are so many exceptions to rules by virtue of holidays and professional idiosyncrasy that you can't count on getting anything done except from Monday to Friday, between 9.30am and 1pm. **Delis** and **butchers** are not allowed to sell fresh meat during summer afternoons (though some flout this rule); similarly, **fishmongers** are only open until they sell out (usually by noon). **Pharmacies** open Monday to Friday, with a duty pharmacist open on Saturdays. **Travel agencies** at the busiest resorts are open from about 9am to 10pm Monday to Saturday, with some Sunday hours as well.

Most **government agencies** are open to the public on weekdays from 8am to 2pm. In general, however, you'd be optimistic to show up after 1pm expecting to be served the same day, as queues can be long.

**Monasteries** are generally open from approximately 9am to 1pm and 5 to 8pm (3.30 to 6.30pm in winter) for limited visits.

Opening hours of **ancient sites** and **museums** vary; as far as possible, times are quoted in the text, but these change with exasperating frequency, and at smaller sites may be subject to the availability of a local site guard. Unless specified, the times quoted are generally summer hours, in effect from around late May to the end of September. Reckon on later opening and earlier closing in winter. Hours will be reduced on the numerous public holidays and festivals. The most important holidays, when almost everything will be closed, are marked 'PH' on pages 63–65.

All the major **ancient sites**, like most **museums**, charge **entrance fees** ranging from €2 to €12, with an average fee of around €3. Entrance to all state-run sites and museums is **free** on Sundays and public holidays from November to March, although they will be shut on public holidays.

## Phones

All Greek numbers require the dialling of all ten digits, including the area code. Land lines begin with 2; mobiles with 6. All landline exchanges are digital, and you should have few problems reaching any number from overseas or within Greece.

**Call boxes**, poorly maintained and sited at the noisiest street corners, usually work only with phonecards (tilekártes), available in denominations starting at €4, from kiosks and newsagents, though call box payphones are now appearing. Call boxes cannot be rung back; however, the green **countertop cardphones** kept by some hotels can. Other options for local calls include **counter coin-op phones** in bars, kafenía and hotel lobbies; these take small coins and can usually be rung back.

Local or intercity calls to land lines are cheap on OTE (Hellenic Telecommunications) tilekártes, but if you plan on making lots of international calls, you'll want a **calling card**, all of which involve calling a free access number from either certain phone boxes or a fixed line (not a mobile) and then entering a twelve-digit code. OTE has its own scheme, but competitors generally prove cheaper. Always tell the card vendor where you intend to call, to get the card best suited for you. Hotels sometimes

## Phone codes and numbers

### Phoning Greece from abroad
Dial ☎0030 + the full number

### Phoning abroad from Greece
Dial the country code (below) + area code (minus any initial 0) + number

| Australia | ☎0061 | UK | ☎0044 |
|---|---|---|---|
| New Zealand | ☎0064 | Ireland | ☎00353 |
| Canada | ☎001 | USA | ☎001 |
| South Africa | ☎0027 | | |

### Greek phone prefixes
| Local call rate | ☎0801 |
|---|---|
| Toll-free/Freefone | ☎0800 |

### Useful Greek telephone numbers
| Ambulance | ☎166 | Police/Emergency | ☎100 |
|---|---|---|---|
| Fire brigade, urban | ☎199 | Speaking clock | ☎141 |
| Forest fire reporting | ☎191 | Tourist police | ☎171 (Athens); |
| Operator | ☎132 (Domestic) | ☎210 171 (elsewhere) | |
| Operator | ☎139 (International) | | |

impose a surcharge for calling from their rooms, so check first.

Three **mobile phone networks** operate in Greece: Vodafone, Cosmote and Q-Telecom/WIND Hellas. **Coverage** countrywide is good – there's even a signal in the Athens metro – though there are a few "dead" zones in the mountains, or on really remote islets. Contract-free plans are heavily promoted in Greece, and if you're here for more than a week or so, buying a **pay-as-you-go** SIM card (for €15–20) from any of the mobile phone outlets will pay for itself very quickly, and you can reuse the same number on your next visit. Top-up cards – starting from €8–10 – are available at all *períptera* (kiosks). UK providers may tell you that another SIM can't be fitted without a hefty surcharge to unlock your phone, but you are legally entitled to the unblock code from the manufacturer after (usually) six months of use. Otherwise, have a mobile shop in Greece unblock the phone for a small charge. North American users will only be able to use tri-band or quad-band phones in Greece. Roaming with your UK provider within the EU will now land you with charges capped at €0.51 equivalent per minute (or €0.26 to receive calls).

## Photography

Memory cards and sticks for **digital cameras** are widely available, and photo shops can print out images or download them onto CD. Fuji and Kodak **print films** are reasonably priced and easy to have processed. APS film is also widely sold and processed. Kodak and Fuji slide films can be purchased in larger centres but often cannot be processed there.

It's free to **take photos** of open-air sites, though museum photography and the use of videos or tripods anywhere requires an extra fee and written permit. This usually has to be arranged in writing from the nearest Department of Antiquities (*Eforía Arheotíton*). Beware of taking pictures near military sites – see p.67.

## Time

Greek summer time begins at 3am on the last Sunday in March, when the clocks go forward one hour, and ends at 2am on the last Sunday in October, when they go back. This change is not well publicized locally, and visitors miss planes and ferries every year. Greek time is always two hours ahead of Britain. For North America, the difference is seven hours for Eastern Standard Time, ten hours for Pacific Standard Time, with daylight saving starting 2–3 weeks earlier and ending a week later than in Europe.

## Toilets

Public toilets are usually in parks or squares, often subterranean; otherwise try a bus station. Except in tourist areas, public toilets tend to be filthy – it's best to use those in restaurants and bars. Remember that throughout Greece you drop paper in the adjacent wastebins, not the toilet bowl.

## Tourist information

The **National Tourist Organization of Greece** (Ellinikós Organismós Tourismoú, or EOT; GNTO abroad, Ⓦwww.gnto.gr) maintains offices in most European capitals, plus major cities in North America and Australia (see below). It publishes an array of free, glossy, regional pamphlets, invariably several years out of date, fine for getting a picture of where you want to go, but low on useful facts.

In Greece, you will find official **EOT offices** in many of the larger towns and resorts where, in addition to the usual leaflets, you can find weekly **schedules** for the inter-island **ferries** – rarely entirely accurate, but useful as a guideline. EOT staff may be able to advise on **bus** and **train** departures as well as current opening hours for local sites and museums, and can occasionally assist with accommodation.

Where there is no EOT office, you can get information from **municipally-run tourist offices** – these can be more highly motivated and helpful than EOT branches. In the absence of any of these, you can visit the **Tourist Police**, essentially a division (often just a single room) of the local police. They can sometimes provide you with lists of rooms to let, which they regulate, but they're really the place to go if you have a **serious complaint** about a taxi, or an accommodation or eating establishment.

### Greek national tourist offices abroad

Australia & New Zealand 51 Pitt St, Sydney, NSW 2000 ☎02/9241 1663, Ⓔhto@tpg.com.au.
Canada 91 Scollard St, 2nd Floor, Toronto, ON M5R 1GR ☎416/968-2220, Ⓔgrnto.tor@sympatico.ca.
UK 4 Conduit St, London W1R 0DJ ☎020/7495 4300, ⒺEOT-greektouristoffice@btinternet.com.
USA 645 5th Ave, New York, NY 10022 ☎212/421-5777, Ⓔinfo@greektourism.com.

## Travellers with disabilities

Unfortunately, many of the delights of Greece like stepped alleys and ancient monuments are inaccessible or hazardous for anyone with mobility impairments. Access to all but the newest public buildings and hotels can also be difficult. In general the **disabled** are not especially well catered for in Greece – with the notable exception of Kos. Few street corners have wheelchair ramps, beeps for the sight-impaired are rare at pedestrian crossings, and outside Athens few buses are of the "kneeling" type. Only Athens airport, its metro and airline staff in general (who are used to handling wheelchairs) are disabled-friendly. However, as relevant EU-wide legislation is implemented, the situation should improve.

Some advance planning will make a trauma-free holiday in Greece more likely. The Greek National Tourist Office is helpful as long as you have specific questions; they also publish a useful questionnaire that you might send to hotels or self-catering accommodation. Before purchasing **travel insurance**, ensure that pre-existing medical conditions are not excluded. A **medical certificate** of your fitness to travel is also extremely useful; some airlines or insurance companies may insist on it.

## Travelling with children

**Children** are worshipped and indulged, demonstrably to excess, and present few problems when travelling. They are not segregated from adults at meal times, and early on in life are inducted into the typical late-night routine – kids at tavernas are expected to eat (and up to their capabilities, talk) like adults. Outside of certain all-inclusive resorts with childrens' programmes, however, there are very few amusements specifically for them apart from a few water parks. Luxury hotels are more likely to offer some kind of **baby-sitting or crèche service**.

Most domestic ferry-boat companies and airlines offer child **discounts**, ranging from fifty to one hundred percent depending on their age; hotels and rooms won't charge extra for infants, and levy a modest supplement for "third" beds which the child occupies by him/herself.

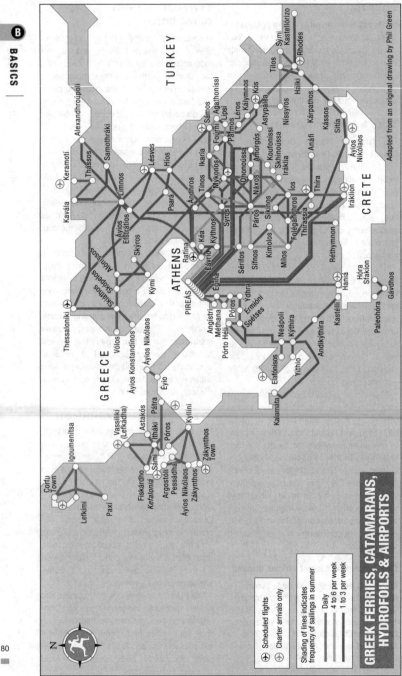

GREEK FERRIES, CATAMARANS, HYDROFOILS & AIRPORTS

⊕ Scheduled flights
⊕ Charter arrivals only

Shading of lines indicates
frequency of sailings in summer

Daily
4 to 6 per week
1 to 3 per week

Adapted from an original drawing by Phil Green

# Guide

# Guide

# 1

# The Argo-Saronic

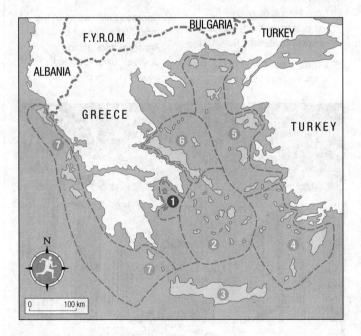

CHAPTER 1 # Highlights

✳ **Temple of Aphaea, Égina**
The best-preserved Archaic
temple on any island, in
an evocative setting on a
wooded hill with magnificent
views towards Athens.
See p.92

✳ **Angístri Island** Little known
to outsiders, this dot of
land is less than an hour
from Athens by hydrofoil,
yet preserves the feel of an
unspoilt hideaway. See p.93

✳ **Póros Town** Climb to the
clocktower of this small
island's capital for a view
over the Argo-Saronic
Gulf and the Peloponnese.
See p.96

✳ **Ýdhra Town** A perfect
horseshoe-shaped harbour
surrounded by grand
eighteenth-century
mansions and traffic-free
streets. See p.101

✳ **Spétses** Enjoy some of the
most alluring beaches in the
Argo-Saronics along
Spétses' pine-speckled
coastline. See p.111

▲ Temple of Aphaea, Égina

# The Argo-Saronic

The rocky, partly volcanic **Argo-Saronic** islands, most of them barely an olive's throw from the mainland, differ to a surprising extent not just from the land they face but also from one another. Less unexpected – given their proximity to Athens and their beauty – is their massive popularity, with Égina (Aegina) almost becoming a city suburb at weekends. Póros, Ýdhra (Hydra) and Spétses are scarcely different in summer, though their visitors include a higher proportion of foreign tourists. More than any other group, these islands are best out of season and midweek, when visiting populations (and prices) fall dramatically and the port towns return to a quieter, more provincial pace. You'll also notice a significant difference between Ýdhra and Spétses, the furthest of the islands, and those closer to Athens – partly perhaps because of the distance, and because they're accessible only by hydrofoil and catamaran rather than the cheaper conventional ferries, they're markedly more expensive and exclusive, with significant ex-pat populations.

The northernmost island of the Argo-Saronic group, **Salamína**, is effectively a suburb of Pireás. Its narrow strait, barely a kilometre across (where, in 480 BC, the Greek navy trounced the Persian fleet, see p.87), is crossed by a constant stream of ferries, but there's little to attract you on the other side, and the island is covered only briefly here. **Égina**, important in antiquity and more or less continually inhabited since then, is infinitely preferable: the most fertile of the group, it is famous for its pistachio nuts and home to one of the finest ancient temples in Greece. Tiny **Angístri** is often treated as little more than an adjunct of Égina, but it's a lovely place in its own right, ideal for a few days' complete relaxation. The three southerly islands – green **Póros**, tiny, car-free **Ýdhra** and upmarket **Spétses** – are pine-covered to various degrees, comparatively infertile, and rely on water piped or transported in rusting freighters from the mainland. Accordingly, they were not extensively settled until medieval times, when refugees from the mainland established themselves here, adopting seagoing commerce (and piracy) as livelihoods. Today, foreigners and Athenians have replaced locals in the depopulated harbour towns; windsurfers, water-taxis and yachts are faint echoes of the massed warships, schooners and *kaḯkia* once at anchor.

For all of these islands, **hydrofoil** services are faster and more frequent than ferries, though they cost around twice as much. Friday evening and Saturday morning sailings, as well as the returns on Sunday night, can be very busy, and if you hope to bring a vehicle for the weekend, reserve your trip well in advance.

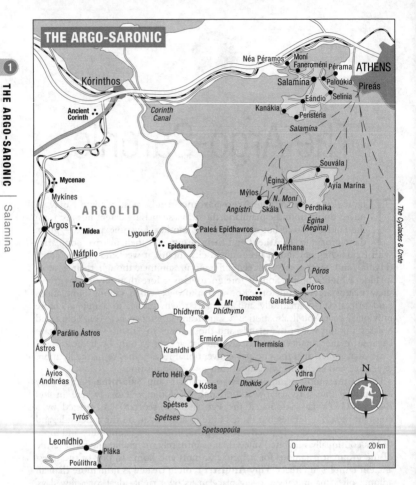

The Cyclades & Crete

# Salamína

**Salamína** is the quickest possible island-hop from Pireás, and indeed much of its population commutes to the city to work. This makes it incredibly easy to get to, and if you have an afternoon to kill it's an enjoyable boat ride. The island itself is highly developed, has few tourist facilities, and is close enough to the Athenian dockyards to make swimming unappealing. The island's port is at **Paloúkia**, facing the mainland, and a short hop across a narrow isthmus to **SALAMÍNA TOWN** on the west coast. Buses run every fifteen minutes between the two, through continuous suburban development. From the ferry dock they also run hourly to numerous other destinations on the island. Getting here from Athens is easy enough – there are hourly small passenger boats from Pireás (departing from the same area as other Argo-Saronic ferries, close to Gate E8; 45min; €2.60), and a constant stream of small boats and roll-on, roll-off car ferries from **Pérama**, on the mainland directly opposite (5min; €1). Pérama is easily reached by bus: #843 from Pireás, G18 or B18 from Omónia in central Athens.

## The Battle of Salamis

Perhaps the main reason for heading to Salamína is for the boat trip itself, through an extraordinary industrial seascape of docks and shipworks. The waters you cross were the site of one of the most significant **sea battles** of ancient times; some would say of all time, given that this was a decisive blow in preventing a Persian invasion and allowing the development of Classical Athens, and with it modern Western culture.

In 480 BC, the Greeks were in full retreat from the vast Persian army under Xerxes following the defeat of the Spartans at Thermopylae (of *300* fame). Many Greek cities, including Athens, had been sacked and burned by the invaders – indeed smoke from the ruins on the Acropolis probably formed a backdrop to the **Battle of Salamis**. The Greeks were by no means united, but Athenian leader Themistocles managed to persuade (or in some cases trick) them into making a stand at Salamis. The Greeks had roughly 370 triremes supplied by around twenty cities, the bulk from Athens, Corinth and Aegina; the Persian fleet was twice the size, with heavier ships, but even more diverse, with many from subject nations whose loyalty was questionable.

Through false information and strategic retreats, the Greeks managed first to tire many of the Persian crews – who rowed all night to cut off a non-existent escape attempt – and then to lure them into the narrow strait off Salamína. Crowded in and unable to manoeuvre, and with the wind in the wrong direction, the Persians found themselves at the mercy of the more nimble Greek triremes, and the battle eventually became a rout. Some two hundred Persian ships were sunk, against forty-odd on the Greek side, and few of their heavily armoured crews or marines survived. Although Xerxes' army was still dominant on the mainland, loss of the fleet made re-supplying such vast numbers all but impossible: by the end of the following year the Persians had also been defeated on land, and Greek ships had taken the war across the Aegean, freeing islands and the Greek cities of Asia Minor from Persian rule.

The route from Pireás roughly follows the course of the Persians as they sailed into the strait. Xerxes himself had a golden throne placed on Mount Egaléo, the hill above modern Pérama, from which he observed the destruction. The Greek fleet was drawn up along the shore of the island opposite Pérama, and in particular in the bay around Paloúkia and on the long beach to your left as you approach, where nowadays ships are beached for breaking. Their attacks forced the Persians toward the mainland shore where they became trapped – in their desperation to escape, Persian ships are said to have turned on each other.

Salamína Town itself is a substantial but not terribly attractive place: there are plenty of cafés, but these are separated from the waterfront and fishing harbour by busy main roads. Five kilometres or so beyond, **Eándio** has the island's cleanest and most attractive beaches. A similar distance from Salamína Town to the north, the **monastery of Faneroméni** (daily 8.30am–12.30pm & 4pm–sunset) is a working nunnery with impressive frescoes, beautifully sited amidst pine woods overlooking the mainland. Alternatively, south of Paloúkia lies the resort of **Selínia**, facing back towards Athens. There are numerous good seafront tavernas here, though the outlook is rather industrial. All three of these have hourly buses from Paloúkia.

# Égina (Aegina)

A substantial and attractive island with a proud history, less than an hour from Pireás, Égina is not surprisingly a popular weekend escape from Athens. Despite the holiday homes, though, it retains a laid-back, island atmosphere, especially if you visit midweek or out of season. Famous for its **pistachio orchards** – the

ÉGINA (AEGINA)

nuts are hawked from stalls all around the harbour – the island can also boast substantial ancient remains, the finest of which is the beautiful fifth-century BC **Temple of Aphaea**, commanding superb views towards Athens from high above the northeast coast, close to the resort-port of **Ayía Marína**.

Inhabited from the earliest times, ancient **Aegina** was a significant regional power as early as the Bronze Age, when it fell under the influence of Minoan Crete, and later a fierce rival of Classical Athens. It traded to the limits of the known world, maintained a sophisticated silver coinage system (the first in Greece) and fostered prominent athletes and craftsmen. The Aeginian fleet played a major role in the Battle of Salamis (see p.87). Thereafter, however, the islanders made the political mistake of siding with the Spartans. Athens used this as a pretext to act on long-standing jealousy; her fleets defeated those of the islanders in two separate sea battles and, after the second, the population was expelled and replaced by more tractable colonists.

Subsequent history was less distinguished, with a familiar pattern of occupation – by Romans, Franks, Venetians, Catalans and Ottomans – before the War of Independence brought a brief period of glory as seat of government for the fledgling Greek nation, from 1826 to 1828. For many decades afterwards Égina was a penal island, and you can still see the **enormous jail** undergoing restoration on the edge of town; the building was originally an **orphanage**, founded by first president Kapodhistrias in 1828.

## Égina Town

**ÉGINA TOWN**, the island's capital, makes an attractive base, with some grand old buildings around a large, busy harbour. The Neoclassical architecture is matched by a sophisticated ethos: by island standards this is a large town, with plenty of shopping, a lively, well-stocked bazaar, a semi-permanent yacht-dwelling contingent and no shortage of attractive places to eat and drink.

## Arrival and information

On arrival, you'll find yourself docking pretty much at the heart of town. The **bus station** is on Platía Ethneyersías, immediately north, with excellent services to most villages; buy your tickets beforehand at the little booth. The **taxi** rank is at the base of the jetty, opposite the row of **cabins** selling tickets for the various catamarans, **ferries and hydrofoils**; some hydrofoils and ferries from Pireás continue to Angístri, but the most frequent service is with the *Angístri Express*, which ties up among the pleasure and fishing boats to the south. The **post office** is at the rear of the platía, and numerous banks have **ATMs** here and around the harbour. Several places on and behind the main waterfront **rent cars**, scooters, motorbikes and mountain bikes – Égina is large and hilly enough to make a motor worthwhile for anything other than a pedal to the local beaches: Trust (T22970 27010), one of the first you come to behind the harbour, has the best prices, though some of their mopeds are fairly battered.

There's no **tourist office**, but Wwww.aegina.com.gr is a useful resource, while Aegina Island Holidays (T22970 26430, Wwww.aeginaislandgreece.com), on the waterfront near the church of Panayítsa, offers excursions to the mainland and islands, including to the Epidaurus festival, as well as help with accommodation should you need it. **Internet** access is available at a couple of the harbour-front cafés and at *Avli* (see p.91), but is faster and more reliable at Global Internet Café at Fanerómenis 7, just off the southern end of the waterfront. **Foreign-language papers** are stocked by Kalezis, midway along the waterfront, and at Kendrou Typou, inland on Eákou at the corner of Spýrou Ródhi.

## Accommodation

As on most of the Argo-Saronics, **accommodation** is at a premium at weekends, but rates can drop appreciably midweek and out of season. With the exceptions noted, most lodgings are subject to a certain amount of traffic noise, and facilities, including bathrooms, can be pretty rudimentary.

**Artemis** Kanári 20, behind Platía Ethneyersías (bus station square) T22970 25195, Wwww .artemishotel-aegina.com. Rather plain, old-fashioned rooms (with fridges, TV and a/c) but an attractive, quiet location; upper floor rooms at the front have balconies with great views over a pistachio orchard towards the sea. ❸

**Brown** Southern waterfront, past Panayítsa church T22970 22271, Wwww.hotelbrown.gr. The town's top offering, this B-class/3-star hotel opposite the southerly town beach, housed in a former sponge factory dating from 1886, earns its rating from its vast common areas (terrace bar, buffet-breakfast salon). The best and calmest units are the garden bungalows; the galleried family suites (❼) sleep four. B&B ❹

**Eginitiko Arhontiko** Cnr Thomaïdhou and Ayíou Nikólaou, by the Markellos Tower T22970 24968, Wwww.aeginitikoarchontiko.gr. Spectacular converted ochre-and-orange Neoclassical mansion,

with period furnishings. The suite (❻) has painted ceilings; other rooms are attractive and traditional (apart from the a/c, TV and fridge) but very basic. Breakfast is served in a pretty conservatory. B&B ❹

**Elektra** Leonárdhou Ladhá 25, northwest of Platía Ethneyersías T22970 26715, Wwww .aegina-electra.gr. Quiet establishment with compact but comfortable rooms with small balconies; near the more easily spotted *Hotel Marmarinos*. ❸

**Pavlou** Behind Panayítsa church at Eyinítou 21 T22970 22795. Old-school rooms establishment with a/c and some double beds in the mosaic-floored rooms; some have their baths across the hall. ❸

**Plaza** Kazantzáki 4 T22970 25600. One of a series of small waterfront hotels immediately north of Platía Ethneyersías, close to the town beach. En-suite rooms, with fridges and a/c, are pretty basic and can suffer from traffic noise, but there are great sea views from those at the front, and little balconies from which to appreciate them. ❸

## The Town

The harbour **waterfront** combines the workaday with the picturesque. Fishermen talk and tend their nets, *kaïkia* sell produce from the mainland and the seascape – of other Argo-Saronic isles and Peloponnesian mountains – is one of the finest in Greece. Sights in town are few, but it's well worth seeking out the restored **Pýrgos Markéllou** or Markellos Tower, an extraordinary miniature castle which was the seat of the first Greek government after independence. Despite appearances, it was built only around 1800 by members of the Friendly Society (see p.621) and the local politician Spyros Markellos. You can't go inside except during the occasional special exhibition, but walking there, through the cramped inland streets, is enjoyable in itself.

The site of **Ancient Aegina** (daily 8.30am–3pm, museum closed Mon; €3) lies north of the centre on a promontory known as **Kolóna**, after the lone column that stands there. The extensive remains, centring on a Temple of Apollo at the highest point, are well signed, and some reconstruction makes it easier to make out the various layers of settlement from different eras. Near the entrance, a small but worthwhile **archeological museum** houses finds from the site, along with information on the island's ancient history. Highlights of the display include a room of Minoan-influenced Middle Bronze Age pottery, rescued from a nearby building site.

On the north edge of town, between the port and Kolóna, there's a tiny but popular **beach** with remarkably shallow water. This was the site of the ancient city's harbour, of which various underwater remains are clearly visible. You can also swim to the south of town, but there are more enticing spots further north – immediately beyond Kolóna there's an attractive bay with a small, sandy **beach**, while other small coves lie off the road heading further out of town in this direction. Just a couple, **Kamares Paradise** and **Prosínemo**, have any facilities, with loungers and beach bars; the former is more attractive. As you head out this way, a plaque marks the house in the suburb of Livádhi where **Nikos Kazantzakis** lived in the 1940s and 1950s and wrote his most celebrated book, *Zorba the Greek*. A few kilometres further on, admirably signposted and marked by a giant bronze sculpture on the seafront outside, is the **Mousío Khrístou Kaprálou/Christos Kapralos Museum** (June–Oct Tues–Sun 10am–2pm & 6–8pm, Nov–May Fri–Sun 10am–2pm; €2), housed in the prominent Greek artist's former studios. The influence of Henry Moore is evident in the hefty wood, terracotta and bronze pieces on display, and there's a replica of his famous frieze *Monument of the Battle of the Pindus*, the original of which now adorns a hall in the Greek Parliament building.

### Eating, drinking and entertainment

There are plenty of good places to eat and drink in Égina, particularly at the south end of pedestrianized Panayióti Irióti behind the fish market, and at the far ends of the waterfront – fussy Athenian patronage keeps the standards fairly high. The cafés near the ferry jetty and in the centre of the waterfront tend to be less good value. Numerous bakeries can be found in the back streets - Papayionis, by Trust motorbike hire up the first alley off the seafront, is excellent.

Athenians are also partly responsible for a surprisingly ample choice of **nightlife** given a town of about nine thousand souls. There are three summer open-air **cinemas** – Anesis on Eákou towards the Pýrgos Markéllou, Olympia on Faneroménis opposite the football ground, and Akroyiali out beyond this on the Pérdhika road; indoor Titina, opposite the Pýrgos Markéllou, is open year-round. For kids, **Water Park**, in the village of Fáros on the coast a kilometre south of town, is fun, with some medium-size slides, pools, bar and restaurant; entry fees vary, but a full day for an adult is around €10. Live **Greek music** is played by the house band at *En Egini*, Spýrou Ródhi 44 (☎22970 22922 or 69446 77 788, ⓦwww.enaegini.gr), every weekend; they also host big name visiting artists – look out for posters or check the website to see what's on, and book if you want to secure a table. *Ellinikon* is a big, enjoyable, somewhat touristy club on the southern fringe of town, near the Cine Akroyiali; *Oinon Music Club*, a little further out in the same direction, is rather more laid back.

**Agora** (also known as Yeladhakis) Rear of fish market. The best of three rival seafood ouzerís here (though the others are very good too). Not the most attractive location, but serves wonderful, inexpensive, authentic Greek food: accordingly it's usually mobbed and you may have to wait for a table. Summer seating in the cobbled lane, winter up in the loft inside.

**Avli** Panayióti Irióti 17. Always busy: in the morning this offers some of the least expensive breakfasts in town, later it becomes a full-service taverna, and in the early hours it transforms into a popular bar with Latin/jazz sounds. Summer seating in the *avlí* (courtyard), and a cosy interior with fireplace for winter.

**Babis** Southern end of the waterfront at corner of Fanerómenis, beyond *Hotel Brown*. Modern ouzerí with a seafront terrace and trendy Athenian crowd; excellent food, relatively high prices.

**Flisvos** North waterfront by town beach. Towards the end of a line of similar establishments, an excellent spot for grilled fresh fish and a few meat dishes, at fair prices.

**Ippokambos** Fanerómenis 9, a couple of blocks inland from the southern end of the waterfront. An attractive, slightly upmarket *mezedhopolío* run by Lebanese George, with rich fare including dishes such as pork roulade and stuffed squid. Open 7.30pm–1am.

**Pelaïsos** Waterfront just south of the market. The best value of a cluster of Greek-patronized taverna-ouzerís in this area, with a good mix of platters, but limited seating. Open from breakfast through till late.

## Paleohóra and the Temple of Aphaea

Two main routes lead east across the island towards Ayía Marína and the Temple of Aphaea: you can head directly inland from Égina Town across the centre of the island or follow the north coast road via **Souvála**. Along this north coast there are plenty of scruffy beaches and clusters of second-home development, between which is a surprisingly industrial landscape, with boatyards and working ports. Souvála itself is something of an Athenian resort, with a couple of direct daily ferries to Pireás and seafront restaurants and cafés all around the harbour. There are plenty of hotels too – should you want to stay try the *Hotel Saronikos* (℡22970 52224 or 694 77 79 995; ❸), overlooking the harbour from the far side, with newly refurbished rooms and apartments with kitchen. There's a small sandy beach just beyond here.

On the inland route you'll pass the whitewashed modern convent of **Áyios Nektários**, whose vast church is said to be the largest in Greece. The convent was founded by Saint Nektarios, who died in 1920 and was canonized in 1961. His tomb lies in the chapel of the original monastery, Ayía Triádha. Miracles surrounded Nektarios from the moment of his death, when the nurses put some of his clothing on an adjacent bed, occupied by a man who was paralysed; the patient promptly leapt up, praising God.

### Paleohóra

On the hillside opposite **Áyios Nektários** is the ghost-town of **Paleohóra**, the island capital through the Middle Ages. Established in early Christian times as a refuge against piracy, it thrived under the Venetians (1451–1540) but was destroyed by Barbarossa in 1537. The Turks took over and rebuilt the town, but it was again destroyed, this time by the Venetians, in 1654, and finally abandoned altogether in the early nineteenth century. The place now consists of some thirty stone chapels dotted across a rocky outcrop, an extraordinary sight from a distance. Little remains of the town itself – when the islanders left, they simply dismantled their houses and moved the masonry to newly founded Égina Town.

You can drive right up to the unenclosed site (free), where a helpful map shows the churches and the paths that lead up the hill between them. Many of the churches are semi-derelict or locked, but plenty are open too, and several preserve remains of frescoes, including Timios Stavros, right by the entrance, and Metamorfosi, Ayios Euthymios and Ayios Ioannis, on the lower path leading away from the entry. Despite the apparent isolation, many have candles burning inside too, and prayers left alongside the icons. If you climb right to the top you're rewarded with wonderful views in all directions – you can also appreciate the defensive qualities of the site, from which both coasts can be watched, yet which is almost invisible from the sea.

### The Temple of Aphaea

The Doric **Temple of Aphaea** (summer daily 8am–7pm, winter Tues–Sun 8am–5pm; €4) stands on a pine-covered hill 12km east of Égina Town, with stunning views all around: Athens, Cape Soúnio, the Peloponnese and Ýdhra are all easily made out. It is one of the most complete and visually complex ancient buildings in Greece, its superimposed arrays of columns and lintels evocative of an Escher drawing. Built between 500 and 480 BC to replace two destroyed sixth-century predecessors, it slightly pre-dates the Parthenon. The dedication is unusual: Aphaea was a Cretan nymph who, fleeing from the lust of King Minos, fell into the sea, was caught by some fishermen and brought to ancient Aegina, the only known locus of her cult, and one observed here since 1300 BC. As recently as two centuries ago, the temple's pediments, depicting two battles at Troy, were intact and essentially in perfect condition. However, like the Elgin marbles, they were "purchased" from the Turks – this time by Ludwig I of Bavaria – and they currently reside in Munich's Glyptothek museum. There's excellent, informative signage and a small **museum** (Tues–Sun 8am–2.15pm) with a great deal of information about the history and architecture of the temple as well as numerous statues and architectural features rescued from it.

At least six daily **buses** from Égina Town to Ayía Marína stop at the temple, or you can walk up from Ayía Marína along a well-signed path.

## The east: Ayía Marína to Mount Óros

The island's major beach resort, **AYÍA MARÍNA**, lies steeply below the temple on the east coast. It has clearly seen better days, as the number of empty premises and the ugly, half-built hotel overshadowing the beach attest, but package tourism (predominantly Scandinavian) is picking up again, and it can be a lively and enjoyable place in a bucket-and-spade sort of way, with plenty of hotels and rooms, and a main street lined with shops, bars and pubs. There's a good, clean, sandy beach that shelves very gently, and plenty of places to eat, many of them catering to day-trippers – several direct boats arrive from Pireás daily. *O Faros* taverna, right by the tiny fishing harbour, has a lovely location with ducks and geese wandering through, and good no-nonsense Greek food. If you want to stay, *Saronis* (T22970 32386; ❸) is a large place whose simple rooms offer a/c (some have kitchens) and substantial balconies overlooking the sandy beach; overlooking the sea on the other side of town, the *Argo Spa Hotel* (T22970 32266, Wwww.argohotel.com; ❻) has a pool and small "spa" (sauna, hot tub) and often offers good, all-in deals.

Beyond the resort, the paved road continues south 8km to **PÓRTES**, a hamlet with a distinctly end-of-the-road feel. Three little fish **tavernas** overlook the water here: *Galinopetra*, by the tiny harbour, is the most basic, *Thanasis* next up is the most ambitious, whilst *Akroyiali* to the south falls somewhere in between. All offer fish and *mezédhes*. Beyond *Akroyiali* stretches a partly sandy beach with decent snorkelling and a summer *kantína*.

From here, the road climbs steeply inland, heading back towards Égina Town via the villages of Anitséou (with a taverna), just below a major saddle on the flank of Mount Óros, and **Pahiá Ráhi**. The latter, with fine views eastwards, has been almost entirely rebuilt in traditional style by foreign and Athenian owners. South of the saddle between Pahiá Ráhi and Anitséou, signposted 400m off the paved road, are the foundations of the shrine of **Ellaníou Dhiós**, with the monastery of Taxiárhis squatting amid the massive masonry. The 532-metre summit of **Mount Óros**, an hour's walk from the highest point of the road, is capped by the modern chapel of Análipsi (Ascension) and has views across the entire island and much of the Argo-Saronic Gulf.

Gerald Thompson's *A Walking Guide to Aegina*, available locally, details a series of walks across the range of mountains and wooded valleys between Mount Óros and the Aphaea temple and down to Souvála, all avoiding main roads.

## Marathónas to Pérdhika

The road south of Égina Town, along the west coast of the island, is flat and easy, served by regular buses (8–9 daily). Sprawling **MARATHÓNAS**, 5km from Égina, has the biggest if not the prettiest of the west coast's sandy beaches, along with a scattering of rooms, tavernas and cafés along the shore. The next settlement, **Eyinítissa**, has a popular, sheltered cove backed by eucalypts and a beach bar.

**PÉRDHIKA**, at the end of the coastal road, scenically set on a little bay packed with yachts, is the most picturesque village on the island. It also has the best range of non-package holiday **accommodation** outside Égina Town: good options include *Hotel Hippocampus* (T22970 61363, Wwww.hippocampus-hotel-greece.com; ③); *Antzi Studios* (T22970 61233, Wwww.antzistudios.gr; ③, or ⑤ for greatly preferable new units with separate kitchen), a large complex with a pool; and pink-painted *Villa Rodanthos* (T22970 61400, Wwww.villarodanthos.gr; ③).

The pedestrianized waterfront esplanade at the southern edge of Pérdhika, overlooking Moní islet and the Peloponnese, is the heart of tourist life. Half a dozen good **tavernas** compete for your trade: *Saronis* is a little cheaper and gets considerable local patronage; *To Proreon*, with its potted-plant decor, has the most attractive atmosphere; while *Andonis*, an Athenian hangout, is the most popular fish taverna of the bunch. Among several **café-bars**, mostly at the far end, *Hermes* is the main late-night spot.

The only other diversion at Pérdhika is a trip to the pale-limestone offshore islet of **Moní** (10min; several departures daily in summer; €5 return). There are no facilities on the island, most of which is fenced off as a nature conservation area, but it's worth the trip for a swim in wonderfully clear water, since Pérdhika Bay itself is shallow and yacht-tainted, though you can swim from the rocky shore further round.

# Angístri

**Angístri**, fifteen minutes by fast boat from Égina, is a tiny island, obscure enough to be overlooked by most island-hoppers, though the visitors it does have are a diverse mix: Athenian weekenders, retirees who bought and restored property here years ago, plus a few British and Scandinavian package holiday-makers. There's a small, not terribly attractive strip of development on the north coast, facing Égina, but the rest of the island is pine-covered, timeless and beautiful – albeit with very few beaches. It's also strangely schizophrenic: holiday weekends can see hordes of young Greeks camping out on otherwise empty

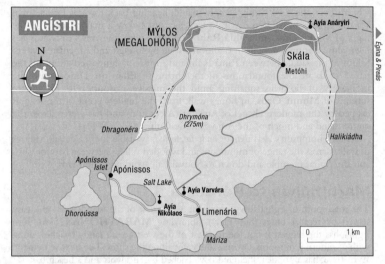

beaches, while in Skála a few small, classy hotels are juxtaposed with cafés serving English breakfasts to the package-trippers.

## Skála

**SKÁLA** and Mýlos, two small ports just a couple of kilometres apart, dominate the north coast. Both are served by the *Angístri Express* from Égina. Skála is the main tourist centre and also the landing place for the big ferries, its sandy beach backed by a straggle of modern development. The beach, and most of the new development, lies to the right from the jetty, beyond the big church, but there are some far more attractive **places to stay**, looking out over a rocky coastline, if you turn left. Of the places towards the beach, the *Aktaion Hotel* (☎22970 91222, ⓦwww.stayinagistri.gr; ❸), visible from the jetty, is the best option, with a swimming pool, restaurant and well-appointed rooms and apartments. Places to the left (south) offer peace and an unobstructed view of the water: try the *Alkyoni Hotel* (☎22970 91377, ⓦwww.alkyoni.com; ❸), with large stone-floored rooms and a lovely coffee/breakfast bar, or the slightly pricier ⚘ *Rosy's Little Village* (☎22970 91610, ⓦwww.rosyslittlevillage.com; ❸), with direct access to its own rocky swimming spot, free kayaks and bikes for guests, and a small sail-boat and motorboat for hire; both offer air conditioning, TV and balconies. *Rosy's* also has a pleasant **restaurant**, and there are plenty more to choose from around the beach: *Yiorgos*, directly above the jetty, and *To Kyma*, in the midst of the beachfront cafés, are both recommended for good-value, old-fashioned Greek meals. Thanks to the weekending Athenian youth, there are lively bars and cafés here too, and an unexpectedly busy **nightlife**. **Internet** access is offered at several of the beach cafés: *Quattro* trumps the others by bringing a laptop to your table. To carry on to the early morning, head for *Taboo*, about 500m out of town on the main road to Mýlos. Everything else you might need is also easily found, including a couple of good bakeries: in summer, there's even an open-air cinema here.

From the paved road's end just beyond the *Alkyoni Hotel*, a marked path leads along the clifftop to secluded **Halikiádha**, a pebble beach, predominantly nudist, backed by crumbling cliffs. At busy weekends there may be crowds of young

Greeks camping nearby; the rest of the time it's almost deserted. The slightly scary scramble down is rewarded by the island's best swimming.

## Metóhi and Mýlos

METÓHI, the hillside hamlet just above Skála, was once the island's main village, but now consists chiefly of holiday homes. If you can face the steep climb there are wonderful views, as well as the excellent *Taverna Parnassos* (whose roof terrace has the best views of all) and comfortable modern studios with kitchens at *Metohi Studios* (☎22970 91382; ❸).

The least attractive aspect of Angístri is the windblown road along the coast to MÝLOS (Megalohóri), the main port of call for the hydrofoils, barely half an hour's walk away. A bus runs regularly along this road, timed to match the Flying Dolphin timetable. Mýlos itself has an attractive, traditional village centre with a church and platía, though lack of a beach means few people stay here. Access to the rest of the island is easy, however, and there are plenty of rooms and **tavernas**. Of the latter, check out *Sailor* and *Fotis*; *Fotis* is also the local butcher, so the meat here is particularly good. For somewhere to **stay**, try *Meltemi Studios* (☎22970 91057; ❸), in a prime position overlooking the harbour, or the modern block of *Studios Mare* (☎22970 91012; ❸), in a quiet spot on the far edge of the village, up from the harbour.

## The rest of the island

**Scooters** and **mountain bikes** are available for rent from several outlets in Skála and Mýlos (Moto Kostas in Skála is particularly helpful); it is less than 10km to the furthest point of the island, so in cooler weather you can comfortably cross Angístri by pedal power – albeit with a couple of steep climbs – or on foot from Metóhi along a winding dirt track through the pines. In summer, the island **bus** connects Skála and Mýlos with Limenária three or four times a day (more at weekends). The broad, paved west-coast road takes you past the turning for **Dhragonéra**, a beautiful but rocky pine-fringed beach with a dramatic panorama across to the mainland; there's a summer *kantína* here and other small coves accessible across the rocks. Despite the warning signs, many people camp in the woods around these beaches.

LIMENÁRIA, a small farming community at the edge of a fertile plateau in the southeast corner of the island, is still largely unaffected by tourism. The single, central **taverna** – *O Tasos* – is popular at weekends, but pricier than you'd expect for the location; they also sell local produce. The closest swimming is a few hundred metres east down a cement drive, then steps, at **Máriza**, where a diminutive concrete lido gives access to deep, crystalline water. A broader paved road leads 2km west, past a shallow salt marsh, to the little anchorage of **Apónissos**, connected via a small causeway to an eponymous islet (private, off limits), with the larger island of **Dhoroússa** looming beyond. The *Aponisos Taverna* here (summer only) has a matchless seaside setting, but the only swimming is in a tiny, hot and stagnant area to the right of the harbour.

# Póros

Separated from the mainland by a 350-metre strait, **Póros** ("the ford") barely qualifies as an island at all. Popular with Brits and Scandinavians – more than any other Argo-Saronic island, Póros attracts package-holiday operators – it is also

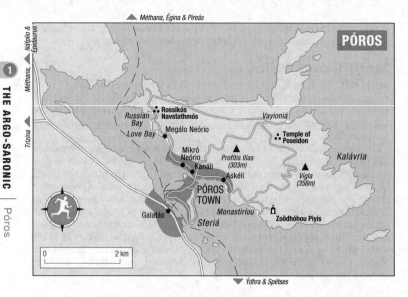

Méthana, Égina & Pireás

Náfplio & Epidaurus

Méthana,

Trizína

POROS

Rossikós Navstathmós

Russian Bay

Vayioniá

Love Bay

Megálo Neório

Temple of Poseidon

Mikró Neório

Profítis Ilías (303m)

Kalávria

Kanáli

Askéli

Vígla (358m)

PÓROS TOWN

Galatás

Monastiríou

Zoödhóhou Piyís

Sferiá

0          2 km

Ýdhra & Spétses

busy with weekending Athenians, who can get here by road (via Galatás) or on cheap ferries from Pireás. There are in fact two islands, **Sferiá** (Póros Town) and the far larger **Kalávria**, separated from each other by a miniature canal, now silting up, spanned by a bridge. The town is a busy place, with constant traffic of shipping and people: if your stay is longer than a couple of nights you may want to base yourself on Kalávria for a little more peace, coming into town for the food, nightlife and shopping.

In addition to regular ferry and hydrofoil connections with Pireás and the other Argo-Saronics, Póros has frequent, almost round-the-clock passenger boats shuttling across from the workaday mainland port of **Galatás** in the Peloponnese (5min; €0.70, €1 after midnight, pay on the boat), plus a car ferry every half hour. These permit interesting excursions – locally to ancient Troezen and the nearby Devil's Bridge, for example, or to Náfplio or Epidaurus (see box, p.99). Local travel agents run tours to these places, or simply rent a car in Galatás.

## Póros Town

**PÓROS TOWN** rises steeply across the western half of tiny volcanic Sferiá, a landmark clocktower at its summit. There's a two-room **archeological museum** on the waterfront (Tues–Sun 8.30am–3pm; €2) whose local finds will fill a spare half-hour, but otherwise few sights. This is a place to eat, drink, shop and watch the world go by. Away from the waterfront you'll quickly get lost in the labyrinth of steep, narrow streets, but nowhere is far away and most of the restaurants reasonably well signed. For a fine view over the rooftops and the strait, climb up to the **clocktower** (signed Roloï) – the tower itself is structurally suspect and fenced off, but you can still enjoy the outlook.

In any event, most things are on the waterfront. Small passenger boats tie up among the yachts and other small vessels on the southerly side facing Galatás, hydrofoils next to them, ferries further round the promontory to the north, and car ferries from Galatás right at the northern end. Close to the ferry and hydrofoil docking points are several **travel agents**, including Marinos Tours (☏22980 23423, ⒲www.marinostours.gr), for Hellenic

Seaways hydrofoil tickets and local **maps**, and Askeli Travel (☎22980 24900, ⓦwww.poros-accommodation.gr), for conventional ferry tickets.

**Platía Iroön**, the triangular "square" close to the hydrofoil dock, facing across to Galatás, is, as much as anywhere, the centre of town: here you'll find a couple of **banks** (with **ATM**s) and the **post office**. Heading east from the platía (away from the ferries) you pass the small fish market, then the Town Hall on **Platía Dhimarhíou**, the museum, and on out of town past restaurants, bars and clubs. In the other direction the coast road loops north round the promontory, past the various ferry docks and travel agents, and eventually over the bridge to Kalávria. **Internet** access and foreign-language **newspapers** are available at the newsagent/bookshop Kendro Typou, opposite where the ferries dock, and there are further internet cafés – with rather more comfortable seating – nearby toward the Galatás car ferries. **Buses** depart to Kalávria, west to Russian Bay or east to the monastery, hourly on the hour from the road across from Platía Iroön; there are also occasional **boat trips** around the island departing from the waterfront nearby and a *trenaki*, setting out from the car park by the Galatás ferry dock, whose trips include a regular evening haul all the way up to the Temple of Poseidon. Travel agents in town can rent you a **quad-bike or scooter**, but much the best service and prices are from Fotis (☎22980 25873); their office is just over the bridge, on the road towards Askéli (with a branch in Askéli too), but if you call they can deliver a bike to you. Finally, Póros Town even has two **launderettes**, Suzi's to the north just off the waterfront by the OTE (telephone company office), and To Apsolo, behind the southeastern waterfront a couple of blocks beyond *Taverna Naftis*.

## Accommodation

**Rooms** in Póros Town itself can be in very short supply at weekends and holiday times, when prices are inevitably high (they can be dramatically lower out of season); some noise is always likely too. At busy times it can be worth checking the agencies mentioned above, or the extensive listings at ⓦwww .poros.com.gr. The greatest concentration is found near the Galatás car-ferry dock, where a number of very basic places hang out "rooms" signs. Over on

▲ The waterfront, Póros Town

**Kalávria** (see box below) there's considerably more choice, with plenty of apartments and small hotels in the touristy enclaves of Askéli – close to good beaches – or less attractive Mikró Neório.

**Dimitra** Behind Dionysos (see next listing) ☎22980 25901, ⓦwww.poros.com.gr/dimitra. Quaintly furnished but very comfortable rooms, plus studios with full kitchen, two beds and sofa-bed. No other facilities and little atmosphere, but a friendly welcome. ❸

**Dionysos** Waterfront directly opposite the Galatás car-ferry dock ☎22980 23511, ⓦwww .hoteldionysos.com. An imposing old mansion that's rather less fancy than the exterior might lead you to believe; the plain rooms are comfortable enough, though, and there's a pleasant café with internet access. ❹

**Manessi** Waterfront where the Pireás ferries dock ☎22980 22273, ⓦwww.manessi .com. Classily refurbished in 2007/08, with lots of dark wood and designery touches. The larger rooms have impressive power showers, while those at the front have fabulous views; new windows mean they're well soundproofed too. ❹

**Níkos Douros** Various locations in the backstreets, including immediately above *Karavolos* taverna (see opposite ) ☎22980 22633. Rooms in a number of houses in town, which means facilities and quality vary, but all seem clean and comfortable, with a/c and TV, and prices are good. Try to see the room before you check in. ❸

**Villa Tryfon** Near the main square at the top of the hill ☎22980 25854, ⓦwww.poros.com.gr /tryfon-villa). Small apartments with air conditioning and kitchen, mostly with bay-view balconies and cheerful blue-and-white decor. ❸

## Eating, drinking and nightlife

The central waterfront is mostly given over to competing cafés, bars and souvenir shops: the better **tavernas** are found towards the southeastern end of the waterfront or up in the steep streets of the hilltop town. There are also some very good restaurants over on Kalávria.

The southeastern end of the waterfront is also the place for better-value **cafés** – *Mostra* and *Palio Syntrivani*, on Platía Dhimarhíou, for example, or *Iy Platia* and *Remezzo*, next to the archeological museum, all of which are open from breakfast till late. **Nightlife** is highly seasonal, but the better **bars** and **clubs** are in this direction too, becoming livelier as you head out along the coast road: possibilities down here include *Malibu*, a bar popular with ex-pats and tourists that's a good place to start your evening, *Orion*, a club playing mostly Greek tunes, bar/club *Maskes* and large dance club *Sirocco*, the latter right round on the uninhabited

---

### Accommodation in Kalávria

The bulk of the accommodation on Kalávria is in small apartment complexes, many with pools. These are perhaps more easily booked through agencies or online (see p.97). A few hotels are also worth noting, however.

**Pavlou** Right on the beach in Megálo Neório ☎22980 22734, ⓦwww .pavlouhotel.gr. Family-run hotel with pool, tennis court and restaurant, right on one of the island's best beaches. The decor is plain but comfortable, with big balconies, half of which have great sea views. Breakfast included. ❹

**Poros Image** Neório ☎22980 22216, ⓦwww.porosimage.gr. Not quite as fancy as its designer exterior and website might suggest, this is nonetheless an elegantly refurbished hotel with great views from almost every room back across the bay towards Póros Town, from the waterfront between Mikró and Megálo Neório. Half-board option best avoided. ❻

**Sirene** Above the beach at Monastiríou ☎22980 22741. Large, modern hotel with pool and tennis courts, spectacularly sited on a steep slope above the sea, with a small private beach below. The stunning location ensures fabulous views from the balconies, though the rooms themselves are curiously dowdy and old-fashioned. ❻

## Excursions to the Peloponnese

Once you've made the crossing from Póros to Galatás, you'll see hire cars on offer starting from around €25 a day, and in a day you can easily reach numerous attractions on the Argolid peninsula. Closest at hand is ancient **Troezen**, an unenclosed site near the modern village of Trizína. Legendary birthplace of Theseus, Troezen is a scattered site most easily understood if you purchase a map in the village – this also recounts the stories of Theseus's life. A short walk up a gorge from the site takes you to the spectacular **Dhiavoloyéfyro**, the Devil's Bridge, a natural rock arch spanning the chasm.

**Epidaurus** (Epídhavros; daily summer 8am–7pm, winter 8am–5pm; €6), one of the finest ancient monuments in Greece, is only about 50km further. Most famous for its fourth-century BC theatre, with extraordinary acoustics, it is also an extensive sanctuary to Asklepios, god of healing. The theatre is used for productions of Classical Greek drama on Friday and Saturday nights from June to August as part of the annual Hellenic Festival (@www.greekfestival.gr, or organised excursions from many island travel agents).

Further afield, the rest of the Peloponnese is also accessible on a more extended trip, or in a long day you could also make it to one of the most rewarding destinations, **Náfplio**. A gorgeous nineteenth-century town in a stunning coastal setting protected by forbidding fortresses, Náfplio has plenty of excellent restaurants and cafés.

side of Sferiá. For a quieter night, the open-air Cine Diana is at the opposite end of town, on the northern waterfront towards the Galatás ferries.

**Karavolos** Above and directly behind the open-air Cine Diana. The name means snail, and you'll find these on the menu along with other typical ouzerí fare; portions are large and prices fair. Evening only.

**Kathestos** Waterfront between the Town Hall and museum. One of several touristy places on a strip where the waiters compete furiously for your custom. Better-than-average seafood.

**Kyma** Waterfront just beyond the archeological museum. Simple, good value kebab place.

🏃 **Kyriakos** In the alley running behind the fish market, from Platía Iroön to Platía Dhimar-híou. Old-fashioned, lunchtime-only *mayireftá* establishment popular with locals. Take a look at the kitchen to see what's been prepared that day – when it's all gone, they close.

**Luna Piena** Platía Iroön. Greek-influenced Italian food, a step up in price and quality from its neighbours; try the excellent spaghetti with king prawns, for example.

**Naftis** Southeastern waterfront three blocks beyond the museum. Excellent psarotaverna with an attractive waterside terrace overlooking the yachts. As the evening wears on, the owners have been known to put on an impromptu Greek dancing display.

🏃 **Platanos** Main square of the upper town by the church of Ayíou Yeoryíou, most easily found by following one of the stepped streets up behind the Town Hall. One of several evening-only tavernas around the town square, serving inexpensive, earthy rural food (the owners also have a butcher's shop) on a vine-covered terrace, washed down with powerful retsina.

## Kalávria: beaches and temples

Crossing the **bridge to Kalávria**, the turning immediately on the left heads for beaches at Neório and Russian Bay. Carry straight on and you'll see the island's only **petrol station**, at the bottom of a street on your left. This road is the end (or start) of the circular route around Kalávria via the Temple of Poseidon. Carrying straight on again you pass an excellent **bakery**, and then the road starts to climb round to the right towards Askéli and the road round the island.

The area around the canal is overdeveloped and unattractive, but heading left (west), there are at least some good restaurants; *Aspro Gato* (the White Cat), on the beach in **Mikró Neório**, for example, serves good seafood on a waterfront terrace with great views back over Póros Town. The first place worth a stop in its own right, though, is **Megálo Neório**, arguably the island's most pleasant resort, small-scale, with a sandy beach, an excellent waterski centre with courses to professional level (☎22980 42540, ⑳www.passage.gr) and some fine beachside tavernas, such as the one attached to the *Hotel Pavlou*. **Love Bay**, next along, has a lovely sandy beach, unfortunately tiny and always packed; there's a friendly seasonal *kantína*, and kayaks and snorkel gear can be hired here. On the bus you can carry on past here as far as the **Rossikós Navstathmós** on Russian Bay, a crumbling Russian naval base dating from the early nineteenth century. There's a hard-packed, mostly shadeless beach here, with lots of small craft anchored offshore. With your own transport, you can carry on round the coast on a newly paved road that eventually joins up with the road down to Vayioniá (see below); it's a pretty drive, mostly high above the coast, and there are a couple of places en route where you can just about scramble down to swim from a rocky shore, but no development at all.

East of the canal, **Askéli**, with its strip of hotels and villas, has some more good places to eat and a narrow, crowded beach; there's a watersports centre here where you can hire kayaks and small sailing boats, as well as take ringo rides and the like. The bus in this direction terminates at the eighteenth-century **monastery of Zoödhóhou Piyís** (daily sunrise–1.30pm & 4.30pm–sunset) next to the island's only spring. Steps from the bus stop lead down to the pleasant sandy beach of **Monastiríou**, overlooked by pine-covered slopes. Perhaps the island's best beach, it is, surprisingly, usually one of the less crowded, though hardly empty as the two **tavernas** here will testify.

Above the monastery a good paved road winds upward to circle round inland Kalávria and back towards Póros Town. The rest of the island is covered in pine forest and barely inhabited, though there are a couple of fertile plateaus on the northern side with olive terraces, vineyards and magnificent panoramic views. From a saddle between the island's two highest peaks the road descends past the well-signed foundations of a sixth-century BC **Temple of Poseidon** (daily 8am–3pm; free). It was here that Demosthenes, fleeing from the Macedonians after encouraging the resistance of Athens to their rule, took poison rather than surrender. The temple lay at the heart of ancient Kalaureia, and it's an extensive site, but despite plenty of new signage and an ongoing Swedish excavation there's not a great deal to see above ground level – many of the stones were carted off to be used as building materials in the seventeenth and eighteenth centuries (much of it ended up on Ýdhra), and some of the more interesting sections are roped off while they are excavated.

Beyond the temple a road leads down to **Vayioniá**, port of the ancient shrine. This is a beautiful spot with a seasonal snack bar, and just about the only accessible beach on the island's north shore, though sand and room for sunbathing are limited. There's a good taverna, *Paradisos*, on the road just beyond the turning down to Vayioniá, serving local wines from the surrounding area, Foússa.

# Ýdhra (Hydra)

The island of **Ýdhra** is one of the most atmospheric and refreshing destinations in Greece. Its harbour and main town preserved as a national monument, it feels like a Greek island should, entirely traffic-free (even bicycles are banned) with a bustling harbour and narrow stone streets climbing steeply above it. Away from the main settlement the rest of the island is roadless, rugged and barely inhabited. The charm hasn't gone unnoticed – Ýdhra became fashionable as early as the 1950s, and in the Sixties characters ranging from Greek painter Nikos Hatzikyriakos-Ghikas to Canadian songster Leonard Cohen bought and restored grand old houses here.

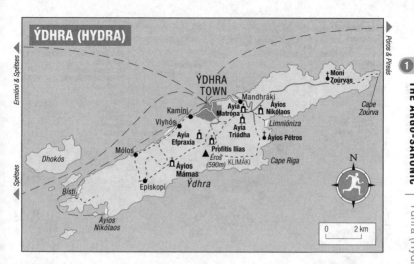

There's still a sizeable expat community, which contributes to a relatively sophisticated atmosphere, and also noticeably high prices. But even the seasonal and weekend crowds, and a very limited number of beaches, can't seriously detract from the appeal. When the town is overrun, it's easy enough to leave it all behind on foot or by excursion boat.

## Ýdhra Town

**ÝDHRA TOWN** and port, with tiers of substantial grey-stone mansions and humbler white-walled, red-tiled houses rising from a perfect horseshoe harbour, form a beautiful spectacle. The waterfront mansions were built mostly during the eighteenth century on the accumulated wealth of a remarkable merchant fleet, which traded as far afield as America and – during the Napoleonic Wars – broke the British blockade to sell grain to France. Fortunes were made, and the island also enjoyed a special relationship with the Ottoman Porte, governing itself and paying no tax in return for providing sailors to the sultan's navy. These conditions naturally attracted Greek immigrants from the less privileged mainland, and by the 1820s the town's population was nearly 20,000 – an incredible figure when you reflect that today it is under 3000. During the War of Independence, Ýdhra's merchants provided many of the ships for the Greek forces and consequently many of the commanders.

### Arrival and information

The town is fairly compact, but away from the waterfront, streets and alleyways are steep and labyrinthine; the best **map** is that issued by Saitis Tours next to the Alpha Bank (☎22980 52184), also agents for the Euroseas **catamaran**. Tickets for Hellenic Seaways **hydrofoils** and conventional ferries are sold on the eastern front, upstairs right opposite their anchorage (☎22980 54007). Several **banks** with **ATM**s can be found round the waterfront, the **post office** is on the market square just inland, and numerous places offer **internet** access – closest to the harbour is the shop immediately behind the waterfront Alpha Bank. Upstairs at the same address is the place to buy foreign **newspapers**. Water taxis and **excursion boats** tie up at various points around the harbour.

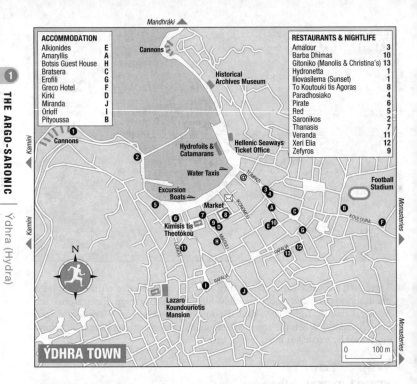

ACCOMMODATION
Alkionides          E
Amaryllis           A
Botsis Guest House  H
Bratsera            C
Erofili             G
Greco Hotel         F
Kirki               D
Miranda             J
Órloff              i
Pityoussa           B

RESTAURANTS & NIGHTLIFE
Amalour                         3
Barba Dhimas                   10
Gitoniko (Manolis & Christina's) 13
Hydronetta                      1
Iliovasilema (Sunset)           1
To Koutouki tis Agoras          8
Paradhosiako                    4
Pirate                          6
Red                             5
Saronikos                       2
Thanasis                        7
Veranda                        11
Xeri Elia                      12
Zefyros                         9

ÝDHRA TOWN

## Accommodation

The preservation order's ban on construction in town has not prevented the refurbishment of old houses for **accommodation**, and there are an increasing number of comfortable rooms. Prices tend to be high and there are rarely any bargains, though midweek or out of season you should be able to negotiate significant reductions on the official fee. The nature of the old buildings and the closely packed streets mean that some noise is inevitable, especially near the waterfront. Addresses and street signs are almost nonexistent, so ask for directions when you book. The pricier places may provide a **mule** to carry your luggage (or you can hire one), though nowhere in town is very far; if you're staying out of town, you'll probably need a water-taxi.

**Alkionides** 120m up the harbour, on next street parallel to Alpha Bank (past the movies) ☎22980 54055, ⓦwww.alkionidespension .com. Pleasant pension, quietly tucked away yet central, with an attractive courtyard and helpful management; all rooms have TV, fridge and tea and coffee-maker. ➍

**Amaryllis** 100m inland from the harbour, up street by Alpha Bank ☎22980 53611, ⓦwww .amarillishydra.gr. Nondescript 1960s building that somehow evaded the preservation code, yet it proves a decent small hotel whose rather old-fashioned rooms have good facilities including a/c and wireless internet, plus small balconies. ➎

**Botsis Guest House** 70m from harbour, up street between market and church ☎22980 52395, ⓦwww.botsis.com. Simple but pleasant rooms; all have balconies a/c, TV and fridge, and some at the back have substantial outdoor terraces. There's also a studio apartment. ➌

**Bratsera** 150m inland from the harbour, past the *Amaryllis* ☎22980 53971, ⓦwww .bratserahotel.com. Easily the best on the island, this four-star hotel occupies a stylishly renovated former sponge factory, and the extensive common areas (including bar, restaurant, conference room and courtyard pool) serve as a museum of the industry with photos and artefacts. Lovely rooms have flagstone floors and beamed ceilings, though only superior and above have balconies. Open mid-March to Oct. **7**

**Pension Erofili** Tucked away in a small street, just beyond *Bratsera* ☎ 22980 54049, ⓦwww .pensionerofili.gr. Fairly basic rooms around a courtyard, but quiet, friendly and relatively inexpensive – buffet breakfast available at extra cost. **3**

**Greco Hotel** On the southeast edge of town, just beyond *Pityoussa* ☎ 22980 53200, ⓦwww .grecohotel.gr. Large (by local standards) hotel in a former bakery – the rooms are slightly sterile and dated, but it's friendly, quiet and comfortable and there's an excellent buffet breakfast included. **5**

**Kirki** 60m from harbour, up street between market and church ☎ 22980 53181, ⓦwww.hydrakirki.gr. Unprepossessing entry leads to a delightful old house, with a small courtyard garden and simple, island-style rooms; all have a/c and balconies, though the attractive large terraces at the back do get some early morning noise from the market. **4**

**Miranda** 200m inland along main lane from mid-quay ☎ 22980 52230, ⓦwww.mirandahotel.gr.

An 1810 mansion converted into one of the most popular hotels here, with wood floors and fridges. Rooms vary; best are nos. 2 and 3, both with painted, coffered ceilings and large sea-view terraces. Large breakfasts in the shaded courtyard are another big plus; there is a basement bar for winter. **6**

**Orloff** On the largest inland square, near *Miranda* ☎ 22980 52564, ⓦwww.orloff.gr. Lovely mansion restored as a boutique hotel, with blue-hued, high-ceilinged rooms and suites. High enough in town for partial sea views, with a very secluded courtyard where a superior buffet breakfast is served. **7**

🏃 **Pityoussa** On the southeast edge of town, beyond *Amaryllis* ☎ 22980 52810, ⓦwww .piteoussa.com. Named after the three giant pines out front, this small inn is exceptional value, with recently refurbished units equipped with CD and DVD players and Korres toiletries in the marble-floored bathrooms. Downstairs rooms are larger, but all have balconies and designer touches. **4**

## The Town

At each side of the harbour, cannons facing out to sea and statues of the heroes of independence remind you of Ýdhra's place in history. Between them, the **mansions** of the wealthy eighteenth-century merchant families are still the great monuments of the town; some are labelled at the entrance with "*Oikía*" ("Residence of …") followed by the family name. It's well worth spending some time simply wandering the picturesque old inland streets – one thing you may notice while doing so is that even more than most Greek island towns, Ýdhra is overrun with wild cats, probably because there are so many "cat ladies" who feed them.

Among the finest of the old homes are the two Koundouriotis mansions. This ship-owning family was one of Ýdhra's most influential, and the mansions were built by two brothers, Yioryios, a leading politician of the fledgling Greek nation and grandfather of Pavlos, president of Republican Greece in the 1920s, and Lazaro, prominent in the independence wars. The **Lazaros Koundouriotis Museum** (Tues–Sun 9am–4pm; €4) is the large yellow building high on the western side of town. The hot climb up the stepped alleyways is rewarded with great views down over the town and port, and a lovingly restored interior that looks ready to move into. The red-tiled floors, panelled wooden ceilings and period furnishings outshine the contents of the museum – paintings, folk costume and independence paraphernalia. The **Yioryios Koundouriotis mansion** is periodically open for art exhibitions.

Across on the eastern waterfront, another of the great houses is now the **Historical Archives Museum** (daily 9.30am–4pm; €5), with a small, crowded and enjoyable display of clothing, period engravings, and ships' prows and sidearms from the independence struggle. The **Melina Mercouri Centre**, next door, often has interesting temporary art exhibitions. The most obvious and important of Ýdhra's many churches is **Kímisis tís Theotókou** by the port, with a distinctive clocktower and a cloistered courtyard housing the small but

▲ Ýdhra Town's peaceful preserved harbour

rich collection of the **ecclesiastical museum** (Tues–Sun 10am–5pm; €2) – silver-bound books, icons, vestments, bejewelled crosses and the like.

### Eating, drinking and nightlife

The permanently busy quayside **cafés** and **bars** offer an incomparable people- and harbour-watching experience – albeit at a price – but there are few worthwhile restaurants on the harbour. If you want something to take down to the beach with you, there's an excellent **bakery**, with *tyrópittes* and cakes, tucked into the western corner of the harbour by the *Pirate* bar. **Nightlife** is tame on the whole, though a number of bars do play music into the early hours; there's also an open-air **cinema** in summer, on the narrow street leading to the *Alkionides* hotel.

### Tavernas and ouzerís

**Barba Dhimas** About 125m inland, in the alley to the right of *Amaryllis* hotel. A small, well-priced taverna with decent *mezédhes*, small fish and even snail casserole.

**Gitoniko (Manolis & Christina's)** Hidden away inland, near Áyios Konstandínos church; get there on the street past the movies, or past *Barba Dhimas*. Very friendly taverna with excellent, well-priced *mayireftá* at lunch – which runs out early – plus grills (including succulent fish) in the evening; extensive roof-terrace in summer.

**Iliovasilema (Sunset)** Behind the cannons, west promontory above *Hydronetta*. Incomparable setting for an end-of-holiday treat or romantic tryst; delicious modern Greek and Italian cuisine

that will set you back about €35 per person including wine.

**To Koutouki tis Agoras** Rear of market. Rickety-tabled, inexpensive tradesmen's ouzerí whose titbits, ranging from *pastourmás* (cured meat) to octopus, can be exceptional. At its best in the early evening.

**Paradhosiako** Between Amalour and *Amaryllis* hotel. Upmarket *mezedhopolío*, with some unusual dishes like *domatekeftédhes* (tomato patties).

**Thanasis** Barely 20m from the harbour, on the lane leading to *Miranda* hotel. Simple and very popular kebab and *yíros* place, which also serves excellent salads and light meals.

**Veranda** Up a steep alley behind the clocktower. White linen, elegant glassware and a scintillating view over the rooftops towards the harbour is what you pay for here; the Italian-influenced menu is sometimes overambitious. If in doubt, stick to pasta.

**Xeri Elia** In a vine-shaded platía immediately beyond Gitoniko. Large, busy taverna in a lovely setting – all the standards and good seafood.

**Zefyros** Just beyond *Thanasis*, on the lane leading to *Miranda* hotel. One of several decent options for simple taverna food in this street, with tables in a sheltered courtyard.

### Bars and cafés

**Amalour** 80m inland from the harbour, up street by Alpha Bank. Laid-back bar with an eclectic playlist and 30-to-40-something crowd; sometimes hosts special events or theme nights.

**Hydronetta** Tucked under the cannons on the west side of the promontory. The classic sunset-watching bar, where the music carries on into the small hours. Limited seating gives it an exclusive, chill-out vibe.

**Pirate** Corner of waterfront by clocktower. Café by day and an increasingly lively bar as the evening wears on, with a young crowd and Western music. Among the best prices on the waterfront for coffee, breakfast and sandwiches.

**Red** Waterfront just beyond *Pirate*. Late-night place playing sixties and seventies rock.

**Saronikos** Western end of the waterfront. Cool café by day, with free wi-fi; predominantly modern Greek sounds until the early hours.

## The north coast: beaches

There's only one paved road on Ýdhra, leading east from the harbour to the beach at Mandhráki just a couple of kilometres away. Even that's a hot and shadeless walk where you're likely to meet the municipal rubbish truck (one of the island's handful of authorised motor vehicles), so most people rely on the small **boats** that shuttle constantly from the harbour to various beaches around the island, at prices ranging from about €2.50 per person one-way to Mandhráki to €10 return to Bísti. You can also hire private water-taxis – good value for groups at around €12 per boat to Vlyhós or €60 to Bísti, for example – or even mules for land-based travel.

**MANDHRÁKI** is dominated by the *Miramare Hotel* (☎22980 52300, ⓦwww.miramare-hotel.net; ❺), whose beachside bungalows are not great value. Despite appearances the sandy beach is open to all, with windsurfing, waterskiing, pedaloes to hire and floating trampolines, while a decent bar-restaurant occupies the imposing former shipyard of independence war hero Admiral Miaoulis. On a pebbly cove immediately west, *Mandraki 1800* is one of the better rural **tavernas** on the island, with slightly pricey ouzerí fare.

Heading out of Ýdhra Town to the west, a paved coastal path leads towards **KAMÍNI**, about a twenty-minute walk. There are several spots en route where you can clamber down to swim from the rocks in crystal clear water, while picturesque Kamíni itself has a shingly beach (just beyond the village and harbour, with no facilities) and a couple of good tavernas and rooms establishments. Of the latter, waterfront ⚐ *Antonia* (☎22980 52481; ❹) has just one delightfully old-fashioned room and one apartment for up to five people, both with balconies hanging right over the sea; *Eleni Petrolekka*, immediately behind (☎22980 52701; ❸) also offers simple but comfortable accommodation. 🍴 *Taverna tis Kondylenias*, by the little harbour, is famous for its seafood and wonderful sunset views, while *Christina's*, a short way inland, is plainer and slightly cheaper.

If you carry on walking – and again, there are plentiful boats to all these places – you'll pass the popular swimming cove at **Kastéllo** on the way to **VLYHÓS**, a small hamlet with a rebuilt nineteenth-century bridge and a shingle beach with loungers and umbrellas; there's pleasant swimming in the lee of an offshore islet here. In peak season there's a taverna and a couple of bar-cafés as well as a single rooms establishment, *Antigone* (☎22980 53228, ✉antigone@freemail.gr; ❹).

Beyond Vlyhós the walking gets much tougher as the path tracks high above the bay of Mólos, where the beach looks tempting but is hard to reach, and then circles back inland. For the fine coves at the western tip, Bísti and Áyios Nikólaos, boat is really your only option. **Bísti** has a smallish, white-pebbled beach surrounded by pine trees that offer shade; **Áyios Nikólaos** is larger and sandier, but with less shade and fewer boats. A path leads over the cape between the two; both have seasonal snack bars as well as loungers and kayaks to rent.

## Interior and south: treks and monasteries

The interior of Ýdhra is mountainous and little-visited, so with a little walking you can find a dramatically different kind of island – one of rural cottages, terraces of grain to feed the donkeys, hilltop monasteries and pine forest.

To explore it, follow the street up past the *Miranda* hotel or head around the eastern edge of town past the Piteoussa: as you start to climb out of town, a left turn leads to Áyios Nikólaos (see below). If you stay on the right, you reach a path that winds up the mountain for about an hour to either the **monastery of Profítis Ilías** or (slightly lower) the **convent of Ayía Efpraxía**. What must be the longest stairway in Greece (or alternatively a zigzag path) constitutes the final approach to **Profítis Ilías** (closed noon–4pm, but water and *loukoúm* are hospitably left at the gate). If you want to go further, a rather tougher, harder-to-follow trail continues left behind the monastery to a saddle overlooking the south coast. From here a pathless scramble brings you within twenty minutes to the 590-metre summit of **Mount Éros**, the Argo-Saronic islands' highest point, but the path itself branches: right to the chapel of Áyios Mámas, on whose feast day of September 2nd there's a pilgrimage of people and animals to be blessed; left eventually circles down to the sea at the tiny hamlet of **Klimáki**, a couple of hours' walk in all.

The alternate route out of town towards deserted **Áyios Nikólaos** monastery offers spectacular views back down over Ýdhra before reaching, at the top, a broad, easy dirt track heading straight across a high plateau towards the monastery. En route you pass between the monasteries of Ayía Triádha and Ayía Matróna, both of which are usually locked. Just beyond Áyios Nikólaos is a small settlement, from where you can in theory head down to **Limnióniza**, an hour and a quarter from Ýdhra Town, the best and most scenic cove on the south coast. However, it's a steep scramble on a path which is hard to find, and the pine forest that once grew here has been devastated by fire. There are no boats back unless you arrange to be picked up by water-taxi; an expensive option since it means an almost complete circuit of the island. The path through the hamlet continues above the coast to **Hoúnda Ríga**, Cape Riga, with fine views, and then, less obviously, on towards Klimáki. A far easier alternative is to follow the broad track down from Áyios Nikólaos to Mandhráki, where you can have a swim before taking the boat back to town.

A good path also leads east from Áyios Nikólaos towards **Moní Zoúrvas** and the eastern tip of the island; about three hours in all from town. Perhaps the best way to do this trip is to take an early water-taxi to Cape Zoúrva, Ýdhra's eastern extremity, from where you can walk all the way back to town along the island's spine. There are several small chapels along the way.

# Spétses

**Spétses** is probably the best-known of the Argo-Saronic islands, largely thanks to John Fowles, who lived here in the early 1950s and used the place, thinly disguised as Phraxos, as the setting for his cult novel *The Magus*. A popular, upmarket escape for Athenians, the island had a brief vogue as a package destination but never really developed the mass infrastructure – or the convenient beaches – to match. Today, the town is much the biggest in the Saronic islands, spreading for several kilometres along the northeast coast, but new development is mainly second homes and small apartments and villas; the rest of the island is almost entirely uninhabited, with pine forest inland and numerous excellent small beaches around the coast.

## Spétses Town

**SPÉTSES TOWN** shares with Ýdhra a history of late eighteenth-century mercantile adventure and prosperity, and a leading role in the War of Independence, which made its foremost citizens the aristocrats of the new Greek state. Plenty of fine old homes and public buildings survive, but here there's been little restriction on new building, which spreads along the shore in both directions. And although most cars are banned in town you won't notice it, as they're replaced by thousands of mopeds and scooters that pay little attention to whether a street is pedestrianized or not. In short, it's much less pretty than Ýdhra Town, but also a great deal more lively and earthy; full of pricey shops, bars and restaurants.

### Arrival and orientation

Spétses splits into three main areas. Ferries and hydrofoils will drop you pretty much in the **heart of town** at the cannon-studded main harbour known as the **Dápia**: ahead of you is the main town square, with the busy shopping streets of the old town tucked in behind it; left along the seafront lies the **town beach** of Áyios Mámas. Continue in this direction (east) around the point and you'll reach the second area, the **Old Harbour**, the upmarket focus of the island's nightlife, where private yachts moor up. West of Dápia is **Kounoupítsa**, with more of a suburban feel – much of the simpler accommodation is here, and there are small beaches and waterfront tavernas. It's a big place: if you're staying in Kounoupítsa and want to walk to one of the bars in Baltíza (at the far end of the Old Harbour), it will take at least forty minutes.

To get around the island there are two **bus** services with frequent departures in summer: from the waterfront by the *Hotel Poseidonion* (the large building undergoing restoration, on the front west of Dápia) to Kounoupítsa (€1), Ligonéri (€1.20) and Vréllos (€1.50); and from Áyios Mámas to Áyii Anáryiri (€3) and Ayía Paraskévi (€3.50). Alternatively, dozens of places in town rent **mountain bikes** (around €6 a day) and **scooters** (€15), or there are *kaïkia* (€9 return to Áyii Anáryiri) and private **water-taxis** (€15–80 per boatload depending on destination) for beaches or round-the-island trips; they also shuttle to Kósta and Pórto Héli on the mainland. Bike Center, about halfway along the shopping street behind

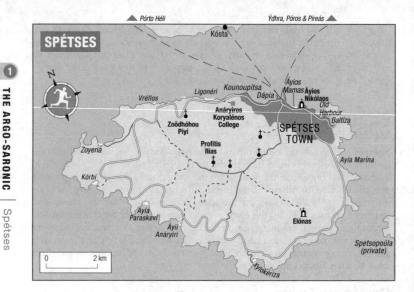

the seafront hotels, has good mountain **bikes**, and for scooters try Stanathiotis on the main street inland, Botasi. These two streets are handy to know, as Spétses is large and confusing, and if you venture into the back streets you're almost bound to get lost at least temporarily. From the Dápia, with the water at your back, turn left. First right is Botasi, heading uphill and eventually out of town; straight ahead, behind the seafront, are the shopping streets with Platía Oroloyíou ("Clocktower Square") immediately behind, surrounded by touristy restaurants.

### Information

Around the harbour you'll see numerous **travel agencies** that can help with accommodation and local maps as well as tickets. Bardakos (☎22980 73141), on the east side of the Dápia, is the agent for Hellenic Seaways, while on the seafront immediately to the east are Mimoza Travel (☎22980 75170), for the Eurofast catamaran, along with Alasia Travel (☎22980 74098, ⊛www.alasiatravel.gr) and Kastro Travel (☎22980 75152, ⊛www.kastro-margarita.com), both of which are agents for a number of good rooms places. The same is true of the Yachting Club (☎22980 73400, ⊛www.spetsesyc.gr), on the opposite side of the Dápia. There are **banks** with ATMs all around the Dápia. **Internet** cafés are surprisingly rare, though: *Café 1800*, on the waterfront towards Kounoupítsa, is the biggest, though connections are very slow; *Amore*, on the seafront east of the Dápia (also entered from the shopping street behind), has wireless if you have your own laptop, or pricey coin-operated machines – great view too.

### Accommodation

**Accommodation**, especially at the cheaper end of the range, tends to be widely scattered. On busy weekends and in August it can be in short supply, so it may make life easier to arrange it through one of the agencies above, who will also be able to arrange transport to get you there. The rest of the season, though, you're likely to be met off the hydrofoil by people offering rooms. In town prices range from high, at comfortable studio complexes, to jaw-droppingly expensive at some of the boutique hotels; at quiet times, big discounts can be negotiated.

Economou Mansion Kounoupítsa shoreline ☎22980 73400, ⊛www.spetsesyc.gr. Grand restored inn, occupying part of an 1851 property; no children allowed. The ground floor of the main house has six well-converted rooms retaining period features; an outbuilding hosts two luxury sea-view suites. Breakfast (included) is served by the fair-sized pool. ❼

Kastro Apartments towards Kounoupítsa, behind *Café 1800* ☎22980 75152, ⊛www.kastrospetses .com. Attractive complex of studios and duplex apartments around a small pool, all with kitchen. ❺

Klimis Waterfront 200m east of the Dápia ☎22980 72334, Ⓔklimishotel@hol.gr. The last of a series of small hotels along the front, *Klimis* may be a little run down, but is convenient, open all year and excellent value given its position, with wonderful views from the balconied rooms at the front and some kind of sea view from almost every room. Downstairs there's a superb, old-fashioned *zaharoplastío* with excellent ice cream, and where breakfast (included) is served. ❹

Roumani On the Dápia ☎22980 72244, ⊛www .hotelroumani.gr. Prime location right on the Dápia, which means rooms at the front have stunning views – though they can also be noisy and are overdue for a refurb. Hence the reasonable prices. ❹

Villa Christina 200m inland from the Dápia, just off Botasi ☎22980 72218, ⊛www .villachristinahotel.com. Friendly, well-maintained restored inn occupying a rambling old building with two courtyards, in a quiet location though no sea views. A/c rooms and studios (with kitchens) for up to four people; breakfast in the courtyard usually included. ❸

Villa Orizontes 500m inland, directly uphill from the back of Platía Oroloyíou, right at the top of town – look for the large veranda and blue shutters ☎22980 72509, ⊛www.villaorizontes.gr. Simple hotel in a quiet spot, high up, with a variety of different-sized rooms and apartments with fridge, a/c and TV; more than half have knockout views across town and out to sea. ❸

Zoe's Club 200m east of the Dápia, on a quiet inland corner (left from the back of Platía Oroloyíou) ☎22980 74447, ⊛www.zoesclub.gr. The pick of the luxury places, with lovely, designer-decorated studios, apartments and houses around a large pool; all have flat-screen satellite TV, DVD players and espresso machines in the fully-equipped kitchens, and almost all have a great sea view. Fully booked for Aug and summer weekends and almost empty the rest of the time, though few bargains even then. ❼

## The Town

For most visitors, shopping, eating and drinking are the principal attractions of Spétses, but it's a very enjoyable place to wander, with majestic old houses and gardens scattered through the narrow streets. One of the grandest, the Hatzi-yannis Mexis family mansion above the east side of town, now houses an enjoyable **local museum** (Tues–Sun 8.30am–2.30pm; €3). Apart from the house itself, highlights include magnificent polychrome wooden ships' prows from the revolutionary fleet, as well as its flag, plus (out of sight in a plain wooden ossuary) the bones of local heroine Laskarina Bouboulina, a wealthy widow who commanded her own small fleet in the War of Independence, reputedly seduced her lovers at gunpoint, and was shot in 1825 by the father of a girl her son had eloped with.

**Bouboulina's Mansion**, signed not far behind the Dápia, is also a private **museum**. Entertaining guided tours (30min; €5) – the only admission permitted – are given in English up to a dozen times daily; times are posted outside and on boards around town. You'll hear the story of how she spent much of her fortune on ships and men for the independence struggle, while highlights among the arms, furniture, pictures and correspondence are a gorgeous wooden ceiling in the main room and a model of Bouboulina's flagship, the *Agamemnon*. The family still live in part of the mansion; they remained prominent in Greek public (especially naval) life for many years. One of Bouboulina's great-granddaughters was also a heroine of the resistance, executed by the Germans during the occupa-tion in World War II.

Almost alongside the Bouboulina mansion, but not open to the public, the kitsch, Neoclassical former residence of **Sotirios Anaryiros**, the island's great nineteenth-century benefactor, is gradually crumbling away. An enormously rich self-made man who made his fortune in America, his enduring legacy is that he replanted the island's pine forests, depleted by generations of shipbuilders. He also built the massive waterfront **Hotel Poseidonion** and endowed **Anáryiros Koryalénos College**, a curious Greek recreation of an English public school, where John Fowles taught (see below).

The twenty-minute walk along the front to the **Old Harbour** is worthwhile too. There are bars and cafés here where you can sit and admire the visiting yachts and also the relics of its days as a working port, with rusty tankers and traditional boatyards. The harbour is overlooked by the monastic church of **Áyios Nikólaos** with its graceful belfry and some vast pebble mosaics out front; inside, Paul-Marie Bonaparte, nephew of Napoleon and casualty of the Greek War of Independence in 1827, was embalmed for five years in a barrel of rum until his body could be repatriated to France.

## Eating, drinking and nightlife

Brace yourself for some of the steepest **food** and **drink** prices in the Greek islands outside of Mýkonos and Rhodes – especially in the cafés around the Dápia and romantic spots around the old harbour. Late-night **nightlife** is mostly centred on Baltíza, the furthest of the inlets at the old harbour – the biggest of the clubs, playing a mix of dance music for a fairly moneyed crowd, are *Privilege*, a vaulted structure on the far side, and *Fortezza*, and there are plenty of quieter bars like *Remezzo*. These places are very seasonal, and even in summer only really come to life at the weekend. Closer to town, Áyios Mámas beach also has a couple of lively music bars. Two cinemas operate in summer, close to the main square – Titania (with a roof for shelter, but open sides) and open-air, rooftop Marina.

## Tavernas and ouzerís

**Akrogialia** On the waterfront, west towards Kounoupítsa. Excellent seafood taverna with reasonable prices and a wonderful setting, with candlelit tables and the water lapping almost to your feet as you eat.

**Cockatoo** In a narrow alley just off the waterfront, between Dápia and Platía Oroloyíou. Basic kebab and *yíros* place, serving probably the cheapest food in town – not to be confused with its nearby, more expensive namesake on touristy Platía Oroloyíou.

**Exedra** Old Harbour. A smarter, older crowd enjoy standard dishes like *moussakás* and *angináres ala políta*, and fresh fish in an unbeatable waterside seating. Despite the upmarket image, prices are little higher than at neighbouring establishments.

**Kafeneíon** Dápia, by Alpha Bank. Pebble mosaics underfoot and sepia photos indicate that this was the island's first watering hole; start the day with well-priced English breakfast, and tame sparrows begging for crumbs, progressing later to a full range of *mezédhes*, or just a drink whilst waiting for a hydrofoil.

**Lazaros** A stiff climb 500m inland from the Dápia, above the dry stream-bed. Cavernous interior with an old jukebox, dangling gourds and wine barrels; it serves a limited but savoury menu of grills, goat in lemon sauce, superior *taramás* and decent barrelled wine. Evening only, late March–early Oct.

**To Liotrivi** Old Harbour. The "old olive oil press" offers an upmarket, modern Mediterranean menu – grilled prawns, king prawns, *scallopine al limone* – to a Latin and jazz soundtrack. Some tables enjoy a stunning position on a jetty that extends right out into the harbour.

**To Nero tis Agapis** Kounoupítsa waterfront. Virtually adjacent to *Patralis* (next listing) and with a similar seafood-based menu (excellent seafood spaghetti), "The Water of Love" could hardly be a greater contrast in style and decor – self-consciously modern, island-style, with decent music and enthusiastic young staff.

**Patralis** Kounoupítsa waterfront, 300m before the *Spetses* hotel ☎ 22980 74441, ⊛ www.patralis.gr. Upmarket, old-fashioned, bourgeois *psarotaverna*. Very popular with Greek visitors, which can mean slow service and a wait for a table, but excellent fish dishes and good barrelled wine if you don't like the prices on the extensive wine list. Better value for fish and sea views than the Old Harbour.

**Stelios** Waterfront east of Dápia, before Áyios Mámas beach. One of several unfussy tavernas in this strip, serving well-prepared standard Greek dishes and *mayireftá* – *yemistá*, *yiouvétsi*, and the like. Some of the least expensive seafront food in town.

**Trehantiri** Terrace overlooking the outer section of the Old Harbour. Traditional Greek dishes with a modern twist attract a youngish crowd; seafood spaghetti, risottos, daily fish specials.

## Bars and cafés

**Balkoni** Waterfront east of Dápia, by *Stelios* hotel/ restaurant. The elegant alternative to nearby *Socrates*; sip your wine or cocktails on a candlelit seafront balcony.

**Mama's Beach Café** Behind Áyios Mámas beach. Lively café and lunch spot by day, while at night the upstairs music bar (playing summer party stuff) takes over.

**To Posto** Waterfront east of Dápia, by Mimoza Travel. Ice-cream parlour serving good, Italian-style gelati.

**Socrates** Waterfront east of Dápia; main entry on shopping street behind. Bar with pub-like atmosphere and big-screen sports.

**Bar Spetsa** Áyios Mámas, behind *Mama's Beach Café*. Chilled out late-night bar playing decent retro rock.

## Around the island

A single paved road circles Spétses, mostly high above a rocky coast but with access to beaches at various points. Circling anti-clockwise, the first tempting spot, just twenty-minutes' walk west of town or with a frequent bus service, is **College Beach** (so called because just inland is the college where John Fowles was unhappily employed and set part of *The Magus*; it is now a conference centre), with lots of facilities including loungers, bars and a waterski outfit that also rents jet-skis. College Beach is often known as **Ligonéri**, but strictly speaking Ligonéri (the end of the road for most buses) consists of a couple of stony coves slightly further on, a bit of a scramble down from the road, with a cave spring just inland, protected by a chapel. Next up in this direction is **Vréllos**, in a pretty, wooded bay. The beach itself is small and pebbly but thanks to paved access and a beach cocktail bar pumping out loud Greek rock it's almost always packed at weekends; some of the Ligonéri buses continue this far. At the western extremity of the island, **Zoyeriá** is reached down a track that soon degenerates into a path (which doesn't stop locals riding their scooters) past a series of rocky coves – following this you eventually climb over a small headland to arrive at a sandy beach with a large taverna. Many of the patrons here arrive the easy way, by boat, and the food is simple but far better than you'd expect in this isolated location; try the grilled chicken or *soutzoukákia*.

Perhaps the best two beaches on the island occupy adjacent bays on the south coast, where they can be reached by the bus that circles the island in the other direction (clockwise) or by excursion boat. **Ayía Paraskeví**, end of the line for the bus, is the sandier and prettier – indeed it probably has the best sand on the island – with a seasonal beach *kantína* and taverna. **Áyii Anáryiri**, though, is larger and more popular: a long, sheltered, mostly sandy bay, with a watersports centre offering kayaks, pedaloes, windsurfers and catamarans to rent, as well as a waterski boat. *Manolis Taverna* here, with tables set out in the shade at the back of the beach, is good. En route, the bus leaves town via **Ayía Marína** or Paradise Beach: a busy, almost suburban beach, in walking distance of the eastern edge of town, it is packed with loungers and a popular bar-restaurant and a water-sports operation offering kayaks and waterski and ringo rides. There are views offshore towards the tempting but off-limits islet of **Spetsopoúla**, the private property of the heirs of shipping magnate Stavros Niarchos. Five kilometres or so further is **Xylokériza**, where a long, steep concrete track leads down to a cove of pale-coloured pebbles. There's no sand at all here, but it's a beautiful spot and rarely crowded, with a substantial seasonal café.

**On foot,** you can head up through town and strike directly across the island to many of the beaches, with fine views along the way. Follow Botasi out of town, past the *Lazaros* taverna, and as you leave town a sign (the only one you'll see) points you up along a paved road. Don't be tempted to take a shortcut around the hairpins here; they rarely work. The paving soon runs out, but a good broad track heads up towards the heights. At the top there are no signs at all: one track heads directly down the other side, to rejoin the road halfway between **Áyii Anáryiri and Xylokériza** (the other end of this track is optimistically signposted "Profitis Ilías 5", but in practice is virtually impassable, on two wheels or four). The better option is to turn right along the spine of the island, with increasingly impressive views across towards the mainland over both coasts; before long there's an obvious (unsigned) path heading down towards **Áyii Anáryiri**. Continue beyond this and there's a less obvious path to **Ayía Paraskeví**, while the main trail curls back around towards the north, eventually descending to the coast road near Vréllos.

# Travel details

Services from Pireás leave from between gates E8 and E9. There are ticket booths here, and there's rarely any need to book ahead, except on the most popular weekends or if you plan to take a car. The summaries below are for summer weekday services: sailings are more frequent at weekends (Fri–Sun), less so from mid-Sept to June. No hydrofoils or catamarans connect Égina with the rest of the islands, and no conventional ferries go to Ýdhra or Spétses. A number of the ferries from Póros stop at Méthana on the mainland, while some hydrofoils and cats call at Ermióni, between Ýdhra and Spétses, or Pórto Héli, beyond Spétses. Company contact details for Pireás (local island agencies are given in the island accounts):
**Aegean Flying Dolphins** (to Égina and Angístri) ☏ 210 41 21 654, ⊕ www.aegeanflyingdolphins.gr.
**Alexandros** (fast ferry to Souvála and Ayía Marína, Égina) ☏ 210 48 21 002, ⊕ www.alexcruises.com.
**Ayios Nektarios Eginas** (ferry to Égina) ☏ 210 42 25 625.
**Euroseas** (Eurofast catamaran to Ýdhra, Spétses and Pórto Héli) ☏ 210 41 13 108, ⊕ www.euroseas.com.
**Hellenic Seaways** (ferries, hydrofoils and Flying Cat to all points) ☏ 210 41 99 000, ⊕ www .hellenicseaways.gr.
**Nova** (ferry to Égina) ☏ 210 41 26 181.

## Ferries

Hellenic Seaways ferry unless otherwise stated.

**Angístri** to: Pireás (2 daily; 1hr 30min).
**Égina (Égina Town)** to: Angístri (Angístri Express 4 daily Mon–Fri, 2 daily weekends; 15min); Pireás (10–12 daily with Hellenic Seaways; 3 daily with Ayios Nektarios Eginas; 4 daily with Nova; 1hr–1hr 30min); Póros (4 daily; 1hr 15min); Ýdhra and Spétses (1 daily; 2hr 15min–3hr 15min).
**Égina (Souvála)** to: Pireás (Alexandros 3 daily; 1hr).
**Égina (Ayía Marína)** to: Pireás (Alexandros 2–3 daily; 1hr).
**Póros** to: Égina and Pireás (3 daily; 1hr 15min–2hr 30min); Galatás (constant passenger shuttle and roll-on roll-off car ferry every 30min 6am– 10.40pm; 5min).

## Hydrofoils and Flying Cat

**Angístri** to: Pireás (Aegean Flying Dolphins; 6 daily, more at weekends; 45min).
**Égina** to: Angístri (Aegean Flying Dolphins; 4 daily; 15min); Pireás (Hellenic Seaways and Aegean Flying Dolphins; half-hourly, 7am–8pm; 40min).
**Póros** to: Pireás (Hellenic Seaways; 6 daily; 1hr); Spétses (4 daily; 1hr 30min); Ýdhra (6 daily; 35min).
**Ýdhra** to: Pireás (Hellenic Seaways and Euroseas; 9 daily; 1hr 20min); Póros (6 daily; 35min); Spétses (6 daily; 45min).
**Spétses** to: Pireás (Hellenic Seaways and Euroseas; 7 daily; 2hr 25min); Póros (4 daily; 1hr 30min); Ýdhra (6 daily; 45min).

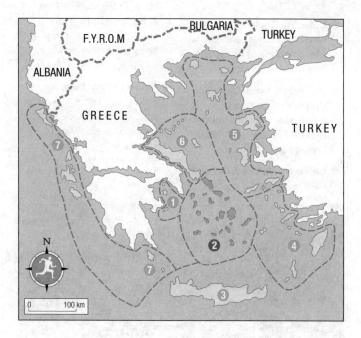

# 2

# The Cyclades

CHAPTER 2 # Highlights

* **Beaches of Mílos** These spectacular beaches are distinguished by multicoloured rocks and volcanically heated sand. See pp.139–140

* **Mýkonos Town** Labyrinthine lanes filled with restaurants, boutiques and nightlife. See p.158

* **Delos** The Cyclades' sacred centre and holiest ancient site, birthplace of Apollo and Artemis. See p.162

* **Ermoúpoli, Sýros** Once Greece's busiest port, the elegant capital of the Cyclades is now a UNESCO heritage site. See p.165

* **Church of Ekatondapylianí, Parikía, Páros** An imposing and ornate Byzantine church incorporating an impressive number of architectural styles. See p.173

* **Mount Zás, Náxos** The Cyclades' highest mountain on the Cyclades' largest island, with the group's finest panorama. See p.188

* **Hóra, Folégandhros** Free of traffic and sitting atop a spectacular cliff, this capital has a handsome old *kástro*. See p.205

* **Caldera of Santoríni** A geological wonder, this crater left by a colossal volcanic explosion averages eight kilometres in diameter. See p.207 & 216

▲ Ermoúpoli harbour, Sýros

# The Cyclades

Named, most probably, from the circle they form around the sacred island of Delos, the **Cyclades** (Kykládhes) offer Greece's best island-hopping. Each island has a strong, distinct character based on traditions, customs, topography and its historical development. Most are compact enough for a few days' exploration to show you a major part of their scenery and personality in a way that is impossible in Crete, Rhodes, or most of the Ionian islands.

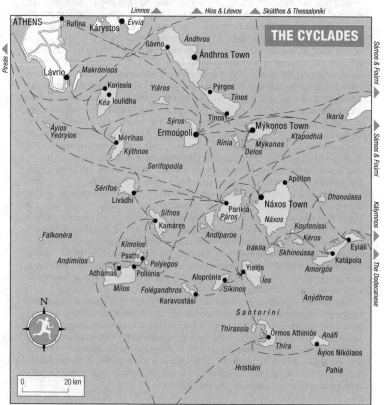

The islands do have some features in common; the majority (Ándhros, Kéa, Náxos and Tínos excepted) are arid and rocky, and most also share the "Cycladic" style of brilliant-white Cubist architecture, a feature of which is the central **kástro** of the old towns. The typical *kástro* has just one or two entrances, and a continuous outer ring of houses with all their doors and windows on the inner side, so forming a single protective perimeter wall – typically, the two-storey houses have a separate owner for each storey. The extent and impact of tourism, though, is markedly haphazard, so that although some English is spoken on most islands, a slight detour from the beaten track – from Íos to Síkinos, for example – can have you reaching for your Greek phrasebook.

## Some history

The known history of the Cyclades starts with **obsidian**, the black, sharp-edged volcanic glass used for making cutting implements and weapons. Shards originating from Mílos and dating to 11,000 BC have been found in the Paleolithic Frágkhthi cave in the Peloponnese, demonstrating early seaborne trade. Fragments of bone from Kýthnos indicate the presence of hunter-gatherers around 7500 to 6500 BC, but the first settlements are Mesolithic, from Sáliagos island near Páros and from Kéa, around 4300 BC, with remnants indicating copper-based metallurgy. The Greek Bronze Age started in the islands and with it came the **Cycladic civilization**, most notable for its sought-after geometric, minimalist female figurines made from marble from Páros or Náxos. **Mining** for copper, silver and gold, combined with the islands' strategic position between mainland Greece and Asia Minor, made trading important, and by 2000 BC the Cretan Minoans had become influential in the area, particularly on Santoríni – though this influence came to an end with a catastrophic volcanic eruption around 1600 BC. After the subsequent Mycenaean period, the Ionians arrived in the tenth century BC and within two hundred years the first cities had appeared. **Delos** became a great religious centre, for the island group and beyond.

During and after the Persian wars, the islands suffered both from their enemies and allies as Athens gradually stripped away the wealth and influence of the **Delian Confederacy**. They only regained prosperity during the Hellenistic period, as demonstrated by the construction of numerous large and impressive towers. The subsequent intervention of the Romans converted Delos into a successful commercial centre, until a series of raiders from the east destroyed its influence. Under **Byzantine** rule, with little control or support from distant Constantinople, the islands were vulnerable to pirates, and settlements moved from the coast to inland capitals. With the destruction of Constantinople by the Crusaders in 1204, the islands came under **Venetian** control, and the Cyclades was divided up by adventurers such as Marcos Sanudo who set up the Náxos-based Duchy of the Aegean. Settlements returned to the coast, substantial fortifications were built there, and Catholicism prospered. Most of the islands were taken by the **Ottomans** in the 1530s, though Tínos held out until 1715; however the Ottomans only demanded tax from the islands and interfered little in other matters, allowing the Orthodox church a resurgence against the former Catholic majority.

The **revolution** against the Ottoman empire in 1821 was marked by varying degrees of support from the different islands, and by the arrival of numerous refugees from other, Greek-speaking parts of the empire. The Cyclades became part of the Greek state in 1832 and **Sýros**, in particular, prospered, as the state's largest port and second largest city and a major industrial base. However, the development of Pireás, and the 1893 opening of the Corinth Canal led to a sharp decline in the islands. In the first half of the twentieth century, mining was the main source of income for a number of islands, succeeded by tourism in the second half.

## Watersports in the Cyclades

More and more **watersports** facilities are opening up across the islands, offering a generally good level of teaching and equipment to rent. Prices start from around €25 for an hour's windsurfing lesson and equipment rental, from €50 for a day's "Discover Scuba", and from €300 for a PADI open-water diving course. One of the best areas for **diving** is in the waters off the northeast coast of Mílos (see p.141), with Andíparos (see p.180), Mýkonos (see p.160), Kýthnos (see p.123) and Santoríni (see p.214) also offering facilities. **Kiteboarders** and **windsurfers** will probably head for Poúnda or Sánta María in Páros (see p.175 and see p.176), Kalafáti in Mykonos (see p.161), or southwest Náxos (see p.185).

But whatever the level of tourist development, there are only three islands where it completely dominates their character in season: **Íos**, the original hippie island and still a paradise for hard-drinking backpackers, **Thíra**, the major island in the volcanic cluster of **Santoríni** and a dramatic natural backdrop for luxury cruise liners, and **Mýkonos**, by far the most popular of the group, with its teeming old town, selection of gay, nude and gay-nude beaches, and sophisticated restaurants, clubs and hotels. After these, **Páros**, **Náxos** and **Mílos** are the most popular, their beaches and main towns packed at the height of the season, which means late July to late August in the Cyclades. The once-tranquil **Minor Cyclades** southeast of Náxos have become fashionable destinations for well-heeled Athenians in recent years, as have nearby **Amorgós**, and **Folégandhros** to the west. To avoid the hordes altogether – except in the Greek summer holidays, when escape is impossible – the most promising islands are **Síkinos**, **Kímolos** or **Anáfi**. For a different view of the Cyclades, visit **Tínos** and its imposing pilgrimage church, a major spiritual centre of Greek Orthodoxy, or **Sýros** with its elegant townscape and (like Tínos) large Catholic minority. Due to their closeness to Athens, adjacent **Ándhros** and **Kéa** are predictably popular – and relatively expensive – weekend havens for Greeks, as are to a lesser extent **Kýthnos** and **Sérifos**, while **Sífnos** remains a popular destination for upmarket tourists of all nationalities. The one major ancient site is **Delos** (Dhílos), certainly worth making time for; the commercial and religious centre of the Classical Greek world, it's visited most easily on a day-trip from Mýkonos. When it comes to **moving on**, many of the islands – in particular Mílos, Páros, Náxos and Thíra – are handily connected with Crete (easier in late July and August), while from Tínos, Mýkonos, Sýros, Páros, Náxos or Thíra you can reach the Dodecanese by direct boat. Similarly, you can regularly get from Mýkonos, Náxos, Sýros and Páros to Ikaría and Sámos (in the eastern Aegean).

One consideration for the timing of your visit is that the Cyclades, particularly in early spring or late autumn, often get frustratingly **stormy**, and it's also the group worst affected by the *meltémi*, which scatters sand and tables with ease throughout much of July and August. Delayed or cancelled ferries (even in the height of the tourist season) are not uncommon, so if you're heading back to Athens to catch a flight, leave yourself a day or two's leeway.

# Kéa (Tziá)

**Kéa**, the nearest of the Cyclades to the mainland, is extremely popular with Athenian families in August and at weekends year-round. Their impact has spread beyond the small resorts, and much of the coastline is peppered with holiday homes and scarred with access roads. There is a preponderance of

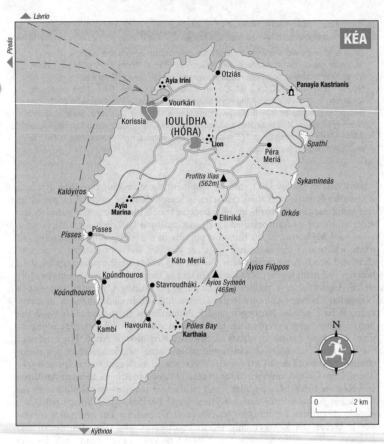

Kéa map showing Lávrio, Pireás, Kýthnos ferry routes; Ayia Iríni, Otziás, Panayia Kastrianís, Vourkári, Korissía, IOULÍDHA (HÓRA), Lion, Péra Meriá, Spathí, Profítis Ilías (562m), Sykamineás, Kalóyiros, Ayia Marína, Elliniká, Orkós, Písses, Káto Meriá, Áyios Filíppos, Koúndhouros, Stavroudháki, Áyios Symeón (465m), Kambí, Havouná, Póles Bay, Karthaía.

expensive apartments and villa accommodation and not as many good tavernas as you might expect (plus virtually no nightlife) because so many visitors self-cater. Outside August, Kéa, with its rocky, forbidding perimeter and inland oak and almond groves, is an enticing destination for those who enjoy a rural ramble, although its tourist infrastructure is poor.

As ancient Keos, the island and its strategic, well-placed harbour supported four cities – a pre-eminence that continued until the nineteenth century when Sýros became the main Greek port. Tourists account for the bulk of the sea traffic with regular (in season) **ferry connections** to and from Lávrio on the mainland, plus sporadic ferries to and from Sýros, Kýthnos and Mílos. Agents in Athens usually won't sell ferry tickets from Lávrio to Kéa, so you will probably need to get these in Lávrio.

## The northwest coast: Korissía to Otziás

The small northern ferry and hydrofoil port of **KORISSÍA** has fallen victim to uneven expansion and is rather dusty and unattractive; if you don't like its looks upon disembarking, try to get a bus to Otziás (6km), Ioulídha (6km) or Písses (16km). Buses may meet the boats; during July and August there's a regular fixed schedule around the island, but at other times public transport can be very elusive. There are a few taxis on Kéa, and one car-rental outfit at the port that is unable to offer full insurance.

The ill-equipped seafront **tourist information** office opens sporadically; next-door Mouzaki (☎22880 21428) are agents only for the *Marmari Express* to Lávrio and unhelpful otherwise. Meltemi (☎22880 21920), the general ferry agency – including the Goutos Lines Lávrio ferries (*Myrina Express* and *Macedon*) – can be more useful. **Accommodation**, in general, is not of a high standard; year-round possibilities near the port are the somewhat noisy *Karthea* (☎22880 21222; ❺) which does, however, have single rooms, or the friendly *Nikitas* pension (☎22880 21193; ❸) with plain, comfortable studios well inland and to the right of the stream-bed. Near the eastern end of the beach, on the road to Vourkári, the comfortable *Hotel Brillante Zoi* (aka Lamberi Zoi, ☎22880 22685, ⓦwww.hotelbrillante.gr; ❻) has the quietest rooms at the back, away from the road. A little further along is the cool, contemporary *Keos Katoikies* (☎22880 84002, ⓦwww.keos.gr; ❼) offering a dramatic setting overlooking the bay. For **eating**, a series of nondescript tavernas along the harbour waterfront serves standard but overpriced Greek dishes.

There's good swimming at **Yialiskári**, a small, eucalyptus-fringed beach between Korissía and Vourkári; beyond the beach, the nearby *Tastra* beach bar-café is something of a hub for nightlife on the island, luring revellers from Korissía and Ioulídha. About 300m beyond, a cluster of accommodation up the steep hillside include the *Gialiskari* rooms (☎22880 21197; ❸) just above the road.

**VOURKÁRI**, strung out around the next bay, a couple of kilometres further northeast, is arguably more attractive than Korissía, serving as a hangout for the yachting set. A few expensive **tavernas**, including the nationally renowned *Yiannis Maroulis* and *Konstantina Marouli*, serve up beautifully prepared fresh seafood, and there's a good ouzerí – *Strofi tou Mimi* – located where the road cuts inland towards Otziás. Despite a few nondescript bars, the nightlife here, as on the rest of the island, consists primarily of hanging out late in tavernas.

Another 4km further, past the **Ayía Iríni** ruins of a Minoan palace that lie virtually unnoticed on the peninsula north of the island's main harbour, **OTZIÁS** has a small beach that's a bit better than the one at Korissía, though more exposed to prevailing winds; facilities are limited to a couple of tavernas and a fair number of apartments for rent. Kéa's only functioning monastery, the eighteenth-century **Panayías Kastrianís**, is 7km along a surfaced road from Otziás. Although more remarkable for its fine setting on a high bluff than for any intrinsic interest, the hostel at the monastery (☎22880 24348; ❷) is the cheapest accommodation on the island, albeit rather basic, isolated and not dependably open. From here you can take the pleasant walk on dirt tracks and occasional paths to the island's capital, Ioulídha, in another two hours.

## Ioulídha

**IOULÍDHA** (aka Hóra), with its numerous red-tiled roofs, Neoclassical buildings and winding flagstoned paths, beautifully situated in an amphitheatric fold in the hills, is by no means a typical Cycladic town, but is architecturally the most interesting settlement on the island. Accordingly it has numerous bars and bistros, much patronized in August and at weekends, but during other times it's quiet, its atmospheric, labyrinthine lanes excluding vehicles. It is accessible from Korissía by paved road or from Otziás on foot via ancient stone paths that connected the towns during the island's heyday.

The **archeological museum** (Tues–Sun 8.30am–3pm; free) displays surprisingly extensive finds from the four ancient city-states of Kéa, although the best items were long ago spirited away to Athens. The lower reaches of the town stretch across a spur to the **kástro**, a tumbledown Venetian fortress incorporating stones from an ancient temple of Apollo. Fifteen-minutes' walk northeast, on the path toward Otziás, you pass the **Lion of Kéa**, a sixth-century BC sculpture carved out of an outcrop of rock, 6m long and 3m high. There are steps right down to the lion, but the effect is most striking from a distance.

Along with a **post office** and **bank agent**, there are a couple of **accommodations**, including the attractive *Hotel Serie* (T22880 22355, Wwww.serie.gr; ⑤). Choices for **eating and drinking** tend to be of a higher quality than in Korissía, but unless you arrive during a busy season, you may find many places closed. *Piatsa*, just as you enter the lower town from the car park, has a variety of tasty dishes while, up on the platía, *Rolando's* offers a range of fish plates; neighbouring *Kalofagadon* is the best place for a full-blown meat feast. The aptly named *Panorama* serves up pastries and coffee and is a good place to watch the sun set. Once a hub of nightlife, the central town now shuts down early, though the mayor, Antonakis Zoulos, is one of the most accomplished traditional violinists in Greece, so you could ask at the town hall where he'll be performing next. Full-on *bouzoúki* nights occur regularly at bars, cafés and tavernas in town or back at the port.

## Southern Kéa

About 8km southwest of Ioulídha, reached via a 1.2km dirt track off the paved road, a crumbling, square Hellenistic watchtower from the fourth century BC sprouts dramatically from the grounds of the dwarfed nineteenth-century **Ayía Marína** monastery church. Beyond, the paved main road twists around the startling scenic head of the lovely agricultural valley at **PÍSSES**, emerging at a large beach. There are several tavernas, plus a pleasant **campsite**, *Camping Kea*, which has good turfy ground and also runs studios (T22880 31302; May–Sept; ⑧) further inland. Of the tavernas, the best is *Akroyiali*, with a good range of dishes and some decent house wine, as well as rooms to rent upstairs (T22880 31301; ②).

Beyond Písses, the asphalt peters out at the end of the five-kilometre road south to **KOÚNDHOUROS**, a sheltered bay popular with yachters, and now with house-building developers; there's a taverna behind the largest of several sandy coves, none of which are cleaner or bigger than the beach at Písses. At the south end of the bay, *St George Bungalows* (T22880 31277, Estgeorge _bungalows@yahoo.gr; ④) has well-kept rooms at reasonable prices, as well as its own taverna which is recommended. A further 2km south, at **Kambí**, there's a nice little beach and a good taverna of the same name.

Besides the very scant ruins of ancient Poiessa near Písses, the only remains of any real significance from Kéa's past are fragments of temples of Apollo and Athena at **ancient Karthaia**, tucked away on the southeastern edge of the island above Póles Bay, with an excellent deserted twin beach that's easiest reached by boat – it may be possible to hire a traditional sailboat in Vourkári to take you. Otherwise, it's a good three-hour round-trip walk from the hamlets of Stavroudháki or Havouná, off the paved road linking Ioulídha, Mt Profítis Ilías (the island's 562m summit), Astrás, Elliniká, Káto Meriá and Havouná. The road is worth following along the island's summit from Ioulídha; affording fine views over the thousands of magnificent oaks which are Kéa's most distinctive feature. Unsurfaced roads connect Stavroudháki with Kambí and Koúndhouros.

# Kýthnos (Thermiá)

One of the lesser known and most low key of the larger Cyclades, **Kýthnos** is a good antidote to the exploitation that may be encountered elsewhere. Few foreigners visit, and the island – known for much of its history as Thermiá, after its renowned hot springs – is quieter than Kéa, particularly to the south where hikes from Dhryopídha, with its colourfully tiled roofs, to coastal coves are the primary diversion. It's a place where Athenians come to buy land for villas, go spear-fishing and sprawl on sunbed-free beaches without having to jostle for space. You could use it as a first or last island stop; in August there are several **ferry connections** a week with Kéa and Lávrio, and frequent ferry and catamaran services to and from Sérifos, Sífnos, Mílos, Kímolos and Pireás.

## Mérihas and around

Boats dock on the west coast at **MÉRIHAS**, an attractive ferry and fishing port with many of the island's facilities, including a helpful but high-season-only tourist information kiosk. The closest beach of any repute is **Episkopí**, a 500-metre stretch of averagely clean grey sand with the *Pountaki* beach bar/taverna,

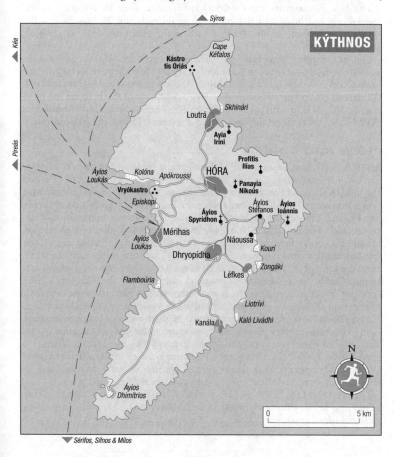

thirty-minutes' walk north of the town; you can shorten this on coast-hugging trails and tracks below the road. Far better are the popular beaches of **Apókroussi**, which has a canteen, and **Kolóna**, a very picturesque sand spit joining Kýthnos to the islet of Áyios Loukás. About an hour's walk northwest of Episkopí, these are more easily reached by boat trip from Mérihas, and get busy once the boats arrive. Between Episkopí and Apókroussi lie the ruined temples, towers, walls and reservoirs of the tenth-century BC fortified town of **Vryókastro** – in 2002 a hoard of some 1500 votive items was discovered here.

**Accommodation** owners may meet the ferries in high season. The numerous rooms to let tend to be large and equipped for visiting Athenian families, so can be on the expensive side for fewer persons – although with some opportunity for bargaining during the week. Out of season, owners are often not on the premises, but a contact phone number is usually posted. The rooms and studios *Panayiota* (☎22810 32268; May–Oct; ❸), in several locations, are a popular choice – the owner's shop is just behind the small bridge on the seafront. The *Panorama* studios (☎22810 32184; May–Oct; ❸) up steep steps behind the harbour have panoramic views over the bay. There is further accommodation opposite the ferry, on the street behind the bridge, and along the Dhryopídha road beyond the petrol station and bakery.

The best **restaurants** are *Ostria*, a classic fish taverna by the jetty, *Gialos*, specializing in lamb dishes, behind the central beach, and *To Kandouni*, on the opposite waterfront to the ferry, a grill with specialities such as *sfoungáto* (baked omelette).

The **bus service**, principally to Hóra and Loutrá, Dhryopídha and Kanála, runs around six times daily in summer, less reliably from September to June; car and motorbike rental is available through Antonis Lavrentzakis (☎22810 32104, ✉anlarent@otenet.gr), who has the ferry agency above the harbour road and may be able to help with accommodation (❹). There is an Emboriki **bank** and **ATM** a short way above the agency, and a second ATM on the harbour road.

## Hóra and Loutrá

**HÓRA** lies 7.5km northeast of Mérihas, in the middle of the island. Though the town is unpromising at first sight, wander into the narrow streets beyond the initial square and you'll find a wonderful network of alleyways, painted with white flowers and lined with real ones, weaving their way past shops, churches and through tiny squares with colourful cafés. The only accommodation is the comfortable *Filoxenia* (☎22810 31644, ⊕www.filoxenia-kythnos.gr; ❹) studios, arranged around a flowery courtyard next to the A. Kanellopoulou square. You can **eat** at the friendly *To Kentro* taverna (good for meat feasts) near the small, central square of Ayía Triádha, at *To Steki tou Detzi* (evenings only) grill a few minutes further in, or at *Messaria* (evenings only), next to the *Filoxenia*; a Hóra speciality is rabbit in wine sauce. For refreshments, try the *Apocalypse* café, next to the main church of – appropriately enough – Áyios Ioánnis Theológos, which has an elaborate wooden iconostasis carved by the brother of the current priest. The nineteenth-century church also has a much older icon, of the three matriarchs, said to have been found floating in the sea by local fishermen. There is a **post office** (Mon–Fri 9.30am–2pm). Hóra had Greece's first **wind-farm** (now derelict and replaced by a single, second-generation wind turbine) and its second solar-farm, and these provide part of the island's electricity.

The resort of **LOUTRÁ** (4.5km north of Hóra and named after its sulfur, saline and ferrous thermal baths) is unexciting, its nineteenth-century spa (designed by Schiller, the architect of many of Greece's finest Neoclassical

▲ Hóra, a classic white village, Kýthnos

public buildings) long since replaced by a sterile modern construction and its harbour by a marina. There are plenty of seafront cafés, bars and tavernas offering facilities to yachting crews, including the *Poco Loco* internet café and car and bike rental. Aqua Team (☎22810 31333, ⓦwww.aquakythnos.com) offer PADI, ANDI and IAHD diving courses, plus mountain-bike rental. **Hotels** include *Meltemi* (☎22810 31271, ⓦwww.meltemihotel-kythnos.gr; ❹, apartments ⑤) and the very comfortable *Porto Klaras* (☎22810 31276, ⓦwww.porto-klaras.gr; April–Oct; ⑤), with sea views and beautifully furnished rooms, studios and apartments. Other rooms and studios tend to open only for the brief July–August peak season. You can visit the state-run *Xenia Anagenissis* baths complex (☎22810 31217), where a twenty-minute bath plus basic check-up – blood pressure, heart rate and weight – costs about €10. The small bay of Ayía Iríni, just 1km east of Loutrá, and north of the church from which it takes its name, is a more pleasant place to swim; en route is the *Vrachia* taverna with excellent fish, oven-cooked Greek staples, and lower prices than the marina area. In the 1862 anti-monarchist revolution, King Otto's forces gained a Pyrrhic naval victory over Sýros rebels in the bay, an event now known as the "Kythniaká" – a memorial marks the event. Just north of Loutrá, at Maroula, Mesolithic graves dating to about the eighth millennium BC suggest Kýthnos may have been one of the earliest inhabited Cycladic islands; other sites indicate copper mining and smelting. About a ninety-minute walk from Loutrá, on Cape Kéfalos, lie the picturesque ruins of the medieval capital **Kástro tís Oriás** (aka Kefalíkastro or Kástro toú Áï Yióryi), once home to around 5000 people and 100 churches, but abandoned by the mid-seventeenth century.

## Dhryopídha and southern Kýthnos

From Hóra it's possible to **walk** south to **DHRYOPÍDHA** (Sýllaka), mainly on dirt track. It takes about ninety minutes, following a walled lane that leaves Hóra heading due south, crossing a couple of deep valleys. After the first valley, the church of Áyios Trýfonas offers the first shade; as you climb out of the second valley, a side trail leads to the triple-naved **chapel of Áyios Spyrídhon**, which has recycled Byzantine columns. Just beyond this, you meet the partly surfaced road between Dhryopídha and Áyios Stéfanos beach.

More visually appealing than Hóra by virtue of spanning a well-watered valley, Dhryopídha (Sýllaka), with its red-tiled roofs, is reminiscent of Spain or Tuscany. It was once the island's capital, built around one of Greece's largest **caves**, the Katafýki (open evenings). Tucked away behind the cathedral is a tiny **folklore museum** (open evenings, erratically). Beside the cathedral is the *Dryopis,* first of a number of small café/snack-bars in the narrow street. Some people let rooms in their houses, but the nearest official accommodation is 6km south at coastal Kanála.

**KANÁLA** is a relaxed alternative to Loutrá, with the Panayía Kanála church set in a tiny but pleasant pine woodland and home to a miracle-working icon by the seventeenth-century Cretan master, Skordhilis. There is accommodation in the older settlement up on the promontory, such as the *Oneiro/Antamoma* (☎22810 32152; ③) and *Nikos Bouritis* (☎22810 32350; ③) studios, the latter above a minimarket and with a garden; tavernas include the hospitable *Ofiousa*, with a terrace overlooking the larger western beach, **Megáli Ámmos**. Arranged around a pleasant seafront courtyard at the far end of the beach are the comfortable *Akrogialia* (☎22810 32366; May–Oct; ⑤) studios. From Kanála, a succession of small coves – Kaló Livádhi, Liotrívi, Lefkés, Zongáki, Kourí, Náoussa – extends up the east coast as far as the coastal hamlet of Áyios Stéfanos.

Southwest of Dhryopídha, reached by a turning off the road to Kanála, **Flamboúria** is the most presentable beach on the west coast. The double bay of **Áyios Dhimitríos** further south, although not too exciting, has a couple of tavernas and the *Akroyiali* (☎22810 32208; ③) rooms to rent in high season.

# Sérifos

**Sérifos** has long languished outside the mainstream of history and modern tourism. Little has happened here since Perseus returned with Medusa's head in time to save his mother, Danaë, from being ravished by the local king Polydectes – turning him, his court and the green island into stone. Many would-be visitors are deterred by the apparently barren, hilly interior, which, with the stark, rocky coastline, makes Sérifos appear uninhabited until the ferry turns into postcard-picturesque Livádhi Bay.

Although paved roads have recently made the interior more accessible, the island is best recommended for serious **walkers**, who can head for several small villages in the under-explored interior, plus some isolated coves. Many people still keep livestock and produce their own wines, and some gather the wild narcissus for export. A central government proposal to install a large number of giant wind-turbines to provide Athens with electricity has gone down badly with islanders resident in Hóra who, because of the town's protected status, are not themselves allowed to install solar heating.

## Livádhi and the main beaches

Most visitors stay in the port, **LIVÁDHI**, set in a wide greenery-fringed bay and handy for most of the island's beaches. The usually calm bay here is a magnet for island-hopping yachts, here to take on fresh water which, despite appearances, Sérifos has in abundance. Livádhi and the neighbouring cove of Livadhákia are certainly the easiest places to find rooms and any amenities you might need, which are scarce elsewhere.

### Arrival and information

Helpful Serifos Travel (☎22810 51448, ⊛www.serifos-travel.com), near the jetty, sells **boat** tickets and has **internet** access. The **bus stop** and timetable are at the base of the yacht and fishing-boat jetty; **buses** connect Livádhi with Hóra, 2km away, 27–30 times a day in summer, otherwise 7–10 times; in high season buses run a circular route via Panayía, Galaní, Kéndharhos, Áyios Ioánnis and Psilí

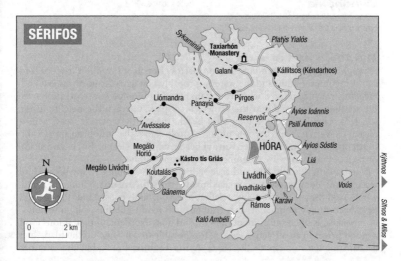

Ámmos, or vice versa (6–7 times), and to Méga Livádhi and Koutalás in the southwest (2 times); outside high season there are just two daily trips to Panayía, Galaní and Kéndarhos.

You can rent a **bike** or **car** from Blue Bird (⊤22810 51511, ⓦwww .rentacar-bluebird.gr), next to the filling station on the main street, or from Serifos Travel. There are a couple of **ATM**s along the seafront, and **internet** access is also available at the *Malabar* pub, inside the shopping arcade.

## Accommodation

Proprietors don't always meet ferries, with the exception of *Coralli Camping* and the *Dorkas/Aegean* in Livadhákia, which often send minibuses. In high season you may need to be briskly off the boat to get a decent bed; the most rewarding hunting grounds are on the headland above the ferry dock in Livádhi itself, or at Livadhákia, a ten-minute walk away. Unlike many islands, much of the accommodation is open year-round.

### Livádhi

**Areti** On the headland overlooking the bay ⊤22810 51479. Attractively positioned hotel with a lovely communal terrace at the back overlooking a tiny beach and the entrance to the bay. They also have studios and apartments. April–Oct. ❹

**Cristi** Next to the *Areti* ⊤22810 51775. Hospitable modern pension in good location. Some rooms have private balconies, others share a veranda; some have sea views. ❹

**Margarita** Beachfront at the far (northeast) end of the bay ⊤22810 51321. Basic, family-run rooms with verandas in a peaceful spot. ❷

**Naias** On the headland, between Livádhi and Livadhákia ⊤22810 51749, ⓦwww.naiasserifos.gr. A slightly dated, but comfortable, good-value hotel. All rooms with balconies, some with sea views. ❹

### Livadhákia

**Alexandros & Vassilia ("A&B")** On the beach, behind the taverna of the same name ⊤22810 51119. Cluster of spotless, balconied doubles (❹) and apartments (❻). Easter–Oct.

**Coralli Camping Bungalows** Behind the beach ⊤22810 51500, ⓦwww.coralli.gr. Bungalows (❹) on the campsite, with its communal pool, restaurant and bar. Also run the newer 4–6-person *Coralli Studios* (❻) closer to town.

**Dorkas/Aegean** On and above main road through Livadhákia ⊤22810 51422, ⓦwww .dorkas-aigaonnis.com. Stylish, comfortable rooms, plus spacious new apartments higher on the hillside with large balconies and sea views. March–Oct. ❹

**Helios** Inland side of main road through Livadhákia ⊤22810 51066. Welcoming bougainvillea-draped family-run pension with comfortable rooms. ❸

**Vaso** Seaward side of main road through Livadhákia ⊤22810 51346. Spacious rooms, some with kitchens. ❸

### The town and around

Though attractive, the sand of the long, narrow **beach** at Livádhi is hard-packed and sometimes muddy, and the water is probably best at its far northeastern end. Heading away from the dock, turn left up the main business street, or climb over the southerly headland past the cemetery car park, to reach the neighbouring, superior, **Livadhákia**, a golden-sand beach, shaded by tamarisk trees, with a pleasant taverna. A further ten-minutes' stroll across the low headland to the south brings you to the smaller **Karávi** beach, which is cleaner, but has no shade or facilities and extensive ongoing development behind.

North of the Livádhi Bay and accessible by bus in summer – or a 45-minute walk (3km) along a (mostly) surfaced road – is **Psilí Ámmos**, a long, sheltered, white-sand beach, backed by a large reservoir, and considered the island's best. Accordingly popular, its two rival tavernas tend to be full in high season – 🍴 *Stefanakos* is open for more of the year and does excellent, unpretentious food at good prices in an attractive garden. It is possible to continue on the road, then by path for ten minutes to the larger **Áyios Ioánnis** beach, but this is rather exposed, and only the far south end is inviting. Theoretically, both beaches are visited by *kaïkia* from Livádhi, as are nearby sea caves, but don't rely on this. Additionally, and plainly visible from arriving ferries, two more sandy coves, **Liá** (naturist) and **Áyios Sóstis**, hide at the far eastern flank of the island opposite the islet Voús; they are popular with the locals, but accessible on foot only, by dirt track and path off the road to Psilí Ámmos.

### Eating and drinking

As on most islands, **tavernas** near the quay tend to be slightly pricier; further up the beach meals get less expensive. The ouzerí *Meltemi* is popular, whilst a little further along the bay, the *Takis* taverna is another good choice, with its tables on the sand. Cheaper options, on the northern half of the beach, include *Fagopoti o Nikoulais* with excellent *mezédhes*, and, at the extreme northeast end of the beach, *Margarita's* with a homely feel and courtyard seating.

**Nightlife** is surprisingly lively, and mostly clustered in or near a seafront mini-mall behind the main group of restaurants, so you should be able to quickly find something to suit your taste. *Passaggio* and next-door *Karnayio* are popular night-time spots playing excellent and varied music. One street back, *Metalleio* is a more full-on evening restaurant/night-time dance bar that gets into the swing after midnight. For something more Greek, try *Alter Ego* behind the shopping arcade.

## Hóra

**HÓRA** is a pleasant if steep forty-minute walk (if you're travelling light) up a cobbled way, with the *kalderími* (footpath) leading off from a bend in the road about 800m from Livádhi Beach.

Quiet and atmospheric, it is one of the least spoilt villages of the Cyclades. The best sights are in the precarious upper town: follow signs to the *kástro* to reach the top via steep and occasionally overgrown stairways. Tiny churches cling to the cliff-edges, and from Áyios Konstandínos on the summit there are breathtaking views across the valleys below.

The central platía, Ayíou Athanasíou, just northwest of the summit, has an attractive church and a small but colourful Neoclassical town hall. It is also home to *Stou Stratou*, an atmospheric café with a poetry-filled menu (ⓦwww .stoustratou.com), and to *Zorba's* ouzerí/snack-bar, which offer nice alternatives to eating on the busy seafront down below. A couple of minutes below the square, a circular loop of road has more tavernas, cafés and shops, as well as the main bus-stop. The *Apanemia* rooms (ⓣ22810 51517; ❸), with good views, are 200m along the street leading down from the Hora supermarket; this shop is an agency for ferries. There are several windmills in varying states of repair, and a small archeological collection (Tues–Sun, 8.30am–3pm; free). The island's **post office** is found in the lowest quarter.

The most dramatic **walk route** (signed "2") from Hóra goes up from the windmills and sweeps across the hillside on a broad, paved *kalderími* that leads to the church of Áyios Yeóryios before joining the Megálo Livádhi road near the heliport. From here you can continue on walk "4" to Panayía village.

## Northern Sérifos

The road northwest then north from Hóra leads to the fine villages of Panayía (after 6km) and Galaní (a further 3.5km). The tenth-century church at **Panayía** is usually locked, but comes alive on its feast day of Xilopanayía (Aug 16). Traditionally, the first couple to dance around the adjacent olive tree would be the first to marry that year, but this led to unseemly brawls, so the priest always goes first these days. **Galaní,** named after ancient galena mines, is the start of walk "6", which leads to the remote and often windswept beach of **Sykamiá**, with a seasonal taverna but no camping allowed; walk "5" continues from there to Panayía. A better bet for a swim is the more sheltered cove of **Platýs Yialós** at the extreme northern tip of the island, reached by a partly paved road. The neighbouring beach has the *Nikoulias* taverna (T22810 52174; ❸) that may have a couple of basic rooms available in season.

Immediately before the Platýs Yialós turn is the fortified fifteenth- to seventeenth-century **monastery of Taxiarhón**, once home to sixty monks but no longer permanently inhabited. Treasures of the monastic church include an ivory-inlaid bishop's throne, silver lamps from Egypt (to where many Serifots emigrated during the nineteenth century) and the finely carved *témblon*.

Three kilometres further is the island's northernmost village, **KÉNDARHOS** (Kállitsos), also reached by a ninety-minute path ("1") from Hóra, marked by red paint splodges along a donkey track that forks off above the cemetery. From Kéndarhos (no facilities), the paved road leads clockwise to Psilí Ámmos beach.

## Southwestern Sérifos

Heading north from Hóra to Panayía, you reach a junction in the road. Turn left for **Megálo Horió** (Mía Horió) – the site of ancient Seriphos, which offers little for the casual tourist. A 4km detour off this road, **Avéssalos** is one of the island's least explored beaches, making up for its relatively uninspiring landscape with sheer peace and quiet. **Megálo Livádhi**, further on from Megálo Horió, is a remote beach resort 10km west of Hóra, with two lovely tavernas whose tables are practically on the beach; the *Marditsa* taverna (T22810 51003; ❸) has some simple rooms behind the beach. Iron and copper ores were once exported from here, via a loading bridge that still hangs over the water, but cheaper African deposits sent the mines into decline. Today most of the idle machinery rusts away, though some gravel-crushing still goes on. At the north end of the beach, there's a monument to four workers killed in 1916 during a protest against unfair conditions.

An alternative turning just below Megálo Horió leads 3.5km to the small mining and fishing port of **Koutalás**, a pretty sweep of bay with a church-tipped rock and a long if narrow beach. It has become rather a ghost settlement, and the workers' restaurants have all closed down, but there is one snack-bar/taverna, catering mainly to yachting crews. Above the port are the scant ruins of the medieval **Kástro tís Griás**. The winding track above the village leads east to Livádhi, and apart from the nearby spacious **Gánema** beach, which has a taverna of the same name, there are no places to buy refreshments on the two-hour journey back. A side-track en route leads down to the very pretty but shadeless **Kaló Ambéli** Beach.

# Sífnos

**Sífnos** is prettier, tidier and more cultivated than its northern neighbours and has some fine architecture. This means it's also much more popular; in July and August, available rooms are in short supply. Take any you can find as you arrive, or have a prebooked reservation. In keeping with the island's somewhat upmarket clientele, camping rough is forbidden, while nude sunbathing is not always tolerated.

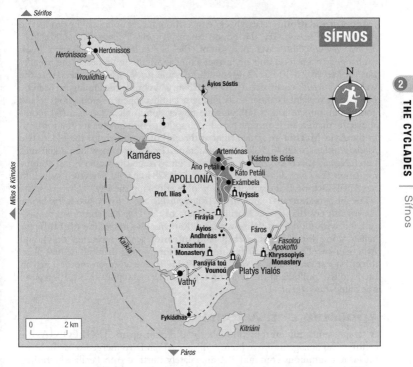

The island's modest size makes it eminently explorable. The **bus service** is excellent, most of the roads good, and there's a vast network of paths that are mostly easy to follow. Sífnos has a strong tradition of pottery (as early as the third century BC) and has long been esteemed for its distinctive cuisine, intrinsically linked to the development of pottery, which allowed for more sophisticated baked foods. The island is perhaps best appreciated today, however, for its many beautifully situated **churches** and **monasteries**, or for the beautiful scenery around **Vathý** in the far southwest (see p.134).

**Ferry connections** are more frequent to Sífnos than to the other more northerly islands. The *Panagia Hozoviotissa* plies a regular shuttle via Kýthnos and Sérifos, then on to Mílos and Kímolos, and is joined by a couple of other ferries in high season; some itineraries continue east to Folégandhros, Síkinos, Íos and Thíra, while catamarans link Sífnos with Sérifos, Páros, Mílos, Folégandhros and Thíra on an almost daily basis in season. Links with the central Cyclades are far less frequent, with twice-weekly high-season ferries to Páros or Sýros.

## Kamáres

**KAMÁRES**, the island's port, with a pleasant beach, is tucked away in a long, steep-sided valley that cuts into the cliffs of the island's western side. A still-compact resort, though with concrete blocks of accommodations edging up to the base of the hill-slopes, Kamáres' seafront road is crammed with bars, travel agencies, ice-cream shops and restaurants. Proprietors tend not to meet boats; while hunting for a room, you can store luggage at the Aegean Thesaurus **travel agency** (☎22840 33527) right by the ferry dock, who also book accommodation across the island.

**Accommodation** is relatively expensive, though bargaining can be productive outside peak season. Try the good, reasonably priced *Hotel Stavros* (T22840 33383, Wwww.sifnostravel.com; ❹) on the harbourfront, who have a book exchange in their reception, or, further along above the town beach, the friendly *Boulis Hotel* (T22840 32122, Wwww.hotelboulis.gr; ❺). Behind the *Boulis*, the welcoming *Makis* **campsite** (T22840 32366, Wwww.makiscamping.gr; March–Nov) has excellent facilities – including a laundry open to non-guests – and good-value on-site rooms (❸), plus the newer, comfortable *Leonidas* (❹) rooms above the main road. Continue past the campsite to find quieter accommodation in the **Ayía Marína** area; turn right at the end of the beach for the older-style *Mosha Pension* (T22840 31269, Wwww.ensifno.gr; ❸) or its new, upmarket sister hotel, *Nymfes* (B&B ❺), next door; or turn left to reach the westernmost accommodation, the Cycladic-style *Delphini* hotel (T22840 33740, Wwww.hoteldelfini .gr; April–Oct; B&B ❻), which has a pool overlooking the bay.

The best **restaurants** are *Meropi Kambourakis*, ideal for a pre-ferry lunch; *Argyris* fish taverna in Ayía Marína en route to the *Delphini*; and *Simos*, family-run and with food from their own farm. Kamáres also has a little **nightlife**; try *Yamas*, good for a sunset cocktail and **internet** access (evenings only), and Athenian-owned *Follie-Follie* for breakfast or for evening drinks. The best place to **rent a car or bike** is at No.1 (T22840 33791, Wwww.protomotocar.gr), on the road to Apollonía at the junction for Ayía Marína. Opposite No.1 is a good bookshop-newsagent.

## Apollonía and Artemónas

A steep twenty-minute bus ride takes you 5.5km up to **APOLLONÍA**, the centre of an amalgam of five hilltop villages which have merged over the years into one continuous community: immediately north is Áno Petáli which then runs into Artemónas, about fifteen minutes away on foot. With white buildings, stepped paths, belfries and flower-draped balconies, it is very scenic, though not self-consciously so.

### Arrival and information

Apollonía's central Platía Iróön looks rather abandoned, but beside it are the **post office** and the **bus stop** for Kamáres; stops for other places are at the junction above, by the *Anthousa* hotel. There are two **pharmacies**, three **banks** and four **ATM**s near the junction; the police station is located on the main road leading north out of town. A few minutes along the road to Faros is the **internet café**, "*8*", and you can rent **bikes** at Moto Apollo, beside the Eko petrol station just beyond – though the island's hidden landscapes are best explored on foot.

### Accommodation

All the central places can be noisy when the nearby clubs are open during the summer and at weekends – rooms in adjacent *Áno Petáli*, on the northern pedestrian street to Artemónas, are generally quieter. The Aegean Thesaurus travel agency (T22840 33151, Wwww.thesaurus.gr), or Room Rental Association (T22840 31333) may be able to help find accommodation not listed below.

**Anthoussa Hotel** Central road junction T22840 31431. A dessert-lovers' paradise, with comfortable rooms and extremely good home-made cakes, chocolates and ice cream. ❹
**Evangelia Kouki** Áno Petáli T22840 31263 Attractive, terraced rooms in a quiet area on the pedestrian street leading to Artemónas. April–Oct. ❸

**Giamaki** Just off the main southern pedestrian street T22840 33973, F22840 33923. Conveniently positioned near the centre, the rooms are spacious, and there's a pleasant communal terrace. ❸

Mrs Dina Cathedral area ☏22840 31125. A variety of rooms and studios in a peaceful position with panoramic views, accessed via the first alley left above the cathedral. Open May–Oct. ❹

Myrto Bungalows Artemónas ☏22840 32055, ⓦwww.bungalows-myrto.gr. Comfortable studios, some with rural views, on the narrow street southwest of the main square towards the Áyios Pétros cemetery. ❺

Petali Village Áno Petáli ☏22840 33024, ⓦwww.hotelpetali.gr.com. A luxurious hotel in a quiet position. B&B ❻

Sifnos Main pedestrian street ☏22840 31624, ⓦwww.sifnoshotel.com. Very friendly hotel, with the most traditional architecture, and a good restaurant underneath. ❹

## The Town

Sights in town include numerous churches, while on the central **Platía Iróön** the **folk museum** (officially daily 9.30am–2pm & 6–10pm, but often closed; €1), with its collection of textiles, lace, costumes and weaponry, is worth a visit. Radiating out from above the platía is a network of stepped marble pedestrian streets, the busiest of which is flagstoned Stylianoú Prókou, which leads off to the south, lined with restaurants, bars, fancy shops and churches, including the balconied cathedral, **Áyios Spyrídhon**, towards the top; **Áyios Athanásios**, next to Platía Triandafýlou, has frescoes and a wooden *témblon*. The main pedestrian street north from the platía leads past the eighteenth-century church of **Panayía Ouranoforía** (aka Yeraniofórou), incorporating fragments of a seventh-century BC temple of Apollo and a relief of St George over the door, and via Áno Petáli to Artemónas.

**ARTEMÓNAS**, north of Apollonía and served by frequent buses (the central bus depot is here), is worth a morning's exploration for its churches and elegant Venetian and Neoclassical houses. **Panayía Gourniá** has vivid frescoes; the clustered-dome church of **Kohí** was built over an ancient temple of Artemis (also the basis of the village's name); and seventeenth-century **Áyios Yeóryios** contains fine icons.

### Eating and drinking

There are a number of **restaurants** in Apollonía: on the main pedestrian street, the charmingly decorated *Odos Oneiron* offers eclectic upscale dishes; the *Sifnos* hotel café/taverna does something for nearly every taste and is open all day. There are several tavernas up in the backstreets: *To Apostoli to Koutouki* is quite good for standard Greek fare and reasonable. At the eastern end of the Artemónas main square is the excellent 🎗 *Margarita* ouzerí, with traditional *mezédhes*. The *Khryso* taverna in the upper part of the village is hard to find (go up beside the *Margarita*, towards the Panayía toú Bali church, and then follow

---

### Walks in the interior

Apollonía is a good base from which to start your **explorations** of more remote Sifnos. Taking the path out from Katavatí (the district south of Apollonía) you'll pass, after a few minutes, the beautiful empty **monastery of Firáyia** and – fifteen minutes along the modern road – the path climbing up to **Áyios Andhréas**, from where there are tremendous views over the neighbouring islands. Just below the church is an enormous Bronze Age/Mycenaean **archeological site**, which is being made more visitor-friendly.

Even better is the all-trail walk to Vathý, around three hours from Katavatí via Taxiárhes and Áyios Nikólaos. Part way along, you can detour on a conspicuous side trail up to the **monastery of Profítis Ilías**, on the very summit (682m) of the island, with a vaulted refectory and extensive views.

occasional signs), but very popular with the locals at weekends, and well-priced. There is an excellent bakery, *To Stavri,* on the Iröön square. To the south of Apollonía, in Katavatí, the *Strofi* taverna is recommended.

Most of the **nightlife** can be found on the main pedestrian street south of the square, at *Botsi* (relaxed), *Volto* (current hits) or the long-standing *Argo* (classic to modern rock). The *Camel Club,* on the road to Fáros, is another popular place for late-night action. For rebétika music there's the *Aloni,* just above the crossroad to Kástro, with chart music.

## The north

Artemónas is the point of departure for **Herónissos**, an isolated hamlet with a few tavernas and rooms, around a small beach in a very deep inlet at the northwestern tip of the island. The 14km road is surfaced and there are three buses a day – there may also be occasional boat trips in season from Kamáres. It is possible to walk back to Artemónas – but the start of the partly marked path is not obvious – look behind and left of the Áyios Prokópios church. The best **taverna** is *Ammoudia* (aka *Nikos*), which also does breakfasts (welcome if you've caught the early bus). **Rooms** include those above the small shop near the church, and – in summer – those above the *Romantza* taverna (℡22840 33139; ❷) at the bus stop. A dirt track and path from the bus stop car park lead to the small Áyios Yeóryios monastery on the island's northernmost point, from where there are lovely views across to Sérifos. The church has an attractive carved plaque of its saint.

En route to Heronissos is the isolated west coast beach of **Vroulídhia**, accessed by a 2.5km dirt road and with a good snack-bar. On the northeast coast, thirty-minutes' walk from the road at Katavatós, is the isolated but very picturesquely sited church of Áyios Sóstis, near ancient silver and lead mines – legend tells of a stash of gold hidden nearby by money-grabbing merchants that was lost into the sea in an apocalyptic earthquake.

## The east coast

Most of Sífnos's coastal settlements are along the less precipitous eastern shore, within a modest distance of Apollonía and its surrounding cultivated plateau. These all have reasonable bus services and a certain amount of food and accommodation. **Kástro** may be more appealing than the resorts of **Fáros** and **Platýs Yialós**, which can get very overcrowded in July and August.

### Kástro

**KÁSTRO** can be reached on foot from Apollonía in 45 minutes, all but the last ten on a clear path threading its way east via the hamlet of Káto Petáli. Built on a rocky outcrop with a steep drop to the sea on three sides, the ancient capital of the island retains much of its medieval character. It's essentially a sinuous main street along the ridge, the houses on either side forming the outer defence wall. There are some fine sixteenth- and seventeenth-century churches with ornamental floors; Venetian coats of arms, ancient wall fragments and cunningly recycled Classical columns can still be seen on some of the older dwellings, while the occasional ancient sarcophagus perches incongruously on the pavement. In addition, there are the remains of the ancient acropolis, as well as a small **archeological museum** (Tues–Sun, officially 8am–2.30pm; free) installed in a former Catholic church in the higher part of the village; the museum has a small but varied collection of items, mainly from the Hellenistic and Roman periods, including coins, pottery, stelae and carved marble fragments.

For **accommodation**, the modernized *Aris & Maria* rooms and studios (☎22840 31161, ◉www.arismaria-traditional.com; ❸) are open all year – the reception is near the archeological museum. More basic, but boasting gorgeous views, *Maximos* (☎22840 33692; ❸) has a couple of rooms next to his jewellery shop, on the eastern side. Eating out is not cheap, and drinking even less so, with some expensive cafés near the bus-stop; the *Remezzo* café inside the walls is better priced and has good views.

You can walk along Kástro's northeastern peripheral path overlooking the picture-postcard church of the **Eptá Martýres** (Seven Martyrs) which juts out into the sea. There's nothing approximating a useable **beach** near Kástro; though for a swim you can use the Eptá Martýres rocks, or possibly the unattractive rocky cove of scruffy **Serália** (just below Kástro, to the south) or the shore at **Panayía Pouláti**, 1.3km to the northwest.

## Fáros and around

To the south of Kástro, the small resort of **FÁROS**, with bus links to Apollonía, is a possible fall-back base, though the beaches are small. The main beach is muddy, shadeless and crowded, and Fasoloú, 400m walk to the southeast past the headland, is only slightly better, much of it having been turned into a car park, though it has some tamarisk trees. Head off west through the older part of the village, and the small Glyfó beach has only pedestrian access, although new housing developments just behind may spell its doom. Fáros has **accommodation** such as the *Captain George* rooms (☎22840 71489; Easter–Oct; ❹) amongst olives behind the beach (ask at Franziskos Kakaki's seafront shop-café) or the nearby *Sifneiko Arhontiko* hotel (☎22840 71454, ◉sifneicoarxontiko@gmail.com; April–Sept; ❹). Behind Fasoloú, the spacious and comfortable 🗡 *Fassolou* studios (☎22840 71490, ◉www.fassolou-studios.gr; Easter–Sept; ❹) offer excellent views; on the eastern headland between Fáros and Fasoloú is Villa Maria (☎22840 71107, ◉www .en.sifnosvillamaria.gr; ❹) in a pretty garden. *To Kyma* is a pleasant seafront **taverna** in Fáros, while *Zambelis* at Fasoloú has been recommended.

Continuing from Glyfó, a fifteen-minute hillside path leads to the longer beach of **Apokoftó**, with a couple of good tavernas – the *Tsapis* and the *Chrysopigi* (*Lebessis*) – and, up an access road, to the *Hotel Flora* (☎22840 71278; April–Oct; ❹), which has superb views. The shore tends to accumulate seaweed, however, and a rock reef must be negotiated to get into the water. Flanking Apokoftó to the south, marooned on a sea-washed promontory, the seventeenth-century **Khryssopiyís monastery** features on every EOT poster of the island. According to legend, the cleft in the rock (under the entrance bridge) appeared when two village girls, fleeing to the spit to escape the attentions of menacing pirates, prayed to the Virgin to defend their virtue. The main festival takes place forty days after Easter and involves the spectacular arrival of a holy icon on a large high-speed ferry, and its (often dramatic) transfer to a small boat to be brought ashore.

## Platýs Yialós

From Apollonía, there are frequent high-season buses to the resort of **PLATÝS YIALÓS**, 12km away, near the southern tip of the island. Despite claims to be the longest beach in the Cyclades – slightly at odds with the claim by nearby Vathý (see p.134) to have the longest beach *on the island* – the sand can get very crowded. Diversions include numerous pottery workshops, but some are put off by the continuous row of buildings which directly line the entire stretch of beach, and by the strong winds that can plague it.

**Rooms** include the welcoming *Angeliki* (☎22840 71288, ◉www.sifnosageliki .com; May–Sept ❹), near the final bus stop #5, which is reasonably priced;

*Nikoleta* (☎22840 71436; May–Oct; ⑤), nearby, has attractive, well-equipped studios. A little inland, at bus stop #1, by the hairpin bends of the entrance road, the luxurious *Alexandros* hotel (☎22840 71333, ⓦwww.hotelalexandros.gr; Easter–Sept; B&B ❼) has mosquito screens and a pool. The local **campsite** (☎22840 71286) is rather uninspiring – a stiff 550m hike inland, shadeless and on sloping, stony ground. Among several **tavernas**, *Kapnisis* is one of the most popular, and *Koutouki tou Psara* at bus stop #3 is recommended for fish. A five-minute walk over the southwestern headland brings you to **Lazárou Beach**, a tiny bay entirely occupied by a bar and restaurant behind the water's edge.

## Vathý

A fishing village on the shore of an almost circular, almost enclosed bay, **VATHÝ** is the most attractive base on the island, with little to do but relax on the beach or in a beachfront taverna. Even the surfaced road and the opening of a luxury hotel, frequented by celebrities and politicians, seems not to have destroyed the character of this previously remote spot. **Rooms** include the attractive studios at the *Nikos* (☎22840 71512, ⓦwww.sifnosrooms.com; April–Nov; ❹) or next door at the *Virginia* (☎22840 71101, ⓦwww.vathysifnos.gr; ❹), just before the jetty and the tiny **monastery of the Archangel Gabriel**. Said to have the largest pool in the Cyclades, *Elies Resort* (☎22840 34000, ⓦwww .eliesresorts.com; B&B ❽) offers minimalist luxury. For **food**, *Manolis* (☎22840 71111; April–Oct; ❹) does excellent grills and has rooms/studios around a garden behind; *Okeanida* has good *mezédhes*, while 🍴 *To Tsikali* on the seafront beyond the monastery has home-made cheese, *mezédhes*, chunky chips and rabbit dishes.

There are regular **buses** (8 daily in high season, 2–4 daily at other times), and *kaïkia* may run in summer from Kamáres. It is possible to walk to Platýs Yialós in 90 minutes, but the path is not well marked. Another path, southwards, leads in 75 minutes to the isolated, sheltered **Fykiádhas Beach** (no facilities, though there is a rainwater supply at the Áyios Yeóryios monastery). From this beach, a path leads onwards in two hours to Platýs Yialós.

# Mílos

Volcanic **Mílos** is geologically diverse with weird rock formations, hot springs, good beaches and sensational views. Minoan settlers were attracted by obsidian, and other products of its volcanic soil made it one of the most important of the Cyclades in the ancient world. Today, the quarrying of baryte, bentonite, gypsum, kaolin, perlite, pozzolana, microcrystalline quartz and sulfur has left huge scars on the landscape but given the island a relative prosperity and independence. With some 74 **beaches**, more than any other island in the Cyclades, Mílos hasn't had to tart itself up to court tourism – indeed, the wealthy mining companies who employ a quarter of the population are happy to see tourism stay at low levels.

You get a good preview of the island's **geological wonders** as your ferry enters Mílos Bay, a striking natural harbour, shaped by a series of explosions in the ancient past. Off the north coast, accessible only by excursion boat, the Glaroníssia (Seagull Isles) are formed of prismatic andesite columns resembling massed organ pipes, and there are more strange formations round the coast, such as Kléftiko in the southwest, and Sarakíniko and Papáfranga in the north. Inland, there are thermal springs, and frequent odd, volcanic outcrops. Like most

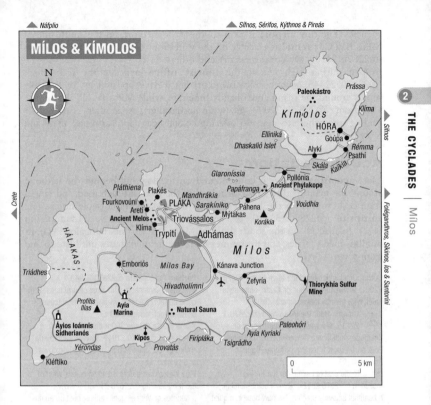

MÍLOS & KÍMOLOS

N

volcanic islands, Mílos is quite fertile; away from the southwestern 748m summit of **Profítis Ilías** and the lower eastern hills, a gently undulating countryside is intensively cultivated to produce grain, hay and orchard fruits. The island of Kímolos, just off Mílos, is covered on p.141.

## Adhámas

The lively main port of **ADHÁMAS** (locally Adhámandas) was founded by refugees from a failed rebellion in Crete in 1841. Despite the marble-paved esplanade around its natural headland, it is architecturally disappointing compared to some of the Cycladic ports.

### Arrival and information

The ill-defined **main square** is just inland of the esplanade, at the junction of the Pláka road and the Mílos Bay coastal road; nearby are several **banks**, a **post office** and a couple of **internet cafés** (on the right at the start of the Pláka road) such as *Netrino*. **Bus services** start from here – there are surprisingly few in low season: seven a day to Pláka, and just twice daily (inconveniently early morning and early afternoon) to Pollónia and Zefyría, and nothing on Sundays. In high season there are daily services to Pláka (17), Pollónia (9), Paleohori via Zefyría (8), the campsite (11 with 8 going on to Hivadholímni), Provatás (8), and Sarakíniko (2–3). The **taxi** rank is nearby – call ☎22870 22219 to book – the fare to Pollónia is around €12. Some visitors arrive by twice-daily plane from Athens; there is no Olympic Airways office in town, so get tickets from agencies. The tiny **airport** is 5km southeast of the port, on the south side of Mílos Bay. **Car rental** is available on the waterfront near the jetty, from Tomaso (☎22870 24100, ⓦwww.tomaso.gr), and others.

Open during high season, the **tourist office** opposite the ferry dock (☎22870 22445, ⓦwww.milos-island.gr) has a daily updated list of available rooms around the island and a handy brochure, while Milos Travel, also on the waterfront (☎22870 22000, ⓦwww.milostravel.gr), is another resource for finding somewhere to stay, also offering coastal boat trips, car rental, maps and ferry tickets.

## Accommodation

Most **accommodation** is concentrated on the low hill behind the harbour, around the main road to Pláka, or inland of the eastern beach road, and ranges from basic rooms on the hill to spacious studios and comfortable hotels. The **campsite** (☎22870 31410, ⓦwww.miloscamping.gr) above Hivadholímni beach (see p.139) on the south shore of Mílos Bay also has bungalows (❸); its minibus meets ferries, and in summer there are frequent buses until late to and from town.

**Delfini** One block behind the town beach ☎22870 22001, ⓦwww.delfinimilos.gr. Clean, older-style hotel, with friendly management. ❹

🎿 **Giannis** Near the Pláka road ☎22870 22216, ⓦwww.giannisapartments.gr. Spacious studios in a flower-covered building. Free port/airport transfers possible. Open April–Oct. ❸

**Ostria** To the east of town (near the mining museum) ☎22870 28127, ⓦwww.ostria-hotel.gr. A beautiful and very comfortable new hotel in a quiet position. ❻

**Portiani** Main square ☎22870 22940, ⓔsirmalen@otenet.gr. The most central hotel, with good buffet breakfasts, wi-fi and a spectacular seaview roof-terrace. B&B ❻

**Santa Maria Village** 300m behind the eastern beach road ☎22840 21949, ⓦwww.santamaria -milos.gr. Complex with a variety of bungalows and studios. ❼

**Villa Notos** Just before the town beach, west of the ferry landing ☎22870 21943, ⓦwww .villanotos.gr. Very elegant studios, built up against the hill. Open April–Nov. ❽

### The Town

On the seafront east of town, about 1.5km from the centre, the well-organized **Mining Museum of Mílos** (ⓦwww.milosminingmuseum.gr; summer daily 9am–2pm & 6–9pm, winter Tues–Sat 8am–2.30pm; €3) gives an interesting insight into how mining has shaped the island, with an extensive collection of mining equipment, mineral samples and geological maps of Mílos, plus informative displays on the extraction, processing and uses of minerals and on reclamation of the exhausted sites. The museum is funded by S&B, one of the largest mining companies, but is well worth a visit at the start of your stay in order to make more sense of the island's appearance and economy. A short distance before the museum, an ad hoc **fish market** operates behind the beach. Near the quayside, the small but interesting **ecclesiastical museum** (mornings and evenings; free) is housed in the ninth-century Ayía Triádha church and has a good collection of liturgical paraphernalia and rare icons.

In season there are **boat tours** around the island's bizarre coastline, passing the Glaroníssia and making several stops at otherwise inaccessible swimming spots like the magnificent Kléftiko, on the way to Kímolos where they often stop for a late lunch. Weather permitting, the boats normally leave at 9am from the Adhámas quayside, and return at 6pm. Tickets cost around €25 per person, without lunch. Australian-Greek-run Sea Kayak Mílos (☎&ⓕ22870 23597,

@www.seakayakgreece.com; April–Oct) in Triovássalos offers guided **kayak trips** around the island, with the chance to stop for a swim.

### Eating and drinking

*Kinigos*, near the jetty, is a popular place to **eat**, with a varied menu, and excellent people-watching potential. Of the three adjacent tavernas along the seafront towards the long tamarisk-lined Papakinoú beach south of town, *Savvas O Thessalonikiós*, specializing in fish, is the most popular. A short way up the Pláka road, *Pitsounakia* is a well-priced meat *psistariá* with a pleasant courtyard; further along the same road is the garden taverna *Barco*, popular with the locals for its *mezédhes*.

For **nightlife**, apart from the obvious string of cafés along the main seafront drag, **music bars** *Akri* and *Vipera Lebetina* are perched on the cliffs above the jetty and are very popular; behind Papanikoú beach, *Aproopto* is another current hot spot, while *Malion* has some live music, including *bouzouki*. Lovers of ice cream should try the waterfront *Angeliki*, or *Rapsis* to the left of the start of the Pláka road, both with their own extremely good home-made products.

## Pláka and around

Four kilometres northwest of Adhámas, a cluster of traditional villages huddles beneath a small crag. This area has been the island's focus of habitation and culture since Classical times, and forms the focus of its appeal today.

**PLÁKA (MÍLOS)** is the largest of these communities and the official capital of the island. Behind the lower car park, at the top of the approach boulevard through the newer district, the attractive **archeological museum** (Tues–Sun 8.30am–3pm – it does not always look open, even when it is; €3) contains numerous obsidian implements, plus a whole wing of finds from ancient Phylakope (see p.140), whose highlights include a votive lamp in the form of a bull and a rather Minoan-looking terracotta goddess. Labelling is scant, but you'll recognize the plaster-cast copy of the Hellenistic *Venus de Milo*, the original of which was found on the island in 1820. Several versions circulate of its immediate post-discovery history – it is not clear whether it was discovered with the arms already separated from the torso, or if they were broken off in a skirmish between French sailors and locals. Whatever the case, this was the last the Greeks saw of *Venus* until a copy was belatedly sent from the Louvre in Paris. Up in a mansion of the old quarter, the recently renovated **Folk Museum** (Tues–Sat 10am–2pm & 6–9pm, Sun 10am–2pm; €3) has a well-presented array of artefacts related to the history of arts, crafts and daily life on Mílos.

A step-street beginning near the *Foras* taverna leads up to the old Venetian **kástro**, its upper slopes clad in stone and cement to channel precious rainwater into cisterns. En route to the summit, where the ancient Melians made their last stand against the Athenians before the massacre of 416 BC, is the large **Panayía Thalassítra**. The smaller church of Kimisis tís Panayía offers one of the best views in the Aegean, particularly at sunset.

### Practicalities

Pláka has a **post office** and a **motorbike-rental** outfit near the archeological museum. There are **rooms** available scattered around the village, with those on the west side offering spectacular views. Among the nicest of these are the pretty *Kastro Milos* studios (℡22870 21702, @www.kastromilos.gr; ❺) high on the kástro. The *Spiti tis Makhis* (℡22870 41353; ❹), below the *Plakiani Gonia* taverna, has refurbished rooms in the house where the *Venus de Milo* was allegedly hidden following its discovery; it also has plenty of parking space.

*Maria's Rooms* (℡22870 21572; ❸) are charming, if basic, studios just west of the archeological museum – further along the same street are more options, including the *Halara* studios (℡22870 22092, ✉studioshalara@yahoo.gr; ❹) at the very edge of the village and with sunset views, while a number of modern accommodation blocks overlook the busy approach road. There are some good places for **eating** near the start of the Kástro path, including the *Foras mezedhopolío*; the nearby *Palaios* café does excellent ice cream.

## Trypití

On a long ridge 1km south of Pláka, the narrow, attractive village of **TRYPITÍ** ("perforated"), which takes its name from the cliffside tombs nearby, is less busy with traffic than lower Pláka. There are **rooms**, including several sixteenth-century windmills (⊛www.milos-island.gr/windmill/windmills.html; ❻), on the eastern side. The best places to **eat** are rustic *Glaronisia*, serving traditional taverna fare, and *Ergina*, which features cuttlefish and oven-roasted goat; for coffee and evening drinks, the stylish *Remvi Café* just past the bus stop has great views.

From Adhámas it's possible to walk up a dirt track with tantalizing fragments of the original broad paved *kalderími*, to join the surfaced road near the Klíma–Trypití junction; in reverse, follow the signs for Skinopí.

### Catacombs, ancient Melos and Klíma

From Pláka's archeological museum, signs point you towards the **early Christian catacombs** (Tues–Sun 8am–5pm; free – but undergoing long-term safety work and likely to be closed), 1km south of Pláka and just 400m from Trypití village; steps lead down from the road to the inconspicuous entrance. Some 5000 bodies were buried in three tomb-lined corridors with side galleries, stretching 200m into the soft volcanic rock, making these the largest catacombs in Greece; however only the first 50m is illuminated and accessible by boardwalk. Don't miss the ruins of **ancient Melos** (located just above the catacombs), which extend down from Pláka almost to the sea. There are huge Dorian walls, the usual column fragments lying around and, best of all, a well-preserved Roman **amphitheatre** (unrestricted access). Only seven rows of seats remain intact, but these look out evocatively over Klíma to the bay. En route to the theatre from the surfaced road is the signposted spot where the *Venus de Milo* was found in what may have been the compound's gymnasium. The small Profitis Ilías church perched on a nearby outcrop, on the ruins of an ancient temple, has excellent views over the bay.

At the very bottom of the valley, and accessed via a road from the southern end of Trypití or steps down from near the catacombs, **KLÍMA** is the most photogenic of the island's fishing hamlets, with its picturesque boathouses tucked underneath the principal living areas. There's little beach to speak of and only one place to stay – the *Panorama* (℡22870 21623, ⊛www.panorama-milos .gr; ❸), on the hillside above, with a balcony taverna – the owner was a cruise-ship chef and is a mine of local information.

**Pláthiena**, 45-minutes' walk northwest of Pláka (driveable via a partly surfaced road from Plakés), is the closest proper beach, and thus extremely popular in summer. There are no facilities, but the beach is fairly well protected and partly shaded by tamarisks.

## Southern Mílos

The main road to the south of the island splits at **Kánava junction**, near the large power station. The left (east) fork leads to **Zefyría**, in a broad cultivated plateau; it was briefly the medieval capital until an eighteenth-century earthquake (and subsequent plague) drove out the population. There is little to see of the old town, but there is a magnificent seventeenth-century church, built over one a millennium older. The building is in fact made up of two interconnected churches side by side, the larger dedicated to the Panayía Portianí, with beautifully painted walls and ceilings, the smaller to Áyios Harálambos. The original *témblon* was transferred to the Kímisi tís Theotókou church in Adhámas, in 1864. The very friendly Cretan priest in the little office nearby may be available to unlock the door.

Head east from Zefyría for 7km on a dirt road to reach the disused **sulphur mine** (Theorykhía) at Paliórema beach with multicoloured rocks and an emerald green sea.

South of Zefyría, it's a further 8km down a winding, surfaced road to the coarse sand of **Paleohóri**, one of the island's better beaches, the main beach's western end warmed by underground vulcanism. A little rock tunnel leads west through from here to a second beach, which is backed by extraordinarily coloured cliffs, and where clothing is optional and steam vents heat the shallow water. There are a number of **places to stay**, such as the inland *Paleochori Studios* (T22870 31267, Wwww.sitemaker.gr/paleochori; •), or the purpose-built rooms behind the seafront *Artemis* restaurant (T22870 31222; •) nearer the beach. There are several **tavernas**, with the *Sirocco* using the hot volcanic sand to cook food. **Ayía Kyriakí** beach, just to the west of Paleohóri, also has a taverna, plus some tamarisk shade.

The westerly road from the Kánava junction leads past the airport entrance to **Hivadholímni**, the best beach on Mílos bay itself. The campsite (see p.136) is just above, so beach camping is frowned upon. Behind the beach is a salty lagoon, with the clams ("hivádhia") that give the beach its name.

Just after the campsite, and before Hivadholímni, you can fork south to **Provatás**, a short beach, closed off by multicoloured cliffs to the east. It's easy to get to and hasn't escaped development: there are two rooms establishments plus, closer to the shore, a luxury complex, *Golden Milos Beach* (T22870 31307, Wwww.milos-beach.gr; •). The best value for food and accommodation is the *Maïstrali* (T22870 31164; •), with private rooms and restaurant.

Several kilometres before Provatás, an initially-surfaced road forks east to the trendy and very popular beach of **Firipláka**, although the road also runs to a huge quarry and has 24-hour lorry traffic. East of Firipláka, sandy **Tsigrádho** beach is excellent for swimming, but it's only accessible by boat, or by means of a rope hanging down a crevice in the cliff face, so is usually uncrowded.

At the hamlet of **Kípos**, 4km west of Provatás, a sign points below left to a small **medieval chapel** dedicated to the Kímisis (Assumption). It sits atop foundations far older – probably fifth century – as evidenced by the early Christian reliefs stacked along the west wall and a carved, cruciform baptismal font in the *ierón* behind the altar screen. At one time a spring gushed from the low-tunnel cave beside the font – miraculous on arid Mílos. The unsigned surfaced road from just before the church winds down to a taverna and jetty at the rock-strewn Kípos beach, disfigured by an ugly, stepped concrete platform – from where there are summer boat trips around this part of the island. After Kípos there is a small crater-like valley, dramatically filled with huge, jumbled boulders. Beyond here, the surfaced road ends, although a dirt road continues into Hálakas.

For the most part **Hálakas**, the southwestern peninsula centred on the wilderness of 748-metre Profítis Ilías, is uninhabited and little built upon, with the exception of the monastery of **Áyios Ioánnis Sidherianós**. Beyond the monastery church at Ayía Marína, the roads are unsurfaced: **Emboriós** on the east side of the peninsula has a fine beach and an excellent local taverna with the *Embourios* rooms (☎22870 23918, ✉info@embourios.gr; ❸). On the mostly rugged west coast, **Triádhes** and **Ammoudharáki** are a couple of the finest and least spoilt beaches in the Cyclades, but you'll have to bring your own provisions. **Kléftiko** in the southwest corner is only reachable by boat (from Kípos via Yérondas, or from Adhámas, but repays the effort to get there with its stunning rock formations, semi-submerged tunnels and colourful coral.

## The north coast

From either Adhámas or the Pláka area, good roads run roughly parallel to the **north coast** which, despite being windswept and little inhabited, is not devoid of geological interest. **Mandhrákia**, reached from Triovássalos, is another boathouse settlement, and **Sarakíniko**, to the east, is an astonishing sculpted inlet with a sandy sea bed and gleaming white rocks popular with sunbathing local youth; there's a shipwreck a little further east. Nearby **Mýtakas** is a beach and fishing boat mooring, accessible via a 500m dirt road, with dramatic views west along the rocky coastline. A few kilometres further east, the little hamlet of **Páhena** is not shown on all maps, though it has another, smaller beach and plenty of seasonal rooms (though little else by way of facilities) – try *Terry's Travel* above the harbour in Adhámas (☎22870 22640, Ⓦwww.terrysmilostravel.com; ❸), or the *Papafraga (Veletas)* rooms and studios (☎22870 41424; ❹) at Páhena.

Still heading east, you reach another of Mílos's coastal wonders, **Papáfranga**, a short ravine into which the sea flows under a rock arch – the tiny beach at its inland end is accessed by rock-carved steps. Immediately west and parallel is a second ravine, with a large sea cave inhabited by birds and smelling of volcanic hydrogen sulphide at its head. To the right of the Papáfranga car park, the remains of three superimposed Neolithic settlements – including a large and dramatic section of walling – crown a small knoll at **Fylakopí** (ancient Phylakope); archeological excavation continues.

▲ Sculpted rocks at Sarakíniko beach, Mílos

### Pollónia

**POLLÓNIA**, 12km northeast of Adhámas, is immensely popular with windsurfers, and the presence of a couple of diving centres has further increased its popularity among watersports enthusiasts. The village is essentially a small harbour in a semi-circular bay with a long, curved, tamarisk-lined beach; the original settlement huddles on the small southern promontory, where the church of Ayía Paraskeví has beautiful ceiling paintings. On the quay are several **tavernas**, including the stylish *Gialos* with a small but well-thought-out menu, plus a few cafés such as that of the *Flora* bakery. For nightlife, try the *8 Beaufort* bar-café, playing a wide variety of music.

Some older **accommodation** sits inland of the quay, with the slight drawback of occasional noise and dust from quarry trucks. Among the best are the recently refurbished *Kapetan Tasos Apartments* (☎22870 41287, Ⓦwww.kapetantasos.gr; ❺). To the north, the bay is protected by a low spit of land known as Pelekoúdha, a quieter area where self-catering units are multiplying rapidly.

At the western end of Pelekoúda, the very friendly ☀ *Andreas* (☎22870 41262, Ⓦwww.andreas-rooms.gr; ❹) has triple studios with stunning views and easy access to the quiet neighbouring bay, plus their own boat, *Perseas*, for trips to nearby islands. Attractive studios at the northeast corner include the *Apollon* (☎22870 41347; April–Oct; ❹), with rooms (some with hydromassage showers), a restaurant overlooking Kímolos and a well-equipped dive centre (☎22870 41451, Ⓦwww.apollon-diving.eu) offering PADI courses, snorkelling trips and equipment rental (April–Nov). Nearby is the comfortably spacious *Villa Tania* (☎22870 41062, Ⓦwww.taniamilos.gr; May–Sept; B&B ❺), and, two blocks west, the laid-back and very pretty *Nefeli* rooms and studios (☎22870 41466, Ⓦwww.milos-nefelistudios.gr, information also at Zakharopetra shop in Adhámas; April–Nov ❹). Pollónia has no bank or post office, but the friendly Axios Rent a Car office (☎&Ⓕ22870 41234) can advise you on accommodation matters; they also sell secondhand English books. You might be tempted to visit the large beach at **Voúdhia**, 3km east, with more of the island's hot springs, although its close proximity to huge mining works means the access road has 24-hour heavy lorry traffic and there is almost no parking for the beach, which lend it the desolate air of a *Mad Max* location.

Taking the **ferry to Kímolos** may be the main reason you're here. The *Panagia Faneromeni* car ferry (☎22870 51184, Ⓦwww.kimolos-link.gr) makes the trip about 4–6 times Mon–Fri year-round (less at weekends); a passenger ticket is €1.80.

# Kímolos

Of the three islands off the coast of Mílos, only **Kímolos** is inhabited. Volcanic like Mílos, it profits from its geology and used to export chalk (*kimolía* in Greek) until the supply was exhausted. Fuller's earth is still extracted locally, and the fine dust of this clay is a familiar sight on the northeast corner of the island, where mining still outstrips fishing and farming as an occupation. Rugged and little cultivated in the scenic interior, it has some fertile land on the southeast coast where wells provide water, and this is where the population of about eight hundred is concentrated.

Kímolos is sleepy from September to June, and even in August sees few visitors, just as well since there are fewer than 170 beds on the whole island, and little in the way of other amenities; those visitors who venture here come for the tranquillity and the walking.

# Psathí and Hóra

Whether you arrive by ferry, or by *kaïki* from Pollónia, you'll dock at the tiny port of **PSATHÍ**, which is pretty much a nonevent except for the excellent *To Kyma* ("The Wave") **taverna** midway along the beach, specializing in tasty seafood. **Ferry tickets** for onward journeys – unless bought in advance up in Hóra – are only sold outside the café at the end of the jetty, an hour or so before the anticipated arrival of the boat. The *Panagia Faneromeni* comes and goes from Pollónia on Mílos (see p.141), whilst some larger ferries call briefly on their way to and from Mílos. The capital, Hóra, can be reached by foot in about fifteen minutes from the port.

Around the bay, there are a few old windmills, with dazzlingly white **HÓRA** perched on the ridge above them. This magnificent, two-gated, sixteenth-century **kástro** was built against marauding pirates; nowadays the perimeter houses are still intact and inhabited, though its heart is a jumble of ruins. Just outside the *kástro* to the north stands the conspicuously unwhitewashed, late sixteenth-century church of **Khryssóstomos**, the oldest and most beautiful on the island. Near the church is the **archeological museum** (irregular hours) with pottery from the Geometric to the Roman period. In a restored house near the eastern gateway is the excellent, privately run **Folk and Maritime Museum** (T22870 51118; summer).

There are a few adequate **rooms** near the port, but halfway between the port and town is the hospitable *Villa Maria* (T22870 51752, Wwww.hellasislands.gr /kimolos/villa-maria; ❸) rooms and studios, open all year. Other accommodation options include the *Petraki* rooms (T22870 51314; ❷), tucked away in the maze of backstreets, or those of Apostolos Ventouris (T22870 51329; ❷) above his *kafenío* nearby. The *Sofia* (T22870 51219; ❺) has studios with sea views, close to the church. For **meals**, aside from a couple of basic *psistariés* and a café–bar, the aptly named *Panorama*, near the east gate of the *kástro*, is the most elaborate and consistently open taverna. *Meltemi*, to the west of the village, is another good taverna, which also has some rooms (T22870 51360; ❸). Other facilities include a couple of ship agencies and a **post office** in the west of the village, as well as an **ATM**.

East of Hóra, a ten-minute walk brings you to **GOÚPA**, a traditional fishing village with a few **tavernas**. At its base, **Rémma** beach remains unspoilt, as does **Klíma**, just off the main dirt road to Prássa to the north.

## Around the island

The hamlet of **ALYKÍ** on the south coast is about thirty-minutes' walk on the paved road that forks left from Psathí; it is named after the saltpan that sprawls behind a rather mediocre beach offering no shade or shelter, but with the **rooms** of *Sardi* (T22870 51458; ❸) and *Pasamichalis* (T22870 51340; ❸), as well as a few simple **tavernas**. You can stroll west one cove to **Bonátsa** for better sand and shallow water, though you won't escape the winds. Passing another cove you come to the even more attractive beach of **Kalamítsi**, with better shade and a decent taverna. To the east, between Alykí and Psathí, the smaller, more secluded beach of **Skála** is better for camping, which is generally tolerated here.

The 700-metre coarse-sand beach of **Ellinika** is a 45-minute walk west of Alykí; starting on the road, bear left just before two chapels on a slope onto a narrower track, which runs through the fields at the bottom of the valley. Divided by a low bluff, the beach is bracketed by two capes and looks out over Dhaskalió islet and across to harder-to-reach **Kambána** beach, home of nesting turtles. Elliniká tends to catch heavy weather in the afternoon, and there are no facilities here.

Another road leads northeast from Hóra to a beach and radioactive springs at **Prássa**, 7km away. The route takes in impressive views across the straits to Políegos, and there are several shady, peaceful coves where it's possible to camp out. Innumerable paths, many well-maintained, invite exploration of the interior of the island – a locally produced information booklet may be available at some accommodation. In the northwest, on Kímolos's 361m summit, are the scant ruins of a Venetian fortress known as **Paleókastro**.

# Ándhros

**Ándhros**, the second largest and northernmost of the Cyclades, is also one of the most verdant, making it a great place for serious walkers. Thinly populated but prosperous, its fertile, well-watered valleys and hillsides have sprouted scores of Athenian holiday villas – some of the more recent of these have turned villages into scattered settlements with no nucleus, creating a weekender mentality manifest in noisy Friday- and Sunday-evening traffic jams at the ferry dock. The island doesn't cater extensively for independent travellers, and it can be difficult to find a bed during August, especially at weekends.

On the positive side, the permanent population is distinctly hospitable. Together with the attractive capital, Hóra, and some idiosyncratic reminders of the Venetian period, such as the *peristereónes* (dovecote towers) and the *frákhtes* (dry-stone walls, here raised to the status of an art form), this friendliness lends Ándhros its charm. In addition, the island has numerous beaches, including some of Greece's best, with more than sixteen on the northwest and north coast only accessible by boat or long dirt track. For walkers, the island has twelve numbered, waymarked paths, varying from 1.7 to 11.5km, though not all are well-maintained and some need transport arrangements for the return.

**Ferries** connect the island with Rafína on the mainland, only an hour from Athens or thirty minutes from the airport by bus, and, in season, you can loop back onto the central Cycladic routes via Mýkonos, Tínos or Sýros.

## Northern Ándhros

The busy western side of northern Ándhros has several resorts, centred on **Gávrio**, the main port, and **Batsí**; the northeastern side of the island, by contrast, is a remote area with little habitation and difficult access.

### Gávrio

All ferries and catamarans arrive at the main port, **GÁVRIO**, a pleasant small town and resort in an oval bay. **Buses** run from the port via Batsí to Hóra at least six times a day in high season, with a few heading from Gávrio to Órmos Korthíou (either direct or with a change at Stavropédha). However, since buses may wait for delayed ferries, the timetabling in this direction can be very unreliable. A tiny converted dovecote houses a sporadically functioning **tourist office**, and there are several ferry **ticket agents**, including Batis (℡22820 71489), Kyklades Travel (℡22820 72363) and Porto Andros (℡22820 71222), near the centre, with **banks** and three **ATMs** at the start of the waterfront, and a **post office** at the other end. There are **internet** facilities at the *Aponemo* bar (open evenings), on the side road south of town signposted to the *Andros Holidays Hotel*.

The cheapest **accommodation** is in Gávrio's central *Galaxias* (℡22820 71005; ➌), which serves as a late-arrival fall-back. The pleasant **campsite**

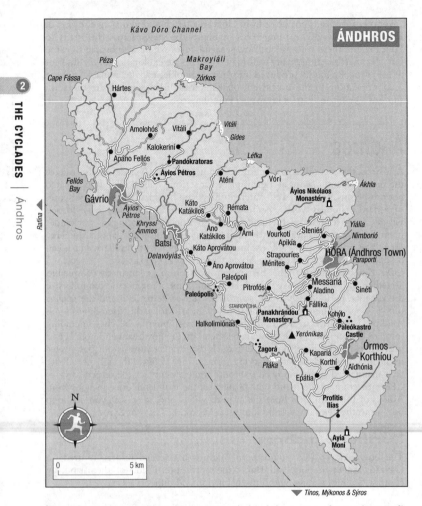

**ÁNDHROS**

Kávo Dóro Channel

Péza
Cape Fássa
Hártes

Makroyiáli Bay
Zórkos

Amolohós   Vitáli   Vitáli
Gídes
Kalokerini
Apáno Fellós   ✝Pandokratoras   Léfka
Áyios Pétros
Aténi   Vóri
Ákhla
Áyios Nikólaos Monastéry
Fellós Bay
Gávrio   Káto Katákilos   Rémata
Áyios Pétros
Khryssi Ámmos   Áno Katákilos   Arni
Vourkotí   Steniés   Yiália   Nimborió
Batsí   Apikia   HÓRA (Ándhros Town)
Delavóyias   Káto Aprovátou   Strapouríes   Paraporti
Áno Aprovátou   Ménites
Paleópoli   Messariá   Sinéti
Pitrofós   Aladino
Paleópolis   STAVROPÉDHA   Fállika
Panakhrándou Monastery   Kohýlo
Halkolimiónas   Paleókastro Castle
▲Yerónikas   Órmos Korthíou
Zagorá   Kapariá
Korthí   Aïdhónia
Pláka
Epátia

Profítis Ilias

Ayia Moní

N

0        5 km

Rafina ◄

◄ Tínos, Mýkonos & Sýros

(☎22820 71444; May–Sept/Oct) is 300m behind the centre of town, has a café and can provide a lift from the port.

There is beach adjacent to the town, but to the southeast there are more attractive alternatives such as **Áyios Pétros,** accessible by a 2km roadside pavement, where you'll also find the area's better accommodation. One of the nearest of these is *Aktio* (☎22820 71607,Ⓦwww.aktiostudios.gr; ➎) with large studios, good discounts and some wheelchair access, near the BP station, while the *Andros Holidays Hotel* (☎22820 71384, Ⓔandroshols@otenet.gr; April–Oct; ➐), on the headland side road south of town, has lovely sea views. Three kilometres south down the coast, between the smaller, pretty Khryssí Ámmos and longer Psilí Ámmos beaches, is the upmarket *Perrakis Hotel* (☎22820 71456, Ⓦwww.hotelperrakis.gr;April–Oct; ➏) – information is available from their café on Gávrio waterfront.

**Restaurants** worth trying include the popular *Konaki mezedhopolío* or the *Asteria psistariá*, on the seafront just east of the *Galaxias*. **Nightlife** revolves around a string of cafés and bars, both along the harbour front and at Áyios Pétros, where the excellent *Yiannouli* taverna is worth checking out for lunch. Gávrio is the easiest place on the island for **car rental**, with several competing establishments including Colours (☎22820 29185) and Tasos (☎22820 71040) on the seafront.

Around 5km northwest of the port are two **beaches**: beautiful Fellós has some holiday homes and a taverna, *Steki tou Andreas*, while Kourtáli is hidden beyond the headland and popular with rough campers. Beyond the village of Páno Fellós, the road continues, partly surfaced, to the north coast at broad Zórkos beach, where there is a seasonal taverna; the countryside is mostly empty except for a scattering of semi-deserted, once Albanian-speaking hamlets.

Head northeast and inland from Gávrio on the road to Áyios Pétros village and you will see a remarkable 20m-high, cylindrical **stone tower**, built between 400 and 300 BC and probably connected with the ancient iron mines visible below. Unfortunately the access path to the tower itself is now both overgrown and blocked by beehives. Continue on the road past Áyios Pétros, towards the pretty agricultural settlements of Kalokeriní and Vitáli, to reach the romantic monastery ruins of Byzantine **Pandokrátoras** (Sotíros) set by rushy springs in an otherwise bleak fire-ravaged landscape.

## Batsí

Most visitors head 8km south to **BATSÍ**, the island's main resort, its hotels, rooms and bars set around a fine natural harbour. The beautiful though often crowded beach curves round the bay, and the sea is cold, calm, sandy and clean (except near the jetty). Most facilities cluster around the bend of the seafront road near the fishing jetty which is being expanded into a marina. In season, it is possible to **hire a boat** from Riva (☎22820 24412), or join fishing trips locally. South of town, a coastal road leads 1.5km through the Káto Stivári area to the small, picturesque cove at Ayía Marína.

**Hotels** in Batsí range from the central, comfortable *Chryssi Akti* (☎22820 41236, ⓦwww.hotel-chryssiakti.gr; ❹) behind the main beach, to the pretty, upmarket, water's-edge *Aneroussa Beach Hotel* (☎22820 41044, ⓔanerouss @otenet.gr; April–Oct; ❻), at Ayía Marína. Besides these there are plenty of other rooms, such as the popular, sea-view 🍴 *Anemos* (☎22820 41287, ⓔanemosst@internet.gr.; ❸) studios near the start of the Ayía Marína road, or the *Agia Marína* fish taverna and studios (☎22820 41963; ❸) at the eponymous beach. At the upper, inland, southeastern end of the village are the *Amorani* (☎22820 41706, ⓦwww.amorani-studios.gr.; ❹) rooms, mostly with kitchens.

Among **restaurants**, the *O, Ti Kalo* is situated in a shady raised street near the jetty and run by the same family as the *Anemos*; the well-priced *Corsair* ouzerí is on the upper access road in the south of the village; and the 🍴 *Steki tis Yevsis*, next to the *Chryssi Akti*, specializes in tasty home-caught fish. There is a cluster of **café-bars** in the centre, plus a half-a-dozen or so loud indoor bars featuring the standard foreign/Greek musical mix; behind the north end of the beach is an open-air summer cinema. The restored *Emelos kafenío*, behind the excellent *Tountas* bakery, has **internet** access. Local produce is available from the women's co-operative Arkhontissa tou Aigiou shop, next to the taxi rank. **Car rental**, ferry tickets, accommodation and guided walks can be arranged through Colours (☎22820 41252, ⓔandrostr@otenet.gr), just above the centre. The tiny **bank**, just beyond the *Dodoni* ice-cream parlour, has an **ATM**.

## Inland villages

From Batsí you're within walking distance of some pleasant inland villages. At **KÁTO KATÁKILOS**, one hour inland, there are a couple of seasonal

**tavernas**; a rough track leads after another hour to **Aténi**, a hamlet in a lush, remote valley, then 3.5km further east to the beautiful Léfka beach. The main road east out of Káto Katákilos leads past the hamlet of **Rémata** 6.5km) with its restored nineteenth-century **Lebesis olive press** (April–Oct, Tues–Sun, 10am–6pm; Nov–March, weekends only, 10am–2pm). The main road continues up the mountain to **ÁRNI** after a further 4km, a beautiful place – once the main village of the island – whose trees are sometimes shrouded in mist. A long, 7km earth road down from Árni to the eastern coast of the island, leads to the secluded, sheltered beach of **Vóri** with its clean, coarse sand and romantic landscape featuring several shipwrecks.

South of Batsí, along the main road below the **Aprovátou** villages, are rooms such as the *Hotel Galini* (☎22820 41472, ⓦwww.andros.gr/galini; April–Oct; ❸), opposite the Kelaria supermarket, plus café-tavernas. **Áno Aprovátou**, accessed via a winding hill road, has the taverna *Balkoni tou Aigaiou* ("*Balcony of the Aegean*") with good, well-priced rural food and panoramic views. At **Paleópoli**, 8km from Batsí, there is a small museum (Tues-Sun, 8.30am-3pm; free) containing well-labelled marble statuary/carvings, coins and domestic items from the nearby archeological site. The ancient city of Paleópolis flourished from the sixth century BC to the end of the sixth century AD, covering a large area just southwest of the modern village. A pleasant walk is signed ("beach") from the main road café, and heads via the Káto Paleópoli church down to the pebble beach, passing fragments of ancient walls and tombs, and with beautiful views back up to the village. You can return via a stony path up from the southeastern end of the beach. There are also **archeological sites** at Ypsilí, Strófilas and Zagorá on west-coast headlands near Paleópoli, but access is not easy.

## Hóra

A bus service links west-coast Gávrio and Batsí with east-coast **HÓRA** (also known as **ÁNDHROS TOWN**), 32km from Gávrio. Stretched along a rocky spur that divides a huge bay, the capital is the most attractive town on the island. Paved in marble and schist from the still-active local quarries, the buildings near the bus station are grand nineteenth-century affairs, and the squares with their ornate wall fountains and gateways are equally elegant. The old port, Plakoúra, on the west side of the headland, has a yacht supply station and a former ferry landing from where occasional boats run to the isolated Ákhla beach in summer. More locally, there are beaches on both sides of the town headland, Nimborió to the north and the better, undeveloped Parapórti to the southeast, though both are exposed to the *meltémi* winds in summer – these winds are the reason Gávrio became the island's main port.

From the Theófilou Kaïri square, right at the end of Hóra's main street, Embiríkou (aka "Agorá"), you pass through an archway and down through the residential area of Paleá Póli past the town **theatre** to **Platía Ríva**, with its Soviet-donated statue of an unknown sailor scanning the sea. These replaced houses destroyed by German munitions in World War II; also damaged was the now-precarious arched stone bridge that stretches across to an islet with the remnants of a thirteenth-century Venetian *kástro*. Inside the modern **archeological museum** (Tues–Sun 8.30am–3pm; €2, but likely to be closed for refurbishment until at least 2009), on the main street near Kaïri – are well-laid-out and labelled displays, with instructive models. Its prize item is the fourth-century *Hermes of Andros*, reclaimed from a prominent position in the Athens archeological museum. Behind the museum, down the step-street B. & E. Goulandhrí, is the **Museum of Contemporary Art**

(@www.moca-andros.gr; June–Sept Wed–Mon 10am–2pm, 6–8pm, Oct–May Sat–Mon 10am–2pm; June–Sept €6, Oct–May €3) which has a sculpture garden and a permanent collection with works by Picasso, Matisse, Kandinsky, Chagall and others, as well as temporary shows. The **Folklore and Christian Art Museum** (Aug Mon–Sat 7–9pm, Sun 11am–1pm; Sept–July Sat 7–9pm, Sun 11am–1pm; €3) is in the old Mandzavelaki ice-factory, just behind (left) the *Paradise* hotel. Near the bus station is an open-air **cinema**.

### Practicalities

The few **hotels** in town are on the expensive side and tend to be busy with holidaying Greeks. The *Paradise* hotel (℡22820 22187, @www.paradiseandros.gr; B&B ❼), with its swimming pool and tennis court, is upmarket, but right beside the main road at the entrance to town. In town, on Embiríkou, in restored mansions, are the *Xenonas Niki* (℡22820 29155, @xenonas.niki@gmail.com; ❻) at the Kaïri end, and the grand *Archontiko Eleni* (℡22820 23471, @www.elenimansion.gr; ❼) near the opposite end. Most **rooms** are clustered behind the long **Nimborió** beach northwest of town; those towards the far end include the attractive rooms of *Villa Stella* (℡22820 22471, @www.pension-stella.gr; ❸) – not only with its own café, but next door to a *Dodoni* ice-cream parlour; to the south, tucked away at the old Plakoúra harbour at the town end of Nimborió, are the *Karaoulanis* (℡22820 24412, @www.androsrooms.gr; ❸) studios and apartments – they also own a nearby diving supplies centre.

For **eating**, *Plátanos* at Platía Kaïri has a generous *mezédhes* selection that can be enjoyed with an ouzo under the plane trees, while *Skalakia*, on steps beside the park below the main church, a couple of minutes from the bus station, also does excellent *mezédhes* at reasonable prices. The nicest fish taverna is *Ononas*, adjacent to – and owned by – the *Karaulanis* (as above). The café *Kokkini Piperia* beside the bus station has a terrace with beautiful views out over the green Megálos Potamós valley, while the *Art Café* (@www.androsartcafe.gr) at Embiríkou 49 has **internet** and wi-fi facilities.

Nimborió beach is the epicentre of the island's **nightlife**, such as it is, with a few thumping discos that start with Western music and shift into Greek pop into the early hours of the morning. Hóra has a **post office**, several **banks** and **ATMs**, a couple of **ferry agents**, all on the main street, and the **motorbike** and **motor-boat rentals** of Riva (℡22820 24412) behind the beach.

## Villages around Hóra

Hiking is particularly inviting south and west from Hóra, where there are lush little river valleys. One obvious destination is **MÉNITES**, a hill village 6km away via Káto Ypsiloú and Lámyra, up a green valley choked with trees and straddled by stone walls. The large church of the **Kímisis tís Panayía** may have been the location of a temple of Dionysos, where water was turned into wine. Water still flows continuously from the row of springs below it and nearby are the *Piges-Karydies* and *Fountana* café-tavernas. Southwest of Ménites is the village of Áno Pitrofós, with a restored nineteenth-century **olive press** (April–Oct Wed–Mon 10am–2pm; Nov–March Sat & Sun 10am–2pm).

Heading from here back to Hóra, you pass the medieval village of **MESARIÁ**, the Byzantine economic centre of the island, with the deserted twelfth-century Byzantine church of **Taxiárhis Mikhaïl** below it , the picturesque setting for a nine-day festival of the Virgin Mary that begins on August 15. The finest monastery on the island, (Panayía) **Panakhrándou**, is only an hour's (steep) walk away, via the village of Fállika: founded around 961 and with an icon said to be by St Luke, it's still defended by massive walls but is occupied these days by just one monk. From the entrance door, a long passageway leads in past gushing springs to the atmospheric church. Panakhrándou clings to the steep hillside below water-seeping cliffs on the ridge southwest of Hóra, to which you can return directly with a healthy two- to three-hour walk down the valley, guided by red dots. It is driveable, from the eastern side of the ridge via Mésa Vouní, however when nearly at the monastery, you may wish to park then walk down the very steep final section of the road for spectacular views of the building below you.

Hidden over the ridge directly north of Hóra, the prosperous nineteenth-century village of **STENIÉS**, an hour's hike away (occasional buses from Hóra), was built by early shipowners; just below, at **Yiália**, there's a sand and pebble beach with a good fish taverna, *Ta Yialia*, and the *Tzoumezi* rooms (T22820 23130; ❸) nearby. Upper Steniés has the crumbling, seventeenth-century **Bísti-Mouvelá fortified house**, signed on the left a few hundred metres before the upper car park. On the road to Strapouriés is an excellent taverna, *Bozakis*, which boasts a view all the way down to the coast and good food. The tidy village of **APIKÍA**, beyond Steniés, bottles Sariza-brand mineral water for a living. There are rooms, including the central *Pigi Sariza Hotel* (T22820 23799, Wwww.andros.gr/pighi-sariza; ❺). Next door is *Tassos*, one of the few village **tavernas**, which has a lovely garden setting and specialities such as goat and rabbit. An uphill turn at the southwestern end of the village, leads, via a signed fifteen-minute path, to the **Rematiá Pytháras**, a pretty wooded stream with small waterfalls. The road continues to Vourkotí (said to be the highest village in the Cyclades) and then becomes a broad, mostly unused highway, via Árni, to the west coast. There are some wonderful views of the northeast coast from along this road, particularly where it crosses the Kouvára ridge at 700m, but it can get very windy.

## Southern Ándhros

If you're exploring the south of the island from Hóra, the road runs through the dramatic Dipotámata valley; at the seaward end, with your own transport, the sheltered cove of **Sinéti** south of Hóra is worth a detour, though the access road is steep. The higher valley hides thirty watermills, one of which is signed "Neromylos no. 5": the building is not open, but you can look underneath to see the horizontal turbine wheel. Two kilometres further, the entry road to Kohýlo village forks: the left goes 2km (partly surfaced) to **PALEÓKASTRO** (aka Kástro Faneroménis, Kohýlou Epáno Kástro), a ruined Venetian castle perched on a rocky crest at 586m, with amazing views overlooking Kórthi Bay. Legend has it that an old woman, who betrayed the stronghold to the Turks, jumped from the top in remorse, and she remains as a column of rock in the sea off Griás Pídhima beach where she landed. It is possible to walk from Hóra, via Sinéti, Dipotámata and Kohýlo to Órmos Korthíou.

A short distance further south, the resort of **ÓRMOS KORTHÍOU** (Kórthi Bay) is a small town, with a new seafront esplanade, waking up to its tourist potential and popular with windsurfers. Set on a large bay, isolated from the rest of the island by the high ridge and relatively unspoilt, it is pleasant enough to merit a stay at the austere-looking *Hotel Korthion* (T22820 61218, Wwww .andros.gr/manesis/; ❹) by the bus stop, or at rooms such as the nearby *Villa Korthi* (T22820 61122; ❺) or at the *Villa Mina* (T22820 61049, 694 41 06 234; ❺) apartments, between the two jetties at the northern end of the harbour. There are also several tavernas at the waterfront. The well-priced *zaharoplastío* near the sporadically open information kiosk has good ice cream and cakes, while the friendly *Centro* café near the roundabout is good for people-watching, or relaxing after the beach. Most facilities are on Odhós Yeoryíou Psálti, parallel to the esplanade: **internet** and pool are available at the *Blue Games* café, while the bank only opens a couple of mornings a week (Mon, Thurs), but has an **ATM**. The Doropigi travel office is a **ferry agent**. Griás Pídhima beach is accessible via signed road and dirt track from near the northern end of the esplanade, while Kandoúni beach covers the southern half of the main bay.

On the Hóra road is a remarkable building, a **tavlómylos** or board mill (not open to the public), a cylindrical stone-built structure, with the top part open to the wind and containing a horizontal wheel with vertical sails.

A string of very pretty villages decorate a winding side road along the southern side of the Kórthi valley; perhaps the most attractive is the nearest to the sea, **Aïdhóna**, with a covered spring – Kríni Potamós – that includes part of the carved *témblon* from the nearby church of Áyii Pándes. Follow the path up from the spring, and through the village, for several ancient churches, although the island's oldest church, sixth-century Áyios Ioánnis, is in the next village, Kórthi.

# Tínos

**Tínos** still feels like one of the most Greek of the larger islands in the Cyclades. A few foreigners have discovered its beaches and unspoilt villages, but most visitors are Greek, here to see the church of **Panayía Evangelístria**, a grandiose shrine erected on the spot where a miraculous icon with healing powers was found in 1822. A local nun, now canonized as Ayía Pelayía, was directed in a

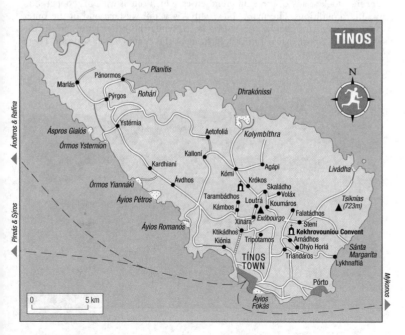

vision to unearth the relic just as the War of Independence was getting under way, a timely coincidence that served to underscore the links between the Orthodox Church and Greek nationalism. Today, there are two major annual pilgrimages, on March 25 and August 15, when Tínos is inundated by the faithful, and at 11am, the icon bearing the Virgin's image is carried in state down to the harbour.

The Ottoman tenure here was the most fleeting in the Aegean. **Exóbourgo**, the craggy mount dominating southern Tínos and surrounded by most of the island's sixty-odd villages, is studded with the ruins of a Venetian citadel that defied the Turks until 1715, long after the rest of Greece had fallen. An enduring legacy of the long Venetian rule is a persistent **Catholic minority**, which accounts for almost half the population, and a sectarian rivalry said to be responsible for the numerous belltowers scattered throughout the island – Orthodox and Catholic parishes vying to build the tallest. Hills are dotted with distinctive and ornate **dovecotes**, even more in evidence here than on Ándhros. Aside from all this, the inland village architecture is striking, and there's a flourishing folk-art tradition that finds expression in the abundant local marble. The islanders have remained open and hospitable to the relatively few foreigners and the steady stream of Greek visitors who touch down here, and any mercenary inclinations seem to be satisfied by booming sales in religious paraphernalia to the faithful.

## Tínos Town

Like Náxos Town and Ermoúpoli, **Tínos Town** is large and commercial, its unique mixture of religion and commerce aimed mainly at a unique type of modern pilgrim.

### Arrival and information

**Ferries** dock at any of three different jetties; which one is used may depend on weather conditions. The main "New Jetty" is at the western end of the outer port (Éxo Limáni), below the *Asteria* hotel, while the other jetties are in the eastern inner port (Mesa Limáni), in front of the central, older seafront. There

▲ Island-hopping Panagia Hozoviotissa

are at least two boats a day from Pireás via Sýros going on to Mýkonos, and several from Rafína via Ándhros, as well as a useful catamaran, and less frequent ferry connections to Páros, Náxos and Thíra. When you're leaving, ask your ticket agent which jetty to head for. **Buses** leave from a small parking area on the inner quay, to Pánormos, Kalloní, Stení, Pórto and Kiónia (timetables available here; buses only early morning/early afternoon outside high season, and no buses after 7.30pm). A **hire-car** or **motorbike** may be a more reliable means of exploring – Vidalis at Zanáki Alavánou 16 and elsewhere (Ⓕ22830 23400, Ⓦwww.vidalis-rentacar.gr), is a good rental agency.

Windmills Travel (Ⓣ22830 23398, Ⓦwww.windmillstravel.com), on the front towards the new jetty, can help with information as well as **tour bookings** and hotel bookings both here and on Mýkonos; they sometimes stay open for late ferry arrivals and also have a book exchange. In season an excursion boat does day-trips taking in Delos (see p.162) and Mýkonos (Tues–Sun; €25 round trip); this makes it possible to see Delos without the expense of staying overnight in Mýkonos, but only allows you two-and-a-half hours at the site. The **tourist police** are located on the road to the west of the new jetty.

## Accommodation

To have any chance of securing a reasonably priced **room** around the pilgrimage day of March 25 (Aug 15 is hopeless), you must arrive several days in advance. At other times, there's plenty of choice, though you'll still be competing with out-of-season pilgrims, Athenian tourists and the ill and disabled seeking a miracle cure. The accommodation listed below is open from mid-April to October only, unless stated otherwise.

Anna's Rooms Road to Kiónia Ⓣ22830 22877, Ⓦwww.tinos.nl. Excellent, family-run apartments set in a large garden just 10min walk out of town. ❹

Asteria Leofóros Stavroú-Kioníou, behind new jetty Ⓣ22830 22132. Friendly, older-style hotel with the nearest accommodation to the new jetty and a good fall-back option. ❹

Avra Towards eastern end of waterfront Ⓣ22830 22242, Ⓔavrahotel@yahoo.co.uk. Neoclassical building with spacious rooms, some with balconies, and attractive plant-filled communal area. B&B ❹

Favie Suzanne Antoníou Sókhou 22 Ⓣ22830 22693, Ⓦwww.faviesuzanne.gr. An attractive hotel about 200m from the waterfront. B&B ❻

Tinion Hotel Alavánou 1, on waterfront Ⓣ22830 22261, Ⓦwww.tinionhotel.gr. Stylish 1920s hotel just back from the waterfront. Spacious rooms, some with balconies. Discount for readers of this book. ❹

Tinos Camping Ten-minute walk south of port Ⓣ22830 22344, Ⓦwww.camping.gr/tinos.html. En-suite rooms and studios, set on one of the nicer campsites in the Cyclades. Follow the signs from the port. ❸

## The Town

Trafficking in devotional articles certainly dominates the streets leading up from the busy waterfront to the Neoclassical church of **Panayía Evangelístria** (officially daily 8am–8pm) that towers above. Evangelistrías in particular overflows with holy-water vessels, votive candles and plastic icons, while parallel Megaloháris, which points a slightly more direct approach to the church, is relatively clear of shops, making room for the long, thick pad that has been bolted to the street in sympathy for the most religious devotees who crawl to the church uphill on their knees from the harbour. In keeping with the times, those supplicants unable to get to Tínos can now send prayers by email. Approached via a massive marble staircase, the famous **icon** inside the church is all but buried under a dazzling array of jewels; below is the crypt (where the icon was discovered) and a mausoleum for the sailors drowned when the Greek warship *Elli*, at anchor off Tínos during a pilgrimage, was torpedoed by an

Italian submarine on August 15, 1940. Museums around the courtyard display more objects donated by the faithful, as well as icons, paintings and work by local marble sculptors.

The shrine aside – and all the attendant stalls, shops and bustle – the port is busy but none too exciting, with just scattered inland patches of nineteenth-century buildings. You might make time for the **archeological museum** (Tues–Sun 8.30am–3pm; €2) on the way up to the church, whose collection includes a fascinating sundial from the local Roman sanctuary of Poseidon and Amphitrite (see below).

### Eating and drinking

As usual, many of the seafront **restaurants** are overpriced and indifferent. However, about midway along the port, behind the *Leto* hotel, there is a cluster of excellent tavernas, including *Epineio*, with good-value, tasty Greek dishes and excellent seafood. A small vine-covered alleyway leads from here to Palládha, a public square with a farmers' **market** every morning with local fruit and vegetables, and lined with yet more good choices, such as *Palea Palladha*, justifiably proud of its grilled *loukániko* (spicy sausage), sharp local feta and smooth house wine. At the end of the alleyway there's a small traditional bakery, *Psomi Horiatiko*. For late-night snacks, try *Edesma* (meaning "food") just off Palládha, which stays open till 5am. At the new jetty, *Mariners* does very good pizzas while you're waiting for your ferry, and may be prepared to store luggage while you look for accommodation.

There are a few **bars**, mostly in a huddle near the new quay. Sleek *Fevgatos* has sophisticated decor, *Koursaros* on the corner of Aktí Ellís plays classic rock at a comfortable volume, while *Pyrsos* is pretty lively with a mixture of international hits and Greek music. The very Greek *Kaktos* is up on the bypass, with a restored windmill and has dancing on a terrace with ocean views, while *Sivilla* blends Greek and world music in a cosy setting.

## Southern beaches

**Kiónia**, 3km northwest of Tínos Town (hourly buses in summer), is the site of the **Sanctuary of Poseidon and Amphitrite** (Tues–Sun 8.30am–3pm; free), which was discovered in 1902; the excavations yielded principally columns (*kiónia* in Greek), but also a temple, baths, a fountain and hostels for the ancient pilgrims. The **beach** is functional enough, lined with rooms to rent and snack-bars, but beyond the large, comfortable *Tinos Beach* hotel (☎22830 22626, Ⓦwww.tinosbeach.gr; ❼) – the last bus stop – you can follow an unpaved road to a series of sandy coves. There is further accommodation up the concrete roads in the valley behind the beach, including the well-equipped *Panorama* (☎22830 24904, Ⓦwww.apartmentspanorama.gr; ❺) studios and apartments.

The Áyios Fokás beach beyond the headland east of town starts off rocky but improves if you walk 500m further along. At Áyios Sostís, the *Cavos* studios and bungalows (☎22830 24224, Ⓦwww.cavos-tinos.com; ❻) are well situated for the beach. Further east, **Pórto** (six buses daily) boasts two good beaches; just behind Áyios Ioánnis beach are the very smart, spacious studios *Porto Raphael* (☎22830 23913, Ⓦwww.portoraphael.gr; ❻).

## Northern Tínos

A good beginning to a foray into the interior is to take the route from the back left of the Evangelistrías, going right then left soon after; this crosses the bypass and heads uphill as an old walled path. It climbs for ninety minutes through appealing countryside to **KTIKÁDHOS**, a fine village with a good, vine-shaded sea-view taverna, *Drosia*. The lower church, Ypapandís, has even better views. You can either flag down a bus on the main road or stay with the trail until Xinára (see below).

Heading northwest from the main road junction beyond Ktikádhos, there are some fine **dovecotes** near Tarambádhos – you can follow a signed path through the village if you want to get close, but the best view is from the main road just beyond.

The road stays high, with long descending side-routes to **beaches**. At a crossroads a few kilometres further, left goes 3km down to **Áyios Romanós beach**, a long stretch of tamarisk-backed sand. There is access at the start of the beach, then the road heads inland and uphill, before a side-turning descends extremely steeply to the far end of the beach. There are studios at *Meltemi* (T22830 24315, Etomeltemi@gmail.com; ❺), near the first car park. Beyond Ávdhos, with its weird, eroded giant boulder and square-based ancient tower hidden among modern animal sheds, is **KARDHIANÍ**, 17km from town, one of the most strikingly set and beautiful villages on the island, with views across to Sýros from amid a dense oasis. In the lower eastern part are the *Perívoli* café-taverna and, more centrally, a traditional *kafenío*. Just beyond Ystérnia village is the turning for **Órmos Ysterníon**, a smaller beach with a lot of holiday homes, and very pretty little Skhináki beach at the far end. Just over the headland to the northeast is Áspros Yialós beach. There are three tavernas and a café, and accommodation includes the *Anemoessa* (T22830 31223, Wwww.anemoessa.gr; ❹) with rooms on the seafront and comfortable studios a few minutes inland. The bay is also connected to Ystérnia by a broad, partly marble-paved *kalderími*, much of which survives.

Five daily buses along this route finish up at **PÝRGOS**, a few kilometres beyond Ystérnia and in the middle of the island's marble-quarrying district. A beautiful village, its local artisans are renowned throughout Greece for their skill in producing marble ornamentation; ornate fanlights and bas-relief plaques crafted here adorn houses throughout Tínos. Pýrgos is also home to the School of Arts, and the overpriced **museum of Tinian artists** (daily 10.30am–1.30pm & 5.30–7pm; €5) contains numerous representative works from some of the island's finest artists. Nearby, the **Yiannoulis Halepas museum** (same hours and ticket) is devoted exclusively to the work of the artist who was born in this house in 1851 and is generally recognized as the most important Neoclassical Greek sculptor. There are *kafenía* and eating places on the attractive shady platía, including the imaginative *Ta Myronia* **taverna** and the *Rodaria zaharoplastío*.

The marble products were once exported from **PÁNORMOS** harbour, 4km northeast, which has a tiny, commercialized beach, a line of cafés, good fish tavernas such as *Markos* and *Paleta*, and some good-value rooms and studios at *Elena* (T22830 31694; ❸) right on the waterfront. The tiny island it faces is called Planítis, "the Planet". Better **beaches** nearby, accessible on foot or *kaïki*, are Róhari to the southeast, and Ayía Thálassa and Kavalourkó on the northwest side of the bay with deep clear waters and massive waves.

## Around Exóbourgo

The ring of villages around **Exóbourgo** (Xómbourgo) mountain is another focus of interest on Tínos. The fortified pinnacle itself (570m), with ancient foundations as well as the ruins of three Venetian churches and a fountain, is reached by steep steps from **XINÁRA** (near the island's major road junction), the seat of the island's Roman Catholic bishop for 1350 years. Most villages in north-central Tínos have mixed populations, but Xinára and its immediate neighbours are purely Catholic; the inland villages also tend to have a more sheltered position, with better farmland nearby – the Venetians' way of rewarding converts and their descendants. An alternative, shorter access path to the summit is from the Ierás Kardhiás (Sacred Heart) monastery to the east. Just south of Xinára, **TRIPÓTAMOS** is a completely Orthodox village with possibly the finest architecture in this region – and has been pounced on by foreigners keen to restore its historic properties.

At **LOUTRÁ**, the next community north of Xinára, there's an Ursuline convent, and a good **folk art museum** (summer only, daily 10.30am–3.30pm; free) in the old Jesuit monastery. From Krókos, 1km northwest of Loutrá, which has a scenically situated taverna, it's a forty-minute walk via Skaládhos to tiny **VÓLAX**, one of the most remote villages on the island, a windswept oasis surrounded by giant granite boulders. Here, a handful of elderly Catholic basketweavers fashion some of the best examples in Greece – on sale at the central shop, Petrino. There is a small **folklore museum** (free, but ask in the village for the key), and the small outdoor Fontaine Theatre, which in August hosts visiting theatre groups from all over Greece. There are a couple of places to eat, including the excellent ⅍ *Rokos* **taverna**, which offers local food.

At Kómi, 5km beyond Krókos, you can take a detour for **KOLYMBÍTHRA**, a magnificent double beach: one part wild, huge and windswept (temporary residence to migrating pink flamingos during May), the other sheltered and with a couple of tavernas including *Viktoria* (☎22830 51309, ⓦwww .tinos-victoria.com; Easter–Oct), which also has sea-view rooms (③) and **internet** access. The bus to Kalloní goes on to Kolymbíthra twice a day in season; out of season you'll have to get off at Kómi and walk 4km.

From either Skaládho or Volák you go on to Koúmaros, where another long stairway leads up to Exóbourgo, or skirt the pinnacle towards the agricultural villages of **FALATÁDHOS** and **STENÍ**, which appear as white speckles against the fertile Livádha valley. Falatádhos has a number of whitewashed churches, including **Áyios Ioánnis**, which is notable for its marble decoration. There is also a **house of exhibitions** (changing hours; free), which shows contemporary art in summer. The village has a number of excellent restaurants including *Lefkes* taverna with home-grown organic produce and *To Katoï*, specializing in grilled meats and *kokorétsi*. From Stení, which has fewer amenities but plenty of postcard-perfect whitewashed buildings to admire, you can catch the bus back to the harbour. On the way down, try to stop off at one of the beautiful settlements just below the important twelfth-century **convent of Kekhrovouníou**, where Ayía Pelayía had her vision. Particularly worth visiting are **Triandáros** and **Dhýo Horiá**, which has a fine main square where cave-fountains burble. If you have your own transport, there are quite wide and fairly negotiable tracks down to some lovely secluded bays on the east of the island from the area of Stení. One such is **Sánta Margaríta**; given the lack of tourist development here, it's a good idea to take something to drink.

# Mýkonos

Originally visited only as a stop on the way to ancient Delos, **Mýkonos** has become easily the most popular, the most high profile and the most expensive of the Cyclades. Boosted by direct air links with Europe and domestic flights from Athens, it sees more than a million tourists pass through in a good year (half of them in Aug alone), producing some spectacular overcrowding in summer on Mýkonos's 75 square kilometres. But if you don't mind the crowds,

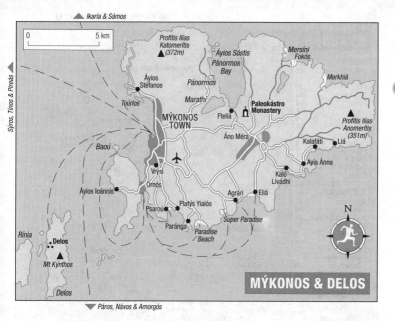

or you come in the shoulder season, the prosperous capital is still one of the most photogenic island towns, its whitewashed houses concealing hundreds of little churches, shrines and chapels.

The sophisticated nightlife is hectic, amply stimulated by Mýkonos's former reputation as *the* gay resort of the Mediterranean – today, gay tourists are in the minority on the island until September, when the gay clientele is present in full force. The locals take it all in their stride, ever conscious of the important revenue generated by their laissez-faire attitude. When islanders first opened up to the artsy tourists who began appearing on Mýkonos in the 1960s, they assumed their eccentric visitors were sharing cigarettes due to lack of funds. Since then, a lot of the innocence has evaporated, and you shouldn't come for scenery, solitude or tradition, but Mýkonos offers lively beaches and the party lifestyle, as well as easy access to Delos island.

## Mýkonos Town and around

Don't let the crowds put you off exploring **MÝKONOS TOWN**, the arche-typal postcard image of the Cyclades. In summer most people head out to the beaches during the day, so early morning or late afternoon are the best times to wander the maze of narrow streets. The labyrinthine design was supposedly to confuse the pirates who plagued Mýkonos in the eighteenth and early nineteenth centuries, and it has the same effect on today's visitors.

### Arrival and information

There is some accommodation information at the **airport** (3km southeast of town) and at the **new port** where large cruise ships dock (2.5km north of town in Toúrlos), but unless you know where you're going it's easier to take a bus or taxi into town and sort things out there. The vast majority of visitors arrive by ferry at the "old port" **jetty** at the north end of town, where a veritable horde of room-owners pounces on the newly arrived.

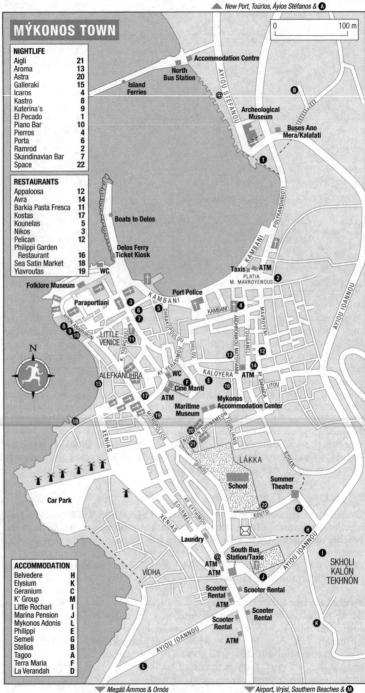

## MÝKONOS TOWN

New Port, Toúrlos, Áyios Stéfanos & **A**

0        100 m

**NIGHTLIFE**

| | |
|---|---|
| Aigli | 21 |
| Aroma | 13 |
| Astra | 20 |
| Galleraki | 15 |
| Icaros | 4 |
| Kastro | 8 |
| Katerina's | 9 |
| El Pecado | 1 |
| Piano Bar | 10 |
| Pierros | 4 |
| Porta | 6 |
| Ramrod | 2 |
| Skandinavian Bar | 7 |
| Space | 22 |

**RESTAURANTS**

| | |
|---|---|
| Appaloosa | 12 |
| Avra | 14 |
| Barkia Pasta Fresca | 11 |
| Kostas | 17 |
| Kounelas | 5 |
| Nikos | 3 |
| Pelican | 12 |
| Philippi Garden Restaurant | 16 |
| Sea Satin Market | 18 |
| Yiavroutas | 19 |

**ACCOMMODATION**

| | |
|---|---|
| Belvedere | H |
| Elysium | K |
| Geranium | C |
| K' Group | M |
| Little Rochari | I |
| Marina Pension | J |
| Mykonos Adonis | L |
| Philippi | E |
| Semeli | G |
| Stelios | B |
| Tagoo | A |
| Terra Maria | F |
| La Verandah | D |

Accommodation Centre

North Bus Station

Island Ferries

Archeological Museum

Buses Ano Mera/Kalafati

Boats to Delos

Delos Ferry Ticket Kiosk

WC

Folklore Museum

Paraportianí

Taxis    ATM

PLATIA M. MAVROYENOUS

Port Police

LITTLE VENICE

ALEFKÁNDHRA

WC

Cine Manti

ATM

Maritime Museum

Mykonos Accommodation Center

ATM

LÁKKA

Car Park

Summer Theatre

School

Laundry

South Bus Station/Taxis

ATM
ATM

Scooter Rental

Scooter Rental

ATM

Scooter Rental

Scooter Rental

ATM

VÍDHA

SKHOLI KALÓN TEKHNÓN

Áno Méra & By-pass

Megáli Ámmos & Ornós

Airport, Vrýsi, Southern Beaches & **M**

N

The **north bus station** for Toúrlos, Kalafáti, Eliá and Áno Méra is located by the old port; the **south bus station** for the popular southwestern beaches is just outside the pedestrianized area at the other end of town. Nearby the latter, are the **post office**, Olympic Airways office, a host of **internet** cafés, and numerous **car and motorbike rental** agencies. Car parking is difficult in town, so car-rental agencies like Fabrika (☎22890 28028, ✉fabrikas@mail.gr) offer private parking on-site for customers. **Buses** to all the most popular beaches and resorts run frequently until the early hours in high season. **Taxis** run from Platía Mavroyénous on the main seafront and from the south bus station; the rates are fixed and quite reasonable; try Mykonos Radio Taxi (☎22890 22400). Be aware that some taxi drivers may try and get you to pay the full fare per person; this is not legal, and you should refuse. There are countless advertiser-based tourist **publications** circulating throughout Mýkonos during high season, the best of which is the free *Mykonos Sky Map*, available from some agents and hotels.

Catamaran and ferry tickets are sold at several separate **travel agencies** on the harbour front. Check out the various possibilities, and if your boat leaves from the new port, catch the bus up from the old ferry landing across from the Eurobank.

## Accommodation

The scrum of room-owners by the old port jetty can be intimidating, so if you arrive by boat press on 100m further, where a row of offices deals with official **hotels**, rented **rooms** and **camping** information. Alternatively, go into the heart of town to the helpful Mykonos Accommodation Center (☎22890 23160, ⓦwww.mykonos-accommodation.com) on Enóplon Dhynaméon near the maritime museum.

Accommodation **prices** in Mýkonos rocket in the high season to a greater degree than almost anywhere else in Greece. For this reason, it may well be worth considering camping in high season – there are two campsites southeast of town (see p.160), both of which can rent out tents. *Mykonos Camping* (☎22890 24578, ⓦwww.mycamp.gr; May–Oct) above Paránga beach is smaller and has a more pleasant setting than nearby *Paradise Camping* on Paradise Beach (☎22890 22129, ⓦwww.paradisemykonos.com), though the latter also has bungalows (❺). Both are packed in season, and dance music from the 24-hour bars on Paradise beach makes sleep difficult. Hourly bus services to Paránga and Paradise beaches continue into the early hours, but can get uncomfortably overcrowded.

Belvedere Off Ayíou Ioánnou ☎22890 25122, ⓦwww.belvederehotel.com. Upmarket hotel with stunning rooms, views, a pool and new gym, in a quiet area of town. It also has its own Japanese restaurant, *Matsuhisa* (June–Sept). Wi-fi available in rooms. Easter–Oct. ❼

Elysium Steep side street off Ayíou Ioánnou, Skholí Kalón Tekhnón area ☎22890 23952, ⓦwww .elysiumhotel.com. Almost exclusively gay hotel with beautiful views, boasting a poolside bar that's a popular setting for a late-afternoon cocktail. Internet access in rooms. May–Oct. B&B ❻

Geranium On hillside southeast of town ☎22890 22867, ⓦwww.geraniumhotel.com. Very stylish, minimalist gay hotel with rooms, studios and a villa. Pool and bar with nude sunbathing area if you're beautiful enough. ❼

K' Group Vrýsi ☎22890 23415, ⓦwww .myconiancollection.gr. A cluster of hotels, *Kalypso, Kochyli, Korali* and *Kyma*, about 1km south of town. Many of the comfortable rooms have wonderful views of town, and there's a pool and restaurant. Often has availability when smaller places are fully booked. B&B ❼

Little Rochari Skholí Kalón Tekhnón 32 ☎22890 79650, ⓦwww.littlerochari.com. Well-run, friendly hotel, with pool and parking. Sister to the larger *Rochari Hotel*. April–Oct. B&B ❻

Marina Pension Off Ayíou Ioánnou ☎22890 24960, ✉marina@mykonos-web.com. Nice neat rooms arranged around courtyard on the southern edge of town. May–Oct. ❺

Mykonos Adonis Near the waterfront, south of town ☎22890 22434, ⓦwww.mykonosadonis.gr.

Beautiful hotel in the Vídha area, with views of the windmills from some of its nicely appointed rooms. B&B ❽

**Philippi** Kaloyéra 25 ☎22890 22294, ⓦphilippi-hotel.com. Clean, comfortable rooms set around a quiet garden right in the middle of the bustling old town. April–Oct. ❹

**Semeli** Off Ayíou Ioánnou ☎22890 27466, ⓦwww.semelihotel.gr. Luxurious hotel above town with pool, whirlpool and very tastefully decorated rooms. Extensive spa facilities and wi-fi available, as well as parking. B&B ❽

**Stelios** Above the old port ☎22890 24641. Excellent-value pension in prime location. Take the steps leading up from the OTE office. ❺

**Tagoo** Tangoú ☎22890 22611, ⓦwww.hoteltagoo.gr. Well-priced and popular hotel overlooking the sea, about 700m walk north of the archeological museum. Attentive service, spacious rooms, wi-fi available, and roof pool with panoramic views. Their studios (ⓦwww.tagoostudios.gr) are 400m further to the north. April–Oct. ❺

**Terra Maria** Kaloyéra 18 ☎22890 24212, ⓦwww.terramariahotel.gr. Long-established central hotel with rooms with small balconies overlooking the next-door open-air cinema. Wi-fi available. Prices negotiable. ❺

**La Veranda** On hillside east of town ☎22890 23670, ℮laveranda@panafonet.gr. A laid-back, upmarket hotel, recently renovated, with rooms and studios set around a small pool. ❺

## The Town

Getting lost in the convoluted streets and alleys is half the fun of Mýkonos, although there are a few places worth seeking out. Coming from the ferry quay you'll pass the **archeological museum** (Tues–Sun 8.30am–3pm; €2) on your way into town, which displays some good Delos pottery, and artefacts from the cemeteries on Rínia island; the town also boasts a **maritime museum** (on Enóplon Dhynaméon) displaying various nautical artefacts, including a lighthouse re-erected in the back garden (Tues–Sun 10.30am–1pm & 6.30–9pm; €3). Next door is **Lena's House** (Mon–Sat 6–9pm, Sun 5–7pm; free), a completely restored and furnished middle-class home from the nineteenth century. Near the base of the Delos jetty, the **folklore museum** (Mon–Sat 5.30–8.30pm, Sun 6.30–8.30pm; free), housed in an eighteenth-century mansion – one of the town's oldest – crams in a larger-than-usual collection of bric-a-brac, including a basement dedicated to Mýkonos's maritime past. The museum shares the promontory with Mýkonos's oldest and best-known church, **Paraportianí** (usually closed), a fascinating asymmetrical hodgepodge of four chapels amalgamated into one (and a serious gay-cruising area after dark).

Beyond the church, the shoreline leads to the area known as **Little Venice** because of the high, arcaded Venetian houses built right up to the water's edge on its southwest side. Together with the adjoining **Alefkándhra** district, this is a dense area packed with art galleries, trendy bars, shops and clubs. Behind Platía Alefkándhra sit Mýkonos's Roman Catholic and Greek Orthodox **cathedrals**. Beyond, the famous **windmills** look over the area, a little shabby but ripe for photo opportunities. South of here, sleepier **Vídha**, which runs along a tiny beach, has seen the recent arrival of accommodation spilling over from the rest of town.

### Eating

Even **light meals** and **snacks** can be expensive in Mýkonos, but there are numerous snack-bars, in particular near the south bus station. The area around Alefkándhra is a promising place to head for a full **meal**; if you're looking for late-night coffee, try *Kavos*, open 24 hours right by the town beach. Supermarkets of any size are absent from the centre of town.

**Appaloosa** Mavroyénous 11, Platía Gouménio. Cosmopolitan restaurant and bar with well-prepared Mexican and international food.

**Avra** Kaloyéra 10. Reliable Greek and fusion cooking, with a choice of terrace or garden seating.

Barkia Pasta Fresca Yioryoúli. Lively home-made pizza and pasta restaurant.

Kostas Mitropoléos. Friendly taverna behind Platía Alefkándhra, with competitive prices, and a good wine list including barrelled wine.

Kounelas Svorónou. Seafood taverna, very popular with the locals, tucked away in a narrow street near *Nikos* taverna.

Nikos Inland from the Delos jetty, on Platía Ayías Monís. One of the most famous tavernas on the island. Every inch of its side of the square is packed with customers, which can have a detrimental effect on service.

Pelican Platía Gouménio off Kaloyéra. Popular taverna serving Greek staples and good pasta dishes. Not the cheapest, but one of the nicest settings in a vine-covered square.

Philippi Garden Restaurant Off Kaloyéra. Exclusive restaurant in romantic setting serving home-grown vegetarian food, as well as superb seafood and traditional local dishes.

Sea Satin Market Below the windmills, next to the *Caprice* bar. Expensive, beautifully located restaurant right on the water with excellent seafood and grills, and a clubby vibe after midnight.

Yiavroutas Off Mitropoléos. Small, unpretentious, family-run place serving excellent-value Greek dishes and good barrelled wine. Also open most of the night, if you're in need of fuel.

## Nightlife

**Nightlife** in town is every bit as good as it's cracked up to be, and every bit as pricey – some clubs have high cover charges. Start with cocktails in Little Venice or head for the bars that line Andhroníkou and Enóplon Dhynaméon.

Aigli En. Dhynaméon. More sophisticated, ideal for cocktails and people-watching.

Aroma Matoyiánni. Well-positioned for early evening drinks and morning-after breakfasts.

Astra En. Dhynaméon, Fashionable, upmarket meeting-place with a variety of music.

Galleraki Skárpa, Alefkándhra. Good for an afternoon drink with views of Little Venice.

Katerina's Anáryiron, Little Venice. A relaxed vibe and sunset views from the balconies.

El Pecado/Remezzo Polykandhrióti. Stylish lounge-style club, often with Latin American music, on the waterfront near the archeological museum.

Skandinavian Bar Áyios Ioánnis Barkiá. For affordable serious drinking, head for the *Skandinavian*, which thumps out dance music and cocktails until the early hours.

Space Platía Lákka. The largest dance club in town.

## Gay venues

Almost everywhere in Mýkonos town is, at the very least, gay-friendly. Although there are no huge **gay clubs** on Mýkonos, there is a good batch of excellent, comparatively laid-back bars in town, both for dancing and drinking, and bar-hopping is definitely the way to go, usually starting in the Little Venice area in time for the dramatic sunsets. Near midnight, the action (and the men) migrate to Platía Mavroyénous, where the more dedicated clubs get going in the early hours and continue through to dawn. During daylight, head for Super Paradise and Eliá beaches, or take a gay cruise-boat from Platýs Yialós.

Icaros Matoyiánni, near Platía Mavroyénous. Late-night shows and a roof terrace, for the younger crowd.

Kastro Anáryiron, Little Venice. Laid-back, with relaxing classical music and sunset views.

Piano Bar (Montparnasse) Anáryiron, Little Venice. With great cocktails, a balcony over the sea and nightly cabaret acts, this is a very good place to warm up.

Pierros/Pierros Café Matoyiánni, near Platía Mavroyénous. Legendary dance club that's thrived since the 1960s, with drag shows and heavy dance music.

Porta Áyios Ioánnis Mykónou 5. Split-level, in a narrow street near *Nikos* taverna. A lively, crowded, cruisier place to head to as the evening gets going.

Ramrod At the back of Mavroyénous. Pumping music, dancing, drag acts and sunset terrace.

## The beaches

The closest **beaches** to town are those to the north, at **Toúrlos** (only 2km away but horrid) and **Áyios Stéfanos** (3km, much better), both developed resorts and connected by a very regular bus service to Mýkonos Town. There are tavernas and rooms (as well as package hotels) at Áyios Stéfanos, away from the beach. Mýkonos's most popular beaches stretch south and east from town, divided by rocky headlands and small, unexceptional patches of resort development. You'll need your own transport, or a bus or *kaïkia*, to get to most of them.

## The west and southwest

The undistinguished but popular beaches of the southwestern resorts are tucked into pretty bays. The nearest to town, 1km away, is **Megáli Ámmos**, a good but often windy beach backed by flat rocks and pricey rooms, but nearby Kórfos Bay is unpleasant, thanks to the town dump and machine noise. Buses serve **Ornós**, a package resort on a low-lying area between the rest of the island and the Áyios Ioánnis peninsula. The south side has a reasonable beach, plus *kaïkia* to other beaches, a handful of tavernas, and numerous accommodation options: try the comfortable *Best Western Dionysos* (℡22890 23313, ⊛www.dionysoshotel.com; May–Oct; B&B ❻), which has a pool and is much cheaper outside high season. Buses continue 2km west to **Áyios Ioánnis**, the island's westernmost bay and small, namesake church, overlooking Delos – the tiny public beach achieved a moment of fame as a location for the film *Shirley Valentine*; there are a few, high-class hotels, and the much smaller *Apollonia* (℡22890 27890, ⊛www .apollonia-resort.gr; April–Oct; B&B ❽), set in a very pretty garden. Accessed by a 500m dirt track northwest from Áyios Ioánnis is the small but popular gay beach at **Kápari**, with good views of Delos and the sunset.

## The south coast

The western half of the south coast is the busiest part of the island. *Kaïkia* head from town to all of its beaches, and buses to many of them, but you certainly won't be alone – on any sunny day in season both beaches and transport range from busy to overcrowded. Car drivers will find that parking spaces at most beaches are inadequate and turning difficult. You might begin with **Platýs Yialós**, 4km south of town: one of the longest-established resorts on the island, the sand is monopolized by end-to-end hotels, and almost every room is prebooked between June and September. **Psaroú**, just a steep, hairpin, access road away to the west, is much prettier – 150m of white sand backed by foliage and reeds. On the waterfront, you'll find *N'Ammos*, an elegant fish **restaurant** popular with Athenians. You'll need to reserve well in advance to secure **rooms** between mid-June and mid-September. Try *Soula* (℡22890 22006, ⊛www.soula-rooms.gr; ❺), pretty studios in a calm garden just behind the beach. Other facilities include the Mykonos Diving Center (℡22890 24808, ⊛www.dive.gr), offering diving courses from beginner to advanced, including night dives for certified divers and snorkelling trips. Waterskiing and windsurfer rental is also possible.

Just over the headland to the east of Platýs Yialós, though accessed by a different, winding road (from near the airport, and off the Paradise beach road), is **Paránga**, actually two beaches separated by a smaller headland, the first of which is quieter than its neighbour, which is home to a loud beach bar and *Mykonos Camping* (see p.157). A short distance from the latter is the small *San Giorgio* (℡22890 27474, ⊛www.sangiorgio.gr; May–Oct; B&B ❽) hotel complex.

Next is the golden crescent of **Paradise beach** (officially Kalamopódhi). Here, as on many of Mýkonos's most popular beaches, it can be difficult to find an opening big enough to fit a towel in high season, and any space clear of people is likely to be taken up by straw umbrellas, rentable (usually along with two accompanying loungers) for about €5. Behind the beach are *Dive Adventures* (℡22890 26539, ⊛www.diveadventures.gr & ⊛www.divemykonos.gr; April–Oct), offering introductory scuba and a full range of PADI. Other facilities include shops, self-service restaurants, the noisy 24-hour beach bars of *Paradise Camping*, while at the far end is *Cavo Paradiso* (Ⓦwww.cavoparadiso.gr), the after-hours club where die-hard party animals of all persuasions come together, often united by world-famous DJs. The next bay east contains **Super Paradise** (officially Plindhrí) **beach**, accessible by *kaïki*, or by a surfaced but extremely steep access road. One of the most fun beaches on the island, it has a decent taverna and two bars at opposite ends of the beach pumping out cheesy summer hits. The eastern half of the beach is mixed, getting progressively more gay as you walk towards the beach bar perched in the hills, below which the beach is almost exclusively gay and nudist.

One of the more scenically attractive beaches on Mýkonos is **Eliá**, the last port of call for the *kaïkia* and with a road from Áno Méra. A broad, sandy stretch, with plenty of parking and a mountainous backdrop at the eastern end, it's the longest beach on the island, though divided by a rocky area, and almost exclusively gay later in the season, with nudity at the far end. Chill-out music is played at the *Elia Pool Bar Restaurant*, while jet-ski, waterski and parachute boating are available for the more active. The more secluded **Agrári** beach is 300m to the west. East from the Eliá road is **Kaló Livádhi** (seasonal bus service), a rather featureless beach fronting an agricultural valley scattered with little farmhouses; the *Sol y Mar* restaurant draws the crowds, while the *Sol y Sombra* trattoria-pizzeria is at the far end.

### The east and north

The main road southeast from Áno Méra (see below; local bus service) leads to **Ayía Ánna**, on a double-headed headland (Dhivoúnia & Tarsonás), with a shingle beach and taverna, just before the larger, more attractive **Kalafáti**. The latter's sand beach supports an increasing number of hotels, notably the huge complex of the *Contiki Resort* (*Aphrodite Beach*), aimed at the 18-35 market, and good fish tavernas such as the *Aneplora* and *Thalassa*. It's also popular with windsurfers: Planet Windsurfing (Ⓦwww.planetwindsurfing.com) offers hire and courses. Seasonal excursion boats run to **Tragoníssi**, the islet just offshore, for spectacular coastal scenery, seals and wild birds. The rest of the east coast is more difficult to reach: there are some emptier beaches, such as Merkhiá, Fokós and Mersíni, really only worth the effort if you crave more space. Liá, roughly 4.6km east by road from Áno Méra, is smaller than Kalafáti, but pleasant, with clear water, plus a good, traditional fish taverna of the same name.

The **north coast** suffers persistent battering from the *meltémi*, plus tar and litter pollution, and for the most part is bare, brown and exposed. The deep inlet of **Pánormos Bay** is the exception to this, with the lovely, relatively sheltered beaches of **Pánormos** and **Áyios Sóstis** along its north-western edge beyond the Marathi reservoir; although not served by buses, they are becoming increasingly popular, but remain among the less crowded on the island. Just behind Pánormos is the very attractive *Albatros Club Hotel* (☎22890 25130, Ⓦwww .albatros-mykonos.com; May–Oct; B&B ❹) with both hotel-style and traditional rooms available; the beach has the *Panormos* bar-restaurant with excellent seafood, pasta and daiquiris. At the southern, inner end of the bay, Fteliá is a windsurfers' beach.

## Áno Méra

The access point for Eliá and beaches eastward is **ÁNO MÉRA**, the only other major residential settlement on the island, scattered over a large and fertile agricultural plateau. The main sight is the red-roofed sixteenth-century

**monastery of Panayía Tourlianí** (closed 1–2pm), next to the main square, where a collection of Cretan icons and the unusual eighteenth-century carved marble belltower are worth seeing.

The square outside the monastery has an air of impermanence, being surrounded by single-storey **restaurants**; however, the most popular eating place, for its wide range of Mediterranean dishes and even more extensive wine-list, is *Daniele,* just outside town on the Hóra road, near the late twelfth-century **Paleokástro monastery** (aka **Dárga**). There are a couple of **hotels**; on the south side is the large, ageing *Ano Mera* (☎22890 71230, Ⓦwwwmykonos-hotel.gr; April–Oct; B&B ❻), while the attractive new *Anatolia* (☎22890 71906, Ⓦwww.hotelanatolia.gr; Easter–Oct; B&B; ❼), on the Kalafáti road, has a pool, gym, jacuzzi and sauna.

# Delos (Dhílos)

The remains of **ancient Delos**, though now just home to lizards and day-tripper tourists, manage to convey the past grandeur of this small, sacred isle a few kilometres west of Mýkonos. The ancient town lies on the west coast on flat, sometimes marshy ground that rises in the south to **Mount Kýnthos**. From the 113m summit there's a magnificent view across the nearby Cyclades.

The first **excursion boats** to Delos leave the small port near the west end of Mýkonos harbour daily at 8.30am (€12.50 round trip), except on Mondays when the site is closed. You may have to return on the same boat, but in season each does the trip several times and you can choose what time you leave. The last return is usually about 3pm, and you'll need to arrive early if you want to make a thorough tour of the site. In season a daily *kaïki* makes return trips from the Mýkonos beaches (€10) with pick-up points at Platýs Yialós and Ornós, but only allows you three hours on the island. Check ahead with operators of Delos excursion boats or look for posters advertising evening concerts and other special performances that occasionally animate the ancient site in season.

▲ Temple of the Egyptian Gods, Delos

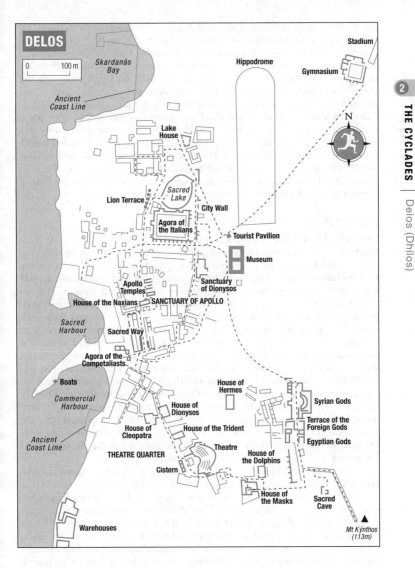

**DELOS**

0    100 m

Skardanás Bay

Ancient Coast Line

Stadium

Hippodrome

Gymnasium

Lake House

N

Sacred Lake

Lion Terrace

City Wall

Agora of the Italians

Tourist Pavilion

Museum

Apollo Temples

Sanctuary of Dionysos

House of the Naxians    SANCTUARY OF APOLLO

Sacred Harbour

Sacred Way

Agora of the Competaliasts

Boats

Commercial Harbour

House of Hermes

House of Dionysos

Syrian Gods

Terrace of the Foreign Gods

House of Cleopatra

House of the Trident

Egyptian Gods

Ancient Coast Line

Theatre

THEATRE QUARTER

Cistern

House of the Dolphins

House of the Masks

Sacred Cave

Warehouses

Mt Kýnthos (113m)

**Day trips** are also possible from Tínos, although they will only allow about two-and-a-half hours at the site.

## Some history

Delos's ancient fame was due to the fact that Leto gave birth to the divine twins Artemis and Apollo on the island, although its fine, sheltered harbour and central position in the Aegean did nothing to hamper development from around 2500 BC. When the Ionians colonized the island about 1000 BC it was already a cult centre, and by the seventh century BC it had become the commercial and religious centre of the **Amphictionic League**. Unfortunately Delos attracted the attention of Athens, which sought dominion over this prestigious island; the wealth of the Delian Confederacy, founded after the Persian Wars to protect the Aegean cities, was harnessed to Athenian ends, and for a while Athens controlled the Sanctuary of Apollo. Athenian attempts to "purify" the island began with a decree (426 BC) that no one could die or give birth on Delos – the sick and the pregnant were shipped to the neighbouring island of Rínia – and culminated in the simple expedient of banishing the native population.

Delos reached its peak in the third and second centuries BC, after being declared a free port by its Roman overlords; by the start of the first century BC, its population was around 30,000. In the end, though, its undefended wealth brought ruin: first Mithridates, of Pontus (88 BC) then his ally Athenodorus (69 BC) plundered the treasures, and the island never recovered. By the third century AD, Rome could not even sell it, and for centuries every passing seafarer stopped to collect a few prizes. Archeological excavations began in 1872.

## The site

As you land at **the site** (Tues–Sun 8.30am–3pm; €5), the Sacred Harbour (now filled-in with twentieth-century excavation debris) is on your left, the Commercial Harbour on your right and straight ahead lies the **Agora of the Competaliasts**. These were Roman merchants or freed slaves who worshipped the Lares Competales, the guardian spirits of crossroads; offerings to Hermes would once have been placed in the middle of the agora (market square), their positions now marked by a round and a square base. The **Sacred Way** leads north from the far left corner; it used to be lined with statues and the grandiose monuments of rival kings. Along it you reach three marble steps leading into the **Sanctuary of Apollo**. On your left is the Stoa of the Naxians, while against the north wall of the House of the Naxians, to the right, a huge statue of Apollo (c.600 BC) stood in ancient times. In 417 BC the Athenian general Nikias led a procession of priests across a bridge of boats from Rínia to dedicate a bronze palm tree; when it was later blown over in a gale it took the statue with it. Three **Temples to Apollo** stand in a row to the right along the Sacred Way: the massive Delian Temple, the Athenian, and the Porinos, the earliest dating from the sixth century BC. To the east towards the museum is the **Sanctuary of Dionysos**, with its marble phalluses on tall pillars.

On the right, behind the small Letoön temple, is the huge **Agora of the Italians**, while on the left are replicas of the famous **lions**, their lean bodies masterfully executed by Naxians in the seventh century BC to ward off intruders who would have been unfamiliar with the fearful creatures. Of the original lions, at least three have disappeared and one – looted by Venetians in the seventeenth century and ineptly reheaded – adorns the Arsenale in Venice. The remaining originals are in the site **museum** (same hours); otherwise, the best finds from the site have gone to Athens, but the museum is still worth a visit for its marble statuary, mosaic fragments and an extensive collection of phallic artefacts. Opposite the lions, tamarisk trees ring the site of the **Sacred Lake** (now drained) where Leto gave birth, clinging to a palm tree. On the other side of the lake is the City Wall, built – in 69 BC – too late to protect the treasures.

Set out in the other direction from the Agora of the Competaliasts and you enter the residential area, known as the **Theatre Quarter**. Many of the walls and roads remain, but there is none of the domestic minutiae that brings other such sites to life. The remnants of impressive private mansions are now named after their colourful main **mosaic** – Dionysos, Trident, Masks and Dolphins. The **theatre** itself seated 5500 spectators, and, though much ravaged, offers some fine views, but just below it and structurally almost as spectacular is a huge underground cistern with arched roof supports. Behind the theatre, a path leads towards the Sanctuaries of the Egyptian and Syrian Gods, then steeply up Mount Kýnthos for a **Sanctuary of Zeus and Athena** with spectacular views back down over the ruins and out to the surrounding Cyclades. Near the base of the final peak path, a small side path leads to the **Antron of Kynthos** or the "Grotto of Hercules", a rock cleft covered with a remarkable roof of giant stone slabs angled against each other, and a possible pre-Delian sacrificial site.

# Sýros

Don't be put off by first impressions of **Sýros**. From the ferry it can seem rather industrial, but once past the Neório shipyard which dominates the harbour entrance things improve quickly. It remains a working island with only a relatively recent history of tourism, making it among the most Greek of the Cyclades. The most populous island in the group, Sýros may also come as a refreshing change from its more touristy neighbours, though outsiders do come to the island (there's a thriving permanent foreign community), the beaches are busy and the villages sprawl widely with new development.

## Ermoúpoli

The main town and port of **ERMOÚPOLI** is one of the most striking in the Cyclades. A UNESCO World Heritage Site, it possesses an elegant collection of grand town houses which rise majestically from the bustling, café-lined waterfront. The town was founded during the War of Independence by refugees from Psará and Híos, and grew in importance to become Greece's chief port in the nineteenth century. Although Pireás outstripped it long ago, Ermoúpoli is still the largest town in the Cyclades, and the archipelago's capital. Medieval Sýros was largely a Catholic island, but an influx of Orthodox refugees during the War of Independence created two distinct communities; now almost equal in numbers, the two groups today still live in their respective quarters occupying two hills that rise up from the sea. They do, however, commonly celebrate each others' festivals, lending a vibrant mix of culture that gives the island its colour.

### Arrival and information

Sýros is a major crossover point on the **ferry** routes, and most people arrive by boat to be met by the usual horde of locals offering rooms. There is no bus service from the **airport**, and you will have to take a taxi (☎22810 86222). On the waterfront there are several **travel agencies**

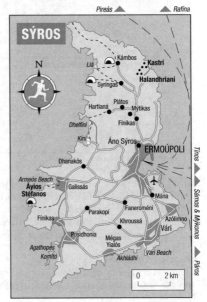

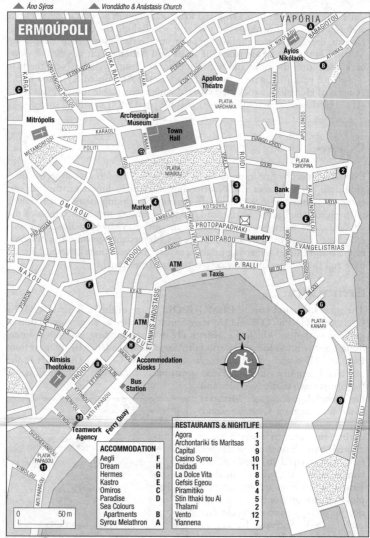

▲ Áno Sýros    ▲ Vrondádho & Anástasis Church

**ERMOÚPOLI**

VAPÓRIA

Áyios
Nikólaos

Apollon
Theatre

PLATIA
VARDHAKA

Mitrópolis

Archeological
Museum

Town
Hall

PLATIA
MIAOULI

Bank

Market

PLATIA
TSIROPINA

Laundry

ATM

Taxis

PLATIA
KANARI

N

Kimisis
Theotokou

Accommodation
Kiosks

Bus
Station

Teamwork
Agency

Ferry Quay

PLATIA
PAPAGOU

0        50 m

| ACCOMMODATION | |
|---|---|
| Aegli | F |
| Dream | H |
| Hermes | G |
| Kastro | E |
| Omiros | C |
| Paradise | D |
| Sea Colours Apartments | B |
| Syrou Melathron | A |

| RESTAURANTS & NIGHTLIFE | |
|---|---|
| Agora | 1 |
| Archontariki tis Maritsas | 3 |
| Capital | 9 |
| Casino Syrou | 10 |
| Daidadi | 11 |
| La Dolce Vita | 8 |
| Gefsis Egeou | 6 |
| Piramitiko | 4 |
| Stin Ithaki tou Ai | 5 |
| Thalami | 2 |
| Vento | 12 |
| Yiannena | 7 |

▼ ⑫, Neório Shipyard & Southern Villages

that sell boat tickets, and you'll also find the **bus station** and some **banks** here.
Alpha (☎22810 42801), based in Galissás, can provide both **car** and **motorbike**
**rental**. Laundry facilities are available at Kimos, Protopapadháki 34, opposite
the *Megaron* café-bar and the **post office**. *In Spot* on the seafront (Papágou 4)
near the bus station, offers **internet** 24 hours a day.

### Accommodation

TeamWork agency (☎22810 83400, ⓦwww.teamwork.gr), at Aktí Papágou 18
on the waterfront, is a useful source of information and is able to help with your

accommodation needs. In the summer you might try one of the accommodation kiosks on the waterfront.

**Aegli** Kleisthénous 14 ☏22810 79279, ⊛www
.lux-hotels.com/aegli. Comfortable rooms, some
with balconies, in an old building a few streets
behind the port. The roof terrace has wonderful
views of the town. B&B **④**

**Dream** Off Náxou ☏22810 84356. Decent, basic
rooms just back from the waterfront, some with
balconies, run by a charming family. **③**

**Hermes** Platía Kanári ☏22810 88011, ⊛www
.hermes-syros.com. Smart hotel in a prime
location, overlooking the port. All rooms have sea
views, and the hotel is home to a very popular
seafront restaurant. **⑥**

**Kastro** Kalomenopoúlou 12 ☏22810 88064,
⊛www.greek-tourism.gr. Spacious rooms in a
beautiful old mansion near the main square, with
access to a communal kitchen. **③**

**Omiros** Omírou 43 ☏22810 84910, ©omirosho
@otenet.gr/www.webhotel.gr. One of the most
romantic options on Sýros, on a quiet road above
the Mitrópolis, in the direction of Áno Sýros.
Classically styled rooms set in an elegant
nineteenth-century mansion once owned by Tinoan
sculptor Vitalis. **⑤**

**Paradise** Omírou 3 ☏22810 83204, ⊛www
.hotel-paradise-syros.com. Clean basic en-suite
rooms in a quiet part of town. All rooms have
access to a pleasant shaded courtyard, whilst
rooms on the top floor have good views. **③**

**Sea Colours Apartments** Athinás 10 (book through
TeamWork Agency; see p.166). Traditionally
decorated apartments for 2–6 people, just above
the swimming platforms of Áyios Nikólaos, 5min
walk from the Platía Miaoúli. **④**

**Syrou Melathron** Babayiótou 5 ☏22810 85963,
⊛www.syroumelathron.gr. Rather regal hotel set in
a restored 1856 mansion in the quieter Áyios
Nikólaos area of town. Has suites as well as
spacious rooms, some with sea views. **⑦**

## The Town

Ermoúpoli itself is worth at least a night's stay, its grandiose buildings a relic of its days as a major port. The long, central **Platía Miaoúli** is named after an admiral of the War of Independence whose statue stands there, and in the evenings the population parades in front of its arcades. Up the stepped street (Benáki) to the left of the town hall is the small **archeological museum** (Tues–Sun 8.30am–3pm; free), with three rooms of finds from Sýros, Páros and Amorgós. To the left of the clocktower more steps climb up to **Vrondádho**, the hill that hosts the Orthodox quarter. The wonderful church of the **Anástasis** stands atop the hill, with its domed roof and panoramic views over Tínos and Mýkonos.

Up from the right of the square is the **Apollon Theatre**, a copy of Milan's La Scala, which occasionally hosts performances. Further on up, the handsome Neoclassical Orthodox church of **Áyios Nikólaos** (8am–1pm, 5pm–7pm) was built in 1848–70, with an impressive marble iconostasis and a tiny ecclesiastical museum of uncertain opening hours under its southwest corner. Beyond it to the right is **Vapória**, where the island's wealthiest shipowners, merchants and bankers built their mansions. A *trenaki* runs a twenty-minute tour (€4) of the town's main sights, starting from the *Dodoni* ice-cream parlour in the old *Limen-arkhío* at Platía Kanári.

On the taller hill to the left from the main square is the intricate medieval quarter of **Áno Sýros**, with a clutch of Catholic churches below the cathedral of St George. It takes about 45 minutes of steep walking up *Omírou*, which becomes *Kárga*, to reach this quarter (or a rare bus from the main station), passing the Orthodox and Catholic cemeteries on the way – the former full of grand shipowners' mausoleums, the latter with more modest monuments and French and Italian inscriptions. There are fine views of the town below, and, close by, the **Capuchin monastery of St Jean**, founded in 1535 to do duty as a poorhouse. Once up here it's worth visiting the local art and church exhibitions at the **Markos Vamvakaris museum** (daily 10.30am–1pm & 7–10pm; €1.50), and the **Byzantine museum** attached to the monastery.

Heading west from Ermoúpoli, on the road leading from the ferry quay to Kíni, accessible by bus, the **industrial museum** (Mon & Wed–Sun 10am–2pm, also Thurs–Sun 6–9pm; €2.50, Wed free) traces the history of the island's shipbuilding, mining and many other industries through a well-labelled series of artefacts and exhibitions.

### Eating

As well as being home to a number of excellent **restaurants**, there are numerous shops along the waterfront selling the *loukoúmia* (Turkish delight), *mandoláta* (nougat) and *halvadhópita* (soft nougat between disc-shaped wafers) for which the island is famed.

**Archontariki tis Maritsas** Roïdi 8. One block east of the main platía, next to *Stin Ithaki*. Very popular rustic taverna tucked away on a side street behind the port. Serves local specialities, including a casserole of mushrooms and ham baked in cheese.

**Daidadi** Platía Papágou. Home-made Italian-style ice cream – possibly the best in the Cyclades.

**La Dolce Vita** Filíni. One of the best, though not the cheapest, restaurants on the island, it occupies a nice spot on steps just north of the ferries. Serves creative Greek-Italian fusion cooking. Closed Sun.

**Gefsis Egeou** Vokotópoulou. Good-value taverna ("Taste of the Aegean"), near the Emboriki bank,

serving Greek food with some decent vegetarian options.

**Stin Ithaki tou Ai** Stefánou. Welcoming taverna on a small bougainvillea-covered street, serving traditional local dishes such as fried tomatoes, as well as a good *souvláki*.

**Thalami** Just off Platía Tsiropína. Top-notch seafood restaurant in a splendid nineteenth-century villa right on the water's edge and with views of Vapória.

**Yiannena** Platía Kanári. Popular, friendly spot, next to the *Hermes* hotel, with a French bistro feel. Serves great seafood and other Greek standards.

### Nightlife

Sýros still honours its contribution to the development of **rebétika**; *bouzoúki*-great Markos Vamvakaris hailed from here, and a platía in Áno Sýros has been named after him on which there is a tiny, sporadically open **museum** in his honour. **Taverna-clubs**, with music at weekends, now take their place beside a batch of more conventional disco-clubs, and there are several other (often expensive) *bouzoúki* bars scattered around the island, mostly strung along routes to beach resorts (see posters and local press for details). The eastern seafront has a rash of lively **bars** in apparent competition for the title of trendiest, but with little to choose between them.

**Agora** Platía Miaoúli. Pleasant, relaxed bar and club with large candlelit garden. Plays an eclectic mix of mostly traditional music to a chilled-out crowd.

**Capital** On waterfront past Platía Kanári. Lively club in the old Port Authority building.

**Casino Syrou** Opposite ferry dock. Large casino open till 6am for those who have money to burn (and are sufficiently well dressed).

**Piramatiko** Platía Miaoúli. Busy, sophisticated bar, playing a loud and varied mix from indie to house.

**Vento** On road to the airport. Huge dance club about 3km out of town which gets going around 4am. Take a taxi, but check it's open in town before heading out.

## Southern Sýros

The southern half of the island has gently rural scenery and a scattered series of pleasant, unpretentious beach resorts with comfortable accommodation. **Buses** ply the main loop road south (to Galissás, Fínikas, Mégas Yialós, Akhládi, Vári and Azólimno) hourly in high season, running until late.

## Galissás

The first stop, **GALISSÁS**, was formerly a village, but became popular with backpackers attracted by the island's best **campsite**, *Two Hearts* (☎22810 42052, ⓦwww.twohearts-camping.com). The site has good facilities and sends minibuses to most boats. There is also a surplus of **rooms**, which makes bargaining possible, and some bona fide hotels, including the *Semiramis* (☎22810 42067, ⓦwww .hotel-semiramis.com; B&B ❹), the *Françoise* (☎22810 42000, ⓦwww.francoise -hotel.com; B&B ❹), and the excellent *Benois* (☎22810 42833, ⓦwww.benois.gr; B&B ❹), with a beautiful pool and **internet** access. Self-catering rooms, around a small pool, are available at *Galissas Studios* (☎22810 42801, ⓦwww.galissas -studios.gr/com; ❸), who also have car and bike rental, and offer free port/airport transfers. Among the many **eating** choices, *To Iliovasilema*, next to *Benois*, is a small taverna with an inventive menu, and *Kavos*, part of a luxury complex, the *Dolphin Bay* hotel (☎22810 42924, ⓦwww.dolphin-bay.gr; April–Oct; B&B ❻), has impressive views overlooking the bay. If you feel the urge to escape, you can rent a scooter, or walk ten minutes around or over the southern headland to the small nudist beach of **Armeós**. A longer walk (1hr 15min plus) goes, rather steeply, over the ridge to the southeast and down to the **sea-cave** of Áyios Stéfanos containing a small church. Note that buses out can be erratically routed out of season; to be sure of making your connection you should wait at the Galissás high-road stop, not down by the beach.

## Fínikas

A rural forty-minute walk, a ten-minute bus ride south from Galissás brings you to the more mainstream resort of **FÍNIKAS**, purported to have been settled originally by the Phoenicians (although an alternative derivation could be from *fínikas* – "palm tree" in Greek). The **beach** is rather narrow and gritty, right next to the road but protected to some extent by a row of tamarisk trees; the pick of the **hotels** is the friendly *Cyclades* (☎22810 42255, ⓦwww.hotelcyclades.com; B&B ❹), with the reasonable *Kyma* taverna just in front. There are numerous rooms – and new homes development – to the southwest, behind Limanáki and towards Kókkina. The fish taverna *Barbalias* on the western seafront is recommended, and is opposite the bus stop and an **ATM**.

Fínikas is separated by a small headland from its neighbour **POSIDHONÍA** (or Delagrazzia after the local Madonna della Gratzia church), a nicer spot with some idiosyncratically ornate mansions and a bright-blue church right on the edge of the village. It's worth walking ten minutes further south, past the naval yacht club and its patrol boat, to **Agathopés**, with a sandy beach and a little islet, Skhinónisi, just offshore. **Komitó**, at the end of the road leading south from Agathopés, is little more than a stony beach fronting an olive grove. **Accommodation** around Posidhonía ranges from the smart *Possidonion* hotel (☎22810 42100, ⓦwww.syros-hotels.gr; ❹) on the northern seafront to basic rooms inland. *Meltemi*, on the road to Agathopés, is a good seafood **taverna**.

## The south coast

From Posidhonía the road swings southeast to **MÉGAS YIALÓS**, a diffuse, elongated resort. There are two beaches – the long, narrow eastern beach is lined with shady trees and there are pedal boats for hire. Accommodation behind the western beach includes the clean and comfortable *Mike and Bill's* (☎22810 43531, ⓦwww.syrosmikeandbill.gr; ❹) rooms, whilst the nearby *Alexandra* hotel (☎22810 42540, ⓦwww.hotelalexandra.gr; ❺) enjoys lovely views. The cove of **AKHLÁDHI** is family-friendly and boasts the small, good-value *Hotel Emily*

(☎22810 61400; ❹), on the seafront, and one taverna. **VÁRI**, just beyond, is more – though not much more – of a town, with its own small fishing fleet. Beach-goers, generally a younger crowd than on the other beaches, are very close to tavernas and **rooms** behind, but it is the most sheltered of the island's bays, something to remember when the *meltémi* is up. The beachfront *Kamelo* hotel (☎22810 61217, ❺lorian10@otenet.gr; B&B ❹) provides the best value, while the *En Plo* **beach bar** is a fun spot in season.

The final resort on the circular tour is **AZÓLIMNO**, accessed by a narrow road from Vári, or a wider one from the northern end. A small beach with tamarisk trees is overlooked by **studios**, such as *Armenaki* (☎22810 61810, ❺armen954@otenet.gr; ❹) near the southern end of the bay, or the *Hotel Santa Maria* (☎22810 61803, ❿www.users.hol.gr/~santamaria/; ❹) inland on the northwest exit road. For eating, try the fish **taverna** *Papagiannis* just behind the beach.

## Northern Sýros

Closest to the capital, and a few kilometres north of Galissás, and reached by bus in twenty minutes (hourly in high season), is the twin-beach coastal settlement of **KÍNI**. Good accommodation can be found at the *Sunset Hotel* (☎22810 71211, ❺enxensyr@otenet.gr; ❸), with the excellent *Zalounis* taverna just below. **Dhelfíni**, just to the north, is also a fine pebbly beach, dramatically accessed on a coastal path, or longer, inland road.

Further to the north, the land is barren and high, with few settlements. The main route north from Áno Sýros is quite easily negotiable by bike, provided you don't mind the hills; en route, the village of **Mýtikas** has a decent taverna just off the road. A few kilometres further on, the road forks, with the left turn leading, after another left, to the small hamlet of **Sýringas**, below which is the interesting Lendínos cave (45min walk). Straight on leads to **Kámbos**, where there's another cave, Mendóni, near the path leading down to Liá beach; the right fork eventually descends to the northeast coast and the early-Cycladic cemetery at **Halandhrianí**. Most of the finds from the nineteenth-century excavation of the site are now in Athens, though there is still an unexcavated settlement here. On **Kastrí** hill, to the north, are the remains of one of the Cyclades' most ancient fortified habitations dating from the third millennium BC.

# Páros and Andíparos

With a gentle and undramatic landscape arranged around the single peak of Profítis Ilías, **Páros** has a little of everything one expects from a Greek island: old villages, monasteries, fishing harbours, a labyrinthine capital, nice beaches and varied nightlife. Parikía, the capital, is a major hub of inter-island ferry services, so that if you wait long enough you can get to just about any island in the Aegean. However, the island can be touristy and expensive, and it can be more difficult finding rooms and beach space here in August, when the other settlements, the port of **Náoussa** and the satellite island of **Andíparos**, handle the overflow. The August 15 festival here is one of the best such observances in Greece, with a parade of flare-lit fishing boats and fireworks delighting as many Greeks as foreigners, though it's a real feat to secure accommodation around this time.

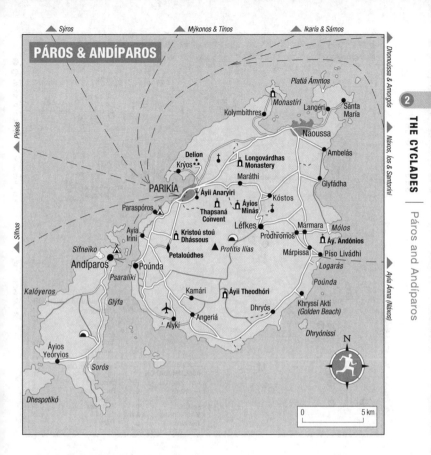

## Parikía and around

Bustling **PARIKÍA** sets the tone architecturally for the rest of Páros, its ranks of typically Cycladic white houses punctuated by the occasional Venetian-style building and church domes.

### Arrival and information

**Ferries** dock in Parikía by the windmill; the **bus station** is 100m or so to the right (west). Bus routes extend to Náoussa in the north, Poúnda (for Andíparos) in the west, Alykí in the south and Dhryós on the island's east coast (with another very useful service between Dhryós and Náoussa). Be aware that there are two places called Poúnda on Páros, one being the west-coast port, the other a beach on the way to east-coast Dhryós (see p.177). Buses to Náoussa carry on running hourly through the night in high season, while other services stop around midnight. The small **airport**, with domestic flights to Athens, is around 12km south of town, close to Alykí.

    **Motorbikes** are common and are available for rent at several places in town; **car rental** is available from European (℡22840 21771, ⓦwww.paroscars.de) and Avant Travel (℡22840 22302, ⓦwww.europcar-paros.com), on the western and eastern waterfronts respectively. Driving and parking rules are enforced:

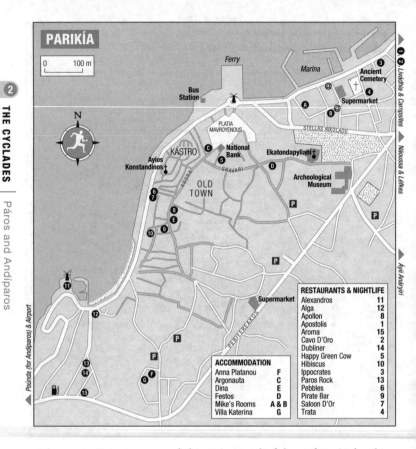

PARIKÍA

0    100 m

N

Ferry

Marina

Bus
Station

Ancient
Cemetery

Supermarket

PLATIA
MAVROYENOUS

KÁSTRO

National
Bank

STELLAS NIKOLAOU

Ayios
Konstandinos †

GRAVARI

Ekatondapyliani †

OLD
TOWN

Archeological
Museum

AGORA

Supermarket

PERIFEREAKOS

Pounda (for Andíparos) & Airport

① ② Livádhia & Campsites
Náoussa & Léfkes
Ávii Anáryiri

**RESTAURANTS & NIGHTLIFE**

| | |
|---|---|
| Alexandros | 11 |
| Alga | 12 |
| Apollon | 8 |
| Apostolis | 1 |
| Aroma | 15 |
| Cavo D'Oro | 2 |
| Dubliner | 14 |
| Happy Green Cow | 5 |
| Hibiscus | 10 |
| Ippocrates | 3 |
| Paros Rock | 13 |
| Pebbles | 6 |
| Pirate Bar | 9 |
| Saloon D'Or | 7 |
| Trata | 4 |

**ACCOMMODATION**

| | |
|---|---|
| Anna Platanou | F |
| Argonauta | C |
| Dina | E |
| Festos | D |
| Mike's Rooms | A & B |
| Villa Katerina | G |

various streets are one-way, and the western end of the seafront is closed to traffic during summer evenings.

Polos Tours, left of the windmill, is one of the more friendly **travel agencies**, issuing air tickets for Olympic, and acting as agents for virtually all the boats. Luggage can be left at various travel agents (look for the signs) along the water-front. There are **internet** cafés: *Marina* on the waterfront, and *Planet Café*, near *Mike's Rooms*.

Continue inland from the **windmill** past the taxi station to reach **Platía Mavroyénous (Ethnikís Andístasis)**, around which you'll find a maze of houses – designed to thwart both the wind and pirates – and the telephone office, police station and banks.

### Accommodation

You'll be met off the ferry by locals offering **accommodation**, even at the most unlikely hours, although you'll have to be quick to grab a room in summer. Many rooms and hotels are to the left of the windmill, and some can be a long walk. Of the two **campsites** nearest to town, *Koula Camping* (☎22840 22081, ⓦwww.campingkoula.gr; April–Oct), 900m along the seafront east of the bus stop, is a reasonable choice for a night or two, with a seasonal café-restaurant and mini-bungalows (**❶**), whilst *Krios Camping* (**☎**22840 21705, **Ⓦ**www.krios-camping.gr), across the bay to the north, has a nice beach, a pool and a regular minibus into town.

**Anna Platanou** 800m southwest of the port **☎**22840 21751, **Ⓦ**www.annaplatanou.gr. This smart, family-run hotel has clean refurbished rooms with kettles. Ten-percent discount for Rough Guide readers. The family also have larger studios, and apartments at the junction of the Alykí-Poúnda roads. Port transfers available. April–Oct. **❹**

**Argonauta** Corner of Platía Mavroyénous near the National Bank **☎**22840 21440, **Ⓦ**www.argonauta .gr. Friendly hotel, refurbished in 2007, with smart rooms arranged around a beautiful courtyard. There is a good restaurant underneath. April–Oct. **❹**

**Dina** Ágora, opposite Ayía Triádha church **☎**22840 21325, **Ⓦ**www.hoteldina.com. Pleasant, central little hotel set in a quiet spot. May–Oct. **❸**

**Festos** Grávari, west of Ekatondapyliani **☎**22840 21635, **Ⓔ**consolas@hol.gr. Friendly hostel with clean doubles and communal courtyard on a quiet backstreet inland. B&B **❸**

**Mike's Rooms** Opposite ferry dock **☎**22840 22856, **Ⓦ**www.roomsmike.com. Clean, comfortable studios and hospitable staff. Mike – a tirelessly enthusiastic source of information and assistance – has further accommodation, including very nice studios near Dhelfíni beach. Credit cards taken. **❹**

**Villa Katerina** Next door to *Anna Platanou* **☎**22840 21864, **Ⓦ**www.villakaterina.gr. Bright, family-friendly doubles, studios and apartments in a peaceful location. **❹**

## The Town

Just beyond the central clutter of the ferry port, to the southeast of the windmill, Parikía has one of the most architecturally interesting churches in the Aegean – the **Ekatondapyliani**, or "The One Hundred Gated". What's visible today was designed and supervised by Isidore of Miletus in the sixth century, but construction was actually carried out by his pupil Ignatius. Legend tells that it was so beautiful on completion that the master, consumed with jealousy, grappled with the apprentice on the rooftop and both fell to their deaths. They are portrayed kneeling at the column bases across the courtyard, the old master tugging at his beard in repentance and his rueful pupil clutching a broken head. The church was substantially altered after a severe earthquake in the eighth century, but its essentially Byzantine aspect remains, its shape an imperfect Greek cross. Enclosed by a great front wall to protect its icons from pirates, it is in fact three interlocking churches; the oldest, the chapel of Áyios Nikólaos to the left of the apse, is an adaptation of a pagan building dating from the early fourth century BC. To the right of the courtyard, the **Byzantine museum** (daily 10am–2pm & 6–9pm; €2) displays a collection of icons. Behind Ekatondapyliani, the **archeological museum** (Tues–Sun 8am–3pm; €3) has a fair collection of antique bits and pieces, its prize exhibits a fifth-century winged Nike and a piece of the Parian Chronicle, a social and cultural history of Greece up to 264 BC engraved in marble.

On the seafront near the marina are the exposed, excavated ruins of an **ancient cemetery** used from the eighth century BC until the third century AD; all around the bay and within 1km of the seafront is a sprinkling of **archeological sites** from the ancient city, including the ruins of a Hellenistic sculpture and pottery workshop, a Delion Apollo sanctuary, and some fragmentary mosaics (at the start of the Áyii Anáryiri road).

These sights apart, the real attraction of Parikía is simply to wander the town itself, especially along the meandering **old market street**, Agorá, and adjoining Grávari. Arcaded lanes lead past Venetian-influenced villas, traditional island dwellings, ornate wall-fountains and trendy shops. The town culminates in a seaward Venetian **kástro** (1260), whose surviving east wall incorporates a fifth-century BC round tower and is constructed using masonry pillaged from a nearby temple of Athena. Part of the temple's base is still visible next to the beautiful, arcaded church of Áyios Konstandínos and Ayía Eléni which crowns the highest point, from where the fortified hill drops sharply to the quay in a series of hanging gardens.

## Eating

Most of the **eating** establishments in Parikía are along the waterfront to the west of the windmill. The Parian Products Farmers' Union, near the police station, is a lovely wine and cheese shop perfect for stocking up for a beach picnic, while the Ragousis Bakery, behind the National Bank, is a good place for sandwiches and pastries. For snacks, there is a cluster of fast-food outlets near the ferry dock, whilst hidden in the backstreets, and along the seafront to the west, there are plenty of small crêperies and cafés.

**Apollon** Off Ágora. Set in a converted 1920s olive press on the tiny backstreets near the market, this is one of the island's best restaurants. Considering its popularity, its prices are reasonable.

**Apostolis** Livádhia seafront. Popular, well-priced, unpretentious seafood taverna, metres from the beach, with good food.

**Aroma** Perifereakós (ring-road). Greek and local dishes, expertly prepared and available to be chosen in the kitchen. The *Siroco's* supermarket next door has a remarkably extensive international selection of alcohol.

**Cavo D'Oro** Livádhia seafront, just north of the stream-bridge. Italian restaurant with a large choice of wood-oven pizza and pasta near *Koula Camping*. They also do takeaway.

**Happy Green Cow** On the side street behind the National Bank. Remarkably eclectic vegetarian (and chicken) restaurant. Not cheap, but very imaginative, with unexpected ingredients.

**Hibiscus** On waterfront south of windmill. One of the oldest restaurants on the island, it serves generous-sized, wood-oven-baked pizzas in a great spot overlooking the sea.

**Ippocrates** On seafront beyond ancient cemetery. Great-value taverna specializing in fresh seafood.

**Trata** Behind ancient cemetery. Family-run taverna serving tasty seafood and grilled meats on a vine-covered patio.

## Nightlife

Parikía has a wealth of **pubs**, **bars** and low-key **discos**. The most popular cocktail bars extend along the seafront, mostly to the south of the windmill, tucked into a series of open squares and offering staggered "happy hours", so that you can drink cheaply for much of the evening, and there are music clubs along the riverbed street at the western end of the seafront. There's also a thriving cultural centre, Archilochos (near Ekatondapylianí), which caters mostly to local artwork exhibitions, but which has occasional **film** screenings – there are also two open-air cinemas, Neo Rex and Paros, where foreign films are shown in season.

**Alexandros** Southern end of quay. A reasonably-priced choice for a sophisticated evening drink in a fabulously romantic spot around a windmill. Wonderful sunset views.

**Alga** Seafront south of windmill. Hip dance bar further along the bay with outdoor seating and DJs playing anything from R&B and house to seventies rock.

**Dubliner/Paros Rock** Just off seafront. Large, brash dance complex set back from the main drag, comprising four loud bars, a snack section, disco and seating area.

**Pebbles** Seafront south of windmill. Upstairs bar playing classical and lounge music, with good sunset views.

**Pirate Bar** One block inland from seafront. Popular, established jazz and blues bar near the town hall.

**Saloon D'Or** Seafront south of windmill. Rowdy but fun spot on the main drag, with cheap drinks and mainstream music.

## Around Parikía

If you're staying in Parikía, you'll want to get out at some stage, if only to the beach. The shortest **excursion** is the 2.5km along the road starting from the northern end of the ring-road, up to the **Áyii Anáryiri** monastery. Perched on the bluff above town, this makes a great picnic spot, with cypress groves, a gushing fountain and some splendid views.

The **beaches** immediately north and south of the harbour are not among Páros's best. In fact, you might prefer to avoid the northern stretch altogether and walk **south** along the asphalt road instead. The first unsurfaced side-track leads to the small, sheltered Dhelfíni beach; fifteen minutes further on is **PARASPÓROS**, with an attractively landscaped and relatively quiet **campsite** (☎22840 21100) and beach near the remains of an ancient temple to Asklepios, the god of healing and son of Apollo. Continuing for 45 minutes (or a short hop by bus) brings you to arguably the best of the bunch, **AYÍA IRÍNI**, with good sand and a taverna next to a farm and shady olive grove.

In the same general direction, but a much longer two-hour haul each way, is **PETALOÚDHES**, the "Valley of the Butterflies", a walled-in private oasis where millions of Jersey tiger moths perch on the foliage in early summer (June–Sept 9am–1pm & 4–8pm; €3). The trip can be combined with a visit to the eighteenth-century nunnery of **Khristoú stoú Dhássous** (Áyios Arsenios), at the crest of a ridge 1km to the north. Only women are allowed in the sanctuary, although men can wait in the courtyard. The succession of narrow roads and donkey paths linking both places begins just south of Parikía. Petaloúdhes can also be reached from Parikía by bus (in summer) or on an overpriced excursion by mule.

## The southwest of the island

There's little to stop for southwest of Parikía until **POÚNDA**, 6km away. Here you can catch the **ferry to Andíparos** (see p.178) or try the watersports: Paros Kite Pro Center (☎22840 92229, ⓦwww.paroskite-procenter .com) offers all levels of kitesurfing and equipment rental, while Paros Dive (☎6976 738687, ⓦwww.parosdive.com) offers PADI courses. The small **airport** is further south, on the road to **ALYKÍ**, a resort on a pretty bay with two sections of beach. Hotels include the friendly, beachfront *Galatis* (☎22840 91355, ⓦwww.galatishotel.com; April–Nov; B&B ❺) with pool, restaurant and (mostly) sea-view rooms. Near the airport is the private Skorpios Cycladic Folk Museum (May–Sept, 10am–2pm; free) with a collection of model boats and reconstructions of various Parian buildings.

## Náoussa and around

The second port of Páros, **NÁOUSSA**, is a decent alternative to Parikía, popular with a laid-back younger crowd. Although a major resort town, with modern concrete hotels and attendant trappings, it has developed around a charming little port where fishermen tenderize octopuses by thrashing them against the walls, and you can wander among winding, narrow alleys and simple Cycladic houses. The local **festivals** – an annual Fish and Wine Festival on July 2, and an August 23 commemoration of a naval victory over the Turks – are still celebrated with enthusiasm, the latter sometimes brought forward to coincide with the August 15 festival of the Panayía. Most people are here for the local beaches (see p.176) and relaxed nightlife; there's really only one cultural attraction, a **museum** (daily 9am–1.30pm & 7–9pm; free) in the monastery of Áyios Athanásios, with an interesting collection of Byzantine and post-Byzantine icons from the churches and monasteries around Náoussa. To the east, at Áyii Anáryiri, the Moraïtis **winery** (Mon–Sat, 9am–3pm; ⓦwww.paroswine.gr) is open for tours and tasting.

The town is more fashionable than Parikía, and accommodation can be expensive. Nissiotissa Tours (℡22840 51480), off the left side of the main square, specializes in transport but can help you find a room. On the western side, the *Sea House* (℡22840 52198, ⓦwww.seahouse.gr; ❺), on the rocks above Pipéri beach, was the first place in Náoussa to let **rooms** and has one of the best locations. If you don't mind a five-minute climb, family-run *Katerina Rooms* (℡22840 51642, ⓦwww.katerinastudios.gr; ❹) have beautiful uninterrupted sea views. Out of season you should haggle for reduced prices at the basic but well-located *Stella* (℡22840 51317, ⓦwww.hotelstella.gr; ❹), with rooms arranged around its own garden, several blocks inland from the old harbour. Most elegant is the spotlessly cool boutique **hotel** *Heaven* (℡22840 51549, ⓦwww.heaven-naoussa.gr; B&B ❺), which is also set back away from the harbour. Further eastwards along the bay is the peaceful *Captain Dounas* (℡22840 52525, ⓦwww.dounas.com; B&B ❼), with studios and large family-friendly apartments and a pool. A good-value **hostel**, the *Young Inn* (℡6942 834911, ⓦwww.young-inn.com; from €8 per bed), behind the main church, has **internet** facilities. There are a couple of **campsites** outside town, including the *Surfing Beach Village* at Sánta María, northeast of Náoussa; it runs courtesy minibuses to and from Parikía.

Most of the harbour **tavernas** are reasonable, specializing in fresh fish and seafood, though there are more varied menus in the places along the main road leading inland from just beside the little bridge over the canal, such as *Vengera* on the main square and *Open Garden* near the bus stop. There are some excellent **bars** clustered around the old harbour, making bar-hopping easy: *Linardo* and *Agosta* play dance music, whilst *Café del Mar* has one of the best settings with its busy tables stretching out to the edge of the sea. Nearby *Shark* is another recommended spot. There are several big clubs up from the bus station, including *Vareladikos,* popular with a younger, late-night crowd. Once a week in summer, hordes of people take the 3.30am bus to the *Beach Bar* at *Sánta María Camping* for a weekly beach party – keep an eye out for flyers.

### Local beaches

**Pipéri beach** is a couple of minutes' walk west of Náoussa's harbour; there are other good-to-excellent beaches within walking distance, and a summer *kaïki* service to connect them for about €6 round trip. To the northwest, 4km on the road around the bay brings you to **Kolymbíthres**, where there are three tavernas and the wind- and sea-sculpted rock formations from which the place draws its name. A few minutes beyond, **Monastíri beach**, below the abandoned Pródhromos monastery, is similarly attractive, and partly gay/nudist. If you go up the hill after Monastíri onto the rocky promontory, the island gradually shelves into the sea via a series of flattish rock ledges, making a fine secluded spot for diving and snorkelling, as long as the sea is calm. Go northeast of town and the sands are better still: the barren Viglákia headland is dotted with good surfing beaches. Eastern **Langéri** is backed by dunes and **Platiá Ámmos** perches on the northeastern tip of the island. The best surfing is at **Sánta María**, a trendy beach 6km by road from Náoussa: *Surfing Beach Village* (℡22840 52491, ⓦwww.surfbeach.gr; ❹) offers camping, bungalows, diving and windsurfing, while Surfistas (℡694 6506340, ⓦwww.surfistas.gr) offers board rental and windsurfing. The beach has a couple of tavernas, including the pleasant *Aristofanes.*

## The east coast

**AMBELÁS** hamlet, a few kilometres southeast of Náoussa, marks the start of a longer trek down the **east coast**. Ambelás itself has a good beach, a small taverna and some rooms and hotels, of which the *Hotel Christiana* (☎22840 51573, ⓦwww.christianahotel.gr; ❹) is good value, with great fresh fish and local wine in the restaurant and extremely friendly proprietors; they have both rooms and apartments. From here a rough track leads south, passing several undeveloped stretches on the way; after about an hour you reach **Mólos beach**, impressive and not particularly crowded. **MÁRMARA**, twenty minutes further on, has some rooms to let and makes an attractive place to stay, though the marble that the village is built from and named after has largely been whitewashed over. If Mármara doesn't appeal, then serene **MÁRPISSA**, just to the south – a maze of winding alleys and ageing archways overhung by floral balconies, all clinging precariously to the hillside – might. *Afendakis* (☎22840 41141, ⓦwww.hotel-afendakis.gr; ❹) has clean, modern rooms and apartments, and you can while away a spare hour climbing up the conical Kéfalos hill, on whose fortified summit the last Venetian lords of Páros were overpowered by the Ottomans in 1537. Today the monastery of **Áyios Andónios** occupies the site, but the grounds are locked (the key may be available in Márpissa before setting out). The largest resort on this coast, **PÍSO LIVÁDHI**, was once a quiet fishing village, but is now dominated by package-holiday facilities; the main reason to visit is to catch a (seasonal) *kaïki* to Ayía Ánna on Náxos. *Hotel Andromachi* (☎22840 41387; B&B ❸) is a good place behind the beach, as is the *Akteon Hotel* (☎22840 41873, 🅵22840 41733; ❹) at the tamarisk-shaded **Logarás beach** next door, or ask at the friendly Perantinos Travel Agency (☎22840 41135) near the bus stop. For a meal try *Vrochas* **taverna**, and head to the *Anchorage* café/bar for afternoon snacks or night-time cocktails.

Between here and Dhryós to the south are several sandy coves – Tzirdhákia, Mezádha and Poúnda (not to be confused with the port of the same name on the opposite coast) – prone to pummelling by the *meltémi*, yet all favoured to varying degrees by campers and windsurfers. Also among these, **KHRYSSÍ AKTÍ** (Golden Beach) now has many tavernas, room complexes and hotels, such as the *Golden Beach Hotel*, right on the beach (☎22840 41366, ⓦwww.goldenbeach.gr; April–Oct; B&B ❺), with large rooms and apartments, watersports, and a restaurant supplied by their own farm. There are tavernas at Logarás, but other facilities are concentrated in **DHRYÓS**, the focal point of this part of the island and the last settlement of any size. Aside from an abundant water supply and surrounding orchards, the village is mostly modern and characterless, lacking even a well-defined platía. You'd do better to follow the signs to the attractive, and relatively quiet Dhryós beach, just behind which are the pleasant *Tarsa* (☎22840 41170, ⓦwww.parosweb.gr/tarsa/; May–Oct; ❹) studios.

## The inland villages

The road runs west from Píso Livádhi back to the capital. A **medieval flagstoned path** once linked both sides of the island, and parts of it survive in the east between Mármara and the villages around Léfkes. **PRÓDHROMOS**, encountered first, is an old fortified farming settlement with defensive walls girding its nearby monastery, while **LÉFKES** itself, an hour up the track, is perhaps the most unspoilt settlement on Páros. The town, whose name means "poplars", flourished from the seventeenth century on, its population swollen by refugees fleeing from coastal piracy; indeed it was the island's capital during most of the Ottoman period. Léfkes's marbled alleyways and amphitheatrical setting are unparalleled – and undisturbed by motorbikes, which are forbidden in the middle of town. The central **church** that dominates the town's landscape is made largely of local marble and contains an impressive collection of icons, though it is usually closed; the views over the hill-hugging cemetery behind it and across the interior to the sea are some of the best on the island. Despite the few rooms, a disco (*Akrovatis*), a taverna on the outskirts and the presence of the *Lefkes Village* (☎22840 41827, ⓦwww.lefkesvillage.gr; ➐), a beautiful, oversized hotel with stunning views – the area around the main square has steadfastly resisted change; the central *kafenío* and bakery observe their siestas religiously, and the reserved local residents seem happy for tourists to remain along the coastal resorts.

Thirty minutes further on, through olive groves, the path reaches **KÓSTOS**, a simple village and a good place for lunch in a taverna. Any traces of path disappear at **MARÁTHI**, from where Parian marble was supplied to much of Europe. Considered second only to Carrara marble, the last slabs were mined here by the French in the nineteenth century for Napoleon's tomb. Just east of the village, marked paths lead to two huge entrances of **ancient marble mines**. From Maráthi, it's easy enough to pick up the bus on to Parikía, but if you want to continue hiking, strike south for the monastery of **Áyios Minás**, twenty minutes away. Various Classical and Byzantine masonry fragments are worked into the walls of this sixteenth-century foundation, and the friendly custodians can put you on the right track up to the convent of **Thapsaná**, 4km from Parikía. From here, other paths lead either back to Parikía (two hours altogether from Áyios Minás), or on up to the island's 762m summit for views over the Cyclades.

## Andíparos

**Andíparos** is no longer a secret destination: the waterfront is lined with new hotels and apartments, and in high season it can be full, though in recent years families have displaced the former young, international crowd. However, the island has retained its friendly small-island atmosphere and has a lot going for it, including good sandy beaches and a remarkable cave; also, rooms and hotels are less expensive than on Páros. To the northeast, between Páros and Andíparos, is the tiny islet of Sáliangos, significant as the oldest known site of human settlement (4300–3700 BC) in the Cyclades.

Most of the population of one thousand live in the large low-lying northern town, across the narrow straits from Páros, the new development on the outskirts concealing an attractive traditional settlement around the *kástro*. A long, flagstoned pedestrian street forms its backbone, leading from the jetty to the Cycladic houses around the outer wall of the *kástro*, which was built by Leonardo Loredano in the 1440s as a fortified settlement safe from pirate raids – the Loredano coat of arms can still be seen on a house in the courtyard. The only way into the courtyard is through a pointed archway from the *platía*, where several cafés are shaded by a giant eucalyptus. Inside, more whitewashed houses surround two churches and a cistern built into the surviving base of the central tower.

Andíparos's **beaches** begin right outside town: **Psaralíki**, just to the south with golden sand and tamarisks for shade, is much better than Sifnéïko (aka "Sunset") on the opposite side of the island. Villa development is starting to follow the surfaced road down the east coast, but has yet to get out of hand. **Glýfa**, 4km down, is another good beach and, in the southeast of the island, **Sorós beach** is seeing increasing development of rooms and tavernas, but still has plenty of space. On the southwest coast there are some fine small sandy coves at **Áyios Yeóryios**, the end of the road, and another long stretch of sand at **Kalóyeros**. *Kaïkia* make daily trips round the island and, less frequently, to the uninhabited but archeologically rich island of Dhespotikó, opposite Áyios Yeóryios.

The great **cave** (summer daily 10.45am–3.45pm; €3) in the south of the island is the chief attraction for day-trippers. In these eerie chambers the Marquis de

▲ Great cave, Andíparos

Nointel, Louis XIV's ambassador to Constantinople, celebrated Christmas Mass in 1673 while a retinue of five hundred, including painters, pirates, Jesuits and Turks, looked on; at the exact moment of midnight explosives were detonated to emphasize the enormity of the event. Although electric light and cement steps have diminished its mystery and grandeur, the cave remains impressive. Tour buses (€3 round trip) and public buses (€1 one-way) run from the port every hour in season; bus services and opening hours are reduced out of season, and in winter you'll have to fetch the key for the cave from the mayor or village council (☎22840 61218).

## Practicalities

To get here, you have a choice of **boats** from Parikía (hourly in season, weather permitting; 40min), arriving at the jetty opposite the main street, or the car ferry from Poúnda (every 30min; 10min), arriving 150m to the south.

There are plenty of **hotels** along the waterfront, including *Anargyros* (☎22840 61204; ❸), which has good, basic rooms. Of the more upmarket places to the north of the jetty, *Mantalena* (☎22840 61206, ⓦwww.hotelmantalena.gr; ❹–❺) offers large rooms and balconies – plus some apartments in the old town – while *Artemis* (☎22840 61460, ⓦwww.artemisantiparos.com; ❻) has spotless contemporary studios and apartments. Inland there are some cheaper rooms, as well as the *Hotel Galini* (☎22840 61420; ❸) to the left of the main street. The popular **campsite** (☎22840 61221) is a ten-minute walk northeast along a track, next to its own nudist beach; the water here is shallow enough for campers to wade across to the neighbouring islet of Dhipló. At the southwestern tip of the island, **Áyios Yeóryios** is laid out behind a long, mostly narrow stretch of beach on a huge grid plan for a resort development that never really happened. For peace and quiet, try the *Delfini* (☎22840 24506, ⓦwww.dolphinantiparos.gr; May–Oct; ❹) studios and apartments, which have large verandas and a café for breakfast or lunch. Of the area's several tavernas, seafront *Captain Pipinos* is recommended – the owner runs boat trips across to the Dhespotikó beaches opposite.

The best of Andíparos town's waterfront **tavernas** is *Anargyros*, below the hotel of the same name. The main street leads up beside it; *Klimataria*, 100m inland off to the left, has tables in a pleasant garden, though it's only open at night. There are plenty of **bars** around the eucalyptus-filled platía, where a festive atmosphere prevails at night. *Café Margarita* is a pleasant street-side hangout on the way up to the platía, while the *Nautica* is probably the liveliest of the waterfront spots. For quiet music and views of the mountains try *Yam*, an outdoor restaurant and bar near the *Klimataria*. A **bank**, a **post office**, a cinema and several **travel agents** cluster around the waterfront, and there's a launderette near the windmill. You can rent scooters and **bicycles** at Europcar near the ferry dock. Blue Island Divers (T22840 61493, Wwww.blueisland-divers.gr) on the main street, offer **diving** courses around Andíparos, including snorkelling trips.

# Náxos

**Náxos** is the biggest and most fertile of the Cyclades, with the second largest (and youngest) population. With its green and mountainous highland scenery, it seems immediately distinct from its neighbours. The difference is accentuated by the **unique architecture** of many of the interior villages: the Venetian Duchy of the Aegean, which ruled from 1204 to 1537, left towers and fortified mansions scattered throughout the island, while medieval Cretan refugees bestowed a singular character upon Náxos's eastern settlements.

Today Náxos could easily support itself without tourists by relying on its production of potatoes, olives, grapes and lemons, but it has thrown in its lot with mass tourism, so that parts of the island are now almost as busy as Páros in season. The island has plenty to see if you know where to look: the highest mountains in the Cyclades, intriguing central valleys, a spectacular north coast and long, marvellously sandy beaches in the southwest. It is also renowned for its wines, cheese – sharp *kefalotýri* and milder *graviéra* – and *kítron*, a sweet liqueur available in green, yellow or clear, distilled from the leaves of this citrus tree.

## Náxos Town

A long causeway, built to protect the harbour to the north, connects the town with the islet of Palátia – the place where, according to legend, Theseus was duped by Dionysos into abandoning Ariadne on his way home from Crete. The famous stone **Portára** that has greeted visitors for 2500 years is the portal of a temple of Apollo, built on the orders of the tyrant Lygdamis around 530 BC, but never completed.

Initial impressions suggest that most of the town's life occurs down by the crowded port esplanade or just behind it; a vast network of backstreets and low-arched narrow alleys lead up through the old town, Boúrgos, to the fortified **kástro** from where Marco Sanudo, the thirteenth-century Venetian who established the Duchy of the Aegean, and his successors, ruled over the Cyclades. However, there is a second, more modern, centre of activity to the south, around the main square, Platía Evripéou (aka "Court Square"), with more tavernas, shops, car and bike rentals, and numerous internet cafés.

### Arrival and information

Náxos is served by a tiny **airport**, located among salt marshes and lagoons just a few-minutes' bus ride south from Náxos Town. Large **ferries** dock along the northern harbour pier; all small boats and the useful *Express Skopelitis* ferry use

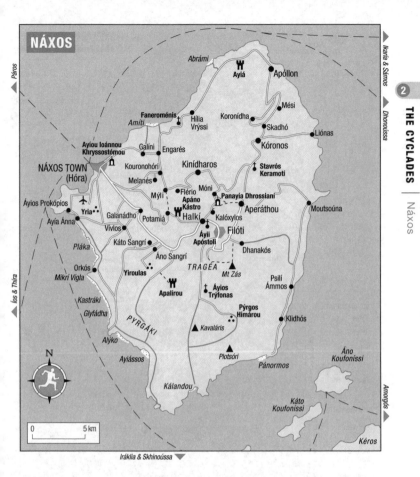

**NÁXOS**

Páros

Ikaría & Sámos

Dhonoússa

Ios & Thíra

Amorgós

Abrámi

Ayiá

Apóllon

Mési

Faneroménis

Hília
Vrýssi

Koronídha

Skadhó

Liónas

Amíti

Galíni

Engarés

Kóronos

Ayíou Ioánnou
Khryssostómou

Kinídharos

Stavrós
Keramotí

NÁXOS TOWN
(Hóra)

Kouronohóri

Melanés

Móni

Ayios Prokópios

Mýli

Flério

Panayía Dhrossianí

Apáno
Kástro

Aperáthou

Moutsoúna

Yría

Halkí

Kalóxylos

Ayía Ánna

Galanádho

Potamiá

Filóti

Vívlos

Pláka

Káto Sangrí

Áno Sangrí

Ayii
Apóstoli

Dhanakós

Orkós

Mikrí Vígla

Yíroulas

TRAGÉA

Mt Zás

Psilí
Ámmos

Kastráki

Apalírou

Ayios
Trýfonas

Glyfádha

Pýrgos
Himárou

Klidhós

PYRGÁKI

Kaváláris

Áno
Koufoníssi

Alýko

Ayiássos

Plotsóri

Pánormos

N

Káto
Koufoníssi

Kálandou

Kéros

0          5 km

Iráklia & Skhinoússa

the nearby jetty in the fishing harbour. The **bus station** is at the landward end of the main dock; buses run 2–5 times a day to the resort of Apóllon, with one of the morning services going via the Engarés-Abrámi route, which is much slower. There are 5–6 buses a day to Aperáthou via Filóti, two of these going on to Moutsoúna on the east coast in summer. Buses run (every 30min 7.30am–2am in summer, three times a day in winter) to Áyios Prokópios, Ayía Ánna and (summer only) beyond the Pláka campsite on Pláka beach, and 4–6 times a day (summer only) to Pyrgáki via Kastráki. Printed timetables are available from the bus station; tickets should be bought before you travel, from the station or nominated shops near the stops and validated in the onboard machine.

**Day-tours** of Náxos (€20) are more convenient and can be booked at **Naxos Tourist Information** (☎22850 25201), on the seafront near the jetty, which offers a wealth of information, accommodation advice, and somewhere to leave your bags (€1.50). Car, bike and cycle rental companies include Mike's (☎22850 24975, ⊛www.naxos-bikes.com) just south of Platía Evripéou. Iris Neubauer at **Naxos Horse Riding** (☎694 88 09 142) organizes three-hour trips in the area for all levels for around €45 per person.

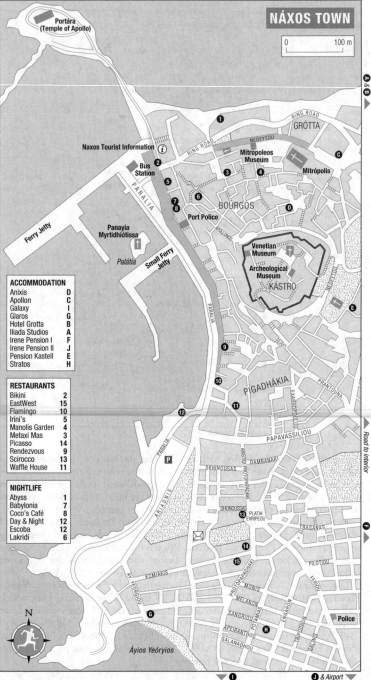

**NÁXOS TOWN**

0     100 m

Portára
(Temple of Apollo)

RING ROAD

GRÓTTA

NEOFYTOU

Naxos Tourist Information ⓘ

Mitropoleos
Museum

RING ROAD

Bus
Station

Mitrópolis

PARALIA

BOURGOS

Port Police

APOLLONOS

Ferry Jetty

Panayía
Myrtidhiótissa

Venetian
Museum

Palátia

Small Ferry
Jetty

Archeological
Museum

KÁSTRO

PARALIA

NEOFYTOU

**ACCOMMODATION**

| Anixis | D |
| Apollon | C |
| Galaxy | I |
| Glaros | G |
| Hotel Grotta | B |
| Iliada Studios | A |
| Irene Pension I | F |
| Irene Pension II | J |
| Pension Kastell | E |
| Stratos | H |

PIGADHÁKIA

PRANTOUNA

EXABBOPOULOU

**RESTAURANTS**

| Bikini | 2 |
| EastWest | 15 |
| Flamingo | 10 |
| Irini's | 5 |
| Manolis Garden | 4 |
| Metaxi Mas | 3 |
| Picasso | 14 |
| Rendezvous | 9 |
| Scirocco | 13 |
| Waffle House | 11 |

PAPAVASSILIOU

Road to interior

PARALIA

P

ARIADNIS

SKHINOUSAS

AGIOI PROTOPAPADAKI

DAMBANAKI

**NIGHTLIFE**

| Abyss | 1 |
| Babylonia | 7 |
| Coco's Café | 8 |
| Day & Night | 12 |
| Escoba | 12 |
| Lakridi | 6 |

DHONOUSSAS

PLATIA
EVRIPEOU

TRAGANAS

FILOTIOU

KOMIAKIS

PROTOPAPADAKI

MONIS

MELANON

FERIOU

ENGARON

TRIPODION

GALINIS

N

AV. YEORYOU

SANGRIOU

POTAMIAS

APEIRANTHOU

GALANADHOU

**Police**

Áyios Yeóryios

## Accommodation

There's plenty of **accommodation** in Náxos, and you should have no problem finding somewhere to stay. Once you've run the gauntlet of touts on the jetty, you would do well to head straight to Naxos Tourist Information (see p.181) who can book **rooms** for you, including at the owner's two hotels. There are three areas in town to look: the old quarter near the *kástro*, where they are hard to find and relatively expensive; up to the northeast of town in Grótta (which can be exposed to the wind); and the southern part of town between the main square, Evripéou, and Áyios Yeóryios beach, where they are most abundant and less expensive, but sometimes with significant night-time noise from clubs and discos. Parking immediately next to accommodation is not always possible.

Anixis Boúrgos ⊤22850 22932, ⓦwww .hotel-anixis.gr. Pleasant, smart rooms set around a garden near the *kástro*, with good views. Two larger studio apartments are also available here, and they have more studio accommodation at Áyios Yeóryios. April–Oct. ❸

Apollon South of Grótta ⊤22850 22468, ⓦwww .naxostownhotels.com. Comfortable, modern doubles, all with balconies, near the Mitropoleos Museum and convenient for the port. ❺

Galaxy Just south of town, near Áyios Yeóryios ⊤22850 22422, ⓦwww.hotel-galaxy.com. Upmarket hotel with pool and large modern rooms and studios with sea views and balconies. B&B ❼

Glaros Áyios Yeóryios ⊤22850 23101, ⓦwww .hotelglaros.com. Comfortable, stylish hotel at the quieter western end of the beach. Most rooms come with sea views, and have wi-fi (there is also an internet room). March–Oct. ❺

Hotel Grotta Kambanelli 7, Grótta ⊤22850 22215, ⓦwww.hotelgrotta.gr. Welcoming hotel in a good location, only a 5min walk from the waterfront.

Offers comfortable rooms, an indoor Jacuzzi, a generous breakfast and free wi-fi. B&B ❺

Iliada Studios Grótta ⊤22850 23303, ⓔiliada @otenet.gr. Quiet studio complex in Grótta on the cliff beyond town, with fabulous views out to sea. Parking. Easter–Oct. ❺

Irene I & II East and southeast of the main square ⊤22850 23169 or 69733 37782, ⓦwww .irenepension-naxos.com. Clean, spacious studios in two locations, the second with a nice pool and sundeck near Áyios Yeóryios. The friendly English-speaking proprietor, Stavros, will meet guests at the port and is an excellent source of information on the island. ❸

Pension Kastell Just south of the *kástro* ⊤22850 23082, ⓦwww.kastell.gr. Friendly pension offering pleasant rooms with balconies and a nice roof garden. Access to the port in 5min around the eastern side of the *kástro*. March–Oct. ❸

Stratos Sangríou ⊤22850 25898, ⓦwww .studios-stratos.com. Very comfortable, attractive studios in two units near Áyios Yeóryios. ❹

## The Town

Only two of the *kástro*'s original seven towers remain, though the **north gate** (approached from Apóllonos and known as the Traní Portá or "Great Gate"), beside the Kríspi (Glezos) tower, survives as a splendid example of a medieval fort entrance. A few of the Venetians' Catholic descendants still live in the old mansions that encircle the site, many with ancient coats of arms above the doorways. One mansion next to the Traní, the **Venetian Museum** (Domus Della-Rocca-Barozzi; daily 10am–3pm & 7–10pm, till 11pm in July–Aug; €5, student €3), is open to the public and offers the best views from the *kástro*, with concerts (see box, p.184); the guided tour includes a tasting from the family's wine cellar. They also offer a two-hour tour of the *kástro* at 11am Tuesday–Sunday in season; €15 includes entrance to all the *kástro* museums.

Catholic buildings in the *kástro* include a seventeenth-century Ursuline convent, and the cathedral, unsubtly restored but still displaying a thirteenth-century crest inside. Nearby was what was to become one of Ottoman Greece's first schools, the French Commercial School; opened by Jesuits in 1627 for Catholic and Orthodox students alike, its pupils included, briefly, Nikos Kazantzakis (see p.233 & p.660). The school building now houses an excellent **archeological museum** (Tues–Sun 8.30am–3pm; €3), with finds from Náxos, Koufoníssi, Kéros and

## Island music

One of the highlights of Náxos Town evenings are the **concerts** of classical, jazz, choral, Byzantine and traditional music held at the Venetian Museum (☏22850 22387, Ⓦwww.naxosisland.gr/venetianmuseum/) in either the garden or the basement, depending on the season and weather. The twice-weekly traditional music evenings feature local musicians, sometimes including bagpipe players, plus Naxian dancing and generous supplies of local wine, *raki* and *kítron*. Nikolaos Karavias, owner of the museum, is a keen proponent of the island folklore and a wonderfully enthusiastic host of the concerts, often leaping on stage himself to play the drums. Tickets should be bought in advance at the museum.

Dhonoússa, including an important collection of Early Cycladic figurines. Archaic and Classical sculpture and pottery dating from Neolithic to Roman times, as well as obsidian knives, spectacular gold rosettes from a tomb, and a large collection of Roman glass, are also on display, though labelling is sparse. On the outdoor terrace, a Hellenistic mosaic floor shows a nereid (sea nymph) surrounded by deer and peacocks. In the centre of the *kástro* are the plain stone remains of a rectangular tower, said to have been the residence of Marco Sanudo.

Further archeology is on view in the remains of the Mycenaean city, a few-minutes' walk east from the harbour. In front of the Orthodox cathedral, the **Mitropoleos Museum** (Tues–Sun 8.30am–3pm; free) has walkways over a recently excavated tumulus cemetery, from the thirteenth to eleventh century BC, with various funerary remnants including a *hermax*, a pile of the stones that were traditionally thrown behind on leaving a cemetery. In the general area, items dating from the early Cycladic period (3200 BC) right through to late Roman (500 AD) have been found.

For a panoramic view over the whole town (and distant Páros), a forty- to sixty-minute walk up from Grótta will take you to the fortified seventeenth-century **Ayíou Ioánnou Khrysostómou** nunnery (not open) on a rocky hillside to the east, with a short detour to the rock-hugging cave-church of **Áyios Ioánnis Theológos** ("Theologáki").

### Eating

The waterfront is crammed with places to **eat**, most of them reasonable. For picnics, there's a good bakery towards the southern end of the harbour front, while for local cheese, wine, *kítron*, spices and other dried foodstuffs, head for Tirokomika Proionia Naxou, a delightful old store on Papavassilíou.

Bikini Opposite ferry dock. This popular crêperie also serves good breakfasts and snacks. Ideal if you're waiting for a ferry.

EastWest Just off A. Protopapadháki, below Platía Evripéou. Extensive menu of well-prepard Indian and Thai food in a relaxed setting.

Flamingo Paralía. Upstairs taverna, with huge, well-priced menu and live traditional music several times a week (and subsequent extra cover charge).

Irini's Paralía. One of the best of the *mezedhopolía/* oven-food tavernas on the waterfront, with some imaginative salads.

Manolis Garden Boúrgos. Popular taverna, located in a large garden in the old town, with small but well-considered menu.

Metaxi Mas Boúrgos. Friendly ouzerí serving excellent, well-priced food on a little street heading up to the *kástro*.

Picasso A. Protopapadháki, southwest corner of Evripéou square. Popular Mexican restaurant, with some good vegetarian options, and another branch on Pláka beach. Evenings only.

Rendezvous Paralía. Busy waterfront café serving tasty cakes and coffee.

Scirocco Platía Evripéou. Well-known restaurant popular with locals and tourists alike for its good-value traditional meals, hence the occasional long queue to get in.

Waffle House Pigadhákia. Excellent, home-made, Italian-style ice cream, to eat in or takeaway. There is a summer branch at Pláka beach.

## Nightlife

Much of the evening action goes on at the south end of the waterfront, where you'll find **café–bars** and **clubs** jostling for business, luring people in with staggeringly huge menus of cheap cocktails. Should that fail to tempt, there's also an open-air **cinema**, the *Cine Astra*, on the road to the airport at the southern end of town; it's a fair walk out, but the Ayía Ánna bus stops here.

Abyss Road to Grótta. The town's biggest club, with dancing to European hits split over two floors.
Babylonia Náxos's first gay bar, discreetly situated on the upper-level of a waterfront building.
Coco's Café Good little cocktail spot on the water-front, playing South American music and serving breakfast through the day.
Day & Night Far southwest end of the harbour. Popular bar turning out European and, later, on

Greek, music every weekend on its packed veranda.
Escoba Just behind *Day & Night*, this place serves yet more great cocktails, and is a little larger, so less of a crush.
Lakridi A tiny jazz bar, which sometimes plays classical music, tucked away on a street behind the port police.

# The southwestern beaches

Of the **beaches** around Náxos Town, **Grótta**, just to the northeast, is easiest to reach; it's not ideal for sunbathing but, for swimmers, the remains of submerged Cycladic buildings are visible. The finest spots, though, are all **south** of town, with the entire southwestern coastline boasting a series of excellent **beaches** accessible in summer by regular buses. **ÁYIOS YEÓRYIOS**, a long sandy bay fringed by the town's southern accommodation area, is within walking distance. There's a line of cafés and tavernas at the northern end of the beach, and a **windsurfing** school: Flisvos Sportsclub (⊕22850 22935, ⊛www.flisvos -sportclub.com) arranges and teaches kitesurfing and windsurfing, and rents catamarans. There is a campsite further south, but there are far more attractive places to camp on Pláka beach (see p.186).

## Ayios Prokopios and Ayía Ánna

Buses take you to **ÁYIOS PROKÓPIOS** beach, a long line of sand with lagoons behind; the village has a southeastern part on the main road and bus route, and a separate western area 1.5km away at the base of the distinct double cone of Stelídha hill. There are plenty of basic tavernas, hotels and rooms, such as the *Adriana* (⊕22850 42804, ⊛www.adrianahotel.com; ❸) with pool, along the road towards Stelídha, as well as the very attractive *Hotel Lianos Village* (⊕22850 26366, ⊛www.lianosvillage.com; B&B ❻), also with pool, nearer to Stelídha. Two excellent traditional restaurants are *Anessio* and *Colosseo*, while the younger, funkier *Kahlua* and *Splash* are good cafés.

Rapid development along this stretch means that this resort has blended into the next one, **AYÍA ÁNNA**, further along the busy road, with accommodation of a similar price and quality. The luxurious sea-view *Iria Beach Hotel* studios (⊕22850 42600, ⊛www.iriabeach-naxos.com; ❼) are a comfortable option, with wi-fi and a gym. Some of the best food in Ayía Anna is at the *Gorgona* taverna (⊕22850 41007, ⊛www.gorgona-naxos.com; ❸), family run and with excellent prices; they also offer rooms, studios and apartments. Further along the coast, away from the built-up area, the beach is sheltered by juniper trees and is naturist.

## Pláka and southwards

Beyond the Ayía Ánna headland, **PLÁKA BEACH**, a vegetation-fringed expanse of white sand, stretches for 5km, with the best sections towards the middle and south, and is accessed by a flat unsurfaced road from the north. Buildings are much more scattered and some parts of the beach are naturist where shielded from the road by dunes past *Plaka* campsite, although they are being edged out by beach umbrellas and sun-loungers. There are two suitably laid-back **campsites** here: *Maragas* (T22850 24552, Wwww.maragascamping .gr), which also has rooms and studios (⑤), and the friendly *Plaka* (T22850 42700, Wwww.plakacamping.gr), about 700m further south, which is smaller and quieter with a comfortable and spacious new studio hotel (April–Oct; ④). Good **tavernas** in the vicinity of Pláka include *Paradiso* near the Ayía Ánna end, *Manolis* at *Maragas*, and *Petrino*, while *Amore Mio* is the most romantic spot for dining, with views of the coast. Naxos Diving (T22850 42072, Wwww .naxosdiving.com; all year) offers PADI courses or wreck, reef, cave and exploration on Náxos and elsewhere in the Cyclades.

At the southern end of Pláka beach is Orkós, before the Mikrí Vígla headland with further hotels, studios and rooms. **KASTRÁKI**, like Mikrí Vígla, is accessed by a surfaced road via Vívlos village; the road runs about 800m behind the beach. The further south you go, the accommodation becomes increasingly high-seasonal. Towards the middle of the beach, *Areti* (T22850 75292; ⑤) has apartments and a restaurant, though the fresh food at the popular nearby *Axiotissa* **taverna** is unbeatable. Beyond Kastráki, Glyfádha beach has lagoons. In summer, this stretch – all the way from Mikrí Vígla down to **Pyrgáki**, where the asphalt ends – attracts camper vans and windsurfers from all over Europe. On the juniper-covered promontory beyond Glyfádha there is a small nudist beach, known locally as "Hawaii Beach" for the vibrant blue colour of its waters. At Pyrgáki's **Alykó beach**, just to the south, the *Finikas* hotel (T22850, Wwww.aparthotelfinikas .gr; ⑤) has rooms and studios around a beautiful pool just behind the sand. Four kilometres further by unsurfaced road is the slightly larger **Ayiássos beach**.

From Kastráki, it's a couple of hours' walk up to the Byzantine castle of **Apalírou**, at 474m, which held out for two months against the besieging Marco Sanudo. The fortifications are relatively intact and the views magnificent. The rest of the **southern coast** – virtually the whole of the southeast of the island – is remote and mountain-studded; you'd have to be a dedicated and well-equipped camper and hiker to get much out of the region.

# Central Náxos and the Tragéa

Although buses bound for Apóllon (in the north) link up the central Naxian villages, the core of the island – between Náxos Town and Aperáthou – is best explored with your own transport or on foot. Much of the region is well off the beaten track, and can provide rewarding excursions if you've had your fill of beaches; Christian Ucke and Dieter Graf's *Walking the Greek Islands: Naxos and the Small Cyclades*, published by Graf Editions (Wwww.graf-editions.de) and available from bookshops such as Zoom in Náxos Town, is a useful guide for hikers. Drivers should note that there are no petrol stations beyond Engarés when heading northeast, nor beyond the two at Halkí when heading into the mountains.

Once out of Náxos Town, head southeast through **Galanádho**, a market village, to reach the twin villages of **SANGRÍ**, on a vast plateau at the head of a long valley, a route which allows a look at the domed eighth-century church of **Áyios Mámas** (1.5km up a dirt road to the left), once the Byzantine cathedral of the island but neglected during the Venetian period and now a sorry sight. **Káto Sangrí** has the ruins of a Venetian castle, next to the Evangelismós church, while **Áno Sangrí** is an attractive little place, all cobbled streets and fragrant courtyards – it's also only about ninety-minutes' walk from the castle of Apalírou (see opposite). Thirty-minutes' stroll away, on a path leading south out of the village, or 3km by surfaced lane, are the partially rebuilt remains of **Yiroulas**, a **Classical temple of Demeter** (Tues–Sun 8.30am–3pm; free) from 530 BC, over which was constructed an early Christian basilica. The attractively laid out site is on a low hill overlooking an appropriately agricultural valley, and has an award-winning museum with further reconstructions.

## The Tragéa

From Sangrí, the road twists northeast into the **Tragéa** region, scattered with olive trees and occupying a vast highland valley. The area is the only part of the Cyclades to have a regular winter snowfall, and the only part with traditional songs about snow. It's a good jumping-off point for all sorts of exploratory rambling.

### Halkí

**HALKÍ**, 16km from Náxos Town, is a fine introduction to what is to come. Set high up, it's a quiet town with some lovely churches, including the **Panayía Protóthronis** church (open mornings), with its eleventh- to thirteenth-century frescoes. Just behind is the restored seventeenth-century Venetian **Grazia-Barozzi Tower**. The *Yiannis* **taverna** is the focal point of village activity and has a good selection of well-prepared local food.

Nearby is the distillery (1896) and shop of Vallindras Naxos Citron, whose charming proprietors explain the process of producing *kítron* followed by a little tasting session. Some two thousand citron plants are still cultivated on the island, mostly around Apóllon and Engarés-Melanés – production of the liqueur usually starts in mid-autumn, and the quantity produced in any particular year depends upon the availability of leaves. The olive plantations surrounding Halkí are crisscrossed by paths and tracks, the groves dotted with numerous **Byzantine chapels** – Áyios Yeóryios Dhiasorítis and Panayía Dhamiótissa (theoretically both are open Mon–Fri 10am–2.30pm) are well-signed from Halkí and the Moní road respectively.

### Moní and Flério

The road from Halkí heads 4km north to **MONÍ**. Just before the village, you pass the sixth-century church of **Panayía Dhrosianí**, a grey-stone building with a few faded frescoes, said to be some of the oldest in Greece; you will find yourself pressed to buy local embroidery and be directed to the donations box. Moní itself enjoys an outstanding view of the Tragéa and surrounding mountains, and has numerous handicraft shops as well as several traditional **tavernas**, of which the *Paradeisos* is most popular.

The main road leads on to **Kinídharos**, with marble quarries above the village and a curious May Day pastime of hoisting donkeys onto house roofs; five kilometres beyond, a signpost points you down to the left, to **FLÉRIO**. The most interesting of the ancient marble quarries of the seventh- to sixth-century BC on Náxos, this is home to two famous **koúri**, left recumbent and unfinished because of flaws in the material. Even so, they're finely detailed figures, over 5m in length. The Koúros Flerioú (Koúros Melánon), from around 570 BC, is a short walk along the stream valley, next to the *Paradise Garden* café; the Koúros Farangioú (Koúros Potamiás) is a steeper walk up the hillside. Just above the car park is a compact, recently excavated and well-labelled **sanctuary**, contemporary with the marble quarries. The bus from Náxos Town is signed "Melanes Kouros".

▲ Unfinished koúros statue, Apóllon, Náxos

## Potamiá

From Flério you could retrace your steps to the road and head back to Hóra via Mýli and the Venetian **fortress-tower** at Kournohóri, both pretty hamlets. On the main road, just after the latter, an unsigned stone path from a small quarry car park leads to a short excavated section of the 11km **terracotta pipe** which supplied Hóra's water until the eighth-century. If you're feeling more adventurous, head south on the footpath that leads over the hill to the Potamiá villages. The first of these, **ÁNO POTAMIÁ**, has a fine taverna and a rocky track back towards the Tragéa. Once past the valley, the landscape becomes craggy and barren, with the forbidding Venetian fortress of **Apáno Kástro** perched on a peak just south of the path. This is believed to have been Sanudo's summer home, but the fortified site was used much earlier, as indicated by the nearby Mycenaean tombs. From the fort, paths lead back to Tsikalarió then Halkí in around an hour. Alternatively, you can continue further northwest down the Potamiá valley towards Hóra, passing first the ruined **Cocco Pýrgos** – said to be haunted by one Constantine Cocco, the victim of a seventeenth-century clan feud – on the way to **MÉSI POTAMIÁ**, joined by some isolated dwellings with its twin village **KÁTO POTAMIÁ** nestling almost invisibly among the greenery flanking the creek. From here it is 7km by road back to Náxos Town.

## Filóti, Mount Zás and around

At the far side of the gorgeous Tragéa valley, **FILÓTI**, the largest village in the region, lies on the northwestern slopes of Mount Zás (or Zeus) which, at 1001m, is the highest point in the Cyclades. Under the shade of the plane trees on the main platía are several pleasant *kafenía*, as well as *Babulas Grill-Restaurant* (☎22850 31426; ❷), which has the best rooms in the village. To get an idea of the old village, climb the steps up the hill starting at the platía.

From Filóti, it's a round-trip walk of three to four hours on partly marked trails to the summit of **Mount Zás**, a climb which rewards you with an astounding panorama of virtually the whole of Náxos and its Cycladic neighbours. The initial path out of the village climbs up to rejoin the Apóllon road. Take the Dhanakós turning to the waymarked final approach trail, which begins beside small Ayía Marína chapel. There is also a marked turn-off steeply down to the 150m-deep Zás Cave, but this is more easily accessed by a separate route (1hr) from Filóti.

A turning at the southern end of Filóti is signposted to the **Pýrgos Himárou** (12.5km, paved), a remote twenty-metre-high Hellenistic watchtower – swathed in scaffolding for the foreseeable future, but impressive nonetheless – and onward (11km, unpaved) to Kalandoú beach on the south coast. En route to the tower, at the Áyios Trýfonas pass, there are some of the best views on Náxos (apart from Mt Zás), including seventeen other Cycladic islands. There are no villages in the south-central part of the island, so bring supplies if you're planning to camp. Over the mountain ridge just to the east of Filóti, the small village of Dhanakós is in a valley full of watermills; a *kalderími* leads up to the spectacular and romantic ruins of the **Khristós Fotodhóti monastery**.

### Aperáthou and the east coast

**APERÁTHOU** (officially Apíranthos), a hilly, winding 8km beyond Filóti, shows the most Cretan influence of all the interior villages. Its location high in the mountains means it is noticeably cooler and greener than the coast. There are two Venetian fortified mansions, Bardáni and Zevgóli, an **ATM**, and several small **museums**: the natural history (April–Oct daily 10.30am–1.30pm; €1.50) and geological (April–Oct daily 10.30am–2pm; €2) are on the main road, the folklore is further inside town. Ask to be pointed to the start of the spectacular **path** up over the Fanári ridge behind; this ends either in Moní or Kalóxylos, depending on whether you fork right or left at the top. Cafés and tavernas on the main street look out over a terraced valley below; the nationally renowned **taverna** *Stou Leftheri*, here, is generally regarded as one of the best restaurants on the island, serving up carefully prepared local dishes and desserts. **Rooms** are available but are not obvious – ask in the cafés or shops – the exception being the *Zorbas Studios* (T22850 61339 or 694 41 01 566; ❸), at the northern end of town.

Aperáthou has a beach annexe 12km east at **Moutsoúna**, under the sheltering prow of Akrotíri Stavrós. Emery – a fine-grained mineral used in the final polishing of marble surfaces – was mined for 2000 years near Aperáthou and Kóronos. From 1926, it was transported down to Moutsoúna by means of an aerial funicular, until the industry collapsed in the 1980s. The harbour has three tavernas, and the sandy cove beyond the dock now features a growing colony of holiday villas and the excellent *Ostria* taverna; there is a second beach, just north, at Azalá. Boat trips are available: around Akrotíri Stavrós, to the nearby uninhabited Makáres islands, or to the Minor Cyclades. A surfaced road heads south along the coast to a remote sandy beach at **Psilí Ámmos** – ideal for self-sufficient campers, but you must take enough water – then on to relatively secluded **Pánormos beach** in the southeastern corner of the island.

## Northern Náxos

The route through the mountains from Aperáthou to Apóllon is very scenic, and the road surface is in reasonable condition all the way. At the Stavrós Keramotí col there are dramatic views down to both sides of the island. Jagged ranges and hairpin bends confront you after **Kóronos** village, where a 9km road off to the right threads through a wooded valley to **Liónas**, a tiny and very Greek port with a pebble beach. The main route continues, past Skadhó, to the remote, emery-miners' village of **KORONÍDHA** – the highest village on the island and the original home of *kítron* liqueur. Alternatively, avoid over 5km of bends by diverting right after Skadhó, through Mési.

Back on the main road, a further series of bends leads down a long valley to **APÓLLON** (Apóllonas), a small resort with two beaches: a tiny and crowded stretch of sand backed by a line of cafés and restaurants, and a longer and quieter stretch of shingle, popular mainly with Greek families. The main hotels are the central *Adonis* (☎22850 67060, ⓦwww.adonis-hotel.com; ❹) and the *Kouros*, behind the long beach (☎22850 67000; ❺). There are studios and rooms available, such as *Flora* (☎22850 67070; ❸), one of the few open outside high season. The only major attraction is a **koúros**, approached by a path from the main road just above the village. Lying *in situ* at a former marble quarry, this largest of Náxos's abandoned stone figures is just over 10m long, but less detailed than those at Flério. Here since 600 BC and probably intended for the Dionysian temple at Ýria, it serves as a reminder of the Naxians' traditional skill; the famous Delian lions (see p.164) are also made of Apollonian marble. Not surprisingly, round-the-island bus tours descend upon the village during the day, when Apóllon is quite a popular little place. The local festival, celebrated on August 28–29, is one of Náxos's best.

The northern coastal road is spectacularly beautiful, going high above the sea for most of the way, making it more like parts of Crete or the mainland than other islands. Eighteen kilometres past the northern cape sprouts the beautiful **Ayiá tower**, another foundation (in 1717) of the Cocco family. There's a tiny hamlet nearby, and, 7km further along, an unsurfaced road leads off to **Abrámi beach**, an idyllic spot with a highly recommended family-run **taverna**, *Efthimios* (☎22850 63244, ⓔabram@can.gr; ❸) with **rooms** to let. Just beyond the hamlet of Hília Vrýsi is the abandoned **monastery of Faneroménis**, built in 1606 and where defending monks are said to have repelled pirates by catapulting beehives at them. Carrying on along the coastal road you will reach the Engarés valley, at the foot of which is another quiet beach, **Amíti**, accessed via one of two dirt tracks, the most obvious being the 2.2km one leading down from Galíni, itself only 7km from Náxos Town. On the final stretch back to the port, you pass a unique eighteenth-century Turkish fountain-house.

# Minor Cyclades

Four of the six small islands in the patch of the Aegean between Náxos and Amorgós have slid from obscurity into fashion in recent years. The group is known commonly as the Minor Cyclades and includes **Iráklia, Skhinoússa, Áno Koufoníssi** and **Dhonoússa**. The islands' popularity has hastened the development of better facilities and higher prices, but with only limited ferry services, they've managed to avoid the mass tourism of the rest of the Cyclades and offer some of the best traditional food. You can even find peace and quiet – what the Greeks call *isykhía* – here in August, when you should make the crossing from Áno Koufoníssi to **Kéros**, with no permanent population but an important archeological site, or **Káto Koufoníssi**, inhabited only by goatherds.

The Pireás-based Blue Star **ferries** call at the islands, often during the night – linking them with Náxos, Amorgós and (sometimes) Páros. However, the small, local *Express Skopelítis* is a more frequent fixture, leaving the smaller ferry quay in Náxos daily to head to most of the islets (Dhonoússa has fewer connexions).

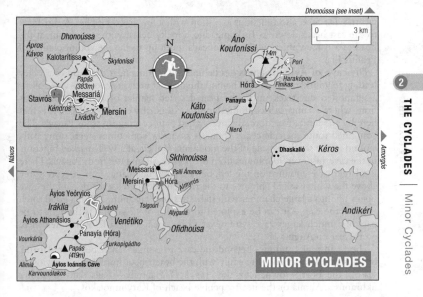

MINOR CYCLADES

## Iráklia

**Iráklia** (locally Iraklía), the westernmost of the Minor Cyclades, and with the least spoiled scenery, has just over a hundred permanent residents. As the first stop on the ferry service from Náxos, the island is hardly undiscovered by tourists, but with fewer amenities than some of its neighbours it retains the feel of a more secluded retreat.

Ferries call at **ÁYIOS YEÓRYIOS**, a small but sprawling settlement behind a sandy tamarisk-backed beach. 🏕 *Anna's Place* (☎22850 71145; ❸) on the hill-slope at the back of the village has great views, rooms with shared cooking facilities in the gardens above, and some luxurious studios, with more of the latter under construction higher up the hill. Both it and the friendly nearby *Alexandra* rooms (☎22850 71482, ✉alexandrasrooms@yahoo.gr; ❸) are open all year. Another accommodation option is the *Maïstrali* taverna (☎22850 71807, ✉nickmaistrali @in.gr; ❷), on the way to *Anna's*, which has rooms near the *Alexandra*. Details of these and other **accommodation** can be found on the island website, Ⓦwww .iraklia.gr. For eating, there are several good tavernas, including the laid-back *Maïstrali* and, near the harbour, the *Perigiali*, which also has a small shop. The **post office**, a short distance above the *Perigiali*, is the agency for ferry **tickets**, but there is no bank/ATM or public transport on the island.

**Livádhi**, the biggest beach on the island, is a 1.5km-walk southeast of the port, and rather disappointing on closer inspection. The *Makuba* taverna, halfway there, runs a rather scruffy, seasonal campsite in the valley behind the beach. The village of Livádhi, deserted since 1940, stands on the hilltop just behind the beach, its houses ruined; among the remains are Hellenistic walls incorporated into a later building, and Venetian fortifications from the time of Marco Sanudo. The *Zografos Rooms* (☎22850 71946, ✉mirtali@otenet.gr; ❹), steeply up the hillside above the road from Livádhi to Panayía, have fine views but are rather remote.

**PANAYÍA (HÓRA)**, an undistinguished hamlet at the foot of Mount Papás, is an hour's walk (4km) inland along the paved road, with a short cut possible up a brief, remaining section of the old *kalderími*. It has no rooms, but the small taverna *Tou Steki* also functions as a shop with a few basic supplies. A dirt track to the east heads down to Turkopigádho, a rocky beach with sea urchins, at the head of a narrow inlet, while a path leads south up to the viewpoint church of Profítis Ilías.

The **cave of Áyios Ioánnis** lies behind the mountain, at the head of a valley leading to Vourkária Bay. From behind the main church in Áyios Yeóryios, follow a signposted dirt track up to the near-deserted hamlet of **Áyios Athanásios** from where a faint path continues up to a col northwest of Mt Papás. It is met here by an alternative, more obvious, signed path coming up from Panayía. The combined route then descends 150m as a narrow, sometimes steep, stony path, around to the southeast side of the mountain. Go left, at a well-marked junction, to the cave, just over 90 minutes from the port or 50 minutes from Panayía. There is a larger cave entrance on the left, but a church bell hangs from a cypress tree above the whitewashed entrance to the right; inside there's a shrine, and the cave opens up into a large chamber with stalactites and stalagmites. With a good torch – and some care – it can be explored to a depth of 120m and is thought to be part of a much larger cave system, yet to be opened up; a festival is held here every year on August 18–19.

The main trail continues beyond the cave to a small sandy beach at **Alimiá**, but this can be reached more easily with the beach-boat from Áyios Yeóryios. In season, the boat – owned by the *Anna's Place* family – sails daily to either Skhinoússa, Alimiá or the nearby pebble beach of Karvounólakos.

## Skhinoússa

A little to the northeast of Iráklia, the island of **Skhinoússa** (locally sometimes Skinoússa) is just beginning to awaken to its tourist potential. Its indented outline, sweeping valleys and partly submerged headlands – such as the sinuous, snake-like islet Ofidhoúsa (Fidoú) – provide some of the most dramatic views in the group. Boats dock at the small port of Mersíni, which has a taverna; a road leads up to **HÓRA** (also called Panayía), the shadeless walk taking about fifteen minutes, with some stony shortcuts for the upper bends. As you enter the village, the agent for Blue Star ferries is on the right (Skopelitis tickets are usually available at the dock just before departure). There are three small supermarkets before the road junction for the tiny settlement of Messariá. There is also another tourist office, Central Travel Agency, at the Almyrós-Lióliou/Livádhi junction at the other end of town, next to the laundry.

**Accommodation** is mostly comfortable rather than luxurious. Just east of the main square, the *Anna* rooms and studios (☎22850 71161; May–Oct; ❷) are quiet and comfortable, whilst the nearby *Iliovasilema Hotel* (☎22850 71948, ⓦwww.iliovasilemahotel.gr; May–Oct; ❹), under the same management, is well-priced and enjoys stunning views of the harbour. At the southern end are the hospitable *Meltemi* rooms (☎22850 71947, ⓦschinousa.gr/meltemi/; Easter–Oct; ❸) and studios, next door to the family taverna, and just out of town is the pleasant *Pension Galini* (☎22850 71983; May–Oct; ❸). All offer transport to and from the port, and the *Iliovasilema* runs beach excursions by minibus in the summer.

The main concentration of **restaurants** and cafés is along the central thoroughfare. Traditional *Panorama* and more trendy and inventive *Margarita* offer diners some of the best views on the island. There is a tiny folk museum (uncertain opening hours), near the Tsigoúri beach track.

There are no fewer than sixteen **beaches** dotted around the island, accessible by a network of dirt tracks. **Tsigoúri** is a ten-minute track walk downhill from northwest Hóra and gradually being developed. The *Grispos Villas* (☎22850 71930, ⓦwww.grisposvillas.com; B&B ❹), perched above at the northwest end, have a good taverna, and new rooms and studios with great views; they also sell ferry tickets in season. On the beach itself is the *Ostria* taverna. The locals' preferred choice of beaches are **Alygariá** to the south, **Psilí Ámmos** to the northeast, and **Almyrós**, half an hour southeast, which has a canteen.

## Áno Koufoníssi, Káto Koufoníssi and Kéros

**Áno Koufoníssi** (usually referred to simply as Koufoníssi) is the flattest, most populous and most developed island of the group. With some of the least-spoilt beaches in the Cyclades, the island is attracting increasing numbers of Greek and foreign holidaymakers; small enough to walk round in a morning, it can feel overcrowded in July and August. The best views are not of Koufoníssi itself, but out across the water to mountainous Kéros island.

The old pedestrian-street of **HÓRA**, crossing a low hill behind the ferry harbour, has been engulfed by new room and hotel development, but the town still has a friendly, small-island atmosphere. To the west (left) of the jetty a dirt road leads to a small bay with fishing boats, to the right is the town and town beach, from where the short main street has several supermarkets and the well-stocked *Yioryioula* bakery-café. The Koufonissia Tours ticket agency (ⓕ22850 71671, Ⓦwww.koufonissiatours.gr) is on the pedestrian street, and there is a **post office** (limited hours) up a street by the *Hotel Roussetos*, with an **ATM**.

At the eastern end of the beach is a further cluster of accommodations, and the road to the eastern beaches. A map by the jetty shows the layout of town, and where to find the island's **rooms**, providing you know the name of the owner rather than that of the accommodation. The hospitable Katerina Prassinos has a variety of rooms, including the upmarket studios and apartments at the ⚶ *Hotel Roussetos* (ⓣ22850 74176; ❺), at the corner of the town beach and start of the main street. Her mother, Maria Prassinou (ⓣ22850 71436; ❸) has a variety of rooms just east of the beach, as well as a couple of old houses to rent (❻). On the pedestrian street of Hóra, the pension *Melissa* (ⓣ22850 71454; May–Oct; ❸), behind a popular taverna, is a good, family-run choice – they have further studios near Fínikas beach. The *Ermes* (ⓣ22850 71693; ❹), has studios, above and behind the post office/ATM. The *Yioryioula* bakery has comfortable rooms at *Hondros Kavos* (ⓣ22850 71707; May–Oct; ❸), located over a popular seafood taverna about fifteen-minutes' walk to the east, near Fínikas beach, with a transfer minibus for the ferry.

Koufoníssi is noted for its fish **tavernas**; *Neo Remezzo*, in the little street directly above the ferry jetty, has excellent food and a cosy atmosphere, while *Capetan Nicolas,* at the bay to the west, is cheaper than most and offers a fine array of seafood; nearby *To Steki Tis Marias* is a good breakfast place with a few rooms (❷), and has views over the narrow channel to Káto Koufoníssi. The most popular nightspot is *Soroccos*, a lively **café-bar** on the eastern seafront with views of Kéros, while a good alternative is *Ta Kalamia* on the main street, with a quieter choice of music.

All the good beaches are in the southeast of the island, getting better as you go east along a semi-paved road that skirts the gradually developing coastline along the edge of low cliffs. **Fínikas**, a fifteen-minute walk from town, is the first of four wide coves with gently shelving golden sand, where there are an increasing number of rooms, and the *Hondros Kavos* taverna. Further east is **Harakópou**, which has a windswept **campsite** (ⓣ22850 71683) with cane shade and a minibus, but limited facilities, situated on the headland before the next beach, **Thános**, where thumping music plays at the beach bar *Fanos*. Next is **Platiá Poúnda**, where caves have been hollowed out of the cliffs. Further east, the path rounds a rocky headland to **Porí**, a much longer and wilder beach, backed by dunes and set in a deep bay. It can be reached more easily from the town by following a dirt road heading inland through the low scrub-covered hills.

**Káto Koufoníssi**, the almost uninhabited island to the southwest, has a seasonal taverna and some more secluded beaches; a high season *kaïki* shuttles people across until late in the evening. A festival is held here on August 15, at the church of the Panayía. The island of **Kéros** is harder to reach, but if there is a willing group of people keen to visit the ancient site, a boat and boatman can be hired for around €50 for the return trip.

## Dhonoússa

**Dhonoússa** is a little out on a limb compared with the other Minor Cyclades, and ferries call less frequently. Island life centres on the pleasant port settlement of **STAVRÓS**, spread out behind the harbour and the village beach.

**Rooms**, most without any signs, tend to be booked up by Greek holiday-makers in August; beyond the beach, try the rooms and studios at *Iliovasilema* (T22850 51570 ; ❸), which also has a good restaurant and is agent for the Blue Star ferries; or nearby *Prasinou* (T22850 51579; ❸), with studios and some beautifully furnished apartments. Next to the *Aposperides* taverna are the *Skopelitis* studios (T22850 52296, Eskopelitis@gmx.net; May–Oct; ❷), set around a flowery garden. There are a few **tavernas** in town; one of the best for *mezédhes* is ⅄ *Captain George*. There is no ATM and the ticket agency above the harbour changes money at unfavourable rates, so you would be wise to bring enough with you.

The hills around Stavrós are low and barren and scarred by bulldozed tracks, but a little walking is repaid with dramatic scenery and a couple of fine beaches. Sunbathers head for **Kéndros**, a long and attractive stretch of sand fifteen minutes over the ridge to the east, although shade is limited; there is a family taverna and a small area for camping, while in July and August, a beach-boat runs from the port. **Mersíni** is an hour's walk from Stavrós and has a small café-taverna at the lower end of the village, the *Tsitsi*, which uses locally sourced products. A nearby path leads down to Livádhi, an idyllic white-sand beach with tamarisks for shade.

The road from Mersíni to **Kalotarítissa**, in the northeast, is paved but has some spectacular views of the coast. You can join the remnants of a zigzag *kalderími* about halfway along. The small village is now mainly holiday homes, with a simple, high-season taverna, two small pebble beaches, and the occasional elderly shepherd. From Kalotarítissa you can follow uphill paths towards 383m Mt Papás, then join dirt roads and paths back to Stavrós.

# Amorgós

**Amorgós**, with its dramatic mountain scenery and laid-back atmosphere, is attracting visitors in increasing numbers; most ferries and catamarans call at both Katápola in the southwest and Eyiáli (Aegiali) in the north – with these destinations, rather than "Amorgós", named on schedules – and there is a bus service (2-6 daily) between these ports. The island can get extremely crowded in midsummer, the numbers swollen by French people paying their respects to the film location of Luc Besson's *The Big Blue*, although fewer venture out to Líveros at the island's western end to see the wreck of the *Olympia* which figures so prominently in the movie. In general it's a low-key, escapist clientele, happy to have found a relatively large, interesting, uncommercialized and hospitable island with excellent walking.

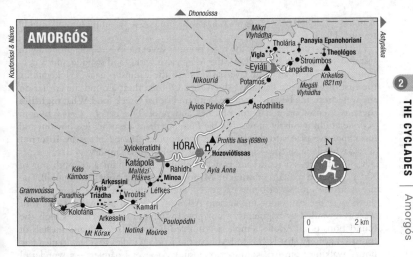

## Katápola and around

**KATÁPOLA**, set at the head of a deep inlet, is actually three separate villages: **Katápola** proper on the south side, **Xylokeratídhi** on the north shore, and **Rahídhi** on the central ridge. There is a beach in front of Rahídhi, but Káto Krotíri beach to the west of Katápola is better, though not up to the standards of Eyiáli in the northeast. In season there is also a regular *kaíki* to nearby beaches at **Maltézi** and **Plákes** (€3 return) and a daily *kaíki* to the islet of **Gramvoússa** off the western end of Amorgós (€8 return).

Prekas (☎22850 71256) in Katápola, just along from the ferry dock, is the one-stop **boat-ticket agency**. There are several **car/bike-rental outfits**, such as Thomas (☎22850 71777, ⓦwww.thomas-rental.gr); the Eko petrol station is partway up the road to Hóra, below a large supermarket. Alternatively, the local bus service is more than adequate in high season, and the walking trails delightful. There are several walking **maps** on sale in shops throughout the island, the most useful published by Anavasi. The **bus** shuttles between Katápola and Hóra, the island capital; several times daily it continues to Ayía Ánna via Hozoviótissas monastery, and 2–7 times weekly (9.45am) out to the "Káto Meriá", made up of the hamlets of Kamári-Vroútsi, Arkessíni and Kolofána.

There are plenty of small **hotels** and **pensions** and, except in high summer when rooms are almost impossible to find, proprietors tend to meet those boats arriving around sunset – though not necessarily those that show up in the small hours. On the waterfront square, the smart, neighbouring *Minoa* and *Landeris* hotels (☎22850 71480, ⓔhotelminoalanderis@yahoo.com; ❹) have some very comfortable, large new rooms, as well as **internet** access. A good place next to the small beach at the western end of Katápola is the friendly *Eleni* rooms and studios (☎22850 71628, ⓔroomseleni@hack-box.net; ❹). Well-signed south of the port you'll find the hospitable *Anna Studios* (☎22850 71218, ⓦwww.studioanna-amorgos.com; ❸), in a garden setting, with mosquito nets and **internet** connections possible. There are several similarly priced pensions a little further east, including *Sofia* (☎22850 71493, ⓦwww.pension-sofia.com; ❸) in its own garden.

The town **campsite** (☎22850 71257; June–Sept) is well signed, just off the beach between Rahídhi and Xylokeratídhi. There's also a newer one, *Camping*

*Kastanis* (T22850 71277, Wwww.kastanis.com.gr), a ten-minute walk uphill towards Hóra.

The family-run *Mourayio* is the most popular **taverna** in Katápola proper, with fish and seafood; alternatively, try the *Minos*, also with good seafood and waterfront views. There are four tavernas close to the campsite near Xylokeratídhi, the first of which is a friendly fish taverna. Of the others around the corner on the waterfront the best is *Vitzentzos*, with traditional Greek food. What **nightlife** there is focuses on a handful of cafés and pubs. The bar *Le Grand Bleu* in Xylokeratídhi regularly shows *The Big Blue*, but there are other less obvious and less expensive places to drink, such as the popular *Moon Bar* nearby. **Internet** access is available at the *Téloneio* café, near the Katápola laundry.

A signed surfaced road runs past the church in Rahídhi and south out of Katápola to the remains of **ancient Minoa**, about a half hour's walk uphill. The site is in the process of being excavated, and is impressive for its size and the views over the bay, Hóra and ancient Arkessíni as much as anything else. Your walk is rewarded by fragments of polygonal wall, four or five courses high, the foundations of an Apollo temple, a crumbled Roman structure and bushels of unsorted pottery shards. Beyond Minoa, the road dwindles to a jeep trail, a few hours' walking from Arkessíni (see opposite) via several hamlets – a wonderful **excursion** with the possibility of catching the bus back.

## Hóra and around

**HÓRA**, accessible by an hour-long walk along the path beginning from behind the *Rahídhi* campsite, is one of the better-preserved settlements in the Cyclades, with a scattering of tourist shops, cafés, tavernas and rooms. Dominated by an upright volcanic rock plug, wrapped with a chapel or two, the thirteenth-century Venetian fortifications look down on nearly thirty other churches, some domed, and a line of decapitated windmills beyond. Of the half-dozen or so **places to stay**, the *Panorama* rooms and studios (T22850 74016, Wwww .panorama-studios.amorgos.net; ④) are a possibility, as is the stunning *Traditional Guest House Amorgos* (T22850 71814, Wwww.amorgos-studios.amorgos.net; ⑥), one of the more beautiful designer hotels in the Cyclades. Hóra is littered with atmospheric little places to **eat** and **drink**: *Liotrivi* restaurant, down the steps from the bus stop, and with a roof terrace, is popular, whilst the small *To Hyma* ouzerí halfway along the main street on the platía is an excellent choice, for its *mezédhes*. Also in the upper square is the island's main **post office**.

From the top of Hóra, near the upper telecoms tower, a wide cobbled *kalderími* drops down to two major attractions, effectively short-cutting the road and taking little longer than the bus to reach them. For the **monastery of Hozoviótissas** (daily 8am–1pm, 5–7pm; donation expected), bear left at an inconspicuous fork, and you'll join the monastery/Ayía Ánna road near the bus-stop junction: the small monastery car park is 300m along to the left. From the car park a path leads rather steeply upwards for 700m, to the spectacular monastery, which appears suddenly as you round a bend, its vast wall gleaming white at the base of a towering orange cliff. Modest dress is required of visitors; the sign advises that trousers are not suitable for women, but you will find that most female Greek visitors wear them. If you arrive during a service, you will need to wait until the end before you can see anything beyond the church. Only a handful of monks occupy the fifty rooms now, but they are quite welcoming considering the number of visitors who file through; you can see the eleventh-century icon around which the monastery was founded, along with other treasures. Legend has it that during the Iconoclastic period, a precious icon of the Virgin was committed to the sea by beleaguered monks at Hózova, in the Middle East, and it washed up safely at the base of the palisade here. The view from the *katholikón*'s terrace is the highlight for most visitors, and to round off the experience, you are ushered into a comfy reception room and treated to a sugary lump of *loukoúmi*, a warming shot of *rakómelo psiméni* (Amorgion raki with honey and spices) and a cool glass of water.

The right-hand trail leads down, within forty minutes, to the pebble **beaches** at **Ayía Ánna**. Skip the first tiny coves, where the car park is larger than the sand, in favour of the path to Kambí Bay, where naturists cavort, almost in scandalous sight of the monastery far above; bring food and water for the day.

## Southwestern Amorgós

For alternatives to Ayía Ánna, head west to **Kamári** hamlet, from where it is a twenty-minute walk (road and path) down to the adjacent beaches of **Notiná**, **Moúros** and **Poulopódhi**. Like most of Amorgós's south-facing beaches, they're clean, with calm water. Adjacent to Kamári is **Vroútsi** hamlet, with a small, traditional taverna, a *kafenío* and a handicrafts shop. Archeology buffs will want to head north from Vroútsi, start of the overgrown hour-long route to **ancient Arkessini**, a collection of tombs, six-metre-high walls and houses out on the cape of Kastrí. The main path from Minoá also passes through Vroútsi, ending next to the well-preserved Hellenistic fort known locally as the "Pýrgos", just outside the rural hamlet of modern **Arkessíni**. The main westward road from Kamári also goes to this hamlet, where rooms and studios are available, including *Marouso* (T22850 72253; ❷) at the minimarket, with a family taverna (June–Oct). In season, there is an afternoon bus back to Hóra and Katápola.

The next settlement, 2.5km further west, is **Kolofána**, with a minimarket, a *kafenío*, and the *T'Apanemo* and *Delfini* tavernas – the latter (T22850 72244; May–Oct; ❷) has newly refurbished rooms and studios arranged around a garden at the back, with rural field and mountain views. From here the surfaced road leads towards the far western tip of the island, branching north to Ayía Paraskeví above **Paradhísa beach**, or west to spectacular **Kalotarítissas Bay**, its tiny fishing jetty and small sand and pebble beach partly enclosed and sheltered by a rocky headland and the islet of Gramvoússa. About 1.8km before Kalotarítissas, the **wreck of the Olympia** is visible down to the right, in **Líveros Bay**.

## Northeastern Amorgós

The energetically inclined can walk the four to five hours from Hóra to Eyiáli, continuing on the faint trail just beyond Hozoviótissas; take water, as there is nowhere to fill up on the way. Along most of the route, you're treated to amazing views of **Nikouriá islet**, nearly joined to the main island, and in former times a leper colony. The only habitations en route are the summer hamlet of **Asfondilítis**, and the two **Potamós** villages (with a café) just above Eyiáli.

### Eyiáli
**EYIÁLI (AEGIALI)** is smaller and more picturesque than Katápola, and so tends to be more popular. For **boat tickets** try Nautilus, just back from the water; there's no bank, but you'll find an **ATM** near the ferry dock. **Car and bike rental** is available from Thomas (T22850 73444, Wwww.thomas-rental .gr); the Elin petrol station is 500m behind the beach, off the Tholária road. **Accommodation** is scattered around the backstreets on the hill behind and is easy to locate; above the jetty is the well-priced and very comfortable *Karkisia* (T22850 73180, Wwww.karkisia-hotel.gr, or contact through

nearby bakery; Easter–Oct; ❹), and behind it the friendly *Pension Christina* (☎22850 73236, ⓦwww.christina-pension.amorgos.net; ❸) with bright, cheerful rooms and studios. The *Mouses tis Amorgos* studios (☎22850 73614; ❹), one row behind the beach, can also be contacted via the supermarket opposite the *Kostaras* restaurant in the square. The largest hotel on the island is the *Aegialis* (☎22850 73393, ⓦwww.amorgos-aegialis.com; ❼), high on the hillside on the far side of the bay, with a pool, very good thalassotherapy (treatments using salt water and natural marine products) spa, gym and above-average restaurant. In the Lakkí area, behind the beach and on the road to Tholária, the friendly official **campsite**, *Aegiali Camping* (☎22850 73500, ⓦwww.aegialicamping.gr; May–Sept), is usually busier than the one in Katápola.

For **eating out**, *Asteria* on the platía has good food at excellent prices, while *Limani* (also called *Katina's*) in a narrow street beyond is very popular and has both traditional Amorgian food and occasional Thai nights. Other places tend to be pricier and of inferior quality, with the exception of the tiny *12 Acropolis* restaurant. *To Steki tou Kritikou* at the start of the beach sometimes has live music, while *Hondros*, with hearty, generous meat and salads, behind the beach, is one of the few places open in the winter.

The main Eyiáli **beach** is more than serviceable, getting less weedy and reefy as you stroll further north, the sand interrupted by the remains of a Roman building, "Derivas", jutting into the sea. A trail here leads over various headlands to three bays: Levrosós, which is sandy, Psilí Ámmos, which is mixed sand and gravel, and shingle Hokhlákas, where naturism is just about tolerated; there are no facilities here so bring along what you need.

### The hill villages

There is a **bus service** up to both Langádha and Tholária, the two villages east of and 200m above Eyiáli Bay, with 3–8 departures daily up and down (a timetable is posted by the harbour bus stop), but it would be a shame to miss out on the beautiful **loop walk** linking them with the port (2–3hr). Head northeast out of Eyiáli and take the first right after the Tholária turning. Join a well-made *kalderími* that climbs up, below the cliff-hung tiny cave-church of Ayía Triádha, to **LANGÁDHA** village. The *Artemis Pension* (☎22850 73315, ⓦwww.artemis-pension.gr; ❸), just before the upper car park, is a friendly place to stay, and owns the good *Loza* taverna in a small nearby square. Beyond Langádha, turn left off the main onward path towards the pretty, monastery-like Panayía Epanohorianí, then continue around the hillside to Tholária (see below). Alternatively, from Langádha, the main path goes to the fascinating church of **Áyios Ioánnis Theológos**, with lower walls and ground plan dating to the fifth century, then becomes a spectacular cliff-edge path (600m drop to the sea) around the base of the island's highest peak, the 823-metre-high **Kríkellos (Kroúkellos)**, to the isolated Stavrós church beyond. Another, steeper walk from Langádha goes south up to the seven ruined windmills at 550m on the main mountain ridge, with an optional detour to the tiny church of Stavrós (another one).

**THOLÁRIA** is named after vaulted Roman tombs found around Vígla, the site of ancient Aegiale – the latter is on a hill opposite the village, but there is little to see beyond the bases of statues and traces of city walls incorporated into later terracing. A descending *kalderími* from the village car park towards Eyiáli divides, the left branch going to the petrol station, the main branch going to the end of the beach. Another path from Tholária winds down behind the hill to a small pebble beach at Mikrí Vlyhádha far below. Tholária has several, good **taverna-cafés**, including, near the church, the *Kali Kardia*, and next door

*Thalassino Oneiro* (☎22850 73345; ❷) with basic rooms, plus the hospitable *Vigla* hotel (☎22850 73288, Ⓦwww.viglamorgos.gr; B&B ❺) by the car park.

# Íos

Though not terribly different – geographically or architecturally – from its immediate neighbours, no other island attracts the same vast crowds of young people as **Íos**. However, it has worked hard to shake off its late-twentieth-century reputation for alcohol and drug excesses and to move the island's tourism upmarket; buildings are now painted white with blue trim, instead of garish psychedelic hues, camping rough is discouraged, and Greece's early closing laws are enforced, so bars no longer stay open all night, though dancing clubs do. The island is still extremely popular with the young backpacker set, who take over the island in July and August, although at other times a large number of young families holiday here.

The only real villages – **Yialós**, **Hóra** and **Mylopótos** – are clustered in a western corner of the island, and development elsewhere is restricted by poor roads. As a result there are still some very quiet beaches with just a few rooms to rent. Yialós itself has one of the best and safest natural harbours in the Cyclades.

Most visitors stay along the arc delineated by the port – at Yialós, where you'll arrive, in Hóra above it, or at the beach at Mylopótos. **Buses** constantly shuttle between Koumbára, Yialós, Hóra and Mylopótos, with a daily service running roughly from 8am to midnight in high season when you should never have to wait more than twenty minutes, but at least once try the short walk up (or down) the stepped path between Yialós and Hóra. There are public and private buses running to the beaches at Manganári and Ayía Theodhóti; they sell return tickets only and are a bit expensive (€6). To rent your **own transport**, try Jacob's Car and Bike Rental (☎22860 91047) in Yialós or Vangelis Bike Rental (☎22860 91919) in Hóra. For a quick escape from the party atmosphere at the height of the season, try one of the daily excursions around quieter nearby beaches on the wooden *Leigh Browne* sailing vessel moored in the harbour (€20). Despite its past popularity, **sleeping on the beach** on Íos is discouraged these days; given the problem of theft, it's best to stick to the official campsites.

## Yialós

From **YIALÓS** quayside, **buses** start just along to the right (southeast), while Yialós **beach** – surprisingly peaceful and uncrowded – is five-minutes' walk in the same direction. You might be tempted to grab a room in Yialós as you arrive: owners meet the ferries, touting the town's **accommodation**, and there are

also a couple of kiosks by the jetty that will book rooms for you. In shoulder season you can bargain for prices considerably lower than those listed below.

**Brothers' Hotel (aka Ta Adelfia)** Down the lane behind the centre of the beach ☎22840 91508, ⓦwww.brothershotel.com. A relaxed family option with comfortable rooms, studios and a small pool. ❹
~~Galini Rooms~~ Down the lane behind the centre of the beach ☎22860 91115, ⓔgaliniios@yahoo.com. A good, quiet choice, in a rural setting just over 200m from the sea. ❹
**Golden Sun** About 300m up the road to Hóra ☎22860 91110, ⓦwwwgoldensun-ios.gr.

Family-owned rooms with a pool and nice views over the bay. B&B. ❹
**Mare-Monte** About halfway down the beach ☎22860 91585, ⓔmaremonte@otenet.gr. Hotel with spacious rooms and a small pool. B&B. ❹
**Yialos Beach** Just behind the hospital ☎22860 91421, ⓦwww.yialosbeach.gr. Stylish hotel with smart doubles and studios set around a pool. ❺

There are more rooms on the stepped path from Yialós to Hóra, although they can be noisy at night. *Ios Camping* (☎22860 91329), at the far south end of the waterfront, is friendly and clean and has a rather luxurious swimming pool. Yialós has other essentials, including an **ATM** near the quay, the large Marinopoulos supermarket and **tavernas**. The *Octopus Tree*, a small *kafenío* by the fishing boats, serves cheap fresh seafood caught by the owner; nearby *Enigma* is a warm, intimate space serving Cypriot cuisine.

From beyond the campsite, a path leads around the coast to little **Valmás Beach**, with a good taverna – a partly asphalt road leads up to emerge by the post office in Hóra. In **KOUMBÁRA**, a twenty-minute stroll over the headland, the scenery is rockier and remoter, with a smaller beach, a cove backed by extraordinary green serpentine cliffs, and a rocky islet to explore. There is accommodation at the large *Koumbara Sunset* hotel (☎22860 91956, ⓦwww.koumbarasunsetresort .com; ❺), popular with Italians, and just before the beach bus stop and bus-turning circle is the *Polidoros* taverna, one of the better places to eat on Ios (though not serving food until around 2pm); the *Koumbara Beach Café*, directly on the beach, serves Italian food; while the excellent *Filippos* fish taverna is on the ridgetop between Koumbára and Yialós.

## Hóra

**HÓRA** (also called Íos Town, but often just "Village"), a twenty-minute walk up behind the port, is one of the more accessible picturesque towns in the Cyclades, filled with meandering arcaded lanes and whitewashed chapels, though it's pretty lively when the younger crowd moves in for the high season, and the laddish logos and inscriptions available on t-shirts and at tattoo parlours are not entirely in keeping with its upmarket aspirations. The main road divides it naturally into two parts: the old town climbing the hillside to the left as you arrive, and the newer development to the right.

The **archeological museum** (Tues–Sun 8.30am–3pm; €2), in the yellow town hall, is part of an attempt to attract a more diverse range of visitors to the island. The **outdoor theatre** of Odyssevs Elytis, behind the windmills, provides a beautiful setting in which to enjoy concerts and plays, details of which can be found at the **travel agent** and information booth next to the archeological museum.

There are plenty of basic **rooms** in the old part, although the bars can make it noisy. If you want quiet, your best strategy is to wend your way up from just above the lower square (by the large church) to the excellent ⚑ *Francesco's* (☎22860 91223, ⓦwww.francescos.net; ❸) which offers the best value on the island, with clean doubles, a small number of dorms (€12 per person) and spectacular views from its bar. Near the bus stop, there's the more grown-up *Mediterraneo* (T22860 91521, Wwww.mediterraneo-ios.com; ⑤), with nice balconied rooms overlooking a pool. In the new quarter, the *Lofos* (T22860 91481, Elofosvillagehotel@yahoo.com; ④), to the right up from the Rollan supermarket, is a good bet, and also runs the *Lofos Village* hotel (contact details as above; ⑦) further up the hill. The friendly *Four Seasons Pension* (T22860 91308, F22860 91136; ②), up from Vangelis Bike Rental, is another quiet, but still central, choice.

Every evening in summer, Hóra is the centre of the island's **nightlife**, its streets throbbing with music from ranks of competing discos and clubs – mostly free, or with a nominal entrance charge, and inexpensive drinks. (Do, however, be wary of drinks that are overly cheap, as a few unscrupulous bars still resort to selling *bómba*, a cheap local drink that gets you drunk fast and makes you sick. If in doubt, ask for spirits by brand name.) Most of the smaller **bars** and pubs are tucked into the thronging narrow streets of the old village on the hill, offering something for everyone, and you'll have no trouble finding them. Evenings tend to start out in places like the *Fun Pub*, which also plays free films and has a pool table, and then progress around midnight to the bars up in the old town where *Rehab*, *Flames* and the *Red Bull Bar* are popular choices. Those looking to carry on eventually stagger down to the main road, where the larger **dance clubs** such as *Skorpion* and *Sweet Irish Dreams* are clustered near the bus stop.

**Eating** is a secondary consideration, but there are plenty of cheap and cheerful *psistariés* and takeaway joints: sound choices include the Italian restaurant *Pinocchio*, *The Nest* taverna and the *Lord Byron mezedhopolío* off the large church square – the latter is open year round and tries hard to recreate a traditional atmosphere, with old rebétika music and some good, unusual Greek food.

## Around the island

The most popular stop on the island's bus routes is **MYLOPÓTAS** (officially Mylopótamos), the site of a magnificent beach with watersport facilities. Due to the large number of young travellers in Íos, **camping** is a popular option. *Far Out Beach Club* (T22860 91468, Wwww.faroutclub.com; April–Sept) is the larger of the campsites, with well-organized facilities, including a pool, laundry, **internet**, **ATM**, and good-value cafeteria. It is, however, very popular and can get noisy and crowded in August; the adjacent hotel, *Far Out Village* (⑥), is under the same ownership. *Stars* (T22860 91302, Wwww.purplepigstars.com) is a friendly, laid-back complex by the road up to Hóra, with bungalows (②) and good camping facilities, including its own club and poolside bar. Nearby is the attractive and luxurious *Dionysos* hotel (T22860 91301, Wwww.dionysos-ios.gr; May–Oct; B&B ⑦). Up the road at the far end of the beach, *Gorgona* apartments (T&F22860 91307; June–Sept; ④), the water's edge *Drakos* (T22860 91281; ④) and the French-run *Hotel Ios Plage* (T22860 91301, Wwww.iosplage.com; June–Sept; B&B ⑤) have reasonable rooms, the *Ios Plage* recently refurbished and with an excellent French cuisine restaurant on its terrace.

On the rocks, beyond the *Ios Plage*, the *Harmony Restaurant* is one of the better places to eat, serving pizzas and Mexican food. The restaurants and self-service cafés behind the beach are uninspiring, and only the *Faros Café* rates a mention for staying open through the night to cater for the crowds returning from Hóra in the early hours. Mylópotos itself has surprisingly little in the way of nightlife.

Meltemi Watersports (T6932 153912, Wwww.meltemiwatersports.com) have outlets on Mylopótas and Manganári beaches, offering rental and **waterskiing**, **windsurfing** and wakeboarding lessons. They also hire out canoes, pedaloes, snorkelling equipment and sailboats, and give a discount for Rough Guide readers.

From Yialós, daily boats depart at around 10am (returning in the late afternoon; €12 return) to **Manganári** on the south coast, where there's a beach and a posh hotel. Most people go from Yialós to Manganári by buses (€6 return), which leave Yialós about 11am and 1pm, calling at Hóra and Mylópotos and returning later in the afternoon. Once predominantly nudist, this is now officially discouraged. There's more to see, and a better atmosphere at **Ayía Theodhóti** up on the east coast. You can get there on a paved road across the island – the daily excursion bus costs €3 return. A couple of kilometres south of Ayía Theodhóti is **Paleókastro**, a ruined Venetian castle which encompasses the remains of a marble-finished town and a Byzantine church. In the unlikely event that the beach – a good one and mainly nudist – is too crowded, try the one at **Psathí**, 14km to the southeast, although you'll need your own transport. Frequented by wealthy Athenians, this small resort has average, but pricey, tavernas, although the *Alonistra* fish taverna is a cheaper, excellent exception. Another decent beach is at **Kálamos**: get off the Manganári bus at the turning for Kálamos, which leaves you with a four-kilometre walk.

"**Homer's**" **tomb** can be reached by motorbike along an unpaved road (turning left from the paved road to Ayía Theodhóti 4.5km from Hóra). An ancient town has long since slipped down the side of the cliff, but the rocky ruins of the entrance to a tomb remain, as well as some graves – one of which is claimed to be Homer's, but which in reality probably dates only to the Byzantine era.

# Síkinos

**Síkinos** has so small a population that the mule ride or walk up from the port to the village was only replaced by a bus late in the 1980s and, until the new jetty was completed at roughly the same time, it was the last major Greek island where ferry passengers were still taken ashore in launches. With no dramatic characteristics, nor any nightlife to speak of, few foreigners make the short trip over here from neighbouring Folégandhros or from sporadically connected Íos Náxos, Páros and Thíra, and this is as near to completely unspoilt rural Greece as you'll find in the islands. There is now a bank with an ATM, and a post office, up in Kástro-Hóra.

## Aloprónia and Kástro-Hóra

Such tourist facilities as exist are concentrated in the little harbour of **ALOPRÓNIA**, with its long sandy beach, breakwaters and jetty. Many of the houses are summer holiday homes owned by expat Sikiniotes now resident in Athens or beyond. Accommodation owners meet the ferries; *Lucas* has water's edge studios (☎22860 51076, ⓦwww.sikinoslucas.gr; ❸) on the opposite side of the bay, as well as rooms and studios among a cluster of buildings by the Eko petrol station (and nearby bus stop), at the back of the village, 700m from the harbour along the road to Kástro-Hóra. Nearer to the Eko is the comfortable and hospitable ⌿ *Hotel Kamares* (☎22860 51234; ❸) and the smaller *Flora* (☎22860 51214, info at the harbour shop; ❸). The much pricier, but luxurious, *Porto Sikinos* complex (☎22860 51220, ⓦwww.portosikinos.gr; May–Oct; ❺) is tucked into the hillside, just beyond the *Flora* shop and *Lucas* taverna. On the jetty side of the bay are two **tavernas** and two **café–bars**: the *Meltemi* has a small menu but well-prepared food; the laid-back *Rock* café, perched above the jetty, has great views.

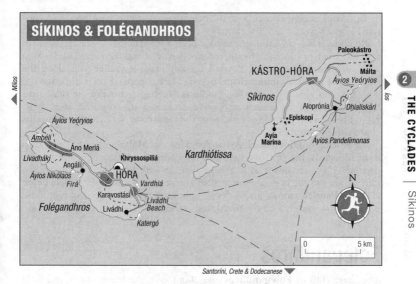

**SÍKINOS & FOLÉGANDHROS**

Santoríni, Crete & Dodecanese ▼

The double village of **KÁSTRO-HÓRA** is served by the single island bus, which shuttles regularly (from around 7.15am–11.45pm) between the harbour and here, with a single evening extension (around sunset) out to Episkopí (see p.204). On the ride up, the scenery turns out to be less desolate than initial views from the ferry suggest, while the village itself, draped across a ridge overlooking the sea, is a delightfully unspoilt settlement. Most of the facilities are in the larger, northeastern Kástro, whereas Hóra (officially Apáno Horió) is mainly residential. The oil-press **museum** (summer daily 5–7pm; free), run privately by a Greek-American, is highly recommended if you want to learn more about one of Greece's most significant crops. A partly ruined fortress-monastery, **Zoödhóhou Piyís** ("Life-giving Spring"), crowns the cliff-edged hill above, and is accessed by a stepped path out of the top of Kástro; the warden opens the church for a couple of hours in the evening from around 6pm – entrance is free, but donations to the restoration fund are very welcome. The architectural highlight of the village is the actual **kástro**, a quadrangle of eighteenth-century mansions arrayed defensively around a blue-domed church. There are only a few **rooms** in town, including a beautiful room and some family apartments at the *Iliovasilema* café/*zaharoplastío* (☎22860 51173, ⓦsikinos-sunset.gr; April–Sept; ❸) at the upper bus stop, between the two villages. The café also makes its own sweets including *pastélli*, a mixture of honey, sesame and orange traditionally given as wedding and baptismal gifts. Rooms are also available at the *Haroula* (☎22860 51212; ❸) and *Kaminia* (☎22860 51253; ❸), in Kástro, and at *Kostas* (☎22860 51064; ❸) in Hóra. You'll find a good selection of **food**, along with fine local wine, at the central *Klimataria* and *To Steki tou Garbi* next door. Both Síkinos and neighbouring Folégandhros have summer **cultural festivals** with various musical and film performances (ⓦwww.mediadellarte.gr).

## Around the island

Ninety-minutes walk northeast from Kástro-Hóra lies **Paleókastro**, the patchy remains of an ancient fortress. In the opposite direction, another ninety-minute walk takes you by old path or higher road through a steeply terraced landscape

203

to **Episkopí**, where elements of an ancient temple-tomb have been incorporated into a seventh-century church – the structure is known formally as the Iróön, though it is now thought to have been a Roman mausoleum rather than a temple of Hera. Note the weathered wooden door, and the cistern under long stone slabs in the courtyard. Beyond Episkopí, take a smaller path along the ridge to the obvious summit chapel of Ayía Marína, perched on a cliff edge and with fabulous views out over Folégandhros. The higher areas of the ridge have faint remnants of an ancient settlement, including an excavated water tank. From Episkopí it is possible to walk along the south coast, via Áyios Pandelímonas church, to Aloprónia.

The beaches of **Dhialiskári**, **Áyios Yeóryios** and **Málta** are reachable by *kaïki* from Aloprónia; the first two have dirt road access, and Áyios Yeóryios has the daytime *Almíra* restaurant. It is also possible to walk to Málta, but the path is unclear towards the end. A more feasible journey by foot is to the pebble beach at **Áyios Pandelímonas**: just under an hour's trail walk southwest of Aloprónia, it is the most sheltered on the island, and is also served by a *kaïki* in season.

# Folégandhros

The sheer cliffs of **Folégandhros** rise 300m from the sea in places, and until the early 1980s they were as effective a deterrent to tourists as they had historically been to pirates. Folégandhros was used as an island of political exile right up until 1974, but life in the high, barren interior has been eased since the junta years by the arrival of electricity and the construction of a road running lengthways from the harbour to Hóra and beyond. Development has been given further impetus by the recent increase in tourism and the commercialization this has brought.

An explosion in accommodation for most budgets, and improvement in ferry arrival times, means there is no longer much local tolerance of sleeping rough on the beaches – although in high summer there may be no accommodation left for late arrivals. Some of the better accommodation has higher prices for upstairs rooms, and unlike nearby Síkinos and Íos many places have mid-season prices as well as high and low. The increased wealth and trendiness of the heterogeneous clientele are reflected in fancy jewellery and clothes shops. Yet away from showcase Hóra and the beaches, the countryside remains mostly pristine, and is largely devoted to the cultivation of barley, the mainstay of many of the Cyclades before the advent of tourism. Donkeys and their paths are also still very much in evidence, since the terrain on much of the island is too steep for vehicle roads.

## Karavostási and around

**KARAVOSTÁSI**, the port whose name simply means "ferry stop", serves as a last-resort base; it has several **hotels** and plenty of rooms but little atmosphere. Best value is *Hotel Aeolos* (☎22860 41205, ⓦwww.aeolos-folegandros.gr; June–Sept; ❹) at mid-beach, while *Vardia Bay* (☎22860 41277, ⓦwww.vardiabay.com; B&B ❻) has rooms and studios in a great location above the jetty. The modern *Vrahos Hotel* (☎22860 41450, ⓦwww.hotel-vrahos.gr; May–Sept; B&B ❻) has nice rooms on the far side of the bay. *Kali Kardhia* taverna above the harbour boasts an excellent traditional menu, and there are a couple of pleasant beach **bars** including the *Syrma* ouzerí, housed in a converted boathouse. There are many buses a day in summer to Hóra, from where further occasional buses run to Áno Meriá or Angáli beach. Spyros's **motorbike rental** (☎22860 41448) is cheaper than its counterparts in Hóra. **Ferry tickets** are available at the Makrati agency.

The closest **beach**, other than the narrow main shingle strip, is the smallish, sand-and-pebble **Vardhiá**, signposted just north over the tiny headland. Some fifteen-minutes' walk south lies **Livádhi**, a rather average beach with tamarisk trees and the island's official **campsite**, *Livadhi Camping* (☎22860 41204; June–Sept), which is friendly, with a café-restaurant. Just before Livádhi, are the prettier, small beaches of Vitséntzou and Poundáki.

Touted as the island's most scenic beach, **Katergó** is a 300-metre stretch of pea-gravel with two offshore islets, on the southeastern tip of the island. Most visitors come on a boat excursion from Karavostási or Angáli, but you can also get there on foot (20min) from the hamlet of Livádhi, itself a fifteen-minute dirt road walk inland from Livádhi beach. Be warned, though, that it's a rather arduous and stony trek, with a final 80m descent on loose-surfaced paths; there is no shade on the walk or the beach. The narrow sea passage between the beach's southern cliffs and the right-hand islet has very strong currents and swimming through is not recommended.

## Hóra

The island's real character and appeal are to be found in the spectacular **HÓRA**, perched on a cliff-edge plateau some 35-minutes' walk from the dock; an hourly high-season **bus** service (6 daily spring & autumn) runs from morning until late at night, with additional services for ferries. Locals and foreigners – hundreds of them in high season – mingle at the cafés and tavernas under the trees of the two adjacent central squares, passing the time undisturbed by traffic, which is banned from the village centre. Towards the northern cliff-edge, and entered through two arcades, the defensive core of the medieval **kástro** is marked by ranks of two-storey residential houses, with almost identical stairways and slightly recessed doors.

▲ Cliff at Hóra, Folégandhros

From the cliff-edge Platía Poúnda, where the bus stops, a path zigzags up – with views along the northern coastline – to the wedding-cake church of **Kímisis Theotókou**, whose unusual design includes two little fake chapels mounted astride the roof. The church, formerly part of a nunnery, is on the gentlest slope of a pyramidal hill with 360m cliffs dropping to the sea on the northwest side and is a favourite spot for watching some of the Aegean's most spectacular sunsets. Beyond and below it hides the **Khryssospiliá**, a large cave with stalactites and inscriptions, once inhabited but now accessible only to climbers; the necessary steps and railings have tumbled away into the sea, although a minor, lower grotto can still be visited by *kaïki* from the port. Towards the top of the hill are a few fragments of the ancient Paleókastro.

### Practicalities

**Accommodation** around Hóra includes both hotels and rooms, with concentrations around the Platía Poúnda bus stop near the eastern entrance to the village and around the southern ring road which becomes the road to Áno Meriá. Of the hotels, the *Polikandia* (T22860 41322, Wwww.polikandia -folegandros.gr; ❺), around a garden just before the bus stop square, is a good, comfortable choice. The luxurious, cliff-edge *Anemomilos Apartments* (T22860 41309, Wwww.anemomilosapartments.com; ❼) are immaculately appointed, with stunning views and a romantic cocktail bar from which to watch the sunset, and a room adapted for wheelchair users.

The only **hotel** actually within old Hóra is the traditional *Castro* (T22860 41230, Wwww.hotel-castro.com; ❹), built in 1500, with rooms including three rather dramatic ones looking precipitously out over the sea. Near the southern ring-road, the new *Chora Resort* (T22860 41590, Wwww.choraresort.com; B&B; ❽), under the same management as the *Vardia Bay*, offers a large pool, fitness centre, designer rooms, minigolf and its own church for weddings and baptisms. The nearby *Aigio* hotel (T22860 41468; April–Sept; ❻) has **internet** facilities and a minibus to meet ferries; the family also has the immaculate *Evgenia/Embati* (April–Oct) rooms(❺) near the bus stop. At the western edge of Hóra, below the road to Áno Meriá, the *Anemoussa* (T22860 41077; ❺) has some of the most spectacular views out over the northern sea.

Hóra's dozen or so **restaurants** are surprisingly varied. The *Folégandhros* ouzerí-snack bar in the first plaza, Platía Dounávi, is a popular hangout with information, board games and **internet** connections. In the adjacent Platía Kondaríni is a dense cluster of busy eating places; while the more laid-back *Pounda*, near the bus stop, has a pleasant shady garden.

Hóra is inevitably beginning to sprawl at the edges, and the burgeoning **nightlife** – a few dance bars along with a number of music pubs and ouzerís – is to the south, away from most accommodation. *Patitiri* and *Greco* are lively bars, while *Kellari* is a rustic and charming wine bar with a more relaxed atmosphere. There's also a **post office**, **ATM** (Platía Dounávi) and **internet** access in the Diaplous and Makrati travel agencies between Dounávi and Poúnda squares.

## The rest of the island

West of Hóra, a paved road threads its way along the spine of the island towards sprawling **ÁNO MERIÁ**, – in fact a multitude of tiny hamlets, and the winter residence for many of Hóra's inhabitants. After 4km you pass its first houses, and then the small **folk museum** (mid-June to mid-Sept daily 5–8pm; donation requested), on a nineteenth-century farm (*thimoniá*) giving an insight into past rural life and with wonderful views of Hóra and its cliffs in the evening sunlight.

Many of the features such as *alónia*, circular threshing floors for winnowing barley and legumes, and *dhendrospítia*, high walls enclosing individual lemon or fruit trees, are still in use today.

About 2km beyond the museum is the *Irina* café (right), and the basic *Nikos* rooms (☏22860 41028; ❷), on the left; some rooms share facilities, and there is a communal kitchen. A little further, beyond the Elémonos church and about 1.5km beyond the museum, are a couple of grocery shops and *Mimis*, the best of the settlement's three tavernas, using locally produced food and open all year. Just beyond is the large parish church of Áyios Yeóryios (1905), with an unusual white, carved iconostasis. At Profítis Ilías a well-concealed bakery shop is along a short lane to the south of the road.

Up to seven times a day in high season, a **bus** trundles out here to drop people off at the long footpaths down to the various beaches on the southwest shore of the island; the end of the line is at **Taxiárhis** (Mitsákis), near the *Iliovasilema* and *Synandisi* (aka *Maria's*) tavernas. Muleteers await the buses here and will, for a fee, transport tourists down dirt roads to the beaches at **Ambéli** and **Áyios Yeóryios**; the former is small and can get crowded, the latter is a much better beach but faces north and is only comfortable when the wind blows from the south. **Livádhaki beach**, accessed by signed path from just beyond Taxiárhis, is an attractive beach with dunes and some tree shade.

A separate bus line from town runs towards Áno Meriá, but turns steeply down to the attractive and popular sheltered south coast beach of **Angáli**, where there are a few tavernas – the *Angali* is very well-priced, with good food. There are a few rooms elsewhere in the western part of the island but the majority are around Angáli, they include *Pano to Kyma* (☏22860 41190; ❸) and *Lydis* (☏22860 41105; June–Sept; ❸) above a small café-shop. Naturists should take the paths which lead twenty minutes east to **Firá** or west to **Áyios Nikólaos** beaches respectively. The latter is particularly fine, with many tamarisks, coarse sand and views back over the island. At Áyios Nikólaos, a lone taverna operates up by the namesake chapel; Firá has no facilities.

# Santoríni (Thíra)

As the ferry manoeuvres into the great caldera of Santoríni, the land seems to rise up and clamp around it. Gaunt, sheer cliffs loom hundreds of metres above the deep blue sea, nothing grows or grazes to soften the awesome view, and the only colours are the reddish-brown, black and grey pumice striations layering the cliff face of Thíra, the largest island in this mini-archipelago, and the location of all but the smallest of its modern settlements. The landscape tells of a history so dramatic and turbulent that legend hangs as fact upon it.

From as early as 3000 BC, the island developed as a sophisticated outpost of Minoan civilization, until sometime between 1647 and 1600 BC (according to latest estimates) when catastrophe struck: the volcano-island erupted, the second largest in human history, ejecting some 60 cubic kilometres of magma. The island's heart sank below the sea, leaving a crater (caldera) 10km in diameter. Earthquakes and tsunami reverberated across the Aegean, Thíra was destroyed, and the great Minoan civilization on Crete was dealt a severe blow by the ensuing ash fallout. At this point, the island's history became linked with legends of Atlantis, the "Happy Isles Submerged by Sea". Plato dated the cataclysm to approximately 9500 BC and was perhaps inspired by folk memories, but he probably intended the story as a metaphorical starting point for his ideas on government.

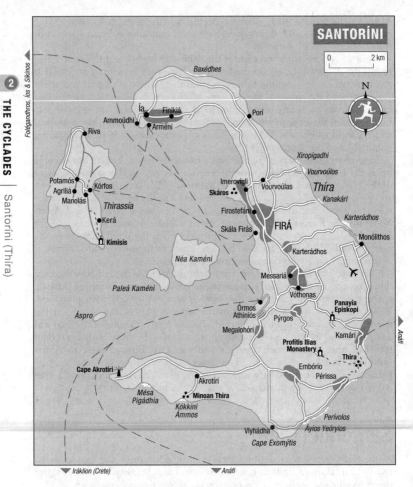

SANTORÍNI

0        2 km

N

Baxédhes

Porí

Ía     Finikiá
Ammoúdhi   Arméní

Ríva

Xiropígadhi
Vourvoúlos

Potamós
Agriliá   Kórfos
Manolás    Thirassía
Kerá

Imerovígli   Vourvoúlas   Thíra
Skáros
Kanakári
Firostefáni
Skála Firás   FIRÁ   Karterádhos

Monólithos

Kímisis

Néa Kaméni

Karterádhos

Paleá Kaméni

Messariá
Vóthonas

Áspro

Órmos
Athiniós
Megalohóri

Pýrgos   Panayía
Epískopí

Kamári

Profítis Ilías
Monastery

Cape Akrotíri

Akrotíri

Thira

Embório
Périssa

Mésa
Pigádhia   Minoan Thira
Kókkini
Ammos

Anáfi

Perívolos
Vlyhádha   Áyios Yeóryios
Cape Exomýtis

Iráklion (Crete)         Anáfi

These apocalyptic events, though, scarcely concern modern tourists, who come here to take in the spectacular views, stretch out on the island's dark-sand beaches and absorb the peculiar, infernal geographic features. The tourism industry has changed traditional island life, creating a rather expensive playground. There is one time-honoured local industry, however, that has benefited from all the outside attention: **wine**. Santoríni is one of Greece's most important producers, and the fresh, dry white wines it is known for (most from the *assýrtiko* grape for which the region is known) are the perfect accompaniment to the seafood served in the many restaurants and tavernas that hug the island's cliffs.

## Arrival

**Ferries** dock at the somewhat grim port of **Órmos Athiniós**. **Skála Firás** and **Ía** in the north are accessible by local ferries, excursion *kaïkia* and cruise ships. **Buses**, astonishingly crammed in summer, connect Athiniós with the island capital Firá and, less frequently, with Ía and the main beaches at Kamári and

Périssa. Disembark quickly and take whatever bus is going, if you want to avoid a long wait or a tedious hike up. You'll be accosted at Athiniós by people offering rooms all over the island; in the summer it might be a good idea to pay attention to them, given the scramble for beds, in Firá especially. There are, however, various scams involving the promise of beds in Firá which turn out to be elsewhere; keep your wits about you, and if in doubt, ask someone else.

Alternatively, from **Skála Firás**, you have the traditional route of 580 steps (about 45min) up to Firá – not too difficult a walk, if you don't mind mule manure (avoid sandals) – or you can go by mule (€4.50, negotiable off-season, watch out for fleas, and scraped knees as you pass close to walls) or cable car (April–Oct daily 6.30am–9/11pm, every 20min; Nov–Mar daily 7.30am–10.30am & 2.30–4.30pm, every 30min; €4, luggage €2 extra), the latter so exhilarating a ride that you may want to take it for fun – though the queues to get on can be over an hour. The overstretched **airport** is on the east side of the island, near Monólithos; there are seven buses a day in summer to the Firá bus station (Ⓦwww.ktel-santorini.gr), between 7.25am and 8.15pm.

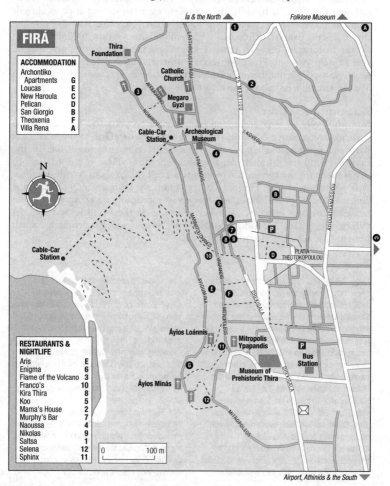

**FIRÁ**

**ACCOMMODATION**
| | |
|---|---|
| Archontiko Apartments | G |
| Loucas | E |
| New Haroula | C |
| Pelican | D |
| San Giorgio | B |
| Theoxenia | F |
| Villa Rena | A |

**RESTAURANTS & NIGHTLIFE**
| | |
|---|---|
| Aris | E |
| Enigma | 6 |
| Flame of the Volcano | 3 |
| Franco's | 10 |
| Kira Thira | 8 |
| Koo | 5 |
| Mama's House | 2 |
| Murphy's Bar | 7 |
| Naoussa | 4 |
| Nikolas | 9 |
| Saltsa | 1 |
| Selena | 12 |
| Sphinx | 11 |

Ía & the North

Folklore Museum

Thira Foundation

Catholic Church

Megaro Gyzi

Cable-Car Station

Archeological Museum

N

Cable-Car Station

PLATIA THEOTOKOPOULOU

Áyios Loánnis

Mitropolis Ypapandis

Bus Station

Museum of Prehistoric Thira

Áyios Minás

0    100 m

Airport, Athiniós & the South

# Firá

Half-rebuilt after a devastating earthquake in 1956, **FIRÁ** (also known as Thíra or Hóra) clings precariously to the edge of the enormous caldera. The rising and setting of the sun are especially beautiful when seen here against the Cycladic buildings lining the clifftop, and are even enough to make battling through the high-season crowds worthwhile.

## Arrival and information

**Buses** leave Firá from just south of Platía Theotokopoúlou to Périssa, Perívolos, Kamári, Monólithos (via the airport), Akrotíri, Órmos Athiniós and the airport. The island's **taxi** base (☎22860 22555) is near the bus station, within steps of the main square. If you want to see the whole island in a couple of days, a rented **motorbike** might do but be aware that local driving standards are often very poor; try Moto Chris at the top of the road that leads down to *Santorini Camping* (see below), while Ancient Thira Tours (☎22860 23915), on the main street in Firá, hire out **mountain bikes** and quads. The Firá branch of Nomikos Travel, opposite the OTE, is friendly and organizes **excursions** and trips to ancient Thíra and Thirassía in conjunction with Kamari Tours (☎22860 31390). The tiny state-run **tourist office** (daily 9am–midnight in season; ☎22860 25490), on the main street between the bus station and the main square, may also be able to help you out. There are several **internet cafés** gathered on the main square, as well as a number of **launderettes** dotted around town, the best being We Do Laundry, just above the road to the campsite.

## Accommodation

Santoríni certainly isn't cheap, and caldera-view properties in Firá tend to be particularly expensive. Adjacent **Imerovígli** and **Firostefáni**, to the north, can have equally stunning views and prices. Prices are more reasonable in the eastern, inland side of town. An alternative location, where you don't have to pay as much for the view, is **Karterádhos**, a small village about twenty-minutes' walk southeast of Firá. The only other option for budget accommodation is *Santorini Camping* (☎22860 22944, ⓦwww.santorinicamping.gr; April–Oct), the nearest **campsite** to town. (The best campsite on the island is near Akrotíri village; see p.216) Considering Santoríni's popularity, it's definitely worth phoning for accommodation in advance.

### Firá

Archontiko Apartments By Áyios Minás church, below the cathedral ☎22860 24376, ⓔarchontikoapartments@hotmail.com. Stunning antique-furnished apartments in a 350-year old stone house perched in a quiet spot over the caldera. May–Oct. ❺

Loucas Below Ypapandís ☎22860 22480, ⓦwww.loucashotel.com. Traditional caldera-side hotel with rooms in barrel-ceilinged caves carved into the cliffside and a beautiful pool. Feb–Oct. ❼

New Haroula On road to the *Santorini Camping* campsite ☎22860 24226, ⓦwww.newharoula.com. Stylish but laid-back family-run hotel with pool and smart doubles. April–Oct. ❺

Pelican On road to campsite ☎22860 23113, ⓦwww.pelicanhotel.gr. Large hotel with spacious rooms near the centre, with free wi-fi. B&B ❻

San Giorgio Tucked away to left of parking below main square ☎22860 23516, ⓦwww.sangiorgiovilla.gr. Hospitable, clean, excellent-value rooms, all with balconies (discount for Rough Guide readers); there's a small pool at the rear. Free transfers. March–Nov. ❹

Theoxenia Ypapandís ☎22860 22740, ⓦwww.theoxenia.net. Stylish boutique hotel with large rooms right in the old town. Guests can also use the caldera-side pool at the nearby *Ariesanna* hotel. B&B ❼

Villa Rena Ten-minutes' walk from town towards the folklore museum ☎22860 28130, ⓦwww.renasplace.gr. Comfortable hotel with a large pool in a quiet spot near the open-air cinema (discount for Rough Guide readers). Minibus transfers available for a charge. April–Oct. ❺

## Firostefáni

**Galini** On waterfront ☏22860 22095, ⊛www
.hotelgalini.gr. Good-value, friendly hotel carved
into the cliff face in a relatively quiet spot 10min
walk from Firá. March–Nov. ❻

**Manos Apartments** On waterfront ☏22860 23202,
⊛www.manos-apartments.gr. Large, cool studios
and apartments with large verandas and great
views. April–Oct. ❽

**Mylos** On main street ☏22860 23884. One of the
cheaper hotel options in Firostefáni; rooms come
with all mod cons and balconies. April–Oct. ❺

## Imerovígli

**Astra** ☏22860 23641, ⊛www.astra.gr. Luxury,
caldera-side apartments and suites, with pool,
steam-room and Jacuzzi. ❽

**Kastro Katerinas** ☏22860 22708, ✉hkaterin
@otenet.gr. Moderately-priced small hotel, with
caldera views from the large balcony/bar area
only. ❻

## Karterádhos

**Pension George** ☏22860 22351, ⊛www
.pensiongeorge.com. Comfortable rooms and
studios, pool and a good welcome, just 15min walk

from Firá. They also have new apartments to the
east, nearer the beach. ❹

## The Town

Firá's dramatic history is explored in a number of museums. Between the
cathedral and bus station, the **Museum of Prehistoric Thira** (Tues–Sun
8.30am–7.30pm; €3, includes entrance to the archeological museum) has informative displays of fossils, Cycladic art and astonishing finds from Akrotíri. The
**archeological museum** (Tues–Sun 8am–5pm; €3, includes entrance to the
above), near the cable car to the north of town, is less well presented, but has a
collection which includes a curious set of erotic Dionysiac figures. The
handsome **Megaro Ghyzi** (Mon–Sat 10.30am–1.30pm & 5–8pm, Sun
10.30am–4.30pm; €3), just north of the archeological museum in an old
mansion owned by the Catholic diocese of Santoríni, has been restored as a
cultural centre, and has a good collection of old prints and maps as well as
photographs of the town before and after the 1956 earthquake. Further north
along the caldera, the **Thíra Foundation** (signed "Wall-paintings of Thera";
daily 10am–8pm; €3), housed in galleries carved into the cliffside, contains
superb life-size colour reproductions of the frescoes of Akrotíri (daily 10am–
8pm; €3). Towards the back of the town, north of the main square, is the
extensive **Lignos Folklore Museum** (daily 10am–2pm; €3), which features a
completely furnished nineteenth-century house with period winery, cavern,
garden and workshops, as well as a gallery and historical archive.

## Eating

Although Firá's **restaurants** are primarily aimed at the tourist market, the food
can be very good; views of the crater will add considerably to the price.

**Aris** Below the *Loucas* hotel. Dependably good Greek
and international food in a relaxed atmosphere, with
a sensational view (and prices to match).

**Flame of the Volcano** Main street, north past the
cable-car station. Reliable family-run restaurant,
the northernmost on the caldera rim.

**Mama's House** North of the main square, on the
road to Ía. A cheap, backpacker-friendly spot with
hearty breakfasts, filling dishes and Aegean views
from its balcony.

**Naoussa** Lagoudera Shopping Centre, on Erythroú
Stavroú. Good traditional Greek and seafood in an
upstairs area.

**Nikolas** Erythroú Stavroú. An old and defiantly
traditional taverna, but it can be hard to get a table.

**Saltsa** Between Firá and Imerovígli. One of
the best restaurants in the area, with
inventive cuisine in an attractive, unpretentious
setting.

**Selena** Below Mitropoléos. Fíra's most famous restaurant, quiet, romantic, and beautifully positioned overlooking the sea, with delicious, inventive food.

**Sphinx** Mitropoléos (Via d'Oro), opposite the cathedral. On terraces overlooking the caldera, and offering exotic pasta dishes with a Greek twist, at a price.

## Drinking and nightlife

Most of the **nightlife** is northwest of the central square on Erythroú Stavroú, often not starting much before midnight and busiest between 1am and 6am. Cover charges can be high. There is an open-air **cinema** near the folklore museum.

**Enigma** Erythroú Stavroú. Long-established dance club with large barrel-roofed hall and outdoor area with a palm-tree bar.

**Franco's** Near the top of the steps down to Skála Firás. Exclusive, expensive cocktail bar in a fabulous location. Classical music, champagne and sunbeds.

**Kira Thira** Erythroú Stavroú. Laid-back with live music, jazz and blues.

**Koo** Erythroú Stavroú. Chill-out or disco, with candles and cocktails.

**Murphy's Bar** Erythroú Stavroú. Reasonably priced Irish pub with all the obligatory hilarity.

# Northern Santoríni

Once outside Firá, the rest of Thíra comes as a surprise. The volcanic soil is highly fertile, with most of the more level areas terraced and cultivated: mainly grapes, but some tomatoes, pistachios and wheat, all still harvested and planted by hand. However the advent of tourism has led to much unsightly ribbon development along the roads, and away from the caldera Santoríni is one of the less attractive Cycladic islands.

A satisfying – if demanding – approach to **Ía**, 12km from Firá in the northwest of the island, is to walk the stretch from **IMEROVÍGLI** (Merovígli), 3km out of Firá, using a spectacular footpath along the lip of the caldera; the walk takes around two hours. Jutting up from the side of the cliff is the conspicuous conical rock of **Skáros**, a Venetian fortress from 1207, and until the eighteenth century the site of an important settlement, although now almost all the structures have succumbed to earthquakes. It can be mounted along a steep but obvious trail for unsurpassed views over the caldera and back to Thíra.

## Ía and around

**ÍA** (Oía), the most photographed town on the island, was once a major fishing port of the Aegean, but it has declined in the wake of economic depression, wars, earthquakes and depleted fish stocks. Partly destroyed in the 1956 earthquake, the town has been sympathetically reconstructed, its multicoloured houses clinging to the cliff face. Apart from the caldera and the town itself, there are a couple of things to see, including the **Naval Museum** (Mon & Wed–Sun 10am–2pm & 5–8pm; €3) and the very modest remains of a Venetian castle. It is a quieter, though still touristy, alternative to Firá, with a **post office** and several **bike-rental** offices, an **easyInternet** café, and a good foreign-language bookshop, Atlantis Books. There are also a couple of travel agencies, including Karvounis (☎22860 71290, ✉mkarvounis@otenet.gr), on the pedestrian street.

Much of the town's **accommodation** is in its restored old houses, including the friendly *Hotel Laouda* (☎22860 71204; ❺) with rooms and studios, perched below the rim, the popular *Hotel Anemones* (☎22860 71220;

April–Oct; B&B ❹) and the *Hotel Fregata* (☎22860 71221; ❺), with its central location and good views; the luxurious *Perivolas Traditional Houses* (☎22860 71308, ⓦwww.perivolas.gr; ❽) are cut into the cliff near a pool suspended at its edge. Well signed from the bus terminal, the excellent *Oia Youth Hostel* (☎22860 71465, ⓦwww.santorinihostel.gr; May–Oct; B&B; €15–17 per person) has a terrace and shady courtyard, laundry, a good café-bar and clean dormitories; excursions are available at reduced prices.

**Restaurant** prices can be as steep as the cliffs, at the western end of town, and in general the further east you go along the central ridge towards the new end of Ía the better the value; try the *Anemomilos* or *Laokastri*. Slightly removed from the sunset tourist stampede, the pleasant *Karma*, serving Eastern cuisine, is on the road leading down to the youth hostel, while, for a splurge, *1800* is regarded by some as the finest restaurant on the island, serving highly refined Mediterranean cuisine. **Nightlife** revolves around sunset-gazing, for which people are coached in from all over the island, creating traffic chaos and driving up prices, though the sunset is little different seen from Ía than from Firá. Public buses are extremely full around this time.

Below the town, two sets of 220-odd steps switchback hundreds of metres down to two small harbours: one to **Ammoúdhi**, for the fishermen, and the other to **Arméni**, where the excursion boats dock. Both have decent fish tavernas, the one in Arméni specializing in grilled octopus lunches. **FINIKIÁ**, 1km east of Ía, is a quieter traditional village. *Lotza Studios* (☎22860 71051, ⓦwww.santorinilotza.gr, or details from Lotza restaurant in Ía; ❹) are located in a 200-year-old house in the middle of the village, while the smarter *Hotel Finikia* (aka *Finikia's Place*; ☎22860 71373, ⓦwww.finikiaplace.gr; April–Oct; B&B ❺), above the village near the main road, has rooms and studios with wi-fi.

## The east coast

Thíra's **beaches**, on the island's east and south coasts, are long black stretches of volcanic sand which get blisteringly hot in the afternoon sun. They're no secret, and in the summer the crowds can be a bit overpowering. Amongst the resorts lie the substantial and beautifully sited remains of **ancient Thira**.

### Kamári

In the southeast, the family resort of **KAMÁRI** is popular with package-tour operators, and hence more touristy. Nonetheless it's quieter (apart from airport noise) and cleaner than most, with a well-maintained seafront promenade, and is home to a diving centre. There's a range of beachfront **accommodation**, including *Hotel Nikolina* (☎22860 32363, ⓔnikolina-htl @hol.gr; April–Oct; ❸), with basic but cheap rooms towards the southern end of the beach, as well as the *White House* (☎69970 91488; ❹) and further north along the beach, the friendly *Sea Side Hotel* (☎22860 33403, ⓦwww.seaside .gr; May–Oct; ❹) above the recommended *Giorgio's* restaurant. *Rose Bay Hotel* (☎22860 33650, ⓦwww.rosebay.gr; April–Oct; B&B ❼) is a much pricier option, with a pleasant pool setting, set back from the beach amongst other luxurious hotels in the north part of town. At the foot of Mt Profítis Ilías, a good choice is the 🍴 *Villa Ostria* (☎22860 31727, ⓦwww.villaostria.gr; ❹), a friendly, family-run oasis of studios and apartments that stands in pleasant contrast to the resort's many large hotel blocks.

*Psistaria Kritikos*, a taverna-grill frequented by locals, is one of the better places to **eat** on the island. It's a long way out of Kamári on the road up to Messariá, and too far to walk, but the bus stops outside. There are plenty of cafés and restaurants behind the beach, though many are expensive or uninspiring. *Saliveros*, in front of the *Hotel Nikolina*, has taverna food at reasonable prices, and *Almira*, next to *Sea Side Rooms*, is a smarter restaurant and only a little more expensive. For a seafood splurge, try *Skaramangas*.

Kamári has little in the way of clubs and nightlife, but there is a good open-air **cinema** near the campsite, which also hosts cultural events. On the seafront, Navy's Diving Centre (☎22860 31006, ⓦwww.navys.gr) offers courses for beginners and volcanic reef diving for certified divers.

### Ancient Thira

Kamári and Périssa – to the southwest – are separated by the Mésa Vounó headland, on which stood **ancient Thira** (Tues–Sun 8.30am–2.30pm; €1.50), the post-eruption settlement dating from 915 BC through to the Venetian period. Excursion minibuses go up from Kamári (€8), spending two hours at the site (ask at Ancient Thira Tours, ☎22860 32474, at the foot of the main hill in Kamári), but you can also ride a donkey up (€20) or walk the interminably looping cobbled road called *Archaias Thiras*, starting from Ancient Thira Tours. A more interesting route is the zigzag path that starts beside the *Antinea* hotel and goes via the whitewashed cliff-set Zoödhóhou Piyís church where a cave contains one of Thíra's few freshwater springs. The path meets the road at a saddle between Mésa Vounó and Profítis Ilías, where a refreshments van sells drinks. The site can also be reached by a stony, shadeless path from Périssa; from either it's less than an hour's walk. From here, the path to the site passes a chapel dating back to the fourth century AD before skirting round to the Temenos of Artemidoros with bas-relief carvings of a dolphin, eagle and lion representing Poseidon, Zeus and Apollo. Next, the trail follows the sacred way of the ancient city through the remains of the agora and past the theatre. Most of the ruins (dating mainly from Hellenistic and Roman times) are difficult to place, but the site is impressively large and the views are awesome.

### Périssa

Things are considerably scruffier at **PÉRISSA**, around the cape. Because of its beach and abundance of cheap rooms, it's crowded with backpackers. *Camping Perissa Beach* (☎22860 81343) is right behind the beach and has plenty of shade but is also next to a couple of noisy late-night bars. There is also a basic youth hostel on the road into Périssa: *Anna* (☎22860 82182, Ⓔannayh@otenet.gr; €8 per person). There are plenty of cheap rooms in the same area and some upmarket hotels behind the beach; the modern *Meltemi Hotel* (☎22860 81325, ⓦwww.meltemivillage.gr; B&B ❼) on the main road, which also runs the nearby water park, is a good choice. The beach itself extends several kilometres to the west, through Perívolos to Áyios Yeóryios, sheltered by the occasional tamarisk tree and with beach bars dotted along at intervals. *Dichtia* ("*Nets*") and *Aquarius* are two excellent restaurants here. Santoríni Diving Centre (☎22860 31006, ⓦwww.divecenter.gr) offers diving courses for beginners, as well as volcanic reef diving for certified divers and snorkelling trips. A new attraction in Périssa is the **Museum of Minerals and Fossils** (summer, daily 10am–2pm; winter Sun only) with exhibits including rare palm tree fossils from pre-eruption Santoríni, and a large collection of minerals from Lávrio.

## Inland Santoríni

West of Kamári is **Panayía Episkopí**, the most important Byzantine monument on the island. Built in the eleventh century, it was the setting of centuries of conflict between Orthodox Greeks and Catholics, but is most notable today for its carved iconostasis of light blue marble with a white grain. Further west, **PÝRGOS** is one of the oldest settlements on the island, a jumble of old houses and alleys that still bear the scars of the 1956 earthquake. It climbs to another Venetian fortress crowned by several churches, and you can clamber around the battlements for sweeping views over the entire island and its Aegean neighbours. A thirty-minute hike up the steep, winding road to the southeast leads to the monastery of **Profítis Ilías** (1771), now sharing its 567m refuge with Greek radio and TV pylons and the antennae of a NATO station. With just one monk remaining to look after the church, the place only really comes to life for the annual Profitis Ilías festival (20 July), when the whole island troops up here to celebrate. The views are rewarding, and from near the entrance to the monastery an old footpath heads across the mountainous ridge in about an hour to ancient Thíra (see opposite). Profitis Ilías and Mésa Vounó are virtually the only remaining visible components of the pre-eruption landscape. By way of contrast, **MESSARIÁ**, north of Pýrgos – has a skyline consisting solely of massive church domes presiding over houses huddled in a ravine. The **Arhondikó Aryírou** (daily 9am–2pm & 4.30–7pm; €4) is a fully restored nineteenth-century mansion, combining Neoclassical elements with island architecture.

South of Pýrgos and towards Megalohóri are scattered a few of Santoríni's most important **wineries**, the largest of which, Boutari (just out of Megalohóri, Ⓦwww.boutari.gr) and Santo (near Pýrgos, Ⓦwww.santowines.gr; April–Nov, 10am–sunset) offer the most comprehensive tours (€2–3), complete with multimedia presentations. Slightly more hidden, on the road to Kamári, are smaller wineries, such as the welcoming Canava Roussos (Ⓦwww.canavaroussos,gr; May–Oct) and Koutsoyianopoulos, with a 300m cave which is home to the **wine museum** (April–Oct, daily noon–8pm; €4 includes tasting; on Friday evenings there are buffet meals with Greek dancing) – which offers a more intimate glimpse at the wine-making process. Whatever the scale of the tour, none is complete without a taste of Santoríni's prized dessert wine, **visánto** (remniscent of the Tuscan *vin santo*), among the finest wines produced in Greece. Tour prices at the smaller wineries (€2–5) usually include tastings, while samples are available from the larger wineries for a nominal fee.

## Akrotíri and the south coast

Evidence of the Minoan colony that once thrived here has been uncovered at the ancient site of Minoan Thira at **Akrotíri** (closed since 2005, for safety work that had not started by 2008, but check with the prehistoric museum in Firá, see p.211), at the southwestern tip of the island. The site was inhabited from the Late Neolithic period through to the seventeenth century BC. Tunnels through the volcanic ash uncovered structures, two and three storeys high, first damaged by earthquake (when it was abandoned), then buried by eruption; only a small fraction of what was the largest Minoan city outside of Crete has been exposed thus far. Many of the lavish frescoes that once adorned the walls are currently exhibited in Athens, though there are excellent reproductions at the Thíra Foundation in Firá (see p.211).

Akrotíri itself can be reached by bus from Firá or Périssa. The newest and best **campsite** on the island, *Caldera View Camping* (T22860 82010), is situated here, as is the *Glaros* **taverna**, on the way to Kókkini Ámmos, which has fine food, though the equally good *Dolphins* is better situated on the water. **Kókkini Ámmos** (Red Beach) is about 500m from the site and is quite spectacular, with high reddish-brown cliffs above sand of the same colour. There's a drinks stall in a cave hollowed into the base of the cliff. It's a better beach than the one below the site, but gets crowded in season.

### The beaches of the south

More secluded black-sand beaches lie under the surreal, pockmarked pumice stone that dominates the lunar coast around **Cape Exomýtis** at the island's southern extremity. Both **Vlyhádha** to the west and **Áyios Yeóryios** to the east of the cape are accessed by decent roads branching off from the main one to Embório, though no buses run here and there are no amenities to speak of. An hour's walk west of ancient Akrotíri, a lighthouse marks the tip of **Cape Akrotíri**, which offers excellent views of the Kaméni islets and Thirassía.

## The Kaméni islets and Thirassía

From either Skála Firás or Ía (Ammoúdhi), boat excursions and local ferries run to the charred volcanic islets of **Paleá Kaméni** (active 46–1458 AD) and **Néa Kaméni** (active 1707–1950). At Paleá Kaméni you can swim (c.150m) from the boat to warm springs with sulfurous mud, and Néa Kaméni (€2 entrance fee), with its own mud-clouded hot springs, features a demanding hike to a smouldering, volcanically active crater. **Day-tours**, arranged through any of the travel companies in Firá and Ía, take in a hike up to the active crater of Néa Kaméni and a possible dip in the mineral-laden springs at Paleá Kaméni, then stay two or three hours on Thirassía. Prices range from €10 for transport on a large ferry to about €30 for a more intimate guided tour on a traditional *kaïki*. The glass-bottom *Calypso* makes the same excursion for €20 and hovers over the volcanic reefs at the end of each journey to allow passengers a peek into the dark depths of Santoríni's flooded crater.

### Moving on

When it comes to **leaving**, especially for summer evening ferry departures, it's best to buy your ticket in advance. Note, too, that although the bus service stops around midnight, a taxi isn't expensive (about €10 from Firá to Athiniós). Incidentally, **ferry information** from any source is notoriously unreliable on Thíra and rival agencies don't inform you of alternatives – Nomikos Travel (T22860 23660), with seven branches, is the largest, though Pelikan (T22860 22220) is also recommended. In any case, it's wise to enquire about your options at several agencies and triple-check departure times before working your way back to the port. If you do get stranded in Athiniós, there's no place to stay, and the tavernas are mediocre, though there is internet access at @thinios.com café.

The boat excursions also continue to the relatively unspoilt islet of **Thirassía** (Wwww.thirasia.gr), which was once part of Thíra until sliced off by an eruption in the third century BC. It's an excellent destination, except during the tour-boat rush of lunch hour. At other times, the island is one of the quietest in the Cyclades, with views as dramatic as any on Thíra. The downside is that there is no sandy beach, no nightlife and nowhere to change money, though there is an **ATM** at the KEP office.

Most tour boats head for the village of **Kórfos**, a stretch of shingle backed by fishermen's houses and high cliffs. It has a few tavernas – including *Tonio* which stays open when the day-trippers have gone – but no rooms. From Kórfos a stepped path climbs up to **MANOLÁS**, nearly 200m above, and where donkeys are still used for transport. Manolás straggles along the edge of the caldera, an untidy but attractive small village that gives an idea of what Thíra was like before tourism arrived there. It has a bakery, a couple of shops and the friendly *Panorama* and *Candouni* tavernas which both do a great octopus *souvláki*, and open for the midday rush. **Rooms** include *Jimmy's* (☎22860 29102; ❹) overlooking the village from the south.

The best **excursion** from Manolás is to follow the unmade road heading south; about halfway along you pass the church of Profitis Ilías on a hilltop to the left. From here an old and overgrown trail descends through the deserted caldera-side village of **Kerá**, before running parallel with the road to the **monastery of the Kímisis** above the southern tip of the island. Minoan remains were excavated in a pumice quarry to the west of here in 1867, several years before the first discoveries at Akrotíri, but there is nothing to be seen today.

**Ferries** run to Thirassía from Órmos Athiniós 5–7 times a week, and 2–3 times daily from Ía (Ammoúdhi); ask at Santo Star (☎22860 23082, Wwww.santostar.gr) in Firá for details. There should be no problem taking a car or rental bike over, but fill up with petrol first.

# Anáfi

A ninety-minute boat ride to the east of Santoríni, **Anáfi** is the last stop for ferries and is something of a travellers' dead end, with no high-season ferries on to Crete or the Dodecanese, and no bank (there is now a single ATM, but bring some cash with you). Not that this is likely to bother most of the visitors, who come here for weeks in midsummer to enjoy the island's beaches.

Although idyllic geographically, Anáfi is a harsh place, its mixed granite and limestone core overlaid by volcanic rock spewed out by Thíra's eruptions. Apart from the few olive trees and vines grown in the valleys, the only plants that seem to thrive are prickly pears.

## The harbour and Hóra

The tiny harbour hamlet of **ÁYIOS NIKÓLAOS** has a taverna, *Akroyiali Popi's*, with a few rooms (☎22860 61218; ❸), and a travel agent selling boat tickets next door, plus a café/snack bar at the inland end. In August there are enough Greek visitors to fill all the rooms on the island, so it's a good idea to book ahead. In season a bus runs from the harbour up to Hóra every two hours or so, 9am to 11pm, to stops at both ends of the village.

**HÓRA** itself, adorning a conical hill, is a stiff 25-minute climb up the obvious broad concrete path which short-cuts the modern road. Exposed and blustery when the *meltémi* is blowing, Hóra can initially seem a rather forbidding ghost town. This impression is slowly dispelled as you discover the hospitable islanders taking their coffee in sheltered, south-facing terraces, or under the barrel vaulting that features in domestic architecture here and in Santoríni, partly due to the lack of timber for making normal roofs.

For accommodation, try *Ta Plagia* (☎22860 61308, ⓦwww.taplagia.gr; B&B ❸), with rooms, studios and family houses, plus good home-made breakfasts and internet facilities, or the *Panorama* (☎22860 61292; May–Oct; ❷) at the east edge of the village, with stunning views south. Also recommended are the rooms of *Illiovasilema* (☎22860 61280; ❹) on the other side of the village (ask at *To Steki* restaurant if you can't find them). Evening **diners** divide their custom between the simple, welcoming ⚵ *To Steki*, with good food, barrel wine and an excellent *raki* served on its terrace, and the more upmarket *Alexandhra's* on the central walkway. Nightlife takes place in *Mylos*, in a converted windmill in the village, and *Argo*, which is also a good spot for breakfast. For exploring Anáfi's roads by **bike**, you can rent one at either *Panorama* (see above) or Rent Moto-Bikes (☎22860 61280) at the other side of the village. There is also a **travel agency**, Jeyzed Travel (☎22860 61253), who sell boat tickets and arrange excursions around the island. Several tiny shops, a bakery and a **post office** round up the list of amenities.

## East along the coast

The glory of Anáfi is a string of south-facing beaches starting under the cliffs at Áyios Nikólaos. These – along with two nearby monasteries – are accessible by road, with four buses a day plying the route from Hóra, although walking is still an option.

### The beaches

Head for **Klisídhi**, east of the harbour, which has 200m of gently shelving sand. Above the reed-and-tamarisk oasis backing the beach, there are two cafés, a taverna, *Margaritas*, which has rooms (☎22860 61237, Ⓔanafi1@hol.gr; ❸), and the comfortable *Villa Apollon* (☎22860 61348, ⓦwww.apollonvillage.com; ❸) with rooms, studios and bungalows on the hillside above. Klisídhi can be reached by road but it's quicker to take the short clifftop path starting behind the power station at the harbour.

From a point on the paved road just east of Hóra, the **main path** skirting the south flank of the island roller-coasters in and out of several agricultural valleys that provide most of Anáfi's produce and fresh water. Just under an hour along, you veer down a side trail to **Roúkounas** with some 500m of broad sand rising to tamarisk-stabilized dunes; unfortunately much of the area behind is used as a toilet by the many rough campers. A single indifferent taverna operates up by the main trail in season; the craggy hill of **Kastélli**, an hour's scramble above the taverna, is the site both of ancient Anáfi and a ruined Venetian castle.

Beyond Roúkounas, it's another half-hour on foot to the first of the exquisite half-dozen **Katelímatsa** coves, of all shapes and sizes, and 45 minutes to **Monastíri** beach, where the bus stops – all without facilities, so come prepared. Nudism is banned on Monastíri, because of its proximity to the monastery.

### The monasteries
Between Katelímatsa and Kálamos, the main route keeps inland, to arrive at the **monastery of Zoödhóhou Piyís**, two-hours' walk from Hóra. The bus stops at a patch of bare ground a few hundred metres before the building. A ruined temple of Apollo is incorporated into the monastery buildings to the side of the main gate, while the courtyard, with a welcome cistern, is the venue for the island's major festivals, celebrated eleven days after Easter and September 7–8. Go left immediately before the monastery to join the spectacular onward path to **Kalamiótissa**, a little monastery perched atop the abrupt limestone pinnacle at the extreme southeast of the island. It takes another hour to reach, but is eminently worthwhile for the stunning scenery and views over the entire south coast – there is no accessible water up here, so bring enough with you.

# Travel details

## Ferries

Most of the Cyclades are served by main-line ferries from Pireás. Boats for Kéa, and seasonally elsewhere, depart from Lávrio. There are regular services from Rafína to Ándhros, Tínos and Mýkonos, with seasonal sailings elsewhere. All three ports are easily reached by bus from Athens. Between May and Sept there are also a few weekly sailings to the most popular islands from Crete and the eastern Aegean.

The frequency of Pireás, Lávrio and Rafína sailings given below is from Jan to Dec, and the timings are for both direct and indirect services. For other islands the listings are intended to give an idea of services from late June to early Sept, when most visitors tour the islands. During other months, expect departures to be at or below the minimum level listed, with some routes cancelled entirely.

The *Blue Star* ships (Ⓦwww.bluestarferries.gr) are usually the fastest for only slightly more than the price of standard tickets – and much less than the cost of catamaran services.

All agents are required to issue computerized tickets, to conform to EU regulations and prevent the ferry overcrowding so common in the past. In high season (particularly Easter, Aug, Sept and elections), popular routes will be booked up well in advance, so it is important to check availability on arrival in Greece and book your outward and final inbound pre-flight tickets well ahead (particularly those returning to Pireás from the most popular islands). That said, agents can be notoriously ill-equipped with advance information on ferry schedules, and purchasing a ticket too far in advance can lead to problems with delayed or cancelled boats. There is usually more space on ferries sailing between islands than to and from Pireás. For catamaran details, see p.221.

**Amorgós** to: Ándhros (2–3 weekly; 8hr); Astypálea (3 weekly; 1hr 30min); Dhonoússa (2–3 weekly; 1hr 10min–1hr 30min); Iráklia (2–3 weekly; 1hr); Koufoníssi (2–3 weekly; 1hr); Mýkonos (2–3 weekly; 6hr); Náxos (6–8 weekly; 4hr); Páros (6–8 weekly; 5hr 30min); Skhinoússa (2–3 weekly; 1hr); Sýros (3–4 weekly; 7hr); Tínos (2–3 weekly; 7hr).

**Anáfi** to: Folégandhros (1 weekly; 4hr 30min); Íos (6–8 weekly; 2hr 30min); Náxos (6–8 weekly; 3hr 30min), Páros (6–8 weekly; 4hr); Síkinos (1 weekly; 4hr); Sýros (1 weekly; 10hr); Thíra (6–8 weekly; 1hr 30min & 2 weekly mail boats; 2hr).

**Ándhros** to: Amorgós (2 weekly; 8hr); Mýkonos (3 daily; 2hr 30min); Náxos (2 weekly; 7hr); Páros (1–4 weekly; 7hr); Sýros (4 weekly; 3hr); Tínos (3 daily; 2hr).

**Dhonoússa** to: Amorgós (3 weekly; 1hr 15min); Iráklia (2–3 weekly; 1hr); Koufoníssi (2–3 weekly; 1hr); Mýkonos (2–3 weekly; 6hr); Náxos (2–3 weekly; 5hr); Páros (2–3 weekly; 5hr 30min); Sýros (2–3 weekly; 7hr 30min); Tínos (2–3 weekly; 6hr 30min).

**Folégandhros** to: Íos (3–6 weekly; 1hr 30min); Kímolos (2 weekly; 2hr 30 min); Kýthnos (2 weekly; 8hr); Mílos (2 weekly; 2hr 30min); Náxos (3–6 weekly; 2hr 30min); Páros (3–6 weekly; 4hr); Sérifos (2 weekly; 5hr 30min); Sífnos (2 weekly; 5hr); Síkinos (6 weekly; 30min); Sýros (2 weekly; 5hr 30min).

**Íos** to: Anáfi (4 weekly; 4hr); Crete, Iráklion (1 weekly; 10hr); Folégandhros (4–5 weekly 1hr); Kímolos (1 weekly; 4hr); Mílos (1 weekly; 4hr); Mýkonos (1 daily; 2hr); Náxos (3 daily; 3hr); Páros (3 daily; 5hr); Sérifos (1 weekly; 5hr); Sífnos (1 weekly; 5hr 30min); Síkinos (4–5 weekly; 30min); Sýros (2–3 weekly; 6hr); Thíra (3 daily; 1hr).

**Iráklia, Koufoníssi, Skhinoússa** to: Amorgós (1 weekly; 1hr 45min); Náxos (1 weekly; 1hr); Páros (1 weekly; 2hr 15min).

**Kéa** to: Folégandhros (1 weekly; 13hr); Kýthnos (1 weekly; 1hr 20min); Mílos (1 weekly; 15hr); Náxos (1 weekly; 9hr); Páros (1 weekly; 8hr); Sýros (1 weekly; 4hr).

**Kímolos** to: Folégandhros (2 weekly; 1hr); Kýthnos (2–5 weekly; 3hr 30min); Mílos, Adhámas (2–8 weekly; 60min); Mílos, Pollónia (4–6 daily; 30min); Sérifos (2–5 weekly; 2hr 30min); Sífnos (2–5 weekly; 2hr); Síkinos (2 weekly; 1hr 30min); Thíra (2 weekly; 3hr).

**Kýthnos** to: Folégandhros (3–4 weekly; 8hr 30min); Íos (1–2 weekly; 8hr); Kéa (1–2 weekly; 1hr 30min); Kímolos (4–8 weekly; 3hr 30min); Mílos (4–8 weekly; 4hr); Sérifos (4–8 weekly; 1hr); Sífnos (4–8 weekly; 1hr 30min); Síkinos (1–2 weekly; 8hr), Sýros (1–2 weekly; 3hr); Thíra (3–4 weekly; 10hr).

**Lávrio** to: Ándhros (0–1 weekly; 10hr); Folégandhros (0–1 weekly; 14hr); Íos (0–1 weekly; 13hr); Kea (14–31 weekly; 50min); Kímolos (0–1 weekly; 16hr); Kýthnos (0–12 weekly; 2hr); Mílos (0–1 weekly; 17hr); Mýkonos (0–1 weekly; 7hr); Náxos (0–1 weekly; 10hr);

**Páros** (0–1 weekly; 9hr); Síkinos (0–1 weekly; 13hr); Sýros (0–3 weekly; 5–7hr); Tínos (0–1 weekly; 6hr).

**Mílos** to: Crete (Iráklion, Áyios Nikólaos, Sitía; 2 weekly; 8–12hr); Folégandhros (2–3 weekly; 1hr); Íos (2–3 weekly; 2hr); Kárpathos and Kássos (2 weekly; 14–17hr); Kímolos (4–6 daily ferries; 30min); Kýthnos (1 daily; 3hr); Rhodes and Hálki (2 weekly; 19–22hr): Sérifos (1 daily; 1hr 30min); Sífnos (1 daily; 2hr); Síkinos (2–3 weekly; 1hr 30min); Sýros (2 weekly; 6hr); Thíra (2–3 weekly; 3hr).

**Mýkonos** to: Ándhros (13–23 weekly; 2hr 30min); Ikaría (7 weekly; 1hr 15min); Íos (1 daily; 2hr); Kós (1 weekly; 8hr); Léros (1 weekly; 6hr); Náxos (1 daily; 3hr); Páros (daily; 1hr 30min); Pátmos (1 weekly; 4hr); Rhodes (1 weekly; 10hr); Sámos (7 weekly; 3hr 40min); Sýros (1 daily; 1hr 15min); Tínos (13–22 weekly; 40min).

**Náxos** to: Amorgós (5–7 weekly; 2–6hr); Anáfi (3 weekly; 7hr); Ándhros (2 weekly; 4hr); Astypálea (1 weekly; 3hr 30min); Crete, Iráklion (1 weekly; 12hr); Dhonoússa (3–6 weekly; 5hr); Folégandhros (2 weekly; 4hr); Ikaría (1 weekly; 3hr 20min); Íos (2–8 weekly; 2hr); Iráklia (2–3 weekly; 1hr 30min); Kárpathos and Kássos (1 weekly; 9–11hr); Koufoníssi (2–3 weekly; 2hr 30min); Páros (15 weekly; 45min–1hr 30min); Sámos (1–2 weekly; 6hr); Síkinos (5 weekly; 3hr); Skhinoússa (2–3 weekly; 2hr); Sýros (6–8 weekly; 3hr); Thíra (at least 3 daily; 2hr 30min); Tínos (4–5 weekly; 4hr).

**Páros** to: Amorgós (4–6 weekly; 4hr); Anáfi (4–6 weekly; 9hr); Ándhros (4 weekly; 5hr); Andíparos (hourly from Parikía, 40min; hourly car ferry from Poúnda, 20min); Astypálea (1–2 weekly; 4hr 30min); Crete, Iráklion (1 weekly; 7hr); Dhonoússa (2–4 weekly; 7hr); Folégandhros (4–6 weekly; 4hr 30min); Íos (2 weekly; 3hr 10min); Kárpathos and Kássos (1 weekly; 22–24hr); Mýkonos (1 weekly; 2hr 40min); Náxos (16 weekly; 40min–1hr 10min); Rhodes (1 weekly; 30hr); Síkinos (4–6 weekly; 4hr); Skhinoússa (2–4 weekly; 6hr); Skiáthos (2–3 weekly; 10hr); Sýros (6–8 weekly; 2hr); Thíra (6 weekly; 3–8hr); Tínos (6–8 weekly; 1hr 30min).

**Pireás** to: Amorgós (3–7 weekly; 8–14hr); Dhonoússa (2–4 weekly; 8–13hr); Folégandhros (2–6 weekly; 12hr); Íos (4–9 weekly; 9–13hr); Iráklia (2–3 weekly; 8–10hr); Kímolos (0–4 weekly; 7–8hr); Koufoníssi (2–3 weekly; 8–11hr); Kýthnos (5–9 weekly; 3–4hr); Mílos (7–11 weekly; 5–10hr); Mýkonos (10–11 weekly; 5–6hr); Náxos (14–18 weekly; 5–8hr); Páros (18–25 weekly; 4–7hr); Sérifos (5–9 weekly; 4–6hr); Sífnos (5–9 weekly; 5–7hr); Síkinos

(2 weekly; 11–13hr); Skhinoússa (2–3 weekly;
8–10hr); Sýros (14–18 weekly; 4–5hr); Thíra
(12–15 weekly; 8–16hr); Tínos (7 weekly; 5hr).
**Rafína** to: Ándhros (15–40 weekly; 2hr);
Folégandhros (0–1 weekly; 14hr); Íos (0–1
weekly; 9hr); Kímolos (0–1 weekly; 16hr); Mílos
(0–1 weekly; 17hr); Mýkonos (13–28 weekly;
5hr); Náxos (0–2 weekly; 6hr); Síkinos (0–1
weekly; 13hr); Sýros (0–1 weekly; 3hr); Tínos
(13–29 weekly; 4hr).
**Sérifos** to: Folégandhros (2–3 weekly; 2hr 30min);
Íos (1 weekly; 6hr 30min); Kímolos (2–5 weekly;
1hr 30min); Kýthnos (5–12 weekly; 30min); Mílos
(5–10 weekly; 1hr 30min); Sífnos (5–12 weekly;
30min); Síkinos (2–3 weekly; 3hr); Sýros (1
weekly; 6hr); Thíra (1 weekly; 7hr 30min).
**Sífnos** to: Folégandhros (2–3 weekly; 2hr); Íos (1
weekly; 6hr 30min); Kímolos (2–5 weekly; 1hr);
Kýthnos (5–12 weekly; 1hr); Mílos (5–10 weekly;
1hr); Páros (twice weekly; 5hr); Sérifos (5–12
weekly; 30min); Síkinos (2–3 weekly; 2hr 30min);
Sýros (2 weekly; 6hr 30min); Thíra (2–3 weekly;
7hr).
**Síkinos** to: Folégandhros (6 weekly; 30min); Íos
(3–6 weekly; 2hr); Kímolos (2 weekly; 2hr);
Kýthnos (2 weekly; 7hr 30min); Mílos (2 weekly;
2hr); Náxos (3–6 weekly; 3hr); Páros (3–6
weekly; 4hr 30min); Sérifos (2 weekly; 5hr);
Sífnos (2 weekly; 4hr 30min); Sýros (2 weekly;
5hr); Thíra (3–6 weekly; 2hr).
**Sýros** to: Amorgós (3 weekly; 7hr); Ándhros (at
least 2 weekly; 3hr 30min); Astypálea (2–3
weekly; 5hr); Folégandhros (1 weekly; 4hr 30min);
Ikaría (7 weekly; 3hr 15min); Íos (2–4 weekly;
7hr); Iráklia (3 weekly; 7hr); Kéa (2–3 weekly;
4hr); Koufoníssi (3 weekly, 7hr 30min); Kýthnos (2
weekly; 3hr); Mílos (2 weekly; 5hr); Kímolos (2
weekly; 5hr); Mýkonos (at least 2 daily; 2hr);
Náxos (at least 2 daily; 3hr); Páros (at least 2
daily; 2hr); Pátmos (1 weekly; 5hr 20min); Sámos
(7 weekly; 6hr 40min); Sérifos (2 weekly; 4hr);
Sífnos (2 weekly; 3hr 30min); Síkinos (1 weekly;
6hr); Skhinoússa (3 weekly; 8hr); Thíra (2–4
weekly; 8hr 30min); Tínos (at least 2 daily; 1hr).
**Thíra** to: Anáfi (4–6 weekly; 2hr, 2 weekly mail
boats); Crete, Áyios Nikólaos, Iráklion, Sitía (1–2
weekly; 4–7hr); Folégandhros (6–8 weekly; 1hr
30min); Íos (at least 3 daily; 1hr); Kárpathos and
Kássos (2 weekly; 10–12hr); Mílos and Kímolos
(2–4 weekly; 2hr); Mýkonos (daily; 2hr 30min);
Náxos (at least 3 daily; 2hr); Páros (at least 3
daily; 3hr); Rhodes and Hálki (2 weekly;
15–18hr); Sérifos (1–2 weekly; 7hr); Sífnos
(4–6 weekly; 7hr); Síkinos (6–8 weekly; 2hr);
Sýros (6–8 weekly; 8hr); Thirassía (1–6 weekly;
30min); Tínos (3–5 weekly; 5hr).

**Tínos** to: Ándhros (at least 2 daily; 1hr); Íos (1
weekly; 8hr); Mýkonos (at least 2 daily; 30min);
Náxos (3–4 weekly; 2hr); Páros (3–4 weekly; 1hr
30min); Sýros (at least 2 daily; 1hr); Thíra (3
weekly; 5hr).

## Catamaran and small-boat services

Catamaran services operate during the summer
season from Pireás and Rafína, replacing winter
ferries on some routes. The Cycladic routes are
covered by Aegean Speed Lines (@www
.aegeanspeedlines.gr), Hellenic Seaways (@www
.hsw.gr), SeaJets (@www.seajets.gr), and NEL
(@www.nel.gr). Catamaran travel is expensive,
but when time is an issue these high-speed craft
are a welcome addition to the conventional fleet.
Journey times are given below for direct routes
only. The slower *Express Skopelitis* plies daily in
season between Náxos and Amorgós,
overnighting at the latter and connecting Iráklia,
Skhinoússa, Koufoníssi and Dhonoússa – for
current info call ☎22850 71256.
**Amorgós** to: Folégandhros (daily); Náxos (daily);
1hr 10min); Páros (daily); Pireás (daily); Sífnos
(daily); Sýros (daily); Thíra (daily; 1hr 20min).
**Folégandhros** to: Amorgós (daily); Náxos (daily);
Páros (daily); Pireás (9 weekly; 3hr 40min);
Sífnos (9 weekly; 55min); Thíra (10 weekly;
55min).
**Íos** to: Crete, Iráklion (6 weekly); Mýkonos (6
weekly); Páros (6 weekly; 1hr 10min); Pireás (13
weekly; 2hr 15min); Thíra (13 weekly; 65min).
**Kímolos** to: Folégandhros (1 weekly; 50min);
Mílos (3 weekly; 55min); Pireás (4 weekly);
Sérifos (1 weekly); Sífnos (3 weekly).
**Mílos** to: Pireás (14 weekly); Sérifos (12 weekly);
Sífnos (12 weekly; 1hr).
**Mýkonos** to: Crete, Iráklion (20 weekly); Íos (6
weekly); Náxos (13 weekly; 1hr); Páros (19
weekly; 1hr); Pireás (25 weekly); Rafína (6
weekly); Sýros (13 weekly; 45min); Thíra (6
weekly); Tínos (13 weekly; 30min).
**Náxos** to: Amorgós (daily; 1hr 10min); Crete,
Iráklion (2 weekly); Folégandhros (daily); Mýkonos
(12 weekly; 1hr); Páros (22 weekly; 40min); Pireás
(19 weekly); Rafína (6 weekly); Sífnos (daily);
Sýros (daily); Thíra (daily); Tínos (12 weekly).
**Páros** to: Amorgós (daily); Crete, Iráklion (6
weekly); Folégandhros (daily); Íos (6 weekly;
65min); Mýkonos (19 weekly); Náxos (21 weekly;
40min); Pireás (26 weekly; 3hr 15min); Rafína (6
weekly); Sífnos (daily); Sýros (daily; 45min); Thíra
(16 weekly; 1hr 30min); Tínos (13 weekly;
55min).
**Pireás** to: Amorgós (1 weekly); Folégandhros
(10 weekly; 3hr 35min); Íos (13 weekly;

3hr 30min); Kímolos (4 weekly; 2hr 45min); Mílos (17 weekly); Mýkonos (26 weekly); Náxos (21 weekly); Páros (25 weekly; 3hr 15min); Rafína (12 weekly); Sérifos (14 weekly; 2hr 40min); Sífnos (22 weekly; 2hr 30min); Sýros (21 weekly; 2hr 55min); Thíra (27 weekly; 4hr 15min); Tínos (17 weekly).

Rafína to: Mýkonos (13 weekly); Náxos (13 weekly); Páros (13 weekly); Pireás (12 weekly); Tínos (13 weekly; 2hr 15min).

Sérifos to: Mílos (11 weekly; 1hr); Pireás (13 weekly; 2hr 35min); Sífnos (13 weekly; 35min).

Sífnos to: Amorgós (1 weekly); Folégandhros (8 weekly; 55min); Mílos (13 weekly; 55min); Náxos (daily); Páros (8 weekly; 1hr); Pireás (21 weekly; 2hr 25min); Sérifos (12 weekly; 35min); Thíra (8 weekly).

Sýros to: Amorgós (daily); Folégandhros (daily); Mýkonos (14 weekly); Náxos (daily); Páros (daily); 50min); Pireás (27 weekly; 2hr 40min); Sífnos (daily); Thíra (daily); Tínos (14 weekly; 35min).

Thíra to: Amorgós (daily; 1hr 20min); Crete, Iráklion (8 weekly; 1hr 50min); Folégandhros (10 weekly; 55min); Íos (13 weekly; 50min); Mýkonos (6 weekly); Náxos (daily); Páros (16 weekly; 1hr 30min); Pireás (25 weekly; 4hr 15min); Sífnos (8 weekly); Sýros (daily).

Tínos to: Crete, Iráklion (2 weekly); Mýkonos (20 weekly; 35min); Náxos (13 weekly); Páros (13 weekly); Pireás (20 weekly); Rafína (6 weekly; 2hr 10min); Sýros (8 weekly).

## Flights

There are airports on Páros, Mýkonos, Thíra, Sýros, Mílos and Náxos. In season, or during storms when ferries are idle, you have little chance of getting a seat on any flight at less than three days' notice, and tickets are predictably expensive. Expect off-season (Oct–April) frequencies to drop by at least eighty percent. Flights are on Olympic unless otherwise stated.

Athens to: Mílos (1–2 daily; 45min); Mýkonos (4–5 daily on Olympic; 3–4 daily on Aegean; 40min); Náxos (6 weekly; 45min); Páros (2–3 daily; 40min); Sýros (3–6 weekly; 35min); Thíra (5–6 daily on Olympic; 3–5 daily on Aegean; 45min).

Mýkonos to: Rhodes (2 weekly; 55min); Thessaloníki (2 weekly on Olympic, 3 weekly on Aegean; 1hr 20min); Thíra (4 weekly; 30min).

Thíra to: Rhodes (2–5 weekly; 50min); Thessaloníki (2 weekly on Olympic, 1 daily on Aegean; 1hr 20min).

# Crete

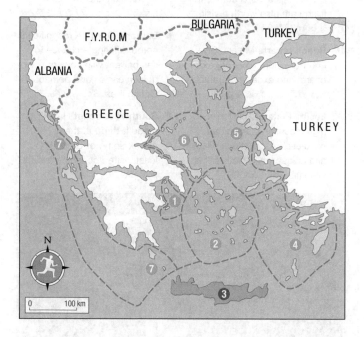

CHAPTER 3 # Highlights

\* **Archeological Museum, Iráklion** The world's foremost Minoan museum. Following a substantial renovation the museum is set to partially reopen in 2009 and fully reopen in 2010. See p.232

\* **Minoan sites** Knossos is the most exciting, but Malia, Phaestos, Zakros and other archeological ruins across the island are also worth a visit. See p.237, 244, 250 & 269

\* **Beach resorts** Mátala, Sitía and Paleohóra have bags of charm and excellent strands. See p.246, p.264 & p.300

\* **Lasíthi Plateau** This fertile high mountain plateau has picturesque agricultural villages and unique white-cloth-sailed windmills. See p.256

\* **The Dhiktean Cave** Mythological birthplace of Zeus, the Dhiktean Cave is stunningly situated on the Lasíthi Plateau. See p.257

\* **Haniá and Réthymnon old towns** Atmospheric city centres where vibrant modern life co-exists with the beautiful architectural legacies of Venetian and Turkish history. See p.277 & p.289

\* **Samariá Gorge** A magnificent gorge, offering a chance to see brilliant wild flowers, golden eagles and perhaps a Cretan ibex. See p.294

\* **Southwest coast** Having made it through the gorge, some of Crete's least visited coastline awaits. See p.297

▲ Mátala, one of Crete's biggest and best beach resorts

# Crete

rete (Kríti) is a great deal more than just another Greek island. In many places, especially in the cities or along the developed north coast, it doesn't feel like an island at all, but rather a substantial land in its own right. Which of course it is – a precipitous, wealthy and at times surprisingly cosmopolitan one with a tremendous and unique history. At the same time, it has everything you could want of a Greek island and more: great beaches, remote hinterlands and hospitable people.

In history, Crete is distinguished above all as the home of Europe's earliest civilization. It was only at the beginning of the twentieth century that the legends of King Minos and of a Cretan society that ruled the Greek world in prehistory were confirmed by excavations at Knossos and Phaestos. Yet the Minoans had a remarkably advanced society, the centre of a maritime trading empire as early as 2000 BC. The artworks produced on Crete at this time are unsurpassed anywhere in the ancient world, and it seems clear that life was good. This apparently peaceful culture survived at least three major natural disasters; each time the palaces were destroyed, and each time they were rebuilt on a grander scale. Only after the last destruction, probably the result of an eruption of Santoríni and subsequent tidal waves and earthquakes, do significant numbers of weapons begin to appear in the ruins. This, together with the appearance of the Greek language, has been interpreted to mean that Mycenaean Greeks had taken control of the island. Nevertheless, for nearly 500 years, by far the longest period of peace the island has seen, Crete was home to a culture well ahead of its time.

The Minoans of Crete probably originally came from Anatolia; at their height they maintained strong links with Egypt and with the people of Asia Minor, and this position as meeting point and strategic fulcrum between east and west has played a major role in Crete's subsequent history. Control of the island passed from Greeks to Romans to Saracens, through the Byzantine empire to Venice, and finally to Turkey for more than two centuries. During World War II, the island was occupied by the Germans and attained the dubious distinction of being the first place to be successfully invaded by paratroops.

Today, with a flourishing agricultural economy, Crete is one of the few Greek islands that could probably support itself without visitors. Nevertheless, tourism is heavily promoted and is making inroads everywhere. The northeast coast in particular is overdeveloped, and though there are parts of the south and west coasts that have not been spoilt, they are getting harder to find. By contrast, the high mountains of the interior are still barely touched, and one of the best things to do on the island is to rent a vehicle and explore the remoter villages.

Every part of Crete has its devotees and it's hard to pick out highlights, but generally if you want to get away from it all you should head west, towards

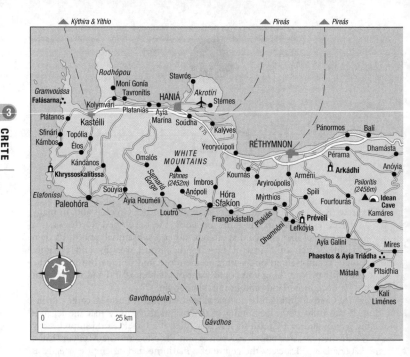

Haniá and the smaller, less well-connected places along the south and west coasts. It is in this part of the island that the White Mountains rise, while below them yawns the famous Samariá Gorge. The far east, around Sitía, is also relatively unscathed, with a string of isolated beaches worth seeking out to the south of overpopular Vaï beach, which lures crowds attracted by its famous palm grove. However, Sitía's new airport, due to open for international flights in 2009, could change things significantly here in the next few years.

Whatever you do, your first priority will probably be to leave Iráklion (Heraklion) as quickly as possible, having paid the obligatory, and rewarding, visit to the revamped archeological museum and nearby Knossos. The other great Minoan sites cluster around the middle of the island: Phaestos and Ayía Triádha to the south (with Roman Gortys to provide contrast), and Malia on the north coast. Almost wherever you go you'll find a reminder of the island's history, whether it's the superbly preserved Minoan town of Gourniá near the cosmopolitan resort of Áyios Nikólaos, the exquisitely sited palace of Zakros in the far east, or the lesser sites scattered around the west. Unexpected highlights include Crete's Venetian forts at Réthymnon and Frangokástello; its hundreds of frescoed Byzantine churches, most famously at Kritsá; and, at Réthymnon and Haniá, the cluttered old Venetian and Turkish quarters.

Crete has by far the longest summers in Greece, and you can get a decent tan here right into October and swim at least from May until November. The one seasonal blight is the *meltémi*, a northerly wind, which regularly blows harder and more continuously here than anywhere else in Greece – the locals may welcome its cooling effects, but it's another reason (along with crowds and heat) to avoid an August visit if you can.

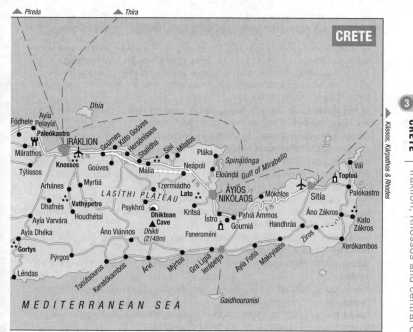

# Iráklion, Knossos and central Crete

Many visitors to Crete arrive in the island's capital, **Iráklion** (Heraklion), but it's not an outstandingly beautiful city, and its central zones are often a maelstrom of traffic-congested thoroughfares. However, it does provide a convenient base for visits to an outstanding **archeological museum** and nearby **Knossos**. On the positive side, the city does have superb fortifications, a fine market, atmospheric old alleys and some interesting lesser museums.

The area immediately around the city is less touristy than you might expect, mainly because there are few decent beaches of any size on this central part of the coast. To the west, mountains drop straight into the sea virtually all the way to Réthymnon, with just two significant coastal settlements: **Ayía Pelayía**, a sizeable resort, and the more attractive **Balí**, which is gradually becoming one as well. Eastwards, the main resorts are at least 30km away, at **Hersónissos** and beyond, although there is a string of rather unattractive developments all the way there. Inland, there's agricultural country, some of the richest on the island, a cluster of Crete's better vineyards and a series of wealthy but rather dull villages. Directly behind the capital rises **Mount**

## Adventure sports

With its temperate climate and varied topography Crete is a great place for **adventure holidays**, and there are now numerous companies across the island offering a wide variety of activities from mountain biking and canyoning to trekking and scuba diving. Here's a selection of what's on offer – other centres and activities are mentioned at destinations throughout this chapter.

**Alpine Travel** ☏28210 50939, ⓦwww.alpine.gr. Hiking, rock climbing, sea kayaking and biking holidays (or combinations of) in Haniá province.

**Cretan Adventures** ☏28103 33772, ⓦwww.cretanadventures.gr. Hiking, horseriding and jeep safaris throughout Crete.

**Driros Beach** ☏699 39 04 302, ⓦwww.spinalonga-windsurf.com. Windsurfing, waterskiing, kayaking and sailing courses at Driros Beach near Eloúnda. Also hires out outboard dinghies.

**Freak Windsurf** ☏28430 61116, ⓦwww.freak-surf.com. Courses and board hire from a reliable company based at Kouremenos, Crete's best windsurfing locale, at the extreme east end of the island.

**Hellas Bike** ☏28210 60858, ⓦwww.hellasbike.net. One-to seven-day bike tours from Ayía Marína in Haniá province, using Scott machines.

**ICNA** ☏6977466900, ⓦwww.icna.gr. Paragliding courses from sites throughout the island.

**Korifi Tours** ☏28930 41440, ⓦwww.korifi.de. Hiking and climbing holidays in central, southern and western Crete.

**Liquid Bungy** ☏693 76 15 191, ⓦwww.bungy.gr. White-knuckle bungee jumping (Europe's second highest) at the Arádhena Gorge, Haniá.

**Melanouri** ☏28920 45040, ⓦwww.melanouri.com. Horseriding holidays (one to seven days) from a stable near Mátala.

**Nature Maniacs** ☏28250 91017, ⓦwww.naturemaniacs.com. Sea-kayaking holidays (one to seven days, or longer) based at Loutró in Haniá.

**Odysseia** ☏28970 51080, ⓦwww.horseriding.gr. One to six day guided and unguided horse treks from their base at Avdhoú near the Lasíthi Plateau.

**Strata Walking Tours** ☏28220 24336, ⓦwww.stratatours.com. Guided trekking holidays in the Kastélli Kissamou area of Haniá.

**Trekking Plan** ☏28210 60861, ⓦwww.cycling.gr. Rock climbing, mountaineering, canyoning, rapelling, kayaking and mountain biking in Haniá province.

**Zoraïda's Horseriding** ☏28250 61745, ⓦwww.zoraidas-horseriding.com. Horseriding holidays and treks from their stables in Yeoryoúpoli, Haniá.

**Ioúktas** with its unmistakably characteristic profile of a recumbent Zeus; to the west the Psilorítis massif spreads around the peak of **Mount Psilorítis** (Ídha), the island's highest mountain. On the south coast there are few roads and little development of any kind, except at **Ayía Galíni** in the southwest, a nominal fishing village which has grown into a popular resort, and beautiful **Mátala**, which has thrown out the hippies that made it famous and, though crowded with package-trippers in high summer, is still an appealing spring and autumn destination. Isolated **Léndas** has to some extent occupied Mátala's old niche, and has a fine beach.

Despite the lack of resorts, there seem constantly to be thousands of people trekking back and forth across the centre of the island. This is largely because of a trio of superb sites in the south: **Phaestos**, second of the Minoan palaces, with its attendant villa at **Ayía Triádha**, and **Gortys**, capital of Roman Crete.

# Iráklion

The best way to approach **IRÁKLION** is by sea, with Mount Ioúktas rising behind it and the Psilorítis range to the west. As you get closer, it's the city walls that first stand out, still dominating and fully encircling the oldest part of town; finally you sail in past the great **Venetian fortress** defending the harbour entrance. Unfortunately, big ships no longer dock in the old port but at great modern concrete wharves alongside, which neatly sums up Iráklion itself. Many of the old parts have been restored and are attractive, but these are offset by the bustle and noise that characterize much of the city today. In more recent times, however, Iráklion's administrators have been giving belated attention to dealing with some of the city's image problems, and large tracts of the centre – particularly the focal Platía Eleftherías and the recently pedestrianized **25-Avgoústou** – have been landscaped and refurbished with the aim of presenting a less daunting prospect to the visitor.

## Arrival

Iráklion **airport** is right on the coast, 4km east of the city. **Bus** #1 leaves for central Platía Eleftherías every few minutes from the car park in front of the terminal; buy your ticket (€0.75) at the booth before boarding. There are also plenty of **taxis** outside (which you'll be forced to use when the buses stop at 11pm), and prices to major destinations are posted here and in the domestic departures hall – it's about €10 to the centre of town, depending on traffic. Get an agreement on the fare before taking a cab and beware if the driver extols the virtues of a particular place to stay and offers to drop you there – he'll usually be getting a kickback from the proprietors. To avoid such hassles ask to be dropped at Platía Eleftherías, from where everything is in easy walking distance.

There are two main **bus stations** (often titled A and B on maps). Bus station A straddles both sides of the main road between the ferry dock and the Venetian harbour, and Station B lies just outside the Haniá Gate. Buses run from here **west** to Réthymnon and Haniá and **east** along the coastal highway to Hersónsissos, Mália, Áyios Nikólaos and Sitía, as well as **southeast** to Ierápetra and points en route. Local bus #2 to Knossos also leaves from here. Buses for the **southwest** (Phaestos, Mátala and Ayía Galíni) and along the inland roads west (Týlissos, Anóyia) operate out of terminal B just outside Pórta Heaníon (Hánia Gate), a very long walk from the centre up Kalokerinoú (or jump on any bus heading down this street). From the wharves where the **ferries** dock, the city rises directly ahead in steep tiers. If you're heading for the centre, the archeological museum or the tourist office, cut straight up the stepped alleys behind the bus station onto Dhoúkos Bofór and to Platía Eleftherías; this will take about fifteen minutes. For accommodation, though, and to get a better idea of the layout of Iráklion's main attractions, it's simplest to follow the main roads by a rather more roundabout route. Head west along the coast, past the major eastbound bus station and on by the Venetian harbour before cutting up towards the centre along 25-Avgoústou.

## Orientation

Virtually everything you're likely to want to see in Iráklion lies within the northeastern corner of the walled city. The most vital thoroughfare, the recently pedestrianized **25-Avgoústou**, links the harbour with the commercial city

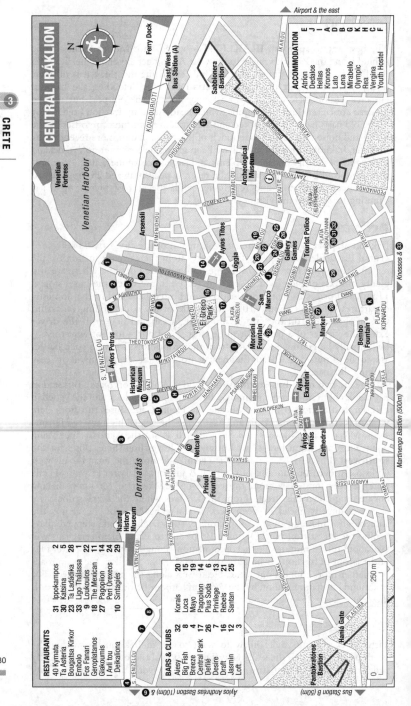

# CENTRAL IRÁKLION

**ACCOMMODATION**
| | |
|---|---|
| Atrion | E |
| Dedalos | J |
| Hellas | I |
| Kronos | A |
| Lato | D |
| Lena | B |
| Mirabello | G |
| Olympic | K |
| Rea | H |
| Vergina | C |
| Youth Hostel | F |

**RESTAURANTS**
| | |
|---|---|
| 40 Kymata | 2 |
| Ta Asteria | 5 |
| Bougatsa Kirkor | |
| Embolo | 1 |
| Fos Fanari | |
| Geroplatanos | 9 |
| Giakoumis | 18 |
| I Avli tou | |
| Deikaliona | 10 |
| Ippokampos | 31 |
| Katsina | 30 |
| Ta Ladádika | 23 |
| Ligo Thalassa | 33 |
| Loukoulos | 22 |
| The Mexican | 11 |
| Pagopiion | 14 |
| Peri Orexeos | 24 |
| Sintagiés | 29 |

**BARS & CLUBS**
| | |
|---|---|
| Aésy | 32 |
| Big Fish | 8 |
| Breeze | 4 |
| Central Park | 17 |
| Defilé | 26 |
| Desire | 7 |
| Draft | 16 |
| Jasmin | 12 |
| Loft | 3 |
| Korais | 20 |
| Loca | 15 |
| Mayo | 19 |
| Pagopiion | 14 |
| Plus Soda | 6 |
| Privilege | 13 |
| Rebels | 21 |
| Santan | 25 |

Airport & the east

Ferry Dock

East/West Bus Station (A)

Venetian Fortress

Venetian Harbour

Dermatás

Sabbionera Bastion

Arsenáli

Archeological Museum

Ayios Titos

Loggia

Ayios Petros

Historical Museum

El Greco Park

San Marco

Morosini Fountain

Gallery Games

Tourist Police

Netcafé

Priouli Fountain

Natural History Museum

Market

Bembo Fountain

Ayia Ekaterini

Ayios Minas

Cathedral

Haniá Gate

Pantokratóros Bastion

Ayios Andhréas Bastion (100m) & 6

Bus Station B (50m)

Martinengo Bastion (500m)

Knossos & 33

0    250 m

centre. At the bottom it is lined with shipping and travel agencies and rental outlets and a few restaurants, but further up these give way to banks and stores. **Platía Venizélou** (or Fountain Square), off to the right, is crowded with cafés and restaurants; behind Venizélou lies **El Greco Park** (actually a rather cramped garden), with more bars, while on the opposite side of 25-Avgoústou are some of the more interesting of Iráklion's older buildings. Further up 25-Avgoústou, **Kalokerinoú** leads down to Haniá Gate and westwards out of the city; straight ahead, **Odhós-1821** is a major shopping street, and adjacent Odhós-1866 is given over to the animated street **market**, perhaps the best on the island. To the left, Dhikeosínis heads for the city's main square, **Platía Eleftherías**, paralleled by the pedestrian alley, Dedhálou, lined with many of the city's swankier fashion stores and the direct link between the two squares. The revamped Eleftherías is very much the traditional centre of the city, both for traffic – which swirls around it constantly – and for life in general; it is ringed by more upmarket tourist cafés and restaurants and comes alive in the evening with crowds of strolling locals.

CRETE | Iráklion

## Information

Iráklion's rather inefficient **tourist office** (Mon–Fri: May–Sept 8.30am–9pm; Oct–April 8.30am–2.30pm; ☎ 2810 246 298, ❷ www.iraklion-city.gr) is located just below Platía Eleftherías, opposite the archeological museum at Zanthoud-hídhou 1. A sub-office at the **airport** (April–Sept daily 8.30am–9pm) is good for basic information and maps. The **tourist police** – more helpful than most – are at Dhikeosínis 10 (☎ 2810 283 190), halfway between Platía Eleftherías and the market.

## Accommodation

Finding a **room** can be difficult in high season. The best place to look for inexpensive places is in the area around Platía Venizélou, along Hándhakos and towards the harbour to the west of 25-Avgoústou. Other concentrations of affordable places are around El Greco Park and in the streets above the Venetian harbour. Better hotels mostly lie closer to Platía Eleftherías, to the south of Platía Venizélou and near the east- and westbound bus stations.

There are no **campsites** near Iráklion. The nearest sites both lie to the east of the city: first comes *Creta Camping* at Káto Goúves (☎ 28970 41400), 16km out, followed by *Caravan Camping* (☎ 28970 22901) at Hersónissos, 28km from the city.

**Atrion** Hronaki 9 ☎ 28102 46000, ❷ www.atrion .gr. Attractive, newish central hotel with well-equipped balcony rooms, satellite TV and free internet connection. ❺
**Dedalos** Dedhálou 15 ☎ 28102 44812, ✉ info @daedalos.gr. Recently refurbished hotel with balcony rooms overlooking a pedestrianized shopping street which is tranquil at night. All rooms are en suite and equipped with TV and a/c. ❸
**Hellas** Hándhakos 24 ☎ 28102 88851. Hostel-type place with simple doubles, and dormitory rooms (€7 per person) favoured by younger travellers. Also has a roof garden and snack-bar. ❷
**Kronos** Agaráthou 2, west of 25-Avgoústou ☎ 281028 2240, ❷ www.kronoshotel.gr. Pleasant,

friendly hotel with en-suite, sea-view balcony rooms. ❸
**Lato** Epomenídhou 15 ☎ 28102 28103, ❷ www.lato.gr. Stylish and luxurious place where a/c rooms have minibar, TV and fine balcony views over the Venetian harbour (the higher floors have better views). B&B ❻
**Lena** Lahana 10 ☎ 28102 23280, ❷ www .lena-hotel.gr. Quiet and efficient small hotel offering a/c en-suite rooms with balcony and TV. ❸
**Mirabello** Theotokopoúlou 20 ☎ 28102 85052, ❷ www.mirabello-hotel.gr. Good-value, family-run hotel featuring en-suite balcony rooms, some with a/c and TV and others sharing bath. In a quiet street just north of El Greco Park. ❸

231

**Olympic** Platía Kornárou ☎ 28102 88861. Overlooking the busy platía and the famous Bembo fountain. One of the many hotels built in the 1960s, but one of the few that has been refurbished; facilities include minibar and strongbox. B&B ❻

**Rea** Kalimeráki 1 ☎ 28102 23638. A friendly, comfortable and clean *pension* in a quiet street. Some rooms with washbasin, others en suite. ❸

**Vergina** Hortátson 32 ☎ 28102 42739. Basic but pleasant rooms with washbasins and shared bath in a quiet street and set around a courtyard with banana trees. ❶

**Youth Hostel** Vyronos 5 ☎ 28102 86281, ℮ heraklioyouthhostel@yahoo.gr. Formerly Iráklion's official youth hostel, now privately operated, this is a reasonable and economical option. There's plenty of space and some beds (albeit illegal) on the roof if you fancy sleeping out under the stars. Private rooms (❷) as well as dormitories (€10 per person); hot showers, breakfast and other meals available.

## The Town

A good place to start your explorations of the town is the focal **Platía Venizélou**, crowded most of the day with locals patronizing its café terraces, and with travellers who've arranged to meet in "Fountain Square". The **Morosini Fountain**, which gives the square its popular name, is not particularly spectacular at first glance, but on closer inspection is really a very beautiful work; it was built by Venetian governor Francesco Morosini in the seventeenth century, incorporating four lions which were some three hundred years old even then. From the platía you can strike up Dhedhálou, a pedestrianized street full of fashion and tourist shops, or continue on 25-Avgoústou to a major traffic junction at Platía Nikifoúrou Foka. To the right, Kalokerinoú leads west out of the city, the market lies straight ahead along Odhós-1866, and Platía Eleftherías is a short walk to the left up Dhikeosínis.

## Platía Eleftherías and the archeological museum

**Platía Eleftherías**, with seats shaded by palms and eucalyptuses, is very much the traditional heart of the city; traffic swirls around it constantly, and on summer evenings strolling crowds come to fill its café terraces. Most of Iráklion's more expensive shops are in the streets leading off the platía.

The **archeological museum** (April–Sept Mon 1–7.30pm, Tues–Sun 8.30am–7.30pm; Oct–March daily 8am–5pm; these times should be confirmed with the tourist office) is nearby. Almost every important prehistoric and Minoan find on Crete is included in this fabulous, if bewilderingly large, collection. Hopefully, the current refurbishment (see box below) will be a huge improvement upon the museum's previously dreary presentation, and it's worth noting that upon reopening some of the items mentioned may not be in the rooms indicated. The museum tends to be crowded, especially when a guided tour stampedes through, but it's worth taking time over. You can't hope to see

### Visiting the archeological museum

The archeological museum closed in 2007 for long-overdue **renovations**. Until it reopens a small selection of the most popular exhibits are displayed in an annexe at the rear of the building (Mon noon–5pm, Tues–Sun 8am–3pm; €5). The museum is scheduled to partly reopen in the spring of 2009 with two galleries displaying the main items from the collection. The complete reopening is scheduled for 2010. Check with the tourist office (ⓦ www.iraklion-city.gr) for the latest information.

everything, nor can we attempt to describe it all (several good museum guides are sold here, the best probably being the glossy ones by J.A. Sakellarakis or Andonis Vasilakis), but highlights include the **"Town Mosaic"** from Knossos in Room 2 (the galleries are arranged basically in chronological order), the famous **inscribed disc** from Phaestos in Room 3 (itself the subject of several books), most of Room 4, especially the magnificent bull's-head **rhyton** (drinking vessel), the **jewellery** in Room 6 (and elsewhere) and the engraved steatite **black vases** in Room 7. Save some of your time and energy for upstairs, where the **Hall of the Frescoes**, with intricately reconstructed fragments of the wall paintings from Knossos and other sites, is especially wonderful.

### The walls and fortifications

The massive **Venetian walls**, in places up to 15m thick, are the most obvious evidence of Iráklion's later history. Though their fabric is incredibly well preserved, access is virtually nonexistent. It is possible to scramble up and walk along them from Áyios Andhréas Bastion over the sea in the west, as far as the Martinengo Bastion where lies the **tomb of Nikos Kazantzakis**, Cretan author of *Zorba the Greek*, whose epitaph reads: "I believe in nothing, I hope for nothing, I am free." At weekends, Iraklians gather here to pay their respects and enjoy a free view of the soccer matches played by one of the city's two teams in the stadium below. If the walls seem altogether too much effort, the **port fortifications** are much easier to see. Stroll out along the jetty (crowded with courting couples at dusk) and you can get inside the sixteenth-century **Venetian fortress** (Tues–Sun 8.30am–3pm; €2) at the harbour entrance, emblazoned with the Venetian Lion of St Mark. Standing atop this, you begin to understand how Iráklion (or Candia as both the city and the island were known to the Venetians) withstood a 22-year siege before finally falling to the Ottomans. On the landward side of the port, the Venetian **arsenáli** (arsenals) can also be seen, their arches rather lost amid the concrete road system all around.

### Churches and other museums

From the harbour, 25-Avgoústou will take you up past most of the town's other highlights. The **church of Áyios Títos**, on the left as you approach Platía Venizélou, borders a pleasant little platía. Byzantine in origin but substantially rebuilt by the Venetians, it looks magnificent principally because, like most of the churches here, it was adapted by the Turks as a mosque and only reconsecrated in 1925; consequently it has been renovated on numerous occasions. On the south side of this platía, abutting 25-Avgoústou, is the Venetian **city hall** with its famous loggia, again almost entirely rebuilt. Just above this, facing Platía Venizélou, stands the **church of San Marco**, its steps usually crowded with sightseers spilling over from the nearby platía. Neither of these last two buildings has found a permanent role in its refurbished state, but both are generally open to house some kind of exhibition or craft show.

Slightly away from the obvious city-centre circuit, but still within the bounds of the walls, there is a clutch of lesser museums worth seeing if you have the time. First of these is the excellent collection of **icons** in the **church of Ayía Ekateríni** (April–Sept Mon–Sat 9.30am–7.30pm; Oct–March Mon–Fri 10am–4pm; €2), an ancient building just below the undistinguished cathedral, off Kalokerinoú. The finest here are six large scenes by Mihaïl Damaskinos (a near contemporary of Cretan painter Doménikos Theotokópoulos, better known as El Greco) who fused Byzantine and Renaissance influences. Supposedly both Damaskinos and El Greco studied at

Ayía Ekateríni in the sixteenth century, before the latter moved to Spain, when it functioned as a sort of monastic art school.

The **Historical Museum** (Mon–Sat 9am–5pm; €5; Ⓦwww.historical -museum.gr) lies some 300m north of here, on the waterfront. Its display of folk costumes and jumble of local memorabilia include the reconstructed studies of both Nikos Kazantzakis and Emanuel Tsouderos (the latter both Cretan statesman and former Greek prime minister). There's enough variety to satisfy just about anyone, including the only El Greco paintings on Crete, the small and uncharacteristic *View of Mount Sinai and the Monastery of St Catherine* and the recently acquired and even smaller *Baptism of Christ*.

To the west, rehoused in a converted old power plant overlooking the bay of Dermatás, is the **Natural History Museum** (Mon–Fri 8.30am–2.30pm, Sun 9am–1pm; €3; Ⓦwww.nhmc.uoc.gr), definitely worth a visit. Currently only two floors of the building have been completed, housing displays covering the ecosystems of the eastern Mediterranean as well as a child-oriented Discovery Centre. As the renovation progresses the building's remaining three floors will include flora and fauna displays and exhibits detailing the island's geological evolution, the arrival of man and the environment as it would have appeared to the Minoans.

## The beaches

Iráklion's **beaches** are some way out, whether east or west of town. In either direction they're easily accessible by bus: #6 heads west from the stop outside the *Astoria* hotel in Platía Eleftherías; #7 east from the stop opposite this, under the trees in the centre of the platía. **Almyrós** (or Ammoudhári) to the west has been subjected to a degree of development, comprising a campsite, several medium-size hotels and one giant one (the *Zeus Beach*, in the shadow of the power station at the far end), which makes the beach hard to get to without walking through or past something built up.

**Amnissós**, to the east, is the better choice, with several tavernas and the added amusement of planes swooping in immediately overhead to land at the nearby airport. This is where most locals go on their afternoons off; the furthest of the beaches is the best, although new hotels are encroaching. Little remains to indicate the once-flourishing port of Knossos here, aside from a rather dull, fenced-in dig. If you're seriously into antiquities, you'll find a more rewarding site in a small Minoan villa, known as **Nírou Háni** (Tues–Sun 8.30am–2pm; free) at Háni Kokkíni, the first of the full-blown resort developments east of Iráklion.

## Eating

Big city though it is, Iráklion often disappoints when it comes to eating, and not many of the central restaurants and tavernas provide good value. The cafés and tavernas of platíes Venizélou and Eleftherías are essential places to sit and watch the world pass by, but their food is expensive and mediocre. One striking exception is *Bougatsa Kirkor*, by the Morosini Fountain in Venizélou, where you can sample authentic Cretan *bougátsa* – a creamy cheese pie sprinkled with sugar and cinnamon. For **snacks** and **takeaways**, a group of *souvláki* and other fast-food stalls cluster around the top of 25-Avgoústou near the entrance to El Greco Park, and are handy if you need somewhere to sit and eat. For *tyrópita* and *spanakópita* (cheese or spinach pies) and other pastries, sweet or savoury, there is no shortage of *zaharoplastía* and places such as *Everest* – just north of the Morosini Fountain – which does takeaways of these as well as lots of other savouries. On and around Platía Dhaskaloyiánni (near the archeological museum) are some authentic and inexpensive ouzerís: try *Ta Asteria* or *40 Kymata* on the platía itself for atmosphere and tasty *mezédhes*.

**I Avli tou Deikaliona** Kalokairinoú 8, at the rear of the Historical Museum ☎ 28102 44215. Popular taverna with a great little terrace fronting the Idomeneus Fountain serving up well-prepared meat and fish dishes. In high summer you may need to book to ensure an outdoor table. Should you despair of getting one the nearby *Paraskevas* with similar fare and terrace is a good substitute.

**Embolo** Miliara 7, south of the central zone. Great little taverna at the end of an alley with terrace under the trees. Run by *lýra* musician Yiannis Stavrakakis, the traditional Cretan food is good and there's often the chance of some live background music.

**Fos Fanari** Marineli 1, opposite the tiny church of Ay. Dimítrios. The first in a row of ouzerís that line this alley off Vironos, sloping down to the harbour, this has good fish dishes and *mezédhes*. The similar neighbouring (and pricier) *Terzáki* is also worth a try.

**Geroplatanos** In the leafy square fronting the church of Ay. Títos. Taking its name from the great old plane tree beneath which its tables are set out, this is one of the most tranquil lunch spots in town and provides the usual taverna staples.

**Giakoumis** Fotiou Theodosaki 5, in the market, ☎ 28102 84039. Established in 1935, this is the city's oldest taverna and locals claim it serves up the best *païdhákia* (lamb chops) on the island – some tribute given the competition. You can wash them down with the *hyma* (house) wine produced by Lyrarakis, a noted Pezá vineyard.

**Ippokampos** Sófokli Venizélou, west of 25-Avgoústou, close to the *Kronos* hotel. The best and least expensive fish in Iráklion, served in unpretentious surroundings. Deservedly popular with locals for lunch *mezédhes* as well as dinner, this place is often crowded late into the evening, and you may have to queue or turn up earlier than the Greeks eat. Has a pleasant shaded terrace over the road on the seafront.

**Katsina** Marineli 12. A simple and friendly ouzerí at the opposite (seaward) end of the alley from *Fos Fanari*. Tasty and economical seafood *mezédhes* served at outdoor tables.

**Ta Ladádika** Tzikritzi 5, near the market. Welcoming little ouzerí in small pedestrianized street with outdoor tables. Excellent *mezédhes* – try their *dolmadhákia* (stuffed vine leaves).

**Ligo Thálassa** At the foot of Marineli near the Venetian fort. This small new ouzerí serves up a good selection of seafood *mezédhes* and has a small terrace facing the harbour.

**Loukoulos** On the alley Koraí, parallel to Dedhálou. With a leafy courtyard terrace and an Italian slant to its international menu, this is one of the better tavernas in Iráklion. However, the pricey food and an expensive wine list seem aimed more at luring Iráklion's smart set than the casual visitor.

**The Mexican** Hándhakos 71. Inexpensive Mexican tacos and beers, complemented by salads and bean dishes.

**Pagopiion** Platía Áyios Títos. This is the mid-priced restaurant of Iráklion's most original bar, serving Cretan and international dishes to a high standard; the wine list includes interesting bottles from little-known but excellent small vineyards around the island. There's also a recommended *mezédhákia* buffet (Sat 12.30–4.30pm) which allows you to fill a plate for €6. A pleasant terrace is also good for lazy breakfasts and snacks.

**Peri Orexeos** Koraí 10 almost opposite *Loukoulos*. This popular small taverna is a good bet for traditional Cretan cooking at reasonable prices.

**Sintagiés** Kozíri 3, just off Platía Dhaskaloyiánni Platía, (☎ 28102 41378). Housed in a charming century-old mansion with many original features, this is an excellent new mid-priced restaurant, where chef Dimitris Pitarokilis creates fusion Cretan-Mediterranean dishes; try the *kotópoulo mesoyeiakó* (chicken with feta, tomatoes and basil). There are also vegetarian options plus a good selection of Cretan wines.

## Drinking, nightlife and entertainment

As a university town, Iráklion has plenty of places to let your hair down. Young Cretans tend to be more into sitting and chatting over background music than energetic dancing; consequently large areas of Koraï and the surrounding streets have been turned into outdoor **lounges** with lines of expansive sofas and armchairs. In addition to the central zone nightlife, venues are also to be found in the suburbs and out along the hotel strip to the west at Amoudhára. A phenomenon over recent years has been the arrival of a new breed of

**kafenío,** aimed at a younger crowd: the drinks are cocktails rather than *rakí,* the music is modern Greek or Western, and there are prices to match. The city's most animated **bars** are located around **Platía Koraï** behind Dhedhálou (up from *Loukoulos* listed on p.235), along the alley of the same name to the west, plus the parallel Milatou, slightly to the north.

## Bars

**Aiesy** Platía Dhaskalyiánnis. This laid-back café-bar casts off its daytime serenity after dark when locals gather to sink into the canvas chairs on the square, to listen to soft rock and sip long drinks.

**Central Park** El Greco Park square. Popular and modish spot for hanging out and (from a kerbside table) watching who's going where and with whom. The nearby *Draft* targets the same clientele.

**Defilé** Platía Koraí. Trendy little bar frequented by students, on a pleasant square just to the north of Dedhálou.

**Jasmin** Ayiostefanitón 6, tucked in an alley on the left midway down Hándhakos. Another good night-time rendezvous, with jazz, soul and Latin music and an outdoor terrace. Also serves 45 different types of tea, including herbal.

**Korais** on the alley Koraí, parallel to Dedhálou. Glitzy open-air café with spacious plant-festooned terraces, overhead movie screens and music – highly popular with Iráklion's smart set.

**Mayo** Milatou 11, just north of Koraí. This new extravaganza of a bar with spotlights, screens and

music under a big canopy terrace is one of the places to be seen if you're part of Iráklion's student set. Its arrival has spawned a whole new set of bars and cafés along the same street.

**Pagopiion** (Ice Factory) Platía Áyios Títos. Stunning bar with arty decor created by photographic artist Chryssy Karelli inside Iráklion's former ice factory. She has preserved much of the old building including a lift for hauling the ice from the basement freezer and a fascistic call to duty in German Gothic script on one wall – a remnant of Nazi occupation of the factory in World War II. Make sure to visit the toilets, which are in an artistic league of their own.

**Rebels** Perdhíkari 3. A chic music bar which has cloned numerous similar places nearby. On weekends in summer this whole zone is the trendiest place to be if you're under 30.

**Santan** Platía Koraí. This café-bar has outdoor tables and serves a wide variety of exotic (and expensive) beers and cocktails. Those on a tight budget can nurse a *frappé* for hours.

### Clubs and discos

For **discos** and **clubs** proper, there is a large selection, playing Western music, interspersed with Greek tunes (not the *bouzoúkia*-type played for tourists). *Privilege* is the most popular, down towards the harbour at the bottom of Dhoúkos Bofór, below the archeological museum. The nearby *Loca* provides competition. Another pleasant music bar with a seafront location is *Loft* with plenty of space to lounge around, overlooking the western end of Dermatás Bay near the Natural History Museum. *Desire, Big Fish* and *Breeze* are similar seafront places further west along the coast road, while *Plus Soda* further out still in Amoudhára is one of the biggest and best of the many clubs in this western beach suburb. One of the Iráklion beach set's favourite summer venues is at Amnissós beach (see p.234). Here two beach clubs, *Akti* and *Wet Wet*, play host to an under-30 crowd who turn up in their droves to swim, drink and dance to DJ rhythms; night-time is slightly more formal when the dress is smarter and people tend not to swim.

## Listings

**Airlines** Aegean, Airport office (☎28103 30475, ⓦwww.aegeanair.com), and Olympic, 25-Avgoústou 27 (☎28102 45644, ⓦwww .olympic-airways.com) are the main scheduled airlines with connecting flights to Athens and other parts of Greece. Charter airlines flying into

Iráklion mostly use local travel agents as their representatives.

**Airport** For airport information call ☎28103 97111. Bus #1 runs from the eastern side of Platía Eleftherías to the airport every few minutes; buy a ticket (€0.75) from a kiosk near the bus stop.

Banks There are ATMs all over town, but the main bank branches are on 25-Avgoústou.

Car and motorbike rental The upper end of 25-Avgoústou is lined with rental companies, but you'll often find good deals on the backstreets nearby; it's always worth asking for discounts. For cars and bikes, good places to start include: Blue Sea, Kosmá Zótou 7, just off the bottom of 25-Avgoústou (☎28102 41097, @www .bluesearentals.com), which gives a twenty percent discount to Rough Guide readers, and Sun Rise, 25-Avgoústou 46 (☎28102 21609, @www .crete-web.gr/rentacar/sunrise). For cars try: Kosmos, 25-Avgoústou 15 (☎28102 41357, @www.cosmos-sa.gr) or the nearby Caravel, 25-Avgoústou 39 (☎28103 35900, @www .caravel.gr); and Ritz in the Hotel Rea, Kalimeráki 1 (☎2810 223 638). All offer free delivery to hotels and airport.

Ferry tickets Available from Minoan Lines, 25-Avgoústou 78 (☎28102 45018, @www .minoan.gr), which handles the islands and Athens; and ANEK Lines, Dhimokratías 11 (☎281022 3067, @www.anek.gr), for Athens only; also try any of the travel agents listed below. Another source for tickets and ferry information is the long-established Paleologos Travel, 25-Avgoústou 5 (☎28103 46185); their comprehensive websites (@www .ferries.gr, @www.greekislands.gr) are excellent.

Hospital The closest is the Venizélou Hospital, on the Knossós road south out of town (☎28102 38835).

Internet Iráklion now has a number of internet cafés located in and around the city centre. Two central places are Netcafé, Odhós-1878 4 (daily 10am–2am) and Gallery Games, Koraï 14.

Laundry Washsalon, Hándhakos 18 (Mon–Sat 8.30am–9pm), is reliable and also does service washes (around €7 for 6kg). The slightly cheaper (around €6 for 6kg) Laundry Perfect at Malikoúti 32, north of the archeological museum, is also good (Mon–Sat 9am–9pm).

Left luggage Offices in (bus) Station A (daily 6.30am–8pm; €1 per bag per day), but not Station B, as well as a commercial agency at Hándhakos 18 (daily 24hr; €1.50 per large locker per day). Blue Sea, Kotzia 3 off Epimenidhou, near the Venetian harbour (daily 7am–11pm), is a reliable and similar outfit and stores bags for €1 per day. You can also leave bags at the youth hostel (even if you don't stay there) for €2 per bag per day. If you want to leave your bag while you go off on a bike for a day or two, the rental company should be prepared to store it.

Newspapers and books For English-language newspapers and novels, Bibliopoleio, almost opposite the Morosini Fountain on Platía Venizélou, is the most central. The excellent Planet International Bookstore, near the seafront at Hándhakos 73, has the island's biggest stock of English-language titles and is a great place to browse.

Pharmacies Plentiful on the main shopping streets – at least one is open 24hr on a rota basis; the others will have a sign on the door indicating which it is. There are traditional herbalists in the market.

Post office Main office in Platía Dhaskaloyiánnis, off Platía Eleftherías (Mon–Fri 7.30am–8pm).

Taxis Major taxi ranks are in Platía Eleftherías, Platía Kornarou and at the bus stations or call ☎28102 10102 or 281021 0168. Prices displayed on boards at the taxi stands.

Toilets In Platía Kornarou (at the southern end of the market) and the public gardens near the cathedral, or at the bus stations.

Travel agencies Budget operators and student specialists include the extremely helpful Blavakis Travel, Platía Kallergón 8, just off 25-Avgoústou by the entrance to El Greco Park (☎28102 82541). For excursions around the island, villa rentals and so on, the bigger operators are probably easier: Creta Travel Bureau, Dhikeosínis 49 (☎28103 00610), or Hilouris Travel, 25-Avgoústou 76 (☎28103 43400).

# Knossos

KNOSSOS, the largest of the **Minoan palaces**, reached its cultural peak more than three thousand years ago, though a town of some importance persisted here well into the Roman era. It lies on a low, largely man-made hill some 5km southeast of Iráklion; the surrounding hillsides are rich in lesser remains spanning 25 centuries, starting at the beginning of the second millennium BC.

Just over a century ago the palace existed only in mythology. Knossos was the court of the legendary King Minos, whose wife Pasiphae bore the Minotaur, half-bull, half-man. Here the labyrinth was constructed by Daedalus to contain the monster, and youths were brought from Athens as human sacrifice until

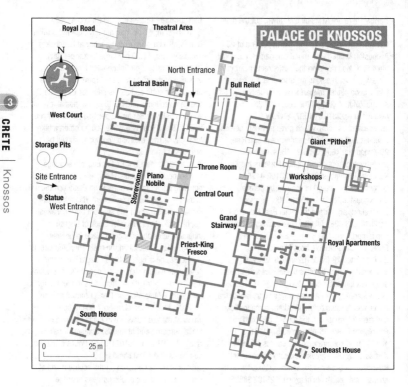

**PALACE OF KNOSSOS**

Royal Road · Theatral Area · North Entrance · Lustral Basin · Bull Relief · West Court · Storage Pits · Giant "Pithoi" · Site Entrance · Piano Nobile · Throne Room · Workshops · Statue · West Entrance · Storerooms · Central Court · Grand Stairway · Royal Apartments · Priest-King Fresco · South House · Southeast House

N

0    25 m

Theseus arrived to slay the beast and, with Ariadne's help, escape its lair. The discovery of the palace, and the interplay of these legends with fact, is among the most amazing tales of modern archeology. Heinrich Schliemann, the German excavator of Troy, suspected that a major Minoan palace lay under the various tumuli here, but was denied the necessary permission to dig by the local Ottoman authorities at the end of the nineteenth century. It was left for Sir Arthur Evans, whose name is indelibly associated with Knossos, to excavate the site, from 1900 onwards.

The #2 and #4 local **buses** set off every ten minutes from Iráklion's city bus stands (adjacent to the eastbound bus station), proceed up 25-Avgoústou (with a stop just south of Platía Venizélou) and out of town on Odhós-1821 and Evans. This is also the route you should take if **driving** (follow the signs from Platía Eleftherías); there's a large free car park downhill on the left, immediately before the site entrance, which will enable you to avoid paying exorbitant rates for the private car parks dotting the road immediately before this (and whose touts will attempt to wave you in). A **taxi** from the centre will cost around €7. At Knossos, outside the fenced site, stands a partly restored Minoan caravanserai where ancient wayfarers would rest and water their animals. Head out onto the road and you'll find no lack of watering holes for modern travellers either – a string of rather pricey tavernas and tacky souvenir stands.

The British School at Athens has a useful website (ⓦ www.bsa.gla.ac.uk /knossos/vrtour) dedicated to Knossos, with detail on its history and excavations in addition to a virtual tour.

# The site

As soon as you enter the **Palace of Knossos** (daily: April–Sept 8am–7.30pm; Oct–March 8.30am–3pm; €6) through the West Court, the ancient ceremonial entrance, it is clear how the legends of the labyrinth grew up around it. Even with a detailed plan, it's almost impossible to find your way around the complex with any success, although a series of **timber walkways** – whose purpose is to protect the monument from the feet of its hundreds of thousands of visitors – now channels visitors around the site, severely restricting the scope for independent exploration. If you're worried about missing the highlights, you can always tag along with one of the constant guided tours for a while, catching the patter and then backtracking to absorb the detail when the crowd has moved on. Outside December to February you won't get the place to yourself, whenever you come, but exploring on your own does give you the opportunity to appreciate individual parts of the palace in the brief lulls between groups.

Knossos was liberally "restored" by Evans, and these restorations have been the source of furious controversy among archeologists ever since. It has become clear that much of Evans's upper level – the so-called *piano nobile* – is pure conjecture. Even so, and putting archeological ethics to one side, his guess as to what the palace might have looked like is certainly as good as anyone's, and it makes the other sites infinitely more meaningful if you have seen Knossos first. Almost as controversial are Evans's designations of the various parts of the palace: he fantasized a royal family living here and in the words of one critic turned the Minoans into "second-millennium BC Victorians". Some sceptical scholars are still not convinced the structure was a palace and argue that the building could well have been a religious centre or shrine. Still, without the restorations, it would be almost impossible to imagine the grandeur of the multistorey palace or to see the ceremonial stairways, strange, top-heavy pillars and gaily painted walls that distinguish the site. For some idea of the size and complexity of the palace in its original state, take a look at the cutaway drawings (wholly imaginary but probably not too far off) on sale outside.

## Royal Apartments

The superb **Royal Apartments** around the central staircase are not guesswork, and they are plainly the finest of the rooms at Knossos. The **Grand Stairway** itself (now closed to public access) is a masterpiece of design: not only a fitting approach to these sumptuously appointed chambers, but also an integral part of the whole plan, its large well bringing light into the lower storeys. Light wells such as these, usually with a courtyard at the bottom, are a constant feature of Knossos and a reminder of just how important creature comforts were to the Minoans, and how skilled they were at providing them.

For evidence of this luxurious lifestyle you need look no further than the **Queen's Suite** (closed at the time of writing for restoration work, but likely to reopen in 2009), off the grand **Hall of the Colonnades** at the bottom of the staircase (reached by descending a timber walkway). Here, the main living room is decorated with the celebrated **dolphin fresco** (a reproduction; the original is now in the Iráklion Archeological Museum, see p.232) and with running friezes of flowers and abstract spirals. On two sides it opens out onto courtyards that let in light and air; the smaller one would probably have been planted with flowers. The room may have been scattered with cushions and hung with plush drapes, while doors and further curtains between the pillars would have allowed for privacy, and provided cool shade in the heat of the day. Remember, though, that all this is speculation and some of it is pure hype; the dolphin fresco, for example, was found on the courtyard floor, not in the room itself, and would have been viewed from an upper balcony as a sort of trompe l'oeil, like looking through a glass-bottomed boat. Whatever the truth, this is an impressive example of Minoan architecture, the more so when you follow the dark passage around to the queen's **bathroom** (now only partially visible behind a screen). Here is a clay tub, protected behind a low wall (and again probably screened by curtains when in use), and the famous "flushing" toilet (a hole in the ground with drains to take the waste away – it was flushed by throwing a bucket of water down).

The much-perused **drainage system** was a series of interconnecting terracotta pipes running underneath most of the palace. Guides to the site never fail to point these out as evidence of the advanced state of Minoan civilization, and they are indeed quite an achievement, in particular the system of baffles and overflows to slow down the runoff and avoid any danger of flooding. Just how much running water there would have been, however, is another matter. Although the water supply was, and is, at the bottom of the hill, the combined efforts of rainwater catchment and hauling water up to the palace can hardly have been sufficient to supply the needs of more than a small elite. The recent discovery of remnants of an aqueduct system carrying water to the palace from springs on nearby Mount Ioúktas (the same source that today provides water for the Morosini Fountain in Iráklion) could mean that this was not the only water supply.

The Grand Stairway ascends to the floor above the queen's domain, and a set of rooms generally regarded as the **King's Quarters** (currently not on view). These are chambers in a considerably sterner vein; the staircase opens into a grandiose reception chamber known as the **Hall of the Royal Guard** (or

▲ Bull relief, Knossos

## Island maps

Along with many other islands in the region Crete isn't that well served by **maps**, and most seem to have a number of significant errors. The best for driving and general use are the German produced Harms-Verlag (ⓦ www.harms-ic-verlag.de), which cover the island (east and west) in two separate maps at a scale of 1:100,000. At a push they can also be used for **hiking**, although the recently produced 1:25,000-scale Crete Hiking Maps series (Anavasi; ⓦ www.mountains.gr) are better. These currently cover only the Lefká Óri (White Mountains), Samariá Gorge and Sfakiá, Mount Psilorítis and Zakros zones, but more are planned. Anavasi has also covered the island with a series of less detailed 1:50,000 maps. Alternatively the Crete Hiking Map (Freytag & Berndt) is a booklet and map pack in German, Greek and English describing twenty walks all over the island ranging from a couple of hours to full-day treks; the accompanying large-scale 1:50,000 map is admirably clear. All the above are widely available from bookshops on the island.

Hall of the Colonnades), its walls decorated in repeated shield patterns. Immediately off here is the **Hall of the Double Axes** (or the King's Room), believed to have been the ruler's personal chamber, a double room that would allow for privacy in one portion while audiences were held in the more public section. Its name comes from the double-axe symbol carved into every block of masonry.

### The Throne Room and the rest of the palace

At the top of the Grand Stairway (you will need to retrace your steps up the timber staircase), you emerge onto the broad **Central Court**, a feature of all the Minoan palaces. Open now, this would once have been enclosed by the walls of the buildings all around. On the far side, in the northwestern corner of the courtyard, is the entrance to another of Knossos's most atmospheric survivals, the **Throne Room**. Here, a worn stone throne – with its hollowed shaping for the posterior – sits against the wall of a surprisingly small chamber; along the walls around it are ranged stone benches, suggesting a king ruling in council, and behind there's a reconstructed fresco of two griffins. Just how much rebuilding took place here can be gauged from the fact that when the throne was unearthed the surrounding ruins cleared its back by only a few centimetres: the ceiling and rooms above are all the creation of Evans's "reconstitution", as he preferred to describe his imaginative reconstructions. Anyway, in all probability in Minoan times this was the seat of a priestess rather than a ruler (there's nothing like it in any other Minoan palace), and its conversion into a throne room seems to have been a late innovation wrought by the invading Mycenaeans, during their short-lived domination prior to the palace's final destruction in the fourteenth century BC. The Throne Room is now closed off with a wooden gate, but you can lean over this for a good view, and in the antechamber there's a wooden copy of the throne on which everyone used to perch to have their picture taken, but this is now also off limits.

The rest you'll see as you wander, contemplating the legends of the place which blur with reality. Try not to miss the giant *pithoi* in the northeast quadrant of the site, an area known as the palace workshops; the storage chambers which you see from behind the Throne Room, and the reproduced frescoes in the reconstructed room above it; the fresco of the Priest-King looking down on the south side of the central court, and the relief of a charging bull on its north side.

This last would have greeted you if you entered the palace through its north door; you can see evidence here of some kind of gatehouse and a lustral bath, a sunken area perhaps used for ceremonial bathing and purification. Just outside this gate is the **theatral area** (another Evans designation), an open space a little like a stepped amphitheatre, which may have been used for ritual performances or dances. From here the **Royal Road**, claimed as the oldest road in Europe, sets out. At one time, this probably ran right across the island; nowadays it ends after about 100m in a brick wall beneath the modern road. Circling back around the outside of the palace, you can get an idea of its scale by looking up at it; on the south side are a couple of small reconstructed Minoan houses which are worth exploring.

## Beyond Knossos

If you have transport, the drive beyond Knossos can be an attractive and enjoyable one, taking minor roads through much greener country, with vineyards draped across low hills and flourishing agricultural communities. If you want specific things to seek out, head first for **MYRTIÁ**, an attractive village with the small **Kazantzakis Museum** (March–Oct daily 9am–7pm; Nov–Feb Sun only 10am–3pm; €3) in a house where the writer's parents once lived. **ARHÁNES**, at the foot of Mount Ioúktas, is a much larger and wealthier farming town that was also quite heavily populated in Minoan times. There are plenty of places to eat on an animated central square, but no places to stay. None of the three archeological sites here is open to the public, but **Anemospiliá**, 2km northwest of the town (directions are available from the archeological museum cited below), can be visited and has caused huge controversy since its excavation in the 1980s: many traditional views of the Minoans, particularly that of Minoan life as peaceful and idyllic, have had to be rethought in the light of the discovery of an apparent human sacrifice. Close to Arhánes' main square, an excellent **archeological museum** (Wed–Mon 8.30am–3pm; free) displays finds from here and other nearby excavations, including the strange ceremonial dagger seemingly used for human sacrifice. From Arhánes you can also drive (or walk with a couple of hours to spare) to the summit of Mount Ioúktas to see the imposing remains of a Minoan **peak sanctuary** and enjoy spectacular panoramic **views** towards Knossos (with which it was linked) and the northern coast beyond. At **VATHÝPETRO**, some 4km south of the mountain, is a **Minoan villa and vineyard** (Tues–Sun 8.30am–2pm; free), which once controlled the rich farmland south of Arhánes. Inside, a remarkable collection of farming implements was found, as well as a unique **wine press**, which remains *in situ*. Substantial amounts of the farm buildings remain, and it's still surrounded by fertile vines (Arhánes is one of Crete's major wine-producing zones) three-and-a-half-thousand years later – making it probably the oldest still-functioning vineyard in Europe, if not the world. Continuing southeast for 2km soon brings you to another agricultural village, **HOUDHÉTSI**, where you'll find the remarkable **Museum of Musical Instruments of the World** (March–Oct daily 8am–4pm; Nov–Feb Sun 10am–3pm; €3; ⓦwww .labyrinthmusic.gr; ☎28107 41027). Founded by Irish *lýra* player Ross Daly, who is famed in Crete and lives in the village, the museum consists of a collection of mainly string and percussion instruments (many very rare) from across the globe. To locate the museum head for *Bar Paranga* at the top (or south end) of the village – the museum is opposite.

# Southwest from Iráklion: sites and beaches

If you take a **tour** from Iráklion (or one of the resorts), you'll probably visit the **Gortys**, **Phaestos** and **Ayía Triádha** sites in a day, with a lunchtime swim at **Mátala** thrown in. Doing it by public transport, you'll be forced into a rather more leisurely pace, but there's still no reason why you shouldn't get to all three and reach Mátala within the day; if necessary, it's easy enough to hitch the final stretch. **Bus services** to the Phaestos site are excellent, with some nine a day to and from Iráklion (fewer Sun), five of which continue to or come from Mátala; there are also services direct to Ayía Galíni. If you're arriving in the afternoon, plan to visit Ayía Triádha first, as it closes early.

## The route to Áyii Dhéka

The road from Iráklion towards Phaestos is a pretty good one by the standards of Cretan mountain roads, albeit rather dull. The country you're heading towards is the richest agricultural land on the island and, right from the start, the villages en route are large and businesslike. In the biggest of them, **Ayía Varvára**, there's a great rock outcrop known as the **Omphalos** (Navel) of Crete, supposedly the very centre of the island.

Past here, you descend rapidly to the fertile fields of the Messará plain, where the road joins the main route across the south near the village of **ÁYII DHÉKA**. For religious Cretans Áyii Dhéka is something of a place of pilgrimage; its name, "The Ten Saints", refers to ten early Christians martyred here under the Romans. The old Byzantine church in the centre of the village preserves the stone block on which they are supposed to have been decapitated, and in a crypt below the modern church on the village's western edge you can see the martyrs' (now empty) tombs. It's an attractive village to wander around, with several places to eat and even some **rooms** – try *Dimitris Taverna* (☎28920 31560; ❷), which has excellent-value en-suite, air-conditioned rooms with views above its restaurant, with an attractive terrace at the rear below.

## Gortys and around

Within easy walking distance of Áyii Dhéka, either through the fields or along the main road, sprawls the site of **Gortys** (daily 8am–7.30pm; €4), ruined capital of the Roman province that included not only Crete but also much of North Africa. After a look at the plan of the extensive site at the entrance, cutting across the fields to the south of the road will give you some idea of the scale of this city, at its zenith in approximately the third century AD. An enormous variety of remains, including an impressive **theatre** and a couple of **temples**, are strewn across your route, and more spectacular discoveries are being unearthed by the archeologists who return to dig each summer. Even in Áyii Dhéka you'll see Roman pillars and statues lying around in people's yards or propping up their walls.

There had been a settlement here from the earliest times and evidence of a Minoan site has been unearthed on the acropolis, but the extant ruins date almost entirely from the Roman era. Only now is the site being systematically excavated by the Italian Archeological School. At the main entrance to the **fenced site**, to the north of the road, are the ruins of the still impressive

**basilica of Áyios Títos**; in the mid-first century the eponymous saint converted the island to Christianity and was its first bishop. Beyond this is the **odeion** which houses the most important discovery on the site, the **Law Code**. These great inscribed blocks of stone were incorporated by the Romans from a much earlier stage of the city's development; they're written in an obscure early Greek-Cretan dialect, and in a style known as *boustrophedon* (ox-ploughed), with the lines reading alternately in opposite directions like the furrows of a ploughed field. At 10m by 3m, this is reputedly the largest Greek inscription ever found. The laws set forth reflect a strictly hierarchical society: five witnesses were needed to convict a free man of a crime, only one for a slave; raping a free man or woman carried a fine of a hundred *staters*, a serf only five. A small **museum** in a loggia (also within the fenced area) holds a number of large and finely worked sculptures found at Gortys, more evidence of the city's importance. Next to the museum is a **café** (same hours as site).

### Míres

Some 20km west of Gortys, **MÍRES** is an important market town and the focal point of transport for the fertile Messará plain: if you're switching buses to get from the beaches on the south coast to the archeological sites or the west, this is where you'll do it. There are good facilities including a **bank**, a few **restaurants** and a couple of **rooms** places, though there's no particular reason to stay unless you are waiting for a bus. A useful **Internet** café, *Net Escape*, near the bus stop will allow you to send a few emails while awaiting onward connections. Heading straight for Phaestos, there's usually no need to stop.

## Phaestos (Festós)

The **Palace of Phaestos** (daily 8am–7.30pm; €4, joint ticket with **Ayía Triádha** €6) was excavated by the Italian Federico Halbherr (also responsible for the early work at Gortys) at almost exactly the same time as Evans was working at Knossos. The style of the excavations, however, could hardly have been more different. Here, to the approval of most traditional archeologists, reconstruction was kept to an absolute minimum – it's all bare foundations, and walls which rise at most 1m above ground level. This means that, despite a magnificent setting overlooking the plain of Messará, the palace at Phaestos is not as immediately arresting as those at Knossos or Malia, but no less fascinating.

It's interesting to speculate why the palace was built halfway up a hill rather than on the plain below – certainly not for defence, for this is in no way a good defensive position. Psychological superiority over the peasants or reasons of health are both possible, but it seems quite likely that it was simply the magnificent view that finally swayed the decision. The site looks over Psilorítis to the north and the huge plain, with the Lasíthi mountains beyond it, to the east. Towards the top of Psilorítis you should be able to make out a small black smudge: the entrance to the Kamáres cave.

On the ground closer at hand, you can hardly fail to notice the strong similarities between Phaestos and the other palaces: the same huge rows of storage jars, the great courtyard with its monumental stairway, and the theatre area. Unique to Phaestos, however, is the third courtyard, in the middle of which are the remains of a **furnace** used for metalworking. Indeed, this eastern corner of the palace seems to have been home to a number of craftsmen, including potters and carpenters. Oddly enough, Phaestos was much less ornately decorated than Knossos; there is no evidence, for example, of any of the dramatic Minoan wall-paintings.

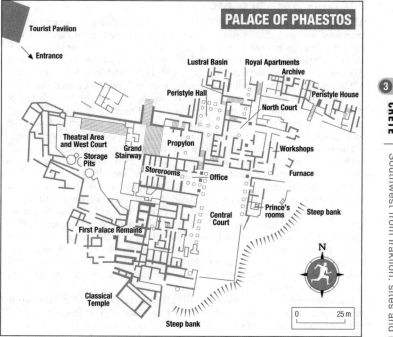

**Tourist Pavilion**

**Entrance**

**Lustral Basin**   **Royal Apartments**
**Archive**
**Peristyle Hall**   **Peristyle House**
**North Court**
**Theatral Area**
**and West Court**   **Propylon**   **Workshops**
**Storage**   **Grand**
**Pits**   **Stairway**
**Storerooms**   **Furnace**
**Office**
**Prince's**   **Steep bank**
**Central**   **rooms**
**First Palace Remains**   **Court**

**N**

**Classical**
**Temple**

0   25 m

**Steep bank**

The nearby village of **ÁYIOS IOÁNNIS**, along the road towards Mátala, has **rooms**, including basic ones at *Taverna Ayios Ioannis* (☎28920 42006; ❶), which serves good charcoal-grilled *kounélli* (rabbit) and lamb from its leafy terrace.

## Ayía Triádha

Some of the finest artworks in the museum at Iráklion came from **Ayía Triádha** (daily: May–Sept 10am–4pm; Oct–April 8.30am–3pm; €4, joint ticket with Phaestos €6), about a 45-minute walk (or short drive) from Phaestos. No one is quite sure what this site is, but the most common theory has it as some kind of royal summer villa. It's smaller than the palaces but, if anything, even more lavishly appointed and beautifully situated. In any event, it's an attractive place to visit, far less crowded than Phaestos, with a wealth of interesting little details. Look out in particular for the row of **stores** in front of what was apparently a marketplace, although recent thinking tends towards the idea that these were constructed after the villa had declined, possibly in the Mycenaean period. The remains of a **paved road** that probably led down to a harbour on the Gulf of Messará can also be seen running alongside the royal villa. The sea itself looks invitingly close, separated from the base of the hill only by Timbáki airfield (mainly used for motor racing these days), but if you try to drive down there, it's almost impossible to find your way around the unmarked dust tracks. There's a fourteenth-century **chapel** – dedicated to Áyios Yeóryios – at the site, worth visiting in its own right for the remains of ancient frescoes (key available from the ticket office).

## Mátala and around

**MÁTALA** has by far the best-known beach in Iráklion province, widely promoted and included in tours mainly because of the famous caves cut into the cliffs above its beautiful sands. These are ancient tombs first used by Romans or early Christians, but more recently inhabited by a sizeable hippie community (including some famous names such as Bob Dylan and Joni Mitchell) in the 1960s and 1970s. You'll still meet people who will assure you that this is *the* travellers' beach on Crete, although today in high season the town is full of package tourists and tries hard to present a more respectable image. The caves have long since been cleared and cleaned up and these days are a fenced-off archeological site (April–Sept daily 10am–7pm; €2), locked up every evening.

The years since the early 1980s have seen the arrival of crowds and the development of hotels, restaurants and clubs to service them; early afternoon, when the tour buses pull in for their swimming stop, sees the beach packed to overflowing. If you're prepared to accept Mátala for what it is – a resort of some size – you'll find the place more than bearable. The town beach is beautiful, and if the crowds get excessive, you can climb over the rocks in about twenty minutes (past more caves, many of which are inhabited through the summer) to another excellent stretch of sand, known locally as "Red Beach". In the evening, when the day-trippers have gone, there are waterside bars and restaurants looking out over invariably spectacular sunsets. If you are arriving **by car**, park either on the road leading into the town or at the beach car park (€1 per day), on the right as you reach the town proper.

The chief problems with staying in Mátala concern prices and crowds: rooms are relatively expensive and oversubscribed, and food is good but not cheap. If you want **accommodation**, a cluster of places lie near to the *Zafiria* hotel (☎28920 45112, ⓦwww.zafiria-matala.com; ❸), just beyond the car park turn-off. Here rooms come with a/c but no TV, and there's a pool. For more economical options try looking in the little street to the left just beyond the *Zafiria* signed "Hotels and Rent Rooms". Here you'll find several rooms for rent, such as *Matala View* (☎28920 45114, ⓦwww.matala-apartments.com; ❷), which also rents studios and apartments sleeping two (❸) or up to four (❹). Nearby, the pleasant, modern and good-value *Fantastik* (☎28920 45362; ❷) has airy air-conditioned en suites with fridge, and the equally good and very friendly 🦌 *Hotel Nikos* (☎28920 45375, ⓦwww.interkriti.net/hotel/matala /nikos/; ❷) has pleasant a/c rooms off a plant-filled patio. If these are full, then everywhere closer in is likely to be as well, so head back out along the main road where places tend to fill up last, or try the **campsite**, *Camping of Matala* (☎28920 45720), next to the beach above the car park; *Kommos Camping* (☎28920 45596) is a nicer site, but a few kilometres out of Mátala and reached by heading back towards Pítsidia and turning left along a signed track.

There are places to **eat and drink** all over the main part of town, and it's worth seeking out the *Skala* fish taverna on the south side of the bay for fresh seafood and a great view, while *Taverna Eleni* is another reliable choice overlooking the beach. Nightlife is generally low-key, conducted in numerous bars which gradually turn up the music volume as the evening wears on. Most of the livelier places are at the southern end of the bay including *Port Side*, a cocktail bar with an enviable beachside location, and *Marinero* and *Tommy's Music Bar* which get lively later on. *Kafe Kantari*, on the square, is another place where people gather after dark. **Internet** access is available inside the stylish *Kafeneio* bar on the main square or at the *Zafiria Café* opposite (and owned by) the hotel of the same name. Impossible to miss are most other facilities, including various stores and a good bookshop (with international press) next to *Kafeneio*. Currency exchange and ATMs, car and bike rental plus travel agents are on or around the main square just off which there's a covered market where tourist tat has almost squeezed out the fruit and veg stalls. The small post office lies 50m to the east of the *Zafiria* hotel facing the entrance to the car park.

### Around Mátala: Pitsídhia and Kalamáki

One way to enjoy a bit more peace is to stay at **PITSÍDHIA**, about 5km inland. This has long been a well-used option, so it's not quite as cheap as you might expect, but there are plenty of rooms, lively places to eat and even music bars. If you decide to stay here, the beach at **KALAMÁKI** is an alternative to Mátala. Both beaches are approximately the same distance to walk, though there is a much better chance of a bus or a lift to Mátala. Kalamáki has developed somewhat, with a number of **rooms** – *Psiloritis* (☎28920 45693; ❶) is a good bet – and a couple of tavernas, but it's still a rather unfinished, soulless little place. The beach stretches for miles, surprisingly wild and windswept, lashed by sometimes dangerously rough surf. At the southern end (more easily reached by a path off the Pitsídhia–Mátala road) lies **Kommos**, once a Minoan port serving Phaestos and now the site of a major archeological excavation. It's not yet open to the public, but you can peer into the fenced-off area to see what's been revealed so far, which is pretty impressive: dwellings, streets, hefty stonework and even the ship sheds where repairs on the Minoan fleet were carried out.

## Iráklion's south coast

South of the Messará plain are two more resorts, **Kalí Liménes** and **Léndas**, with numerous other little beaches along the coast in between, but nothing spectacular. **Public transport** is very limited indeed; you'll almost always have to travel via Míres (see p.244). If you have your own transport, the roads in these parts are all passable and newly sealed, but most are very slow going; the Kófinas hills, which divide the plain from the coast, are surprisingly precipitous.

### Kalí Liménes

While Mátala itself was an important port under the Romans, the chief harbour for Gortys lay on the other side of Cape Líthinon at **KALÍ LIMÉNES**. Nowadays, this is once again a significant port – for oil tankers. This has rather spoilt its chances of becoming a major resort, and there are few proper facilities, but some people like Kalí Liménes: it's certainly off the beaten track and the constant procession of tankers gives you something to look at while beach-lounging. There are a couple of places offering **rooms** – the best is the seafront *Taverna Panorama* (☎28920 97517; May–Oct; ❷), which has a decent **taverna** attached. The coastline is broken up by spectacular cliffs and, as long as there hasn't been a recent oil spill, the beaches are reasonably clean and totally empty.

### Léndas

**LÉNDAS**, further east along the coast, is far more popular, with a couple of buses daily from Iráklion and a partly justified reputation for being peaceful (sullied by considerable summer crowds). Many people who arrive think they've come to the wrong place, as at first sight the village looks shabby, the beach is small, rocky and dirty, and the rooms are frequently all booked. A number of visitors leave without ever correcting that initial impression; the attraction of Léndas is not the village at all but the beach on the other (west) side of the headland. Here lies a vast, excellent sandy strand named **Dhytikós** (or Dhiskós) **beach**, part of it usually taken over by nudists, with a number of taverna/bars overlooking it from the roadside. The beach is a couple of kilometres from Léndas, along a rough track; if you're walking, you can save time by cutting across the headland. A considerably more attractive prospect than staying in Léndas itself is **camping** on the beach to the west of the village or, with luck, getting a **room** at one of the few beach tavernas – try 🏠 *Villa Tsapakis* (☎28920 95378, ⊛www.villa-tsapakis.gr; ❷), with sea-view rooms and reductions for longer stays. They will also change money on a credit card here (a useful service in this part of Crete where banks and ATMs are nonexistent) and have their own decent **taverna**, *Odysseas*, nearby. After you've discovered the beach, even Léndas begins to look more welcoming, and at least it has most of the facilities you'll need, including a couple of minimarkets, both of which will change money, a phone box and a dual-screen **internet** café (enterprisingly named Café Internet) on the main square. Car hire is available at the Villa Tsapakis. Lendas also has numerous places to **eat and drink**: the outstanding 🏠 *Taverna El Greco* (☎28920 95322) with a leafy terrace above the beach on the east side of the village is one of the best restaurants on the whole south coast – their *oktapódhi* (octopus), *kolikythákia* (fried zucchini) or prime Messará beef pepper steak are all recommended. Its popularity means that you may need to book in high season; *Akti* and *Elpida* on the main square are reasonable substitutes.

Once you've come to terms with the place, you can also explore some deserted beaches eastwards, and the scrappy remains of **ancient Lebena** on a hilltop overlooking them. There was an important Asklepion (temple of the god Asklepios) here around some now-diverted warm springs, but only the odd broken column and fragments of mosaic survive in a fenced-off area on the village's northern edge.

# East of Iráklion: the package-tour coast

East of Iráklion, the startling pace of **tourist development** in Crete is all too plain to see. The merest hint of a beach is an excuse to build at least one hotel, and these are outnumbered by the concrete shells of resorts-to-be. It's hard to find a room in this monument to the package-tour industry, and it can be expensive if you do. That said, there are one or two highlights amidst the dross, which are well worth a visit. Beyond the teenage resort of Mália, a fine **Minoan palace** will transport you back three and a half millennia, or, if you're looking for splendid isolation, the twin sea hamlets of **Sísi** and **Mílatos** are refreshingly out of sync with the rest of this coast.

## Goúrnes and Goúves

As a general rule, the further east you go, the better things get: when the road detours all too briefly inland, the more alluring Crete of olive groves and stark mountains asserts itself. You certainly won't see much of it at **GOÚRNES**, 15km from Iráklion, where part of an abandoned former US Air Force base has given way to the newly constructed Cretaquarium Thalassocosmos (daily: June–Sept 9am–9pm; Oct–May 9am–7pm; ⊛www.cretaquarium.gr, ☎28103 37788; €8, under 12s €6), a spectacular and sizeable **marine aquarium** with thirty tanks (some huge) housing a variety of sea creatures including menacing sharks and dazzling jellyfish. Part of the Hellenic Centre for Marine Research, the venture is purely educational, scientific and non-profit making. Most of the island's fish and crustaceans are included among the 250 species and over 2500 specimens on display, and unless you're a marine biologist the audio-guide (€2; easily shared between two or three) is pretty well indispensable and gives loads of fascinating background information on the creatures you're looking at. The aquarium is well signposted on the road leading from Irák lion.

A little way further east lies **Káto Goúves**, where a **campsite**, *Camping Creta* (T 28970 41400), shares a boundary with the former base. From here, however, you can head inland to the old village of **GOÚVES**, a refreshing contrast, and just beyond to the **Skotinó Cave**, one of the largest and most spectacular on the island (about an hour's walk from the coast; open all hours; free).

## Hersónissos (Límin Hersoníssou)

Heading east from Goúves you'll pass the turn-off for the new E75 Hersónissos bypass (avoiding the beach resort's bottleneck), which cuts inland to rejoin the coast road just before Stalídha. Shortly beyond this junction, there's the turning for the direct route up to the Lasíthi Plateau. Carry straight on, though, and you'll roll into the first of the really big resorts, **HERSÓNISSOS**, or, more correctly, Límin Hersoníssou; Hersónissos is the village in the hills just behind, also overrun by tourists.

Hersónissos was once just a small fishing village; today it's the most popular of Crete's package resorts. If what you want is plenty of video-bars, touristy tavernas, restaurants and Eurodisco nightlife, then this is the place to come. The resort has numerous small patches of sand beach between rocky outcrops, but a shortage of places to stay in peak season.

The focal main street, two-kilometre-long Odhós Elefthériou Venizélou, is a seemingly endless ribbon of bars, travel agents, tacky jewellery and beachwear shops, amusement arcades and – during the daytime at least – nose-to-tail traffic jams. North of here, along the modern seafront, a solid line of restaurants and bars is broken only by the occasional souvenir shop; in their midst you'll find a small pyramidal Roman **fountain** with broken mosaics of fishing scenes, the only real relic of the ancient town of Chersonesos. Around the headland above the harbour and in odd places along the seafront, you can see remains of Roman harbour installations, mostly submerged.

Beach and clubs excepted, the distractions of Hersónissos include **Lychnostatis Open-air Museum** (Mon–Fri & Sun 9.30am–2pm; €5), a surprisingly rewarding "museum" of traditional Crete with imaginative reconstructions of island life past and present, on the coast at the eastern edge of the town; there's also a small aquarium, **Aqua World** (April–Oct daily 10am–6pm; €8 adults, €5 under-12s), just off the main road at the west end of town, up the road almost opposite the *Vibe* style bar. To cool down, the watersports paradise **Star Beach Water Park** (daily: April & May 10am–6pm; June–Sept 10am–7pm; free entry but charges for most activities) sits near the beach at the eastern end of the resort or, 3km inland, the competing and more elaborate **Aqua Splash Water Park** (€18 full day, under-12s €12; cut-price late-entry deals). A short distance inland are the three **hill villages** of Koutoulafári, Piskopianó and "old" Hersónissos, which all have a good selection of tavernas, and are worth searching out for accommodation.

### Practicalities

Hersónissos is well provided with all the back-up **services** you need to make a holiday go smoothly. Banks, bike and car rental and post office are all on or just off the main drag, Elefthériou Venizélou, as are the taxi ranks. There are a number of **internet** cafés: Easy Internet Café is one of a number on the water-front near the harbour, while CNet, Papadoyiorgi 10, alongside the church, is a more central option; both have plenty of screens. **Buses** running east and west leave from the main bus stop on Venizélou every thirty minutes.

Finding somewhere to stay here can verge on the impossible in July and August. Much of the **accommodation** is allocated to package-tour operators and what remains for casual visitors is among the priciest on the island. To check for general availability of accommodation, the quickest and best option is to enquire at one of the many travel agencies along Venizélou such as KTEL Tours next to the bus stop and opposite the petrol station in the centre of town.

Despite the vast number of **eating places**, there are few in Hersónissos worth recommending, and the tavernas down on the harbourfront should be avoided. One of the few Greek tavernas that stands out is *Kavouri* along Arhéou Theátrou, but it's fairly expensive; a cheaper in-town alternative for some delicious and inexpensive Cretan cooking is 🎋 *Taverna Creta Giannis*, Kaniadhakí 4, just off the south side of Venizélou slightly east of the church (closes 10pm). Nearby, and also definitely worth a try, is 🎋 *Passage to India*, an authentic and extremely good Indian restaurant; it lies on Petrákis, another side street just off the main street near the church. For an evening stroll you could head a couple of kilometres up the hill to Hersónissos village where *Tria Adelphi* (*The Three Brothers*) is one of the more authentic tavernas clustered around its main square. Both here and in the neighbouring hill village of Koutoulafári, you can have a relaxed evening amongst the narrow streets and small platíes.

Hersonnisos has one of the wildest **nightlife** scenes on the island – just follow the crowds heading for the harbour with its lines of clubs, throbbing music bars and greeters who will try to tempt you inside or squeeze you into a terrace sofa.

## Mália

Eight kilometres east of Hersónissos lies the brash resort town of **MÁLIA.** Like many other places along this coast it is carved up by the package industry, so in peak season finding a place to stay is not always easy. The town's focus is a T-junction (where the **bus** drops you) and from where the beach road – a kilometre-long strip lined with bars, clubs, games arcades, tavernas and souvenir shops – heads north to the sea and beaches. South of this junction the older village presents a slightly saner image of what Mália used to be, but even here rampant commercialism is making inroads. If you must **stay**, there are numerous rooms and *pensions* signposted up in the old town to the south of the main road. Here Platía Ayíou Dhimitríou, a pleasant square beside the church, has a few decent tavernas.

### The Palace of Malia

Much less imposing than either Knossos or Phaestos, the **Palace of Malia** (Tues–Sun 8.30am–3pm; €4), 2km east of Mália town, in some ways surpasses both. For a start, it's a great deal emptier and you can wander among the remains in relative peace. While no reconstruction has been attempted, the palace was never reoccupied after its second destruction in the fifteenth century BC, so the ground plan is virtually intact. It's much easier to comprehend than Knossos and, if you've seen the reconstructions there, it's easy to envisage this seaside palace in its days of glory. There's a real feeling of an ancient civilization with a taste for the good life, basking on the rich agricultural plain between the Lasíthi mountains and the sea.

▲ Hitting the beach road, Mália

From this site came the famous **gold pendant** of two bees (which can be seen in the Iráklion Archeological Museum or on any postcard stand), allegedly part of a hoard that was plundered and whose other treasures can now be found in the British Museum in London. The beautiful leopard-head axe, also in the museum at Iráklion, was another of the treasures found here. At the site, look out for the strange indented stone in the central court (which probably held ritual offerings), for the remains of ceremonial stairways and for the giant *pithoi*, which stand like sentinels around the palace. To the north and west of the main site, archeological digs are still going on as the **large town** which surrounded the palace comes slowly to light, and part of this can now be viewed via an overhead walkway.

Any passing **bus** should stop at the site, or you could even rent a **bike** for a couple of hours as it's a pleasant, flat ride from Mália town. Leaving the archeological zone and turning immediately right, you can follow the road down to a lovely stretch of clean and relatively peaceful **beach**, backed by fields, scrubland and a single makeshift taverna, which serves good fresh fish. From here you can walk back along the shore to Mália or take a bus (every 30min in either direction) from the stop on the main road.

## Sísi and Mílatos

Head **east** from the Palace of Malia, and it's not long before the road leaves the coast, climbing across the hills towards Áyios Nikólaos. If you want to escape the frenetic pace of all that has gone before, try continuing to Sísi or Mílatos. These little shore villages are bypassed by the main road as it cuts inland, and are still very much in the early stages of tourist development. The larger of the two, **SÍSI**, is charmingly situated around a small harbour

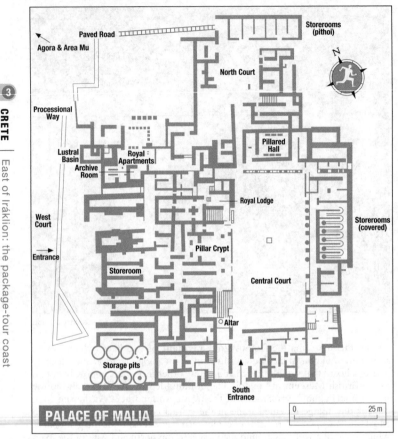

Storerooms
(pithoi)

Paved Road

Agora & Area Mu

North Court

N

Processional
Way

Pillared
Hall

Lustral
Basin

Archive
Room

Royal
Apartments

Royal Lodge

West
Court

Storerooms
(covered)

Entrance

Pillar Crypt

Storeroom

Central Court

Altar

Storage pits

South
Entrance

0          25 m

**PALACE OF MALIA**

overlooked by balcony bars and more tavernas. The opening of the resort's first disco bar (*Faros*) and the large holiday complex (*Kalimera Krita*), a couple of kilometres to the east, are a sure sign that more development is on its way; there's even a **post office**, confirming the resort status. **Accommodation** is mainly in studios and apartments; it's best to ask in the travel agencies and tavernas for details of availability. There's also a shady **campsite** with pool and taverna (☎28410 71247) signposted on the way in. Among a cluster of seafront **tavernas** all specializing in freshly caught fish, the *Fisherman's Place* is worth a try.

In quieter **MÍLATOS**, rooms can be found in the old village, 2km inland, but the seaside settlement – despite a rather pebbly beach – is more desirable. A number of the seafront tavernas let out rooms and, outside the peak season when there's little chance of a bed, the friendly ⚘ *Rooms Taverna Sokrates* (☎28410 81375; ❶–❷) is worth a try and does decent **food**, especially fish, netted by the village boats. Despite their pebbly main **beaches**, the resorts make for a refreshing change of pace, and there are some fine, deep aprons of sand in the rocky coves beyond the resort centres.

# West of Iráklion: around Psilorítis

Most people heading west from Iráklion speed straight out on the **E75 coastal highway**, nonstop to Réthymnon. If you're in a hurry this is not such a bad plan; the road is fast and spectacular, hacked into the sides of mountains which for the most part drop straight to the sea, though there are no more than a couple of places where you might consider stopping. By contrast, the old roads inland are agonizingly slow, but they do pass through a whole string of **attractive villages** beneath the heights of the Psilorítis range. From here you can set out to explore the **mountains** and even walk across them to emerge in villages with views of the south coast.

## The coastal route towards Réthymnon

Leaving the city, the **new highway** runs behind a stretch of highly developed coast, where the hotels compete for shore space with a cement works and power station. As soon as you reach the mountains, though, all this is left behind and there's only the clash of rock and sea to contemplate. As you start to climb, look out for **Paleókastro** hovering beside a bridge which carries the road over a small cove; the castle is so weathered as to be almost invisible against the brownish face of the cliff.

### Ayía Pelayía and Fódhele

Some 3km below the highway, as it rounds the first point, lies the resort of **AYÍA PELAYÍA**. It looks extremely attractive from above but, once there, and especially in July and August, you're likely to find the narrow, taverna-lined beach packed to full capacity. This is not somewhere to roll up in high season without reserved **accommodation**, although in quieter times *Zorba's Apartments* (☎28102 56072, ⓦwww.zorbas.gr; ❸), along the nameless main street behind the beach, or, the nearby *Irini* (☎28108 11455; ❷) are worth a try. On the road above these, the excellent-value *Danai Rooms* (☎28102 85936; ❷), whose air-conditioned, en-suite rooms have kitchenette and fridge, should have space. Opposite *Zorba's Apartments*, the Pangosmio travel agency (☎28108 11402) may be able to come up with something, even at the last minute in high season. Out of season you might find a real bargain apartment and, despite the high-season crowds, the resort maintains a dignity long since lost in Mália and Hersónissos, and even a certain exclusivity; a couple of Crete's most luxurious hotels, including the *Capsis Beach* (☎28108 11112, ⓦwww.capsis.gr; ❸), nestle on the headlands just beyond the main town beach. There are plenty of **minimarkets** for buying picnic food, and **internet** access is available at *Worldc@fé*, next door to *Zorba's Apartments*.

Not far beyond Ayía Pelayía, there's a turning inland to the village of **FÓDHELE**, allegedly El Greco's birthplace. A plaque from the University of Valladolid (in Spain) acknowledges the claim and, true or not, the community has built a small tourist industry on that basis. There are a number of craft shops and some pleasant tavernas where you can sit outside along the river. A peaceful one-kilometre walk (or drive) takes you to the spuriously titled **El Greco's House** (aka Museum of El Greco; May–Oct Tues–Sun 9am–5pm; €1.50), exhibiting a few poor reproductions of his works and not much more, and the more worthwhile and picturesque fourteenth-century Byzantine **church of the Panayía** (officially Tues–Sun 9am–3.30pm but often locked; free) with frescoes, opposite. None of this amounts to very much but it is a pleasant, relatively unspoilt village if you simply want to sit in peace for a while. A couple of **buses** a day run here from Iráklion, and there's the odd tour; if you arrive on a direct bus, the walk back down to the highway (about 3km), where you can flag down a passing service, is not too strenuous.

## Balí and Pánormos

**BALÍ**, on the coast about halfway between Iráklion and Réthymnon, is a charming small resort with a beautiful setting and sandy beaches. The village is built around a trio of small coves, some 2km from the highway (a hot walk from the bus), and is similar to Ayía Pelayía except that the beaches are not quite as good and there are no big hotels, just an ever-growing proliferation of studios, apartment buildings, rooms for rent and a number of smaller hotels. You'll have plenty of company here, and it has to be said that Balí has become a package resort too popular for its own good: the third and best beach, known as "Paradise", no longer really deserves the name; it's a beautiful place to splash about, surrounded by mountains rising straight from the sea, but there's rarely a spare inch on the sand in high season. Should you decide to stay, decent-value rooms are available in the second cove at *Mira Mare* (☎2834094256, Ⓦwww .goldenmemories-crete.com; ❷) and internet access is available at Bali Netcafé close to the third cove's harbour.

Continuing along the coast, the last stop before you emerge on the flat stretch leading to Réthymnon is at **PÁNORMOS**, a good stopover if you're in search of somewhere more peaceful and authentic. The small sandy beach can get crowded when boats bring day-trippers from Réthymnon, but most of the time the attractive village remains relatively unspoilt, and succeeds in clinging to its Cretan identity. There are several decent **tavernas** – ꓴ *Sofoklís* near the harbour is the best of the bunch – and **rooms** places, one large hotel and the very comfortable *Pension Lucy* (☎28340 51328, Ⓦwww.lucy.gr; ❷–❸), which has also sprung a seafront offshoot with balcony studio rooms and apartments.

## Inland towards Mount Psilorítis

Of the **inland routes**, the old main road (via Márathos and Dhamásta) features few places of any size or appeal, though it's a very scenic drive. If you want to dawdle, you're better off on the road which cuts up to **Týlissos** and then goes via **Anóyia**. It's a pleasant ride through fertile valleys filled with olive groves and vineyards, a district (the Malevísi) renowned from Venetian times for the strong, sweet Malmsey wine.

### Týlissos and Anóyia

**TÝLISSOS** has a significant archeological site (daily 8.30am–3pm; €2) where three Minoan houses were excavated; unfortunately, its reputation is based more on what was found here (many pieces in the Iráklion Archeological Museum) and on its significance for archeologists than on anything which remains to be seen. Still, it's worth a look, if you're passing, for a glimpse of Minoan life away from the big palaces, and for the tranquillity of the pine-shaded remains.

**ANÓYIA** is a much more tempting place to stay, especially if the summer heat is becoming oppressive. Spilling prettily down a hillside close below the highest peaks of the mountains, it looks traditional, but closer inspection shows that most of the buildings are actually concrete; the village was destroyed during World War II and the local men rounded up and shot – one of the German reprisals for the abduction of General Kreipe by the Cretan resistance. The town has a reputation as a centre of *lýra* playing (many famous exponents were born here) and also as a **handicrafts** centre (especially for woven and woollen goods), skills acquired both through bitter necessity after most of the men had been killed, and in a conscious attempt to revive the town. At any rate it worked, for the place is thriving today – thanks, it seems, to a buoyant agricultural sector made rich by stockbreeding, and the number of elderly widows keen to subject any visitor to their terrifyingly aggressive sales techniques.

Quite a few people pass through Anóyia during the day, but not many **stay**, even though there are some good *pensions* and rented rooms in the upper half of the town, including flower-bedecked *Rooms Aris* (T28340 31817; ❷) and the nearby *Aristea* (T28340 31459; B&B; ❷), which has an ebullient proprietor, en-suite rooms with spectacular terrace views and rates that include breakfast.

The town has a very different, more traditional ambience at night, and the only problem is likely to be finding a **place to eat**: although there are plenty of snack-bars and so-called tavernas, most have extremely basic menus, more or less limited to spit-barbecued lamb, which is the tasty local speciality served up by the grill places on the lower square. Options in the upper town include *Aetos* on the main street, or a steep hike beyond this to the top of the village will bring you to *Taverna Skalomata* offering well-prepared taverna standards, good barbecued lamb, plus a fine view. Opposite this taverna is Anóyia's solitary internet café, Infocost@.

### Mount Psilorítis and its the Idean cave

Heading for the mountains, a smooth road ascends the 21km from Anóyia to an altitude of 1400m on the **Nídha Plateau** at the base of Mount Psilorítis. Here, the *Taverna Nida* (T28340 31141; April–Sept daily; Oct–May Sat & Sun only) serves up hearty mountain dishes featuring lamb, pork and chicken, and has a couple of simple **rooms** (❶ including breakfast), which makes it a good base for hikes in the surrounding mountains. A short path leads from the taverna to the celebrated **Idean cave** (Idhéon Ándhron), a rival of that on Mount Dhíkti (see p.257) for the title of Zeus's birthplace, and certainly associated from the earliest of times with the cult of Zeus. The remnants of a major archeological dig carried out inside – including a miniature railway used by archeologists to remove tonnes of rock and rubble – still litter the site, giving the place a rather unattractive prospect. When you enter the cave down concrete steps into the depths, it turns out to be a rather shallow affair, with little to see.

The taverna also marks the start of the way to the top of **Mount Psilorítis** (2456m), Crete's highest mountain, a climb that for experienced, properly shod hikers is not at all arduous. The route (now forming a stretch of the E4 Pan-European footpath) is well marked with the usual red dots and paint splashes, and it should be a six- to seven-hour return journey to the **chapel of Tímios Stavrós** ("Holy Cross") at the summit, although in spring, thick snow may slow you down.

If you're prepared to camp on the plateau (it's very cold, but there's plenty of available water) or find rooms at the taverna, you could continue on foot the next day down to the southern slopes of the range. It's a beautiful hike and also relatively easy, four hours or so down a fairly clear path to **Vorízia** where there is no food or accommodation, although **KAMÁRES**, 4km west, has both: for **rooms**, the very cheap, very basic and unsigned (you'll need to ask for it) *Hotel Psiloritis* (T28920 43290; ❶) should have a bed, and the best **place to eat** is the *Taverna Bournelis* at the village's western end. If you're still interested in caves, there's a more rewarding one above Kamáres, a climb of some five hours on a good but aggressively steep path; if you're coming over from Nídha, the cave actually makes a rather shorter detour off the main traverse path. The start of the route is just to the left of the *Taverna Bournelis* and the proprietors here can advise on the ascent (in Greek and German only). There is at least one daily **bus** from here down to Míres and alternative (more difficult) routes to the peak of Psilorítis if you want to approach from this direction.

# Eastern Crete

Eastern Crete is dominated by **Áyios Nikólaos**, a highly developed resort. Far fewer people venture beyond the road south to **Ierápetra** and into the eastern isthmus, where only **Sitía** and the famous beach at **Váï** ever see anything approaching a crowd. Inland, too, there's interest, especially on the extraordinary **Lasíthi Plateau**, which is worth a night's stay if only to observe its abidingly rural life.

## Inland to the Lasíthi Plateau

Leaving the palace at Malia, the highway cuts inland towards **NEÁPOLI**, soon beginning a spectacular climb into the mountains. Set in a high valley, Neápoli is a market town little touched by tourism. Just off a leafy main square there's an excellent **hotel**, 🎿 *Neapolis* (☎28410 33967, ⓦwww.neapolis-hotel.gr; ③), with air-conditioned rooms, some with fine views. On the main square there's a superb little **folk museum** (Mon 9am–2pm, Wed–Sun 9.30am–4.30pm; €1.50) displaying some fascinating photos, utensils and farming equipment from Neápoli's past as well as reconstructions of a bar, schoolroom, cobbler's workshop and domestic kitchen from a bygone age. On the square – and 50m from the museum entrance – *Taverna Yeúseis* is a good place for **food** and has a pleasant shady terrace. Beyond the town, it's about twenty minutes before the road suddenly emerges high above the Gulf of Mirabéllo and Áyios Nikólaos, the island's biggest resort. If you're stopping, Neápoli also marks the second point of access to the **Lasíthi Plateau**.

Scores of bus tours drive up here daily to view the "thousands of white-cloth-sailed windmills" which irrigate the high plain ringed by mountains, and most groups will be disappointed. There are very few working windmills left, and these operate only for limited periods (mainly in June), although most roadside tavernas seem to have adopted many of those made redundant as marketing features. The drive alone is worthwhile, however, and the plain is a fine example of rural Crete at work, every inch devoted to the cultivation of potatoes, apples, pears, figs, olives and a host of other crops; stay in one of the villages for a night or two and you'll see real life return as the tourists leave. There are plenty of easy rambles around the villages as well, through orchards and past the rusting remains of derelict windmills.

You'll find **rooms** in the main village of **TZERMIÁDHO**, where the *Hotel Kourites* (☎28440 22194; ②) is to be found on the eastern edge, in **ÁYIOS YEÓRYIOS** – where there's a **folk museum and crafts centre**, and the economical and friendly *Hotel Dias* (☎28440 31207; ①) – in **MAGOULÁS** where rooms and fine food are on offer at ⚔ *Taverna Dionysos* (☎28440 31672; ❷) and **PSYKHRÓ**, where the *Hotel Zeus* (☎6972981782 or enquire at *Taverna Halavro* close to the cave car park; ❷) lies close to the Dhiktean cave.

## The Dhiktean cave

Psykhró is the most visited village on the plateau, as it's the base for visiting Lasíthi's other chief attraction: the birthplace of Zeus, the **Dhiktean cave** (daily June–Sept 8.30am–7pm; Oct–May 8.30am–3pm; €4; ask for the free information leaflet on the cave). In legend, Zeus's father, the Titan Kronos, was warned that he would be overthrown by a son, and accordingly ate all his offspring; however, when Rhea gave birth to Zeus in the cave, she fed Kronos a stone and left the child concealed, protected by the Kouretes, who beat their shields outside to disguise his cries. The rest, as they say, is history (or at least myth). There's an obvious path running up to the cave from Psykhró, near the start of which (beyond the car park) the mule handlers will attempt to persuade you the ascent is better done on one of their steeds (costing a hefty €10 one way). In reality, it's hardly a particularly long or dauntingly steep hike to the cave entrance.

The cave has been made more "visitor friendly" in recent years, with the introduction of concrete steps in place of slippery stones, and electric lighting instead of torches and candles. Inevitably some of the magic and mystery have been lost, and the guides, who used to make the visit much more interesting with their hilarious and preposterous tales, have now been banned, presumably in the interests of accuracy and decorum. Thus you will now have to pick out for yourself the stalactites and stalagmites formed in the image of the breasts of Rhea where the infant Zeus was suckled, as well as the baby Zeus himself – a feat verging on the impossible for someone lacking a Cretan imagination.

One of the cave guardians, Petros Zarvakis, is also a wildlife expert and leads **guided wild-flower and bird-spotting hikes** (April–Sept) into the mountains surrounding the plain, and also to the summit of Mount Dhíkti; if he is not on duty at the cave entrance or at the taverna (*Taverna Petros* run by his family) in the car park, he can be contacted on ☎28440 31600 or 694 56 16 074. **Buses** run around the plateau to Psykhró direct from Iráklion and from Áyios Nikólaos via Neápoli. Both roads offer spectacular views, coiling through a succession of passes guarded by lines of ruined windmills.

# Áyios Nikólaos and around

**ÁYIOS NIKÓLAOS** ("Ag Nik" to the majority of its British visitors) is set around a supposedly bottomless salt lake, now connected to the sea to form an inner harbour. It is supremely picturesque and has some style and charm, which it exploits to the full.

## Arrival, information and orientation

The **tourist office** (daily May–Oct 8am–9.30pm; ☎28410 22357, Ⓦwww .aghiosnikolaos.gr), situated between the lake and the port, is one of the best on the island for accommodation information. The **bus station** is situated to the northwest end of town near the archeological museum. You'll find the greatest concentration of **stores** and **travel agents** on the hill between the bridge and Platía Venizélou (along the streets 25-Martíou, Koundoúrou and pedestrianized 28-Oktovríou), and the main **ferry agent**, Plora Travel (☎28410 82804), on the corner of 28-Oktovríou and K. Sfakianáki. The **post office** (Mon–Sat

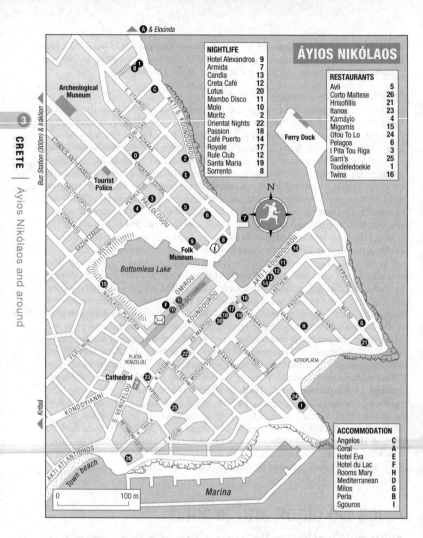

**NIGHTLIFE**

| | |
|---|---|
| Hotel Alexandros | 9 |
| Armida | 7 |
| Candia | 13 |
| Creta Café | 12 |
| Lotus | 20 |
| Mambo Disco | 11 |
| Molo | 10 |
| Moritz | 2 |
| Oriental Nights | 22 |
| Passion | 18 |
| Café Puerto | 14 |
| Royale | 17 |
| Rule Club | 12 |
| Santa Maria | 19 |
| Sorrento | 8 |

**ÁYIOS NIKÓLAOS**

**RESTAURANTS**

| | |
|---|---|
| Avli | 5 |
| Corto Maltese | 26 |
| Hrisofillis | 21 |
| Itanos | 23 |
| Karnáyio | 4 |
| Migomis | 15 |
| Ofou To Lo | 24 |
| Pelagos | 6 |
| I Pita Tou Riga | 3 |
| Sarri's | 25 |
| Toudeledoekie | 1 |
| Twins | 16 |

**ACCOMMODATION**

| | |
|---|---|
| Angelos | C |
| Coral | A |
| Hotel Eva | E |
| Hotel du Lac | F |
| Rooms Mary | H |
| Mediterranean | D |
| Milos | G |
| Perla | B |
| Sgouros | I |

7.30am–2pm) is halfway up 28-Oktovríou on the right. To **hire a motorbike**, **scooter** or **mountain bike** try the reliable Mike Manolis (☎28410 24940), who has a pitch along Modhátsou near the junction with K. Sfakianáki. Good **car-rental** deals are available at Club Cars, 28-Oktovríou 24 (☎28410 25868), near the post office or Economy (☎28410 22013) under the *Hotel Angelos*. Various **boat trips** to points around the gulf (such as Spinalónga and Eloúnda; about €12–17 depending on company) leave from the west side of the harbour. **Internet** access is available at *Peripou*, 28-Oktovríou 25 (daily 9.30am–2am), and *Café du Lac* at no. 17 on the same street.

### Accommodation

Since many of the package companies have pulled out in recent years the town is no longer jammed solid as it once was, though in the peak season you won't have so much choice. One thing in your favour is that there are literally hundreds of **rooms**, scattered all around town. The tourist office normally has a couple of boards with cards and brochures about hotels and rooms, including their prices. If the latter seem very reasonable it is because many are for the low season. The nearest **campsite** is *Gournia Moon*, 17km away (see p.257).

**Angelos** Aktí S. Koundoúrou 16 ☎ 28410 23501. Welcoming small hotel offering excellent a/c balconied rooms with TV and fridge plus fine views over the Gulf. ❸

**Coral** Aktí S. Koundoúrou ☎ 28410 28363, ⓦ www.mhotels.gr. One of Áyios Nikólaos's leading in-town hotels offering a/c rooms with sea view, fridge, balcony and satellite TV, plus a rooftop pool and bar. Out of high season, prices can fall by up to fifty percent. In July–Aug you may need to ask for the room-only price as they will quote you half-board. B&B. ❺

**Hotel Eva** Stratigoú Kóraka 20 ☎ 28410 22587. Decent en-suite a/c rooms with TV and view in a misnamed *pension* close to the centre. ❷

**Hotel du Lac** 28-Octovríou ☎ 28410 22711, ⓦ www.dulachotel.gr. Perhaps the most unexpected bargain in town, with classily renovated rooms and studios in designer style with all facilities including a/c, TV and (in studios) kitchenette in a prime location overlooking the lake. However, it's also in the heart of things, and night-time noise from revellers is the only downside. ❸

**Mediterranean** S. Dhávaki 27 ☎ 28410 23611. Clean, economical en-suite rooms with fridges and fans, and close to the lake. ❷

**Milos** Sarolídi 2 ☎ 28410 23783. Sweet little *pension* east of the Kitroplatía beach, with some of the best rooms in town for the price. The spotless, en-suite balcony rooms (number 2 is a dream) have spectacular sea views over the Gulf. ❷

**Perla** Salaminos 4 ☎ 28410 23379. Decent budget option close to the sea, on a hill to the north of the harbour. En-suite rooms with fans and fridge, and front rooms have sea-view balconies. ❷

**Rooms Mary** Evans 13, near the Kitroplatía ☎ 28410 23760. Very friendly place with a/c (€5 extra) en-suite balcony rooms (some with sea view), access to fridge and use of kitchen. Also has some apartments nearby costing only slightly more. ❷

**Sgouros** Kitroplatía ☎ 28410 28931, ⓦ www .sgourosgrouphotels.com. Good-value modern hotel with a/c balcony rooms overlooking one of the town's beaches, and close to plenty of tavernas. ❸

## The Town

There are no sights as such, but the excellent **archeological museum** (Tues–Sun 8am–5pm; €3) on Paleológou north of the lake, and an interesting Folk museum (Tue–Sun 10am–2pm; €3) near the tourist office (p.257) are both worth seeking out. The lake and port are surrounded by restaurants and bars, which charge above the odds, and whilst the resort is still very popular, some tourists are distinctly surprised to find themselves in a place with no decent beach at all.

There are swimming opportunities further north, however, where the pleasant low-key resort of **Eloúnda** is the gateway to the mysterious islet of **Spinalónga**,

## Diving and sailing in Áyios Nikólaos

The seas around eastern Crete are a diver's paradise. Companies who will help you to find your flippers in this activity – or get you up to the next level – include:

**Creta Underwater Centre** In the *Hotel Mirabello* on the Elounda Road ☎ 28410 82546, ⓦ www.cretaunderwatercenter.com.

**Happy Divers** In front of the *Hotel Coral* ☎ 28410 82546, ⓦ www.cretashappydivers .gr.

**Pelagos** In the *Minos Beach Hotel*, Elounda Road ☎ 28410 24376, ⓦ www.divecrete .com. This company also hires out sailing dinghies by the hour.

All the above are PADI certificated and typical seven-day courses for beginners and advanced divers start at €640 (beginners) or €540 (advanced) which includes airport transfers, hotel accommodation, tuition and dive equipment.

and some great backcountry inland – perfect to explore on a scooter. Inland from Áyios Nikólaos, **Kritsá** with its famous frescoed church and textile sellers is a tour-bus haven, but just a couple of kilometres away, the imposing ruins of **ancient Lato** are usually deserted.

## Eating

At least when it comes to eating there's no chance of missing out, even if some of the prices are fancier than the restaurants. There are tourist-oriented **tavernas** all around the lake and harbour and little to choose between them, apart from the different perspectives you get on the passing fashion show. Have a drink here perhaps, or a mid-morning coffee, and choose somewhere else to eat. The places around the Kitroplatía are generally fairer value, but again you are paying for the location.

Avlí Odhós P. Georgíou 12, two blocks behind the tourist office. Delightful garden ouzerí offering a wide *mezédhes* selection as well as more elaborate dishes. Open eves only.

Corto Maltese Aktí Nearchou 15, near the Marina. New and stylish mid-priced bar-restaurant with a fusion approach to Greek, Cretan and Mediterranean cuisines. Opens for breakfast (with freshly squeezed juices) and lunch and goes on until midnight. Also stocks a wide selection of Greek and Cretan wines and each Thurs evening does a wine-tasting featuring a different vineyard on the island.

Hrisofillís Aktí Themistokleous. Attractive, stylish and creative *mezedhopolío* with reasonably priced fish, meat and veggie *mezédhes* served on a pleasant sea-facing terrace fronting the east side of the Kitroplatía beach.

Itanos Kýprou 1, off the east side of Platía Venizélou. Popular with locals, this traditional taverna serves Cretan food and wine and has a terrace across the road.

Karnáyio Paleológou 21, close to the lake. Atmospheric traditional *kafenío* popular with a younger crowd and serving tasty *mezédhes* – try the *faba* (mashed split peas) – inside or on its pleasant terrace with lake view. A bonus here is some great *lýra* and *lauto* (lute) music most Fri and Sat (not July and Aug).

Café/Restaurant Migomis Nikoláou Plastíra 22 (☎28410 24353). Pleasant café high above the bottomless lake with a stunning view. Perfect (if

pricey) place for breakfast, afternoon or evening drinks. Their next-door restaurant enjoys the same vista and is pricier than the norm, but perhaps worth it if you've booked a frontline table to feast on that view.

Ofou To Lo Kitroplatía. Best of the moderately priced places on the seafront here: the food is consistently good. Try their *loukánika me tirí* (sausages with cheese) starter.

Pelagos Stratigoú Kóraka, just back off the lake behind the tourist office ☎28410 25737. Housed in an elegant mansion, this stylish fish taverna has an attractive leafy garden terrace which complements the excellent food. Pricey, but worth it.

I Pita Tou Riga Paleológou 24, close to the lake. Excellent Lilliputian snack-bar/restaurant serving imaginative fare – salads, filled pitta breads and some Asian dishes; has a small terrace up steps across the road. They'll let you bring your own bottle of wine.

Sarri's Kýprou 15. Great little economical neighbourhood café-diner especially good for breakfast and *souvláki*, all served on a leafy terrace.

Toudeledoekie Aktí S. Koundoúrou 24. Friendly, low-key Dutch-run café with international press to read; great sandwiches and milkshakes by day, chilled bar at night.

Twins Fronting the harbour. Handy pizzeria, fast-food outlet and coffee bar, open all hours. Their "small" pizzas are big enough for two.

## Drinking and nightlife

After you've eaten you can get into the one thing which Áyios Nikólaos undeniably does well: **bars and nightlife**. Not that you really need a guide to this – the bars are hard to avoid, and you can just follow the crowds to the most popular places centred on the harbour and 25-Martíou. For a more relaxed drink you could try *Hotel Alexandros* on Paleológou (behind the tourist office), with a rooftop cocktail bar overlooking the lake, which after dark metamorphoses into a 1960s-to-1980s period music bar. One curiosity worth a look in the harbour itself is *Armida* (April–Oct), a bar inside a beautifully restored century-old wooden trading vessel, serving cocktails and simple *mezédhes*.

**Music bars** with terraces filled with easy chairs and even sofas spread along Aktí I Koundoúrou from the harbour where *Café Puerto*, *Candia* and *Creta Café* play cool sounds to their lounging clientele. Further along a bunch of popular new café bars look out over the ferry dock; *Molo* is a good choice here. There are bars on the opposite side of the harbour too, though fewer of them: *Sorrento* is a long-established haunt of ex-pats and tour reps, loud and fun if that's what you're in the mood for; *Moritz* could hardly be more different, with a dressy clientele and jazz and soft-rock sounds.

Later on it's an easy move to go **dancing** at places like *Rule Club* (above the *Creta Café* on Koundoúrou) and the nearby *Mambo Disco* – the only genuine dance venues. The more raucous music bars and clubs crowd the bottom of 25-Martiou (known as "Soho Street") as it heads up the hill. *Royale*, *Passion* and *Lotus* all go on into the small hours as does *Santa Maria* around the corner on M. Sfakianáki. Further up 25-Martíou at no. 19, *Oriental Nights* is a big, Middle Eastern-themed club.

## The coast north of Áyios Nikólaos

North of Áyios Nikólaos, the swankier hotels are strung out along the coast road, with upmarket restaurants, discos and cocktail bars scattered between them. **ELOÚNDA**, a resort on a more acceptable scale, is about 8km out along this road. **Buses** run regularly, but if you feel like renting a **scooter** it's a spectacular ride, with impeccable views over a gulf dotted with islands and moored supertankers. Ask at the bookshop near the post office, on the central square facing the sea, about the attractive *Milos* and *Delfinia* **rooms**, studios and apartments (T 28410 41641, W www.pediaditis.gr; ❷–❸), which come with sea views and, at the more modern *Milos*, a pool. You could also try the friendly *Pension Oasis* (T 28410 41076, W www.pensionoasis.gr; ❷), which has en-suite rooms with kitchenette and is just off the square, behind the church. There are more options along this road nearby. The seafront *Akti Olous* on the Olous road (T 28410 41270, W www.greekhotels.net/aktiolous; ❹) is one of the better hotel options. If you find that things are tight (which only happens in high summer) ask at one of the many travel agents around the main square for help finding a room or apartment; you could try friendly Olous Travel (T 28410 41324), which also gives out **information** and changes money. If you're looking for reading matter or want to offload or swap your paperbacks Eklektos, Papandreou 13, is a great little English bookshop about 100m uphill from the square in the direction of Áyios Nikólaos; it also stocks *Greek Islands* author Lance Chilton's walking guides and maps for this zone which include rambles around Olous, the Spinalónga peninsula and nearby hill villages.

For **eating**, *Britomares*, in a plum spot in the centre of the harbour, the nearby *Poulis* and the ultra-chic *Ferryman* (tellingly with a menu in English only) are the town's best (and priciest) tavernas, and near to the latter the recently refurbed *Megaro* serves well-prepared seafood and steaks inside or on a pontoon terrace on the water. More economical fish and *mezédhes* are to be had at the simple *Ouzeri Maritsa* below the church tower at the north end of the square. **Nightlife** tends to be generally low-key, and centres on café terraces and cocktail bars around the main square where *Babel* and *Aligos* are among the biggest and loudest. *Katafigio*, right at the start of the Olous road, has live Greek music.

▲ Spinalónga island, a former fortress and leper colony

Just before the centre of the village, a road (signposted) leads downhill to a natural causeway leading to the ancient "sunken city" of **Olous**. Here you'll find restored windmills, a short length of canal, Venetian salt pans and a well-preserved dolphin **mosaic**, inside a former Roman basilica, but nothing of the sunken city itself beyond a couple of walls in about 70cm of water. Swimming here is good, however – but watch out for sea urchins.

From Eloúnda, boats run half-hourly in high season (€10 return) to the fortress-rock of **Spinalónga**. As a bastion of the Venetian defence, this tiny islet withstood the Turkish invaders for 45 years after the mainland had fallen; in more recent decades and until 1957 it served as a leper colony. As you look around at the roofless shells of houses once inhabited by the unfortunate lepers, and the boat which brought you disappears to pick up another group, an unnervingly real sense of the desolation of those years descends.

Back on the mainland, and 5km north of Eloúnda, **PLÁKA** used to be the colony's supply point; now it is a haven from the crowds, with a small pebble beach and a clutch of fish **tavernas**, one of which, *Taverna Spinalonga*, can arrange a boat to take you across to Spinalónga (April–Sept) for about €7 return. The *Spinalonga*'s proprietor Aris also does boat trips to isolated beaches not reachable by road (€15 per person) and all-day fishing trips (€50 per person in a group of four, which includes rod and tackle, drinks and meals and a great evening cook-up of the catch at the taverna). The taverna rents **rooms** (②) and good-value apartments (②) for stays of at least two nights. There are also daily **boat trips** from Áyios Nikólaos to Olous, Eloúnda and Spinalónga (costing around €12–17), usually visiting at least one other island along the way.

**Inland to Kritsá and Lato**

The other excursion everyone takes from Áyios Nikólaos is to **KRITSÁ**, a "traditional" village about 10km inland. Buses run at least every hour from the bus station, and despite the commercialization it's still a good trip. The local **crafts** (weaving, ceramics and embroidery basically, though they sell almost everything here) are fair value, and Michalis Apostolakis's olive woodcarving workshop on the main street is especially worth a look: some of his carvings are worked from wood 500 to 1500 years old. A trip out to Kritsá is also a welcome break from living in the fast lane at "Ag Nik". In fact, if you're looking for somewhere to stay around here, the village has a number of advantages: chiefly availability of **rooms**, better prices and something at least approaching a genuinely Cretan atmosphere; try *Argyro* (☎28410 51174, ⓦwww.argyrorentrooms.gr; ❷), with pleasant rooms – some en suite – around a courtyard on your way into the village. *Pension Kera* (☎28410 51045; ❶), up the main street from where the bus drops you, has the cheapest rooms but although clean, they're pretty basic. The most attractive place to stay, however, is the *The Olive Press* (☎28410 51296, ⓦwww.olivepress.centerall.com; ❸), a Belgian-run venture with two pleasant rooms in a beautifully restored, stone-built olive-oil mill. A little difficult to find, it lies at the very end of the tapestry sellers' street, close to the church of Áyios Yeóryios Harakitis. The small platía at the centre of the village is the focus of life, and there are a number of decent places **to eat** here, too: the central ⚑ *Kafenío Saridhakis* is a wonderfully old-fashioned throwback to a Crete fast disappearing with place to sit out under a plane tree, or you could head for the bakers for tempting *tyrópita* (cheese pies) or currant breads. One of the best-situated tavernas is *Castello*, also in the centre, and there are a few others near where the bus stops.

On the approach road, some 2km before Kritsá, is the lovely Byzantine **church of Panayía Kyrá** (daily 8.30am–5.30pm; €3), inside which survives perhaps the most complete set of Byzantine frescoes in Crete. The fourteenth- and fifteenth-century works have been much retouched, but they're still worth the visit. Excellent (and expensive) reproductions are sold from a shop alongside. Just beyond the church, a surfaced road leads off for 3km to the archeological site of **Lato** (Tues–Sun 8.30am–2.30pm; €2), where the substantial remains of a Doric city are coupled with a grand hilltop setting. The city itself is extensive, but largely neglected, presumably because visitors and archeologists on Crete are more concerned with the Minoan era. If you're interested in knowing more about the site and its history an informative booklet is on sale at the ticket office. Ruins aside, you could come here just for the views: west over Áyios Nikólaos and beyond to the bay and Olous (which was Lato's port), and inland to the Lasíthi mountains.

# The eastern isthmus

The main road south and then east from Áyios Nikólaos is not a wildly exciting one, essentially a drive through barren hills sprinkled with villas and skirting above the occasional sandy cove. The stretch of the E75 northern highway beyond Ístro is undergoing major **engineering works** intended to by-pass the archeological site of Gourniá and the coastal town of Pahía Ámmos, making the route to Ierápetra more direct as well as upgrading the route to Sitía. Five kilometres east of Ístro, along a newly completed stretch of the E75, an exit on the left is signed for the **monastery of Faneroméni**. The way bends around to cross the E75 on a viaduct before heading inland along a track (partly asphalted in its early stage) that climbs dizzily skywards for 6km, giving spectacular views over the Gulf of Mirabéllo along the way. The **view** from the monastery over the gulf is one of the finest in Crete. To get into the rather bleak-looking monastery buildings, knock loudly. You will be shown up to the chapel, built into a cave sanctuary, and the quite brilliant seventeenth-century frescoes.

## Gourniá, Pahiá Ámmos and Mókhlos

Back on the coast road, it's another 2km to the site of **Gourniá** (Tues–Sun 8.30am–3pm; €2), slumped in the saddle between two low peaks. The most completely preserved **Minoan town**, its narrow alleys and stairways intersect a throng of one-roomed houses (of which only the ground-floor walls survive – they would have had at least one upper floor) centred on a main square, and the rather grand house of what may have been a local ruler or governor. Although less impressive than the great palaces, the site is strong on revelations about the lives of the ordinary people – many of the dwellings housed craftsmen (working with wood, metal and clay), who left behind their tools and materials to be found by the excavators. Its desolation today (you are likely to be alone save for a dozing guardian) only serves to heighten the contrast with what must have been a cramped and raucous community 3500 years ago.

It is tempting to cross the road here and take one of the paths through the wild thyme to the sea for a swim. Don't bother – the bay and others along this part of the coastline act as a magnet for every piece of floating detritus dumped off Crete's north coast. There is a larger beach (though with similar problems), and rooms to rent, in the next bay along at **PAHIÁ ÁMMOS**, about twenty-minutes' walk, where there is also an excellent seafront fish taverna, ⚘ *Aiolus*; all the fish (caught with their own boat) plus *kolokithokéftedes* (courgette balls) and *achinosalata* (sea urchin's eggs) are outstanding. In the other direction, there's the campsite of *Gournia Moon* (☎ 28420 93243; May–Sept), with its own small cove and a swimming pool.

This is the narrowest part of the island, and from here a fast road cuts across the isthmus to Ierápetra (see p.272) in the south. In the north, the route on towards Sitía is one of the most exhilarating in Crete. Carved into cliffs and mountain-sides, the road teeters above the coast before plunging inland at Kavoúsi. Of the beaches you see below, only the one at **MÓKHLOS** is at all accessible, some 5km below the main road. This sleepy seaside village has a few rooms, a hotel or two and a number of **tavernas** – *Tò Bogazi* is good – squatting along its tiny harbour; if you find yourself needing a **place to stay**, you could try the rooms at the clean and simple *Pension Hermes* (☎ 28430 94074; ❷) behind the waterfront, which are the cheapest in the village, or *Hotel Sofia* (☎ 28430 94738; ❸) on the harbour itself for a bit more en-suite luxury. Nearer Sitía the familiar olive groves are interspersed with vineyards used for creating wine and sultanas, and in late summer the grapes, spread to dry in the fields and on rooftops, make an extraordinary sight in the varying stages of their slow change from green to gold to brown.

## Sitía

**SITÍA** is the port and main town of the relatively unexploited eastern edge of Crete. It's a pleasantly scenic if unremarkable place, offering a plethora of waterside restaurants, a long sandy beach and a lazy lifestyle little affected even by the thousands of visitors in peak season. There's an almost Latin feel to the town, reflected in (or perhaps caused by) the number of French and Italian tourists, and it's one of those places that grows on you, perhaps inviting a longer stay than intended. For entertainment there's the **beach**, providing good swimming and windsurfing, and in town a mildly interesting **folklore museum** (Mon–Sat 10am–1pm; €2), a Venetian fort and Roman fish tanks to explore, plus an excellent **archeological museum** (Tues–Sun 8.30am–3pm; €2). As part of a government push to increase tourism at this end of the island, a new **airport** (set to open to international flights in 2009) has been constructed on a plateau above the town, and seems likely have a big impact on Sitía itself as well as the surrounding area.

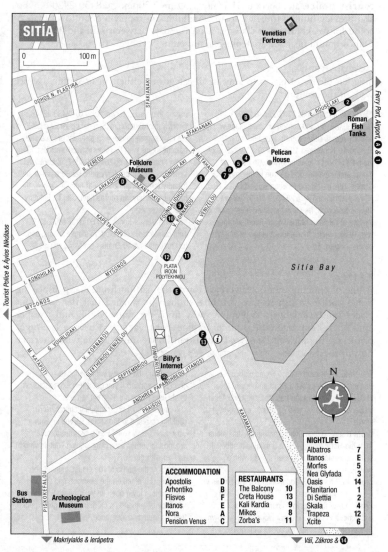

## Arrival and information

The bus drops you at the **bus station** (actually an office on the street; ☎28430 22272) on the southwest fringe of the centre, close to the town's main **supermarket**, useful for stocking up on provisions. **Internet** access is available at Enter Café, on Venizélou 95 to the west of Platía Iroón Polytekhníou (daily 8am–midnight) or at Billy's Internet (daily 10am–10pm), Papandreou 16, near the tourist office. Sitía also has a PADI certificated diving centre, Universal Diver, at Kornárou 140 (☎28430 23489), offering beginners and advanced diving courses.

Should you have problems finding somewhere to stay, the **tourist office** (Mon–Fri 9.30am–2.30pm & 5–9pm, Sat 9am–2.30pm; ☎28430 28300), on the seafront at the start of the beach road, should be able to help, or there's the **tourist police** at Therisou 31 (daily 7.30am–2.30pm; ☎28430 24200), who also provide limited tourist information; both can supply a good town map. A colourful weekly **market** takes place on Tuesdays between 7am and 2pm along Odhós Itanou near the archeological museum.

## Accommodation

Sítia has plenty of places to **stay** in all categories, either on or within a short walk of the seafront.

**Apostolis** Kazantzákis 27 ☎28430 22993. Pleasant, friendly and central en-suite place where balcony rooms come with fridges and fans. ❶
**Arhontiko** Kondhiláki 16 ☎28430 28172. One of the best budget places in town, with attractive rooms and a mature orange tree in the front garden. One of the rooms is en suite. ❷
**Flisvos** Karamanli 4 ☎28430 27135, ⓦwww .flisvos-sitia.com. Newly refurbished hotel fronting the sea at the start of the Beach Road; a/c rooms with TV and fridge face either the sea or a patio garden behind. ❹

**Itanos** Platía Iroon Polytekhníou ☎28430 22146, ⓦwww.itanoshotel.com. Smart, upper-range hotel on the town's main square with pleasant, a/c sea-view balcony rooms with TV. Rates include breakfast. ❹
**Nora** Rouseláki 31 ☎28430 23017, ⓔnorahotel @yahoo.gr. Near the ferry port, this is a small and friendly female-run hotel, with fine views over the harbour and bay; all rooms have a/c, TV, balcony and shower. ❷
**Pension Venus** Kondhiláki 60 ☎28430 24307. This comfortable place offers simple rooms, and has an enthusiastic English-speaking owner. ❶

## Eating

A line of enticing outdoor tavernas crowds the harbourfront, many displaying dishes and fresh fish to lure you in – though be warned that these seafront places can be relatively expensive. Away from the water you'll find cheaper (and often more interesting) places to dine. For breakfast pastries or late night drinks try the pleasant *Trapeza*, Platía Iroon Polytehniou, a café with a terrace on this focal square.

**The Balcony** Kazantzákis & Foundalídhou. Stylish restaurant in the upper floor of an elegant town house. An eclectic menu has Mexican- and Asian-influenced dishes as well as Greek; expensive, but worth it.
**Creta House** Beach Road (Karamanli). Just along from the *Hotel Itanos*, this is a reliable traditional taverna specializing in Cretan dishes, with a harbourside terrace.
**Kali Kardia** Foundalídhou 28, two blocks in from the waterfront. The popular "Good Heart" ouzeri lives up to its name in terms of its welcome, and is an excellent place to wash down fish, cheese and snail *mezédhes* with house

retsina. You'll be mixing with the locals here, and don't be surprised if you get a few extra titbits on the house. Has a small street terrace.
**Mikos** Kornárou 117. Traditional charcoal-grill cooking on a spit in the street, served up with a very strong local wine. Has a seafront terrace around the corner served by jogging waiters who to and fro with dishes.
**Zorba's** At the harbour. The oldest, biggest and most popular place on the seafront, and the only restaurant in town open all year round. Serves up much more authentic food than you might expect from its touristy appearance.

## Drinking and nightlife

Sitía's **nightlife**, mostly conducted at an easy pace, centres on the music bars at the northern end of Venizélou towards the Roman fish tanks and out along the beach road. The first group of bars includes *Albatros Xcite*, *Morfes* and *Skala* – all on the seafront near the jetty – and the somewhat glitzier *Nea Glyfada* a little further on above the duck pond. Above here and entered from Rouselaki, *Di Settia* is a laid-back taverna and music bar with garden. At the opposite end of town the roof garden of the *Hotel Itanos* has a relaxed late-night music bar, while further along the beach road, *Oasis*, has an expansive seafront terrace. For late-night clubbing from midnight on look no further than the town's monster disco-club, *Planitarion*, with sliding glass roof and state-of-the-art techno gadgetry which attracts crowds from all over the east. It lies a couple of kilometres beyond the ferry port, and is best reached by taxi. Sitía's main bash is the summer-long Kornaria **cultural festival** featuring concerts, dance and theatre by Greek and overseas participants (details from the tourist office).

# Onward to Váï beach and Palékastro

Leaving Sitía along the beach, the Váï road climbs above a rocky, unexceptional coastline before reaching a fork to the **monastery of Toploú** (daily 9am–1pm & 2–6pm, Oct–March closes 4pm; €3). The monastery's forbidding exterior reflects a history of resistance to invaders, and doesn't prepare you for the gorgeous flower-decked cloister within. The blue-robed monks keep out of the way as far as possible, but in quieter periods their cells and refectory are left discreetly on view. In the church is one of the masterpieces of Cretan art, the eighteenth-century icon *Lord Thou Art Great* by Ioannis Kornaros, incorporating 61 small scenes full of amazing detail inspired by the Orthodox prayer "Lord thou art great …" In the monastery's shop you can buy enormously expensive reproductions of the work as well as olive oil and wine made by the monks. The monastery, which is enormously wealthy and owns vast tracts of this end of the island, has recently done a controversial deal with an international development company to build a huge one-billion euro 7000-bed **tourist complex** covering much of Cape Sideros to the north of Toploú. Based on five new "Cretan-style villages" with a yacht harbour, conference centres, golf courses and tennis courts, many environmentalists regard the project as a major threat to the delicate ecology of eastern Crete and have taken the case to the Greek high court. Toploú's abbot, Philotheos, who is backing the project, believes it will provide thousands of much-needed jobs. Should the court reject the environmentalists' case (the Athens government is also in support of the project) construction is scheduled to begin in 2009.

**Váï beach** itself features alongside Knossos or the Lasíthi Plateau on almost every Cretan travel agent's list of excursions. Not surprisingly, it is now covered in sunbeds and umbrellas, though it is still a superb beach. Above all, it is famous for its palm trees, and the sudden appearance of the grove is indeed an exotic shock; lying on the fine sand in the early morning, the illusion is of a Caribbean island – a feature seized upon by countless TV-commercial makers seeking an exotic location on the cheap. As everywhere, notices warn that "camping is forbidden by law", and for once the authorities seem to mean it – most campers climb over the headlands to the south or north. If you do sleep out, watch your belongings, since this seems to be the one place on Crete with crime on any scale. There's a compulsory car park (€2.50), a café and an expensive taverna at the beach, plus toilets and showers. Because of its status as a nature reserve there is **no accommodation** here whatsoever; the nearest place offering a bed for the night is Palékastro. By day you can find a bit more solitude by climbing the rocks or swimming to one of the smaller beaches which surround Váï. **Ítanos**, twenty-minutes' walk north by an obvious trail, has a couple of tiny beaches and some modest ruins from the Classical era.

### Palékastro

**PALÉKASTRO**, an attractive farming village some 9km south, makes a good place to stopover. Although its beaches – highly popular with windsurfers – can't begin to compare with those at Váï, you'll find several modest places with **rooms** – among them *Hotel Hellas* (☎28430 61240, ✪www.palaikastro.com; ❷), which offers comfortable en-suite rooms with balcony, TV and fridge and reductions for longer stays. The good-value *Váï* (☎28430 61414; ❶), with rooms above a taverna at the west end of the village, on the Sitía road is another possibility. There are some attractive rooms and apartment options a little further out on the roads leading to the beaches and information on these is available from the tourist office (see p.266). The extensive **beaches** provide plenty of space to **camp** out without the crowds, but you should respect local sensitivities, keeping away from the main strands and responsibly disposing of any rubbish. Add in a **tourist office** (April–Oct daily 9am–10pm; ☎28430 61546) on the main street, a small **folk museum** (May–Oct Tues–Sun 10am–1pm & 5–8.30pm; €1.50), an internet café inside the *Hotel Hellas*, a few **bars** and even a **dance club**, *Design*, just outside the village on the Váï road, and the place begins to seem positively throbbing. There are plenty of **tavernas** both in the village – the taverna of ⚘ *Hotel Hellas* is particularly recommended – and out at the beaches. The sea is a couple of kilometres down a dirt track, effortlessly reached with a **scooter** hired from Moto Kastri (☎28430 61477), on the eastern edge of the village along the Váï road. Palékastro is also the crossroads for the road south to Zákros, and your own transport presents all kinds of beach and exploration possibilities.

### Angáthia and the beaches

**ANGÁTHIA**, smaller and even quieter than its neighbour, lies a kilometre closer to the beaches. Just across the bridge leading into the village on the right, you'll find the good-value *Taverna Vaios* (☎28430 61403; ❷), which has a couple of pleasant sea-view balcony rooms with bath; they have some nearby luxury apartments too (❸), equipped with air conditioning, garden and balcony sea views. The taverna also makes a good lunch stop if you're at the beach. **Chiona beach**, a good stretch of EU blue-flagged pebble and sand, to the south of a flat-topped hill named Kastrí which dominates the coastal landscape, is a kilometre beyond Angáthia and is the beach most people visit, thanks to its car park and nearby tavernas.

South of Chiona beach along a track running beside the sea, about 200m down on the right (signed "Peak Sanctuary"), a walking track will take you to the nearby **Petsofás peak** – a pleasant three-kilometre hike. This was also the site of a Minoan sanctuary, and the view from the summit gives you a great overview of the ancient Minoan town and harbour. Behind Chiona beach lies the main excavation area (known as Roussolákkos and left open) of Palékastro's **Minoan site**, one of the most important in eastern Crete. Only partly excavated, surveys indicate that the largest Minoan town yet found still lies underground, as well as a very large building which could be a palace. Due to the size of the project, work on revealing these will only begin when funding is available.

There are some more excellent beaches nearby where you could easily **camp**. The better sands are around the bay further to the south of Chiona, where for most of the year you can easily claim a cove to yourself. However, the best beach of all, **Kouremenos**, lies to the north of the Kastri bluff and is one of Crete's top **windsurfing** spots. If you fancy riding a few breakers Freak Surf Station (☎28430 61116, Ⓦwww.freak-surf.com) rents out boards and offers courses. The beach's popularity has now attracted a couple of **tavernas**, including *To Botsalo*, with a pleasant terrace shaded by tamarisk trees. For accommodation, just behind the Kouremenos beach and surrounded by olive groves, the welcoming *Marina Village Hotel* (☎28430 61407, Ⓦwww.palaikastro.com /marinavillage; ❸ including breakfast) is a peaceful haven with very nice **rooms** surrounded by a garden with bougainvillea and banana plants.

## Zákros

**ÁNO ZÁKROS** (Upper Zákros) lies a little under 20km from Palékastro. There are several tavernas and a simple hotel, the *Zakros* (☎28430 93379; ❷), which has some rooms with bath and great views from its rear rooms; it also offers guests a free minibus service to the Minoan palace and beach. The palace is actually at Káto ("lower") Zákros, 8km further down towards the sea. Most buses run only to the upper village, but in summer a couple go all the way to the site every day; it's usually not difficult to hitch if your bus does leave you in the village. Two kilometres along the road you can, if on foot, take a short cut through an impressive **gorge** (the "Valley of the Dead", named for ancient Minoan tombs in its sides). The gorge entrance is signed "Dead's Gorge" next to an information board and car-park area with a steep path leading down to the trail, which then follows a stream bed for 4km to reach the sea near the Minoan palace. It's a solitary but magnificent hike, brightened especially in spring with plenty of plant life.

The **Palace of Zakros** (daily: July–Oct 8.30am–5pm, Nov–June 8am–3pm; €3) was an important find for archeologists; it had been occupied only once, between 1600 and 1450 BC, and was abandoned hurriedly and completely. Later, it was forgotten almost entirely and as a result was never plundered. The first major excavation began only in 1960; all sorts of everyday objects, such as tools, raw materials, food and pottery, were thus discovered intact among the ruins, and a great deal was learned from being able to apply modern techniques (and knowledge of the Minoans) to a major dig from the very beginning. None of this is especially evident when you're at the palace, except perhaps in a particularly simple ground plan, so it's as well that it is also a rewarding visit in terms of the setting. Although the site is set back from the sea, in places it is often marshy and waterlogged – partly the result of eastern Crete's slow subsidence, partly the fault of a spring which once supplied fresh water to a cistern beside the royal apartments, and whose outflow is now silted up. In wetter periods, among the remains of narrow streets and small houses of the town outside the palace and higher up, you can keep your feet dry and get an excellent view down over the central court and royal apartments. If you want a more detailed overview of the remains, buy the guide to the site on sale at the entrance.

The delightful village of **KÁTO ZÁKROS** is little more than a collection of tavernas, some of which rent out rooms around a peaceful beach and minuscule fishing anchorage. It's a wonderfully restful place, but is often unable to cope with the volume of visitors seeking accommodation in high season, and as rooms are rarely to be had on spec you'd be wise to ring ahead. Villagers are far more hostile these days to wild camping after years of problems, and you should be sensitive to their concerns. Reliable rooms (sharing bath or en suite) can be found at the simple ⚓ *Poseidon* (☎28430 26896; ❶), which has stunning sea views, and the friendly *George Villas* (☎28430 26883; ❸), 600m behind the archeological site along a driveable track. *Zakros Palace Apartments* (☎28430 29550, ⓦwww.palaikastro.com/katozakrospalace/indexeng.htm; ❸) is an attractive new option on the hill overlooking the bay offering rooms, studios and apartments, all air conditioned with terraces. Otherwise ask at the *Taverna Akrogiali* (☎28430 26893, ⓦwww.katozakros.sitiarealestate.com; ❶–❸) on the seafront, which acts as an agent for many other room options.

## Xérokambos and the southeast

Few tourists venture **south of Zákros**, and indeed there's little in the way of habitation in the whole of the southeastern corner of the island, nor any public transport whatsoever. Even the boulder-strewn dirt roads seem to be left in this condition to discourage casual drivers – a bonus for the walker. With your own transport, however, a little effort is rewarded with scores of excellent beaches – mostly deserted. There's an inland route by which you can circle back north to Sitía, via a newly sealed road after Xérokambos.

### Xérokambos and around

Leave Áno Zákros on the new road towards Káto Zákros and you'll shortly reach a turn-off to the right, with a hand-painted sign for "Ambelos and Liviko View", next to another **Minoan villa** bisected by the road. Recently asphalted, the road descends through olive groves and giant greenhouses to run along a deep ravine. After 10km, and just when you're convinced you're lost, a brilliant turquoise sea and white sandy beaches divided by rocky outcrops appear below.

Tucked in the lee of the foothills of the Sitían Mountains which rise away behind, the tiny hamlet of **Xérokambos** is as tranquil a hideaway as you could wish for. The settlement consists of one street with two tavernas, a couple of minimarkets selling basic food, and a few olive groves strung out along its length. Both **tavernas** will provide information and keys for **rooms** and some nice apartments (if available, which they may not be in Aug). Try phoning ahead to secure space at the excellent ⚓ *Liviko View* (☎28430 27001, ⓔlivikoview@infogreek.gr; ❷), run by a couple of Greek-Australians. Rooms come with air conditioning and balcony sea view, and there are some more expensive apartments (❸) sleeping up to four. The cooking here – with organic ingredients grown on the family farm – is recommended, and at weekends they even put on the occasional *lýra* concert. *Asteras* (☎28430 26787; ❸), with air-conditioned studio rooms set back from the sea, is another possibility. Alternatives for eating and drinking include *Taverna Kostas* (slightly before *Liviko View*) for grilled meat dishes, and the seafront *Akrogiali* for fish. Camping on the main beach is not allowed although you should be able to find secluded places away from here, but drinking water may be a problem.

The main beach – a short walk away along the beach road and one of the best on the island – is a couple of kilometres of pristine shimmering sand that hardly sees a towel or sunbed all year, and if that isn't escapist enough, to the north and especially the south are wonderful isolated coves where you might never see another soul. The crystal-clear waters here are great for snorkelling too – the minimarkets sell the basic equipment. Away from the sea there's little to do, but you could stretch your legs with a walk to the tiny chapel on a low hill to the south of the beach. Surrounding this are the ruins of an extensive Minoan settlement not yet fully explored or documented. For a more ambitious walk you could follow a track which heads south behind the beach for 4km to the deserted village of Ayía Iríni, with plenty of opportunities for a dip along the way. Continuing inland from here along the same track would enable you to climb to the peak of Agridomouri (627m), descending to Kaló Horió on the other side (6km from Ayía Iríni). From Kaló Horió, you could hitch the 11km to Xérokambos via the new road.

Xérokambos has nothing at all in the way of after-dark diversions – not even a bar – but the pitch-black nights here are magical with the opportunity for beach-walking, a midnight swim or simply sipping raki beneath a dome of stars, trying to spot the various constellations.

# Ierápetra and the southeast coast

The main road from Sitía to the south coast is a cross-country, roller-coaster ride between the east and west ranges of the **Sitía mountains**. One of the first places it hits on the south coast is the sprawling resort of **Makryialós** soon followed by the bustling town and resort of **Ierápetra**. More tranquil hideaways lie further west at the charming pint-sized resorts of **Mýrtos** and **Keratókambos** and the slightly less inviting **Árvi** and **Tsoútsouras**.

## Makryialós

Although originally composed of two distinct villages, the larger **MAKRY-IALÓS** (Ⓦwww.makrigialos.gr) has gobbled up its neighbour Análipsi to form a single and unfocused resort, whose only real plus point is a long strand with fine sand which shelves so gently you feel you could walk the two hundred nautical miles to Africa. Unfortunately, since the early 1990s it has been heavily developed, so while still a very pleasant place to stop for a swim or a bite, it's not somewhere that's overflowing with cheap **rooms**. The first budget option is *María Tsanakalioti* (Ⓣ28430 51557, Ⓔdtsanakalioti@hotmail.com; ❷) on the seaward side as you enter the resort from the east; the friendly proprietor offers pleasant studio rooms – some with sea view and terrace – with kitchenette, air conditioning and TV. Nearby and up a track inland signed "María Apartments" lies *Stefanos Rooms* (Ⓣ28430 52062; ❷) offering decent en-suite rooms with fans. A little before these two and signed up a side road (that soon degenerates into a track) 1km inland is the more upmarket ⚑ *White River Cottages* (Ⓣ28430 51694, Ⓔwriver@otenet .gr; ❹), where an abandoned hamlet of traditional stone dwellings (originally Áspro Pótamos or "White River") has been restored as a warren of charming air-conditioned studios and apartments with a focal pool. At the western end of town beyond a steep hill (topped with a sign on the left for a Roman villa), *Taverna-Rooms Oasis* (Ⓣ28430 51918; ❸) fronts the sea at the end of a short track. Offering sea-view en-suite rooms with air conditioning and fridge, downstairs there's an outstanding ⚑ **taverna** which has based its reputation on using only fresh (never frozen) fish, meat and vegetables, and they claim with some justification that their moussaka is the best on the island. Other places to eat include *Faros* and *To Limani*, with great positions overlooking the harbour.

From here to Ierápetra there's little reason to stop; the few beaches are rocky and the coastal plain submerged under ranks of polythene-covered greenhouses. Beside the road leading into Ierápetra are long but exposed stretches of sand, including the appropriately named "Long Beach", where you'll find a

**campsite**, *Camping Koutsounari* (☎ 28420 61213), which offers plenty of shade and has a taverna and minimarket.

## Ierápetra

**IERÁPETRA** itself is a bustling modern supply centre for the region's farmers. It also attracts a fair number of package tourists and the odd backpacker looking for work in the prosperous surrounding agricultural zone, especially out of season. The tavernas along the tree-lined seafront are scenic enough and the EU blue-flagged beach stretches a couple of miles east. But as a town, most people find it pretty uninspiring, despite an ongoing modernization programme, which has cleaned up the centre and revamped the seafront. Although there has been a port here since Roman times, only the **Venetian fort** guarding the harbour and a crumbling Turkish minaret remain as reminders of better days. What little else has been salvaged is in the one-room **archeological museum** (Tues–Sun 8.30am–3pm; €2) near the post office.

One way to escape the urban hubbub for a few hours is to take a boat to the **island of Gaidhouronísi** (aka Chrissi or Donkey Island) some 10km out to sea. It's a real uninhabited desert island 4km long with a cedar forest, fabulous "**Shell Beach**" covered with millions of multicoloured mollusc shells, some good beaches and a couple of tavernas. **Boats** (daily 10.30am & 12.30pm out, 4pm & 7pm return; €20, under-12s €10) leave from the seafront harbour, and you can buy tickets on the boat or in advance from Iris Travel (☎ 28420 25423) at the north end of the seafront. The voyage to the island takes fifty minutes and the boats have an on-board bar.

### Practicalities

In the absence of a tourist office the town hall on the main square, Platía Kanoupáki, or the library next door, should be able to provide a copy of the detailed **town map** (but not much else) which will help you find your way around. Another good source of information is the Ierápetra Express travel agency, 100m north of the town hall on Platía Eleftherías. If you want to stay, head up Kazantzákis from the chaotic bus station, and you'll find a friendly welcome and good-value, apartment-style **rooms** with kitchenette at *Rooms Popy* at no. 27 (☎ 28420 24289; ❶), or nearby in the more luxurious ⚹ *Cretan Villa*, Lakérdha 16 (☎ 28420 28522, ⓦ www.cretan-villa.com; ❸) where sparkling air-conditioned rooms with TV and fridge overlook the flower-bedecked patio of a beautiful 180-year-old house. More central and economical is the *Hotel Ersi*, Platía Eleftherías 20 (☎ 28420 23208; ❷), which will also rent you a seafront apartment nearby for not much more than the cost of a room. The cheapest seafront rooms option is *Katerina* (☎ 28420 28345; ❶–❸) at the eastern end of the strand, offering air-conditioned rooms with TV, fridge and sea view, which also has some bargain rooms sharing a bath.

You'll find places to **eat** and **drink** all along the waterfront, the better of them, such as *Taverna Napoleon*, *Gorgona* and *Babi's*, being towards the Venetian fort. **Nightlife** centres on a clutch of **clubs**, **bars** and fast-food places along central Kyrba, behind the seafront promenade. The town's most central **internet café** is *Internet Café* (daily 9am–10pm) inside the *Cosmos Hotel*, Koundoúrou 16, slightly north of Platía Eleftherías.

## West from Ierápetra

Heading **west** from Ierápetra, the first stretch of coast is grey and dusty, the road jammed with trucks and lined with drab ribbon development and plastic greenhouses. There are a number of small resorts along the beach, though little in the way of public transport. If travelling under your own steam, there is a scenic detour worth taking at Gra Lygiá: the road on the right for Anatolí climbs to Máles, a village clinging to the lower slopes of the **Dhíkti range**. It's a good starting point for **walking** through some stunning mountain terrain (the E4 Pan-European footpath which crosses the island from east to west passes just 3km north of here). Otherwise, the dirt road back down towards the coast (signposted Míthi) has spectacular views over the Libyan Sea, and eventually follows the Mýrtos river valley down to Mýrtos itself.

## Mýrtos and Árvi

**MÝRTOS**, 18km west of Ierápetra, is the first resort that might actually tempt you to stop, and it's certainly the most accessible, just off the main road with numerous daily **buses** from Ierápetra and a couple direct to Iráklion. Although developed to a degree, it nonetheless remains a tranquil and charming white-walled village kept clean as a whistle by its house-proud inhabitants. There are plenty of **rooms** possibilities, amongst which you could try the central, friendly and good-value ↟ *Hotel Mirtos* (☎28420 51227, ⓦwww.mirtoshotel .com; ❷) with comfortable en-suite rooms above an excellent taverna. Nearby, *Rooms Angelos* (☎28420 51091; ❷) and *Nikos House* (☎28420 51116, ⓦwww .nikoshouse.cz in Czech only; ❷) are slightly cheaper options, or try the even less expensive *Rooms Despina* (☎28420 51524; ❶) at the back of the village near the bus stop. A useful travel agent, Prima Tours (☎28420 51035, ⓦwww .sunbudget.net) near the beach to the eastern end of the village, is a good source of **information**, and also **changes money**, rents **cars**, sells boat and plane tickets and can arrange taxis to Iráklion and Haniá airports. Just off the road from Ierápetra a couple of kilometres east of the village (and signed) are a couple of excavated hilltop **Minoan villas** you might want to explore: Néa Mýrtos (aka Fournoú Korifí) and Mýrtos Pýrgos. Some of the finds from these sites – in addition to a folklore section with tools, kitchen and farming implements once used by the villagers – are displayed in a superb village **museum** (April–Oct Mon–Fri 9am–1pm; €1.50), located to the side of the church. A highly popular addition to the museum is a wonderfully detailed **scale model** of the Fournoú Korifi site as it would have looked in Minoan days by a resident English potter, John Atkinson.

After Mýrtos the main road turns inland towards Áno Viánnos, then continues across the island towards Iráklion; several places on the coast are reached by a series of recently asphalted roads replacing the former rough tracks. **ÁRVI** is a resort of similar size to Mýrtos, although it lacks the latter's charm. The beach, flanked by a new harbour development, hardly justifies it, but it's an interesting little excursion (with at least one bus a day) if only to see the bananas and pineapples grown here and to experience the microclimate – noticeably warmer than neighbouring zones, especially in spring or autumn – that encourages them. For **rooms** you could try the *Hotel Ariadne* (☎28950 71300; ❸), the fanciest place in town with balcony sea-view rooms or, beyond the river at the east end of the beach, the cheaper *Taverna Kyma* (☎28950 71344; ❷).

## Beyond Árvi

**KERATÓKAMBOS**, reached on a side road 4km from Áno Viánnos, has a rather stony beach and, although popular with Cretan day-trippers, is a great place to escape the tourist grind. It has a range of **rooms**, though they're not easy to come by in August. Try the *Morning Star* taverna (☎28950 51209; ❷) which has air-conditioned rooms with and without bath, or the comparable *Taverna Kriti* (☎28950 51231; ❸) next door; the **food** at both places is tasty, too.

   **TSOÚTSOUROS** (🅦www.tsoutsouros.com), 10km west as the crow flies and now linked by an eleven-kilometre-long asphalted road to the major highway further north, is similar to its neighbour with a line of tavernas, hotels and rooms places arching behind a seafront and yacht harbour, to the east and west of which are a couple of decent if pebbly, grey-sand **beaches**. **Accommodation** may be available here when the other resorts are full: *Rooms Mihalis* (☎28910 92250; ❶) or the good-value *San Georgio Hotel* (May–Sept ☎28910 92322; ❷) further east are both worth trying. There are no facilities for changing money at either place, although both have a couple of **supermarkets**, handy for gathering picnic ingredients.

   If you hope to continue across the **south** of the island, be warned that there are no buses, despite completion of the road towards Míres after years of work. It's an enjoyable rural drive, but progress can be slow.

# Réthymnon and around

The relatively low, narrow section of Crete which separates the Psilorítis range from the White Mountains in the west seems at first a nondescript, even dull, part of the island. Certainly in scenic terms it has few of the excitements that the west can offer; there are no major archeological sites and many of the villages seem modern and ugly. On the other hand, **Réthymnon** itself is an attractive and lively city, with some excellent beaches nearby. And on the south coast, in particular around **Plakiás**, there are beaches as fine as any Crete can offer and, as you drive towards them, the scenery and villages improve.

## Réthymnon

Since the early 1980s, **Réthymnon** has seen a greater influx of tourists than perhaps anywhere else on Crete, with the development of a whole series of large hotels extending almost 10km along the beach to the east. For once, though, the middle of town has been spared, so that at its heart Réthymnon remains one of the most beautiful of Crete's major cities (only Haniá is a serious rival), with an enduringly provincial air. A wide sandy beach and palm-lined promenade border a labyrinthine tangle of Venetian and Turkish houses lining streets where ancient minarets lend an exotic air to the skyline. Dominating everything from the west is the superbly preserved outline of the **fortress** built by the Venetians after a series of pirate raids had devastated the town.

### Arrival and information

The **bus station** in Réthymnon is by the sea to the west of the town centre just off Periferiakós, the road which skirts the waterfront around the fortress. If you

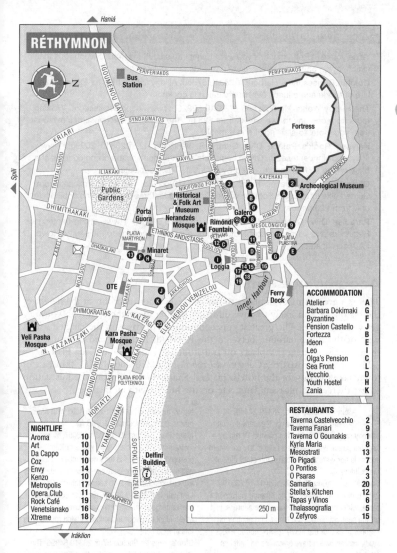

RÉTHYMNON

Haniá

Bus Station

PERIFERIAKOS

PERIFERIAKOS

SYNDAGMATOS

Fortress

PERIFERIAKOS

Spili

IGOUMENOU GAVRIL

KRIARI

TRANTALIDHOU

ILIAKAKI

DHIMITRAKAKI

DIMAKOPOULOU

MAVILI

NIKIFOROU FOKA

KOROMILADOU

KATEHAKI

Public Gardens

Porta Guora

Historical & Folk Art Museum

Nerandzés Mosque

Galero

Rimóndi Fountain

❶

❸
❹
❺

ARKADHIOU

❻
❼ @

❷ Archeological Museum

❺

HIMARAS

MESOLONGIOU

PETIHAKI

❾

ZABELIOU

PLATIA MARTYRON

ETHNIKIS ANDISTASIS

SOULIOU

❶❶
❶❷ C
❶❿ PLATIA PLASTIRA

E

DHASKALAKI

Minaret F H

PALEOLOGOU

SALAMINOS

DAMVERGI

D

Loggia

❶❸

❶❹ ❶❺ ❶❻

❶❼
❶❽
❶❾

E

MIAATSOU

OTE

VERAKARI K

J

K

ARKADHIOU

L

Ferry Dock

Inner Harbour

DHIMOKRATIAS

V. KALERGI

ELEFTHERIOU VENIZELOU

Veli Pasha Mosque

KOUNDOURIOTOU

YERAKARI K

Kara Pasha Mosque

ARKADHIOU

❷⓿

HORTATZI

PLATIA IROON POLYTEKNIOU

K. YIAMBOUDHAKI

SOFOKLI VENIZELOU

Delfini Building
ⓘ

PAPANDHREOU

0       250 m

Iráklion

N

Z

### ACCOMMODATION

| | |
|---|---|
| Atelier | A |
| Barbara Dokimaki | G |
| Byzantine | F |
| Pension Castello | J |
| Fortezza | B |
| Ideon | E |
| Leo | I |
| Olga's Pension | C |
| Sea Front | L |
| Vecchio | D |
| Youth Hostel | H |
| Zania | K |

### RESTAURANTS

| | |
|---|---|
| Taverna Castelvecchio | 2 |
| Taverna Fanari | 9 |
| Taverna O Gounakis | 1 |
| Kyria Maria | 8 |
| Mesostrati | 13 |
| To Pigadi | 7 |
| O Pontios | 4 |
| O Psaras | 3 |
| Samaria | 20 |
| Stella's Kitchen | 12 |
| Tapas y Vinos | 6 |
| Thalassografia | 5 |
| O Zefyros | 15 |

### NIGHTLIFE

| | |
|---|---|
| Aroma | 10 |
| Art | 10 |
| Da Cappo | 10 |
| Coz | 10 |
| Envy | 14 |
| Kenzo | 10 |
| Metropolis | 17 |
| Opera Club | 11 |
| Rock Café | 19 |
| Venetsianako | 16 |
| Xtreme | 18 |

arrive by **ferry**, you'll be more conveniently placed, over at the western edge of the harbour. The **tourist office** (Mon–Fri 8am–2.30pm, Sat 10am–4pm; ☎28310 29148, Ⓦwww.rethymnon.com) is located in the Delfini Building at the eastern end of the town beach and provides maps, timetables and accommodation lists. To access the **internet** head for the *Galero Internet Cafe* (daily 9am–midnight), beside the Rimóndi Fountain in the old town. At the time of writing Réthymnon's daily ferry to Athens had been suspended; it is hoped that a new service will be operating by 2009. For the latest information on this plus tickets and timetables visit or contact the very helpful Ellotia Tours, Arkhadíou 155, behind the seafront (☎28310 51981, Ⓦwww.rethymnoatcrete.com) which is also a reliable source of travel information on the island generally.

## Action in Réthymnon

While you're in Réthymnon, if you want to get into something more adventurous than simply frying on the beach here are a few ideas to get you going:

**Dolphin Cruises** Inner Harbour ☎28310 57666. All day fishing trips for €25 including hire of tackle and a lunch (where the catch is cooked).

**The Happy Walker** Tombázi 56 ☎28310 52920, ⓦwww.happywalker.com. Walking tours from one day to two weeks from €28 (for the day-hike which includes minibus from your hotel to start point and a meal).

**Kalypso Rock's Palace Dive Centre** S. Venizélou 42 ☎28310 20990, ⓦwww .kalypsodivingcenter.com. Offers beginners and advanced scuba diving courses at a base on the south coast (reached by minibus). PADI certificated.

**Olympic Bike** Adelianos Kampos 32 ☎28310 72383, ⓦwww.olympicbike.com. Guided bike tours using Scott machines from €139 for three one-day trips or bike hire only from €20 per day.

**Paradise Dive Centre** Petres Geraniou ☎28310 26317, ⓦwww.diving-center.gr. Beginners and advanced scuba diving based near Yeoryoúpoli to the west of town. PADI certificated.

# Accommodation

There's a great number of places to stay in Réthymnon, and only at the height of the season are you likely to have difficulty finding somewhere, though you may get weary looking. The greatest concentration of **rooms** is in the tangled streets west of the inner harbour, between the Rimóndi Fountain and the museums; there are also quite a few places on and around Arkadhíou and Platía Plastíra.

The nearest **campsite**, *Camping Elizabeth* (☎28310 28694), lies 4km east of town; take the bus for the hotels (marked *Scaleta/El Greco*) from the bus station to get there. It's a pleasant, large site on the beach, with all facilities.

**Atelier** Himáras 32 ☎28310 24440, ⓔatelier@ret.forthnet.gr. Pleasant en-suite balcony rooms with fridge and plasma TV run by a talented potter, who has her studio in the basement and sells her wares in a shop on the other side of the building. ➋

**Barbara Dokimaki** Platía Plastíra 14 ☎28310 24581, ⓔalicedokk@yahoo.com. Strange warren of a place, with one entrance at the above address, just off the seafront behind the *Ideon*, and another on Dambérgi; ask for the newly refurbished top-floor studio rooms, which have balconies and kitchenettes. ➋

**Byzantine** Vospórou 26, near the Porta Guora ☎28310 55609, ⓦwww.byzantineret.gr. Pleasant en-suite rooms with fans in a renovated Byzantine palace with elegant interior courtyard. ➌

**Pension Castello** Karaoli 10 ☎28310 23570, ⓔcastelo2@otenet.gr. A very pleasant small *pension* in a 300-year-old Venetian-Turkish mansion; a/c en-suite rooms with fridge and a delightful patio garden. ➌

**Fortezza** Melissinoú 16, near the fortress ☎28310 55551, ⓦwww.fortezza.gr. Stylish,

top-of-the-range but great-value hotel with a/c rooms, pool and restaurant. B&B ➍

**Ideon** Platía Plastíra 10 ☎28310 28667, ⓦwww .hotelideon.gr. High-class hotel with a brilliant position just north of the ferry dock; little chance of getting one of their balcony sea-view, en-suite rooms without prebooking in high season, though. B&B ➎

**Leo** Vafé 2 ☎28310 26197, ⓦwww.leohotel.gr. Has undergone an extensive makeover and now offers eight luxurious individually styled rooms with lots of mod cons. ➎

**Olga's Pension** Soulíou 57 ☎28310 54896. The star attraction at this very friendly *pension* on one of Réthymnon's most touristy streets is the resplendent flower-filled roof garden. Offers a variety of rooms (some en suite) as well as studios with sea view. ➊

**Sea Front** Arkadhíou 159 ☎28310 51981, ⓦwww.rethymnoatcrete.com. En-suite rooms with sea views and balconies in an attractively refurbished mansion with ceiling fans. The welcoming owners also have a number of good-value apartments (➌) nearby. Rough Guide readers can claim a ten percent discount. ➋

Vecchio Daliani 4, near the Rimondi Fountain. ☏ 28310 54985, ⓦ www.vecchio.gr. Elegant Venetian mansion tastefully transformed into an enchanting small hotel with a/c rooms (some with balcony) set around a pool. B&B. ❸

Youth Hostel Tombázi 41 ☏ 28310 22848, ⓦ www.yhrethymno.com. The cheapest beds (€9) in town. Large, clean, very friendly and popular, it has food, showers, clothes-washing facilities, internet access and a multilingual library. ❶

Zania Pávlou Vlástou 3 ☏ 28310 28169. *Pension* right on the corner of Arkadhíou in a well-adapted and atmospheric Venetian mansion, but with only a few airy, high-ceilinged rooms with a/c and fridge; bathrooms are shared. ❷

## The Town

With a **beach** right in the heart of town, it's tempting not to stir at all from the sands, but Réthymnon repays at least some gentle exploration. For a start, you could try checking out the further reaches of the beach itself. The waters protected by the breakwaters in front of town have their disadvantages – notably crowds and dubious hygiene – but less sheltered sands stretch for miles to the east, crowded at first but progressively less so if you're prepared to walk a bit.

Away from the beach, you don't have far to go for the most atmospheric part of town, immediately behind the **inner harbour**. Almost anywhere here, you'll find unexpected old buildings, wall fountains, overhanging wooden balconies, heavy, carved doors and rickety shops, many still with local craftsmen sitting out front, gossiping as they ply their trades. Many of these workshops house *lýra* makers, the "national" instrument of Crete, and they will be only too pleased to show you their beautiful creations should you show an interest. Look out also for the **Venetian loggia** which houses a shop selling high-quality and expensive reproductions of Classical art; the **Rimóndi Fountain**, another of the more elegant Venetian survivals; and the **Nerandzés mosque**, the best preserved in Réthymnon but currently serving as a music school and closed to the public. When (seemingly endless) repairs are completed it should again be possible to climb the spiral staircase to the top of the **minaret** for a stunning

▲ Réthymnon harbour

view over the town. Simply by walking past these three, you'll have seen many of the liveliest parts of Réthymnon. Ethnikís Andístasis, the street leading straight up from the fountain, is the town's **market** area.

The old city ends at the Porta Guora at the top of Ethnikís Andístasis, the only surviving remnant of the city walls. Almost opposite are the quiet and shady **public gardens**. These are a soothing place to stroll, and in the latter half of July the **Réthymnon Wine Festival** is staged here. Though touristy, it's a thoroughly enjoyable event, with spectacular local dancing as the evening progresses and the barrels empty. The entrance fee includes all the wine you can drink, though you'll need to bring your own cup or buy one of the souvenir glasses and carafes on sale outside the gardens.

### The museums and fortress

A little further up the street from the Nerandzés mosque at M. Vernárdhou 28, a beautifully restored seventeenth-century Venetian mansion is the home of the small but tremendously enjoyable **Historical and Folk Art Museum** (Mon–Sat 9am–2pm; €3). Gathered within four, cool, airy rooms are musical instruments, old photos, basketry, farm implements, an explanation of traditional ceramic and breadmaking techniques, smiths' tools, traditional costumes and jewellery, lace, weaving and embroidery (look out for a traditional-style tapestry made in 1941 depicting German parachutists landing at Máleme), pottery, knives and old wooden chests. It makes for a fascinating insight into a fast-disappearing lifestyle, which survived virtually unchanged from Venetian times to the 1960s.

Heading in the other direction from the fountain you'll come to the **archeological museum** (Tues–Sun 9.30am–2pm; €3), which occupies a building almost directly opposite the entrance to the fortress. This was built by the Turks as an extra defence, and later served as a prison; it's now entirely modern inside: cool, spacious and airy. Unfortunately, the collection is not particularly exciting, and really only worth seeing if you're going to miss the bigger museums elsewhere on the island.

The massive **Venetian fortress** (daily 8am–8pm; closes 6pm Nov–Mar; €3.10) is a must, however. Said to be the largest Venetian castle ever built, this was a response, in the last quarter of the sixteenth century, to a series of **pirate raids** (by Barbarossa among others) that had devastated the town. Inside is now a vast open space dotted with the remains of all sorts of barracks, arsenals, officers' houses, earthworks and deep shafts, and at the centre a large domed **mosque** complete with surviving *mihrab* (a niche indicating the direction of Mecca). The fortress was designed to be large enough for the entire population to take shelter within the walls. Although much is ruined, it remains thoroughly atmospheric, and you can look out from the walls over the town and harbour, or in the other direction along the coast to the west. It's also worth walking around the outside of the fortress, preferably at sunset, to get an impression of its fearsome defences, plus great views along the coast; there's a pleasant resting point around the far side at the *Sunset* taverna.

## Eating

The most touristy **restaurants** are arrayed immediately behind the town beach – the vast majority of them overpriced and of dubious quality. Around the inner **harbour** there's a second, rather more expensive, group of tavernas, specializing in fish, though occasionally the intimate atmosphere in these places is spoilt by the odours from the harbour itself. The most inviting and best-value places to eat tend to be scattered in less obvious parts of the old town.

Taverna Castelvecchio Himáras 29. This long-established family taverna next to the fortress has a pleasant terrace with view over the town and offers some vegetarian choices.

Taverna Fanari Makedhonías 5, slightly west of Platía Plastíra. A good-value little seafront taverna serving up tasty lamb and chicken dishes.

Taverna O Gounakis Koronaiou Panou. Hearty, no-frills traditional cooking by a family who leave the stove to perform *lýra* every night, and when things get really lively the dancing starts.

Kyria Maria Moskhovítou 20, tucked down an alley behind the Rimóndi Fountain. Pleasant, unassuming little taverna for good-value fish and meat dishes; after the meal, everyone gets a couple of Maria's delicious *tyropitákia* with honey on the house.

Mesostrati Yerakári 1. Tucked behind the church on Platía Martíron, this is a pleasant little neighbourhood ouzerí/taverna serving well-prepared Cretan country dishes on a small terrace. It's frequented by some of Réthymnon's (and Crete's) top *lýra* and lauto players who often hold impromptu jam sessions.

To Pigadi Xanthoúdhidhou 31, slightly west of the Rimóndi Fountain. In a street containing a cluster of upmarket restaurants with overinflated rates, this place stands out for its excellent, reasonably priced food and efficient service. The attractive terrace's main feature – an ancient well (*pigádi*) – has also inspired its name.

O Pontios Melissinoú 34. A good lunchtime stop close to the archeological museum, this is a simple place with surprisingly good food, outdoor tables and an enthusiastic female proprietor.

O Psaras Corner of Nikiforou Foka and Kironaiou. An economical and unpretentious fish taverna (although less fish and more meat is served in summer) with tables on a terrace beside a church.

Samaria Venizélou, on the seafront facing the town beach. One of the few seafront tavernas that maintains some integrity (and reasonable prices) and is patronized by locals.

Stella's Kitchen Souliou 55. Great-value little diner serving healthy, home-baked food and six daily specials (at least two of which are vegetarian); there's a leafy terrace roof garden and they also do breakfasts. Closes 9pm.

Tapas y Vinos Melissinou 14. An expatriate *malagueña* (from Málaga) has given Réthymnon its first genuine Spanish tapas bar complete with a great tapas range, excellent jamón serrano (cured ham) and superb Spanish wines.

Thalassografia Kefalogianidon 33 ☏ 28310 52569. Best approached from the car park fronting the fortress entrance (although there are steps up from the road below), this superb "new style" taverna perched on a cliff overlooking the sea is currently one of the in places for Rethimni-otes to dine out (making booking advisable). Tables have sensational views, service is slick and recommended dishes include *arní sti stamna* (jugged lamb) and *loukánika krasata* (sausages in wine).

O Zefyros At the inner harbour. One of the less outrageously pricey fish places here and maintains reasonable standards.

## Nightlife

**Nightlife** is concentrated in the same general areas as the tavernas. At the west end of Venizélou, in the streets behind the inner harbour, a small cluster of noisy music bars – *Rock Cafe*, *Envy*, *Xtreme* and *Metropolis* – keep the action going until the small hours. Not far away on Salaminos, *Opera Club* is one of the town's bigger dance clubs with an eclectic mix of Greek and western rock and lots of strobe pyrotechnics. A relatively new bar scene popular with the local student community has taken root around Platía Plastíra, above the inner harbour, where music bars include *Venetsianako*, *Art*, *Da Cappo*, *Coz*, *Kenzo* and *Aroma*, all with expansive terraces.

# Around Réthymnon

While some of Crete's most drastic resort development spreads ever eastwards out of Réthymnon, to the west a sandy coastline, not yet greatly exploited, runs all the way to the borders of Haniá province. But of all the short trips that can be made, the best-known and still the most worthwhile is to the **monastery of Arkádhi**.

## Southeast to Arkádhi

The **monastery of Arkádhi** (daily 9am–8pm; €2), some 25km southeast of the city and immaculately situated in the foothills of the Psilorítis range, is also something of a national Cretan shrine. During the 1866 rebellion against the Turks, the monastery became a rebel strongpoint in which, as the Turks gained the upper hand, hundreds of Cretan independence fighters and their families took refuge. Surrounded and on the point of defeat, the defenders ignited a powder magazine just as the Turks entered. Hundreds (some sources claim thousands) were killed, Cretan and Turk alike, and the tragedy did much to promote international sympathy for the cause of Cretan independence. Nowadays, you can peer into the roofless vault where the explosion occurred and wander about the rest of the well-restored grounds. Outside the entrance a modern monument displays the skulls of many of the victims. The sixteenth-century **church** survived, and is one of the finest Venetian structures left on Crete; other buildings house a small **museum** devoted to the exploits of the defenders of the (Orthodox) faith. The monastery is easy to visit by public bus or on a tour.

## West along the coast

Leaving Réthymnon to the west, the main road climbs for a while above a rocky coastline before descending (after some 5km) to the sea, where it runs alongside sandy **beaches** for perhaps another 7km. An occasional hotel offers accommodation, but on the whole there's nothing but a line of straggly bushes between the road and the windswept sands. If you have your own vehicle, there are plenty of places to stop for a swim, with rarely anyone else around – but beware of some very strong currents.

One worthwhile detour inland is to **ARYIROÚPOLIS**, a picturesque village perched above the Mousselás river valley and the seat of ancient Lappa, a Greek and Roman town of some repute. The village is famous for its **springs**, which gush dramatically from the hillside and provide most of Réthymnon's water supply. Among a number of **places to stay** near the springs in the lower village, *Rooms Argiroupolis* (☎28310 81148, ✉mrom@mia.gr; B&B; ❷) has en-suite rooms in a garden setting. In the livelier upper village there's *Rooms Zografakis* (☎28310 81269, ⓦwww.ezografakis.gr; B&B; ❷), or – with great views from its air-conditioned rooms and taverna terrace – the friendly and excellent-value ✻ *Agnantema* (☎28310 81172; ❷). Information on a number of attractive and good value apartments around the village (available for stays of two nights or more) is available from Lappa Avocado (see below). For **places to eat**, you're spoilt for choice, with five tavernas at the springs (try *Vieux Moulin* with an attractive terrace) and three bars (serving *mezédhes*) in the upper village, together with tavernas at *Zografakis* and *Agnantema*, the latter enjoying a spectacular terrace view down the river valley. The best taverna by far in these parts lies 4km north of the village on the road to Episkopí: ✻ *O Kipos Tis Arkoúdainas* (☎28310 61607) serves up creative lamb and pork dishes and has a delightful tree-shaded garden. A shop under the arch in the main square, named Lappa Avocado (☎28310 81070) and selling local products of the region including olive oil and avocado-based skin products, can provide a free **map** detailing a surprising number of churches, caves and ancient remains to see in and around the village, including an outstanding third-century **Roman mosaic**. An interesting **folklore museum** (daily 10am–7pm; free) – signed from the main square – is worth a look for its collection of tapestries, farm implements, photos and ephemera collected by the Zografakis family who have lived here for

# Beach life

Greece, with some 16,000km of coastline – half on its myriad islands – is enviably well endowed with beaches, lapped by some of the Mediterranean's cleanest water. Indeed, despite the country's monumental heritage, the appeal of basking on a sun-soaked strand draws more visitors than anything else. Ranging from discreet pebble coves to grand sweeps of sand, the beaches of the Aegean and Ionian seas offer everything from windsurfing and non-stop bars to calm waters ideal for family holidays. Although the better-known spots are packed during summer, a little legwork (or a water-taxi) can bring you to a secluded patch of shore.

Agnóndas beach, Skópelos ▲

Kiteboarding off Prassoníssi, Rhodes ▼

# Family fun

On many islands, family-orientated resorts fill with Greeks in July and August, plus foreign tourists throughout the warm months. The sand at these locations tends to shelve gently, making ideal paddling conditions for children; as in the rest of the Mediterranean, the lack of a tide also makes for calm waters. Self-contained communities, they offer everything from sportswear shops and music bars to organized boat trips and cultural excursions.

# Watersports

With warm water temperatures throughout the season and reliable summer winds, many island beaches pitch a broad selection of watersports including inflatable-banana rides, parasailing, waterskiing and sea-kayaking. Renowned windsurfing havens include Prasoníssi on Rhodes, southern Kárpathos, Kokkári on Sámos, Kamári on Kós and Lefkádha's Vassilikí. Scuba diving is also increasingly popular, following a 2006 relaxation in laws restricting the sport. Small motorboats and dinghies can be rented on spec almost everywhere, though yachting requires more planning and expertise.

# Nude beaches

Although nude bathing is illegal nearly everywhere, at many shorelines the practice has become common, tolerated by both local businesses and the authorities. Naturists gather in fairly isolated locations such as Corfu's Myrtiótissa beach and gay Super Paradise on Mýkonos, but also at surprisingly accessible bays like Tzamadhoú on Sámos or Skópelos's Velanió beach.

# Nature

Thanks to the dry climate, island beaches are often stark, although pines and tamarisk trees offer some shade. Nature-lovers, especially hikers, will be rewarded after trail-walks with unspoilt coves, perfect for a refreshing dip; bird-watchers will find that coastal wetlands such as Corfu's Korissíon lagoon and Skála Kallonís on Lésvos harbour an astonishing variety of species; and conservationists can visit the Ionian-island nesting grounds for endangered loggerhead turtles.

Volcanic sand or pebble beaches, often backed by dark lava-scapes or pale pumice-cliffs, indicate local volcanic activity – Mávra Vólia on Híos and Hokhláki on Níssyros consist of black-to-purplish-red igneous pebbles in various sizes, while volcanic-sand bays elsewhere on Níssyros, Tílos, Límnos and Lésvos tend to be anything from

▲ Diving near Paleokastritsa, Corfu

▼ Falásarna beach, Crete

## Relaxing beaches

▶▶ **Paleohóri, Mílos** Triple strand with a naturist zone, steam vents and rock overhangs for shade. See p.139.

▶▶ **Falásarna, Crete** Close to a tropical fantasy: successive crescents of fine yellow sand, gently shelving turquoise water, and an ancient city to explore. See p.299.

▶▶ **Livádhi Yeranoú, Pátmos** Swim out to Áyios Yeóryios islet, then lounge under the line of tamarisks or head for the excellent taverna. See p.401.

▶▶ **Megálo Seïtáni, Sámos** You have to walk or water-taxi to this huge, sandy beach in a nature reserve; monk seals are occasionally seen nearby. See p.427.

▶▶ **Yialós, Lefkádha** A stunning, deserted coarse-sand beach on the island's west coast. See p.564.

purply-red to light brown. The sole-scorching black-sand beaches on the flat eastern side of Santoríni are a legacy of that island's volcano, which erupted cataclysmically around 1640 BC. At some coves, especially on Ikaría, Lésvos and Mílos, **thermal springs or steam vents** still bubble and hiss away.

# Free for all

More popular beaches are carpeted with **sunbeds and umbrellas**, whose rental charge varies from €4 to a whopping €11 per pair per day. You are not obliged to use them; Greek law states that from the maximum storm tidemark down to the water is public land, and plenty of folk spread their towels in this zone. Similarly, there are **no strictly private** beaches in Greece; even mega-hotels are obliged to provide access to "their" beach along the side of the property.

The volcanic pebbles of Hokhláki, Níssyros ▲

Lounging on Skiáthos ▼

## Activities beaches

▶▶ **Paradise, Mýkonos** Home to one of Greece's most established scuba operators; the nearby reefs and wrecks have colourful marine life. See p.160.

▶▶ **Faliráki, Rhodes** The Dodecanese's parasailing capital; the sedate can watch from the excellent sands. See p.332.

▶▶ **Thermá Lefkádhos, Ikaría** Not really a beach, but a shoreline "corral" of boulders forming a giant hot-spring-fed pool to bob in. See p.431.

▶▶ **Skála Kallonís, Lésvos** The beach itself is sandy, the water ridiculously shallow; the big attraction is the bird-rich saltmarsh inland. See p.465.

▶▶ **Vromólimnos, Skiáthos** The Sporades' premier youth beach, with a lively bar and a multinational crowd doing surreal "water aerobics" at August parties. See p.501.

countless generations. There are numerous fine **walks** in the surrounding hills, on which the proprietor of Lappa Avocado, who speaks English, can advise. Although little over 20km from Réthymnon and easy to get to with your own transport, Aryiroúpolis is also served by **buses** from Réthymnon's bus station (Mon–Fri only), currently leaving at 11.30am and 2.30pm, and in the reverse direction (from the upper village) at 7am, 12.30pm and 3.30pm.

## Yeoryoúpoli and around

Back on the coastal route, **YEORYOÚPOLI**, just across the provincial border in Haniá, is the best choice if you are looking for a place to stop. Here the beach is cleaner, wider and further from the road, and though Yeoryoúpoli is very much a resort, packed with rooms to rent, small hotels, apartment buildings, tavernas and travel agencies, everything remains on a small scale. As long as you don't expect to find too many vestiges of traditional Crete, it's a very pleasant place to pass a few days. For **accommodation**, most of the beachfront places are exclusively for package tourists, so it's best to head along the roads down towards the beach from the central platía. Here, you'll find *Andy's Rooms* (T 28250 61394; ❸) and *Zorbas* (T 28250 61381, W www.zorbas-geo.com; ❸), more or less opposite each other, both with comfortable air-conditioned rooms and small apartments, most with balconies; *Zorbas* also has a good taverna and tiny courtyard swimming pool. *Hotel Nicolas* (T 28250 61375, W hotelnicolas .georgioupoli.net; ❸), on the road into town, has pleasant, recently refurbished rooms. In the other direction, on the far side of the bridge across the river, *Anna* (T 28250 61556, W www.annashouse.gr; ❷/❹) offers some of the best-value rooms in town – simple places in a garden setting – as well as a new complex of stylish studios and apartments (sleeping up to seven) around a large pool. *Taverna Paradise* (T 28250 61313; ❷), towards the river from the square, has more rooms, studios and apartments, as well as a good taverna set in lush gardens; *Taverna Babis*, down towards the beach, is also good for plain Greek **food**, as is *Sirtaki*, near the bridge. **Internet** access is available at Planet Internet, just off the main square. Near here too are all the other facilities you might need – banks, shops, car and bike hire and travel agencies. Ethon (T 28250 61432, W www.ethon.gr), on the corner of the square, can organise just about any tour you can imagine; more adventurous alternatives are Adventure Bikes (T 28250 61830, W www.adventurebikes.org), who organise easy bike tours all around the western end of the island with transport to get you up the steep bits, or Zoraïda's (T 28250 61745, W www.zoraidas-horseriding.com), for **horseriding**, including organised rides along the beach or up to Lake Kournás.

**Kournás**, Crete's only freshwater lake, is set deep in a bowl of hills just 4km inland from Yeoryioúpolo. Whether you undertake it on foot, on horseback, by bike or with the *trenaki* that chugs up from the beach daily, it's a worthwhile excursion. The best route is via the village of **MATHÉS** where *Taverna Mathes* offers great terrace views and good food and the *Villa Kapasa* (T 28250 61050, W www.villa-kapasas.com; ❷) has very comfortable en-suite rooms around a garden. From here a path leads to the lake's northern edge, and a path heading round the shore. Beside the lake there are several more tavernas with rooms to rent (bring mosquito repellent), while a few kilometres uphill in **KOURNÁS** village, the *Kali Kardia* taverna on the main street is a wonderful place to sample the local lamb and *loukánika* (sausages).

West of Yeoryoúpoli, the main road heads inland, away from a cluster of coastal villages beyond Vámos. It thus misses the quiet, rural Dhrápano peninsula, some spectacular views over the sapphire Bay of Soúdha and several quiet beaches.

Kefalás, Pláka and nearby Kókkino Horió, location for the film of *Zorba the Greek*, are all postcard-picturesque, with spectacular locations high above the east coast. On the exposed north coast there are good beaches at **Almyrídha** and **Kalýves**, and off the road between them. Both have been discovered by package operators; accommodation is mostly in apartments and rooms are scarce, although there are a few mid-range and more upmarket hotels. Almyrídha is the more pleasant, with a string of good fish tavernas (try *Dimitri's*) along the beach that make for an enjoyable lunch stop. If you want to stay here *Marilena's Pension* (☎28250 32202; ❷) is on the seafront to the east.

# South from Réthymnon

There are a couple of alternative routes south from Réthymnon, but the main one heads straight out from the centre of town, an initially featureless road due south across the middle of the island towards **Ayía Galíni**. About 23km out, a turning cuts off to the right for **Plakiás** and **Mýrthios**, following the course of the spectacular Kourtaliótiko ravine.

## Plakiás and the south coast

**PLAKIÁS** has undergone something of a boom in recent years and is no longer the pristine village all too many people arriving here expect. That said, it's still quite low-key, with a satisfactory beach and a string of good tavernas around the dock. There are hundreds of **rooms**, but at the height of summer you'll need to arrive early if you hope to find one; the last to fill are generally those furthest inland, heading towards the youth hostel. Good places to try include *Gio-ma Taverna* (☎28320 32003, ⊛www.gioma.gr; ❷), on the seafront by the harbour with sea-view rooms and studios, or the excellent balcony rooms at *Ippokambos* (☎28320 31525, ✉amoutsos@otenet.gr; ❷), slightly inland on the road to the enjoyably relaxed **youth hostel** (☎28320 32118, ⊛www.yhplakias.com; dorms ❶), which is 500m inland and signed from the seafront. The bougainvillea draped *Pension Afrodite* (☎28320 31266, ✉kasel@hol.gr; ❷) is a quiet spot with pleasant apartments, off the road to the hostel. More accommodation options can be found online at ⊛www.plakias-filoxenia.gr.

Once you've found a room there's not a lot else to discover here. Every facility you're likely to need is strung out along the waterfront or on the few short streets off it, including a **post office** (Mon–Fri 7.30am–2pm), **bike rental**, ATMs and **money exchange**, several **supermarkets** and even a **laundry**. Places to eat are plentiful too. If you want to do some diving the PADI-certificated Kalypso Rock's Palace Diving Centre (☎28310, 20990, ⊛www.kalypsodivingcenter .com) has a base close to the resort and offers advanced and learner courses.

The attractive **tavernas** on the waterfront in the centre are a little expensive; the pick of them – with inviting terraces – are *Sofia* near the bus stop and *Gio-ma*, overlooking the harbour at the western end of the seafront, for fish. You'll eat cheaper further inland: seek out *Taverna Medousa* – a splendid traditional taverna – at the east end of town, reached up the road inland past the post office and then right. On the way here you'll pass *Nikos Souvlaki*, which dishes up the least expensive meals in town – excellent *souvláki* or even fish and chips – often accompanied by live *bouzoúki* music in the evenings. Beyond the harbour at the west end of town, *Psarotaverna Tassomanolis* is one of a line of waterfront places enjoying spectacular sunsets; it specializes in fish caught by the proprietor from his own boat.

## Mýrthios

For a stay of more than a day or two, **MÝRTHIOS**, in the hills behind Plakiás, also deserves consideration. Originally put on the map for legions of younger travellers by a legendary youth hostel (now closed), these days it's distinctly pricey, but there are some great apartments and wonderful views, and you'll generally find locals still outnumbering the tourists. To **stay**, check out the classy *Anna Apartments* (℡697 33 24 775, Ⓦwww.annaview.com; ❸), while for **food** the long-established 🍴 *Taverna Plateia* on the square in the centre of the village has had a complete makeover but still serves up excellent traditional Cretan cooking and great wines, and has arguably the most spectacular terrace view of any taverna on the island. A car is an advantage here, although the Plakiás bus will usually loop through Mýrthios (be sure to check – otherwise, it's less than ten-minutes' walk uphill from the junction). It takes twenty minutes to walk down to the beach at Plakiás, a little longer to Dhamnóni.

## Dhamnóni and Skhinariá

Some of the most tempting **beaches** in central Crete hide just to the east of Plakiás, though unfortunately they're now a very poorly kept secret. These three splashes of yellow sand, divided by rocky promontories, are within easy walking distance and together go by the name **Dhamnóni**. At the first, Dhamnóni proper, there's a taverna with showers and a wonderfully long strip of sand, but there's also a lot of new development including a number of nearby rooms for rent and a huge and ugly Swiss-owned holiday village, which has colonized half of the main beach. At the far end, you'll generally find a few people who've dispensed with their clothes, while the little cove which shelters the middle of the three beaches (barely accessible except on foot) is entirely nudist. Beyond this, **Ammoúdhi** beach has another taverna, *Ammoudi* (℡28320 31355, Ⓦwww.ammoudi.gr; B&B ❸), with good if slightly pricey rooms for rent, and more of a family atmosphere. **Skhinariá** beach, just around the corner, is a considerable distance by road via the village of Lefkóyia. A popular diving spot, in summer it attracts Greek families, but is otherwise quiet. There's a decent (daytime) taverna here, *Lybian Star*.

## Préveli and "Palm Beach"

Next in line along the coast is **PRÉVELI**, some 6km southeast of Lefkóyia, served by two daily **buses** from Réthymnon (check current times with any tourist office). It takes its name from a **monastery** (April & May daily 8am–7pm; June–Oct Mon–Sat 8am–1.30pm & 3.30–7.30pm, Sun 8am–7.30pm; in winter, knock for admission; Ⓦwww.preveli.org; €2.50) set high above the sea which, like every other in Crete, has a proud history of resistance, in this case accentuated by its role in World War II as a shelter for marooned Allied soldiers awaiting evacuation. There are fine views and a new monument – to the left as you approach – commemorating the rescue operations and depicting a startling life-size, rifle-toting abbot and an Allied soldier cast in bronze. The evacuations took place from "**Palm Beach**", a sandy cove with a small date-palm grove and a solitary drink stand where a stream (actually the Megapótamos river) feeds a little oasis. The beach usually attracts a summer camping community (now officially discouraged by the authorities) and is also the target of day-trip boats from Plakiás and Ayía Galíni. Sadly, these groups between them deposit heaps of rubbish, often leaving this lovely place filthy, and despite an ongoing clean-up campaign it seems barely worth the effort. The easiest way to get to "Palm Beach" from the monastery is to follow a newly asphalted road that leaves the main road 1km before the monastery itself. This leads, after a further kilometre, to a **pay car park** (€1.50) where you'll need to leave any transport. From here, a marked path clambers steeply down over the rocks – about a ten-minute descent to the beach (but a sweaty twenty-minute haul back up). Should you not wish to return this way (although you'll have little option if you've brought transport), you can avoid the arduous, steep climb by taking a track on the east side of the beach which follows the river valley 2km back to a stone bridge, where there are cafés. You should be able to get one of the two daily buses to drop you at this bridge. All this said, **boat trips** from Plakiás and Ayía Galíni will get you here with a great deal less fuss.

## Spíli and Ayía Galíni

Back on the main road south, the pleasant country town of **SPÍLI** lies about 30km from Réthymnon. A popular coffee break for coach tours passing this way, Spíli warrants a visit and there's some good hiking country in the nearby hills. Sheltered under a cliff are narrow alleys of ancient houses, all leading up from a platía with a famous 24-spouted **fountain** that replaced a Venetian original. If you have your own transport, it's a worthwhile place to stay, peacefully rural at night but with several good **rooms** for rent. Try the *Green Hotel* (☎28320 22225, ⓦwww.greenhotel.gr; ❷), on the main road, or the charming ⚲ *Rooms Herakles* (☎28320 22111, Ⓔheraclespapadakis@hotmail.com; ❷, reductions for more than one night) with air-conditioned ensuite balcony rooms just behind; the genial eponymous proprietor will provide information on the town to non-guests, can advise on some superb **walks** in the surrounding hills and rents out **mountain bikes**. There are two **banks** along the main street (with ATMs) and **internet** access is possible at *Cafe Babis* close to the fountain.

The ultimate destination for most people on this road is **AYÍA GALÍNI**, a picturesque "fishing village" so busy in high season that you can't see it for the tour buses, hotel billboards and package tourists. It also has a beach that is much too small for the crowds that congregate here. Even so, there are a few saving graces – mainly some excellent restaurants and bars, a lively nightlife scene, plenty of rooms and a friendly atmosphere that survives and even thrives on all the visitors. Out of season, when the climate is mild, it can be quite enjoyable too, and from November to April, despite competition from immigrant workers, a number of long-term travellers spend the winter packing tomatoes or polishing cucumbers here. If you want somewhere to stay, start looking at the top end of town, around the main road: the economical and great value *Hotel Minos* (☎28320 91292; ❶), with en-suite rooms with superb views, is a good place to start, with the nearby *Hotel Idi* (☎28320 91152; ❷) and *Hotel Hariklia* (☎28320 91257, ⓦwww.agia-galini.com; ❷) as back-ups, and close to the foot of the hill leading to the harbour, *Neos Ikaros* (☎28320 91447, ⓦwww.neosikaros.gr; ❸) is a more upmarket option with superb garden pool. There are dozens of other possibilities, and usually something can be found even at the height of summer. *Camping Agia Galini* (April-Oct ☎28320 91386) is sited to the east, near the mouth of the Plátis river. There are plenty of places to eat – although of fairly indifferent quality – lining the central "Taverna Street" and along the harbourfront; *Onar* is perhaps the most reliable of the former and *Bozos* of the places nearer the water. Internet access is available at the *Café Zanzibar* next to the bus stop.

The coastal plain east of Ayía Galíni, hidden under acres of polythene green-houses and burgeoning concrete sprawl, must be among the ugliest regions in

Crete, and **Timbáki** the dreariest town. Since this is the way to Phaestos and back to Iráklion, you may have no choice but to grin and bear it.

## The Amári valley

An alternative route south from Réthymnon, and a far less travelled one, is the road which turns off on the eastern fringe of town to run via the **Amári valley**. Very few buses go this way, but if you're driving it's well worth the extra time. There's little specifically to see or do (though a number of richly frescoed Byzantine churches are hidden away en route – all the villages mentioned below have at least one), but it's an impressive drive under the flanks of the mountains and a reminder of how, in places, rural Crete continues to exist regardless of visitors. The countryside here is delightfully green even in summer, with rich groves of olive and assorted fruit trees, and if you **stay** (there are rooms in Amári, Thrónos, Yerákari, Fourfourás and Kourítes), you'll find the nights are cool and quiet. It may seem odd that many of the villages along the way are modern: they were systematically destroyed by the German army in reprisal for the 1944 kidnapping of General Kreipe and many have poignant roadside monuments commemorating these tragic events.

(see p.280)

### Hikes in and around the Amári valley

A good base for touring the Amári valley is Thrónos, a sizeable village at the valley's northern end with an inviting place to stay, *Rooms Aravanes* (see below). The proprietor here – Lambros Papoutsakis – is a keen walker and conducts guided treks to the peak of Mount Psilorítis, which at 2456m is Crete's highest. Although he does guide groups up in the daytime, his preferred approach is during the full moons of June, July and August, which avoids the extreme summer temperatures. Phone in advance for details; it's not a difficult climb, but you'll need sturdy footwear and a sleeping bag. For these night walks, the group starts out by jeep in the early evening to reach the start point on the mountain. After a meal cooked in the open and a short nap, the ascent begins in bright moonlight. The summit is reached at around dawn, and the sunrise is always spectacular: on clear days the mountain offers a breathtaking view of the whole island and its four seas spreading in all directions. On the route down the hike takes in a visit to a goatherd's *mitato* (stone mountain hut) where you see and sample delicious cheese made on the spot. The price (in a minimum group size of eight) is €50 per person, which includes transport, food and drink.

Other hikes from Thrónos include a relatively easy path leading north through the foothills in a couple of hours to the monastery of Arkádhi (see p.280). The first 3km are now along a newly asphalted road (the former track), and the walking route then heads off to the east of this to reach the monastery where you can pick up buses. South from Thrónos is an extremely easy stroll on a paved road running back into the main valley via Kalóyeros. Fifteen-minutes' walk beyond Kalóyeros, a narrow path on the left leads uphill to the small stone church of Áyios Ioánnis Theológos, whose fine but decayed frescoes date from 1347 – the church should be open. This walk can be extended into a two-hour trek back to Thrónos; a map detailing this (and information on the other walks described here) is available from *Rooms Aravanes* (☎28330 22760, ✉thronosm@otenet.gr; ❷), which offers terrace balcony rooms in its main guesthouse or even more attractive rooms with terraces in a nearby and refurbished stone-built house. The *Aravanes*'s small shop also sells mountain herbs collected by the proprietor as well as his home-made honey.

# Haniá and the west

The substantial attractions of Crete's westernmost quarter are enhanced by its relative lack of visitors, and despite the now-rapid spread of tourist development, the west is likely to remain one of the emptier parts of the island. This is partly because there are no big sandy beaches to accommodate resort hotels, and partly because it's so far from the great archeological sites. But for mountains and empty (if often pebbly) beaches, it's unrivalled.

Haniá itself is an excellent reason to come here, but the immediately adjacent coast, especially to the west of the city, is overdeveloped and not particularly exciting; if you want beaches head for the south coast or the far west. Here, **Paleohóra** is the only place which could really be described as a resort, and even this is on a thoroughly human scale; others are emptier still. Elsewhere on the south coast, **Ayía Rouméli** and **Loutró** can be reached only on foot or by boat; **Hóra Sfakíon** sees hordes passing through but few who stay; **Frangokástello**, nearby, has a beautiful castle and the first stirrings of development. Behind these lie the **White Mountains** (Lefká Óri) and the famed walk through the **Samariá Gorge**. In the far west, great beaches at Falásarna and Elafoníssi are mostly visited only as day trips.

## Haniá

**HANIÁ**, as any of its residents will tell you, is spiritually the capital of Crete, even if the official title was passed back (in 1971) to Iráklion. It is also the island's most attractive city, especially if you can catch it in spring, when the White Mountains' snowcapped peaks seem to hover above the roofs. Although it is for the most part a modern city, you might never know it as a tourist. Surrounding the harbour is a wonderful jumble of half-derelict **Venetian streets** that survived the wartime bombardments, and it is here that life for the visitor is concentrated. Restoration and gentrification, consequences of the tourist boom, have made inroads of late, but it remains an atmospheric place.

### Arrival, information and orientation

Large as it is, Haniá is easy to handle once you've reached the centre; you may get lost wandering among the narrow alleys of the old city but that's a relatively small area, and you're never far from the sea or from some other obvious landmark. The **bus station** is on Kydhonías, within easy walking distance of the centre – turn right out of the station, then left down the side of Platía 1866, and you'll emerge at a major road junction opposite the top of Halídhon, the main street of the old quarter leading straight down to the Venetian harbour. Arriving by **ferry**, you'll anchor about 10km east of Haniá at the port of Soúdha: there are frequent buses from here which will drop you by the **market** on the fringes of the old town, or you can take a taxi (around €8); there are also KTEL buses to Réthymnon and Kastélli meeting most ferries. From the **airport** (15km east of town on the Akrotíri peninsula), taxis (around €12) will almost certainly be your only option, though it's worth a quick check to see if any sort of bus is meeting your flight. The very helpful **tourist office** is in the *dhimarhío* (town hall) at Kydhonías 29 (Mon–Fri 8am–2.30pm; ☎28210 36155,

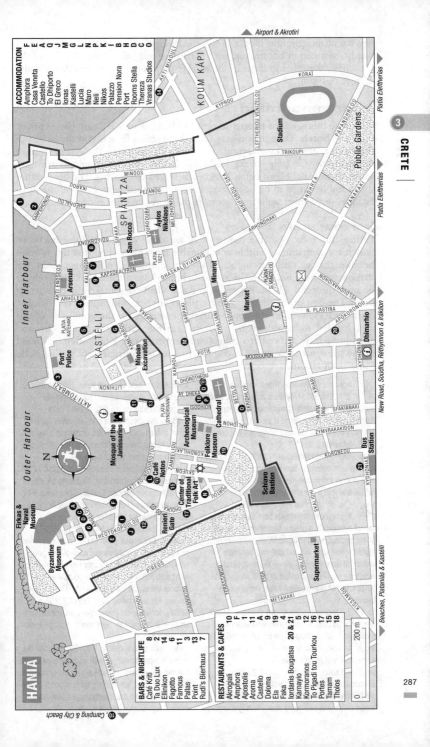

# HANIÁ

**ACCOMMODATION**
| | |
|---|---|
| Amphora | F |
| Casa Veneta | E |
| Castello | A |
| To Dhiporto | Q |
| El Greco | J |
| Ionas | M |
| Kastelli | G |
| Lucia | L |
| Maro | N |
| Neli | P |
| Nikos | K |
| Palazzo | I |
| Pension Nora | B |
| Port | H |
| Rooms Stella | D |
| Thereza | C |
| Vranas Studios | O |

**BARS & NIGHTLIFE**
| | |
|---|---|
| Café Kriti | 8 |
| Ta Duo Lux | 2 |
| Ellinikon | 14 |
| Fagotto | 6 |
| Famous | 11 |
| Pallas | 3 |
| Point | 13 |
| Rudi's Bierhaus | 7 |

**RESTAURANTS & CAFÉS**
| | |
|---|---|
| Akrogiali | 10 |
| Amphora | F |
| Apostolis | 1 |
| Aroma | A |
| Castello | 9 |
| Doloma | 19 |
| Ela | 4 |
| Faka | |
| Iordanis Bougatsa | 20 & 21 |
| Karnayio | 5 |
| Kormoranos | 12 |
| To Pigadi tou Tourkou | 16 |
| Portes | 17 |
| Tamam | 15 |
| Tholos | 18 |

Airport & Akrotiri

KOUM KÁPI

Platía Eleftherías

Platía Eleftherías

New Road, Soúdha, Réthymnon & Iráklion

Beaches, Plataniás & Kastélli

Camping & City Beach

**3**

**CRETE**

287

Inner Harbour

Outer Harbour

SPLÁNTZA

KASTÉLLI

Firkás & Naval Museum

Byzantine Museum

Mosque of the Janissaries

Archeological Museum

Folklore Museum

Schiavo Bastion

Cathedral

Market

Stadium

Public Gardens

Bus Station

Supermarket

San Rocco

Áyios Nikólaos

Arsenáli

Port Police

Minoan Excavation

Minaret

Café Notos

Renieri Gate

Center of Traditional Folk Art

Dhimarhío

N

0       200 m

@www.chania.gr), four blocks east of the bus station; in summer they run two handy information booths, one on the harbour just behind the Mosque of the Janissaries, the other in front of the market (both open June–Sept daily 10am–2pm & 6–10pm).

## Accommodation

There are thousands of **rooms** to rent in Haniá, as well as a number of pricey boutique **hotels**. Though you may face a long search for a bed at the height of the season, eventually everyone does seem to find something. The nearest **campsite** is *Camping Hania* (☏28210 31138, @www.camping-chania.gr), some 4km west of Haniá behind the beach, served by local bus. The site is rather small, and hemmed in by new development, but it has a pool and all the usual facilities just a short walk from some of the better beaches.

### Harbour area

Perhaps the most desirable rooms of all are those overlooking the **harbour**, which are sometimes available at reasonable rates: be warned that this is often because they're noisy at night. Most are approached not direct from the harbourside itself but from the streets behind; those further back are likely to be more peaceful. Theotokopoúlou and the alleys off it make a good starting point. The best of the more expensive places are here, too, equally set back but often with views from the upper storeys. In recent years the popularity of this area has led to anyone with a room near the harbour tarting it up and attempting to rent it out at a ridiculously inflated price. You'll often be touted in the street for these and it's wise not to commit yourself until you've made some comparisons.

**Amphora** 2 Párodos Theotokopoúlou 20 ☏28210 93224, @www.amphora.gr. Traditional hotel in a beautifully renovated Venetian mansion; worth the expense if you get a view, but probably not for the cheaper rooms without one. Good restaurant below. ❺

**Casa Veneta** Theotokopoúlou 57 ☏28210 90007, @www.casa-veneta.gr. Very well-equipped, comfortable studios and apartments behind a Venetian facade and with a friendly owner; good value. ❹

**Castello** Angélou 2 ☏28210 92800, @www.castello-chania.com. First of a little row of *pensions* in a great situation on the far side of the harbour near the Naval Museum; newly refurbished rooms have a/c and galleried beds and almost all have stunning views; prices depend on size, from small rooms to family suite with private terrace, but all are excellent value. Popular café below. ❸

**El Greco** Theotokopoúlou 47–49 ☏28210 94030, @www.elgreco.gr. Comfortable hotel with nicely furnished if rather compact rooms which include fridge, a/c and TV. Some have balconies and there's a seasonal roof terrace. B&B ❹

**Lucia** Aktí Koundouriótou ☏28210 90302, @www.loukiahotel.gr. Harbourfront hotel with a/c balcony rooms; furnishing is basic at best, hence much less expensive than you might expect

for one of the best views in town, and – thanks to double-glazing – reasonably soundproof. ❸

**Maro** B Párodos Portoú 5 ☏28210 97913. Probably the cheapest en-suite rooms in the old town, hidden away in a quiet, unmarked alley off Portou not far from the Schiavo bastion. Basic but friendly and clean; a/c €2 extra. ❷

**Pension Nora** Theotokopoúlou 60 ☏28210 72265, @pensionnora@yahoo.co.uk. Charming a/c rooms in a ramshackle wooden Turkish house, some very basic with shared bath, others relatively fancy, so look first. Pleasant breakfast café below. ❷

**Palazzo** Theotokopoúlou 54 ☏28210 93227, @www.palazzohotel.gr. An old mansion converted to a hotel, with wood-beamed ceilings and dark wood floors. Good-sized, simply furnished rooms, most with balconies, plus a roof terrace with harbour views and tasty breakfasts. ❹

**Rooms Stella** Angélou 10 ☏28210 73756. Creaky, eccentric old house above an eclectic gift shop, with pleasant en-suite rooms equipped with a/c and fridge. ❸

**Thereza** Angélou 8 ☏28210 92798. Beautiful old house in a great position, with stunning views from the roof terrace and en-suite a/c rooms (some with TV); classy decor, too. Slightly more expensive than its neighbours but deservedly so; unlikely to have room in high season unless you book. ❹

## The old town: east of Halídhon

In the eastern half of the old town, rooms are far more scattered, usually cheaper, and in the height of the season your chances are much better over here. **Kastélli**, immediately east of the harbour, has some lovely places with views from the heights. Take one of the alleys leading left off Kanevárou if you want to try these, although since they are popular, they're often booked up.

**To Dhiporto** Betólo 41 ☎28210 40570, ⓦwww.todiporto.gr. Pleasant, good-value en-suite rooms, all with a/c, TV and fridge; some triples and singles too. ❸

**Ionas** Sarpáki, cnr Sórvolou ☎28210 55090, ⓦwww.ionashotel.com. Small boutique hotel in a lovingly restored Venetian mansion. Very comfortable rooms and beautiful architectural detail, though service occasionally lacking. ❻

🏃 **Kastelli** Kanevárou 39 ☎28210 57057, ⓦwww.kastelistudios.gr. A comfortable, modern, reasonably priced *pension* that's very quiet at the back. All rooms come with fans or a/c and plug-in mosquito repellents. The owner is exceptionally helpful and also has a few apartments and a beautiful house (for up to five people) to rent. ❷

**Neli** Isódhion 21–23 ☎28210 55533, ⓦwww.nelistudios.com. Larger and fancier than it appears from outside, this hotel rambles through three lovingly restored old buildings, with stylishly decorated, fully equipped rooms with balconies, a/c and cooking facilities. ❺

**Nikos** Dhaskaloyiánnis 58 ☎28210 54783. Built on top of a Minoan ruin (visible through a basement window), this is one of several rooms places along this street near the inner harbour; good-value, relatively modern rooms, all with a/c, shower and fridge. The same owner has economical studios nearby with fully-equipped kitchens. ❷

**Port** Sífaka 73, just off Dhaskaloyiánnis ☎28210 59484. Clean, quiet, modern place with good-size, en-suite rooms with a/c. ❸

**Vranas Studios** Ayíon Dhéka, cnr Sarpáki ☎28210 58618, ⓦwww.vranas.gr. Pleasant, spacious, studio-style rooms with TV, a/c, fridge and kitchenette. ❹

# The City

**Haniá** has been occupied almost continuously since Neolithic times, so in some ways it is surprising that there's so little specifically to see or do. It is, however, fascinating simply to amble around, stumbling upon surviving fragments of city wall, the remains of **ancient Kydonia**, which are being excavated, and odd segments of Venetian or Turkish masonry. A few small museums help add focus to your wanderings.

## Kastélli and the harbour

The **port** area is, as ever, the place to start, the oldest and the most interesting part of town. It's at its busiest and most attractive at night, when the lights from bars and restaurants reflect in the water and crowds of visitors and locals turn out to promenade. By day, things are quieter. Straight ahead from Platía Syndriváni (also known as Harbour Square) lies the curious domed shape of the **Mosque of the Janissaries**, built in 1645 (though heavily restored since) and the oldest Ottoman building on the island. It is usually open as a gallery, housing temporary exhibitions.

The little hill that rises behind the mosque is **Kastélli**, site of the earliest habitation and core of the Minoan, Venetian and Turkish towns. There's not a great deal left, but archeologists believe that they may have found the remains of a Minoan palace (logically, there must have been one at this end of the island), and the "lost" city of Kydonia, in the **excavations** being carried out – and open to view – along Kanevárou. It's also here that you'll find traces of the oldest **walls**; there were two rings, one defending Kastélli alone, a later set encompassing the whole of the medieval city. Beneath the hill, on the inner (eastern) harbour, the arches of sixteenth-century **Venetian arsenals**, a couple of them beautifully restored (and one housing a reconstructed Minoan ship), survive alongside remains of the outer walls.

Following the esplanade around in the other direction leads to a hefty bastion which now houses Crete's **Naval Museum** (April–Oct daily 9am–4pm, Nov–March daily 9am–2pm; €3). The collection consists of model ships and other naval ephemera tracing the history of Greek navigation, plus a section on the 1941 **Battle of Crete** with fascinating artefacts, and poignant photos depicting the suffering here under the Nazis. From the **Fírkas**, the fortress behind the museum, the modern Greek flag was first flown on Crete, in 1913.

Walking around the outside of these restored bulwarks you'll find a free car park (also the starting point for *trenaki* tours of the new town), from where you can follow the sea wall round towards the town beach. Turn inland, along Pireós, to see the the best-preserved, weighty and threatening stretch of the old city walls from the outside. Following the walls around on the inside is rather trickier, but far more enjoyable. This is where you'll stumble on some of the most picturesque little alleyways and finest Venetian houses in Haniá. Just behind the Naval Museum at the top of Theotokopoúlou lies the **Byzantine Museum** (Tues–Sun 8.30am–7.30pm; €2, combined ticket with archeological museum €3), with a small but interesting collection of mosaics, icons and jewellery from the various periods of Byzantine rule. Continue up Theotoko-poúlou and explore the alleys off it to discover some of the most attractive parts of the old town, with widespread restoration and plenty of fascinating small shops. Keep your eyes open for details on the houses, such as old wooden balconies or stone coats of arms. The arch of the **Renieri Gate**, at the bottom of Moschón, is particularly elegant. There are also lots of interesting art and craft stores around here, along Theotokopóulou and the many alleys that run off it down towards the harbour.

Between the Renieri Gate and Hálidhon are more such streets and alleys, though here the emphasis is more on tavernas, bars and cafés. This area was the medieval Jewish ghetto, and at the end of a small alley off the west side of Kóndhilaki is Haniá's fifteenth-century Etz Hayyim **synagogue** (Mon–Fri 9am–12.30pm & 6–8pm; prayers daily at 9am; free; ⓦ www.etz-hayyim-hania .org), recently renovated. All but one of the city's Jews were rounded up by the Nazi occupation forces in 1944, but they met their end (along with around five hundred members of the captured Cretan resistance) when the transport ship taking them to Auschwitz was torpedoed by a British submarine off the island of Mílos. Look out too for the **Centre of Traditional Folk Art and Culture**, at Skúfon 20. This is actually a shop rather than a museum, but it displays the amazing embroideries created by the owner, Maria, and model ships made by her son. These are not for sale, though you can order copies of the simpler embroideries (from around €5000, to reflect the weeks of work involved), and there are plenty of smaller gift items available.

### Halídhon and beyond

Behind the harbour lie the less picturesque but more lively sections of the old city. First, a short way up Halídhon on the right, is Haniá's **Archeological Museum** (Mon 1–7.30pm, Tues–Sun 8am–7.30pm; €2, combined ticket with Byzantine Museum €3), housed in the Venetian-built church of San Francesco. Damaged as it is, especially from the outside, this remains a beautiful building and it contains a fine little display, covering the local area from Minoan through to Roman times. In the garden, a huge fountain and the base of a minaret survive from the period when the Ottomans converted the church into a mosque; around them are scattered various other sculptures and architectural remnants. The nearby **Folklore Museum** (Mon–Sat 9.30am–3pm & 6–9pm; €2) is worth a look as much for its setting, on a fine courtyard that is also home to Haniá's Roman Catholic church, as for its contents.

The **cathedral**, ordinary and relatively modern, is just a few steps further up Halídhon on the left. Around the cathedral square are busy cafés and some of the more animated shopping areas, leading up to the back of the market: **Odhós Skrídhlof** ("Leather Street") still has numerous traditional leathermakers plying their trade among the tackier souvenirs. In the direction of the Spiántza quarter, further east behind the market, are ancient alleys with tumbledown Venetian stonework and overhanging wooden balconies; though gentrification is spreading apace, much of the quarter has yet to feel the effect of the city's modern popularity. There are a couple more **minarets** too, one on Dhaliáni, and the other attached to the church of Áyios Nikólaos, currently undergoing restoration. Nearby Platía 1821 is a fine traditional square to stop for a coffee.

## The beaches

Haniá's beaches all lie to the west of the city. For the crowded but clean **city beach** this means no more than a ten-minute walk, following the shoreline from the Naval Museum, but for more extensive spaces you're better off taking the local bus (#21) out along the coast road. This leaves from the east side of Platía 1866 and runs along the coast as far as **Kalamáki beach**. Kalamáki and the previous stop, **Oásis beach**, are again pretty crowded but they're a considerable improvement over the beach in Haniá itself. In between, you'll find plenty of alternatives, though some of these are quite a walk from the bus stop. Further afield there are even finer beaches at **Ayía Marína** (see p.294) to the west, or **Kalathás** and **Stavrós** (p.293) out on the Akrotíri peninsula, all of which can be reached by KTEL buses from the main station.

## Eating

You're never far from something to **eat** in Haniá, and the harbour itself is encircled by a succession of restaurants, tavernas and cafés. These tend to be pricey, though, and the quality at many leaves a lot to be desired. Away from the water, there are plenty of slightly cheaper possibilities on Kondhiláki, Kanevárou and the streets off Halídhon. For snacks or lighter meals, the cafés around the harbour generally serve cocktails and fresh juices at exorbitant prices, though breakfast can be good value. For more traditional places, try around the market and along Dhaskaloyiánnis (Synganaki here is a good traditional bakery serving *tyrópita* and the like, with a cake shop next door). Fast food is also increasingly widespread.

### Restaurants

**Akrogiali** Aktí Papanikolí 19, behind the city beach ☎ 28210 73110. Excellent, reasonably priced seafront fish taverna, with a summer terrace, that's well worth the 15min walk or short taxi ride. Always packed with locals, so may be worth booking – though there are plenty of alternatives along the same street.

**Amphora** Aktí Koundouriótou, under the *Hotel Amphora*. One of the most reliable places on the outer harbour, with good, simple Greek food.

**Apostolis** Aktí Enóseos 6 & 10, inner harbour. The fish tavernas at the inner end of the harbour are rated much more highly by locals than those

further round – some locals claim *Apostolis 2*, practically the last, and just a couple of doors down from its seemingly identical sister restaurant, is the best of all. The fish is excellent, but pricey.

**Doloma** Kapsokályvon 5, near the Arsenali. Excellent little taverna with a shady terrace serving well-prepared and economical Cretan dishes.

**Ela** Top of Kondhiláki. Standard taverna food enlivened by live Greek music, in a romantically semi-ruinous old mansion.

**Faka** Arholéon 15. Set back from the harbour, so significantly less touristy and less expensive than many near neighbours, *Faka* serves excellent traditional local food, often with live Greek music. Check out the daily specials, made using local seasonal ingredients.

**Karnayio** Platía Kateháki 8 ☎ 28210 53366. Not right on the water, but one of the best harbour restaurants nonetheless. Excellent fish, traditional Cretan cooking and a fine selection of wines – all served on an inviting terrace – make this a winner.

**To Pigadi tou Tourkou** Sarpáki 1. Greco-Moroccan restaurant with an interesting menu combining the two cuisines along with dishes from the Middle East.

**Portes** Portoú 48. A small group of restaurants nestles under the walls along Portoú. Portes is smarter than most, with a particularly adventurous menu putting a modern twist on age-old dishes: rabbit with prunes, cuttlefish with fennel, and traditional pies with unusual fillings.

**Tamam** Zambelíou. Excellent, fashionable place where the adventurous Greek menu includes much vegetarian food. Unfortunately there are only a few cramped tables in the alley outside, and inside it can get very hot. Service sometimes slow.

**Tholos** Ayíon Dhéka 36. Slightly north of the cathedral, *Tholos* is another "restaurant in a ruin", this time Venetian/Turkish, with a wide selection of Cretan specialities.

## Cafés

**Aroma** Aktí Tombázi 4. Pleasant café with a great harbour view to savour over lazy breakfasts or late drinks. *Mousses*, nearby at the corner of Kanevárou, is equally good, and open 24hr.

**Castello** Angélou 2. Slow, relaxed terrace bar beneath the rooms place of the same name; good for breakfast, and where locals (especially expats) sit whiling the day away or playing *tavli* (backgammon).

**Iordanis Bougatsa** Branches at Kydhonías 96 and Apokorónou 24. Specializes in traditional creamy *bougátsa*, a sugar-coated cream-cheese pie to eat in or takeaway.

**Kormoranos** Theotokopoúlou. A bakery/café/ouzerí occupying two small sites on opposite sides of the street. Pastries washed down by juices, herb teas and coffee during the day, and an ouzerí serving delicious *meze* to go with your drinks at night.

## Bars and nightlife

As you might expect, the harbour area contains dozens of beautifully set but touristy **bars**. Locals head east, to Koum Kápi and the scores of bars and cafés lining Aktí Miaoúli, the seafront outside the walls – these are heaving by 11pm. Sometime after midnight, action will move on to the **clubs**, and where these are depends on the time of year. In summer, many of the downtown venues close down and the action moves to the vibrant club scene on the coast west of town. The top places here include *Destijl* and *Vareladiko* in Ayía Marína, and *Mylos* in Plataniás. Over winter, *Vareladiko* operates from a waterfront warehouse by the Port Police.

For other events, such as **Greek music** concerts, look out for posters, especially in front of the market: some of these take place in the open-air auditorium in the public gardens, but most – and the most authentic – are at out-of-town restaurants. The hoardings in front of the market also have **movie** posters: there are open-air screenings at Attikon, on Venizélou out towards Akrotíri, about 1km from the centre, and occasionally in the public gardens.

**Ta Duo Lux** Sarpidhónos. Comfy bar-café in a street full of similar places that attract a slightly older crowd than nearby Aktí Miaoúli.

**Ellinikon** Aktí Miaoúli. One of the more popular and consistent of the bars on this coastal strip, packed nightly with young locals: if this doesn't appeal, take your pick from its dozens of neighbours.

**Fagotto** Angélou 16. Pleasant, laid-back jazz bar off the quieter end of the harbour, often with live performances.

**Famous** Aktí Tombázi, above *Aroma*. Live Greek-music venue, occasionally with big-name performers.

**Café Kriti** Kalergón 22, corner of Andhroyíou. Greek music and dancing virtually every night at what is basically an old-fashioned *kafenío*.

**Pallas** Aktí Tombázi 15, near Port Police. Quiet upstairs café/cocktail bar with a roof terrace that's ideally placed to admire the sunset over the harbour.

**Point** Platía Syndriváni, above *Mousses* café. Chilled bar that gets wilder as the night goes on.

**Rudi's Bierhaus** Kalergón 16. Haniá's beer shrine: Austrian – and long-time Haniá resident – Rudi Riegler's bar stocks more than a hundred of Europe's finest. Excellent *mezédhes* to accompany them.

## Listings

**Airlines** Olympic (☎28210 63264) and Aegean (☎28210 63366) both have offices at the airport.

**Banks and exchange** The main branch of the National Bank of Greece is directly opposite the market with two ATMs, and there's a cluster of banks with more ATMs around the top of Halídhon. You'll also find plenty of out-of-hours exchange places on Halídhon, in the travel agencies.

**Bike and car rental** For bikes, Summertime, Dhaskaloyiánnis 7, slightly northeast of the market (☎28210 45797, ✆www.strentals.gr), has a huge range, including mountain bikes. For cars, two reliable local companies are Hermes, Tzanakáki 52 (☎28210 54418), and Tellus Rent a Car, Halídhon 108, opposite Platía 1866 (☎28210 91500). *Rough Guide* readers get 25 percent off normal rates from El Greco Cars at the *El Greco* hotel (☎28210 60883, ✆www.elgreco.gr; see p.288).

**Boat trips** A number of boats run trips from the harbour (around €10 for 2hr), mainly to the nearby islands of Áyii Theódori and Lazarétta, for swimming and *krí-krí* (ibex) spotting: you're unlikely to escape the attentions of their stalls around the harbour. Alternatives include sunset cruises and all-day trips to the Rodhópou peninsula.

**Diving** Blue Adventures Diving, Arholéon 11, near the inner harbour (☎28210 40608, ✆www.blueadventuresdiving.gr), runs daily diving and snorkelling trips.

**Ferry tickets** From any travel agent, or the ANEK line office (on Venizélou, right opposite the market; ☎28210 27500); Hellenic Seaways are at Platía 1866 14 (☎28210 75444).

**Internet** There are plenty of internet cafés including Vranas, Ayíon Dhéka beneath *Vranas Studios* (see p.289) and Café Notos, on the outer harbour under the *Hotel Lucia*.

**Laundry** Speedy Laundry (☎28210 88411), junction of Koronéou and Korkídhi, just west of Platía 1866, will collect and deliver your load if you call; the Old Town Laundromat, Karaóli 40; Oscar, Kanevárou, just off Platía Syndriváni.

**Left luggage** The bus station has a left-luggage office (6am–8.30pm; €1–2 per item per day depending on size).

**Market and supermarkets** To buy food, head for the entertaining market, which has fresh fruit and vegetables, meat and fish, bakers, dairy stalls and general stores for cooked meats, tins, etc; on Sat mornings there's a wonderful line of stalls along Minóos, inside the eastern city wall, where local farmers sell their produce. Several small stores by the harbour platía sell cold drinks and food; they are expensive but open late. Small supermarkets can be found on Platía 1866, and the larger Champion supermarket is at the top of Pireos, outside the western wall, close to the Schiavo bastion.

**Post office** The main post office is on Tzanakáki (Mon–Fri 7.30am–8pm, Sat 9am–1pm).

**Taxis** The main taxi ranks are on Platía 1866. For radio taxis try ☎28210 18300, ☎28210 94300 or 28210 98700.

**Travel agencies** Plenty, concentrated around the top of Halídhon and on Platía 1866, as well as around the bus station. Try Tellus Travel, Halídhon 108 (☎28210 91500, ✆www.tellustravel.gr), or in the old town El Greco Travel, Theotokopoúlou 50 (☎28210 86015, ✆www.elgreco.gr).

**Waterpark** Limnoupolis (✆www.limnoupolis.gr) is located close to the village of Varipetro, 8km southwest of the city, with slides taking advantage of a natural hillside. There's a regular bus service from the bus station.

# Around Haniá: the Akrotíri and Rodhópou peninsulas

North of Haniá, the **Akrotíri peninsula** loops around, protecting the Bay of Soúdha. The bay itself, and the southern side of the peninsula overlooking it, are packed with NATO military hardware, with bases surrounding the airport. The peninsula's northwestern coastline, however, is fast developing into a luxury suburb; the excellent beach of **Kalathás**, near Horafákia, is ringed by villas and apartments. **STAVRÓS**, further out, has not yet suffered this fate, and its **beach** is absolutely superb if you like the calm, shallow water of an almost completely enclosed lagoon. It's not very large, so it does get crowded, but rarely overpoweringly so. There's a makeshift taverna/*souvláki* stand on the beach, and a couple of tavernas across the road, but for accommodation you need to search slightly south of here, in the area around **Blue Beach**, where there are plenty of apartment buildings but very little availability in summer: one to try is *Zorba's Apartments* (☎28210 39010, ⓦwww.hotel-zorbas.gr; ❸), for slightly dated studios and apartments round a pool very near Blue Beach.

Inland are the **monasteries** of **Ayía Triádha** (daily 7.30am–2pm & 5–7pm; €2) and **Gouvernétou** (Easter–Sept Mon, Tues & Thurs 9am–noon & 5–8pm, Sat & Sun 5–11am & 5–8pm; Oct–Easter afternoon hours are 4–7pm; free). Ayía Triádha is much more accessible and has a beautiful seventeenth-century church inside its pink-and-ochre cloister. It is also a thriving and commercial place, producing and selling its own organic olive oil, for example. Gouvernétou, by contrast, is isolated, contemplative and strict; visitors are expected to respect this. There are fine frescoes in the ancient church, and from just beyond the monastery you can clamber down a craggy path to the amazing abandoned ruins of the **monastery of Katholikó**, built into a craggy ravine, and the remains of its narrow harbour.

## West to Rodhópou

The coast to the west of Haniá was the scene of most of the fighting during the German invasion in 1941, and at Máleme there's a big German cemetery; the Allied cemetery is in the other direction, on the coast just outside Soúdha. There are also beaches and considerable tourist development along much of this shore. **Ayía Marína** has a fine sandy beach and an island offshore said to be a sea monster petrified by Zeus before it could swallow Crete. Seen from the west, its "mouth" still gapes open.

Between **Plataniás** and **Kolymvári** an almost unbroken strand unfurls, exposed when the wind blows and by no means all sandy, but deserted for long stretches between villages. The road here runs through mixed groves of calamus reed (Crete's bamboo) and oranges; the windbreaks fashioned from the reeds protect the ripening oranges from the *meltémi*. At Kolymvári, the road to Kastélli cuts across the base of another mountainous peninsula, **Rodhópou**. Just off the main road here is a monastery, **Goniá** (summer Mon–Fri & Sun 8am–12.30pm & 4.30–8pm, Sat 4–8pm; winter afternoon hours 3.30–5.30pm; free; respectable dress required), with a view most luxury hotels would envy. Every monk in Crete can tell tales of his valiant ancestry of resistance to invaders, but here the Turkish cannon balls are still lodged in the walls to prove it, a relic of which the good fathers are far more proud than any of the icons.

# South to the Samariá Gorge

From Haniá the spectacular **Samariá Gorge**, which, at 16km, claims to be Europe's longest, can be visited as a day-trip or as part of a longer excursion to the south. The **gorge** begins at the *xylóskalo*, or "wooden staircase", a stepped path plunging steeply down from the southern lip of the Omalós plain. Here, at the head of the track, opposite the sheer rock face of Mount Gíngilos, the crowds pouring out of buses disperse rapidly as keen walkers march purposefully down while others dally over breakfast, contemplating the sunrise. The descent is at first through almost alpine scenery: pine forest, wild flowers and greenery – a verdant shock in the spring, when the stream is at its liveliest. Small churches and viewpoints dot the route, and about halfway down you pass the abandoned village of **Samariá**, now home to a wardens' station, with picnic

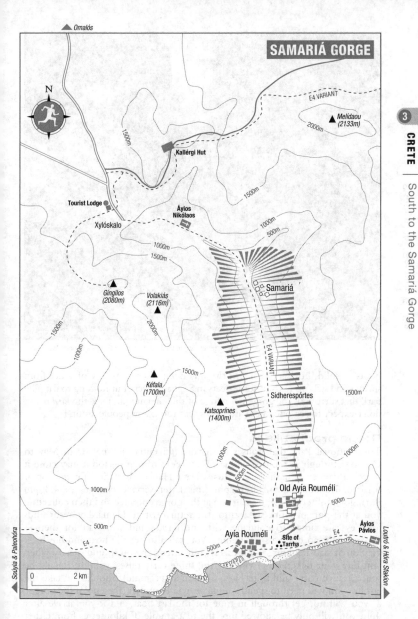

**Omalós**

**Melídaou (2133m)**

E4 VARIANT

**Kallérgi Hut**

**Tourist Lodge**

**Xylóskalo**

**Áyios Nikólaos**

**Gíngilos (2080m)**

**Volakiás (2116m)**

**Samariá**

E4 VARIANT

**Kéfala (1700m)**

**Katsoprínes (1400m)**

**Sidherespórtes**

**Old Ayía Rouméli**

**Ayía Rouméli**

**Site of Tarrha**

**Áyios Pávlos**

E4

Soúyia & Paleohóra

Loutró & Hóra Sfakíon

0    2 km

facilities and filthy toilets. Further down, the path levels out and the gorge walls close in until, at the narrowest point (the *sidherespórtes* or "iron gates"), one can practically touch both tortured rock faces at once and, looking up, see them rising sheer for almost a thousand feet.

At an average pace, with regular stops, the walk down takes five or six hours (though you can do it far quicker), and the upward trek considerably longer. It's strenuous – you'll know all about it next day – the path is rough, and walking

295

▲ A group approaches the Samariá Gorge's famous Iron Gates

boots or solid shoes are vital. On the way down there is plenty of water from springs and streams (except some years in Sept and Oct), but nothing to eat. The park that surrounds the gorge is a refuge of the Cretan wild ibex, the *krí-krí*, but don't expect to see one; there are usually far too many people around.

### Gorge practicalities

The National Park that houses the gorge (€5 entry) is open from May to October, though in the first and last few weeks of that period it may close if there's a danger of flash floods. **Buses** leave Haniá bus station for the top at 6.15am, 7.30am, 8.30am and 2pm (this latter service changes to 4.30pm during school terms), depositing you at the gorge entrance and then collecting you at the port of Hóra Sfakíon for the return trip to Haniá. The return bus journeys are timed to coincide with the ferries and will wait for them – theoretically, no one gets left behind. You can also get the boat and bus back via Soúyia or Paleohóra, and if this is your intention you should specify when you buy your ticket: otherwise, for the three early buses, you'll normally be sold a return trip (valid from Hóra Sfakíon at any time). Should you take the last bus you will need to spend a night at Ayía Rouméli (the end of the gorge), as you will not get through in time for the last boat, and if you arrive after 4pm you will only be allowed into the first couple of kilometres from either end. The wardens ensure that no one remains in the gorge overnight, where camping is strictly forbidden.

It's well worth catching the earliest bus to avoid the full heat of the day while walking through the gorge, though be warned that you will not be alone – there are often as many as five coachloads setting off before dawn for the nail-biting climb into the White Mountains. There are also direct early-morning buses from Iráklion, Réthymnon, Soúyia and Paleohóra as well as bus **tours** from virtually everywhere on the island, adding up to a thousand-plus walkers on most days during high season.

## Omalós

One way to avoid an early start from the north coast would be to stay at the elevated village of **OMALÓS**, in the middle of the mountain plain from which the gorge descends. The climate is cooler here all year round and the many paths into the hills surrounding the plateau are a welcome bonus; in season a profusion of wild flowers and birdlife is to be seen. There are plenty of **tavernas** and some surprisingly fancy **rooms** with all facilities; the *Hotel Neos Omalos* (☎28210 67269, ⓦ www.neos-omalos.gr; ❷) is perhaps the best, but the slightly cheaper neighbouring *Hotel Gingilos* (☎28210 67181; ❷) is also very friendly. Both have tavernas and offer lifts to the top of the gorge in the morning if you stay overnight. However, since the village is some way from the start of the path, and the first buses arrive as the sun rises, it's almost impossible to get a head start on the crowds. Some people sleep out at the top (where there's a bar-restaurant in the *Tourist Lodge* and kiosks serving drinks and sandwiches), but a night under the stars here can be a bitterly cold experience. The one significant advantage to staying up here would be if you wanted to undertake some other **climbs** in the White Mountains, in which case the **Kallérgi mountain hut** (☎28210 33199 or 693 66 57 954; €12 per person) is about ninety-minutes' hike (signed) from Omalós or the top of the gorge.

# Villages of the southwest coast

When you finally emerge from the gorge, it's not long before you reach the singularly unattractive village of **AYÍA ROUMÉLI**, which is all but abandoned until you come to the beach, a mirage of iced drinks and a cluster of tavernas with **rooms** for rent. One of the best of these is *Tara* (☎28250 91231, ⓦ www.agiaroumeli.gr; ❷), with rooms above the taverna and also at the seafront *Calypso*, while *Livikon* (☎28250 91363; ❷), at the back of the village, is one of the more peaceful places. On arrival, it's best to buy your boat tickets straightaway to be sure of getting the sailing you want (though in theory they guarantee that no one will be left behind, and that the buses will wait for the boat). If you plan to stay on the south coast, you should get going as soon as possible for the best chance of finding a room somewhere more attractive than Ayía Rouméli. From May to October there are three boats daily to Loutró and Hóra Sfakíon (Mon–Thurs 11.30am, 3.45pm & 6pm; Fri–Sun 9.30am, 3.45pm & 6pm), plus a daily sailing to Soúyia and Paleohóra (Mon–Thurs 4.45pm, Fri–Sun 5.30pm).

## Loutró

For tranquillity, it's hard to beat **LOUTRÓ**, two-thirds of the way from Ayía Rouméli to Hóra Sfakíon, and accessible only by boat or on foot. The chief disadvantage of Loutró is its lack of a real beach; the pebbly bay in front of the village soon gets crowded, so many people swim from the rocks roundabout. If you're prepared to walk, however, there are plenty of lovely **beaches** along the coast in each direction; these can also be reached by hired **canoe**, and some (particularly Sweetwater to the east and Mármara to the west) by regular excursion boats. For walkers, the **coastal trail** through Loutró covers the entire distance between Ayía Rouméli and Hóra Sfakíon (now part of the E4 Pan-European footpath), and there's also a daunting zigzag path up the cliff behind to the mountain village of **Anópoli**.

Loutró itself has a number of excellent **tavernas** and a fair few **rooms**, though not always enough of the latter in peak season. The best known and most comfortable are the ⌖ *Blue House* (☎28250 91127; ❸), with comfortable, sea-front en-suite rooms and a wonderful (slightly pricier) top-floor extension as well as a great taverna, and the *Hotel Porto Loutro* (☎28250 91433, ⓦwww .hotelportoloutro.com ❹), the only place with any pretensions at all, whose comfortable rooms spread across several cubist white buildings. Thanks to its position right at the eastern end of the seafront, the simple rooms at *Rooms Nikolas* (☎28250 91352 ❸) are probably the quietest you'll find. *Rooms Manousoudaki* (☎28250 91348 ❷), set further back in the village, behind the church, is simpler and cheaper, and its air-conditioned en-suite rooms with fridge may be available when seafront places have all sold out. You'll find links to much of the local accommodation at ⓦwww.loutro.net/accommodation. Of the **places to eat**, the *Blue House* is again good, as are *Ilios*, for fish caught from their own boat, *Limani*, for charcoal grills, and ⌖ *Notos* for excellent *mezédhes*.

## Hóra Sfakíon and beyond

**HÓRA SFAKÍON**, the ancient capital of the Sfakiá region, is the main terminus for gorge walkers, with a regular boat service along the coast to and from Ayía Rouméli, and buses back to Haniá and elsewhere. It also has the most regular ferry service to the island of Gavdhós (see p.303). Thousands of people pass through daily, and almost every facility is provided for them (though the local ATMs are notoriously unreliable). Relatively few stay, however, although there are plenty of great-value **rooms** and some excellent **tavernas**. Good choices if you do stop over include the *Hotel Stavris* (☎28250 91220, ⓦwww.hotel-stavris-chora-sfakion.com; ❶) for plain but comfortable en-suite rooms (and smarter apartments on the edge of town); the seafront *Livikon* (☎28250 91211, ⓦwww.sfakia-livikon.com; ❷), with great views from the upper floor rooms though some noise from the tavernas below; or the *Hotel Xenia* (☎28250 91202 ⓦwww.xenia-crete.com; ❸), with the best rooms and the best location in town.

Though there are a couple of pebbly coves, what is missing in Hóra Sfakíon is a decent beach. You could walk (or for much of the year take an excursion boat) west to Sweetwater, or there are numerous opportunities for a dip along the coast road east towards Plakiás. The most memorable spot in this direction is **FRANGOKÁSTELLO**, named after a crumbling Venetian attempt to bring law and order to a district that went on to defy both Turks and Germans. The four-square, crenellated thirteenth-century **castle**, isolated a few kilometres below a chiselled wall of mountains, looks as though it's been spirited out of the High Atlas or Tibet. The place is said to be haunted by ghosts of Greek rebels massacred here in 1829: every May, these *dhrossoulítes* ("dewy ones") march at dawn across the coastal plain and disappear into the sea near the fort. The rest of the time Frangokástello is peaceful enough, with a lovely beach and a number of tavernas and rooms scattered for some distance along the coast. The greatest concentration is immediately below the castle – try *Maria's Studios* (☎28250 92159, ⓦwww.marias-studios.net; ❷) or the more basic *Kali Kardia* (☎28250 92123, ⓦwww.kali-kardia.eu; ❶). Unfortunately there's very little transport in this direction – just one bus a day from Haniá to Frangokástello and Skalóti, 5km further on.

# Kastélli and the western tip

Apart from being Crete's most westerly town, and the end of the main coastal highway, **KASTÉLLI** (Kíssamos, or Kastélli Kissámou as it's variously known) has little obvious appeal. It's a busy town with a rocky central **beach** (there's also a small sandy beach to the west) visited mainly by people using the boat that runs weekly to the island of Kýthira and the Peloponnese. The very ordinariness of Kastélli, however, can be attractive: life goes on pretty much regardless of outsiders, and there's every facility you might need. The town was important in antiquity, when the Greco-Roman city-state of **Kísamos** was a major regional power. The most important remnants of this have been gathered into a superb 2006-opened **museum** (Tues–Sun 8.30am–3pm; free) on the main square, Platía Kastellíou. The highlights are the stunning Roman-era **mosaics** on the upper floor. Mosaic production was a local speciality, and many more are being excavated around town, where it is hoped that some will be put on display *in situ*.

As regards **practicalities**, almost everything you need is also on or near Platía Kastellíou. The bus station is here, as are a couple of cafés; banks, shops and travel agencies (for ferry tickets or car rental) lie east of the square along Skalídhi; another group can be found around nearby Platía Venizélou, on the main road through town. The **ferry port** is some 3km west of town – a significant walk if you're heavily laden, or a cheap taxi ride; there are daily boat trips from here to beautiful beaches at Gramvoússa and Bálos Bay, at the far northwestern tip of Crete. For **rooms**, *Vergerakis* (aka *Jimmy's*; ☎28220 22663; ❶) is right by Platía Kastellíou, but you'll find better facilities and location if you head downhill to the shore. Here the excellent *Galini Beach Hotel* (☎28220 23288, ⓦwww.galinibeach.com; B&B ❸), whose sparkling air-conditioned, sea-view rooms come with balconies and bountiful breakfasts, lies at the pebbly, eastern end of the seafront near the sports stadium. Behind the central seafront, *Argo* (☎28220 23322, ⓦwww.papadaki.biz; ❷) has plainer rooms with air conditioning, TV, fridge and balcony.

Here on the beach promenade are a number of **tavernas** – *Papadakis* and *Aretousa* are both recommended. Around them are numerous cafés and **bars**, popular with young locals and hence livelier than you might expect, particularly at weekends.

## Falásarna to Elafoníssi

To the west of Kastélli lies some of Crete's loneliest and finest coastline. The first place of note is **FALÁSARNA**, where the scant ruins of an ancient city are ignored by most visitors in favour of some of the best beaches on Crete, wide and sandy with clean water, though far from undiscovered. There's a handful of **tavernas** and an increasing number of **rooms** for rent: *Sunset* (☎28220 41204, ⓦwww.sunsethotel.biz; ❶), at the end of the paved road near the archeological site, is among the better choices for both; *Pension Anastasia Stathis* (☎28220 41480, ⓦwww.stathisanastasia.com; ❷), one of many you'll pass on the way down, offers rather more spacious, modern rooms. Plenty of people **camp** out here too; if you join them, take any litter away with you. Rubbish, occasional tar and crowds of locals on summer weekends can always be escaped if you're prepared to walk, and the beaches are worth it. The nearest town is **Plátanos**, 5km up a paved road, where you'll find supermarkets and a bank with **ATM**.

Further south, the western coastline is far less discovered. **SFINÁRI** is a sleepy village with a number of rooms to rent on the road down to a quiet beach,

## A round trip

If you have transport, a circular drive from Kastélli, via the west coast and back by the inland route through Élos and Topólia, makes for a stunningly scenic circuit. Near the sea, villages cling to the high mountainsides, apparently halted by some miracle in the midst of calamitous seaward slides. Around them, olives ripen on the terraced slopes, the sea glittering far below. Inland, especially at **ÉLOS**, the main crop is the chestnut, whose huge old trees shade the village streets.

South of **TOPÓLIA**, the chapel of Ayía Sofía is sheltered inside a cave which has been used as a shrine since Neolithic times. Between Élos and Topólia, a spectacular paved road continues through the high mountains towards Paleohóra. On a motorbike, with a sense of adventure and plenty of fuel, it's great: the bus doesn't come this way, villagers still stare at the sight of a tourist, and a host of small, seasonal streams cascades beside or under the asphalt.

sandy in patches. At the bottom are a couple of tavernas; try *Captain Fidias*, which offers free camping and sunloungers to clients.

**KÁMBOS** is similar, but even less visited, its beach a good hour's walk down a well-marked gorge path – a branch of the E4 – starting from the village square (or a very steep drive). **Accommodation** is available at *Rooms Hartzulakis* (☎28220 44445; ●) on the edge of the village, which also has a taverna with great views and details of local walking routes. Beyond them both is the **monastery of Khryssoskalítissa** (daily 8am–8pm, €2), increasingly visited by tours from Haniá and Paleohóra, but well worth the effort for its isolation.

Some 5km beyond Khryssoskalítissa, the tiny uninhabited islet of **Elafonísi** lies marooned on the edge of a gloriously scenic turquoise lagoon that shares its name. It's all too easy to get here, a fact reflected in the huge number of visitors who do, by car, with coach tours, or on a boat from Paleohóra. The pinky-white sand, the warm, clear lagoon and the islet to which you can easily wade still look magnificent, but you certainly won't have them to yourself. There are a number of stalls selling cold drinks and basic food, while 1km or so up the road are a couple of taverna/rooms places – *Elafonisi* (☎28220 61274; ●) is the best of them, with its own excellent taverna that uses many home-grown ingredients. Perhaps the best option, though, is to bring your own supplies and picnic on the beach.

## Paleohóra

The easiest route to the far southwest leaves the north coast at Tavronítis, 22km west of Haniá, heading for Paleohóra; several buses follow this route from Haniá every day, and although this road also has to wind through the western outriders of the White Mountains, it lacks the excitement of the alternatives to either side. **KÁNDANOS**, at the 58-kilometre mark, has been entirely rebuilt since it was destroyed by the Germans for its fierce resistance to their occupation. The original sign erected when the deed was done is preserved on the war memorial in the central square: "Here stood Kándanos, destroyed in retribution for the murder of 25 German soldiers, and never to be rebuilt again." The pleasantly easy-going and once-again substantial village had the last laugh.

When the beach at **PALEOHÓRA** finally appears below, it is a welcome sight. The little town is built across the base of a peninsula, its harbour and a beach known as Pebble Beach on the eastern side, the wide sands (Sandy Beach) on the west. Above, on the outcrop, ruined Venetian ramparts stand sentinel. Though a resort of some size, Paleohóra remains thoroughly enjoyable, with a main street that closes to traffic in the evenings so diners can spill out of the restaurants, and with a pleasantly chaotic social life. When you tire of beach life there are plenty of alternative entertainments, from dolphin-watching trips to excursions into the hills to Azoyirés, or a five-to-six-hour hike along the coastal path to Soúyia.

### Information and orientation

You'll find the helpful **tourist office** (Mon & Wed–Sun 10am–1pm & 6–9pm; ℡ 28230 41507) in a cabin on Pebble Beach, close to the ferry harbour. They have full accommodation lists and provide a map which is useful for finding food and accommodation locations.

When the tourist office is closed, try Notos Travel (℡ 28230 42110), on Venizélou, a friendly source of information on almost everything to do in Paleohóra, from renting apartments, cars and bikes to local walks. There are plenty of other travel agents along and around central Odhós Venizélos, and almost everything else you're likely to need is located nearby. **Banks** (with ATMs), a **laundry**, **mountain-bike** and **car-rental** companies and **internet** access (at Er@to Cafe or Notos Travel) are all along Venizélou, while the **post office** is on the road behind Sandy Beach. There are three **pharmacies** on Kontekáki (the road running from east to west at the south end of Venizélou) and there's a **health centre** in the street parallel to Venizélos to the west.

**Boats** run from Paleohóra to Elafoníssi and along the coast to Soúyia and Ayía Rouméli; they also run to the island of **Gávdhos**, some 50km south (see p.303). Notos Travel and E-Motion (℡ 28230 41755), by the ferry dock, sell tickets for all boats. They also have information about other trips – to walk the **Samariá Gorge**, for example, although you can also do that independently by catching the bus leaving daily at 6am throughout the summer, and a boat back from Ayía Rouméli.

### Accommodation

There are hundreds of **places to stay** in Paleohóra, though not always many vacancies in high season. There's also a fair-sized **campsite**, *Camping Paleohora* (℡ 28230 41120), 2km north of Pebble Beach.

**Castello Rooms** Overlooking the southern end of Sandy Beach ℡ 28230 41143. Exceptionally friendly place, most of whose simple rooms have balconies overlooking the beach; if yours doesn't, you can enjoy the view from the excellent café. The alleys behind here, beneath the castle, have many more simple rooms places. ❷
**Homestay Anonymous** Backstreet off Odhós Venizélos, near the centre of town ℡ 28230 42098, ⓦ www.cityofpaleochora.gr. Among the least expensive places in town, and something of a travellers' meeting place, with simple, en-suite rooms around a courtyard garden and a very friendly atmosphere. ❶
**Sandy Beach Hotel** Seafront at the southern end of Sandy Beach ℡ 28230 42138. The town's chicest hotel option, its a/c balcony rooms equipped with fridge, TV and sea view. ❸

**Scorpios** North end of Pebble Beach ℡ 28230 41058, ⓦ www.scorpios-rooms.gr. One of many rooms options behind Pebble Beach; comfortable, balcony rooms, most with sea views, and quieter than most thanks to a position near the end of the beach. ❷
**The Third Eye** Backstreet behind south end of Sandy Beach ℡ 28230 41234, ⓦ www.thethirdeye -paleochora.info. Inexpensive, no-frills rooms above Crete's best vegetarian restaurant. ❷
**Villa Marise** and **Europa Studios** Sandy Beach just north of the Post Office ℡ 28230 41162, ⓦ www.villamarise.com. One of the best locations in town, right on the sandy beach, for two neigh-bouring blocks that share a pool and have a variety of well-equipped rooms, apartments and studios for up to six people. ❸–❹

## Eating, drinking and nightlife

**Tavernas**, **bars** and **cafés** are liberally scattered throughout Paleohóra, particularly along the roads behind the two beaches. **Nightlife** is enjoyable, if tame – there are plenty of bars and even small clubs, but on the whole they reflect the local mood and keep the noise levels low. The greatest concentration of bars is around the junction of Kontekáki and Venizélou. Cine Attikon, tucked away in the northern backstreets, is a great little open-air **cinema**: most of their films are in English and programmes (which change daily) are posted outside the town hall and on fliers around town.

**Atoli** Southern end of Sandy Beach. Lively café-bar – a good spot to catch the sunset – that has occasional live music, both traditional and modern.

**Caravella** Overlooking the harbour. Paleohóra's flagship seafood restaurant: the cooking and service are outstanding, as is their chilled *hýma* (barrelled wine) from a vineyard in the Kastélli Kissámou area.

**Nostos** Pebble Beach by the tourist office. Open as a café and bar throughout the day, Nostos is also the liveliest late-night joint in town, with a chilled club atmosphere.

**Paleohora Club** Far north end of Pebble Beach close to the campsite. The one real dance place, far enough from town to be able to make some noise, though still fairly restrained and mainstream.

**Pizzeria Niki** Off the south side of Kontekáki. Good pizzas from a wood-fired oven, served in a pleasant courtyard.

**The Third Eye**, see p.301. The summer of love still lives at *The Third Eye*, where the excellent vegetarian food includes plenty of Asian spices and ingredients you won't find anywhere else on the island.

**The Wave** South end of Pebble Beach. Good fish and straightforward Greek dishes, served on a seaside terrace.

# Soúyia

It's a winding, spectacular and lonely drive from Paleohóra to **SOÚYIA**, which can also be approached directly from the north coast, or by boat. A small village slowly on its way to becoming a resort, Soúyia is not, in all honesty, a particularly attractive place. The exceptionally slow pace of life here does help it grow on you however, and there's an enormous swathe of bay with a long, grey pebble beach and sparkling water. At the far end of this bay most summers there's something of a nudist and camping community – known locally as the Bay of Pigs. Otherwise, sights are few – the local church has a sixth-century Byzantine mosaic as the foundation – but there are a couple of fabulous walks: down the beautiful **Ayía Iríni Gorge** or a wonderful hour-long hike over to the nearby ancient site of **Lissós** with temples and mosaics.

Surprisingly few facilities are on offer apart from food and accommodation – no fuel for example – though there is an ATM, a couple of minimarkets and the occasional organised excursion. **Rooms** are scattered around the road on the way in and along the seafront: the latter tend to be both pricier and noisier. There are links to many, and a handy map, at ⓦwww.sougia.info. One of the many places on the road as it comes into Soúyia is *Captain George* (ⓣ28230 51133 or 694 76 05 802; ❷), where there are some larger apartments, or the peaceful *El Greco*, set further back (ⓣ28230 51186; ❷); both offer balcony rooms with fridge and (some) kitchenette. Nearby, the newly built *Hotel Syia* (ⓣ28230 51174; ❹) has usurped the seafront *Hotel Santa Irene* (ⓣ28230 51342; ❸) as the fanciest place in town; its spacious *rooms* are more modern and more elegant, though it can't compete on location.

**Bus tickets** are sold at the beachfront booth opposite the *Hotel Santa Irene*, where you can also book taxis: there's an early morning bus to Omalós for the Samariá Gorge. **Ferries** depart from the little harbour at the west end of the bay, where a kiosk opens to sell tickets about ten minutes before departure. **Taxi boats** to local beaches (get one to bring you home from Lissós, for example) can be arranged through one of the minimarkets or at *Captain George*. For **food**, *Rembetiko* has a pleasant garden terrace just off the main street, while the seafront is packed with possibilities. The German-run *Omikron* taverna has a more northern-European ambience and offers some vegetarian choices; *Café Lotos* provides **internet** access.

## Gávdhos

The island of **GÁVDHOS**, some 50km of rough sea south of Paleohóra, is the most southerly land mass in Europe. Gávdhos is small (about 10km by 7km) and barren, but it has one major attraction: the enduring **isolation** which its inaccessible position has helped preserve. Still in the infancy of tourist development, Gávdhos remains truly remote except in August, when thousands of Greek visitors descend. Things are changing, with newly asphalted roads heading out from an enlarged harbour and an electricity plant under construction, but for the moment, if all you want is a beach to yourself and a taverna to grill your fish, this remains the place for you. Most people who come here still camp out by the beach so, although the season is getting longer – July and September are also increasingly busy – it is still usually possible to turn up on spec and find a bed. Travel agents in Paleohóra (see p.301) or Hóra Sfakíon (p.298) will arrange a room if you want one and also provide current ferry information. There's a semi-permanent community of campers and would-be "Robinson Crusoes" resident on the island year-round, swelling to thousands in August – but just six indigenous families.

Largely because water is often difficult to obtain, most people choose to base themselves near to one of the three largest beaches; at the most popular of all, **SARAKÍNIKO**, there's a slew of beachfront tavernas in addition to a squatters' community spreading a shanty town of unsightly breezeblock summer dwellings behind the beach. For **rooms** *Taverna Gerti & Manolis* (☎28230 41103; ❷) is reliable, while *Sarakiniko Studios* (☎28230 42182, ⓦ www.gavdostudios.gr; B&B; ❸) is a step upmarket. The latter's proprietors will collect you from the harbour and they have a **campsite** for pitching tents. Good **places to eat** at Sarakíniko include *Gerti & Manolis* (as above) for fresh fish and *Karapistolas* for Middle Eastern specialities, while the friendly *Sorolop* has a pleasant "community" feel, with people hanging around to play chess or Scrabble after eating. At **Áyios Ioánnis**, one of the other beach settlements 2km to the northwest (where's there's a thriving hippy and nudist community), a solitary, unnamed taverna is also an excellent place for fresh fish. The third choice is pebbly **Kórfos**, south of the port and capital at Karabé. *Yioryios and Maria's* (☎28230 42166, ⓦ www.gavdos-online.com; B&B; ❸) is an excellent taverna with comfortable rooms. Although many people still bring as much food as they can with them on the boat, there are now well-stocked **minimarkets** at Sarakíniko and Áyios Ioánnis.

Check **ferries** in advance, as the schedules have changed in recent years, and be aware that in bad weather the ferry will not go at all – in winter you could potentially be stranded for some time. The summer timetable currently sees departures from Paleohóra at 8am on Monday and Tuesday, and from Hóra Sfakíon at 11.30am on Friday and Sunday, with an additional Saturday service in July and August. At Karabé, beaten-up local buses head north towards Sarakíniko and south to Kórfos, or if you've booked a room you'll probably be met by a pick-up.

# Travel details

## Buses

The following are the main routes only showing the frequency of weekday services; weekend services will be less frequent. For the latest timetables and complete route and fare information for the island, visit ⓦ www.bus-service-crete-ktel.com.

**Áyios Nikólaos** to: Eloúnda (20 daily; 20min); Iráklion (at least 20 daily, 6 via Iráklion Airport 6.15am–9.30pm; 1hr 30min); Kritsá (9 daily 6am–8.15pm; 20min); Lasíthi plateau (2 daily; 2hr); Pláka (7 daily 6am–7pm; 30min); Sitía (7 daily 6.15am–8.30pm; 1hr 45min).

**Haniá** to: Elafonísi (daily at 9am; 3hr); Falásarna (3 daily 8.30am–3.30pm; 1hr 30min); Frangokástello (daily at 2pm; 2hr 30min); Hóra Sfakíon (3 daily 8.30am–2pm; 2hr); Iráklion via Réthymnon (16 daily 5.30am–9pm; 3hr); Kastélli (14 daily 6.30am–9pm; 1hr); Omalós (Samariá Gorge; 4 daily 6.15am–2pm; 1hr); Paleohóra (4 daily 5am–4pm; 1hr 30min); Soúyia (2 daily 5am & 1.45pm; 2hr); Stavrós (5 daily 6.50am–8.15pm; 30min).

**Iráklion** to: Ayía Galíni (7 daily 6.30am–4.30pm; 2hr 15min); Áyios Nikólaos (26 daily 6.30am–9.30pm; 1hr 30min); Haniá (16 daily 5.30am–9pm; 3hr); Mátala (5 daily 7.30am–3.30pm; 2hr 30min); Anóyia (5 daily 6.30am–4.30pm); Phaestos (8 daily 7.30am–4.30pm; 1hr 30min); Ierápetra (8 daily 6.45am–7.30pm; 2hr 30min).

**Kastélli** to: Haniá (14 daily 6.30am–9.30pm; 1hr 15min).

**Réthymnon** to: Arkádhi monastery (3 daily; 40min); Ayía Galíni via Spíli (5 daily 5.30am–2.15pm; 45min–1hr 30min); Haniá (16 daily 7am–10.30pm; 1hr 30min–3hr); Iráklion (18 daily 6.30am–10.15pm; 1hr 30min–2hr); Plakiás (6 daily 6.15am–7.30pm; 50min).

## Ferries

For the latest timetables for domestic and international ferries to and from Crete visit

ⓦ www.cretetravel.com, ⓦ www.ferries.gr or www.greekislands.gr.

**Áyios Nikólaos and Sitía** 2–3 sailings a week to Pireás (12–15hr); 2–3 ferries a week to Kássos (4hr), Kárpathos (6hr), Hálki (9hr 30min) and Rhodes (11hr); 2–3 weekly to Mílos (8hr).

**Haniá** Daily overnight to Pireás (8hr 30min), extra daytime sailing in July and Aug.

**Hóra Sfakíon** 5 ferries daily to Loutró/Ayía Rouméli (1hr/2hr 30min); 3–4 weekly to Gávdhos (1hr 30min) in season.

**Iráklion** 2 ferries daily to Pireás (9hr); 1 daily fast catamaran to Thíra (2hr), also fast boats and hydrofoils (2hr 30min); 4–5 weekly ferries to Páros, Mýkonos, Íos and Náxos in season; twice weekly to Tínos & weekly to Skíathos.

**Kastélli** Weekly (8am Thurs) to Andikýthira (2hr) Kýthira (4hr) and Yíthio (8hr).

**Paleohóra** 2–3 boats a week in season to Gávdhos. Also daily sailings to Elafoníssi and Soúyia/Ayía Rouméli.

**Réthymnon** Daily ferries to Pireás (10hr) currently suspended see; seasonal day-trips to Thíra.

**South Coast** Summer: 3 daily Hóra Sfakíon, Loutró, Ayía Rouméli; 1 daily Paleohóra, Soúyia, Ayía Rouméli; 2/3 weekly Hóra Sfakíon to Gávdhos; 2 weekly Paleohóra to Gávdhos.

## Flights

**Haniá** to: Athens (5 daily on Olympic; 4 daily on Aegean; 50min); Thessaloníki (1 daily on Olympic, 3 weekly on Aegean; 1hr 30min).

**Iráklion** to: Athens (12 daily with Olympic and Aegean; 50min); Rhodes (at least 2 daily on Olympic and Sky Express; 1hr); Thessaloníki (at least 2 daily on Olympic, Aegean or Sky Express; 1hr 15min).

**Sitía** to: Alexandhroúpoli in Thrace (3 weekly on Olympic); Athens (3 weekly on Olympic); Préveza in northwest Greece (3 weekly on Olympic).

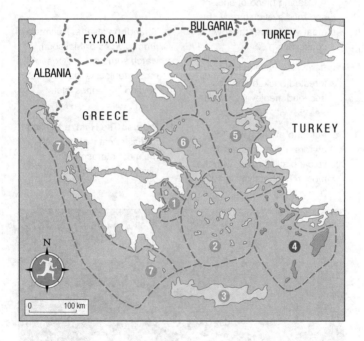

# 4

# The Dodecanese

# CHAPTER 4

# Highlights

* **Northern Kárpathos** Old walking trails take you between isolated villages. See p.318

* **Ródhos Old Town** Superbly preserved medieval streets, inextricably linked with the Knights of Saint John. See p.324

* **Lindos Acropolis, Rhodes** A pleasing blend of ancient and medieval culture, with great views over the town and coast. See p.334

* **Sými** Hike or bike the forested backcountry to frescoed medieval chapels. See pp.353–354

* **Volcano at Níssyros** The craters of the dormant volcano still hiccup, with the most recent activity in 1933. See p.364

* **Brós Thermá, Kós** Relax in shoreline hot springs, which flow into the sea, protected by a boulder ring. See p.373

* **Hóra, Astypálea** The windswept island capital, wrapped around a beautiful Venetian *kástro*, perches dramatically above the sea. See p.379

* **Télendhos straits, Kálymnos** From Myrtiés or Massoúri, watch some of the Aegean's most fabulous sunsets beyond Télendhos islet. See p.388

* **Pátmos** The Hóra, a fortified monastery at its heart, is the most atmospheric village in this archipelago. See p.399

▲ Hóra of Astypálea

# The Dodecanese

T he furthest island group from the Greek mainland, the Dodecanese (Dhodhekánisos) lie against the Turkish coast – some almost within hailing distance of Anatolia. Because of their position en route to the Middle East, these islands – too rich and strategic to be ignored, but never powerful enough to rule themselves – have had a turbulent history. They were the scene of ferocious battles between German and British forces in 1943–44 – the Germans held several islands until May 1945 – and were only finally included in the modern Greek state in 1948 after centuries of rule by Crusaders, Ottomans and Italians. Although relations between Greece and Turkey are currently at their best ever, the Greek military retains numerous military bases and watch-points, which proliferated after the 1996 crisis over the disputed double islet of Ímia.

Whatever the rigours of the various occupations, their legacy includes a wonderful blend of **architectural styles** and **cultures**; almost every island has Classical remains, a Crusaders' castle, a clutch of vernacular villages and whimsical or grandiose public buildings. For these last the Italians, who held the Dodecanese from 1912 to 1943, are responsible. Determined to turn them into a showplace for Fascism, they undertook ambitious public works, excavations and reconstruction; if historical accuracy was often sacrificed on the altar of visual propaganda, only an expert is apt to complain. A more sinister aspect of the Italian administration was attempted forcible Latinization of the populace: the Greek language and Orthodox religious observance were banned in progressively stricter phases between the mid-1920s and 1936. The most tangible reminder of this policy is the (rapidly dwindling) number of older people who can still converse – and write – as fluently in Italian as in Greek.

The islands themselves display a marked topographic and economic schizo-phrenia. The dry limestone outcrops of **Kastellórizo**, **Sými**, **Hálki**, **Kássos** and **Kálymnos** always relied on the sea for their livelihoods, and the wealth generated by maritime culture – especially during the nineteenth century – engendered attractive port towns. The relatively fertile giants **Rhodes** (Ródhos) and **Kós** have recently seen their traditional agricultural economies almost totally displaced by a tourist industry focused on good beaches and nightlife, as well as some of the more compelling monuments in the Aegean. **Kárpathos** is more variegated, its forested north grafted onto a rocky limestone south; **Tílos**, despite its lack of trees, has ample water, though the green volcano-island of **Níssyros** does not. **Léros** shelters softer contours and more amenable terrain than its map outline would suggest, while **Pátmos** and

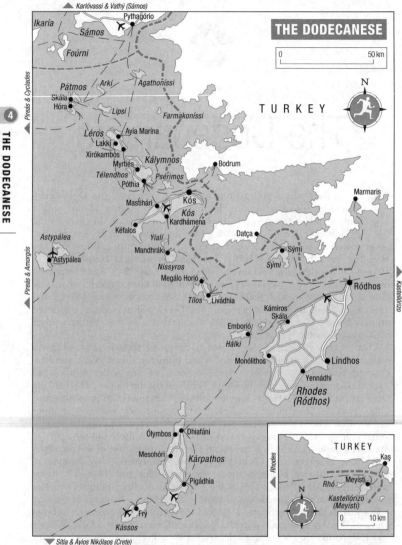

THE DODECANESE

**Astypálea** at the fringes of the archipelago offer architecture and landscapes more reminiscent of the Cyclades.

The largest islands in the group are connected by regular ferries and catamarans, as well as flights; only Kastellórizo and Tílos are relatively difficult to reach. Rhodes is the main **transport** hub, with connections for Crete, the northeastern Aegean, the Cyclades and the mainland too. Kálymnos, with a useful small ferry based there, is an important secondary terminus, as is Kós, endpoint of a useful hydrofoil service. Two local catamarans, mostly based on Rhodes (but occasionally overnighting on Pátmos or Léros), conveniently supplement larger ferries calling at uncivil hours.

# Kássos

Like Psará in the northeast Aegean, **Kássos** contributed its large fleet to the Greek revolution, and suffered appalling consequences. In May 1824, an Ottoman fleet sent by Egyptian governor Ibrahim Pasha besieged the island; on June 7, aided perhaps by a traitor fingering the weak point in Kássos's defences, the invaders descended on the populated north-coastal plain, slaughtered most of the 11,000 inhabitants and put houses, farms and trees to the torch.

Barren and depopulated ever since, Kássos attracts few visitors, despite air links with Rhodes and Kárpathos, and being a stop on ferry lines from those isles to Crete. Sheer gorges slash through lunar terrain relieved only by fenced small-holdings of midget-olive trees; spring grain crops briefly soften usually fallow terraces, and livestock somehow survives on a thin furze of scrub. The remaining population occupies five **villages** facing Kárpathos, leaving most of the island uninhabited and uncultivated, with crumbling old houses poignantly recalling better days.

Especially after the 1824 events, Kassiots distinguished themselves as skilled pilots, and the sailing tradition endures; you might see a *kaïki* fetching the largely Kassiot crew from a passing freighter for a three-hour "home furlough". Ironically, in view of Ibrahim Pasha's origins, islanders were also instrumental in digging the Suez Canal, and there was for decades a substantial Kassiot community in Port Said. These days, evidence of emigration to the USA abounds: American-logo T-shirts and baseball caps are *de rigueur* in summer, and the conversation of vacationing expatriates is spiked with east-coast American-isms. That said, island pride is strong, traditions are preserved and summer festivals are authentic.

Kássos arrival can be tricky, since in extreme wind conditions, **ferries** can't dock at Frý (pronounced "free"). In such cases, you disembark at Kárpathos and fly the remaining distance in a 38-seater aircraft, or use one of the Finíki (Kárpathos)-based excursion *kaïkia* which can manoeuvre into Boúka port in most weathers. The **airport** lies 1km west of Frý, an easy enough walk, otherwise a cheap ride in one of the island's three taxis. Except from June to September – when a single **scooter/quad rental** outfit (☎22450 41746 or 697 79 98 676) operates, a Mercedes van provides a regular bus service, and boat excursions are offered – the only way to explore Kássos is on foot. Place-name signposting is in Greek only, and in Kassiot dialect at that – clearly nobody's expecting many non-Kassiot-diaspora visitors, though tourist facilities have improved greatly in recent years.

## Frý

Most of the capital **FRÝ's** appeal is confined to the wedge-shaped **Boúka** fishing port, protected by two crab-claws of breakwater and overlooked by Áyios Spyrídhon cathedral. Inland, Frý is engagingly unpretentious, even down-at-heel in spots; there are few concessions to tourism, though some attempts have been made to prettify a scruffy little town that's quite desolate out of season. Ignore the obvious, shabby central hotel in favour of better-value, quieter, remoter **accommodation** such as basic, seaside *Flisvos* (☎22450 41284; ❷), 150m east of the new harbour, with shared kitchen; *Captain's House* (☎22450 41801, ✉hpetros@otenet.gr; ❹), galleried trad-style studios above Kassian Travel, near the police station; *Angelica's* overlooking Boúka (☎22450 41268, ⓦwww.angelicas.gr; ❹), four apartments in a converted mansion; or, best of all, ⚡ *Evita Village*, 200m uphill from Emboriós suburb (☎22450 41731,

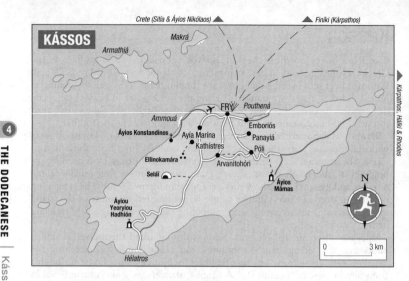

Crete (Sitía & Áyios Nikólaos)

Finíki (Kárpathos)

**KÁSSOS**

Makrá

Armathiá

Ammouá

FRÝ  Pouthená

Áyios Konstandínos

Ayía Marína

Kathístres

Emboriós

Panayiá

Póli

Ellinokamára

Arvanitohóri

Selái

Áyios
Mámas

Áyiou
Yeoryíou
Hadhíon

N

0    3 km

Hélatros

Kárpathos, Háiki & Rhodes

ⓦ www.evita-village.gr; ❹), a complex of impeccable, 2007-built studios. There
are two stand-alone **ATMs**, a **post office** plus a wi-fi/ADSL **internet** café,
*ACS*, nearby.

Outside of peak season, Frý supports just one full-service **taverna**: *O Mylos*,
overlooking the ferry port; luckily it's excellent, with *mayireftá* at lunch and
grills by night. During summer, tavernas at Boúka include *Iy Orea Bouka* for
Kassiot dishes and lamb specialists *To Koutouki*, while *Emborios* on the
eponymous cove can sometimes match *Mylos* for quality and value. Several bar-
kafenía-ouzerí perched above Boúka are the focus of low-key **nightlife**.

### Local beaches

Frý's **town beach** is at **Ammouá**, a thirty-minute walk beyond the airstrip
along the coastal track. This sandy cove, just before Áyios Konstandínos chapel,
is often caked with seaweed and tar, but persevere five minutes more and you'll
find cleaner pea-gravel coves. The determined swim off the little patch of sand
at **Emboriós**, fifteen minutes from Frý, along with the resident ducks; there's
a more private pebble stretch off to the right. But having got this far, continue
ten minutes along the shore, first along an old track, then on a path past the
last house, for a final scramble to the base of the **Pouthená ravine**, where
there's another secluded pebble cove. In high season, boats sail to far better
beaches on two islets visible to the northwest, **Armáthia** and **Makrá**.
Armáthia has five white-sand beaches to choose from (Mármara the most
famous, and best sheltered), while Makrá has just one large cove. Armáthia was
inhabited until the 1960s but now there are no amenities on either islet, so
bring all you need.

## The villages and Áyios Mámas

At the edges of the agricultural plain inland from Frý cluster several villages,
linked to each other by road; all can be toured on foot in a single day. Larger
and yet more rural than Frý, **AYÍA MARÍNA**, 1500m inland and uphill, is
most attractive seen from the south, arrayed above olive groves; its two belfried
churches are the focus of the island's liveliest **festivals**, on July 16–17 and

September 13–14. Fifteen minutes beyond the hamlet of **Kathístres**, a further 500m southwest, the cave of **Ellinokamára** has a late Classical, polygonal wall blocking the entrance; its ancient function is uncertain, perhaps a cult shrine or tomb complex. To reach it, turn south at the two restored windmills in Ayía Marína, then right (west) at the phone-box junction; carry on, straight and down (not level and left) until you see a red-dirt path going up to a crude, stone-built pastoral hut. Some modern masonry walls enclose the start of this path, but once at the hut (the cave is more or less underneath it) you're compelled to hop a fence to visit – there are no gates. From the first turn on the Hélatros-bound road, another, fainter path continues to the larger, more natural cave of **Seláï**, with impressive stalactites in the rear chamber.

Generally Kássos **walking trails** are limited and unmarked, with no shade and few reliable water sources. An exception is the forty-minute path from the village of **Arvanitohóri to Póli**, which is clearly walled in and enjoyable, shortcutting the road effectively – it starts at the base of the village, where two trees occupy planter-wells. **PÓLI**, impoverished and agricultural, has a badly deteriorated ancient and medieval acropolis – a few stretches of fortification remain – and marks the start of a four-kilometre paved road southeast to **Áyios Mámas**, signposted as "Áï Mámas", one of two important rural monasteries (with the island's oldest church), perched spectacularly overlooking the sea. Alternatively, from Póli you can descend – again on a walled-in path for the first twenty minutes, then track – to **PANAYÍA**, famous for its now-neglected sea-captains' mansions and for eighteenth-century **Panayía toú Yióryi**, focus of an August 14–15 festival rivalling Ayía Marína's. Nearby stands an intriguing Siamese-sextuplet chapel complex, logically enough called **Éxi Ekklisíes** (Six Churches), originally built to expel female sprites haunting the place.

## Ayíou Yeoryíou Hadhión and Hélatros

Between Ayía Marína and Arvanitohóri, another paved road veers southwest towards the rural monastery of **Ayíou Yeoryíou Hadhión**. There's not much joy to be had in walking this, so take a taxi, rent a scooter or hitch a lift in at least one direction. The start of the route skirts a dramatic gorge, beyond which you're unlikely to see another living thing aside from goats, sheep or an occasional Eleonora's falcon. Soon the Mediterranean appears; when you reach a fork, take the upper, right-hand turning, following phone lines and signs for "Áï Yeóryi", 12km from Frý. Cistern water is always available in the monastery grounds, which really only come to life around the April 23 festival.

From the monastery it's another 2.5km on paved road to **Hélatros**, a lonely cove at the mouth of one of the larger, more forbidding Kassiot canyons. Only the right-hand 80m of this sand-and-pea-gravel beach is usable, but the water is pristine and – except for the occasional fishing boat or yacht – you'll be alone outside July/August. The lower, left-hand option at the fork is the direct, dirt-surface track to Hélatros; this is only 700m shorter but perfectly passable by scooter, and varies the return to town.

# Kárpathos

A long, narrow island between Rhodes and Crete, wild **Kárpathos** has always been an underpopulated backwater, although it's the third largest of the Dodecanese. A habitually cloud-capped **mountainous spine** rises to over

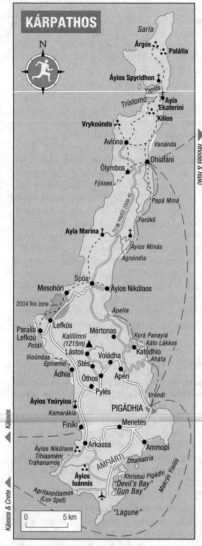

1200m, dividing the lower-lying south from an exceptionally rugged north. A magnificent, windswept **coastline** of cliffs and promontories attracts numerous package tourists, who pretty well monopolize several resorts in the southern part of the island, pushing independent travellers up to the remote **north**, where facilities are basic. Most visitors come for a glimpse of the far north's traditional village life, and for various secluded **beaches** lapped by proverbial crystalline water. Taverna **prices** (in the south anyway) have, however, soared to beyond-Rhodes levels, offsetting reasonable room rates.

Kárpathos's **interior** isn't always that alluring: the central and northern forests have been scorched by repeated fires, while agriculture plays a slighter role than on any other Greek island of this size. The Karpathians are too well off to engage in much farming; emigration to North America and the resulting remittances have transformed the island into one of Greece's wealthiest parts.

Although the Minoans and Mycenaeans established trading posts on what they called Krapathos, the island's four Classical cities figure little in ancient **history**. Kárpathos was held by the Genoese and Venetians after the Byzantine collapse and so has no castle of the Knights of St John, nor any surviving medieval fortresses of note. The Ottomans never bothered to settle or even garrison it properly; instead they just installed a civil governor, charging the Greek population plus a few scattered Muslim gendarmes with his safety during the many pirate attacks.

## Pigádhia (Kárpathos Town)

The island capital of **PIGÁDHIA** (or Kárpathos) nestles at the south end of scenic **Vróndi Bay**, whose sickle of sand extends 3km northwest. The town itself, curling around the quay and jetty where ferries and excursion boats dock, is as drab as its setting is beautiful; an ever-growing number of concrete blocks leaves the impression of a vast construction site, making the Italian-era port police and county-government buildings heirlooms by comparison. While there's nothing special to see, Pigádhia does offer most conceivable facilities,

albeit with a package-tourism slant. The name of the main commercial street –
Apodhímon Karpathíon ("Karpathians Overseas") – speaks volumes about the
pivotal role of emigrants and emigration here. Another local quirk is a conspicuous community of several hundred **Egyptians** from the Damietta area, who
have two coffee-houses to themselves (but as yet no mosque), and are locally
esteemed as masons, fishermen and carpenters.

### Arrival, information and accommodation

The principal **travel agent** is Possi Travel (☎22450 22235) on the front, selling
air tickets plus passages on all boats. The **post office** is on Ethnikís Andístasis
up from Platía 5-Oktovríou; there are several bank **ATMs**. *Café Galileo* (all
year), on Apodhímon Karpathíon, offers **internet** and wi-fi access; it's very
lively at night with windsurfers and locals.

Most **ferries** are met by people offering self-catering **studios**. Unless you've
booked in advance, you might consider such offers – the best location is the
hillside above the bus terminal and central car park. More comfortable places lie
north, behind Vróndi beach either side of the ruined fifth-century basilica of Ayía
Fotiní, but tend to be occupied by package clients. Better hillside premises
include *Amarillis Studios* (☎22450 22375, ✉johnvolada@in.gr; ❸), with enormous,

## Getting around Kárpathos

Regular **buses** serve Pylés, via Apérí, Voládha and Óthos, as well as Ammopí,
Menetés, Arkássa, Finíki and (less frequently) Mesohóri via Paralía Lefkoú and Kyrá
Panayía; the Pigádhia "station" is a car park at the western edge of town, beyond the
post office. Set-rate, unmetered **taxis** have a terminal two blocks inland from the
fountain along Dhimokratías (table of current fares posted).

A dozen outfits **rent cars**, though in season you may have to try every one to find
an available vehicle, and rates are well over the norm. Tried-and-true agencies
include Circle (☎22450 22690) near the post office; Avis (☎22450 22702), at the
north edge of town; Drive/Budget (☎22450 23873), 2km out behind Vróndi beach;
The Best, near *Sunrise Hotel* (☎22450 23655); and Billy's (☎22450 22921). You can
save €30 return in taxi transfers by renting a car from and to the **airport** (17km away)
which should be arranged in advance, though a new enlarged terminal (open 2009)
may include staffed car-hire booths. Moto Carpathos (☎22450 22382), at the west
edge of town, and Euromoto (☎22450 23238) have the largest fleet of **scooters**.
Tanks on smaller scooters are barely big enough to permit a circuit of the south, let
alone heading north beyond Spóa; the only **fuel** on Kárpathos is obtained from two
pairs of stations just to the north and south of town. The Spóa–Ólymbos road has
been regraded to allow passage of ordinary cars, and should be paved some time in
2009. **Jeeps** are only really necessary to reach a few remote beaches served by
atrocious tracks.

Despite road improvements, reaching northern Kárpathos by **boat** is still an attractive option. The excursion boat *Chrisovalandou III* offers all-in day-tours to Dhiafáni
and Ólymbos for €23 maximum (pay on board); you can use this boat to travel one-
way (1hr 20min–1hr 30min) between the north and the south in either direction (€10).
Some seasons a second craft offers competing service. Departures are typically
8.30am northbound, 4–4.30pm southbound. There's also Captain Andoni's tiny mail
*kaïki Chrisovalandou I*, which reverses this pattern: southbound from Dhiafáni Mon,
Wed, Thurs at 8am, northbound from Pigádhia same days at 3pm (EU subsidized fare
€3; 1hr). On Thurs eve or Fri am, weather depending, the same craft goes down to
Pigádhia for €10, returning Sun evening for the same fare. You can of course use the
mainline ferries between the two ports for about €6. Various agencies also offer trips
to isolated east coast beaches, which may not include lunch.

air-conditioned units, and the helpful *Elias Rooms* (☎22450 22446 or 697 85 87 924, ⓦwww.eliasrooms.com; ❸; May–Sept) just above the *Hotel Karpathos*, with variable, mostly en-suite rooms in a converted older house. Up an alley beyond Avis at the start of Vróndi, *Paradise Studios* (☎22450 22949; ❸) offers seven simple but practical, good sized air-conditioned studios in a quiet, aesthetic orchard setting. The only comfortable hotel catering to independent travellers is helpful *Atlantis*, opposite the Italian "palace" (☎22450 22777, ⓦwww .atlantishotelkarpathos.gr; B&B ❹).

### Eating, drinking and nightlife

Many Pigádhia-waterfront **tavernas**, where tacky photo-menus and defrosted *yíros* and chips reign supreme, are undistinguished and overpriced; quality and value improve significantly as you head east towards the ferry dock. Near the end of the strip stand characterful *Anna*, good for fair-priced, non-farmed fish with heaped salads; and next door the best all-rounder, *Iy Orea Karpathos*, with palatable local bulk wine, *trahanádhes* soup, spicy sausages, marinated artichokes and great spinach pie – locals use it as an ouzerí, ordering just *mezédhes*. There's competition from *To Spitikon*, the first place in from the seafront fountain, with a large range of salads, island specialities and *mayireftá*, though portion sizes are erratic. Also a block inland, *Mezedhopolio To Ellinikon* (all year) caters to a local clientele with hot and cold *orektiká*, meat and good desserts. If *yíros* and chips it must be, then the best place for the fresh kind, own-sourced, is *Ovelistirio tis Erasmias*, opposite the taxi rank. *Enigma* offers background **music** from a perch overlooking the bay, while *Oxygen* is the most durable indoor midnight-to-dawn **dance club**.

## Southern and western Kárpathos

The southern extremity of Kárpathos, near the airport, is flattish, desolate and windswept. There are a few undeveloped sandy beaches along the southeast coast in **Amfiárti** district, but most are only attractive to foreign **windsurfers** who take advantage of the prevailing northwesterlies, especially during the annual summer European championships. The most established surf school here is Pro Center Kárpathos (☎22450 91063 or 697 78 86 289, ⓦwww .Chris-Schill.com), which has the advantage of three separate bays near the airport, catering to different ability levels; smaller, more personal Soultravels (☎694 29 42 090, ⓦwww.soultravels.ch) occupies an adjacent cove.

Non-surfers will be more interested in sheltered, sand-and-gravel **Khristoú Pigádhi beach**, just over 2km north of the airport, with a 500-metre access road, a *kantína* and a nudist annexe just south. Beyond the headland bounding Khristoú Pigádhi to the north, with a separate 900-metre access drive, stretches **Dhamatría beach**, sandier but more exposed. Here, up the slope, you'll find the peaceful *Hotel Poseidon* (☎22450 91066; B&B ❸), with a full-service taverna.

Most people go no further than **AMMOPÍ** (alias "Amoopi"), 7km south of Pigádhia, the biggest of Kárpathos's purpose-built resorts. Three sand-and-gravel, tree- or cliff-fringed coves are fringed by half a dozen tavernas and rather more **hotels** and studios. The quietest of these are the well-designed ⚘ *Vardes Studios* (☎22450 81111 or 697 21 52 901, ⓦwww.hotelvardes.com; ❸), with distant sea views, an orchard setting and house fruit and jam at breakfast. Among **tavernas**, best is *Esperida*, about halfway along the approach road, coping efficiently with crowds scoffing local cheese, wine and sausage, roast aubergine, and pickled wild vegetables.

West out of Pigádhia the road climbs steeply 9km to **MENETÉS**, draped in the lee of a ridge, with some handsome old houses and a spectacularly sited – if hideous – church. The most distinctive local **taverna**, east beyond the World War II resistance monument memorial, is 🍴 *Pelayia* (all year) in Kritháres district, offering local marinated "sardines" (really the larger *ménoula*), cheese, wild greens and live music some nights.

### Arkássa, Finíki and Ádhia

Beyond Menetés, you descend to **ARKÁSSA**, on the slopes of a ravine, with excellent views to Kássos en route. A few hundred metres south of where the ravine meets the sea, a signposted cement side-road leads briefly to the white-washed chapel of **Ayía Sofía**. Remains of a much larger, surrounding Byzantine basilica feature several mosaic floors with geometric patterns; the best one's inside a vaulted cistern at one corner. The Paleókastro headland beyond was the site of Mycenaean Arkessia; the walk up is scarcely worth it for the sake of a few stretches of polygonal wall and a couple of tumbled columns.

Despite just one good nearby beach, Arkássa has been heavily developed, with **hotels** and often mediocre **tavernas** aimed at the package tour market sprouting along the rocky coastline. Independent travellers could try **Áyios Nikólaos beach**, a rare 100-metre stretch of sand signposted just south. Here you'll find *Montemar Studios* (☎22450 61394; ❹) with units in two grades, and – right behind the beach – the *Glaros* (☎22450 61015, ✉mikefrangos @hotmail.com; ❹), with five studios and an attached **taverna**, run by returned Karpathian-Virginians. Beyond Áyios Nikólaos, the road dwindles to dirt track as it passes remote, sandy **Tihiasméni** and **Trahanamós** beaches en route to **Cape Áyios Theódhoros**, over 6km from Arkássa, with its eponymous little monastery and difficult-to-reach cove.

The tiny fishing port of **FINÍKI**, 2km north, offers a minuscule beach and four weekly excursions in season to Kássos. Comfortable **accommodation** is provided by well-designed and -built *Arhontiko Studios* on the main bypass road (☎22450 61473, ⓦwww.hotelarhontiko.com; ❸). Best of three port **tavernas** is locally attended *Marina* (all year), good for fish.

Some 7km north of Finíki along the coast road, Karpathian forest resumes at **ÁDHIA** hamlet, where the appropriately named *Pine Tree Restaurant* offers home-baked bread, lentil soup and octopus *makaronádha* (plus other *mayireftá*) washed down by sweet Óthos wine. They also have **accommodation** overlooking the orchard and the sea (☎697 73 69 948, ⓦwww.pinetreerestaurantkarpathos.cjb .net; ❷). Easy paths lead twenty minutes west to tiny **Epínemo beach** (and 10min further to larger **Ilioúndas**), while a meatier **hike** up the **Flaskiá gorge** towards Mt Kallílímni starts from the main-road bridge (signposted for Lastós; 2hr 20min one-way).

### Paralía Lefkoú and Mesohóri

Dense forest continues much of the way to the turning for the attractive resort of **PARALÍA LEFKOÚ**. Three **car-rental** outfits – Lefkos (☎22450 71057), Hot Wheels (☎22450 71085) and Drive (☎22450 71415) – make this a feasible touring base, when you're not flopped on one of the three local beaches (**Yialoú Horáfi**, **Panayiás tó Limáni** and **Frangolimniónas**) separated by a striking topography of cliffs, islets and sandspits. Badly crumbled medieval fortifications separate the two northerly bays, and indeed the whole area is archeologically protected. The most impressive monument, well signposted inland off the northerly access road, is the "**Roman cistern**" (free, unenclosed), actually a catacomb complex.

There are more than two dozen places to stay, and perhaps half as many tavernas, but package companies monopolize the better **accommodation** from June to September. About the only exception is spartan *Sunweek Studios* (☎22450 71025; ❷), on the promontory dividing Yialoú Horáfi from Panayiás tó Limáni. You'll have better luck at **Potáli**, the stonier fourth bay just south of the access road; here go for quiet and spacious *Akrogiali Studios* (☎22450 71263; ❸), with balconies overlooking the beach, or the smaller *Lefkosia Studios* near the road (☎22450 71176 or 22450 71148; ❸). **Tavernas** at Yialoú Horáfi can disappoint: the best options are *Mihalis* at the base of the promontory, with vegetarian platters, or the kindly *Blue Sea* with its pizzas, meaty *mayireftá* and pancake breakfasts.

Back on the main road, you climb northeast through fire-wrecked pine forest to **MESOHÓRI**. The village tumbles seaward along narrow, stepped alleys, coming to a halt at the edge of a bluff dotted with three tiny, ancient chapels, separated from the village proper by extensive orchards. These are nurtured by the fountain (the best water on the island) beneath the church of **Panayía Vryssianí**, wedged against the mountainside just east. On the stair-street leading to this is a good, reasonably priced **taverna**, the *Dhramoundana*, featuring local capers, sausages and the local marinated "sardines". The paved main road continues over the island's watershed to Spóa, overlooking the east coast.

## Central Kárpathos

**Central Kárpathos** supports a group of villages blessed with commanding hillside settings, ample running water and a cool climate, even in August. Nearly everyone here has "done time" in North America – number plates on expensive imported gas-guzzlers tell you exactly where – before returning home with their nest eggs; the area has the highest per capita income in Greece. West-facing **PYLÉS** is the most attractive, set above another spring-fed oasis, while **ÓTHOS**, noted for its bread, sausages and sweet, tawny-amber wine, is the highest (around 400m) and chilliest, on the flanks of 1215-metre Mount Kalilímni.

Northeast of Óthos, at the high point of the road, a paved side-turning leads towards **Kalilímni summit**; after 4.6km, bear left off the pavement (right goes to the air force relay station) and continue 1km on a dirt track to *Iy Kali Kardhia/O Thanassis* **taverna/rooms** (☎697 24 67 688; ❶), the sole local amenity. Only on this fertile, poplar-studded upland (850m elevation) does a pastoral and agricultural life just hang on, away from beach tourism; reserve a meal or even a bed with Thanassis and make a day of it by **climbing the peak** (3hr return).

Downhill and east of Óthos nestles **VOLÁDHA**, with its tiny Venetian citadel and two nocturnal tavernas. From the smart track-and-soccer stadium below **APÉRI**, the largest, lowest and wealthiest settlement, a paved five-kilometre road leads to **Aháta** pebble beach (shower and a pricey taverna), 150m of pebbles flanked by dramatic palisades.

Beyond Apéri, the road up the **east coast** passes above more **beaches** often visited by boat trips from Pigádhia. A paved, twisty side road via Katódhio hamlet leads first to a further turning (2km of rough, steep dirt track; jeep required) to **Káto Lákkos**, 150m of scenic sand and gravel favoured by naturists, and then after 4km on the main pavement to **Kyrá Panayiá**. Numerous villas and rooms huddle in the ravine behind 150m of fine gravel and sheltered, turquoise water; the beach taverna is, alas, mediocre. **Ápella** is the best of the beaches you can reach by road, though there's a final short path from the single, good-value *Apella Beach Taverna Studios* (☎697 24 23 741; ❸) to the scenic 300-metre gravel strand, with another naturist cove a scramble southeast. The route ends at **SPÓA**, high above the shore just east of the island's spine, with a snack-bar and *kafenío* at the edge of the village, which might make better meal stops than the overpriced taverna down at **Áyios Nikólaos**, 5km below, with an average beach.

## Northern Kárpathos

Although it's now far easier to reach **northern Kárpathos** from Spóa, arrival **by sea** is the cheapest option without a hire car, as taxis remain exorbitant (about €100 from the airport). Main-line ferries call at Dhiafáni at least twice weekly in season, while foot passengers can use the smaller boat services from **Pigádhia** (see box, p.313). Excursion-boat arrivals are met at Dhiafáni for an eight-kilometre bus transfer up to traditional **Ólymbos** village, the main local attraction along with good walking opportunities. The paving of the road in from Spóa will, however, sharply curtail the day-trip industry, and should encourage a more thoughtful type of tourism. If you can't tear yourself away from the sea, coastal **Dhiafáni** makes a better base, with excellent beaches to either side.

### Ólymbos

Founded as a pirate-safe refuge during Byzantine times, windswept **ÓLYMBOS** straddles a long ridge below slopes studded with ruined windmills. Two restored ones, beyond the main church, grind wheat and barley in late summer only, though one is kept under sail during any tourist season. The village has long attracted foreign and Greek ethnologists for **traditional dress**, **crafts**, **dialect and music** long since vanished elsewhere in Greece – and dwindling by the year here too. Nowadays it's only older women and those working in several tourist shops who wear striking, colourful apparel – while assiduously flogging trinkets mostly imported from China, India or Bulgaria. Women play a prominent role in daily rural life: tending gardens, carrying goods on their shoulders or herding goats. Nearly all Ólymbos men historically emigrated to Baltimore or work outside the village, sending money home and returning only on holidays. (In recent years, this pattern has begun shifting as many women and children go to Rhodes, Pireás or further afield for a decent education, with the menfolk staying in northern Kárpathos, working.) The long-isolated villagers speak a unique dialect, said to maintain traces of its Doric and Phrygian origins – "Ólymbos" is pronounced "Élymbos" locally. Many houses are decorated with legendary and historical themes executed in relief plaster, mostly the work of **Vassilis Hatzivassilis** (1918–2005), also an accomplished naïve painter; a **museum** (daily 10am–4pm; €3) in one of his decorated houses displays most of his portable works. Live folk music is still played regularly, especially at festival times (Easter and Aug 15), when visitors have little hope of finding a bed.

The best **accommodation** in Ólymbos is ☂ *Anemos* (☎693 28 58 901 or Gabriella on ☎22450 51509, ⓦwww.geocities.com/escape2olympos/; ❸), a traditional house past the church divided into studios with knockout views. Honourable mentions go to friendly *Rooms Olymbos* (☎22450 51009; ❷), near the village entrance, which has modern units with baths and unplumbed ones with traditional furnishings (and an excellent, inexpensive, home-cooking ☂ **restaurant**), plus the en-suite *Hotel Astro* (☎22450 51421 or 697 37 69 522; B&B; ❸) managed by the two sisters who run *Café-Restaurant Zefiros*, where breakfast is taken. *Restaurant Olymbos* has an annexe at Ávlona, *Restaurant Avlona*, on the through road, featuring artichoke hearts with eggs in spring; with four en-suite rooms (☎694 60 18 521; ❷), it makes an ideal base for walkers. The local signature dish is *makaroúnes*, home-made pasta with onions and cheese. In spring, *myrgouátana*, a rock-dwelling marine invertebrate (tastier than it sounds), is served up breaded and sautéed as *mezédhes* in Ólymbos *kafenía*.

## Local hikes

From the village, the superb west coast beach at **Fýsses** is a sharp drop below, served by jeep track. Most local **hikes**, however, head more gently north or east on waymarked paths. Easiest is the ninety-minute walk back down to Dhiafáni, beginning just below the two working windmills. The way is well marked, with water en route twenty minutes along, eventually dropping to a ravine amid extensive forest, though the final half-hour is unfortunately bulldozed riverbed.

Another trail heads north via sparsely inhabited **AVLÓNA** (1hr 30min; population 10), set on a high upland devoted to grain, to the ruins and beach at **Vrykoúnda** ("Vrougoúnda" in dialect). From Avlóna it's just under an hour more descending moderately, then steeply, on an ancient, marked, walled-in path taking off from the valley-floor track. Your destination offers traces of Hellenistic/Roman *brykous* – mostly masonry courses and rock-cut tombs – the remote cave-shrine of John the Baptist on the promontory (focus of a major Aug 28–29 festival) and good swimming at pebble coves to one side.

**Trístomo**, a Byzantine anchorage in the far northeast of Kárpathos, can also be reached (2hr 30min) on a magnificent cobbled way beginning above Avlóna via the abandoned agricultural hamlets of Ahordhéa and Kílios. The views en route, and the path itself, are the thing, as Trístomo itself is dreary, with no special attractions or facilities – not even a beach – and just one eccentric elderly couple in residence. Rather than retrace your steps, you can hook up, via a shortish link trail east from Trístomo, with a spectacular **coastal path back to Vanánda** (3hr 30min); once clear of abandoned agricultural valleys and over a pine-tufted pass, it's often a corniche route through the trees, with distant glimpses of Dhiafáni and no real challenge except at the steep rock-stairs known as Xylóskala.

From **Avlóna**, there's also a fine marked path directly down to **Vanánda** (1hr 20min); take a dirt track southeast past the remote church of Áyios Ioánnis to find the true trailhead. The route, partly on *kalderími*, shuns another jeep track heading directly to Dhiafáni in favour of a trail east through a secluded, lushly vegetated valley draining to Vanánda (see below), with the occasional palm tree (and May orchids) lending an exotic touch.

### Dhiafáni and beaches

The pace of life in **DHIAFÁNI** is slow outside high summer; the only "attraction" is a small **monk seal information office** inland from the quay. Seasonal boat trips are offered to remoter local **beaches**, as well as to uninhabited **Saría islet** (typically Wed or Thurs, 10am out, 4.30pm back; €28 with lunch; Captain Andoni's subsidized *kaïki* on Tues is much cheaper at €6 return); passengers hike the trans-island path to the Byzantine site of Palátia with its odd domed structures, below which you swim and have barbecued lunch before returning. The closest cove is stony **Vanánda**; follow the pleasant signposted path north through the pines for thirty minutes, shortcutting the more recent road. Naturist **Papá Miná**, with a few trees and cliff-shade, lies an hour's walk distant via the cairned trail taking off from the road to the ferry dock. An ordinary car can drive most of the 4.3km there, with the last 300m on foot;

with more caution you can get a car to 250-metre long, naturist **Forókli** (5.5km below the Spóa–Ólymbos road). But you really need a jeep to reach **Áyios Minás** (seasonal taverna; bear left at fork partway along) or equally pristine **Agnóndia** (bear right).

You can buy ferry tickets and change money at the small **travel agency** (there's no ATM); a few hotels now accept credit cards. Dhiafáni has abundant sleeping and eating opportunities, though aggressive touts on the quay are worth ignoring. In terms of **accommodation**, top of the heap in all senses is hospitable George and Anna Niotis's *Hotel Studios Glaros* (T22450 51501 or 694 79 44 601, Wwww.hotel-glaros.gr; ❸) up the south slope, with sixteen huge, tiered units, some sleeping four. Worthy alternatives, 300m along the road west more or less opposite each other, are the pleasant, ground-floor *Dolphins/ Dhelfinia Studios* (T22450 51354; ❷) under the eponymous restaurant, or the air-conditioned *Hotel Nikos* (T22450 51410, Wwww.nikoshotel.gr; ❷). Among **tavernas**, *Dolphins/Dhelfinia* does good fish, and vegetables from the garden below, while vine-shrouded, backstreet *Iy Anixi* offers no touting, not much spoken English and a few inexpensive, homestyle *mayireftá* daily. Behind the seafront fountain, favourite meeting places are Italian-run 🍴 *Iy Gorgona* (Wwww.gorgonakarpathos.it), featuring light dishes, wonderful desserts, proper coffees and *limoncello* digestif, and 🍴 *Korali* (*Mihalis & Popi's*) across the lane, which serves good grills, fish, salads and Cretan *tsikoudhiá*, and doubles as the liveliest **nightspot**.

# Rhodes (Ródhos)

It's no surprise that **Rhodes** is among the most visited Greek islands. Not only is its southeast coast adorned with numerous sandy **beaches**, but the capital's nucleus is a beautiful **medieval city**, legacy of the crusading Knights of St John, who used the island as their main base from 1309 until 1522. This showpiece can be jampacked with over a million tourists in a good season, booked into often luxurious digs, versus about 120,000 permanent inhabitants (including thousands of foreigners).

Ródhos Town's medieval **Old Town** is very much the main event, followed by **Líndhos**, with its ancient acropolis and (off-seasonally) atmospheric village. The southeastern **beaches** – particularly around **Afándou**, **Kálathos** and **Yennádhi** – and isolated monuments of the partly forested interior, such as castles near **Monólithos** and **Kritinía**, and frescoed churches at **Thárri**, **Asklipió** and **Áyios Yeóryios Várdhas**, are also worth pointing a car towards. The far south cape, **Prassoníssi**, is one of the best windsurfing spots in Europe.

## Some history

Blessed with an equable climate and strategic position, Rhodes was important from earliest times despite a lack of good harbours. The best natural port served the ancient town of **Lindos** which, together with the other Dorian city-states **Kameiros** and **Ialyssos**, united in 408 BC to found a new capital, **Rodos** (Rhodes), at the windswept northern tip of the island. The cities allied themselves with Alexander, the Persians, Athenians or Spartans as conditions suited them, generally escaping retribution for backing the wrong side by a combination of seafaring audacity, sycophancy and burgeoning wealth as a trade centre. Following the failed siege of Macedonian general Demetrios Polyorketes in 305 BC, Rhodes prospered even further, displacing Athens as the major venue for rhetoric and the arts in the east Mediterranean.

Decline set in when the island became involved in the Roman civil wars and was sacked by Cassius; by late imperial times, it was a backwater, and victim of numerous barbarian raids during the Byzantine period. The Byzantines ceded Rhodes to the Genoese, who (after a three-year resistance) in turn surrendered it to the Knights of St John. The second great siege of Rhodes, during 1522–23, saw Ottoman Sultan Süleyman the Magnificent oust the stubborn knights; Rhodes once again lapsed into relative obscurity, though heavily colonized and garrisoned, until its seizure by the Italians in 1912.

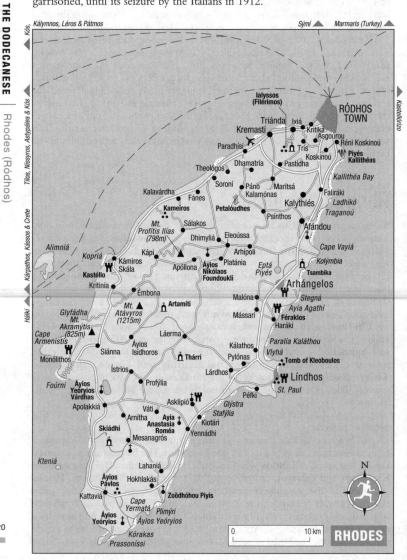

▲ Rhodes's medieval old town

## Arrival, information and transport

All international and inter-island **ferries and catamarans** dock at the middle of Ródhos Town's three ports, **Kolóna harbour**; excursion craft, the *Sea Star* and *Symi II* catamarans and **hydrofoils** use the yacht harbour of **Mandhráki**. Its entrance was supposedly once straddled by the Colossus, an ancient statue of Apollo commemorating the end of the 305 BC siege; today two columns (one currently removed for refurbishment) topped by bronze deer serve as replacements.

The **airport** lies 14km southwest of town, right by Paradhísi village; the new **north terminal** is for international departures only, the adjacent **south terminal** still handles all arrivals and domestic departures. There's a **bus** stopping outside between the two terminals (turn left out of arrivals; into town frequently 6.30am–midnight; €2.20), probably a better bet than a **taxi** (midnight blue, white on top) into town, which should cost €16–23, depending on your exact destination and on time of day. Rhodian taxi drivers have a poor reputation – overcharging of new arrivals is routine, as is refusing to take you to your chosen hotel, while steering you to accommodation giving them kickbacks; most won't enter the Old Town either. Other **buses** for the west and east coasts leave from adjacent terminals on Avérof just outside the Italian-built New Market (a tourist trap, eminently missable except for the wonderful rotunda of the old fish market inside).

All non-resident **traffic** is supposedly banned within the medieval walls, though barriers at each gate are currently unstaffed and unenforced. **Parking** anywhere near the Old Town is a challenge; the closest most will get is along Filellínon, between the Ayíou Athanasíou and Koskinoú gates. Neohóri, the northern extension of the New Town, is a nightmare, with just about everywhere subject to **pay-and-display** during business hours (Mon–Sat 9am–2.30pm & 5–9pm; minimum tariff €1.50). If you don't see a ticket machine and blue markings, or a "P Free/*Eléfthero*" sign, it's probably a residents-only zone – traffic police are industrious, and fines steep. You can sometimes find **unmetered** parking spots near the Casino, between Elli Ronda and Evangelismós basilica (white markings), or around Ekatón Hourmadhiés/"100 Palms" (officially Platía Gavriél Harítou).

Near the taxi rank at Platía Rimínis there's a **municipal tourist office** (June–Sept Mon–Sat 8am–9.30pm, Sun 9am–3pm), while some way up Papágou on the corner of Makaríou the **EOT office** (Mon–Fri 8.30am–2.45pm) dispenses bus and ferry schedules, plus a list of standard taxi fares, complete with complaint form (see warning on p.321).

## Ródhos Town

**Ancient Rodos**, which lies beneath most of the modern city, was laid out during the fifth century BC by Hippodamos of Miletos in the grid layout then in vogue, with planned residential and commercial quarters. Its perimeter walls totalled almost 15km, enclosing nearly double the area of the present town, and the Hellenistic population was over 100,000 – a staggering figure for late antiquity, as against 50,631 at the 2001 census.

The contemporary town divides into two unequal parts: the compact walled **Old Town**, and the **New Town**, which sprawls around it in three directions. The latter dates from the Ottoman occupation, when Greek Orthodox residents – forbidden to dwell in the old city – founded several suburb villages or *marásia*, long since merged. Commercialization is predictably rampant in the walled town, and in the modern district of **Neohóri** ("Niohóri" in dialect), west of Mandhráki yacht harbour: a sprawl of mostly elderly hotels, souvenir shops, designer outlets, mediocre restaurants, car rental or travel agencies and bars – easily thirty in every category.

### Accommodation

**Hotels and pensions** at all price levels abound in the Old Town; there are also some attractive, more modern possibilities in Neohóri. During busy seasons, or late at night, it's prudent to **reserve** well in advance – only the worst unlicensed accommodation is touted by desperate proprietors at the ferry and catamaran quays.

### Old Town

**Andreas** Omírou 28D ☎22410 34156, ⓦwww.hotelandreas.com. This perennially popular (reservations mandatory) spot with switched-on, international management is one of the more imaginative old-Turkish-mansion restoration-pensions. Rooms with a/c (including family-size and a spectacular "penthouse") all have dedicated baths, though some are down a corridor. Terrace bar with free wi-fi signal and views for excellent breakfasts (extra) and evening drinks; two-night minimum stay. Open all year. ❸

**Apollo Tourist House** Omírou 28C ☎22410 32003, ⓦwww.apollo-touristhouse.com. Five unique wood-trimmed, pastel-hued en-suite doubles, with raised bed platforms and central

heating; best is the galleried north-facing one. Congenial English management. April–Oct; winter by arrangement. ❹

**Avalon** Háritos 9 ☎22410 31438, ⓦwww.avalonrhodes.gr. Converted in 2007, this fourteenth-century manor house offers six unique luxury suites (some quads, four with fireplaces) with plasma TV and internet. Breakfast in your unit or down in the vaulted bar. Rack rates are nutty – €350–500 – but internet specials or booking through the recommended agent (see p.332) makes it more affordable. Open all year.

**Marco Polo Mansion** Ayíou Fanouríou 42 ☎22410 25562, ⓦwww.marcopolomansion.gr. Superb conversion of another old Turkish mansion, with a *hamam* on site; all rooms are en

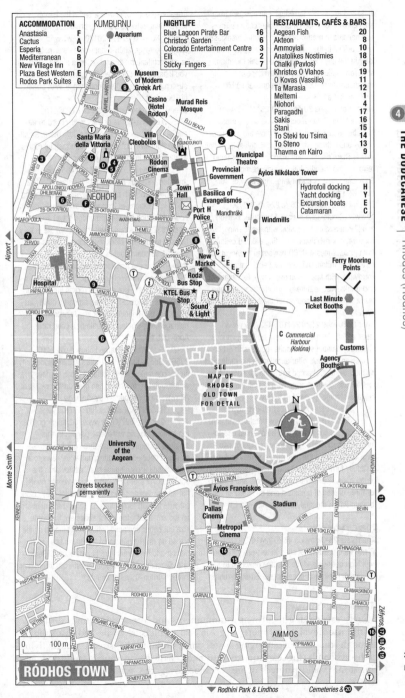

**ACCOMMODATION**

| | |
|---|---|
| Anastasia | F |
| Cactus | A |
| Esperia | C |
| Mediterranean | B |
| New Village Inn | D |
| Plaza Best Western | E |
| Rodos Park Suites | G |

**NIGHTLIFE**

| | |
|---|---|
| Blue Lagoon Pirate Bar | 16 |
| Christos' Garden | 6 |
| Colorado Entertainment Centre | 3 |
| Elli | 2 |
| Sticky Fingers | 7 |

**RESTAURANTS, CAFÉS & BARS**

| | |
|---|---|
| Aegean Fish | 20 |
| Akteon | 8 |
| Ammoyiali | 10 |
| Anatolikes Nostimies | 18 |
| Chalki (Pavlos) | 5 |
| Khristos O Vlahos | 19 |
| O Kovas (Vassilis) | 11 |
| Ta Marasia | 12 |
| Meltemi | 1 |
| Niohori | 4 |
| Paragadhi | 17 |
| Sakis | 16 |
| Stani | 15 |
| To Steki tou Tsima | 14 |
| To Steno | 13 |
| Thavma en Kairo | 9 |

| | |
|---|---|
| Hydrofoil docking | H |
| Yacht docking | Y |
| Excursion boats | E |
| Catamaran | C |

KUMBURNU

Aquarium

Museum of Modern Greek Art

Casino (Hotel Rodon)

Murad Reis Mosque

Santa Maria della Vittoria

Villa Cleobolus

Rodon Cinema

Municipal Theatre

Provincial Government

Áyios Nikólaos Tower

NEOHORI

Town Hall

Basilica of Evangelismós

Port Police

Mandhráki

Windmills

Hospital

New Market

Roda Bus Stop

KTEL Bus Stop

Sound & Light

Ferry Mooring Points

Last Minute Ticket Booths

Commercial Harbour (Kolóna)

Customs

Agency Booths

SEE MAP OF RHODES OLD TOWN FOR DETAIL

N

University of the Aegean

Áyios Frangískos

Streets blocked permanently

Stadium

Pallas Cinema

Metropol Cinema

AMMOS

0    100 m

**RÓDHOS TOWN**

Airport

Monte Smith

Zéfyros

Rodhíni Park & Líndhos

Cemeteries & 20

suite and exquisitely furnished with antiques from the nearby eponymous gallery, plus cotton pillows and handmade mattresses. Large buffet breakfasts are provided in the garden snack bar, open to all later in the day (see p.329). One-week minimum stay, reservations and credit card deposit mandatory. April–Oct. Garden rooms are a bit cheaper, but all ⑤.

**Niki's** Sofokléous 39 ☎22410 25115, ⓦwww .nikishotel.gr. Some rooms can be on the small side, but all are en suite, most have a/c, and upper-storey ones (three with private balconies) have fine views. There's a washing machine, two common terraces and friendly, helpful management. Someone will wait up for late-night arrivals. All year. B&B ③

**Nikos Takis** Panetíou 26 ☎22410 70773, ⓦwww.nikostakishotel.com. Miniature "fashion hotel" in a restored mansion with just seven somewhat garish units (including painted ceilings), from junior suites with CD players to "honeymoon" suites with fridge, DVD and TV. Pebble-mosaic courtyard, with fine views over town, for breakfast and drinks. Also features a ground-floor boutique featuring the haute couture of the two designer owners. ⑦

**Spot** Perikléous 21 ☎22410 34737, ⓦwww .spothotelrhodes.gr. In a modern building, various cheerfully painted a/c en-suite rooms with art or textiles on the walls offer excellent value (unlimited buffet breakfast, charged extra, in rear patio). Also roof terrace, internet area, wi-fi signal and free luggage storage. Open March–Nov. ③

🏃 **Via-Via** Lysipoú 2, alley off Pythagóra ☎22410 77027, ⓦwww.hotel-via-via.com. Efficiently but congenially run hotel; most one-to-four-person rooms, all a/c, are en suite but two have baths across the hall. All are simply and tastefully furnished with bedding and throw rugs in pastel hues. Roof terrace with pergola and divans for three grades of breakfast and an eyeful of the Ibrahim Pasha mosque opposite. All year. ④

## Neohóri

**Anastasia** 28-Oktovríou 46 ☎22410 28007, ⓦwww.anastasia-hotel.com. Italian-era mansion with high ceilings and tiled floors converted to a congenial, family-run guest house. En-suite rooms

are simple but a/c; there's a bar in the garden, with its resident tortoises. All year; breakfast extra. ③

**Cactus** Kó 14 ☎22410 26100, ⓦwww .cactus-hotel.gr. 2006-redone three-star hotel of some architectural distinction, with a pool – though you'll hardly need it as you're opposite the best stretch of Élli beach. Very good value, with buffet breakfast, at ⑤.

**Esperia** Yeoryíou Gríva 7 ☎22410 23941, ⓦwww.esperia-hotels.gr. Very well-priced three-star in a quiet spot overlooking a little plaza. Small-to-medium size, but salubrious and tasteful rooms with showers in the baths. All year. ④

**Mediterranean** Kó 35 ☎22410 24661, ⓦwww .mediterranean.gr. Beachfront four-star hotel in a prime location, with phased renovations beginning 2009; less expensive than you'd think, especially if booked through the recommended travel agent (see p.332). The street-level snack-bar/café is very popular around the clock with non-residents. All year, ⑥ standard double, ⑧.

**New Village Inn** Konstandopédhos 10 ☎22410 34937, ⓦwww.newvillageinn.gr. Whitewashed, somewhat grotto-like en-suite rooms (upper-floor units have balconies), arrayed around a courtyard breakfast-bar. Friendly Greek and American management; singles available at a good rate. April–Oct. ③

**Plaza Best Western** Ierou Lóhou 7 ☎22410 22501. One of the better 4-stars within Rhodes city limits, convenient for Mandhráki. Pool, garden, sauna, Jacuzzi, buffet English breakfast, restaurant. All year; good discounts Nov–April. ⑥

🏃 **Rodos Park Suites** Ríga Fereoú 12 ☎22410 89700, ⓦwww.rodospark.gr. The top-ranked lodging within the city limits, this smallish boutique hotel has three grades of standard doubles and suites, half with views to a quiet hillsite archeological site, half towards the pool area. All share the same wood-veneer floors, flat-screen TVs and cool blue-and-steel-grey colour scheme for soft furnishings; doubles' balconies are on the small side, the junior suites are the same size but better equipped, while the standard suites are 40 sq m. The basement "wellness spa" and two on-site restaurants are big attractions. Rack rate ⑦ rooms, ⑧ suites, but substantial internet or through-Triton-Travel discounts.

## The Old Town

Merely cataloguing its principal monuments and attractions cannot do justice to the **medieval city**. There's a great deal of pleasure to be had just slipping through the eleven surviving gates and strolling the streets under flying archways built for earthquake resistance, past warm-toned sandstone and limestone walls painted ochre or blue, over the *votsalotó* (pebble-mosaic)

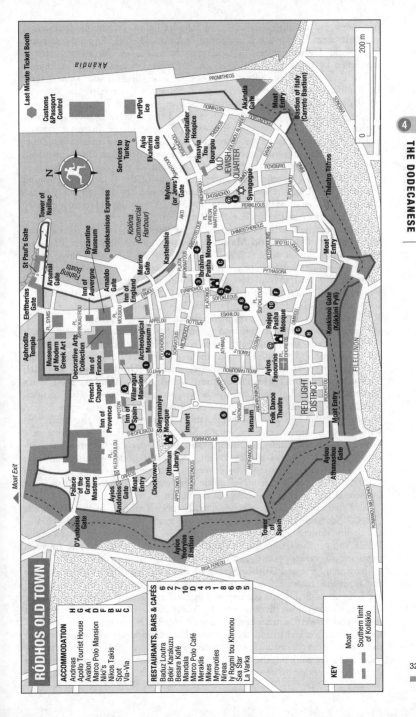

# RÓDHOS OLD TOWN

**ACCOMMODATION**

| | |
|---|---|
| Andreas | H |
| Apollo Tourist House | G |
| Avalon | A |
| Marco Polo Mansion | D |
| Niki's | F |
| Nikos Takis | B |
| Spot | E |
| Via-Via | C |

**RESTAURANTS, BARS & CAFÉS**

| | |
|---|---|
| Baduz Loutra | 6 |
| Bekir Karakuzu | 2 |
| Besara Kafé | 7 |
| Mandala | 10 |
| Marco Polo Café | D |
| Meraklis | 4 |
| Mikes | 3 |
| Myrovolies | 1 |
| Nireas | 8 |
| Iy Rogmi tou Khronou | 6 |
| Sea Star | 9 |
| La Varka | 5 |

**KEY**

Moat

Southern limit
of Kollákio

200 m

0

*Akándia*

*Moat Exit*

Last Minute Ticket Booth

Customs
&Passport
Control

PortPolice

N

pavements. As a walled medieval city, Rhodes invites favourable comparison with Jerusalem, Dubrovnik, Carcassonne or Ávila, and UNESCO has designated it a World Heritage Site. All structural alterations are (in theory) strictly controlled by the archeological service, but unlike its rivals, this old town is essentially a large village: vibrant (or "noisy", depending on your values), dirty or bombed out in spots, bristling with obtrusive TV aerials, and with an emphatically "lived-in" feel away from the tourist zones.

The Knights of St John frequently adhered to the city's classical grid-plan: Pythagóra, Omírou, Sokrátous and Ayíou Fanouríou are important streets exactly following ancient predecessors. The foundations of ancient buildings, well below present ground level, are on view everywhere. The Ottomans added little to the urban fabric other than a handful of purpose-built mosques, minarets and the graceful clocktower just south of the Palace of the Grand Masters. Though not of strategic importance, the old city suffered heavy bomb damage at the hands of the Allies from 1943 to 1945 owing to German military installations in the adjacent commercial harbour.

Dominating the northernmost sector of the fourteenth-century fortifications is the **Palace of the Grand Masters** (summer Mon 12.30–7.10pm, Tues–Sun 8am–7.10pm; winter Mon 12.30–2.40pm, Tues–Sun 8.30am–2.40pm; €6, or €10 for a joint ticket for all museums in this section). Destroyed by an 1856, lightning-triggered ammunition depot explosion, it was reconstructed by the Italians as a summer home for Mussolini and Vittore Emmanuele III ("King of Italy and Albania, Emperor of Ethiopia") – neither of whom ever visited Rhodes. The exterior, based on medieval engravings and accounts, is passably authentic, but inside, free rein was given to Fascist delusions of grandeur: a marble staircase leads up to rooms paved with Hellenistic mosaics from Kós, and the clunky period furnishings rival many a northern European palace. The ground floor contains splendid galleries entitled **Rhodes from the 4th Century until the Turkish Conquest** and **Ancient Rhodes, 2400 Years** (same hours and admission), jointly the best museums in town. The medieval collection highlights the importance of Christian Rhodes as a trade centre, placing the island in a trans-Mediterranean context. The Knights are represented with a display on their sugar-refining industry and a gravestone of a Grand Master; precious manuscripts and books precede a wing of post-Byzantine icons. Across the courtyard, "Ancient Rhodes" overshadows the official archeological museum by covering, thematically, everyday life around 250 BC; highlights include a Hellenistic floor mosaic of a comedic mask and a household idol of Hecate, goddess of the occult.

From stairs by the palace, there's sporadic **access** to part of the **city walls** (Tues & Sat 8am–11am; €2) as far as the Koskinoú gate, worth it for views of the skyline punctuated with minarets, palm trees and the brooding mass of the Palace. You can walk through **St Paul's Gate** and out to the Naillac Tower (a popular dusk vantage point), and traverse almost all of the grassy moat.

The heavily restored **Gothic Street of the Knights** (Odhós Ippotón) leads east from Platía Kleovoúlou in front of the palace; the "Inns" lining it lodged the Knights of St John, according to linguistic and ethnic affiliation, until the Ottoman Turks forced them to leave for Malta after a six-month siege in which the defenders were outnumbered thirty to one. Today the Inns house government offices, foreign consulates or cultural institutions vaguely appropriate to their past, with occasional exhibitions (especially in the fifteenth-century Villaragut Mansion), but the overall effect of the Italian renovation is sterile and stagey (indeed, nearby streets were used to film both *Pascali's Island* and more recently *El Greco*).

At the bottom of the hill, the Knights' Hospital has been refurbished as the **archeological museum** (summer Tues–Sun 8am–7.10pm, winter Tues–Sun 8.30am–2.40pm; €3 or joint ticket), though the arches and echoing halls of the building somewhat overshadow its contents – largely painted pottery dating from the ninth through the fifth centuries BC. Behind the second-storey sculpture garden, the Hellenistic statue gallery is less arcane; in a rear corner stands *Aphrodite Adioumene*, the so-called "Marine Venus", beloved of Lawrence Durrell but lent a rather sinister aspect by her sea-dissolved face – in contrast to the friendlier *Aphrodite Bathing*. Virtually next door is the **Decorative Arts Collection** (Tues–Sun 8.30am–2.40pm; €2 or joint ticket), gleaned from old houses across the Dodecanese; the most compelling artefacts are carved cupboard doors and chest lids painted with mythological or historical episodes.

Across the way stands the **Byzantine museum** (Tues–Sun 8.30am–2.40pm; €2 or joint ticket), housed in the old cathedral of the Knights, adapted from the Byzantine shrine of Panayía toú Kástrou. Medieval icons and frescoes lifted from crumbling chapels on Rhodes and Hálki, as well as photos of art still *in situ*, constitute the exhibits. Highlight of the permanent collection is a complete fresco cycle from the domes and squinches of Thárri monastery (see p.338) from 1624, removed in 1967 to reveal much older work beneath.

## Turkish and Jewish Rhodes

Heading south from the Palace of the Grand Masters, it's hard to miss the most conspicuous Turkish monument in Rhodes, the rust-coloured, candy-striped **Süleymaniye Mosque**. Rebuilt in the nineteenth century on foundations three hundred years older, it's currently shut like most local Ottoman monuments. The Old Town is in fact well sown with mosques and *mescids* (the Islamic equivalent of a chapel), many converted from Byzantine churches after the 1522 conquest, when the Christians were expelled from the medieval precinct. A few, such as the purpose-built (1531) **Ibrahim Pasha Mosque** on Plátonos, are still used by the sizeable Turkish-speaking minority here. Their most enduring civic contributions are, opposite the Süleymaniye, the **Ottoman Library** (Mon–Sat 9.30am–4pm; tip custodian), with a rich collection of early medieval manuscripts and Korans; an **imaret** (mess-hall) at Sokrátous 179, now an exceptionally pleasant café (*Palio Syssitio*), with temporary **exhibits** (Tues–Sat 10am–2pm; free) across the courtyard; and the imposing 1558 **Mustafa Hamam** (Turkish bath) on Platía Aríonos (Mon–Fri 10am–5pm, Sat 8am–5pm, last admission 4pm; €5). Bring everything you need – soap, shampoo, towel, loofah – to enjoy separate, *au naturel* men's and women's sections. Heading downhill from the Süleymaniye Mosque, you reach **Odhós Sokrátous**, since time immemorial the main commercial thoroughfare, and now the "Via Turista", packed with fur and jewellery stores pitched at cruise-ship tourists. Beyond the tiled central fountain in Platía Ippokrátous, Odhós Aristotélous leads to **Platía tón Evréon Martýron** ("Square of the Jewish Martyrs"), named in memory of the large local community almost totally annihilated during the summer of 1944; a black granite, multilingual column honours them. Of four synagogues that once graced the nearby Jewish quarter, only ornate, arcaded, pebble-floored **Kal Kadosh Shalom** (Mon–Fri & Sun 10am–3pm; donation) on Odhós Simíou, just to the south, survives. It's maintained essentially as another memorial to the approximately 2100 Jews of Rhodes and Kós sent to the concentration camps in July 1944; plaques in French commemorate the dead. To one side, a well-labelled, three-room **museum**, set up by a Los Angeles attorney of Jewish Rhodian descent, thematically chronicles the community's life on Rhodes (Ladino language, football clubs, change from oriental to Italian dress) and its far-flung diaspora in the Americas and Africa.

## Neohóri

**Kumburnú**, the pointy bit of **Neohóri**, is surrounded by a continuous beach (loungers, parasols and showers), particularly at **Élli**, the more sheltered east-facing section. Despite its proximity to the city, the water offshore is exceptionally clean owing to strong sweeping currents some fathoms down. At the northernmost point of the island, the **Aquarium** (daily: April–Sept 9am–8.30pm; Oct–March 9am–4.30pm; €5) offers displays on the history and function of the building, a monk seal buried as an ancient family's pet, a stuffed Cuvier's beaked whale and a subterranean maze of fish tanks (whose labels and tenants don't always match). Immediately south, on "100 Palms" Square, in the Nestorídhio Mélathro, is the **Museum of Modern Greek Art** (Tues–Sat 8am–2pm & Fri 5–8pm; €3), the most important collection of twentieth-century Greek painting outside Athens: all the heavy hitters – Hatzikyriakos-Ghikas, Spyros Vassiliou, Yiannis Tsarouhis, surrealist Nikos Engonopoulos, naïve artist Theophilos, neo-Byzantinist Fotis Kontoglou – are amply represented. Some of Kontoglou's greatest frescoes dating from 1951–61, can be found in the **Evangelismós basilica** at Mandhráki, in particular an *Annunciation* on the north wall, a *Virgin Platytéra* in the conch, and a psalmody on the south wall, from 1951–61. What used to be the main, cramped home of the museum, on Platía Sýmis 2 in the Old Town, is now the **annexe** (same hours, shared ticket), devoted to maps and prints, medieval watchtower and special exhibits. Both premises have excellent gift shops. East of "100 Palms", the Italian-built Albergo delle Rose has become the **Casino**, Greece's third largest (€15 24hr admission ticket; Mon–Thurs 3pm–6am, Fri noon–Mon 6am continuously; minimum age 23). Continue in the same direction to the 2008-refurbished **Murad Reis Mosque** and its atmospheric, eucalyptus-shaded Muslim cemetery, just past the **Villa Cleobolus** (really just a cottage), where Lawrence Durrell lived from 1945 to 1947.

About 2km southwest of Mandhráki, sparse, unenclosed remains of the **acropolis of Hellenistic Rhodes** – a restored theatre and stadium, plus three columns of a temple to **Apollo Pythios** – perch atop Monte Smith, the hill of Áyios Stéfanos renamed for a British admiral during the Napoleonic Wars. Other signposted reminders of the ancient city include the foundations of an **Aphrodite temple** in the old town's Platía Sýmis; gauging the distance between it and the acropolis gives you a fair idea of ancient Rhodes' vast extent.

## The cemeteries

The vast **municipal cemeteries** at Korakónero, just inland from Zéfyros beach 2km southeast of the centre, might not immediately strike one as a hot tourist destination, but if you have any interest in Rhodes' recent past, they prove strangely compelling. This is one of the very few remaining spots in the Balkans – certainly the only one in Greece – where the dead of four faiths lie in proximity, albeit separated by high walls. The easterly **Greek Orthodox section** is, of course, the largest and holds the fewest surprises. The small **Catholic section** is not only the last home of various north European expatriates, but also demonstrates that – contrary to received wisdom – a fair number of Italians elected to accept Greek nationality and stay on after the 1948 unification with Greece, and that a few native Greeks had renounced the Orthodox faith. There's also a massive Italian mausoleum at the rear, covering the years 1912–41, and another French one commemorating the victims of the cruiser

*Indien*, sunk near Kastellórizo in 1915. The **Jewish section** (Mon–Fri 8am–1pm) has, for reasons made clear on p.327, seen little activity since 1944, and is full of memorials in French to those who were deported. Immediately opposite its gate, across the busy road, is a small **Allied War graves** plot with 142 burials from 1941 to 1946, some moved here from inconvenient sites on other Dodecanese islands; there's admirable documentation and a guest register to sign by the gate. Just south of the Jewish section, the **"Muslim" section** (ie Turkish) is the most heavily used and best maintained of the three minority cemeteries.

## Eating and drinking

**Eating** well for a reasonable price in and around Ródhos Town is a challenge, but not an insurmountable one. As a general rule, the further south in the Old Town and (once outside it) towards Zéfyros beach you go, the better value you'll find. Unless otherwise stated, establishments operate year round.

### Old Town

**Mandala** Sofokléous 38. Part-Swedish-run, popular garden bistro-café doing generic Med-lite salads and pasta dishes; after hours it's more of a bar with good beer and occasional live acoustic music on Sat evening and Sun noon. Open 2pm–3am, from 7pm only low season; tables inside by the wood stove in winter.

**Marco Polo Café** Ayíou Fanouríou 42. What started as the breakfast venue for the eponymous hotel (see p.322) has become the sleeper hit of the Old Town. Traditional adapted recipes, adeptly blending subtle flavours, include pilaf with lamb and raisins, turnovers with *pastourmá*, and *psaronéfri* with *manoúri* cheese, fig and red peppercorn sauce. Excellent wine list and desserts of the day; last orders 11pm. April–Oct.

**O Meraklis** Aristotélous 30. One of the last Rhodian rough edges not yet filed smooth, this *pátsatzídhiko* (tripe-and-trotter-soup kitchen) caters for a pre-dawn clientele of clubbers from the Miltiádhou lanes, Turkish shopkeepers, gangsters and nightclub singers. Great free entertainment, including famously rude staff, and the soup's good, too: the traditional Greek working man's breakfast and hangover cure. Open 1–8am only, at its peak 3–4am.

**Mikes** (pronounced "mee-kess") Nameless alley behind Sokrátous 17. Inexpensive but salubrious hole-in-the-wall, serving only grilled fish, a few shellfish appetizers, salads and wine; outdoor tables, galley-like kitchen. Daily April–Nov.

**Myrovolies** Láhitos 19. Popular if pricey ouzerí featuring hearty pork and mushroom dishes, with patio and indoor seating. Live music three nights a week; budget €25–28 a head with a few drinks.

**Nireas** Sofokléous 22 ⓦ www.nireas-rhodes.gr. A kindly managing family, fair prices for the Old Town and atmospheric indoor/outdoor seating make this a good choice for a treat. Food is all-fresh fish and shellfish, with, unusually, a range of Italian desserts too. Around €70 for two including dessert and wine.

**Sea Star** Sofokléous 24. The least expensive quality seafood outlet after *Mikes* serves a limited but delicious menu of scaly fish, shellfish and *mezédhes* like *kápari* and salt-cured mackerel. Indoor seating in winter, otherwise outside on the little square.

**La Varka** Sofokléous 5. Hole-in-the-wall ouzerí with sought-after outside seating, plus a 2008-expanded interior for cooler months; good salads, *pikilíes* for 2 at €30, grilled *thrápsalo*, fried or salt-cured seafood titbits, cheapish ouzo and *soúma* by the carafe. Daily 11.30am–1am.

### Neohóri

**Akteon** Platía Eleftherías. Café in a graceful Italian building by the law courts; moderate prices for Rhodes, and great people-watching under the trees.

**Ammoyiali** Voríou Ipírou 17, cnr Kennedy. Probably the most visually stunning restaurant interior in town, Asian-themed (one of the owners is a Tai Chi professor), plus an airy terrace; the food – great preliminary nibbles, Med-fusion starters, meat and fish mains – nearly matches it. Allow €40–45 a head including the stiffly priced wine list. Dinner all year, lunch high season only.

**Chalki (Pavlos)** Kathopoúli 30. Ancient bottles of who-knows-what provide the decor in this little ouzerí doing good vegetarian *mezédhes* and a limited range of mains (including seafood), washed down by ouzo and CAIR wine. Average portions, but quite cheap. Evenings only.

**O Kovas (Vassilis)** Kolokotróni 66, 80m east of Kanadhá. Sympathetic, inexpensive canteen with a daily-changing menu of *mayireftá* goat stew with celery, *fáva*, baked *biftékia*, big salads and decent bulk wine. Busiest at lunch, when they run out of the best dishes by 2.30pm, and at night, with meat on the grill. Vine-shaded conservatory seating between the auto-repair shops.

**Ta Marasia** Platía Ayíou Ioánni 155. Ouzerí operating out of a 1923-vintage house, with plenty for vegetarians – aubergine *bourékia*, grilled oyster mushrooms, stuffed squash blossoms – plus seafood platters like urchins, *soupiá krasáta* and *rengosaláta*, or a full meat list, with decent bulk wine.

🏃 **Meltemi** Platía Koundourióti 8, Élli beach. Classy beachside ouzerí offering such delights as *karavidhópsyha* (crayfish nuggets), octopus croquettes, chunky hummus, and superb roast aubergine with beans and onions to a local crowd; pleasant winter salon inside. Open all day.

**Niohori** Ioánni Kazoúli 29, by the Franciscan monastery. Alias "Kiki's" after the jolly proprietress, this homely, inexpensive local is tops for meat grills, sourced from their own butcher/farm; shame about the prefab chips though. There's usually a cooked vegetable dish like okra for the salad-averse.

**Stani** Ayías Anastasías 28, cnr Paleón Patrón Yermanoú, out the Koskinoú Gate. Central outlet of a Rhodian Turkish confectioners' chain, scooping two dozen flavours of Rhodes' best ice cream – queues all day (until 1am) tell you this is the place.

**To Steki tou Tsima** Peloponnísou 22, around the corner from *Stani*. Seafood ouzerí, featuring titbits like *foúskes* (fresh marine invertebrates), *spiniálo* (a pickled version of same) and small fish not prone to farming. No airs or graces, just patently fresh ingredients. Mon–Sat evening and Sun noon.

🏃 **To Steno** Ayíon Anaryíron 29, 400m southwest of Ayíou Athanasíou Gate. Traditional "cult" taverna-ouzerí with indoor/outdoor seating by season, attracting a mix of locals, expats and some savvy tourists. The well-priced menu encompasses sausages, *pitaroúdhia* (courgette croquettes), *hórta*, assorted *ospriá* like chickpeas, squash flowers in autumn, and simple seafood like *soupiá*, squid and *marídhes*. Daily supper only.

**Thavma en Kairo** Eleftheriou Venizelou 16–18 ☏22410 39805, Ⓦwww.restaurantwonder.com. Swedish-run high-end restaurant occupying a elegant Belle Époque mansion overlooking parkland. The small-portioned food is Mediterranean-Greek with a strong seafood presence and Asian flavours; bills run to around €30 a head even before you've hit the vast and pricey selection of beers, wines and cocktails. From 7pm Mon–Sat. Credit cards taken.

### Zéfyros and around

**Aegean Fish** Klavdhíou Pépper 1, opposite street market. The cheapest seafood on Rhodes: choose your fish from the retail counter, have it weighed and cleaned, take it to the grill (free), sit at wooden tables in this vast premises and enjoy. Limited array of starters, beer and soft drinks as accompaniment; Mon-Sat lunchtime only.

**Anatolikes Nostimies** Klavdhíou Pépper 109, Zéfyros Beach. The name means "Anatolian Delicacies": Thracian Pomak/Middle Eastern dips and starters, plus beef-based kebabs. Beach-hut atmosphere, but friendly, popular and reasonably priced; post-prandial hubble-bubble on request. Daily noon–midnight.

**Khristos (O Vlahos)** Klavdhíou Pépper 165, bend before Zéfyros Beach. Enduringly popular *estiatório* where civil servants from the nearby tax office lunch at outdoor seating. Great *tzatzíki*, plus vegetable-strong *mayireftá* (cuttlefish with spinach, pork stew, fish soup, aubergine imam) that sell out quickly.

**Paragadhi** Cnr Klavdhíou Pépper and Avstralías. Seafood/fish restaurant that's the haunt of the Rhodian *beau monde*. Reasonable *mezédhes* and wine prices are offset by somewhat bumped-up fish rates; their *risótto thalassinoú* is excellent if not absolutely authentic. Large parties must book weekend nights (☏22410 37775); closed Sun evening & (usually) Mon noon.

**Sakis** Kanadhá 95, cnr Apostólou Papaïoánnou; Ⓦwww.tavernasakis.gr. A friendly old favourite with pleasant patio and indoor seating, equally popular with Rhodians and foreigners. Known for its shellfish (such as limpets and snails), meat (chops, Cypriot *seftaliés*) and the usual starters. Daily 5pm–1am, also Sun lunch.

### Nightlife and entertainment

In the **Old Town**, an entire alley (Miltiádhou) off Apellóu is home to a score of loud, annually changing **music bars** and **clubs**, extending towards Plátonos and Platía Dhamayítou, and frequented mostly by Greeks (in winter too); there are persistent touts, though they tend to ignore foreigners. Another nucleus of activity is around Platía Aríonos and Menekléous, where six clubs cater to a slightly older, mixed-nationality crowd – here *Baduz Loutra* has hard rock and funk nights Wednesday to Saturday, while neighbouring *Rogmi tou Khairou* hosts live bands one or two nights weekly. Together these have rather eclipsed the forty or so surviving, theme-night and gimmick-slanted bars and clubs in **Neohóri**, in the area bounded by Alexándhrou Dhiákou, Orfanídhou, Lohagoú Fanouráki and Nikifórou Mandhilará.

Two a/c **cinemas** showing first-run action movies operate year round: the Metropol multiplex, at the corner of Venetokléon and Výronos, southeast of the Old Town opposite the stadium, and the nearby Pallas multiplex on Dhimokratías. The Rodon open-air cinema behind the town hall is only used for special events, such as the excellent mid-to-late-June **film festival** (@www.ecofilms .gr). Quality live **summer music acts**, mostly Greek (watch for posters), appear in the open-air Théatro Tafros, in the grassy moat between the Akándia and Koskinoú gates.

**Bekir Karakuzu** Sokrátous 76. The last traditional Turkish *kafenío* in the Old Town, this has bags of atmosphere, with an Oriental-fantasy interior with ornate *votsalotó* floor. Yoghurt, *loukoúmi*, *alisfakiá* tea and coffees are on the expensive side – consider it admission to an informal museum. 11am–midnight.

**Besara Kafé** Sofokléous 11–13, Old Town. Congenial breakfast-snack café-cum-low-key bar run by Australian-Texan Besara Harris, with a mixed clientele and live jazz two nights weekly Oct–May.

**Blue Lagoon Pirate Bar** 25-Martíou 2, Neohóri. One of the better theme bars, with pirate kitsch, palm trees, waterfalls, live turtles and parrots, and a shipwrecked galleon. The flagship outfit of a small, changing chain of clubs (see @www .lepalais.gr). Open 8.30am–3am April–Oct.

**Christos' Garden** Dhilberáki 59, Neohóri. This combination art gallery/bar/café occupies a carefully restored old house and courtyard with pebble-mosaic floors throughout.

**Colorado Entertainment Centre** Orfanídhou 57, cnr Aktí Miaoúli, Neohóri. A triple venue: "Colorado Live" has an in-house band, "Studio Fame" is a club, and "Heaven" upstairs is a chill-out bar.

**Elli** Platía Koundourióti, Élli beach. The upper floor of the Italian-era Ronda bathing establishment is home to a seasonally changing repertoire of clubs, from ballroom dancing to Latin music.

**Sticky Fingers** Anthoúla Zérvou 6, Neohóri. Durable (founded mid-1980s) music bar with live rock several nights a week from 10.30pm onwards, Fri & Sat only off-season. Typical admission €15.

# Listings

**Car rental** Rack rates weigh in at €45–55 per day, but can be bargained to €22–33 a day, all-inclusive, in low season and/or for long periods. Especially recommended is Drive/Budget (@www.driverentacar .gr), who change their cars every 12–18 months; they've several premises across the island, including at the airport (T22410 81011); their central, long-hours reservation number is T22410 68243. Other durable outfits in Neohóri include Just, Mandhilará 70 (T22410 31811, @www.just-rentacar.gr) and Kosmos, Papaloúka 31 (T22410 74374, @www .cosmos-sa.gr). Major international chains at the airport include Alamo/National (T22410 81600); Avis (T22410 82896) and plus Sixt (T22410 81995).

**Exchange** Conventional banks (Alpha is open Sat morning & evenings) with ATMs crowd Platía Kýprou in Neohóri; a few exchange bureaux keep longer hours. In the Old Town, there are ATMs near the museums, and along Sokrátous.

**Ferry agents** ANES (T22410 37769) for catama-rans and hydrofoil to Sými; Dodhekanisos Navtiliaki

(T22410 70590) for the *Dodekanisos Express/ Dodekanisos Pride* catamarans; Tsangaris (T22410 36170) for GA boats; Skevos (T22410 22461) for Blue Star; Zorpidhis (T22410 20625), for LANE; Sea Star and *Panayia Spiliani* (T22410 78052). Any changes should be shown on the EOT office's fairly reliable handouts.

**Hospital/clinic** The new state hospital, well out of town to the south, is still understaffed and has a deservedly poor reputation; especially if you're insured, head for the well-signed Euromedica clinic in Koskinoú, 6.5km south (24hr; English-speaking staff; T22410 45000) for their ambulances).

**Internet cafés** The most central and competitive are *On the Spot Net* (inside the *Spot Hotel*, 8am–midnight), and *Mango Bar* (same hours; closed late Oct–Easter) at Platía Dhoriéos 3, Old Town. Wi-fi signal is widely advertised in cafés.

**Motorbike rental** Low-displacement scooters make little impact on Rhodes; sturdier Yamaha 125s are suitable for two people. Recommended

Neohóri outlets include Margaritis, Ioánni Kazoúli 23, with a range of models up to 500cc, plus mountain bikes; or Kiriakos, Apodhímon Amerikís 16, which will deliver to the Old Town and shuttle you back once you've finished.

**Scuba diving** The better of two operators touting at Mandhráki quay is Waterhoppers (✆www .waterhoppers.com); local dives have got more exciting since the opening of new deep-wall areas at Ladhikó and near Líndhos.

**Travel agencies** In Neohóri, conveniently located Triton Holidays at Plastíra 9 (☎22410 21690, ✆www.tritondmc.gr) is excellent for all local travel

arrangements, including Drive/Budget car rental, domestic catamaran, ferry and air tickets for every company, plus the catamaran to Turkey or charters to the UK. They also have accommodation affiliates across the Dodecanese (including all listed Rhodes luxury hotels), bookable at very attractive rates. French-run Passion Sailing Cruises (Ayíou Fanouríou 64 ☎22410 73006, ✆www .aegeanpassion.com) offers a bespoke service for skippered cruises, as well as bareboat charter. Yann and Servanne have years in the business and their enthusiasm is palpable.

# The east coast

Heading down the east coast from the capital, the first tempting stop – 7km along – is the former spa at **Piyés Kallithéas**, a prize example of orientalized Art Deco from 1929, the work of a young Pietro Lombardi who, in his old age, designed Strasbourg's European Parliament building. Accessed via a short side road through pines, the complex (daily 8am–8pm; €2.50) has an upmarket bar serving from inside artifical grottoes at the swimming lido, just below the dome of the **Mikrí Rotónda** in its clump of palms. The main **Megáli Rotónda** higher up is now a small **museum**, with changing modern art exhibits and a permanent collection of stills from 1961's *The Guns of Navarone* (partly filmed here) and the spa in its postwar heyday. Southwest of the spa complex, several well-signed coves, furnished with sunbeds and snack bars (the best of these *Oasis*, with caper-garnished salads and well-fried *marídhes*), are framed by rock formations that often interpose themselves between the water and the sand. Off to the left (north) of the *Oasis* lido is a recognized **gay nude-bathing** zone.

## Faliráki and Afándou

Some 2km further south, the northerly zone of **Faliráki** – a half-dozen high-rise hotels pitched at families – sits uneasily alongside the cheap-and-nasty southern zone, notorious for its drink-fuelled brawls, rapes and a 2003 murder. Following that casualty, police forcefully curbed the local club-crawling culture, and the place is now a shadow of its former self, with the mayhem moved on to such spots as Mália, Crete and Laganás, Zákynthos.

Faliráki's sandy sweep is closed off on the south by the cape of **Ladhikó**. On its north flank nestles the scenic bay of "**Anthony Quinn**", named in honour of the late actor whom Greeks took to their hearts following his roles in *Zorba the Greek* and *The Guns of Navarone*. The main cove, south of the promotory, actually has better swimming and a reasonable full-service taverna.

South of Ladhikó, the coastline is adorned, as far as Líndhos, by striking turrets of wedding-cake-like limestone formations, punctuating long stretches of beach. The first is the pebble-and-sand expanse of **Afándou Bay**, the least developed large beach on the east coast, with just a few showers and clusters of relatively inexpensive sunbeds. Spare a moment, heading down the main access road to mid-beach, for the atmospheric sixteenth-century church of **Panayía Katholikí**, paved with a *votsalotó* floor throughout and incorporating fragments of a much older basilica; recently cleaned frescoes include an almond-eyed *Virgin Enthroned* on the left of the *témblon*. Immediately opposite is a very popular **taverna**, doing grills, salad and dips: *Estiatorio Katholiki* (Mon–Sat supper, Sun lunch also). For overpriced but excellent fish, and not much else other than a few dips and vegetable starters, head for *Kostas Avandís*, south along the beach.

The most distinctive bit of Afándou Bay is the far north end, known as **Traganoú** beach (and signposted as such from the main highway). Beyond the army officers' R&R post of Erimókastro, which overlooks the protected gravel-pebble cove here, are the Traganospília, a trio of **caves** with both land and sea entrance, and freshwater seeps which make the sea cooler than you'd expect. Showers, sunbeds and snacks are offered by a single *kantína*.

### Tsambíka to Vlyhá

The enormous promontory of **Tsambíka**, 26km south of town, offers unrivalled views from up top along some 50km of coastline. From the main highway, a steep, 1500-metre cement drive leads to a small car park from where steps mount to the summit. On its September 8 festival childless women climb up – on their hands and knees in the final stretches – to the otherwise unremarkable **monastery** here to be cured of their barrenness; any children born afterwards are dedicated to the Virgin with the names Tsambikos or Tsambika, particular to the Dodecanese. Shallow **Tsambíka Bay**, south of the headland (2km access road), has an excellent if packed beach, protected by its owners, the Orthodox Church, from permanent development – there are just eight *kantínas*. For a proper **taverna**, try the polite *Panorama Tsambikas*, up the main highway south of the beach turning, with good grills and *mezédhes*.

The next beach south is **Stegná**, reached by a steep road east just before the comparatively nondescript inland village Arhángelos, overlooked by a crumbling castle. Behind the fine-gravel shore stands a mix of summer cottages for locals and German-monopolized **accommodation**. Much the best of several **tavernas** is ⭐ *To Periyali* down by the fish anchorage, where Greeks go for seafood, hand-cut round chips, home-made *yaprákia* and substantial salads ("Periyali" has caper greens and grilled aubergine) washed down by good bulk wine; the travertine-clad loos must be the wackiest, yet most charming, on the island.

Another overnight base on this coast, English-dominated this time, is **HARÁKI**, a pleasant if undistinguished two-street fishing port with mostly self-catering **accommodation** (generally ❸) overlooked by the stubby ruins of **Feraklós castle**, the last Knights' citadel to fall to the Turks. You can swim off the town beach in front of the waterfront cafés and **tavernas** (best of these is *Maria's*), but most people head northwest to sunbed-carpeted **Ayía Agathí** beach, or down the coast 8km to **Paralía Kaláthou**, with its vast, less claustrophobic stretch of sand and fine gravel. One of the few developments there is inobtrusive, Tardis-like *Atrium Palace* (☎22440 31601, ⓦwww.atrium.gr; ❽ – €230 and up), its expensively landscaped grounds dotted with pools and its lawns extending to the beach; the remoter villa wings, towards the spa, are best.

Just beyond the little naval base here is another, smaller, cove, **Vlyhá**, overlooked by twin tiered boutique hotels (May–Oct): the *Lindos Mare* (☎22440 31130, ⓦwww.lindosmare.gr; ❽ – €240–420) and 2008-opened *Lindos Blu* (☎22440 32110, ⓦwww.lindosblu.gr; ❽ – €420 & up). The former, despite having 142 designer units (a third of them suites, not all sea-view), manages to feel small-scale; a funicular takes you down through lush grounds from the large pool to the beach. The latter has similar decor and a spa, but has even more on-site restaurants, all-sea-view units, and is for adults only – villas/maisonettes have private pools.

## Líndhos

**LÍNDHOS**, the island's number-two tourist attraction, erupts from barren surroundings 12km south of Haráki. Like Ródhos Old Town, its charm is heavily undermined by commercialism and crowds. At noon dozens of tour coaches barricade the outskirts; in the village itself, those few vernacular houses not snapped up by package operators have, since the 1960s, been bought and refurbished by British, Germans and Italians. The old *agorá* or serpentine high street presents a series of fairly indistinguishable bars, crêperies, mediocre restaurants and travel agents. Although high-rise hotels and all vehicular traffic are banned, the result is a labyrinthine theme park, hot and airless from June to August, but eerily deserted in winter.

Nonetheless, if you arrive outside peak season, when the lanes between the immaculately whitewashed houses are relatively empty, you can still appreciate the village's beautiful, atmospheric setting. The belfried, post-Byzantine **Panayía church** (Mon–Sat 9am–3pm & 6.30–8pm, Sun 9am–3pm) is covered inside with well-preserved eighteenth-century frescoes. The most imposing **medieval captains' residences** are built around *votsalotó* courtyards, their monumental doorways often fringed by intricate stone braids or cables supposedly corresponding in number to the fleet owned.

On the bluff looming above the town, the ancient **acropolis** (part scaffolded for restoration) with its Doric Temple of Athena and imposing Hellenistic stoa is found inside the **Knights' castle** (mid-June to mid-Sept Mon 12.30–7.10pm, Tues–Sun 8am–7.10pm; spring/autumn closes 6.10pm; winter Tues–Sun 8.30am–2.40pm; €6) – a surprisingly felicitous blend of ancient and medieval. Though the ancient city of Lindos and its original temple dated from at least 1100 BC, the present structure was begun by local ruler Kleoboulos in the sixth century BC. Its unusual southwest-to-northeast orientation was dictated by the limited triangular area of flat ground on the summit. Visiting sites as close as possible to dawn or dusk is always good advice, here even more so for the sake of sweeping views: north to Tsambíka and Feraklós, south to the gaunt cliffs hemming in St Paul's Bay.

Líndhos's north **beach**, once the principal ancient harbour, is overcrowded; quieter options lie one cove beyond at **Pállas beach**, with its nudist annexe around the headland. South of the acropolis huddles the small, perfectly sheltered **St Paul's harbour**, with excellent swimming; the apostle purportedly landed here in 58 AD on a mission to evangelize the island. According to legend, the ship bringing Paul to Rhodes was threatened by a storm and unable to find the main, north harbour; a miraculous bolt of lightning split the rocks asunder, creating this almost landlocked bay expressly for the saint's benefit.

### Practicalities

If you're not met at the bus stop under the giant fig tree by proprietors touting **accommodation**, Lindos Suntours (☎22440 31333, ⓦwww.lindosuntours.gr) can arrange a room or even a villa for a small fee; just watch that you're not shoved into a windowless cell – ventilation is paramount here. The only real hotel in Líndhos, among the most exclusive on the island, is 🍴 *Melenos* (☎22440 32222, ⓦwww.melenoslindos.com; Easter–Oct; ❽ – €400–900), discreetly sited on the second lane above the north beach, by the school. No expense has been spared in laying out the twelve luxurious suites with semi-private, *votsalotó* terraces and tasteful furnishings; there's also a swanky garden-bar and restaurant. Most local **restaurants** serve bland, absurdly priced food, with a rapid turnover in ownership. You may as well plump for 🍴 *Mavrikos* on the fig-tree square, founded 1933 and in the same family ever since. Starters such as *yígandes* in carob syrup, sweet marinated sardines, or beets in goat-cheese sauce, are accomplished, as are fish mains such as skate timbale with sweetened balsamic, or superior traditional recipes like *dolmádhes* and *tyrokafterí*; choosing from the excellent (and expensive) Greek wine list will add €18 minimum a bottle to the typical food charge of €23–28 per person. For **snacks** and desserts, try *Il Forno*, an Italian-run bakery, and *Gelo Blu*, best of several gelaterie, also serving decadent cakes and juices. The better-equipped of two **internet** cafés is helpful *Lindianet*; The Link is a unique combination of laundry and secondhand bookshop (daily in season 9am–8pm); and there are four bank **ATMs**. Líndhos also has a **spa** (Mon–Sat 1pm–9pm), offering the usual range of services except massage (there are too many freelancers on the beaches).

## The west coast

Rhodes' windward **west coast** is damper, more fertile and more forested than the rest of the island; beaches, however, are exposed and often rocky. None of this has deterred development and, as on the east coast, the first few kilometres of the busy main road have been surrendered entirely to tourism. From Rhodes Town limits down to the airport, the shore is lined with generic Mediterranean hotels, though **Triánda**, **Kremastí** and **Paradhísi** are still nominally villages, with real centres.

There's little inducement to stop until you reach the site of ancient **KAMEIROS**, which together with Lindos and Ialyssos united to found the powerful city-state of Rhodes. Soon eclipsed by the new capital, Kameiros was abandoned and only rediscovered in 1859, leaving a particularly well-preserved Doric townscape in a beautiful hillside setting (Tues–Sun: summer 8am–7.10pm; winter 8.30am–2.40pm; €4). You can make out the foundations of two small temples, the re-erected pillars of a Hellenistic house, a Classical fountain, and the stoa of the upper agora, complete with a water cistern. Kameiros had no fortifications, nor even an acropolis – partly owing to the gentle slope of the site, and also to the likely settlement here by peaceable Minoans.

At the tiny anchorage of **KÁMIROS SKÁLA** (aka Skála Kamírou), 15km south, there are five touristy **restaurants**, the best being *Loukas* nearest the quay, with big salads and no hype or picture-menus. A weekday *kaïki* leaves for the island of Hálki (see p.340) at 2.30pm, weather permitting; on Sundays (and usually Wednesdays) there are journeys at 9am and 6pm. With transport, proceed 400m southwest to off-puttingly named **Paralía Kopriá** ("Manure Beach"), where *Psarotaverna Johnny's* has good fish and *mezédhes*.

Some 2km south of Skála, **Kástro Kritiniás** (locally dubbed "Kastéllo") is – from afar – the most impressive of the Knights' rural strongholds, and the paved access road is too narrow and steep for tour buses. Close up it proves to be no more than a shell, albeit a glorious one, with fine views west to Hálki, Alimniá, Tílos and Níssyros. The castle's church was restored in 2008 to eventually house a museum, and a ticket booth was installed, but thus far neither function.

Beyond the quiet hillside village of Kritiniá itself, the main road winds south through dense forests below mounts Akramýtis and Atávyros to **SIÁNNA**, famous for its aromatic honey and *soúma*, similar to Italian grappa but far smoother. You can make a road circuit of Mount Akramýtis by using the paved back-road signposted for the rural chapel and festival grounds of Zoödhóhou Piyís – keep going until you emerge on the Monólithos–Foúrni road. The tiered, flat-roofed houses of **MONÓLITHOS**, 4km southwest of Siánna, don't themselves justify the long trip out, but the view over the Aegean is striking and you could base yourself at the *Hotel Thomas* (☎22460 61291 or 697 30 38 494; ❷), whose fair-sized rooms belie a grim exterior. The best of several **tavernas** is welcoming *O Palios Monolithos* (all year, weekends only off season) opposite the church: mains are a bit pricey but it's known for grilled meat and starters like wild mushrooms, *tyrokafterí* and mixed *dolmádhes*, accompanied by good bread and non-CAIR bulk wine. Local diversions include yet another **Knights' castle**, 2km west of town, photogenically perched on its own pinnacle but enclosing very little, and the sand-and-gravel beaches at **Foúrni**, five paved but curvy kilometres below the castle.

# The interior

**Inland Rhodes** is hilly and still part-forested, despite the ongoing efforts of arsonists. You'll need a vehicle to take in the soft-contoured, undulating scenery, along with the last vestiges of agrarian life in the villages; no single spot justifies the expense of a taxi or battling with inconveniently sparse bus schedules. Most people under retirement age are away working in the tourist industry, returning only at weekends and during winter.

## Ialyssos to Maritsá

Starting from the west-coast highway, turn inland at the central junction in Triánda for the side road (5km) up to the scanty acropolis of ancient **Ialyssos** (summer Tues–Sat 8am–7.10pm, Sun 8.30am–2.40pm; winter Tues–Sun 8.30am–2.40pm; €3) on flat-topped, strategic Filérimos hill; from here Süleyman the Magnificent directed the 1522 siege of Rhodes. Filérimos means "lover of solitude", after tenth-century Byzantine hermits who dwelt here; **Filérimos monastery**, restored successively by Italians and British, is the most substantial structure. Directly in front of the church sprawl the foundations of third-century temples to Zeus and Athena, built atop a far older Phoenician shrine; below this lies the partly subterranean church of **Aï-Yeórgis Hostós**, a vaulted structure with faint fourteenth- and fifteenth-century frescoes. Southwest of all this, a **Via Crucis**, its fourteen stations marked out in copper plaques during the Italian era, leads to an enormous (18m-high) concrete crucifix, a 1995 replacement of an Italian-built one destroyed during the war to deny Allied airmen a navigational aid; you're allowed to climb up, then out onto the cross-arms as a supplement to the already amazing view. Illuminated at night, the crucifix is clearly visible from Sými and – perhaps more pertinently – "infidel" Turkey across the straits.

The only much-promoted tourist "attraction" in the island's interior, **Petaloúdhes** ("Butterfly Valley") (daily: May–Sept 9am–6pm; April & Oct 9am–5pm; €0–5 by season), is reached by a seven-kilometre side road bearing inland between Paradhísi and Theológos. It's actually a rest stop for Jersey tiger moths; only from mid-June through September (when full admission is charged) do they congregate here, attracted for unknown reasons by the abundant *Liquidambar orientalis* trees growing abundantly in this stream canyon. The moths, which roost in droves on the tree trunks and cannot eat during this final phase of their life cycle, rest to conserve energy, and die of starvation soon after mating. When stationary, the moths are a well-camouflaged black and yellow, but they flash cherry-red overwings in flight.

Some 2km before Petaloúdhes, the **microwinery** (15,000–20,000 bottles annually) of Anastasia Triandafyllou merits a stop for its ten varieties, including Athiri whites, Muscat rosé, sweet dessert wine and Cabernet or Mandhilari reds (daily 8.30am–7pm). The best nearby **taverna** is at the edge of **PSÍNTHOS** village, where ⚓ *Piyi Fasouli* serves excellent grills and appetizers as well as a few tasty *mayireftá* at tables overlooking the namesake spring. Afterwards, follow signs downstream to visit an aquarium dedicated to captive specimens of

*Ladigesocypris ghigii* (**gizáni** in Greek), a rare, now-protected fish of Rhodian mountain streams, about the size of a sand smelt.

From Psínthos centre a winding secondary road leads north to **MARITSÁ**, not much to look at by day but an extraordinary scene after dark when seven **tavernas** and **ouzerís** of all pretensions come to life along the high street. The simplest – and arguably the best, near the top of the grade – is always-packed *To Koutouki*, where €10 (drink extra) nets you whatever half-dozen platters chef Ioannis Velis decides to serve. This changes daily, and could be cumined chicken fillet, *pansétta*, assorted *ospriá*, lamb or salads.

## Eptá Piyés to Profítis Ilías

Heading inland from Kolýmbia junction on the main east-coast highway, it's 4km to **Eptá Piyés** ("Seven Springs"), an oasis with a tiny irrigation dam created by the Italians. A trail and a rather claustrophobic Italian aqueduct-tunnel both lead from the vicinity of the springs to the reservoir. Continuing on the same road, you reach neglected Italian structures at **ELEOÚSSA** (built as the planned agricultural colony of Campochiaro in 1935–36) after another 9km, in the shade of dense forest. Among a handful of **tavernas** here, *To Steki* is a good, cheap lunch-stop while touring, with salads and chops. From the vast Art Deco pool just west of the village, stocked with more endangered *gizáni* fish, keep straight 3km further to the late Byzantine church of **Áyios Nikólaos Foundouklí** ("St Nicholas of the Hazelnuts"). Interior frescoes, dating from the thirteenth to the fifteenth centuries, could use a good cleaning, but scenes from the life of Christ are recognizable.

Continuing west from the church brings you to **Profítis Ilías** hamlet, where the Italian, 1929-vintage chalet-hotel ⚒ *Elafos Hotel* (☎ 22460 22402, ⓦ www.elafoshotel.gr; doubles ④, suites ⑥) has high-ceilinged rooms with retro charm, and arcaded ground-floor common areas including a restaurant and a sauna. It looks out from deep woods just north of the 780-metre peak, Rhodes' third-highest point but off-limits as a military area, although there is good, gentle strolling below and around the summit. The closest serious independent **restaurants** are about 5km away on the south flank of the mountain in **APÓLLONA**, a foodie destination especially by night or off-season (when they're most likely to be open); best of several choices here is *Paradhosiako Mayerio Paranga*, at the east edge of the village. There's more **accommodation** north and downhill from Profítis Ilías in **SÁLAKOS** at the simpler but again Italian-era (1926) *Hotel-Café Nymph* (☎ 22460 22206, ⓦ www.nymph.gr; ③) just south of the village, with air-conditioned, antique-tile-floored rooms.

## Atávyros villages

All tracks and roads west across Profítis Ilías converge on the road from Kalavárdha bound for **ÉMBONA**, a large, architecturally nondescript village backed up against the north slope of 1215-metre **Mount Atávyros**. Émbona lies at the heart of the island's most important wine-producing districts, and CAIR – the Italian-founded vintners' co-operative – produces a choice of acceptable mid-range varieties. However, products of the smaller, family-run **Emery winery** (daily 9.30am–3.30pm; ⓦ www.emery.gr) at the northern outskirts are more highly regarded. You can carry on clockwise around the peak to less visited **ÁYIOS ISÍDHOROS**, with nearly as many vines, a more open feel and the trailhead for the five-hour return **ascent of Atávyros**. This placard-documented path, beginning at the northeast edge of the village and well marked with paint splodges, is the safest and easiest way up the mountain, though the slopes are sullied by a wind-power farm, a radar "golf ball" up top and the tracks built to install these.

## Thárri monastery

The rough road from Áyios Isídhoros 12km east to Láerma, and the vast, sad tableau of 2008-burnt trees all around that village, is worth enduring if you've any interest in Byzantine monuments – though there's easier, all-paved access along a road starting 2km east of Apóllona. The monastery of **Thárri**, regrettably still in the fire zone 5km south of Láerma, is the oldest religious foundation on the island, re-established as a vital community in 1990 by charismatic abbot Amfilohios. In the striking *katholikón* (daily, all day), successive cleanings have restored damp-smudged frescoes dated 1300–1450 to their former exquisite glory. The most distinct, in the transept, depict the Evangelists Mark and Matthew, plus the Archangel Gabriel, while the nave has various acts of Christ, including the *Storm on the Sea of Galilee*, *Meeting the Samaritan Woman at the Well* and *Healing the Cripple*.

# The far south

South of a line connecting Monólithos and Lárdhos, you might think you'd strayed onto another island; gone are most mega-hotels, with second-home villa developments more a feature of the landscape. Only a few weekly buses serve the depopulated villages here (Yennádhi has much better frequencies); tavernas dot the village centres and popular beaches, but aside from Lárdhos, Péfki and Kiotári, there's scant accommodation.

Dense beachfront development flanks **LÁRDHOS**, solidly on the tourist circuit despite the village's inland position. The beach 2km away is gravelly and heavily impinged upon by hotels; Glýstra cove, 3km south, proves a small, more sheltered crescent that gets crowded in season. The best **accommodation** hereabouts is *Lindian Village* (☎ 22440 35900, ⓦ www.lindianvillage.gr; ❽ – €500 & up), an attractively designed bungalow complex with three grades of units (suites have their own plunge-pools), several gourmet restaurants, a spa/gym and private beach. Four kilometres east of Lárdhos, **PÉFKI** (Péfkos) began life as the garden annexe and overflow of Líndhos, but is now a burgeoning resort in its own right; the sea is clearer than at Lárdhos, with small, secluded **beaches** tucked at the base of low cliffs (the biggest, in western Péfki, is **Lothiáriko**). Among **tavernas**, *Kavos* at the east edge of town has the Greekest menu and the choicest setting.

## Asklipió

Nine kilometres beyond Lárdhos, a side road heads 3.5km inland to **ASKLIPIÓ**, a sleepy village enlivened by a crumbling Knights' castle and Byzantine **Kímisis Theotókou church** (daily: summer 9am–6pm, spring/autumn 9am–5pm; €1.50). This dates from 1060, and has a pebble-floored ground plan similar to Thárri's, though two apses were added during the eighteenth century. Frescoes inside are in better condition thanks to the drier local climate, and also a bit later, though the final work at Thárri and the earliest here were possibly executed by the same hand.

The format and themes of the **frescoes** are unusual in Greece. Didactic "cartoon strips" often extend completely around the church, featuring Old Testament stories alongside the more usual lives of Christ and the Virgin. There's a complete Genesis sequence, from the *Creation* to the *Expulsion from Eden*; note the comically menacing octopus among the fishes in the panel of the Fifth Day, and Eve being fashioned from Adam's rib. An *Apocalypse* takes up most of the south transept, while an enormous *Archangel Michael* dominates the north transept, with sword in right hand and a small soul to be judged in his left. Two adjacent buildings house an ecclesiastical exhibit, and a more interesting folklore gallery in an ex-olive mill, full of rural craft tools and antiquated, belt-driven machinery.

### Kiotári, Yennádhi, Váti and Profýlia

Back on the coast road, **KIOTÁRI** beachfront district has mushroomed as a package venue for Germans and Italians since the Orthodox Church sold its vast holdings here. You could stop for an expensive (€25–30 a head plus drink) meal at bistro-bar *Mourella* on the beachfront road, or **stay** at superior ☆ *Paraktio Apartments* (☎22440 47278, ⓦwww.paraktio.com; ❸ studio, ❹ apt) on the main highway, with direct beach access and a café. But you'll likely continue 4km to **YENNÁDHI**, the only sizeable settlement on this coast, whose rather drab outskirts mask the attractive older village core inland, now half-populated by ethnic Albanians. Most local **tavernas** stand just behind the dark-sand-and-gravel **beach** extending kilometres in either direction, clean and with the usual amenities laid on. Other amenities include an **ATM**, post office, car rental and some **accommodation** – pick of this being *Effie's Dreams* at the northern end of things (☎22440 43410, ⓦwww.effiesdreams.com; all year; ❸), overlooking a fountain-fed oasis. There's a bar and **internet** café downstairs from the serviceable studios. The Greek-Australian owners can help locate the key-keeper for sixth-to-fifteenth-century **Ayía Anastasía Roméa**, the village cemetery-church 300m northwest through the oasis. Though the present, barrel-vaulted structure dates from the late fifteenth century, it's built on sixth-century foundations – and covered inside with post-Byzantine **frescoes** in a naïve style not seen elsewhere on the island. On the ceiling are scenes from the life of Christ and the young Virgin, and the martyrdom of Anastasia; in the conch of the apse there's a Virgin *Platytera* and *Communion of the Apostles*, while on the west wall's *Last Judgment*, Jews and Beelzebub are shown together in the River of Fire draining into Hell's Mouth.

From Yennádhi, a good road heads 7km inland, past baby pines slowly greening up a fire-blasted landscape, to **VÁTI**, where the best of three local **tavernas** is 2007-opened, roadside *Pelikanos* (all year). The nearby village of **PROFÝLIA** – accessed by the newest and best road on the island – offers *Tò Limeri tou Listi* (closed Mon low season), though the food isn't quite up to the setting and friendly service. Its tables share a terrace with the little sixteenth-century **chapel of Áyios Yeóryios and Arhángelos** (always open), whose warm contemporary frescoes show protagonists in period dress.

### The southern tip

Some 10km south of Yennádhi, then 2km inland, **LAHANIÁ** village was abandoned after a postwar earthquake, though since the 1980s its older houses have been mostly occupied and renovated by foreigners. On the main platía at the lower, eastern end of the village, ☆ *Platanos* **taverna** has superb *mezédhes* platters like hummus and *dolmadhákia*, and seating between the church and two wonderful Ottoman fountains. You can **rent** one of the old **houses** when their leaseholders are away: ask at *Platanos* or ring ☎694 41 60 128.

From Lahaniá a good road heads 9km northwest to picturesque hilltop **MESANAGRÓS**, which already existed by the fifth century AD, judging from a ruined basilica at the village outskirts. A smaller thirteenth-century chapel sits amid foundations of the larger, earlier church, with a *votsalotó* floor and barrel arches (key from the nearby *kafenío*). You can also go directly from Lahaniá to **Plimýri**, an attractive sandy bay backed by dunes and the church of **Zoödhóhou Piyís** (May–Oct Sun noon–5pm), ancient columns upholding its vaulted porch, with swimming marred only by strong afternoon winds. The sole facility, by the church, is a popular fish **taverna**, *Plimiri Beach*, 1980s-style in the best sense, with friendly per-kilo prices, devout observance of the tao of chips, a few starters and maybe a cherry liqueur on the house.

**Áyios Pávlos**, 5km beyond the Plimýri turning, is a now-derelict Italian model farm complex (1936), complete with belfried church. From here an unmarked, fair-quality dirt road leads southeast 5km to the little monastery of **Áyios Yeóryios**, which lends its name to the local beaches. Heading straight another 1500m brings you to the broadest sandy bay, just beyond dunes and low junipers, extending for 2km south of **Cape Yermatá**. Though it's one of the last turtle-nesting sites in the Dodecanese, efforts to protect it came to naught, and building is beginning on the cape. Bearing right at the monastery and continuing 2km on a rougher track – best have a jeep – takes you to a more sheltered fantasy cove, with higher dunes and gently shelving sea.

Beyond Áyios Pávlos the road curves around to **KATTAVIÁ**, nearly 90km from the capital, lost amid grain fields; the village, like so many hereabouts, is seasonally occupied by returning immigrants from Australia or North America. There are some **rooms** to rent, a vital **filling station** and several **tavernas** at the junction that doubles as the platía.

From Kattaviá a road goes to **Prassoníssi** ("Leek Island"), Rhodes' southernmost extremity and a European **windsurfing** mecca. The sandspit tethering Prassoníssi to Rhodes was breached by currents to form a channel in 1996, but enough remains to create flat water on the east side and up to two-metre waves on the west, ideal for all levels. Of two **windsurfing schools** operating here, Polish-run Prasonisi Center (late April–Oct; ☎22440 91044, ⓦwww.prasoniscenter.com) is keener and friendlier. They're geared up for one-week packages, lodging their clients in Yennádhi and Kattaviá as well as at *Oasis*, marginally the better of two **taverna-rooms** outfits here.

Beyond Kattaviá, the highway loops to emerge onto the deserted, sandy southwest coast just below workaday, agricultural **APOLAKKIÁ**, equipped with nondescript tavernas but no accommodation. Northwest, the road leads to Monólithos, while the northeasterly bearing leads quickly and pleasantly back to Yennádhi via Váti. Due north, near an irrigation reservoir, the tiny Byzantine chapel of **Áyios Yeóryios Várdhas** (unlocked) deserves a four-kilometre detour (with your own transport) for the sake of its thirteenth-to-fourteenth-century frescoes, smudged but wide-eyed and warmly naïve in style. These include a fine *Entry to Jerusalem* and *Presentation of Jesus* on the right (south) vault and an expressive *Panayía Glykofiloússa* (*Virgin Kissing the Christ Child*) on the left wall, plus what seem to be personifications of Faith, Hope and Charity also on the left wall, behind the *témblon*.

# Hálki

**Hálki**, a waterless limestone speck just west of Rhodes, is a fully fledged member of the Dodecanese, though all but a few hundred of the then three-thousand-strong population emigrated (mostly to Rhodes or Florida) following Italian restrictions on sponge-fishing in 1916. Despite a renaissance through tourism, the island is tranquil compared to its neighbour, albeit with a distinctly stage-set atmosphere; foreigners vastly outnumber locals (400–800 depending on the season). Besides people, Hálki shelters about five thousand sheep and goats, plus a sizable fishing fleet which sends most of its catch to Rhodes – together, the only significant livelihoods aside from tourism.

Hálki first attracted postwar foreign attention in 1983, when **UNESCO** designated it the "isle of peace and friendship" and the seat of regular international conferences. Some 150 derelict houses in Emborió were to be restored at UNESCO's expense as accommodation for delegates, but by 1987 just one hotel had been completed, and the only sign of "peace and friendship" were bureaucrats staging periodic, alcohol-fuelled musical binges disguised as "ecological seminars". Confronted with an apparent scam, the islanders sent UNESCO packing and engaged two UK package operators to complete restorations and bring in paying guests. There are now six tour companies present, and most of the ruins have been refurbished to host their clients.

## Emborió

The skyline of **EMBORIÓ**, Hálki's port and sole habitation, is pierced by the tallest freestanding **clocktower** in the Dodecanese and – a bit further north – by the **belfry** of Áyios Nikólaos with its fine *votsalotó* courtyard. The waterfront has been paved with fieldstones, generally prettified and declared off-limits to vehicles in season. Emborió's restored houses (and a boutique hotel) are largely block-booked from May to late September by tour companies and interest groups; independent travellers will be lucky to find anything on spec. Recommended **accommodation** to be prebooked includes the delightful, en-suite ⚓ *Captain's House* (☎22460 45201, captainshouse@ath.forthnet.gr; ❷), with a shady garden and the feel of an old French country hotel; Frances Mayes' *Mouthouria House* (☎22460 45061, ✉francesm@otenet.gr; €210–500 per week, sleeps 4); the two luxury apartments at *Villa Praxithea* (☎697 24 27 272, ⓦwww.villapraxithea.com; sleeps 6–8; ❻ for 2; minimum 1-week stay), with private lido; and the municipally owned, 2007-refurbished *Hiona Art Hotel* (☎22460 45244, ⓦwww.hionaart.gr; rooms & suites ❻) in the old sponge factory on the south side of the bay, with its own lido, gym and conference facilities. Among six full-service **tavernas** along the waterfront, *Remezzo* is

▲ Emborió quayside, Hálki

excellent for *mayireftá* and pizzas, *Maria* behind the post office is the cheap-and-cheerful option (quality varies), while *Avra* is conscientiously run by Greeks from Caucasian Georgia. Among a similar number of quayside **bars** and **cafés**, *Theodosia's* (or "The Parrot Café" after its resident bird), at the base of the jetty, has puddings and home-made ice cream to die for, as well as good breakfasts. In September the **Hálki Festival** hosts performances by top Greek musical names. There's a **post office**, a stand-alone **ATM**, four well-stocked stores, a bakery, plus a sixteen-seat **bus** that shuttles between the waterfront, Póndamos and Ftenáya. The more useful of two **travel agencies**, Zifos (℡22460 45028, ✉zifos-travel@rho.forthnet.gr) sells all boat tickets and also flogs a selection of apartments unfilled by tour companies.

## The rest of the island

Three kilometres west of Emborió looms the old pirate-safe village of **HORIÓ**, abandoned in the 1950s but still crowned by its Knights' castle. The provision of power lines and a few cottage restorations implied that Horió might go the way of Emborió, but the archeological service has put its foot down, so deserted it remains. Except during the major August 14–15 festival, the church here is kept locked to protect its frescoes. Across the valley, little **Stavrós monastery** hosts another big bash on September 14. There's little else inland, though you can cross the island on an eight-kilometre road, the extension of the cement "Tarpon Springs Boulevard" donated by the expatriate community in Florida. At the end (1 bus daily) you'll reach the monastery of **Ayíou Ioánnou Prodhrómou** (festival Aug 28–29; *kantína* otherwise), with some charm in its array of cells (you can stay the night) around a courtyard dominated by a huge juniper. The terrain en route is bleak, but compensated for by views over half the Dodecanese and Turkey.

Longish but narrow **Póndamos**, fifteen-minutes' walk west of Emborió, is the only sandy beach on Hálki, subject to scouring by storms. The lone facility is somewhat pricey *Nick's Pondamos Taverna*, serving lunch daily, plus supper two random evenings weekly; they also offer four basic, terrazzo-floored, sea-view rooms (☎22460 45295; ❷). A few-minutes' well-signposted path-walk behind the *Hiona Art Hotel*, a tiny pebble cove and the gravel sunbed-lido at **Ftenáya** are also heavily subscribed; a paved lane also leads to its decent **taverna-bar** (*Tou Vangelí*) with good seafood and *ouzomezédhes*. Small, pebbly **Yialí**, west of and considerably below Horió via jeep track, lies an hour's hike away from Póndamos.

Better swimming can be had by taking **boat excursions** to remoter beaches from Emborió quay. Directly below Horió's castle, **Trahiá** consists of two coves to either side of an isthmus; you can (just) reach this overland by rough path from Yialí. North-coast beaches figuring as excursion-boat destinations include the Aréta fjord, **Áyios Yeóryios** just beyond and the remote double bay of **Dhýo Yialí**.

### Hike to Aréta from Emborió

Of these, **Aréta** is the most attractive, and the only one accessible overland (1hr 30min one-way) by experienced hillwalkers equipped with the locally sold *Halki, Island of Peace and Friendship* **map** based on the old Italian topographical survey sheet. Begin along the cemented track towards Kánia; above the municipal cisterns, the way starts at a roadside power pole near a small pastoral shed. Go north through a crude gate, then take the path climbing to a second gate. Beyond this, you're in open country, with the trail fairly distinct, and marked by occasional cairns. The route skirts a large stone pen, then threads between terraces of stunted olives; this is **Petrólakko** ("Petrolaco" on the Italian map).

The path resumes climbing, right under the island's summit ridge with some shallow caves, slipping through a wall and, about an hour along, entering a vast, slightly inclined plateau. Near a second wall, Tílos pops into view, and 300m to the left stands a rock outcrop resembling a pimple or a mole. Once through a third wall, the path drops gradually and then more sharply, zigzagging past a livestock corral built under some rock formations. The obvious nearby canyon draining seaward is **Kelliá** ("Cellia" on the map) – avoid it. The correct, cairned trail heads northwest, then almost west, across the top of the gulch leading down to Aréta. Go through two more gates, then curl along the left (west) flank of the canyon, dropping to sea level in easy stages; memorize landmarks here carefully, as it's easy to get lost on the way back. The final approach is via a recessed rock-stair, manageable by any fit person.

**Aréta fjord** is an impressive, cliff-girt place where seabirds roost and soar. There's some morning and afternoon shade, but only a brackish well for the inquisitive sheep with whom you may share the small-pebble beach, so bring plenty of water.

### Alimniá islet

Another potential outing visits **ALIMNIÁ** (Alimiá) islet, halfway between Hálki and Rhodes. Despite well-water and greenery, plus a better harbour than Hálki's, the village here, overlooked by some palm trees and a Knights' castle, lay abandoned by the 1960s. The inhabitants were initially deported in April 1944 after being caught assisting British commandos sent to sabotage German submarines using the deep harbour here. The seven commandos themselves were captured by the Nazis and bundled off to Thessaloníki, where six were summarily executed as spies rather than treated as regular POWs; future UN Secretary General Kurt Waldheim countersigned their death sentences.

Despite its historical interest, Alimniá is not a place to be stuck for the duration of a day excursion – overpriced, even considering that they include lunch. Upon anchoring, there's a mad scramble for precious spots on the tiny beaches of the bay's south shore. Beyond little Áyios Minás monastery, snorkellers glimpse the **submarine pens**; Italian barracks near the mooring point are bullet-pocked. The **old village** behind a salt marsh consists mostly of derelict shepherds' huts; near the church a grander building sports crude paintings of ships and submarines sketched by bored German soldiers. The battered **castle** is a 45-minute hike up from the anchorage along poor paths, though worth the climb.

# Kastellórizo (Meyísti)

Despite **Kastellórizo**'s official name, Meyísti ("Biggest" – of a local archipelago of islets), it's actually among the smallest of the Dodecanese, more than 100km from Rhodes but barely more than a nautical mile off the Turkish coast. At night its lights are quite outnumbered by those of Turkish Kaş opposite, with which Kastellórizo has excellent relations.

During the island's **heyday** (1860–1910) 10,000 people lived here, supported by schooners transporting timber from the Anatolian mainland. But events during the next two decades – a French 1915–21 occupation, attracting destructive shelling from Ottoman territory, the subsequent Italian occupation, and the post-1923 frontier between Kastellórizo and republican Turkey, combined with the expulsion of all Anatolian Greeks – dealt the local fleet (which had failed to convert to steam power) a fatal blow. In the 1930s Kastellórizo enjoyed a brief role as a major stopover point for French and British seaplanes en route to the Middle East, but World War II events ended any hopes of the island's continued viability.

When Italy capitulated to the Allies in September 1943, about 1500 Commonwealth commandos occupied Kastellórizo, most of them departing in November after the German capture of the other Dodecanese – and leaving the island vulnerable to looters, both Greek and British. In early July 1944, a harbour fuel dump caught (or was set on) fire and an adjacent arsenal **exploded**, demolishing half the 900 houses on Kastellórizo. Most islanders had already left for Rhodes, Australia and North America. Today there are just 342 registered inhabitants (about 250 of them permanent), maintained by remittances from more than 30,000 emigrants, and subsidies from the Greek government to prevent the island reverting to Turkey should numbers diminish further.

Yet Kastellórizo has a future of sorts, thanks partly to repatriating "Kassies" returning each summer to renovate their crumbling ancestral houses as second homes. An airport functions, the harbour has been improved, and the island should soon become an **official Greek port of entry**, eliminating problems for yachties and travellers crossing from Turkey.

The biggest boost in Kastellorizo's fortunes, however, was providing the location for the Italian film **Mediterraneo**, winner of the 1992 Best Foreign Film Oscar, resulting in numerous Italian visitors (though the island in fact gets a variety of tourists). They either love Kastellórizo and stay a week, or crave escape after a day; detractors dismiss it as a human zoo maintained by the Greek government to placate nationalists, while partisans celebrate an atmospheric, barely commercialized outpost of Hellenism.

## Kastellórizo Town

The island's population is concentrated in the northern settlement of **KASTELLÓRIZO** – supposedly the finest natural harbour between Beirut

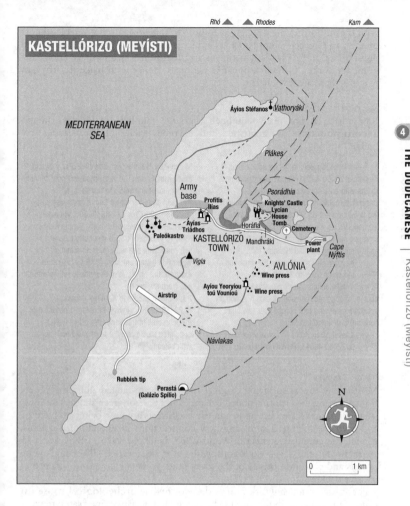

and Fethiye on the Turkish coast – and its "suburb" of Mandhráki, just over the fire-blasted hill with a half-ruined Knights' castle. In summer, it's what Greeks call a *klouví* (bird cage) – the sort of place where, after two strolls up and down the pedestrianized quay, you'll have a nodding acquaintance with your fellow visitors and all the island's characters.

## Arrival, information and transport

A single **ATM** stands on the east quay; the **post office** is on the far side of the bay. The sole **travel** agency is Papoutsis (☎22410 70630 or 693 72 12 530), selling all sea and air tickets. A **minibus** shuttles once between town and airstrip at flight times (€1.80); excess passengers are accommodated in the lone **taxi**, which may make multiple journeys at €6 per passenger.

It's possible to arrange a shuttle to **Turkey** on a local boat, most reliably on Monday or Friday (8am departure). The standard day-return fee is €18, plus any required visa costs on the Turkish side (if you stay overnight); leave your passport with the authorities the day before. Although Kastellórizo is not yet a legal port of entry to Greece – a border "post" is being built – police cannot legally deny disembarkation to EU/EEA nationals arriving from Kaş, an official entry/exit point for Turkey. In theory, non-EU nationals cannot even make day-trips; in practice, there are few checks.

## Accommodation

Kastellórizo is not really equipped for large numbers of visitors, though **accommodation** has gentrified and become pricier of late, leaving few budget options.

**Asimina Pension** Behind the arcaded Italian market ☎22460 49361. Simple wood-trimmed rooms with en-suite baths. ❷

**Caretta Pension** Apply in the gift shop behind the Italian market ☎22460 49056, ⓦwww .kastellorizo.de. Large-roomed if basic, multi-storeyed old-house conversion (❷); a fine restored apartment for two is also available (❹).

**Karnayo** Off the platía at the west end of the south quay ☎22460 49266, ⓔkarnayo@otenet.gr. An excellent mid-range choice, offering a/c rooms or studios (❸) and an apartment sleeping four spread over two quiet, sensitively restored buildings.

**Kastellorizo Hotel** Middle of west quay ☎22460 49044, ⓦwww.kastellorizohotel.gr;

March–Nov. Has the best amenities of any digs in town, with its own lido, a thalasso-spa-pool, friendly management and suites in two sizes. ❺

**Pension Mediterraneo** End of northwest quay ☎22460 49007 or 697 36 76 038, ⓦwww .mediterraneo-kastelorizo.com. Simple rooms (B&B ❹), furnished with mosquito nets and wall art, some with sea view, plus an arcaded, waterside basement suite (B&B ❻) worth the extra for the privilege of essentially rolling into the sea from the door.

**Poseidon** Adjacent to *Karnayo* apartment ☎22460 49257, ⓦwww.Kastelorizo-poseidon.gr. Purpose-built in trad style, this offers well-appointed studios similar to its neighbour, some with balcony. ❸

## The Town

Most of the town's surviving original **mansions** are ranged along the waterfront, sporting tiled roofs, wooden balconies and blue or green shutters on long, narrow windows. Derelict houses in the backstreets are now being attended to, and even the hillside is sprouting new constructions in untraditional colours, though the cumulative effect of World War I shelling, a 1926 earthquake, 1943 air-raids and the 1944 explosions will never be reversed. Black-and-white posters and postcards for sale of the town in its prime are poignant evidence of its later decline.

The castle's outer bulwark houses the worthwhile **archeological museum** (Tues–Sun 8.30am–3pm; free), its displays including Byzantine plates, frescoes rescued from decaying rural churches and a reconstruction of an ancient basilica on the site of today's gaudy, crumbling Áyios Yeóryios Santrapé church at Horáfia. Just below and beyond the museum, in the cliff-face opposite Psorádhia islet, is Greece's only **Lycian house-tomb**, signposted from the shoreline walkway. The 1755 mosque, also below the castle in waterfront Kávos district, is home to the **Historical Collection** (Tues–Sun 8.30am–3pm; free), with ethnographic items, local costumes, printable recipes and folk-song lyrics, and a good photographic archive marred only by a tendentious video blaming British and Italian bombing for the town's destruction.

### Eating, drinking and nightlife

Apart from fish, goat meat and wild-fig preserves, plus produce smuggled over from Kaş, Kastellórizo has to import food and drinking water from Rhodes; this plus the island's celebrity status means taverna **prices** are higher than you might expect. Incidentally, the mains **water** here – contaminated by goat droppings – is not safe to drink. Recommendable waterfront **tavernas** include cheap, cheerful and popular *Iy Ypomoni* (dinner only), two doors to the left of the arcaded market, with a limited seafood menu, and inexpensive 🍴 *Akrothalassi* dishing out large, good-value grills and salads near the west end of the quay – popular at lunch too, as they've the only shaded quayside seating. Inland (adorned with film posters – it was the *Mediterraneo* film-crew's canteen), *Ta Platania* (June to mid-Oct), on the Horáfia platía, is good for daily-changing *mayireftá* and desserts, though no cheaper than waterfront establishments. There are more puddings and good breakfasts at *Zaharoplastio Iy Meyísti*, back on the waterfront.

**Nightlife** spills out of the half-dozen *barákia* lining the quay. *Faros* near the mosque is a cool place with a roof terrace and noise levels kept under control; it's also a "day-bar" with sunbeds on the quay. *Mythos*, towards the ferry jetty, also has an extensive snack menu – handy when all bona-fide tavernas are booked in midsummer – while *Radio Café* next door offers **internet** access and *ouzomezédhes*.

# The rest of the island

Kastellórizo's austere **hinterland** is predominantly bare rock, flecked with stunted vegetation; incredibly, until 1900 this was carefully tended, producing abundant wine of some quality. A rudimentary paved road system links points between Mandhráki and the airstrip, plus there's a dirt track towards Áyios Stéfanos, but there aren't many specific attractions and no scooters for rent. Karstic cliffs drop sheer to the sea, offering no anchorage except at the main town, Mandhráki and Návlakas fjord (see p.348).

## Rural monasteries and ancient monuments

Heat permitting, hike up the obvious, zigzag stair-path from town, then south through scrub to the sadly dilapidated monastery of **Ayíou Yeoryíou toú Vounioú**, thirty minutes from Horáfia's platía. The sixteenth-to-eighteenth-century church (obtain key from annually changing keeper in town) has fine rib-vaulting, an ancient *votsalotó* floor and a carved *témblon*, as well as a rare fresco of Christ emerging from the tomb in the left of the *ierón*. But the most unusual feature is a crypt incorporating the subterranean chapel of **Áyios Harálambos**, with a dark niche-fresco of the saint; access is via a steep, narrow passage descending from the church floor – bring a torch. Just beyond, east of the old path (not the new track), there's a sixth-century BC **wine press** carved into the rock; another one, its cavities and sluices the best preserved of several such presses on the island, can be seen by varying the return to town and using a secondary path from the monastery to Horáfia via Avlónia – only five minutes longer.

Alternatively, a fifteen-minute track-walk west of the port leads to peaceful **Ayías Triádhos monastery**, perched on the saddle with the telecom tower, and an army base. After twenty minutes, the onward path reaches ancient **Paleókastro** citadel, a warren of vaulted chambers, tunnels and cisterns plus another little monastery. From any of the heights above town there are tremendous views over sixty kilometres of Anatolian coast, including dozens of islets large and small, Greek and Turkish.

## The shoreline – and Rhó islet

**Swimming** is complicated by a total absence of beaches and an abundance of sea urchins and razor-sharp limestone reefs; the safest entries near town lie beyond the graveyard at Mandhráki and the cement jetty below the power plant at road's end – or people just dive from the lidos on the northwest quay. Once clear of the shore, you're rewarded by clear waters with a rich variety of marine life and amphora shards testifying to the local ancient wine trade. **Taxi-boats** can take you to otherwise inaccessible coves such as **Plákes**, with superb swimming off, and sunbathing on, the flat surfaces of this ex-quarry.

From Ayíou Yeoryíou toú Vounioú, continue forty minutes further on foot, first on a modern bulldozer track, then on the original, French-built *kalderími*, to **Návlakas fjord**, a favourite mooring spot for yachts and fishing boats. The French, using local labour, opened this route in early 1917 to facilitate offloading the components of a 120-millimetre gun battery, which eventually silenced Ottoman artillery on the mainland. Uniquely on Kastellórizo, Návlakas is sea-urchin-free, with freshwater seeps keeping the temperature brisk; there's superb snorkelling to 20-metre depths off the south wall.

Further along the southeast coast, accessible by boat excursion (usually 9.30am; 1hr 30min return; €10) from town, **Perastá grotto** (Galázio Spílio) deserves a visit for its stalactites and strange blue-light effects; the low entrance, negotiable only by inflatable raft, gives little hint of the enormous chamber within, with monk seals occasionally sheltering in an adjacent cave.

Perastá boat trips are sometimes extended (at double the cost, ca. 5hr) to include **Rhó islet**, where until her death, *Iý Kyrá tís Rhó* (**The Lady of Rhó**), aka Dhespina Akhladhioti (1898?–1982), hoisted the Greek flag daily in defiance of the Turks across the way. In her waning years, an honorary salary, a commemorative postage stamp and television appearances lent her glory and fame which she revelled in; by most accounts she was a miserly curmudgeon, known to have refused passing sailors emergency rations of fresh water.

Her **tomb** is the first thing you see on arrival at the sandy, northwestern harbour; from here a path heads 25 minutes southeast to the islet's southerly port, past the side trail to an intact Hellenistic **fortress** on the island's summit. Rhó has no facilities – just a few soldiers to prevent Turkish landings or goat-poaching – so bring supplies.

# Sými

**Sými**'s most pressing problem, lack of fresh water, is in some ways its saving grace. As with other dry, rocky Dodecanese islands, **water** must be imported from Rhodes, pending completion of a reservoir in the distant future. Consequently, the island can't support more than a few large hotels; instead, hundreds of people are shipped in for seasonal day-trips from Rhodes. This arrangement suits both the Symiots and those visitors lucky enough to stay longer; many foreigners return regularly, or even own houses here. The island, long fashionable among Italians, Brits and Danes, entered domestic Greek consciousness in a big way after 2005 when it featured in the Turkish TV serial *The Frontiers of Love*. With fame has come fortune – it's an expensive resort, with restaurant meals and bar drinks at Rhodian prices.

Once beyond the inhabited areas, you'll find an attractive island that has retained some **forest** of junipers, valonea oaks and even a few pines – ideal walking country in spring or autumn (though not midsummer, when temperatures are among the highest in Greece). Dozens of privately owned tiny **monasteries** dot the landscape; though generally locked except on their patron saint's day, freshwater cisterns are usually accessible.

## Sými Town

**SÝMI**, the capital and only town, comprises **Yialós**, the excellent natural port, linked to **Horió**, on the hillside above, by two massive stair-paths, the **Kalí Stráta** and **Katarráktes**. Arriving by sea, the town's exquisite Neoclassical mansions slowly reveal themselves as your vessel rounds the promontories guarding the deeply inset harbour. Incredibly, around 1895 the place was more populous (25,000) than Ródhos Town, its wealth generated by shipbuilding and sponge-diving, skills nurtured since ancient times. Under the Ottomans, Sými enjoyed considerable autonomy, in exchange for a yearly tribute in sponges to the sultan; but the 1913 Italian-imposed frontier, the 1919–22 Greco-Turkish war, the advent of synthetic sponges and the gradual replacement of crews by Kalymniots shattered the local economy. Vestiges of past nautical glories remain in still-active boatyards at Pédhi and Haráni, but today's souvenir sponges come entirely from overseas and – an ongoing restoration boom notwithstanding – magnificent nineteenth-century mansions still stand roofless and empty.

The approximately 2500 remaining Symiots are scattered fairly evenly across a mixture of Neoclassical and vernacular island dwellings; many outsiders prefer to build from scratch at the edge of town, rather than renovate derelict shells

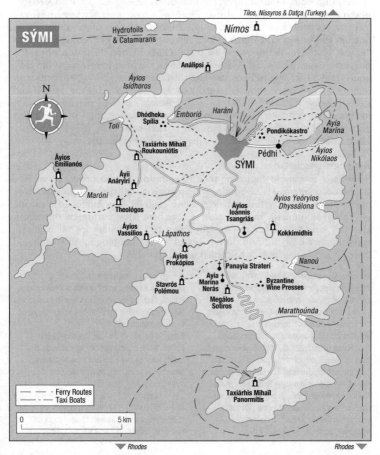

accessible only by donkey or on foot. As on Kastellórizo, a September 1944 ammunition blast – this time set off by the retreating Germans – levelled hundreds of houses up in Horió. The official German surrender of the Dodecanese to the Allies, the last Axis territory to yield, was signed in Yialós on May 8, 1945: a plaque marks the spot at *Restaurant Les Catherinettes*.

## Arrival, information and transport

One **conventional craft** (*Symi II*, 1hr 50min; some cars taken) and a **hydrofoil** (*Aegli*, 1hr; double the price) each run at least daily to Sými from Mandhráki in Ródhos Town. The *Aegli* docks at Yialós's south quay, conveniently near the **taxi rank** and **bus stop**, while the *Symi II* and all other vessels anchor at the north quay by the clocktower. Almost daily, the cheap, locally based *Protevs* and the *Dodekanisos Express/Pride* chip in with various links to Rhodes and other Dodecanese. All these boats use the central Kolóna harbour of Rhodes. Among **ferry agents**, ANES, for *Protevs/Symi II/Aegli* tickets, maintains booths on each quay and an office in the marketplace lanes (☎22460 71444), while *Dodekanisos Express/Pride* and the very rare long-distance ferry are handled by Symi Tours nearby (☎22460 71307).

There's no official tourist office, but the island's English-language **advertiser-newspaper** and associated **website** *The Symi Visitor* (free; ⓦwww.symivisitor .com) are useful, and the Symi Visitor Accommodation office above Pahos Kafenio sells **books and maps** of local interest. The **post office** is in the Italian "palace" on the north quay; there are three **ATMs**. During the season a **bus** (€1) shuttles between Yialós and Pédhi via Horió on the hour (returning at the half-hour) until 11/11.30pm. There are also six **taxis** (allow €5 Yialós–Horió with baggage), two pricey **scooter** rental outletss – Katsaras by the bridge and customs house (☎22460 72203) is more reasonable than exorbitant Glaros on the north quay (☎22460 71926) – and **car rental** (a whopping €58–70 per day) from Symi Tours (ⓦwww.symitours.com). **Taxi-boat** fares (€7–10, no one-ways) make a scooter – or walking – that much more attractive.

## Accommodation

Sými has a reasonable choice of **accommodation** for independent travellers, at least compared to Hálki. Studios and apartments, rather than simple doubles, predominate; you may find vacancies more easily in July/August than during spring and autumn, the most pleasant seasons here. Most outfits stay open from Easter to early November, to catch the Panormítis monastery festival. Asphyxiating summer heat and non-universality of air conditioning mean you should go for north-facing and/or balconied units if possible.

**Albatros** Marketplace ☎22460 71707, ⓦwww .albatrosymi.gr. Partial sea views from this exquisite small hotel with a/c and a pleasant second-floor breakfast salon. The website is also the booking venue for a number of magnificent Neoclassical villas divided into apartments. ❸
**Aliki** Haráni quay ☎22460 71665, ⓦwww.hotelaliki .gr. A complete overhaul of an 1895 mansion, and Sými's most exclusive hotel. The tasteful rooms have wood floors and some antique furnishings, plus a/c and large bathrooms, though only some have sea views or balconies. Standard rooms ❻, suites ❼.
**Les Catherinettes** Above the eponymous restaurant, north quay ☎22460 71671,

ⓔmarina-epe@rho.forthnet.r. Spotless en-suite pension in a historic building with painted ceilings, fridges, fans and sea-view balconies in most rooms (❸). They also offer three studios in Haráni, plus a family apartment (❹).
**Fiona** At the top of the Kalí Stráta ☎22460 72088. Mock-traditional hotel whose large airy rooms have double beds and stunning views; breakfast is taken on a common balcony. Also three studios next door. ❹
**Iapetos Village** Just back from Yialós Platía ☎22460 72777, ⓦwww.iapetos-village.gr. 2008-inaugurated complex of huge (80 sq m), balconied maisonettes plus a few studios that's

made an impression locally with its roofed-over pool and lushly landscaped grounds complete with palm trees. Though units have full kitchens, a good breakfast is offered either in cool basement premises or by the pool bar; wi-fi signal. Studio **⑥**, maisonette **⑦**.

**Katerina Tsakiris** Hillside between Yialós and Horió ☎22460 71813 or 694 51 30 112. Just a handful of rather plain if a/c en-suite rooms with separate self-catering kitchen facilities and a grandstand view over the harbour; reservations essential. **③**

**Niriides Apartments** Haráni–Emborió road, 2km from Yialós ☎22460 71784, @www.niriideshotel .com. Spacious, quiet, plain units sleeping four, spread over four hillside buildings. All have phone, TV and optional a/c. Friendly management, on-site "lounge-café", internet booking discount. **⑥**

**Odyssia Apartments** Haráni far quay ☎22460 72642. The best shoreline views from this quiet yet convenient spot, though the apartments themselves are on the spartan, blonde-pine/white-tile side.

A mix of studios and three/four person galleried units; sweetshop/café on the the ground floor. **⑥**

**Symi Villas** ☎22460 71819, @www.symi-villas .gr. Jean Manship manages four traditional houses in Horió, suitable for two to six people, with stunning views. **③–⑥**

🛏 **Symi Visitor Accommodation** ☎22460 71785, @www.symivisitor.com. Managed by Wendy Wilcox and Adriana Shum, who offer a variety of restored properties from simple studios (**③**) to family mansions for €400; average price about €115 for four people. Be aware that these are second homes let in their owners' absence, so come with full kitchens, book/DVD collections – and possible quirks.

🛏 **Villa Agapi** Behind Yialós platía; enquire at *Kandrimi* bar ☎22460 71381, ☎693 64 21 215 or @www.symigreece.com/agapi.htm. Exceptionally well-appointed three-bedroom, two-bath house sleeping six. €175 a night for the entire two-storey house; weekly rates.

## The Town

At the architecturally protected **port**, sponge and souvenir stalls on the north quay throng with Rhodes-based trippers between 10am and 3pm, when excursion craft disgorging them envelop the shoreline with exhaust fumes. But just uphill, away from the water, the pace of village life takes over, with livestock and chickens roaming free. The Kalí Stráta and Katarráktes effectively deter most day-trippers and are especially dramatic towards sunset; owl-haunted ruins along the lower Kalí Stráta are lonely and sinister after dark, though these too are now being renovated.

A series of arrows through **Horió** leads to the excellent local **museum** (Tues–Sun 8.30am–2.30pm; €2). Housed in a fine old mansion at the back of the village, the collection highlights Byzantine and medieval Sými, particularly frescoes in isolated, often locked churches. The nearby **Hatziagapitos mansion** serves as an annexe; here, wonderful carved wooden chests are the main displays, along with allegorical wall-paintings including a female figure (perhaps Learning personified) making a gift of a book to a young lad. At the very pinnacle of things, a **Knights' castle** occupies the site of Sými's ancient acropolis, so you glimpse a stretch of Classical polygonal wall on one side. The **church of the Assumption**, inside the fortifications, replaces one blown to bits when the Germans detonated the munitions cached there. One of the bells in the new belfry is the nose-cone of a thousand-pound bomb, hung as a memorial.

## Eating and drinking

At most places on the north and west quays of the port, ingredients, prices and attitudes have been warped by the day-trip trade. Elsewhere, you've a fair range of choice among *koultouriárika* **tavernas**, old-style *mayireftá* places, genuine ouzerís and cafés both traditional and modern.

### Restaurants

**Dhimitris** South quay, heading out of Yialós. Family-run ouzerí with exotic seafood items like

*hokhlióalo* (sea snails), *fouskóalo* and the miniature local shrimps, along with the usual sausages, chops and vegetarian starters.

**O Meraklis** Rear of Yialós bazaar. Polite service and fair portions of *mayireftá*, fresh fish and *mezédhes* make this a reliable year-round bet. A meal might include beans, beets, dips, and roast lamb with potatoes as a tender main course.

🏃 **Mythos Meze** South quay, Yialós. Roof-terrace supper venue (late May to late Sept) in the former summer cinema, serving some of the best-value cooking on the island. Chef-owner Stavros has scaled back his tasting menu a bit, banishing some of the more *outré* dishes, but it still features recipes such as *psaronéfri* with mushrooms and sweet wine sauce, lamb *stifádho*, feta *saganáki* in fig sauce, and good desserts like lemon pie or panna cotta. His original premises near the bus stop is now *Mythos Fish*, stressing à la carte seafood, open a longer season and some lunches too. Allow €25–30 a head plus drink at either; book for both premises on ☎22460 71488.

**Muses** Yialós platía, south side. Lovely seating under trailing vines, similar ambitions, quality and prices to *Mythos*.

**Syllogos** Just south of Platía Syllógou, Horió. Vast but not impersonal place with indoor/outdoor seating, great for taverna standards like *skordhaliá*, *arní lemonáto*, fried fish and aubergine *imám*, with good *hýma* wine on offer – only skimpy portion sizes deprive it of an author pick symbol.

**Yiorgos** Top of Kalí Stráta, Horió. Jolly, much-loved Sými institution, with summer seating on a pebble-mosaic courtyard. Service can be slipshod and food quality fluctuates, but perennial dishes include feta-stuffed peppers, beans with sausage, chicken in mushroom-wine sauce, and a full range of grills. Open random lunchtimes in season, supper all year (winter indoors).

## Cafés & sweets

**Lefteris** Top of the Kalí Stráta, second shopfront on Platía Syllógou, Horió. The local characters' *kafenío*, attended by all. Coffee or ice cream at any hour; also simple *mezédhes*.

**Nikolas** Back alley near Yíalos bridge. The first-ever *zaharoplastío* on the island, and still the only one doing its sweeties on site rather than importing from Rhodes.

🏃 **Pahos** West quay near Yialós bridge (no sign). Classic *kafenío*, in operation since World War II, and still the spot for an evening oúzo or coffee and people-watching. Pahos himself has retired and can often be found sitting out front as a customer; otherwise it's hardly changed – including the prices, significantly lower than elsewhere.

**Sunrise Café/Anatoli Iliou** East edge Horió, just past *Hotel Horio*. Cozy English/German-run place doing well-priced drinks, breakfast and light snacks; open all day until the small hours.

### Nightlife and events

**Nightlife** is divided between Horió and Yialós, with a slight bias towards the latter. Convivial *The 2 As* (that's owners Alex and Astrid) is heart and soul of the bar scene in Horió, catering to a mixed clientele with 1960s music; *Kali Strata* at the top of said stairs has the best views and a jazz/world soundtrack. Down at Yialós, *Katoï* on the south quay pulls in locals and was the busiest here in 2008; nearby *Harani Club* plays Greek or international music depending on the crowd, while in the same alley, *Vapori* offers free newspapers, breakfasts and internet access with wi-fi signal. On the far side of Yialós platía in the shade of huge spreading ficus trees, *Evoi Evan* is open from breakfast until late, with a cavernous interior and slightly more reasonable drink prices than elsewhere.

There are also year-round Friday-night **movie screenings** in various venues, while the July-to-early-September **Sými Festival** presents a mix of classical and popular Greek performances in the respective platíes of Yialós and Horió.

## Around the island

Sými has no large sandy **beaches**, but instead various pebbly stretches at the heads of deep, protected bays that indent the coastline. **PÉDHI**, 1km east of Horió, retains some of its past as a fishing hamlet, with the plain behind – the island's largest – supporting a few vegetable gardens. The beach is medicore, though, and patronage from yachts (for whom an unsightly marina is being built) and the *Pedhi Beach* hotel has bumped up prices at local **tavernas**, of which the most reasonable and authentic is fish specialist *Tolis* (no sign up), tucked away by the boatyard at the north corner of the bay. Many will opt for either a sporadic taxi-boat or a fifteen-minute path walk from the brackish springs by the church, along the south shore of the almost landlocked bay, to **Áyios Nikólaos**. The only all-sand cove on Sými, this offers sheltered swimming, shady tamarisks, a bar, beach volleyball and an overpriced taverna. Alternatively, a paint-splodge-marked path on the north side of the inlet leads in half an hour to **Ayía Marína**, where there's a minuscule beach, a shingle lido with sunbeds, an uneven taverna-bar and a monastery-capped islet to which you can easily swim. You can return directly to town by using the onward trail through the gate at the far end of the "beach"; it's well marked but rough, so allow an hour to emerge at the **Pondikókastro**, a round Hellenistic funerary monument, just before a line of windmills at the east end of Horió.

Around Yialós, tiny, man-made **Symi Paradise** "beach" lies ten minutes beyond the Haráni boatyards, with an eponymous restaurant, coarse-shingle shore (shaded all afternoon) and frankly poor swimming. You can continue along the paved coast road, or cut inland from the Yialós platía past the abandoned desalination plant to quiet **Emborió** (Nimborió) Bay, with a good taverna, a coarse-shingle beach, and tranquil swimming. Inland from here lie Byzantine mosaic fragments (follow signs to "Early Christian Basilica") under a protective shelter next to Siamese-triplet chapels. Much has been obliterated, but you can discern a man leading a camel, a partridge and a stag in flight from a boar. A faint trail leads 100m further to the partly fenced **Dhódheka Spília** catacomb complex. On the other side of the hill from Emborió, small, pebbly **Tolí Bay** is now reachable by dirt track from the paved road to Roukouniótis monstery; a taverna was set to commence operation there in 2009.

## Remoter bays and monasteries

Plenty of other, more **secluded coves** are accessible to energetic walkers (who should furnish themselves with the "Walker's Map of Symi", packaged along with Lance Chilton's *Walks in Symi*), or those prepared to pay for taxi-boats (daily outbound 10am–1pm, returning 4–6pm). These are the most popular method of reaching the large southern bay of Nanoú, and the only method of getting to the spectacular fjord of **Áyios Yeóryios Dhyssálona**. Dhyssálona – which served as a location for *The Guns of Navarone* – lacks a taverna and lies in afternoon shade, while **Marathoúnda** (usually reached by road) is fringed by coarse pebbles, though it has an excellent, popular, eponymous **taverna**, with fish at or below town prices and good starters.

**Nanoú** is the most popular destination for day-trips, its 200-metre beach consisting of gravel, sand and small pebbles, with good snorkelling, a scenic backdrop of pines and a reasonable, seafood-strong **taverna** (also with a dish of the day) just behind. It's also possible to reach Nanoú overland, descending through a scenic, forested gorge for 45 minutes from Panayía Straterí chapel on the main trans-island road (allow 1hr up); most of the old path from Horió to Panayía Straterí still exists, making a marvellous traverse of about three hours in total, leaving time for a meal and swim before the boat trip back to Yialós.

Another meaty hike crosses the island from Horió in ninety minutes to scenic **Áyios Vassílios** gulf (or 40min from the road's end along a paint-splodge-marked path), with a namesake little monastery above **Lápathos beach**; partly cleaned frescoes in the monastery (which has accessible water) include a *Crucifixion*, *Transfiguration*, *Calvary* and *Raising of Lazarus* as an upper series, with the life of the saint in the lower. It's three hours one-way, partly through forest, from Yialós to **Áyios Emilianós** at the island's extreme west end, where another tiny monastery (no art) is tethered to the body of Sými by a causeway. On the way there you'll pass **Taxiárhis Mihaïl Roukouniótis** monastery (ring inner doorbell 9–11am & 5–6pm), Sými's oldest, with naïve eighteenth-century frescoes and the current *katholikón* superimposed on a lower, abandoned thirteenth-century structure, with an intriguing fresco of St Lawrence.

More and better frescoes are scattered across the island – especially at hilltop, 1697-vintage **Kokkimídhis monastery** (usually open), reached by a steep track off the Panormítis road, with a complete cycle showing the acts of the Archangel and the risen Christ. At fourteenth-century **Áyios Prokópios** (usually open), just off the same road before Panayía Straterí, there's a fine *Crucifixion*, *Resurrection*, martial saints and a deesis (the Virgin and John the Baptist flanking Christ) in the apse; **Ayía Marína Nerás** church (always open) further along the same road beyond Panayía Straterí, has naïve if damaged fifteenth-century images of the *Crucifixion*, the *Angel at the Tomb* and a *Nativity* with the Virgin nursing. Nearby **Megálos Sotíros** (often locked, key from Kalodoukas Tours), just before the drop down the escarpment, shelters fine frescoes from 1727 including a *Deposition*, with Joseph of Arimathaea holding a winding sheet to receive the dead Christ, and a *Resurrection* with Jesus seemingly doing a jig on the sepulchre. Across the road, a signposted trail leads to some worthwhile, reconstructed Byzantine **wine presses**.

### Panormítis monastery

The Archangel (*Taxiárhis* in Greek), patron of the island, is honoured at giant **Taxiárhis Mihaïl Panormítis** monastery in the far south, the first port of call for many excursion boats from Rhodes. These allow only a thirty-minute tour; for more time, come from Yialós by scooter (the road down from the central escarpment is steep, with nine hairpin bends) or bus (2–3 daily).

Panormítis was thoroughly pillaged during World War II, so – except for its lofty belfry – don't expect much of the building or its contents. An appealing *votsalotó* courtyard surrounds the central *katholikón*, lit by an improbable number of oil lamps. It's also graced by a fine *témblon* and of course the cult icon, though frescoes are mediocre. One of two small **museums** (€1.50 admits to both) contains a strange mix of precious antiques, exotic junk, votive offerings, models of ships named *Taxiarhis* or *Panormitis* and a chair piled with messages-in-bottles brought here by Aegean currents – supposedly if the bottle or toy boat arrived, the sender got their prayer answered. There's a **shop/kafenío**, a **bakery** and a **taverna** popular with passengers on the many yachts calling here. A memorial commemorates three Greeks, including the monastery's abbot, executed on February 11, 1944 by the Germans for aiding British commandos.

# Tílos

The small, usually quiet island of **Tílos**, with an official population of about five hundred (dwindling to 100 in winter), is among the least frequented and most unpredictably connected of the Dodecanese. It's a great place to rest on the beach or go walking, and while there's nothing very striking at first glance, after a few days you may have stumbled on several small Knights' **castles** studding the crags, or found some of the inconspicuous, often frescoed, often locked **medieval chapels** (ring Pandelis Yiannourakis on ☎22460 44240 for admission) clinging to the hillsides.

Tílos shares the characteristics of its closest neighbours: limestone **mountains** like those of Hálki, plus volcanic lowlands, pumice beds and red-lava sand as on Níssyros. Though rugged and scrubby on its heights, the island has ample **water** – from springs or pumped up from the agricultural plains – and clusters of oak and terebinth near the cultivated areas. From many points you've startling views across to Kós, Sými, Turkey, Níssyros, Hálki, Rhodes and even (weather permitting) Kárpathos. Stranded midway between Kós and Rhodes, Tílos has always been a backwater, and has the least developed nautical tradition of the Dodecanese. With ample groundwater and rich volcanic soil, the islanders could afford to turn their backs on the sea, and made Tílos the **breadbasket** of the Dodecanese. Until the 1970s, approaching travellers were greeted by the sight of shimmering fields of grain bowing in the wind; today the hillside terraces languish abandoned, evidence of typical small-island depopulation.

Recent changes on Tílos, however, threaten the things that many visitors value; besides burgeoning **development** at Livádhia, a hyperactive road-bulldozing programme has scarred nearly every mountain in the east of the

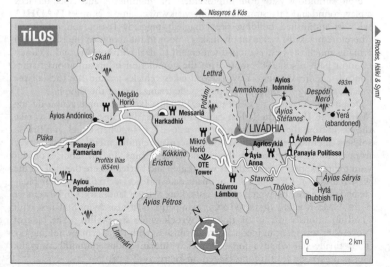

island. Thankfully, the remotest beaches are located in terrain too steep to create vehicle access without prohibitive expense, and a project – currently suspended – exists to protect much of coastal and mountain Tílos as a **national park**. In June 2008, Tílos acquired a bit of notoriety by hosting Greece's **first same-sex civil marriage** ceremonies (a gay and a lesbian couple), conducted by PASOK Mayor Tassos Aliferis in defiance of the central government's interpretation of the 1982 law governing civil unions.

### Transport and information

Tílos's main road runs 7km from **Livádhia**, the port village, to **Megálo Horió**, the capital and only other significant habitation. A blue-and-white **bus** links the two, theoretically coinciding with seaborne arrivals; otherwise it makes up to five runs daily between Livádhia and Éristos. There is just one **taxi**, so you might want to **rent a car** from Livádhia outlets such as Drive (℡ 22460 44173) and Tilos Travel (see below). Stefanakis, also in Livádhia (℡ 22460 44310), has a monopoly on **ferry** and **hydrofoil tickets**; Tilos Travel is arguably more helpful (℡ 22460 44294 or 694 65 59 697, ⊛ www.tilostravel.co.uk), offering a good accommodation booking service, used-book swap and scooter- as well as car-rental. The unreliable, expensive *Sea Star* **catamaran** has its own office by the church (℡ 22460 44000); the single **filling station** lies between Livádhia and Megálo Horió. There's a **post office** in Livádhia, a single bank **ATM**, several **internet** cafés (try *Balthazar* or *Croma Bar*), usually with wi-fi signal, and two well-stocked **supermarkets**.

Many visitors come specifically to **walk**, assisted by the accurate **map** prepared originally by Baz Ward and sold locally – or by certified walking guides Iain and Lyn Fulton (℡ 694 60 54 593 or ⊛ www.tilostrails.com), who may take you on itineraries not described or mapped in existing literature. A half-dozen sections of deteriorating trail or *kalderími* have been surveyed in preparation for consolidation.

## Livádhia

Despite ambitious waterfront improvement programmes – landscaped terraces, a playground and a flagstoned shoreline walkway of almost 2km – **LIVÁDHIA** with its unfinished building sites, higgledy-piggledy layout and overdrawn (therefore brackish) water supply makes a poor introduction to the island. Yet it remains much the best-equipped settlement to deal with tourists, and is closest to most path-hikes. 2009 should see the completion of an ambitious traffic-control scheme, whereby a bypass road takes vehicles around the back of the village, allowing (in theory) complete pedestrianization of the shoreline.

Despite its currently peaceful profile, Livádhia Bay saw ample action during **World War II** after the Italian capitulation. The Allies first attempted to take the island from the Germans on October 26–27, 1944, when Greek and British soldiers disembarked from HMS *Sirus*; German reinforcements quickly arrived from Rhodes and reversed the Anglo-Greek gains. In the course of this counterattack, two Greek fighters were killed and buried where they fell on the west hillside on October 28, a resonant date indeed (see p.624) – their blue-striped white **tombs**, which can be visited, are a major landmark. On November 5, the HMS *Kimberly* destroyed a German patrol boat near Áyios Stéfanos; with good directions you can still find the **wreck** while **snorkelling**. The bulk of November was spent in inconclusive skirmishes, with the Germans holding on; Tílos finally fell when a force of mostly Indian troops, outnumbering the German garrison four to one, landed on February 27–28, 1945.

## Accommodation

Simple doubles, some studio format, still predominate among **accommodation**, though larger apartments are appearing. There are generally enough beds available, but at peak season it's worth advance booking.

**Anna's Studios** On the west hillside above the jetty ☏ 22460 44334, ⊛ www.annas-studios.com. Immaculate units with pastel-hued furnishings, priced according to size. ❸

**Blue Sky** Right above ferry jetty ☏ 22460 44294. Well-appointed, 2002-built, galleried apartments managed by Tilos Travel. ❸

**Dream Island Apartments** About two-thirds of way around the bay ☏ 22460 70707, ⊛ www .dreamisland.gr. A mix of one- and two-bedroom apartments, all with at least oblique sea views; decor is modern in cool colours. No breakfast, but on-site bar. One-bed ❺

**Eleni Beach Hotel** About halfway around the bay ☏ 22460 44062, ⊛ www .elenihoteltilos.gr. Expanded in 2007 to three wings, its airy, white-decor rooms with bug screens and wi-fi signal offer the best value on the shoreline; wheelchair access and private beach facilities. ❸

**Elli Bay Hotel Apartments** Near *Mihalis* taverna ☏ 22460 44435, ⊛ www.ellibay.com. 2008-opened, Cycladic-style seafront complex with mock-antique furnished units and compact kitchens. B&B ❹

**Faros Hotel** At the extreme northeast end of the bay ☏ 22460 44068, ⓔ dimkouk@otenet.gr. Widely praised for its calm, well-cared-for rooms and hospitable managing family; also has an acceptable restaurant (with resident parrot) and a tiny private beach. ❸

**Ilidi Rock** On the west hillside (contacts as for *Irini Hotel*). State-of-the-art studios with wi-fi, a conference centre, gym, private beach; some apartments sleep four and one wing has disabled access. Breakfast served summer only. ❹

**Irini Hotel** 200m inland from the middle of the beach ☏ 22410 44293, ⊛ www.tilosholidays.gr. A lushly landscaped low-rise hotel, where a large pool, good breakfasts, wi-fi signal and pleasant gardens make up for somewhat small, mock-antique furnished rooms. ❸

**Tilos Fantasy** South inland on hillside ☏ 22460 44425, ☏ www.tilosfantasy.gr. Despite the silly name, these are more than decent, if a bit IKEA-decor, 2008-opened studios in a quiet location, though the grounds are still a bit barren. ❸

## Eating, drinking and nightlife

Less than half of Livádhia's dozen or so peak-season **tavernas** merit consideration, and in spring or autumn you must book timed seatings at the more Anglophilic restaurants – unheard of on other islands. Among more authentic spots are *Mihalis* at the east end of the shopping street, with no-nonsense roast goat and fish as well as good vegetable platters and non-CAIR bulk wine served at garden tables; *To Armenon* on the shore road, a professionally run and salubrious beach-taverna-cum-ouzerí, with large portions of octopus salad, white beans, meaty mains and fish platters washed down by Alfa beer on tap; nearby *Oneiro/Dream*, with a limited menu of excellent grills but overpriced bulk wine; and Brazilian-managed *Luna Mare* beyond this pair, doing flat crispy pizzas, pasta dishes and good risottos with (that island rarity) top-flight service.

Among **cafés**, *Iy Omonia* (aka *Tou Mihali*), under trees strung with light bulbs overlooking the park, is the enduringly popular traditional venue for a sundowner, breakfast or a drink while waiting for a ferry; its inexpensive, tasty, generous *mezédhes* will stand in for a formal meal. The jetty-café *Remezzo* also does excellent *ouzomezédhes*. Organized **nightlife** in or near Livádhia relies mostly on small music bars like *To Mikro Café* and *Café Ino*, two restored shoreline cottages, though 2008 saw *Luna Mare* hosting **live music** nightly, with resident and guest guitarists performing. There's also a regular Thursday-evening folk/blues gig at the *Faros Hotel*'s restaurant.

## Walks and beaches near Livádhia

From Livádhia you can walk an hour north along an obvious trail to the pebble bay of **Lethrá**; about two-thirds of the way along, you pass the side-path to the tiny red-sand beach of **Ammóhosti**, though it's no secret and you're unlikely to have it to yourself.

It takes about as long to hike south on separate itineraries to the secluded coves of **Stavrós** or **Thólos**. The track to the former, soon a trail, begins between the *Tilos Mare Hotel* and the *Castellania Apartments*; once up to the saddle with its paved road, you've a sharp drop to the beach. Ignore the cairns in the ravine bed; the true path is up on the right bank, indicated by red-painted surveyor's marks. The route to Thólos begins by the cemetery and the chapel of **Áyios Pandelímon**, then curls under the seemingly impregnable castle of **Agriosykiá**; from the saddle on the paved road overlooking the descent to Thólos (25min; also red-marked), a cairned route leads northwest to the citadel in twenty minutes. Head east a couple of curves along that paved road to the trailhead for **Áyios Séryis Bay**, the most pristine of Tílos's beaches but the hardest to reach (30min from the road).

It's less than an hour's walk west, with some surviving path sections shortcutting the road curves, to the ghost village of **Mikró Horió**, whose 1200 inhabitants left for Livádhia during the 1950s. The only intact structures are churches (locked to protect their frescoes) and an old house restored as a small-hours **music bar** (July–Aug). From the north end of the village below the ruined castle, a path leads down within twenty minutes to the paved road, then crosses it to resume (after a section of bulldozer track) as a partly vegetation-obstructed trail through the scenic, steep-sided **Potámi canyon**; do not follow any cairns directing you up and right, as that path fizzles out high up on the hillside. Under an hour, past a fairly reliable spring, should see you to Lethrá Bay; you can make a loop return to Livádhia via the more trodden coastal path.

## Megálo Horió and Éristos

The rest of Tílos's inhabitants live in or near the village of **MEGÁLO HORIÓ**, which enjoys sweeping views over the vast agricultural plain stretching down to Éristos (see opposite), and is overlooked in turn by a prominent **Knights' castle**, built atop ancient Tílos, whose recycled masonry remains evident. You reach it by a stiff, thirty-minute climb that begins on the lane behind the Ikonomou supermarket before threading its way through a vast jumble of cisterns, house foundations and derelict chapels – the remains of much larger medieval Megálo Horió. Towards the northeast end of the village is one of Tílos's few unlocked churches: **Áyios Ioánnis Thelógos**, with engaging sixteenth-to-seventeenth-century frescoes. Other monumental interest is provided by the handsome, post-Byzantine parish **church of Taxiárhis**, built on the site of a temple to Apollo and Athena, and the **chuch of the Panayía** near the top of the village, both with extensive *votsalotó* courtyards. Two more nearby fortresses stare out across the plain: the easterly one of Messariá marks the location of the **Harkadhió cave** (closed), where Pleiocene midget-elephant bones were discovered in 1971. The bones themselves may eventually be displayed in a purpose-built museum near the cave.

**Accommodation** in Megálo Horió comprises the central *Milios Apartments* (T 22460 44204; ❷) and *Studios Ta Elefandakia* (T 22460 44213; ❷), set among attractive gardens by the car park; a more comfortable choice is British-run *Eden Villas* in the valley leading north towards Skáfi beach (T 22460 44094, W www.eden-villas.com), two well-sited three-bedroom villas with pool and free wi-fi (€1300 per week peak season; all year, long winter lets). The lone **taverna**, *Kastro*, is somewhat glum but serves own-raised meat, goat cheese and home-made *dolmádhes*; Athenian-run *Kafenio Ilakati* (July–Sept evenings only) further uphill does desserts and drinks.

Below Megálo Horió, signs direct you 3km south to long, pink-grey-sand **Éristos beach**, allegedly the island's best (and home to summer colonies of campers), though a reef must be crossed entering the water. The far south end, where the reef recedes, is nudist, as are the two secluded all-naturist coves at **Kókkino** beyond the headland (accessible by path from the obvious military pillbox). On the secondary, parallel road down to Éristos, *En Plo* is the best nearby venue for a **snack**, while the *Eristos Beach Hotel* (☎22460 44025; ❸) offers big balconies, a pleasant pool and larger apartments fitting four.

## The far northwest

The main road beyond Megálo Horió hits the coast again at somewhat grim **ÁYIOS ANDÓNIOS**, which has an exposed, truncated beach; the better of the two **tavernas** is *Dhelfíni*, packed at weekends but frequented otherwise mainly by local fishermen. There's better, warm-water swimming at isolated, sandy **Pláka beach**, 2km west of Áyios Andónios, where people camp rough despite a total lack of facilities.

The paved road ends 8km west of Megálo Horió at fortified **Ayíou Pandelímona monastery** (daily: May–Sept 10am–7pm, may close briefly at noon; Oct–April 10am–4pm), founded in the fifteenth century for the sake of its miraculous spring, still the best water on the island. A fitfully operating drinks café hosts the island's major **festival** of July 25–27. The monastery's tower-gate and oasis setting, high above the forbidding west coast, are its most memorable features, though a photogenic inner courtyard boasts a *votsalotó* surface, and the church a fine tesselated mosaic floor. On the south *katholikón* wall, an early eighteenth-century fresco shows the founder-builder holding a model of the monastery, while behind the ornate altar screen hides another rare fresco of the Holy Trinity.

The public bus calls at the monastery only on Sunday as part of a tour, so you'll need transport to get here. To vary the return to Megálo Horió, take a taxi out then walk back much of the way on a signposted path; it's shown on both our and Baz Ward's map (see p.356), and was part-cleaned in 2008.

### Ayíou Pandelímona to Éristos

Committed and experienced hill-walkers can tackle the challenging path (not on the local map) around the southwest flank of Profítis Ilías (651m), Tílos's highest mountain, finishing several hours later at Éristos. This begins (unsigned) beside the monastery; it's a well-surveyed route – one of the six set for revamping – with no real exposure or sharp drops, and extensive surviving patches of old *kalderími* still *in situ*. But there's only one water source, rather demoralizing scree at the start, and the feel of a remote traverse on a much larger island.

The scree-slides have obliterated the original course of the trail, as shown on old Italian ordnance survey maps; the first 25 minutes are thus a bit further inland than you'd expect, with a tough climb past or even over the loose scree, until the grade slackens and you're back onto proper path. With the worst over, you then negotiate three successive, gentle passes; the second is the highest on this part of the route, and you glimpse the sea swirling around Tílos's southwesterly cape far below. An hour along should find you at the top of the first small ravine draining to Limenári Bay, with a claw-like promontory visible beyond. Twenty minutes later you reach the lone spring en route, inside a stone pen; the spout-water should be potable, though there's often a dead goat near (or in) the trough.

Continue descending, over less obvious sections, past a dilapidated chapel, to cross the bed of the main ravine descending to **Limenári**, one hour forty minutes out – barely halfway to Éristos, if you're thinking of detouring for a swim.

Now you climb in earnest to a final saddle, partly along a corniche path, to the southernmost point of the way, two hours and twenty minutes away from the monastery; bear northeast for the more gradual, final descent to your goal. Just under three hours along, the surveyed trail meets a track system, where a little sign cheerily (and optimistically) informs those coming the opposite direction that it's three hours to the monastery. This is your last chance for a private swim, at **Áyios Pétros** cove. Use an obvious side-turning from the main track system to reach Éristos, three-and-a-quarter walking hours after leaving Ayíou Pandelímona. However, with rest stops, you'd be prudent to allow four-and-a-half to five hours.

# Níssyros

Volcanic **Níssyros** is noticeably greener than its neighbours Tílos and Hálki, and unlike them has proven wealthy enough to retain more than eight hundred of its population year-round. While remittances from abroad (particularly New York) are significant, most of the island's income is derived from the offshore islet of **Yialí**, a vast lump of pumice to the north that's slowly being quarried away by Lava Ltd. The concession fee collected from Lava by the municipality has engendered a little Alaska-style welfare statelet, with a huge public payroll and vast per-capita income. Accordingly, the Nissyrians bother little with agriculture other than keeping cows and pigs; the hillside terraces carved out for grain and grapes mostly lie fallow, though a small amount of wine and *koukouzína* (distilled spirit) is made.

The island's peculiar geology is potentially a source of other benefits: the Greek power company DEI sunk exploratory **geothermal** wells between 1988 and 1992, attempting to convince the islanders of the benefits of cheap electricity. But locals were suspicious, mindful of DEI's poor track record on Mílos island, which resulted (as it eventually did here too) in noxious fumes, industrial litter and land expropriation. In 1993, a local referendum voted massively against the project, as did (by a closer margin) a 1997 poll, after which DEI took the hint and packed up. A desalination plant scarcely provides enough fresh water; the relatively few tourists (mostly German) who stay the night, as opposed to day-trippers from Kós, still find peaceful villages with few concrete eyesores and a friendly if rather tight-knit population.

Níssyros also offers good **walking** opportunities through a countryside studded with oak and terebinth, on a network of trails fitfully marked and maintained; the pigs gorge themselves on the abundant acorns, and pork figures prominently on local menus. Autumn is a wonderful time to visit, especially for the wonderful local figs (the Turks knew the island as *İncirli*, "fig place").

## Mandhráki

**MANDHRÁKI** is the deceptively large port and capital, with blue patches of sea visible at the end of narrow stone-paved lanes lined with whitewashed houses, whose brightly painted balconies and shutters are mandated by law. Except for the tattier fringes near the ferry dock, where multiple souvenir shops and bad tavernas pitched at day-trippers leave a poor first impression, the town, arrayed around the *kámbos* (community orchard) and overlooked by two

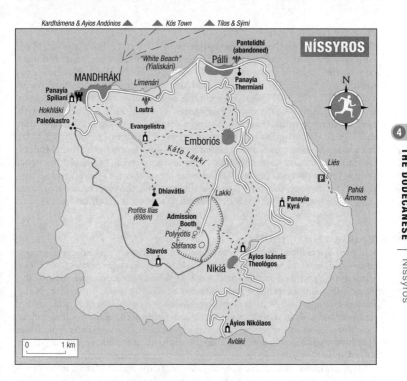

**NÍSSYROS**

Pantelídhi
(abandoned)

Pálli

Panayía
Thermianí

"White Beach"
(Yialiskári)

MANDHRÁKI

Limenári

Panayía
Spilianí

Hokhláki

Loutrá

Paleókastro

Evangelistra

Emboriós

Kátō Lakkí

Liés

Dhiavátis

Lakkí

Pahiá
Ámmos

Profítis Ilías
(698m)

Admission
Booth

Panayía
Kyrá

Polyvótis

Stéfanos

Stavrós

Áyios Ioánnis
Theológos

Nikiá

Áyios Nikólaos

Avláki

0      1 km

N

4

fortresses, is attractive and village-like – a fact not lost on many outsiders engaged in restorations.

Into a corner of the nearer, fourteenth-century **Knights' castle** is wedged little **Panayía Spilianí monastery** (daylight hours), built here in accordance with an islander's vision of the Virgin; raiding Saracens overlooked vast quantities of silver sheathing a collection of Byzantine icons. During 1996–97, the Langadháki district just below was rocked by several **earthquakes**, damaging many venerable houses (mostly repaired now); the seismic threat is ever present, quite literally cutting the ground out from under those who erroneously dub the volcano "extinct".

As a defensive bastion, the seventh-century-BC Doric **Paleókastro** (unrestricted access), twenty-minutes' well-signposted walk out of Langadháki, is infinitely more impressive, ranking as one of the more underrated ancient sites in Greece. You can clamber up onto the massive, polygonal-block walls by means of a broad staircase beside the still-intact gateway.

### Information and transport

The most useful of Mandhráki's four **travel agencies** are Kendris (☎22420 31227), near the town hall, handling ANES and Blue Star ferries, and Dhiakomihalis (☎22240 31459), which represents ANES and the *Panayia Spiliani*, and rents cars. There's a **post office** near the pharmacy, a stand-alone **ATM** at the harbour and high-speed/wi-fi **internet** access at *Proveza* café-bar, in Lefkandió district. Also at the jetty-base is the **bus stop**, with up to five daily departures to the hill villages and six to Pálli. Otherwise, use two set-rate **taxis** and two outlets for **scooter rental**, the more economical being Manos K (☎22420 31029) on the harbour, also renting **cars**.

## Accommodation

With few exceptions, **accommodation** is of a basic, 1980s-vintage standard. Among a few port hotels on your left as you disembark, the best value and most comfortable are those of the well-kept *Romantzo* (☎22420 31340; ❷), whose best, top-floor rooms have renewed baths and air conditioning; the municipal *Xenon Polyvotis* (☎22420 31011; ❷), whose biggish, neutral rooms mostly have knockout sea views; and the slightly overpriced *Haritos* (☎22420 31322; all year; ❸), with marble-trimmed baths, veneer floors and a seaside hot-spring pool (11am–4pm & 7–10pm; €3 non-guests). In the town centre, the *Porfyris* (☎22420 31376; ❹) has a large swimming pool and breakfast terrace; most rooms, with a/c and fridges, overlook the sea and *kámbos*, though the bathrooms need an overhaul. Otherwise, splurge on a restoration project making some use of Níssyros's considerable architectural heritage: on the shore lane near the windmill, the two comfortable suites at ✴ *Ta Liotridia* (☎22420 31580, ✉liotridia@nisyrosnet.gr; ❼) host up to four, with fine sea views and volcanic-stone-and-wood decor.

## Eating and nightlife

Culinary **specialities** include *pittiá* (chickpea croquettes), pickled caper greens, honey and *soumádha*, wild-almond syrup sold in recycled wine bottles (dilute four parts to one, consume within three months). When eating out, give most of the shoddy shoreline **tavernas** a miss in favour of more genuine haunts. Top of the heap is evenings-only ✴ *Mezedhopolio Ankyrovoli* at Áyios Sávvas quay, with indoor and outdoor seating, rebétika soundtrack and well-priced, hearty food including rich, pork-based *boukouniés* and plenty for vegetarians, along with Attica bulk wine. Runners-up include *Kleanthis* in Lefkandió district, best for fish, or *Taverna Nissiros* inland, the oldest eatery in town, always busy despite average-quality grills.

Main **nightlife** venues are several cafés on ficus-shaded Platía Ilikioméni – most characterful is *Antrikos*, while *Rendezvous* does sweets – and a few *barákia* on the shore at Lefkandió district, the most popular being musical *Enallax* and the striking, ex-olive-press bar of the *Liotridia* inn.

## The coast

**Beaches** on Níssyros are in even shorter supply than water, such that excursions are offered to a sandy cove on **Áyios Andónios islet** opposite. Closer to hand, the short, black-rock beach of **Hokhláki**, behind the Knights' castle, is unusable if the wind is up. It's best to head east along the main road, passing the old-fashioned spa of **Loutrá** (hot baths 6–7am, 9am–noon & 6–8pm; bring towel; €3 per 20min). For excellent **meals**, continue east to ✴ *Limenari* (aka *Makis & Ourania*; lunch & supper), perched scenically in a terraced valley above the namesake bay, with fair prices for big portions of home-style food.

A kilometre or so further, 4km from Mandhráki, the fishing village of **PÁLLI** makes a good retreat when the port fills with trippers. **Tavernas** have multiplied, but some are overpriced, so best stick with long-running *Ellinis*, with spit-roasted meat by night, grilled fish in season and simple rooms upstairs (☎22420 31453; ❷). An economical **scooter-rental** outlet (Captains) and an excellent **bakery** cranking out brown bread and pies (branch in Mandhráki) make Pálli also worth considering as a base. There's more **accommodation** at *Frantzis Studios* by the bakery (☎22420 31240; ❷), with well-kept units in slightly scruffy grounds. A tamarisk-shaded, dark-sand **beach**, kept well groomed, extends east to the abandoned Pantelídhi spa, behind which the little grotto-chapel of **Panayía Thermianí** is tucked inside the vaulted remains of a Roman baths complex.

To reach Níssyros's **best beaches**, continue in this direction, along an initially bleak shoreline to the delightful cove of **Liés**, with a snack-bar (July–Aug only). Just past here the paved road ends at a car park 5km beyond Pálli; in summer taxi boats from Mandhráki call here too. Another fifteen minutes by trail over the headland brings you to the idyllic, 300-metre expanse of **Pahiá Ámmos**, with grey-pink sand heaped in dunes, limited shade at the far end and a large colony of rough campers and naturists in summer.

## The interior

Níssyros's central, dormant **volcano** lends the island its special character and nurtures its abundant vegetation – no stay would be complete without a visit. Tours from Kós tend to monopolize the crater floor (and most of the island's coaches) between 11am and 2pm, so if you want solitude, use early-morning or late-afternoon scheduled buses to Nikiá (a few continue to the crater floor), a scooter or your own two feet to get there.

The road up from Pálli winds first past the all-but-abandoned village of **EMBORIÓS**, where pigs and free-ranging cattle (a major driving hazard) far outnumber people (winter population 5), though the place is being bought up and restored by Athenians and foreigners. New owners often discover natural volcanic saunas in the basements of the crumbling houses; at the outskirts of the village there's a signposted public **steam bath** in a grotto, its entrance outlined in white paint. If you're descending to Pálli from here, an old cobbled way starting at the sharp bend below the sauna offers an attractive short cut of the four-kilometre road, while another *kalderími* drops from behind the little platía to within a fifteen-minute walk of the craters. Also just off the platía, by the church, is the better and more reliably open of two **tavernas**: ⚲ *Apyria/Triandafyllos* (all year, supper only; book on ☎ 22420 31377), with spit-roasted suckling pig in summer – otherwise grills and *mezédhes*.

Some 3km past Emboriós, a paved drive leads down to **Panayía Kyrá**, the island's oldest and most venerable monastery, worth a stop (and dealing with the somewhat cantankerous warden) for its enchanting, arcaded festival courtyard as much as its church. **NIKIÁ**, the larger village on the east side of

▲ Platía Pórta, Nikiá

the caldera, is – with thirty year-round inhabitants – more of a going concern, and its spectacular situation 14km from Mandhráki offers views out to Tílos as well as across the volcano. The sole **taverna**, at the village entrance, is pricey *Andriotis* (Easter–Oct), with a good if limited menu and chocolatey desserts. On the engagingly round platía called Pórta, ringed by stone seating and marked out in white paint for folk dances, are two cafés. From the bus turn-around area, a 45-minute trail descends to the crater floor; a few minutes downhill, detour briefly to the eyrie-like monastery of **Áyios Ioánnis Theológos**, whose festival grounds come to life at the September 25–26 evening festival. Driving directly to the volcanic area means using the road that veers off just past Emboriós.

### The volcano

However you approach the volcano, a sulphurous stench wafts out to meet you as trees and pasture, then clumps of oregano, gradually yield to lifeless, caked powder. The sunken main crater of **Stéfanos** presents a striated moonscape of grey, white, brown and pale yellow; there is another, less-visited double crater (dubbed **Polyvótis**) to the west, arguably more dramatic, with a clear trail leading up to it from the snack-bar. The perimeters of both are punctuated with tiny, steam-puffing blowholes, around which form little pincushions of sulphur crystals. Since the millennium, boiling mud-pots have surfaced towards the eastern side of Stéfanos (danger of falling through the crater-floor at their edges); sound effects are akin to a huge cauldron bubbling away below you. In legend this is the groaning of Polyvotis, a titan crushed here by Poseidon under a huge rock torn from Kós. When tour groups appear, a small, tree-shaded **snack-bar** operates in the centre of the volcanic zone, and a booth on the access road charges admission (€1.50).

### Island walks

Since DEI's 1991 destruction of the ancient *kalderími* between the volcano and Mandhráki, finding pleasant walks back towards town from Nikiá, Emboriós or the volcano requires a bit of imagination – though surviving paths are marked with red paint-dots and/or wooden signposts – and possession of Beate and Jürgen Franke's GPS-drawn topographical **map** (download from Ⓦwww.bjfranke.privat.t-online.de/.)

### Volcano to Mandhráki or Profítis Ilías via Evangelístra

About 1km north of the volcano admission booth, a clear, crudely marked path climbs to a pass, then maintains altitude along the north flank of **Káto Lákki** gulch, emerging after ninety minutes at the important monastery of **Evangelístra** with its giant terebinth tree just outside. Beyond Evangelístra, you must walk about a kilometre on the paved access road before the old path kicks in for the final half-hour down to Mandhráki. Look sharp at curves to find the old walled-in path which initially just short-cuts the road, and then for quite a long stretch loops above the port well away from the road, finally curling around to emerge above the local school.

Evangelístra also marks the start of the two-hour, round-trip detour up **Profítis Ilías** (698m), the island's summit. From the terebinth-tree roundabout head west about 150m, then left on the start of the rough path, marked with cairns and white-painted arrows or crosses. A few minutes before the shrine on the peak, tiny **Dhiavátis** monastery, tucked into a small hollow with huge trees, makes a good picnic spot or emergency bivouac.

### Evangelístra or Nikiá to Emboriós

Just before the **Evangelístra** terebinth tree, another paint-splodged path heads right or northeast towards Emboriós, mostly along the north flank of Káto Lákki. This route takes 45 minutes and is shown correctly on the downloadable map; despite haphazard marking and cleaning the trail is still rough or even nonexistent in parts, but remains an enjoyable and useful link. You'll enter the village from above, near the cemetery and small castle; it's marginally easier to find the way in reverse.

By contrast, **Nikiá to Emboriós** takes just under ninety minutes, with a short stretch of road-walking towards the end, but the trail has been long abandoned and is not shown on the German-made map. Descend from Nikiá towards the volcano and bear right in the direction of Theológos monastery, but then take the left fork by the wooden gate before reaching it. The path ambles along through neglected terraces, without much altitude change, occasionally obstructed by landslide debris and thick vegetation; you'll eventually emerge after 50–55 minutes by some utility poles on the modern Emboriós-Nikiá road, just opposite the drive serving a small army watchpost. There's no old secondary trail parallel to the road; you must asphalt-tramp for about 1km (15min) to the turnoff for Lakkí, where the onward trail continues conspicuously uphill into Emboriós.

# Kós

After Rhodes, **Kós** is the second largest and second most visited Dodecanese. Here too the harbour is guarded by an imposing castle of the Knights of St John, the streets are lined with Italian-built public buildings, and minarets and palm trees punctuate extensive Hellenistic and Roman remains. Although its hinterland mostly lacks the wild beauty of Rhodes' interior, Kós is the most fertile of this archipelago, blessed with rich soil and abundant ground water.

But mass **tourism** has largely displaced the old agrarian way of life; all-inclusive complexes comprising tens of thousands of beds are a blight that contribute little to the local economy, and have forced many restaurants (though fortunately not the best ones) and more modest hotels to close. Except in Kós Town and Mastihári, there are few independent travellers, and from mid-July to mid-September you'll be lucky to find a room without reserving far in advance. The tourist industry is juxtaposed rather bizarrely with cows munching amid baled hay near olive groves, and Greek Army tanks exercising in the volcanic badlands around the airport. Like Tílos further south, Kós never had to earn its living from the sea and consequently has little in the way of a maritime tradition or a contemporary fishing fleet. All these peculiarities acknowledged, Kós is still worth a few days' time while island-hopping: its few **mountain villages** are appealing, the tourist infrastructure excellent and **swimming** opportunities limitless – about half the island's perimeter is fringed by beaches of various sizes, colours and consistencies.

## Kós Town

**KÓS TOWN**, home to over half of the island's population of just over 28,000, radiates out from the harbour and feels remarkably uncluttered thanks to its

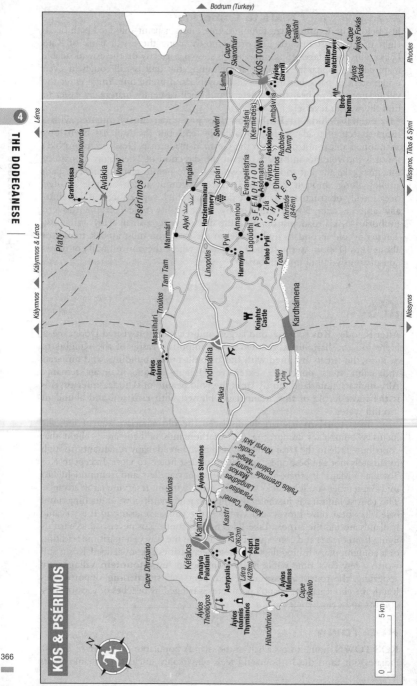

## KÓS & PSÉRIMOS

Bodrum (Turkey)

◄ Léros

◄ Kálymnos & Léros

◄ Kálymnos

Rhodes ►

Níssyros, Tílos & Sými ►

Níssyros ►

Cape Psalídhi
Cape
Ayios Fokás
KÓS TOWN
Military
Watchtower
Cape
Skandhári
Lámbi
Ayios
Gavriíl
Ayios
Fokás
Brós
Thermá
Platáni
(Kermédes)
Asklepíon
Selvéri
Zipári
Rubbish
Dump
Ámbavris
Evangelístria
Ayios
Dhimítrios
A S F E N D H I O U
Amanioú
Zía
Dhíkeos
Khristós
(846m)
Hatziemmanuil
Winery
Tingáki
Alykí
Lagoúdhi
Marmári
Pylí
Paleó Pylí
Psérimos
Linópotis
Harmýlio
Tolári
Tam Tam
Troúlos
Kardhámena
Platý
Avláki
Vathý
Grafiótissa
Marathoúnda
Knights'
Castle
Mastihári
Ayios
Ioánnis
Andimáhia
Jeeps
Only
Pláka
Límniónas
Ayios
Stéfanos
Kéfalos
Kamári
Kastrí
 Psalís Gremmós Langádhes
Kamíla "Camel"
"Paradise"
Markos "Sunny"
Polemi "Magic"
"Exotic"
Knysí Aktí
Cape Dhrépano
Panayía
Palatianí
Astypalia
Zíni
(362m)
Aspri
Pétra
Látra
(428m)
Ayios
Mámas
Cape
Kríkello
Ayios
Theológos
Ayios Ioánnis
Thymianós
Hilandhríou

5 km

0

N

sprawling layout. The Knights' castle is the first thing you see on arrival; by contrast, the town's Hellenistic and Roman remains were only revealed by an earthquake in 1933, and excavated by the Italians, who also planned the "garden suburbs" extending either side of the central grid. Elsewhere, sizeable expanses of open space or archeological zone alternate with a hotchpotch of Ottoman monuments and later mock-medieval, Art Deco-ish and Rationalist buildings, designed in two phases either side of the earthquake and incorporating as ever a "Foro Italico" – the Italian administrative complex next to the castle – and a Casa del Fascio (Fascist Headquarters), with the inevitable speaker's tower for haranguing party rallies gathered on the central square below.

### Arrival, transport and information

Large **ferries** and **catamarans** anchor at a special dock by one corner of the castle; **excursion boats** to neighbouring islands sail right in and berth all along Aktí Koundouriótou; **hydrofoils** tie up south of the castle at their own jetty, on Aktí Miaoúli. Virtually all ferry, catamaran and *kaïki* agents sit within 50m of each other at the waterfront end of pedestrianized **Vassiléos Pávlou**. Among those representative of ferries and hydrofoils, not just expensive excursions, are Kentriko (for Blue Star) by the DEAS terminal (℡22420 28914); Exas (for most everyone else) opposite the National Bank at Andóni Ioannídhi 4 (℡22420 29900); and Hermes at Vasiléos Pávlou 2 (℡22420 26607) for the *Panayia Spiliani* to Níssyros, catamarans, hydrofoils and boats to Turkey.

The **airport** is 24km southwest of Kós Town in the centre of the island; Aegean Airways operates a shuttle bus to the town terminal by the Casa Romana, but other flight arrivals may have to either take a taxi, or flag down an orange-and-cream-coloured KTEL bus at the giant roundabout outside the airport gate – they pass here en route to Mastihári, Kardhámena and Kéfalos as well as Kós Town. **KTEL buses** use a series of stops around a triangular park 400m back from the water, with an information booth adjacent at Kleopátras 7 (tickets on the bus). The municipality also runs a frequent **local bus service**, DEAS, through the beach suburbs and up to the Asklepíon, with a ticket and information office at Aktí Koundouriótou 7. Push- or **mountain-bike rental** are popular options for getting around, given the island's relative flatness and Kós Town's bike-lane system; if you want a **motor scooter**, try Moto Harley at Kanári 42, or Moto Service at Harmylíou 7. Budget at Vassiléos Pávlou 31 (℡22420 28882 or 694 45 00 062) and in Psalídhi suburb (℡22420 28882), opposite the *Grecotel Imperial*, has a reputation for good-condition **cars**, as does AutoWay at Vassiléos Yeoryíou 22 (℡22420 25326, ⓦwww.autowaykos.gr). The main **taxi** stand is at the east end of Koundouriótou.

Driving or pedalling around Kós Town can be complicated, given a fairly comprehensive one-way system and a wide-ranging pedestrian-only zone. At the back of the harbour, the round Platía Iróön Polytekhníou – informally known as "Dolphin Square" after its central sculpture – effectively marks one end of the tourist esplanade, Finíkon or "Palm Avenue" the other. For **drivers**, Ippokrátous is the only unrestricted street penetrating the commercial district from the northeast shore esplanade, while Elefthateríou Venizélou and its contin-uation, Artemisías, provide the best means of moving west to east. From the waterfront, Megálou Alexándhrou, or Koraí then Grigoríou toú Pémptou, are the quickest ways of getting out to the main island trunk road. **Parking** is strictly controlled (watch for kerbside signs) and fees are payable Monday to

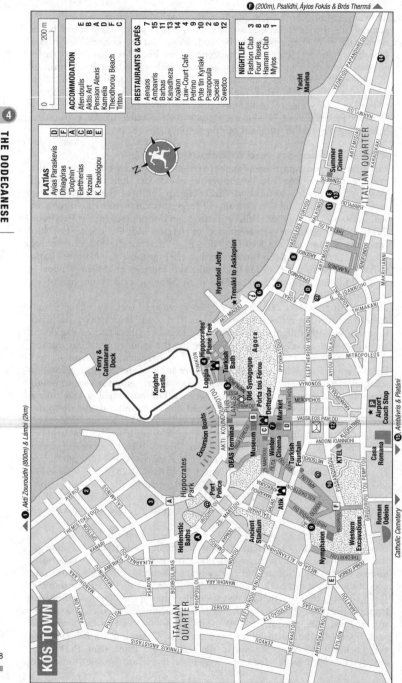

## KÓS TOWN

(200m), Psalidhi, Áyios Fokás & Brós Thermá ▲

Yacht
Marina

**ITALIAN QUARTER**

Summer
Cinema

NIGHTLIFE
Fashion Club ...... 3
Four Roses ........ 8
Hamam Club ..... 5
Mylos ............... 1

PLATÍAS
Ayías Paraskevís ... D
Dhiagóras ........... F
"Dolphin" ............ A
Eleftherías .......... C
Kazoúli .............. B
K. Paeológou ....... E

ACCOMMODATION
Afendoulis ........... E
Aktis Art ............. B
Pension Alexis ...... A
Kamelia ............... D
Theodhorou Beach . F
Triton ................. C

RESTAURANTS & CAFÉS
Aenaos ............... 7
Ambavris ............ 15
Barbas ............... 11
Kanadhéza .......... 13
Koakon ............... 14
Law-Court Café ..... 4
Petrino .............. 9
Pote tin Kyriakí .... 10
Psaropoúla ......... 2
Special .............. 6
Swedco .............. 12

Hydrofoil Jetty

★ Trenáki to Asklepíon

Agora

Hippocrates'
Plane Tree

Turkish
Bath

Loggia

Old Synagogue

Pórta toú Fórou

Deftardar

Knights'
Castle

Ferry &
Catamaran
Dock

Excursion Boats

DEAS Terminal

Museum

Winter
Cinema

Turkish
Fountain

Market

Port
Police

Hippocrates
Park

Hellenistic
Baths

Ancient
Stadium

Nymphaion

Western
Excavations

Casa
Romana

★ P
Airport
Coach Stop

KTEL

Roman
Odeion

**ITALIAN QUARTER**

0                    200 m

▲ Akti Zouroúdhi (800m) & Lámbi (2km)

◀ Villages, Airport & Asklepíon

Catholic Cemetery ▶

Ambávris & Platáni ▶

Friday, 8am to 9pm; buy hourly scratch-card tickets from kiosks or the DEAS office on the front.

The municipal **tourist office** at Vassiléos Yeoryíou 3 (May–Sept Mon–Fri 7.30am–2.45pm & 5–8pm, Sat 9am–2pm; Oct–April Mon–Fri 8am–2.30pm) stocks local maps, bus timetables and seagoing schedules; there's also Newsstand **book shop/newsagent** just behind the archeological museum on Platía Kazoúli, and the bookshop inside the Politistiko Polykendro at the corner of Korytsás and Aryirokástrou also has some English-language titles. Road Editions' 1:60,000 **map** no. 205 is widely available; otherwise, the most accurate one, for both the island and the town, is published by Pandelis Vayianos. Bank **ATMs** are numerous; the best-equipped of several **internet cafés** are E-global at Artemisías 2, and Cafe del Mare at Megálou Alexándhrou 4a.

## Accommodation

If you're in transit, you're effectively obliged to stay in Kós Town, and even given a few days on the island, it still makes a sensible base, with the majority of car- and bike-hire agencies, the best range of restaurants and the hub of public transport. Be wary of **touts** who besiege every arriving sea-craft – their rooms are apt to be unlicensed, remote and of dubious cleanliness. They may further claim to represent the establishments listed below, and then take you elsewhere.

**Afendoulis** Evrypýlou 1 ☏ 22420 25321, ⓦ www.afendoulishotel.com. Large, balconied en-suite rooms – including a few family quads – with fridge and a/c. Alexis Zikas, brother Ippokrates and wife Dionysia really look after their guests, winning a loyal repeat clientele. Wi-fi in most common areas; breakfast at any reasonable hour. March 15–Nov 15; credit cards accepted. ❸

**Aktis Art** Vassiléos Yeoryíou 7 ☏ 22420 47200, ⓦ www.kosaktis.gr. Designer hotel whose futuristic standard doubles or suites, in brown, grey and beige, all face the water. Bathrooms are naturally lit and have butler sinks. There's wi-fi, gym, conference area, seaside bar and affiliated restaurant. All year. ❻

**Pension Alexis** Irodhótou 9, cnr Omírou ☏ 22420 25594. Popular, friendly budget option across from the Roman agora with wood-floored rooms that share bathrooms and a self-catering kitchen. Run by the sister and

niece of Alexis of the *Afendoulis*. March to early Nov. ❷

**Kamelia** Artemisías 3 ☏ 22420 28983. Rear-facing rooms at this well-kept two-star hotel have a quiet orchard view; tends to get overflow from the *Afendoulis*. May–Sept. ❸

**Theodorou Beach** 1200m from the centre, towards Psalídhi ☏ 22420 22280, ⓦ www .theodorouhotel.com. Generous-sized units with disabled access, including suites and a wing of self-catering studios. A leafy environment includes a lawn-pool at the back and a small "private" beach with the *Nostos* day-and-night café-bar. ❹

**Triton** Vassiléos Yeoryíou 4 ☏ 22420 20040, ⓦ www.maritina.gr. The "other" moderately upmarket, town-centre seafront hotel, part of a small local chain, with veneered floored rooms (not all with sea view) in a netutral decor. Bathrooms somewhat small; the ground floor *Avanti* Italian restaurant and breakfast café is popular. ❹

## The Town

The **castle** (April–Oct Tues–Sun 8am–6pm, Nov–March 8.30am–2.30pm; €3), called "Nerantziás" locally, is reached via a causeway over its former moat, now filled in as an avenue and planted with palms (hence its Greek name, Finíkon). The existing double citadel, built in stages between 1450 and 1514, replaced a fourteenth-century fort deemed incapable of withstanding advances in medieval artillery; you can walk around most of the perimeter. A fair proportion of ancient Koan masonry is stacked inside or has been recycled into the walls, where the escutcheons of several Grand Masters of the Knights of St John can be seen. There are dozens of cannonballs lying about, few if any fired in anger, since this castle surrendered without resistance in accordance with the terms ending the marathon 1522 siege of Rhodes. The biggest explosion here ever was orchestrated for the grand finale of Werner Herzog's first black-and-white feature, *Signs of Life* (1968), in which a low-ranking Wehrmacht officer goes berserk in 1944 and torches an ammunition dump inside the castle.

Immediately opposite the causeway stands the riven trunk of **Hippocrates' plane tree**, its branches propped up by scaffolding; at seven hundred years of age, it's not really elderly enough to have seen the great healer, though it's certainly one of the oldest trees in Europe. Adjacent are two **Ottoman fountains** (a dry hexagonal one and a working one feeding an ancient sarcophagus) and the eighteenth-century **Hassan Pasha mosque**, also known as the Loggia Mosque; its ground floor – like that of the **Defterdar mosque** on central Platía Eleftherías – is taken up by rows of shops.

Also on Platía Eleftherías stands the Italian-built **archeological museum** (Tues–Sun 8.30am–2.30pm; €3), with a predictable Latin bias. Four statue galleries surround an atrium with a mosaic of Hippocrates welcoming Asklepios to Kós; the most famous item, purportedly a statue of Hippocrates, is indeed Hellenistic, but most of the other famous works – Hermes seated with a lamb, Artemis hunting, Hygeia offering an egg to Asklepios's serpent, a boxer with his arms bound in rope, statues of wealthy townspeople – are emphatically Roman.

The largest single section of ancient Kós is the **agora** (closed for works), a confusing jumble of ruins owing to repeated earthquakes between the second and sixth centuries AD. More comprehensible are the so-called **western excavations**, lent definition by two intersecting marble-paved streets and the Xystos or colonnade of a covered running track. In the same area lie several interesting **floor mosaics** (most famously Europa being abducted by Zeus-as-a-bull), all viewable under protective canopies. To the south, across Grigoríou toú Pémptou, are a Roman-era **odeion**, garishly restored both during the 1930s and again in 2000, and the **Casa Romana** (shut for works indefinitely), a third-century-AD house whose surviving patches of mosaic floors show panthers, tigers and assorted sea creatures.

▲ Art Deco school, Kós Town

Kós also retains a thoroughly commercialized **old town**, lining the pedestrianized street between the Italian market hall on Platía Eleftherías and Platía Dhiagóras with its isolated minaret overlooking the western archeological zone. One of the few areas to survive the 1933 earthquake, today it's crammed with expensive tourist boutiques, cafés and snack-bars. About the only genuinely old thing remaining is a capped Turkish fountain with a calligraphic inscription, where Apéllou meets Odhós Venizélou.

## Eating and drinking

Despite an overwhelming first impression of Euro-stodge cuisine, it's easy to eat well and even reasonably in Kós Town, as long as you search inland, away from the harbour. Koan **wine-making** has been revived recently; the Hatziemmanouil label (red, white, rosé) is particularly worth sampling, and its **winery** (see map, p.366) can be visited (☎22420 68888).

### Cafés

**Aenaos** Platía Eleftherías. Join the largely local crowd at this café under the Defterdar mosque, and people-watch while refilling your Greek coffee from the traditional *bríki* used to brew it. Also a variety of teas and flavoured hot chocolates.

**Law-court Café** Some of the cheapest and best-brewed coffees in Kós are available (along with cold drinks) under the arches at the rear of the courthouse, a few paces from Hippocrates' plane tree; no place for civil-servant clientele.

**Special (Arvanitakis)** Vassiléos Yeoryíou. Hole-in-the-wall *zaharoplastio* with dynamite gelato.

**Swedco** Vassiléos Pávlou 20. Ultra-sleek outlet of the Rhodes café chain, with (pricey) sandwiches, hot drinks and decadent desserts.

### Restaurants

**Ambavris** 500m south of the edge of town along the road from near Casa Romana, in the eponymous suburb village. Skip the English-only à la carte menu, take the hint about "Mezedes" and let the house bring on their best. This changes seasonally but won't much exceed €25 (drink extra) for six plates – typically *pinigoúri* (bulgar pilaf), *pikhtí* (brawn), little fish, spicy *loukánika*, stuffed squash flowers and *fáva*. May–Oct evenings only.

**Barbas** Evrypýlou 6, opposite *Hotel Afendoulis*. Excellent grills as well as the odd seafood choice

like octopus salad, at cozy outdoor seating. April–Oct.

**Kanadheza** Evrypýlou, cnr Artemisías. Creditable pizzas as well as grills and some *mayireftá*, served at indoor/outdoor tables. All year.

**Koakon** (aka Andonis) Artemisías 56. Versatile all-rounder, handling grilled meat and fish, *mezédhes* and a few daily *mayireftá* with equal aplomb, without the usual multinational flags and photo-menus. All year.

**Petrino** Platía Theológou 1 ☎22420 27251. The town's most elegant *koultouriárika* taverna, and accordingly expensive at €30–35 each for the works, booze extra. You can push the total down a bit by sticking to *orektiká* and the house wine. Extensive garden seating, and two cozy indoor salons, allow all-year operation (supper only); large groups should reserve.

**Pote tin Kyriaki** Pissándhrou 9. Kós's sole genuine ouzerí, whose creatively assembled menu (in school copy-books) has delights such as shrimps, fried mussels or *gávros*, *monastiriakí* (Cretan "monk's") salad), as well as grilled chops and *loukánika*. Summer Mon–Sat evenings only, winter Thurs–Sat evenings plus lunch.

**Psaropoula** Avérof 17. Long the town's best-value fish/seafood specialist, with many Greeks in attendance; open all year.

## Nightlife and entertainment

The most durable **clubs** are *Four Roses* on the corner of Arseníou and Vassiléos Yeoryíou, and cavernous *Fashion Club* on the west side of the inner port, noted for its light shows. The **"Pub Lanes"**, officially Nafklírou and Dhiákou, are the place for 120-decibel techno and house; bar identities change each season, however, and it's become very listless and naff. The most stable and classy venue here is *Hamam Club*, installed in an ex-Turkish bath, with its original oriental decor, chill-out sofas and outdoor seating before a midnight noise curfew moves everyone indoors. There are newer, **better nightlife areas** around Platía

Dhiagóra (mostly Greeks) and out at Aktí Zouroúdhi, where *Mylos* – built around an old windmill on the beach – is currently the top day-and-night-bar, with both live music and DJs. Otherwise there is one active **cinema**, the Orfeas, with summer and winter (Oct–May) premises as shown on the map on p.368; the indoor premises also host special events.

## The Asklepion and Platáni

Native son **Hippocrates** is justly celebrated on Kós; not only does he have a tree, a street, a park, a statue and an international medical institute named after him, but his purported **Asklepion** (May–Oct Tues–Sun 8am–6pm, Nov–April 8.30am–2.30pm; €3), 4km south of town and one of three in Greece, is a major attraction. A green-and-white *trenáki* shuttles to the site regularly from near the tourist office; otherwise take a DEAS bus to Platáni (see below), from where the ruins are a further fifteen-minute walk.

The Asklepion was actually founded just after Hippocrates' death, but the methods used and taught here were probably his. Both a sanctuary of Asklepios (god of healing, son of Apollo) and a renowned curative centre, its magnificent setting on three artificial terraces overlooking Anatolia reflects early concern with the therapeutic environment. Until recently, springs provided the site with a constant supply of pure water, and stretches of clay piping are still visible, embedded in the ground.

Today, little remains standing, owing to periodic earthquakes and the Knights filching masonry for building their castle. The lower terrace never had many buildings, being instead the venue for the observance of the Asklepieia – quadrennial athletic/musical competitions in honour of the god. Sacrifices to Asklepios were conducted at an **altar**, the oldest structure here, whose foundations are found near the middle of the second terrace. Just east, the Corinthian columns of a second-century-AD **Roman temple** were partially re-erected by nationalistic Italians. A monumental **staircase** leads from the altar to a second-century-BC **Doric temple** of Asklepios on the highest terrace, the last and grandest are a succession of the deity's local shrines.

En route to the Asklepion, **PLATÁNI** (also Kermedés, from the Turkish Germe) village is, along with Kós Town, home to the island's dwindling community of ethnic Turks. Until 1964 there were nearly three thousand of them, but successive Cyprus crises and the worsening of relations between Greece and Turkey prompted mass emigration to Anatolia, and a drop in the Muslim population to well below a thousand. Several creditable Turkish-run

---

### Hippocrates

**Hippocrates** (c.460–370 BC) is generally regarded as the father of scientific medicine, though the Hippocratic oath, anyway much altered from its original form, probably has nothing to do with him. Hippocrates was certainly born on Kós, probably at Astypalia near present-day Kéfalos, but otherwise confirmed details of his life are few; probably he was a great physician who travelled throughout the Classical Greek world, but spent at least part of his career teaching and practising on his native island. Numerous medical writings have been (often dubiously) attributed to Hippocrates; *Airs, Waters and Places*, a treatise on the importance of environment on health, is generally thought to be his, but others are reckoned to be a compilation found in a medical library in Alexandria during the second century BC. This emphasis on good air and water, and the holistic approach of ancient Greek medicine, now seems positively contemporary.

**tavernas** cluster near the main crossroads junction, with a working Ottoman fountain: *Arap* (summer only); *Asklipios* (aka Ali's) and *Sherif*, adjacent across the way (also summer only); and *Gin's Place* (all year), each offering Anatolian-style *mezédhes* and kebabs better than most fare in Kós Town. Afterwards, retire across from *Arap* to *Zaharoplastio Iy Paradhosi* for the best ice cream on the island.

Just outside Platáni on the road back to the port, the island's neglected **Jewish cemetery** lies in a dark conifer grove, 300m beyond the well-kept Muslim graveyard. Dates on the Hebrew-Italian-script headstones stop abruptly after 1940, after which presumably none of the 120 local Jews died a natural death prior to their deportation in July 1944. Their former **synagogue**, a wonderfully orientalized Art Deco Italian-designed specimen from 1934, at Alexándhrou Dhiákou 4, is now an events hall; a plaque commemorates its former use.

## Eastern Kós

To reach anything resembling a deserted **beach** near the capital, you'll need to use the DEAS bus line connecting the various resorts either side of town, or else rent a vehicle; designated cycle-paths extend as far east as **Cape Psalídhi**, either side of which lie many of Kós's luxury **hotels**. The two best of these lie adjacent at the end of the "strip". The *Grecotel Kos Imperial* (☎22420 58000, ⓦww.grecotel.com; ❽ but frequent web specials ❻), is a superbly designed garden complex with tropical-river novelty pool and spa, where standard doubles and bungalows share decor (including music systems) and size (large). The more overtly family- (and package-) orientated *Oceanis Beach Resort* (☎22420 24641, ⓦwww.oceanis-hotel.gr; ❺) has three pools (two saltwater), kids' club, on-site windsurf school, and a similar garden environment.

The easterly bus line usually terminates at **Áyios Fokás**, 8km southeast of Kós Town, but sometimes continues an extra 4km almost to remote **Brós Thermá** (last service around 6pm). With your own transport you negotiate a dirt track for the final kilometre to these massively popular **hot springs**, best experienced at sunset or on moonlit nights. They issue from a grotto and flow through a trench into a shoreline pool formed by boulders, heating the seawater to an enjoyable temperature. Winter storms disrupt the boulder wall, rebuilt every April, so that the pool changes from year to year. Just uphill, long-running *Psarotaverna Therma* does pricey fish and a few *mezédhes*.

### Tingáki and Marmári

The two neighbouring beach resorts of Tingáki and Marmári are separated by the **Alykí** salt marsh, which retains water – and throngs of migratory birds, including flamingos – until June after a wet winter. There's almost always a breeze along this coast, attracting windsurfers; the profiles of Kálymnos, Psérimos and Turkey's Bodrum peninsula all make for spectacular offshore scenery. If you're aiming for either resort from town, especially on a two-wheeler, it's safest and most pleasant to go via the minor road from the southwest corner of town (follow initial signage for the Vassiliadhi supermarket); the entire way to Tingáki is paved, and involves the same distance as using the main trunk road and marked turn-off. Similarly, a grid of paved rural lanes links the inland portions of Tingáki and Marmári.

Brit-popular **TINGÁKI** lies 12km west of the harbour; oddly, there's little **accommodation** near the beach – most surviving medium-sized hotels and more numerous studios are scattered inland through fields and cow pastures. The best local **taverna** here, with pleasant seating indoors and out, is ⚘ *Ambeli* (May–Oct daily; Nov–April Fri/Sat evening, Sun lunch; book peak season on ☎22420 69682), well signposted 2.5km east of the main beachfront crossroads.

Featured dishes include *pinigoúri, bekrí mezé, pikhtí, yaprákia* (the local *dolmádhes*) and *arnáki ambelourgoú*, washed down with wine from their own vineyard. Among **car-rental** outfits, Sevi (☎22420 68299) can be recommended. The beach itself is white sand, long and narrow – improving, and veering away from the frontage road, as you head southwest.

**MARMÁRI**, 15km from town, has a smaller built-up area than Tingáki, and the beach is broader, especially to the west where it forms little dunes. Most German-slanted hotels here are all-inclusive; an exception, on the main access road down from the trunk road, is *Esperia* (☎22420 42010, ⓦwww .hotelesperiakos.gr; May–Oct; ④), with well-landscaped grounds and two grades of rooms. Between Tingáki and Marmári stands **Salt Lake Riding Centre** (☎694 41 04 446; May–Oct), just back from the sea on the west side of Alykí salt marsh. This has fifteen horses and ponies available for rides along the beach – including the most popular sunset ride – or up into the hills.

## The Asfendhioú villages

The inland villages of **Mount Dhíkeos**, a handful of settlements collectively referred to as **Asfendhioú**, nestle amid the island's only natural forest. Together these communities give a good idea of what Kós looked like before tourism and ready-mix concrete arrived, and all have been severely depopulated by the mad rush to the coast. They are accessible via the curvy side road from Zipári, 8km from Kós Town; an inconspicuously marked minor road to Lagoúdhi; or by the shorter access road for Pylí.

The first Asfendhioú village you reach up the Zipári road is **Evangelístria**, where a major crossroads by the eponymous parish church leads to Lagoúdhi and Amanioú (west), Asómatos (east) and Ziá (uphill). **ZIÁ**'s spectacular sunsets make it the target of up to six evening tour buses daily, though the village has barely a dozen resident families, and its tattiness – particularly the kitsch rugs for sale in hideous hues and patterns – increases annually. The best of the dozen **tavernas** here is Greek-patronized ⚑ *Oromedon* (all year), serving good *pinigoúri*, mushrooms and local sausage on a roof terrace. Secluded *Kefalovrissi* (unpredictable hours; ring ☎22420 69605) near the top of the village, is good for *mezédhes* plus selected daily mains like *pansétta* or *bakaliáros*.

Ziá is also the trailhead for the ascent of 846-metre **Khristós peak**, a minimum two-and-a-half-hour round trip, initially on track but thereafter mostly by path through stands of juniper. The route is fairly obvious, and the views, over half the Dodecanese and Turkey's Knidos peninsula, from the pillbox-like summit chapel of **Metamórfosis** amply reward the effort. Up top, you can also ponder the symbolism of a giant crucifix fashioned out of PVC sewer pipe and filled with concrete.

East of Ziá or Evangelístria, roads converge at **ASÓMATOS**, home to about twenty villagers and various outsiders restoring abandoned houses; the evening view from the gaily painted church of **Arhángelos** with its *votsalotó* courtyard rivals that of Zía, though there are no amenities. **ÁYIOS DHIMÍTRIOS** (aka Haïhoútes), 2km beyond along a paved road, is ruined except for a few restored houses next to the attractive church; in its narthex, a small photo-display documents a much larger population until World War II, when the village was a centre of resistance to the occupation. You can continue 3.5km further to the junction with the road descending from the rubbish tip to Platáni.

## Pylí

The medieval ruined town and contemporary village of **PYLÍ** can both be reached via the road through Lagoúdhi and Amanioú, or from beside the duck-patrolled Linopótis pond on the main island trunk road, across from which indoor-outdoor ⚒ *Ouzeri Limni* (aka *Karamolengos;* noon–11pm except Tues, all year) is well worth an evening drive from elsewhere (at lunchtime road-noise is offputting). They've got the broadest variety of ouzo, *tsikoudhiá* and *tsípouro* in the islands, platters in three sizes for all appetites, and a broad range of dishes from *atherína* and fresh *bakaliáros* to baked chickpeas and grills.

In the upper Pylí's two neighbourhoods, 100m west of the partly pedestrianized square and church, *Iy Palia Piyi* taverna serves inexpensive *soutzoukákia* grilled with onions, home-made *tzatzíki*, fried-vegetable *mezédhes* and local sweet red wine in a superb setting, beside a giant, lion-spouted cistern-fountain (the *piyí*). Pylí's other attraction is the **Harmýlio** ("Tomb of Harmylos"), signposted near the top of the village as "Heroon of Charmylos". This fenced-off, subterranean, niched vault was probably a Hellenistic family tomb; immediately above, traces of an ancient temple have been incorporated into the medieval chapel of Stavrós.

**Paleó** (medieval) **Pylí**, 3km southeast of its modern descendant, was the Byzantine capital of Kós. Head there via Amanioú, keeping straight at the junction where signs point left to Ziá and Lagoúdhi. In any case, the castle is obvious on its rock, straight ahead; the paved road ends next to a spring, opposite which a stair-path leads within fifteen minutes to the roof of the fort. En route you pass the remains of the abandoned town tumbling southwards down the slope, as well as two fourteenth-to-fifteenth-century chapels (and an earlier locked one) with fresco fragments; the lowest church, **Arhángelos**, has the best-preserved ones, mostly scenes from the life of Christ, including a fine *Betrayal* in the north vault. Outside are the remains of a graceful Latin arcade of a type usually only seen on Rhodes or Cyprus.

## Western Kós

Near the desolate centre of the island, well sown with military installations, a pair of giant, adjacent roundabouts by the airport funnel traffic northwest towards **Mastihári**, northeast back towards town, southwest towards **Kéfalos**, and southeast to **Kardhámena**. Most visitors are bound for the south coast **beaches**, reached from the Kéfalos-bound turning.

### Mastihári, Andimáhia and Kardhámena

The least "packaged" and least expensive of the north-shore resorts, **MASTIHÁRI** has a shortish, broad beach extending west, with less frequented dunes (and no sunbeds) towards the far end. The fifth-century basilica of **Áyios Ioánnis** lies about 1.5km down the west beach, following the shoreline promenade; it's fairly typical of Kós's numerous early Christian sites, the results of Paul's evangelizing, with a row of column bases separating a pair of side aisles from the nave, a tripartite narthex, and a baptistry tacked onto the north side of the building.

Quiet beachfront **accommodation** includes simple *Hotel Kyma* (☎22420 59045; ②) or *Hotel Fenareti* (☎22420 59024) further up the slope, with rooms (②) and studios (③) in a peaceful garden environment. *O Makis*, one street inland from the quay, and *Kali Kardia*, at the base of the jetty, are the best of a half-dozen **tavernas**, well regarded for fresh fish, *mezédhes* and (at *Kali Kardia*) *mayireftá* and desserts. Mastihári is also the port for roll-on-roll-off **ferries** (current information on ☎22420 59124) and smaller **jet-boats** to Kálymnos; there are three and five well-spaced daily departures respectively in each direction most of the year, the jet-boats timed more or less to coincide with flight arrivals from Athens.

The workaday village of **ANDIMÁHIA**, 5km southeast of Mastihári, straggles over several ridges; the only concession to tourism, besides a single **windmill** kitted out as a museum (sporadic hours; €1.50), is a line of snack bars at the southwestern edge, easily accessible from the airport (across the road and car park) if your outbound flight is delayed. East of Andimáhia, reached via a marked, 2.8-kilometre side road, an enormous, triangular **Knights' castle** (unrestricted access, occasional concert venue) overlooks the straits to Níssyros. Its **Áyios Nikólaos** chapel features an interesting fresco of Áyios Khristóforos (St Christopher) carrying the Christ child.

**KARDHÁMENA**, 31km from Kós Town, is the island's largest package resort after the capital itself, with locals outnumbered twenty to one in a (now rare) busy season by boozing-and-bonking visitors (mostly heavily tattooed young Brits). A beach stretches to either side of the town – sandier to the southwest, but intermittently reefy and hemmed in by a road going northeast towards Tolári and Kós's largest all-inclusive complex – but runaway local development has banished any redeeming qualities the place might have had.

The resort is most useful as a place to catch a boat to **Níssyros**. There are two daily sailings in season: the morning excursion *kaïki* at 9.30am, and another, less expensive, unpublicized one – either the *Ayios Konstandinos* or the *Nissyros* – at anywhere from 2.30 to 7pm depending on the day.

### South coast beaches

The portion of Kós southwest of the airport and Andimáhia boasts the most scenic and secluded beaches on the island, plus a number of minor ancient sites. Though given fanciful English names and shown separately on tourist maps, these **south-facing beaches** form essentially one long stretch at the base of a cliff, most with jet-skis for rent and sunbeds. "**Magic**", officially Polémi, is the longest, broadest and wildest, with a proper taverna above the car park, no jet-skis and a nudist zone ("**Exotic**") at the east end. "**Sunny**", signposted as Psilós Gremmós and easily walkable from "Magic", has another taverna and jet-skis; **Langádhes** is the cleanest and most picturesque, with junipers tumbling off its dunes and more jet-skis. "**Paradise**", alias "**Bubble Beach**" because of volcanic gas-vents in the tidal zone, is small and oversubscribed, with wall-to-wall sunbeds. Jet-ski-free "**Camel**" (Kamíla) is the shortest and loneliest, protected somewhat by the steep, unpaved drive in past its hillside taverna; the shore here is pure, fine sand, with good snorkelling either side of the cove.

Uninterrupted beach resumes past **Áyios Stéfanos** headland, overshadowed by a holiday complex, and extends 3km west through Kamári resort (see below). A marked public access road leads down to beaches either side of a small peninsula, crowned with the remains of two triple-aisled, sixth-century **basilicas**. Though the best preserved of several such on the island, most columns have been toppled, and wonderful bird mosaics languish under a permanent layer of protective gravel. The basilicas overlook tiny, striking **Kastrí** islet with its little chapel; in theory it's an easy swim (sometimes wading) across from the westerly beach, with decent snorkelling around the rock formations, but in practice you must run a gauntlet of boats from the local watersports outfit.

### The far west

Essentially the shore annexe of Kéfalos, **KAMÁRI** is a sprawling package resort and watersports venue of scattered breeze-blocks, with more families and oldies than at Kardhámena. Probably the best of a pretty Anglicised bunch of **tavernas** is *Stamatia*, by the central shoreline junction. **KÉFALOS** itself, 43km from Kós Town and terminus for buses, covers a bluff looking down the length of the island. Aside from some lively **cafés** at the south end, it's a dull village mainly of note as a staging point for expeditions into the rugged **peninsula** terminating dramatically at **Cape Kríkello**.

The main highlights of a visit there, along the ridge road south, include **Panayía Palatianí** Byzantine church amid the ruins of a much larger ancient temple, 1km beyond the village, and the Classical theatre (unrestricted access) – two rows of seats remaining – and Hellenistic temple of **ancient Astypalia**, 500m further via the side-path starting from an unmarked but unlocked gate. A paved road west just beyond Astypalia leads to often windy **Áyios Theológos beach**, 7km from Kéfalos; the *Ayios Theologos* **taverna** here is popular at weekends, despite ruthlessly exploiting its monopoly and a snacky menu (fish on request). Keeping to the main paved road to its end brings you to the appealing (but usually locked) monastery of **Áyios Ioánnis Thymianós**, also 7km from Kéfalos; an onward unmarked dirt track leads just under 4km to clothing-optional **Hilandhríou beach**, 300m-plus of fine sand with no reliable facilities.

# Psérimos

**Psérimos**, with remote beaches of various shapes and sizes to walk to, could be an idyllic little island were it not so close to Kós and Kálymnos. Throughout the season, these larger neighbours dispatch so many daily excursion boats that a second jetty has been built to accommodate them at little **AVLÁKIA** port. In midsummer, hundreds of day-trippers blanket the main sandy beach which curves in front of Avlákia's thirty-odd houses and huge communal olive grove; even during May or late September you're guaranteed at least eighty outsiders daily (versus a permanent population of 25). There are three other, variably attractive beaches to hide away on: clean **Vathý** (sand and gravel), a well-marked, thirty-minute path-walk east, starting from behind the *Taverna Iy Pserimos*; grubbier **Marathoúnda** (pebble), a 45-minute walk north on the main trans-island track; and best of all **Grafiótissa**, a 300-metre-long beach of near-Caribbean quality at the base of low cliffs. This lies half an hour's walk west of town, more or less following the coast; the way is cross-country around illegally fenced hillside plots, until a trail kicks in at a large, lone tree by a stone corral.

Even during high season there won't be many other overnighters, since there's a limited number of beds. The pick of several small **rooms** establishments is *Tripolitis* (T 22430 23196; May–Oct; ❶), upstairs from English-speaking *Anna's* café/snack-bar; otherwise try the rooms above *Taverna Manola* on the opposite end of the beach (T 22430 51540; ❶), or the co-managed, somewhat superior *Studios Kalliston* adjacent (❸). There's just one limited-stock shop, since most of the island's supplies are brought in from Kálymnos. **Eating out** won't break the bank, and there's often fresh fish in the handful of tavernas; many have contracts with tour boats, but *Taverna Manola* doesn't, and despite a bar-like appearance (it provides the main **nightlife**) it proves adept at ouzerí fare and seafood.

Most boats **based** at Kós harbour operate triangle tours to Platý islet and somewhere on Kálymnos as well as Psérimos, with only a brief stop at the latter. If you want to spend the entire day here, you'll have to depart Póthia (Kálymnos) at 9.30am daily on the roll-on-roll-off *Maniaï*, returning at 5–6pm (€6.60 round trip); some years there may also be a daily service on the *Kalymnos Star/ Kalymnos Dolphin*.

# Astypálea

Geographically, historically and architecturally, **Astypálea** (alias Astropália) really belongs to the Cyclades – on a clear day you can see Anáfi or Amorgós far more easily than any of the other Dodecanese. Its inhabitants are descendants of medieval colonists from the Cyclades, and the island looks and feels more like one of these than its neighbours to the east. Supposedly, Astypálea was reassigned to the Ottomans after the Greek Revolution only because the Great Powers had such a poor map at the 1830 and 1832 peace conferences.

Despite an evocative butterfly shape, Astypálea may not immediately strike you as especially beautiful. Many **beaches** along the bleak, heavily indented coastline have reef underfoot and periodic dumpings of seaweed. Windswept heights are covered in thornbush or dwarf juniper, yet the sage *alisfakiá*, brewed as a tea, flourishes too. Hundreds of sheep and goats (source of the excellent local **cheese**) manage to survive – unlike snakes, which are (uniquely in the Aegean) entirely absent (migrating cranes supposedly ate them all). Citrus groves and vegetable patches in the valleys signal a relative abundance of water, hoarded in a reservoir. Besides cheese, Astypálea is renowned for its **honey**, **fish** and **lobster**.

**Ferry links** with Pireás and the Cyclades have improved, though arrival/departure times remain grim (typically 3am/5am) and service to the Dodecanese other than Kálymnos is spotty. Thus you may need or want to take advantage of **flights** to Léros, Kós or Rhodes. There is no **package tourism** on Astypálea, and its remoteness discourages casual trade, but motivated people descend during the short, intense **midsummer season** (mid-July to early

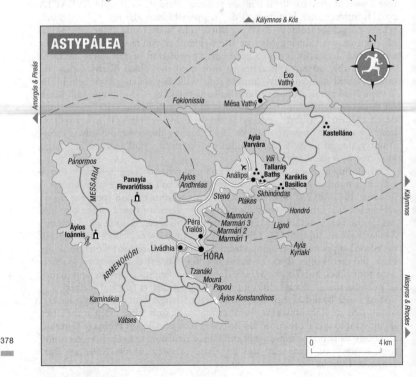

Sept), when 1500 permanent inhabitants are vastly outnumbered by visitors. Most arrivals are Athenians, French or Italians, supplemented by large numbers of yachties and foreign second-home owners in picturesque Hóra. At such times you won't find a bed without reserving well in advance, and camping rough is expressly frowned upon.

## Péra Yialós and Hóra

The main harbour of **PÉRA YIALÓS** or Skála dates from the Italian era (Astypálea was the first Dodecanese island occupied by the Italians) and most of the settlement between the quay and the line of eight windmills is even more recent. Its only real bright spot is a small **archeological museum** (June–Sept Tues–Sun 10am–1pm & 6.30–10pm; Oct–May Tues–Sun 8.30am–2.30pm; free), its single gallery crammed with local finds spanning the Bronze Age to medieval times.

As you climb up towards **HÓRA**, however, the neighbourhoods get progressively older and more attractive, their steep streets enlivened by photogenic *poúndia*, or colourful wooden balconies-with-stairways attached to whitewashed houses. Building styles here owe much to colonists from Mýkonos and Tínos who were brought over to repopulate the island in 1413. It all culminates in the thirteenth-century **kástro** (always open; free), one of the finest in the Aegean, erected not by the Knights of St John but by the Venetian Quirini clan and subsequently modified by the Ottomans after 1537. Until well into the twentieth century more than three hundred people dwelt inside, but depopulation and a severe 1956 earthquake combined to leave only a desolate shell. The fine rib vaulting over the main west gate supports the church of **Evangelístria Kastrianí**, one of two here, the other being **Áyios Yeóryios** (both usually locked). The *kástro* interior is undergoing a major consolidation and restoration project, so about half of it is off-limits at any given time.

### Arrival, information and transport

All **ferries** except the *Nissos Kalymnos* call at northerly Áyios Andhréas port, 7km away. In summer there's a shuttle bus; otherwise the two **buses** ply the paved road between Hóra, Péra Yialós, Livádhia and Analípsi (July–Aug frequently 8am–11pm; out of season 3–4 daily). Análipsi-bound buses usually don't dovetail well with arriving/departing flights, so ask your chosen accommodation or car-rental outfit (see below) to fetch you. The one set-rate **taxi** can't cope with passenger numbers in season, although fares are reasonable (€7 from Skála to the airport). Various places offer **scooters** (cheap), plus **cars** and **jeeps** (expensive), the most reliable being Lakis and Manolis (☎22430 61263), at Skála dock, Tomaso next door (☎22430 61000), and Vergoulis (☎22430 61351) near the museum. Also near the museum, Astypalea Tours (☎22430 61571) represents the *Nissos Kalymnos*; Paradisos under the namesake hotel (☎22430 61224) handles Blue Star. Road Editions publishes the best island **map**, worth snagging in advance; others sold locally are grossly inaccurate, even by Greek island standards, though rural junctions are adequately signposted on the ground. The **post office** and most shops are in Hóra, though the island's only **ATM** is down in Péra Yialós.

### Accommodation

**Accommodation** in Péra Yialós ranges from spartan, 1970s-vintage rooms to new luxury complexes; Hóra has a slightly more high-end slant. For the atmospheric restored studios or entire houses (❸–❹) up in **Hóra**, enquire at Kostas Vaïkousis' antique shop on Skála's quay or reserve on ☎22430 61430 or

697 74 77 800. 🏛 *Studios Kilindra* (☎22430 61966, ⓦwww.astipalea.com.gr; April–Dec; ⑥), on the quiet west slope of Hóra, are rather plusher, with galleried maisonettes, a swimming pool and good breakfasts – units accommodate two to three people. Almost as luxurious, at the the start of the road to Livádhia, are tasteful, flagstoned-terrace *Kallichoron Studios* (☎22430 61934, ⓦwww.astypalea.com; all year; ⑤), also with one-bed apartments (⑥), all with views of Hóra. About halfway along the road from Hóra to Livádhia, non-a/c *Provarma Studios* (☎22430 61096; June to early Sept; ③), comprise southwest-facing galleried studios with large balconies.

The best accommodation in **Péra Yialós** is the *Hotel Thalassa* (☎22430 59840, ⓦwww.stampalia.gr; all year; B&B ⑥), one of the last buildings on the way to Análipsi, consisting entirely of suites and studios. The less remote *Akti Rooms* (☎22430 61114, ⓦwww.aktirooms.gr; ④) is better value, with on-site car rental and a popular restaurant. The en-suite *Rooms Australia*, above the eponymous restaurant (☎22430 61275 or 22430 61067; ③) have fans or air conditioning; the same family offers compact studios closer to the water, with heating and double glazing (④). A basic **campsite** (☎22430 61900; July–Aug) operates amongst calamus reeds and tamarisks behind Dhéftero Marmári Bay, about 4km along the road to Análipsi, but (like much of the island) it can be mosquito-plagued after a wet winter.

### Eating and drinking

During August, nearly thirty **tavernas** and **beach snack-bars** operate across the island, few of them memorable and most out for a quick buck. Among the more reliable **Péra Yialós** options, *Akroyiali* has only slightly better-than-average food but fills nightly due to its fair prices and unbeatable setting with tables on the sand. The *Astropalia* (closes end Sept), just off the road to Hóra, does good, if somewhat pricey, fish and little else. Best of the lot, with even better seafood, and superbly prepared home-grown vegetable dishes, is homely, 1971-founded 🏛 *Australia* (April–Nov), just inland from the head of the bay. On the far (west) side of the bay, you'll find more polished presentation and higher prices at *Maïstrali* (*Tou Penindara*; all year), the place for lobster, scaly fish or *mayireftá* from a broad menu. Under *Hotel Astynea*, the *Dapia Café* is good for full breakfasts, crêpes and novelty teas; a few steps down, on the corner, *Iy Vouli* (*O Mihalis*) is tops for inexpensive home-made desserts and warm *píttes* plus morning coffees. The only serious taverna up in **Hóra** is *Barbarossa* (all year, dinner only) near the *dhimarhío*, popular for its pleasant interior, desserts and rich meaty dishes of the day (though the salads are a disappointment).

### Nightlife

Except for *Yialos* music café near *Akroyiali*, most **nightlife** happens up in Hóra, where the esplanade between the windmills and the base of the *kástro* forms one solid café-bar. Of these, standouts are music bar *Notos*, tucked in by the triple chapel, with desserts as well, and nearby, unsigned *Tou Nikola* (*Iy Myli*) on a corner, with the island's characters in residence and home-made *glyká koutalioú* dished out amidst wonderfully kitsch Greek-royalist decor. These are joined in season by *Kastro*, good for conversation-level music, near which a July–August outdoor **cinema** operates.

## Southwestern Astypálea

A twenty-minute walk (or short bus journey) from Hóra brings you to **LIVÁDHIA**, a fertile valley draining to a popular, serviceable **beach** with a collection of restaurants and cafés immediately behind. You can rent a **studio** just inland – for example at *O Manganas* (℡22430 61468; ❹), on the frontage road (they've even tiny washing machines in the units), or *Venetos Studios* (℡22430 61490 or 694 43 01 381; May–Sept; ❸), at the base of the westerly hillside, comprising several buildings scattered in a pleasant orchard. Better than either, however, is the 2007-built ⌁ *Kalderimi* complex on the road bend just above (℡22430 59843, ⓦwww.kalderimi.gr; ❺), a cluster of eleven impeccably appointed mock-trad a/c cottages (some fitting families) with CD players, internet and satellite TV. Among the half-dozen **tavernas**, ⌁ *To Yerani* (May–Oct) is renowned for its excellent *mayireftá*; they also offer quality rooms, with modern furnishings and marble floors (℡22430 61484; ❸). *Astropelos* on the beach is open later in the season, with good vegetable dishes, but outrageously priced seafood.

If the busy beach here doesn't suit, continue southwest fifteen minutes on foot to three small fine-pebble coves at **Tzanáki**, packed with naturists in midsummer. Beyond these, **Papoú** is an 80-metre fine-gravel strand accessible overland by a horrifically steep side track, and then a final path approach around a fenced-off farm. The third large bay beyond Livádhia, more usually reached by motorbike, is **Áyios Konstandínos**, a partly shaded, sand-and-gravel cove with a good seasonal taverna. Further afield, the lonely beaches of **Vátses** and **Kaminákia** are visited by a seasonal excursion boat from Péra Yialós. By land, **Vátses** has the easier dirt road in, some 25 minutes by scooter from Livádhia; it's one of the sandier island beaches, with a basic *kantína*, but often windy. The track to **Kaminákia**, 8.5km from Livádhia, is rough and steep for the final 2km – best to go in a jeep – but the sheltered, clean and scenic cove, Astypálea's best, repays the effort. A good **taverna** (*Linda*, July–Sept) oversees a handful of sunbeds and offers honest, rustic fare (salads, fresh fish and a dish of the day).

### Áyios Ioánnis monastery and around

One favourite outing is the two-hour walk or half-hour motorbike trip from Hóra to **Áyios Ioánnis**, just under 10km distant. Proceed northwest along the signposted, initially paved road beginning from the windmills, passing high above the reservoir, then keep left when a side track goes right towards Panayía Flevariótissa. Beyond this point the main track curls north at the base of a ridge, where the overflow of two springs may seep across the road. Once past the half-dozen isolated farms in **Messariá** valley, go through the left-hand gate at the next junction, and soon the securely walled orchards of the uninhabited farm-monastery **Áyios Ioánnis** appear.

From the balcony of the church, Anáfi floats on the horizon, and a steep, faint path drops to the base of a ten-metre **waterfall**; alas, bathing pools here have silted up, and the cascade itself – apparently tapped for irrigation – tends to be dry most months. Below, a pathless trek down the canyon ends at fine, pebbly Áyios Ioánnis **beach**, potentially the last stop for southwesterly boat excursions.

## Northeastern Astypálea

Northeast of the harbour are the three coves known as **Próto** (First), **Dhéftero** (Second) and **Tríto** (Third) **Mármari**. The first is home to the power plant and boatyards, the next hosts the campsite, while the third, relatively attractive, also marks the start of the path east to the decent but unfortunately named **Mamoúni** ("bug" or "critter" in Greek) coves. Beyond Tríto Mármari, the main beach at **Stenó** ("narrow", after the isthmus here), with sandy shore and shallows, a few tamarisks and a seasonal *kantína*, is the best.

**ANÁLIPSI**, widely known as Maltezána after medieval Maltese pirates, is 9km from Péra Yialós. Although the second-largest settlement on Astypálea, there's surprisingly little for visitors save a narrow, exposed, packed-sand beach (there are better ones east of the main bay at **Skhinóndas**, and west at **Plákes**) and a nice view south to islets. Despite this, blocks of **rooms/ studios** (July–Aug only) sprout in ranks well back from the sea, spurred by the proximity of the airport. A more reliable exception, and the island's largest hotel, is the 48-unit (including five for families) *Maltezana Beach* (T 22430 61558, W www.maltezanabeach.gr; Easter to mid-Sept; ➏ std, ➐ family), with large, well-appointed bungalow-rooms, pool and on-site restaurant. Among several **tavernas** here, the most consistently open (Feb–Christmas) is *Analipsi* (aka *Ilias-Irini's*) by the jetty, which doubles as the fishermen's *kafenío*. The food – fried squid, bean soup – is simple but wholesome; confirm prices and portion size of the often frozen seafood. Behind calamus reeds and eucalyptus near the fishing jetty lie well-preserved mosaic floors at the Byzantine **Tallarás baths**, though sadly they're now under a layer of protective gravel (photos in Skála's museum); view exposed ones at the **Karéklis basilica** 1km east (geometric and animal designs) or at fifth-century **Ayía Varvára** basilica, an equal distance north (abstract and vegetal motifs) – easiest access is past the last house and windmill. On the headland near Karéklis, a memorial obelisk commemorates French sailors who died after scuttling their frigate *Bisson*, trapped by the Ottoman navy here on November 6, 1827, during the Greek War of Independence.

The motorable track ends 23km from Hóra at **Mésa Vathý** (erroneously labelled on many maps as Éxo Vathý), a sleepy fishing hamlet with a single **taverna** (*Iy Galini*) and superb yacht anchorage at this landlocked inlet ending in a marsh, sporadically home to those snake-eating cranes. Frankly, though, it's not really worth the long, bumpy trip out on a scooter, and to rub salt in the wound, the menu's seafood is usually frozen (if local).

# Kálymnos

Most of **Kálymnos's** 17,000-strong population lives in or around the large port of **Póthia**, whose historical prosperity was based on its **sponge industry**. Unfortunately, almost all of the eastern Mediterranean's sponges were devastated by a mysterious disease in 1986, and only a few boats of the thirty-strong fleet are still in use; most of the sponges processed and sold in the warehouses behind the harbour are imported from Asia and the Caribbean. You will see numbers of elderly (and middle-aged) men with severe mobility problems, stark evidence of the havoc wrought in their youth by the "bends" before divers understood its crippling effects (see box, p.385).

In response to the sponge blight (and a repeat outbreak in 1999), the island established a **tourist industry** – confined to one series of beach resorts – and also adapted most sponge boats for deep-sea fishing. But mass tourism proved as fickle as sponges, and essentially collapsed after the millennium. The then-unfinished airport near Árgos village (not built for jets anyway), and the ongoing need for tedious transfers from Kós, was the main excuse for most package companies leaving. Subsequently, the island re-invented itself as an off-season **hiking** and **rock-climbing** destination – it has some of the best cliffs in Greece, and a respectable surviving path network – and began promoting **scuba diving** and **sea kayaking** through a late-summer festival.

Kálymnos essentially consists of two cultivated, inhabited valleys sandwiched between three **limestone** ridges, harsh in the full glare of noon but magically tinted towards dusk. The **climate** is claimed to be drier and healthier than that of neighbouring Kós or Léros, since the quick-draining limestone strata, riddled with caves, doesn't retain as much moisture. This rock does, however, admit seawater, which has tainted Póthia's wells; drinking **water** must be trucked in from the Vathýs valley, and there are also potable springs at Kamári, Potamí district of Póthia and Hóra.

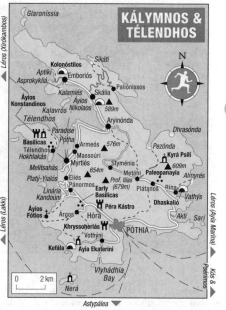

Despite its hostile geology, Kálymnos's position and excellent harbours ensured its prominence from ancient times, especially during the **Byzantine era**, and there are more ruined early basilicas here than on any other island in the Dodecanese. Another local Byzantine legacy is the survival of peculiar medieval names (eg Skévos, Sakellários and Mikés for men, Themélina, Petránda and Sevastí for women) found nowhere else in Greece.

## Póthia

**PÓTHIA**, without being conventionally picturesque, is colourful and authentically Greek, its houses marching up the valley inland or arrayed in tiers along the surrounding hillsides. With nearly 16,000 inhabitants, it has overtaken Kós Town as the second-largest Dodecanesian municipality after Ródhos Town, and your first impression may be of the phenomenal noise engendered by motorbike traffic and cranked-up sound systems of the half-dozen waterfront cafés. Things get even louder on **Easter Sunday** evening, when teams stationed on the heights engage in an organized dynamite-throwing contest, with feasting and general merriment after the inevitable casualties are taken to hospital.

### Arrival, information and transport

All boat and hydrofoil agents, plus a municipal **tourist information** booth (sporadic hours in season; otherwise ⓦwww.kalymnos-isl.gr), line the waterfront as you bear right out of the pier-area gate, where **taxis** also await arrivals. The best **map**, seldom sold on Kálymnos, is Anavasi's 1:25,000 #10.32, which shows all walking routes. Useful **agencies** include Mangos (☎22430 28777), for Blue Star and hydrofoils; Sofia Kouremeti (☎22430 23700) for GA and *Dodekanisos Express/Pride*; and Kalymna Yachting (☎22430 28200) for the *Nissos Kalymnos* and *Kalymnos Star/Dolphin*. Olympic Airways is represented by Kapellas, Patriárhou Maxímou 12 (☎22430 29265), 200m inland from the quay; the **airport** is 6km west by Árgos village. The two best **internet** cafés are Heaven, opposite the yacht anchorage, and giant Neon in Khristós district.

▲ Sponges on sale, Kálymnos

**Buses** run as far as Emboriós in the northwest and Vathýs in the east, from two terminals beside the municipal "palace", with schedules posted near many stops, and fairly frequent departures (to west coast resorts at least) in season. Tickets (€0.80–2) must be bought beforehand from authorized kiosks, and cancelled on board. Otherwise, use shared **taxis** from Platía Kýprou (pricier than KTEL buses, less than a normal taxi), or rent a **scooter** from Kostas (☎22430 50110) near the port police, or Nomikos Kardoulias (☎22430 51780), just back from the waterfront in Khristós district. **Car rental** is also available on the quay (Spiros Kypraios, ☎2430 51470; Budget, ☎22430 51780 or 697 28 34 628), though the island's compact enough that only groups will need one.

### Accommodation

**Accommodation** is rarely a problem, with a high-season booking office on the quay; as on Kós, beware of touts flogging substandard, unlicensed or remote premises. The town's quietest and most elegant hotel, near the archeological museum, is garden-set ⚜ *Villa Melina* (☎22430 22682, villa-melina.com; all year; B&B ❸), an early-twentieth-century mansion with high-ceilinged, bug-screened, wood-floored rooms, a modern annexe of studios and apartments, plus a breakfast patio, an engaging managing family and a large saltwater swimming pool. Less characterful alternatives include, on Áyios Nikólaos's southwest quay, *Arhondiko* (☎22430 24051; all year; ❷), another refurbished mansion whose plain rooms have TV and fridge, or – high up in Amoudhára district west of the harbour – the well-kept *Hotel Panorama* (☎22430 23138; April–Oct; ❸), with balconied view-rooms and a pleasant breakfast salon.

### The Town

Perhaps the most rewarding way to explore Póthia is by wandering the **backstreets**, where elegant **Neoclassical houses**, painted the traditional pink or ochre, are surrounded by surprisingly large gardens, and craftsmen ply their trade in a genuine workaday bazaar. They particularly excel in iron-working,

## Sponges and sponge-diving

**Sponges** are colonies of microscopic marine organisms which excrete a fibrous skeleton, increasing in size by about thirty percent annually. When alive, they are almost black in colour, and can be seen throughout the Aegean as melon-sized blobs, anchored to rocks in three to ten metres of water. However, these are mostly "wild" sponges, impossible to clean or shape with shears; Kalymnian divers are after the so-called "tame" sponges, which are much softer, more pliable, and dwell at greater depths – typically thirty to forty metres.

Before the late nineteenth century, sponge-fishers **free-dived** for their quarry; weighted with a specially shaped rock, the *skandhalópetra*, they descended to the seabed to hand-collect or spear as many sponges as possible on a single breath before being hauled to the surface by a safety line. The industrial revolution signalled momentous changes: divers were fitted with heavy, insulated suits – the *skáfandhro* – and breathing apparatus supplied by an air-feed line connected to primitive, hand-operated compressors on board the factory boats. They could now attain depths of up to 70m, but this resulted in the first cases of the "bends", or **nitrogen embolism**. Divers working at any depth over 10m and at pressures of several atmospheres would rise too quickly to the surface, so that the dissolved air in their bloodstream bubbled out of solution – with catastrophic results. From the late nineteenth century until well into the twentieth, roughly half of the sponge divers who left with the fleets in spring never returned in autumn: buried at sea, or in a lonely grave in some remote islet, sometimes while still alive up to their necks so that the hot sand might provide slight relief from the excruciating pain of nitrogen bubbles in the joints.

Not until World War I was the physiological basis of the malady well understood; by then thousands of Kalymnians had died, with many survivors paralyzed, deaf or blind. The *skáfandhro*, despite being the obvious culprit and having been banned elsewhere in the Mediterranean, returned to use until after World War II. The first **decompression chambers**, and commercial diving schools imparting systematic knowledge of safe diving practices, were only available in Greece from the 1950s. Now, new technology enabled the seabed to be stripped with ruthless efficiency; the sponge fleets were forced to hunt further from home, finally ending up in Egyptian and Libyan waters until the Nasser and Gaddafi regimes imposed punitive duties in 1962 and 1972 respectively.

Even the "tame" sponge is unusable until **processed**. First they have the smelly organic matter and external membrane thrashed out of them, traditionally by being trodden on the boat deck; next they are tossed in a rotary vat with hot sea-water for a day or so, to complete the process. In Póthia you can visit a few **workshops** (the best is on the shore road opposite Ayía Iríni, in Vouvális district) where the sponge-vats still spin; in the old days, the divers simply made a "necklace" of their catch and trailed it in the sea behind the boat. A third, optional processing step is bleaching the sponges with nitric acid to a pale yellow colour in accord with modern tastes. But bleaching weakens the fibres, so it's best to buy the more durable, natural-brown ones. In line with the risks, and competition from the production of synthetics, natural sponges are not cheap, even on Kálymnos. The enduring appeal of natural sponges – aside from the mystique of their gathering, and supporting a traditional lifestyle, however harsh – is that they're simply more durable, absorbent and softer than synthetic products, and lend themselves to a wide range of uses, from make-up artistry to canvas-painting to window-washing.

and all but the humblest dwellings in eastern Evangelístria district are adorned by splendidly ornate banisters, balcony railings and fanlights.

The best of two local museums is the **Municipal Nautical and Folklore Museum** (daily 10am–1pm; €1.50), on the seaward side of Khristós cathedral. A large photo shows Póthia in the 1880s, with no quay, jetty, roads or sumptuous mansions, and with most of the population still up in Hóra, while other images document sponge fishing and the Allied liberation of 1945. You can also see horribly primitive divers' breathing apparatuses, and "cages" designed to keep propellers from cutting air lines, a constant danger. Eventually (nobody knows when), a new annexe to the soporific existing **archeological museum** in Evangelístria (Tues–Sun 9am–2pm) will open, featuring a dazzling array of Roman and Byzantine finds.

### Eating and drinking

The most obvious place to eat is the line of generally mediocre seafood **tavernas** northeast along the waterfront past the Italian-built municipal "palace". An exception is friendly, family-run *To Steki ton Navtikon*, with good fresh and cured seafood. Much the best-value meals, however, are scoffed at ✴ *Kafenes*, on Khristós esplanade opposite the county "palace", always full thanks to generous, tasty salads, seafood, local goat cheese and bulk wine. *Taverna Pandelis*, tucked inconspicuously into a cul-de-sac behind waterfront *Olympic Hotel*, is tops for meat grills and *mezédhes*, with wild scaly fish and shellfish off-menu – ask for the daily catch. Wood-fired pizzas are served at *Pizza Porto* and *Pizza Imia* at mid-quay. Greek sweetmeat fans should make for the traditional *Zaharoplastio O Mihalaras* in "restaurant row", or their more modern annexe near the ferry jetty. **Nightlife**, except for *Blue Note* bar near *Pandelis*, is resolutely quayside café/*frappádhika*-based; for more ambitious seasonal venues outside town, watch for posters. Adjacent summer (Oasis) and winter (Splendid) **cinemas** function behind the traditional, column-facaded café-tearoom *Ai Musai*, on the front.

## Medieval monuments around Póthia

In the suburb of Mýli, 1.2km northwest of Póthia, stands the Knights' **Kástro Khryssoheriás** (unrestricted access), whose whitewashed battlements offer wonderful views southeast over town to Kós and north towards Hóra and Péra Kástro. The former Kalymnian capital of **HÓRA** (aka Horió), 1.5km further along the main road, is still a large, busy village, guarding a critical pass in local geography. Steep steps lead up from its eastern edge to the nocturnally illuminated Byzantine citadel-town of **Péra Kástro** (Mon–Fri 9am–1pm; free), appropriated by the Knights of St John and inhabited until the late 1700s. Inside the massive gate and perimeter walls you'll find nine **medieval chapels**, of which Áyios Nikólaos, Ayía Ánna, Timíou Stavroú and Metamórfosis contain fifteenth-to-sixteenth-century fresco fragments.

Some 200m beyond the turning for Árgos en route to the northwest coast, two early Byzantine **basilicas** are among the biggest, and easiest to find, of a vast number on Kálymnos. The more impressive of the pair, accessed by steps on the left just as the highway begins to descend, is **Khristós tís Ierousalím**, probably dating from the late fourth century, with a fully preserved apse.

## West coast resorts: Brostá

From the basilicas, the main road leads to the half-dozen consecutive **beach resorts** collectively referred to as "Brostá" by islanders. **KANDOÚNI**, some 200m of brown, hard-packed sand favoured by the locals, is the shore annexe of the agricultural villages of Pánormos and Eliés. For a pleasant local walk, best towards sunset, take the obvious path from below the large monastery of Stavroú at Kandoúni to the little monastery of **Áyios Fótios** (45min each way), tucked under cliffs towards the westernmost point of the island.

**Accommodation** includes the well-appointed *Kalydna Island Hotel* (☎22430 47880, ⓦwww.kalydnaislandhotel.gr; ❹), and **nightlife** (try *Café del Mar* and *Domus* on the beach) is fairly active, but most will prefer **LINÁRIA**, the north end of the same bay. A smaller cove set apart from Kandoúni by the Patélla outcrop, this has better sand, and lodging at *Skopellos Studios* (☎22430 47155; ❸), below the hillside church. Of two shoreline full-service **tavernas** here, seafood-strong *Mamouzelos* (alias *Yiorgos*; supper only) offers big portions of excellent food let down by bumped-up prices and rude service. *To Steki tis Fanis*, in an old mansion up on the hillside, has local specialities such as *mermizéli* (salad of greens, *kopanistí* and barley rusks) and ample vegetarian starters, but mains quality varies.

The next beach north, **PLATÝ-YIALÓS**, again a bit shorter than Kandoúni, is arguably Kálymnos's best: cleaner than its neighbours, more secluded, and placed scenically at the base of a cliff, opposite Ayía Kyriakí islet. A lone **taverna** (*Kyma/Wave*) at the road's end serves simple, inexpensive lunches and sunset drinks (it closes shortly after). **Staying** locally, the blue-and-white *Mousselis Studios* (☎22430 48307, ⓦwww.mousellis.gr; ❹), just up the road from the beach, accommodate two to six people, with weekly half board rates available.

The main road climbs from Pánormos up to Kamári pass, before descending in zigzags to seaside **MYRTIÉS**, 8km from Póthia. Together with **MASSOÚRI** (1km north via an upper bypass road, part of a giant, circular one-way system) and **ARMEÓS** (2km north and terminus for most buses), Myrtiés was hardest hit by the Kalymnian tourism slump, so vacant and for-sale premises abound. Thriving exceptions include ⚓ *Akroyali* (☎22430 47521 or 693 89 13 210, ⓔacroyali@klm.forthnet.gr; ❸), well designed beachside apartments in Massoúri sleeping two adults and two kids which require advance booking; the *Apollonia* studio-format hotel nearby, with blander decor (☎22430 48094; March–Nov; ❸); jointly operated Avis/Alfa (☎22430 47430, ⓦwww.kalymnosrent.com) **renting cars and bikes**; and a daily *kaïki* from Myrtiés to Xirókambos on Léros. The best surviving **taverna**, in Armeós, is the friendly if pricey meat specialist *Tsopanakos* (all year), serving fresh meat and cheese dishes from island-grazed goats. There's also some Greek-pitched **nightlife**, with live music at *Kastelli Club*. Armeós is also the local mecca for European **rock-climbers**, with many of the most popular cliffs overhead (look for the route-inscribed columns at their base) and a small equipment shop (Climber's Nest) catering to them.

The **beach** at Myrtiés is narrow, pebbly and cramped by development, though it does improve as you approach Massoúri, where *Stavedo Beach Bar* (ⓦwww .stavedo.com) offers a range of **watersports**. The closest all-sand beach to Myrtiés lies 500m south, at **Melitsáhas** cove, where one of three **tavernas**, *Iy Dhrossia* (aka *O Andonis*; all year), is noted for seafood and scaly fish. On-spec **accommodation** is easy to find; try spacious *Maria's Studios* (☎22430 48135 or 22430 28528; ❷) on the hillside, or attractively tiered *Vassilis Studios* opposite (☎22430 47751; ❸). Possibly this coast's most appealing feature is its setting, opposite evocatively shaped Télendhos islet (see p.388), which frames some of the most dramatic **sunsets** in Greece.

## Northern Kálymnos

Some 5km beyond Massoúri, **ARYINÓNDA** has a clean pebble beach, two **tavernas** (*Katerina* has **rooms**; ☎22430 40036; ❷) and sunbeds. It's also the trailhead for the spectacular two-and-a-half-hour traverse **walk** over two gentle passes to Metóhi in the Vathýs valley. From the bus stop and paved car-park area and cistern-spring, head southeast on a path between rock walls which soon climbs the south flank of the ravine here, sporadically marked by paint dots; the route is shown correctly on the Anavasi map. Walkers need a sun hat, stout boots and a litre or two of water, as the next source is in Plátanos hamlet (opposite a small, good **taverna**), beyond Metóhi; **drivers** can use the paved road up from Aryinónda to complete a 42-kilometre loop around Kálymnos.

The end of the bus line, **EMBORIÓS**, 20km from the port, offers a gravel-and-sand beach, accommodation and several **tavernas**, including *Harry's Paradise*, with garden apartments (☎ 22430 40061; a/c; ❸). If the twice-daily **bus** service fails you, there is a **shuttle boat** back to Myrtiés at 4pm (leaving the latter at 10am). There are also better, if unamenitied **beaches** between here and Skália, such as **Kalamiés** (with a taverna) and **Áyios Nikólaos**.

Just past Skália, a very rough dirt track zigzags east over the ridge some 5km to the popular yacht anchorage of **Paliónissos**, more usually visited by boat excursion from Rína (see opposite). It's a chore to reach on an ordinary scooter; many leave these up on the pass by the church and finish the journey on the cairned, blue-paint-dotted trail beginning opposite. However you arrive, there's a ten-minute final walk from track's end to the coarse-shingle, 90-metre beach here, threading through the little eponymous hamlet (population 5); the only facility is Nikolaos Makarounas' **taverna** *Paradise* (all day school hols, otherwise supper and weekends), something of a yachties' cult destination. **Sikáti Bay**, clearly visible to the left (north) of the zigzag road down from the saddle, is sandy but exposed to washed-up debris.

One cove beyond Emboriós lies goat-patrolled **Asprokykliá beach**, much the same quality as Emboriós'. Follow the rough dirt track above Asprokykliá to the isthmus by the fish farm, then walk fifteen minutes north on path and track to **Aptíki**, a smallish but perfectly formed pea-gravel cove. There's World War II-vintage debris to see when snorkelling, and perhaps moray eels or skates.

## Télendhos

The trip across the straits to the striking islet of **TÉLENDHOS** is arguably the best reason to come to Myrtiés; little boat-buses shuttle to and fro regularly (every 30min 8am–midnight; €1.50), occasionally dodging numerous sea kayaks. According to local legend, Télendhos is a petrified princess, gazing out to sea in the wake of her ill-starred affair with the prince of Kastélli in Armeós; the woman's-head profile is most evident at dusk. The hardly less romantic geological explanation has the islet sundered from Kálymnos by a cataclysmic earthquake in 554 AD; traces of a submerged town are said to lie at the bottom of the straits.

Home to about fifteen permanent inhabitants, Télendhos is car-free and blissfully tranquil, even more so since certain package operators gave up allotments here. For cultural edification you'll find the ruined thirteenth-century monastery of **Áyios Vassílios** and an enormous basilica of **Ayía Triádha** up on the ridge, part way along the flagstoned, ten-minute path to Hokhlakás pebble **beach**, which is small but very scenic, with sunbeds for rent and a **restaurant**, *Hohlakas Sunset*, by Ayía Triádha. Pótha and nudist "Paradise" on the other side of the islet are preferred by some: they're sandy and with calm water, but no afternoon sun.

There are nine places to eat and a roughly equal number of places to **stay**, many linked to the tavernas. Best bets include *Pension Studios Rita* (☎ 22430 47914; April to late Oct), its rooms (❶) and renovated-house studios (❷) managed by *Rita's Café*; the simple en-suite rooms above *Zorba's* (☎ 22430 48660; ❶); the high-standard *Rinio Studios* (☎ 22430 23851; ❷), set a bit inland;

or, north beyond Áyios Vassílios, Greek-Australian-run ☂ *On the Rocks* (☎22430 48260, ⓦwww.otr.telendos.com; April–Nov; ❸), three superbly appointed rooms and a more remote studio with double glazing, satellite TV, bug screens, fridges and internet, as well as kayaks on the beach out front. It's fairly easy to get a room at the large, friendly *Hotel Porto Potha* (☎22430 47321, ⓦwww .telendoshotel.gr; April to late Oct; ❸), at the edge of things but with a large pool, "private" beach and eight self-catering studios. Recommended **tavernas** include *Barba Stathis* (aka *Tassia's*), en route to Hokhlakás, with a few hot dishes each day; *Zorba's*, doing excellent goat or fresh squid; *Plaka*, next to *On the Rocks*, good for inexpensive meat; and the slightly pricey, full-service taverna at *On the Rocks* itself, with lovely home-made desserts, and a bar that's the heart of local **nightlife**. At one corner of the premises the chapel of Áyios Harálambos occupies a former Byzantine bathhouse; energetic types can walk just under an hour on a waymarked path up to the chapel of **Áyios Konstandínos** inside Byzantine fortifications, with fine views.

## Vathýs and around

The first 4km east from Póthia are vastly unpromising (power plant, rubbish tip, gasworks, cement quarries, fish farms), until you round a bend and the ten-kilometre ride ends dramatically at **VATHÝS**, a long, fertile valley whose orange and tangerine groves provide a startling contrast to the mineral greys and ochres higher up on Kálymnos. At the fjord port of **RÍNA**, most local tavernas are overpriced, geared toward the yachtie crowd; best are *The Harbors*, the first place on the right at road's end, with shambolic service but good fish, and the more upmarket but good-value *To Limanaki tou Vathy* near the lido, with tasty octopus and aubergine dishes.

The steep-sided inlet is beachless; the closest pebble-coves reachable overland are **Aktí**, 3km back towards Póthia, a functional pebble strand with sunbeds and a snack-bar; secluded **Mikrés Almyrés**, forty minutes away by rough path as traced on the Anávasi map (where the cove is unlabelled); and **Pezónda**, a little further north with a phenomenal amount of submerged World War II debris, reached by steep cement track (and then a 45min walk northwest) starting from Metóhi hamlet.

At track's end another path heads east in fifteen minutes to the amazingly set little **Kyrá Psilí monastery**, tucked into an overhang in the 609-metre mountain above, the second highest on Kálymnos. Accordingly there are superb views northwest at dusk as far as Ikaría and Mount Kérkis on Sámos, taking in intervening islands like Arkí and Foúrni. Incidentally, the name Kyrá Psilí ("The Tall Lady") has nothing to do with the altitude but is an epithet of the Virgin inherited from her predecessors, Aphrodite and Cybele. Most of Vathýs's historic **Byzantine churches** are locked; one exception, north of the road before Plátanos, is ruined **Paleopanayía**, with vivid sixth-century floor mosaics.

It's possible to **walk** back to Póthia along the old direct *kalderími* that existed before the coastal highway – a two-hour jaunt beginning at a fenced-in olive grove by two water cisterns above Plátanos hamlet. Without the Anavasi map, the route is tricky to find in this direction, so many people start in Póthia at the church of Ayía Triádha behind the *Villa Melina* hotel – look for red paint splodges at the start. In theory – and in possession of the Anavasi map – one can do a **day-long circuit**, returning from Áyios Nikólaos chapel west of Metóhi, via Profítis Ilías and a gorge, to Horió.

## The southwest

As you climb southwest out of Póthia towards Áyios Sávvas monastery, the most worthwhile halt is the **Folklore Museum-Traditional House of Kalymnos** (daily 9am–9pm; €1.50), a treasure trove of old furnishings and costumes. Some 6km southwest of Póthia, small **Vlyhádhia Bay** is reached via the nondescript village of Vothýni. The sand-and-pebble **beach** here isn't really worth a trip, since the bay is apt to be stagnant and reliable amenities are limited to a single beachside **snack bar**. A local diver has assembled an impressive **Museum of Submarine Finds** (Mon–Sat 9am–7pm, Sun 10am–2pm; free), which besides sponges and shells displays a reconstructed ancient wreck with amphorae and World War II debris. Most of the Kalymnian coast is now legal for **scuba diving**; the most reputable local dive operator, Pegasus Diving Club (℡ 22430 22034, Ⓦ www.kalymnosdiving .com), works out of Póthia.

From Vothýni a different road leads west past Ayía Ekateríni convent to within a few-minutes' trail walk of the **Kefála cave** (daily 9am–dusk), the most impressive of half a dozen caverns around the island. The cavern was inhabited in pre-history, and later served as a sanctuary of Zeus (fancifully identified with an imposing stalagmite in the biggest of six vividly coloured chambers). Beyond the cave, the trail system – challenging at times – leads past **Áyios Andhréas monastery**, above **Pithári Bay** with its outsize jetty and eventually to **Áyios Konstandínos monastery** prior to arrival in Árgos village (bus service) – allow two hours from Kefála.

# Léros

**Léros** is so indented with deep, sheltered anchorages that between 1928 and 1948 it harboured, in turn, much of the Italian, German and British Mediterranean fleets. Unfortunately, these magnificent bays seem to absorb rather than reflect light, and the island's **fertility** – with orchards and vegetable gardens a-plenty – make Léros seem scruffy compared to the crisp lines of its more barren neighbours. Such characteristics, plus a lack of spectacularly good beaches, meant that until the late 1980s just a few hundred Italians who grew up on Léros, and not many more Greeks, visited each summer. Since then the tourist profile has broadened to include Scandanavians and Brits, and the season has lengthened, but numbers have levelled off as the airport can't accommodate jets.

For decades, the local economy relied on prisons and sanatoria in former Italian military buildings, directly or indirectly employing a third of the population. During the civil war and the later junta,

leftists were confined to a notorious **detention centre** at Parthéni, and from 1948 on several **hospitals** essentially warehoused many of Greece's intractable psychiatric cases and mentally handicapped children. In 1989, a major scandal erupted concerning the asylums, with EU funds found to have been embezzled and inmates kept in degrading conditions. Most wards were eventually closed, with patients dispersed to sheltered housing and seven hundred carers (who can't be made redundant) left idle. Some of the slack was taken up by tourism, some by the opening of a major nursing college.

Equally obvious today is the legacy of the **Battle of Léros** on November 12–16, 1943, when German paratroops displaced a Commonwealth division that had occupied the island following the Italian capitulation. Bomb nose-cones and shell casings turn up as gaily painted garden ornaments in the courtyards of churches and tavernas, or do duty as gateposts. Each year for three days following September 26, memorial services and a naval festival commemorate the sinking of the Greek battleship *Queen Olga* and the British *Intrepid* during intense German air-raids in the two months prior to the battle.

Unusually for a small island, Léros has abundant ground **water**, channelled into several cisterns (only the two on the Plátanos upper bypass are potable). These, plus damp ground staked with avenues of Italian-planted eucalyptus, make for horrendously active mosquitoes.

Léros has a reasonably reliable **bus** service, plus several **motor-** and **mountain-bike** rental outlets; Motoland (Pandélli, ☎22470 24103; Álinda, ☎22470 24584) also offers **cars**. If you rent a **scooter**, take care – Lerian roads are particularly narrow, potholed and gravel-strewn, and the low-slung, fat-tyred bikes on offer don't cope well.

## Lakkí and Xirókambos

All large **ferries**, the *Nissos Kalymnos* and the *Dodekanisos Pride* catamaran arrive at **LAKKÍ** port, built in 1935–38 as a model town to house 7500 civilian dependants of an adjacent Italian naval base. Boulevards, generous even for today's traffic, are lined with Stream Line Modern edifices (see box, p.392) such as the round-fronted cinema, the church, the primary school, a shopping centre and the derelict *Leros Palace Hotel*. A restoration programme should see most of these marvellous buildings refurbished by 2009. The nearest approximation of a beach is sand-and-gravel **Kouloúki**, 500m west, supporting a seasonal taverna and ample trees for shade. You can carry on for a kilometre or so to **Merikiá**, a slight improvement, also with two **tavernas**, and the only real local attraction – Léros's **War Museum** (daily 10am–1pm; €3), a huge quantity of barely labelled World War II documents and military hardware crammed into an enormous Italian-built subterranean complex; at the end a somewhat histrionic film using archival footage makes some sense of it all.

Buses don't meet the ferries – instead a **taxi** squadron charges set fares to standard destinations; rent **cars or bikes** from Koumoulis (☎22470 22330), near the cinema. Few people stay at any of Lakkí's handful of drab hotels, preferring to head straight for Pandélli, Álinda or Vromólithos (see p.393). Neither will surplus-to-requirements pizza parlours, snack bars and *yirádhika* appeal much – there's just one proper **taverna**, *To Petrino*, next to the **post office**. Other amenities include three **ATMs**, and Aegean Travel just inland (☎22470 26000), agent for Blue Star and the catamaran – other boat tickets are sold from a booth on the jetty.

**XIRÓKAMBOS**, nearly 5km from Lakkí in the far south of the island, is the arrival point for the *kaïki* from Myrtiés on Kálymnos. It's essentially a fishing

## Italian architecture in the Dodecanese

The three-decade Italian tenure in the Dodecanese left a significant architectural heritage which has only recently begun to be appreciated. Many structures were long allowed to deteriorate, if not actually abandoned, this neglect apparently a deliberate policy of Greeks who would just as soon forget the entire Italian legacy, but since the late 1990s maintenance work has been fitfully undertaken.

These buildings are often erroneously dubbed "Art Deco"; while some certainly contain elements of that style, most are properly classed as **Rationalist** (or in the case of Léros, **Stream Line Modern**). They drew on various post-World-War I architectural, artistic and political trends across Europe, particularly its immediate predecessor, Novecento (a sort of Neoclassicism), the collectivist ideologies of the time, and the paintings of Giorgio di Chirico. The school's purest expressions tended to have grid-arrays of windows (or sometimes walls entirely of glass), arcades of tall, narrow arches at ground level, rounded-off bulwarks on the facade, and either a uniform brick surface or grooved/patterned concrete. Surviving examples of this design can still be found in places as disparate as Moscow or London (underground stations and blocks of flats), Los Angeles (apartment buildings) and Ethiopia (cinemas), as well as in Italy and Greece.

Italy initially attempted – under the governorship of Mario Lago (1924–36) – to create a hybrid of Rationalist style and local vernacular elements in the Dodecanese, both real and semi-mythical, evoking a supposed generic "Mediterranean-ness". Every Italian-claimed island got at least one specimen in this "**protectorate**" style, usually the gendarme station, post office, covered market or governor's mansion, but only on the most populous or strategic islands of Rhodes, Kós, Kálymnos and Léros were plans drawn up for sweeping urban re-ordering.

The 1936–1941 term of office of Cesare Maria de Vecchi, second governor of the Dodecanese, was marked by intensified Fascist imperial ideology, an increased reference to the Latin heritage of the islands (the Romans and their purported successors the Knights) and the replacement of the "protectorate" style with that of the "**conqueror**". This involved "**purification**", the stripping of many public buildings in Rhodes (though not, curiously, in Kós) of their orientalist ornamentation, its replacement with a cladding of poros stone to match medieval buildings in the old town, plus a monumental severity – blending Neoclassicism and modernism – and rigid symmetry to match various institutional buildings (especially Fascist Party headquarters) and public squares across Italy.

port where folk also happen to swim – the beach is poor to mediocre, improving as you head west. Top **accommodation** is the *Hotel Efstathia* (☏22470 24099; ❸), actually studio apartments with huge, well-furnished doubles (though bathrooms are basic) as well as family four-plexes facing a large pool. *To Aloni*, with decent *mayireftá*, is the best of three **tavernas** along the shore road. The island's **campsite** (☏22470 23372; mid-May to early Oct), with an in-house **scuba** centre (Panos on ☏694 42 38 490), occupies an olive grove at the village of **LEPÍDHA**, 750m back up the road to Lakkí. Dives explore Leros's wealth of wrecks from ancient times to World War II, plus natural drop-offs and reefs. Just north of the campsite, an access drive (signposted "Ancient Fort") leads up to a tiny **acropolis** with stretches of ancient masonry behind the modern summit chapel.

## Pandélli and Vromólithos

Just under 3km north of Lakkí, Pandélli and Vromólithos form an attractive and scenic joint resort. **PANDÉLLI** is a working port, the cement jetty benefiting local fishermen rather than yachts, which in high season must anchor offshore. A small but reef-free, pea-gravel **beach** is complemented by a relative abundance of non-block-booked **accommodation**, such as *Pension Happiness* (☎22470 23498; ❷), where the road down from Plátanos meets the sea. For a higher standard, try Australian-Greek-run *Niki Studios* (☎22470 25600; ❸) at the base of the road up to the castle, which has double units and quad apartments (both a/c), with partial sea views, or, further up the castle road, the ☀ *Windmills/Anemomyli* (☎22470 25549; May–Oct; ❹), two galleried windmill apartments and a long cottage, all with stone floors and great views from rear terraces. Up on the ridge dividing Pandélli from Vromólithos in Spília district, the *Hotel Rodon* (☎22470 23524; ❸) comprises studios and larger apartments, with knock-out views. On summer nights there may be a faint strain of **music** from *Café del Mar*, perched on a rock terrace below; the other long-standing local bar is civilized, English-Danish-run *Savana*, at the opposite end of Pandélli, with excellent tunes (you can request your favourites). It stands beyond a row of decidedly patchy waterfront **tavernas**, the best of which are *Psaropoula* (all year), with good, non-farmed fish and *mayireftá*, and *Tou Mihali*, a corner *kafenío* where expertly fried *gópes* or *sargoudháki*, mixed salads and good wine are scoffed by a largely local crowd. Up in Spília, next to the *Hotel Rodon*, ☀ *Mezedhopolio O Dimitris O Karaflas* (all year) is one of the best-sited ouzerís on the island, with ample portions of delicacies such as chunky local sausages, onion rings and *floyéres*, or dairy-based dips like *galotýri* and *batíris*.

**VROMÓLITHOS** has the best easily accessible beach on the island, car-free and hemmed in by oak-studded hills. The shore is gravel and coarse sand, and the sea is clean, but you have to cross rock seabed at most points before reaching deeper water; there's a more secluded, sandier cove southeast towards **Tourkopígadho**, and an even better duo at the end of the side-road to **Aï Yiórgi**. Two **tavernas** behind Vromólithos beach trade more on their location than their cuisine but **accommodation** here can be better than at Pandélli. Prime choices are *Tony's Beach*, spacious studio units set in extensive waterside grounds (☎22470 24742, ⊛ www.tonysbeachstudios.gr; May–Sept; ❹), and the stone-floored units at *Glaros*, just inland with garden views (☎22470 24358; May–Oct; ❹).

## Plátanos and Ayía Marína

The Neoclassical and vernacular houses of **PLÁTANOS**, 1km west of Pandélli, are draped gracefully along a saddle between two heights, one of them crowned by the inevitable Knights' castle or **kástro** (daily 8.30am–12.30pm, also May–Oct Wed, Sat & Sun 3.30–6.30pm). This is reached either by a zigzagging road peeling off the Pandélli-bound road, or via a stair-path from the central square; the views from the top of the caper-festooned battlements are especially dramatic at sunset. The medieval church of **Panayía toú Kástrou** inside the gate houses a small ecclesiasical museum, though its carved *témblon* and naïve oratory are more remarkable than the sparse exhibits. The **archeological museum** (Tues–Sun 8am–2.30pm; free), down the road to Ayía Marína, is more interesting, compensating for a dearth of artefacts with a comprehensible gallop through Lerian history. Plátanos is not really a place to stay or eat, though it has a **post office** down the road towards Ayía Marína and a few **ATMs**. A single **bus** (schedule posted at stop opposite the island's main **taxi** rank) runs several times daily between Parthéni and Xirókambos.

Plátanos merges seamlessly with **AYÍA MARÍNA**, 1km north on the shore of a fine bay, graced by a small, Italian-built public market building and customs house. Travelling to Léros on an excursion boat from Lipsí, the *Dodekanisos Express*, or a hydrofoil, this will be your port of entry – unless high winds force a diversion to Lakkí. At the western edge of things the superior ⚓ *Ouzeri* (*Nero-Mylos*), out by the wave-lapped windmill (March–Nov; reservations mandatory July–Aug; ☎22470 24894) has the most romantic setting on the island, the best music, and some of the tastiest **food**. Specialities include expertly home-made *garidhopílafo* (shrimp-rice), grilled *mastéllo* cheese, seasonal fresh fish, and *kolokythokeftédhes* (courgette patties). Lively (for Léros) **nightlife** is provided by several bars between the police station and the customs house, such as ultra-sleek *Thalassa* and *Enallaktiko*, with a few **internet** terminals. Kastis Travel nearby (☎22470 22140) handles all ticket sales for hydrofoils and the *Dodekanisos Express*, and there are two **ATMs**. The locally berthed *Barbarossa* comes recommended as a **day-trip** boat (☎697 87 93 670).

## Álinda and around

**ÁLINDA**, 3km northwest of Ayía Marína, is the longest-established resort on Léros, with development fringing a long, narrow strip of pea-gravel beach. It's also the first area to open in spring, and the last to shut in autumn. Worthwhile **accommodation** includes, just back from mid-beach, *Hotel Alinda* (*Xenonas Mavrakis;* ☎22470 23266, ⊛www.alindahotel.gr; ❸), with the very good, affiliated *Taverna Alinda* and sunken Byzantine mosaic out front, plus well-kept air conditionar rooms with fridges, and the marvellously atmospheric ⚓ *Archontiko Angelou* well inland (☎22470 22749, ⊛www.hotel-angelou-leros.com; May to mid-Oct; ❻), with Victorian bath fittings, beamed ceilings and antique furnishings. The other reliable beachfront **restaurant** is somewhat pricey *Giusi e Marcello* (supper only), with pasta, meat and Italian wines. At **KRITHÓNI**, 1.5km south, luxury is available at the island's top accommodation: ⚓ *Crithoni's Paradise* (☎22470 25120, ⊛www.crithonisparadisehotel.com; all year; ❻), a 2006-redone low-rise complex whose vast common areas include a large pool, gym, sauna and wi-fi zone; rooms and baths are fair-sized, the top-floor units with bay views.

The **Allied War Graves Cemetery**, mostly containing Commonwealth casualties of the November 1943 battle, occupies a walled enclosure at the south end of the beach; immaculately maintained, it serves as a moving counterpoint to beachside life outside. The other principal sight at Álinda is the **Historical and Ethnographic Museum** (May–Sept Tues–Sun 9am–1pm & 6–8pm; €3) housed in the castle-like mansion of Paris Bellenis (1871–1957). Most of the top floor is devoted to the Battle of Léros: relics from the sunken *Queen Olga*, a wheel from a Junkers bomber, a stove made from a bomb casing. There's also a grisly mocked-up clinic (mostly gynaecological tools), assorted rural implements, costumes and antiques. Photos trace the sad decline of many monuments: a fine market *halle* in Plátanos was thoughtlessly demolished in 1903, and a soaring medieval aqueduct supplying the *kástro* was a casualty of the November 1943 battle. One room is devoted to Communist artist Kyriakos Tsakiris (1915–98), interned here by the junta, with works executed on stones, shells and wood, plus pen-and-ink studies for the Ayía Kiourá frescoes (see opposite) and sketches of daily life at Parthéni camp.

Other **beaches** near Álinda include **Dhýo Liskária**, a series of gravel coves at the far northeast of the bay (snack bar/café), and pebbly **Kryfós** cove, 25 minutes' scramble north on a faint path whose start is marked by paint dots. There's only a cave for shade there, and no nudism if island families have got there first by boat. **Goúrna**, the turning for which lies 1km or so off the trans-island road, is Léros's longest sandy beach, hard-packed and gently shelving, if wind-buffeted; a few sunbeds are provided by the hospitable *Gourna* **taverna**, which has grills, wild fish and good *mezédhes*.

## The far north

Seven kilometres from Álinda along the main route north, a marked side-track leads left to the purported **Temple of Artemis**, on a slight rise west of the airport runway. In ancient times, Léros was sacred to the goddess, and the temple here was supposedly inhabited by guinea fowl – the grief-stricken sisters of Meleager, metamorphosed thus by Artemis following their brother's death. All that remains now are some jumbled, knee-high walls, almost certainly (as signposted) an ancient fortress, but the view is superb. The real site of the temple is unknown, but was probably nearer the stagnant, reed-fringed bay below – marshes and river-mouths were the usual site of Artemis temples – or perhaps under the **airport** runway. The tiny terminal itself is no place to be stuck a minute longer than necessary; if your midday flight to Astypálea or Rhodes is delayed (likely), the only diversion lies across the road at overpriced *Taverna To Arhondiko* – eat elsewhere beforehand and just have a coffee here.

The onward route skims the shores of bleak **Parthéni Bay**, with its yacht dry-dock and dreary, Italian-built army base (the 1946–51 and 1967–74 political prison). The camp, however, left one outstanding cultural legacy: the chapel of **Ayía Kiourá** (always open), reached by a one-kilometre marked access road. During the junta era, Kyriakos Tsakiris and two other prisoners decorated this otherwise unremarkable church with striking murals – squarely in the tradition of Diego Rivera's 1930s Leftist art – rather than conventional frescoes. The Orthodox Church has always abhorred these images – a local monk obliterated several in the 1980s – but Ayía Kiourá is now a protected monument. Most of the scattered murals (whose quality varies) dwell on the Passion, in a calculated dig at their jailers. The best are a *Dormition of the Virgin* over the central door; a *Deposition* on the north wall, with four women cradling an elongated Christ; and a decidedly heterodox *Last Supper* over the southwest door, where protagonists Judas and Christ stand and stare at you, while the other disciples (some with head in hands) look on in dismay. The paved road ends 11km from Álinda at **Blefoútis** and its huge, almost landlocked bay. The small **beach** (the rough Lerian norm) has tamarisks to shelter under and an adequate **taverna**, *Iy Thea Artemi*.

# Pátmos

Arguably the most beautiful, certainly the best known of the smaller Dodecanese (thanks in part to Friedrich Hölderlin's epic poem eulogizing it), **Pátmos** has a distinctive, immediately palpable atmosphere. In a cave here St John the Divine (in Greek, *O Theológos* or "The Theologian", after whom about half the island's men are named) set down the New Testament's Book of Revelation. The **monastery** honouring him dominates Pátmos, its fortified bulk towering over everything else, and its monks ran the island unchallenged for centuries. Their influence remains, although Pátmos now has several nudist beaches, something unthinkable up to the 1990s.

Despite the island's firm presence on cruise and yachting circuits, **day-trippers** still exceed overnighters, and Pátmos feels an altogether different place once the last cruise-ship or excursion boat has left after sunset. Among those staying, no one nationality predominates, lending Pátmos a **cosmopolitan** feel almost

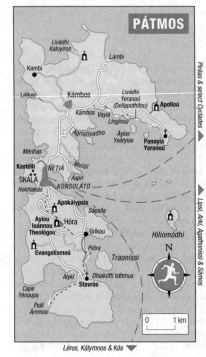

PÁTMOS

Livádhi
Kaloyíron
Lámbi
Kambí
Léfkes    Kámbos          Livádhi
                          Yeranoú
                          (Dellapothítou)  Apolloú
          Kámbos Vayiá
                 Lingínou
          Agriolívadho  Áyios
                        Yeóryios  Panayiá
Mérihas                           Yeranoú
Kastélli   NÉTIA   Melóï
SKÁLA              Asprí
Hokhlakás  KONSOLÁTO
        Apokàlypsis
                  Sápsila
Ayíou
Ioánnou   Hóra
Theológou      Gríkou    Hiliomódhi
        Pétra                 N
Evangelismoú
              Traoníssi
        Alykí  Dhiakófti Isthmus
Cape        Stavrós
Yénoupa
Psilí
Ammos

Pitéas & select Cyclades
Lipsí, Arkí, Agathoníssi & Sámos

0        1 km

Léros, Kálymnos & Kós ▼

unique in the Dodecanese. The steady clientele can be very **posh** indeed – the late Agha Khan's extended family and the ex-Yugoslav royal family maintain properties here, while the Belgian and (deposed) Greek royal families are repeat visitors. While there are several bars and clubs around the main port and up in **Hóra**, drunken rowdiness is all but unknown. Package clients never outnumber **independent visitors**, and are pretty much confined to Gríkou and a few hotels at Skála and Kámbos; outside these areas, touristic development is subdued if not deliberately retarded, thanks to the lack of an airport. On outlying beaches, little has superficially changed since the 1980s, though "For Sale" signs on every field or farmhouse, plus villa developments closer to Skála, suggest such days are numbered.

## Skála and around

**SKÁLA**, where most of the island's 3200 official residents live, seems initially to contradict any solemn, otherworldly image of Pátmos; the commercial district with its gift boutiques is incongruously sophisticated for such a small town. During peak season, the quay and inland lanes throng with trippers souvenir-hunting or being shepherded onto coaches for the short ride up to the monastery; after dark there's still traffic in of visitors on shore-leave from the huge, humming cruisers that weigh anchor around midnight. In winter (which here means by Oct 7), Skála becomes a ghost town as most shops and restaurants close, their owners and staff returning to Rhodes or Athens.

Hóra, overhead up the mountain, would be a more attractive base, but has little accommodation. And given time, 1820s-built Skála reveals more enticing corners in the residential fringes to its east and west, where vernacular mansions hem in pedestrian lanes creeping up the hillsides. At the summit of the westerly rise, **Kastélli**, lie extensive masonry courses from the island's ancient acropolis, enclosing a more recent chapel.

### Information and transport

Almost everything of note can be found within, or within sight of, the Italian-built municipal "palace": all arriving sea-craft anchor opposite, the **port police** occupy the east end, the **post office** one of its corners, the main **bus stop**, with a posted timetable, and **taxi rank** are in front, and three **ATMs** stand nearby. There's no **tourist office**, but ⓦwww.patmos-island.com and ⓦwww .patmosweb.gr are both useful. **Scooter rental** outfits such as Billis (☎22470 32218) and Aris (☎22470 32542) are numerous, as are car-hire outlets (Aris, as above; Stratas ☎22470 32580; Avis ☎22470 33025); **drivers** must use **car parks** at Hókhlakas, behind the town beach or off the road to Hóra. **Excursion**

**boats** to Psilí Ámmos and Arkí/Maráthi leave at 9.30–10am (7.30–10am to Léros and Lipsí depending on day/season) from in front of Astoria Travel and Apollon Travel, the two **agencies** handling hydrofoil tickets; Apollon (☎22470 31324) is also the central rep for Blue Star Ferries. GA Ferries (☎22470 31217) and the *Nissos Kalymnos* (☎22470 31314) have separate agencies on, or just off, the central waterfront square; several outlets sell tickets for the *Dodekanisos Express/Pride* catamarans. Best of several **internet cafés** is *Millennium*, upstairs in a fine old building just behind the little park inland from the port.

## Accommodation

Pátmos's vernacular architecture is quite distinctive, but you wouldn't know it from the island's bland, often overpriced **accommodation** with quasi-monastic 1980s-vintage interiors. Numerous touts, some with shuttle vans, meet all arriving sea-craft; their offerings tend to be a long walk distant and/or inland – not necessarily a bad thing, as nowhere is hopelessly remote, and anywhere on the waterfront, which doubles as the main road between Grikou and Kámbos, will be noisy.

Besides central Skála, you could end up in **Konsoláto** district, east near the fishing anchorage, with fairly decent digs, but the worst noise from fishing boats and ferries coming and going from 1 to 4am. **Nétia**, the unglamorous area northwest between the power plant and Mérihas cove, is actually not a bad choice as a base. Pebbly **Hokhlakás Bay**, a ten-minute walk southwest starting from the central market street, is the quietest, with wonderful sunset views. **Melóï cove**, 1.5km northwest, has a good beach and hosts the reed-shaded **campsite**, *Stefanos-Flowers* (☎22470 31821; May–Oct). Unless otherwise stated, assume Easter–mid-October operation.

**Asteri** Nétia, nr Mérihas cove ☎22470 32465, ✆www.asteripatmos.gr. The best in Nétia: large sea-view lounge and variably sized rooms (two with wheelchair access, many with a/c) unimprovably set on a knoll overlooking the bay. Breakfasts feature own-grown produce, and there's a private car park and wi-fi throughout. B&B ❹

**Blue Bay** 150m beyond Konsoláto on Gríkou Rd ☎22470 31165, ✆www .bluebay.50g.com. Probably the best-value, quietest choice for this area, with helpful Australian-Greek management, sea-view rooms with fridges, balconies and a/c, plus a small internet café. Credit cards accepted for stays of over two days. B&B ❺

**Captain's House** Konsoláto ☎22470 31793, ✆www.captains-house.gr. The rear wing, with quiet rooms, overlooks a fair-sized pool and shady terrace. Friendly management, nice furnishings and on-site car rental. B&B ❺

**Doriza Bay** Hokhlakás, south hillside ☎22470 33123, ✆www.dorizabay.com. This hillside annexe of *Porto Scoutari* has the best sunsets in Skála. There's a wing of standard rooms with a breakfast salon, and galleried maisonettes (including some two-bedroom apartments) across the way. Off-street scooter parking. ❺–❼

**Effie** On hillside above the beach car park, centre ☎22470 32500, ✆www.effiehotel.gr. Two-wing

hotel with bland, white-tile/light-pine heated a/c rooms and private parking. Uniquely in Skála, open all year. B&B ❸

**Galini** End of cul-de-sac in from ferry quay ☎22470 31240, ✆www.galinipatmos.gr. Excellent-value hotel, with furnishings in the large rooms, most of which have balconies. ❹

**Hellenis** Just north of new yacht marina, Netiá ☎22470 31275, ✆www.patmosweb.gr /hellinishotel.htm. Bright, airy common areas (including breakfast out front), a lift (rather superfluous for just two stories) and better-than-average rooms with fridges and baths. The same management has six superior apartments in contemporary style out back. ❹

**Maria** Hokhlakás flatlands, 150m from sea ☎22470 31201, ✆hotelmariapatmos.com. Quietly set small hotel where the pleasant front garden, a/c, lobby internet facility and big sea-view balconies offset tiny bathrooms. B&B ❹

**Porto Scoutari** Melóï hillside ☎22470 33124, ✆www.portoscoutari.com. Pátmos's premier hotel, this bungalow complex overlooks the beach and islets. The common areas and spacious a/c units, with TV and phone, arrayed around a large pool and small spa, had their antique furnishings completely redone in 2007. The big attraction for most guests, however, (including frequent wedding parties) is the personal attention of the staff and owner Elina Scoutari. **⑧**, offers at **⑥** **Romeos Hokhlakás** South hillside ☎22470 31962, ⌨www.hotelromeos.com. Tiered bungalow-hotel with poolside breakfast service and sizable, brown-tile-floored units of decidedly 1980s vintage; usually a vacancy despite package patronage. **⑥**

**Yvonni Studios** Hokhlakás, north hillside ☎22470 33066, ⌨www.12net.gr/yvonni. Basic but salubrious mid-sized pine-and-white-tile units with fridges, a/c and oblique sea views over a hillside garden. Walk-ins should call at the gift shop next to the *Nissos Kalymnos* agency. **⑧**

## Eating, drinking and nightlife

Among the all-too-numerous snack stalls and *yirádhika* in Skála are just a handful of recommendable full-service **restaurants**. Otherwise, you're best off heading slightly out of town; **beach tavernas** excel on Pátmos. The focus of in-town *frappádhika* life is the square in from the Italian "palace", but the most durable **café-bar** is wood-panelled, barn-like *Café Arion* further along, where all sorts sit outside, dance inside or prop up the long bar. Fake *gelato* abounds; for the real thing head for Italian-run *Gelateria De Santis* in the lane behind, with *gelato* and *granita* in improbable flavours. Other **nightlife** venues change almost annually; two constants are hippy-ish *Koukoumavla* in Konsoláta, with garden seating, wacky decor and crafts on sale, and the northernmost building in Nétia, *Anemos*, a restored old house with music and beer. The annual **Festival of Religious Music** (late Aug/early Sept) is held in the grounds of the Apokálypsis monastery, featuring performers primarily from Greece, Russia and Bulgaria.

**Benetos** Sápsila cove, 2km southeast of Skála; reserve in summer ☎22470 33089. Idyllic conservatory seating and a Mediterranean fusion menu encompassing the likes of smoked sardine, bean and salmon croustade, *astakomakaronádha* and decadent desserts; budget €35–40 for three courses plus drink. June–early Oct, Tues–Sun supper only.

**To Hiliomodhi** Start of Hóra Rs. Cheap and crowded ouzerí offering vegetarian *mezédhes* and seafood delicacies such as limpets (served live) or grilled octopus, with summer seating in a pedestrian lane and decent *hýma* wine from Mégara. All year.

**Kyma** Áspri cove, south of Melóï. Waterside fish specialist scoring for its romantic setting as much as its food. Mid-June to Aug 31 only.

**Melloi (Stefanos)** Melóï beach. Decent, reasonably priced *mayireftá*, best at lunch (though it gets coach tours), working a long season.

**Ostria** Behind excursion-boat quay. Another mid-priced, evergreen ouzerí where the food's not always superlative, but (late ferry arrivals take note) they're the only place serving after 11pm. All year.

**Tzivaeri** behind Theológos town beach. Quality outfit featuring delicate Cretan-style *mezédhes* and live music from the owner. Dinner only, all year.

🏃 **Vegghera** Opposite yacht marina; reserve on ☎22470 32988. The best all-rounder, with flawlessly presented stuffed scorpion fish, vegetarian or seafood salads, superb desserts, and per-head bills of €40–45 plus drink. Easter to early Sept, dinner only.

## The monasteries and Hóra

Top of your sightseeing agenda is likely to be **Ayíou Ioánnou Theológou** (St John) **monastery** in hilltop Hóra. Coach tours pack the place around midday, so go early or late. The best **dates** to visit, besides the famous Easter observances, are September 25–26 (Feast of John the Theologian) and October 20–21 (Feast of Khristodhoulos), both featuring solemn liturgies and processions of the appropriate icon. Up to eleven public **buses** serve Hóra daily, or you can take a forty-minute **walk** along a beautiful old cobbled path. Proceed through Skála towards Hokhlakás, and once past the telecoms building bear left onto a lane starting opposite the ironmonger's; follow this uphill to its end on the main road – immediately opposite you'll see the cobbles. Just over halfway, pause at the **Apokálypsis monastery**

▲ Monk by the narthex of Ayíou Ioánnou Theológou monastery, Pátmos

(daily 8am–1.30pm, also Tues, Thurs & Sun 4–6pm; free) built around the cave where St John heard the voice of God issuing from a cleft in the rock, and where he sat dictating to his disciple Prohoros. In the cave wall, the presumed nightly resting place of the saint's head is fenced off and outlined in beaten silver.

This is merely a foretaste of Ayíou Ioánnou Theológou monastery (same hours). In 1088, the soldier-cleric **Ioannis "The Blessed" Khristodhoulos** (1021–93) was granted title to Pátmos by Byzantine emperor Alexios Komnenos; within three years he and his followers had completed most of the existing monastery, the threats of piracy and the Selçuk Turks dictating a heavily fortified style. A warren of courtyards, chapels, stairways, arcades, and roof terraces, it offers a rare glimpse of a Patmian interior. Off to one side, the **treasury** (same hours; €6) doesn't quite justify its entrance fee with its admittedly magnificent array of religious treasure, mostly medieval icons of the Cretan school. Pride of place goes to an unusual mosaic icon of Áyios Nikólaos, and the eleventh-century parchment chrysobull (edict) of Emperor Alexios Komnenos, granting the island to Khristodhoulos (another popular local name for males).

### Hóra

St John's promise of shelter from pirates spurred the growth of **HÓRA** immediately outside the stout fortifications. It remains architecturally homogeneous, with cobbled lanes sheltering dozens of shipowners' mansions from the island's seventeenth-to-eighteenth-century heyday. High, windowless walls and imposing wooden doors betray nothing of the painted ceilings, *votsalotó* terraces, flagstone kitchens and carved furniture inside. Inevitably, touristic tattiness disfigures the main approaches to the monastery, but elsewhere are lanes that rarely see traffic, and by night, when the ramparts are startlingly floodlit, it's hard to think of a more beautiful Dodecanesian village. Neither should you miss the view from **Platía Ló(t)za**, particularly at dawn or dusk. Landmasses to the north, going clockwise, include Ikaría, Thýmena, Foúrni, Sámos, Arkí and double-humped Samsun Da (ancient Mount Mykale) in Turkey.

Numerous "minor" churches and monasteries around Hóra contain beautiful icons and examples of local woodcarving; almost all are locked to prevent thefts, but key-keepers generally live nearby. Among the best are the church of

## Saint John on Pátmos

Pátmos has been intimately associated with Christianity since **John the Evangelist** – later John the Divine – was exiled here from Ephesus by the Roman emperor Domitian in about 95 AD. While John was on Pátmos, supposedly dwelling in a hillside grotto, an otherworldly voice from a cleft in the ceiling bid him set down in writing what he heard. By the time John was allowed to return home, that disturbing finale to the New Testament, the **Book of Revelations** (aka the Apocalypse), had been disseminated as a pastoral letter to the Seven Churches of Asia Minor.

Revelations, whoever really wrote it, followed the standard Judeo-Christian tradition of apocalyptic books, with titanic battles in heaven and on earth, supernatural visions, plus lurid descriptions of the fates awaiting the saved and the damned following the **Last Judgement**. Of all the chapters of the Bible, Revelations is the most amenable to subjective application by cranks, and was employed as a rhetorical and theological weapon within a century of appearing. Its vivid imagery lent itself to depiction in frescoes adorning the refectories of numerous Byzantine monasteries and the narthexes of Orthodox churches, conveying a salutary message to illiterate medieval parishioners.

In addition to transcribing the Apocalypse, John supposedly wrote his Gospel on Pátmos, and also combatted paganism in the person of an evil local wizard, **Kynops**. In an episode related by John's disciple Prohoros, Kynops challenged the saint to a duel of miracles; the magician's stock trick involved retrieving effigies of the deceased from the seabed, so John responded by petrifying Kynops while he was under water. A buoy just off Theológos beach in Skála today marks a submerged rock that is supposedly the remains of the wizard. All mechanical efforts to remove this marine hazard have failed, and it is claimed that fish caught nearby taste bad. In the far southwest of the island, a foul-smelling volcanic cave has also been identified as a lair of the magician, whose name lives on as Cape Yénoupa (the modern form of "Kynops").

Forever after in the Orthodox world, heights amidst desolate and especially **volcanic topography** have become associated with John, and Pátmos with its eerie landscape of minatory igneous outcrops is an excellent case in point. Other nearby examples include the isle of Níssyros, where one of the saint's monasteries overlooks the volcano's caldera, and Lésvos, where another monastery dedicated to him sits atop an extinct volcano, gazing at basalt-strewn wastelands.

**Dhiasózousa**; the convent of **Zoödhóhou Piyís** (daily 9am–1pm & 4–7pm) well southwest of the village, and the convent of **Evangelismoú**, at the edge of Hóra in the same direction (daily 9–11am) – follow the wall-arrows.

The best of Hóra's few **tavernas** is late-serving *Pantheon* (Easter–Jan 1) at the start of the monastery approach, where good atmosphere and music, a lovely old interior or terrace views over the village and friendly management offset somewhat run-of-the-mill, pricey *mezédhes*; *Loza*, just below the eponymous platía, offers snacks, crêpes and desserts as well as hot and alcoholic drinks. There are, though, few places to **stay** if you're not one of the lucky outsiders who've bought up and restored almost half of the mansions since the 1960s. Even in spring or autumn, book well ahead at the spare *dhomátia* of Yeoryia Triandafyllou (☎22470 31963; ❸) on the south flank of the village, en suite with a communal terrace and self-catering kitchen, or the more comfortable *Epavli Apartments* at the east edge of Hóra, on the ring road (☎22470 31261, ⓦwww.12net.gr/epavli; ❻), a restored building with superb views, good bathrooms and raised bed-platforms.

## The rest of the island

Pátmos, a local guidebook once proclaimed, "is immense for those who know how to wander in space and time"; lesser mortals get around on foot or by motor vehicle. Unfortunately, most paths have been destroyed by road-building and property development; the single **bus** offers reliable service between Skála, Hóra, Kámbos and Gríkou.

After its extraordinary atmosphere and scenery, **beaches** are Patmos's main attraction. From Konsoláto, a principal road heads east to uninspiring **Sápsila beach**, home not only to *Benetos* taverna (see p.398) but also to ⚘ *Studios Mathios* (☎22470 32583, ⓦwww.mathiosapartments.gr; ❹), superior rural accommodation with creative decor, extensive gardens and welcoming proprietors in Iakoumina and Theologos. The onward road, and another from Hóra, converge at the sandiest part of overdeveloped and cheerless **GRÍKOU** – shut tight as a drum come mid-September. The beach itself, far from the island's best, forms a narrow strip of hard-packed sand, yielding to sand and gravel, then large pebbles at **Pétra** immediately south, where rock outcrops at the far end are colonized by nudists. Its near side features about the best rural **taverna** on Pátmos, ⚘ *Ktima Petra* (Easter–Oct 7; book summer on ☎22470 33207), with brown bread, lush salads, home-made *dolmádhes*, carefully cooked *mayireftá*, plus grills after dark. En route to Pétra, you pass hillside *Flisvos* (*Floros*), now rather eclipsed by *Ktima Petra* but known for inexpensive, savoury *mayireftá*. They also have basic **rooms** (☎22470 31380; ❸) and fancier apartments (❹).

From Hóra – but *not* Pétra, beyond which the track deteriorates – you can ride a scooter as far as the car park just past the Dhiakoftí isthmus and its boatyard, amidst which *Tarsanas* is an unlikely hit **taverna**, with mountainous salads and quiche-like *píttes* as well as some Greek standards, a favourite (all-year) "power lunch" spot for locals. From road's end a 25-minute walk southwest on a bona fide path leads to **Psilí Ámmos**. Although the only pure-sand cove on the island, it's not the best beach – often windy and flotsam-strewn – but has shade lent by tamarisks, nudism on the southern half and a good **taverna** serving goat culled from their own flocks. Summer *kaïki* service (dear at €15) to here from Skála departs by 10am and returns at 4 or 5pm.

## Northern Pátmos

There are more good beaches **north** of Skála, tucked into the startling eastern shoreline (west-facing bays are generally unusable owing to the prevailing wind and washed-up debris); most are accessible from side roads off the main road. **Melóï** is handy and quite appealing, with tamarisks behind the slender belt of sand, and good snorkelling offshore. The first beach beyond Melóï, **Agriolívadho** (Agriolivádhi), has mostly sand at its broad centre, watersports, and a good fish-**taverna**, *O Glaros*, on the south hillside. Hilltop **KÁMBOS** is the island's only other real village, the focus of scattered farms in little surrounding oases; Pátmos is lucky enough to be able to tap a vein of water from Turkey, with a public fountain just before Kámbos. The best of two **tavernas** at the crossroads is ⚘ *Panagos* (all year), superb for traditional *mayireftá* like baked fish and *revýthia*, with yogurt dessert; don't miss the archival photos inside. Kámbos **beach**, 600m downhill, is pretty lively considering its remote location, with non-motorized watersports and two tavernas, though its appeal is dented by the road running just behind.

East of Kámbos, less busy coves include pebble/coarse-sand **Vayiá** (snack bar); nudist, double-bay **Lingínou** (with a *kantína*), accessed by paths only, and long, sand-and-gravel **Livádhi Yeranoú** (aka **Livádhi Dellapothítou**), the latter with tamarisks, an islet to swim out to and a creditable **taverna** (May–Sept) doing just seafood, chops, *tzatzíki*, *hórta* and salads. Another road from Kámbos leads north to **Lámbi Bay**, best for swimming when the wind is from the south, and renowned for its multicoloured volcanic stones. A good **taverna**, *Leonidas* (Easter–Oct 15), up at Koumariá pass overlooking the bay, has terrace seating and big portions of grilled chops; down on the shore, *Lambi* (same months), founded in 1958, is better for fish though the menu is very brief off-season.

Only on south-wind days might you be tempted by **Livádhi Kaloyíron** or **Léfkes** beaches, both beyond Kámbos via different roads. Both have basic *kantínes*; Livádhi is perhaps more scenic, with an old monastery and lovingly tended market gardens just inland.

# Lipsí

**LIPSÍ** is the largest, most interesting and most populated of the islets north and east of Pátmos – and the one with the most significant tourist trade. Returning clients of a now-vanished British package company, Italian, Dutch and French regulars, plus the island's appearance on ferry routes and catamaran/hydrofoil lines make showing up in peak season without reservations unwise.

During quieter months, however, Lipsí still provides an idyllic halt, its sleepy pace almost making plausible a dubious link with **Calypso**, the nymph who held Odysseus in thrall. Like most nearby small islets, Lipsí was once a dependency of the monastery on Pátmos, and is still conspicuously sown with blue-domed churches. Deep wells water small farms and vineyards, but there is only one flowing spring, and livestock-grazing appearances are deceptive – four times the full-time population of about 750 live overseas (mostly in Australia and Ohio), and much of eastern Lipsí is for sale as real estate.

More recently, however, the island acquired a definite – and unwanted – link with **Dhekaeftá Noemvríou/17 November**, Greece's (and Europe's) longest-lived terrorist organization. In July 2002, the national anti-terrorist squad swooped on Lipsí and apprehended the group's supremo, Alexandhros Yiotopoulos, as he was leaving en route to exile in Turkey. He had been living here for 17 years in a hilltop villa, now abandoned following his December 2003 life sentencing; ironically Yiotopoulos was much liked by locals for his generosity, sociability and willingness to help with bureaucratic problems.

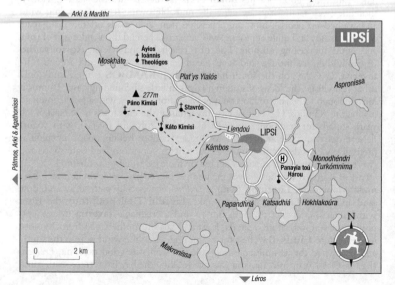

## The port settlement

The hilltop centre of the harbour village, the only significant habitation, is a 600-metre walk from the northwest end of the quay, where catamarans, hydrofoils, the largest excursion boats and all ferries **dock**; smaller excursion boats use the inner jetty cutting the swell into the easterly fishing anchorage. All seagoing **tickets** are sold just before departures from an office inside the jetty café *Okeanis*, while at the head of the harbour there's a bank with **ATM**. The *Calypso Snack Bar* has **wi-fi signal**, and there are two **internet** terminals in the upper village. The **post office** is on the attractive cathedral platía, reached by pedestrian stairs, near a hilariously eclectic **ecclesiastical museum** (daily in theory 9am–2.30pm; free) featuring such "relics" as earth collected from Mount Tabor and water from the River Jordan, as well as archeological finds and two letters from Greek revolutionary hero Admiral Miaoulis.

### Accommodation

Both quantity and quality of **accommodation** has improved in recent years, keeping pace with the island's growing profile; all of it is in, or just outside, town. Assume Easter-to-October opening unless otherwise stated.

**Aphrodite** Just inland from Liendoú beach ☎22470 41000, ⊛www.hotel-aphroditi.gr. Studio-bungalow complex, with large units and a bar across the road from the sand. Open all year, in theory. B&B ❹

**Galini Apartments** Above the ferry jetty ☎22470 41212. The first building you see on disembarking, and a prime budget choice in all respects, run by the hospitable Matsouris family. Nikos may take guests fishing on request. ❸

**Helios Apartments** Just off the road to Hokhlakoúra and Katsadhiá ☎694 54 60 534, ⊛www .helioslipsi.gr. These five variably sized units, some galleried – but with no sea view – are tastefully decorated with terracotta tiles, rounded corners and quality furnishings like wrought-iron beds. ❹

🏃 **Nefeli Hotel** Overlooking Kámbos beach ☎22470 41120, ⊛www.nefelihotels.com.

Indisputably the top digs on the island, this 2008-built bungalow-hotel complex offers a range of huge studios plus one- and two-bedroom apartments in the same pastel colour scheme, though all have unique floor plans. Ground-floor studios are cave-like, breezier upstairs units are preferable. B&B ❺–❻

🏃 **Poseidon Apartments** 150m along the quay ☎22470 41130, ⊛www .lipsi-poseidon.gr. Impeccable, roomy, 2007-built studios plus a one-bedroom apartment; the decor may be IKEA-on-steroids but everything has been thought of. On the ground floor, handy scooter rental and a convenient *psistariá* with roast chicken. ❹

**Rena's Rooms** Overlooking Liendoú beach ☎22470 41110 or 697 9316512. Good, solid choice with terrazzo floors, communal veranda, very helpful management and a small kitchen; nos. 3, 4 and 5 (single) are the best. April–Dec. ❸

### Eating and drinking

Of the nine full-service **tavernas**, mostly on or just behind the quay, best are *O Yiannis* (early May to early Oct), an excellent all-rounder with meat/seafood grills, *mayireftá* and inexpensive dishes of the day; nearby 🏃 *To Pefko* (May to late Sept), strong on baked aubergine recipes and lamb-based hotpots like *ambelourgoú*, plus efficient service; good-value 🏃 *Karnayio* on the far side of the bay, open all year at lunch too, serving hefty salads and good helpings of *mayireftá* like pork with celery and carrots; and, up opposite the post office, *Taverna du Moulin*, with more hearty lashings of *mayireftá* at shaded tables, as well as inexpensive breakfasts. On the waterfront, *kafenía* and ouzerís with idiosyncratic decor (especially the stacked bottles of *Asprakis*, aka *Vasso*) offer al fresco twilight drinks and *mezédhes* – an atmospheric and almost obligatory pre-supper ritual – or even a full meal. Nearby rivals *Nikos* and *Sofoklis* operate all year, the latter having a slight edge in quality and music. The classiest **snack-café** is the *Kaïris Bakery* behind the landscaped park, open until late with table service for desserts and drinks. The most durable **bar** is aptly named *The Rock*, with a congenial crowd, boulder-like host Babis and good tunes; in summer only, livelier *Meltemi* operates across the bay.

## Around the island

None of Lipsí's **beaches** is more than an hour's walk from the port. The closest, and sandiest, are crowded **Liendoú** (effectively the town beach) and **Kámbos**, but many prefer attractive **Katsadhiá** (sand) and **Papandhriá** (coarse sand-and-gravel), adjacent coves 2km south of the port. A musical **taverna-café**, *Dilaila* (June 1–Sept 15) overlooks Katsadhiá – pricier than the island norm, but worth it for such delights as salad with bits of local cheese, chunky aubergine dip or *fáva* and marinated fish dishes; from 11pm to 4am it's a **music bar**.

Another paved road leads 4km west from town to protected **Platýs Yialós**, a shallow, sandy bay with a single **taverna** (mid-June to late Sept), continuing to sumpy Moskháto fjord (no beach). From May to October, two to three van-type **minibuses** ply from the port to all points noted above (there are also two **taxis**); otherwise rent a **scooter** from one of two outlets and point them towards isolated east coast beaches without facilities. Of these, **Hokhlakoúra** consists of coarse shingle (finer pebbles at mid-strand); nearby **Turkómnima** is sandy and much shadier, if mercilessly exposed to the *meltémi*. A different road system, ending in a rough, non-motorable track, then a final fifteen-minute path scramble through goat-gates, brings you to remote **Monodhéndhri** on the northeast coast, very scenic with its photogenic lone juniper tree and the striking Aspiníssia islets. The obvious beach is only adequate, but there are superior, secluded coves to the right, with nudist practice everywhere here.

The road network, paved or otherwise, rather limits genuine path **walks** through the undulating countryside. The most challenging route heads west, high above the coast, from the far end of Kámbos Bay to **Kímisi Bay** (3hr round trip), where the **monk Philippos**, long a cult figure among foreign visitors, once lived in a tiny hermitage above the shore, next to the single island spring. A stepped path up from the good **beach** here climbs to **Páno Kímisi** monastery, Philippos's quarters before 1983. A particularly steep, ugly road arrived from the north in the 1990s, disturbing his solitude; Philippos moved to town and died, aged 85, in 2002, though a stone memorial and various photographs at the hermitage commemorate him.

## Arkí and Maráthi

About two-thirds the size of Lipsí, **Arkí** is far more primitive, lacking proper shops or anything like a coherent village. Just 45 permanent inhabitants eke out a living here, mostly fishing or goat/sheep-herding, though servicing yachts attracted by the superb anchorage at Avgoústa Bay ("Port Augusta" on nautical charts) – named for the half-ruined Hellenistic/Byzantine **Avgoustínis fortress** overhead – is also important. Arkí is a stop on the *Nissos Kalymnos*, which can be used to make cheap day-trips from Pátmos; post/shopping *kaïkia* (3 weekly) or excursion boats (1hr 15min from Pátmos) dock at the inner quay. Two **tavernas** on the flagstoned harbourside platía – *Nikolas* (℡22470 32477; B&B ❸) and *O Trypas* (aka *Tou Manoli*; ℡22470 32230; ❷) – provide **accommodation**; *O Trypas* is perhaps better value with mock-trad, stone-floored units up the hill. *Nikolas* has home-made puddings and *mayireftá* provided by a mother/son team, while *O Trypas* does very decent fish meals or *mezédhes*, and doubles as the happening **music pub**. Perhaps the most accomplished seafood grills are at *Apolavsi*, one inlet southeast at **Dhídhymi Ormí**; yachties (and land-lubbers) in the know come here for garden vegetables, slow-cooked fish, octopus and *mezédhes* at attractive prices.

Excursion-boat clients swim at the "Blue Lagoon" of **Tiganákia** at the southeast tip of the island, but other **beaches** on Arkí take resourcefulness to find. The more obvious are the carefully nurtured sandy cove at **Pateliá** by the outer jetty, or tiny **Limnári** pebble-bay (fitting five bathers at a pinch) on the northeast coast, a 25-minute walk away via the highest house in the settlement.

The nearest large, sandy, tamarisk-shaded beach lies ten boat-minutes away on **Maráthi**, the only inhabited islet (permanent population 3) of the mini-archipelago around Arkí. Three **taverna-rooms** along the 150-metre, east-facing beach – packed in summer – cater both to day-trippers and a growing number of overnighters. *Marathi* (T 22470 31580 or 697 3962462; most of year; ❷) has waterside seating, simple, adequate rooms and barefoot proprietor Mihalis, who emphasizes his comic-book-pirate persona with a Jolly Roger and speedboat named *Piratis*. The middle outfit, *Stavrangos* (T 22470 32900 or 694 55 19 221; May–Oct; ❷), offers just four rooms inland, while *Pantelis* (T 22470 32609, E pmarathi@internet.gr; May–Oct; ❸) at the far end, is the most elaborate and "resort"-like establishment here. All tavernas feature local free-range goat on the menu – at bumped-up prices (*Marathi* is marginally the cheapest).

Both Arkí and Maráthi are most frequently visited by all-day **"Five Islands Tours"** from Lipsí, where the more congenial of two excursion boats/captains is the *Rena I* or *II* skippered by John Paradhisi (book on T 697 7918560).

## Agathoníssi

The small, steep-sided, waterless islet of **Agathoníssi** (aka **Gaïdharo** after its map-outline resemblance to a donkey) is too remote – much closer to Turkey than Pátmos, in fact – to be a popular day-trip target, though some are very rarely offered from Sámos, where many islanders spend the winter. Intrepid Greeks and Italians form its main tourist clientele, along with a daily quota of yachts attracted by excellent anchorage. Even though the *Nissos Kalymnos* (and a summer catamaran) appear regularly, schedules mean you should count on staying at least two days. Despite the lack of springs (cisterns are ubiquitous, topped up by water tankers), the island is greener and more fertile than apparent from the sea; lentisc, carob and scrub oak on the heights overlook two arable plains in the west. Less than a hundred people live here full time, down from several hundred before World War II, but those who've remained make a go of stock-raising or fishing (or rather, fish-farming), and there are few abandoned or neglected dwellings. The islanders are well outnumbered by their goats and cattle, and lately by dozens – sometimes hundreds – of **illegal immigrants** on any given summer day, for whom Agathoníssi is a main destination. The landscape is littered with their discarded life-jackets and drip-dry nylon clothing; unscrupulous Turkish captains often scuttle the smuggling boats, obliging the Greek authorities to fish their erstwhile cargo out of the sea and send them on to Pátmos, then Athens.

Most of the population lives in **Megálo Horió** hamlet, just visible on the ridge above the harbour hamlet of **ÁYIOS YEÓRYIOS (Aï-Yeóryi)** and at eye level with tiny **Mikró Horió** opposite. Except for a small shop and two café-restaurants working peak-season nights only in Megálo Horió, all amenities are in the port. **Accommodation** vacancies are not a problem except from late July to mid-August, especially around the date of the local festival (July 26–27). The best of five establishments, with little to distinguish them other than location (all ❷) – are, in descending order of preference, vine-patioed, seafront *Rooms Maria Kamitsi* (T 22470 29065, or 693 25 75 121), with fridges, a/c and shared kitchen; basic but quiet seafront *Rooms Theoloyia Yiameou* (T 22470 29005), also with kitchen facilities; and newer *To Agnandi* above the *Memento Bar* (T 22470 29019 or 697 48 14 013). You'll almost certainly try all three full-service **tavernas**:

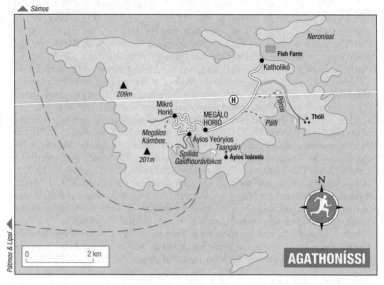

*George's* for good-value *mayireftá*, especially goat; *Limanaki* (also a shop) by the yacht berthing, is the best for grilled fish, and the Greeks' preferred hangout; while *Seagull/Glaros* next along draws crowds by night for its romantic waterside tables, although the food's not nearly as good value or as well executed as elsewhere. There's no **post office** or **ATM**; **tickets** for the *Nissos Kalymnos* must be bought in advance at a booth opposite *Café Yetoussa*, one of two **bars** (the other is popular *Memento*, with a wooden deck over the water).

With **no rental scooters**, exploring involves **walking** along the cement-road network, or following a very few tracks and paths – bring plenty of water along (the mains supply is drinkable). If you won't swim at the port, which has the largest sandy **beach**, track-hike ten minutes southwest to shingle-gravel **Spiliás**, or continue another quarter-hour by path over the ridge to **Gaïdhourávlakos**, another gravel cove. It's possible to vary the return by heading inland on a trail up the ravine to Megálos Kámbos, Mikró Horió and thence the port (45min). Bays in the east of the island, all reached by the paved road system (occasionally supplemented or short-cut by trails), include tiny **Póros** (45min distant), fine sand with lentisc-tree shade at the back; **Thóli** (25min further) in the far southeast, with good snorkelling and some morning shade; and **Pálli** on the opposite shore of the same bay, a small but pristine fine-pebble cove reached by fifteen-minute walk down from the trans-island road. Just above Thóli stands an arcaded **Byzantine structure**, probably a combination granary and trading post, and by far the most venerable sight on Agathoníssi.

# Travel details

To simplify the lists on the right, subsidized long-haul routes are summarized and not repeated. These provide a weekly link between Rhodes, Kós, Kálymnos, Sámos, Híos and Thessaloníki in each direction, plus another weekly link from Rhodes to Alexandhroúpoli and back via Kós, Kálymnos, Sámos, Híos, Lésvos and Límnos.

## Nissos Kalymnos

The small, reliable (if often late) Nissos Kalymnos (cars carried) is the lifeline of the islands between Kálymnos and Sámos, visiting them all several times weekly between mid-March and mid-Jan:
**Mon, Wed, Fri & Sun** Leaves Kálymnos 7am for Léros (Lakkí), Lipsí, Pátmos, Arkí, Agathoníssi, Sámos (Pythagório) arrives 2.30pm. Turns around immediately and retraces steps through the same islands in reverse order, arriving Kálymnos 11pm.
**Tues, Thurs & Sat** Leaves Kálymnos 7am, arrives Astypálea 10.15am, turns around immediately to arrive Kálymnos at 1.30pm.

## Protevs (Proteus)

From April to Oct, the small, slow but reliable Protevs serves as a counterpart to the Nissos Kalymnos in the southern Dodecanese. Its schedule (confirm on @www.anes.gr) is:
**Tues** Leaves Rhodes in morning, arrives Kastellórizo after noon, returns to Rhodes, evening trip to Sými.
**Wed** Noon departure from Sými to Tilos, Níssyros and Kós, after a morning round trip Sými–Rhodes–Sými.
**Thurs & Sat** Early morning departure from Kós to Níssyros, Tilos, Sými and Rhodes, from where there's a 2pm trip out to Kastellórizo and back, returning near midnight.
**Fri** Late afternoon departure from Sými to Tilos, Níssyros and Kós.
**Sun & Mon** Idle except for the odd trip Rhodes–Sými or vice versa.

## Large ferries and local kaïkia

**Astypálea** 3 weekly to Amorgós, Náxos, minor Cyclades, Páros and Pireás on Blue Star; 1 weekly to Kálymnos, Kós, Níssyros, Tilos, Rhodes and Pireás on Blue Star.
**Hálki** 2–3 weekly to Ródhos Town, Kárpathos (both ports), Kássos, Crete (Sitía & Áyios Nikólaos or Iráklio), Santoríni and Mílos on LANE. Daily kaïki (daily 6 or 8am, also Wed/Sun afternoon departures) to Rhodes (Kámiros Skála); ring ☎697 34 60 968 for latest info.
**Kálymnos** Similar frequencies to Kós, plus 3 daily roll-on-roll-off ferries, well-spaced, to Mastihári; 5 passenger-only speedboats (Kalymnos Star or Kalymnos Dolphin) daily to Mastihári; daily morning kaïki to Psérimos, plus 1 noon speedboat; and a daily kaïki from Myrtiés to Xirókambos on Léros.
**Kárpathos** (both ports) and **Kássos** 2–3 weekly with each other, Hálki, Crete (Áyios Nikólaos & Sitía), Mílos, Santoríni and Ródhos Town, on LANE; 1 weekly to Rhodes, Kós, Sýros and Pireás on Blue Star.
**Kós** At least daily to Rhodes, Kálymnos, Léros, Pátmos and Pireás on GA or Blue Star; 2 weekly to Sýros on Blue Star; 2 weekly to Tilos, Níssyros and

Kálymnos on Blue Star; 5 weekly on Panayia Spiliani mid-afternoon to Níssyros; daily afternoon small kaïki from Kardhámena to Níssyros.
**Léros** At least daily to Pireás, Pátmos, Kálymnos, Kós and Rhodes on GA or Blue Star; 2 weekly to Sýros on Blue Star; 1–2 weekly to Mýkonos on GA; 4 weekly mid-afternoon on Patmos Star (2 cars carried) kaïki to Lipsí and Pátmos; daily excursion boats from Ayía Marína to Lipsí and Léros (2pm), and from Xirókambos to Myrtiés on Kálymnos (time for 2009 unknown).
**Lipsí** 2 weekly to Kós, Kálymnos, Léros, Pátmos, Mýkonos or Sými, and Pireás on GA; daily mid-afternoon on Patmos Star (2 cars carried) kaïki to Pátmos.
**Níssyros** and **Tilos** 2 weekly with each other, Rhodes, Kós, Kálymnos and Pireás on Blue Star. Excursion boats between Níssyros and Kós as follows: to Kardhámena and Kós Town nearly daily at 3.30–4pm (these are seasonal). Níssyros-based Panayia Spiliani (2–3 cars carried) leaves 5 days weekly at 7.30am (Sat 9am) for Kós Town, while the Ayios Konstandinos and/or Nisyros (foot pax only) goes 4–6 times weekly at 7am to Kardhámena. 2 weekly on Panayia Spiliani from Níssyros to Tilos, Hálki, Rhodes and back the same day.
**Pátmos** Near-identical ferry service as Léros, plus additional tourist kaïkia to Sámos (Pythagório); daily at 9am or 10am on Patmos Star to Lipsí, continuing 4 days weekly to Léros; to Arkí and Maráthi 4 weekly.
**Rhodes** At least daily to Kós and Pireás on GA or Blue Star; 4–6 weekly to Kálymnos, Léros and Pátmos on GA or Blue Star; 2–3 weekly to Hálki, Kárpathos, Kássos, Crete (Sitía & Áyios Nikólaos or Iráklio), Santoríni and Mílos on LANE; 1–2 weekly to Tilos, Níssyros, Astypálea on Blue Star; 2 weekly to Sýros and Mýkonos on Blue Star.
**Sými** 2–3 daily on catamaran, conventional boat or hydrofoil run by ANES (@www.anes.gr) to Rhodes; 1–2 weekly to Rhodes, Kós, Kálymnos, Léros, Lipsí, Pátmos and Pireás on GA.

## Catamarans

Three long-distance catamarans ply the Dodecanese: The Dodekanisos Express, the co-owned Dodekanisos Pride (@www.12ne.gr for both) and the Sea Star.

### Dodekanisos Express

The Dodekanisos Express, based on Rhodes, carries 4–5 cars and a slightly higher number of two-wheelers; it's a sleek Norwegian-built craft, with a limited amount of aft deck space.
High-season schedules are as follows: Tues–Sun, 8.30am departure from Rhodes to Sými (not Tues), Kós, Kálymnos, Léros, Lipsí (not Wed/Thurs) and

Pátmos; it returns from Pátmos at 1.30–1.45pm via the same islands, arriving at Rhodes 6.30–6.45pm. On Mon it makes a single journey to Kastellórizo, arriving 11am, returning at 4pm. In spring or autumn there is no Kastellórizo service, and services beyond Léros are just 3 weekly.

### Dodekanisos Pride

The *Express*'s sister ship, *Dodekanisos Pride*, is similar in build but has far more complicated movements, and tends to run only late June to end Aug. High-season schedule patterns are as follows: Sat–Sun departs Rhodes at 8 or 10am for Hálki, Tílos, Níssyros and Kós, returning via the same islands at 3.30pm; Sun does an evening out-and-back to Sými. Mon departs Rhodes 8.30am for Sými, Kós and Kálymnos, returning via same islands immediately, then leaving Rhodes 3pm for same islands plus Léros, where it overnights. Tues, returns early am via same islands to Rhodes, whence it departs 3pm for Sými, Kós, Kálymnos, Léros, Agathoníssi and Pátmos, where it overnights. Wed, returns early am via same islands to Rhodes, whence it departs 3pm for Sými, Kós, Kálymnos, Léros and Pátmos for another overnight. Thurs, departs early am via same islands to Rhodes, where it turns around 3pm for Sými, Kós, Kálymnos and Léros to overnight. Fri, returns early am via same islands to Rhodes, with 3pm turnaround to Sými, Kós and Kálymnos, where it overnights before heading back to Rhodes via the same islands early Sat am.

### Sea Star

The deeply unreliable (and deeply overpriced) *Sea Star* does not carry vehicles and serves mainly the route Rhodes–Tílos–Rhodes, with up to 3 weekly diversions via Sými. Schedules are so inconsistent that it's impossible to predict future ones, other than saying it should do at least a daily trip in each direction (1hr 20min), with multiple trips on Sun.

### Hydrofoils

Currently just one scheduled hydrofoil, based at Pythagório, Sámos, and run by Aegean Flying Dolphins, serves the northern Dodecanese between mid-May and mid-Oct, providing an 8am service out of Pythagório as far as Kós, arriving at 11.30am and returning at 2.30pm, calling at Pátmos, Lipsí, Léros and Kálymnos en route in both directions.

### International ferries

NB In all cases port taxes are included but cost of Turkish visas, required by most nationals, is not.
Kálymnos to Bodrum, Turkey (1hr 45min), departing at 7–8am; €30 day-return, though discount "specials" 2 days weekly.

Kós At least daily April–Nov to Bodrum, Turkey (30–45min). Greek boat or hydrofoil leaves 9am & 4pm; additional out-and-back 10am/5pm Fri & Sun, 3 extra departures Tues (market day) and Sat 9.30am/4.30pm to Turgut Reis. Fares €20–25 day return/one-way, €50 open return. Only the Turkish boat (*Fahri Kaptan*) carries cars (€100) and is pricier for foot passengers, but provides the sole service (3 weekly, Tues guaranteed) Dec–March.
Kastellórizo 2 weekly (Mon & Fri) to Kaş, Turkey (20min); €15 one-way/day return; €32 maximum (bargain with boatman if necessary) if you begin travel from the Turkish side.
Rhodes April–Nov to Marmaris, Turkey, by daily Greek catamaran at 8am, Mon–Sat; Turkish catamaran at 4.30pm (each 1hr); prices same at €56 day return, €75 open return, €48 one-way. 1 weekly car ferry, usually Thurs at 2pm, runs much of year. Late May to early Oct, 3–5 weekly to Fethiye, Turkey, by hydrofoil at 4.30pm (1hr 30min); €60 one-way, €90 open return. Sea Dreams at Grigoríou Lambráki 46 in Neohóri (☎22410 74235) is the central agent for Marmaris service, Bluebonnet at Karpáthou 4 (☎22410 78780) for the Fethiye run, though other agencies (such as Triton Travel) will sell you passage.
Sými Up to 3 weekly *kaïkia* (1hr 20min, €40 return plus $12 Turkish tax) and 1 hydrofoil or catamaran (40min, €30 return plus Turkish tax) to Datça; Sat most reliable day.

### Flights

NB: All are on Olympic Aviation/Olympic Airways unless stated otherwise.
Astypálea 4–5 weekly to Athens; 2–3 weekly to Léros, Kós and Rhodes on the same plane.
Kálymnos 1 daily to Athens.
Kárpathos 2 daily to Rhodes; 6–9 weekly to Kássos and Sitía (Crete); daily to Athens.
Kássos 9 weekly to Kárpathos, Sitía (Crete) and Rhodes.
Kastellórizo (Meyísti) 4–6 weekly to Rhodes.
Kós 3 daily to Athens on Olympic, 2–4 daily on Aegean; 2 weekly to Thessaloníki on Aegean; 2–3 weekly to Astypálea, Léros and Rhodes; 3 weekly on Sky Express to Iráklio, Crete.
Léros 1 daily to Athens; 2–3 weekly to Astypálea, Kós and Rhodes.
Rhodes Olympic: 4–5 daily to Athens; 2 daily to Iráklio; 2–3 weekly to Kós, Léros and Astypálea on same plane; 2 weekly to Sámos and Híos; 5 weekly to Lésvos and Límnos; 8–9 weekly to Thessaloníki; 9 weekly to Kárpathos, Kássos & Sitía on same plane. Aegean: 4–7 daily to Athens; 1–2 daily to Thessaloníki. Sky Express: daily to Iráklio; 3 weekly to Kalamáta; 3 weekly to Mýkonos & daily to Santoríni June to early Oct only.

# The East and North Aegean

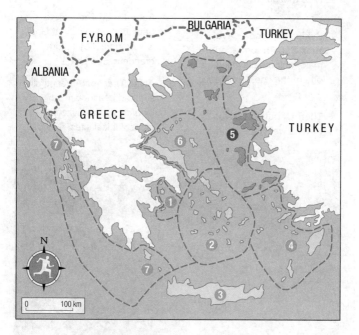

CHAPTER 5     # Highlights

▲ Alykí beach, Thássos

# The East and North Aegean

The seven substantial islands and four minor islets scattered off the Aegean coast of Asia Minor form a rather arbitrary archipelago. While there are similarities in architecture and landscape, the strong individual character of each island is far more striking. Despite their proximity to modern Turkey, only Lésvos, Límnos and Híos bear significant signs of an **Ottoman** heritage in the form of old mosques, hamams and fountains, plus some domestic architecture betraying obvious influences from Constantinople, Macedonia and further north in the Balkans. But the enduring Greekness of these islands is testimony to a four-millennium-long **Hellenic** presence in Asia Minor, which ended only in 1923.

This heritage has been duly referred to by Greece in an intermittent propaganda war with Turkey over the sovereignty of these far-flung outposts – as well as the disputed boundary between them and the Turkish mainland. **Tensions** here have occasionally been worse than in the Dodecanese, aggravated by suspected undersea oil deposits in the straits between the islands and Anatolia. The Turks have also persistently demanded that Límnos, astride the sea lanes to the Dardanelles, be demilitarized, and only since 2001 has Greece shown signs of complying, with garrisons also much reduced on Sámos and Lésvos.

Ironically, this conflict gave these long-neglected islands a new lease of life from the 1960s onward, insomuch as their sudden **strategic importance** prompted infrastructure improvements to support garrisoning, and gave a mild spur to local economies, engaged in providing goods and services to soldiers, something pre-dating mass tourism. Yet EU-funded studies around the millennium showed that, in terms of per-capita income, the "northeast Aegean" still ranked along with Epirus on mainland Greece, Apuglia in Italy and Extremadura in Spain as one of the **poorest regions** in western Europe. At first, this might seem an incredible or sensational judgement, given the lucrative tourist-takings on Sámos or the shipping-based remittance economy of Híos, but forays off the beaten track through the more backward and depressed corners of Ikaría, Lésvos or Límnos will still uncover early-twentieth-century lifestyles which are pulling the average down.

As in the Dodecanese, local agencies do a thriving business shuttling passengers between the easternmost islands and the **Turkish coast** with its

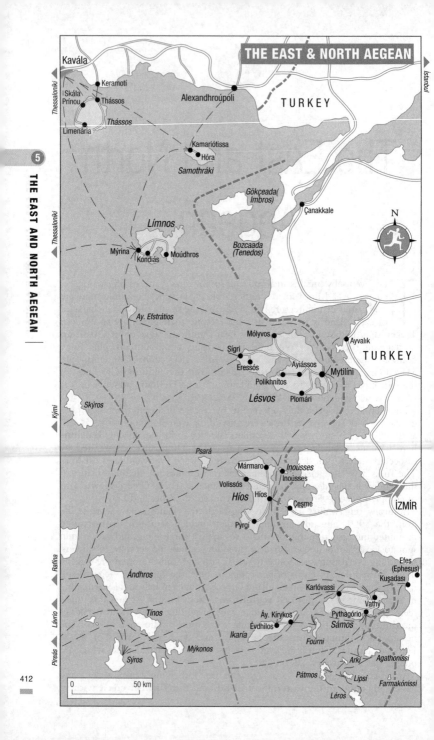

THE EAST & NORTH AEGEAN

Kavála

Keramotí

Skála
Prinou
Thássos

Limenária

Thássos

Thessaloníki

Thessaloníki

Kými

Rafína

Lávrio

Piraiás

Alexandhroúpoli

TURKEY

İstanbul

Kamariótissa
Hóra
Samothráki

Gökçeada
(İmbros)

Çanakkale

N

Límnos

Mýrina
Kondiás
Moúdhros

Bozcaada
(Tenedos)

Ay. Efstrátios

Skýros

Mólyvos

Sígri
Eressós

Ayiássos
Polikhnítos
Lésvos
Plomári

Ayvalık

TURKEY

Mytilíni

İZMİR

Psará

Mármaro
Inoússes
Inoússes

Volissós
Híos
Híos
Çeşme

Pyrgí

Ándhros

Tínos

Ay. Kírykos
Évdhilos
Ikaría

Mýkonos

Sýros

Karlóvassi

Vathý

Pythagório
Sámos

Efes
(Ephesus)

Kuşadası

Foúrni

Arkí

Agathoníssi

Pátmos

Lipsí

Farmakónissi

Léros

0        50 km

archeological sites and busy resorts. Most main **port-towns** here are urbanized provincial capitals and far from picturesque; suppress any initial impulse to take the next boat out, and discover the worthwhile interiors. Also bear in mind that the **tourist season** this far north is short – late June to early September – with many establishments shut outside this period, except on Sámos and Lésvos.

Verdant **Sámos** ranks as the most visited island of the group but, once you leave its crowded resorts behind, is still arguably the most beautiful, even after a devastating fire in 2000. **Ikaría** to the west remains relatively unspoilt, if a minority choice, and nearby **Foúrni** is (except in summer) a haven for determined solitaries, as are the Híos satellites **Psará** and **Inoússes**. **Híos** proper offers far more cultural interest than its neighbours to the south, but far fewer tourist facilities. **Lésvos** may not impress initially, though once you get a feel for its old-fashioned Anatolian ambience you may find it hard to leave. By contrast, few foreigners visit **Áyios Efstrátios**, for good reason. **Límnos** to the north is much busier, its most popular villages and beaches – and attractive harbour capital – residing in its western half. In the far north Aegean, Samothráki and Thássos are relatively isolated and easier to visit from northern Greece, which administers them. **Samothráki** (officially in Thrace) has one of the most dramatic seaward approaches of any Greek island, and one of the more important ancient sites. **Thássos** (technically part of eastern Macedonia) is more varied, with sandy beaches, mountain villages and minor archeological sites.

# Sámos

Lush, seductive and shaped like a pregnant guppy, **Sámos** seems to swim away from Asia Minor, to which the island was joined until Ice Age cataclysms sundered it from Mount Mykáli (Mycale) on the Turkish mainland. The resulting 2500-metre strait provides the narrowest maritime distance between Greece and Turkey, except at Kastellórizo. In its variety of mountainous terrain, beaches and vegetation, Sámos has the feel of a much larger island, and before recent development and wildfires took their toll, it was indisputably among the most beautiful in the Aegean; much of value remains, testimony to its ample natural endowments.

Sámos was during the Archaic era among the **wealthiest** islands in the Aegean and, under the patronage of tyrant Polykrates, home to a thriving intellectual community that included Epikouros, Pythagoras, Aristarkhos and Aesop. Decline set in as Classical Athens was on the rise, though Sámos's status improved in Byzantine times when it formed its own imperial administrative district. Late in the fifteenth century, the ruling Genoese **abandoned** the island to the mercies of pirates, and Sámos remained almost uninhabited until 1562, when it was repopulated with Greek Orthodox settlers recruited from various corners of the empire (later joined by many Asia Minor refugees after 1923).

The new Samians **fought** fiercely for independence during the **1820s**, but despite their sinking a Turkish fleet in the narrow strait and annihilating a landing army, the Great Powers handed the island back to the Ottomans in 1830, with the consoling proviso that it be semi-autonomous, ruled by an appointed Christian prince. This period, known as the **Iyimonía** (Hegemony), was marked by a renaissance in fortunes, courtesy of the hemp, leather-tanning

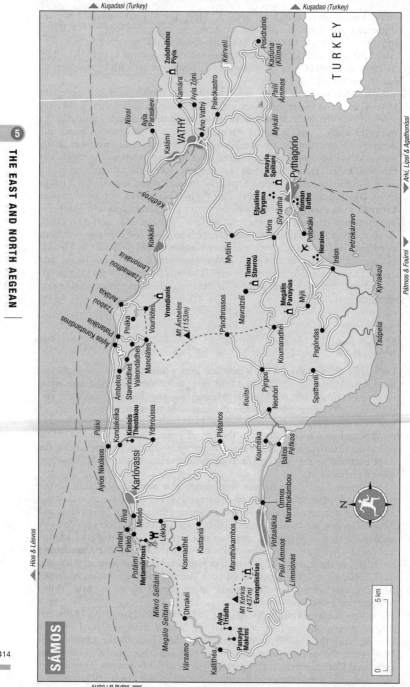

SÁMOS

▲ Kuşadası (Turkey)          ▲ Kuşadası (Turkey)

T U R K E Y

▲ Híos & Lésvos

▲ Ikaría & Foúrni

▶ Pátmos & Foúrni

▶ Arkí, Lipsí & Agathoníssi

Posidhónio

Kérveli

Kaddúna (Klíma)

Psilí Ámmos

Zoödhóhou
Piyís

Kamára

Ayía Zóni

Paleókastro

Ayía
Paraskeví

Níssi

Kalámi

VATHÝ

Áno Vathý

Mykáli

Panayía
Spilianí

Pythagório

Kédhros

Kokkári

Tzamadhoú

Lemonákia

Efpalínio
Órygma

Glyfádha

Roman
Baths

Hóra

Potokáki

Heraion

Iréon

Petrokáravo

Mytilíni

Tzabou
Platanákia

Áyios Konstandínos

Vrondianís

Vourliótes

Pnáka

Mt Ámbelos
(1153m)

Pándhrossos

Timíou
Stavroú

Megális
Panayías

Mýli

Kyriakoú

Tsópela

Mavratzéi

Koumaradhéi

Pagóndas

Spatharéi

Stavrinídhes

Valeondádhes

Manolátes

Ambelos

Kondakéika

Kímisis
Theotókou

Ydhroússa

Pýrgos

Neohóri

Koútsi

Áyios Nikólaos

Karlóvassi

Platanos

Piáki

Koumbéika

Balos

Péfkos

Ormos
Marathókambou

Votsalákia

Psilí Ámmos

Limniónas

Marathókambos

Kastaniá

Kosmadhéi

Dhrakéi

Mt Kérkis
(1437m)

Evangelístria

Ayía
Triádha

Panayía
Makriní

Kallithéa

Vársamo

Mikró Seïtáni

Megálo Seïtáni

Metamórfosis

Potámi

Léka

Lékka

Meséo

Ríva

Limáni
Paleó

N

0        5 km

and (especially) tobacco trades. However, union with Greece in 1912, the ravages of a bitter World War II occupation and mass emigration effectively reversed this recovery until tourism appeared on the horizon during the 1980s.

The heterogeneous descent of today's islanders largely explains an enduring identity crisis and a rather thin topsoil of **indigenous culture**. Most village names are either clan surnames, or adjectives indicating origins elsewhere. There is no distinctly Samian music, dance or dress, and little that's original in the cuisine and architecture. The economy relies on **package tourism**, with Kokkári, Pythagório and the southwestern coasts pretty much surrendered to holiday-makers, although the more rugged west and northwest have retained their undeveloped grandeur. Low-key nightlife, a world away from that in the Dodecanese and Cyclades, and phalanxes of self-catering villas hint at the sedate (mostly Dutch, central European, Scandanavian and Brit), couples-orientated custom expected.

Not coincidentally, the most heavily developed areas have been most afflicted by repeated **wildfires**, most recently in July 2000, which destroyed a quarter of the island's forest and orchards, and more than ninety dwellings; taking into account other areas torched since 1987, Sámos is now about half denuded. Some stands of magnificent black pines survive on the heights, with Calabrian pine lower down, but in the centre and south of the island, the deforestation is total. Volunteer-staffed fire-lookouts have since sprouted, but as ever in such cases the trees will be a half-century in returning.

## Arrival and getting around

Sámos's **airport** (five car rental booths, one ATM near check-in) lies 14km southwest of Vathý and 3km west of Pythagório. There is no airport bus; **taxi** fares to all points are posted on placards, and in summer taxis to the airport or ferry docks must be booked in advance. There are three **ferry ports**: Karlóvassi in the west, plus Vathý and Pythagório in the east, making the island a major travel hub. All ferries between Pireás and Sámos call at both Karlóvassi and Vathý, as does the small, locally based *Samos Spirit*, linking the island with Foúrni and Ikaría. Vathý also receives most of the sailings between northern Greece and the Dodecanese, via major intervening islands, plus small boats from Kuşadasi. Pythagório sees four regular weekly ferry connections from Kálymnos in the Dodecanese (and intervening islands), as well as a **hydrofoil service** to all Dodecanese down to Kós.

The **bus terminals** in Pythagório and Vathý lie (just) within walking distance of the ferry dock; at Karlóvassi, you can take a taxi or an occasional shuttle bus the 3km into town. The weekday KTEL service is adequate along the Pythagório–Vathý and Vathý–Kokkári–Karlóvassi routes, and cheap at under €1.50 for Vathý–Kokkári, but poor at weekends or for other destinations; it's easy to find a good deal all season at numerous car- and motorbike-rental outlets.

## Vathý

Lining the steep northeastern shore of a deep bay, beachless **VATHÝ** (often confusingly referred to as "Sámos") is a busy provincial town which grew from a minor anchorage after 1830, when it replaced Hóra as the island's capital. It's an unlikely, rather ungraceful resort, where numerous hotels have closed or become apartments since the 1990s, and holds little of interest aside from an excellent museum, some Neoclassical mansions and the hillstde suburb of **Áno Vathý**.

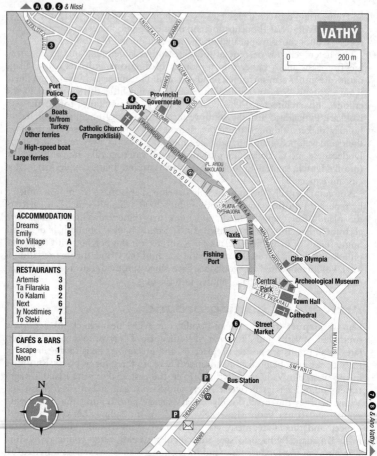

▲ **Ⓐ, ❶, ❷** & Nissi

**VATHÝ**

0                    200 m

Port
Police ⒼＣ

Boats
to/from
Turkey

Other ferries

High-speed boat

Large ferries

ENDHEKALÍOU

GIMMÍNO

Ⓑ

KEFALOPOÚLOU

Ⓓ

Ⓐ

**Provincial**
❹ **Governorate** Ⓓ
**Laundry**

Catholic Church
(Frangoklisiá)

IVANÍ

KORYVÍDOU

ÁRTOS

KALÓMRI

LOBÓMEN

THEMISTOKLÍ SOFOÚLI

PL. AYÍOU
NIKOLÁOU

@

KAPETÁN STAMÁTI

**ACCOMMODATION**

| | |
|---|---|
| Dreams | **D** |
| Emily | **B** |
| Ino Village | **A** |
| Samos | **C** |

PLATÍA
PYTHAGÓRA

Taxis ★

**Fishing
Port**

❺

**RESTAURANTS**

| | |
|---|---|
| Artemis | 3 |
| Ta Filarakia | 8 |
| To Kalami | 2 |
| Next | 6 |
| Iy Nostimies | 7 |
| To Steki | 4 |

**Cine Olympia**

Central
Park **Archeological Museum**

ALEX PÁSKHALI **Town Hall**

**Cathedral**

**CAFÉS & BARS**

| | |
|---|---|
| Escape | 1 |
| Neon | 5 |

❻

ⓘ

**Street
Market**

YIANKOÚ KATEGÁKI

MÝKALIS

SMÝRNIS

Ⓟ **Bus Station**

THEMISTOKLÍ SOFOÚLI

@

Ⓟ

KANÁRI

**N**

❼, ❽ & Áno Vathý ►

▼ Kokkári, Museum of Samos Wines, Pythgório & Cine Crystal Plex

## Arrival, information and transport

From the **ferry dock**, the shore boulevard – Themistoklí Sofoúli – describes a 1300-metre arc around the bay. About 400m along is pedestrianized **Platía Pythagóra**, distinguished by its lion statue; about 800m along there's a major turning inland to the **KTEL** terminal, a perennially bus-cluttered intersection by the ticket office. If you've arrived with your own vehicle, use the free **parking** lots on the shoreline near the KTEL turning – there's never any street parking to be had.

The most comprehensive waterfront **ferry/travel agent** is By Ship, with one branch at the base of the jetty (☎22730 80445), another about 300m southeast (☎22730 25065). Helpful ITSA (☎22730 23605), also at the jetty base, are main agents for Kallisti Ferries. Among ten **scooter- and car-rental** agencies, three to try are Aramis/Sixt (☎22730 23253) at Themistoklí Sofoúli 7, Avis/Reliable (☎22730 80445), both with branches island-wide, and Auto Union at Themistoklí Sofoúli 79 (☎22730 27444), which negotiates good long-term rates and will deliver cars to the airport. Other amenities include

416

the **post office**, inconveniently remote on Themistoklí Sofoúli; six waterfront **ATMs**; and a few **internet cafés**, such as Net House on the front near the KTEL. The **tourist information office** (May–Oct Mon–Fri 9am–2pm) at Themistoklí Sofoúli 107 is minimally helpful.

## Accommodation

Budget **accommodation** clusters in the hillside district of **Katsoúni**, above the ferry dock; except in August, you'll have little trouble finding vacancies. More comfortable hotels are found on or near the shore, from the ferry dock north into **Kalámi** district.

**Dreams** Up a stair-lane at Áreos 9, Katsoúni ☎22730 24350. Well-kept, en-suite rooms with fridges and double beds at this all-year-operating *pension*. ❷

**Emily** Top of Grámmou, cnr 11-Noemvríou, Katsoúni ☎22730 24691, ✉emilyhotel@hotmail.com. Small, well-run two-star hotel with cheerful rooms – there's even wall art – and a roof garden.❸

**Ino Village** 400m beyond hospital, Kalámi ☎22730 23241, ⦿www.inovillagehotel.com.

Surprisingly affordable three-star hotel with views, a big pool and a decent on-site restaurant. ❸

**Samos** Base of ferry dock ☎22730 28377. This is a 2007-refurbished, obvious, C-class behemoth that's a firm favourite despite the rooms being a bit small (and the breakfast very perfunctory). Double-glazing against traffic noise, rooftop pool-terrace, popular café out front. All year. ❹

**Trova** Manóli Kalomíri 26, Katsoúni ☎22730 27759. Just five en-suite rooms at this all-year *pension*; shared kitchen. ❷

## The town and archeological museum

A prominent waterfront curiosity near the ferry jetty is the old French **Catholic church**, labelled "Ecclesia Catolica" but universally known as the **Frangoklisiá**. Since 1974, when the last nuns departed Sámos after having schooled the elite for nearly a century, the church is open at best once weekly, when a priest arrives from Sýros to celebrate mass for interested tourists and the half-dozen or so Samian Catholics.

The best inland target on foot, a twenty-minute walk south and 150m above sea level, is the atmospheric hill village of **ÁNO VATHÝ**, a nominally protected but increasingly threatened community of tottering, canal-tile-roofed houses being steadily replaced by bad-taste blocks of flats or defaced with aluminium windows and modern tiles. Best of several **churches** is quadruple-domed **Aï Yannáki** (sometimes open; key from Mrs Vassiliki at the first house to the west) in the vale separating the village's two hillside neighbourhoods, with an intriguing ground plan that compensates for its scandalously deteriorated condition. Few of the eighteenth-century frescoes have survived the damp, but one – a rare image of the dead Christ in His tomb, the "Utter Humiliation" in Orthodox iconography (akin to the West's Man of Sorrows) – can be found at the rear left of the unlit interior; be sure to bring a torch. In the conch of the apse is an equally uncommon depiction of Christ Arkhierévs (Archpriest), flanked by angels.

The only real must is the excellent **archeological museum** (Tues–Sun 8.30am–3pm; €3), set behind the small central park beside the nineteenth-century town hall. The collections are housed in both the old Paskhallion building and a modern wing just opposite, specially constructed to house the star exhibit: a majestic, five-metre-tall *kouros* discovered out at the Heraion sanctuary. The largest free-standing effigy surviving from ancient Greece, this *kouros* was dedicated to Apollo, but found next to a devotional mirror to Mut (the Egyptian equivalent of Hera) from a Nile workshop.

In the Paskhallion, more votive offerings of **Egyptian** design – a hippo, a dancer in Nilotic dress, Horus-as-Falcon, an Osiris figurine – prove trade and pilgrimage links between Sámos and the Nile valley going back to the eighth century BC. The **Mesopotamian** and **Anatolian** origins of other artwork confirm an exotic trend, most tellingly in a case full of ivory miniatures: Perseus and Medusa in relief, a kneeling, perfectly formed mini-*kouros*, a pouncing lion and a bull's-head drinking horn. The most famous local artefacts are numerous bronze **griffin-heads**, for which Sámos was the major centre of production in the seventh century BC; they were mounted on the edge of cauldrons to ward off evil spirits. There's also an unlabelled **hoard of gold byzants**, some of more than three hundred imperial coins from the fifth to seventh centuries AD, found inside a bronze urn in 1984 by a Dutch archeologist wading in the shallows at a remote bay – one of the largest such troves ever discovered.

### Eating, drinking and nightlife

Obvious **tavernas** along Themiskolí Sofoúli between the ferry dock and the "Lion Square" are worth shunning in favour of remoter and/or inland choices below, all open year round. Vathý's perennial **nightlife** venue is a "strip" at the start of Kefalopoúlou north of the jetty, its annually changing bars with seaside (or sea-view) terraces; the most reliable contenders are *Escape* at no.9, *Ble* next door and Indonesian-themed *Sayang* across the street. Plushly fitted Cine Olympia, inland on Yimnasiárhou Katevéni, offers a variable programme of **films** (subject to unpredictable closure months), in competition with newer Crystal Plex at the head of the bay (mostly action/capers). The **Museum of Samos Wines** (Mon–Sat 8am–8pm; €2), run by the local co-op 300m past the Crystal Plex, is rather a failure as a museum with no labelling or anything on the interesting history of the local industry, but for the admission fee you can sample most of the island's wines.

**Artemis** Kefalopoúlou 4, just north of the ferry jetty. Excellent all-rounder, tellingly busy with locals at lunch, doing excellent, affordable seafood and starters like *fáva*, *hórta*, *seláhi* and *foúskes* as well as the usual mains. Good bulk *robóla* wine from the hill villages. Pleasant indoor/outdoor seating by season.

**Neon** Themistoklí Sofoúli, beside Eurobank. A traditional *kafenío* that's the best place for an early-evening tipple-with-seafood-*mezédhes*; there's no menu, but the waiter brings a big platter of whatever's cooking for a set price (which shouldn't be much more than €6 per head with drink).

**Next** Themistoklí Sofoúli 97. Much the best of Vathý's four pizza-pasta joints, also with good salads, all at reasonable prices. Outdoor – and elegantly rustic indoor – seating.

**ly Nostimies (tou Tassou)** Áno Vathý, next to the school and community offfice. Popular, fairly inexpensive *ouzerí* with seasonally variable menu: autumn through spring features seafood titbits like shredded steamed skate with *skordhaliá*, or meat with poppy greens; summer, when service can suffer, sees more conventional grilled chops and *koliós* (mackerel). Try also their *bouyiourdí* or pepper-and-cheese hotpot. Daily dinner except Sun; also some lunches Oct–May.

**Ta Filarakia** Ayía Matróna, Áno Vathý. The village characters' hangout, with the music (rebétika and *kapsoúrika tragoúdhia*) cranked up loud. The food – typically just a dish or two of the day, plus grills and fry-ups – varies in quality but can be surprisingly good, and always cheap (best stick to bottled wine, though).

**To Kalami** (aka **Triandafyllos**) Kefalopoúlou, about 3km into Kalámi. Despite its location in an unpromisingly touristy enclave, this has a friendly managing family, decent food and live music of middling quality twice weekly. Open Easter–Oct, also off-season weekends.

**To Steki** Shopping centre behind the Catholic church. Family-run *inomayirío* that's tops for dishes like bean soup at lunch; also good fish like *gávros*, and decent bulk wine.

## Beaches and monasteries around Vathý

Some modest **beaches** around Vathý compensate for lack of same in the capital, though you'll need your own transport to visit them, as you do for the two

**monasteries** of Vlamarí. Heading north out of town, the narrow, tour-bus-clogged street threads through beachless **Kalámi** – formerly the summer retreat of rich Vathýots, now home to package hotels – before ending after 7km at the pebbly bay and fishing port of **AYÍA PARASKEVÍ** (aka Nissí), with good, if rather unsecluded, swimming.

Two kilometres east of and above Vathý spreads the vast inland plateau of **Vlamarí**, devoted to vineyards and flanked by the hamlets of **Ayía Zóni** and **Kamára** (plus numerous bad-taste modern villas). Ayía Zóni is flanked by a fortified monastery, in the throes of restoration 2008–09, its *katholikón* with smoke-smudged frescoes. From Kamára you can head east on a zigzag road climbing to ridge-top **Zoödhóhou Piyís convent** (open except 2–5pm) for superb views across the end of the island to Turkey; the dome of its *katholikón* (where the nuns' chanting is excellent) is upheld by four ancient columns from Miletus in Asia Minor.

As you head southeast from Vathý along the main island loop road, the triple chapel at **Trís Ekklisíes** marks an important junction, with another fork 100m along. Bearing left twice takes you through the hilltop village of **Paleókastro**, 3km beyond which is another junction; forking left yet again brings you after another 3km to striking **Kérveli Bay**, with a small but popular pebble beach and a mediocre taverna. The best local **food** and lodging is just above: the B-class *Kerveli Village* **hotel** (T 22730 23006, W www.kerveli.gr; ⑤), above the last road curve descending to the beach, is reckoned one of the best in eastern Sámos, with sympathetic architecture, on-site car rental, pool, tennis court and private lido. Another 300m uphill, ⚟ *Iy Kryfí Folia* ("The Hidden Nest"; May to early Oct) is as described: a secluded oasis offering simple but inexpensive and sustaining fare such as *kalamári* rings, the best lamb chops on Sámos and roast goat – ring T 22730 25194 to preorder your goat.

Bearing right at the junction before Paleókastro leads to the beaches of Mykáli and Psilí Ámmos. **Mykáli**, a kilometre or so of windswept sand and gravel, has no outstanding tavernas, and two all-inclusive hotels for Italians, but a third alternative – *Zefiros Beach* (T 22730 28532, W www.zefirosbeach.gr; ④) – is good for families, with ample watersports facilities off its patch of beach. **Psilí Ámmos**, further east around the headland, is a crowded, sandy cove backed by several **tavernas**, best of these being *Psili Ammos*, on the far right as you face the sea, with good seafood, salads and meat grills. If you swim to the islet, beware strong eastbound currents in the narrow straits.

## Pythagório and its antiquities

Most traffic south of Vathý heads for **PYTHAGÓRIO**, the island's premier resort, renamed in 1955 to honour Pythagoras, ancient mathematician, philosopher and initiator of a rather subversive cult. Until then it was known as Tigáni (Frying Pan) – in midsummer you'll learn why at what can be a rather tacky resort. Sixth-century BC tyrant Polykrates had his capital here, whose sporadic excavation has made modern Pythagório expand northeast and uphill. The village core of cobbled lanes and stone-walled mansions abuts a cosy **harbour**, fitting almost perfectly into the confines of Polykrates' ancient jetty (traces of it still visible), but today devoted almost entirely to pleasure craft and overpriced café-bars.

A 2005-built **archeological museum** at the start of the Vathý road, featuring finds from the ancient city, seems destined never to open. Sámos's most complete **castle**, the nineteenth-century *pýrgos* of local chieftain Lykourgos Logothetis, overlooks both town and the shoreline where he, together with a certain "Kapetan Stamatis" and Admiral Kanaris, oversaw decisive naval and land victories against the Turks in the summer of 1824. The final battle was won on Transfiguration Day (Aug 6) – thus the dedication of the church by the castle – with an annual fireworks show commemorating the triumph. Also next to the castle are the remains of an early Christian basilica, occupying the grounds of a slightly larger Roman villa.

Other antiquities include **Roman baths**, signposted as "Thermai", 400m west of town (Tues–Sun 8.45am–2.30pm; free); considerably more interesting is the well-signposted **Efpalínio Órygma** (Tues–Sun 8.45am–2.15pm; €4), a 1036-metre aqueduct bored through the mountain just north of Pythagório. Designed by one Eupalinos of Mégara, and built by slave labour at the behest of Polykrates, it guaranteed the ancient town a siege-proof water supply, and remained in use until late Byzantine times. Visits consist of traversing a hewn rock ledge used to transport the spoil from the water channel far below; there are guard-grilles over the worst drops, and lighting for the first 650m. Although the work-crews started digging from opposite sides of the mountain, the eight-metre horizontal deviation from true, about halfway along, is remarkably slight, and the vertical error nil: a tribute to the competence of ancient surveyors.

On the way up to the Efpalínio Órygma is the well-marked turning for the monastery of **Panayía Spilianí**. The monastery itself, now bereft of nuns or monks, has been insensitively restored and the grounds are crammed with souvenir kiosks, but behind the courtyard, the *raison d'être* of the place is still magnificent: a cool, illuminated, hundred-metre **cave**, at the drippy end of which is a subterranean shrine to the Virgin (open daylight hours; free). This was supposedly the residence of the ancient oracular priestess Phyto, and a hiding place from medieval pirates.

### Practicalities

The **bus stop** lies just west of the intersection of the main thoroughfare, Lykoúrgou Logothéti, and the road to Vathý; the **taxi** rank is at the harbour end of Lykoúrgou Logothéti, while the **tourist information** booth (June–Sept daily 8.30am–9.30pm; ℡22730 62274) is a few paces along. Several **ATMs** line the same street; the **post office** is near the bus stop. The flattish country just west is ideal for **cycling**, a popular activity; if instead you want to rent a **motorbike**, several outfits on Logothéti will oblige you. These are interspersed with numerous **car rental** outlets (try Nicos ℡22730 61094, Ⓦwww.nicos-rentals.gr, or Yes ℡69748 40060, Ⓦwww.rentacar.gr, both on Logothéti), though street **parking** in Pythagório is impossible – use the pricey car park near the main T-junction, or the free one just west behind the town beach.

**Accommodation** proprietors meet all arriving ferries and hydrofoils, even in peak season – some touted prices seem too good to be true, but it's free to look, and no location is that inconvenient. Quietly located at the seaward end of Pythagóra, south of Lykoúrgou Logothéti, the modest *Tsambika* (℡22730 61642; ❷) or the more comfortable *Dora*, a block west (℡22730 61456; ❸), are worth contacting in advance. A peaceful area is the hillside north of Platía Irínis, where *Studios Galini* (℡22730 61167 or 210 98 42 248 in winter; ❹) has high-quality self-catering units with ceiling fans, balconies and kindly English-speaking management.

**Eating out** can be frustrating in Pythagório, with good value and sound ingredients often completely alien concepts. Bright spots include, at the far north end of the quay, then inland, *Dolichi* (supper only), serving upscale Greek/Mediterranean fusion cuisine in a space doubling as an art gallery; 2007-revamped *Remataki* just beyond; and *Viva* at the base of the jetty for well-priced pizza and pasta. In terms of **nightlife**, the top outing is to *Amadeus* (closed Mon) just in from the jetty, with quality live Greek acts at bearable amplification. **Outdoor-cinema** aficionados will love the Rex, one of the best-maintained in the islands, at the outskirts of Mytiliní village, 7km northwest; they screen quality first-run films, with free *loukoumádhes* (sweet fritters) and cheap pizza at intermission.

## Potokáki, Heraion and Iréon

The local, variable beach stretches several kilometres west of the Logothetis castle, punctuated partway along by the end of the airport runway, and the cluster of nondescript hotels known as **POTOKÁKI**. Just before the turn-off to the heart of the beach sprawls the luxury *Doryssa Seaside Resort* complex (☎22730 61360, ⓦwww.doryssa-bay.gr; ❸), which includes a hotel wing with Philippe-Starck-ish rooms and a meticulously concocted fake village; no two of its cosier bungalows are alike, and there's even a platía with a (pricey) café. Although you'll have to contend with the hotel crowds and low-flying jets, the sand-and-pebble **beach** here is well groomed, the water clean and sports available.

Under layers of alluvial mud, plus today's runway, lies the processional Sacred Way joining ancient Samos with the **Heraion**, a massive shrine of the **Mother Goddess** (daily: June–Sept 8am–7.30pm; Oct–May 8.30am–3pm; €3). Much touted in tourist literature, this assumes humbler dimensions – one surviving column and low foundations – upon approach. Yet once inside the precinct you sense the former grandeur of the temple, never completed owing to Polykrates' untimely death at the hands of the Persians. The site chosen, near the mouth of the still-active Imvrassós stream, was Hera's legendary birthplace and site of her trysts with Zeus; in the far corner of the fenced-in zone you tread a large, exposed patch of the Sacred Way.

Modern **IRÉON** nearby is at first glance a nondescript, grid-plan resort behind a coarse-shingle beach, where the water can be cold owing to the outflow of the Imvrassós. Nonetheless the place has fanatical devotees who patronize studios and small hotels, mostly within sight of the more characterful pedestrianized waterfront, and after dark it has a friendly, more relaxed feel than Pythagório, with much better **tavernas** worth a special drive. Ones along the shore are especially busy on summer nights around the **full moon**, when Iréon is the best spot on the island to watch it rise out of the sea.

### Iréon eating

**Aegeon (Markos)** Waterfront, halfway along. Probably the most accomplished, and Greek-patronized, taverna, with fresh wild fish at normal prices, good starters like potato salad and mushroom soufflé, and an averagely varied and priced wine list. On moonlit nights you should book on ☎22730 95271.

**Angyra** Corner premises 2 blocks inland. Welcoming, super-hygienic, seafood-strong ouzerí where five platters and a *karafáki* (enough for two) won't much top €30.

**Glaros** Inconspicuous shack on shore, about two-thirds of the way along. Cult eatery where the atmosphere and prices are excellent, though if Mamma isn't in the kitchen that day doing the likes of fish soup and okra, the fare is penitentially plain and restricted to grills, salads, (over)fried vegetables and bulk wine.

**Ioannis O Psaras** Lane perpendicular to the shore, opposite Pro-Po lottery stall. Service can be shambolic but as the name implies, they serve only fresh, own-caught fish – which sells out quickly.

# Southern Sámos

Since a circum-island bus rarely passes through or near the following places, you really need your own vehicle to explore them. Three Samian "**pottery villages**", in addition to the usual wares, specialize in the *Koúpa toú Pythagóra* or "Pythagorean cup", supposedly designed by the sage to leak over the user's lap if they were overfilled. The biggest concentration of retail outlets is at **KOUMARADHÉÏ**, about 7km west of Hóra, just before which is one of the most strikingly set and ambitiously appointed **drink-and-snack** outfits on the island, *Meteoron*, with sweeping views. From the village you can descend to the sixteenth-century monastery of **Megális Panayías** (Wed–Mon 10am–1pm & 5.30–8pm), containing very damp-smudged frescoes, then carry on via **MÝLI**, with most of Sámos's citrus groves, to **PAGÓNDAS**, a large hillside community with its main square hosting a lively Pentecost Sunday-evening festival, and an unusual communal fountain house on the southerly hillside. From there, a scenic road curls 15km around deforested hillside to **PÝRGOS**, at the head of a ravine draining southwest and the centre of Samian honey production; the best **taverna** here is central *Koutouki tou Barba Dhimitri* (all year, supper only) with a good range of vegetarian *mezédhes* and grills in an upscale environment. A short distance down the gorge, **Koútsi** is a small roadside oasis of plane trees (supposedly seventeen) shading a gushing spring and an eponymous, unreliably open **taverna**.

The rugged coast south of the Pagóndas–Pýrgos route is largely inaccessible and fire-scarred, glimpsed by most visitors for the first and last time from the descending plane bringing them to Sámos. **Tsópela**, a scenic sand-and-gravel cove at a gorge mouth, is the most renowned **beach** here with marked track access and a good rustic **taverna** in a surviving pine grove, with fish and a dish or two of the day; with care, ordinary cars regularly make the six-kilometre descent. A separate track system – with a branch in from Iréon, either requiring a jeep – leads to **Kyriakoú**, better and longer as a beach but with no facilities.

The western reaches of this shoreline are approached via handsome **KOUMÉÏKA**, with a massive inscribed marble fountain and a pair of *kafenía*-snack bars on its photogenic square. Below extends the long pebbly bay at **Bállos**, with sand and rock overhangs at the far east end. Bállos itself is merely a collection of summer houses, several places to stay (mostly contracted to package operators) and a few **tavernas**, all on the shore road. The best **accommodation** for walk-ins is *Hotel Amfilissos* (☎22730 31669; ❹), while good-value grills and a few seafood items are served at simple *Paralia* (May–early Oct). From Kouméïka, the paved side road going west just before the village is a very useful short cut for travelling towards Órmos Marathokámbou (see p.426) and beyond.

A separate road from Kouméïka leads to **Péfkos**, at first glance a grubby, narrow beach with no reliable facilities behind. But persevere towards the west, and you'll discover tiny pebble coves tucked in amongst rock overhangs and a much longer, idyllic strand reached by a track from Péfkos main bay through olive groves – all, of course, clothing optional.

## Plátanos

Continuing along the island's loop road back northeast towards Karlóvassi, it's worth detouring up to **PLÁTANOS**, on the flanks of Mount Karvoúnis; at 520m this is one of Sámos's highest villages, with sweeping views west and south. The name comes from the three stout plane trees (*plátanos* in Greek) on its platía, whose spring-water in the arcaded fountain-house is immortalized in one of the most popular Samian folk songs; there are also a few **tavernas** here – the most accomplished being *Leon*, with live music some nights. The only special sight is the double-naved thirteenth-century **church of Kímisis Theotókou** (key at house opposite west entrance) in the village centre; the Byzantine Nicaean emperors built it thus, making provision for the Catholic rite of their allies, the Genoese garrison.

## Kokkári and around

Leaving Vathý on the north-coast section of the island loop road, you've little to stop for until **KOKKÁRI**, Sámos's second major tourist centre. The town's coastal profile, covering two knolls behind mirror-image headlands called Dhídhymi (Twins), remains unchanged, and one or two fishermen still doggedly untangle nets on the quay, but its identity has been altered beyond recognition by inland expansion across old vineyards and along the west beach. Since the exposed, coarse-pebble **beaches** here are buffeted by near-constant winds, locals have made a virtue of necessity by developing the place as a successful **windsurfing** resort – just west of town a **school** (℡ 22730 92102, Ⓦ www.samoswindsurfing.gr) thrives.

### Practicalities

**Buses** stop on the through road, by the church. Other amenities on the same road include a few **ATMs**, branches of all major Samian **travel agents**, and a **newsstand/foreign-language bookstore**, Lexis; on a seaward lane stands a **post office** in a Portakabin. A **shop** to single out, several cuts above the usual tourist tat, is Charles Vergara's Lapis Lazuli near the river mouth, setting not only that alluring stone in gold, silver or just necklaces, but also tourmaline, malachite and others at fair prices.

As at Pythagório, a fair proportion of Kokkári's **accommodation** is booked solid by tour companies. Exceptions include, towards the south end of the west beach, English-run *Tsamadou Hotel* (℡ 22730 92314, Ⓦ www.tsamadou.com; ❸), its simple air-conditioned rooms with fridge; the nearby, popular *Athena Hotel*, just across the road from the beach (℡ 22730 92030; ❹), with a pool if it's too windy; or (on the fishing port), *Pension Alkyonis* (℡ 22730 92225; ❸). **Tavernas** lining the north waterfront have a nice view and little else to recommend them, with one exception cited below. The shoreline is better for **nightlife**, either at the "Bar Square" just left of the rivermouth, or a bit further on at *Cavos*, going since 1982, with breakfast and snacks as well.

### Eating

**Ammos Plaz** West beach. Long-established full-service taverna offering fair-priced *mayireftá* (moussakás, stews) and fish – they've a loyal repeat clientele, and in high season you must book well in advance (℡ 22730 92463) for seaside tables.

🏃 **Iy Byra** Opposite main church. Limited but superbly executed, reasonably priced range of light *mezédhes* like *domatokeftédhes* and *keftedhákia*, plus maybe seafood titbits. Packed every night, less so at midday.

**Jasmin Garden** The downstairs diner of *Tsamadou Hotel*. Generic southeast Asian fare like spring rolls, satay chicken, Thai soups and noodle or fried-rice dishes won't satisfy purists but it's well-priced, savoury and the only such food on the island. Daily in season, Sat pm/Sun lunch winter.

**Piccolo Porto** North waterfront. Inconspicuous hole-in-the-wall doing excellent wood-oven pizzas. Dinner only.

🏃 **Tarsanas** 100m down the lane from west beach, near headland. Wonderful terrazzo-floored 1980s throwback doing pizzas, a couple of dishes of the day like *briám* or *dolmádhes*, and their own dynamite red wine. Supper only except peak season.

## West of Kokkári: the coast

The closest sheltered **beaches** are about thirty-minutes' walk west, all carpeted with sunbeds and permanently anchored umbrellas. The first, **Lemonákia**, is a bit close to the road, though popular with patrons of the four-star *Arion* (☎22370 92020, ⓦwww.arion-hotel.gr; ❼) a bit inland, a well-designed bungalow/hotel-wing complex on an unburnt patch of hillside, with dazzlingly white, minimalist rooms. The graceful crescent of **Tzamadhoú**, 1km beyond, has path-only access, with the eastern third of the beach (saucer-shaped pebbles) a well-established nudist zone with gay and straight patronage. Beyond two indifferent beach tavernas is another upmarket hotel, ☖ *Armonía Bay* (☎22730 92279, ⓦwww.armoniabay.gr; ❻), literally on top of the action yet secluded and tastefully done up with marble-clad baths and pleasant common areas.

Some 3km beyond Tzamadhoú, **AVLÁKIA** is a quiet shoreline hamlet mostly frequented by Greeks in summer, but offering two excellent **tavernas**, both with some of the best views on the island: reliable *To Delfíni*, where Kyra Alexandra is the heart and soul of the place, strong on fresh little fish, *hórta* and chips; or a few paces north, multilingual Claudio's ☖ *Doña Rosa*, delivering Greek standards with an Italian flair: competent *fáva*, rocket salad, Calabrian chili garnish, *lovash* bread, fish or meat, washed down by a good wine list including Italian labels. The nearest beach, 2km further with a steep lane down, is **Tzaboú**, probably the most scenic north-coast beach with its rock formations but mercilessly buffeted by the prevailing wind most days – and the snack-bar tries to charge €6 for parking. There's a nudist annexe, with separate path access from Avlákia, off to the right.

The next settlement of **Platanákia**, essentially a handful of buildings at a bridge by the turning for Manolátes, is actually the eastern quarter of **ÁYIOS KONSTANDÍNOS**, whose surf-pounded esplanade has been prettified. However, there are no significant beaches within walking distance, so the collection of warm-toned stone buildings, with few modern intrusions, constitutes a peaceful alternative to Kokkári, only seeing much trade in spring or autumn when Dutch hikers frequent the place. They **stay** at *Hotel Iro* (☎22730 94013, ⓦwww.hotel-iro.gr; ❸), or *Hotel Apartments Agios Konstantinos* (☎22730 94000; ❸), both on the street linking Platanákia to the sea. **Eating** out, you're spoilt for choice; besides *To Kyma* at the east end of the quay (Easter–Sept), with good bulk wine, rich *mayireftá* and olive paté with the bread, there's cheap-and-cheerful *mayireftá* specialist *Akroyiali* at mid-quay, open all day much of the year, or *Aeolos* (May–Sept) at the far west end of the esplanade, with terrific fish or grilled meat and a few daily oven dishes, served at tables adjoining a tiny pebble cove.

Beyond this point, the mountains loom in against the sea, and the terrain doesn't relent until **Kondakéïka**; its diminutive shore annexe of **Áyios Nikólaos** has a good venue for fish meals in *Iy Psaradhes* (☎22730 32489; Easter–Oct), with a terrace lapped by the waves – you'll need to book in season as it has appeared (deservedly) in so many guides. A passable pebble beach, **Piáki**, lies ten-minutes' walk east past the last studio units. Áyios Nikólaos is also home to a thriving **New Age retreat centre**, *Villa Eva* (☎22730 30020, ⓦwww.villaeva-samos.gr; May–Oct), with reiki, yoga and Sufi seminars.

From Kondakéïka, a road – first paved, then good dirt – leads inland for 2.5km to the signposted Byzantine church of **Kímisis Theotókou**. The second oldest and most artistically noteworthy on Sámos, it has extensive frescoes contemporaneous with the building (late twelfth/early thirteenth century). The deceptively simple exterior gives little hint of the glorious barrel-vaulted interior (unlocked), its decoration still vivid except where damp has blurred the images. On the north wall are the soldier-saints Demetrios, George and the two Theodores, along with Constantine and Helen, plus a Virgin and Child. The south wall is mostly taken up by prophets reading their texts, as well as a fine Archangel Michael, but the most unusual image lies behind the altar-screen, on the north wall. Here the early bishop Peter of Alexandria engages in dialogue with a youthful, beardless, dishevelled Christ ("Who has torn your robe?" "The foolish and abominable Arius.") The fresco and exchange made clear to simple parishioners the presumed damage to the Body of Christ done by the Arian heresy of the early fourth century.

## Northern hill villages

Inland between Kokkári and Kondakéïka, an idyllic landscape of pine, cypress and orchards is overawed by dramatic mountains; except for some streaks of damage reaching the sea between Lemonákia and Tzaboú, and the destruction of **Vrondianís monastery** (being rebuilt) near Vourliótes, it miraculously escaped the 2000 fire. Despite bulldozer vandalism, some of the trail system linking the various **hill villages** is still intact, and walkers can return to the main highway to catch a bus back to base. Those with transport should leave it at Vourliótes and execute a **three-hour loop** via Manolátes, north and down to Aïdhónia, then back up east to your starting point. There is some waymarking, and the final stretch of trail has been rehabilitated.

**VOURLIÓTES**, closest to Kokkári, has beaked chimneys and brightly painted shutters sprouting from its typical tile-roofed houses. But restaurateur greed has ruined the formerly photogenic central square by chopping down old mulberries and cramming in more tables; it's best to pass over the **tavernas** there in favour of ⚓ *Iy Pera Vrysi* (March–Nov) at the village entrance, with a huge range of well-priced, imaginative *mezédhes* like spinach croquettes or chicken livers, and local *robóla* wine, or – beyond the platía – *Galazio Pigadhi*, serving up rabbit stew, *soutzoukákia* and eggplant dishes at limited pavement seating (book on ☎22730 93480) under a kangaroo vine. On the drive up to Vourliótes, you could also detour to five-house **PNÁKA** hamlet with its

▲ Sámos, vineyards and farm below Manolátes

gushing spring, beside which an eponymous **taverna** – not nearly as accomplished as the Vourliótes duo – compensates with the most idyllic setting on the island.

**MANOLÁTES**, further uphill and an hour-plus walk from Vourliótes via a deep river canyon, also has several **tavernas**, as ever with inland locales better value than those at coastal resorts (though two high-quality **raku-ceramic workshops** are anything but cheap). Worth singling out are *Despina*, serving dishes of the day, *revythokeftédhes* and good *tzatziki* in a gazebo by the central fountain, and ⊁ *AAA* downhill, under new management from 2008 and making a good fist of such dishes as *yiouvarlákia*, grilled *mastéllo*, an idiosyncratic version of eggplant *imám* and dry red wine from Stavrinídhes; it's a tad pricier than its neighbours but worth the difference.

Manolátes is the trailhead for the five-hour round-trip up **Mount Ámbelos** (Karvoúnis; 1153m), the island's second-highest summit. The trail has been cut perilously in three places by a jeep track (which you may be forced to follow briefly) a few minutes along, and there are broad swaths of fire damage, but overall the scenery, including some surviving 25-metre-tall black pines, is still alluring away from the burn zones.

From Manolátes you can no longer easily continue on foot to Stavrinídhes, the next village, but should plunge straight down, partly on a cobbled path, through the shady valley known as **Aïdhónia** (Nightingales), towards Platanákia and its bus stop, or the loop back to Vourliótes noted above.

## Karlóvassi

**KARLÓVASSI**, 31km west of Vathý and Sámos's second town, is sleepier and more old-fashioned than the capital, despite having roughly the same population. It's a useful base for enjoying western Sámos's excellent **beaches** or taking a number of rewarding **walks**. The name, despite a vehement denial of Ottoman legacy elsewhere on Sámos, appears to be a corruption of the Turkish for "snowy plain" – the conspicuous saddle of Mount Kérkis overhead. The town divides into five straggly neighbourhoods: Néo, well inland, whose growth was spurred by the influx of post-1923 refugees; Meséo, across the usually dry riverbed, tilting appealingly off a knoll and then blending with the shoreline district of Ríva; and picturesque Paleó (or Áno), above Limáni, the small harbour district.

Most tourists stay at or near **Limáni**, which has most tourist facilities. **Hotels** here tend to have road noise and not much view; an exception, part of a small local chain, is the *Samaina Port* (☎22730 30850, ⓦwww.samainahotels.gr; ❸), where **rooms**, all on the inland pedestrian lane behind the through road, are quieter – try *Vangelis Feloukatzis* (☎22730 33293; ❷). The port itself is a pleasant place with a working boatyard at the west end and **ferry-ticket agencies** along the approach road. *Frappádhika* and bars line the pedestrianized quay, where the only reliable **eatery**, towards the east end, is ⊁ *Tsipouradiko Ta Tsoungrismata*, with excellent, non-greasy platters of squid with parsley and onions or abundant servings of *gávros* and *sardhélles* washed down by beer or oúzo. Local university students support some nightlife, for example long-running venue *Popcorn* with DJed events at weekends, in an old customs warehouse.

Immediately overhead is the partly hidden hamlet of **Paleó**, its hundred or so houses draped either side of a leafy ravine, with two competing tavernas – *O Grados* is economical, simple and open all year. **MESÉO**, just east, has three all-year **tavernas** on central Platía 8-Maïoú, of which the most ambitious is *Dionysos* (large parties book on ☎22730 30120), with creative dishes, pleasant indoor/outdoor tables and a wine list aspiring to Athenian sophistication. Quick-serving

*Iy Platía* across the way is busy with locals at lunchtime for the sake of traditional *mayireftá* and a few grills, though quality varies. In between these two, *To Meseo* is probably the best value of the trio, with *mayireftá* such as goat in red sauce.

Following the kilometre-long street linking this square to **RÍVA**, you pass one of the huge, early twentieth-century **churches**, topped with twin belfries and a blue-and-white dome, that dot the coastal plain here. Just at the intersection with the shore road, you'll find the very popular, sunset-view ouzerí *To Kyma* (April–Sept), where Ethiopian proprietress Berhane adds a welcome Middle Eastern/East African touch to the range of seafood and vegetarian dishes such as *alí saláta*, with sun-dried tomatoes, cashews and courgettes; expect a wait for tables (no reservations taken). Otherwise, Ríva has little of interest besides derelict stone-built warehouses, tanneries and mansions, reminders of the defunct leather industry that flourished here until the 1960s. As for **Néo**, you'll almost certainly visit one of several **ATMs**, the **post office** or the **taxi rank** on the main square, just off which is a traditional *kafenío* doing snacks, *Kleanthis*. The **KTEL bus stop** is at the northeast end of the market district, on the roundabout by the university HQ, main **car park** and clinic.

## Western Sámos

The closest **beach** to Karlóvassi is **Potámi**, forty-minutes' walk away via the coast road from Limáni or an hour by a more scenic, high trail from Paleó. This broad arc of sand and pebbles, presided over on the east by the strikingly hideous clifftop chapel of Áyios Nikólaos from 1971, gets crowded at summer weekends, when effectively the entire town descends on the place. There are a few **rooms**, though folk camp rough along the lower reaches of the river that gives the beach its name. A streamside path leads twenty minutes inland, past the eleventh-century church of **Metamórfosis** – the oldest on Sámos – to a point where the river disappears into a small gorge (a guard-railed but still vertiginous stairway takes you up and left here). Otherwise, you must swim and wade 100m in heart-stoppingly cold water through a series of fern-tufted rock pools before reaching a low but vigorous waterfall; bring shoes with good tread and perhaps even rope if you want to explore above the first cascade. Just above the Metamórfosis church, a clear if precipitous path leads up to a small, contemporaneous **Byzantine fortress**. There's little to see inside other than a subterranean cistern and badly crumbled lower curtain wall, but the views in all directions are terrific; in October the place is carpeted with pink autumn crocuses.

The **coast beyond Potámi** ranks among the most beautiful and unspoilt on Sámos; since the early 1980s it has served as a protected refuge for the rare **monk seal**, still glimpsed occasionally by lucky hikers or bathers. Some twenty minutes along the dirt track at the west end of Potámi Bay takes you to the well-cairned side trail running parallel to the water. After twenty minutes more you'll arrive at **Mikró Seïtáni**, a small pebble cove guarded by sculpted rock walls. A full hour's walk from the trailhead, through olive terraces, brings you to **Megálo Seïtáni**, the island's finest sand beach, at the mouth of the intimidating Kakopérato gorge. Bring food, water and something to shade yourself, though not necessarily a swimsuit – there's no dress code at either of the Seïtáni bays. During peak season, there are a couple of daily **water-taxi** services from Karlóvassi port for non-walkers.

### Southwestern beach resorts

The first substantial place you reach on the island loop road south of Karlóvassi is **Marathókambos**, an amphitheatrical village overlooking the eponymous gulf; it has no tourist facilities, and by taking the bypass road you'll avoid the village's traffic bottlenecks – and save about 4km. Its port, **ÓRMOS MARATHOKÁMBOU**, 18km from Karlóvassi, has become something of a resort, though with ample character in its backstreets. The harbour is the starting point for several weekly *kaïki* **day-trips** to the nearby islet of Samiopoúla, inaccessible parts of the south coast and sometimes (by hydrofoil as well) Foúrni. Otherwise, the main focus of attention is the pedestrianized quay, home to several **tavernas**, of which the best is *Iy Trata* at the far east end of things, just off the pedestrian zone. **Accommodation** includes *Studios Avra* (☎22730 37221; ❸), unimprovably perched above the jetty, or good-value *Hotel Kerkis Bay* (☎ 22730 37202, Ⓦwww.kerkis-bay.com; ❸), one block inland from mid-quay.

The **beach** immediately east of Órmos is hardly the best; for better ones continue 2km west to **VOTSALÁKIA** (signposted as "Kámbos"), Sámos's most family-pitched resort, straggling a further 2km behind the island's longest (if not its most beautiful) beach. But for many, Votsalákia is still an improvement on the Pythagório area, and Mount Kérkis looming overhead rarely fails to impress (see below). For **accommodation**, try *Elsa Hiou*'s rooms behind her *Evoinos* taverna near mid-strand (☎22730 37791 or 694 67 92 923; ❸); *Emmanouil Dhespotakis* has numerous premises towards the quieter, more scenic western end of things (☎22730 31258; ❸–❹). Also nearby are two **tavernas** with wood-fired ovens: *Loukoullos*, overlooking the sea, best at night with an engaging owner, and *Akroyialia* (*Anna's*), about the oldest eatery here (1979), where tasty recipes offset small portions and bumped-up prices. Branches of nearly all the main Vathý **travel agencies** offer **vehicle rental**, and there are two stand-alone **ATMs**; during summer a **bus** calls several times daily from Karlóvassi.

*Loukoullos* marks the start of the access track to **Fournáki**, a series of sand-and-pebble **nudist coves** backed by low cliffs – sun traps in spring or autumn. Alternatively, continue 3km further to 600-metre-long **Psilí Ámmos**, not to be confused with its namesake beach in southeastern Sámos. The sea shelves ridiculously gently here – 100m out you're still just knee-deep – and more cliffs shelter clusters of naturists at the east end. Development comprises just three studio complexes in the pines at mid-beach, and two **tavernas** up on the approach road. Access to **Limniónas**, a smaller cove 2km further west, passes the *Limnionas Bay Hotel* (☎22730 37057; ❺), the best local **accommodation**, with tiered units arrayed around a garden and pool. Yachts and *kaïkia* occasionally call at the protected bay, which offers decent swimming at the east end, away from a rock shelf in the middle.

## Mount Kérkis and around

A limestone/volcanic oddity in a predominantly schist landscape, **Mount Kérkis** (Kerketévs) – the Aegean's second highest summit after Mount Sáos on Samothráki – attracts legends and speculation as easily as the cloud pennants that usually wreath it. Hermits colonized and sanctified the mountain's many caves in Byzantine times; resistance guerrillas controlled it during World War II; and mariners still regard it with superstitious awe, especially when mysterious lights – presumed to be the spirits of the departed hermits, or the aura of some forgotten holy icon – are glimpsed at night near the cave-mouths.

Gazing up from a supine seaside position, you may be inspired to **climb the peak**. The classic route begins from Votsalákia, along the paved but narrow lane leading inland towards Evangelistrías convent. After a 45-minute walk through olive groves, the path begins, more or less following power lines up to the convent. A friendly nun may proffer an ouzo and point you up the paint-marked trail, continuing even more steeply up to the peak. The views are tremendous, though the climb itself is humdrum once you're out of the trees. About an hour before the top there's a chapel with an attached cottage for sheltering in emergencies, and just beyond, a welcome spring. All told, it's a seven-hour return outing from Votsalákia, not counting rest stops.

Less ambitious walkers might want to circle the mountain's flank, first by vehicle and then by foot. The road beyond Limniónas to Kallithéa and Dhrakéï, back-of-beyond villages with views across to Ikaría, is paved all the way to Dhrakéï. The bus service is better during term time, when a vehicle leaves Karlóvassi (Mon–Fri 1.20pm) bound for Kallithéa; during summer it only operates two days a week (Mon to Dhrakéï, Fri to Kallithéa).

From **DHRAKÉÏ**, a lovely trail – minimally disrupted by a track – descends ninety minutes through forest to Megálo Seïtáni, from where it's easy to continue on to Karlóvassi within another two-and-a-half hours. People climbing up from Seïtáni must either retrace their steps, summon a taxi or stay at a few unofficial **rooms** establishments (summer only; try those of Athena Halepi, ☎22730 37861; ②) in Dhrakéï, and dine at one of four **taverna-kafenía**. In **KALLITHÉA**, 7km southwest, there's only a simple *psistariá* on the tiny square. From Kallithéa, a newer track (from beside the cemetery) and an older trail both lead up within 45 minutes to a spring, rural chapel and plane tree on the west flank of Kérkis, with path-only continuation for another thirty minutes to a pair of faintly frescoed cave-churches. **Panayía Makriní** stands at the mouth of a high, wide but shallow grotto, whose balcony affords terrific views. By contrast, **Ayía Triádha**, a ten-minute scramble overhead, has most of its structure made up of cave wall; just adjacent, another long, narrow, volcanic cavern can be explored with a torch some hundred metres into the mountain.

After these subterranean exertions, the closest spot for a swim is **Vársamo** (Válsamo) cove, 4km below Kallithéa and reached via a well-signposted if rough dirt road. The **beach** consists of multicoloured volcanic pebbles, with two caves to shelter in, and a basic but not especially cheap **taverna** (June–Sept) just inland, which also offers **rooms** (☎22730 37847; ①).

# Ikaría

**Ikaría**, a narrow, windswept landmass between Sámos and Mýkonos, is comparatively little visited and invariably underestimated by travel writers (like Lawrence Durrell) who haven't even shown up. The name supposedly derives from Icarus, who in legend fell into the sea just offshore after the wax bindings on his wings melted. (First Test Pilot Icarus has been adopted as the patron of the Greek Air Force – on reflection, a rather inauspicious choice.) For years the only substantial tourism was generated by a few **hot springs** on the southeast coast; since the early 1990s, however, tourist facilities of some quantity and quality have sprung up in and around Armenistís, the only resort of note. Overseas flights still don't land, as the airport at the northeast tip can't accommodate jets.

Ikaría, along with Thessaly, Lésvos and the Ionian islands, has traditionally been one of the **Greek Left**'s strongholds. This dates from long periods of right-wing domination in Greece, when (as in Byzantine times) the island was used as a place of **exile** for political dissidents, particularly Communists, who from 1946 to 1949 outnumbered native islanders. This house-arrest policy backfired, with the transportees (including Mikis Theodhorakis in

# IKARÍA & FOÚRNI

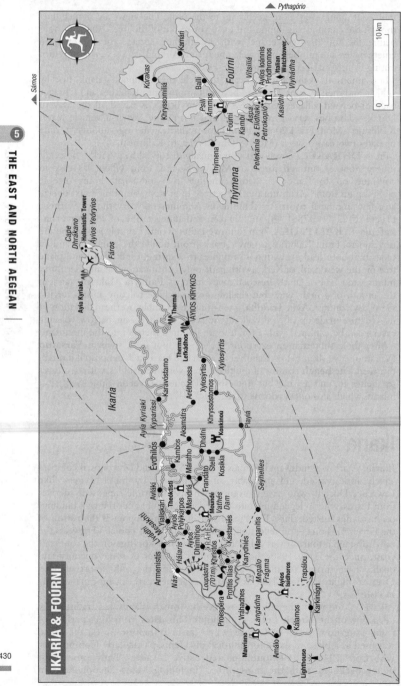

▲ Pythagório

▲ Sámos

▲ Syros, Mýkonos & Tínos

0  10 km

1946–47) favourably impressing their hosts as the most noble figures they had ever encountered, worthy of emulation. Earlier in the twentieth century, many Ikarians had emigrated to North America and ironically their capitalist remittances kept the island going for decades. Nowadays posters urge you to attend anti-racist summer camps on Páros or help fund a Zapatista teacher-training school in Chiapas. Athens has always reacted to such contrarian stances with punitive neglect, which only made the islanders more self-sufficient and idiosyncratic. Local pride dictates that outside opinion matters little, and many Ikarians – dressed in grubby, out-of-date American garb – exhibit a lack of obsequiousness and a studied **eccentricity**, which some visitors mistake for hostility.

For many the place is an acquired taste, contrasting strongly (for better or worse) with Sámos; heaps of construction waste, rusting machinery and automobile carcasses lend the place a scruffy air. Except for forested portions in the northwest (now fire-denuded near the shore), it's not a strikingly beautiful island, with most of the landscape being scrub-covered granite and schist put to use as building material. The mostly desolate south coast is overawed by steep cliffs, while the less sheer north face is furrowed by deep canyons creating hairpin road-bends extreme even by Greek-island standards. Neither are there many picturesque villages, since the rural stone-roofed houses are usually scattered next to their famous apricot orchards and vineyards, with the community store or *kafenío* often pointedly inconspicuous.

## Áyios Kírykos and around

A few weekly ferries on the Pireás–Cyclades–Sámos line call at the south-coast port and capital of **ÁYIOS KÍRYKOS**, about 2km southwest of the main thermal resort. Because of the spa trade, beds are at a premium in late summer; arriving in the evening from Sámos, accept any reasonable offers of rooms, or – if in a group – offers of a taxi-ride to the north coast, which should cost about €55 to Armenistís. A bus crosses the island from the seafront (July–Sept 10, Mon–Fri noon) to Évdhilos, usually changing vehicles there for Armenistís. The only conventional attraction is the 2007-refurbished **archeological museum** housed in a former school in the back streets (Tues–Sun 10am–1pm; €3), highlighting finds from Dhrákano (see p.432).

The spa of **Thérma**, 1km northeast of the port, saw its heyday in the 1960s, and now relies on a mostly elderly, health-service-subsidized clientele from July to early October. Of more general interest is the *spílio* or **natural sauna** on the shore (7.30am–noon & 5.30–8pm; €3), co-housed with plunge pools under the cave roof. Other good bets for informal soaks are the seaside, open-air pool (35–40°C) of the **Asklipioú hot springs**, reached by steps down from the Áyios Kírykos courthouse, or (better) the natural, shoreline hot springs at **Thérma Lefkádhos**, 2km southwest of Áyios Kírykos, where 50–58°C water mixes with the sea to a pleasant temperature inside a ring of giant volcanic boulders (signposted path down to the shore).

### Fáros and Dhrákano

A more conventional **beach** – the longest on the south coast – is at **Fáros**, 10.5km northeast of Áyios Kírykos along a good road, which also serves the airport. A colony of summer cottages shelters under tamarisks along the sand-and-gravel strand, with a reefy zone to cross before deep water. Three **tavernas** here are better than most in Áyios Kírykos; of these *Leonidas* (all year) is popular, but pricey, especially the seafood – *O Grigoris* is more dour but better in quality.

From a signposted point just inland from Fáros beach, a dirt track leads 2km to the trailhead for the round **Hellenistic watchtower** at **Cape Dhrákano**, much the oldest (and most impressive) ancient ruin on the island (closed for restoration), part of a much larger, now mostly crumbled fort extending half way to the cape and its pretty rustic chapel of **Áyios Yeóryios**. Right below this to the north, perfectly sheltered in most weathers, is a fantasy-image sand **beach**, with assorted rocks and islets off the cape-tip for contrast.

### Practicalities

Rare hydrofoils, the *Samos Spirit* and *Samos Sun* use the small east jetty; large ferries dock at the main west pier. Several **ATMs**, a **post office** on the road out of town and three **travel agents** – Icariada (℡22750 22277) for hydrofoils and catamarans, Roustas (℡22750 23691) for Hellenic Seaways or Saos, and Lakios (℡22750 22426) for *Samos Spirit* – round up the list of essentials. You can **rent motorbikes** and **cars** from Dolihi Tours/Lemy (℡22750 23230) and Glaros ℡22750 23637), both by the east jetty.

Among several **hotels**, most useful (and consistently open) is friendly, en-suite *Akti* (℡22750 22694, ⓦwww.pensionakti.gr; a/c; all year; ❸), on a knoll above the east quay, with wi-fi signal, fluent English-speaking management and views of Foúrni from the café-garden. Otherwise, directly behind the base of the large-ferry jetty and two blocks inland there's *Hotel Maria-Elena* (℡22750 22835; ❸), a large modern block in a quiet setting. With a car you might consider heading out to Fáros, where *Evon's Rooms* (℡22750 32580, ⓦwww.evonsrooms.com; ❸–❺) are attractively appointed, especially the pricier galleried top-floor units, and have private parking.

Restaurants are limited, seasonally operational (such as Iy Klimataria and Tzivaeri) and mostly uninspired; avoid exorbitant Stou Tsouri on the front and head instead for popular, back-street Filoti (all year), serving big pizzas and salads at loft seating. With a car, you're best off heading to Thérma for fish at *Avra* on the shore, or 5km west to **XYLOSÝRTI** where *Arodhou* (daily from 2.30pm, closed Mon low season), next to Ayía Paraskeví church, does excellent *mezédhes*; *Toula's* en route, by the main village church, is also worth a try for simpler ad-hoc dishes. On the front, *Casino* is the last remaining traditional **kafenío**; two summer **clubs** operate at the start of the road to Thermá Lefkádhos.

## Évdhilos and around

The twisting, 37-kilometre road from Áyios Kírykos to Évdhilos is one of the most hair-raising in the islands (especially as a passenger), and Ikaría's longitudinal ridge often wears a streamer of cloud, even when the rest of the Aegean is clear. Although **ÉVDHILOS** is the island's second town and a more regular ferry stop on the Sámos–Cyclades–Pireás line, it's less equipped to deal with visitors than Áyios Kírykos. Best of three **hotels** is *Kerame* (℡22750 31426, ⓦwww.atheras-kerame.gr; ❹), with studio units 1km east overlooking the eponymous beach. A **post office** on the through road and a pair of **ATMs** are also useful. The **boat-ticket** trade is divided between agencies Blue Nice (℡22750 31990) and Roustas (℡22750 32293); you can **rent cars** from MAV (℡22750 31354). Among numerous harbourside sweet shops, *kafenía* and **restaurants**, *Coralli* on the west quay is the best value, but for more interesting food head either 1km west of the harbour to **FÝTEMA** hamlet. Here the more reliable of two **tavernas**, on the rocky shore beyond the football pitch, is welcoming ⚓ *Kalypso* (daily May–Oct, by arrangement otherwise on ℡22750 31387), with excellent, reasonable vegetable dishes and fish. Alternatively, 9k

▲ Kámbos beach

southeast and inland in lushly set **PÉRA ARETHOÚSSA** is local-meat-and-rabbit specialist *Iy Plaka* (daily peak season, weekend dinners otherwise).

**KÁMBOS**, 1.5km west of Fýtema, offers a small hilltop **museum** with finds from nearby ancient Oinoe; the twelfth-century church of **Ayía Iríni** stands adjacent, with column stumps and mosaic patches of a fourth-century basilica defining the entry courtyard. Lower down still are the sparse ruins of a **Byzantine palace** used to house exiled nobles, signposted as "odeion", which earlier structure it encloses. An unmarked track below the palace leads to a 250-metre-long sandy **beach** with a *kantína* and sunbeds. *Rooms Dhionysos* (☎22750 31300 or 22750 31688; ❷), on the paved drive to the west end of the beach, are available from the green-doored store run by Vassilis Kambouris, who also acts as the unofficial and enthusiastic tourism officer for this part of Ikaría.

**AVLÁKI**, the next coastal settlement west, offers two decent **tavernas**, the more distinctive, 300m up the road towards Theóktisti, being fair-priced ☀ *Tou Ilia* (June–Sept daily, otherwise weekends). The only real ouzerí on the north coast, it's very proud of its own-sourced (or -fished) raw materials, and has a lovely sea-view courtyard.

### Inland to the south coast

From Kámbos, a twisty road leads up 4km – as does an easier road from Avláki, in 3km – to Ikaría's outstanding medieval monument, the **monastery of Theóktisti**, looking over pines to the coast from its perch under a chaos of slanted granite slabs (under one of which is tucked the much-photographed chapel of **Theoskepastí**). The *katholikón* features damaged but worthwhile naïve frescoes dated to 1688; there's also a pleasant *kafenío* on site. For proper meals nearby, head 2km south to **MÁRATHO**, where unreliably open *Marinakis* (check on ☎22750 31182) purveys the Ikarian version of "slow food". At **PIYÍ**, on the Kámbos–Theóktisti road, stands the organic ☀ *Karimalis Winery* (☎22750 31151, ⓦwww.ikarianwine.gr), open for tours and also offering several restored ancient, family-sized cottages as accommodation by the week, during which cooking courses and wine seminars are offered.

By following the road heading south and inland from Évdhilos's main church, signposted for Manganítis, you first reach, after 4km, **AKAMÁTRA**, arguably the most conventionally attractive of the hill villages, with a pair of nocturnal **tavernas**. Some 11km further is the marked side-track to the Byzantine castle of **Koskiná** (Nikariás). Any vehicle can cover the 2km to the start of a short walk up to the tenth-century fort, perched on a distinctive conical hill, with an arched gateway and vaulted chapel incorporating ancient masonry.

Beyond this turning, the paved route creeps over the island watershed before dropping steadily towards the south coast; with your own vehicle this is a quicker and much less curvy way back to Áyios Kírykos compared to going via Karavóstomo. It's an eminently scenic route worth taking for its own sake, the narrow road threading corniche-like through oaks at the pass, and then olives at Playiá village on the steep southern slope of the island. Out to sea the islands of Pátmos and Dhonoússa are generally visible, and on really clear days Náxos and Amorgós as well. The principal potential detour, 2km past the castle turning, is the road right (west) to the secluded pebble beach of **Seyhélles** ("Seychelles"), the best on this generally inhospitable coast, with the final approach by ten-minute hike.

## Armenistís and around

Most visitors congregate at **ARMENISTÍS**, 51km from Áyios Kírykos via Évdhilos, and for good reason: this little resort lies below Ikaría's greatest (if slightly fire-diminished) forest, with two enormous, sandy **beaches** battered by seasonal surf – **Livádhi** and **Mesaktí** – five and fifteen-minutes' walk east respectively, the latter with several reed-roofed *kantínas*. The sea between here and Mýkonos is the windiest patch in the Aegean, generating a fairly consistent summer surf. The waves, which attract Athenian boogie-boarders, are complicated by strong lateral currents, and regular summer drownings have (at Livádhi) prompted a lifeguard service and a string of safety buoys.

Armenistís itself is spectacularly set, facing northeast along the length of Ikaría towards sun- and moonrise, with Mount Kérkis on Sámos visible on a clear day. A dwindling proportion of older, schist-roofed houses and ex-warehouses, plus boats hauled up in a central sandy cove, lend the place the air of a Cornish fishing village, though in fact it started out as a smuggler's depot, with warehouses but no dwellings. Despite an ongoing building boom just west, it remains manageable, even if gentrification (and a package presence) set in long ago. Just east of Mesaktí, the fishing settlement of **YIALISKÁRI**, with a few more facilities (including *pensions* taking the summer overflow), looks out past pines to a picturesque jetty church.

### Accommodation

There are easily a score of *dhomátia* in the Armenistís area, as well as three **hotels**, mostly working a May-to-September season. Among the latter, the *Erofili Beach*, at the entrance to town (℡22750 71058, @www.erofili.gr; ❻), is considered about the island's best, though the common area and pool perched dramatically over Livádhi beach impress more than the rooms. On the western edge of Armenistís, good-value ⚓ *Daidalos* (℡22750 71390, @www .daidaloshotel.gr; ❹) has a more artistic flavour, with another eyrie-pool, unusually appointed rooms and a shady breakfast terrace. Among **rooms**, the *Kirki* by the *Erofili Beach* (℡22750 71254 or ask at *Dhefini* taverna; ❸) is spartan but en suite, with large private balconies and sea views; along the shore lane, *Paskhalia Rooms* (℡22750 71302; Easter–Oct; ❷) are on the small side but with air conditioning, TV and fridge, while at the far end of Livádhi beach, ☘ *Valeta Apartments* (☎22750 71252, @www.valeta.gr; May–Oct; ❹) offer the best standard and setting outside of the hotels, with both studios and quads.

### Eating, drinking and nightlife

There are five full-service **tavernas** in Armenistís proper, of which two have a consistently good reputation. *Dhelfíni*, its terrace hovering above the fishing-boat cove, is a cheap-ish-and-cheerful favourite – come early or very late for a table, and a mix of grills or *mayireftá*. *Paskhalia* (aka *Vlahos* after the helpful managing family), under the eponymous rooms, serves more elaborate food at its sea-view terrace, and is a reliable venue for breakfast and works late into the season. At the far end of Livádhi, *Atsahas* is acceptable as a beach taverna, with generous, slightly oily vegetarian platters. Of two *zaharoplastía*, go for ☘ *Paradhosiaka Glyka* (*Kioulanis*), featuring addictive *karydhópita* with goats'-milk, mastic-flavoured ice cream.

**Yialiskári** offers another pair of tavernas above the boat-launching slips: ☘ *Kelaris* (aka *tis Eleftherias*) tops for well-executed *mayireftá* and the freshest fish locally, and nearby, German-co-managed *Symposio*, good for non-stodgy *mayireftá*, organic wine and meat grills. Small **summer-clubs** like *Casmir* and *Pleiades* operate in the river reeds behind Livádhi, though most nightlife involves extended sessions in **café-bars** at Yialiskári, the north end of Armenistís quay – or up in Ráhes (see p.436).

### Information, transport – and getting away

The only **internet** café is Internet Point, at the west edge of the resort. There are at least three **scooter/mountain-bike rental** agencies; among five

### Walking in western Ikaría

Despite bulldozers and forest fires having reduced the number of attractive possibilities, **walking** between Ráhes and both coasts on old paths is a favourite visitor activity. A locally produced, accurate map-guide, *The Round of Ráhes on Foot*, shows most asphalt roads, tracks and trails in the west of the island, as well as a **loop-hike** taking in the best of the Ráhes villages. The well-marked route sticks partly to surviving paths; the authors suggest a full day for the circuit, with ample rests, though total walking time won't exceed six hours. The highlight is the section from Khristós to Kastaniés, which takes in the Hárakos ravine with its Spanédhon watermill.

More **advanced outings** involve descending the Hálaris canyon to Nás, or crossing the island to Manganítis via Ráhes. In either case you'll still need to follow the first portion of the "Round of Ráhes", beginning at the Livádhi river bridge by the nightclubs, climbing up to Áyios Dhimítrios within eighty minutes and to Khristós within 1hr 45min. From Khristós a well-marked trail, broad and fitted with wooden railings in places, leads down in forty minutes to the massive nineteenth-century Loupástra bridge in the Hálaris canyon. Backtracking slightly, a narrower path follows the canyon's right bank initially downstream, then climbing back to Áyios Dhimítrios (40min), with another left-and-down option just before towards Nás (another 40min).

Thus those wishing to traverse across Ikaría are best advised to keep on a "Round of Ráhes" sub-route from Khristós to Karydhiés, from where a historic path crosses the lunar Ammoudhiá uplands before dropping spectacularly southeast to Manganítis on the south coast, a generous half-day's outing from Armenistís. Alternatively, with an initial vehicle transfer, you can descend from Áyios Isídhoros monastery to either Karkinágri or Trapálou on the south coast.

**car-rental** outlets, Aventura (☎22750 71117) and Dolihi Tours/Lemy (☎22750 71122) are the most prominent, with branches for drop-offs in Évdhilos and Áyios Kirykos respectively. They're handy for ferry departures (tickets from Nas Travel, co-housed with Lemy; ☎22750 71396) towards Sámos at an ungodly hour. Indeed, getting away when you need to is problematic, since taxis and buses can prove elusive – with the exception of the fairly frequent (late June to early Sept) shuttle van linking Armenistís with Yialiskári, Nás and Ráhes. Theoretically, long-distance **buses** head for Évdhilos twice daily (once Sat/Sun) mid-July to early September; Áyios Kírykos has only one through service year-round in the morning, though this fills with school kids in term-time. If you've a ferry to catch, it's more sensible to prebook a **taxi**: a list of all drivers' phones is posted at the entrance to Armenistís.

### The Ráhes villages

Armenistís was originally the port of four inland hamlets – Áyios Dhimítrios, Áyios Polýkarpos, Kastaniés and Khristós – collectively known as **Ráhes**. Curiously, these already served as "hill station" resorts during the 1920s and 1930s, with three hotels and the only tourism on the island, being relatively easy to reach by boat from Piraeus (and then mule-ride uphill). Despite the modern, paved access roads through the pines, the settlements retain a certain Shangri-La quality, with older residents speaking a positively Homeric dialect. On an island not short of foibles, **KHRISTÓS** (Khristós Rahón in full) is particularly strange inasmuch as most locals sleep until 11am or so, shop until about 4pm, then have another nap until 8pm, whereupon they rise and spend most of the night shopping, eating and drinking, in particular excellent home-brewed **wine** traditionally kept in goatskins. In fact all villages west of Évdhilos adhere to this schedule, defying edicts to bring them into line with the rest of Greece. The local **festival**, with merrymaking and (it is said) controlled substances a-plenty, is on August 6, though better ones take place the same day at Stávlos, or at Áyios Isídhoros monastery (May 14). Whit Monday at Kastaniés is fairly typical of minor observances: it lasts from 11pm until 3am, with overdone goat *soúvla* and rough wine on sale, and locals dancing free-style *harsilamás* to a three-man acoustic band.

On or near the schist-paved, pedestrianized *agorá* of Khristós, there's a **post office**, plenty of rustic **bars** (4pm–3am) and a few sweet shops. In accordance with the prevailing nocturnalism, **eating** lunch here is a non-starter; *Kapilio* on the pedestrian zone is a good, inexpensive carnivorous supper option, though *Platanos* just downhill in **ÁYIOS DHIMÍTRIOS** is reckoned the best locally, while *Aoratos* bar-restaurant is the place to be in **ÁYIOS POLÝKARPOS**.

### Nás

Following altercations with locals, hippies and beachside naturists have shifted themselves 3km west of Armenistís by paved road to **NÁS**, a tree- (and rough-camper-) clogged river canyon ending at a deceptively sheltered sand-and-pebble beach. This little bay is almost completely enclosed by weirdly sculpted rock formations, but for the same reasons as at Mesaktí it's unwise to swim outside the cove's natural limits – marked here also with a line of buoys. The crumbling foundations of the fifth-century BC temple of **Artemis Tavropoleio** (Artemis in Bull-Headdress) overlook the permanent deep pool at the mouth of the river. Back at the top of the stone-paved stairs leading down to the beach from the road are several **tavernas**, most of them offering rooms. Among **accommodation**, the rambling *Artemis* (☎22750 71485; ❷ rooms, ❸ studios) overlooks the river canyon, while ✴ *Thea* (☎22750 71491; ❷) faces out to sea. The latter offers the most accomplished cooking in the area, working weekends October to May as well, with lots of vegetarian options like *soufikó* (the local ratatouille) and pumpkin-filled *pítta*.

### The southwest coast

With your own transport, you can visit several villages at the southwest tip of the island. **VRAHÁDHES**, with two *kafenía* and a natural-balcony setting, makes a good first or last stop on a tour. A sharp drop below it, the impact of the empty convent of **Mavrianoú** lies mostly in its setting amid gardens overlooking the sea. Nearby **AMÁLO** has two summer-only tavernas; just inland, **Langádha** is not a village but a hidden valley containing an enormous *exohikó kéndro* (rural taverna) that hosts an August 14–15 *paniyíri*, the island's biggest, once dubbed by an Athens newspaper *Iy Panayía toú Raver*.

It's a sturdy motorbike that reaches somewhat anticlimactic **KARKINÁGRI**, at the base of cliffs near the southern extremity of Ikaría. You'll find two sleepy, seasonal **tavernas** and two **rooms** establishments near the jetty. Before the road in was opened (the continuation to Manganítis and Áyios Kírykos has been abandoned at a difficult-to-dynamite rock-face), the village's only easy link with the outside world was by ferry or *kaïki*. There is still a thrice-weekly post-and-shopping boat from Karkinágri (via Manganítis; Mon, Wed & Fri at 7am, returning from Áyios Kírykos at 1pm), an invaluable facility if you've just made a trek across the island ending here.

## Satellite islands: Thýmena and Foúrni

The straits between Sámos and Ikaría are speckled with a mini-archipelago of several islets – once haunted by pirates from various corners of the Mediterranean – of which Thýmena and Foúrni are inhabited. Most westerly **Thýmena** has one tiny hillside settlement; *kaïkia* call regularly at the quay below on their way between Ikaría or Sámos and Foúrni, but there are no tourist attractions, save one large beach south of "town". **FOÚRNI** itself is home to a huge fishing fleet and one of the more thriving boatyards in the Aegean; thanks in part to these its population (officially c.1600) is stable, unlike so many small Greek islands.

The small **ferry** *Samos Spirit* and *kaïki Samos Sun* are based much of the week at Foúrni, making early-morning shopping-and-post departures to Sámos and Ikaría, returning in the afternoon. Larger main-line ferries that call periodically every few days are likewise run for the benefit of the islanders. The only way to visit Foúrni on a **day-trip** is by using one of the several weekly morning departures of the *Samos Sun* from Áyios Kírykos, or unreliable excursions from Órmos Marathokámbou on Sámos.

Apart from remote **Khryssomiliá** hamlet in the north, reached by the island's longest (18km) road, Foúrni's inhabitants are concentrated in the **port** and **Kambí** hamlet just south. The harbour community is larger than it seems from the sea, with a friendly ambience reminiscent of 1970s Greece; the historical pirate connection is reflected in the municipality's official name, *Foúrni Korseón* (Fourni of the Corsairs).

### Foúrni port practicalities

The central "high street", field-stoned and mulberry-shaded, ends well inland at a little **platía** with two giant plane trees, a bakery (one of two) and popular *Kafenio Iy Dhrosia*; between them stands a Hellenistic sarcophagus found in a nearby field. Nearby there's a **post office** and stand-alone **ATM**, plus several well-stocked shops and two outlets for **scooter hire**. The bakeries sell the famous local **thyme honey**: strongly flavoured, very expensive and available after any rainy winter.

Manolis and Patra Markakis (☎22750 51268, ⓦwww.fourni-patrasrooms .gr), immediately left of the *kaïki* quay, manage popular **accommodation** options, ranging from wood-floored, antique-bed rooms, some with balconies (❶), to fourteen superb 🏠 hillside apartments, most sleeping up to four, in a tiered complex (❸). When they're full, plump for *Bilios Resort*, apartments high up the south hillside (☎22750 51113, ⓔbilioshotel@axiotis-group.com; ❸), or the 2007-built *Archipelagos Hotel* by the fishing port (☎22750 51250, ⓦwww .archipelagoshotel.gr; ❹), with quality fittings in its eighteen doubles and suites and an on-site restaurant during summer.

Waterfront **tavernas**, sadly, have seen their prices climb and quality dip sharply, with the exception of *Ta Dhelfinakia*, ace for *kalamária* (the local speciality *astakós* or Aegean lobster is now pretty well out of reach price-wise); generally you're better off on the mulberry high street at either *To Koutouki tou Psarrakou*, the local characters' hangout doing good *mayireftá* and roasts accompanied by Cretan bulk wine and liqueur from the Peloponnese, or *Iy Kali Kardhia*, serving similar food just past the sarcophagus square. For breakfast and desserts, repair to the tamarisk terrace of *To Arhondiko tis Kyras Kokonas*, under the *Markakis* inn. There's surprisingly lively **nightlife** at a handful of music cafés and ouzerís around the port end of the mulberry high street.

## Southern Foúrni

A fifteen-minute walk south from the primary school on a flagstone lane, skirting the cemetery and then slipping over the restored-windmill ridge, brings you to **KAMBÍ**, a scattered community overlooking a pair of sandy, tamarisk-shaded coves. There are two cheap and sustaining **tavernas**: ramshackle, 1970s-style *Kambi (Sklavos)*, with tables on the sand, good fish soup but somewhat erratic pricing, and slightly more accomplished *O Yiorgos*, just up a valley inland. If you fancy **staying**, try *Studios Rena* (☎22750 51364; ❷), stacked in three tiers on the north hillside, or *Buzakos Apartments*, up the valley past *O Yiorgos* (☎697 79 45 877; ❷).

A path system starting at Kambí's last house continues south around the headland to other, more secluded bays of varying sizes and beach consistencies, which like Kambí cove are favourite anchorages for passing yachts, but unlike Kambí have substantial summer communities of rough campers and naturists. In order of appearance they are sand-and-pebble **Áspa** (15min along, with a tiny spring seeping from the rocks just before), **Pelekanía** (5min more, brackish well) and (5min further still) **Elidháki** – both of these coarse pebble, the latter also with paved road access. The trail is slippery and steep just before Áspa; some may prefer to arrive by motorbike as far as Elidháki, or on a taxi-boat service. The side-road serving Elidháki from the main island ridge-road also has an option for **Petrokopió** (Marmári) cove, named after its role as a quarry for ancient Ephesus in Asia Minor. The quarry itself with obvious chisel-marks, and abandoned half-worked stones down by the shore, proves impressive; the beach is made of the same stone.

The main ridge-road drops to the hamlet and monastery of **Áyios Yiánnis Pródhromos**, 8km from the port (no facilities). From behind the unreliable monastery spring, an obvious path goes uphill then down, within fifteen minutes, to secluded **Kasídhi**: pristine (except for occasional goats), deserted and clothing-optional. Those on a scooter may prefer sandy, popular **Vlyhádha**, a double cove with its own 1300-metre access track, or less crowded, sand-and-fine-gravel **Vitsiliá** on the east coast, again with its own paved track access beside the Vlyhádha turning. Like most remoter Foúrni beaches, none of these coves have amenities.

### Northern Foúrni

Heading north from Foúrni harbour via steps, then path, you'll find a pair of slightly sullied beaches. **Psilí Ámmos**, in front of a derelict fish-processing plant and equally defunct café at the end with tamarisks, is superior to **Kálamos** further along, dominated by a military watchpoint; both now have track access and (in the former case) a fishermen's jetty.

In the extreme north of the island, remote, time-warped **KHRYSSOMILIÁ** is not very tourist-friendly, with a scrappy beach, little accommodation and just one listless **taverna**. The rough road there is finally being paved (taxi boats and the *Samos Sun* call here too), but you're still better off pointing a rental scooter towards **KAMÁRI**, just over halfway along – its beach still isn't up to much, though *Almyra* here is the most accomplished out-of-town **taverna** on the island. Without transport, it's possible to **walk** between town and Kamári on the old *kalderími*, which goes via the ridge-top monastery of Panayía.

# Híos

"Craggy Híos", as **Homer** aptly described his putative birthplace, has a turbulent history and a strong identity. This large island has always been prosperous: in medieval times through the export of **mastic resin** – a trade controlled by Genoese overlords between 1346 and 1566 – and later by the Ottomans, who dubbed the place Sakız Adası ("Resin Island"). Since union with Greece in 1912, several shipping dynasties have emerged here, continuing to generate wealth. Participation in maritime life is widespread, with someone in almost every family spending time in the merchant navy.

Unfortunately, the island has suffered more than its share of **catastrophes** since the 1800s. The Ottomans perpetrated their most infamous, if not their worst, anti-revolutionary atrocity here in March 1822, massacring 30,000 Hiots and enslaving or exiling even more. In 1881, much of Híos was destroyed by a violent earthquake, and throughout the 1980s the island's natural beauty was compromised by devastating forest fires, compounding the effect of generations of tree-felling by boat-builders. Over half of the majestic pines are now gone, with substantial patches of woods persisting only in the far northeast and the centre of Híos (though reafforestation is beginning to take effect).

For many years the more powerful ship-owning dynasts, local government and the military authorities discouraged **tourism**, but a 1980s shipping crisis and the saturation of other, more obviously "marketable" islands eroded resistance. Yet two decades after the first charters arrived, there are still scarcely five thousand guest beds on Híos, mostly in the capital or the nearby beach resorts of Karfás and Ayía Ermióni. You often get the feeling, as an outsider, of intruding on the workings of a private club which just happens to have an "open" day. Although the airport can now safely accommodate jets, there are still no direct flights from most countries, including Britain. Despite this, various foreigners have discovered a Híos beyond its rather daunting port capital: fascinating **villages**, important **Byzantine monuments** and a respectable, if remote, complement of **beaches**. The local scene has a distinctly modern flavour – courtesy of numerous returned Greek-Americans and Greek-Canadians – and English is widely spoken.

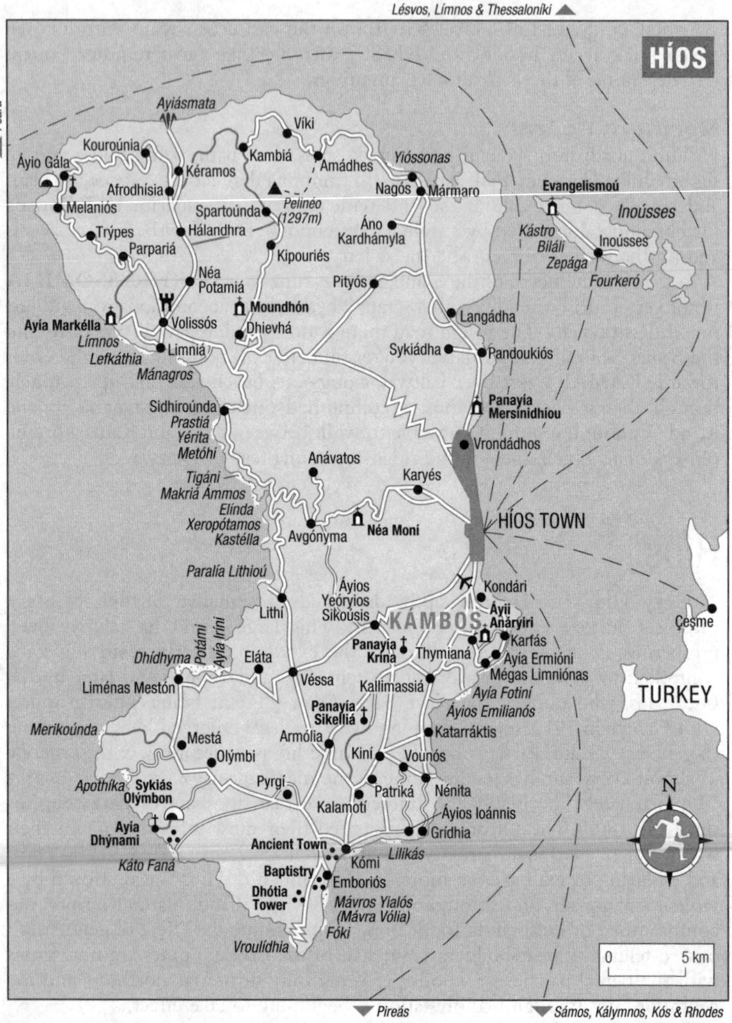
Lésvos, Límnos & Thessaloníki
HÍOS
Psará
Ayiásmata
Víki
Kouroúnia
Kambiá
Amádhes
Yióssonas
Áyio Gála
Kéramos
Nagós
Mármaro
Afrodhísia
Evangelismoú
Melaniós
Spartoúnda
Pelinéo (1297m)
Inoússes
Trýpes
Hálandhra
Áno Kardhámyla
Kástro
Biláli
Zepága
Inoússes
Parpariá
Kipouriés
Fourkeró
Néa Potamiá
Pityós
Moundhón
Langádha
Ayía Markélla
Volissós
Dhievhá
Límnos
Lefkáthia
Limniá
Sykiádha
Pandoukiós
Mánagros
Sidhiroúnda
Panayía Mersinidhíou
Prastiá
Yérita
Vrondádhos
Metóhi
Anávatos
Tigáni
Karyés
Makriá Ámmos
Elínda
HÍOS TOWN
Xeropótamos
Néa Moní
Kastélla
Avgónyma
Paralía Lithioú
Áyios Yeóryios Sikoúsis
Kondári
Lithí
Áyii Anáryiri
KÁMBOS
Çeşme
Potámi
Ayía Iríni
Karfás
Panayía Krína
Thymianá
Ayía Ermióni
Dhídhyma
Eláta
Mégas Limniónas
Liménas Mestón
Véssa
Kallimassiá
Ayía Fotiní
TURKEY
Panayía Sikelliá
Áyios Emilianós
Merikoúnda
Katarráktis
Mestá
Armólia
Olýmbi
Kiní
Vounós
Apothíka
Sykiás Olýmbon
Pyrgí
Patriká
Nénita
N
Kalamotí
Áyios Ioánnis
Ayía Dhýnami
Grídhia
Ancient Town
Lilikás
Káto Faná
Kómi
Baptistry
Emboriós
Dhótia Tower
Mávros Yialós (Mávra Vólia)
Fóki
Vroulídhia
0
5 km
Pireás
Sámos, Kálymnos, Kós & Rhodes

## Híos Town

**HÍOS TOWN**, a brash, concrete-laced commercial centre with little predating the 1881 quake, will come as a shock after modest island capitals elsewhere. Yet in many ways it's the most satisfactory of the east Aegean ports, with a large and fascinating **marketplace**, several **museums**, an **old quarter** and some good, authentic **tavernas**. Although a sprawling place of about 30,000 souls, most things of interest lie within a few hundred metres of the water, fringed by Leofóros Egéou.

### Arrival, information and transport

**Ferries** and *kaïkia* dock at various points along the northerly Neoríon quay, as mapped opposite. The poky **airport** (two car-hire booths) lies 3km south along the coast at **Kondári**, a €4 taxi-ride away; otherwise any blue urban **bus** labelled "ΚΟΝΤΑΡΙ ΚΑΡΦΑΣ" should pass the conspicuous stop opposite the airport, bound for the town terminal on the north side of the central park. **Ferry agents** cluster along the north end of waterfront Egéou and its continuation Neoríon: NEL (℡22710 23971) is a few paces south of the KTEL station; Mihalakis Travel just behind (℡22710 22034) does Hellenic Seaways and LANE; Triaina (℡22710 29292) represents Saos Ferries; Travelshop (℡22710 43981) handles the local ferry to Psará; Kanaris Tours (℡22710 42490) represents the Turkish afternoon boat to Çeşme (Turkey); while Sunrise Tours at Kanári 28 (℡22710 23558) is the central agency for the faster morning boat to Turkey and the most regular boat to Inoússes. The municipal **tourist office** (April–Oct daily 7am–8pm; Nov–March Mon–Fri 7am–3.30pm; ℡22710 44389) is at Kanári 18; commercial **maps** and an extremely limited stock of English-language **books** are found at Newsstand, at the first "kink" in Egéou. The most reliable **internet** café is Enter, just seaward of the *Fedra Hotel*. The **post office** is on Omírou; **ATMs** are legion.

Long-distance **KTEL buses** leave from just behind the passenger waiting-room on Egéou. While services to the south of Híos are adequate, those bound elsewhere are almost nonexistent, and to explore properly you'll need to rent a

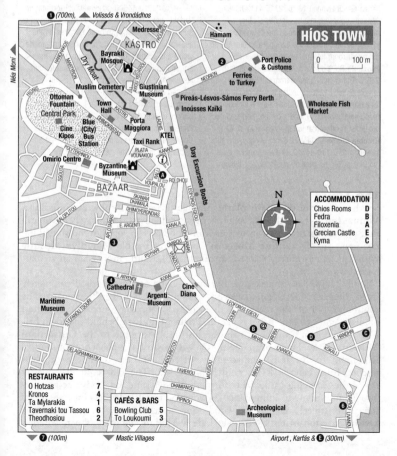

powerful motorbike or a car, or share a **taxi** (bright red here, not grey as in most of Greece; the main rank is on the central platía). Two independent or small-chain **car-rental** agencies sit at Evyenías Handhrí 5–7, behind the eyesore *Chandris Hotel*; of these, Vassilakis/Reliable Rent a Car (☎22710 29300 or 694 43 34 898), with a branch at Mégas Limniónas (☎22710 31728), is recommended. **Parking** is impossible except near the archeological museum, and in the moat west of the *kástro*.

## Accommodation

Híos Town has a fair quantity of affordable **accommodation**, rarely full. Most places line the front or the perpendicular alleys and parallel streets behind, and almost all are plagued by traffic noise to some degree – we've listed the more peaceful establishments.

**Chios Rooms** Egéou 110, cnr Kokáli ☎22710 20198 or 697 28 33 841, ⊛www .chiosrooms.gr. Don and Dina's lovingly restored tile- or wood-floored, high-ceilinged rooms, some en suite and relatively quiet for a seafront location. Best is the penthouse "suite" with private terrace. ❷

**Fedra** Mihaïl Livanoú 13 ☎22710 41130. Well-appointed pension in a nineteenth-century mansion, with stone arches in the downstairs winter bar; in summer the bar operates outside, so get a rear room to avoid nocturnal noise. ❹

**Filoxenia** Roïdhou 2, cnr Voupálou 8 ☎22710 22813. Better than it looks from outside, this rambling, early 1900s building is wrapped around an atrium-airshaft. Room furnishings – including round double beds, TV, and a/c – are part-updated; breakfast is offered at the mezzanine level. ❸

**Grecian Castle** Bella Vista shore avenue, en route to airport ☎22710 44740, ⊛www.greciancastle .gr. Occupying the shell of an old factory, this is

Híos Town's top-rated (4-star) digs. Lovely grounds and a sea-view pool, but the smallish main-wing rooms, despite their marble floors, wood ceilings and bug screens, don't justify their ❻ rates; the rear "villa" suites at ❼ are more pleasant.

**Kyma** East end of Evyenías Handhrí ☎22710 44500, ⓔkyma@chi.forthnet.gr. Variable hotel rooms in a Neoclassical mansion or a modern extension, with huge terraces on the sea-facing side; most units have new handmade wood-and-leather furniture, though a few rooms are still antiquated. But owner Theo's splendid service and big breakfasts (in a salon with painted ceilings) really make the place. The old wing saw a critical moment in modern Greek history in Sept 1922, when Colonel Nikolaos Plastiras commandeered it as his HQ after the Greek defeat in Asia Minor, and announced the deposition of King Constantine I. B&B ❹

## The Town

South and east of the **main platía**, officially Plastíra but known universally as **Vounakíou**, extends the marvellously lively tradesmen's **bazaar**, where you can find everything from parrots to cast-iron woodstoves. Opposite the Vounakíou taxi rank, the **"Byzantine Museum"**, occupying the old **Mecidiye Mosque** with its leaning minaret (closed for renovation), is little more than an archeological warehouse.

Until the 1881 earthquake, the Byzantine-Genoese **Kástro** stood completely intact; thereafter developers razed the seaward walls, filled in the moat to the south and sold off the real estate thus created along the waterfront. The most dramatic entry to the citadel is via the **Porta Maggiora** behind the town hall. The top floor of a medieval mansion just inside is home to the **Giustiniani Museum** (Tues–Sun 8.30am–3pm; €2), with a satisfying collection of unusual icons and twelve fourteenth-century frescoes of Old Testament prophets rescued from Panayía Krína church (see p.447). The old residential quarter inside the surviving castle walls, formerly the Muslim and Jewish neighbourhoods (now home to immigrants), is worth a brief wander, less for the sake of the main street's dilapidated wood- and plaster-houses than for assorted **Ottoman monuments**. These include a Muslim cemetery, the minaretless

Bayraklı mosque, two ruined hamams – one being restored – a *medresse* in the courtyard of Áyios Yeóryios church and several inscribed **fountains**, the most ornate of which – with four facets – stands outside opposite the central park.

Further afield, three other museums beckon. The **Maritime Museum** at Stefánou Tsoúri 20 (Mon–Sat 10am–1pm; free) consists principally of model ships and nautical oil paintings, all rather overshadowed by the mansion containing them. In the foyer are enshrined the knife and glass-globe grenade of Admiral Kanaris, who partly avenged the 1822 massacre by ramming and sinking the Ottoman fleet's flagship, thus dispatching Admiral Kara Ali, architect of the atrocities. The central **Argenti Folklore Museum** (Mon–Thurs 8am–2pm, Fri 8am–2pm & 5–7.30pm, Sat 8am–12.30pm; €2), on the top floor of the Koráï Library at Koráï 2, features ponderous genealogical portraits of the endowing family, an adjoining wing of costumes and rural impedimenta, plus multiple replicas of Delacroix's *Massacre at Hios*, a painting which did much to arouse sympathy for the cause of Greek independence.

The **archeological museum** on Mihálon (June–Aug daily 8am–7pm; Sept–May Tues–Sun 8.30am–3pm; €3) has a wide-ranging, well-lit collection from Neolithic to Roman times. Highlights include limestone column bases from the Apollo temple at Faná in the shape of lions' claws; numerous statuettes and reliefs of Cybele (an Asiatic goddess especially honoured here); Archaic faience miniatures from Emborió in the shape of a cat, a hawk and a flautist; a terracotta dwarf riding a boar; and figurines (some with articulated limbs) of *hierodouloi* or sacred prostitutes, presumably from an Aphrodite shrine. Most famous is an inscribed edict of Alexander the Great from 322 BC, setting out relations between himself and the Hiots.

## Eating

**Eating out** in Híos Town can be better than the fast-food joints, touristy fake ouzerís and multiple *barákia* on the waterfront would initially suggest. Brusque service, however, is near-universal – brace yourself.

**O Hotzas** Yeoryíou Kondhýli 3, cnr Stefánou Tsoúri. Oldest and most popular (thanks to its summer garden) taverna in town, with fourth-generation chef Ioannis Linos presiding. Menu (and quality) varies seasonally, but expect a mix of vegetarian dishes and *lahanodolmádhes*, sausages, baby fish and *mydhopílafo* (rice and mussels) accompanied by own-brand ouzo or retsina. Dinner only; closed Sun.

**Kronos** Filíppou Aryéndi 2, cnr Aplotariás. The island's best, and own-made ice cream, purveyed since 1929. Limited seating or takeaway. Noon–midnight.

**Ta Mylarakia** At the four restored windmills in Tambákika district, just before the hospital ☎22710 40412. A large if erratically priced seafood selection, every kind of Hiot ouzo (Tetteri Penindari is the best) and limited seating at the

island's most romantic waterside setting. Reservations advisable in summer. Dinner daily all year, lunch also Oct–April.

**Tavernaki tou Tassou** Stávrou Livanoú 8, Bélla Vísta district. Superb all-rounder with creative salads, better-than-average bean dishes, *dolmádhes*, snails, good chips, a strong line in seafood, good barrel wine, and maybe a *mastíha* digestif on the house. Open lunch and supper most of the year, with good service, seaview summer garden seating and a heated gazebo for winter.

**Theodhosiou** Neoríon 33. The oldest of three ouzerís on this quay, occupying a domed, arcaded building. A fair amount of meat grills for this type of place, plus various seafood standards. Generally, avoid fried platters in favour of grilled or boiled ones. Dinner only; closed Sun.

## Drinking, nightlife and entertainment

Some 1400 local university students help keep things lively, especially along the waterfront between the two "kinks" in Egéou. Shooting **pool** is big here; many bars have several tables. One, *Bowling Club* at the east end of Egéou, has seven

**bowling** alleys as well. **Film** fans are well served by Cine Kipos (late June to early Sept), in one corner of the central park, with quality/art-house first-run screenings; from October the action shifts to Cine Diana, under the eponymous hotel. On the south side of the park, the Omirio cultural centre and events hall hosts changing exhibitions; big-name (foreign) acts often come here after Athens concerts. Just off Aplotariás in a converted warehouse, *To Loukoumi* is another occasional events venue but mostly functions as a Nov–April day-café and nocturnal bar (shut Sun).

## ⑤ Beaches near Híos Town

The locals swim at tiny pebble coves near **Vrondádhos**, north of Híos Town, or from the grubby town beach in **Bélla Vísta**, but really the closest decent option is at **Karfás**, 7km south beyond the airport and served by frequent blue buses. Most large Hiot resort **hotels** are planted here, to the considerable detriment of the 500-metre-long beach itself, sandy only at the south end. The main bright spot is a unique **pension**, ☀ *Markos' Place* (☎ 22710 31990 or 697 32 39 706, ⓦ www.marcos-place.gr; April–Nov; ❷), occupying the disestablished monastery of Áyios Yeóryios and Áyios Pandelímon, on the hillside south of the bay. Markos Kostalas has created a peaceful, leafy environment much loved by special-activity groups. Guests are lodged in the former pilgrims' cells, with a kitchen available or superior breakfasts provided by arrangement; individuals are more than welcome, as are families (in two quads), though reservations are advisable and the minimum stay is four days.

The shoreline **restaurants** aren't brilliant; it's better to strike inland for eating opportunities. The closest venue is attractive **THYMIANÁ** village, where central, family-run ☀ *To Talimi* serves excellent home-style *mayireftá* like *yiouvarlákia*, *kókoras krasáto* or bean-and-artichoke salad at friendly prices. *Ouzeri To Apomero* (daily all year), in hillside **Spiládhia** district west of the airport (bear off the Pyrgí road towards Áyios Theodhósios and follow luminous green signs), has terrace seating with an eyeful of the Çeşme peninsula and unusual dishes such as Cretan sausages and battered artichoke hearts. Between Thymianá and Neohóri, *Fakiris Taverna* (all year; weekends only in winter) offers home-marinated aubergine and artichokes, goat baked in tomato sauce and excellent wood-fired pizzas along with well-executed seafood and pork-based *bekrí mezé*. To find it, head south on the road to Kalimassiá, then turn west onto the Ayíou Trýfonos road, just before Neohóri, and proceed about 1km.

Some 2km further along the coast from Karfás, **AYÍA ERMIÓNI** is a fishing anchorage surrounded by a handful of tavernas (none stands out) and apartments to rent. The nearest proper **beach** is at **Mégas Limniónas**, a few hundred metres further on, smaller than Karfás but more scenic, with low cliffs as a backdrop; here *Ankyra* is a reliable if not wildly exciting **taverna**. Both Ayía Ermióni and Mégas Limniónas are served by extensions of blue-bus routes to either Karfás or Thymianá. From the latter, you can (with your own transport) continue 3km south towards Kalimassiá to the turning for **Ayía Fotiní**, a 600-metre pebble **beach** with exceptionally clean water. Cars are excluded from the shore area; the pedestrian esplanade is lined with various rooms (the best of these is central *Apartments Iro* (☎ 22710 51166; ❹), large self-catering studios with sea views, air conditioning and dedicated parking, plus there's **car hire** locally. Some **tavernas** cluster where the side road meets the sea, but there's far better food, especially fish, at **KATARRÁKTIS** (return to the Kalimassiá road), where *O Tsambos* is the best and cheapest of several contenders.

There are no beaches of any note in the vicinity, all the way down to the southeastern tip of the island. Beyond Nénita and Vounós villages, you emerge on the coast again at **GRÍDHIA**, a scruffy place with one noteworthy **taverna** just past the little monastery of Panayía Agridhiótissa: *Snack Bar Iy Agridhioditssa* (all year), doing top-drawer *mezédhes* and fresh sardines under the tamarisks of the sea-view terrace, plus grills by night.

## Southern Híos

Besides olive groves, southern Híos's gently rolling countryside is home to the **mastic bush** (*Pistacia lentisca*). It's found across much of Aegean Greece, but only here – pruned to an umbrella shape to facilitate harvesting – does it produce aromatic resin of any quality or quantity, scraped from incisions made on the trunk during summer. For centuries it was used as a base for paints, cosmetics and the chewable jelly beans that became an addictive staple in Ottoman harems. Indeed, the interruption of the flow of mastic from Híos to Istanbul by the revolt of spring 1822 was a main cause of the brutal Ottoman reaction.

The wealth engendered by the mastic trade supported twenty **mastihohoriá** (mastic villages) from the time the Genoese set up a monopoly in the substance during the fourteenth century, but the demise of imperial Turkey and the development of petroleum-based products knocked the bottom out of the mastic market. Now it's just a curiosity, to be chewed – try the sweetened Elma-brand gum – or drunk as *mastíha* liqueur. It has had medicinal applications since ancient times; contemporary advocates claim that mastic boosts the immune system and thins the blood. High-end cosmetics, toothpaste and mouthwash are now sold at the Mastiha Shop at Egéou 36 in Híos Town.

These days, however, the *mastihohoriá* live mainly off their tangerines, apricots and olives. The villages, the only settlements on Híos spared by the Ottomans in 1822, are architecturally unique, designed by the Genoese but retaining a distinctly Middle Eastern feel. The basic plan involves a rectangular warren of tall houses, with the outer row doubling as perimeter fortification, and breached by a limited number of gateways. More recent additions, whether in traditional architectural style or not, straggle outside the original defences.

### Armólia, Olýmbi, Mestá

**ARMÓLIA**, 20km from town, is the smallest and least imposing of the mastic villages; its main virtue is its pottery industry. **PYRGÍ**, 5km further south, is the most colourful, its houses elaborately embossed with *xystá*, patterns cut into whitewash to reveal a layer of black volcanic sand underneath; in autumn, strings of sun-drying tomatoes add a further splash of colour. On the northeast corner of the central square the twelfth-century Byzantine church of **Áyii Apóstoli** (erratic hours), embellished with much later frescoes, is tucked under an arcade. In the medieval core you'll find an **ATM**, a **post office** and an array of **cafés** and *souvláki* stalls on the central platía. **OLÝMBI**, 7km further west along the same bus route, is one of the less visited mastic villages, but not devoid of interest. The characteristic **tower-keep**, which at Pyrgí stands half-inhabited away from the modernized main square, here looms bang in the middle of the platía, its ground floor occupied by the community *kafenío* on one side, and a **taverna-bar** on the other. **Accommodation** is offered at restored *Chrysanthi Apartments* (☎22710 76196, ⓦwww.chrysanthi.gr; ❹), three units suitable for two to five persons.

Sombre, monochrome **MESTÁ**, 4km west of Olýmbi, is considered the finest of the villages; despite more snack-bars and trinket shops than strictly necessary,

▲ Xystá facades on the platía, Pyrgí

it remains just the right side of twee. From its main square, dominated by the **church of the Taxiárhis** with its two icons of the Archangel – one dressed in Byzantine robes, the other in Genoese armour – a maze of dim lanes, with anti-seismic tunnels, leads off in all directions. Most streets end in blind alleys, except those leading to the six portals; the northeast one still has its original iron gate. Top-drawer **accommodation** is provided by the scattered *Medieval Castle Suites* (☏22710 76345, ⓦwww.medievalcastlesuites.com; ❹–❻), with the reception in a lane just off the square. Humbler rooms in other restored traditional houses are managed by Dhimitris Pipidhis (☏22710 76029; ❸); alternatively, three separate studio apartments managed by Anna Floradhi's gift shop (☏22710 76455; ❸) are more modernized. Of two **taverna-cafés** sharing table-space on the main platía, *Mesaionas* (*Kyra Dhespina*) is better value and has the more helpful proprietor (she also has rooms: ☏22710 76494; ❸).

### The mastic coast – and the Sykiás Olýmbon cave

The closest good, protected **beach** to Mestá lies 4.7km southwest by paved, narrow road at **Apothíka**. Others, east of unused Liménas Mestón port, include **Dhídhyma** (4km away), a double cove with an islet protecting it; **Potámi**, with a namesake stream feeding it; and less scenic **Ayía Iríni** (8km), with a reliably open **taverna**. All these little bays (except for Apothíka) will catch surf and flotsam when the north wind is up.

From Olýmbi, a paved road heads 6km to the well-signed cave of **Sykiás Olýmbon** (June–Aug Tues–Sun 10am–8pm, Sept 11am–6pm; admission in groups of 25 or less every 30min; €5). For years it was just a hole in the ground where villagers disposed of dead animals, but from 1985 on speleologists explored it properly. The cavern, with a constant temperature of 18°C, evolved in two phases between 150 million and 50 million years ago, and has a maximum depth of 57m (though tours only visit the top 30m). Its formations, with fanciful names like Chinese Forest, Medusa and Organ Pipes, are among the most beautiful in the Mediterranean. Before or after your subterranean tour, you can continue another 1500m on a dirt track to the little cape-top monastery of **Ayía Dhýnami** and two sheltered swimming **coves**.

Pyrgí is closest to the two major beach resorts in this corner of the island. The nearest, 6km distant, is **EMBORIÓS**, an almost landlocked harbour with four passable **tavernas**; *Porto Emborios* has the edge with almost year-round operation, fair prices, home-made desserts and good seafood. Ancient **Emboreios** on the hill to the northeast has been rehabilitated as an "archeological park" (summer daily 9am–3pm, winter closed Mon; €2). Down in modern Emboriós a cruciform early Christian **baptistry** is signposted in a field just inland; it's protected by a later, round structure (locked but everything's visible through the grating).

For **swimming**, follow the road to an oversubscribed car park and the beach of **Mávros Yialós** (Mávra Vólia), then continue by flagstoned walkway over the headland to the more dramatic pebble strand (part nudist) of purple-grey volcanic stones, **Fóki**, twice as long and backed by impressive cliffs. If you want sand (and amenities) go to **KÓMI**, 3km northeast, also accessible from Armólia via Kalamotí; there are a few **tavernas** (most reliably open *Bella Mare* and *Nostalgia*, both offering sunbeds for patrons), café-bars and seasonal apartments behind the pedestrianized beachfront.

## Central Híos

The portion of Híos extending west and southwest from Híos Town matches the south in terms of interesting **monuments**, and good roads make touring under your own steam an easy matter. There are also several **beaches** on the far shore of the island which, though not necessarily the best on Híos, are fine for a dip en route.

### The Kámbos and its churches

The **Kámbos**, a vast fertile plain carpeted with citrus groves, extends southwest from Híos Town almost as far as the village of Halkió. The district was originally settled by the Genoese during the fourteenth century, and remained a preserve of the local aristocracy until 1822. Exploring by two-wheeler may be less frustrating than going by car, since the web of narrow, poorly marked lanes sandwiched between high walls guarantees disorientation and frequent backtracking. Behind the walls you catch fleeting glimpses of ornate old mansions built from locally quarried sandstone; courtyards are paved in pebbles or alternating light and dark tiles, and most still contain a pergola-shaded irrigation pond filled by a *mánganos* or donkey-powered waterwheel, used before the advent of electric pumps to draw water from wells 30m deep.

Many of the sumptuous dwellings, constructed in a hybrid Italo-Turco-Greek style, have languished derelict since 1881, but numbers have been converted for use as private estates or unique **accommodation**. The best of these are *Mavrokordatiko* (☎22710 32900, ⓦwww.mavrokordatiko.com; B&B ④), about 1.5km south of the airport, with enormous heated, wood-panelled rooms, and ⚹ *Arhondiko Perleas* (☎22710 32217, ⓦwww.perleas.gr; B&B ⑥) on the Vitiádhou road, set in a huge organic citrus ranch, with a well-regarded in-house restaurant.

Not strictly speaking in Kámbos, but most easily reached from it en route to the *mastihohoriá*, is an outstanding rural Byzantine monument. The eleventh-century hillside church of **Panayía Krína** is worth the challenge of negotiating a maze of paved but poorly marked lanes beyond Vavýli village, 9km from town. It's being comprehensively restored and should open as a tourist attraction in

2009; all of the late-medieval frescoes have been removed, some displayed in Híos Town's Giustiniani Museum. The remaining twelfth-century layer includes some fine saints, a *Resurrection* and a *Communion of the Apostles*, originally lit only by a twelve-windowed drum, echoed somewhat clumsily by the lantern added later over the narthex.

The monastic church of **Panayía Sikelliá** is easier to find, visible from afar in its dramatic clifftop setting south of Tholopotámi, beyond which the three-kilometre dirt access road leading to it is well signposted. Roughly contemporaneous with Panayía Krína, Sikelliá is best visited near sunset, when the cloisonné surface of its blind arches acquires a golden tone. There's nothing much to see inside other than a fine, carved *témblon* and a peculiar, late fresco of John the Divine, so it's not essential to time your visit to coincide with that of the key-keeper, who may appear at dusk. The monastery outbuildings, save for a perimeter wall and a few fortifications above, have long since vanished, but it's worth climbing the latter for views over the adjacent ravine and the entire south of the island.

## Néa Moní

Almost exactly in the middle of the island, the monastery of **Néa Moní** was founded by the Byzantine Emperor Constantine Monomahos ("The Dueller") IX in 1042 on the spot where a wonder-working icon had been discovered. It ranks among the most important monuments on any of the Greek islands; the mosaics, together with those of Dháfni and Ósios Loukás on the mainland, are the finest surviving art of their era in Greece, and the setting – high in partly forested mountains 15km west of the port – is equally memorable.

However, EU part-funded **restoration** work proceeds at a snail's pace, with no end date in sight; the *katholikón* exterior is cocooned in scaffolding, while the interior is regrettably off-limits indefinitely. Accordingly it's not worth shelling out especially for a taxi at the moment, but do stop in briefly if touring with a bike or car.

Once a powerful community of six hundred monks, Néa Moní was pillaged in 1822 and most of its residents (including 3500 civilians sheltering here) were put to the sword. The 1881 tremor caused comprehensive damage, wrecking many of its outbuildings, while exactly a century later a forest fire threatened to engulf the place until the resident icon was paraded along the perimeter wall, miraculously repelling the flames.

Just inside the **main gate** (daily 8am–1pm & 4–8pm, 5–8pm in summer) stands a **chapel/ossuary** containing some of the bones of the 1822 victims; axe-clefts in children's skulls attest to the savagery of the attackers. The *katholikón*, its cupola resting on an octagonal drum, is of a design seen elsewhere only in Cyprus; once restoration is complete, the famous **mosaics** should reappear in all their glory. The narthex contains portrayals of various local saints sandwiched between *Christ Washing the Disciples' Feet* and the *Betrayal*, in which Judas's kiss has unfortunately been obliterated, but Peter is clearly visible lopping off the ear of the high priest's servant. In the dome, which once contained a complete life cycle of Christ, only the *Baptism*, part of the *Crucifixion*, the *Descent from the Cross*, the *Resurrection* and the evangelists Mark and John survived the earthquake.

## The west coast

Some 5km west of Néa Moní sits **AVGÓNYMA**, a cluster of dwellings on a knoll overlooking the coast; the name means "Clutch of Eggs", an apt description when viewed from the ridge above. Since the 1980s, the place has been restored as a summer haven by descendants of the original villagers, though the permanent population is just seven. A returned Greek-American family runs a reasonable, simple **taverna**, *O Pyrgos* (all year), in an arcaded mansion on the main square. The classiest **accommodation** option is *Spitakia*, a cluster of small restored houses sleeping up to five people (☎22710 20513 or 22710 81200, Ⓦwww.spitakia.gr; ❹–❺), though *O Pyrgos* also keeps more modernized units in the village (☎22710 42175; ❸).

A side road continues another 4km north to **ANÁVATOS**, whose empty, dun-coloured dwellings, soaring above pistachio orchards, are almost indistinguishable from the 300-metre-high bluff on which they're built. During the 1822 insurrection, some four hundred islanders threw themselves over this cliff rather than surrender to the besieging Ottomans. Anávatos can now only muster two permanent inhabitants; given a lack of accommodation, one mediocre snack bar, plus an eerie, traumatized atmosphere, it's no place to linger, though you can visit the *kástro*, restored by the archeological service which controls the village.

West of Avgónyma, the main road descends 6km to the sea in well-graded loops. Turning right (north) at the junction leads first to the beach at **Elínda**, alluring from afar but rocky and often murky up close; it's better to continue towards more secluded, mixed sand-and-gravel coves to either side of Metóhi – best of these are **Tigáni** and **Makriá Ámmos**, the latter nudist. Semi-fortified **SIDHIROÚNDA**, the only village hereabouts, enjoys a spectacular hilltop setting overlooking the sea; both view and architecture – including gates and towers – surpass Avgónyma's. There's a competent **taverna**, *Mylos*, at the village entrance, while you can enjoy Sidhiroúnda's famous sunsets from the imaginatively named *Sunset Cafe*.

All along this coast stand round **watchtowers** erected by the Genoese to look out for pirates – the second swimmable cove you reach after turning left from the junction bears the name **Kastélla** (officially Trahíli), again mixed sand and gravel. The first cove, more protected and popular, is **Xeropótamos**. Friendly **LITHÍ** village perches on a forested ledge overlooking the sea 9km south of the junction. There are **tavernas** and *kafenía* in the centre, but most visitors head 2km downhill to **Paralía Lithioú**, a popular weekend target of Hiot townies thanks to its large but hard-packed, windswept beach. The better of two adjacent, pricey fish **tavernas** is *Ta Tria Adherfia*.

South of Lithí 5km, valley-bottom **VÉSSA** is, like Sidhiroúnda, an unsung gem: more open and less casbah-like than Mestá or Pyrgí, but still homogeneous, its tawny buildings arrayed in a vast grid punctuated by numerous belfries and arcaded passages. There's a *kafenío* installed on the ground floor of the tower-mansion on the main through road, while across the square *Kostas* (aka *Frosso's*) does excellent *yíros*, *loukániko* and *souvláki*.

## Northern Híos

**Northern Híos** never really recovered from the 1822 massacre, and between Pityós and Volissós the forest's recovery from 1980s **fires** has been partly reversed by a bad 2007 blaze. Most villages usually lie deserted, with about a third of the former population living in Híos Town, returning occasionally for major festivals or to tend smallholdings; others, based in Athens or North America, visit their ancestral homes for just a few midsummer weeks.

### The road to Kardhámyla

Blue urban buses from Híos Town serve **VRONDÁDHOS**, an elongated coastal suburb that's a favourite residence of the many local seafarers. Homer is alleged to have lived and taught here, and in terraced parkland just above the little fishing port and pebble beach you can visit his purported lectern, more likely an ancient altar of Cybele. Accordingly most buses heading here are labelled, "the Teacher's Rock".

Some 14km out of town, the tiny bayside hamlet of **PANDOUKIÓS** has an excellent if pricey waterside **taverna**, *Kourtesis*, where lobster can often be had. But **LANGÁDHA**, 2.5km beyond, is probably the first point on the eastern coast road you'd be tempted to stop, though there is no proper beach nearby. Set at the mouth of a deep valley, this attractive little harbour settlement looks across its bay to a pine grove, and beyond to Turkey. Night-time/weekend visitors come for the sustaining, reasonable **seafood** at the best of three quayside **tavernas**: ★ *Tou Kopelou*, better known as *Stelios's*.

Just beyond Langádha a side road leads 5km up and inland to **PITYÓS**, an oasis in a mountain pass presided over by a small, round castle; people come here from some distance to **eat** at *Makellos*, a shrine of local cuisine on the southwest edge of the village (late June to early Sept daily lunch/dinner; rest of year Fri–Sun evenings only). Continuing 4km further brings you to a junction that allows quick access to the west of the island.

### Kardhámyla and around

Most traffic proceeds to **ÁNO KARDHÁMYLA** and **KÁTO KARDHÁ-MYLA**, the latter 37km out of Híos Town. Positioned at opposite edges of a fertile plain rimmed by mountains, they initially come as welcome relief from Homer's crags. Káto, better known as **MÁRMARO**, is larger – indeed, the island's second town – with a **bank**, **post office** and **filling station**. However, there is little to attract casual visitors other than some Neoclassical architecture; the mercilessly exposed port is strictly businesslike, and there are few tourist facilities. A sterling exception is *Hotel Kardamyla* (☎22720 23353; ❺ Aug, ❹ otherwise), co-managed with Híos Town's *Hotel Kyma*, offering spacious, fan-equipped **rooms** and a few suites. The in-house restaurant is a reliable lunch venue (July & Aug). Worthwhile independent **tavernas** include *Ouzeri Barba Yiannis* (all year), beside the port authority, and newer *Thalasses*, more upmarket but good value.

For better swimming head west 5km to **Nagós**, a pebble bay at the foot of an oasis, at the end of the summer-only bus line. The place name is a corruption of *naos*, after a Poseidon temple that once stood near uphill springs enclosed in a rock overhang, but no trace of it survives today. Down at the shore the swimming is good, though the water's chilly; there are mediocre **tavernas** (there's a better one inland, by the spring) and a few **dhomátia**. Your only chance of relative solitude in midsummer lies 1km west at **Yióssonas**, a much longer if less sheltered and rockier beach, with no facilities.

### Northwestern villages

Few outsiders venture beyond Yióssonas, and no buses cover the distance between Mármaro and Kambiá village, 20km west. Along the way, Amádhes and Víki are attractive enough villages at the base of 1297-metre **Pelinéo**, the island's summit, most easily **climbed** from **Amádhes** – a five-hour round trip. **Kambiá**, overlooking a ravine with a ruined castle, has very much an end-of-the-line feel, although a partly paved road heads 5km south towards Spartoúnda, where a completely paved road resumes for the remaining 15km to the intersection with the main trans-island road bound for Volissós. About halfway along, well signposted outside the village of **KIPOURIÉS**, are two **tavernas** in a fountain-nourished oasis, the more accomplished being *To Mayerio tis Kyrarinis*, specializing in elaborate local recipes and desserts (daily summer, sporadically off season; ring ☏ 22740 22016 to check).

About 5km south of Kipouriés, you can make a detour to the engagingly set sixteenth-century **monastery of Moundhón**, second in rank to Néa Moní before its partial destruction in 1822. For admittance to the locked church, seek out the warden, Yiorgos Fokas, in Dhievhá village (☏ 22740 22011). Best of the naïve interior frescoes is one depicting the *Ouranódhromos Klímax* (Stairway to Heaven, not to be confused with Led Zeppelin's): a trial-by-ascent, in which ungodly priests are beset by demons hurling them into the mouth of a great serpent symbolizing the Devil, while the righteous clergy are assisted upwards by angels. In an era when illiteracy was the norm, such panels were intended quite literally to scare the hell out of simple parishioners.

## Volissós and around

**VOLISSÓS**, 42km from Híos Town by the most direct road (but just 44km by the much easier route via Avgónyma), was once the market town for a dozen remote hill villages beyond. Its old stone houses still curl appealingly beneath a crumbling hilltop Byzantine-Genoese **fort**. Volissós can seem depressing at first, with the bulk of its 250 mostly elderly permanent inhabitants living in newer buildings around the main square, but impressions improve with time. This backwater ethos may not last; the upper quarters are in the grip of a restoration mania, most in good taste, with ruins changing hands for stratospheric prices.

Grouped around the platía you'll find a **post office**, an **ATM** and three mediocre **tavernas**. A pair of **filling stations** operate 2.5km out of town, the only ones hereabouts; if reliant on public transport, plan on overnighting since the bus only ventures out here on Sundays on a day-trip basis, plus on three weekly workdays in the early afternoon (unless you care to travel at 4.30am). This should cause no dismay, since the area has some of the best beaches and more interesting **accommodation** on Híos. The most reasonable and longest established of a few restoration projects are sixteen old houses, mostly in Pýrgos district, available through ⅍ *Volissos Travel* (☏ 22740 21413 or 693 69 75 470, ⓦ www.volissostravel.gr; May–Oct; ❹ may include car hire). Units usually accommodate two people – all have terraces, fully equipped kitchens, air conditioning and features such as tree trunks upholding sleeping lofts, reflecting proprietress Stella's background as a sculptor.

**LIMNIÁ** (or Limiá), the port of Volissós (though the *kaïki* service to Psará has been suspended), lies 2km south, bracketed by the local beaches. The most consistent **taverna** here is *O Zikos* (all year) at the far end of the quay, with good grills and a fine house salad featuring sun-dried tomatoes, plus occasional seafood. A 1.5-kilometre drive or walk southeast over the headland brings you to **Mánagros**, a seemingly endless sand-and-pebble beach. More intimate, sandy **Lefkáthia** lies just a ten-minute stroll along the cement drive over the headland north of the harbour; amenities are limited to a seasonal snack shack on the sand, and Ioannis Zorbas's garden-set **apartments** (☏ 22740 21436, ⓦ www.chioszorbas.gr; ❹), where the concrete drive joins an asphalt road down from Volissós.

This is bound for **Límnos**, the next protected cove 400m east of Lefkáthia, where *Taverna Iy Limnos* features fish grills and specials like *kokorás krasáto*, and the spruce *Latini Apartments* (☏ 22740 21461; ❸) are graced with multiple stone-paved terraces. **Ayía Markélla**, 5km further northwest of Límnos, has a long **beach** (with a mediocre taverna) fronting the eponymous, barracks-like pilgrimage **monastery** of Híos's patron saint (festival July 22). The dirt road beyond Ayía Markélla is passable with care by any vehicle, and emerges on the paved road running high above the northwest coast. Turn left for remote **ÁYIO GÁLA**, notable for a **grotto-church** complex built into a stream-lapped palisade at the bottom of the village. Signs ("Panayía Ayiogaloúsena") point the way, but for off-season access you'll need to find the key-keeper (ask at the central *kafenío*), and descend via a flight of stairs starting beside a eucalyptus tree. Of two churches inside the cavern, the larger one is fifteenth-century but seems newer owing to a 1993 external renovation. Beyond, however, a fantastically intricate *témblon* vies for your attention with a tinier, older chapel, built entirely within the cavern. Its frescoes are badly smudged, except for a wonderfully mysterious and mournful Virgin, surely the saddest in Christendom, holding a knowing Child. Still further inside, a **cave system** with all the usual formations has limited admission hours (June–Aug Fri–Sun 11am–6pm; €5).

## Satellite islands: Psará and Inoússes

There's a single settlement, with beaches and an isolated rural monastery, on both of Híos's satellite islets, but each is surprisingly different from the other, and of course from their large neighbour. **Inoússes**, the nearer and smaller, has a daily *kaïki* service from Híos Town in season, sometimes permitting day-trips; **Psará** has equally regular small-ferry services, but is too remote for day-trips.

### Psará

The birthplace of revolutionary war hero Admiral Konstantinos Kanaris, **Psará** devoted its merchant fleets – the third largest in 1820s Greece – to the cause of independence, and paid dearly for it. Vexed beyond endurance, the Turks landed overwhelming forces in 1824 to stamp out this nest of resistance. Perhaps 3000 of the 30,000 inhabitants escaped in small boats to be rescued by a French fleet, but the majority retreated to a hilltop powder magazine and blew it (and themselves) up rather than surrender. The nationalist poet Dhionysios Solomos immortalized the incident in famous stanzas:

On the Black Ridge of Psará,
Glory walks alone.
She meditates on her heroes
And wears in her hair a wreath
Made from a few dry weeds
Left on the barren ground.

Today, it's a sad, bleak place fully living up to its name ("the mottled things" in ancient Greek), never really having recovered from the holocaust. The Turks burned whatever houses and vegetation the blast had missed, and the official population now barely exceeds four hundred. A 1980s revitalization project instigated by a French-Greek descendant of Kanaris saw the port improved, mains electricity and potable water provided, a secondary school opened, and cultural links between France and the island established, though this never resulted in a tourist boom. 2008 did, however, see the institution of a summer cultural festival in early August, which may continue.

Since few buildings in the east-facing harbour community pre-date the twentieth century, a strange hotchpotch of ecclesiastical and secular architecture greets you on disembarking. There's a distinctly southern feel, more like the Dodecanese or the Cyclades, and some peculiar churches, no two alike in style. **Accommodation** ranges from a handful of fairly basic rooms to three more professional outfits: *Psara Studios* (T22740 61233; ❹) and *Apartments Restalia* (T22740 61201; ❷–❹), both a bit stark but with balconies and kitchens, or the

*EOT xenónas* (☎22740 61293; ❹), multi-bedded rooms in a restored prison. A few **tavernas** (the most distinguished being *Spitalia* in a restored medieval hospital), a **post office**, bakery and shop complete the amenities; there's no full-service bank.

Psará's **beaches** are decent, improving the further northeast you walk from the port. You quickly pass **Káto Yialós**, **Katsoúni** and **Lazarétto** with its off-putting power station, before reaching **Lákka** ("narrow ravine"), fifteen minutes along, apparently named after its grooved rock formations in which you may have to shelter – much of this coast is windswept, with a heavy swell offshore. **Límnos**, 25 minutes from the port along the coastal path, is big and attractive, but there's no reliable **taverna** here, or indeed at any of the beaches. The only other thing to do on Psará is to follow the paved road north across the island to **Kímisis (Assumption) monastery**; uninhabited since the 1970s, this comes to life only during the first week of August, when its revered icon is carried in ceremonial procession to town and back on the eve of August 5.

## Inoússes

**Inoússes** has a permanent population of about three hundred – less than half its 1930s figure – and a very different history from Psará. For generations this islet, first settled around 1750 by Hiot shepherds, provided Greece with many of her wealthiest shipping families: various members of the Livanos, Lemos and Pateras clans were born here. This helps explain the large villas and visiting summer gin-palaces in an otherwise sleepy Greek backwater – as well as a **maritime museum** (daily 10am–1pm; €2) near the quay, endowed by various shipping magnates. At the west end of the quay, the bigwigs have also funded a nautical academy, which trains future members of the merchant navy.

On Mondays, Fridays and Sundays you can make an inexpensive **day-trip** to Inoússes from Híos with the locals' ferry *Inousses II*; on most other days of the week this arrives at 1 or 3pm, returning 8am the next day. Otherwise, during the tourist season you must take one of the double-priced excursions offered from Híos.

Two church-tipped, privately owned islets guard the unusually well-protected harbour; the **town** of Inoússes is surprisingly large, draped over hillsides enclosing a ravine. Despite the wealthy reputation, its appearance is unpretentious, the houses displaying a mix of vernacular and modest Neoclassical style. There is just one, fairly comfortable, **hotel**, the *Thalassoporos* (☎22720 55475; ❹), on the main easterly hillside lane, but no *dhomátia*. **Restaurants** are similarly limited; the most reliable option is *Taverna Pateronisso*, at the base of the disembarkation jetty, though every season a few simple ouzerís towards the nautical academy try their luck. **Café-bars** such as *Naftikos Omilos* provide a semblance of nightlife. By the museum you'll find a **post office** and a **bank**.

The southern slope of this tranquil island is surprisingly green and well tended; there are no springs, so water comes from a mix of fresh and brackish wells, as well as a reservoir. The sea is extremely clean and calm on the sheltered southerly shore; among its beaches, choose from **Zepága**, **Biláli** or **Kástro**, respectively five, twenty and thirty-minutes' walk west of the port. More secluded **Fourkeró** (or Farkeró) lies 25 minutes east: first along a cement drive ending at a seaside chapel, then by path past pine groves and over a ridge. As on Psará, there are no reliable facilities at any of the beaches.

# Lésvos (Mytilíni)

**Lésvos**, the third-largest Greek island after Crete and Évvia, is the birthplace of the ancient bards Sappho, Aesop, Arion and – more recently – the Greek primitive artist Theophilos, the Nobel laureate poet Odysseus Elytis and the novelist Stratis Myrivilis. Despite these **artistic associations**, the island may not initially strike one as particularly beautiful or interesting; much of the landscape is rocky, volcanic terrain, encompassing vast grain fields, salt pans or even near-desert. But there are also oak and pine forests as well as endless olive groves, some more than five centuries old. With its balmy climate and suggestive contours, Lésvos tends to grow on you with prolonged exposure.

Lovers of medieval and Ottoman **architecture** certainly won't be disappointed. Castles survive at Mytilíni Town, Mólyvos, Eressós, Sígri and near Ándissa; most date from the late fourteenth century, when Lésvos was given as a dowry to a Genoese prince of the Gattilusi clan following his marriage to the sister of one of the last Byzantine emperors. Apart from Crete and Évvia, Lésvos was the only Greek island where Muslims settled significantly in rural villages (they usually stuck to the safety of towns), which explains the occasional Ottoman bridge, box-like mosque or crumbling minaret in the middle of nowhere. Again unusually for the Aegean islands, eighteenth-century Ottoman reforms encouraged the emergence of a Greek Orthodox land- and industry-owning aristocracy, who built imposing mansions and tower-houses, a few of which survive. The worthies in Mytilíni Town erected Belle Époque townhouses to French Second Empire models; many have been pressed into service as government buildings or even restored as hotels.

The first two centuries of **Ottoman rule** were particularly harsh, with much of the Orthodox population sold into slavery or deported to the imperial capital – replaced by more tractable Muslim colonists – and most physical evidence of the Genoese or Byzantine period demolished. Out in the countryside, Turks and Greeks got along, relatively speaking, right up until 1923; the Ottoman authorities favoured Greek *kahayiádhes* (overseers) to keep the peons in line. However, large numbers of the lower social classes, oppressed by the pashas and their Greek lackeys, fled across to Asia Minor during the nineteenth century, only to return again after the exchange of populations.

A resulting quirk is a tendency to **vote Communist** (with usually at least one Red MP in office), a legacy of the Ottoman-era quasi-feudalism, 1880s conflicts between small and large olive producers, and further disruption occasioned by the arrival of many refugees, reinforcing the share-cropping system which prevailed in the countryside until the 1930s. But whatever their politics, you'll find the islanders fairly religious, with old-fashioned (if occasionally rough-edged) manners and – by Greek-island standards – a strong sense of community.

Social **idiosyncrasies** persist: anyone who has attended one of the village *paniyíria*, with hours of music and tables groaning with food and drink, will not be surprised to learn that Lésvos has the highest alcoholism rate (and some of the worst driving habits) in Greece. Breeding livestock, especially horses, remains important, and signs reading "Forbidden to Tether Animals Here" are still common, as are herds of apparently unattended donkeys wandering about. Much of the olive acreage is still inaccessible to vehicles, and the harvest can only be hauled out by donkeys – who are loaded en masse onto the back of trucks to be transported to the point where the road fizzles out. Organic production has been embraced enthusiastically as a way of making Lésvos agricultural products more competitive – *Violoyikó Ktíma* (Organic Plot) or *Violoyikí Kaliéryia* (Organic Cultivation) signs abound.

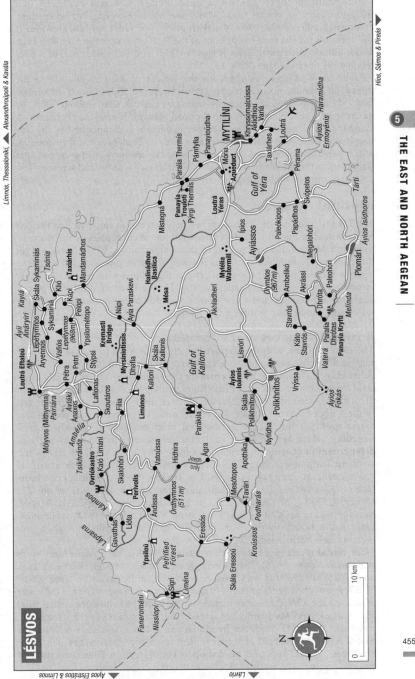

LÉSVOS

Limnos, Thessaloníki, Alexandhroúpoli & Kavála

Híos, Sámos & Psará

Ávios Efstrátios & Límnos

Lávrio

455

MYTILÍNI

Gulf of Yéra

Gulf of Kalloní

Olýmbos (967m)

Órdhymnos (511m)

Lepétymnos (968m)

Petrified Forest

Áyii Anáryiri
Kayiá
Skála Sykaminiás
Sykaminiá
Kápi
Tsónia
Klió
Pélopi
Ypsilométopo
Mandamádhos
Taxiárhis
Kremastí Bridge
Lepétymnos
Argénnos
Vafiós
Petrí
Stýpsi
Pétra
Lafiónas
Anaxos
Avláki
Skoutáros
Loutrá Eftaloú
Mólyvos (Mithymna)
Psiriára
Mýrsiniótissa
Dháfia
Kalloní
Limónos
Fília
Kaló Limáni
Skalohóri
Ovriókastro
Perivolís
Vatoússa
Hídhira
Ándissa
Ypsiloú
Sígri
Líota
Gavathás
Limóna
Eressós
Skála Eressoú
Mesótopos
Tavári
Agra
Jeeps only
Parákila
Apóthika
Polihnítou
Polihnítos
Nyfídha
Vrýssa
Ayios Ioánnis
Skála Kalloní
Lisvóri
Misteghná
Paralía Thermís
Pámfylla
Panayioúdha
Mória
Aqueduct
Khryssomaloússa
Aklidhíou
Variá
Loutrá
Taxiárhes
Pérama
Panayía Trouloti
Pyrgí Thermís
Ípios
Ayiássos
Loutrá Yéras
Nápi
Ayía Paraskeví
Mésa
Akhladhéri
Ambelikó
Stavrós
Káto Stavrós
Vaterá
Paralía Dhrótas
Panayía Kryfti
Melínda
Paleohóri
Dhróta
Akrási
Megalohóri
Paleókipos
Papádhos
Sképelos
Halinádhou Basilica
Mylélia Watermill
Ayios Fokás
 Tsíkhránda
Ambélia
Kambos
Lapsárna
Kroússos
Podharás
Faneroméni
Nissiópi
Tárti
Ayios Isídhoros
Plomári
Ermoyénis
Ayios
Haramídha

Ortelius / Théssalonique

N

10 km

0

Historically, the olive plantations, ouzo distilleries, animal husbandry and fishing industry supported those who chose not to emigrate, but when these enterprises stalled in the 1980s, **tourism** made appreciable inroads. However, it still accounts for less than ten percent of the local economy: there are few large hotels outside the capital, Skála Kalloní or Mólyvos, and visitor numbers have levelled off since the late 1990s.

Public buses observe schedules for the benefit of villagers coming to the capital on errands, not day-tripping tourists. Accomplishing such excursions from Mytilíni is impossible anyway, owing to Lésvos's **size** – about 70km by 45km at its widest points – though the road network is now mostly improved, along with its signposting. Moreover, the topography is complicated by the two deeply indented gulfs of Kalloní and Yéra, with no bridges across their mouths, which means that both bus and car journeys will involve a change or transit at Kalloní, near the middle of the island. It's best to pick a resort and stay for a few days, exploring its immediate surroundings.

## Mytilíni Town

**MYTILÍNI**, the port and capital, sprawls between and around two bays divided by a fortified promontory, and in Greek fashion often doubles as the name of the island. Many visitors are put off by the combination of urban bustle and (in the traditionally humbler northern districts) slight seediness, and contrive to leave as soon as possible; the town returns the compliment by being a fairly impractical and occasionally expensive base. However, several diversions, particularly the marketplace and a few museums within a few-minutes' walk of the waterfront, can occupy you for a few hours.

### Arrival, transport and information

There's no bus link with the **airport** (which has an ATM in arrivals, and three car rental booths), so you may need to take a **taxi** the 7km into Mytilíni Town. As on Híos, there are two **bus terminals**: the *yperastykó* (standard KTEL) buses leave from a small station near Platía Konstandinopóleos at the southern end of the harbour, while the *astykó* (blue bus) service departs from a stand at the top of the harbour. Drivers should use the enormous free public **car park** a few blocks south of the KTEL, or the oval plaza near the new archeological museum – there are no other easily available spaces. If you're driving out, **8-Noemvríou** starting just behind the ferry quay, is the quickest way to the northern harbour of Epáno Skála and beyond to the Mandamádhos road. If you're intent on getting over to Ayvalık in **Turkey**, you've a choice of two boats (*Jale* or *Konstandinos I*); most likely **agencies** are Picolo Travel at no. 73a (☎22510 27000), or Dimakis Tours at Koundouriótou 73 (☎22510 27865). Saos Ferries are handled by Fun Tours at no. 87 (☎22510 40802), while NEL Lines has a booth in the harbour zone (☎22510 42239), though nearly everyone sells their tickets.

**Car rental** is arrangeable through reputable franchises like Payless/Auto Moto at Koundouriótou 49 (☎22510 43555, ✉automoto@otenet.gr), Budget/Sixt at no. 47 (☎22510 29600, ⓦwww.lesvosholidays.com), or Best at no. 87–89 (☎22510 37337, ⓦwww.best-rentacar.com) – though it may be cheaper to rent at the resort of your choice. Other amenities include the **post office** behind the central park, and numerous **ATMs** starting just outside the port gate. Before leaving town, you might visit **EOT regional headquarters** at James Aristárhou 6 (Mon–Fri 8am–2.30pm) to get hold of their excellent town and island **maps**, plus other brochures, or the Newsstand **bookshop** at Vostáni 6 for a limited selection of English literature. The **website** ⓦwww.lesvos.com is also highly useful.

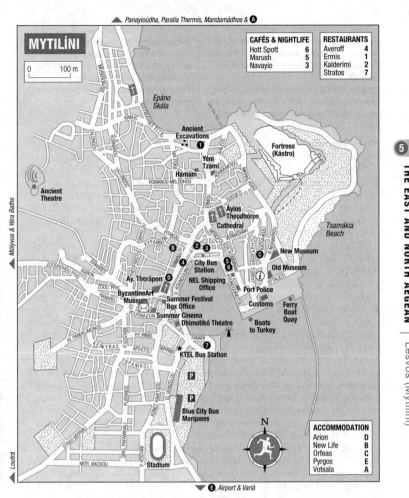

**MYTILÍNI**

0    100 m

| CAFÉS & NIGHTLIFE | | RESTAURANTS | |
|---|---|---|---|
| Hott Spott | 6 | Averoff | 4 |
| Marush | 5 | Ermis | 1 |
| Navayio | 3 | Kalderimi | 2 |
| | | Stratos | 7 |

Panayioúdha, Paralía Thermís, Mandamádhos & **A**

Epáno Skála

Ancient Excavations **1**

Yéni Tzamí

Hamam

Fortress (Kástro)

Ancient Theatre

 Áyios Theodhóros

Cathedral

Tsamákia Beach

City Bus Station

Ay. Therápon **D**

NEL Shipping Office

New Museum

Old Museum

ByzantineArt Museum

Summer Festival Box Office

Summer Cinema

Dhimotikó Théatro

Port Police

Customs

Ferry Boat Quay

Boats to Turkey

KTEL Bus Station **7**

FANARI

P

P

Blue City Bus Marquees

Stadium

N

**B**, Airport & Variá

Mólyvos & Yéra Baths

Ancient Theatre

Loutrá

| ACCOMMODATION | |
|---|---|
| Arion | D |
| New Life | B |
| Orfeas | C |
| Pyrgos | E |
| Votsala | A |

## Accommodation

Finding **accommodation** can be frustrating: waterfront hotels are noisy and overpriced, but supply usually exceeds demand for the better-value rooms in the backstreets.

**Loriet/Laureate** At Variá shore, 4km south of town ☎22510 43111, ⓦwww.loriet-hotel.com. Sophisticated accommodation comprises a nineteenth-century mansion and modern wings, gardens and a 25-metre saltwater pool with a bar area. Rooms vary from blandly modern, marble-trimmed studios (less grim than they seem from outside) to massive suites in the "Big House" with retro decor and big bathrooms (plus three smaller ones under the roofline). Booking advisable year-round; on-site restaurant. Studios ⑤, suites ⑧

**New Life** End of Olýmbou, cul-de-sac off Ermoú ☎22510 42650 or 693 22 79 057. Polished-wood-floored, en-suite rooms (some a/c) in an old mansion with a garden, or similarly priced ones, but with bizarre modern murals, in the co-managed *Arion* down the street at Aríonos 4, Áyios Therápon church. ③, also monthly rates.

**Orfeas** Katsakoúli 3 ☎22510 28523, ⓦwww .orfeas-hotel.com. Probably the quietest of the in-town hotels (rear rooms facing the garden even calmer), yet handy for the archeological museum

457

and port, this well-restored nineteenth-century building has somewhat small a/c doubles (triples are larger), but cheerfully hued modern furnishings. Some balconies; lift; breakfast indoors or on the patio. ❹

**Pyrgos** Eleftheríou Venizélou 49 ☎ 22510 25069, ⓦwww.pyrgoshotel.gr. Premier in-town restoration accommodation, with utterly over-the-top kitsch

decor in the common areas: Second Empire salon furniture, painted ceilings, the lot. However the rooms are perfectly acceptable: most have a balcony, all differ in colour scheme, some have tubs in the baths and there are three round units in the tower. Also offers "American" breakfast and secure parking at the rear. ❻

## The Town

On the promontory sits the Byzantine-Genoese-Ottoman **fortress** (Tues–Sun 8.30am–2.30pm; €2), its mixed pedigree reflected in the Ottoman-Turkish inscription immediately above the Byzantine double eagle at the southern outer gate. Inside you can make out the variably preserved ruins of the Gattilusi palace, a Turkish *medresse* (Koranic academy), a dervish cell and a Byzantine cistern. Just below the fortress, at **Tsamákia**, is the mediocre, fee-entry town "beach".

Inland, the town skyline is dominated in turn by the Germanic-Gothic belfry spire of **Áyios Athanásios cathedral** and the mammary dome of **Áyios Therápon**, both expressions of the (post)-Baroque taste of the nineteenth-century Ottoman Greek bourgeoisie. The interior decor of Áyios Therápon in particular seems more appropriate to an opera house than a church, with gilt a-plenty in the vaulting and ornate column capitals. They stand more or less at opposite ends of the **bazaar**, whose main street, Ermoú, links the town centre with the little-used north harbour of **Epáno Skála**, following the course of a canal that joined the two ports until the Byzantine era. On its way there Ermoú passes various expensive antique shops near the roofless, derelict **Yéni Tzamí** at the heart of the old Muslim quarter, just a few steps east of a superb Turkish **hamam**, restored to its former glory but – like the mosque – closed unless a special exhibit is being held. Between Ermoú and the castle lies a maze of atmospheric lanes lined with Belle Époque mansions and humbler vernacular dwellings; more ornate townhouses are found in the southerly districts of **Sourádha** and **Kióski**, towards the airport.

Mytilíni's excellent **archeological collection**, the only real must-see, is housed in two separate **galleries** (Tues–Sun 8.30am–3pm; €3), a few hundred metres apart. The newer, upper museum, at the base of 8-Noemvríou, is devoted to finds from wealthy Roman Mytilene, in particular three rooms of well-displayed mosaics from second/third-century AD villas. Highlights include a crude but engaging scene of Orpheus charming all manner of beasts and birds, two fishermen surrounded by clearly recognizable (and edible) sea creatures, and the arrival of baby Telephos, son of Auge and Hercules, in a seaborne box, again with amazed fishermen presiding. Earlier eras are represented in the older wing (same hours, same ticket), located in a former mansion just behind the ferry dock. The ground floor has Neolithic finds from Áyios Vartholoméos cave and Bronze Age Thermí, but the star, late Classical exhibits upstairs include minutely detailed terracotta figurines: a pair of acrobats, two *kourotrophoi* figures (goddesses suckling infants, predecessors of all Byzantine Galaktotrofoússa icons), children playing with a ball or dogs, and Aphrodite riding a dolphin. A rear annexe contains stone-cut inscriptions of various edicts and treaties, plus a Roman sculpture of a drunken satyr asleep on a wineskin.

The well-lit and well-laid-out **Byzantine Art Museum** (Mon–Sat 9am–1pm, €2), just opposite the entrance to Áyios Therápon, contains various icons rescued from rural island churches. The most noteworthy exhibit, and the oldest, is a fourteenth-century icon of Christ *Pandokrátor*; other highlights include a sultanic *firmáni* or grant of privileges to a local bishop, a rare sixteenth-century three-dimensional icon of *The Crucifixion* and a canvas of the *Kímisis* (*Assumption*) by Theophilos (see p.460).

### Eating, drinking and nightlife

Mytilíni Town offers more dining choices than the obvious, touristy, seafood **tavernas** on the southerly Fanári quay. For **snacks** and **drinks**, *Navayio* at the head of the harbour is the favourite, with an unbeatable combo **breakfast** at a fair price. The trendy northeast quay is the main venue for informal **nightlife** at *frappádhika*-cum-bars; most durable are *Marush* and *Hott Spott*, interspersed with other annually changing outfits (one the former premises of the Banque Ottomane Imperiale). Otherwise, watch as usual for flybills advertising out-of-town nocturnal events in summer. The summer **cinema** Pallas is on Vournázon near the park; the winter cinema, Arion, is near the KTEL.

**Averoff** West quay. Lodestar of *mayireftá* (including early-morning *patsás*); popular for lunch before an afternoon ferry departure.

**Ermis** Epáno Skála. Best-value, and friendliest, of a few ouzerís in this district. A 1999 refit didn't much affect its Belle Époque decor (panelled ceiling, giant mirrors, faded oil paintings), or its claimed two centuries of purveying titbits to a jolly, varied crowd in the pleasant courtyard. Open daily.

**Kalderimi** Three premises around Thássou 2. One of the few surviving bazaar ouzerís, with seating under the shade of vines; the food is abundant if a bit plainly presented. Closed Sun.

**Stratos** Far end Fanári quay. Marginally the best of the seafood tavernas here, and it doesn't tout aggressively.

## Around Mytilíni

The road heading **north** from Mytilíni towards Mandamádhos follows a rather nondescript coastline, but offers startling views across the straits to Turkey. The most appealing spot en route is **PANAYIOÚDHA**, 8km away, with a church resembling a miniature Áyios Therápon, and waterside **tavernas** buzzing at weekends. Best, most popular and priciest of these is *Kostaras*, one of the first establishments you encounter coming from Mytilíni. At the far end of the flagstoned pedestrian quay, the simple *Akroyiali* is homelier and excellent value.

Just past Panayioúdha you can detour to **MÓRIA**, and thence to a valley 1km south, site of a second-century-AD Roman **aqueduct** that used to bring water from the foothills of Mount Ólymbos; the eleven remaining spans of its 26-kilometre extent are intact to varying degrees (more so after 2001 restoration), lofty and impressive. A little further along the coastal road at **Pámfylla** and **Pýrgi Thermís** you glimpse various *pýrgi* (tower-mansions), relics of the nineteenth-century gentry. Also near Pýrgi Thermís stands the well-preserved, well-signposted Byzantine church of **Panayía Troulotí**, one of the few Byzantine monuments to escape Ottoman ravages. A small, domed, cross-in-square structure, built in stages from the ninth to fourteenth centuries, this may only have the narthex open, but through the door you can see extensive fresco fragments on the piers. Just 500m further at **PARALÍA THERMÍS**, the Roman/Byzantine **hamam** has been allowed to decay in favour of an ugly, sterile modern facility adjacent, though it still supplies the hot water, and you can stick your head in to admire the vaulted brickwork. You're a bit far (12km) from town, but there's a sophisticated, quiet, seafront B-class **hotel** here, the *Votsala* (☎22510 71231, ⓦ www.votsalahotel.com; ❸), with watersports off the somewhat scrappy beach, well-tended gardens but no TV in the rooms.

Heading **south** instead, beyond the airport and Krátigos village, the paved road loops around to **Haramídha**, 14km from town and the closest decent (pebble) **beach**; the eastern bay has a few **tavernas**, the best of these being *Theodhora Gklava (Grioules)*, with vegetarian and seafood *mezédhes*. **Áyios Ermoyénis**, 3km west and directly accessible from Mytilíni via Loutrá village, is more scenic and sandy, but small and surprisingly crowded at weekends. The patron saint's chapel perches on the cliff separating two small, sandy coves from a larger, less usable easterly bay accessed by a separate track; there's a popular, eponymous **taverna** by the parking area, renowned for its salt-cured and fresh fish platters.

For other pleasant immersions near Mytilíni, make for **Loutrá Yéras**, 8km along the main road to Kalloní. These **public baths** (daily: April–May & Oct 8am–6pm; June–Sept 8am–7pm; Nov–March 9am–5pm; €2.50) are just the thing if you've spent a sleepless night on a ferry, with two ornate spouts that feed 38°C water to marble-lined pools in vaulted chambers; there are separate facilities for men and women (the ladies' pool is a tad smaller, but has lovely masonry), and skinny-dipping is, unexpectedly in prudish Greece, obligatory.

### The Variá museums

The most rewarding single targets near Mytilíni are a pair of museums at **VARIÁ**, 5km south of town (hourly buses). The **Theophilos Museum** (daily 10am–4pm; €2) honours the painter, born here in 1873, with four rooms of wonderful, little-known compositions commissioned by his patron Thériade (see opposite) during the years immediately preceding Theophilos's death. A wealth of detail is evident in elegiac scenes of fishing, reaping, olive-picking and baking from the pastoral Lésvos which Theophilos obviously knew best; there are droll touches also, such as a cat slinking off with a fish in *The Fishmongers*. The *Sheikh-ul-Islam* with his hubble-bubble (Room 2) seems drawn from life, as does a highly secular Madonna merely titled *Mother*

#### Theophilos Hadzimihaïl (1873–1934): the Rousseau of Greece?

The "naïve" painter **Theophilos Hadzimihaïl** was born and died in Mytilíni Town, and both his eccentricities and talents were remarkable from an early age. After a failed apprenticeship as a shoemaker, he ran away to Smyrna, then to Mount Pílio on the Greek mainland in 1894 after allegedly killing a Turk. Wandering across the country from Pílio to Athens and the Peloponnese, Theophilos became one of the prize eccentrics of Belle Époque Greece, dressing up as Alexander the Great or various revolutionary war heroes, complete with *tsaroúhia* (pom-pommed shoes) and *fustanélla* (pleated skirt). A recluse who (it is claimed) neither drank, swore, smoked nor attended church, Theophilos was ill and living in severely reduced circumstances back on Lésvos when he was introduced to Thériade in 1919; the latter, virtually alone among critics of the time, recognized his peculiar genius and ensured that Theophilos was supported both morally and materially for the rest of his life.

With their childlike perspective, vivid colour scheme and idealized mythical and rural subjects, Theophilos's works are unmistakeable. Relatively few of his works survive today, because he executed commissions for a pittance on ephemeral surfaces such as *kafenío* counters, horsecarts, or the walls of long-vanished houses. Facile comparisons are often made between Theophilos and Henri Rousseau, the roughly contemporaneous French "primitive" painter. Unlike "Le Douanier", however, Theophilos followed no other profession, eking out a precarious living from his art alone. And while Rousseau revelled in exoticism, Theophilos's work was principally and profoundly rooted in Greek mythology, history and daily life.

*with Child* (also Room 2). But in classical scenes – Sappho and Alkaeos, a landscape series of Egypt, Asia Minor and the Holy Land, and episodes from wars historical and contemporary – Theophilos was on shakier ground; *Abyssinians Hunting an Italian Horseman* has clearly been conflated with New World Indians chasing down a conquistador. The sole concessions to modernity are the aeroplanes sketched in as an afterthought over various island landscapes.

The adjacent, imposing **Thériade Museum** (Tues–Sun 9am–2pm & 5–8pm; €2) is the legacy of another native son, Stratis Eleftheriades (1897–1983). Leaving the island aged 18 for Paris, he Gallicized his name to Thériade and eventually became a renowned avant-garde art publisher, enlisting some of the leading artists of the twentieth century in his ventures. The displays comprise two floors of lithographs, engravings, ink drawings, wood-block prints and watercolours by the likes of Miró, Chagall, Picasso, Giacometti, Matisse, Le Corbusier, Léger, Rouault and Villon, either annotated by the painters themselves or commissioned as illustrations for the works of prominent poets and authors: an astonishing collection for a relatively remote Aegean island, deserving leisurely perusal. Highlights include Miró's cheerfully lurid lithos for Alfred Jarry's *Ubu Roi* and *L'Enfance d'Ubu*; Matisse's *Jazz* series from 1947; Léger's uncompleted 1958 homage to Paris, *La Ville*; Chagall's surprisingly coarse, sometimes Brueghel-esque *Biblical Cycle* water-colours; and reproductions of illuminated medieval manuscripts from issues of *Verve*, the art quarterly which Thériade published from 1937 to 1971. There is also more by Theophilos, notably *The Lion Wrestler* and *The Outdoor Barbers*.

## Southern Lésvos

Southern Lésvos is indented by two great inlets, the gulfs of **Kalloní** and **Yéra**: the first curving in a northeasterly direction, the latter northwesterly, creating a fan-shaped peninsula at the heart of which looms 967-metre **Mount Ólymbos**. Both shallow gulfs are landlocked by very narrow outlets to the open sea, which don't – and probably never will – have bridges spanning them. This is the most verdant and productive olive-oil territory on Lésvos, and stacks of pressing-mills stab the skyline.

**PÉRAMA**, its oddly atttractive townscape dotted with disused olive-oil warehouses, is one of the larger places on the Gulf of Yéra, and has a regular *kaïki* service (no cars carried) linking it with Koundoroudhiá and blue city buses to/from Mytilíni on the far side. The most likely reason to show up is for one of the better **taverna-ouzerís** in the region: 𝕁 *Balouhanas* (all year; lunch and dinner), the northernmost establishment on the front, with a wooden, cane-roofed conservatory jutting out over the water plus outdoor tables. The name's a corruption of *balıkhane* or "fish-market" in Turkish, and seafood is a strong point, whether grilled or made into croquettes, as are regional *mezédhes* and own-made desserts.

### Plomári and around

Due south of Mount Ólymbos, at the edge of the "fan", **PLOMÁRI** is the only sizeable coastal settlement hereabouts, and indeed the second-largest municipality on Lésvos. It presents an unlikely juxtaposition of scenic appeal and its famous ouzo industry, courtesy of several local **distilleries**; the largest and oldest, *Varvayianni* (Ⓦ www.barbayanni-ouzo.com), offers free tours (and tasting) during working hours, plus a fascinating display of old alembics, presses, storage jars and archival material. Best venue for a tipple afterwards are the old *kafenía* on central Platía Beniamín.

Despite a resounding lack of good **beaches** within walking distance, Plomári is popular with Scandinavian tourists, but you can usually find a **room** (prominently signposted) at the edge of the old, charmingly dilapidated town, or 1km west in **Ammoudhélli** suburb, which has a small pea-gravel beach. A good on-spec bet is *Pension Lida* above the inland Platía Beniamín (℡ 22520 32507; ❸), a restoration inn occupying two old mansions, with sea-view balconies for most units (some not en suite); in Ammoudhéli try *Irini Apartments* (℡ 22520 32875; ❸) or *Marcia Rooms* (℡ 22520 32755; ❸), both with partial sea views. Rustling up a decent meal presents more difficulties; the line of obvious **tavernas** on the shore either side of the **post office** (**ATMs** too) are all much of a muchness. Imperial (℡ 22520 32896) is the most prominent local **car- rental** outlet.

**Áyios Isídhoros**, 3km east, is where most tourists actually stay; best of the **hotels** here, at the highest point in the settlement, is *Sandy Bay* (℡ 22520 32825, Ⓦ www.sandybay.br; B&B ❹), with well-appointed rooms (though no balcony partitions) and a pleasant lawn around the pool. For a shoreline location, try *Pebble Beach* (℡ 22520 31651; B&B ❹), where many rooms overlook a slightly reefy section of beach – though avoid those near the bar if you value sleep. For **eating** out, the clear winner is *Taverna tou Panaï* (all year) in an olive grove just by the northerly town limits sign; here you'll find salubrious meat, seafood and *mayireftá* dishes, and mostly Greeks in attendance.

**Melínda**, a 700-metre sand-and-shingle beach at the mouth of a canyon lush with olive trees, lies 6km west of Plomári by paved road. It's an alluring place, with sweeping views west towards the Vaterá coast and the cape of Áyios Fokás, and south (in clear conditions) to northern Híos, Psará and the Turkish Karaburun peninsula. Of several inexpensive taverna-rooms outfits, ramshackle *Maria's* (℡ 22520 93239; ❷) offers basic **lodging** and more elaborate **meals**. The Gannosis family's *Melinda Studios* (℡ 22520 93282 or 694 95 50 629; ❷) two doors along, has better accommodation (though no meals), as does *Melinda* (aka *Dhimitris Psaros*; ℡ 22520 93234; ❷) at the west end of the strand.

One of the best excursions beyond Melínda is to the **Panayía Kryftí hot springs**. From the first curve of the paved road up to Paleohóri, a dirt track goes 2.8km to a dead-end with parking space, with the final 400m on a downhill path to the little chapel just above a protected inlet. On the far side of this you'll see a rectangular cement tank, just big enough for two people, containing water at a pleasant 37–38°C.

Even more unspoiled than Melínda (thanks to a formerly dreadful 10km side road in, now paved except for the last 3km), **TÁRTI**, some 22km in total from Plomári, is a 400-metre-wide cove guarded by rocky capes. Of the three beachfront **tavernas** here, two work late into September; *dhomátia* (eg Vangellis Asmanis, ℡ 22510 83577; ❷) flank the final approach road should you want to **stay**.

### Ayiássos and Mylélia

**AYIÁSSOS**, nestled in a remote, wooded valley under the crest of Mount Ólymbos, is the most beautiful hill town on Lésvos, its narrow cobbled streets lined by ranks of tiled-roof houses, built in part from proceeds of the trade in *tsoupiá* (olive sacks). On the usual, northerly approach, there's no hint of the enormous village until you see huge knots of parked cars at the southern edge of town, 26km from Mytilíni. From this point, keen walkers can follow marked paths/tracks three hours to the **Ólymbos summit**. Approaching from Plomári, there's asphalt road and public transport only up to Megalohóri, with a good dirt surface and your own conveyance thereafter up to some air-force radar balls, where paving resumes. The area between Megalo-hóri and the summit ridge was damaged by a 1994 forest fire, though once over the other side dense woods of unscathed oak and chestnut take over from scorched pine.

Most visitors proceed past endless ranks of kitsch wooden and ceramic souvenirs or carved "Byzantine" furniture, aimed mostly at Greeks, and the central church of the **Panayía Vrefokratoússa** – built in the twelfth century to house an icon supposedly painted by the Evangelist Luke – to the old bazaar, with its *kafenía*, yoghurt/cheese shops and butchers' stalls. With such a venerable icon as a focus, the local August 15 *paniyíri* is one of the liveliest on Lésvos. **Restaurants** include *Dhouladhelli*, on the right at the Y-junction as you enter the village from its south end, or idiosyncratic *Ouzerí To Stavrí*, at the extreme north end of the village in Stavrí district.

Headed for Ayiássos with your own transport, you might visit the **Mylélia water mill** (daily 9am–6pm; ⊛www.mylelia.gr), its inconspciuous access track taking off 1km west of the turning for Ípios. The name means "place of the mills", and there were once several hereabouts. As the last survivor, restored to working order, the keeper will show you the mill race and paddle-wheel, as well as the flour making its spasmodic exit, after which you're free to buy gourmet pastas and other products at the shop. Since its 1990s restoration, Mylélia has branched out into cheeses, jams, vinegar, salted fish, even cooking courses – and their products are sold in every Lésvos resort as well as overseas.

### Vaterá, Skála Polikhnítou – and spas en route

A different bus route from Mytilíni leads to Vaterá beach via the inland villages of Polikhnítos and Vrýssa. If you're after a hot bath, head for the vaulted, well-restored **spa** complex 1.5km east of **Polikhnítos** (daily: April–Oct 9am–8pm; Nov–March 2–7pm; €3); there are separate, warm-hued chambers for each sex. These are preferable to the erratically managed, indifferently maintained hot springs at **Áyios Ioánnis**, 3km below the village of Lisvóri (daily 8.30–midnight; €3), where the better Ottoman bath-house is often booked by groups.

**VRÝSSA** has a **natural history museum** (daily 9.30am–5pm; €1.50) documenting local paleontological finds – though it's not exactly required viewing until or unless the gallery is expanded. In 1997 Athenian paleontologist Michael Dermitzakis confirmed what farmers unearthing bones had long suspected when he pronounced the area a treasure trove of **fossils**, including those of two-million-year-old gigantic horses, mastodons, monkeys and tortoises the size of a Volkswagen Beetle. Until 20,000 years ago, Lésvos (like all other east Aegean islands) was joined to the Asian mainland, and the gulf of Vaterá was a subtropical freshwater lake; the animals in question came to drink, died nearby and were trapped and preserved by successive volcanic flows.

**VATERÁ**, 9km south of Polikhnítos, is a seven-kilometre-long sand beach, backed by vegetated hills; the sea here is delightfully calm and clean, the strand itself among the best on Lésvos. Development, mostly seasonal villas and apartments for locals, straggles for several kilometres to either side of the central T-junction; at the west end of the strip is one of the few consistently attended and professionally run **hotels**, *Vatera Beach* (☎22520 61212, ⊛www.vaterabeach.gr; ❹ but 20 percent web discount), with air conditioning and fridges in the rooms. It also has a good **restaurant** with own-grown produce and shoreline tables looking 3km west to the cape of **Áyios Fokás**, where only the foundations remain of a temple of Dionysos and a superimposed early Christian basilica. The little tamarisk-shaded anchorage here has a fair-priced fish **taverna**, *Akrotiri/Angelerou* (April–Oct), better than most at Vaterá, and as good as those at **SKÁLA POLIKHNÍTOU**, 4km northwest of Polikhnítos itself, where *T'Asteria*, *Iliovasilema* and *Akroyiali* can all be recommended. Skála itself is pleasantly workaday, with only a short, narrow beach that morphs into a better one at **Nyfídha**, 3km west.

East from Vaterá, a mostly paved road leads via Stavrós and Akrássi to either Ayiássos or Plomári within ninety minutes, making day-trips feasible. When going north towards Kallóni, use the completely paved, fast short-cut via the naval base and seashore hamlet – with a good eponymous **taverna** – at **Akhladherí**.

# Western Lésvos

The main road west of Loutrá Yéras is surprisingly devoid of habitation, with with little of interest before you glimpse the Gulf of Kallóni. Beyond it lies a mostly treeless, craggy region whose fertile valleys offer a sharp contrast to the bare ridges. River mouths form little oases behind a handful of beach **resorts** like Skála Kallonís, Sígri and Skála Eressoú. A few **monasteries** along the road west of Kallóni, plus occasionally striking inland villages, provide monumental interest.

An ancient Aphrodite temple at **Mésa** (Méson), is 1km north of the main road, and signposted just east of the Akhladherí turn-off. At the site (periodically closed for excavations), just eleventh-century BC foundations and a few column stumps remain, plus the ruins of a fourteenth-century Genoese basilica wedged inside; it was once by the sea, but a nearby stream silted things up in the intervening millennia. It doesn't merit a special trip, merely a short detour if you're passing by with your own transport.

### Ayía Paraskeví and around

More rewardingly, bear northeast towards **AYÍA PARASKEVÍ** village, midway between two more important (and photogenic) monuments from diverse eras: the Paleo-Christian, three-aisled basilica of **Halinádhou**, its dozen basalt columns amidst pine-and-olive scenery, and the large medieval bridge of **Kremastí**, the largest and best preserved such in the east Aegean, 3km west of Ayía Paraskeví. The village itself can offer, at the southern outskirts, the

## The olives of Lésvos

No other Greek island is as dominated by **olive production** as Lésvos, which is blanketed by approximately 11 million olive trees. Most of these vast groves date from after a lethal frost in 1851, though a few hardy survivors are thought to be over five hundred years old. During the first three centuries after the Ottoman conquest, production of olive oil was a monopoly of the ruling pasha, but following eighteenth-century reforms in the Ottoman Empire, extensive tracts of Lésvos (and thus the lucrative oil trade) passed into the hands of the new Greek bourgeoisie, who greatly expanded the industry.

As in most of Greece, olives are harvested on Lésvos between late November and late December, the best ones coming from steep hillside plantations between Plomári and Ayiássos. Each grower's batch is brought to the local *trivío* (mill) – ideally within 24 hours of picking – pressed separately and tested for quality. Good first-pressing oil, some forty percent of that available in the fruit, is greenish and low in linoleic acid (by EU law, less than one-percent acidity is required to earn the label "extra virgin"). The remaining oil, much of it from the kernels and other waste mash, is used for inferior blended oils and for soap production. In general, Greek oil tends to exceed Spanish or Italian in quality, owing to hotter, drier summers which promote low acid levels in the olives.

eminently worthwhile **Mousío Viomihanikís Elaeouryías Lésvou/Lesvos Museum of the Olive-Pressing Industry** (daily except Tues 10am–6pm, closes 5pm Oct 16–Feb 28; €3), housed in the restored communal olive mill. This, built by public subscription in the 1920s, only ceased working under the junta; the industrial machinery has been lovingly refurbished and its function explained, while former outbuildings and warehouses are used as venues for secondary exhibits and short explanatory films.

### Kalloní and Skála Kallonís

**KALLONÍ** is a lively agricultural and market town in the middle of the island, with various shops and services (including a **post office** and three **ATMs**). Some 3km south lies **SKÁLA KALLONÍS**, an unlikely package resort backing a long, sandy but absurdly shallow beach on the lake-like gulf whose water can be turbid. It's mainly distinguished as a **bird-watching** centre during the March–May nesting season in the adjacent salt marshes. The pick of a half-dozen **hotels** west of town is the garden-set *Aegeon* (☎22530 22398, ⓦwww .aegeon-lesvos.gr; ❹), with above-average furnishings for its class, a large pool and friendly owners. The local speciality is the gulf's celebrated, plankton-nurtured **sardines**, best eaten fresh-grilled from August to October (though they're available salt-cured all year round); **tavernas** near the in-town fishing jetty include *Medusa*, tops for sardines, and *Omiros*, a decent, inexpensive option conveniently behind the west beach.

### Inland monasteries and villages

West of Kalloní, the road winds 4km uphill to **Limónos monastery**, founded in 1527 by the monk Ignatios, whose cell is maintained in the surviving medieval north wing. It's a rambling, three-storeyed complex around a vast, plant-filled courtyard, home to just a handful of monks and lay workers. The *katholikón*, with its ornate carved-wood ceiling and archways, is traditionally off-limits to women; a sacred spring flows from below the south foundation wall. Only a ground-floor **ecclesiastical museum** (daily 9.30am–6.30pm, may close 3pm off-season; €1.50) currently functions, with the more interesting ethnographic gallery upstairs closed. You can however see an overflow of farm implements in a storeroom below, next to a chamber where giant *pithária* (urns) for grain and olive oil are embedded in the floor.

Beyond Limónos, the main westbound road passes through **FÍLIA**, with its truncated minaret and pre-1923 mosque, where you can turn off for a broad, paved shortcut to Skoutáros and northern Lésvos. Most traffic continues through to **SKALOHÓRI**, with another battered minaret, a central **kafenío-taverna** (best at lunchtime) and houses stacked in neat tiers at the head of a valley facing the sea and the sunset. A dirt track from the north edge of the village descends about 3km to **Kálo Limáni** ("Good Harbour"), the anchorage on the east side of an isthmus-hamlet, with on the west a somewhat exposed sandy beach and a cult **taverna-ba**r, *Ta Kokkina*, with a good menu of Greek music.

The beautiful landlocked settlement of **VATOÚSSA** offers a **folklore/ historical museum** in the ancestral mansion of Grigorios Gogos, as well as excellent **grills** on the lower platía at *Renna* (alias *Tryfon*). Just beyond Vatoússa a paved side-road leads 7km to the outskirts of **HÍDHIRA**, where the **Methymneos Winery** (daily July–Sept 30 9am–6pm, otherwise by appointment on ☎22530 51518, ⓦwww.methymneos.gr) has successfully revived the local ancient grape variety, decimated by phylloxera some decades ago. Because of the altitude (300m) and sulphur-rich soil (you're in a volcanic caldera), their velvety, high-alcohol, oak-aged red can be produced organically; 2007 saw the introduction of bottled white wines. Proprietor Ioannis Lambrou gives a highly worthwhile twenty-minute tour of the state-of-the-art premises, in English. Afterwards, have a *mezédhes* **snack** at one of the village's several *kafenía*, for example *Vangelis* (on the platía) or *Thanasis*.

Some 8km beyond Vatoússa, a short track leads down to the thirteenth-century monastery of **Perivolís** (daily 10am–1pm & 5–6pm; donation, no photos), built amid a riverside orchard (*perivóli*), with fine if damp-damaged sixteenth-century frescoes in the narthex. An apocalyptic panel worthy of Bosch (*The Earth and Sea Yield up their Dead*) shows the Whore of Babylon riding her chimera and assorted sea monsters disgorging their victims; just to the right, towards the main door, the Three Magi approach the Virgin enthroned with the Christ Child. On the north side there's a highly unusual iconography of Abraham, the Virgin, and the Penitent Thief of Calvary in Paradise, with the Four Rivers of Paradise gushing forth under their feet; just right are assembled the Hebrew kings of the Old Testament.

### Ándissa and around

**ÁNDISSA**, 3km further on, nestles under this parched region's only substantial pine grove; at the edge of the village a sign implores you to "Come Visit Our Square", not a bad idea for the sake of a handful of **tavernas** (the best being *Pedhinon*) and *kafenía* sheltering under three sizeable plane trees. Directly below Ándissa a paved road leads 6km north to **Gavathás**, a shortish, partly protected **beach** with a few places to **eat** and **stay** – among these *Pension Restaurant Paradise* (☏22530 56376; ❷), serving good fish and locally grown vegetables. A side road leads one headland east to huge, duney, surf-battered **Kámbos** beach, as well as signposted "Ancient Antissa", actually **Ovriókastro**, the most derelict of the island's Genoese castles, evocatively placed with a good stretch of coast to either side. In legend the head of Orpheus, torn off by Thracian Maenads, washed ashore here with his lyre, still singing – and imparting lyric gifts to the ancient islanders.

In the opposite direction, from behind Gavathás beach, an inconspicuous but initially paved road leads up to the hillside oasis village of **LIÓTA** (Lygerí on some maps), with a small Byzantine chapel and two simple summertime **tavernas** nearby. From near the chapel, the road (now dirt) continues to the vastly sandy, but unamenitied beach of **Lápsarna**, from where it's 9km back to Ándissa.

Just west of Ándissa there's an important junction. Keeping straight leads you past the still-functioning, double-gated monastery of **Ypsilou**, founded in 1101 atop an outrider of extinct Órdhymnos volcano. The *katholikón*, tucked in one corner of a large, irregular courtyard, has a fine wood-lattice ceiling but has had its frescoes repainted to detrimental effect. Exhibits in the upstairs museum (donation) encompass a fine collection of *epitáfios* (Good Friday) shrouds, ancient manuscripts, portable icons and – oddest of all – a *Deposition* painted in Renaissance style by a sixteenth-century Turk. Ypsilou's patron saint is John the Divine, a frequent dedication for monasteries overlooking apocalyptic landscapes like the surrounding boulder-strewn hills.

Just west begins the five-kilometre side road to the main concentration of Lésvos's overrated **petrified forest** (daily: June–Sept 8am–sunset, Oct–May 8am–4pm; €2), a fenced-in "reserve" toured along 3km of walkways. For once, contemporary Greek arsonists cannot be blamed for the state of the trees, created by the combined action of volcanic ash from Órdhymnos and hot springs some fifteen to twenty million years ago. The mostly horizontal sequoia trunks average 1m or less in length, save for a few poster-worthy exceptions; another more accessible (and free) cluster is found south of Sígri.

## Sígri

**SÍGRI**, near the western tip of Lésvos, has an appropriately end-of-the-line feel; its bay is guarded both by an Ottoman castle and the long island of **Nissiopí**, which protects the place somewhat from prevailing winds. Until the early 1990s Sígri was an important NATO naval base; civilian ferries call here unreliably depending on the year. The eighteenth-century **castle** (built atop an earlier one) sports the reigning sultan's monogram over the entrance, something rarely seen outside İstanbul, evidence of the high regard in which this strategic port with a good water supply was held. The odd-looking church of **Ayía Triádha** is in fact a converted **mosque**, with a huge water cistern taking up the ground floor; this supplied, among other things, the half-ruined **hamam** just south. At the top of town stands the well-executed but overpriced **Natural History Museum of the Lésvos Petrified Forest** (daily: May 15–Oct 15 8.30am–8pm; Oct 16–May 14 8.30am–4.30pm; €5), which covers pan-Aegean geology with samples and maps (including, ominously, seismic patterns), as well as the expected quota of petrified logs and plant fossils from when the surrounding hills were far more vegetated. Sígri itself presents an odd mix of vernacular and concrete dwellings, while the town **beach**, south of the castle headland, is long, narrow and protected, with a **taverna**. There are much better beaches at **Faneroméni**, 3.5km north by coastal dirt track from the northern outskirts of town, or at **Liména** (part naturist), 2km south, just below the fifteen-kilometre dirt track to Eressós; neither has any facilities.

Package companies have vanished, so **accommodation** is fairly easy to find by direct booking; two of the best are *Evangelia* (☎694 49 43 063, ⓦsigri-lesvos.co.uk/evan2.html; ②–③), with studios and apartments and some units looking across the bay, and *Pyrgospito/Towerhouse* (☎22530 22909, ⓦwww.lesvos-towerhouse.gr; ⑤–⑥), four antique-furnished apartments in a Belle Époque folly 500m outside of the village, in a landscaped hillside setting with pool. Among a half-dozen **tavernas**, the *Cavo d'Oro/Blue Wave* (no sign) by the harbour is a classic for lobster and scaly fish; most of the restaurants around the nearby platía are run-of-the-mill in comparison. **Nightlife** is provided by durable *Notia* (June–Sept), with frequent live jazz sessions.

The nearest of several **beaches**, south of the castle headland, is somewhat narrow and backed by a little-used road to Eressós; the far superior, if unamenitied, one of **Faneroméni** lies 3.5km north by a coastal dirt track from the northern outskirts of town. A shorter but equally good strand, **Liména**, can be found 2km south of Sígri at another creek mouth, just off the rough one-lane, fifteen-kilometre track to Eressós (passable with care in an ordinary car most years, in 35min).

## Skála Eressoú and around

Most visitors to western Lésvos park themselves at **SKÁLA ERESSOÚ**, reached via a southerly turning between Ándissa and Ypsiloú. Its three-kilometre **beach** rivals Vatera's, and consequently the resort just trails Mólyvos, Pétra and Plomári for visitor numbers. Behind stretches the largest and most attractive agricultural plain on Lésvos, a welcome green contrast to the volcanic ridges above.

There's not much to central Skála – just a roughly rectangular grid of perhaps five streets by twelve, angling up to the oldest cottages on the slope of Vígla hill

▲ Wood taverna deck, Skála Eressoú, Lésvos

above the east end of the beach. The waterfront pedestrian lane is divided midway by a café-lined, circular platía with a bust of **Theophrastos**. This renowned botanist hailed from **ancient Eressos** atop Vígla hill – the remaining citadel wall is still visible from a distance. The ruins themselves prove scanty, but it's worth the scramble up for the views – you can spy the ancient jetty submerged beyond the modern fishing anchorage.

Another famous native of ancient Eressós, honoured by a stylized statue on the platía, was **Sappho** (c.615–562 BC), poetess and reputed lesbian. There are thus always conspicuous numbers of gay women about (especially during the annual September festival), particularly in the clothing-optional zone of the **beach** west of the river mouth, home to a small community of terrapins. Ancient Eressós lasted into the Byzantine era, whose main legacy is the **Áyios Andhréas** basilica behind the modern church – foundations and a fragmentary, if restored, floor mosaic remain. The tomb of the saint, an early Cretan bishop (not the patron of Scotland), huddles just beyond.

If you're **returning to the main island crossroads** at Kallóni, you can loop back from Eressós along the western shore of the Gulf of Kallóni via Mesótopos, Ágra and Parákila villages (you can climb the isolated minaret at Parákila), much quicker than returning via Ándissa and Skalohóri. Just off this paved road there's an excellent **beach** at **Kroússos**, with a cult ⚑ **taverna** installed in an immobilized bus at the east end; here Kyra-Maria lays on home-style food (good white bulk wine, snails, chickpea soup, *dolmádhes*, beans, maybe sea urchin roe) a world away from resort platters, at attractive prices.

### Practicalities

Skála has countless **rooms** and **apartments** (❷–❹), but those near the sea fill quickly and can be noisy; in peak season you should aim for something quiet and inland, overlooking a garden or fields. Attempts to promote Skála as a family resort have been stymied by its enduring reputation as the premier **lesbian watering hole** of Europe, engendered by the Sappho connection and helped along by some sensational documentaries on UK television. Lesbians remain the most consistent and loyal customers, with locals reluctant to bite the hand that feeds, but most package companies have dropped the place, making vacancies easier to find. Still, it's wise to entrust the search to Sappho Travel (℡22530 52202 or 22530 52140, ⓦwww.lesvos.co.uk), which also serves as a car-rental station, ferry agent and air-ticket source.

Otherwise, there are few bona fide **hotels** in the village, some of which are **women-only** – for example the seafront, 2007-redone *Sappho the Eressia* (℡22530 53233, ⓦwww.sappho-hotel.com; ❸), with wi-fi and a pleasant ground-floor snack bar, and *Mascot* (book through Sappho Travel; ❹), three blocks inland. A straight alternative is the popular if basic *Kyma* (℡22530 5355; ❹), at the east end of the front, with seven of ten rooms facing the sea, and wi-fi in the lobby.

Most **tavernas**, with elevated wooden dining platforms, crowd the beach; in the wake of a post-millennium tourism slump, they've been subjected to harsh winnowing. Worthy survivors include *Kyani Sardhini/Blue Sardine*, a creditable seafood ouzerí at the far west end of the front, or nearby *Soulatsos*, one of the more reliable and popular grill-and-*mezédhes* outfits. *Margaritari* on the east quay is the venue for somewhat pricey puddings, including Austrian strudel.

With about seven clubs/bars to choose from in peak season, local **nightlife** is the best on the island. Gay women favour *Sappho Garden of the Arts* inland, often with live events; *Parasol* and *Cooya Caribu* are straighter café-bars on the east esplanade, while well-established *Primitive*, west of town past the bridge over the terrapin-filled river, is unbeatable for theme parties. There's also a central, open-air **cinema** (July to early Sept), called (predictably) Sappho. Skála has a **post office**, an **ATM**, and a seafront **internet café** on the east walkway and two bars with wi-fi. An alternative local car rental agency is Igfa (Alamo/National reps; ℡22530 53001).

# Northern Lésvos

The road **north from Kalloní** curls up a piney ridge, then down the other side into countryside stippled with poplars and blanketed by olive groves. Long before you can discern any other architectural detail, **Mólyvos castle's** cockscomb silhouette indicates your approach to the oldest-established destination on Lésvos.

## Mólyvos (Míthymna)

**MÓLYVOS** (officially Míthymna after its ancient predecessor), 61km from Mytilíni, is arguably the island's most beautiful village, with tiers of sturdy, red-tiled houses, some standing with their rear walls defensively towards the sea, mounting the slopes between the picturesque harbour and the Byzantine-Genoese **castle** (closed for restoration). A score of weathered Turkish fountains, a mosque and hamam grace flower-fragrant, cobbled alleyways, reflecting the fact that before 1923 Muslims constituted more than a third of the local population and owned many of the finest dwellings. The **Komninaki Kralli mansion**, high up in the town, is particularly worth a look (daily 9am–5pm; free); the lower floor houses a well-signposted "School of Fine Arts", but the wall- and ceiling-murals on the upper storey (dated 1833) compare with those of the Vareltzídena mansion in Pétra (see p.471). Panels in the smallest room portray dervish musicians and women dancing to shaum and drum, while other murals depict stylized versions of Constantinople and Mytilíni Town; you can tell the men's and women's quarters apart by the wider recessed "throne" provided for the latter.

Modern dwellings and hotels have been banned from the old core, but this hasn't prevented a steady drain of all authentic life from the upper **bazaar**; perhaps four or five "ordinary" shops ply their trade amongst souvenir shops vastly surplus to requirements. Once an exclusive resort, Mólyvos is now firmly middle of the road, with the usual silly T-shirts and other trinkets carpeting every vertical surface of a stage-set, albeit an attractive one, for package tourism. The shingly **town beach** is mediocre, improving considerably as you head towards the sandy southern end of the bay, called **Psiriára**, with its clothing-optional zone. Advertised **boat excursions** to remote bays like Tsónia seem a frank admission of this failing; there are also frequent shuttle buses in season, linking all points between Ánaxos and Eftaloú.

### Arrival and information

The municipal **tourist office** (summer Mon–Sat 10am–3pm, Sun 10am–2.30pm; ☎22530 71347, ⓦwww.mithymna.gr) by the **bus** stop, **taxi** rank and main **car park** at the southeast edge of town (a big, newer lot has opened above the port, joining an existing one up by the castle) keeps lists of rented **rooms**. Nearby you'll find three **ATMs**, plus numerous **motor-bike** and **car-rental** places, including Kosmos (☎22530 71710), Best (☎22530 72145) and Avis (☎22530 71797), all offering the option of pick-up here and drop-off in Mytilíni or the airport. The main **post office** is near the top of the upper commercial street; Centraal and Resalto, down near the harbour, are the principal **internet** cafés, with ADSL connection.

### Accommodation

The main sea-level thoroughfare of Miháïl Goútou links the tourist office with the harbour; just seaward stand a number of bona fide **hotels** or **pensions** not completely taken over by packages. These include the *Hermes* on the beach (☎22530 71250, ⓦwww.hermeshotel-molivos.com; ❸), with variable, marble-floored rooms, and the *Molyvos I* next door (☎22530 71496, ⓦwww.molyvos-hotels.com; ❹), with large balconied rooms, and breakfast served on the flagstoned terrace under the palms. For more comfort, head 1km south of town to the friendly 🍴 *Delfinia* (☎22530 71315, ⓦwww .hoteldelfinia.com; all year; ❺–❼, internet discounts), with rooms and bungalows set in 87 acres of greenery, a castle-view pool, tennis courts and direct access to Psiriára beach.

**Rooms** are scattered along the lanes leading uphill from the upper market thoroughfare. Best of these are *Studios Voula* below the castle car park (☎22530 71719 or 694 52 41 994), which has studios (❸) and a restored four-person house (❺), both with knockout views. Families should consider the restored *Captain's House* offered by Theo and Melinda (☎22530 71241, ⓦwww.lesvosvacations.com), up by the Komninaki Kralli mansion; it sleeps up to six, with seasonal rates of €90–140 for the entire premises. The municipal **campsite**, *Camping Methymna* (late June–Sept), lies 2km northeast of town on the Eftaloú road.

### Eating, drinking and nightlife

The sea-view **tavernas** on both lower and upper market lanes are for the most part much of a muchness, where you pay primarily for the view; best head for the fishing port, where 🍴 *The Captain's Table* (supper only) offers squirming fresh seafood, meat grills and vegetarian *mezédhes*, washed down by their very palatable, own-label wine. *To Ouzadhiko tou Baboukou* (all year), around the corner on the south quay, has an impressive array of ouzos, a bohemian atmosphere and competent, well-priced (for the location) renditions of the usual *mezédhes*. *Babís*, at the town approaches with semi-rural seating, is the place to head for good grills and a few *mayireftá* of the day. For **snacks**, municipally run *Iy Agora* (*To Dhimotiko Kafenio*), just downhill from the converted mosque/conference centre, has a lovely wood interior, a panoramic balcony, subsidized and thus inexpensive ouzo-*mezédhes* combos and larger platters from a limited menu.

**Nightlife** revolves around several musical bars: most durable is youth-orientated, tropical-themed *Congas* (May–Sept) down by the shore, with DJ events, sunset snacks and theme nights. Just above the harbour, *Molly's Bar* is the thirty-somethings' preferred hangout, with taped music at a conversational level and a cosy balcony, while *Bazaar* opposite is the main indoor dance hall. There's also a well-regarded outdoor **cinema** (June–Sept) next to the taxi rank.

### Pétra, Ánaxos and Ambélia

Given political and practical limits to expansion in Mólyvos, many package companies have shifted emphasis to **PÉTRA**, 5km due south. The modern outskirts sprawl untidily behind its broad sand beach, but two attractive nuclei of old stone houses, some with Levantine-style balconies overhanging the street, extend back from the part-pedestrianized seafront square. Pétra takes its name from the giant, unmissable rock monolith inland, enhanced by the eighteenth-century church of the **Panayía Glykofiloússa**, reached via 114 rock-hewn steps. Other local attractions include the sixteenth-century church of **Áyios Nikólaos**, with three phases of well-preserved frescoes up to 1721, and the intricately decorated **Vareltzídhena mansion** (Tues–Sun 8am–2.30pm; free), with naïve, late-eighteenth-century wall paintings of courting couples, a bear being trained, sailing ships and a stylized view of a naval engagement at Constantinople.

In addition to a couple of **ATMs**, Pétra's amenities include a **post office**, next to Áyios Nikólaos, and a number of **scooter** or **car-rental** places such as Homerus (℡22530 41577) on the north side of town, or Budget (c/o Nirvana Travel, ℡22530 41991). Most small **hotels** and studios are block-booked, so on-spec arrivals might contact the **Women's Agricultural Tourism Cooperative** on the south side of the seafront square (℡22530 41238, Ⓔwomes@otenet.gr), which arranges rooms or studios (❷–❸) in scattered premises. For more comfort, try the *Hotel Michaelía* behind the south waterfront (℡22530 41730; ❹), with decent buffet breakfasts, or the three-star *Clara Hotel-Bungalows* at Avláki, 2km south (℡22530 41 532, Ⓦwww.clarahotel.gr; ❻), the first and still one of the best luxury complexes near Pétra, with a pool and tennis court. All of the large, tastefully furnished units, a mix of standard rooms, studios and suites, face the sea and Mólyvos.

The excellent, well-priced Women's Coop **restaurant** serves grills and *mayireftá* at rooftop seating. Alternatives include cheap-and-cheerful grill *Kostas*, on a little square east of the monolith; characterful *Rigas* (evenings only), Pétra's oldest ouzerí, further inland; and *Tsalikis Café* on the square for excellent own-made ice cream. You may prefer to leave town – either to ✻ *Taverna Petri* (all day May to mid-Oct) in **PETRÍ** village 3km inland, with superb home-recipe *mayireftá*, meat grills and a view-terrace, or to tiny **Avláki** beach and its competent, signposted **taverna/ouzerí**, 1.5km southwest en route to Ánaxos.

**ÁNAXOS**, 3km south of Pétra, is a higgledy-piggledy package resort fringing by far the cleanest **beach** and seawater in the area: 1km of sand well sown with sunbeds and a handful of **tavernas**. From anywhere along here you enjoy beautiful sunsets between and beyond three offshore islets.

For something utterly different, drivers can head 1km south, then 3km west along a well-signposted side road (then right at the only fork) to **Ambélia**, a 700-metre sand-and-pebble bay. There are some large rocks in the shallows, and often washed-up seaweed, but generally the place is clean, with a cultivated valley for a backdrop. Facilities are limited to a single **taverna** (*George's*), where decently prepared vegetables and fish in season belie the dubious appearance of the kitchen.

### Eftaloú and its spa

**EFTALOÚ**, though technically part of Mólvos, almost counts as a separate resort 2–3km northeast, with numerous fancy **hotels** and bungalow complexes. The friendliest and best value (though tour-dominated like the others) is *Eftalou* (T22530 71584, Wwww.eftalouhotel.com; ❹), with a pool, well-tended garden and loyal repeat clientele. A worthwhile **taverna** within sight of the spa is *Iy Eftalou*, with a shady courtyard, large meat grills, fish and *mayireftá*, if sometimes glum service.

The **Loutrá Eftaloú** thermal baths lie 5km east of Mólyvos, at the end of the paved road (and occasional summer shuttle-bus service). Patronize the hot pool under the Ottoman-era domed structure, not the sterile modern tub-rooms (daily: May & Oct 9am–1pm & 3–7pm; June–Sept 10am–2pm & 4–8pm; Dec–April variable access; €3.50 for group pool). The spa is well looked after, with the water mixed up to a toasty 43°C, so you'll need to cool down regularly; outside stretches the long, good pebble beach of **Áyii Anáryiri**, broken up by little headlands, with the two remotest coves nudist. There's a fetchingly positioned **taverna** here, the *Khrysi Akti*, which also lets small en-suite **rooms** (T22530 71879; ❷) in the old spa-patrons' inn, built around a church.

### Around Mount Lepétymnos

East of Mólyvos, the villages of 968-metre, poplar-tufted **Mount Lepétymnos** provide a day's rewarding exploration. The main paved road around Lepétymnos first heads 5km east to **VAFIÓS**, with its clutch of three fairly comparable **tavernas** with views (*Vafios, Ilias, Petrino*) – *Petrino* is the cheapest, and open winter weekends too – before curling north around the base of the mountain. The exquisite hill village of **SYKAMINIÁ** (Sykamiá, Skamniá) was the 1892 birthplace of novelist Stratis Myrivilis; below the platía, with its two *kafenía* and views north to Turkey, one of the imposing basalt-built houses is marked as his childhood home.

A marked trail shortcuts the twisting road down to **SKÁLA SYKAMINIÁS**, easily the most picturesque fishing port on Lésvos. Myrivilis used it as the setting for his best-known work, *The Mermaid Madonna*, and the tiny rock-top chapel at the end of the jetty will be instantly recognizable to anyone who has read the book. Skála has ample **accommodation**, including the central, partly air-conditioned *Gorgona* (T22530 55301; ❸), with a shaded breakfast terrace, and several **tavernas**. *Iy Skamnia* (*Iy Mouria tou Myrivili*) has seating under the mulberry tree in which Myrivilis used to sleep on hot summer nights, though *Anemoessa* (by the chapel, open winter weekends too) has the edge quality-wise, with good stuffed squash blossoms complementing fresh seafood. The only local **beach** is the pebble-on-sand-base one of Kayiá 1.5km east, where *Poseidon* **taverna** operates in season. A fairly rough, roller-coaster track follows the shore west from Skála for 9km back to the baths at Eftaloú, its condition not deterring a steady stream of vehicles.

Some 5km east from upper Sykaminiá, you reach **KLIÓ**, whose single main street leads down to a platía with a plane tree, fountain, *kafenía* and more views

# Greek **cuisine**

Although standards like kalamári and moussaka often dominate taverna menus, Greek cooking is more complex and varied than these ubiquitous cliché dishes might suggest. Modern Greeks are rediscovering their rich rural culinary heritage: initially simple and functional, relying on local products, later expanding under the influence of elaborate recipes brought by immigrants from Asia Minor. The resulting cuisine relies on fresh raw ingredients, subtle herbal fillips and preparation by charcoal grilling or in wood-burning ovens. Myriad regional specialities are proudly touted: anything from whole pickled caper sprigs to smoked eels, molluscs bottled in brine to soft sheep's cheese, thyme honey to wild almond syrup.

# Eat your greens

Wild or cultivated **vegetables** are the bedrock of Greek cuisine. During the cooler months, street markets overflow with **leafy greens**: purslane, rocket, various chicories, chards and the edible weeds known as *hórta*. These and other garden vegetables end up in salads, *píttes* (baked pies), fritters and casseroles. *Briám* or *tourloú* is a ratatouille of courgettes, potatoes, aubergines and tomatoes; chickpeas are stewed or formed into *revythokeftédhes* (coarse falafels). The versatile aubergine gets fried in slices, stuffed and baked, or puréed. Chips are a staple; any restaurant keen on its reputation prepares them fresh, daily.

## Olives and olive oil

**Olive oil** is a universal ingredient; traditionally every family, even city-dwelling, got its own from trees on a country property. **Olives** are harvested between November and January, beaten off the trees early on, or harvested ripe from the ground. There are over a dozen varieties, coloured from green to black to purple: some are used mainly for oil, but others are reserved for eating, particularly in the ubiquitous *horiátiki* or "peasant" salad.

## Meat and cheese

Formerly reserved for festive meals, **meat** now figures almost daily in local diets. Besides chops and *pansétta* (spare ribs), **pork** appears as locally made *loukánika* (sausages), the legendary take-away snack *souvláki*, or stewed with celery or plums. Many casserole dishes are meat-based; standards include the perennial favourites moussaka and *stifádho* (stew). **Goat**, whether stewed, baked or grilled,

Vegetable market ▲

Olives ready for the press ▼

is the healthiest meat around, free-range and redolent of the herby hillside on which it grazed. Those herbs reappear at taverna **grills**, where the proprietor bastes your order, sizzling over olive- or oak-wood coals, with a "broom" of thyme or oregano.

Greeks are, perhaps surprisingly, Europe's biggest **cheese** consumers and every region of Greece produces it, feta merely being the most famous. Consistency varies from hard blocks of *kéfalograviéra* meant for grating over pasta to pyramids of soft cheeses like sweet *manoúri* or *anthótyro* and savoury *dhermatísio*, used for spreading or stuffing. Special treats include Hiot cow's-milk *mastéllo*, served grilled, or the wine-marinated *krasotýri* from Kós.

▲ Kebabs sizzle on spits

▼ A large bream served at the table

## Fish and seafood

Besides premium, often farmed **fish** like bream and bass, there are more affordable, seasonally available species. Delicacies include springtime shrimp and sole, and anchovies, *atherína* (sand smelt) and sardines in late summer, all best flash-fried. Everywhere, fried *gópes* (bogue), *soupiá* (cuttlefish) with rice and spinach, and grilled or wine-stewed octopus are good year-round choices. **Shellfish** such as *petalídhes* (limpets), *yialisterés* (smooth Venus), *kydhónia* (cockles) and *petrosolínes* (razor clams) should be eaten alive to avoid poisoning – if they twitch when drizzled with lemon juice, they're fine.

## Ouzo

**Ouzo**, the quintessential Greek apéritif, is produced by distilling the fermented grape-mash residue left after wine-pressing. The resulting liquid, originally called **rakí**, grew in popularity during the nineteenth century, when distilleries appeared in

Smyrna, Constantinople and Lésvos. The word ouzo derives from the Italian label *uso Massalia* applied to early *rakí* shipments leaving the Ottoman Empire for Marseille. Today it means *rakí* flavoured with various **aromatic spices**, usually star anise or fennel, both containing anethole, which causes ouzo to turn milky white when water is added.

## Greek coffee

**Greek coffee** is essentially the same drink that's prepared across the Middle East and Balkans; indeed the term "Turkish coffee" was used in Greece until the Cyprus crises of 1954–74 prompted renaming. It's made with fine-ground robusta beans (not the arabica used in filter coffee), sugar to taste and water, combined in a long-handled vessel known as a **bríki**. Allowing it to surge, but not boil, twice before decanting produces the prized **kaïmáki** (froth), a test of properly made coffee. Once you've finished your cup – except for the residue at the bottom – cover it with the saucer, invert, and swirl. The resulting patterns on the cup-side can be used to tell your fortune by the local *kafetzoúles*, ladies well-versed in this divinatory art.

Greek coffee ▲

Wine on display, Kefaloniá ▼

## Greek wine

Quality **wine-making** is a big part of the Greek culinary renaissance; local vintners have a distinguished pedigree going back four thousand years, but production remains low. If you think that Greek wine begins and ends with retsina, think again – top-drawer vintages are every bit as sophisticated (and pricey) as their French, Australian or South American counterparts. See p.55 for a summary of Greek wine domaines.

across to Turkey. The village is set attractively on a slope, down which a wide, paved six-kilometre road descends to **Tsónia** beach, 600m of beautiful pink volcanic sand. *Oniro* at the more protected north end is by far the more popular of two **tavernas**. Just south of Klió, a right (west) fork toward Kápi allows you to complete a loop of the mountain. **PELÓPI** is the ancestral village of unsuccessful 1988 US presidential candidate Michael Dukakis (who finally visited the island in 2000); the main street is now named after him, and the main walkers' path up to the peak is signposted from here. Garden-lush **YPSILOMÉTOPO**, 5km further along, is punctuated by a minaret (but no mosque) and hosts revels on July 16–17, the feast of Ayía Marína.

Like Pelópi, the westernmost foothill villages of **Petrí** and **Stýpsi** also make good jump-off points for rambles along Lepétymnos' steadily dwindling network of **trails**; across northern Lévos you'll see advertisements for **donkey- or mule-trekking**, which has become more popular than **walking**. During the 1990s, the Mytilíni EOT marked several long-distance routes across the island with yellow diamonds, documenting them in its brochure "Trekking Trails on Lesvos". However, these rely almost exclusively on vehicle tracks or roads, and are considered locally as something of a bad joke; the most worthwhile and path-like of these itineraries, besides the summit trail from Pelópi, are the coastal track from Pétra to Ambélia and the Kápi–Sykaminiá–Skála Sykaminiá traverse. A much better printed **guide** is the locally (and internationally) sold, self-published one by Mike Maunder, *On Foot in North Lesvos*, which details some rambles on the hillsides.

# Límnos

**Límnos** is a sizeable agricultural and military island whose remoteness and peculiar ferry schedules protected it until the mid-1990s from most aspects of the holiday trade. Conventional tourism was late in coming because hoteliers lived primarily off the visiting relatives of the numerous soldiers stationed here; most summer visitors are still Greek, particularly from Thessaloníki, though Danes, Brits, Austrians, Czechs and Italians now arrive by charter flights. Bucolic Límnos has become positively trendy of late: there are upscale souvenir shops, old village houses restored by mainlanders (and foreigners) as seasonal retreats, and a noon-to-small-hours music bar during summer at nearly every beach.

The island has long been the focus of **disputes** between the Greek and Turkish governments; Turkey has a perennial demand that Límnos be demilitarized, and Turkish aircraft regularly intrude Greek air space overhead, prompting immediate responses from the Greek Air Force squadron based here. Límnos's **garrison** ran to 25,000 soldiers at the nadir of Greco-Turkish relations during the 1970s and 1980s, though it is now down to about 6000, and set to fall further if/when Greece abolishes conscription and most of the remaining army camps (but not the air base) close. For years security considerations meant there was no remotely decent **map** of Límnos, but the military has finally relented and allowed Road Editions to produce an unusually accurate 1:50,000 product.

The **bays** of **Bourniá** and **Moúdhros**, the latter one of the largest natural harbours in the Aegean, divide Límnos almost in two. The west of the island is dramatically hilly, with abundant basalt put to good use as street cobbles and house masonry. The east is low-lying and speckled with seasonal salt marshes,

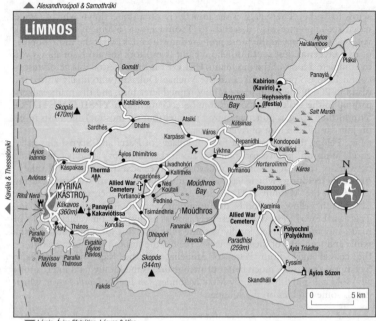

▲ Alexandhroúpoli & Samothráki

**LÍMNOS**

Gomáti

Áyios Harálambos

Pláka

Panayiá

Kabirion (Kavírio)

Katálakkos

Bourniá Bay

Hephaestia (Ifestía)

Salt Marsh

Skopiá (470m)

Atsikí

Kótsinas

Sardhés

Dháfni

Város

Karpássi

Repanídhi

Kondopoúli

Kalliópi

Kornós

Áyios Ioánnis

Áyios Dhimítrios

Lýkhna

Hortarolímni

Kéros

Káspakas

Thermá

Livadhohóri

Kallithéa

Romanoú

Roussopoúli

Avlónas

MÝRINA (KÁSTRO)

Angariónes

Néa Koútali

Moúdhros Bay

Allied War Cemetery

Portianoú

Pedhinó

Kamínia

Ríha Nerá

Kákavos (360m)

Panayía Kakaviótissa

Tsimándhria

Moúdhros

Allied War Cemetery

Polyochni (Polyókhni)

Platý

Thános

Kondiás

Fanaráki

Dhiapóri

Paradhísi (259m)

Ayía Triádha

Paralía Platý

Evgátis (Áyios Pávlos)

Havoúli

Playísou Mólos

Paralía Thánous

Skopós (344m)

Fyssíni

Áyios Sózon

Fakós

Skandháli

N

0      5 km

▼ Lávrio, Áyios Efstrátios, Lésvos & Híos

where it's not occupied by cattle, combine harvesters and vast corn fields. Like most volcanic islands, Límnos produces excellent wine – good dry white, rosé and retsina – plus ouzo. The Limnians proudly tout an abundance of **natural food products**, including thyme honey and sheep's cheese, and indeed the population is almost self-sufficient in foodstuffs. Despite off-islander slander, Límnos is not flat, barren or treeless; the rolling hills are well vegetated except on their heights, with substantial clumps of almond, jujube, myrtle, oak, poplar and mulberry trees. This far north, snow falls annually and stays on the ground, responsible for both novelty postcards of a white Límnos and a healthy hydrology, with irrigation water pumped from deep wells, and a few potable springs in the western half. Various streambeds bring sand to long, sandy **beaches** around the coast, where it's easy to find a stretch to yourself. Most bays shelve gently, making them ideal for children and quick to warm up in spring, with no cool currents except near the river mouths.

## Mýrina

**MÝRINA** (aka Kástro), the port-capital on the west coast, has the ethos of a provincial market town rather than a resort. With about five thousand inhabitants, it's pleasantly low-key, if not especially picturesque, apart from a core neighbourhood of old stone houses dating from the Ottoman era, and the ornate Neoclassical mansions of Romeïkós Yialós.

### Arrival, information and transport

The civilian **airport** lies 18km east of Mýrina, almost at the geographic centre of the island, sharing a runway with an enormous air-force base; there are three **car rental** booths, an **ATM**, a few **taxis** outside – and no shuttle bus into town. **Ferries** dock at the southern edge of Mýrina, in the shadow of the castle; the newer jetty on the far side of the bay serves commercial lorries only. There are separate **agencies** for the sailings of NEL ferries (Pravlis Travel, ☎ 22540 24617) and Saos Ferries (☎ 22540 29571).

The **bus station** is on Platía Eleftheríou Venizélou, at the north end of Kydhá. One look at the sparse schedules (a single daily afternoon departure to most points) will convince you of the need to **rent a vehicle** from outlets clustered around the harbour area. Cars, motorbikes and bicycles can be rented from Limnos Car Rental (☎ 22540 23777, airport ☎ 694 54 95 104), Myrina Rent a Car (☎ 22540 24476), Petrides Travel (☎ 22540 22039, airport ☎ 22540 24787) and Holiday (☎ 22540 23280, airport ☎ 693 24 81 056); rates for bikes are only slightly above the island norm, but cars are exorbitant. A motorbike (most obviously from Moto Lemnos, ☎ 22540 25002, in from the jetty clocktower) is generally enough to explore the coast and the interior of the closer villages, as there are few steep gradients but many perilously narrow streets. A 2006-built **bypass road** via Néa Mádhitos district and the commercial port has relieved most of Mýrina's traffic bottlenecks; **parking**, however, remains nightmarish, with spaces possible only at the outskirts.

Most bank **ATMs** cluster around a platía about halfway along Kydhá; the main **taxi** rank is here too, while the **post office** is around the corner on Garou-falídhi. Among three **internet** cafés, the most convenient and pleasant is Excite just back from the harbour roundabout.

## Accommodation

Despite Límnos's steady gentrification, and explicit discouragement of backpackers, one may still be met off the boat with offers of a **room** or **studio**; there are officially two dozen or so licensed establishments in Mýrina, especially in the northern districts of **Rihá Nerá** and **Áyios Pandelímonas**. Otherwise there are adequate in-town **hotels** plus upmarket complexes at nearby beaches. At **Romeïkós Yialós** a few restored old buildings serve as small inns, though many are affected by noise from the seafront bars. There's no official **campsite**, though a few tents sprout furtively at Kéros (see p.479).

▲ Romeïkós Yialós, from the Byzantine castle

Apollo Pavilion On Frýnis ☎22540 23712. Hidden away in a peaceful cul-de-sac about halfway along Garoufalídhou, this offers three-bed a/c studios with TV and mini-kitchen. Most units, part-refurbished in 2007, have balconies, with views of either the castle or the mountains. Open all year. ❸
Arhondiko Cnr Sakhtoúri and Filellínon, Romeïkós Yialós ☎22540 29800, ✍www.guestinn.com. Límnos's first hotel, this 1851-built mansion was reopened in 2003 as three floors of small-to-medium-sized, wood-trimmed rooms with all mod cons (but no balconies). There's a pleasant ground-floor bar/breakfast lounge, though bathrooms are already dated and a major overhaul is scheduled. ❹
Ifestos Ethnikís Andístasis 17, Andhróni district, inland from Rihá Nerá ☎22540 24960. Quiet, professionally run two-star hotel, with pleasant common areas. Slightly small rooms have a/c, fridges, balconies and a mix of sea or hill views. ❹
Nefeli Suites Castle approach, Romeïkós Yialós ☎22540 23551, ✉info@nefeli-lemnos.gr. These apartments include four-plexes suitable for families, though no balconies. Enjoy the view instead from the terrace-café on the west side of the building. Limited parking. ❹
Porto Myrina Avlónas beach, 1.5km north of Rihá Nerá ☎22540 24805. The island's best beachfront lodging, though its five-star rating is really one too many. Standard rooms and free-standing bungalows surround an Artemis temple found during construction; vast common areas include tennis courts, a football pitch, one of the largest (salt-water) pools in Greece, and summer water-sports on the beach. Open May–Oct 15. ❻–❼

## The Town

Mýrina's main attraction is its **Byzantine castle** (unrestricted access), perched on a craggy headland between the ferry dock and Romeïkós Yialós, the town's beach-lined esplanade backed by ornate Neoclassical mansions. Ruinous despite later Genoese and Ottoman additions, the fortress is flatteringly lit at night and warrants a climb towards sunset for views over the town, the entire west coast and – in clear conditions – Mount Áthos, 35 nautical miles west. Miniature, skittish deer imported from Rhodes, and fed by the municipality, patrol the castle grounds to the amusement of visitors. Behind the hospital in a small park is another diminutive, signposted fort, the **Dápia**, built by the Russian Orloff brothers during their abortive 1770 invasion. The fort failed spectacularly in its avowed purpose to besiege and bombard the main castle, as did the entire rebellion, and Ottoman reprisals on the island were severe. Despite an appreciable pre-1923 Turkish population, few explicitly **Islamic monuments** have survived. A dilapidated octagonal structure with an inscription over the door, probably the *tekke* or lodge of a dervish order, hides behind the Co-op supermarket on the main harbour platía, while an unassuming **fountain** at the harbour end of the main drag, Kydhá, retains its calligraphic inscription and is still highly prized for drinking water.

Shops and amenities are mostly found along **Kydhá** and its continuation **Karatzá** – which meanders north from the harbour to Romeïkós Yialós – or **Garoufalídhi**, its perpendicular offshoot, roughly halfway along. As town beaches go, **Romeïkós Yialós** and **Néa Mádhitos** (ex-Toúrkikos Yialós), its counterpart to the southeast of the harbour, are not bad; **Rihá Nerá**, the next bay north of Romeïkós Yialós, is even better, shallow as the name suggests and well attended by families, with watersports on offer.

The **archeological museum** (Tues–Sun 8.30am–3pm; €2) occupies the former Ottoman governor's mansion right behind Romeïkós Yialós, not far from the site of Bronze Age Myrina. Finds from all of the island's major sites are assiduously labelled in Greek, Italian and English, and the entire premises is exemplary in terms of presentation – the obvious drawback being that the best items have been spirited away to Athens, leaving a collection that's often of specialist interest. The star upper-storey exhibits are votive lamps in the shape of sirens, found in an Archaic sanctuary at Hephaestia (Ifestía), much imitated in modern local jewellery. Rather less vicious than Homer's creatures, they are identified more invitingly as the "muses of the underworld, creatures of super-human wisdom, incarnations of nostalgia for paradise". There are also numerous representations of the goddess Cybele/Artemis, who was revered across the island; her shrines were typically situated near a fauna-rich river mouth – on Límnos at Avlónas, now inside the grounds of the *Porto Myrina* resort. An entire room is devoted to metalwork, of which the most impressive items are gold jewellery and bronze objects, both practical (cheese graters, door-knockers) and whimsical-naturalistic (a snail, a vulture).

### Eating, drinking and nightlife

**Seafood** is excellent on Límnos, owing to the island's proximity to the Darda-nelles and seasonal fish migrations. For waterside dining, *To Limanaki* is among the most popular of several establishments around the little fishing harbour, with strong ouzo in bulk and big portions, but also lax service and tricky fish pricing – *O Glaros* nearby is reckoned more professional and accomplished. About halfway along Kydhá, *O Platanos* serves traditional *mayireftá* to big crowds on an atmospheric little square beneath two plane trees. Most restaurants along Romeïkós Yialós offer poor value; the tree-shaded tables of *Iy Tzitzifies* (May–Oct) at Rihá Nerá are a far better option for daily-changing *mayireftá* and a few fish dishes.

Romeïkós Yialós is, however, the hub of *frappádhika* action and where **nightlife** kicks off with a sunset drink in the shadow of the castle; the two are combined nicely at *Karagiozis* at no. 32, by the bridge (11am–late). Choices elsewhere are limited, for example to stunningly appointed *Alexandros* at the base of the jetty; the closest after-hours beach bar is *Kioski* (July–Aug), on the sand at Avlónas. There's also the Maroula **cinema-theatre** on Garoufalídhi.

## Western Límnos

Beyond Mýrina's respectable town beaches, the closest good sand lies 3km north at **Avlónas**, unspoilt except for the local power plant a bit inland. Just beyond, the road splits: the right-hand turning wends its way through **Káspakas**, its north-facing houses in neat tiers and a potable spring (but no taverna) on its platía, before plunging down to **Áyios Ioánnis**, also reached directly by the left-hand bypass. There are **studios** here, plus a few tavernas, most distinctive the one (late June to late Aug) featuring seating in the shade of piled-up volcanic boulders. The nearby **beaches** – buffeted by southwesterly winds – are not the best, and the shore is densely built up with villas.

Just east, the old Ottoman baths at **Thérma**, complete with calligraphic plaques, have been restored as an eye-wateringly expensive contemporary health spa (ⓦ www.thermaspa.gr), with all conceivable treatments available – or you can just have a hydromassage soak (daily 10am–2pm & 5–9pm; €12). Unusually for a hot spring, the water is non-sulphurous and the tastiest on the island, so there is always a knot of cars parked nearby under the trees while their owners fill jerry cans with warm water from a **public fountain** – again with a bilingual Greek/Ottoman Turkish inscription.

South of Thérma, reached from the easterly bypass of Mýrina, is the iconic poster image of Límnos: the **chapel of Panayía Kakaviótissa**, tucked into a volcanic cave on the flank of Mt Kákavos (360m). The recommended map shows the dirt track heading east to the trailhead, from where it's twenty-minutes' hike through lava crags to the shrine. Go in the afternoon for the best light.

Some 7km north of Thérma, **SARDHÉS** is the highest village on the island, with wonderfully broody sunsets, clusters of handsome houses, and a celebrated central taverna, ✻ *Man-Télla* (all year, lunch and dinner). Portions are large and the food (meat and *mezédhes*, no fish) rich, so arrive hungry; book for summertime dinner (☎22540 61349) in the pleasant courtyard.

Beyond Sardhés, 5km below Katálakkos, lies the spectacular, well-signposted **dune environment at Gomáti**, one of the largest such in Greece. There are two zones reached by separate dirt tracks: one at a river mouth, with a bird-rich marsh, and the other to the northwest, with a beach bar and sunbeds. Despite wind exposure, the latter portion especially is a popular outing locally.

### Platý to Néa Koútali

**PLATÝ**, 2km southeast of Mýrina, has had its profile spoilt by the modern villa construction that is blighting many Limnian villages, but it does have two nocturnal **tavernas**. The better of these is *O Sozos*, just off the main platía (groups reserve in season on ☎22540 25085), featuring huge, well-priced grills, salads and a few *mayireftá* like *dolmádhes*, washed down by *tsípouro* and local bulk wine. The long sandy **beach**, 700m below, is popular, with non-motorized **watersports** available at the south end through Babis, below the *Lemnos Village* complex. Near mid-strand, *Grigoris* proves a reliable, popular beachside taverna, with fish occasionally. The highest standard **hotel** in the area, if not all of Límnos, is ✻ *Villa Afroditi* (☎22540 23141, ✉contact@afroditivillas.gr; mid-May to early Oct; ❺–❻), with its spectacular topiary, pleasant pool bar, and one of the best buffet breakfasts in the islands. Completely refurbished in 2007, with a new wing added, it comprises standard doubles and two-room apartments. If they're full, try the nearby hillside *Panorama Studios* (☎22540 22 487; May–Sept; ❹), well-kept units for two to four people, with sea views and easy parking. If Platý beach gets too crowded – likely in August – there's another cove, **Playísou Mólos**, less than 2km away, heading south past the *Lemnos Village*. The water shelves sharply with rocks in the shallows, but the bay is very scenic, with a little islet to give it definition.

**THÁNOS**, 2km further southeast, proves bigger and more architecturally characterful, with Nikos Dhimou's high-standard mock-trad **bungalows** at the east edge (☎22540 25284; ❹). **Paralía Thánous**, 1.5km below, is among the most scenic of southwestern beaches, flanked by volcanic crags and looking out to Áyios Efstrátios island. There's good-value **accommodation** at *Villa Thanos Beach* (☎22540 23496 or 697 37 10 543; ❸), with a lush front garden, plus good food (if surly service) at *Yiannakaros* taverna. Beyond Thános, the road curls over to the enormous beach at **Evgátis** (**Áyios Pávlos**), reckoned the island's best, with more igneous pinnacles for definition and Áyios Efstrátios still on the horizon. Three music bar/*kantínas* offer sunbeds, while 2007-expanded *Evgatis Hotel* across the road (☎22540 51700; ❹) has a full-service **taverna**.

Some 3km further along (11km from Mýrina), **KONDIÁS** is the island's third-largest settlement, cradled between hills tufted with Límnos's biggest pine forest. Stone-built, often elaborate houses combine with the setting to make Kondiás an attractive inland village, a fact not lost on the Greeks and foreigners restoring those houses with varying degrees of taste. Cultural interest is lent by the central **Pinakothíki Valkanikís Tékhnis/Balkan Art Gallery** (daily except Fri 10am–2pm & 7.30–9.30pm; €2), the result of a 2005 residential programme whereby prominent painters from across the Balkans – especially Bulgarian Svetlin Russev – donated works as the core collection; a repeat event is planned. Short-term facilities are limited to *Iy Galini* **taverna**, where seating under mulberries makes up for average food; you'll eat better 2.5km away at **TSIMÁNDHRIA**, where *Iy Kali Kardhia* on the central square dishes up cheap, salubrious grills and a few seafood dishes; at **PALEÓ PEDHINÓ**, 5km northeast, where *Petrino Horio* (dinner only, June–Aug) offers fine meat and an enchanting setting on the flagstoned platía of this mostly abandoned village; or 1km further at **NÉA KOÚTALI**, where *Iy Glaroupoula* (lunch too), despite a position three blocks inland, is *the* place for a seafood blowout.

## Eastern Límnos

The shores of **Moúdhros Bay**, glimpsed south of the trans-island road, are muddy and best avoided by serious bathers. The bay itself enjoyed strategic importance during World War I, culminating in Allied acceptance of the Ottoman surrender aboard the British warship HMS *Agamemnon* on October 30, 1918. **MOÚDHROS**, the second-largest town on Límnos, was (until recently) quite literally a God-forsaken place, owing to an incident late in Ottoman rule. Certain locals killed some Muslims and threw them down a well on property belonging to the Athonite monastery of Koutloumousioú; the Ottoman authorities, holding the monks responsible, slaughtered any Koutloumousiot brethren they found on the island and set the local monastery alight. Two monks managed to escape to Áthos, where every August 23 a curse was chanted, condemning Moúdhros's inhabitants to "never sleep again"; the Athonite brothers finally relented in July 2001. It's still a dreary place, with only the wonderfully kitsch, two-belfried **Evangelismós church**, and perhaps the two restaurants attached to the overpriced hotels, to recommend it. The closest decent **beaches** are at **Havoúli**, 4km south by dirt track, and **Fanaráki** 4km west, but both have muddy sand and don't really face open sea; far superior is **Ayía Triádha**, accessed off the Polyókhni (see p.480) road, with blonde sand heaped in dunes and a *kantína*.

**KALLIÓPI**, 8km northeast of Moúdhros via attractive **KONDOPOÚLI** (platía ouzerí and *souvladzídhika*), has smart **rooms** (*Keros* ☎22540 41059; ❹) at the start of the road down to **Kéros beach**, popular despite being exposed and often dirty. A 1500-metre stretch of sand with dunes and a small pine grove, plus shallow water, it attracts foreigners with camper vans and windsurfers as well as Greeks; a small *kantína* keeps sunbeds during July and August only. For more solitutude, head to road's end at Pláka village, with a good nearby **beach** and **taverna** at **Áyios Harálambos**, facing Samothráki.

West of Kondopoúli, reached via Repanídhi, the hard-packed beach at **KÓTSINAS** (follow signs to "Kótsinas Fortress") is set in the protected western limb of Bourniá Bay. The nearby anchorage offers two busy, seafood-strong **tavernas**, of which pricier *To Mourayio* is worth the difference for more careful cooking and better service compared to rival *To Koralli*. On a knoll overlooking the jetty stands a corroded, sword-brandishing statue of **Maroula**, a Genoese-era heroine who briefly delayed the Ottoman conquest, and a large church of **Zoödhóhou Piyís** (the Life-Giving Spring), with intriguing kitsch icons, a vaulted wooden ceiling and antique floor tiles. Out front, 63 steps lead down through an illuminated tunnel in the rock to the potable (if slightly mineral) spring in question, oozing into a cool, vaulted chamber.

### The war cemeteries

About 800m along the Roussopoúli road from Moúdhros, you pass an Allied **military cemetery** (unlocked) maintained by the Commonwealth War Graves Commission, its neat lawns and rows of white headstones incongruous in such parched surroundings. During 1915, Moúdhros Bay was the principal staging area for the disastrous Gallipoli campaign. Of approximately 36,000 Allied dead, 887 are buried here – mainly battle casualties, who died after having been evacuated to the base hospital at Moúdhros. Though the deceased are mostly British, there is also a French cenotaph, and – speaking volumes about imperial sociology – a mass "Musalman" grave for Egyptian and Indian troops in one corner, with a Koranic inscription.

There are more graves at another immaculately maintained cemetery behind the hilltop church in **Portianoú**. Follow a narrow street marked by a blue-on-white sign reading "ANZAC ST", then bear left onto a rough lane, avoiding the way up to the church, to discover the meticulously tended cemetery, edged by pines. Amongst the 348 buried here are two Canadian nurses, three Egyptian labourers, three Maori troops and a Levantine or Jewish Ottoman officer. East of Portianoú and Paleó Pedhinó, signposted on a headland, lies the last and strangest of Límnos's military cemeteries: about forty 1920–21 graves of **Kuban Cossacks**, White Army refugees from the Russian civil war.

### Ancient sites

Traces of the most advanced Neolithic Aegean civilization have been unearthed at **Polyochni (Polyókhni)**, 10km east of Moúdhros, on a bluff overlooking a long, narrow beach. Since 1930, Italian excavations have uncovered five layers of settlement, the oldest from late in the fourth millennium BC, pre-dating Troy on the Turkish coast opposite. The town met a sudden, violent end from war or earthquake in about 2100 BC. The **ruins** (Tues–Sun 8.30am–3pm; free) are well labelled but mostly of specialist interest, though a small, well-presented museum behind the entrance helps bring the place to life.

Hephaestia and Kabirion, Límnos's other significant ancient sites, are remote and only reachable with your own transport. **Hephaestia** (present-day Ifestía; Tues–Sun 8.30am–3pm), 4.5km from Kondopoúli by rough, signposted track, offers an admirably reconstructed theatre, overlooking its former harbour; the name comes from the god Hephaestos, rescued and revered by the ancient Limnians after he crash-landed on the island, hurled from Mt Olympos by Hera. **Kabirion**, also signposted as "Kabeiroi" (modern Kavírion), on the opposite shore of Tigáni Bay and accessed by a paved road, remains more evocative. The **ruins** (Tues–Sun 8.30am–3pm; free) are of a sanctuary connected with the cult of the Samothracian Kabiroi (see p.483), though the site here is probably older. Little survives other than eleven column stumps staking out a *stoa*, behind the *telestirio* or shrine where the cult mysteries took place. A nearby sea grotto has been identified as the Homeric **Spiliá toú Filoktíti**, where Trojan war hero Philoktetes was abandoned by his comrades-in-arms until his stinking, gangrenous leg had healed by application of *límnia yí*, a poultice of volcanic mud still prized on the island. Landward access to the cave is via steps leading down from the caretaker's shelter, though final access (from a little passage on the right as you face the sea) involves some wading.

# Áyios Efstrátios (Aï Strátis)

**Áyios Efstrátios** is one of the quietest and loneliest islands in the Aegean, with a registered population of around 370 (but just 200 full-time residents); it was only permanently settled during the sixteenth century, and land is still largely owned by three monasteries on Mount Áthos. Historically, the only outsiders to visit were those compelled to do so – politically prisoners exiled here both during the 1930s and the civil war years.

ÁYIOS EFSTRÁTIOS village – the island's only habitation – is among the ugliest in Greece. Devastation caused by an earthquake on February 20, 1968, which killed 22 and injured hundreds, was compounded by the reconstruction plan: the contract went to a junta-linked company, who prevented survivors from returning to their old homes and used army bulldozers to raze even those structures – comprising one of the more beautiful ports in these islands – that could have been repaired. From the hillside, some two dozen surviving houses of the old village overlook grim rows of prefabs, a sad monument to the corruption of the junta years.

Architecture apart, Áyios Efstrátios still functions as a traditional fishing and farming community, with the prefabs set at the mouth of a wooded stream valley draining to the sandy harbour beach. Tourist amenities consist of just two basic **tavernas** (one operating July–Aug only), plus four **pensions**. Best of these, in one of the surviving old houses, is *Xenonas Aï-Stratis* (☎22540 93329; ❹); *Andonis Paneras* (☎22540 93209; ❸), *Stavros Katakouzinos* (☎22540 93362; ❸) and *Apostolos Paneras* (☎22540 93343; ❸) have more conventional rooms in prefabs. Stiff prices for such an out-of-the-way place reflect Aï Strátis's trendiness with Greeks, and you may not find a vacancy in midsummer.

Beyond the village – there are few vehicles and no paved roads – the hilly **landscape**, dotted with a surprising number of oak trees, is deserted apart from rabbits, sheep, an occasional shepherd, and some good **beaches**. **Alonítsi**, on the north coast – ninety-minutes' walk from the port following a track due east and over a low ridge – is a 1500-metre stretch of sand with rolling breakers and views across to Límnos. South of the harbour lie a series of grey-sand beaches, most with wells and drinkable water, accessible by roundabout tracks. **Áyios Dhimítrios**, an hour-plus distant, and **Lidharió**, ninety minutes away at the end of a wooded valley, are the most popular.

**Ferries** on the Kavála/Alexandhroúpoli–Límnos–Lávrio line call at Áyios Efstrátios several times weekly much of the year; in summer a small Límnos-based ferry, the *Aiolis*, sails every weekday at 2.30pm from Límnos, returning the next day at 6.30am. Despite improvements, Aï Strátis still has a very exposed mooring, and in bad weather you could end up stranded here far longer than you bargained for. If an indefinite stay does not appeal, visit from Límnos on one of the admittedly overpriced **day-trips** (€35 return; Wed, Sun & often Fri).

# Samothráki (Samothrace)

**Samothráki** has one of the most dramatic profiles of all the Greek islands, second only to Thíra (Santorini): its dark mass of granite rises abruptly from the sea, culminating in the 1611-metre **Mount Fengári**. Seafarers have always been guided by its imposing outline, clearly visible from the mainland, and its summit provided a vantage point for Poseidon to watch over the siege of Troy. Landing is subject to the notoriously unpredictable weather, but that did not deter pilgrims who, for hundreds of years in Antiquity, journeyed to the island to visit the **Sanctuary of the Great Gods** and were initiated into its mysteries. The sanctuary remains the main archeological attraction of the island which, too remote for most tourists, combines earthy simplicity with natural grandeur. The tourist season is relatively short – essentially (late) July and August – but you will find some facilities open as early as Easter and one or two all year round.

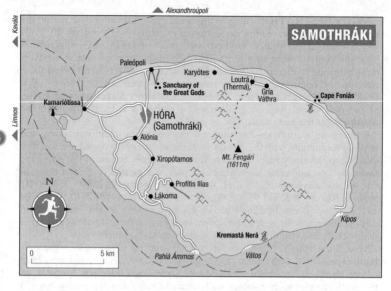

Alexandhroúpoli

Kavála

Límnos

SAMOTHRÁKI

Paleópoli

Karyótes

Loutrá
(Thermá),
Gría
Váthra

Cape Foniás

Sanctuary of
the Great Gods

Kamariótissa

HÓRA
(Samothráki)

Alónia

Xiropótamos

Mt. Fengári
(1611m)

Profítis Ilías

Lákoma

Kípos

N

Kremastá Nerá

0        5 km

Pahiá Ámmos

Vátos

## Kamariótissa

Ferries and hydrofoils dock at the dull village of **KAMARIÓTISSA**. While
you're unlikely to want to spend much time here, it does make a convenient
base, as some of Samothráki's best **hotels** lie along or just behind the tree-lined
seafront and various **rooms** for rent can be found in the maze of streets behind;
owners often meet incoming vessels. Accommodation can be pricey for what
you get, and bargaining is not always productive, especially in midsummer. Along
the shore, some way east of where you arrive, is *Kyma* (☎25510 41263; ❷),
where rooms overlooking the pebbly beach can get noise from the establishments below. Occupying a bluff to the northeast, the slightly impersonal *Aeolos*
(☎25510 41595; ❹) has a large pool and quiet, spacious rooms; Samothráki's
most comfortable accommodation, it offers good half-board deals out of season.
The spacious new *Kyrkos* apartments (☎25510 41620; ❸), 500m from the port,
just off the road to Hóra, can also be booked through their car rental agency
(see below). Bars and cafés on the harbour front serve snacks and breakfasts –
lively *Aktaion* also has internet – while the best of the **tavernas** is the *Iy Klimataria*, towards the northeast end, serving fresh fish and meat.

   **Motorbikes** and **cars** – in short supply in season – are the only way of
getting to the south and far east of the island. Reserve a bike in advance from
Hanou Brothers (☎25510 41511) or a car from Niki Tours (☎25510 41465),
or either one from Kyrkos car rental (☎25510 69728). A car is preferable, as
Samothracian roads are often dangerously windswept for bikes. The only
fuelling station on the entire island is 1km above the port, en route to Hóra. A
fairly reliable timetable for island **buses** is also posted at the port; these travel
up to eight times daily in season (twice weekly in winter) along the north coast
to Loutrá (Thermá) via Paleópoli, near the site of the Sanctuary, or Karyótes, or
directly inland seven times daily to the largest village, Hóra. A converted
container opposite the docks acts as a ticket and information offices for **ferries
and hydrofoils**. Kamariótissa also has two **banks** with **ATMs**, and the island's
only **post office**.

## Hóra

**HÓRA**, also known as **Samothráki**, is the island's capital. Far larger than the portion visible from out at sea would suggest, it's an attractive town of Thracian-style stone houses, some whitewashed, clustered around a hollow in the western flanks of Mount Fengári. It is dominated by the Genoese Gateluzzi fort, of which little survives other than the gateway. Half an hour or so can be whiled away at the charming **folklore museum** (erratic opening hours; free), which contains a motley collection of clothing, domestic items and miscellany.

Hóra has no reliable short-term **accommodation**, though various *kafenía* along the winding commercial street offer unadvertised rooms. On the atmospheric, irregularly shaped platía, a couple of summer-only **tavernas**, *Iy Platia* and the down-to-earth 🍴 *To Kastro*, provide the best suppers on the island, with such delicacies as stuffed squid and *mýdhia saganáki* (mussels with cheese). There are several convivial year-round **cafés**, such as *Kalderimi*.

## The Sanctuary of the Great Gods

Hidden in a stony but thickly wooded ravine between the tiny hamlet of **PALEÓPOLI** – 6km northeast from Kamariótissa, and 3km directly north from Hóra – and the plunging northwestern ridge of Mount Fengári, lie the remains of the **Sanctuary of the Great Gods**. Buses from Kamariótissa stop nearby, opposite a small car park on the seashore. From the late Bronze Age until the early Byzantine era, the mysteries and sacrifices of the cult of the Great Gods were performed on Samothráki, in ancient Thracian until the second century BC. Little is known of this dialect except that it was a very old Indo-European tongue, related to and eventually replaced by ancient Greek. The spiritual focus of the northern Aegean, the importance of the island was second only in all the ancient world to the Mysteries of Eleusis.

The religion of the Great Gods revolved around a hierarchy of ancient Thracian fertility figures: the Great Mother Axieros, a subordinate male deity known as Kadmilos, and the potent and ominous twin demons the Kabiroi, originally the local heroes Dardanos and Aeton. When the Aeolian colonists arrived (traditionally c.700 BC) they simply merged the resident deities with their own – the Great Mother became Cybele, while her consort Hermes and the Kabiroi were fused interchangeably with the *Dioskouroi* Castor and Pollux, patrons of seafarers. Around the nucleus of a sacred precinct the newcomers made the beginnings of what is now the sanctuary.

Despite their long observance, the mysteries of the cult were never explicitly recorded, since ancient writers feared incurring the wrath of the Kabiroi (who could reputedly brew up sudden, deadly storms), but it has been established that two levels of initiation were involved. Both ceremonies, in direct opposition to the elitism of Eleusis, were open to all, including women and slaves. The lower level of initiation, or *myesis*, may, as is speculated at Eleusis, have involved a ritual simulation of the life, death and rebirth cycle; in any case, it's known that it ended with joyous feasting, and it can be conjectured, since so many clay torches have been found, that it took place at night. The higher level of initiation, or *epopteia*, carried the unusual requirement of a moral standard – the connection of theology with morality, so strong in the later Judeo-Christian tradition, was rarely made by the early Greeks. This second level involved a full confession followed by absolution and baptism in bull's blood.

The only **accommodation** near the sanctuary is in diminutive **PALEÓPOLI**, where the old and basic *Xenia Hotel* (☎25510 41166 or 25510 41230; ④) offers a downmarket alternative to the smart but overpriced

▲ Sanctuary of the Great Gods

*Kastro Hotel* (☎25510 89400, ⓦwww.kastrohotel.gr; ❺), which comes with pool, restaurant and sea views. Basic but en-suite rooms (❸) are also available on the seashore below the *Kastro*.

## The site

The well-labelled **site** (daily 8am–7.30pm, closes 3pm in winter; €3 combined ticket with museum) strongly evokes its proud past while commanding views of the mountains and the sea. For an explanatory introduction, it is better first to visit the **archeological museum** (Tues–Sun 8am–7.30pm, closes 3pm in winter), whose exhibits span all eras of habitation, from the Archaic to the Byzantine. Highlights include a **frieze** of dancing girls from the propylaion of the Temenos, entablatures from different buildings, and Roman votive offerings such as coloured glass vials from the necropolis of the ancient town east of the sanctuary. You can also see a reproduction of the exquisitely sculpted marble statue, the *Winged Victory of Samothrace*, which once stood breasting the wind at the prow of a marble ship in the Nymphaeum (see opposite). Discovered in 1863 by a French diplomat to the Sublime Porte, it was carried off to the Louvre, where it is a major draw, and the well-crafted copy was graciously donated to this museum a mere century later.

The **Anaktoron**, or hall of initiation for the first level of the mysteries, dates in its present form from Roman times. Its inner sanctum was marked by a warning stele, now in the museum, and at the southeast corner you can make out the **Priestly Quarters**, an antechamber where candidates for initiation donned white gowns. Next to it is the **Arsinoeion**, the largest circular ancient building known in Greece, used for libations and sacrifices. Within its rotunda are the fourth-century BC walls of a double precinct where a rock altar, the earliest preserved ruin on the site, has been uncovered. A little further south, on the same side of the path, you come to the **Temenos**, a rectangular area open to the sky where the feasting probably took place, and, edging its rear corner, the conspicuous **Hieron**, the site's most immediately impressive structure. Five columns and an architrave of the facade of this large Doric edifice, which hosted the higher level of initiation, have been re-erected; dating in part from the fourth century BC, it was heavily restored in Roman times. The stone steps have been replaced by modern blocks, but Roman benches for spectators remain *in situ*, along with the sacred stones where confession was heard. To the west of the path you can just discern the outline of the theatre, while just above it, tucked under the ridge, is the **Nymphaeum (Fountain) of Nike**, which the *Winged Victory* used to preside over. West of the theatre, occupying a high terrace, are remains of the main *stoa*; immediately north of this is an elaborate medieval fortification made entirely of antique material.

## Loutrá and further east

With its running streams, giant plane trees and namesake hot springs, **LOUTRÁ** (aka **THERMÁ**), 6km east of Paleópoli, is a pleasant place to stay, although in late July and August it is packed, mainly with an incongruous mixture of foreign hippies and elderly Greeks, here to take the sulphurous waters. Far more appealing than the grim baths themselves, the low waterfalls and rock pools of **Gría Váthra** are signposted 1.5km up the paved side road leading east from the main Thermá access drive.

Loutrá is the prime base for the tough six-hour climb up the 1611-metre **Mount Fengári** (known to the ancients as **Sáos**, a name found on some maps to this day), the highest peak in the Aegean islands; the path starts at the top of the village, beside a concrete water tank and a huge plane tree. Tell your accommodation proprietors that you're going. Fengári is Greek for "moon" and, according to legend, if you reach the top on the night of a full moon your wish will come true – most of those foolhardy enough to attempt this will just hope to get back down safely.

Loutrá is a rather dispersed place, with its winding dead-end streets, all ghostly quiet in winter, and its miniature harbour – built as an alternative to Kamariótissa, but never used. **Accommodation** includes the B&B *Kaviros Hotel* (☎25510 98277; ❸), just east of the "centre", and, further downhill, 700m from the beach, the slightly cheaper *Mariva Bungalows* (☎25510 98258; ❸). Of the **tavernas**, *Paradhisos* has the best setting, up under the trees. A few seasonal eateries, like leafy *To Perivoli T'ouranou*, are dotted along the side road to Gría Váthra.

Beyond Loutrá the wooded coastline holds two municipal **campsites**. *Platia* (☎25510 98244), 1.5km from the village, is large but has no facilities except toilets, while *Voradhes* (☎25510 98258), 3km out, has hot water, electricity, a small shop, restaurant and bar. The Loutrá bus may go to either site if you ask nicely.

**Beaches** on Samothráki's north shore are mostly clean but uniformly pebbly and exposed, but it's still worth continuing along the road east from Loutrá for the views and one or two minor sights. At **Cape Foniás** there's a ruined Gateluzzi watchtower and, 45-minutes' walk inland along the stream, there are **waterfalls** and refreshingly cold pools, though the signposted description of "canyon" is exaggerated. Some 15km from Loutrá along a fine corniche road is **Kípos beach**, a long strand facing the Turkish island of Gökçeada (Ímvros to the Greeks) and backed by open pasture and picturesque crags. The water is clean and there's a rock overhang for shelter at one end, a spring, shower and seasonal drinks *kantína*, serving basic snacks.

## The south coast

The warmer south flank of the island, its fertile farmland dotted with olive groves, boasts fine views out to sea – as far as Gökçeada on a clear day. Up to three daily buses go from Kamariótissa via the sleepy village of Lákoma as far as **PROFÍTIS**

**ILÍAS**, an attractive hill village. The best of its good **tavernas**, *Paradhisos*, has a wonderful terrace, and there's also some basic **accommodation**.

From **Lákoma** itself, which has an admirable ouzerí, *O Mavros*, it's less than 2km down to the eponymous beach, where *To Akroyiali* fish taverna (☎ 25510 95123; ❸) has some **rooms**. A further 6km east lies **Pahiá Ámmos**, a long, clean beach with the *Delfini* taverna-rooms outfit (☎ 25510 94235; ❸) at the west end. The nearest (meagre) supplies are in Lákoma, but this doesn't deter big summer crowds who also arrive by excursion *kaïkia*. These continue east to **Vátos**, a secluded beach (nudity tolerated) that's also accessible by land, the **Kremastá Nerá** coastal waterfalls, and finally round to Kípos beach (see p.485).

# Thássos

Just 12km from the mainland, **Thássos** has long been a popular resort island for northern Greeks, and since the early 1990s has also attracted a cosmopolitan mix of tourists, particularly Germans and Scandinavians on packages, as well as an increasing number of people from eastern Europe. They are all entertained

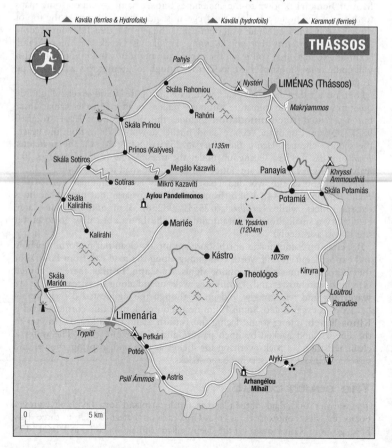

by vast numbers of *bouzoúkia* (music halls) and tavernas that lay on music at weekends (and during the week in July and Aug), while nature-lovers can find some areas of outstanding beauty, especially inland. Moreover, the island's traditional industries have managed to survive the onslaught of modernity. The elite of Thássos still make a substantial living from the pure-white **marble** that constitutes two-thirds of the land mass, found only here and quarried at dozens of sites in the hills between Liménas and Panayía. Olives, especially the oil, honey, fruit and nuts (often sold candied) are also important products. The spirit *tsípouro*, rather than wine, is the main local tipple; pear extract, onions or spices like cinnamon and anise are added to home-made batches.

Inhabited since the Stone Age, Thássos was settled by Parians in the seventh century BC, attracted by **gold** deposits between modern Liménas and Kínyra. Buoyed by revenues from these, and from **silver** mines under Thassian control on the mainland opposite, the ancient city-state here became the seat of a medium-sized seafaring empire. Commercial acumen did not spell military invincibility, however; the Persians under Darius swept the Thassian fleets from the seas in 492 BC, and in 462 BC Athens permanently deprived Thássos of its autonomy after a three-year siege. The main port continued to thrive into Roman times, but lapsed into Byzantine and medieval obscurity.

Sadly, the salient fact of more recent history has been a series of devastating, deliberately set **fires** in the 1980s and 1990s. Only the northeastern quadrant of the island, plus the area around Astrís and Alykí, escaped, though the surviving forest is still home to numerous pine martens.

Thássos is small enough to circumnavigate in one full day by rented motorbike or car. KTEL's buses will do the driving for you – albeit with little chance for stopping – with their complete circuit four times daily. **Car rental** is offered by the major international chains and local Potos Car Rental (☎25930 23969), with branches in all main resorts; try bargaining in the shoulder seasons. On the other hand, don't bother showing up in Thássos between early October and late April, as the weather can be dodgy and most facilities, including hotels, will be shut.

## Liménas

Largely modern **LIMÉNAS** (also signposted as Limín or Thássos) is the island's capital, though not the only port. At first glance Liménas seems an unlikely resort, plagued as it is with surprisingly clogged vehicles, but it is partly redeemed by its picturesque fishing harbour and the substantial remains of the ancient city which appear above and below the streets.

### Arrival and information

Kavála-based **ferries** stop 12km down the coast at Skála Prínou, with a KTEL bus on hand to meet most arrivals except the last. The KTEL office is on the front, opposite the hydrofoil berth; the service is good, with several daily **buses** to Panayía and Skála Potamiás, Limenária via Potós, Theológos, Kínyra and Alykí. The **taxi** rank is just in front of the bus stop. **Bikes** can be rented from Thomai Tsipou (☎25930 22815), back from the front. Thassos Tours (☎25930 23250) and Indispensible Holiday Services (☎25930 22041, ⓔihs @kav.forthnet.gr) provide various services. Several banks have **ATMs**.

### Accommodation

While few **hotels enjoy** any tranquillity or decent views (and most are shut Oct–April), some are reasonable enough, and relatively quiet **rooms** are available just behind the town beach. The closest **campsite** is the pretty basic one at Nystéri cove, 2.5km west.

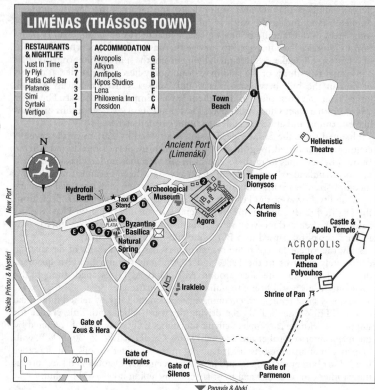

LIMÉNAS (THÁSSOS TOWN)

**RESTAURANTS & NIGHTLIFE**
| | |
|---|---|
| Just In Time | 5 |
| Iy Piyí | 7 |
| Platia Café Bar | 4 |
| Platanos | 3 |
| Simi | 2 |
| Syrtaki | 1 |
| Vertigo | 6 |

**ACCOMMODATION**
| | |
|---|---|
| Akropolis | G |
| Alkyon | E |
| Amfipolis | B |
| Kipos Studios | D |
| Lena | F |
| Philoxenia Inn | C |
| Possidon | A |

Town Beach

Hellenistic Theatre

Ancient Port (Limenáki)

Hydrofoil Berth

★ Taxi Stand

Archeological Museum

Temple of Dionysos

Artemis Shrine

Castle & Apollo Temple

ACROPOLIS

Byzantine Basilica

Agora

Temple of Athena Polyouhos

Natural Spring

Shrine of Pan

Irakleio

Gate of Zeus & Hera

Gate of Hercules

Gate of Silenos

Gate of Parmenon

0        200 m

N

▼ Panayía & Alykí

---

**Akropolis** ☎25930 22488. Occupying a fine traditional house with flagstone floors and a rear garden-bar, but subject to traffic noise. ❸

**Alkyon** ☎25930 22148. Certainly the most pleasant harbour hotel; English tea and breakfast plus friendly, voluble management make it a home away from home for independent British travellers. Open most of the year; ask also about their cottage in Sotíras and beach villa at Astrís. B&B ❸

**Amfipolis** ☎25930 23101. Housed in a folly, this atmospheric hotel is the most exclusive accommodation outfit – and guests pay dearly for the privilege. It also has a stylish drinks terrace. ❺

**Kipos Studios** ☎25930 22469, ⓦwww .kipos-apartments.gr. In a quiet cul-de-sac next to Iy Piyí taverna, this has cool lower-ground-floor

doubles and four-person galleried apartments, plus a pool in the garden. ❸

**Lena** ☎25930 23565, ⓔhotellena @hotmail.com. The best-value hotel in town, with compact but comfy rooms near the post office; run by a welcoming American ex-pat. ❷

**Philoxenia Inn** ☎25930 23331, ⓦwww .philoxeniainn.gr. Quietly situated behind the archeological museum, this has immaculate rooms with fridges, designated breakfast areas and a garden with a small pool. ❹

**Possidon** ☎25930 22690, ⓦwww .thassos-possidon.com. Unattractive concrete block on the seafront with nicely refurbished rooms. Somewhat overpriced but the only place guaranteed to be open all year. ❹

## The Town

Thanks to its mineral wealth and safe harbour, **ancient Thassos** prospered from Classical to Roman times. The largest excavated area is the agora, a little way back from the fishing harbour. The site (free) is fenced but not always locked, and is most enjoyably seen towards dusk. Two Roman stoas are prominent, but you can also make out shops, monuments, passageways and sanctuaries from the remodelled Classical city. At the far end, a fifth-century BC passageway leads through to an elaborate sanctuary of Artemis, a substantial stretch of Roman road and a few seats of the odeion. The nearby **archeological museum** (Tues–Sun 9am–3pm; €2) contains small but absorbing displays on prehistoric finds, archeological methods and ancient games. Pride of place goes to the four-metre-tall, seventh-century BC *kouros* carrying a ram, found on the acropolis.

From a **temple of Dionysos** behind the fishing port, a path curls up to a **Hellenistic theatre**, fabulously positioned above a broad sweep of sea. Sadly, it's only open for performances of the **summer festival** (Ⓦwww.thassos-festival.gr). From just before the theatre, the trail winds on the right up to the **acropolis**, where a Venetian-Byzantine-Genoese fort arose between the thirteenth and fifteenth centuries, constructed from recycled masonry of an Apollo temple. You can continue, following the remains of a massive circuit of fifth-century walls, to a high terrace supporting the foundations of the Athena Polyouhos (Athena Patroness of the City) temple, with Cyclopean walls.

From the temple's southern end, a short path leads to a cavity in the rock outcrop that was a shrine of Pan, shown in faint relief playing his pipes. Following the path to the left around the summit brings you to a precipitous rock-hewn stairway with a metal handrail, which provided a discreet escape route to the Gate of Parmenon, the only gate in the fortifications to have retained its lintel; it name comes from an ancient inscription ("Parmenon Made Me") on a nearby wall slab. From here a track, then a paved lane, descend through the southerly neighbourhoods of the modern town, completing a satisfying one-hour circuit.

### Eating, drinking and nightlife

Given the cheap-and-cheerful-package ethos, cuisine is not Liménas's strong point. The picturesque **tavernas** around the old harbour are predictably touristy – sophisticated ✻ *Simi* is by far the best, open all year, and serves memorably good wine. Another good option is *Syrtaki*, at the far eastern end of the crowded town beach. In the town centre, a dependable favourite for *mayireftá* is *Iy Piyi*, at the south corner of the main square, while *Platanos*, with a pleasant terrace opposite the ferry docks, is the place to head for breakfast. By contrast, there's plenty of choice in local **bars**: *Vertigo* near the *Hotel Alkyon* is popular with Greeks and tourists alike for its rocking ambience; across the road, *Just In Time* is another lively café-bar; *Platia Café Bar*, back on the square, also has a decent atmosphere.

## Around the coast

Whether you plan to circumnavigate the island clockwise, or in the opposite direction, plan on a lunch stop at **Alykí**, roughly a third of the way along in the circuit described below, and the most photogenic spot along the coast.

### Panayía, Potamiá and Mount Ypsárion

The first beach east of Liménas, **Makrýammos**, is a purpose-built, controlled-access compound for package tourists, so carry on to **PANAYÍA**, the attractive hillside village overlooking Potamiá Bay. It's a large, thriving place where life revolves around the central square with its large plane trees, fountain and slate-roofed houses. Top **accommodation** choice in both senses is the *Hotel Thassos Inn* (Ⓣ25930 61612; ❹), up in the Tris Piyés district near the Kímisis church, with fine views over the rooftops. Down on the main road, beside the municipal car park, the clean *Pension Stathmos* (Ⓣ25930 61666; ❸) is the quietest of several nearby, with stunning views out the back; there are also high-standard rooms (☎25930 61981; ❷) below the school basketball courts. Avoid the tout-infested competing **tavernas** on the square; for a lower-key approach, try *Iy Thea*, a view-terrace *psistariá* at the southeast edge of town en route to Potamiá, or the nearby *Lykhnari zaharoplastío*, which serves great cakes and has a back garden.

**POTAMIÁ** itself, much lower down in the river valley, is far less prepossessing – with modern red tiles instead of slates on the roofs – and thus little visited, though it has a lively winter carnival. It also offers the modest **Polygnotos Vayis Museum** (Tues–Sat 9.30am–12.30pm, Sun 10am–1pm; summer also Tues–Sat 6–9pm,; free), devoted to the locally born sculptor; though Vayis emigrated to America when young, he bequeathed most of his works to the Greek state. Potamiá also marks the start of the preferred route up to the 1204-metre summit of **Mount Ypsárion**. Follow the bulldozer track to the big spring near the head of the valley extending west of the village (the last source of water), where you'll see the first red-painted arrows on trees. Beyond this point, cairns mark the correct turnings in a modern track system; forty minutes above the spring, take an older, wide track, which ends ten minutes later at a narrow ravine with a stream and the current trailhead. The path is steep, strenuous and unmaintained, and you'll be dependent on cairns and painted arrows. Go early in the day or season, and allow four hours up from Potamiá, and nearly as much for the descent.

### Skála Potamiás and Khryssí Ammoudhiá

The onward road from Potamiá is lined with rooms for rent and apartment-type accommodation. A side road some 12km from Liménas takes you down to **SKÁLA POTAMIÁS**, at the southern end of the bay, where some fairly uninspired **tavernas** line the harbour front; an honourable exception is the *Kramboussa*, which serves acceptable *mayireftá* and grills. From here a road off to the left brings you to sand dunes extending all the way to the far northern end of the bay. In *Eric's Bar*, on the main road just outside the village, Stratos Papafilippou has made a career of his uncanny resemblance to footballer Eric Cantona; a full English breakfast is available, you can watch Premiership matches on satellite TV and there is a heated outdoor swimming pool.

The best places to **stay** are either above the plane-shaded traffic turnaround area by the port, beyond the tavernas – where the *Hera* (☎25930 61467; ❷), just on the left looking inland, or the *Delfini* (☎25930 61275; ❷), 200m straight back, are peaceful but basic – or, for almost double the price, the *Miramare* further up the same lane (☎25930 77209, ⊛www.hotelmiramare.gr; ❹) has a swimming pool and well-manicured gardens.

The north end of this beach – **Khryssí Ammoudhiá**, better known as "**Golden Beach**" – is quite built-up but pleasant nonetheless; a direct road (plied by infrequent buses) spirals for 5km down from Panayía. Once there, choose between the self-catering *Villa Emerald* (☎25930 61979; ❹) or the *Golden Sand* (☎25930 61771; ❸), nearer the sands. The *Golden Beach* **campsite** (☎25930 61472) is the only official one on this side of the island. As for food, the best *mezédhes* and main courses are to be had at *Sotiris* taverna. **Water taxis** come here from Liménas twice daily in summer, at 10am and 4.30pm (€7).

### Kínyra and Alykí

The dispersed hamlet of **KÍNYRA**, some 24km south of Liménas, marks the start of the burnt zone which overlooks it, though recovery is under way; it has a poor beach, a couple of grocery stores and several small **hotels**. Those not block-booked include *Villa Athina* (☎25930 41214; ❷) at the north end of things, whose top-floor rooms see the water over the olive trees, and the welcoming *Pension Marina* (℡25930 31384; ❷). *Yiorgos* and *Faros* are the best **tavernas** here. Kínyra is convenient for the superior **beaches** of Loutroú (1km south) and partly nudist Paradise (3km along) – officially called Makrýammos Kinýron – both of which can be reached down poorly signposted dirt tracks. The latter ranks as most scenic of all Thassian beaches, with still-forested cliffs inland, a namesake islet offshore beyond the extensive shallows and much cleaner water than at Khryssí Ammoudhiá. A couple of mediocre snack-bars behind the sand overcharge bathers.

The south-facing coast of Thássos has the balance of the island's best beaches. **ALYKÍ** hamlet, 35km from Liménas and just below the main road, faces a perfect double bay, which almost pinches off a headland. Uniquely, it retains its original whitewashed, slate-roofed architecture, since the presence of extensive antiquities here has led to a ban on any modern construction. Those ruins include an ancient temple to an unknown deity, and two exquisite early Christian basilicas out on the headland, with a few columns re-erected. The sand-and-pebble west bay gets oversubscribed in peak season, though you can always head off to the less crowded, rocky east cove, or snorkel in the crystal-clear waters off the marble formations on the headland's far side. A lively bar and a row of water-edge **tavernas** compete for your custom, with *To Limanaki/The Little Mole* winning, if only for its more varied menu. At secluded **Kékes** beach, in a pine grove 1km further along the coast, traditional taverna *Skidhia* offers en-suite, air-conditioned **rooms** in plain but comfortable bungalows (℡25930 31528; ❸).

## Arhangélou Mihaïl to Potós

Some 5km west of Alykí, the **convent of Arhangélou Mihaïl** (open reasonable daylight hours) clings spectacularly to a cliff on the seaward side of the road. Though founded in the twelfth century above the spot where a spring had gushed forth, the convent has been hideously renovated by the nuns, resident here since 1974. A dependency of Filothéou on Mount Athos, its prize relic is a purported nail from the Crucifixion.

At the extreme south tip of Thássos, 9km further west, **ASTRÍS** (Astrídha) can muster two uninspiring medium-sized hotels, a few rooms and a good beach. Just 1km west is another better but crowded beach, **Psilí Ámmos**, with watersports on offer. A few kilometres further, **POTÓS** is the island's prime Germanophone package venue, its centre claustrophobically dense, with the few non-block-booked rooms overlooking cramped alleys. However, the kilometre-long beach is still unspoilt. For a less touristy place to eat, the **taverna** *Piatsa*, one of the cheaper and better places, is tucked away at the southern end of the seafront, in a semi-pedestrianized street; next door, *Michael's Place* has great ice cream and breakfasts. Along the harbour front a string of varyingly trendy **bars and cafés** offers viable alternatives. There are plenty of rental outlets for **cars**, scooters and mountain bikes, including the headquarters of Potos Rent a Car. **Pefkári**, with its manicured beach and namesake pine grove, 1km west, is essentially an annexe of Potós, with a few mid-range **accommodation** options such as *Prasino Veloudho* (℡25930 52001, ✉nikolis7@hol.gr; ❸) and the more upmarket *Thassos* (℡25930 51596, ✉thassoshotel@msn.com; ❹). The **campsite**, *Pefkari* (℡25930 51190; June–Sept), with its attractive wooded location and clean facilities, is one of the best on Thássos.

## Limenária and the west coast

**LIMENÁRIA**, the island's second town, was built to house German mining executives brought in by the Ottomans between 1890 and 1905. Their remaining mansions, scattered on the slopes above the harbour, lend some character, but despite attempts at embellishing the waterfront, it's not the most attractive place on Thássos, though it is handy for its **banks** and **ATMs**, **post office** and seasonal hydrofoil connections. The best **accommodation** is the *Hotel George* (☎25930 51413; ❹), with bright and modern rooms at the lower end of the main street leading down to the harbour front. At the east end of the quay, in some 1960s blocks, are a cluster of very basic hotels such as the *Sgouridis* (☎25930 51241; ❸). There are also plenty of **rooms** on offer. For eating and drinking, choose from among half-a-dozen each of bars and eateries along the front, of which *Mouragio* is the only one that comes close to having some charm.

The nearest good beach is **Trypití**, a couple of kilometres west – turn left into the pines at the start of a curve right. All development – mostly package villas – is well inland from the broad, 800-metre long strand, although there are umbrellas and sun loungers for rent. The cleft that the name refers to (literally "pierced" in Greek) is a slender tunnel through the headland at the west end of the beach, leading to a tiny three-boat anchorage.

Continuing clockwise from Limenária to Liménas, there's progressively less to stop off for as the western coast is the most exposed and scenically least impressive. The various *skáles* (harbours) such as Skála Kaliráhis and Skála Sotíros – originally the ports for namesake inland villages – are bleak, straggly and windy. **Skála Marión**, 13km from Limenária, is the exception: an attractive little bay, with fishing boats hauled up on the sandy foreshore, and the admittedly modern low-rise village arrayed in a U-shape all around. There are **rooms** available, a few tavernas and, most importantly, two fine beaches on either side. **Skála Prínou** has little to recommend it, other than ferry connections to Kavála. Buses are usually timed to coincide with the ferries, but if you want to stay, there are several hotels, numerous rooms, quayside tavernas and an EOT **campsite** (☎25930 71171; June–Sept) 1km south of the ferry dock. **Skála Rahoníou**, between here and Liménas, has more accommodation (including the *Perseus* campsite) and fish restaurants, as well as proximity to **Pahýs beach**, 9km short of Liménas, by far the best strand on the northwest coast. Narrow dirt tracks lead past various tavernas through surviving pines to the sand, partly shaded in the morning.

## The interior

Few people get around to exploring inland Thássos – with the post-fire scrub still struggling to revive, it's not always rewarding – but there are several worthwhile excursions to or around the **hill villages**, besides the aforementioned trek up Mount Ypsárion from Potamiá (see p.490).

From Potós you can head 10km along a well-surfaced but poorly signposted road to **THEOLÓGOS**, founded in the sixteenth century by refugees from Constantinople and the island's capital under the Ottomans. Its houses, most with oversized chimneys and slate roofs, straggle in long tiers to either side of the main street, surrounded by generous kitchen gardens or walled courtyards. A stroll along the single high street, with its couple of *kafenía*, a soldiers' bar, a sandalmaker and a traditional bakery, is rewarding and quickly dispels the off-putting effect of vigorous advertising at the outskirts for "Greek Nights" at local tavernas. Two that eschew musical gimmicks and rely on their good food are the long-running *Psistaria Lambiris*, at the entrance into town, and 🍴 *Kleoniki/ Tou Iatrou*, in the very centre, on the right-hand side past the bus stop and police station. They're at their best in the evening when the roasting spits, loaded with goat and suckling pig, start turning.

Despite its proximity as the crow flies, there's no straightforward way from Theológos to **KÁSTRO**, the most naturally protected of the anti-pirate redoubts; especially with a car, it's best to descend to Potós before heading up a rough, seventeen-kilometre dirt track from Limenária. Thirty ancient houses and a church surround a rocky pinnacle, fortified by the Byzantines and the Genoese, which has a sheer drop on three sides. Summer occupation by shepherds is becoming the norm after total abandonment in the nineteenth century, when mining jobs at Limenária proved irresistible. There's only one *kafenío*, on the ground floor of the former school, with one telephone, no mains electricity and far more sheep than people.

From Skála Marión an unmarked but paved road (slipping under the main highway bridge to the north) proceeds 11km inland through gnarled old olive trees to well-preserved **MARIÉS** at the top of a wooded stream valley; of two tavernas here, the well-signed one to the right, *Bethel*, is preferable. From Skála Sotíros, a very steep road heads 3.5km up to **SOTÍRAS**, the only interior village with an unobstructed view of sunset over the Aegean and thus popular with foreigners, who've bought up about half of the houses for restoration. On the ridge opposite are exploratory shafts left by the miners, whose ruined lodge looms above the church. On the plane-shaded square below the old fountain, *O Platanos* taverna is congenially run by Maria and Manolis, who offer grills plus one *mayireftá* dish-of-the-day, good bulk wine and sometimes their potent, home-made *tsípouro*, but only in July and August.

From Prínos (Kalýves) on the coast road, you've a six-kilometre journey inland to the Kazavíti villages, shrouded in greenery that escaped the fires; they're (poorly) signposted and mapped officially as Megálo and Mikró Prínos but still universally known by their Ottoman name. **MIKRÓ KAZAVÍTI** marks the start of the track south for **MEGÁLO KAZAVÍTI**, where the magnificent platía, one of the prettiest spots on the whole island, is home to a couple of decent, normal-priced **tavernas**, while *Vassilis*, below in a beautifully restored house, is regarded as a cut above. Some 4km up from its *skála* (harbour), **RAHÓNI** is well set at the head of a denuded valley. The road up to the square has plenty of simple tavernas, such as *Iy Dhrosia*.

# Travel details

## Conventional ferries and kaïkia

To simplify the following lists we've excluded certain peripheral services on north-to-south routes. These are the 2 weekly Saos Ferries departures between Sámos (Vathý or Karlóvassi), Áyios Kírykos (1 weekly), Híos, Lésvos, Límnos and Kavála each direction (19–20hr), the weekly sailing between Rhodes and Thessaloníki via Kós, Kálymnos, Sámos, and back (27hr each way); and the weekly sailing between Rhodes and Alexandhroúpoli via the same islands, and back (28hr each way).

**Áyios Efstrátios** 4 weekly on Saos Ferries to Límnos, Kavála and Lávrio; 1–2 weekly on Saos to Sígri (Lésvos) and/or Psará; 5 weekly, early morning, by small local ferry to Límnos.

**Foúrni** 3 weekly to Sámos (northern ports), Áyios Kírykos and Pireás, on Kallisti Ferries; Tues, Thurs, Sat 7.30am on the *kaïki Samos Sun* to Karlóvassi,

returning 2.15pm; Mon, Wed, Fri 7.30am on same craft to Áyios Kírykos, returning 3pm; 5–6 weekly on the *Samos Spirit* (7.30am) to Karlóvassi & Vathý, returning 2.15pm.

**Híos** 6 weekly on NEL Lines to Pireás (10hr) and Lésvos (3hr 30min), daily to same destinations on Hellenic Seaways (5hr/2hr); 1 weekly to Límnos on NEL. Daily 1pm or 3pm *kaïki* to Inoússes except Sun morning, and Tues in off-season; 6 weekly on *Nisos Thira* – between 1.30 and 9.30pm – from Híos Town to Psará (3hr).

**Ikaría** 3 weekly from Áyios Kírykos to Sámos (both northern ports), Foúrni and Pireás, on Kallisti Ferries; daily *kaïki* (*Samos Sun*) or small ferry (*Samos Spirit*) from Áyios Kírykos to Foúrni, mid-to-late afternoon; 3 weekly *kaïkia*, typically Mon, Wed & Fri mornings, from Manganítis to Áyios Kírykos.

**Lésvos (Mytilíni Town)** 6 weekly on NEL Lines to Pireás (13hr), daily on Hellenic Seaways (8hr

30min); 6 weekly to Híos (3hr 30min), daily on Hellenic Seaways (2hr); 1–2 weekly on NEL to Límnos (5hr 30min); 1 weekly to Thessaloníki on NEL (13hr 30min).

**Lésvos (Sígri)** 2 weekly to Áyios Efstrátios, Límnos, Kavála, and Lávrio on Saos Ferries.

**Límnos** 3 weekly on NEL Lines to Lésvos (Mytilíni) & Híos; 4 weekly to Áyios Efstrátios & Lávrio on Saos Ferries; 2 weekly to Kavála on Saos; 2 weekly to Thessaloníki on NEL or Saos; 1 weekly to Piraeus on NEL; 1 weekly to Samothráki on Saos.

**Sámos (Pythagório)** 4 weekly (Mon, Wed, Fri & Sun afternoon) on *Nissos Kalymnos* to Agathónissi, Arkí, Lipsí, Pátmos, Léros and Kálymnos, with onward connections to southern Dodecanese (see p.407 for the full schedule).

**Sámos (Vathý & Karlóvassi)** 3 weekly on Kallisti Ferries, to Ikaría (Áyios Kírykos and Pireás (11–14hr), usually calling at Foúrni too.

**Samothráki** 2–3 daily to Alexandhroúpoli (2hr 30min) in season, dropping to 5–6 weekly in winter; 2 weekly late spring and early autumn, up to 3 weekly in July & Aug, to Kavála; 1 weekly direct to Límnos during July and Aug.

**Thássos** At least 7 daily in summer (2–4 daily Oct–May), from Skála Prínou to Kavála (1hr 15min); 8–12 daily year round from Liménas to Keramotí (40min).

## Hydrofoils and catamarans

**Aegean Flying Dolphins** Operates daily out of Pythagório (Sámos) once daily at 8am to Pátmos, Lipsí, Léros (Ayía Marína), Kálymnos and Kós, arriving 11.30am and returning at 2pm. Advertised midsummer detours to Foúrni and Ikaría (Áyios Kírykos) rarely run owing to weather conditions.

**Kallisti Ferries'** *Corsica Express* plies 3 days weekly, usually at 3.30pm, on the route Vathý–Karlóvassi–Évdhilos–Mýkonos–Tínos–Piréas, with Foúrni added once weekly (7–8hr total journey time).

**Hellenic Seaways'** *Nisos Mykonos* provides a competing service 6 days weekly Vathý–Karlóvassi–Évdhilos and often Mýkonos–Sýros too, leaving towards Pireás 10.30pm except Sun at 2pm.

**Samothráki** to: Alexandhroúpoli (April–Sept 1–2 daily; 1hr 10min).

**Thássos (Liménas)** to: Kavála (April–Oct 8–15 times daily; 40min).

**Thássos (Skála Prinou)** to: Kavála (April–Oct 2–4 daily; 30min).

## International ferries

**Híos–Çeşme (Turkey)** 2–13 boats weekly at 8.30am and/or 4.30–5pm, depending on season. Passenger fares on the Greek boat (*San Nicholas*) or

Turkish vessel (*Ertürk II*) are nominally about €40 return, including Greek taxes (no Turkish tax), but "special offers" of €30 are frequent, plus €10 coach transfer to İzmir; one-way €25. Small cars €65–70 one-way, €110 return, plus small Greek tax. Journey time 30min (*San Nicholas*) or 45min (*Ertürk II*).

**Mytilíni (Lésvos)–Ayvalık/Dikili (Turkey)** Daily May–Oct; winter link sporadic. Two craft, the Turkish *Jale* and the Greek Costar Line's *Konstandinos I*, depart Mytilíni 8.30–9am most days. Passenger rates €25 one-way or round trip, all taxes inclusive. Dikili services run Tues, Thurs & Sat, for €35 return. Small cars (each boat carries two) €60 one-way, €90 return. Journey time 1hr 20min to Ayvalık, 1hr 30min to Dikili.

**Mytilíni (Lésvos)–Foça (Turkey)** May to Oct, Tues/Thurs 9am, Fri/Sun eve on the Turyol speedboat; no cars carried, €38 return, €25 one-way.

**Vathý (Sámos)–Kuşadası (Turkey)** 2 daily, early May to late Oct (maximum 1 weekly in winter). Greek boat at 8.30am; afternoon (4.45pm) Turkish boats (usually 2 craft in season). Rates are €43 one-way including taxes, €47 day return including taxes, €65 open return including taxes. Cars are ferried only on the *Samos Spirit*'s Mon & Fri am departures (€100 one-way, €150 return for a small car). Journey time 1hr 30min.

## Flights

**NB:** All flights on Olympic Airlines/Aviation unless otherwise specified. Frequencies are for June–Oct.

**Híos** to: Athens (2–3 daily on Olympic, 2 daily on Aegean; 45–50min); Límnos (2 weekly, both via Lésvos; 1hr 35min); Rhodes (2 weekly, 1 via Sámos; 55min–1hr 45min); Thessaloníki (5 weekly, 2 via Lésvos/Límnos; 1hr 10min–2hr 45min).

**Ikaría** to: Athens (4–6 weekly; 50min); Iráklio Crete, (1 weekly on Sky Express; 40min).

**Lésvos** to: Athens (2–4 daily on Olympic, 3 daily on Aegean; 50min–1hr); Híos (2 weekly, 30min); Límnos (5 weekly; 40min); Rhodes (2 weekly, via Sámos; 1hr 40min); Sámos (2 weekly, 1 direct; 45min–1hr 30min); Thessaloníki (1–2 daily, 5 weekly via Límnos, on Olympic; 4–6 weekly direct on Aegean; 55min–1hr 50min).

**Límnos** to: Athens (2 daily on Olympic, 1 daily on Aegean; 45–55min); Lésvos (5 weekly; 40min); Rhodes (5 weekly; 2hr 5min–3hr 40min); Thessaloníki (6 weekly; 45min).

**Sámos** to: Athens (3–4 daily on Olympic, 2 daily on Aegean; 50–60min); Iráklio, Crete (2 weekly on Sky Express; 1hr); Lésvos (2 weekly, 1 via Híos; 50min–1hr 30min); Límnos (2 weekly, via Lésvos/Híos; 1hr 35min–1hr 55min); Rhodes (2 weekly; 45min); Thessaloníki (3 weekly direct, 2 via intervening islands; 1hr 20min–3hr 45min).

# 6

# The Sporades and Évvia

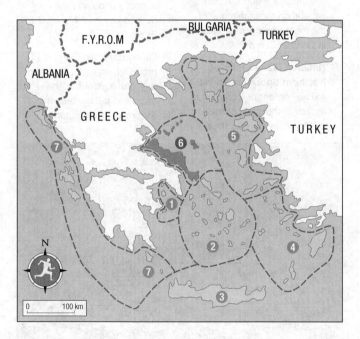

# CHAPTER 6 Highlights

* **Laláría beach, Skiáthos**
  White oval stones and
  turquoise waters, backed
  by steep cliffs and a natural
  rock arch, form a photogenic
  contrast to the island's
  other, mostly sandy, bays.
  See p.501

* **Skópelos Town** Wooden
  shutters, ornate balconies,
  domed churches, atmospheric
  passageways and luxuriant
  vegetation make this one of
  the most alluring island towns
  in Greece. See p.504

* **National Marine Park of
  Northern Sporades** Spend
  a day – or longer – on a boat
  exploring the islets of this
  pristine reserve, with their

  wildlife, monasteries and
  secluded bays. See p.512

* **Skýros** An outrageously
  pagan carnival, a striking
  hillside Hóra and traditional
  interiors are all found on one
  of the least spoiled islands in
  the Aegean. See pp.514–515

* **Dhimosári Gorge, southern
  Évvia** Traverse the wildest
  corner of the island on
  a mostly cobbled path
  descending from Mount Óhi.
  See p.523

* **Límni, northern Évvia** A
  proud, characterful port with
  beautiful horizons to the west
  and clean pebble beaches
  either side. See p.524

▲ Skýros Hóro and citadel from west

# The Sporades and Évvia

The three northern **Sporades**, as their name suggests, are scattered off the central mainland, hilly terrain betraying their status as extensions of Mount Pílio right opposite on the mainland; they're also culturally, historically and administratively very much part of Magnisía province, centred on Vólos, the main port for these islands. Archetypal Aegean-holiday venues, with fine beaches, lush vegetation and transparent sea, they're all packed out in midsummer. **Skiáthos**, nearest to Pílio, is the busiest of the trio thanks to excellent sandy beaches, nightlife and an airport, but **Skópelos**, with extensive pine forests and idyllic pebble bays, is catching up fast. The quietest, remotest and least developed, **Alónissos**, is part of a National Marine Park, attracting more nature-lovers than night-owls.

**Skýros**, the fourth inhabited Sporade, lies well southeast, and has little historical connection with the others. It has best succeeded in retaining its traditional culture, though tourism (and real estate sales) are accelerating. While the dramatically set *hóra* remains a "normal" village, its main street is well used to visitors, and popular beach resorts lie downhill.

Between Skýros and central Greece, enormous **Évvia** (the classical Euboea) extends for nearly 200km alongside the mainland. Although in spots one of the most dramatic Greek islands, with forested mountains and rugged stretches of little-developed coast, it attracts fewer foreign tourists, perhaps because it lacks that mid-Aegean feel. Nonetheless, mainlanders throng the island, erecting holiday homes around several seaside resorts.

The northern Sporades are well connected by **bus** and **ferry** with Athens (via Áyios Konstandínos or Vólos), and less often by boat from Thessaloníki; it's easy to island-hop between them. The only reliable ferry connection to Skýros is from Kými on Évvia, though some years the same boat may provide a peak-season link with Alónissos. Evvia is joined to central Greece by two bridges at Halkídha, and by local ferries from several strategic points on the mainland. Only Skiáthos and Skýros have **airports**. Many people come to the forested Sporades to hike; the best **maps** are those published for each island by Anavasi, available in Athens, Vólos and on the islands themselves for €5–7.50.

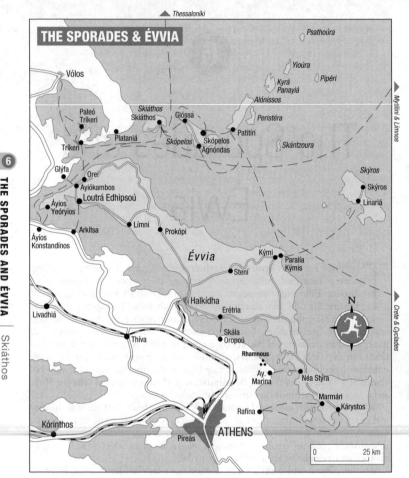

THE SPORADES & ÉVVIA

Thessaloníki

Vólos

Paleó
Trikeri

Skiáthos
Skiáthos

Platanía

Glóssa

Skópelos
Skópelos

Psathoúra

Yioúra

Kyrá
Panayiá

Pipéri

Alónissos

Peristéra

Patitíri

Skántzoura

Mytilíni & Límnos

Trikeri

Skópelos

Agnóndas

Glýfa

Oreí

Ayiókambos
Loutrá Edhipsoú

Áyios
Yeóryios

Límni

Prokópi

Skýros

Skýros

Linariá

Crete & Cyclades

Áyios
Konstandínos

Arkítsa

Évvia

Kými

Paralía
Kýmis

Stení

Livadhiá

Thíva

Halkídha

Erétria

Skála
Oropoú

Rhamnous

Ay.
Marína

Néa Stýra

Marmári

Kárystos

Kórinthos

Rafína

ATHENS

Pireás

N

0        25 km

# Skiáthos

Undulating green countryside, some fine rural monasteries and the main town's labyrinthine old quarter certainly rate, but the real business of **Skiáthos** is yacht flotillas – there's a sizeable marina and drydock towards the airport, logical outgrowth of the traditional *kaïki*-building trade – and **beaches**: the best, if most oversubscribed, in the Sporades. There are over fifty strands (plus a few more on satellite islets), still not enough to absorb legions of visitors; the island's five thousand inhabitants are vastly outnumbered all season – in spring and autumn by Brits, during summer by Italians and Greeks. The main road along the south and southeast coasts serves an almost unbroken line of villas, hotels, mini-markets and restaurants; although they've not impinged much on Skiáthos's natural beauty, they make it difficult to find anything particularly Greek here. But by **hiking** or using a **4WD vehicle**, you can find relative solitude, refreshing vistas and charming medieval monuments in the island's north.

# Skiáthos Town

**SKIÁTHOS TOWN**, the main habitation and harbour, clambers over various hillsides and promontories. Above the picturesque old port, the southwesterly old quarter, with its old gardened houses, maze-like lanes, shady platíes and the graceful belfries of Trís Ierárhes and Ayía Triádha churches, rewards random strolling, though tourist development (and the German burning of the town in Aug 1944 in reprisal for persistent resistance activities) has scarred the flatter northeastern districts around main drag Alexándhrou Papadhiamándi, where most services, tackier shops, and "English" pubs are found.

There aren't many specific sights, though the **Alexandros Papadiamantis Museum** (Tues–Sun 9.30am–1.30pm & 5–8pm; €1) on Mitropolítou Ananíou, housed in the nineteenth-century home of one of Greece's best-known writers, is worth a look. The upper storey has been maintained as it was when the writer lived (and died) here, while the ground floor operates as a bookshop-cum-exhibition-area. **Galerie Varsakis antique shop** (open long hours) on Platía Trión Ierarhón just in from the old port has one of the best **folklore displays** in Greece, and many older items would do Athens' Benáki Museum proud; the proprietor neither wants nor – given his stratospheric prices – expects to sell most of these, which include textiles, handicrafts, copperware, rural tools and jewellery.

## Arrival, transport and information

**Exiting** the **ferry harbour**, the main **taxi** rank is 50m right of the gate; the **bus** stop is at the yacht end of the quay, by the landscaped platía. In between are numerous **rental outlets** offering bicycles, motorbikes, cars and motorboats; Aegean Car Rental (☎24270 22430 or 694 42 24 376, ⓦwww.heliotropio.gr), a few steps northeast along the quay, is recommended. Parking in town is impossible, except out past the yacht anchorage and at the southwest edge near the health centre. You can get your bearings on an anticlockwise **boat trip** around the island (€20 per person; out 10am, back 5pm, 4–5 photo/swim stops, lunch at Megálos Asélinos), departing from the old port, beyond the Boúrtzi ex-islet and its causeway linking it to the quay. A shorter jaunt from the old port heads for **Tsougriá** islet (opposite Skiáthos Town, with two beaches and a taverna).

Most other facilities are on Alexándhrou Papadhiamándi, including the **post office** and **several ATMs**. One block in from the old port on Nífonos, Enter has both wi-fi signal and high-speed **internet** terminals. The Hellenic Seaways **ferry agent** (☎24270 22209) is at the base of Papadhiamándi; GA is handled by Dhioyenis Theodhorou (☎24270 22204), 100m further right.

## Accommodation

Town **accommodation** is heavily booked during summer, though you can usually find a *dhomátio*, albeit pricier (minimum ❹) than elsewhere; at other times, supply exceeds demand and rates dip. The quayside room-owners' association kiosk operates long hours in high season; otherwise bookings can be made through several tourist agencies.

Small town **hotels** include jointly run *Bourtzi* (☎24270 21304, ⓦwww.hotelbourtzi.gr; ❹) at Moraïtou 8, and *Pothos* (☎24270 22694; ❹), on Evangelistrías, both immaculate with delightful gardens; the former has a swimming pool, the latter a shady patio. In the old quarter at 25-Martíou 30, *Mato* (☎24270 22186; ❺) has old-fashioned, mock-rustic communal areas and some tour presence. Noisier, though with sea views, is the waterfront *Meltemi* (☎24270 22493, ⓔmeltemi@skiathos.gr; ❹), with breakfast available in the eponymous snack-bar out front.

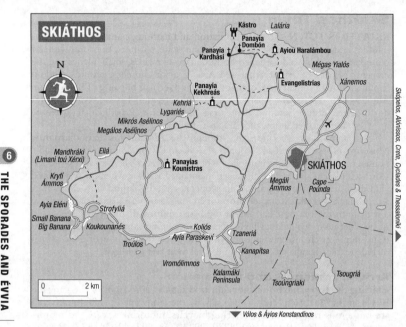

Skópelos, Alónissos, Crete, Cyclades & Thessaloníki

▼ Vólos & Áyios Konstandínos

Indisputably the best standard in the town environs, 1km southwest at **Megáli Ámmos**, is offered by 2007-refurbished 🪂 *Aegean Suites* (☎24270 24068, Ⓦwww.aegeansuites.com; ❽ – €430–630 ), 21 luxury hillside units averaging 55 square metres, all with bug screens, wi-fi signal and sound systems, differing only in the degree of sea view. The large pool is bracketed by a breakfast gazebo and "live cooking" restaurant; there's ample off-road parking, and the elevated setting cuts down on road noise.

## Eating and drinking

Most full-service **tavernas** (as opposed to fast-food joints) cluster around Platía Trión Ierarhón or flank the old harbour. Live *bouzoúki* or guitar serenades with your meal are the norm. The best fish restaurants – priced accordingly (€55–60 per kilo) – line the far end of the old port.

🪂 **Alexandhros** Kapodhistríou, well signposted from Platía Trión Ierarhón. Decent *mezédhes*, excellent lamb chops (or *mayireftá*), home-made crème caramel, all at reasonable prices, and Greek sing-alongs with the ad hoc musicians make this a winner, let down only by poor bulk wine. Summer tables under the mulberry tree; winter seating indoors in an old stone-built salon.

🪂 **Amfiliki** Opposite the health centre, southwest shore of old town. All the standard taverna recipes, salubriously prepared – as tempting aromas wafting from the kitchen up front tell you. They're tops for seafood dishes like *seláhi* (skate) parsley and onion salad, or *bráska kípo* – monkfish covered in spicy tomato sauce.

Just forty seats overlooking the sea, so reserve in season on ☎24270 22839. Open all year, with fireplace going as needed.

**Bakaliko** Airport road. Probably the most accomplished of three restaurants here in a strip more known for nightlife, with mock decor of a traditional Greek grocer's, unusual takes on traditional recipes and unimprovable seating cantilevered over the water. Moderately priced; live acoustic Greek music some nights.

**Maria's** Behind apse of Trís Ierarhes church. Specialists in pizza, pasta and creative salads, but worth visiting for its riotously eclectic interior decor alone, though in summer you'll prefer to sit out on the balcony, or down in the courtyard. One of the cheaper places, at about €40 for two people with a mountainous double salad, pizza and house wine. Dinner only.

**Mesoyia** Beyond and northwest of Platía Trión Ierarhón. Cheap-and-cheerful outfit, with some Greek patronage, featuring the usual grilled and *mayireftá* suspects, plus daily changing seafood. Some corners – such as tinned *dolmádhes* – may be too sharply cut, but overall it's still worth showing up. Tables in the lane in summer; indoors during the cooler months.

## Nightlife

Non-naff **bars**, well attended by a trendy multinational clientele, have two main nuclei: overlooking the old port, and out on the "club strip" at the start of the airport road beyond the yacht marina, featuring a mix of Latin, blues, rock and Greek sounds. At the former locale, four contiguous, essentially identical **bars** (*7 Steps, Rock and Roll, Slip Inn, Cassablanca*) with scatter cushions and fashion victims on display line the stairway up from the quay. "Club strip" venues are more annually changeable, but currently *Red Marrakesh* with its billowy curtains, purple lighting scheme and hubble-bubbles to smoke on a deck jutting out over the shallows is typical. *Kentavros*, near the Papadiamantis Museum, an evergreen, much-loved jazz and blues bar, is a worthy exception to this polarisation; the summer **cinema**, Attikon, is next door. Another seasonal venue is the Boúrtzi, whose fortress grounds host occasional **theatrical** and **musical** performances.

## Around the island

With 25 numbered stops along the way, the island **bus** shuttles at least hourly in summer (every 15min at peak times) until late between town and Koukounariés, a major resort 12km west. But you'll need your own transport to explore the hinterland, overgrown with pine, lentisc, holm oak, heather and arbutus – all regrown forest or maquis as it's been frequently **burned** by arsonists. Thanks to the humid climate and springs fed from the mainland, vegetation regenerates quickly, but camping rough is strictly forbidden (as it is throughout the Sporades).

### Nearby beaches

Many northeast-coast **beaches** aren't accessible unless you take an excursion *kaïki*, hire a jeep, or embark on fairly long treks. In any case, the south coast is better protected from the prevailing northerly *meltémi*, and its beaches are just a few steps from the bus stops. All the more popular coves have at least a drinks/snacks *kantína*, while a few support full-service tavernas.

Famous **Laláría** beach, featured on all postcard-stands, nestles near the northernmost point of Skiáthos, only accessible by taxi- or excursion-boat from town. Consisting of white pebbles, with steep cliffs rising behind and an artistic natural arch, it's undeniably beautiful; three **sea-grottoes** just east rate a stop on most "round-the-island" trips. About 3.5km north of Skiáthos Town, reached by vehicle followed by a steep ten-minute path down, **Mégas Yialós** – 250m of coarse sand and gravel – is lovely and naturist, though a lack of shade and facilities (an eponymous taverna is 400m up the access road) discourages casual visits. You can drive right up to **Xánemos**, at the end of the airport runway, not too bad despite being a bit exposed; its 200m of sand come with showers, sunbeds and a *kantína*.

On the southeast coast, beaches before the **Kalamáki peninsula** are no great shakes, but on the promontory itself are excellent **Tzaneriá** on the east and **Vromólimnos** on the west. At Tzaneriá (bus stop no. 12), Manthos's friendly, PADI-affiliated Dolphin Diving Centre (☎694 49 99 181, ⓦwww .ddiving.gr) offers a variety of **scuba dives** (at 9.30am & 1pm) around the coast. Vromólimnos has **windsurfing** and **water-skiing** facilities, plus very lively August parties by (and in) the water, though only one beach bar is currently operating.

Mega-hotels dominate the beaches between Vromólimnos and Troúlos; just before the latter, a side-road leads 3.5km north through a lush valley to **Megálos Asélinos**, an exposed, coarse-sand beach with a bar, tour-beset taverna and showers. The fork in the paved road leading to Panayías Kounístras continues to quieter **Mikrós Asélinos** just east.

### Koukounariés and around

Beaches around **KOUKOUNARIÉS**, the island's third settlement after Troúlos, are excellent if you don't mind sharing them. The 1200-metre-long main bay of clear, gradually deepening water is backed by acres of stone pines; wooden walkways traverse the sand to a series of *kantínas*. The approach road runs behind a small lake, **Strofyliá**, behind the grove – all of it a protected reserve – past **hotels**, **apartments** and **restaurants**, as well as a decent **campsite**, *Koukounaries* (☏ 24270 49250; May 15–Sept 15). The best-value accommodation locally, albeit inland northeast of the lake, is 2007-opened *Mandraki Village* (☏ 24270 49670, ⓦ www.mandraki-skiathos.gr; ❼), with tasteful, pastel-coloured family quads and junior suites (worth small price difference) with bigger baths, a small pool, well-landscaped grounds and a competent (if luridly coloured) on-site restaurant. All usual **watersports** are available at the beach, plus **horseriding** with the conspicuous Skiathos Riding Centre (May–Oct; ☏ 24270 49548, ⓦ www.skiathos-horse -riding.gr) in the forested dunes to the north.

Signposted across the headland, "**Big Banana**" beach (officially **Krassás**) is trendy and road-accessible, with **wall-to-wall sunbeds**, two buzzing bars and watersports; a headland (and steep 400m path) separates it from partly gay, all-nude "**Small Banana**", named like its fellow not for the appendages on display but the yellow crescents of sand. A separate track system leads 1km to more family-orientated **Ayía Eléni** (snack bar), and then past **Kryfí Ámmos** beach into a unique, **dune-forest** system also traversed by paths north from Koukounariés. Side-turnings lead to either excellent **Mandhráki** (aka **Limáni tou Xérxi**), 500m of blonde sand with a characterful if not especially cheap fish-fryer snack bar, and equally alluring **Eliá (alias Gournés)**, with another eatery, sunbeds and a naturist zone.

### The monasteries and Kástro

From town, you arrive at eighteenth-century **Evangelistrías monastery** (daily 10.30am–2.30pm & 5–8pm) by motorized transport in ten minutes or on foot in just over an hour, using the path short-cut shown on the Anavasi map. Founded by Athonite monks, and supposedly scene of the first (1807) unfurling of the Greek flag, it's beautifully set; inside there's an eclectic **museum** (same hours, €3) comprising ecclesiastical and rural-folklore galleries, musical instruments, and a vast collection of documents, posters and photos from the Balkan Wars donated by the Potamianos family.

Below Evangelistrías, another **path** starting beside a watermill, then rough track, continue to restored **Ayíou Haralámbou** monastery, full of cats and chickens kept by the caretaker. Out the back gate, a faint trail heads west up to a pass, where a broader path drops to **Panayía Dombón** chapel and then to **Panayía Kardhási** on the way to Kástro (see p.503). Motorists can reach Kástro from Evangelistrías by heading southwest to Stavrós junction (*Platanos* taverna just before being the only facility en route) and then turning north; foot passengers can disembark from one of the tour *kaïkia* at the beach below it, or – if already at Evangelistrías – use the *kalderími* indicated on the recommended map from a point just southwest to emerge on the main Kástro-bound road. Another path shortcut, not shown on any commercial map, is possible from Kardhási to **Áyios Ioánnis**, the last chapel before Kástro proper.

**Kástro**, 8km from the south-coast road (final approach from a car park by broad, 10min path), straggles over a windswept headland, reached by stone steps replacing the former drawbridge leading to the gatehouse. This sixteenth-century fortified settlement, established for security from pirate raids, was abandoned after 1830, when the new Greek state stamped hard on piracy and the population left to build the modern town on the site of ancient Skiáthos. The crumbled ruins are overgrown, and just four **churches** survive, the largest (Yénnisi toú Khristoú) retaining original frescoes. From both the gatehouse and car park, paths descend east to a good sandy **beach**, wonderful in June or September, but overrun in summer despite its remoteness; a wooden bridge crosses the stream here to a friendly, not too overpriced, limited-menu **taverna**.

Returning from Kástro, about 3km south, is the rough, steep track down to seventeenth-century **Panayía Kekhreás (Kehriás)** monastery, oldest on the island, with superb frescoes from 1745 under its pink-and-blue cupola. The track continues a bit further down the canyon, past watermills, towards sand-and-pebble **Kehriá** beach, but the final approach is on foot; this tiny beach (snack bar), and its neighbour **Lygariés** (200m of sand, full-service taverna), are usually reached by a much better, separate track system from the south-coast highway.

# Skópelos

Its extensive pine forests mostly still unburnt, **Skópelos** is bigger and more rugged than Skiáthos and almost as popular, but its concessions to tourism are lower key and in better taste. Besides conifers there are olive groves, and orchards of plums (**prunes** are a local speciality), apricots, pears and almonds. **Skópelos (Hóra)** and **Glóssa**, the two main towns, are easily the prettiest in the Sporades, their hillside houses distinguished by painted wooden trim and grey slate roofs. The island has appreciable ground water, but less than Skiáthos, heavily mineral-tainted from the tap (there are potable springs at Karyá and en route to Mount Paloúki's monasteries) and not really enough to support the villa projects burgeoning across the bay from the *hóra*.

Foreign **occupiers** at various stages of the island's history have included Romans, Venetians, French and, of course, the Ottomans. The Ottoman pirate-admiral Barbarossa – actually a Greek renegade from Lésvos – slaughtered the entire population during the sixteenth century. Unlike Skiáthos and Alónissos, Skópelos – nearly as active in the resistance – escaped German wartime reprisals owing to protection from the resident, philhellenic Austrian regional commander, who had lived here as a deep-cover spy from 1937–39 and returned after the war to drink with the

local fishermen and live out his days on nearby Mount Pílio. Today, Greek visitor numbers match foreign (mostly British, Scandinavian, Italian and French) ones, owing to the lack of an airport.

Skópelos should offer better **walking** than it does, with the trail network becoming overgrown or bulldozed into tracks. Long-time Skópelos resident Heather Parsons battles to maintain paths and leads spring/autumn walks along what remains (☎694 52 49 328, ⓦwww.skopelos-walks.com), as well as publishing a hiking guide. That said, the **countryside** – especially the southwest coast – remains spectacular, and served as main location for the **film** version of *Mamma Mia!* during September 2007 (something the island has not been slow to capitalize on).

## Skópelos Town

**SKÓPELOS TOWN** (Hóra) pours off a hill on the west flank of a wide, oval bay; a cascade of handsome mansions and slate-domed churches below the ruined Venetian **kástro** is revealed slowly as the boat rounds the north headland with its postcard-fixture church of Panayítsa toú Pýrgou. This is just one of a reputed 123 shrines scattered across town, most locked except on their saint's day. Away from the requisite waterside commercial strip, the *hóra* is endearingly time-warped – indeed among the most unspoilt in the islands – with wonderfully idiosyncratic shops of a sort long vanished elsewhere, and vernacular domestic architecture unadulterated with tasteless monstrosities. The disorganized **folklore museum** (daily 10am–2.30pm & 6–10pm; €2) musters a motley collection of weaving, embroidery and costumes; informative panels explaining local customs and the religious calendar redeem it. The **Photographic Centre** opens only for temporary exhibits, though there's a permanent display of 1950s photos in the municipal quayside *kafenío*.

### Arrival, transport and information

The **new port** is towards the east end of the tree-lined quay, with two ticket **agencies** (Lemonis for GA ☎24240 22363; Hellenic Seaways, straight out of the gate, ☎24240 22767). Both the **taxi** stand and **KTEL stop** are 100m to the left of the port as you exit; **buses** (4–8 daily by season) ply the main paved road between here and Loutráki via Glóssa and all the main beaches. Drivers should use the free municipal **car park** beside the KTEL terminal. Several **car-and-scooter-rental** outlets, such as Magic (☎22420 23250, ⓦwww.skopeloscars .com), Discovery (☎24240 23033, ⓦwww.skopelos.net/discovery) and Alpha/Avis (☎24240 23170, ⓦwww.alpha-rentals.gr) cluster near the start of the road towards Glóssa or around the corner opposite the town beach. **Boat cruises** cost €20 for a trip around the island; those heading to the Sporades National Marine Park (see p.512) are a con, only going as far as the channel between Alónissos and Peristéra – if you want to visit, start from Alónissos. Quayside **ATMs** abound, while the **post office** is on Dhoulídhi, a lane east of the platía ("Souvlaki Square") graced with plane trees, in from the port; nearby Orange is the best **internet** café (wi-fi and high-speed terminals), though En Plo and Anemos cafés at the kink in the waterfront also have wi-fi signal. There's no tourist office, but ⓦwww.skopelos.net and ⓦwww.skopelosweb.gr are useful.

### Accommodation

There are numerous **rooms** (❸–❹) for rent in the backstreets, as well as entire houses; these – plus apartments and hotels – are best arranged through helpful Madro Travel, by the old port (☎24240 22145, ⓦwww.madrotravel.com), also good for boat excursions. Unless you've booked through them or an overseas operator, you're unlikely to find high-season space in the comfortable hillside **hotels** with pools.

**Adonis** Opposite ferry quay and car park ☎24240 22231. Just ten rooms (five facing the front) at this adequate hotel, handy if you're arriving late at night on a ferry from Vólos or Skiáthos. All year. ❸

**Georgios L.** Northwest promenade, by Panayítsa toú Pýrgou ☎24240 22308, ⓦwww.skopelos.net /georgios/. Bland, 1970s-vintage hotel, but all rooms (part a/c) have a sea view, there's parking nearby and internet terminals in the ground-floor café. ❹

**Kapetanios** Up from ferry jetty ☎24240 22110. Just a short walk inland, this quiet, garden-set, 1970s-built hotel stretches over two wings. ❸

**Kyr Sotos** Just in from mid-quay ☎24240 22549, ⓦwww.skopelos.net/sotos/. Rambling, restored old-house *pension* with wood-floored, a/c, en-suite rooms that are justifiably a favourite budget option. Go for the quieter rear units facing the courtyard, especially no. 4, with its fireplace. Open all year. ❷

🏃 **Mando** ☎24240 23917, ⓦwww.skopelos .net/mando/ Easily the best accommodation at Stáfylos (see p.506), very friendly and quiet with stone-floored, a/c rooms set among manicured lawns, a short way up from its own lido. Also a family suite with fireplace. ❺

🏃 **Skopelos Village** 600m around bay from ferry dock ☎24240 22517, ⓦwww .skopelosvillage.gr. Self-catering complex, its units range from studios up to three-bed apartments with mock-Victorian bathroom fixtures, set among landscaped grounds with two pools (one for laps only); the plushest local option, popular with families and package companies – and if photos in the sea-view *Agioli* nouvelle cuisine restaurant are reliable, the cast of *Mamma Mia* as well. April to mid-Oct. Studios ❺, apartments ❻–❽

**Thea Home** On ring road ☎24240 22859, ⓦwww.skopelosweb.gr/theahome/. Studios and larger apartments with white-tile-and-pine decor, fridges, phones and TV, most with balconies with sweeping sea views; easy street parking. Breakfast (extra) offered on a pleasant patio. April–Oct. ❹

## Eating and drinking

In-town **tavernas** range from acceptable *yirádhika* on plane-tree-shaded "Souvlaki Square" to excellent, photo-menu-free eateries on the northwest quay, by way of forgettable tourist traps at mid-quay and *koultouriárika* outfits inland.

🏃 **Englezos** Northwest quay ⓦwww.englezos .gr. 2007-opened all-rounder that's worth the 15 percent extra for Greek island standards with a highly original twist. The menu changes seasonally and annually, but might include eggplant croquettes with mint and cheese, samphire, creative salads, and lamb joint with cubed potatoes, accompanied by good bulk wine from Anhíalos and perfumed brandy as a nightcap.

**Gorgones** Inland, beside well-signed *Oionos Blue Bar*. The only genuine ouzerí in town, with tables indoors and out in the lane. The menu – stressing chops and seafood – is fine, the prices fair, only erratic service letting it down. All year.

**Klimataria** Next to the *dhimarhío*. Reasonable (for Skópelos) fish by the kilo like *mousmoúlia*, scorpion fish and stewed grouper; a few *mayireftá* and *mezédhes* too.

🏃 **Ta Kymata (Angelos)** Last building, northwest quay. About the oldest taverna on Skópelos, a shrine of quality *mayireftá* such as *exohikó* (lamb and vegetables in a filo triangle) and *mezédhes* like fresh beets with their own greens.

**Molos** Northwest quay, between *Englezos* and *Klimataria*. May not have the panache of its neighbours, but still a solid choice with good salads, well-priced lamb and pork dishes, Dimitra white wine from Anhíalos and probably a dessert on the house.

**Nastas** Near T-junction on Glóssa road. Greek-patronized ouzerí that's really more seafood taverna, strong on fish and lobster. Portions aren't huge but quality is high and service assiduous. All year; out under the mulberries in summer, in the wood-floored salon during winter.

**Perivoli** Up a lane from the plane-tree platía with its *yirádhika*. Courtyard taverna preparing Greek recipes with a cordon bleu twist; wine by the glass.

## Nightlife

**Nightlife** in Skópelos is more of the musical-**bar** than the dance-club variety, though a few of the latter (such as *Eleotrivio*) occupy old olive mills or warehouses on Dhoulídi, the post-office street.

Anatoli Veteran rebétika musician Yiorgos Xintaris performs (and sells a worthwhile CD) at this unsigned outfit on top of the *kástro*. Only operates late June to early Sept, when his sons (who accompany him) return from university in Athens. Large parties should book on ☎ 24240 22851.

Merkourio (Mercurius) Mixed musical offerings at this Greek-favoured terrace bar by Áyios Merkoúrios church.

Oionos Blue Bar Old-house bar inland from mid-quay with a jazz, blues and world-music playlist, plus a staggering variety of imported beers and whiskies.

Platanos Evergreen bar on the northwest quay, with jazz and world-music soundtrack. Great too for a morning coffee or breakfast and people-watching under the namesake plane tree outside.

## Around Hóra

On the slopes of Mount Paloúki east of the bay stand three historic monasteries; without wheeled transport, access is simplest via a track from Áyios Andónios chapel behind the football pitch, which goes first to Metamórfosis; from there what's left of the old *kalderími* system effectively shortcuts the roads to Evange-listrías and Prodhrómou. **Evangelistrías** (daily 8am–1pm & 5–8pm), visible from town and founded 1712 as an ecclesiastical academy, is notable more for the fine glazed tiles and *témblon* in the *katholikón*, and relief carving around its windows and doors, than its two rather dim nuns belying the scholarly tradition here. More secluded **Prodhrómou** (same hours), occupied by three elderly but more switched-on sisters, was largely destroyed in the 1965 quake but retains some fine icons. Sixteenth-century **Metamórfosis**, an Athonite dependency at the top of a verdant ravine, is being restored, worth braving the surly caretaker monk for a look at its floral courtyard and colourful dome held up by four dark coral-rock columns.

Some 4km south of town, **Stáfylos** is the closest decent beach, though small and seasonally crowded, with a spring and a single **taverna**, *Pefkos*, that's merely adequate with its limited seafood menu and bulk-pack *mezédhes*. You're best off walking five minutes east over the headland to larger, more scenic, sand-and-fine-gravel **Velanió**, 600m long with an official naturist zone and a summer-only *kantína* renting sunbeds.

Northwest of Skópelos Town, reached by taxi-boats and a paved road, **Glystéri** is a small sand-and-pebble beach with sunbeds, its *Palio Karnayio* **taverna** much frequented at weekends. A side-turning, 1km out of town, from the Glystéri road leads west via the lush, well-watered Karyá valley to the east flank of 681-metre **Mount Dhélfi** and a major junction just below Áyios Riyínos pass; bear right for 1km to the well-marked trailhead to the **Sendoúkia**, three cyst-type Helle-nistic graves with their lids ajar, a twelve-minute walk distant first on path, then a cairned cross-country route. Only hard-core antiquities buffs will enthuse, but the views over Alónissos and minor islets, especially at dusk, are fabulous.

## The south and west coast

About 7km due south of Hóra lies the elephant's-foot-shaped bay of **AGNÓNDAS**, the island's back-up harbour when the main port is storm-shut, and designated port of call for boats to the Cyclades, Thessaloníki and Crete. **Accommodation** includes *Pavlina Apartments* (☎ 24240 23272, ✉ pavlinaskopelos@mail.gr; ③) behind the short pebble beach, offering four high-ceilinged, wood-trimmed one- and two-bedroomed units. Among three **tavernas**, waterfront seafood specialist *Pavlos* (March–Oct) has fair fish prices, *mezédhes* like *tsitsírava* and Apostolakis bulk wine. At **LIMNONÁRI** just west, 300m of white sand bracketed by the steep-sided bay, *Limnonari Beach Restaurant* serves delicious spiral *striftés tyrópittes* and rents **rooms** (☎ 24240 23046; ④).

The first bay on the west-facing coast, **PÁNORMOS** is the biggest resort outside Skópelos Town, with abundant lodgings, four **tavernas** (*Asterias* is competent), yacht anchorage in contiguous **Bló** inlet and **watersports**, including small-boat hire (☎694 43 28 821, ⓦwww.holidayislands.com/boathire). The main gravel beach shelves steeply, but there are smaller, sandier bays close by. Among **accommodation**, the well-kept *Panormos Beach Hotel* (☎24240 22711, ⓦwww.skopelosweb.gr/panormosbeach; ❺) has fine views and a huge lawn studded with fruit trees; 1km beyond it, isolated ⚶ *Adrina Beach* (☎24240 24250, ⓦwww.adrina.gr; late May to Sept; min four-day stay; ❻) comprises ivy-clad bungalows, a sea-water pool, on-site taverna and private beach.

Just around the corner, **Miliá** comprises two 400-metre sweeps of tiny pebbles opposite Dhassía islet divided by a headland with a sometimes obtrusively noisy beach bar at the south cove. Parking for it is impossible in season unless you patronize the **taverna** with its private lot, worth doing for their fresh small fish or squid, hand-cut chips and simple vegetable starters. If you're really taken with the place, **stay** at nearby *Milia Studios* (☎24242 23998; ❺), with breakfast supplied to the rooms, galleried quads as well and – besides *Adrina Beach* – the only true beachfront digs on the island. That said, some will prefer **Kastáni** immediately north, 150m of fine sand and arguably the island's best beach, with a naturist zone and a peak-season *kantína*.

**Élios (Néo Klíma)**, 4km north of the Kastáni turning, was established by the junta to house residents of the earthquake-damaged villages above it; it's a dreary place, redeemed mainly by adjacent, scenic **Hóvolo** beach, 350m of pebbles backed by cliffs. The only other memorable local beach, 2km northwest and down from a petrol station, is secluded **Armenópetra**, so named for its ship-shaped rock formation. A similar distance further along, the renovated village of **Palió Klíma** marks the start of a beautiful 45-minute **trail** to Glóssa, via the foreigner-owned hamlet of **Áyii Anáryiri** and the island's oldest settlement, **Athéato** (Mahalás), slowly being restored by outsiders.

## Glóssa, Loutráki and around

Skópelos's second town, **GLÓSSA**, 26km from Hóra near the northwest tip of the island, is much more countrified, with lush gardens amidst a mix of vernacular

▲ Hóvolo beach and Dhassía islet, Skópelos

houses and unfortunate modern additions arrayed in stepped tiers on the hillside. Along narrow, mostly car-free lanes are several *psistariés*, an **ATM** and a few (sometimes substandard) **dhomátia**; an exception, *Kostas and Nina's Place* (☎24240 33686; ❸) has simple, clean rooms and studios. The well-signposted central *koultouriárika* **taverna**, *To Agnandi*, serves upmarket (and pricey) takes on traditional recipes – pork with prunes or *hortokeftédhes* (vegetable croquettes) – at both indoor and roof-terrace seating, though locals prefer *To Steki tou Mastora* at the church by the outskirts, doing whole roast lamb or goat on the spit in summer.

Hydrofoils, catamarans and some ferries call at diminutive **LOUTRÁKI** port ("Glóssa" on ferry and hydrofoil schedules; the harbour **agent** is Triandafyllou, ☎24240 33435), reached from Glóssa proper down a serpentine 3km road (or a much shorter *kalderími*). There's not much here aside from lots of **yachts** at anchor and a narrow pebble beach. If you need to **stay**, there are various **rooms** (❸), such as *Orfanos* (☎24240 33695), or the more comfortable *Selinounda Hotel* (☎24240 34073; ❹) up the road. Three quayside **tavernas** aren't worth a special drive but will do for a meal before a boat ride.

**Beaches** near Glóssa are all on the northeast-facing coast, reached by partly paved roads. **Perivolioú**, 7km away and about 100m long, is the best: scenic, coarsely sandy and with rock overhangs for shade, though prone to surf. A good motorable track continues 1.5km east to **Hondroyiórgis** beach, similar though marred by rocks in the water, before looping back to Glóssa. From 250m east of where this track returns, a paved, narrow road leads 5.3km to photogenic **Áyios Ioánnis Kastrí** church, perched on a rock monolith (steps lead up). A short, steep path leads southeast to a small sandy cove.

# Alónissos

Thanks to remoteness, no airport and often sparse ferry/catamaran connections, **Alónissos** attracts fewer foreign visitors than Skópelos or Skiáthos. There is, however, a significant British and Italian presence (the latter mostly in all-inclusive hotels), while Greeks descend in force all summer; second-home owners fill a broad spectrum of nationalities. The resulting scene is trendy but low key, with art exhibits, a homeopathic academy and resident herbalists.

Alónissos is the largest and only permanently inhabited member of a mini-archipelago (of which more on p.512) at the east end of the Sporades. It's more **rugged** and **wild** than its neighbours, but no less green, and has spring water;

---

### Hiking on Alónissos

Although its often harsh, rugged landscape might suggest otherwise, of all the Sporades Alónissos caters best to **hikers**. Fourteen routes have been surveyed and numbered, with path-starts admirably signposted and all itineraries figuring prominently on the Anavasi **map**. In 2007, an EU grant helped clean and refurbish certain trails. Many admittedly provide just short walks from a beach to a village or the main road, but some can be combined to make meaty circular treks. The best in that category are trail #11 from Áyios Dhimítrios, up the Kastanórema and then back along the coast (2hr 30min), or trails #13 plus #12, Melegákia to Áyios Konstandínos and Áyios Yeóryios (just over 2hr, including some road-walking to return to start). Island resident Chris Browne's comprehensive walking guide to Alónissos and three neighbouring islets, *Alonnisos Through the Souls of Your Feet*, is obtainable through ⓦwww.travelleur.com.

ALÓNISSOS & PERISTÉRA

0          5 km

N

Kyrá Panayiá, Yioúra & Psathoúra ▲

TOUR BOAT ROUTE

Yérakas

Melegákia

Kastanórema

Áyios Konstandínos †    † Áyios Yeóryios    ● Áyios/ Dhimítrios

● Kalamákia

Alónissos    Glyfa
            ● Stení Vála

Áyios Petros

Peristéra

Leftó Yialós
● Miliá    Tzortzí Yialós

● Kokkinókastro

Yiália
Vrysítsa

Miliá  Khryssí Miliá

PALEÁ ALÓNISSOS    ● Vótsi
(Hóra)    ● Roussoúm Yialós

Mikrós Mourtiás    PATITÍRI
Megálos Mourtiás
Výthisma

Marpoúnda

▼ Skópelos, Skiáthos, Vólos, Áy. Konstandínos & Paralía Kými (seasonal)

pine forest, olive groves and fruit orchards cover the southern half, while a dense maquis of arbutus, heather, kermes oak and lentisc cloaks the north. A salubriously dry climate once made the island's **wine** notable, until 1950s phylloxera wiped out the vineyards (resistant vines now support a modest revival); the famous local June **apricots** were unaffected. Some of Greece's cleanest sea surrounds Alónissos, though **beaches** tend to be functional rather than picturesque.

Known in ancient times as Ikos, and during the medieval period as Hiliadhrómia (both names assiduously exploited by local businesses), Alónissos was, like its neighbours, a Byzantine and Ottoman backwater, with a Venetian tenure during the fifteenth and sixteenth centuries. Alónissos suffered significant German reprisals in August 1944, with a stele in its hilltop *hóra* commemorating firing-squad victims. The most significant event in more recent **history** was the March 9, 1965 earthquake, which shattered that lovely village.

## Patitíri

The port and de-facto capital, **PATITÍRI**, occupies a sheltered bay flanked by steep, pine-tufted cliffs and ringed by bars, cafés and tavernas. It's a bit soulless – some "shoebox" prefab earthquake housing still lurks in the backstreets – but it has tried to compensate with a stone-paved waterfront and general tidy-up. The waterfront **MOM Information Centre** (daily 10am–4pm & 6–10pm; free;

@www.mom.gr), just above the Alkyon ticket agency, has models and multi-media displays about the endangered **monk seal** (see box, p.513). In an unmissable stone building on the southern side of the cove, the **Costas and Angela Mavrikis Museum** (daily 11am–7pm; €3 includes drink at café) is crammed with local artwork, traditional costumes, reconstructed island interiors, war memorabilia, wine-making equipment, and exhibits on piracy and seafaring. At the top of town by the main roundabout, one business well worth patronizing is **Ikos**, the Women's Agricultural Cooperative, selling a variety of edible goodies including pickled *tsitsírava*.

### Practicalities

**Orientation** is straightforward, with two shopping streets forging inland from the quay (the rightmost straight, the left-hand one in roundabout fashion) to unite as the road to Hóra. **Buses** and four **taxis** stop adjacent on the waterfront end of the right-hand shopping street, which hosts the single **ATM** and the **post office**. There are many outlets for hiring **scooters and cars** along the quay and up either commercial street, including National/Alamo (℡24240 66242) and AutoStop (℡24240 65888); waterfront offices also rent **motorboats and dinghies**. Two **agencies** divide the shipping trade: Alonissos Travel (℡24240 66000) for GA ferries/catamarans, Alkyon Travel (℡24240 65220) for all Hellenic Seaways ferries, catamarans and hydrofoils.

Most Alónissos **accommodation** is in Patitíri or immediately around; you may be approached with offers as you disembark at the port. Albedo Travel (℡24240 65804, @www.albedotravel.com) handles hotels, studios and villas, while the local room-owners' association booth (℡24240 66188) on the waterfront can also find you a room (mostly ❸) in Patitíri or nearby Vótsi. The best budget option is *Pension Pleiades* (℡24240 65235; ❸) up behind Albedo Travel, with rooms and two apartments. Fully fledged hotels include *Liadromia* (℡24240 65521, @liadromia@alonissos.com; doubles ❹, suites ❺), with pastel-tinted, engagingly furnished units, reached by steps near the post office, and hillside Nereides southwest of town at the forest edge (℡24240 65643; ❺), with a pool and gaily coloured studios and apartments.

Waterfront **restaurants** are nothing special; an exception is locally patronized *Archipelagos,* with good *mezédhes*. Another recommended, if pricier, ouzerí is friendly *To Kamaki* (dinner only except Fri/Sat), 150m up towards the post office from the waterfront; portions are not huge but the menu encompasses unusual dishes like crab croquettes, skate and *tsitsírava* shoots. Much the best option is the *Hotel Nereides* ⚓ restaurant, best for *mayireftá* with lots for vegetarians and their own red wine from Neméa grapes. About the best *gelato* in the Sporades is found at the Italian-run stall forty paces up from the taxi rank, towards the post office. **Nightlife** is low-key, mostly confined to the seafront cafés; Hóra is livelier after dark, especially in summer.

## Hóra (Paleá Alónissos)

**HÓRA (Paleá Alónissos)** was damaged by the Sporades-wide March 1965 quake, and during the junta most of the reluctant population was compulsorily moved to Patitíri; the issue was essentially forced in 1977 by the school's closure and cutting off of electricity. Outsiders, mostly Germans (now selling up), plus Brits and Athenians, acquired the abandoned houses for a song and restored them in variable taste; only a few locals still live here, which gives the village a very twee, un-Greek atmosphere, abetted by multiple knick-knack and crafts shops – the most genuine souvenirs are locally made feta and rice pudding from Maria Anagnostou's small grocery. But it's undeniably picturesque, with great views as far as Mount Áthos in clear conditions. For much of the year there are far more hedgehogs than people about; the place only really comes to life – noisily so – in midsummer.

Hóra can be **reached** from Patitíri by a fine, signposted *kalderími* (45min uphill, 30min down); alternatively, there's a frequent bus service (10min; €1.30) most of the day. For **accommodation**, *Konstantina's Studios* (☎24240 66165; ❹) is a renovated building with eight studios and one apartment, all enjoying exceptional views, while the beam-ceilinged *Fantasia House* (☎24240 65186; ❸), just up from the bus stop, has a pleasant view-terrace. More upmarket are the exquisitely restored *Elma's Houses* at the far end of the village (☎24240 66108, ⓦwww .elmashouses.com; ❻), two units fitting four each, furnished from the affiliated Gorgona antique shop. **Restaurants**, sadly, are either vastly overpriced or (on the old central square) not very accomplished; the best value, at the north edge of town, is traditional grill *Aloni*. At the far end of Hóra's main street, *Hayiati* is unbeatable for coffees and traditional sweets like *kazandibí*, fairly priced considering the incomparable view to Skópelos. *Arhondostasi* at the agora's near end is the "other" patisserie, with occasional live Greek acoustic music; *Panselinos* bar on the bus-stop platía also serves creditable snacks.

## The rest of the island

The **roads** between Patitíri, most beaches, Stení Vála and Áyios Dhimítrios are paved, and other dirt roads serving minor beaches – with some exceptions – are in good condition. There's an infrequent (3–4 daily) **bus service** along the Hóra–Patitíri–Stení Vála route; a few pricey morning **water-taxis** operate in high season from near the hydrofoil berth in Patitíri north to the remoter east-coast beaches, returning late afternoon.

### Southern and eastern beaches

In southern Alónissos, **Marpoúnda** beach is effectively monopolized by an all-inclusive Italian complex; turn right instead before Marpoúnda on a rough but passable dirt track towards **Výthisma.** Use the secondary path descending from the power pole by the parking area, not the broad main track which is washed out at the bottom. The 200-metre sand-and-pebble stretch is pretty, but without facilities or shade. Further along the coast, pebbly and crowded **Megálos Mourtiás** (two tavernas) is reached by paved road (2km) from Hóra; **Mikrós Mourtiás** just west, served by marked path (40min from Hóra) and a dirt track, is more secluded and naturist, but only the left-hand forty metres is usable. Immediately north of Hóra, visible tucked into their respective finger-like inlets, compact **Vrysítsa** and **Yiália** (with a picturesque windmill) both have more sand than pebbles, but no facilities and are prone to *meltémi*-borne debris.

The first two bays northwest of Patitíri are auxiliary fishing ports more than beaches; **ROUSSOÚM YIALÓS** does have a small pebbly strand, a few **dhomátia** and a **taverna**, *Remezzo* (all year), a good all-rounder doing unusual salads, fish and *mayireftá*. Bigger **VÓTSI** beyond – almost a proper village – can offer three **tavernas**, homeliest, most reasonable and best being ✻ *Iy Mouria*, dishing up big salads, squid and *mayireftá* washed down with bulk retsina and red wine; they have simple **rooms** (☎24240 65273; ❸) too. Neither **Miliá** nor **Khryssí Miliá** are memorable as beaches, though on the slopes just before Miliá is top-standard **accommodation**: ✻ *Milia Bay Hotel Apartments* (☎24240 66032, ⓦwww.milia-bay.gr; April–Oct; studios ❻, apartments ❼), whose units offer sea views over lovingly landscaped grounds and a pool area. The first indisputably good – and most scenic – east-coast **beach** is **Kokkinókastro**, whose flanking headland is the site of ancient Ikos (inaccessible by land). Pebbles on a red-sand base (without facilities) extend both sides of the promontory; access to the northerly one is allowed through an unfenced private estate. Of the next two pebble coves along, **Leftó Yialós** pips **Tzortzí Yialós** as about the best Alonissan beach, attracting both midday cruise *kaïkia* and customers to two good **tavernas**. The better is ⚓ *Elaionas* (May–Sept), enchantingly set in the olive grove of the name, with unusual platters like *tsitsírava* and *xynógalo*, and daily specials.

### Stení Vála and around

**STENÍ VÁLA**, about halfway up the east coast, attracts many yacht flotillas combing the Sporades; facilities include a shop, a couple of café-bars, a few **rooms** (the plushest being *Agnantema Villas* ☎24240 65155, ⓦwww .agnantema.gr; ⑥), with antique furnishings and knockout views, plus three **tavernas**, of which *Steni Vala* (aka *Tassia*; open most of year) is noted for *mayireftá*. Greek/South-African-run Ikion Diving (☎24240 65158, ⓦwww.ikiondiving .gr) anticipates an expansion of legal scuba zones for 2009 from the present two islets; the area is full of ancient and Byzantine wrecks which must first be vetted by the archeological service. There's a long pebble beach – **Glýfa** – just north, and a better, partly sandy one, **Áyios Pétros**, a ten-minute path-walk south.

**KALAMÁKIA**, the next hamlet north along the coast road, hasn't a beach but it does have a fishing-port feel and a reliable **taverna/rooms**, *Margarita* (☎24240 65738; May–Oct; ③), with good fish and *mezédhes*. The sealed road ends at **Áyios Dhimítrios**, where boats **anchor off** a curving pebbly, unshaded beach (there's no proper harbour) with a snack-bar and sunbed rental.

# The National Marine Park of Alónissos-Northern Sporades

The 1992-founded **National Marine Park** protects monk seals, dolphins, wild goats and rare seabirds in an area encompassing Alónissos plus a dozen **islets** speckling the Aegean to the east. None of these (save one) have any permanent population, but a few can be visited by June-to-September excursion boats, weather permitting; the 25-metre wooden *kaïki Planitis* run by Alonissos Travel (see p.510) is recommended (all-day cruises from €45–50). **Pipéri** islet forms the core zone of the park – an off-limits seabird and monk-seal refuge, approachable only by government-authorized scientists. **Peristéra**, opposite Alónissos, is uninhabited, though some Alonissans cross to tend olive groves in the south; since a ban on campfires was imposed, it's little visited by excursion craft except for a brief swim-stop at the end of a cruise. Well-watered **Kyrá Panayiá**, the next islet out, belongs to Meyístis Lávras monastery on Mount Áthos; there's a tenth-century monastery here too, its old bakery and wine/olive presses restored in the 1990s, inhabited by one farmer-monk. Boats are allowed to anchor at two bays, southerly Áyios Pétros (good snorkelling over ancient potsherds) and northerly Planítis, for passengers to walk up to the monastery. Nearby **Yioúra** has a Neolithically inhabited stalactite cave which sheltered Homer's Cyclops, plus the main wild-goat population, but you won't see either as *kaïkia* must keep 400m clear of the shore. Tiny, northernmost **Psathoúra** is dominated by its powerful lighthouse, the tallest in the Aegean; excursions – only calling here in high season for an extra charge, when passenger numbers and day-length make it feasible – stop for a swim at a pristine, white-sand beach. Flat, green **Skánt-zoura**, off southeast towards Skýros and too remote for tours to visit, has a single empty monastery and populations of Eleonora's falcon and Audouin's gull.

## The Mediterranean monk seal

The **Mediterranean monk seal** (*Monachus monachus*) has the dubious distinction of being the most endangered European mammal – fewer than 350 survive, the majority around the Atlantic island of Madeira but also off North Africa. A small population occupies the Ionian and Aegean seas of Greece; the largest community, of fifty to sixty, lives and breeds around the islets of the Sporades marine park.

Females have one **pup** about every two years, which can live for 45 years, attaining 2m in length and over 200 kilos as **adults**. Formerly pups were reared in the open, but disturbance by man led to whelping seals retreating to isolated sea caves with partly submerged entrances. Without spending weeks on a local boat, your chances of seeing a seal are slim (marine-park cruises are far more likely to spot dolphins); if seals are spotted (usually dozing on the shore or swimming in the open sea), keep a deferential distance.

Monk seals can swim 200km a day in search of food – and compete with fishermen in the overfished Aegean, often destroying nets. Until recently fishermen routinely killed seals; this occasionally still happens, but the establishment of the **National Marine Park of Alónissos-Northern Sporades** has helped by banning September–November fishing northeast of Alónissos and prohibiting it altogether within 1.5 nautical miles of Pipéri. These measures have won local support through the efforts of the **Hellenic Society for the Protection of the Monk Seal** (HSPMS), based at Stení Vála, even among Sporadean fishermen, who realize that the restrictions should exclude industrial-scale trawlers from elsewhere and help restore local fish stocks. The HSPMS has reared several abandoned seal pups (bad weather often separates them from their mothers), subsequently released in the sea around Alónissos.

# Skýros

Despite its airport and natural beauty, **Skýros** until recently had a low tourist profile, thanks to few major sites or resorts and problematic land-and-sea access from Athens, plus its economic reliance on about nine hundred naval and air force personnel. Times have changed, with Italians and French especially showing up overland, Dutch flying in on charters, and trendy Athenians and Thessalonians taking advantage of domestic flights. The New Age Skyros Centre, pitched mostly at Brits, has also effectively publicized the place, though the tourist season is still too short to properly support young islanders.

The popular theory that Skýros was originally two islands seems unlikely, but certainly the character of its two parts differs. The fertile north, **Merói**, has a gentler landscape, retaining much of its original pine forest, while the more barren, rocky south, **Vounó**, is mountainous (though it has several of Skýros's many springs), quarried for marble and home to semi-wild herds of the local pony (see p.517). Voúno belongs mostly to Athonite monastery Meyístis Lávras, which has sharply polarized the population with its proposal to erect 111, enormously tall power-generating **wind turbines**, potentially the largest such installation in the world.

Local **beaches** are generally serviceable rather than film-set-worthy like those on Skópelos; west-coast ones tend to attract seaborne rubbish. Sandier east-coast beaches cluster around Skýros Town, which makes staying there or immediately nearby the most obvious choice. Good, isolated beaches in the island's north are under threat of being expropriated by the air force, which otherwise maintains a low profile, though pilots and their families keep many tavernas and bars hopping during the off-season.

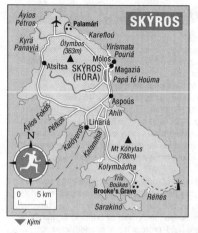

All this notwithstanding, Skýros still ranks as one of the most interesting Greek islands. A central Aegean position guaranteed that it was settled from prehistory; by the late sixth century BC it was a vital Athenian outpost, and it served as an equally important naval base for the Byzantines. Venetian rule lasted three centuries, without however producing Catholic converts as elsewhere; the highly stratified local class system had its roots instead in a nucleus of exiled Byzantine nobles, with Skyrian sailors – or pirates, as the occasion demanded – being a particularly high-status group. Whatever the ruling power, the island remained an important staging-post on the sea-lanes to Constaninople, with many foreign consuls here in the 1700s and 1800s.

Skýros has a long tradition of **woodcarving** in mulberry, its apotheosis the *salonáki skyrianó* (a set of sitting-room furniture), as well as collecting improbably exotic **ceramicware**, obtained through purchase or piracy. A very few old men still wear the traditional cap, vest, baggy trousers and *trohádhia* (sandals), while some elderly women still wear the requisite yellow scarves and embroidered skirts, but this is dying out. And then there's **Carnival** (see box below).

## Linariá

**Ferries** dock at **LINARIÁ**, a functional port on the southwest-facing coast, tolerable enough for an hour or two while waiting for a boat. **Taxis** and buses meet arrivals for the trip to Skýros Town (10km), the latter continuing to Magaziá and Mólos in high season. **Accommodation** (convenient for the occasional morning departure), consists of *King Lykomides* (☎22220 93249, ❸), spotless, air-conditioned *dhomátia* with little balconies above the harbour, or – behind this

### Carnival on Skýros

Skýros has a particularly outrageous *apokriátika* (pre-Lenten) **carnival**, featuring its famous **goat dance**, performed by grouped masked revellers in the streets of Hóra. The leaders of each troupe are the **yéri**, menacing figures (usually men but sometimes sturdy women) dressed in goat-pelt capes, weighed down by huge garlands of sheep bells, their faces concealed by kid-skin masks, and brandishing shepherd's crooks. Accompanying them are their "brides", men in drag known as **korélles** (maidens), and **frángi** (maskers in assorted "Western" garb). When two such groups meet, the *yéri* compete to see who can ring their bells longest and loudest with arduous body movements, or even get into brawls using their crooks as cudgels. For the full story, see Joy Coulentianou's *The Goat Dance of Skyros*, available in Athens from Ekdotiki Ermis (Ⓦwww.ermis-ekdotiki.gr).

These rites take place on each of the four **weekends** before Clean Monday (see p.63), but the final one is more for the benefit of tourists, both Greek and foreign. The Skyrians are less exhausted and really let their (goat) hair down for each other during the preceding three weeks. Most local hotels open for the duration, and you have to book rooms around Christmas.

– *Linaria Bay Hotel* (☎22220 93274; ❹), a mixture of rooms and apartments. The best of four quayside **tavernas** is *O Maïstros*, hidden behind a plane tree, with good vegetarian *mezédhes* and fresh fish. **Nightlife** means hillside *Kavos Bar*, a short walk up the hóra-bound road, which does light snacks by day too and greets the evening ferry with a rousing musical fanfare. In high season, **excursion** *kaïkia* (€30 including lunch) offer trips from Liniariá to the islet of **Sarakinó**, with its white-sand beach at Glyfádha, also stopping at various sea-caves.

## Skýros Town

**SKÝROS TOWN (Hóra)**, with its somewhat Cycladic, flat-roofed architecture, covers the leeward, southwest slope of a pinnacle rising precipitously from the coast; in legend, King Lykomedes raised the young Achilles in his palace here, and also pushed Theseus to his death from the summit. Given its workaday atmosphere, the town doesn't feel like a resort, but away from the scruffier outskirts it's decidedly picturesque, with covered passageways, churches and distinct historical quarters (the highest neighbourhoods, logically, being upper-class). On the climb up, you may glimpse traditional house interiors with gleaming copperware, painted ceramic plates and antique embroideries decorating chimney hoods, a matter of intense pride for residents. Arrival at the Byzantine-Venetian **kástro** erected atop the ancient **acropolis**, enclosing an originally Byzantine **monastery of Áyios Yeóryios**, will be sadly anticlimactic, as it's all closed due to 2001 earthquake damage, with no re-opening foreseen.

Taking the descending, left-hand fork in Hóra's central lane brings you to a round platía at the north edge of town with its nude bronze statue of "Immortal Poetry"; this is actually a **memorial to Rupert Brooke**, the British poet adopted as a paragon of patriotic youth by Kitchener and later Churchill, despite his socialist and internationalist views. Brooke arrived as a naval officer off the south of the island on April 17, 1915, dying six days later of blood poisoning on a French hospital ship. He's become a local hero despite his limited acquaintance with Skýros, and lies buried in an olive grove above the bay of Trís Boúkes (see p.518).

Just below the Brooke statue, the **archeological museum** (Tues–Sun 8.30am–3pm; €2) has a modest collection from local excavations, especially Palamári (see p.517); highlights include a Geometric-era ceramic rhyton in the form of a Skyrian pony (see p.517) and a vase-rim with eight birds being beset by snakes. Nearby, in an early nineteenth-century mansion built over a bastion in the ancient walls, is the more compelling private **Manos Faltaïts Museum** (daily 10am–noon & 5.30–8pm/6–9pm in summer; €2 admission, €5 includes guided tour; ⓦwww.faltaits.gr). It's an Aladdin's cave of curious industrial and household items like a Kavála tobacco press and dismountable furniture, a mocked-up typical Skyrian house interior, traditional costumes of each social class, rare documents and Skyrian pottery – covetable examples, made by Faltaïts himself, are sold in the gift shop.

### Practicalities

The **bus** (2–3 services daily) leaves you by the school, 200m below the main square, beyond which only rogue scooterists drive; other drivers use the signposted **car park** on the far side of the village. The **post office** and **lone ATM** are each on or near the platía; the most reliable **internet** café is Mano. com, on the *agorá* street. There's no tourist office, but municipal **website** ⓦwww.skyros.gr is useful. Skyros Travel (☎22220 91600, ⓦwww.skyrostravel .com), on the same commercial lane, **hires cars and scooters** trading as Pegasus Rentals (though there are three other outlets for bikes), does excursions and has limited accommodation; the **ferry-boat agency** is across the way (T 22220 91790). If you arrive by plane (the **airport** is 11km distant), only Pegasus has a booth in arrivals, though competitors like Theseus-Yiannakakis (T 22220 91459) will bring you a car – otherwise budget €15 for a taxi transfer.

You may be met off the bus with offers of **rooms**, perhaps in a traditional Skyrian house like those of Anna Stergiou (T 22220 91657) and Maria Mavroyiorgi (T 22220 91440), both clean, cosy and ❸. The island's plushest hotel, ⚘ *Nefeli* (T 22220 91964, Ⓦ www.skyros-nefeli.gr; ❻), on the main road before the square, offers cutting-edge designer rooms in various grades, or traditional studios in the "Petrino" wing, arrayed around a large salt-water pool. Alternatively, a bit further south out of town are the *Atherinis Apartments* (T 22220 93510, Ⓦ www.simplelifeskyros.com; ❸), a mix of self-catering rooms and larger units in a garden setting, with half-board available, though they're usually the venue for Jan Smith's reiki courses.

The platía and the *agorá* lane climbing north from it host a variety of *kafenía* and *yirádhika*, and a few outstanding full-service, all-year **tavernas**. Top of the heap in all senses – it's the highest establishment – is ⚘ *O Pappous ki Ego* (dinner only), an atmospheric ouzerí in a former pharmacy with a good range of *mezédhes* and quality Greek music on the stereo (but live rebétika Fri/Sat off-season, €5 extra; book on T 22220 93200); specialities include wild mushrooms and cuttlefish in anise sauce. Popular *Maryetis* slightly down the same lane is tops for grilled fish and good bulk wine from Thessaly, though *mayireftá* can be uneven. *Tó Konatsi*, just downhill from the platía, is another, slightly cheaper ouzerí, off to a good start under new management since 2007.

**Nightlife** is bar-based until very late, when the few out-of-town clubs get going. Besides the obvious, loud, Greek-rock **bars** overlooking the platía, further up the *agorá* there's summer-only *Kalypso* (jazz and blues); *Akamatra*, a versatile place with conversational-level music; and *Kalitekhnikon/Artistiko* near *Maryetis*, a veritable sardine tin of a pub, with a quality Greek soundtrack. The most durable summer-only **clubs** are *Skyropoula*, south of Magaziá on the coast road, and *Stone* further south at Basáles cove.

## Magaziá, Mólos, Pouriá and Yirísmata

A direct stairway and a roundabout road descend from the statue platía to the coastal hamlet of **MAGAZIÁ**. From Magaziá, an 800-metre sandy beach – rather sullied initially by an artificial reef offshore – extends to adjacent **MÓLOS**; since the 1990s, though, a real-estate boom between the inland road and the beach has amalgamated the two. Magaziá is livelier, with a better selection of rooms; more scattered Mólos has a good range of studios and better sand.

The narrow lane down to Magaziá beach's south end holds a clutch of **rooms** for rent, the best and most helpful of which is *Perigiali* (T 22220 92075, Ⓦ www .perigiali.com; all year), a mix of studios (❺) and well-furnished air-conditioned rooms (❹) with phone, overlooking a large garden where breakfast is offered. Other top choices include spacious *Paliopyrgos Studios* (T 22220 91014; ❸), up on the road between Magaziá and the *kástro*, or bungalow complex *Angela* (T 22220 91764; ❹) near the supermarket in Mólos, just behind the beach.

Local beachfront **tavernas** often compare favourably with those in town. In Magaziá, popular *Stefanos* (April–Oct) is reliable for *mayireftá*, while at the south end of Mólos, *Tsipouradhiko Iy Istories tou Barba* (all year), installed in a restored rural cottage, has good grilled seafood and chunky *mezédhes* at slightly bumped-up prices, accompanied by good recorded Greek music.

Beyond Mólos, the beach becomes punctuated by weirdly eroded rock outcrops as you approach **Pouriá**, opposite several offshore islets, one (**Áyios**

## Skyrian ponies

Skýros has a race of **native pony**, related to the breeds found on Exmoor and Dartmoor. They are thought to be the diminutive steeds depicted in the Parthenon frieze; according to legend Achilles went off to fight at Troy mounted on a chestnut specimen. In more recent times they were used for summer threshing; communally owned, they were left to graze wild ten months of the year on Vounó, from where each family in turn rounded up the ponies they needed. Currently only about 150 individuals survive, and the breed is **threatened** by the decline of local agriculture, indifference and cross-breeding; this figure includes about twenty sterile mules fathered by donkeys, who can prevent pure-blood stallions from mating. To be classed as a true Skyrian pony, the animal must be 98–115cm in height, and 130cm maximum from shoulder to tail. The largest concentration of the appealing beasts can be seen at Amanda and Stathis's **Skyrian Horse Project** (T22220 92918; daily 11am–1pm & 6.30–8pm), behind the main Mólos super-market. Donations are gratefully accepted as they get no official support for their efforts to maintain a healthy and genetically viable pony population.

Ermoláos) serving as venue for a lively festival on July 25–26. Much of the erosion is man-made, as the **rocks** were **quarried** by the Romans; one squared-off monolith, by the cape with its snack-bar/windmill, shelters a chapel of **Áyios Nikólaos** tucked into a corner. Roads north through Mólos end at **Yirísmata**, a long, sandy if exposed beach with a popular **taverna**, *Stelios* (all year, in winter weekends only).

## Around the rest of the island

In **Merói**, the first points of interest – heading anticlockwise from Hóra along its mostly paved loop road – are secluded **Kareflóu** beach (no facilities) and **Palamári** (Mon–Fri 7.30am–2.30pm; free), an early Bronze Age settlement overlooking its own sandy harbour-**beach**; walkways have been prepared, and much of the landward fortification walls exposed. The closest amenity is an excellent, reasonably priced **taverna** at the airport turning, *To Perasma* (all year), where half the local air force tucks into the family's own meat and cheese dishes. West, then north of here – the last 2.5km on track – **Áyios Pétros** is among the most scenic of the remoter beaches, though without facilities (a taverna's 1km away) and a reef to cross into deeper water. The paved circular route hits the coast again at **Kyrá Panayiá** beach (summer taverna) before continuing to **Atsítsa**, home of the Skyros Centre, and a good pottery kiln. It's an attractively pine-fringed bay with a seafood **taverna** (*Andonis*) and a few inland **dhomátia**, but only a small rocky beach. From here, you can either head back to town on a good dirt road through the woods, or carry on along asphalt to **Áyios Fokás**, a poor beach with a decent taverna-rooms establishment, *Kali* (T693 70 90 848; ❸). The road between here and deeply indented **Péfkos**, the best of the southwest-coast bays, should be paved by now; there's a **taverna**, *Stamatia*, by the jetty, and simple **rooms** run by Makis Mavromihalis (T693 88 18 886; ❷) at one end of the long, sandy beach.

South from Magaziá, on the coastal bypass road, there's an undeveloped nudist beach, **Papá tó Hoúma**, directly below Hóra's *kástro*, though reaching it requires acrobatics as the path down is washed out. Some 4km further, the next significant beach is 200-metre, sandy **Aspoús**, where roadside facilities include the *Ahillion* hotel (T22220 93300; all year; ❺) and an excellent, all-year **taverna**, *Lambros*, grilled fish, vegetable and chops specialists, with an inviting interior and efficient, polite service. From Aspoús, a minor paved road heads southeast – past **Fléa** hamlet with its **taverna** *Mouries* (May–Oct & Carnival), serving local lamb and wine under the namesake mulberries – to Kalamítsa beach, a narrow pebble strand (**Kolymbádha** 4.5km south is better). At Kalamítsa there's *O Pappous ki Ego stin Thalassa*, summer annexe of the Hóra premises, with weekend music, and the possibility of continuing into **Vounó**, where the only paved roads lead eventually to military facilities – and Rupert Brooke's grave at **Trís Boúkes**.

# Évvia (Euboea)

Looming across a narrow gulf from central Greece, **Évvia** – the second-largest Greek island after Crete – seems more like an extension of the mainland to which it was once joined. At **Halkídha**, the old drawbridge spans a mere forty-metre channel where Évvia was mythically split from Attica and Thessaly by a blow from Poseidon's trident (earthquakes and subsidence being more pedestrian explanations). The south of the island is far closer to Athens than it is to the northern part, and in summer Évvia can seem merely a beach annexe for Athens and the mainland towns across the Gulf.

Nevertheless, Évvia *is* an island, often a very beautiful one, which has largely remained out of the mainstream of tourism. A marked **Albanian influence** in the south, and scattered **Frankish** watchtowers across the island, lend a distinctive flavour. The **Ottomans** had a keen appreciation of the island's wealth; their last garrison was not evicted until 1833, hanging on in defiance of the treaty awarding Évvia to the new Greek state, and substantial Muslim communities remained in the northwest half of the island until 1923. Évvia has always been prized for its exceptional **fertility**, producing grain, corn, cotton, kitchen vegetables and livestock. The classical name, Euboea, means "rich in cattle", but nowadays goat and lamb are more common, and highly rated, as is the local retsina (though wine in northern Évvia is flavoured with herbs, not resin).

The rolling countryside of the **north** is a more conventionally scenic region, with combines whirling on sloping grain fields between olive groves and pine forest. The **northeast coast** is rugged and sometimes inaccessible, its few sandy beaches surf-pounded and often debris-strewn; the **southwest shore** is gentler and more sheltered, though much disfigured by heavy industry. The **centre** of the island, between Halkídha and the easterly port of Kými, is mountainous and dramatic, while the far **southeast** is more arid and isolated. **There are bus services** to Kárystos in the southeast, and Límni and Loutrá Edhipsoú in the northwest, but explorations are best conducted by car.

## Halkídha

Évvia's capital, **HALKÍDHA** (ancient Chalkis) has a population of over 50,000. A shipyard, rail-sidings and cement works hardly make it enticing – you can if desired bypass most of the town on a modern suspension bridge – but some charm remains in the old Ottoman **Kástro** district, around the seventeenth-century Karababá fortress on the mainland side and along the waterfront overlooking the narrow **Évripos** (Euripus) channel, whose strange currents have baffled scientists for centuries. Below the old bridge spanning it, the gulf-water swirls by like a river; every few hours the current reverses. Aristotle is said to have thrown himself into the waters in despair at his inability to understand what was happening; there is still no entirely satisfactory explanation.

The **kástro** – on the right as you head inland along Kótsou from the Euripos bridge – is dominated by a handsome fifteenth-century **mosque** (locked), now a warehouse of Byzantine artefacts; out front is an exceptionally ornate carved **Ottoman fountain**. Beyond lies unusual **Ayía Paraskeví basilica** (open for services); its oddness is due to its conversion into a Gothic cathedral by the Crusaders in the fourteenth century. The *kástro's* residential districts have yet to be gentrified, being in part a shanty town for gypsies and Greek Muslim minorities. Further northeast, the **archeological museum** at Venizélou 13 (Tues–Sun 8.30am–3pm; €2) has a good display of finds from across the island. Just south of the old market, the 2006-opened **Folklore Museum** (Wed–Sun 10am–1pm, also Wed 6–8pm; €3) occupies the old jail. The main reminder of Halkídha's once-thriving Jewish community, dating back 2500 years, is their handsome nineteenth-century **synagogue** at Kótsou 27.

## Practicalities

**Trains** arrive on the mainland side of the channel, beneath Karababá; given numerous, quick rail links with Athens, there's little reason to stay overnight. If necessary, the *Kentrikon* hotel (☎22210 22375; ❹), at Angéli Govíou 5 on the town side of the bridge, offers reasonable value. The **KTEL** is an inconvenient 1500m away at the east edge of town (take a taxi); you should get a bus to any destination as long as you show up by 2pm, later for Kými or Límni.

Halkídha is noted for its seafood, especially **shellfish**; waterfront

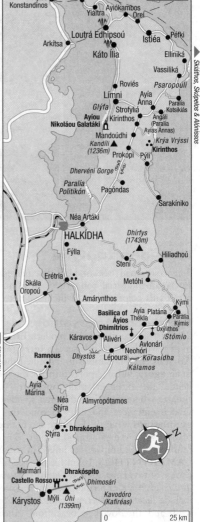

**restaurants**, while popular at weekends with Athenians, aren't necessarily the best-value options. An exception is 🍴 *Apanemo* (☎22210 22614), at the far north end of the shoreline, in Fanári district, just before the lighthouse, which has tables on the sand and requires booking in summer. Inland you might try durable and cheerful *Tsaf* at Papanastasíou 3, off Platía Agorás, or less expensive *O Yiannis*, nearby at Frízi 8, both serving all manner of seafood; *Yiannis's* limited *mezédhes* menu is offset by a good wine list.

▲ The suspension bridge connecting Halkídha, Évvia, to the mainland

## Halkídha to Kými

The coast road east of Halkídha makes an almost libellous introduction to Évvia; an industrial zone yields to nondescript suburb-villages, succeeded by gated villa colonies and all-inclusive hotel compounds for package tourists.

### Erétria and Amárynthos

The first substantial town is modern **ERÉTRIA**, a dull resort on a grid plan; for most travellers its main asset is a **ferry** service across to Skála Oropoú in Attica. **Ancient Eretria** is more distinguished, though town-centre remains are confined to an **agora** and an Apollo **temple**; the more compelling northwest excavations behind the excellent small **museum** (Tues–Sun 8.30am–3pm; €2) include a **theatre** where steps from the orchestra descend to an underground vault used for sudden entrances and exits. Beyond this are the **House of Mosaics** and a **gymnasium**. One of the more interesting **hotels** is *Island of Dreams* (☎22290 61224, ⓦwww.dreamsisland.com.gr; ⓖ), comprising bungalows and standard rooms on a landscaped islet linked by causeway to the end of the bay.

**AMÁRYNTHOS**, 10km further, is a smaller and more pleasant resort with a choice of **tavernas**, such as *Ouzeri di Stefano* or *Theodoros* on the waterfront, and *To Limanaki* 300m further west on the shore. Sound **accommodation** options include *Iliaktidhes Hotel Apartments* (☎22290 37215; all year; ❹), just off the main road, and the low-key, beachfront *Artemis Hotel* (☎22290 36168, ⓦwww.artemis-hotel.gr; all year; ❺), with an indoor/outdoor café and wi-fi signal.

Beyond Amárynthos an exceptionally dreary landscape, made worse by a 2007 fire and enlivened only by some medieval towers, unfolds past Alivéri to Lépoura, with its strategic fork in the road system.

### Lépoura to Kými

Heading north from Lépoura towards Kými, the first potential detour, after 5km at Neohóri, is east to secluded beaches at **Kálamos** (7km) and **Korasídha** (11km); **accommodation** at Kálamos includes pleasant *To Egeon* (☎22230 41865; ❸), which has a downstairs **restaurant**. At **Háni Avlonaríou**, 6km past

Neohóri, stands the thirteenth-century **Áyios Dhimítrios basilica**, Évvia's largest and finest (key at the café next door). This region is well endowed with Byzantine chapels, the best being shed-like **Ayía Thékla**, tucked in a vale below the modern church near the eponymous hamlet; slightly later than Áyios Dhimítrios, its interior fresco fragments depict large-eyed faces.

The inland road passing Ayía Thékla continues to upper **KÝMI**, on a green ridge overlooking the sea, while Paralía Kýmis, the ferry port, lies 4km below, via a winding road. All buses from Halkídha leave you in the upper town, except for those connecting with Skýros ferries. Just below town, on the harbour-bound road, a **folklore museum** (daily 10am–1pm and 6–8.30pm; €2) houses costumes, rural implements and old photos recording the doings of Kymians both locally and in the US, home to a huge emigrant community. Among them was Dr George Papanikolaou, deviser of the "Pap" cervical smear test, and a statue honours him up on the platía, with its **post office** and **ATMs**. Kými's only proper **taverna**, just below the museum, is *Tou Hari*.

The coast road bears right north of Háni Avlonaríou, meeting the sea at **Stómio,** a rivermouth beach by straggly seaside **PLATÁNA** (tavernas). Functional **PARALÍA KÝMIS** port lies 3km beyond; despite the name it has no beach, and isn't a congenial place to stay, which you shouldn't need to do as there's always an early-evening ferry to Skýros. For a lunch **taverna**, head to *Ouzeri Iy Skyros*, 150m north of the jetty with its **ticket agency** (☏22220 22020).

## Southeastern Évvia

So narrow that you sometimes spot the sea on both sides, lightly populated **southeastern Évvia** is often bleak and windswept, geologically resembling Ándhros with its slates and marble. Also like Ándhros, it was settled by Albanian migrants from the early fifteenth century onwards, and **Arvanítika** – medieval Albanian – was long the first language of remoter villages here.

Just southeast of Lépoura, **Lake Dhýstos** has been largely reclaimed as farmland, but **migratory birds** still frequent its shallow marshes – about 7km along, a sign points to an observation area. Atop conical Kastrí hill on the east shore are sparse fifth-century-BC ruins of **ancient Dystos** and a medieval citadel.

With your own transport, it's worth stopping at the north edge of **STÝRA** (35km from Lépoura), where three **dhrakóspita** ("dragon houses") are signposted and reachable by track. So named because only such beings were thought capable of installing the enormous masonry blocks, their origins and purpose remain obscure. One cogent theory suggests they are sixth-to-fourth-century BC temples built by immigrants or slaves from Asia Minor working in nearby quarries.

The shore annexe of **NÉA STÝRA**, 3.5km downhill, is a dull, Greek-frequented resort, worth knowing about only for its handy ferry connection to Ayía Marína. Much the same is true of **MARMÁRI**, 20km south, except here the link is with Rafína. The road between upper Stýra and Marmári is under (re)construction, slowing progress until 2010.

### Kárystos and around

First impressions of **KÁRYSTOS** are of a boring grid (courtesy of an 1843 Bavarian town-planner), ending fairly abruptly to east and west, studded with modern construction. But soon you'll notice graceful, nineteenth-century Neoclassical buildings in the centre, some endearingly old-fashioned shops and tavernas, and its magnificent setting on a wide bay, with good (if often windy) beaches flanking it. The town feels bigger and livelier than the official population of about three thousand, and it grows on many visitors, who stay longer than intended. Only a fenced-in **Roman heroön** at the corner of Theohári Kotsíka and Sakhtoúri bears out Kárystos's ancient provenance; the other obvious old structure is the thirteenth-century, waterfront **Boúrtzi** (locked except for special events), all that's left of once-extensive fortifications. Opposite this small Venetian tower (incorporating masonry from the heroön), in the Yiokálio Centre, a small but well-explained **archeological museum** (Tues–Sun 8.30am–3pm; €2) displays statues, temple carvings and votive objects from the region.

## Practicalities

No **ferries** serve Kárystos directly; Marmári, 13km west, acts as its passenger port. There's also no bus shuttle between them – the car-less should arrange to share a taxi. The **KTEL** station is at the west end of Kriezótou, a block in from the water; the **post office** and **ATMs** lie within sight of central, waterfront Platía Amalías. There's no tourist office, but helpful South Evia Tours at Platía Amalías 7 (☎22240 26200, ⓦwww.eviatravel.gr) sells ferry tickets, rents cars and bikes, finds lodging, sells maps and arranges excursions.

There's ever-increasing **accommodation** at outlying beaches and inland (most easily booked through South Evia Tours) but central hotels are limited to rambling *Galaxy* (☎22240 22600; all year; ❸) at the west end of waterfront Kriezótou, a veritable 1970s time capsule with its vinyl sofas, lino floors and floral bath tiles, but friendly and with lobby wi-fi signal; or quieter ⚓ *Karystion* (☎22240 22391, ⓦwww.karystion.gr; March–Oct; B&B ❺), 150m east of the Boúrtzi, with filling breakfasts, renovated sea-view rooms and direct access to the adjacent beach. Near the *Karystion* at Sakhtoúri 42, *Vassillis Rooms*, in a garden setting, are a decent alternative (☎22240 22071; ❸).

There's far more choice when eating out; central **tavernas** include *Kavo Doro*, in a lane between Kriezótou and parallel Sakhtoúri one block west of the square, for *mayireftá*; or a line of *psistariés* on Theohári Kotsíka, of which *Panouryias* at no. 9 and *Karystaki* at no. 3 are popular. But much the best hereabouts is ⚓ *To Koutouki (Hondhronastos)* at Sakhtoúri 75 (Oct–May), a terrazzo-floored *estiatório* mustering just six tables laden with bean soup, *lahanodolmádhes*, chops and *fáva*, plus *halvás* on the house. Further afield (May–Oct only), *Ta Kalamia*, at the start of the west beach, is popular at lunchtime, while 2km east at **KÁTO AETÓS**, seaside *To Kyma* is much-visited for evening meals and Sunday lunches. Local bulk **wines** are well worth sampling, especially at the late-August Wine Festival.

## Mount Óhi and the Dhimosári Gorge

Just inland from Kárystos, **Mount Óhi** (1399m) is Évvia's third-highest peak and the focus of trails of sufficient quality to attract overseas trekkers. Some 3km north, **MÝLI**, a fair-sized village around a spring-fed oasis with a few tavernas, is a natural first stop. Medieval **Castello Rosso (Kokkinókastro)** lies a twenty-minute climb from the main church; inside, the castle is ruinous, except for an Orthodox **chapel** built over the water cistern, but sweeping views make the trip worthwhile.

From Mýli, it's a three-hour-plus **hike** up the bare slopes of Óhi, mostly by a good path shortcutting the road; about forty minutes along are various finished and half-finished cipollino marble **columns**, abandoned almost two thousand years ago. The Romans loved the stuff and extensively quarried southern Évvia, shipping the marble back to Italy. The path reaches an alpine club shelter (springwater outside; ☎22240 24414 to get the keys), just below the summit, and another schist-slab **dhrakóspito**, more impressive than the Stýra trio (see p.521), seemingly sprouting from the mountainside.

From here, you either retrace your steps all the way to Mýli, or just slightly west towards Petrokánalo ridge, where you're poised to tackle the one unmissable excursion of southeastern Évvia: the three-hour onward traverse of the **Dhimosári Gorge**. The descent northeast, mostly in deep shade past various springs and watermills, is on path (often *kalderími*) as far as the farming hamlet of Lenoséi, then track to **Kallianós** village, with another path just before the latter down to a beach. You'll have to arrange a taxi beforehand, or trust to hitching back to Kárystos, as there's no bus.

## Northwestern Évvia

At bustling Néa Artáki, 5km north of Halkídha, a side-road (daily bus) leads east to **STENÍ**, a village-cum-hill-station at the foot of Mount Dhírfys. Of two **hotels**, the *Steni* (☎22280 51221; ❸) – with newer bathrooms and sumptuous common areas – is preferable. Eight **tavernas** specializing in meaty fare line the roadside and two adorn the village-centre platía, where *O Vrahos* is the most atmospheric, with seating under a mulberry. There are hiking trails up Dhírfys, Évvia's highest summit, but being badly track-damaged they can't compare to trekking around Mount Óhi. Of more interest is the very useful, scenic **road link to Kými**, all paved except for 8km just before Metóhi; it's 51km or 95-minutes' drive (follow signposting for Metóhi if starting from Kými).

Beyond Psahná, the main road snakes steeply over a forested ridge and then down through the **Dhervéni Gorge**, gateway to **Évvia's northwest**. **PROKÓPI** just beyond, in a broad wooded upland, is famous for its hideous 1960s pilgrimage **church of St John the Russian**, actually a Ukrainian soldier captured by the Ottomans early in the eighteenth century and taken to central Anatolia, where he died. His mummified body began to work miracles, leading to canonization; the saint's relics were brought here from Cappadocian Prokópi (today Ürgüp) in the 1923 population exchange.

Evvian Prokópi was part of **Ahmétaga**, the Turkish fiefdom bought in 1832 by English Philhellene nobleman Edward Noel, a relative of Lady Byron. His direct descendant Philip Noel-Baker now lives in the manor-house of the estate (☎694 42 02 112, ⓦwww.candili.gr) overlooking the village, with the tastefully converted outbuildings operating as **accommodation** and a course centre (yoga, ceramics, etc); with space for 25, groups and families may rent the entire premises (half/full board available).

From Mandoúdhi, 8km north of Prokópi, the closest decent – if shortish – **beach** is **Paralía Kírinthos**, better known as **KRÝA VRÝSSI** (accessed from **Kírinthos** hamlet, 3km beyond Mandoúdhi), where a tiny landscaped platía supports seasonal tavernas and cafés. Dutch-run **hotel** *Kirinthos* (☎22270 23660; ❸), with some rooms enjoying sea views, primarily operates as a craft centre.

At **Strofyliá**, 8km beyond Mandoúdhi, the left fork leads west to Límni (see p.524). The right-hand turning arrives after 7.5km at **AYÍA ÁNNA**, its worth-while **Folklore Museum** (Wed–Sun 10am–1pm & 5–7pm; €3) well signposted at the southeast edge of the village; displays include exquisite local weavings, rural impedimenta and photographic documentation of festivals which ceased after the 1920s. Most travellers are interested in the turn-off for **Angáli beach**, a long and dark swath of sand 4km below. For **accommodation**, the *Agali Hotel* (☎22270 97103; ❹) is congenial, at the protected north end of the pedestrianized esplanade lined with cafés, bars and tavernas. **Horseriding** is offered by Atio stables (☎694 52 91 110), hidden in the pines inland.

Towards the northernmost cape of Évvia, the next appealing – if small – beach is **Elliniká**, with a picturesque, church-capped islet offshore; the final approach road has **studios** – such as *Egeo* (☎22260 42262; ❹) – and a few **tavernas**. Beyond Elliniká, the main road (and bus line) curl southwest towards **PÉFKI**, a seaside resort with multinational clientele now leavening the historical Greek contingent; it straggles 2km along a mediocre beach, behind which are **hotels** such as 2006-renovated *Galini* (☎22260 41208; all year; ❺) and more modest *Myrtia* (☎22260 41202; April–Sept; ❹).

**Oreí**, the next resort 14km southwest via inland Istiéa, faces the sunset; in a quayside glass case is a fine Hellenistic statue of a bull, recovered from the sea in 1965. Nearby **Néos Pýrgos** beach has a better selection of **rooms** and restaurants, though Oreí sees a regular summer jet-boat bound for Vólos. Some 7km west, **AYIÓKAMBOS** has regular **ferry** connections to Glýfa on the mainland, and proves surprisingly pleasant, with a patch of beach, two or three **tavernas** and **dhomátia**.

## Límni and around

Límni, a well-preserved Neoclassical town built from nineteenth-century shipping-based wealth, is the most appealing settlement on Évvia, with congenial beach suburbs just northwest and a remarkable convent nearby. Further along the scenic coast road, Loutrá Edhipsoú is one of Greece's most popular **spa** towns, its thermal springs exploited since antiquity. Both Límni and Loutrá Edhipsoú are termini of separate Halkídha-based KTEL services, though the bus also links them.

### Límni

Some 13km southwest of Strofyliá, tile-roofed **LÍMNI** (ancient Elymnia) is a delightful, sheltered port, with magnificent views west to the mainland. The worthwhile **museum** (Mon–Sat 9am–1pm, Sun 10.30am–1pm; €2) has archeological finds, including a late Roman mosaic on the ground floor, and a rich historical/ethnographic collection upstairs: a mocked-up rural kitchen, photos of events and personalities and costumed mannequins.

**Buses** stop in front of quayside *Tsambanis Kafenio* (the ticket office), one of eight waterfront **cafés** and **bars**; the **post office** and two **ATMs** are found inland. In-town **rooms** and **hotels** can disappoint; a 2007-opened exception, on a calmer junction near the east end of the front, is the heated, air-conditioned *Graegos Studios* (☎22270 31117, ⓦwww.graegos.com; all year; ❸). Other possibilities lie 2km northwest at **SPIÁDHA**, the hamlet behind the good pebble strand of **Kohýli**, where *Livadhitis Studios* (☎22270 31640; ❸) has a prime location on a quiet beachfront cul-de-sac; on the inland side of the main road, *Ostria* (☎22270 32247, ⓦwww.ostria-apartments.gr; all year; B&B; ❺) is overpriced, though its pool-bar across the road abuts the best stretch of beach. Adjacent is the purpose-built theatre hosting the annual summer **Elymnia Festival**. **KHRÓNIA**, the next village 1km along, has another possibility in *Dennis House* (☎22270 31787 or 694 52 94 040; all year; ❸), down on the shore, good value for ample parking, sweeping balcony views and large (if rather well-worn) studios. Some 4.5km separate Khrónia from **ROVIÉS**, famous for its olives and a medieval tower but now a busy resort; much the best choice here is unsigned, family-friendly ⚘ *Eleonas* (☎22270 71619, ⓦwww.eleonashotel .com; most of year; ❺), secluded up in its namesake olive ranch – besides tasteful doubles, there's a wing of quad apartments (€170) and an on-site restaurant.

Back in Límni itself, forego the obvious central-waterfront **tavernas and ouzerís** in favour of *To Pyrofani* (*Livadhitis*) at the west end of the quay, a bit pricey for modest mains portion sizes but high quality and with big salads and nice touches like sides of sweet cabbage, or at the opposite end, always crowded *To Pikandiko*, a *yirádhiko* with daily specials like kebab, *splinándero* (innards) and *provatína* (mutton) in addition to the usual fare, with seating indoors and out. Inland favourites include cheap-and-cheerful *Lithostroto* one lane up from the platía, with seafood platters, meat grills and even *patsás*, or local *koultouriárika* entrant *Stous Efta Anemous* (dinner only; closed Tues Oct–May), with generic

Mediterranean food like pizza, pasta with salmon, salads and a few grills served in a garden or (in winter) inside by a roaring fire.

### Ayíou Nikoláou Galatáki

Nearly 9km south of Límni, **Ayíou Nikoláou Galatáki** (daily: winter 8am–noon & 2–5pm; summer 8am–noon & 4–8pm; no photos) perches superbly on the wooded slopes of Mount Kandíli, overlooking the Evvian Gulf. Though much rebuilt since its original Byzantine foundation atop a Poseidon temple, the convent retains a thirteenth-century anti-pirate tower and a crypt. One of six nuns will show you narthex **frescoes** dating from a sixteenth-century renovation. Especially vivid, on the right, is the *Entry of the Righteous into Paradise*: the virtuous ascend a perilous ladder to be crowned by angels and received by Christ, while the wicked miss the rungs and fall into the maw of Leviathan. Further to the right, a chapel portrays grisly martyrdoms.

Below Ayíou Nikoláou Galatáki are pebble-and-sand beaches at **Glýfa**, the most secluded on this coast. Several in succession lead up to the very base of Mount Kandíli: some reachable by paths, the last few only by boat. The shore is remarkably clean, considering the number of people illegally camping rough; there's a single roadside spring, 800m before the road turns inland to the monastery.

### Loutrá Edhipsoú

It's 22km from Roviés to **LOUTRÁ EDHIPSOÚ**, one of Greece's most popular **spa** towns (**ferry** links with Arkítsa). If your wallet doesn't stretch to services at the *Thermae Sylla Spa* (such as a 45min "oriental bath" for €123 or four-handed massage for €136) – you can bathe **for free** at the adjacent public **beach**, where geothermal water pours into an artificial set of cascades. There are more free, open-air **hot springs** at **Káto Ília**, 8km east, where sulphurous water boils up at 65 degrees on the pebble beach, then is channelled at more bearable temperatures into ad hoc pits dug by shovel-wielding locals.

Numerous architecturally remarkable seafront **hotels** stand to the right as you leave the ferry port; outside peak season, good deals can be had, and all have some sort of spa facility on-site. The Rationalist-International-style *Aegli* (☏22260 22215; May–Oct; ❹), with a restaurant opposite, is one good choice, while the *Avra* next door (☏22260 22226, ⓦwww.avraspahotel.gr; all year; ❻), also 1920s-vintage, proves considerably more luxurious, with a historically VIP clientele. The only plusher option is 1897-built, 1998-overhauled *Thermae Sylla* (☏22260 60100, ⓦwww.thermaesylla.gr; all year; ❽) all the way along the promenade, an elegant French-style pentagonal complex; non-guests can use their 34°C indoor pool for €25. For affordable relative elegance, try 1908-inaugurated *Istiaia* between the *Avra* and the *Thermae Sylla* (☏22260 22309; April to early Nov; ❹), with high-ceilinged, laminate-floored rooms (if basic baths), and a pleasant ground-floor wine bar. About the best independent **taverna** is *Smpanios* right opposite the ferry dock, specializing in reasonable grilled sardines, the usual *mezédhes* and local rosé wine.

# Travel details

## From the mainland

Conventional car ferries to the northern Sporades from Vólos run year-round: 2–3 daily May–Oct, 1 otherwise. Full journey time to Alónissos (not served with every departure, or every day off-season) is 5hr, to Skiáthos 2hr 30min. In Vólos, Sporades Travel at Argonaftón 33 (☏24210 23400) is the central agent for Hellenic Seaways, which currently has a monopoly on all sea traffic out of this port. There are also 2–3 weekly car ferries from Áyios Konstandínos, often to Skiáthos and Skópelos only (3–5hr), continuing to Thessaloníki, before returning along the same route. Hydrofoils/catamarans/"jet ferries" from Vólos or Áyios Konstandínos to the Sporades ply reliably only between late June and early Sept. Frequencies range from 3 daily out of Vólos in peak season, down to 1 off-peak. Journey times vary from

1hr 30min to Skiáthos to 3hr for Alónissos. From Áyios Konstandínos, there are at least 2 daily departures for all three islands, the "jet ferries" carrying cars. Journey times vary from 2hr to Skiáthos to 4hr for Alónissos. The two agencies in Áyios Konstandínos are Bilalis (℡ 22350 31614, ⓦ www.bta.gr), for some Hellenic Seaways departures, and Alkyon (℡ 22350 32444, ⓦ www .alkyontravel.com) handling other Hellenic Seaways sailings plus GA boats.

## Skiáthos, Skópelos and Alónissos

### Long-distance ferries

Skiáthos/Skópelos/Alónissos to: Iráklion, Thessaloníki and select Cyclades – typically Tínos, Mýkonos, Páros, Náxos, Íos and Thíra (1–2 weekly June–Sept on GA Ferries).

### Flights

Skiáthos to: Athens (April–Oct 1 daily, otherwise 2 weekly; 30min).

## Skýros

### Local ferries

The car ferry *Achilleas* between Kými (Évvia) and Liniará (Skýros) takes 1hr 45min. Services are twice daily from mid-June to early Sept from Kými (mid-morning and early evening), and once daily (usually early evening) the rest of the year; from Liniará departures all year are early morning, with extra peak-season ones at mid-afternoon. At Carnival time there may be up to 3 daily departures each direction. In 2008, during summer school

holidays only, there was a twice-weekly link from Skýros (via Kými) to Alónissos and Skópelos, though whether this will continue is uncertain. Download current timetables from ⓦ www.sne.gr. There is a connecting bus service for the later boat out of Kými from Athens' Liossíon 260 terminal.

### Flights

Skýros to: Athens (2–3 weekly; 40min); Thessaloníki (2–3 weekly; 40min).

## Évvia

### Buses

Athens (Liossíon 260 terminal) to: Halkídha (every 30min 5.30am–9pm; 1hr 15min); Kými (5 daily; 3hr 15min).
Halkídha to: Kárystos (2–3 daily; 3hr); Kými (8 daily; 2hr); Límni (3–4 daily; 2hr); Loutrá Edhipsoú (3–4 daily; 2hr 30min).

### Trains

Athens (Laríssis station) to: Halkídha (20 daily 6am–11pm; 1hr 30min).

### Ferries

Ayiókambos to: Glýfa (13–16 daily summer, 7 daily winter; 25min; information ℡ 22260 31245).

Erétria to: Skála Oropoú (every 20min 6am–8.30pm most of year; 20min; information ℡ 22290 62201).
Loutrá Edhipsoú to: Arkítsa (roughly hourly mid-June to mid-Sept, at least every 2hr otherwise, dawn to 9pm; 45min; information ℡ 22260 23800/330).
Marmári to: Rafína (5–6 daily April–Oct, 3–4 Nov–March; 1hr; information ℡ 22240 31341).
NB: Connecting buses link Athens with Rafína (every 30min; 1hr), Ayía Marína (5–6 daily; 1hr 15min) and Skála Oropoú (hourly; 1hr), using the Mavromatéon terminal, and with Arkítsa and Glýfa from the Liossíon 260 terminal.
Néa Stýra to: Ayía Marína (5–9 daily; 45min; information ℡ 22240 41533).

**7**

# The Ionian islands

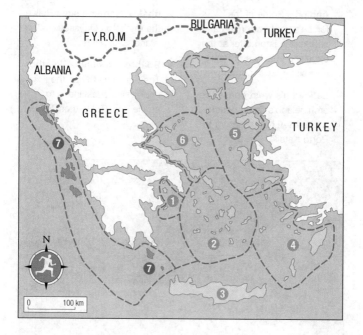

CHAPTER 7 # Highlights

▲ Yialós beach, Lefkádha

# 7

# The Ionian islands

T he six core Ionian islands, shepherding their satellites down the west coast of the mainland, float on the haze of the Ionian sea, their green, even lush, silhouettes coming as a shock to those more used to the stark outlines of the Aegean. The fertility of the land is a direct result of the heavy rains that sweep over the archipelago – and especially Corfu – from October to May, so if you visit at this time, come prepared.

The islands were the Homeric realm of Odysseus, centred on Ithaca (modern Itháki), and here alone of all modern Greek territory the Ottomans never held sway – except on Lefkádha. After the fall of Byzantium, possession passed to the **Venetians,** and the islands became a keystone in Venice's maritime empire from 1386 until its collapse in 1797. Most of the population remained immune to the establishment of Italian as the official language and the arrival of Roman Catholicism, but Venetian influence remains evident in the architecture of the island capitals, despite damage from a series of earthquakes.

On Corfu, the Venetian legacy is mixed with that of the **British**, who imposed a military "protectorate" over the Ionian islands at the close of the Napoleonic Wars, before ceding the archipelago to Greece in 1864. There is, however, no question of the islanders' essential Greekness: the poet Dhionyssios Solomos, author of the national anthem, hailed from the Ionians, as did Nikos Mantzelos, who provided the music, and the first Greek president, Ioannis Kapodhistrias.

**Tourism** is the dominant influence these days, as it has been for decades on **Corfu** (Kérkyra), which was one of the first Greek islands established on the package-holiday circuit, though the general downturn since the millennium means it does not feel as swamped as in the past. Nevertheless, parts of its coastline are among the few stretches in Greece with development to match the Spanish *costas*, although the island is large enough to contain parts as beautiful as anywhere in the group. The southern half of **Zákynthos** (Zante) – which with Corfu has the Ionians' most oversubscribed beaches – has also gone down the same tourist path, but elsewhere the island's pace and scale of development is a lot less intense. Little **Paxí** lacks the water to support large-scale hotels and has limited facilities tucked into just three villages, meaning it gets totally packed in season, when connections to Corfu and the mainland peak. Perhaps the most rewarding trio for island-hopping are **Kefaloniá**, **Itháki** and **Lefkádha**. The latter is connected to the mainland by a causeway and iron bridge but still has quite a low-key straggle of tourist centres and only two major resorts, despite boasting some excellent beaches, strung along its stunning west coast. Kefaloniá offers a series of "real towns" and a life in large part independent of tourism, as well as a selection of worthwhile attractions. Finally Itháki, Odysseus's rugged capital, is protected from a tourist influx by an absence

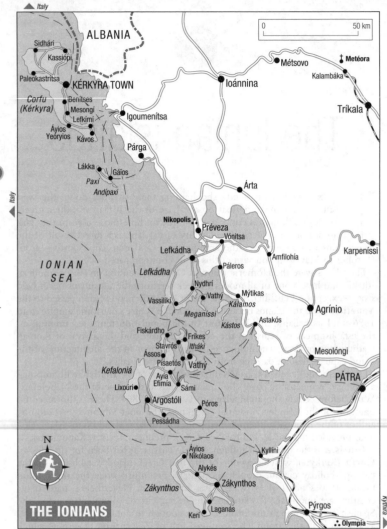

of sand. The Ionian islands' claims to Homeric significance are manifested in the countless bars, restaurants and streets named after characters in *The Odyssey*, including the "nimble-witted" hero himself, Penelope, Nausicaa, Calypso and the Cyclops.

Although officially counted among the Ionians and constituting the seventh of the traditional *eptánisos* (heptanese or "seven islands"), rugged **Kýthira** is quite separate from the six main islands on several counts. It is geographically 200km removed and only accessible from the southern Peloponnese, it shares the drier and warmer climate of southern Greece, and it remains quite a touristic backwater.

# Corfu (Kérkyra)

Dangling between the heel of Italy and the west coast of mainland Greece, green, mountainous **Corfu (Kérkyra)** was one of the first Greek islands to attract mass tourism in the 1960s. Indiscriminate exploitation turned parts into eyesores, but much of the island still consists of olive groves, mountains or woodland. The majority of package holidays are based in the most developed resorts, but unspoiled terrain is often only a few-minutes' walk away.

Corfu is thought to have been the model for Prospero and Miranda's place of exile in Shakespeare's *The Tempest*, and was certainly known to writers such as Spenser and Milton and – more recently – Edward Lear and Henry Miller, plus Gerald and Lawrence Durrell. Lawrence Durrell's *Prospero's Cell* evokes the island's "delectable landscape", still evident in some of the best beaches of the whole archipelago.

The staggering amount of accommodation (over five thousand places) on the island means that competition keeps prices down even in high season, at least in many resorts outside of Kérkyra Town. Prices at restaurants and in shops also tend to be a little lower than average for the Ionians.

## Igoumenítsa

**IGOUMENÍTSA**, directly opposite central Corfu in the mainland region of Ipirus, is the third busiest passenger port in Greece and, when the last section of the cross-country Via Egnatia is completed, will become the country's number-one cargo port. It is the major link with the mainland for both Corfu and Paxí, as well as being a key stop on ferry routes between Italy and Pátra. **Domestic ferries** dock at the open quay north of the secured international terminal; different boats operate their own ticketing systems, with the name of the ferry posted on one of two ticket kiosks opposite the loading ramps. **Ferries** to Corfu Town's New Port run every fifteen minutes to one hour from 4.30am to 10pm daily year round, with at least one crossing daily to Paxí. The town is an important crossroads for **bus services**, with connections to Athens and Thessaloníki, inland to Ioánnina and south to Párga and Préveza; the KTEL **station** is inland from the Corfu/Paxí ferry dock, on the corner of Minermoú and Arhilóhou. Buses to Athens stop at 6pm and to Ioánnina at 8pm, while the one Thessaloníki bus leaves at 11.45am (Mon–Sat).

There's little in this busy industrial port to detain you; the main shopping street, Kýprou, is a short walk away from the southeast corner of the town's main square, Platía Dimarhíou, which stands two blocks back and a few blocks east of the port. Should bad connections or a tiring journey force you to **stay** in Igoumenítsa, you'll find that hotels are plentiful, though not particularly appealing; most are to be found either on or just back from the seafront. The best budget hotel, with simple en-suite rooms, is the *Stavrodhromi* (℡26650 22343; ❷) at Soulíou 14, the street leading diagonally uphill and northeast from the Platía Dimarhíou. A smarter seafront option close to the port is *Oscar*, Ayíon Apostólon 149 (℡26650 23338; ❹), while the closest **campsite** is the *Drepano* (℡26650 24442; April–Oct), out at Dhrépano beach, 5km west.

A short walk away from the Corfu dock west along the seafront will bring you to a marina used by visiting yachts and fringed with an elegant promenade. Here on Antístasis, you'll find some stylish **bars**, catering to high-spending Greeks who hang out at nightspots like *Art* and *Memphis*. Also nearby are some of the better **restaurants**, such as the *Petros* and *Emilios psistariés*. Another direction to head in search of food is the north end of the front, where several fish tavernas and ouzerís come to life in the evening. There are **banks** and 24-hour ATMs opposite the ferry docks on Apostólon, as well as **international ferry offices**, and a **post office** on Evangelistrías, just behind the north end of the seafront.

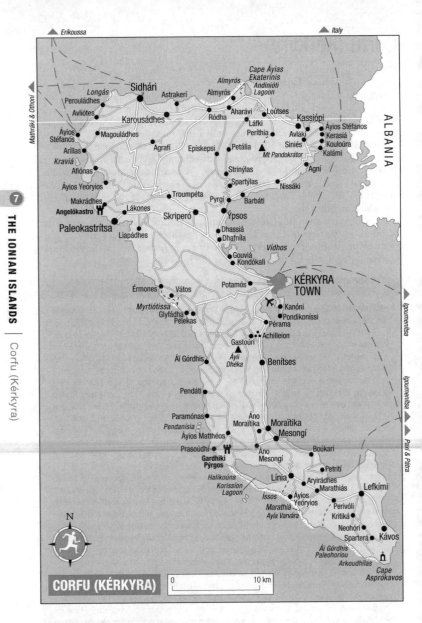

**CORFU (KÉRKYRA)**

0                    10 km

## Kérkyra (Corfu) Town

The capital, **KÉRKYRA (CORFU) TOWN**, has been one of the most elegant
island capitals in the whole of Greece since it was spruced up for the EU summit
in 1994. Although many of its finest buildings were destroyed by Nazi bombers
in World War II, two massive forts, the sixteenth-century church of Áyios
Spyrídhon and buildings dating from French and British administrations remain

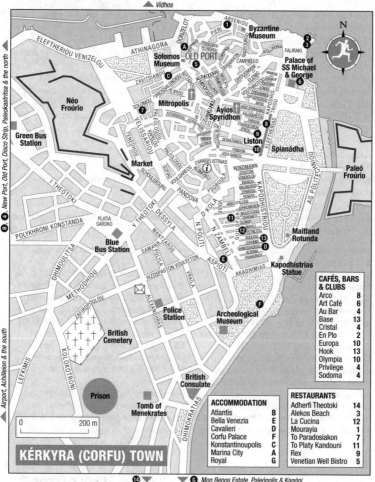

▲ Vídhos

**KÉRKYRA (CORFU) TOWN**

0 — 200 m

| CAFÉS, BARS & CLUBS | |
|---|---|
| Arco | 8 |
| Art Café | 6 |
| Au Bar | 4 |
| Base | 13 |
| Cristal | 4 |
| En Plo | 2 |
| Europa | 10 |
| Hook | 13 |
| Olympia | 10 |
| Privilege | 4 |
| Sodoma | 4 |

| ACCOMMODATION | |
|---|---|
| Atlantis | B |
| Bella Venezia | E |
| Cavalieri | D |
| Corfu Palace | F |
| Konstantinoupolis | C |
| Marina City | A |
| Royal | G |

| RESTAURANTS | |
|---|---|
| Adherfi Theotoki | 14 |
| Alekos Beach | 3 |
| La Cucina | 12 |
| Mourayia | 1 |
| To Paradosiakon | 7 |
| To Platy Kandouni | 11 |
| Rex | 9 |
| Venetian Well Bistro | 5 |

Map labels: Byzantine Museum, Palace of SS Michael & George, Solomos Museum, OLD PORT, Néo Froúrio, Green Bus Station, Market, Mitrópolis, Áyios Spyrídhon, Listón, Spianádha, Paleó Froúrio, Maitland Rotunda, Kapodhistrias Statue, Blue Bus Station, Police Station, Archeological Museum, British Cemetery, Prison, Tomb of Menekrates, British Consulate

Side margin: ◀ **B. ④.** New Port, Old Port, Disco Strip, Paleokastritsa & the north ◀ Airport, Achilleion & the south

⑭ ▼     ▼ **⑥**, Mon Repos Estate, Paleópolis & Kanóni

**7**

**THE IONIAN ISLANDS** | Corfu (Kérkyra)

intact. As the island's major port of entry by ferry or plane, Kérkyra Town can get packed in summer.

### Arrival, information and services

**Ferries** and hydrofoils to and from Italy, the mainland (Igoumenítsa and Pátra) and Paxí dock at the New Port (Néo Limáni) west of the Néo Froúrio (New Fort). The Old Port (Paleó Limáni), east of the New Port, is used only for day excursions. Most of the ferry offices are on the main road opposite the New Port; ferries to Italy or south towards Pátra become very busy in summer and booking is advisable. The port authority (domestic ☎26610 32655, international ☎26610 30481) can advise on services.

The **airport** is 2km south of the city centre. There are no airport buses, although local **blue buses** #5 and #6 can be flagged at the junction where the airport approach drive meets the main road (500m from terminal). It's a thirty-minute walk on flat terrain into town (follow the road running beside the

533

*Hotel Bretagne* opposite the junction for the shortest route or turn right then follow the sea road). **Taxis** charge a rather steep €10 and, in the unlikely circumstances that none are waiting, you can phone ☎26610 33811 for a radio cab.

A new **tourist office** (daily Mon–Fri 8am–2pm; ☎26610 37520, ✉e.o.t.corfu @otenet.gr) had taken over premises opposite the town hall on Evangelistrías in 2008 but was experiencing staffing problems so hours should be treated with caution. The **post office** (Mon–Fri 7.30am–8pm) is on the corner of Alexándhras and Zafirópoulou. Of the town's several internet cafés, the best value is *X-plore*, N. Lefteriti 4, a couple of blocks north of Platía Saróko (often anglicized to San Rocco, though it is officially named Platía Yeoryíou Theotóki).

## Accommodation

**Accommodation** in Kérkyra Town is busy all year round, and not always the best value when compared to the rest of the island. For rooms you can try the Room Owners' Association, near the tourist office at D. Theotóki 2A (Mon–Fri 9am–1.30pm, plus summer Tues, Thurs & Fri 6–8pm; ☎26610 26133, ✉oitkcrf@otenet.gr). Budget travellers might be better off heading straight for the nearest **campsite** at Dhassiá (see p.539).

**Atlantis** Xenofóndos Stratigoú 48 ☎26610 35560, ✉atlanker@mail.otenet.gr. Large and spacious air-con hotel in the New Port; its functional 1960s ambience rather lacks character. ⑤

**Bella Venezia** Zambéli 4 ☎26610 46500, ⓦwww.bellaveneziahotel.com. Smart, yellow Neoclassical building, with an elegant yet cosy atmosphere. Just behind the *Cavalieri*, with all the *Cavalieri*'s comforts, but cheaper. ⑤

**Cavalieri** Kapodhistríou 4 ☎26610 39041, ⓦwww.cavalieri-hotel.com. Smart and friendly, with all mod cons, great views and a roof bar open to the public. ⑥

**Corfu Palace Hotel** Leofóros Dhimokratías 2 ☎26610 39485, ⓦwww.corfupalace.com. Luxury hotel with pools, landscaped gardens and excellent rooms, each with a marble bath. The smartest place on the island. ⑧

**Konstantinoupolis** Zavitsiánou 1 ☎26610 48716, ⓦwww.konstantinoupolis.com.gr. Classy hotel in the Old Port with tasteful decoration and comfortable rooms. Good discounts out of high season. ⑤

**Marina City Hotel** Dónzelot 15 ☎26610 39505, ✉hotel_astron@hol.gr. The smartest option in the Old Port, the former *Astron* was completely refurbished in 2008. All rooms now have flat screen TVs, free wi-fi, fridges and plush new furniture. ④

**Royal** Kanni ☎26610 39915. Splendidly located on a hill 3km south of town and extremely good value. There's a pool and all rooms have balconies with bay views. ④

## The Town

Kérkyra Town comprises a number of distinct areas. The **Historic Centre**, the area enclosed by the Old Port and the two forts, consists of several smaller districts: **Campiello**, the oldest, sits on the hill above the harbour; **Kofinéta** stretches towards the Spianádha (Esplanade); **Áyii Apóstoli** runs west of the Mitrópolis (Orthodox cathedral); while tucked in beside the Néo Froúrio are **Ténedhos** and what remains of the old **Jewish quarter**. These districts form the core of the Old Town, and their tall, narrow alleys conceal some of Corfu's most beautiful architecture.

The **New Town** comprises all the areas that surround the Historic Centre. **Mandoúki**, beyond the Old Port, is the commercial and dormitory area for the port, and is worth exploring as a living quarter of the city, away from the tourism racket. The town's **commercial area** lies inland from the Spianádha, roughly between Yeoryíou Theotóki, Alexándhras and Kapodhistríou streets, with the most shops and boutiques around Voulgaréos, Yeoryíou Theotóki and off **Platía Saróko**. Tucked below the southern ramparts of the Néo Froúrio is the old morning **market**, which sells fish and farm produce.

## The Historic Centre

The most obvious sights are the forts, the **Paleó Froúrio** and **Néo Froúrio**, whose designations (*paleó* – "old", *néo* – "new") are a little misleading, since what you see of the older structure was begun by the Byzantines in the mid-twelfth century, just a hundred years before the Venetians began work on the newer citadel. They have both been damaged and modified by various occupiers and besiegers, the last contribution being the Neoclassical shrine of **St George**, built by the British in the middle of Paleó Froúrio during the 1840s. Looming above the Old Port, the Néo Froúrio (daily: summer 8am–7.30pm; winter 8am–3pm; €2) is the more architecturally interesting of the two. The entrance, at the back of the fort, gives onto cellars, dungeons and battlements, with excellent views over the town and bay; there's a small gallery and café at the summit. The Paleó Froúrio (same hours as Néo Froúrio; €4) is not as well preserved and contains some incongruous modern structures, but has an interesting Byzantine museum just inside the gate, and even more stunning views from the central Land Tower. It also hosts daily son et lumière shows.

Just west of the Paleó Froúrio, the **Listón**, an arcaded street built during the French occupation by the architect of the Rue de Rivoli in Paris, and the green **Spianádha** (Esplanade) it overlooks, are the focus of town life. The cricket pitch, still in use at the northern end of the Spianádha, is another British legacy, while at the southern end the **Maitland Rotunda** was built to honour the first British High Commissioner of Corfu and the Ionian islands. The neighbouring statue of

## The Ionian School of painting

The Ionian islands have a strong tradition of excellence in the fine arts, particularly iconography. They were in a unique position to bring Greece more in touch with mainstream developments in western European ideas and art, having spent centuries occupied by the Venetians and later the British, rather than by the Turks.

The founder of the **Ionian School of painting** is considered to be **Panayiotis Dhoxaras**, who was born in the Peloponnese in 1662 but, after studying in Venice and Rome, moved to Zákynthos and later lived and worked in Lefkádha and Corfu until his death in 1729. Until the late seventeenth century, religious art in the Ionians, as elsewhere, was dominated by the Cretan School; Crete was another Venetian possession, and there was a great deal of contact between the two islands. Exponents of this school were intent on maintaining the stylistic purity and dignified austerity of the Byzantine tradition. Dhoxaras, however, having absorbed the spirit of Italian Renaissance art, brought a greater degree of naturalism into iconography by showing his subjects, usually saints, in more human poses amid everyday surroundings. He is also credited with introducing the technique of **oil painting** into Greece in place of the older method of mixing pigments with egg yolk. He translated da Vinci's *Treatise on Painting* into Greek and published his own *Manual of Painting*. His most lauded work was the ceiling of Áyios Spyrídhon church in Corfu Town, which succumbed to damp in the mid-nineteenth century and had to be redone by Nikolaos Aspiotis. Originals of his do survive in the Panayía church of Áno Garoúna in Corfu and Áyios Dhimítrios in Lefkádha Town, among other places.

Dhoxaras's work was carried on by his son, Nikolaos, whose best work is the ceiling of Áyios Minás in Lefkádha Town, and over the next two centuries the tradition flourished through the skilled brushwork of a host of talented artists. Among these, **Yioryios Khrysoloras**, another eighteenth-century Corfiot, painted a number of the works on display at Corfu's Byzantine Museum; the Zakynthian **Nikolaos Kandounis** (1768–1834), creator of *The Last Supper* and *Washing of the Feet* at the Panayía Platytéra, was another prolific exponent; and three generations of the Proselandis family, starting with **Pavlos Proselandis** (1784–1837), have left work in various locations.

Ioannis Kapodhistrias celebrates the local hero and statesman (1776–1831) who led the diplomatic efforts for independence and was made Greece's first president in 1827. At the far northern end of the Listón, the nineteenth-century **Palace of SS Michael and George**, a solidly British edifice built as the residence of their High Commissioner (one of the last of whom was the future British prime minister William Gladstone), and later used as a palace by the Greek monarchy. The former state rooms house the **Asiatic Museum** (Tues–Sun 8am–7.30pm; €3) which is a must for aficionados of Oriental culture. Amassed by Corfiot diplomat Gregorios Manos (1850–1929) and others, it includes Noh theatre masks, woodcuts, wood and brass statuettes, samurai weapons and art works from Thailand, Korea and Tibet. The adjoining **Modern Art Gallery** (daily 9am–5pm; €1.50) holds a small collection of contemporary Greek art. It's an interesting diversion, as are the gardens and café–bar secreted behind the palace.

In a nearby backstreet off Arseníou, five minutes from the palace, is the museum dedicated to modern Greece's most famous nineteenth-century poet, **Dhionysios Solomos** (Mon–Sat 9.30am–2pm; €1). Born on Zákynthos, Solomos was author of the poem A *mnos stín Elefthería* ("*Hymn to Liberty*"), which was to become the Greek national anthem. He studied at Corfu's Ionian Academy, and lived in a house on this site for much of his life. Up a short flight of steps on Arseníou, the **Byzantine Museum** (Tues–Sun 9am–3pm; €2) is housed in the restored church of the Panayía Andivouniótissa. It houses church frescoes and sculptures and sections of mosaic floors from the ancient site of Paleópolis, just south of Kérkyra Town. There are also some pre-Christian artefacts, and a collection of icons dating from the fifteenth to nineteenth centuries. A block behind the Listón, down Spyrídhonos, is the sixteenth-century **church of Áyios Spyrídhon** (daily 8am–9pm), whose maroon-domed campanile dominates the town. Here you will find the silver-encrusted coffin of the island's patron saint, **Spyridhon** – Spyros in the diminutive – after whom seemingly half the male population is named. Four times a year (Palm Sunday and the following Sat, Aug 11 and the first Sun in Nov), to the accompaniment of much celebration and feasting, the relics are paraded through the streets of Kérkyra Town. Each of the days commemorates a miraculous deliverance of the island credited to the saint – twice from plague during the seventeenth century, from a famine of the sixteenth century and (a more blessed release than either of those for any Greek) from the Turks in the eighteenth century.

The next most important of the town's many churches, the **Mitrópolis** (Orthodox cathedral), perched at the top of its own square opposite the Old Port, also houses the remains of a saint, in this case St Theodora, the ninth-century wife of Emperor Theophilos. The building dates from 1577, and the plain exterior conceals a splendid iconostasis, as well as some fine icons, including a fine sixteenth-century image of *Saint George Slaying the Dragon*.

### The New Town

There are a couple of noteworthy sights in the new town that surrounds the historic centre. Kérkyra Town's **archeological museum** (Tues–Sun 8.30am–3pm; €3), just round the coast from the southern end of the Spianádha, is the best in the archipelago. The most impressive exhibit is a massive (17m) gorgon pediment excavated from the Doric temple of Artemis at Paleópolis, just south of Kérkyra Town; this dominates an entire room, the gorgon flanked by panthers and mythical battle scenes. The museum also has fragments of Neolithic weapons and cookware, and coins and pots from the period when the island was a colony of ancient Corinth.

Just south of Platía Saróko and signposted on the corner of Methodhíou and Kolokotróni, the well-maintained **British cemetery** features some elaborate civic and military memorials. It's a quiet green space away from the madness of Saróko and, in spring and early summer, it comes alive with dozens of species of orchids and other exotic blooms.

## The outskirts

Each of the following sights on the outskirts of the city is easily seen in a morning or afternoon, and you can conceivably cover several in one day.

Around the bay from the Rotunda and archeological museum, tucked behind Mon Repos beach, the area centred on the **Mon Repos** estate (8am–7.30pm; free) contains the most accessible archeological remains on the island, collectively known as **Paleópolis**. Within the estate, thick woodland conceals two **Doric temples**, dedicated to Hera and Poseidon. The Neoclassical **Mon Repos villa**, built by British High Commissioner Frederic Adam in 1824 and handed over to Greece in 1864, is the birthplace of Britain's Prince Philip and has been converted into the **Paleópolis Museum** (daily 8.30am–7.30pm; €3). As well as various archeological finds from the vicinity, including some fine sculpture, it contains period furniture *in situ*, and temporary modern art exhibitions. Other remains worth a peek outside the confines of the estate include the **Early Christian Basilica** (Tues–Sun 8.30am–3pm; free) opposite the entrance, the **Temple of Artemis**, a few hundred metres west, and the eleventh-century church of **Áyii Iáson and Sosípater**, back towards the seafront on Náfsikas.

The most famous excursion from Kérkyra Town is to the islets of **Vlahérna** and **Pondikoníssi**, 2km south of town below the hill of Kanóni, named after the single cannon trained out to sea atop it. A dedicated bus (#2) leaves Platía Saróko every half-hour, or it's a pleasant walk of under an hour. Reached by a short causeway, the tiny white convent of Vlahérna is one of the most photographed images on Corfu. Pondikoníssi (Mouse Island) can be reached by a short boat trip from the dock at Vlahérna (€2.50 return). Tufted with greenery and the small chapel of Panayía Vlahernón, Vlahérna is identified in legend with a ship from Odysseus's fleet, petrified by Poseidon in revenge for the blinding of his son Polyphemus, the Homeric echoes somewhat marred by the thronging masses and low-flying aircraft from the nearby runway. A quieter destination is **Vídhos**, the wooded island visible from the Old Port, reached from there by an hourly shuttle *kaïki* (€1 return, last boat back 1.30am). It makes a particularly pleasant summer evening excursion, when there is live music at the municipal restaurant near the jetty.

Four kilometres further to the south, past the resort sprawl of Pérama, is a rather more bizarre attraction: the **Achilleion** (daily 8am–7pm; winter closes 4pm; €7), a palace built in a mercifully unique blend of Teutonic and Neoclassical styles in 1890 by Elizabeth, Empress of Austria. Henry Miller considered it "the worst piece of gimcrackery" that he'd ever laid eyes on and thought it "would make an excellent museum for surrealistic art". The house is predictably grandiose, but the gardens are pleasant to walk around and afford splendid views in all directions. Finally, 6km inland from Corfu Town and served by its own dedicated blue bus, is one of Greece's busiest and most high-tech water parks, **Aqualand** (daily: May, June, Sept & Oct 10am–6pm; July & Aug 10am–7pm; €25).

## Eating and drinking

Although there are the inevitable tourist traps, Kérkyra Town offers some excellent, quality restaurants. As well as those listed below, there are several decent *psarotavérnes* on the Garítsa seafront, though you need to be wary of the fish prices.

**Adherfi Theotoki** M. Athanassíou, Garítsa. By far the best of the several establishments tucked behind the seafront park, this popular family taverna serves excellent *mezédhes*, meat and good-value fish dishes.

Alekos Beach Faliráki jetty. Set in the tiny harbour below the palace, with great views, this place offers simple, mostly grilled meat and fish dishes at good prices.

La Cucina Guildford 15. The town's most authentic Italian food, including fine antipasti, seafood or meat spaghetti dishes at a little above taverna prices.

Mourayia Arseníou 15–17. This unassuming, good-value ouzerí near the Byzantine Museum does a range of tasty *mezédhes*, including sausage and seafood such as mussels and shrimp in exquisite sauces. One of the best establishments in town, with views of passing ferries and Vídhos island.

To Paradosiakon Solomoú 20. Behind the Old Port, this friendly place serves good fresh food,

especially home-style oven dishes such as *stifádho* and *kokkinistó*.

To Platy Kandouni Guildford 14. Convivial *mezedhopolío*, serving small but fairly priced portions of dishes like *soupiés* and lamb, which you can wash down with *tsípouro*.

Rex Kapodhistríou 66 (the Listón). Pricey owing to its location, but some of the best food in the centre, especially the delicious oven food, mixing Greek with north European.

Venetian Well Bistro Platía Kremastí. A well-kept secret, tucked away in a tiny square a few alleys to the south of the cathedral, this is the nearest you're likely to get to Greek nouvelle cuisine, with large portions, and exotica such as Iraqi lamb and Albanian calves' livers in ouzo. Very expensive.

## Cafés and nightlife

Kérkyra Town has a plethora of **cafés**, most noticeably lining Listón, the main pedestrianized cruising street. None of these popular establishments is cheap and they look almost identical, but among the more reasonable are the *Europa*, *Olympia* or rockier *Arco*, all guaranteed to be packed from morning till late at night. *En Plo* on Faliráki jetty, however, has an unbeatably brilliant and breezy

## Moving on from Corfu Town

Corfu's **bus** service radiates from the capital. There are **two** terminals: the islandwide green bus service is based on Avramíou (also for Athens and Thessaloníki), and the suburban blue bus system, which also serves nearby resorts such as Benítses and Dhassiá, is based in Platía Saróko. Islandwide services stop between 6 and 9pm, suburban ones at between 9 and 10.30pm. Printed English timetables are available for both and can be picked up at the respective terminals.

Frequent **ferries** run throughout the day from the New Port to Igoumenítsa on the mainland, as well as regular services to Pátra and several Italian ports. All the major lines have franchises on the seafront opposite the port: Agoudimos (☎26610 80030, ⓦwww.agoudimos-lines.com), Anek (☎26610 24503, ⓦwww.anek.gr), Fragline (☎26610 38089, ⓦwww.fragline.gr), Minoan (☎26610 25000, ⓦwww.minoan.gr), Superfast (☎26610 32467, ⓦwww.superfast.com), Ventouris (☎26610 21212, ⓦwww.ventouris.gr) and Snav (☎26610 36439, ⓦwww.snav.it). **Hydrofoil** services to Paxí are run by Ionian Cruises through the Petrakis agency (☎26610 25155, ⓦwww.ionian-cruises.com), who also operate tours to Albania, Párga and other Ionian islands at much cheaper rates than the travel agents in the resorts.

There are daily **flights** to Paxí and varying numbers weekly to Ioánnina, Kefaloniá, Lefkádha, Itháki and Pátra. The seaplane actually takes off from Gouviá marina (see opposite). For further details on all public transportation see "Travel details" p.597.

Increasing numbers of visitors rent their own vehicles to get round the sizeable island. **Cars** can be rented from international agencies at the airport or in town; try Avis, Ethnikís Andístasis 42 (☎26610 24404, airport 26610 42007), behind the new port, Budget, Venizélou 22 (☎26610 28590; airport 26610 44017) or Hertz, Ethnikí Lefkímis (☎26610 38388, airport 26610 35547). Among local companies, Sunrise, Ethnikís Andístasis 14 (☎26610 44325) is reliable and many agents listed throughout the resorts offer competitive deals. **Motorbikes** and **scooters** can be rented from Easy Rider, Venizélou 4 (☎26610 43026) or Atlantis, Xenofóndos Stratigoú 48 (☎26610 40580) both in the New Port.

setting and is much quieter, as is the leafy *Art Café*, behind the Palace of SS Michael and George.

The hippest youth **bars** in town are the trio on Kapodhistríou adjacent to the *Cavalieri* hotel, of which *Hook* is the rockiest and *Base* offers a mixture of pop, rock and dance sounds. The rooftop bar at the *Cavalieri* itself is more middle-of-the-road musically but can be heaven at night.

**Club** action takes place at Corfu's self-proclaimed **disco** strip, a couple of kilometres north of town, past the New Port. This only revs up after midnight, when it becomes classic *kamáki* territory, although in summer many of its macho regulars forsake it for the resorts in order to hunt foreign females. The currently "in" joints are *Privelege*, a standard disco, *Au Bar*, a large indoor club which mixes in some Latin, *Sodoma*, which boasts an impressive lightshow, and *Cristal*, whose DJs favour trance and world music.

Kérkyra Town's two **cinemas** – the winter Orfeus on the corner of Akadhimías and Aspióti and the open-air summer Phoenix down the side street opposite – both show mostly English-language films.

## The northeast and the north coast

The **northeast**, at least beyond the immediate suburbs, is the most typically Greek part of Corfu – it's mountainous, with a rocky coastline chopped into pebbly bays and coves, above wonderfully clear seas. Green **buses** between Kérkyra Town and Kassiópi serve all resorts, along with some blue suburban buses as far as Dhassiá.

### Kérkyra Town to Ýpsos

The landscape just north of Kérkyra Town is an industrial wasteland, and things don't improve much at the first village you come to, **KONDÓKALI**, overrun by package holiday developments. Neighbouring **GOUVIÁ** is home to Corfu's largest yachting marina, as well as the new seaplane service (see box opposite). The village boasts a couple of small **hotels**, most notably the *Hotel Popi Star* (☎26610 91500, ✉popistar@otenet.gr; ❸). For **rooms**, try *Karoukas Travel* (☎26610 91596, ✉karoukas@otenet.gr; ❸). There are a number of decent **restaurants**, including all-purpose tavernas *Vergina* and *Gorgona*, the basic but excellent *Steki psistariá* and pizzerias such as *La Bonita*. For a **drink** and bop, among the slew of nightspots are the Brit-oriented *Irish Knights* bar and the nearby *Kingsize* club, which draws young people from Corfu Town. The very narrow shingle **beach**, barely 5m wide in parts, shelves into sand but given the volume of sea traffic, the water quality is doubtful.

Two kilometres beyond Gouviá the coastline begins to improve at **DHAFNÍLA** and **DHASSIÁ**, set in adjacent wooded bays with pebbly beaches. The latter is much larger and contains nearly all the area's facilities, including a trio of **watersports** enterprises, the most established of which, Corfu Ski Club (☎6942 852188, ⊕www.aqua-striders.com), claims to be the world's first paragliding operator. It is also home to the most respected UK-qualified doctor on the island, Dr John Yannopapas (☎26610 97811), whose surgery is on the main road. Two luxury sister **hotels**, the *Dassia Chandris* and *Corfu Chandris* (both ☎26610 97100–3, ⊕www.chandris.gr; ❼), dominate the resort, with extensive grounds, pools and beach facilities. Down at the beach the twin *Dassia Beach*/*Dassia Margarita* (☎26610 93224, ⊕www.dassiahotels.gr; ❹) is the best bet. Independent **rooms** can be scarce, the most reliable source being Helga Holiday Services (☎26610 97505, ✉helga@otenet.gr). Dhafníla does, however, have the best **campsite** on the island, *Dionysus Camping Village* (☎26610 91417, ⊕www.dionysuscamping.com); tents are pitched under terraced olive trees.

Friendly *Dionysus* also has simple bungalow huts, a pool, shop, bar and restaurant, and offers a ten-percent discount to Rough Guide readers. Two of the best eateries in Dhassiá are *Nikos*, a pleasant fish taverna on the beach, and *Karydia*, a multi-cuisine restaurant on the main road. The ever-popular *EDEM* outdoor disco on the beach draws revellers from far and wide.

**ÝPSOS**, 2km north of Dhassiá, can't really be recommended to anyone but hardened bar-hoppers. The thin pebble beach lies right beside the busy coast road, and the resort is generally pretty tacky. Most **accommodation** is prebooked by package companies, although Pelais Travel (T 26610 97564, W www.pelaistravel.com) can offer rooms. *Camping Ipsos Beach* (T 26610 93246) has a bar and restaurant, and offers standing tents. Ýpsos is also home to one of the island's major **diving centres**, Waterhoppers (T 26610 93867, E diverclub @hotmail.com). **Eating** on the main drag is dominated by fast food, though a more traditional meal and a quieter setting can be found in the *Akrogiali psistariá* and *Asteria* tavernas, both by the marina to the south of the strip, or you can get a decent curry at the *Viceroy*. The northern end is largely devoted to competing **bars** and **discos** including *B52*, popular for its large outdoor dancefloor.

## Mt Pandokrátor

Ýpsos has now engulfed the neighbouring hamlet of Pyrgí, which is the main point of access from the south for the villages and routes leading up to **MOUNT PANDOKRÁTOR**, Corfu's highest mountain; the road, signposted Spartýlas, is 200km beyond the junction in Pyrgí. A popular base for walkers is the village of **STRINÝLAS**, 16km from Pyrgí and served by buses from Corfu Town. Accommodation is basic but easy to come by: the *Elm Tree* taverna, a long-time favourite with walkers, can direct you to rooms. You might also ask at *The Fog* taverna in **Petália**, barely a kilometre further north.

Most visitors with their **own vehicle** approach Mount Pandokrátor from the north coast via the dull, modern village of Néa – the starting point for two basic routes. The more easterly one is via Loútses to the charming ghost village of **Áno Períthia**, from where you are a steep 5km from the summit and can only climb any higher on foot or in a four-wheel drive. Apart from taking a quick peak at the crumbling remains of half a dozen churches, most visitors come to Áno Períthia for its two excellent tavernas, especially ⅍ *Old Perithia*, renowned for succulent goat and home-produced feta cheese.

The main westerly route ascends via **Láfki** to **Petália**, just south of which a paved road leads all the way to the summit, 5km east. You may wish, however, to take a detour further west to admire the three-storey manor in the Venetian village of **Epískepsi**, 5km northwest of Strinýlas and linked to it by a direct footpath. The **summit** itself is crowned by the moderately interesting **Pandokrátoras monastery**, whose main sanctuary, built in the seventeenth century, is open to visitors; nothing remains of the original buildings from three centuries earlier.

Alternative walking or 4WD routes onto the eastern side of the mountain from the northeast coast are via Vinglatoúri, 2km north of Nissáki or via Víngla and Pórta, just west of the coast road north of Kalámi. Anyone interested in walking the Pandokrátor paths is advised to get the **map** of the mountain by island-based cartographer Stephan Jaskulowski or one of Hilary Whitton-Paipeti's walking books, available from the better English language bookshops in Corfu Town.

## North to Áyios Stéfanos

The coast road beyond Ýpsos mounts the slopes of Pandokrátor towards **BARBÁTI**, 4km further on. Here you'll find the sandiest beach on this coast, though its charm has been somewhat diminished recently by the construction of the gargantuan *Riviera Barbati* apartment complex. The beach is a favourite with families, and much **accommodation** is prebooked in advance. However, there are some rooms available on spec – try *Paradise* (☎26630 91320; ❸) or King Travel Agency (☎26630 91719, ⓦwww.corfu-holiday-rentals.com), both up on the main road. For **eating**, *Akrogiali* has good food and great views from a terrace just below the main road, while *Akti Barbati* is a decent beach taverna with a lawn and watersport facilities.

The mountainside becomes steeper and the road higher beyond Barbáti, and the population thins drastically. **NISSÁKI** is a sprawling roadside settlement rather than a village, with a number of coves, the first and last accessible by road, the rest only by track – the furthest dominated by the gigantic and rather soulless *Nissaki Beach Hotel* (☎26630 91232, ⓦwww.nissakibeach.gr; ❺ half-board). There are a couple of shops and a bakery, and a few travel and **accommodation agencies**, most notably the Nissaki Holiday Center (☎26630 91166, ⓦwww.nissakiholidays.com), up by the first junction. The white-pebble cove below boasts three very good tavernas – try the quayside *Mitsos* for fresh fish and salads.

Three pebbly coves no one visiting this coast should miss are Agní, not far past the *Nissaki Beach Hotel*, Kalámi and neighbouring Kouloúra: the first for its trio of fine tavernas, the second for its Durrell connection, the third for its exquisite bay. Crowds flock to **AGNÍ** for the fine eating – 🍴 *Nikolas* is the oldest taverna and just pips *Toula* and *Agni* for quality; delicious home-style dishes such as lamb *kléftiko* are served and it also runs the peaceful *Nikolas House* and other accommodations (☎26630 91243, ⓦwww.agnibay.com; ❹).

**KALÁMI** is on the way to being spoilt, but the village is still small and you can imagine how it would have looked in the year Lawrence Durrell spent here on the eve of World War II. The **White House**, where Durrell wrote *Prospero's Cell*, is now split in two: the ground floor is an excellent taverna; the upper floor is let through CV Travel (see Basics, p.32). Sunshine Travel (☎26630 91170, ⓦwww.sunshineclub.gr) and Kalami Tourist Services (☎26630 91062, ⓦwww.kalamits.com) both have a range of rooms on their books; see if one's going at *Villa Rita* (☎26630 91030; ❸). The **restaurant** at the White House is recommended for its mussels and swordfish with garlic specials, as are *Kalami Beach* and *Thomas' Place*, both above average tavernas on the beach. Two cocktail bars compete for the happy-hour trade.

The tiny harbour of **KOULOÚRA** has managed to keep its charm intact, set at the edge of an unspoilt bay with nothing to distract from the pine trees and *kaïkia*. The fine sole **taverna** here is one of the most idyllic settings for a meal in the whole of Corfu.

### Around the coast to Aharávi

Two kilometres beyond Kouloúra, down a shady lane, the large pebble cove of **Kerasiá** shelters the family-run *Kerasia Taverna*, a pleasant spot to enjoy some fresh fish or a salad. The most attractive resort on this stretch of coast, however, 3km down a lane from Siniés on the main road, is **ÁYIOS STÉFANOS** (officially Áyios Stéfanos Sinión to distinguish it from its namesake in north-western Corfu). Most **accommodation** here is of the upmarket prebooked villa sort, and the village has yet to succumb to any serious development; the only independent rooms and apartments are managed by the *Kochili* taverna (☎26630 81522; ❸). For food, as well as the friendly *Kochili* itself, try the excellent *Fagopotion* **taverna**, which offers finely prepared seafood, or the *Eucalyptus*, over by the tiny beach, which is pricier but serves more adventurous fare such as pork with artichokes. The *Damianos* cocktail bar is the main spot to idle with a drink. Giannis Boats (📞26630 81322, 🌐www.giannisboats.gr) rents out vessels of varying sizes from €50 per day.

A thirty-minute walk from the coastguard station above Áyios Stéfanos, along a newly surfaced road, stretches the beach of **Avláki**, a pebble bay that provides lively conditions for the **windsurfers** who visit the beach's windsurf club. There are two **tavernas**, the *Cavo Barbaro* and *Avlaki*, but the only accommodation is taken by upmarket package companies.

Further round the coast is **KASSIÓPI**, a fishing village that's been transformed into a major party resort. The Roman emperor Tiberius had a villa here, and the village's sixteenth-century Panayía Kassópitra church is said to stand on the site of a temple of Zeus once visited by Nero. Little evidence of Kassiópi's past survives, apart from an abandoned Angevin *kástro* on the headland – most visitors come for the nightlife and the five pebbly beaches. Most non-package **accommodation** in Kassiópi is rented through village agencies; the largest, Travel Corner (📞26630 81220, 🌐www.kassiopi.com), with offices near the square and the harbour, is a good place to start. An independent alternative, the great-value *Kastro* restaurant-cum-pension (📞26630 81045, 📧kyrosai@hol.gr; ❸) overlooks the beach behind the castle, while *Panayiota Apartments* (📞26630 81063, 🌐www.panayotakassiopi.com; ❷) offers bargain studios one block behind Kalamíones beach on the west side. The most popular **restaurants** are multi-cuisine tavernas, which supplement a traditional Greek diet with various international dishes, such as *Janis*, by the corner of Kalamíones beach. Other options include the *Porto* fish restaurant at the harbour and *Sze Chuan* Chinese on the main road.

At night, Kassiópi rocks to the cacophony of its music and video bars: the flashiest is the hi-tech *Eclipse*, which also shows DVDs, closely followed by *Jasmine* and *One For The Road*, all within falling-over distance of the small town square. The *Passion Club* is the liveliest spot down at the otherwise laid-back harbour. The village is also home to one of the most reliable diving operations, Corfu Divers (📞26630 81218, 🌐www.corfudivers.com), which is partly British-run. You can get online at Photonet, a short way west of the square.

The coastline beyond Kassiópi is overgrown and marshy until you get to little-developed **Almyrós beach**, one of the longest on the island, with only a few

▲ Kassiópi harbour

apartment buildings and one huge new resort dotted sporadically behind it. For a peaceful stay you could try *Villa Maria* (☎26630 63359; ❸) and eat at *Avra*, a pleasant taverna further along the beach. The **Andinióti lagoon**, smaller than Korissíon in the south but still a haven for birds and twitchers, backs Cape Ayías Ekaterínis to the east, which marks the northern end of the Corfu Trail (see box, p.552). The beach extends east all the way to **AHARÁVI**, whose wide stretch of the main coast road is vaguely reminiscent of an American Midwest truck stop. The village proper is tucked on the inland side of the road in a quiet crescent of old tavernas, bars and shops. Aharávi makes a quieter beach alternative to the southerly strands, and should also be considered by those seeking alternative routes up onto **Mount Pandokrátor** (see p.540). Roads to small hamlets such as Áyios Martínos and Láfki continue onto the mountain, and even a stroll up from the back of Aharávi will find you on the upper slopes in under an hour. Those with children might also appreciate the proximity of **Hydropolis** water park (summer daily 10.30am–6.30pm; €22, kids €18), just to the east, a less manic version of Aqualand (see p.537).

**Accommodation** isn't always easy to find, but a good place to start is Castaway Travel (☎26630 63541, ⓦwww.corfucastaway.com). One independent hotel is *Dandolo* (☎26630 63557, ⓔdandolo@otenet.gr; ❸), set in lush grounds towards the old village. Of the many **restaurants** on Aharávi's main drag, the *Pump House* steak and pasta joint and *To Ellinikon psistariá*-taverna are the best. Meanwhile the simple *Votsalakia* restaurant, at the western end of the beach, is by far the most genuine seaside eatery, while the *Theritas* taverna in the old village is the most authentic establishment inland. The main drag's bar-restaurants tend to get quite rowdy at night, although the airy *Captain Aris* is a pleasant watering hole. For a quieter drink, head for the friendly *Iy Paskhalia kafenío* or cosy *Harry's Bar*, both in the old village.

### Ródha, Sidhári and Avliótes

Continuing further west, **RÓDHA** has tipped over into overdevelopment, and can't be wholeheartedly recommended for those after a quiet time. Its central crossroads have all the charm of a service station, and the beach is rocky in parts and swampy to the west. "Old Ródha" is a small warren of alleys between the main road and the seafront, where you'll find the best **restaurants** and **bars**: the *Taverna Agra* is the oldest in Ródha and the best place for fish, while the sadly-named *Opa* and *New Port* are reasonable alternatives. For drinks, try *Crusoe's Pub* or *Maggie's Bar*, both with Sky Sports, or the trendier bar-club *Skouna*. If for some reason you decide **to stay**, the friendly seafront *Roda Inn* (☎26630 63358, ⓦwww.rodainn.com; ❷) has good value en-suite rooms. Corfu Nostos Travel on the seafront (☎26630 64602, ⓔe.kostaki@otenet.gr) rents rooms and handles car rental. There are, however, a couple of decent campsites nearby – the smart *Roda Beach Camping* (☎26630 93120) is a little way east of the resort, while the even pleasanter *Karoussades Camping* (☎26630 31415) is to the west, towards Sidhári. Myron's good-rate motorbike rental (☎26630 63477), Voyager boat rental (from €15 per hour; ☎6932 908173) and Costas horseriding (☎694 41 60 011; €20 for 2hr) are all based in Ródha. Several kilometres inland from Ródha, just east of Agrafí, the relatively undiscovered ⚑ *Angonari mezedhopolío* serves an excellent range of dishes and great barrelled wine in a relaxed garden with subtle live music.

The next notable resort, **SIDHÁRI**, is constantly expanding and totally dominated by British-package tourists; its small but pretty town square, with a bandstand set in a small garden, is lost in a welter of bars, shops and joints. The beach is sandy but not terribly clean, and many people tend to head just west to the curious coves, walled by wind-carved sandstone cliffs, around the vaunted Canal d'Amour. The biggest accommodation agency, Vlasseros Travel (℡ 26630 95695), also handles car rental, horseriding and excursions, including day-trips to the Dhiapóndia islands (see below). Sidhári's **campsite**, *Dolphin Camping* (℡ 26630 31846), is over 1km inland from the junction at the western end of town. Most **restaurants** are pitched at those looking for a great night out rather than a quiet meal in a taverna. The best value is to be found at *Bournis,* which also does Mexican, or at *Kavvadias,* both on the eastern stretch of beach. Asian cuisine, such as the Indian food at *Kohenoor,* and cheap full-on English breakfasts are also readily available. There are no quiet bars in Sidhári, and several **night-clubs** vie for late custom, including *IQ, Mojo* and *Ice Club.* Sidhári also has its own modest water park with free entry, a good place to keep the kids happy.

The Sidhári bus usually continues to **AVLIÓTES**, a handsome hill town with the odd *kafenío* and tavernas but few concessions to tourism. The town is note-worthy for two reasons: its accessibility to quiet **Perouládhes** in the very northwest and **Áyios Stéfanos** (see p.546) to the southeast, both only a few kilometres away. Stunning **Longás beach**, bordered by vertical reddish layer-cake cliffs that make for shady mornings, lies below Perouládhes. You can stay 200m back from the beach at *Logas Beach Studios* (℡ 26630 95412, ✉ giorkou@mailbox .gr; ❸) or enjoy a splendid sunset dinner at the clifftop *Panorama* taverna.

## Corfu's satellite islands

Only three of Corfu's quintet of **Dhiapóndia islands**, scattered up to 20km off the northwest coast, are inhabited: **Eríkoussa**, **Othoní** and **Mathráki**. Some travel agencies in the northern resorts offer **day-trips** for sunbathing on Eríkoussa only, while a trip taking in all three islands from Sidhári or Áyios Stéfanos is excellent value. You can also travel independently between the islands on regular *kaïkia*. The thrice-weekly **ferry** from Kérkyra Town is the least efficient way to get there. Each of the islands supports a tiny year-round community but only really comes alive in summer.

Flattish **ERÍKOUSSA** is the sandiest and most visited of the trio. There is an excellent golden sandy beach right by the harbour and quieter **Bragíni beach**, reached by a path across the wooded island interior. The island's cult following keeps its one **hotel**, the *Erikousa* (℡ 26630 71110, ⓦ www .hotelerikousa.gr; ❹), busy throughout the season; the hotel also boasts the only bona fide taverna. **OTHONÍ** is the largest of the islands and has a handful of places to stay and eat in its port, **Ámmos**, which has two pebbly beaches. The sizeable *Hotel Calypso* (℡ 26630 72162; ❸), 200m east of the jetty, has relieved pressure on **accommodation**, while the one smart **restau-rant**, *La Locanda dei Sogni* also has rooms (℡ 26630 71640; ❸). Two tavernas, *New York* and tiny *Lakis*, offer decent but fairly limited menus. The village of **Horió** in the island's centre and sandy but deserted **Fýki Bay** are worth visiting if you stay. Hilly, densely forested and with long empty **Portéllo beach**, beautiful **MATHRÁKI** has the fewest inhabitants of the three islands. However, the island is gradually gearing up towards visitors, and locals Tassos Kassimis (℡ 26630 71700; ❷) and Khristos Aryiros (℡ 26630 71652; ❸) rent **rooms** and **studios** on Portéllo beach. At the harbour, **Plákes**, the *Port Centre* restaurant specializes in freshly caught fish.

## Paleokastrítsa and the northwest coast

The northwest conceals some of the island's most dramatic coastal scenery, the violent interior mountainscapes jutting out of the verdant countryside. The area's honeypot is **Paleokastrítsa**, the single most picturesque resort on Corfu, which suffers from its popularity. Further north, the densely olive-clad hills conceal better, sandier beaches, such as **Áyios Yeóryios** and **Áyios Stéfanos**. Public **transport** all along the west coast is difficult: virtually all buses ply routes from Kérkyra Town to single destinations, and rarely link resorts.

## Paleokastrítsa

**PALEOKASTRÍTSA**, a small village surrounded by dramatic hills and cliffs, has been identified as the Homeric city of Scheria, where Odysseus was washed ashore and escorted by Nausicaa to the palace of her father Alkinous, king of the Phaeacians. It's a stunning site, as you would expect, though one that's long been engulfed by tourism. The focal point of the village is the car park on the seafront, which backs onto the largest and least attractive of three **beaches**, home to sea taxis and *kaïkia*. The second beach, to the right, is stony with clear water, but the best of the three is a small unspoilt strand reached along the path by the *Astakos Taverna*. Protected by cliffs, it's undeveloped apart from the German-run Korfu-Diving Centre (☎26630 41604) at the end of the cove. From the first beach you can get a **boat trip** to some nearby seawater caves, known as the "blue grottoes" (€8 for a 30min trip), which is worth taking for the spectacular coastal views; full day cruises cost €20, including a barbecue. Boats also serve as a taxi service to three neighbouring beaches, Áyia Triánda, Palatákia and Alípa, which all have snack bars. You can also rent your own boat from €40 per day (☎6974 375852, Ⓦwww.ampelakiboats.com;) at Alipa harbour, which is under a kilometre down a side road from the first main beach.

On the rocky bluff above the village, the **Theotókou monastery** (7am–1pm & 3–8pm; free, donations welcome) is believed to have been established in the thirteenth century. There's also a museum, resplendent with icons, jewelled bibles and other impedimenta of Greek Orthodox ritual, though the highlight is the gardens, with spectacular coastal views. Paleokastrítsa's ruined castle, the **Angeló-kastro**, is around 6km up the coast; only approachable by a path from the hamlet of Kríni, it has stunning, almost circular views of the surrounding sea and land. At the time of writing it was officially closed for renovations, although many visitors bypass the sign and ascend the steps anyway – caution is advised if you choose to do so. For a drink or snack with tremendous views on the way up from Paleokastrítsa, it's worth stopping at the excellent *O Boulis* taverna in Lákones or the *Bella Vista* or *Golden Fox* tavernas, between there and Makrádhes.

**Accommodation** isn't hard to find but sprawls a long way back from central Paleokastrítsa, often leaving quite a walk to the beach. A good hotel is the family-run *Odysseus* (☎26630 41209, Ⓦwww.odysseushotel.gr; ❹ half-board), on the road into town, while the modern nearby *Akrotiri Beach* (☎26630 41237, Ⓦwww.akrotiri-beach.com; ❻) is upmarket but unpretentious. Along the first turning back from the centre on the north side of the main road, the friendly family-run *Villa Korina* (☎26630 44064; ❷) has great value **rooms**, as does the *Dolphin Snackbar* (☎26630 41035; ❷), further back above Alípa beach. Michalas tourist bureau (☎26630 41113, Ⓔmichalastravel@ker.forthnet.gr) is another source, as well as offering all the usual services. *Paleokastritsa Camping* (☎26630 41204) is just off the main road, almost a half-hour walk from the centre.

There isn't a huge choice of **restaurants** in the centre of Paleokastrítsa. The *Astakos Taverna* and *Corner Grill* are two traditional places, while the seafront *Smurfs* has a good seafood menu despite the dreadful name. Also recommended is the very smart *Vrahos*, which offers pricey fish and some unusual dishes like artichokes. **Nightlife** hangouts include the restaurant-bars in the centre, and those straggling back up the hill, such as the relaxing *Petrino* bar. By the Lákones turning is Paleokastrítsa's one nightclub, *The Paleo Club*, a small disco-bar with a garden.

### Áyios Yeóryios to Áyios Stéfanos

Like many of the west-coast resorts, **ÁYIOS YEÓRYIOS**, 6km north of Paleokastrítsa, isn't actually based around a village, though it is sometimes referred to as Áyios Yeóryios Pagón after the inland village of Payí to avoid confusion with its southern namesake. The resort has developed in response to the popularity of the large sandy bay, and it's a major **windsurfing** centre, busy even in low season, especially towards the northern end, where boats can also be rented. Contrary to the general trend, more **accommodation** is now block-booked here than in the past, but independent rooms are available at bargain rates in the cute walled-garden complex of *Kóstas Bardhís* (☏26630 96219; ❷), towards the north end of the beach, and at the Arista supermarket (☏26630 96350; ❸) or *Studio Eleana* (☏26630 96366; ❸), both behind the central section of beach. The *San George* campsite (☏26630 51759) is nearly 1km back from the beach towards Kavvadhádhes. *To Vrahos* at the northern end of the beach and *Spiros* halfway along are among the better restaurants, both serving Greek and international cuisine, while gaily-painted *Ostrako* is unbeatable for seafood in the far south. Nearby *Noa Noa* is one of the liveliest nightspots.

The village of **AFIÓNAS**, perched high above the north end of the bay, has been suggested as the likely site of **King Alkinous's castle** – there are vestigial Neolithic remains outside the village – and the walk up to the lighthouse on Cape Aríllas affords excellent views over Áyios Yeóryios and Aríllas Bay to the north. The village itself is very small, but does boast one fine **taverna**, 🍴 *To Panorama*, which serves tasty meals made from organic produce and has great views from its terrace; it has also some good-value rooms (☏26630 51846, ✉panorama_afionas@hotmail.com; ❷).

The northernmost of the west coast's resorts, **ÁYIOS STÉFANOS** is low-key, popular with families and a quiet base from which to explore the northwest and the Dhiapóndia islands, visible on the horizon. Day-trips to Mathráki, Othoní and Eríkoussa (see p.544) run several times a week in season (€15–20 per person), as well as cheaper passenger services (€8–10 return) most days on the Aspiotis lines *kaïki*. Áyios Stéfanos's oldest **hotel**, the *Nafsika* (☏26630 51051, ☻www.nafsikahotel.com; ❸), has a large restaurant, a favourite with villagers, and gardens with a pool and bar. Also behind the main southern beach is the *Hotel San Stefano* (☏26630 51053; ❷), while the *Restaurant Evinos* (☏26630 51766; ❸) has small **apartments** above the northern end of the village. For those on a budget, Peli and Maria's gift shop offers bargain **rooms** (☏26630 51424, ☻www.pelimaria.gr; ❷) and a number of travel agencies handle accommodation, among them San Stefanos (☏26630 51910, ☻www.san-stefano.gr) in the centre; they also rent boats out for €70 per day. Besides the above-mentioned establishments, good options for **eating** include the *Waves* and very reasonable *Mistral* tavernas above the beach, while *O Manthos* taverna serves Corfiot specialities such as *sofríto* and *pastitsádha*. For **nightlife**, lively *Condor* and more laid-back *Summer Dreams* stand out among the handful of music bars.

## Central and southern Corfu

Two natural features divide the centre and south of Corfu. The first is the **plain of Rópa**, whose fertile landscape backs onto some of the best beaches on this coast, such as delightful **Myrtiótissa**. Settlements and development stop a little to the south of Paleokastrítsa and only resume around **Érmones** and **Pélekas** – a quick bus ride across the island from Kérkyra Town. Down to the south, a second dividing point is the **Korissíon lagoon**, the sandy plains and dunes that skirt this natural feature being great places for botanists and ornithologists. Beyond, a single road trails the interior, with sporadic side roads to resorts on either coast. The landscape here is flat, an undistinguished backdrop for a series of increasingly developed beaches and, in the far south, **Kávos**, Corfu's big party resort.

## The west coast from Érmones to Glyfádha

**ÉRMONES**, around 15km south of Paleokastrítsa by road, is one of the busiest resorts on the island, its lush green bay backed by the mountains above the Rópa River. The resort is dominated by the luxury *Ermones Beach* **hotel** (☎26610 94241, ⓦwww.sunmarotelermones.gr; ❼), which provides guests with obligatory full board and a funicular railway down to the beach. Of the two mid-range hotels on the other side of the river, the *Philoxenia* (☎26610 94091, ⓦwww.hotelphiloxenia.com; ❹) is better value, while cheaper rooms can be found at the *Pension Katerina* (☎26610 94615; ❷) and *Georgio's Villas* (☎26610 94950; ❷), further back on the hillside above the road that leads to the beach. Both the *Maria* and *Nafsica* **tavernas** above the beach provide good, filling *mezédhes* and main dishes. Just inland is the Corfu Golf and Country Club (☎26610 94220, ⓦwww.corfugolfclub.com), the only golf club in the archipelago, and reputed to be one of the finest in the Mediterranean.

The nearby small village of **VÁTOS**, on the Glyfádha bus route from Kérkyra Town, has only a shop-cum-café and a quaint church, as all the other facilities are to be found on the main road 1km below. Here, the *Olympic Restaurant and Grill* (☎26610 94318; ❷) has rooms and apartments, as well as the only food, while the *Villa Frederiki* (☎26610 94003; ❷), opposite, consists of two large double studios. The extremely handy, if basic, *Vatos Camping* (☎26610 94393), is 500m further south.

Far preferable to the gravelly sand of Érmones is the idyllic strand of **MYRTIÓTISSA**, signposted just south of the campsite. In *Prospero's Cell*, Lawrence Durrell described Myrtiótissa as "perhaps the loveliest beach in the world"; it was for years a well-guarded secret but is now a firm favourite, especially with nudists, and gets so busy in summer that it supports three *kantínes*, meaning it's at its best well out of high season. Above the north end of the beach is the tiny, whitewashed **Myrtiótissa monastery**, dedicated to Our Lady of the Myrtles. There are a few **rooms**, just off the approach road at the friendly *Myrtia* taverna (☎26610 94113, ⓔsks_mirtia@hotmail.com; ❸), which serves tasty home-style cooking.

## The west coast from Pélekas to the Korissíon lagoon

**PÉLEKAS**, inland and 2km south of Glyfádha, has long been popular for its views – the **Kaiser's Throne** viewing tower, just above the town, was Wilhelm II's favourite spot on the island. As the only inland resort, there are some good **room** deals here, including the friendly *Pension Paradise* (☎26610 94530; ❶), on the way in from Vátos, the *Alexandros* restaurant (☎26610 94215, ⓦwww.alexandrospelekas.com; ❷) and *Thomas* (☎26610 94441; ❸) pension, both on the way towards Kaiser's Throne. Among the **tavernas**, *Pink Panther*, with a refreshing array of peppery sauces, and *Roula's Grill House*, especially good for simple succulent meat, are both highly recommended. Colourful *Zanzibar*, run by a witty Brummie lady, is a pleasant spot for a drink by the diminutive square, whose Odhiyítria church, renovated in 1884, is worth a peek.

Pélekas's sandy **beach** is reached down a short path. Sadly, the beach has been rather spoilt by the monstrous *Pelekas Beach* hotel that now looms over it.

Meanwhile, the inland area around Pélekas holds some of Corfu's most traditional villages. This atmosphere of days gone by is best reflected in **SINARÁDHES**, which has the **Folk Museum of Central Corfu** (Tues–Sun 9.30am–2.30pm; €1.50). The museum comprises an authentic village house, complete with original furniture, fittings and decoration and full of articles and utensils that formed an intrinsic part of daily rural life. You can enjoy a coffee or something stronger at the **café-bar** *Sinarades*, or grab a tasty and inexpensive meal at the friendly *Igoumenos* **psistariá**.

Around 7km south of Pélekas, **AÏ GÓRDHIS** is one of the major party beaches on the island, largely because of the activities organized by the startling **Pink Palace** complex (☎26610 53103, ⓦwww.thepinkpalace.com), which dominates the resort. It has pools, games courts, internet access, restaurants, a shop and a disco. Backpackers cram into communal rooms for up to ten (smaller rooms and singles are also available) for €18–26 a night, including breakfast and an evening buffet. Other accommodation is available on the beach, notably at *Michalis Place* taverna (☎26610 53041; ❸); the neighbouring *Alex in the Garden* **restaurant** is a favourite place to eat. The beachside *Alobar* is the spot for refreshments by day and entertainment by night. Calypso (☎26610 53101, ⓦwww.divingcorfu.com) is a **diving centre**, which offers excellent diving packages with accommodation.

Inland from the resort is the south's largest prominence, the humpback of **Áyii Dhéka** (576m), reached by path from the hamlet of Áno Garoúna; it is the island's second-largest mountain after Pandokrátor. The lower slopes are wooded, and it's possible to glimpse buzzards wheeling on thermals over the higher slopes. The monks at the tiny monastery just below the summit lovingly tend a bountiful orchard.

Around 5km south by road from Aï Górdhis, the fishing hamlet of **PENDÁTI** is still untouched by tourism. There is no accommodation here, but *Angela's* café and minimarket and the *Strofi* grill cater to villagers and the few tourists who wander in. Another 4km on, **PARAMÓNAS** has slowly evolved over the years but remains a low-key resort with some fine **accommodation** deals: at the beach, the *Sunset* taverna (☎26610 75149; ❷) and smart *Paramonas* hotel (☎26610 76595, ⓦwww.paramonas-hotel.com; ❸), just behind it, both offer panoramic sea views, while *Areti Studios* (☎26610 75838; ❸), on the lane in from Pendáti, has a more rural air.

The town of **ÁYIOS MATTHÉOS**, 3km inland, is still chiefly an agricultural centre, although a number of *kafenía* and tavernas offer a warm if slightly bemused welcome to passers-by: head for the *Mouria* snack-bar/grill, or the modern *Steki*, which can rustle up tasty *mezédhes*. On the other side of Mount Prasoúdhi, 2km by road, is the **Gardhíki Pýrgos**, the ruins of a thirteenth-century castle built in this unlikely lowland setting by the despots of Epirus. The road continues on to the northernmost tip of splendid and deserted **Halikoúna beach** on the sea edge of the **Korissíon lagoon**, which, if you don't have your own transport, is most easily reached by walking from the village of Línia (on the Kávos bus route) via **Íssos beach** (see p.550); other, longer routes trail around the north end of the lagoon from Áno Mesongí and Khlomotianá. Over 5km long and 1km wide at its centre, Korissíon is home to turtles, tortoises, lizards and numerous indigenous and migratory birds. For one of the quietest stays on the island, try *Marin Christel Apartments* (☎26610 75947; ❸), just north of Halikoúna beach, or *Logara Apartments* (☎26610 76477; ❹), 500m inland. *Spiros* has the slightly better selection of the two tavernas on this stretch of road. The beach is an idyllic spot for rough camping but only a seasonal canteen operates in the immediate vicinity.

## Benítses to Petrití: the east coast

South of Kérkyra Town, there's nothing to recommend before **BENÍTSES**, a once-notorious bonking-and-boozing resort, whose old town at the north end has long since reverted to a quiet bougainvillea-splashed Greek village. There are a couple of minor attractions, namely the modest ruins of a Roman bathhouse at the back of the village and the small but impressive **shell museum** (March–Oct daily 9am–7pm, closes later in high season; €4). **Rooms** are plentiful, as visitor numbers have never returned to heyday levels: try Best Travel (☎26610 72037). Among **hotels** offering good deals, the central *Hotel Potamaki* (☎26610 71140, ⓦwww.potamakibeachhotel.gr; ❹), is a gigantic 1960s throwback, while the smaller modern *Benitses Arches* (☎26610 72113; ❷) offers quiet rooms set back from the main road. Benítses has its fair share of decent **tavernas**, notably *La Mer de Corfu* and the Corfiot specialist *O Paxinos*, as well as the plush Italian *Avra*. Lively **bars** such as *Lacey's* and *Sunshine* are concentrated behind the crescent-shaped park that separates the old village from the coast road, while larger **nightclubs** like *Casanovas 2000* or *Stadium* are at the southern end of the main strip. Several kilometres south of Benítses, just beyond the short tunnel through the cliff behind the quiet beach of Áyios Ioánnis Peristerón, Aqua Fantastic (☎26610 76026, ⓦwww.aquafantastic-watersports.com) offers jet skiing, parasailing, waterskiing, canoeing and other rides.

   **MORAÏTIKA**'s main street is an ugly strip of bars, restaurants and shops, but its beach is the best between Kérkyra Town and Kávos. Confusingly, the biggest touristic landmark in the area, the *Messonghi Beach* **hotel** complex (☎26610 75830, ⓦwww.messonghibeach.gr; ❺), set in lush landscaped gardens and home to the Nautilus diving centre (daily 5–7pm; ☎26610 83295), actually lies just within the limits of Moraïtika, which is separated from neighbouring Mesongí by the Mesongís River. Other reasonable beachside **hotels** include the *Margarita Beach* (☎26610 75267, ⓦwww.corfu-hotel-margarita.com; ❹) and the plusher *Three Stars* (☎26610 75263; ❹). Budget Ways Travel (☎26610 76768) offers a range of accommodation and there are **rooms** between the main road and beach, such as those at the *Firefly* taverna (☎26610 75850; ❸). Much of the main drag is dominated by souvenir shops and minimarkets, as well as a number of **bars**, including the village's oldest, *Charlie's*, which opened in 1939, and the lively *Very Coco* nightclub. The *Rose Garden* **restaurant** is just off the main road and has a fair mix of vegetarian, Greek and international food, as does the beach restaurant *Kavouria*, where the seafood and special salads are excellent. The village proper, **ÁNO MORAÏTIKA**, is signposted a few-minutes' hike up the steep lanes inland, and is virtually unspoilt. Its tiny houses and alleys are practically drowning in bougainvillea, among which you'll find two **tavernas**: the *Village Taverna* and the *Bella Vista*, the latter of which has a basic menu but justifies its name with a lovely garden, sea views and breezes.

   Commencing barely a hundred metres on from the Moraïtika seafront, **MESONGÍ** continues this stretch of package-tour-oriented coast but is noticeably quieter and has a range of accommodation deals. Both the *Hotel Gemini* (☎26610 75221, ⓦgeminihotel.gr; ❺) and the far better value, British-run *Pantheon Hall* (☎26610 75802, ⓦwww.corfu-summer.com; ❷) have pools and gardens, and en-suite rooms with balconies. Mesongí has a number of good **restaurants**: notably the *Memories* taverna, which specializes in Corfiot dishes and serves its own barrel wine, and the upmarket *Castello*.

   The quiet road from Mesongí to Boúkari follows the seashore for about 3km, often only a few feet above it. **BOÚKARI** itself comprises little more than a

THE IONIAN ISLANDS | Corfu (Kérkyra)

7

handful of tavernas, a shop and a few small, family-run hotels; the 🍴 *Boukari Beach*, 1km north of the tiny harbour, is the best of the **tavernas**, offering fresh fish and live lobster. The very friendly Vlahopoulos family who run the taverna also offer rooms and own two small hotels nearby, the fully renovated *Penelopi,* with smart self-catering suites, and *Villa Alexandra* (☎26620 51269, ⓦwww .boukaribeach.com; ❸). Boúkari is out of the way, but an idyllic little strip of unspoilt coast for anyone fleeing the crowds elsewhere on the island, and inland from here is the unspoiled wooded region around **Aryirádhes**, rarely visited by tourists and a perfect place for quiet walks.

Back on the coastline, the village of **PETRITÍ**, only created in the 1970s when geologists discovered the hill village of Korakádhes was sliding downhill, fronts onto a small but busy harbour. It is mercifully free of noise and commerce, with a beach of rock, mud and sand, set among low olive-covered hills. The *Pension Egrypos* (☎26620 51949, ⓦwww.egrypos.gr; ❸) has **rooms** and a restaurant. At the harbour, a few **tavernas** serve the trickle of sea traffic: *Stamatis* is the best of the bunch. Back from the village, near the hamlet of Vassilátika, is the elegant *Regina* **hotel**, with gardens and pool (☎26620 52132, ⓦwww .reginahotel.de; ❹), mainly occupied by Germans. Barely 2km south of Petrití, the rocky coves of **Nótos beach** are little visited and conceal a wonderful and friendly place to stay in the shape of *Panorama Apartments* (☎26620 51707, ⓦwww.panoramacorfu.gr; ❸), which also has a fine shady restaurant.

## Southern Corfu

Across the island on the west coast, the beach at **ÁYIOS YEÓRYIOS** spreads as far south as Ayía Varvára, and north to encircle the edge of the Korissíon lagoon, around 12km of uninterrupted sand. The resort itself, however, is an unprepossessing seafront sprawl, and tourism here has the most mercenary air of anywhere on the island. British package operators dominate the scene, with bars competing to present bingo, quizzes and video nights. The smart *Golden Sands* (☎26620 51225, ⓦwww.corfugoldensands.com; ❸) has a pool, open-air restaurant and gardens, but the best **hotel** bargain is the smaller *Blue Sea* (☎26620 51624, ⓦwww.bluesea-hotel.com; ❷); both are situated midway along the seafront road. The easiest place to look for good **rooms** is at Star Travel (☎26620 52800, ⓦwww.startravel.com), further north. Most **restaurants** are predictably bland but you can eat well enough at the *Stamatis* and *Splendid* taverna/grill houses. **Nightlife** centres on music and pool bars like the *Gold Hart* and *Bluebell*, although the laid-back *Amazona* cocktail bar and lively *Mad Mike's*, one of the few places off the seafront, have a better atmosphere. Kostas Jet Ski (☎593 66 91 440) offers a range of watersports activities and boat rental through branches at each end of the resort.

A few-minutes' walk north of Áyios Yeóryios, **ÍSSOS** is a far better and quieter beach; the dunes north of Íssos towards the Korissíon lagoon are an unofficial nude bathing area. Facilities around Íssos are sparse: one **taverna**, the *Rousellis Grill*, a few hundred metres from the beach on the lane leading to Línia on the main road; the smart new yellow-and-maroon *Vicky's Apartments* (☎26620 53161; ❹), above a bend in the lane; and the *Friends* snack-bar in Línia itself. The German-run Surf4Fun **windsurfing school** (☎6946 558303, ⓦwww .surf4fun-korfu.de) offers rental and instruction in both windsurfing and kite surfing, while Nikos Sea Sports has other watersports equipment for use.

Far pleasanter than Áyios Yeóryios are the two burgeoning developments of **MARATHIÁ** and **AYÍA VARVÁRA**, both further southeast along the continuous strand, but reached by separate and convoluted inland routes. The most direct route to Marathiá beach is signposted from the tiny village of **Marathiás**, on the main road to Lefkími, a couple of kilometres southeast of Aryirádhes. Around 2km out of Marathiás, the road forks; the right branch leads after 400m to a low cliff with a couple of **tavernas** above the end of a triangular wedge of beach, of which *Akroama* is the better with treats like swordfish and local sausage and has rooms (T 26620 52736; ❷), while the left branch ends up beside another duo of beach restaurants. These are divided by only 300m of sand and the estuary of a small stream, bridged by wooden planks, from the beachfront of Ayía Varvára. Although it is less than 1km along the sand from Marathiá, Ayía Varvára is at least a seven-kilometre drive away. It is signposted from the village of Perivóli, 2km southeast of Marathiás on the main north-south thoroughfare. On the beach, the *Santa Barbara Miaris* (T 26620 22200, E biros@pathfinder.gr; ❷) has good-value **rooms**, including breakfast, and a restaurant, which doubles up as the village's prime watering hole.

Anyone interested in how a Greek town works away from the bustle of tourism shouldn't miss **LEFKÍMI**, towards the island's southern tip. The second-largest settlement after Kérkyra Town, it's the administrative centre for the south of the island as well as the alternative ferry port to or from Igoumenítsa, with half a dozen daily crossings in summer. The town has some fine architecture, including several striking churches: **Áyii Anáryiri** with a huge double belfry, **Áyios Theódhoros**, on a mound above a small square, and **Áyios Arsénios**, with a vast orange dome that can be seen for miles. There are some **rooms** at the *Cheeky Face* taverna (T 26620 22627; ❶), by the bridge over the canal that carries the Himáros River through the lower part of town, and the *Maria Madalena* apartments (T 26620 22386; ❶) further up. For **food** look no further than the home-cooking at the tiny *Maria estiatório*, on the opposite side of the canal to *Cheeky Face*. A few local **bars** are tucked in corners of the upper town, such as *Mersedes* and *Esperos,* which has a leafy garden, or you can sip a coffee at trendy new *Central* café.

There are no ambiguities in **KÁVOS**, 6km south of Lefkími: either you like 24-hour drinking, clubbing, bungee-jumping, go-karts, video bars named after British sitcoms and chips with almost everything, or you should avoid the resort altogether. Kávos stretches over 2km of decent sandy beach, with watersports galore. This is very much Club 18–30 territory, although numbers have dropped of late so unbelievable bargains can be had; look around for signs offering **rooms** for as little as €5 per night or ask at Florida Holidays (T 26620 61350, E ncpandis@otenet.gr). The nearest to genuine Greek **food** you'll find is at the *Two Brothers psistariá*, at the south end of town. Fast food and British-style Asian cuisine are much easier to come by. *Future* is the most lively **club**, with imported north European DJs, followed by *42nd St* and *Sex*. The favourite **bars** here include *Rolling Stone*, *The London Pub*, *The Face*, *SOS* and *Bonkers*, and at night the main drag is one unbroken crowd of young revellers.

Beyond the limits of Kávos, where few visitors stray, a path leaving the road south to the hamlet of Sparterá heads through unspoilt countryside; after around thirty minutes of walking it reaches the cliffs of **Cape Asprókavos** and the crumbling **monastery of Arkoudhílas**. The cape looks out over the straits to Paxí, and down over deserted **Arkoudhílas beach**, which can be reached from Sparterá, a pleasant village 5km by road but only 3km by the signed path from Kávos; its *Fantasia* and *Paradise* tavernas are far more appealing and authentic than any in the resort. Even wilder is **Áï Górdhis Paleohoríou beach**, 3km further on from Sparterá, one of the least visited on the island and not to be confused with the eponymous beach further north; a municipal café

> ## Walking the Corfu Trail
>
> In 2001, years of hard work and planning came to fruition with the opening of the **Corfu Trail**. The trail, 200km in length, covers the whole island from top to bottom, from **Cape Asprókavos** in the south to Áyios Spyrídhon beach, next to **Cape Ayías Ekaterínis** in the far north. The route avoids roads as much as possible and takes walkers across a variety of terrain – from beaches to the highest peaks. The principal places passed en route are Lefkími, Korissíon lagoon, Paramónas, Áyii Dhéka, Pélekas, Paleokastrítsa, Áyios Yeóryios Pagón, Agrós and Mount Pandokrátor.
>
> Paths along the entire route are **waymarked** with yellow aluminium signs. As usual, ramblers are advised to wear headgear and stout footwear and carry ample water and provisions, as well as all-weather kit in all but the high summer months. It is reckoned that strong walkers can cover the route in **ten days**.
>
> Those interested in attempting all or part of the trail should pick up a copy of Hilary Whitton Paipeti's excellent *Companion Guide to the Corfu Trail* (Pedestrian Publications, Corfu; €7.50), which contains detailed **maps** and descriptions of the route, divided into ten daily sectors. A proportion of the profits goes towards maintenance of the trail, and anyone using the trail is asked to contribute €3 for the same reason. You can also log on to Ⓦwww.travelling.gr/corfutrail for information on organized walking packages, including accommodation.

provides the only refreshment. The Cape is also the southern starting point for the **Corfu Trail** (see box above).

# Paxí (Paxos) and Andípaxi

Unusually verdant and still largely unspoilt, **Paxí (Paxos)** has established a firm niche in Greece's tourist hierarchy, despite being the smallest of the main Ionian islands at barely 12km by 4km and having no sandy beaches, no historical sites, and relatively sparse facilities. Yet it has become so popular it is best avoided in high season. It's a particular favourite of yachting flotillas, whose spending habits have brought the island an upmarket reputation, making it just about the most expensive place to visit in the Ionian islands and lending it a rather cliquey air. Most accommodation is block-booked by travel companies, though there are local tour operators whose holiday deals are often a fraction of the price. The few independent rooms get snapped up quickly. The capital, **Gáïos**, is quite cosmopolitan, with delis and boutiques, but northerly **Lákka** and tiny **Longós** are where hardcore Paxophiles head, and by far the best swimming is at Paxí's little sister island, **Andípaxi**.

### Gáïos and around

Most visitors arrive, either by ferry from Igoumenítsa (see p.531) or hydrofoil from Corfu, at the new port, 1km north of **GÁÏOS**, a pleasant town built around a small square on the seafront overlooking two islands, Áyios Nikólaos and Panayía. The island's only museum is the **Folk Museum** (May–Oct daily 10am–2pm & 7–11pm; €2), housed in an old school building on the seafront about 200m south of the square. One room is set up as an eighteenth-century bedroom with some period furniture and costumes. Other items on display from different epochs include kitchen implements, musical instruments, china, stationery and guns.

Given the shortage of rooms, it's advisable to phone ahead: try Gaïos Travel (Ⓣ26620 32033, Ⓦwww.gaiostravel.com) or Bouas Tours (Ⓣ26620 32401,

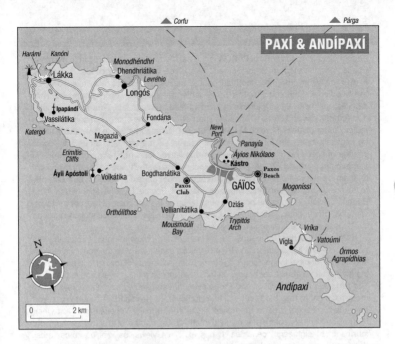

PAXÍ & ANDÍPAXÍ

Ⓦwww.bouastours.gr), both situated on the seafront. Paxí's two most established seasonal **hotels** are both near Gáïos: the *Paxos Beach Hotel* (☎26620 32211, Ⓦwww.paxosbeachhotel.gr; ❺ half-board) which has smart en-suite bungalows on a hillside above a pebbly beach 2km south of town, and the fairly luxurious *Paxos Club* (☎26620 32450, Ⓦwww.paxosclub.gr; ❾), nearly 2km inland from Gáïos.

Gáïos boasts a number of decent **tavernas**, most of which are on the pricey side. The best of the bunch are *Dodo's*, set in a garden inland from the Anemoyiannis statue, which has a full range of *mezédhes* and main courses; *Genesis*, most reasonable of the seafront establishments; and *Vassilis*, which has the best selection and prices of the trio to the left of the road up towards the bus stop. *The Cellar* at the top of the square is the best place for a tasty *souvláki*. *Gonia*, by the Párga kaïki mooring, is the better of the two remaining *kafenía*. Trendier bars include *Remego* on the southern seafront and *Alter Ego* round the quay towards the new port. The *Castello Music Club*, inland beyond the bus stop, is the most established summer disco.

**Inland** are some of the island's oldest settlements, such as Oziás and Vellianitátika, in prime walking country, but with few, if any, facilities. Noel Rochford's book, *Landscapes of Paxos*, lists dozens of walks, and cartographers Elizabeth and Ian Bleasdale's *Paxos Walking Map* is on sale in most travel agencies.

The **coast south** of Gáïos is punctuated by the odd shingly cove, none ideal for swimming, until matters improve towards the tip at **Mogoníssi beach**, which shares some of Andípaxi's sandier geology. There is an eponymous taverna and en route you can take a peek at Fiat supremo Agnelli's distinctive hillside mansion, turrets and all.

### The north of the island

Paxí's one main road runs along the spine of the island, with a turning at the former capital **Magaziá**, leading down to the tiny port of Longós. The main

## Párga

Almost directly opposite Paxí, **PÁRGA** is the most attractive coastal resort in mainland Epirus (Ípiros in modern Greek), spread over three wooded, hilly coves. Historically, it was the Venetians' main foothold on the mainland and was also ruled over by the Napoleonic French, as well as being settled by the Turks, each group leaving its architectural mark. Párga's jumble of low, red-tiled buildings faces out across vegetation-tufted rocks and islets, which are a short swim off some of the best beaches in the region. Unfortunately, it is also Epirus's most popular resort: even in low season it can be hectically busy, and in high summer it heaves. All the same, it can be a welcome change of scene on one of the **day-trips** that leave Gáïos most days of the week in summer (from around €20 per person). You can also use the twice-daily excursion *kaïki* (9.30am & 5.30pm) from Párga as an alternative route to Paxí in summer, as it is happy to take one-way passengers. The crossroads of Spýrou Livadhá and Alexándhrou Bánga, halfway between the port and bus station, is the commercial heart of the town, with post office, banks, ATMs, shops and travel agencies. The **KTEL** station is out on the bypass road, near the end of Spýrou Livadhá.

Of Párga's **beaches**, the pebble strand immediately below the quay is probably the poorest; the smaller **Kryonéri** and **Píso Kryonéri** beaches just to the north are cleaner and quieter; another long strand is **Lýkhnos**, 3km southeast of town. Best, however, is the long, sandy **Váltos beach**, beyond the massive *kástro* that towers above the town. Sea taxis (€2) connect Váltos and Párga every fifteen minutes from 9am onwards for those reluctant to face the twenty-minute slog over the headland. The **kástro** that you pass (8am–midnight; free) is the ruined skeleton of a major Venetian fort, built when Párga was Venice's sole mainland settlement during its rule of the Ionians from the fourteenth to eighteenth centuries. It has excellent views, as well as some rather dangerous unguarded precipices, and makes a good stroll or picnic destination.

Reasonably priced **accommodation** in Párga is notoriously difficult to find from mid-June to late September. Phoning ahead is virtually obligatory, but anyone who finds themselves here without accommodation should first try the Municipal Tourist Office opposite the jetty (℡26840 32107, ⦿www.parga.net). Or you can try one of the friendly rooming houses on the whitewashed lane leading past the *kástro*, such as *Martha's House* (℡26840 31942; ❸). Among the handful of **hotels** not block-booked are the mostly German-patronized *Galini* (℡26840 31581; ❸), set in an orchard below the Váltos road; and the basic but spotless *Golfo Beach* (℡26840 32336; ❹) at Kryonéri, which also has a great restaurant. **Campers** should head for either *Parga Camping* (℡26840 31161), just behind Kryonéri beach, or the newer unobtrusive *Valtos* (May–Sept; ℡26840 31171), at the far end of Váltos beach by the yacht harbour.

Párga's thirty-odd **restaurants** are for the most part rather touristy. One notable exception is the simple and friendly *Oskar* on the westquay, pizza, pasta and salad specialists. The best place on the busier east quay is *To Soúli*, which offers non-greasy *mayireftá* and some grills, the *Eden Bistro* in the inland marketplace is tops for crepes, breakfast and fresh juices, and doubles as a late-night bar.

road continues to Lákka, the island's most idiosyncratic resort, set in a breath-taking horseshoe bay. Buses ply the road between Gáïos and Lákka four or five times a day, most diverting to swing through Longós. The Gáïos–Lákka bus (30min) affords panoramic views, and the route is an excellent walk of under three hours (one-way). A taxi between the two costs around €9.

Approached from the south, **LÁKKA** is an unprepossessing jumble of buildings, but once in its maze of alleys and neo-Venetian buildings, or on the quay with views of distant Corfu, you do get a sense of its charm. Lákka's two **beaches**, Harámi and Kanóni, are none too brilliant for swimming or sunbathing, however. **Accommodation** is plentiful (except in high season) from the area's two biggest agencies: local Routsis (☎26620 31807, ⓦwww.routsis-holidays.com) or the British-owned Planos Holidays (☎26620 31744 or UK 01373 814200, ⓦwww .planos.co.uk), both on the seafront. Paxi's third bona-fide hotel is the snooty and overpriced *Amfitriti Hotel* (☎26620 30011, ⓦwww.amfitriti-hotel.gr; ●). Mercifully, the practice of low-key, freelance camping behind Kanóni has not been affected. There's an embarrassment of good **tavernas**, such as the friendly *Nionios* and neighbouring *Pounentes*, both serving a fine range of Hellenic favourites on the square; the secluded *Ἀ Alexandros*, great for *gourounópoulo* (roast suckling pig) and fresh fish; and more upmarket seafront *La Rosa di Paxos*, which does risottos and ravioli. There's a similar wealth of bars, including the seafront *Harbour Lights* and the friendly *kafenío* of Spyros Petrou – the hub of village life. Lákka is also well situated for **walking**: up onto either promontory, to the lighthouse or Vassilátika, or to Longós and beyond (see box below).

**LONGÓS** is the prettiest village on the island, and perfectly sited for morning sun and idyllic alfresco breakfasts. The village is dominated by the upmarket villa crowd, making the Planos office here (☎26620 31530) the best place to look for independent accommodation. Longós has some of the island's best restaurants: the seafront *Vassilis*, which does terrific fish dishes and tasty starters, *Nassos*, also with a wide variety of fish and seafood, and *O Gios*, a much simpler and cheaper taverna. *To Taxidhi* on the quay is a nice spot for coffee or an early drink, while *Roxi Bar* and *Ores* pander to the night-owls.

Longós has a small, scruffy beach, with sulphur springs favoured by local grannies, but most people swim off **Levrehió beach** in the next bay south, which gets the occasional camper. Islanders are touchy about camping for fear of fires so it's politic to ask at the beach taverna if it's acceptable. Longós is at the bottom of a steep winding hill, making **walking** a chore, but the short circle around neighbouring **Dhendhriátika** provides spectacular views and allows access to the small but excellent **Monodhéndhri beach**, and the walk to **Fondána** and **Magaziá** can be done to coincide with a bus back.

---

### Walks around Lákka

Lákka is perfectly sited for the finest walking on the island. For a simple, short hike, take the track leaving the far end of Harámi beach. This mounts the headland and leads on to the **lighthouse**, where a goat track descends through tough scrub to a sandy open-sea beach with rollers best left to confident swimmers.

Another good walking route heads west into the hills above the village to **Vassilátika**, high on the west coast cliffs, which has stunning views out to sea. From here, the path to the left of the blue-painted stone archway leads on to the most dramatic cliff-edge views (vertigo sufferers beware) and continues to **Magaziá** in the centre of the island, where you can flag down a bus or taxi. There is also the basic *Lilas* **taverna**, if you are in need of a hearty country meal.

The best **walk** on Paxí, however, especially good under a clear early evening sky, is to the church at **Áyii Apóstoli**, almost halfway down the west coast, next to the hamlet of **Voïkátika**, which has a decent taverna. The rough track is signposted a few hundred metres south of Magaziá, and takes less than half an hour on foot. The church and surrounding vineyards overlook the sheer 150-metre **Erimítis cliffs**, which at sunset are transformed into a seaside version of Ayers Rock, turning from dirty white to pink and gold and brown. If you visit Áyii Apóstoli at sunset, take a torch and, after walking back to the trailhead, it's best to return by bus or – more likely – taxi, either of which can be waved down on the main road. The *Sunset* bar, next to the church, can provide a welcome drink to augment the natural splendour and even hosts full-moon parties during the warmer months.

## Andípaxi

A mile south, Paxí's tiny sibling **Andípaxi** has scarcely any accommodation and no facilities beyond several beach tavernas open during the day in season. It is most easily reached by the frequent shuttle *kaïkia* from Gáïos (€6 return). The glass-bottomed boat (€15 return) also takes you to its sea stacks and caves, the most dramatic in the Ionians. Andípaxi's sandy, blue-water coves have been compared with the Caribbean, but you'll have to share them with *kaïkia* and sea taxis from all three villages on Paxi, plus larger craft from Corfu and the mainland resorts.

Boats basically deposit you either at the sandy **Vríka beach** or the longer pebble beach of **Vatoúmi**. Vríka has a taverna at each end, of which *Spiros* (☎26620 31172) has great grilled and oven food and can arrange self-catering accommodation up in **Vígla**, the island's hilltop settlement, on a weekly basis. Vatoúmi also has two restaurants, the justifiably named *Bella Vista* restaurant, perched on a cliff high above the beach, and the newer *Vatoumi*, a little way back from the beach.

For a swim in quieter surroundings, the trick is to head south, away from the pleasure-craft moorings, although path widening has made even the quieter bays more accessible. Paths also lead inland to connect the handful of homes and the southerly lighthouse, but there are no beaches of any size on Andípaxi's western coastline and thick thorny scrub makes it difficult to approach. In the shoulder seasons, there's also the risk of bad weather keeping pleasure craft in port and stranding you on the island.

# Lefkádha (Lefkás)

**Lefkádha** is an oddity, which is exactly why it is some people's favourite Ionian island. Connected to the mainland by a long causeway through lagoons, it barely feels like an island, at least on the busier eastern side – and historically it isn't. It is separated from the mainland by a canal cut by Corinthian colonists in the seventh century BC, which has been redredged (after silting up) on various occasions since, and today is spanned by a 30m pontoon-swivel-bridge. Lefkádha was long an important strategic base, and approaching the causeway you pass a series of fortresses, climaxing in the fourteenth-century castle of **Santa Maura** – the Venetian name for the island. These defences were too close to the mainland to avoid an Ottoman tenure, which began in 1479, but the Venetians wrested back control a couple of centuries later. They were in turn overthrown by Napoleon in 1797 and then the British took over as Ionian protectors in 1810. It wasn't until 1864 that Lefkádha, like the rest of the Ionian archipelago, was reunited with Greece.

The island immediately creates a more positive impression than the mainland just opposite. The whiteness of its rock strata – *lefkás* has the same root as *lefkós*, "white" – is apparent on its partly bare ridges, the highest of which is sadly marred by ugly military and telecom installations. While the marshes and boggy inlets on the east coast can lead to a mosquito problem, the island is a fertile place, supporting cypresses, olive groves and vineyards, particularly on the western slopes. Life in the mountain villages remains relatively untouched, with the older women still wearing traditional local dress – two skirts (one forming a bustle), a dark headscarf and a rigid bodice. The rugged west coast, however, is the star attraction, boasting some of the finest beaches in the archipelago.

Lefkádha has been home to various literati, including two prominent Greek poets, Angelos Sikelianos and Aristotelis Valaoritis, and the American writer Lafcadio Hearn. Support for the arts continues in the form of two well-attended international **festivals** of theatre, music and dance (see box, p.560). On a smaller scale, frequent village celebrations accompanied by *bouzoúki* and clarinet ensure that the strong local wine flows well into the early hours.

Lefkádha remains relatively undeveloped, with just two major resorts: **Vassilikí**, in its vast bay in the south, claims to be Europe's biggest windsurfing centre; **Nydhrí**, on the east coast, overlooks the island's picturesque set of satellite islets, and is the launching point for the barely inhabited island of

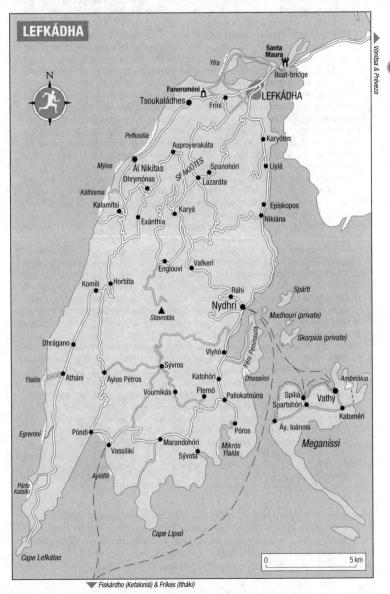

Though the majority of foreign tourists visiting Lefkádha use its airport, few ever see the mainland town of **PRÉVEZA**, 2km to the east. The **airport** actually stands on, and takes its name from, the sandy peninsula of Áktio, off which the Battle of Actium was fought in 31 BC, when the fleet of Octavian decisively defeated that of Antony and Cleopatra. Anyone wishing to stay in Préveza itself is advised to take the Olympic minibus (at Olympic flight times) or a taxi from the airport terminal (around €5 including tunnel toll) or flag down the Lefkádha–Préveza bus at the stop on the main road only a few-minutes' walk away.

Préveza boasts a pleasant seafront and a newly rejuvenated centre, though there are no beaches beyond a thin strip of imported sand. The town is built on a grid system, with most facilities a few-minutes' walking distance from the quay. The old central area is a very attractive warren of alleys, which conceal most of the town's shops and restaurants. It's bookended by two large medieval **forts**, the castles of St George and St Andrew, but both are in use by the armed forces, who have quite a presence in Préveza, and are off-limits to the public. It's also a useful base for visiting **Nikópolis**, the ancient city whose scattered walls and foundations can be seen 7km north of town (site access unrestricted; museum Tues–Sun 8.30am–2.30pm; €3), and the Amvrakikós **wetlands** skirting the **Amvrakikós Gulf** which extends 20km inland from the town. The wetlands are one of the biggest wildlife sanctuaries in Greece, but are only really accessible with your own vehicle.

All **buses** arrive at the KTEL station on Leofóros Irínis, 1km north of the centre on the road to Párga. Services from Athens, Igoumenitsa, Párga, Ioánnina and Thessaloníki are regular if not frequent, and there are four daily services from Lefkádha Town (30min). Those heading south travel via the new tunnel (car toll €3). The municipal tourist office (Mon–Fri 8am–2.30pm) is in the government building at the west end of the seafront, next to the post office.

Because Préveza is very popular with Greek tourists, there is no really cheap **accommodation** in the centre. Of the four central hotels, the smart *Hotel Avra* (☎26820 21230, ⓦwww.epirus.com/hotelavra; ❸), in the middle of the action across the road from the ferry quay, provides the best value, followed by the *Dioni* (☎26820 27381; ❹), a small, comfortable hotel on pedestrianized Platía Papayeoryíou in the centre of town. The nearest **campsite** is *Kalamitsi* (☎26820 22368), around 4km north of town on the main road which skims along a few hundred metres back from the coast.

There are at least a dozen **tavernas** scattered around the inland market lanes in central Préveza, with cafés and bars on the pedestrianized portion of the waterfront boulevard Venizélou. Good eating choices inland include *Psatha*, Dhardhanellíou 4–6 (west of the main shopping strip), for standard oven food; on Grigoríou E, the lane leading seaward from the Venetian clocktower, are several touristy grilled-sardine and bulk-wine specialists; nearby *Iy Trelli Garidha* is better. By night, the bazaar alleys around the clocktower come alive with an assortment of bars, ouzerís and cafés. Two of the best ouzerís for atmosphere and a great selection of inexpensive *mezédhes* are *Kaïxis* at Parthenogoyíou 7 and *To Rembetiko Steki* on Adhrianoupóleos. If you're here in July and August it's worth checking out the programme of concerts and plays put on as part of the **Nikopolía Festival** in Nikópolis.

**Meganíssi**. The completion of the capital's superb **marina** in 2003, however, with a smart reception centre and ample mooring, refuelling and restocking facilities has increased the island's appeal to yachties. There is no tourist office on Lefkádha but for further information you can check out ⓦwww .lefkasgreece.com, the most comprehensive site on the island.

# Lefkádha Town and around

**LEFKÁDHA TOWN** sits at the island's northernmost tip, right where the causeway meets it. Like other capitals in the southern Ionian, it was hit by the earthquakes of 1948 and 1953, and the town was devastated, with the exception of a few **Italianate churches**. As a precaution against further quakes, little was rebuilt above two storeys, and most houses acquired second storeys of wood, giving the western dormitory area an unintentionally quaint look. The town is small – you can cross it on foot in little over ten minutes – and still very attractive, especially around the main square, Platía Ayíou Spyridhónos, and the arcaded high street of Ioánnou Méla. Much of Lefkádha Town is pedestrian-only, mainly because of the narrowness of its lanes. The centre boasts over half a dozen richly decorated private family churches, best visited around services as they are usually locked at other times. Many contain rare works from the Ionian School of painting, including work by its founder, Zakynthian Panayiotis Doxaras.

You can catch a glimpse of the old way of life at the quaint little **Phonograph Museum** (daily 10am–2pm & 7pm–midnight; free), which is dedicated to antique phonographs and bric-a-brac, and sells cassettes of rare traditional music. On the northwestern seafront the modern Cultural Centre houses the newly expanded **archeological museum** (Tues–Sun 8.30am–3pm; €2), which contains interesting, well-labelled displays on aspects of daily life, religious worship and funerary customs in ancient times, as well as a room on prehistory dedicated to the work of eminent German archeologist Wilhelm Dörpfeld. The **municipal art gallery** (daily 9am–1pm & 7–10pm; free) is now also housed in the same complex.

## Practicalities

The new **bus station** is out past the marina, around 1km from the centre of town. It has services to almost every village on the island, with extensive daily schedules to Nydhrí, Vassilikí and Káthisma beaches on the west coast. Car and motorbike rental is useful for exploring; try EuroHire, Golémi 5 (℡26450 26776), near the bus station or I Love Santas (℡26450 25250) next to the *Ionian Star* hotel.

▲ Sunrise over harbour bridge, Lefkádha Town

## Lefkádha summer festivals

Each summer for around fifty years, Lefkádha has hosted two parallel and wide-ranging **cultural festivals**, which these days attract performers and visitors from around the world. These are the International Folklore Festival and Speech & Arts Events. Originally only lasting for two to three weeks in August, they now extend from June to September and are intended to act as a base for artistic efforts on the island year round. They still peak in August, however, adding to the usual high-season demand for accommodation. Troupes come from eastern and western Europe, South America and elsewhere, performing mainly at Santa Maura castle near Lefkádha Town, but also in villages around the island. The island and mainland Greece respond with troupes of their own musicians, dancers and theatrical companies. You can usually enjoy occasional performances of world music and jazz too, as well as art exhibitions and special cinema showings. For details, contact ☎26450 26711 or see ⓦwww.lefkasculturalcenter.gr.

All of the half-dozen **hotels** are in busy areas and none is cheap, but the more expensive ones are glazed against the noise and heat. The *Ionian Star*, Panágou 2 (☎26450 24672, ⓦwww.ionianstar.gr; ❺), has its own pool, a games room and free internet access for guests. The best mid-range hotel is the stylish seafront *Nirikos*, Ayías Mávras (☎26450 24132, ⓦwww.nirikos.gr; ❺), which offers fairly spacious rooms. The *Pension Pyrofani*, just below the square on Dörpfeld (☎26450 25844; ❹), is just as comfortable and almost as pricey. There are simple **rooms** in the dormitory area northwest of Dörpfeld: the Lefkádha Room Owners Association (☎26450 21266; ❷) can help, or try the *Pinelopis Rooms* (☎26450 24175; ❷) at Pinelópis 20, off the seafront two short blocks from the pontoon bridge. Lefkádha Town has no campsite, although there are decent sites at Karyótes and Epískopos, a few kilometres to the south.

The best **restaurants** are hidden in the backstreets: the ⚘ *Regantos* taverna, on Dhimárhou Venióti is the local favourite, serving a delicious array of meat, fish and starters, but only opens in the evenings, when it often has live Lefkadan *kantádhes* (a hybrid of Cretan folk song and Italian opera ballad). At other times, head for the *Eftyhia*, a fine little *estiatório* just off Dörpfeld, or *Romantika* on Mitropóleos, which also has nightly *kantádhes*. Tasty meat, fish and *mezédhes* at very fair prices can be enjoyed at *Agirovoli*, on Golémi.

The most traditional place for a tipple is the *Cafe Karfakis*, on Ioánnou Méla, an old-style *kafenío* with splendid *mezédhes*. Of the **bars** in the main square, the *Cäsbäh* is the most popular, and trendy haunts such as adjacent *Coconut Groove* and *Il Posto* line the seafront west of the bridge. The town's outdoor **cinema**, Eleni, on Faneroménis, has two showings and programmes change daily.

### Around Lefkádha Town

The town has a decent and lengthy shingle and sand beach west of the lagoon at **Yíra**, a thirty-minute walk from the centre. Roughly 4km long, the beach is often virtually deserted even in high season; there's a **taverna** at either end, and a couple of **bars** in the renovated windmills at the western end, as well as the trendy *Club Milos*. The beach's western extension, **Aïyánnis**, is growing in popularity and now has several restaurants, including *Tilegraphos* (☎26450 24881; ❸), which also lets out some **rooms**.

The uninhabited **Faneroméni monastery** (daily 8am–2pm & 4–8pm; free) is reached by any of the west-coast buses, or by a steep hike on foot from town (45min) through the hamlet of Fríni. There's a small museum and chapel, and an ox's yoke and hammer, used when Nazi occupiers forbade the use of bells. There are wonderful views over the town and lagoon from the Fríni road.

The island's **interior**, best reached by bus or car from Lefkádha Town, offers imposing mountainscapes and excellent walking between villages only a few kilometres apart. **KARYÁ** is its centre, and offers some rooms: try the Kakiousis family (☎26450 61136; ❷) or Haritini Vlahou (☎26450 41634; ❶). The leafy town square has a popular taverna, *Iy Klimataria*, just below it and two *psistariés* on it, *Ta Platania*, and the smarter *O Rousos*. Karyá is the centre of the island's lace and weaving industry, with a small but fascinating **folklore museum** set in a lacemaker's home (April–Oct daily 9am–9pm; €2.50). The historic and scenic villages of **Vafkerí** and **Englouví** are within striking distance, with the west-coast hamlets of **Dhrymónas** and **Exánthia** a hike over the hills.

## The east coast to Vassilikí

Lefkádha's east coast is the most accessible and the most developed part of the island. Apart from the campsite at **Karyótes**, *Kariotes Beach* (☎26450 71103), there's little point stopping before the small fishing port of **LIYIÁ**, which has a hotel *Konaki* (☎26450 71127, ⓦwww.hotelkonaki.gr; ❺), as well as a number of restaurants, the best of which is *O Xouras Psarotavérna*. Further on, beyond the *Episcopos Beach* campsite (☎26450 71388), lies **NIKIÁNA**, another fishing village where you'll find the hotel *Pegasos* (☎26450 71766, ⓦwww .hotelpegasos.gr; ❸), as well as the *Christina* pension (☎26450 25194; ❸). In addition, Nikiána has a selection of fine tavernas, notably *Pantazis psistariá*, which also has rooms to let (☎26450 71211; ❸), and *Lefko Akroyiali*, a good fish restaurant further south. Beaches here tend to be pebbly and small.

Most package travellers will find themselves in **NYDHRÍ**, the island's biggest resort by far, with ferry connections to Meganíssi and myriad **boat trips** around the nearby satellite islands and to Itháki and Kefalloniá. The boats line up along the quay each morning, ready for departure between 9 and 10am, returning late afternoon. Tickets are around €10 per person for the local trips, €15–20 for the longer distances. Most craft to the nearby islets are interchangeable: small fibreglass *kaïkia*, with bars and toilets, and open seating areas on the top deck or aft. Where they do differ, however, is in their itinerary – some will take in the sea caves of Meganíssi, others not, so it's advisable to check.

The German archeologist Wilhelm Dörpfeld believed Nydhrí, rather than Itháki, to be the site of Odysseus's capital, and did indeed find Bronze Age tombs on the plain nearby. His theory identifying ancient Ithaca with Lefkádha fell into disfavour after his death in 1940, although his obsessive attempts to give the island some status over its neighbour are honoured by a statue on Nydhrí's quay. Dörpfeld's tomb is tucked away at Ayía Kyriakí on the opposite side of the bay, near the house in which he once lived, visible just above the chapel and lighthouse on the far side of the water.

Nydhrí is an average resort, with a reasonable pebble beach offering watersports and a lovely setting, but the centre is an ugly strip with heavy traffic. The best **place to stay** is the refurbished *Ionian Paradise* (☎26450 92268, ⓦwww .ionianparadise.gr; ❸), set in a lush garden away from the traffic a minute along the Ráhi road, which leads to Nydhrí's very own **waterfall**, a 45-minute walk inland. Rooms are best arranged through any of the resort's many travel agencies – try All Seasons Holidays (☎26450 92623, ⓔallseasons@aias.gr). The town's focus is the Aktí Aristotéli Onássi quay, where most of the rather ritzy **restaurants** and **bars** are found – best of the bunch is the *Barrel* taverna, which offers dishes of reliable quality and quantity. The cheapest places to eat are predictably on the noisy main drag – try *Agrabeli* or *Roza*, an unpretentious little hole-in-the-wall type place that does great grilled *keftédhes* and fish. Nightlife centres on bars like *Iguana* and *The Old Saloon*, and later on the *Sail Inn Club*, which claims to be open for 22 hours of the day – you can have fun trying to work out which two it closes for.

Nydhrí sits at the mouth of a deep inlet stretching to the next village, somnolent **VLYHÓ**, with a few good tavernas and mooring for yachts. Over the Yéni peninsula, across the inlet, is the large **Dhessími Bay**, home to two campsites: *Santa Maura Camping* (☎26450 95007) and *Dessimi Beach Camping* (☎26450 95374), one at each end of the beach but often packed with outsized mobile homes. The ☕ *Pirofani* beach taverna in between them is excellent, dishing up exquisite *mezédhes* such as octopus and *koloukythopittákia*.

The coast road beyond Vlyhó turns inland and climbs the foothills of Mount Stavrotás, through the hamlets of Katohóri and Paliokatoúna to **Póros**, a quiet village with few facilities. Just south of here is the increasingly busy beach resort of **MIKRÓS YIALÓS**, more widely known as Rouda Bay. It boasts a handful of **tavernas**, a few rooms at *Oceanis Studios* (☎26450 95095; ❸), plus the posh *Poros Beach Camping* (☎26450 95452, ⓦwww.porosbeach.com.gr), which has bungalows (❸), shops and a pool. For great food, try the *Rouda Bay* taverna opposite the beach, which also has smart suites (☎26450 95634, ✉manolitsis@otenet.gr; ❹).

A panoramic detour off the main road to quiet **Vournikás** and **Sývros** is recommended to walkers and drivers (the Lefkádha–Vassilikí bus also visits); both places have tavernas and some private rooms. It's around 14km to the next resort, the fjord-like inlet of **SÝVOTA**, 2km down a steep hill (bus twice daily). This is one of the most popular stops for yachting flotillas. There's no beach except for a remote cove, but some fine tavernas, mostly specializing in fish: the ☕ *Palia Apothiki* is the most attractive and serves giant shrimps wrapped in bacon, but the *Delfinia* and *Ionion* also draw numerous customers. Just above the middle of the harbour there are **rooms** of varying sizes at *Sivota Apartments* (☎26450 31347; ❸) or you can ask at any of the seafront supermarkets.

Beyond the Sývota turning, the mountain road dips down towards Kondárena, almost a suburb of **VASSILIKÍ**, the island's premier watersports resort. Winds in the huge bay draw vast numbers of windsurfers, with light morning breezes for learners and tough afternoon blasts for advanced surfers. The largest of the three beach windsurf centres, British-run Club Vassiliki (☎26450 31588, ⓦwww.clubvass.com), offers all-in **windsurfing tuition** and accommodation deals; Wildwind is another UK-based operation (ⓦwww.wildwind.co.uk). Booking your **accommodation** ahead is advisable in high season: *Pension Hollidays* (☎26450 31011; ❸), round the corner from the ferry dock, is a reasonable option with air conditioning and TV in all rooms. In the centre of town you'll find the good-value *Vassiliki Bay Hotel* (☎26450 31077, ⓦwww.vassilikibay.gr; ❸), with full amenities. Rooms and apartments are available along the beach road to Póndi: try the smart and purpose-built *Billy's House* (☎26450 39363; ❸) or ask at the central Samba Tours (☎26450 31520, ⓦwww.sambatours.gr; ❸).Vassilikí's only **campsite**, the large *Camping Vassiliki Beach* (☎26450 31308), is about 500m along the beach road; it has its own restaurant, bar and shop.

Vassilikí's pretty quayside is lined with **tavernas** and bars: the most popular places are *Penguins*, specializing in fish and seafood dishes like *marinara*, and *Alexander*, which has pizza as well as Greek cuisine. Quieter spots round the headland include the *Jasmine Garden* Chinese and the leafy *Apollo* taverna. The best place for a coffee or **drink** is *Livanakis kafenío* (next to the bakery), now modernized but still genuine and cheap. Vassilikí's **nightlife** matches its popularity with high spending youth, although you might say style outstrips content. Bars along the front have different music policies and each attracts its own faithful following. The best bar on the road down to the harbour is

*Abraxas Tunnel*, a cosy hole-in-the-wall place with imported beer. Meanwhile, on the beach, *Remezzo* gets more than its fair share of poseurs and designer beefcakes.

The beach at Vassilikí is stony and poor, but improves 1km on at tiny **Póndi**; most non-windsurfers, however, use the daily *kaïki* trips to nearby Ayiófili or around Cape Lefkátas to the superior beaches at Pórto Katsíki and Egremní on the sandy west coast (see p.564). There's a gradually increasing number of **places to stay** at Póndi, some with great views of the bay and plain behind. One fine spot is the terrace of the *Ponti Beach Hotel* (☎26450 31572; ❺), a rather dated sixties-era hotel very popular with holidaying Greeks, but the restaurant and bar are fair enough. The *Nefeli* (☎26450 31378, ✉clubnefeli @hotmail.com; ❸), right on the beach, is much better value though. The *Panorama* **taverna** serves delights such as garlic prawns and steak Diana.

## The west coast

Around 10km southwest of Lefkádha Town, the road plunges down to the sand-and-pebble **Pefkoúlia beach**, one of the longest on the island, with two tavernas towards the north end, one of which, *Pelagos*, has rooms (☎26450 97070, ✉mypelagos@can.gr; ❸), and there is unofficial camping down at the other end, over 1km away. This part of the island suffered severe structural damage but mercifully no fatalities in the earthquake of summer 2003, which closed the main road, now protected by huge concrete and steel mesh barriers.

Jammed into a gorge between Pefkoúlia and the next beach, Mýlos, is **ÁÏ NIKÍTAS**, the prettiest resort on Lefkádha, a jumble of lanes and small wooden buildings. The back of the village is a dust-blown car park, which has completely taken over the former campsite, but this means that the village itself is now a pedestrian zone, at least in theory. The most attractive **accommodation** is in the ⚘ *Pension Ostria* (☎26450 97483; ❹), a beautiful blue-and-white building above the village, decorated in a mix of beachcomber and ecclesiastical styles. The *Villa Milia* (☎26450 97475; ❸), by the junction, offers cosy rooms and a warm welcome. Other options line the main drag or hide in the alleys running off it; the best bets are the small *Aphrodite* (☎26450 97372; ❷) and quieter *Olive Tree* (☎26450 97453, ⓦwww.olivetreelefkada.com; ❹), which is also signposted from the main road. The best tavernas include the *Sapfo* fish taverna by the sea, the *T'Agnantio*, just above the main street, which serves excellent traditional cuisine, and *O Lefteris*, a good inexpensive restaurant on the main street. *Captain's Corner* near the beach is the liveliest drinking venue, while *En Plo* is a pleasant café-bar overlooking the sea.

Sea taxis (€2 one-way) ply between Áï Nikítas and **Mýlos beach**, or it's a 45-minute walk (or bus ride) to the most popular beach on the coast, **Káthisma**, a shadeless kilometre of fine sand, which becomes nudist and a lot less crowded beyond the large jutting rocks halfway along – freelance camping still goes on at this end too. Of the two tavernas on the beach, choose the barn-like *Kathisma* (☎26450 97050, ⓦwww.kathisma.com; ❹), which also has smart apartments. The *Club Copla* has now established itself as a favourite with the night-time crowd, holding regular parties and raves to a techno soundtrack. Above the beach the upgraded *Sunset* has **rooms** (☎26450 97488, ⓦwww.sunsetstudios .gr; ❺), while the nearby *Hotel Sirius* (☎26450 97025, ⓦwww.hotelsirios.gr; ❹) also commands fine views.

Beyond Káthisma, hairpin bends climb the flank of Mount Méga towards the small village of **KALAMÍTSI**, a much cheaper base for this area. Good-value **rooms** or apartments can be found at the smart *Blue and White House* (☎26450 99413, ⓦwww.bluewhitehouse.com; ❸) and the newer *Pansion Nontas*

(☎26450 99451; ❸). There are also a few decent **tavernas**, including the *Paradeisos*, set in its own garden with fountain, the more basic *Ionio* and, just north of the village, the aptly titled *Panoramic View*. Three kilometres down a newly paved road is the village's quiet sandy beach.

South of Kalamítsi, past the hamlets of **Hortáta**, which boasts the excellent *Lygos* taverna with rooms (☎26450 33395, ✉aglakost@freemail.gr; ❷), and Komíli, the landscape becomes almost primeval. At 38km from Lefkádha Town, **ATHÁNI** is the island's most remote spot to stay, with a couple of good tavernas which both have great-value rooms: ⚓ *Panorama* (☎26450 33291; ❷) and *O Alekos* (☎26450 33484; ❷), the latter only open in high season. Three of the Ionian's choicest **beaches**, where azure and milky turquoise waves buffet strands enclosed by dramatic cliffs, are accessible from Atháni: the nearest, reached by a 4km paved road, is **Yialós**, followed by **Egremní**, down a steep incline unpaved for the last 2km; the former has the *Yialos* café-restaurant and a couple of *kantínes*, the latter just one *kantína*. Further south, an asphalted road leads to the dramatic and popular twin beach of **Pórto Katsíki**, where there are several better-stocked *kantínes* on the cliff above.

Keeping to the main road for 14km from Atháni will bring you to barren **Cape Lefkátas**, which drops abruptly 75m into the sea. Byron's Childe Harold sailed past this point, and "saw the evening star above, Leucadia's far projecting rock of woe: And hail'd the last resort of fruitless love". The fruitless love is a reference to Sappho, who in accordance with the ancient legend that you could cure yourself of unrequited love by leaping into these waters, leapt – and died. In her honour the locals termed the place Kávos tis Kyrás ("lady's cape"), and her act was imitated by the lovelorn youths of Lefkádha for centuries afterwards. And not just by the lovelorn, for the act (known as *katapondismós*) was performed annually by scapegoats – always a criminal or a lunatic – selected by priests from the Apollo temple whose sparse ruins lie close by. Feathers and even live birds were attached to the victims to slow their descent and boats waiting below took the chosen one, dead or alive, away to some place where the evil banished with them could do no further harm. The rite continued into the Roman era, when it degenerated into little more than a fashionable stunt by decadent youth. These days, in a more controlled modern re-enactment, Greek hang-gliders hold a tournament from the cliffs every July.

## Lefkádha's satellites

Lefkádha has four satellite islands clustered off its east coast, although only one, **Meganíssi**, the largest and most interesting, is accessible. **Skorpiós**, owned by the Onassis family, fields armed guards to deter visitors. **Madhourí**, owned by the family of poet Nanos Valaoritis, is private and similarly off-limits, while tiny **Spárti** is a large scrub-covered rock. Day-trips from Nydhrí skirt all three islands, and some stop to allow swimming in coves. Though officially a dependency of Lefkádha, the more remote island of **Kálamos** is only accessible from the mainland.

### Meganíssi

**Meganíssi**, twenty minutes by frequent daily ferries from Nydhrí, is a large island with limited facilities but a magical, if bleak landscape. Ferries stop first at **Spiliá**, ten minutes by foot below **SPARTOHÓRI**, an immaculate village with whitewashed buildings and an abundance of bougainvillea. The locals – many returned émigrés from Australia – live from farming and fishing and are genuinely welcoming. You arrive at a jetty on a pebble beach with a few tavernas and a primitive but free (for a night or two only) campsite behind the excellent *Stars Taverna*. The village proper boasts three restaurants: a pizza place called the *Tropicana*, which can direct you to **rooms** (☎26450 51486; ❷), as can the simple *Gakias* (☎26450 51050; ❸); the trio is completed by the fine traditional taverna *Lakis*. Further west round the coast at Áyios Ioánnis there is a good beach with the *Il Paradiso* taverna and a makeshift campsite, a great spot to unwind in.

The attractive inland village of **Katoméri** is an hour's walk through magnificent country. It has the island's one **hotel**, the *Meganíssi* (☎26450 51240; ❸), a comfortable place with a restaurant and pool, and a few café-bars. Ten-minutes' walk downhill is the main port of **VATHÝ**, with a few accommodation options, including *Different Studios* (☎26450 22170; ❸) and several highly rated restaurants, notably the waterside taverna, *Porto Vathi*, which Lefkadans flock to on ferries for a Sunday fish lunch, and the *Rose Garden*. The *Twins Bar* by the ferry dock is a friendly spot for a drink. After the high-season madness of Nydhrí, Meganíssi's unspoilt landscape is a tonic, and it's easy to organize a **day-trip** from Nydhrí, getting off at Spiliá, walking via Spartohóri to Katoméri for lunch at the *Meganissi* or down at Vathý, from where you can catch the ferry back. Paths lead from Katoméri to remote beaches, including popular **Ambelákia**, but these aren't realistic on a day-trip.

## Kálamos

**KÁLAMOS**, lying the best part of the way towards the mainland from Meganíssi, is another drowned mountain, mostly bare but with some evergreen woods reaching down as far as its pebbly beaches. It's mainly seen as a stopping-off point for bareboat sailors, some of whom favour it above any other small island in the region. The only public transportation link is a *kaïki* from mainland Mýtikas once a day at noon (sometimes more often in high season).

Kálamos has just one village, **HÓRA**, with some **rooms**, although these are often booked through the summer – try calling the Lezentinos family (☎06460 91238; ❷). Hóra is spread out above the small harbour, and is one of the few villages in the area that survived the 1953 earthquake, the epicentre of which was quite close by. Beside the harbour there's the large taverna *Akroyiali* (☎06460 91358; ❷), and a few other basic facilities. There are passable beaches within ten to fifteen-minutes' walk either side of Hóra, and the westerly one has a sporadically opening taverna. Given the lack of accommodation, freelance camping is quite acceptable on these or any of the island's other coves but many of them are only really accessible by sea.

With just one road winding around the 920m top of Mount Vouní, Kálamos provides excellent, if limited, walking terrain. The fortified former capital, **Kástro**, now deserted and overgrown, is near the summit, a ninety-minute walk from Hóra, and its five-bastioned castle is surrounded by derelict buildings. The road also goes to the monastery of **Áyios Yeóryios**, which is open to visitors. The longest walk on the island, to the deserted village of **Pórto Leóne,** is a two-hour hike across the mountainside with fantastic views over Kastós.

# Kefaloniá

**Kefaloniá** is the largest of the Ionian islands – a place that has real towns as well as resorts. Like its neighbours, Kefaloniá was overrun by Italians and Germans in World War II; the "handover" after Italy's capitulation in 1943 led to the massacre of over five thousand Italian troops on the island by invading German forces, as chronicled by Louis de Bernières in his novel, *Captain Corelli's*

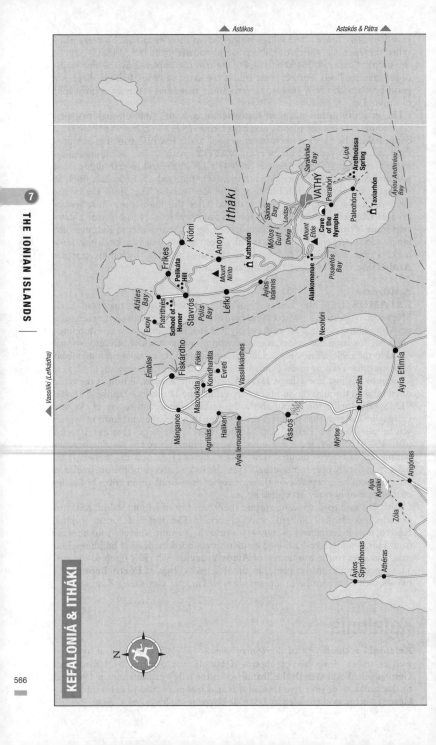

KEFALONIÁ & ITHÁKI

N

▲ Astákos

Astakós & Pátra ▲

◀ Vassilikí (Lefkádha)

Ith-áki

Astakós

Sarakíniko Bay

VATHÝ

Skínos Bay

Loútsa

Perahóri

Lípa

Arethoússa Spring

Paleohóra

Taxiárhon

Ayíou Andhréou Bay

Cave of the Nymphs

Mólos Gulf

Dhexá

Mount Etós

Katharón

Anoyí

Kióni

Fríkes

Pelikáta Hill

Mount Nírito

Ayios Ioánnis

Alálkomenae

Pisaetós Bay

School of Homer

Platrithiés

Stavrós

Lefkí

Afáles Bay

Exoyí

Pólis Bay

Émblisi

Fiskárdho

Fókis

Évreti

Kondharáta

Vassilikiádhes

Neohóri

Mazoukáta

Mánganos

Agriliás

Halikéri

Ayía Ierousalím

Ássos

Mýrtos

Dhívaráta

Ayía Efímia

Angónas

Ayía Kyriáki

Zóla

Ayíos Spyrídhonas

Athéras

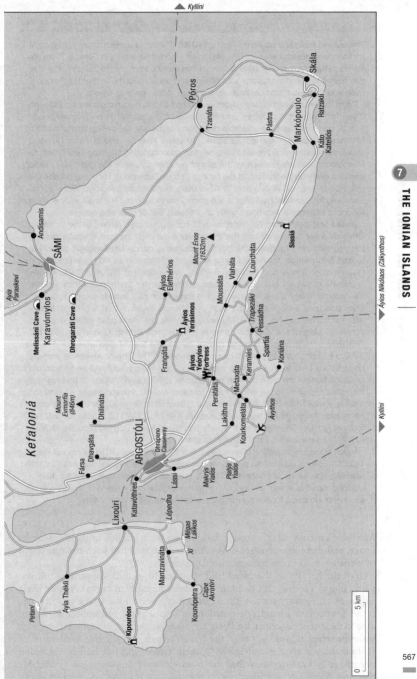

▲ *Kyllíni*

*Kefaloniá*

Póros

Skála

Tzanáta

Ratzaklí

Pástra

Markópoulo

Káto
Kateliós

Andisamis

SÁMI

*Ayía
Paraskeví*

Mount Énos
*(1632m)*

Sissiá ⚓

Melissáni Cave

Karavómylos

Vlaháta

Lourdháta

Ávios
Eleuthérios

Moussáta

Dhrogaráti Cave

*Trapezáki*

Ávios Yerásimos

Pessádha

Frangáta

Spartiá

Koriána

Ávios
Yeóryios
Fortress

Keramiés

Metaxáta

Mount
Evmorfía
*(846m)*

Peratáta

Lakíthra

Kourkomeláta

*Ávithos*

Dhilináta

Dhrápano
Causeway

ARGOSTÓLI

Dhavgáta

Lássi

*Makrýs Yialós*

*Plátys Yialós*

Fársa

Lixoúri

Katavóthres

*Lépedha*

*Mégas
Lákkos*

Mantzaváta

*Xí*

Ayía Thékli

*Pétani*

Kounópetra

Cape
Akrotíri

Kipouréon

▶ *Ávios Nikólaos (Zákynthos)*

▶ *Kyllíni*

0 ____ 5 km

## Pátra

The busiest mainland port after Pireás, **PÁTRA** (Patras) is a major stopping-off point for travellers moving between Italy, the Ionian islands and mainland Greece. There are ferries to Kefaloniá and Itháki and a direct bus service via Kyllíni to Zákynthos. It also has train and bus connections with Athens and services to the rest of the Peloponnese and some northern destinations – though, oddly, no civil airport.

Pátra itself is not particularly attractive and has little to detain the traveller, although if you find yourself in between connections you can easily while away a few hours. Patra's two main sights, visible from most parts of the city, are the *kástro* and basilica of Ayíou Andhréou. Reached via some 190 steps from the end of Ayíou Nikoláou street, the **kástro** ruins are set in a quiet park, commanding stunning views north to Messolóngi, and are sometimes the site of outdoor concerts. The giant jelly-mould **basilica of Ayíou Andhréou**, at the far end of town, opened in 1979 and houses the relics of St Andrew, who is said to have been martyred on this spot. There are no beaches or major historical sites in the immediate vicinity, but Pátra is handy enough for ancient **Olympia**, two hours away by frequent bus or train connections.

**Buses** and **trains** from Athens arrive within a few hundred metres of the ferries on Óthonos & Amalías, in an area that resembles a rail shunting yard. If you're passing through with time to spare, the train station has a handy **left luggage** office. For **tourist information**, the helpful, large Info Center Patras, in an old raisin-processing factory at Óthonos and Amalías 6 (daily 8am–10pm; ☎26104 61740, ⓦwww .infocenterpatras.gr), has a good photographic gallery of the province's attractions, free internet (30min) and, amazingly, free three-hour bike loan (passport required). They also have a kiosk on Platía Trión Symáhon (daily 9am–1pm & 5–8pm). **Banks** with exchange facilities and ATMs abound, while the main **post office** is on the corner of Mézonos and Zaïmi. There is also a small **British Consulate** (☎26102 77079) at Bótsi 2, several hundred metres west of the train station.

Pátra is built on a grid system, much of it one-way. The long cross-streets are very busy, so it's best to try for accommodation off the main roads and away from the seafront. **Hotels** are often booked out, despite standards not being all that high for the rates charged, so expect to have to shop around. Handy places include the *Atlanta*, Zaïmi 10 (☎2610 220 098, ⓔatlanta@pat.forthnet.gr; ⓞ), which offers good off-season discounts and the *Adonis*, Kapsáli 8 (☎2610 224 213, ⓔhoteladonis@pat. forthnet.gr; ⓞ). There is also a **youth hostel** at Iróön Polytekhníou 68 (☎2610 427 278; €9 per bed) but it's 1.5km east of the centre.

Much of the town's **eating** is uninspired, like the cheap *souvláki* joints around Platía Trión Symáhon, with better places well hidden or in the flashier suburbs. Try the seafront *Apanemo*, opposite the fishing harbour at Óthonos & Amalías 107, a seafood taverna noted for its *galaktoboúreko* dessert, or the *Avli tou Yenneou*, another good place for fish on Paraskhoú, not far from the youth hostel.

*Mandolin*. Virtually all of its towns and villages were levelled in the 1953 earthquake, and these masterpieces of Venetian architecture had been the one touch of elegance in a severe, mountainous landscape.

Until the late 1980s, the island paid scant regard to tourism; perhaps this was partly due to a feeling that Kefaloniá could not be easily marketed. A more likely explanation, however, for the island's late emergence on the Greek tourist scene is the Kefalonians' legendary reputation for insular pride and stubbornness, plus a good measure of eccentricity. There are, however, definite attractions here, with some **beaches** as good as any in the Ionian islands, and the fine local wines of Robola. Mercifully, the anticipated "Corelli factor" did not lead to the island becoming either oversubscribed or overexpensive, despite some predictable theming. Moreover, the island seems able to soak up a lot of people without feeling at all crowded, and the magnificent scenery speaks for itself, the escarpments culminating in the 1632-metre bulk of **Mount Énos**, a national park.

For **airport** arrival, see the **Argostóli** section on p.598. Kefaloniá's **bus** system is basic but reliable, and with a little legwork it can be used to get you almost anywhere on the island. Key routes connect Argostóli with the main tourist centres of **Sámi**, **Fiskárdho**, **Skála** and **Póros**. There's a useful connection from Sámi to the tiny resort of **Ayía Efimía**, which also attracts many package travellers. Those with their own transport will not want to miss the chance to explore the delightful **Lixoúri peninsula**. If you're using a motorbike, take care: roads can be very rough off the beaten track – although all the major routes have now been surfaced – and the gradients can sometimes be a bit challenging for underpowered machines. The island has a plethora of **ferry** connections (see p.598) principally from Fiskárdho to Lefkádha and Itháki, and from Sámi to Itháki, Astakós and Pátra, as well as links from Argostóli and Póros to Kyllíni and Pessádha to Zákynthos. Direct sailings between Sámi and one of the Italian ports – usually Brindisi – are offered most years in peak season only, by just one company.

## Sámi and around

Most boats dock at the large and functional port town of **SÁMI**, near the south end of the Itháki straits, more or less on the site of ancient Sami. This was the capital of the island in Homeric times, when Kefaloniá was part of Ithaca's maritime kingdom: today the administrative hierarchy is reversed, Itháki being considered the backwater. With the only ferry link to Pátra, frequent connections to Itháki and direct (albeit erratic) links to Italy, the town is clearly preparing itself for a burgeoning future. The long sandy beach that stretches round the bay is quite adequate; 2km beyond ancient Sami lies a fine pebble beach, **Andísamis**, with the lively *Mojito Beach Bar* providing refreshments and some watersports.

The town has three big **hotels**: the friendly *Athina* (☎26740 23067, ⓦwww .athina-beach-hotel.com; ⑨), is the better of the two at the far end of the beach, actually in Karavómylos, while the *Pericles* (☎26740 22780; ④), which has extensive grounds, two pools and sports facilities, lies over 1km along the Argostóli road. The best mid-range bet is the comfortable seafront *Kastro* (☎26740 22282, ⓦwww.kastrohotel.com; ④), followed by the *Melissani* (☎26740 22464; ④), up behind the main dock. Sámi's **campsite**, *Camping Karavomilos Beach* (☎26740 22480, ⓔvalettas@hol.gr), has over three hundred well-shaded spaces, a taverna, shop and bar, and opens onto the beach – it is by far the better of the island's two official sites.

Sámi's **tavernas** are dotted along the seafront; *Mermaid* and *O Faros*, both with a decent selection of vegetable and meat dishes, including the famous local meat pie, are the best of the central bunch. Better still, head further along the beach to *Dionysos*, where you can sample fresh seafood at low prices and hear live music at weekends. The inevitably renamed *Captain Corelli's* and *Aqua Marina* are the favourite **bars** in the evenings, while the *Asteria bouzoúki* club on the road to Karavómylos can make for a lively and amusing night out. The seafront Sami Center (☎26740 22254) rents out **motorbikes** at fair rates and Island (☎26740 23084, ⓔislecars@otenet.gr) is a reliable local **car rental** company. A seasonal municipal **tourist office** (May–Sept 9am–7pm), a short way back from the dock, can help with orientation.

### The Dhrogaráti and Melissáni caves

The main reason to stay in Sámi is its proximity to the Drogharáti and Melissáni caves; the former is 5km out of town towards Argostóli, the latter 3km north towards Ayía Efimía. A very impressive stalagmite-bedecked chamber, **Dhroga-ráti** (April–Oct daily 9am–8pm; €4) is occasionally used for concerts thanks to its marvellous acoustics. **Melissáni** (daily 8am–7pm; €6) is partly submerged in brackish water, which, amazingly, emerges from an underground fault extending the whole way underneath the island to a point near Argostóli. At that point, known as Katavóthres, the sea gushes endlessly into a subterranean channel – and, until the 1953 earthquake disrupted it – the current was used to drive sea mills. That the water, now as then, still ends up in the cave has been shown with fluorescent tracer dye. The beautiful textures and shades created by the light pouring through the collapsed roof of the cave make it a must.

### Ayía Efimía

**AYÍA EFIMÍA**, 9km north of Sámi, is a friendly little fishing harbour popular with package operators, yet with no major developments. Its two drawbacks are its beaches, or lack thereof – the largest, risibly named Paradise beach, is a pathetic 20m of shingle, although there are other coves to the south – and its poor transport connections (only two daily buses to Sámi and Fiskárdho). It is, however, home to one of the island's few **scuba diving** enterprises, the Aquatic Scuba Diving Club (℗ 26740 62006, Ⓦ www.aquatic.gr). **Accommodation** here is confined to one hotel, the welcoming *Moustakis* (℗ 26740 61030, Ⓦ www.moustakishotel.com; ❹) and a selection of apartments – try Yerasimos Raftopoulos (℗ 26740 61233; ❷). The *Paradise Beach* **taverna**, furthest round the headland past the harbour, is the place for moderately priced island cuisine; the *Pergola* and *To Steki Ton Kalofagadhon* also both offer a wide range of island specialities and standard Greek dishes. Predictably, the café-bar where the film crew and actors used to hang out has been renamed *Captain Corelli's*, while *Strawberry Zaharoplastío* is the place for a filling breakfast. If you are making your own way between here and Sámi, the ⚔ *Ayía Paraskeví* taverna, at the tiny cove of the same name, is famous for its delicious spaghetti with mussel marinade and boasts a great setting.

## Southeast Kefaloniá

Travel **southeast from Sámi** has been made a lot easier by the completion of the asphalt road to **Póros** and the consequent addition of a twice-daily bus route between the two. Continuing south, Póros is connected to **Skála** by another coastal road, which then loops back round to rejoin the main road to Argostóli, from which there is easy access to smaller resorts such as **Káto Kateliós** and **Lourdháta**.

### Póros

**PÓROS** was one of the island's earliest developed resorts, and definitely gives the impression of having seen better days. The town's small huddle of hotels and apartment blocks is almost unique on Kefaloniá, and not enhanced by a scruffy seafront and thin, pebbly beach.

Póros does, however, have a regular ferry link to **Kyllíni** on the Peloponnesian mainland, a viable alternative to the Sámi–Pátra route. Póros is actually made up of two bays: the first, where most tourists are based, and the actual harbour, a few minutes over the headland. There are plenty of rooms, apartments and a few **hotels**. The best deal is at the cosy *Santa Irina* (℗ 26740 72017, ✉ maki@otenet .gr; B&B; ❷), by the crossroads inland, whose low rate includes breakfast, while the nearby *Odysseus Palace* (℗ 26740 72036, Ⓦ www.odysseuspalace.eu; ❺) often gives good discounts. Among **travel agents**, Poros Travel by the ferry dock (℗ 26740 72476) offers a range of accommodation, as well as services such as car rental and ferry bookings. The main seafront has the majority of the **restaurants** and **bars**. The *Fotis Family* taverna serves good food in a pleasant setting and the *Mythos* bar has internet access.

The aforementioned road twists 12km around the rocky coastline from Póros to Skála at the southern extremity of the island. It's a lovely, isolated route, with scarcely a building on the way, save for a small chapel, 3km short of Skála, next to the ruins of a **Roman temple**.

## Skála

In total contrast to Póros, the resort of **SKÁLA** is a low-rise development set among handsome pines above a few kilometres of good sandy beach. A **Roman villa** (daily 10am–2pm & 5am–8pm, longer hours in summer; free) and some mosaics were excavated here in the 1950s, near the site of the *Golden Beach Palace* rooms, and are open to the public.

A faithful return crowd keeps Skála busy until well after Póros has closed for the season, and **accommodation** can be hard to find. There are studios and apartments at *Dionysus Rooms* (☎26710 83283; ❷), a block south of the main street, or a range is available through Etam Travel Service (☎26710 83101, ⓦwww.etam-carhire.gr). Of hotels, the cosy *Captain's Hotel* (☎26710 83389, ⓦwww.captainshouse.net; ❸), on the road parallel to the main street to the east, is comfortable and friendly, while the more upmarket *Tara Beach Hotel* (☎26710 83250, ⓦwww.tarabeach.gr; ❹) has rooms and individual bungalows in lush gardens on the edge of the beach. Skála boasts a number of **tavernas**: *The Old Village* and the *Flamingo* are both good spots with a standard range of Greek and continental cuisine, while, on the beach, *Paspalis* serves fish and home-cooking and *Sunrise* offers pizza as well as Greek food. Drinkers head for *Veto* cocktail **bar** and the beachside *Stavento* restaurant-bar, which plays the coolest sounds. The Dolphin Ski Club (☎6973 234692) has a range of watersports facilities.

## Skála to Lourdháta

Some of the finest sandy beaches on the island are just beyond Skála below the village of Ratzaklí, and around the growing micro-resort of **KÁTO KATELIÓS**, which already has a couple of hotels: the smart *Odyssia* (☎26710 81615; ❹) and the mostly German-occupied *Galini Resort* (☎26710 81582, ⓦwww.galini.de; ❹), which has good deals on **apartments** for four. There are also some rooms and apartments available via the local branch of CBR Travel (☎26710 22770, ⓦwww.cbr-rentacar.com; ❸). Of the half a dozen restaurants and cafés at the seafront, the *Blue Sea* taverna is renowned for the freshness and quality of its fish, the *Ostria* offers a wide selection of dishes, while the *Cozy* bar is the prime drinking location. You can rent boats from the Sea Breeze Club (☎6945 335598) from €70 per day. The coast around Káto Kateliós is also Kefaloniá's key breeding ground for the loggerhead **turtle** (see box, p.586); camping on the nearby beaches is therefore discouraged.

The inland village of **MARKÓPOULO**, claimed by some to be the birth-place of homophonous explorer Marco Polo, witnesses a bizarre snake-handling ritual every year on August 15, the **Assumption of the Virgin festival**. The church where this ritual is enacted stands on the site of an old convent. The story goes that when the convent was attacked by pirates, the nuns prayed to be transformed into **snakes** to avoid being taken prisoner. Their prayers were supposedly answered, and each year the "return" of a swarm of small, harmless snakes is meant to bring the villagers good luck. As Mother Nature is unlikely to keep to such a schedule, some discreet snake-breeding on the part of the village priests must be suspected.

Heading further west, the coastline is largely inaccessible until the village of **Vlaháta**, which has some rooms and restaurants, but there's little point in staying up here, when you can turn 2km down to **Lourdháta**, which has a kilometre-long shingle beach, mixed with imported sand. *Adonis* (☎26710 31206; ❸) and *Ramona* (☎26710 31032; ❸) have **rooms** just outside the village on the approach road, while behind the beach the smart new *Christina Studios* (☎26710 31130, ✉christinastudio@in.gr) and *Thomatos Apartments* (☎26710 31656, ✉critithomatos@yahoo.com; ❹) both offer fully equipped kitchen-studios. Of the smattering of **tavernas**, *Diamond,* on the tiny plane-shaded village square, does a good range of vegetarian items, while further up the hill towards Vlaháta, *Dionysus* serves good taverna standards. At the beach itself, *Patritsia* is good for inexpensive fish and *Lorraine's Magic Hill* has good food and a laid-back feel to it. The *Platanos* café back in the village is a friendly watering hole. Another fine beach, reached by a turning from Moussáta, west of Vlaháta, is **Trapezáki**, an attractive strand with just one restaurant by the small jetty. On the hill about 500m above it the luxurious modern *Trapezaki Bay Hotel* (☎26710 31503, ⓦwww.trapezakibayhotel.gr; ❻) offers all mod cons, including spa and beauty treatments; its policy of keeping the same fixed price all season makes it quite good value at the peak but book well ahead.

## Argostóli and around

**ARGOSTÓLI**, Kefaloniá's capital, is a large and thriving town – virtually a city – with a marvellous site on a bay within a bay. The stone bridge, connecting the two sides of the inner bay, was initially constructed by the British in 1813. Known as Dhrápano owing to its sickle shape, the bridge was closed to traffic indefinitely in 2005, making it a much more pleasant walk than previously. The town was totally rebuilt after the 1953 earthquake, but has an enjoyable atmos-phere that remains defiantly Greek, especially during the evening *vólta* around **Platía Valianoa** (formerly Platía Metaxá) – the nerve centre of town – and along the pedestrianized Lithóstroto, which runs parallel to the seafront.

### Arrival and information

Argostóli's modern **Kefaloniá airport** lies 7km south of town. There are no airport buses, and suburban bus services are so infrequent or remote from the terminal that a taxi (at an inflated flat rate of at least €10) is the only dependable connection. Those arriving in Argostóli by bus from Sámi or elsewhere will wind up at the KTEL **bus station**, a minute from the Dhrépano causeway and ten-minutes' walk south of the main square, Platía Valianoú. KTEL runs bus **tours** of the island every Wednesday and Saturday in season (9am–5pm; €17) from the bus station. Argostóli's friendly **tourist office** (Mon–Fri 7.30am–2.30pm; ☎26710 22248), on Andoníou Trítsi at the north end of the seafront, next to the port authority, has information about rooms, piles of brochures and trail guides, and can advise on transport, sites and all resorts around the island. The island-wide Sunbird agency (☎26710 23723, ⓦwww.sunbird.gr) is a reliable outlet for **car** or **motorbike** rental. Excelixis at Minoös 3, behind the church on Lithóstrotou, has **internet** facilities.

### Accommodation

**Hotels** in Argostóli are mostly mid-range and open all year. In a working town with a large permanent population, **private rooms** aren't too plentiful, but you can call the Room-Owners Association (☎26710 29109) to see what's on offer. A number of travel agencies also offer rooms, apartments and villas: try Ainos

# ARGOSTÓLI

**ACCOMMODATION**
| | |
|---|---|
| Chara | E |
| Ionian Plaza | B |
| Kyknos Studios | A |
| Mirabel | C |
| Olga | D |

**RESTAURANTS**
| | |
|---|---|
| Arhondiko | 4 |
| El Greco | 7 |
| Kiani Akti | 1 |
| Kohenoor | 9 |
| Portside | 6 |
| Tzivras | 11 |

**CAFÉS, BARS & CLUBS**
| | |
|---|---|
| Aristofanis | 12 |
| Bass | 10 |
| Bodega | 5 |
| Finikas | 8 |
| Notes | 2 |
| Pub Old House | 3 |

① , ② & Katovóthres ▲

Lixoúri
Ferry Dock

HAROKOPOU
CHAMPOURI
RIZOSPASTON
MOMFERATOU

Anny
Cinema

Police
Station

Port
Authority

Napier
Gardens

PLATIA
VALIÁNOU

K. VERGÓTI

Nomarhía

Focas-Cosmetatos Foundation

LASSIS

I. ZERVOU

VALIANOU

Archeological
Museum

R. VERGOTI

R. VERGOTI

Theatre

Folklore
Museum

Áyios Spyrídhon

VYRONOS

LITHOSTROTO

Cathedral

LASSIS

YIORYIOU VERGOTI

Áyios Nikólaos

V. VANDHOROU

Bell
Tower

Market

Koútavos
Lagoon

LITHOSTROTO

SITEMBORON

A. TRITSI

DHREPANO CAUSEWAY

DHEVOSSETOU

Lássi & Airport ▲

N

0    50 m

Hospital

Bus Station

▼ Skála, Sámi, Fiskárdho & Botanical Gardens

Travel (☎26710 22333, ⓦwww.ainostravel.gr), opposite the archeological museum, or Myrtos at A. Trítsi 117 (☎26710 25895, ⓔmyrtostr@hol.gr). The town's **campsite**, *Argostoli Camping* (☎26710 23487), lies 2km north of the centre, just beyond the Katovóthres sea mills; there's only an infrequent bus service in high season, so you'll probably have to walk and it's rather basic with limited shade.

Chara Corner Dhevossétou and Y. Vergóti ☎26710 22427. A small and extremely simple rooming house with shared bathrooms very close to the Dhrápano causeway and the bus station, with a friendly owner who offers coffee in the leafy courtyard. The only budget hotel left in town. ❶

Ionian Plaza Platía Valiánou ☎26710 25581, ✺www.ionianplaza.gr. One of the ritziest hotels on the island, and surprisingly cheap for what it is – designer decor down to its chic bathroom fixtures. If it's in your budget, this is a good place for some pampering. ❺

Kyknos Studios M. Yeroulánou 4 ☎26710 23398. Good value modern kitchenettes near Platía Valiánou, all a/c and with TV. ❸

Mirabel Platía Valianou ☎26710 25381-3, ✉mirabel@compulink.gr. Tucked into the southeast corner of the main square, with large and comfortable, a/c, en-suite rooms. Reasonable value for its position. ❹

Olga A. Trítsi 82 ☎026710 24981–4, ✺www .olgahotel.gr. Imposing, seafront hotel with a/c and TV in all rooms, but the rooms do not match the grandeur of the lobby. Sizeable off-season discounts. ❺

## The Town

The **Korgialenio History and Folklore Museum** (Mon–Sat 9am–2pm; €3), on Ilía Zervoú behind the Municipal Theatre, has a rich collection of local religious and cultural artefacts, including photographs taken before and after the earthquake. Insight into how the island's nobility used to live can be gained from a visit to the **Focas-Cosmetats Foundation** (Mon–Sat 9.20am–1pm, plus summer 7–10pm; €3), on Valiánoa opposite the provincial government building. It contains elegant furniture and a collection of lithographs and paintings, including works by nineteenth-century British artists Joseph Cartwright and Edward Lear. The refurbished **Archeological Museum** (Tues–Sun 8.30am–3pm; €3), on nearby R. Vergóti, has a sizeable collection of pottery, jewellery, funerary relics and statuary from prehistoric, through Mycenaean to late Classical times. It is well laid out and labelled, rivalling Kérkyra Town's (see p.536) as the best such museum in the Ionians.

### Eating, drinking and nightlife

Local posers hang out at the café-bars lining the square, while more discerning drinkers head for *Pub Old House*, a relaxed hangout behind the playground on

▲ Lithóstroto, Argostóli

Rizospastón, or the more modern *Bodega* en route to it. *Bass*, by the museum, is the town's big late-night indoor club. The quayside bars, particularly the *Aristofanis Kafenío* by the Dhrápano bridge, are quiet, cheap and have the best views. Argostóli's restaurants range from simple oven-food *estiatória* to high quality and expensive fish tavernas, with the odd ethnic place thrown in.

**Arhondiko** Rizospastón 5. Newly renovated, this friendly spot with a small patio, from which you can hear the *kandádhes* from *The Captain's Table* next door without paying silly prices, offers a range of tasty dishes, including some originals like *biftéki* in Roquefort sauce.

**El Greco** K. Vergóti 3. Tucked just southwest of the main square, this family taverna belies its touristic name by serving some exquisite dishes – try the *poutsin italien* (baked potato and cheese) – in a cosy little garden.

**Kiani Akti** A. Trítsi, 5min walk north of the Lixoúri ferry. Unmissable dining experience on a large wooden deck jutting out above the water. Specializes in seafood such as razor clams in mustard sauce and shrimps in ouzo. Friendly service and reasonable prices.

**Kohenoor** Lavrága, just southeast of the square. British-run curry house with an Indian chef, one of the most authentic in the Ionians. All the favourites like *balti*, *korma* and *vindaloo* dishes are available.

**Portside** A. Trítsi 58. Another friendly place on the front, offering an inexpensive selection of grilled and baked meals and salads, washed down with an excellent, aromatic house wine.

**Tzivras** V. Vandhórou 1. A classic daytime-only *estiatório* (closes 5pm) with an impressive range of staples from the oven, including a lot of vegetarian options such as *briám* (potato and courgette bake), helpings of which tend to be large and should probably be ordered on their own.

## South of Argostóli: beaches and Áyios Yeóryios

Many package travellers will find themselves staying in **LÁSSI**, a short bus ride or twenty-minute walk from town. Lássi sprawls unattractively along a busy main road and it cannot be recommended to the independent traveller, although the *Ionio* family-run taverna is worth a stop for its delicious wrapped snapper. At least it has a couple of good sandy beaches, namely **Makrýs Yialós** and **Platýs Yialós**, although they're right under the airport flight path. Further on, **beaches** such as **Ávythos** are well worth seeking out, although if you're walking beyond the inland town of **Kourkomeláta** there is a real, if occasional, risk of being attacked by farm dogs, particularly during the hunting season (Sept 25–Feb 28). There is very little accommodation in the region, and precious few shops or bars. **Pessádha** has a twice-daily ferry link with Zákynthos in summer, but little else, and be warned that the pathetic bus service from Argostóli is no good for connecting with the boats. You'll have to hitch or take an expensive taxi in most cases.

With a scooter, the best inland excursion is to **ÁYIOS YEÓRYIOS**, the medieval Venetian capital of the island. The old town here supported a population of fifteen thousand until its destruction by an earthquake in the seventeenth century: substantial ruins of its **castle** (Tues–Sun 8.30am–3pm; free), now reopened after extensive renovations, churches and houses can be visited on the hill above the modern village of Peratáta. Byron lived for a few months in the nearby village of Metaxáta and was impressed by the view from the summit in 1823; sadly, as at Mesolóngi, the house where he stayed no longer exists. The *Castle* **café-bar** provides refreshments and great views from near the castle gates. Two kilometres south of Áyios Yeóryios is a fine collection of religious icons and frescoes kept in a restored church that was part of the nunnery of Áyios Andhréas.

## Mount Énos and around

At 15km from a point halfway along the Argostóli–Sámi road, **Mount Énos** isn't really a walking option, but roads nearly reach the official 1632m summit. The mountain has been declared a national park, to protect the *Abies cephalonica* firs (named after the island), which clothe the slopes. There are absolutely no facilities on or up to the mountain, but the views from the highest point in the Ionian islands out over Kefaloniá's neighbours and the mainland are wonderful. Out of summer, watch the weather, which can deteriorate with terrifying speed. Not far before the mountain turning, taking a detour towards Frangáta is doubly rewarded by the huge and lively **Áyios Yerásimos monastery** (daily 9am–1pm & 4–8pm), which hosts two of the island's most important festivals (Aug 15 and Oct 20); the most interesting feature is the double cave beneath the back of the sanctuary, where the eponymous saint meditated for lengthy periods. Right behind the monastery, the **Robola winery** (April–Oct daily 7am–8.30pm; Nov–March Mon–Fri 7am–3pm; ®www.robola.gr) offers a free self-guided tour and generous wine-tasting.

## Lixoúri and its peninsula

Half-hourly ferries (hourly in winter) ply between the capital and **LIXOÚRI** throughout the day until after midnight. The town was flattened by earthquakes, and hasn't risen much above two storeys since. It's a little drab, but has good restaurants, quiet hotels and is favoured by those who want to explore the eerie quake-scapes left in the south and the barren north of the peninsula. **Hotels** are not especially plentiful or cheap, but two comfortable air-conditioned options are *La Cité* (®26710 92701; ❹), four blocks back from the front, and a beach hotel just south of town, *Summery* (®26710 91771, ®www.hotelsummery.gr; ❺). Two agencies offer cheaper accommodation around town and further afield: A.D. Travel (®26710 93142, ®www.adtravel.gr) on the main road through town, and Perdikis Travel (®26710 92503) on the quay. Among the tavernas, ⚵ *Akrogiali* on the seafront is excellent and cheap, drawing admirers from all over the island. *Iy Avli*, on the block behind, serves a variety of dishes in a leafy garden, while *Adonis* is a good basic *psistariá* at the back of the square. *Overdose* is the trendy place to drink on the square, while the old seafront *kafenía* have unfortunately been replaced by youth-orientated cafés such as *Club Vamos*.

Lixoúri's nearest beach, a two-kilometre walk south, is **Lépedha**, composed of rich-red sand and backed by low cliffs, as are **Xí** and **Mégas Lákkos** (the name means "big hole") beaches, both of which are served by bus from Lixoúri and have restaurants and accommodation. Around 4km southwest lies the quieter beach at **Kounópetra**, site of a curious rock formation. Until the 1953 earthquake, this "rocking stone", as the name signifies in Greek, had a strange rhythmic movement that could be measured by placing a knife into a gap between the rock and its base. However, after the quake the rock became motionless. Two kilometres further west, in an area known as Vátsa, the last beach of any size on the southern tip of the peninsula is sandy **Áyios Nikólaos**. The strand is very quiet and has no accommodation, but the friendly ⚵ *Spiaggia* restaurant serves excellent pasta, seaweed salad and seafood.

Those with transport can also strike out for the rugged western coast of the peninsula, first visiting the monastery at **Kipouréon**, then heading north to the spectacular beach at **Petaní**. Here there are two restaurants, the better being the further of the two, *Xouras*, whose friendly Greek-American owner Dina has rooms (®26710 97128, ®petani@in.gr; ❹) or you can stay up on the access road at the *Niforo* apartments (®26710 97350; ❹). Tucked in the fold of the **Áyios Spyrídhonas** inlet, the beach of **Pórto Athéras**, which serves the traditional village of Athéras, a short way inland, is another fine strip of sand with shallow water that's safe for swimming. There is an ouzerí and the *Yialós* **taverna**, whose garden acts as home for families with camper vans and could be used for camping.

# The west coast and the road north

The journey between Argostóli and Fiskárdho is the most spectacular ride in the archipelago. Leaving town, the road rises into the Evmorfia foothills, where you can detour a short way inland to visit the modest **Museum of Natural History** (summer Mon–Fri 9am–1pm & 6–8pm, Sat & Sun 9am–1pm, rest of year Sun–Fri 9am–1pm; €1.50) at **Dhavgáta**. Continuing to rise beyond Agónas, where a steep road twists down to the long, sandy beach of **Ayía Kyriakí** below, the coast road clings to near-sheer cliffs as it heads for **Dhivaráta**, which has a smattering of rooms, such as *Mina Studios* (☎26740 61716, ✉markela1@hol.gr; ❸), a couple of restaurants, and is the stop for dramatically photogenic **Mýrtos beach**. It's a four-kilometre hike down the motorable road, with just a couple of seasonal snack-bars, but from above or below this is the most dramatic beach in the Ionian islands – a splendid strip of pure-white sand and pebbles. Sadly, it's shadeless and gets mighty crowded in high season.

Six kilometres on is the turning for the atmospheric village of **ÁSSOS**, clinging to a small isthmus between the island and a huge hill crowned by a ruined fort. It can get a little claustrophobic, but there's nowhere else quite like it in the Ionians. Accommodation is scarce so it's wise to book: try the neat and friendly *Cosi's Inn* (☎26740 51420, ⊛www.cosisinn.gr; ❸), the posher *Kanakis Apartments* (☎26740 51631, ⊛www.kanakisapartments.gr; ❹) or, more standard, *Andhreas Rokos' rooms* (☎26740 51523; ❷); all three are on the approach road. Ássos has a small pebble beach, and three tavernas on a plane-shaded village square backed by mansions, mostly now restored after being ruined in the quake; the *Nefeli* does a nice line in seafood, *mezédhes* and salads, while the *Platanos Grill* is better for meat.

## Fiskárdho and around

**FISKÁRDHO**, on the northernmost tip of the island, sits on a bed of limestone that buffered it against the worst of the quakes. Two **lighthouses**, Venetian and Victorian, guard the bay, and the ruins on the headland are believed to be from a twelfth-century chapel begun by Norman invader Robert Guiscard, who gave the place its name. The nineteenth-century harbour frontage is intact, and is nowadays occupied by smart restaurants and chic boutiques. There is a new **Environmental and Nautical Museum** (summer Mon–Fri 10am–6pm, Sun 10am–2pm; donations), housed in a renovated Neoclassical mansion on the hill behind the village. The volunteers who curate it conduct valuable ecological research and can also arrange **scuba diving** (☎26740 41182, ⊛www.fnec.gr). Daily **ferries** connect Fiskárdho to Itháki and Lefkádha in season. You can rent motorboats from €45 per day at Regina (☎6938 984647), on the quay.

The island's premier resort, Fiskárdho remains busy through to the end of October, with **accommodation** at a premium. The cheapest rooms are at welcoming *Regina's* (☎26740 41125; ❸), up by the car park, and those of Sotiria Tselenti (☎26740 41204, ⊛www.fiskardo-ellis.gr; ❸), arranged through the bakery 50m back from the tiny square. A splendid if pricey option is the beautifully converted mansion *Archontiko* (☎26740 41342; ❻), above and behind a harbourfront minimarket. Pama Travel (☎26740 41033, ⊛www.pamatravel.com), on the seafront furthest away from the ferry quay, is another source of rooms and costlier apartments. There's a wealth of good but mostly expensive **restaurants**. *Tassia* is famous for a vast range of seafood but check the price of any fish you order carefully, likewise at the *Captain's Table*. Just round the headland past Pama Travel, *Panormos* has much lower prices and a great location. Just off the only square, *Lagoudera* specializes in tasty oven food and now has a second seafront location.

*Irida's* and *Theodora's* are two of the most popular harbourside **bars**. The town's only nightclub spot is *Kastro Club* up at the back of the village.

There are two good pebble beaches close to Fiskárdho – **Émblisi** 1km back out of town and **Fókis** just to the south – and a nature trail on the northern headland. A longer walk starts beyond Fókis beach, cuts up into the hills overlooking Itháki for 4km to **Mazoukáta**, which has a taverna and *kafenío*, before rejoining the main Argostóli–Fiskárdho road at Mánganos 1km further on. An alternative route veers 2km south before Mazoukáta at the partly ruined village of **Tselendáta**, where there are some fine old stone buildings, to the dead-end hamlet of Evretí. From here, where it is claimed Penelope's suitors set their ambush for the returning Odysseus, you can enjoy great views across to both Itháki and Lefkádha. It is worth making the effort to explore the coastal region west of Mánganos. **Alatiés** has a tiny beach tucked in between folds of impressive white volcanic rock but the real gem is the small bay of **Ayía Ierousalím,** whose gravel and sand beach remains quiet even in August. The only development is the extremely friendly ✻ *Odisseas* **taverna** (☎6937 714982; ➋), which has inexpensive rooms and allows camping in its spacious grounds, charging only a small fee for the use of facilities. The family cooks exquisite and very unusual olive bread and other baked goodies, and all the meat is free range, another rarity.

# Itháki

Rugged **Itháki**, Odysseus's legendary homeland, has yielded no substantial archeological discoveries, but it fits Homer's description to perfection: "There are no tracks, nor grasslands … it is a rocky severe island, unsuited for horses, but not so wretched, despite its small size. It is good for goats." In Constantine Cavafy's splendid poem *Ithaca*, the island is symbolized as a journey to life:

When you set out on the voyage to Ithaca
Pray that your journey may be long
Full of adventures, full of knowledge.

Despite the romance of its name, and its proximity to Kefaloniá, very little tourist development has arrived to spoil the place. This is doubtless accounted for in part by a dearth of beaches beyond a few pebbly coves, though the island is good walking country, and indeed the interior with its sites from **The Odyssey** is the real attraction. Most visitors will arrive at **Vathý**, the capital, which enjoys a splendid location, although some arrivees from Kefaloniá will dock at laid-back **Fríkes** or the small port of Pisaetós. An excellent website on the island is ⓦ www.ithacagreece.com.

## Vathý

Ferries from Pátra, Astakós and a minority of those from Kefaloniá land at the main port and capital of **VATHÝ**, a bay within a bay so deep that few realize the mountains out "at sea" are actually the north of the island. This snug town is compact, relatively traffic-free and boasts the most idyllic seafront setting of all the Ionian capitals. Like its southerly neighbours, it was heavily damaged by the 1953 earthquake, but some fine examples of pre-quake architecture remain here and in the northern port of **Kióni**. Vathý has a small **archeological museum** on Kalliníkou (Tues–Sun 8.30am–3pm; free), a short block back from the quay. Near the corner of the quay behind the Agricultural Bank, there is also the moderately interesting **Folklore & Cultural Museum** (summer Mon–Sat 10am–2pm; €1). There are **banks**, a **post office**, police and a medical centre in town.

The oldest of Vathý's **hotels** is the refurbished and air-conditioned *Mentor* (℡26740 32433, ⓦwww.hotelmentor.gr; ❺) in the southeast corner of the harbour. Further on round the bay is the posh *Omirikon* (℡26740 33598; ❻), and, just beyond it, the much better-value ⚘ *Captain Yiannis* (℡26740 33419; ❸), complete with tennis court and pool. The small *Odyssey* (℡26740 32268; ❸) is perched on the hillside a short way up the road to Skínos beach. The best source of rooms, studios or villas is the town's two main quayside travel agents, Polyctor Tours (℡26740 33120, ⓦwww.ithakiholidays.com) and Delas Tours (℡26740 32104, ⓦwww.ithaca.com.gr).

Even though it's tiny, Vathý has a wealth of **tavernas** and **bars**. Many locals head off south around the bay towards the friendly, family-run ⚘ *Paliocaravo* (aka *Gregory's*), popular for its lamb and fish and best of the three fine restaurants in that direction. In town, the excellent *O Nikos*, just off the square, is a good old-fashioned *estiatório*, while *To Kohili* is by far the best of the half-dozen harbourside tavernas serving a good range of *mezédhes*, as well as tasty meat dishes such as lamb *kléftiko*. The town's ancient *kafenío* one street back from the front is the spot for a quiet and inexpensive tipple with the locals. More ambience and eclectic music can be found at *Karamela Café*, opposite the ferry dock.

There are two reasonable pebble **beaches** within fifteen-minutes' walk of Vathý: **Dhéxa**, over the hill above the ferry quay, and tiny **Loútsa**, opposite it around the bay. Better beaches at **Sarakíniko** and **Skínos** are an hour's trek along paved roads leaving the opposite side of the bay. In season, daily *kaïkia* ply between the quay and remote coves.

## Odysseus sights around Vathý

Three of the main **Odysseus** sights are just within walking distance of Vathý: the Arethoússa Spring, the Cave of the Nymphs and ancient Alalkomenae, although the last is best approached by **moped** or **taxi** (no more than €15 round-trip).

### The Arethoússa Spring
The walk to the **Arethoússa Spring** – allegedly the place where Eumaeus, Odysseus's faithful swineherd, brought his pigs to drink – is a three-hour round trip along a track signposted next to the seafront telecoms office. The unspoilt but shadeless landscape and sea views are magnificent, but the walk crosses slippery inclines and might best be avoided if you're nervous of heights.

Near the top of the lane leading to the spring path, a signpost points up to what is said to have been the **Cave of Eumaeus**. The route to the spring continues for a few hundred metres, and then branches off onto a narrow footpath through gorse-covered steep cliffs. Parts of the final downhill track involve scrambling across rock fields (follow the splashes of green paint), and care should be taken around the small but vertiginous ravine that houses the **spring**. The ravine sits below a crag known as **Kórax** (the raven), which matches Homer's description of the meeting between Odysseus and Eumaeus. In summer it's just a dribble of water. You have to return by the same route but you might have time to swim in a small cove a short scramble down from the spring.

### The Cave of the Nymphs
The **Cave of the Nymphs** (Marmarospíli) is about 2.5km up a rough but navigable road signposted on the brow of the hill above Dhéxa beach. The cave

is atmospheric, but it's underwhelming compared to the caverns of neighbouring Kefaloniá and, these days, is illuminated by coloured lights. The claim that this is *The Odyssey*'s Cave of the Nymphs, where the returning Odysseus concealed the gifts given to him by King Alkinous, is enhanced by the proximity of Dhéxa beach, although there is some evidence that the "true" cave was just above the beach, and was unwittingly demolished during quarrying many years ago.

### Alalkomenae

**Alalkomenae**, Heinrich Schliemann's much-vaunted "Castle of Odysseus", is signposted on the Vathý–Pisaetós road, on the saddle between Dhéxa and Pisaetós, with views over both sides of the island. The actual site, however, some 300m uphill, is little more than foundations spread about in the gorse. Schliemann's excavations unearthed a Mycenaean burial chamber and domestic items such as vases, figurines and utensils (displayed in the archeological museum), but the ruins actually date from three centuries after Homer. In fact, the most likely contender for the site of Odysseus's castle is above the village of Stavrós (see below).

The road continues to the harbour of **Pisaetós**, about 2km below, with a large pebble beach that's good for swimming and popular with local rod-and-line fishermen. There is just one *kantína* here, serving those awaiting the regular ferries from Sámi on Kefaloniá.

## Northern Itháki

The main road out of Vathý continues across the isthmus and takes a spectacular route to the northern half of Itháki, serving the villages of **Léfki**, **Stavrós**, **Fríkes** and **Kióni**. There is no regular bus service but it is excellent scooter country; the close proximity of the settlements, small coves and Homeric interest also make it good rambling terrain. Once a day a *kaïki* also visits the last two of those communities – a cheap and scenic ride used by locals and tourists alike to meet the mainline ferries in Vathý. As with the rest of Itháki there is only a limited amount of accommodation.

### Stavrós and around

**STAVRÓS**, the second-largest town on the island, is a steep two kilometres above the nearest beach (Pólis Bay). It's a pleasant enough town nonetheless, with *kafenía* edging a small square dominated by a rather fierce statue of Odysseus. There is even a tiny **museum** (Tues–Sun 8.30am–3pm; free) off the road to Platrithriés, displaying local archeological finds. Stavrós's Homeric site is on the side of **Pelikáta Hill**, where remains of roads, walls and other structures have been suggested as the possible site of Odysseus's castle. Stavrós is useful as a base if both Fríkes and Kióni are full up, and is an obvious stopping-off point for exploring the northern hamlets and the road up to the medieval village of Anoyí. Both Polyctor and Delas handle **accommodation** in Stavrós; the traditional *Petra* taverna (☎26740 31596; ❸) offers rooms. The oldest and best **taverna** is *Fatouros*, and the *Margarita zaharoplastío* is a good place for a drink or to sample the local sweet *rovaní* (syrupy rice cakes).

A scenic mountain road leads 5km southeast from Stavrós to **ANOYÍ**, which translates roughly as "upper ground". Once the second-most important settlement on the island, it is almost deserted today. The centre of the village is dominated by a free-standing Venetian campanile, built to serve the (usually locked) church of the **Panayía**, which comes alive for the annual *paniyíri* on August 14, the eve of the Virgin's Assumption; at other times enquire at the *kafenío* about access to the church, the Byzantine frescoes of which have been heavily restored following centuries of earthquake damage. On the outskirts of the village are the foundations of a ruined **medieval prison**, and in the surrounding countryside are some extremely strange rock formations, the biggest being the eight-metre-high Iraklis (Hercules) rock, just east of the village. The **monastery of Katharón**, 3km further south along the road, has stunning views down over Vathý and the south of the island, and houses an icon of the *Panayía* discovered by peasants clearing scrubland in the area. The monastery celebrates its festival on September 8 with services, processions and music.

Two roads push north of Stavrós: one, to the right, heads 2km down to Fríkes, while the main road, to the left, loops below the hill village of **Exoyí**, and on to **Platrithiés**, where the new *Yefiri* taverna serves a wide range of tasty fare. Just off the start of the road up to Exoyí a signpost points about 1km along a rough track to the supposed **School of Homer**, where excavations still in progress have revealed extensive foundations, a well and ancient steps. The site is unfenced and well worth a detour for its views of **Afáles Bay** as much as the remains. On the outskirts of Platrithiés a track leads down to Afáles, the largest bay on the entire island, with an unspoiled and little-visited pebble-and-sand beach. The landscape around here, thickly forested in parts and dotted with vineyards, provides excellent walking.

### Fríkes

At first sight, tiny **FRÍKES** doesn't appear to have much going for it. Wedged in a valley between two steep hills, it was only settled in the sixteenth century, and emigration in the nineteenth century almost emptied the place – as few as two hundred people live here today – but the protected harbour is a natural year-round port. Consequently, Fríkes stays open for tourism far later in the season than neighbouring Kióni, and has a better range of tavernas. There are no beaches in the village, but plenty of good, if small, pebble strands a short walk away towards Kióni. When the ferries and their cargoes have departed, Fríkes falls quiet and this is its real charm: a downbeat but cool place to lie low.

Fríkes's one **hotel** is the upmarket *Nostos* (℡26740 31644, @www .hotelnostos-ithaki.gr; ❺), which has a pool, or you can try the equally comfy *Aristotelis Apartments* (℡26740 31079, @www.aristotelis-ithaca.gr; ❹). The Gods souvenir shop (℡26740 31021) can help find **rooms**, though in peak season chances are slim. Fríkes has a quartet of good seafront **tavernas**, of which *Rementzo*, with its fresh fish, salads and pizza, and *Ulysses,* specializing in succulent home-style cuisine, stand out. Tucked in the corner of the harbour, the *Isalos* café-bar offers a good ambience, to-die-for cakes and an eclectic taste in music.

### Kióni

**KIÓNI** sits at a dead end 5km southeast of Fríkes. On the same geological base as the northern tip of Kefaloniá, it avoided the very worst of the 1953 earthquakes, and so retains some fine examples of pre-twentieth-century architecture. It's an extremely pretty village, wrapped around a tiny harbour, and tourism here is dominated by British blue-chip travel companies and visiting yachts. The bay has a small **beach**, 1km along its south side, a sand-and-pebble strand below a summer-only snack-bar. Better pebble beaches can be found within walking distance towards Fríkes.

While the best **accommodation** has been snaffled by the Brits, some local businesses have rooms and apartments to let, among them *Captain's Apartments*

(☎26740 31481, ⓦwww.captains-apartments.gr; ❹), set up above the village, and *Maroudas Apartments* (☎26740 31691, ⓔmaroudas@greek-tourism.gr; ❹) closer to the harbour. A quieter option, just a short walk uphill on the main road in the hamlet of Ráhi, are the rooms and studios run by Captain Theofilos Karatzis and his family (☎26740 31679; ❸), which have panoramic views.

Kióni's **restaurants** are dotted around the picturesque harbour, but compare unfavourably with those in Fríkes; *Oasis* has a wide selection and is the best of the bunch, the *Avra* fish taverna is fair enough, while the upmarket *Calypso* taverna has imaginative dishes like pork with artichokes. Village facilities stretch to two well-stocked shops, a post office and a couple of bars and cafés, of which *Spavento* is the place for the best range of sounds.

# Zákynthos (Zante)

**Zákynthos**, southernmost of the six core Ionian islands, is somewhat schizophrenically divided between underdevelopment and indiscriminate commercialization. Much of the island is still green and unspoilt, with only token pockets of tourism, and the main resorts seem to be reaching maximum growth without encroaching too much on the quieter parts.

The island has three distinct zones: the barren, mountainous northwest; the fertile central plain; and the eastern and southern resort-filled coasts. The

biggest resort – rivalling the busiest on Corfu – is **Laganás**, on Laganás Bay in the south, a 24-hour party venue that doesn't give up from Easter until the last flight home in October. There are smaller, quieter resorts north and south of the capital, and the southerly Vassilikós peninsula has some of the best countryside and beaches, including exquisite **Yérakas**.

Although half-built apartment blocks and a few factories are spreading into the central plain, this is where the quieter island begins: farms and vineyards, ancient villages and the ruins of Venetian buildings levelled in the 1948 and 1953 earthquakes. The island still produces fine wines, such as the white Popolaro, as well as sugar-shock-inducing *mandoláto* nougat, whose honey-sweetened form is best. Zákynthos is also the birth-place of *kantádhes*, which can be heard in tavernas in Zákynthos Town and elsewhere. It also harbours one of the key breeding sites of the endangered **logger-head sea turtle** at Laganás Bay (see box, p.586).

# Zákynthos Town

The town, like the island, is known as both **ZÁKYNTHOS** and Zante. This former "Venice of the East" (*Zante, Fior di Levante*, "Flower of the Levant", in an Italian jingle), rebuilt on the old plan after the 1953 earthquake, has bravely tried to recreate some of its style, though reinforced concrete can only do so much.

## Arrival, information and accommodation

Zákynthos is a working town with limited concessions to tourism, although there are hotels and restaurants aplenty, and it's the only place to stay if you want to see the island by public transport. The **bus** station is one block back from the seafront, about halfway along it. **Cars** and **mopeds** can be rented from Eurosky (℡ 26950 26278, ⊛ www.eurosky.gr) at Makrí 6, two blocks south of the main square. On the front nearby, the **tourist police** have a fairly welcoming office (May–Oct daily 8am–10pm; ℡ 26950 24482) in the main police station, which can supply basic information and help people find accommodation. There are a couple of **internet** cafés on pedestrianized Alexándhrou Romá, parallel to the seafront but several blocks back.

The Room Owners Association (℡ 26950 49498) can be contacted for accommodation around town and all over the island. Of the central seafront **hotels**, the *Egli*, on Loútzi (℡ 26950 28317; ❹), has clean, compact rooms, tucked in beside the gargantuan eyesore of the *Strada Marina*. There are quieter hotels in the Repára district beyond Platía Solomoú: try either the *Plaza*, Kolokotróni 2 (℡ 26950 45733; ❸), or the classy and surprisingly inexpensive ⅄ *Palatino*, Kolokotróni 10 (℡ 26950 27780, ⊛ www.palatinohotel.gr; ❹), which has beautifully furnished rooms; both places are near the municipal lido.

## The Town

The town stretches beyond the length of the wide and busy harbour, its main section bookended by the grand **Platía Solomoú** at the north, and the church of **Áyios Dhionýsios** (daily 8am–1pm & 5–10pm), patron saint of the island, at the south. The church is well worth a visit for the dazzling giltwork and fine modern murals inside, and a new **museum**, which has some fine paintings and icons (daily 9am–1pm & 5–9pm; €2). The vestments of St Dhionysios are kept in the restored church of Áyios Nikólaos tou Mólou on Platía Solomoú. The **square** is named after the island's most famous son, the poet Dhionysios Solomos, the father of modernism in Greek literature, who was responsible for establishing demotic Greek (as opposed to the elitist *katharévousa* form) as a literary idiom. He is also the author of the lyrics to the national anthem, an excerpt from which adorns the statue of Liberty in the square. There's an impressive **museum** (daily 9am–2pm; €3) devoted to the life and work of **Solomos** and other Zakynthian luminaries in nearby Platía Ayíou Márkou. It shares its collection with an eponymous museum on Corfu (see p.536), where Solomos spent most of his life.

## Boat trips from Zákynthos

At least ten pleasure craft offer **day-trips** around the island from the quay in Zákynthos Town for around €15. All take in sights such as the **Blue Caves** at Cape Skinári, and moor in **To Naváyio (Shipwreck Bay)** and the **Cape Kerí** caves. You might want to shop around for the trip with the most stops, as eight hours bobbing round the coast can become a bore. Check also that the operators actually take you into the caves.

Platía Solomoú is home to the town's **library**, which has a small collection of pre- and post-quake photography, and the massive **Byzantine Museum** (Tues–Sun 8am–3pm; €3), sometimes referred to as the Zákynthos Museum. The latter is most notable for its collection of artworks from the Ionian School, the region's post-Renaissance art movement, spearheaded by Zakynthian painter Panayiotis Doxaras. The movement was given impetus by Cretan refugees, unable to practise their art under Turkish rule. It also houses some secular painting and a fine model of the town before the earthquake.

Zákynthos's other main attraction is its massive **kástro**, brooding over the hamlet of Bóhali on its bluff above the town. The ruined Venetian fort (daily 8am–7.30pm in summer, 8am–2pm in winter; €1.50) has vestiges of dungeons, armouries and fortifications, plus stunning views in all directions. Its shady carpet of fallen pine needles makes it a great spot to relax or picnic. Below the *kástro* walls, **Bóhali** has a good though expensive taverna with panoramic views.

### Eating, drinking and nightlife

Most of the **restaurants** and bars on the seafront and Platía Ayíou Márkou are bedevilled by traffic, although the seafront *Psaropoula* does fine meat and fish, and the pricey but elegant *Komis*, across the quay from Áyios Dhionýsios, serves unusual seafood dishes and is far enough away from the bustle. First stop though, should be the friendly *Arekia* beyond the lido, which offers a succulent range of dishes and the best nightly *kantádhes* to be heard anywhere. The *Green Boat*, further along, serves up quality meals in a romantic waterside setting. The most popular bars in town are *Base* on Ayíou Márkou, which plays an eclectic dance mix, and the *Jazz Café*, on Tertséti, which, despite the name, is actually a house/techno bar with DJs and a token cover charge.

## The south and west

The busy southern end of the island comprises the **Vassilikós peninsula**, headed by the package resort of **Argási**, and the large sweep of **Laganás Bay**, whose resort of the same name is a major party destination. At the far southwest end of the bay, the landscape ascends into the mountains around **Kerí**, the first of a series of villages along the sparsely inhabited **west coast**.

### Argási

The road heading southeast from Zákynthos passes through **ARGÁSI**, the busiest resort on this coast, but with a beach barely a few feet wide in parts. Although independent travellers would be better off basing themselves at one of the places further down, it could be used as a jumping-off point for the Vassilikós peninsula; there are rooms at the *Pension Vaso* (☎26950 44599; ❸) and *Soula* (☎26950 44864; ❷) just off the main road entering the village, and the seafront boasts some smartish hotels, among them the B&B *Locanda* (☎26950 45386, ⓦwww.locanda.gr; ❹) and the *Iliessa Beach* (☎26950 27800, ⓦwww.iliessa.com; ❹). Beyond a few indigenous tavernas – try *Three Brothers* or *The Big Plate* restaurant – culture is mainly low-brow with set-piece "Greek nights", one notable exception being the *Venetsiana*, which accompanies traditional food with nightly *kantádhes*. Argási is also home to some of the island's biggest and most popular discos on the town side, such as *Byblos* and *Manhattan*, and a host of cheap and cheerful bars in the village.

### The Vassilikós peninsula

The peninsula that stretches southeast of Argási is one of the most attractive parts of the island, with a happy blend of development and natural beauty.

Various maps vaguely identify different inland spots as **Vassilikós** villages, but the real interest lies in the series of small beach resorts, mainly situated on the east coast. The first two are recently developed **Kamínia**, with the comfortable *Levantino* rooms (℡26950 35366, Ⓦwww.levantino.gr; ❹), and the more established **Pórto Zóro**, a better strand with the good-value eponymous hotel (℡26950 35304, Ⓦwww.portozorro.gr; ❸) and restaurant. The only real facilities away from the coast are to be found at the sprawling village of **Áno Vassilikós**, which serves the nearby beaches of **Iónio** and **Banana**. Accommodation possibilities are the *Vassilikos Apartments* (℡26950 35280; ❸), on the main road, and *Angelika* (℡26950 35201; ❷), by the church just off it. Among the **tavernas**, on the main road, *Kostas' Brother* is well worth a try, as is the *Logos* **bar**. Isolated **Áyios Nikólaos** has a good beach and lures day-trippers from Argási, Kalamáki and Laganás with a **free bus** service in season. Its expanding *Vasilikos Beach* (℡26950 35325, Ⓦwww.hotelvasilikosbeach.gr; ❺) complex is the focal point of a fast-emerging hamlet with a few restaurants and rooms – the neat white, friendly *Christina's* (℡26950 39474; ❷) is one of the best deals on the island. St Nicholas Beach Watersports (℡6937 107652) rents equipment for a range of activities, including windsurfing, parasailing and scuba diving.

At the very tip of the peninsula is its star: **Yérakas**, a sublime crescent of golden sand. It's also a key loggerhead turtle breeding ground, and is therefore off-limits between dusk and dawn, as well as being subject to a strict limit of daily visitors, so get there early in high summer. The excellent open-air **Turtle Information Centre** (Ⓦwww.earthseasky.org) provides interesting background on these and other sea creatures. **Accommodation** in the vicinity is best booked through British-based Ⓦwww.ionian-eco-villagers.co.uk. Otherwise, there's little here beyond three tavernas back from the beach – try *To Triodi* for fresh fish and well-prepared meat dishes. The only beach on the west coast of the peninsula really worth visiting, especially in the quieter months, is **Dháfni**; the road to it is now paved and there are a couple of tavernas, such as the fine *Mela Beach*.

### Laganás and Kalamáki

The majority of the hundreds of thousands of people who visit Zákynthos each year find themselves in **LAGANÁS**. The 9km beach in the bay is good, if trampled, and there are entertainments from watersports to ballooning, and even an occasional funfair. Beachfront bars and restaurants stretch for well over a kilometre, the bars and restaurants on the main drag another kilometre inland. Some stay open around the clock; others just play music at deafening volume until dawn. The competing video and music bars can make Laganás at night resemble the set of *Bladerunner*, but that's how its predominantly English visitors like it. **Accommodation** is mostly block-booked by package companies. There's a basic campsite on the southern edge of town, where there are also quietish private rooms, or you can contact the Union of Room Owners (daily 8.30am–2pm & 5–8pm; ℡26950 51590). As for hotels, try the old-fashioned *Byzantio* (℡26950 51136; ❸), near the crossroads, *Pension Tasoula* (℡26950 51560; ❷), between the beach and the campsite, or the larger *Ionis* (℡26950 51141, Ⓦwww.hotelionis.com; ❹), on the main drag towards the beach. *Dionysos*, halfway along the main drag, and *Zougras*, just before the river along the Kalamáki road, are among the more authentic **tavernas**, the latter hosting *kantádhes* most nights. An even better place to hear this music is the sprawling *Sarakina* taverna, which serves tasty dishes such as pork in wine sauce and sends round a free bus to scoop up potential diners and convey them to its leafy location nearly 2km inland. Cheap and filling Chinese and Indian buffets can be had at *Butterfly* or *Estia*, both well back along the main drag. Favourite **bars** here include *Kamikazi* and *Potters Bar*, typical of the English-themed joints that abound; raucous clubs like *Zeros* and *End* boast state-of-the-art sound systems and carry on till dawn.

Neighbouring **KALAMÁKI** has a better beach than Laganás, and is altogether quieter, although it does suffer from some airport noise. There are several sizeable, mostly package-oriented hotels, but the vast *Crystal Beach* (☎26950 42788, ⓦwww.crystalbeachhotel.info; ⑤) keeps some rooms aside, and the islandwide Spring Tours agency (☎26950 43795, ⓦwww.springtours.gr) can also arrange accommodation. The two *Stanis* tavernas have extensive menus of Greek and international dishes, although the beachside version is geared more to lunches and its sibling in town more to evening meals. A fine alternative is *Zepo's*, near the beach. **Nightlife** centres on bars like *Fire* and *Down Under* on the Laganás road, although the *Cave Club,* which lives up to its name, and upmarket *Byzantio* disco, both on the hillside above the village, are more atmospheric spots. Just outside the resort is Nana's Horses (☎26950 23195), which can arrange riding trips.

### Kerí

The village of **KERÍ** is hidden in a fold above the cliffs at the island's southernmost tip. The village retains a number of pre-quake, Venetian buildings, including the church of the **Panayía Kerioú**; the Virgin is said to have saved the island from marauding pirates by hiding it in a sea mist. A rough path leaving the southern end of the village leads 1km on to the lighthouse, with spectacular

---

## Loggerhead turtles

The Ionian islands harbour the Mediterranean's main concentration of **loggerhead sea turtles**, a sensitive species which is, unfortunately, under direct threat from the tourist industry. Easily frightened by noise and lights, these creatures lay their eggs at night on sandy coves and are therefore uneasy cohabitants with rough campers and late-night discos. Each year, many turtles fall prey to motorboat injuries, nests are destroyed by bikes and the newly hatched young die, entangled in deckchairs and umbrellas left out at night.

The Greek government has passed laws designed to protect the loggerheads, including restrictions on camping at some beaches, but local economic interests tend to prefer a beach full of bodies to a sea full of turtles. On Laganás, nesting grounds are concentrated around the fourteen-kilometre bay, and Greek marine zoologists are in angry dispute with those involved in the tourist industry. Other important locations include the turtles' nesting ground just west of Skála on Kefaloniá, although numbers have dwindled to half their former strength, and now only about eight hundred remain. Ultimately, the turtles' best hope for survival may rest in their potential draw as a unique tourist attraction in their own right.

While capitalists and environmentalists are still at, well, loggerheads, the **World Wildlife Fund** has issued guidelines for visitors:

* Don't use the beaches of Laganás and Yérakas between sunset and sunrise.
* Don't stick umbrellas in the sand in the marked nesting zones.
* Take your rubbish away with you – it can obstruct the turtles.
* Don't use lights near the beach at night – they can disturb the turtles, sometimes with fatal consequences.
* Don't take any vehicle onto the protected beaches.
* Don't dig up turtle nests – it's illegal.
* Don't pick up the hatchlings or carry them to the water.
* Don't use speedboats in Laganás Bay – a 9kph speed limit is in force.

views of the sea, rock arches and stacks and a taverna. En route a road branches off to **LÍMNI KERIOÚ** at the southwestern end of Laganás Bay, which has gradually evolved into a laid-back and picturesque resort and is home to the Turtle Beach Diving Centre (☎26950 48768, ⓦwww.diving-center-turtle -beach.com), one of two diving operations here. **Rooms** can be found at the friendly ⚐ *Pension Limni* (☎26950 48716, ⓦwww.pensionlimni.com; ❸), now sporting two smart new blocks, or through the local Room-Owners Association (☎26950 45105). For **food** there is the *Poseidon* overlooking the bay from the far end and the *Keri* restaurant, which has good daily specials.

### Maherádho, Kiliómeno and Kambí

The bus system does not reach the wild western side of the island, but a rental car or sturdy motorbike will get you there. **MAHERÁDHO** boasts impressive pre-earthquake architecture set in beautiful arable uplands, surrounded by olive and fruit groves. The church of **Ayía Mávra** has an impressive free-standing campanile and, inside, a splendid carved iconostasis and icons. The town's major festival – one of the biggest on the island – is the saint's day, which falls on the first Sunday in June. The other notable church in town, that of the Panayía, commands breathtaking views over the central plain.

**KILIÓMENO** is the best place to see surviving pre-earthquake domestic architecture, in the form of the island's traditional two-storey houses. The town was originally named after its church, **Áyios Nikólaos**, whose impressive campanile, begun over a hundred years ago, still lacks a capped roof. The *Alitzerini* taverna (usually supper only) still occupies a cave-like house that dates from 1630 and dishes up superb traditional food. The road from Kiliómeno passes through the nondescript village of Áyios Léon, from where two turnings lead through fertile land and down a newly paved loop road to the impressive rocky coast at **Limniónas**, where there is a tiny bay overlooked by the excellent *Porto Limnionas* taverna.

Further along the main road, another turning leads to the tiny clifftop hamlet of **KAMBÍ**, popular with day-trippers, who come to catch the sunset over the sea; there are extraordinary views to be had of the 300-metre-high cliffs and western horizon from Kambí's three clifftop **tavernas**. The best of the three is named after the imposing concrete **cross** above the village, constructed in memory of islanders killed here during the 1940s, either by royalist soldiers or Nazis. The tiny village of **Mariés**, 5km to the north and set in a wooded green valley, has the only other coastal access on this side of Zákynthos, a seven-kilometre track leading down to the rocky inlet of **Stenítis Bay**, where there's a taverna and yacht dock, and another road to the uninspiring **Vrómi Bay**, from where speedboats run trips to Shipwreck Bay (see p.590). Meanwhile, the main road continues north towards Volímes (see p.589).

## The north

A few kilometres north of the capital the contiguous resorts of **Tsiliví** and **Plános** are the touristic epicentre of this part of the island. Further north they give way to a series of tiny beaches, while picturesque villages punctuate the lush landscape inland. Beyond **Alykés**, as you approach the island's tip at **Cape Skinári**, the coast becomes more rugged, while the mountains inland hide the weaving centre of **Volímes**.

### Tsiliví, Plános and around

North and inland from Zákynthos Town, the roads thread their way through luxuriantly fertile farmland, punctuated with tumulus-like hills. **TSILIVÍ**, 5km north of the capital, is the first beach resort here, and is in effect one with the hamlet of **PLÁNOS** and matches Argási for development. There's a good, basic **campsite**, *Zante Camping* (☎26950 61710), beyond Plános, and, for a prime package-tour location, a surprising variety of accommodation – try the beachside *Anetis Hotel* (☎26950 44590, ✉anetishotel@yahoo.gr; ❸), which has air conditioning and TV in all rooms; *Gregory's* rooms (☎26950 61853; ❷); or contact Tsilivi Travel (☎26950 44194, ✉akis-125@otenet.gr), on the inland road in from town. *The Olive Tree* taverna is the best of a touristy bunch, while the *Passage to India* serves fairly authentic Chinese, as well as Indian. Drinking dens such as the *Mambo Club* and *Planet Pub* tend to be Brit-oriented.

The beaches further along this stretch of coast become progressively quieter and more pleasant, and all have at least some accommodation and restaurants to choose from. Good choices include **Pahiá Ámmos**, with the *Pension Petra* (☎26950 63593, ⓦwww.zakynthos-petra.com; ❸) and *Porto Roulis* fish taverna. In **Dhrossiá**, you can find the *Avouris* (☎26950 61716; ❸) and *Drosia* apartments (☎26950 62256, ⓦwww.drosiaapartments.gr; ❹) and eat at another popular fish taverna, *Andreas*.

### Alykés and its bay

**Órmos Alykón**, 12km north of Tsiliví, is a large sandy bay with lively surf and two of the area's largest resorts. The first, **ALIKANÁS**, is a small but expanding village, much of its accommodation being overseas villa rentals; the second, **ALYKÉS**, named after the spooky salt pans behind the village, has the best beach north of the capital. There are **rooms** near the beach, most easily found through the local branch of Spring Tours (☎26950 83035, ⓦwww.springtours.gr), and a number of **hotels** set back from it, but with sea views – try the *Ionian Star* (☎26950 83416, ⓦwww.ionian-star.gr; ❹) or the *Montreal* (☎26950 83241, ⓦwww.montreal.gr; ❹) – although the best deal is off the crossroads at the chaotic *Eros Piccadilly* (☎26950 83606, ⓦwww.erospiccadilly.com; ❷). There are many eating joints, among the best the *Vineleaf*, which has unusual items such as jalapeño peppers stuffed with cream, and more standard *Fantasia* and *Ponderosa* tavernas.

Alykés is the last true resort on this coast, and the one where the bus service largely gives out, so you really need your own wheels. **Xygiá beach**, 4km north, has sulphur springs flowing into the sea – follow the smell – which provide the odd sensation of swimming in a mix of cool and warm water. The next small beach of **Makrýs Yialós**, which has a good taverna and makeshift campsite, also makes for an extremely pleasant break on a tour of the north. Just to the north of Makrýs Yialós you come to a pretty promontory with a small harbour and the *Mikro Nisi psarotavérna*, beyond and above which there are a couple of places to rent rooms; try *Klimati* (☎26950 31225; ❸) if you fancy a bit of isolation.

**ÁYIOS NIKÓLAOS**, 6km on, is a small working port with a daily summer ferry connection to Pessádha on Kefaloniá but unfortunately there is no bus service, so travellers using the crossing without their own transport are forced to fork out for a taxi or hitch a ride south. Few visitors actually **stay** here, which perhaps explains why it hosts one of the most exclusive establishments in the Ionian, the classy stone *Nobelos* apartments (☎26950 31131, ⓦwww .nobelos.gr; ❽), as well as the more modest *Panorama* (☎26950 31013, ✉panorama@altecnet.gr; ❸). Pre-ferry meals can be had at *La Storia* fish restaurant or *Orizodes* taverna.

Ignore scams claiming that this is the last chance to take a boat to the **Blue Caves**, which are some of the more realistically named of the many contenders in Greece. They're terrific for snorkelling, and when you go for a dip here your skin will appear bright blue. To reach them, follow the road as it snakes onwards from **Áyios Nikólaos** through a landscape of gorse bushes and dry-stone walls until it ends at the lighthouse of **Cape Skinári**, from below which three friendly brothers operate the best and cheapest **boat trips** to the caves (€7.50; €15 combined with Shipwreck Bay). Not far away, steps also lead down to a swimming jetty, near the caves, from behind the two unique rentable **windmills** of ✈ *Anemomilos* (☎26950 31241, ⓦwww.potamitisbros.gr; ❹), belonging to the same welcoming family; they also have more conventional rooms, and run the excellent *To Faros* **taverna**.

### Katastári, Ayía Marína and Volímes

The northern towns and villages are best explored with a car or sturdy motorbike, although there are guided coach tours from the resorts and limited bus services. Two kilometres inland from Alykés, **KATASTÁRI** is the largest settlement after the capital. Precisely because it's not geared towards tourism, it's the best place to see Zakynthian life as it's lived away from the usual racket. Its most impressive edifice is the huge rectangular church of Iperáyia Theotókos, with a twin belfry and small new amphitheatre for festival performances. *To Kendro psistariá* does tasty grills at rock-bottom prices. A couple of kilometres south of Katastári, the tiny hamlet of **Pighadhákia** is the unlikely setting for the **Vertzagio Cultural Museum** (summer daily 9am–3pm & 5–7pm; €3), which houses an interesting array of agricultural and folk artefacts. There is also the diminutive **Áyios Pandeléïmon** chapel, which has the unusual feature of a well, hidden beneath the altar. Just above the chapel, the *Kaki Rahi* taverna provides tasty local cuisine.

    **AYÍA MARÍNA**, a few kilometres southwest of Katastári, has a church with an impressive Baroque altar screen, and a belfry that's being rebuilt from the remnants left after the 1953 earthquake. As in most Zákynthos churches, the bell tower stands detached, in Venetian fashion. Just above Ayía Marína is the *Parthenonas* taverna, rightly boasting one of the best views on the island. From here you can see the whole of the central plain from beyond Alykés in the north to Laganás Bay in the south.

    **VOLÍMES** is the centre of the island's embroidery industry and numerous shops sell artefacts produced here. With your own transport, you could make it

▲ Shipwreck Bay

to the **Anafonítria monastery**, 3km south, thought to have been the cell of the island's patron saint, Dhionysios, whose festivals are celebrated on August 24 and December 17. A paved road leads on to the cliffs overlooking **Shipwreck Bay** (Naváyio), with hair-raising views down to the shipwreck, a cargo ship which was mistaken for a drug-running vessel and run aground by the coast-guard in the 1960s.

# Kýthira and Andikýthira

Isolated at the foot of the Peloponnese, the island of **Kýthira** traditionally belongs to the Ionians, and shares their history of Venetian and, later, British rule. Administratively it is part of Pireás in mainland Attica – like the Argo-Saronic islands. For the most part, similarities end there. The island architecture of whitewashed houses and flat roofs looks more like that of the Cyclades, albeit with an ever-stronger **Venetian** influence. The landscape is different, too: wild scrub- and gorse-covered hills, or moorland sliced by deep valleys and ravines.

Depopulation has left the land underfarmed and the abandoned fields overgrown – since World War II, most of the islanders have left for Athens or Australia, giving Kýthira a reputation for being the classic emigrant island; it is known locally as "Australian Colony" or "Kangaroo Island", and Australia referred to as "Big Kýthira". Many of the villages are deserted, their *platíes* empty and schools and *kafenía* closed. Kýthira was never a rich island, but, along with Monemvasiá, it did once have a military and economic signifi-cance – which it likewise lost with Greek independence and the opening of the Corinth Canal. For the few foreigners who reach Kýthira, it remains something of a refuge, with its undeveloped **beaches** a principal attraction. However, Theo Angelopoulos's film *Taxidhi sta Kythira* ("Journey to Kýthira"), and, to a much greater extent, a 1998 popular Greek television serial filmed on the island, have attracted a huge amount of domestic attention and, conse-quently, holiday-makers from the mainland. Much of the accommodation is now fully booked by Christmas for the entire Greek school summer holiday period; outside of this period some accommodation does not open until June and closes early in September. The Association of Rental Room Owners (T 27360 31855) has a list of places to stay "in villages across the island".

## Arrival and getting around

The huge **harbour** at Dhiakófti is the arrival point for the daily Neápoli ferries (W www.kythira-kithira-kythera.com), as well as the less frequent ones from Yíthio, Kalamáta and Kissamos (Crete). The airport is deep in the interior, 8km southeast of Potamós; the few Olympic Airways flights are met by taxis, as are most high-season boats. Taxis from the port charge around €28 to Kapsáli and €20 to Potamós, but establish a price beforehand. The island's **buses** are mostly used for school runs, but a single service runs Ayía Pelayía–Kapsáli–Dhiakófti, starting at 9am Mondays to Saturdays, returning Dhiakófti–Kapsáli–Ayía Pelayía late mornings or mid-afternoon, depending on the ferry times. The only alternative to taxis is to hitch or, more advisedly, hire a **car** or **scooter**. The roads are now well surfaced all over the island and there are petrol stations on the central road at Potamós, Kondoliánika and Livádhi. Panayotis, now based in Kondoliánika (T 27360 31600, E panayoti @otenet.gr), rents cars, motorbikes, mountain bikes and scooters, as well as canoes and pedalboats; you can call off-season (T 694 42 63 757) and get wheels when most places are closed.

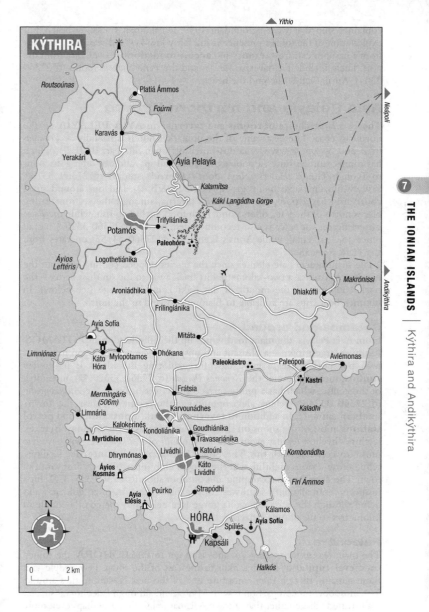

## Dhiakófti

**DHIAKÓFTI**, towards the bottom of the northeast coast, was a relatively inaccessible backwater before the opening of the harbour, constructed by joining the islet of Makrónissi to the shore by a causeway. Perched on nearby Prasónissi island – and slightly disconcerting when arriving by sea – is a Greek container ship that went aground in 1999. Dhiakófti has a sandy beach, but exploitation of the tourist presence is still fairly low-key and seasonal, and apart from a harbour café, **restaurants** and **accommodation** are over 1km from the port. These include fish taverna *Manolis* and the *Porto Diakofti* rooms (☎ 27360 33041; April–Oct; ❻) behind the beach.

## Ayía Pelayía and northern Kýthira

There's a large choice of **rooms** and **tavernas** in **AYÍA PELAYÍA** on the northeast coast. The best value of the upmarket hotels is friendly ⚐ *Venardos* (☎ 27360 34205, ⓦ www.venardos-hotels.gr; open all year; B&B ❼), which has rooms, studios, suites, a pool, gym, sauna and spa, and can offer a discount to Rough Guide readers. Next door's *Filoxenia* studios (☎ 27360 33100, ⓦ www.filoxenia-apartments.gr; April–Oct; B&B ❼), laid out around small courtyards, has a pool. The *Moustakias* taverna, amongst the seafront eating places north of the jetty, offers good, fresh food, including fish, while the *Paleo* ouzerí nearer the jetty is also recommended. Active (☎ 27360 33207) has an office for car rental, while Anna's Rentacar (☎ 27360 34153) operates from the *Hotel Romantica*.

The main beaches are cleaner since the ferries stopped coming here, but the beach at Kalamítsa, a two-kilometre dirt track away to the south, is better – the track continues to the mouth of the Káki Langádha gorge (see below). In summer, boat trips are available to Elafónissos island to the north.

### Potamós and around

From Ayía Pelayía, the main road winds up the hillside towards **POTAMÓS**, Kýthira's largest town – a pleasant and unspoilt place which, if you have your own transport, makes a good base for exploring the island. It has a few **studios**, such as those at the *Xenonas Porfyra* (☎ 27360 33329; ❹), just north of the centre, which has a pretty terrace and courtyard, and the *Alevizopoulos* (☎ 27360 33245, ⓔ elena_alevizopoulou@yahoo.com; ❹), near the town's southern entrance. In addition to **tavernas**, a **bank**, a **post office** and **petrol stations**, most of the shops on the island are here, as is the **Sunday market**, Kýthira's liveliest regular event – either the *Lilis* or *Astikon* cafés will have live music to coincide with this. The *Selana* café-pizzeria has **internet** facilities, while more serious nightlife is at the *Vergadi* club (open all year), just south of town. The *Mare Nostrum* camping and outdoor shop (☎ 27360 33573, ⓔ chronisdiver@hotmail.com), southwest of the platía, can organize guided walks down through the Káki Langádha gorge (see below) to the coast a couple of kilometres south of Ayía Pelayía.

### Paleohóra

The main reason for visiting Potamós is to get to **PALEOHÓRA**, the ruined **medieval capital** of Kýthira, 3km to the east of the town. Few people visit these remains, though they constitute one of the best Byzantine sites around. The most obvious comparison is with Mystra, and although Paleohóra is smaller – a fortified village rather than a town – its natural setting is perhaps even more spectacular. Set on a hilltop at the forked head of the **Káki Langádha gorge**, it is surrounded by a sheer hundred-metre drop on three sides.

The site is lower than the surrounding hills and invisible from the sea and most of the island, which served to protect it from the pirates that plagued Paleohóra through much of its history. The town, then called Áyios Dhimítrios, was built in the thirteenth century by Byzantine nobles from Monemvasiá, and when Mystra fell to the Turks, many of Mystra's noble families sought refuge here. Despite its seemingly concealed and impregnable position, the site was discovered and sacked in 1537 by Barbarossa, commander of the Turkish fleet, and the island's seven thousand inhabitants were killed or sold into slavery.

The town was never rebuilt, and tradition maintains that it is a place of ill fortune, which perhaps explains the emptiness of the surrounding countryside, little of which is farmed today. The hills are dotted with Byzantine **chapels**, which suggests that, in its heyday, the area must have been the centre of medieval Kýthira; it is rumoured to have once had eight hundred inhabitants and 72 churches. Now the principal remains are of the surviving churches, some still with traces of frescoes (but kept firmly locked), and the castle. The site is unenclosed and has never been seriously investigated.

The 4.5km road to Paleohóra is signposted off the main road from Potamós just north of Aroniádhika: the first 2.4km is asphalt, the remainder driveable gravel. By foot, it's more interesting to take the path from the tiny village of Trifyliánika, just outside Potamós – look out for a rusting sign to the right as you enter the village. The path is overgrown in parts and not easy to follow; the ruins only become visible when you join the road above the gorge.

### Karavás

The architecture and setting of **KARAVÁS**, 6km north of Potamós, above a deep, partly wooded valley with a stream, are more reminiscent of the northern Ionian islands. There is nowhere to stay, but a popular **café-bar**, *Amir Ali*, provides a wide range of *mezédhes* (and sometimes live music) in a shady, streamside setting at the northern end of the village, down a narrow lane off the road to Platiá Ámmos. At the northeast end of the village, the new Artopiío tou Karava bakery is in a former agricultural building, with beautifully restored olive press machinery on display; a café is planned.

**Platiá Ámmos**, at the end of the valley, en route to the lighthouse at the island's northern tip, is a small, scattered village behind an attractive sandy beach. On the headland just beyond, the popular *Varkoula* taverna has live rebétika music – Saturdays in winter, daily in summer. You'll also find an ouzerí, café, the *Modeas* restaurant, and several establishments with **rooms**, of which the best is the *Akrotiri* (☎27360 33216; ❸). There is an even more attractive little pebble beach at **Foúrni**, 2km south by dirt road.

## Kapsáli

**KAPSÁLI**, on the south coast, is largely devoted to tourism, and much of it closes down from September to June. Most foreign visitors to Kýthira in summer stay here, and it's a popular port of call for yachts heading from the Aegean to the Ionian islands and Italy, particularly since it is sheltered from the strong north winds of summer. Set behind double pebble-and-sand bays, overlooked by Hóra castle, and backed by high grey cliffs on which the tiny white monastery of Áyios Ioánnis Éngremmos perches, it is certainly picturesque. The larger of its two bays has a line of **tavernas**: *Vlastos* is one of the first to open in the season, with fish, local dishes and its speciality, cockerel (*kókoras*) in wine; *Zeidoros* (☎27360 38212, ✆www.zeidoros.gr), halfway along the seafront, has an exhibition hall in a restored Venetian building, organizes summer concerts, and serves food in the olive garden behind; *Idragogio* at the Hóra end of the beach serves up good veggie options. The *Panorama Club*, near the *Porto Delfino* entrance road junction, sometimes has live music.

The best **accommodation** is in high demand and expensive. Top of the tree is the *Porto Delfino* (☎27360 31940, ⓦwww.portodelfino.gr; April–Oct; ❼); a few hundred metres above the bay are *Kalokerines Katikies* (☎27360 31265; May–Oct; ❻) and *Hotel Raïkos* (☎27360 31629, ⓦwww.raikoshotel .gr; May–Sept; ❽). The attractive ⚡ *Afroditi Apartments* (☎27360 31328; ⓔafrodite@aias.gr; open all year; ❺) has more reasonable rates, a pleasant rear garden and internet facilities for guests. The *Vasili Spitia* (☎27360 31125, ⓦwww.kythirabungalowsvasili.gr; April–Oct; B&B ❺) a short way up the hill, has comfortable rooms and studios, most with sea views, and an attractive breakfast room. A basic **campsite** (☎27360 31580; June–Sept) nestles in the pine trees below the *Porto Delfino* entrance road.

## Hóra

**HÓRA** (or Kýthira Town), a steep two-kilometre haul above Kapsáli, has an equally dramatic position, its Cycladic-style houses tiered on the ridge leading to the Venetian **castle**. Access to the fortress is up a modern pathway, but, to the right of this, the original narrow tunnel entrance is still usable. Within the walls, most of the buildings are in ruins, except the paired churches of Panayía Myrtidhiótissa and the smaller Panayía Orfáni (Catholic and Orthodox respectively, under the Venetian occupation), and the office of the archives of Kýthira opposite. There are spectacular views down to Kapsáli and out to sea to the striking chunk of inaccessible islet known as Avgó (Egg), legendary birthplace of Aphrodite. On the cliffs grow the yellow-flowered everlasting (*sempreviva*), used locally for making small dried flower arrangements. Below the castle are both the remains of older Byzantine walls and, in Mésa Vouryó, numerous well-signed but securely locked Byzantine churches. A small **museum**, at the junction of the Hóra–Kapsáli road, currently closed following 2006 earthquake damage, houses modest remnants (labelled in Greek only) of the island's numerous occupiers, in particular Minoan finds from excavations at Paleópoli and an Archaic stone lion, as well as a selection of gravestones from the English cemetery. The Stavros bookshop, almost opposite, sells a book of walks (mainly in the southern half of the island).

Compared with Kapsáli, Hóra stays quieter in summer and many places have an even shorter season. Facilities include a couple of banks with **ATMs** and a **post office** on the main square, a branch of Panayotis vehicle rental (☎27360 31004) and the office of Kýthira Travel (☎27360 31390, ⓔkkmk @otenet.gr), the island's agent for the Neápoli ferry. A few **tavernas** open in summer, of which *Zorba* is by far the best, but the climb from Kapsáli discourages the crowds. Popular café-bar *Mercato* stays open in the winter and has exhibitions of local art. **Internet** facilities are available at the Photo Cerigo shop just above the square, while the nearest bakery is at Livádhi, 4km north. **Accommodation** is slightly easier to find than in Kapsáli: options include the *Castello* rooms and studios (☎27360 31069, ⓦwww.castelloapts-kythera .gr; ❸) on the Kapsáli side, the *Hotel Margarita* (☎27360 31711, ⓦwww.hotel -margarita.com; B&B ❺) in a beautiful 1840s house below the main street, and the gorgeous *Xenon Nostos* (☎27360 31056, ⓦwww.nostos-kythera.gr; B&B ❺) in a nineteenth-century house at a fork of the main street. The *Xenonas Keiti/Keti/Kaiti* (☎27360 31318; April–Oct; ❹), above the square, and also accessible from the Kapsáli road, has non-smoking rooms in a large, characterful 240-year-old house that has seen General Metaxas and George Papandreou as visitors.

# North and west of Hóra

**LIVÁDHI**, 4km north of Hóra, has rooms and, on the main road, a hotel, the *Aposperídes* (☎27360 31656, @aposperides@freemail.gr; B&B ❹), as well as two tavernas, a supermarket, a bakery and *zaharoplastía*. Livádhi is also home to one of the most efficient travel agencies on the island, Porfyra Travel, which is the main ANEK/ANEN and Olympic Airways agent (☎27360 31888, ⓦwww .kythira.info), with exchange and car rental; they can also arrange accommodation and transfers. There are **internet** facilities at the Polyedro shop; for nightlife, head 5km north to the *Camelot* dance club (open Fri–Sat in low season, daily in high season), near Frátsia.

At **Káto Livádhi**, 1km east of Livádhi, there is a small **museum** of Byzantine and post-Byzantine art (July–Oct Tues–Sun 8am–3pm; Nov–June Mon–Fri 8.30am–2pm; free) next to the large central church. It contains frescoes, painstakingly removed from island churches, dating from the twelfth to the eighteenth centuries, a seventh-century mosaic floor and some portable icons (labelling in Greek only). A few-minutes' walk away there is also a cooperative pottery workshop (open mornings and evenings, with a 2–4pm break) and, on the road to Katoúni, a multiple-arched bridge, said to be the longest stone bridge in Greece and a legacy of the nineteenth century when all the Ionian islands were a British protectorate. The best view of it is from beside *Rena's zaharoplastío* in Livádhi. A popular **taverna** nearby is the *Theofílos*.

From Livádhi, a side road heads west to Kalokerinés, and continues 3.6km further to the island's principal monastery, **Myrtidhíon**, set above the wild and windswept west coast, among a dead forest of pines burned in June 2000. The monastery's main icon is said to date from 1160. Beyond the monastery, a track leads down to a small anchorage at **Limnária**; there are few beaches along this rocky, forbidding shore.

An early left fork off the Myrtidhíon road out of Livádhi brings you through the hamlet of Poúrko and past the unusual Byzantine church of Áyios Dhimitríos. From here, an increasingly steep road leads up to the **Ayía Elésis**, a nineteenth-century monastery marking the martyrdom of the saint on the hilltop in 375 AD, an event depicted in modern wall-paintings inside the church. For many visitors, however, the breathtaking view from the western side of the courtyard is the main reason to visit.

## Mylopótamos, Káto Hóra and the Ayía Sofía cave

North of Livádhi, just beyond Dhókana, it is worth making a detour off the main road for **MYLOPÓTAMOS**, a lovely traditional village and an oasis in summer, set in a wooded valley with a small stream. The *Xenónas Porfyrousa* (☎27360 38281, ⓦwww.porfyrousa.gr; Apr–Oct; B&B ❼) has apartments in an old restored house. The shady *Plátanos* café-taverna makes a pleasant stop for a drink above the village's springs, and the music bar *Kamari* serves snacks and drinks on a lower waterside terrace. Follow the signs for "Katarráktis Neräidha" to find a waterfall, hidden from view by lush vegetation, next to a long-closed café. The valley below the falls contains the remains of the watermill that gave the village its name – this is accessed by a longer path starting beyond the village cemetery, although the partly waymarked path is uncomfortably overgrown with prickly vegetation.

**Káto Hóra** (also called Kástro Mylopotamoú), 500m down the road, was Mylopótamos's predecessor, and remains half-enclosed within the walls of a Venetian fortress – it is signposted only as Áyios Ioánnis Pródhromos, the main church. The fortress is small, full of locked, name-labelled churches, and has a rather domestic appearance: unlike the castle at Hóra, it was built as a place of refuge for the villagers in case of attack, rather than as a base for a Venetian garrison. All the houses within the walls are abandoned – as are many outside – but are open and accessible. The traditional style of two-floored Cycladic *kástro* houses, with separate dwellings on each floor, can be seen in the village's main street. Beyond here, a surfaced but briefly precipitous road continues 5km through spectacular cliffscapes to **Limniónas**, a rocky inlet with a small sand beach; thanks to fires, the surrounding countryside is exposed and barren.

Most visitors come to Mylopótamos to see the **cave of Ayía Sofía**, the largest and most impressive of a number of caverns on the island. A half-hour signposted walk from the village, or a short drive along a dirt road off the Limniónas road, the cave is open from mid-June to mid-September (Mon–Fri 3–8pm, Sat & Sun 11am–5pm; €3). When the cave is closed, you can probably find a guide in Mylopótamos; ask at the village, giving a day's notice if possible. The cave's entrance has been used as a church and has an iconostasis carved from the rock, with important Byzantine frescoes on it. Beyond are a series of chambers reaching 250m into the mountain, although the obligatory thirty-minute guided tour (in Greek and English) only takes in the more interesting outer chambers. These include some startling formations such as the "shark's teeth", but you have to ask to be shown "Aphrodite's chambers".

# The southeast coast

The beach at Kapsáli is decent but not large and gets very crowded in July and August. For quieter, undeveloped beaches, it's better to head out to the southeast coast, towards Avlémonas.

### Firí Ámmos, Kombonádha and Halkós beaches, and Spiliés cave

**Firí Ámmos**, the nearest good sand beach to Kapsáli, is popular but not overcrowded, even in summer. To get there, follow paved roads from Kapsáli or Livádhi as far as the *Filio* taverna (June–Sept), which serves good traditional food and local specialities, in the scattered settlement of Kálamos; the onward road becomes a four-kilometre dirt track to the beach. Firí Ámmos can also be reached by a second dirt track off the Livádhi–Kálamos road, while a longer surfaced road, off the Káto Livádhi–Frátsia road, leads to **Kombonádha**, the next beach north. There are summer cafés at both beaches. Much smaller, but prettier, pebbly **Halkós beach** near the southeast corner of the island is signposted from the crossroads at the entrance to Kálamos. Between Kálamos and Kapsáli, a short surfaced road leads south to **Spiliés** village; immediately before the village a signed earth road leads down to a small gorge and a large stalagmite cave with an open-roofed church dedicated to Ayía Sofía (not to be confused with the sea cave near Mylopótamos).

### Paleópoli and Avlémonas

**PALEÓPOLI**, a hamlet of a few scattered houses, is accessible by asphalt roads from Aroniádhika, Frátsia and Kondoliánika. The area is the site of the ancient city of **Skandia**, and excavations on the headland of **Kastrí** have revealed remains of an important Minoan colony. There's little visible evidence, apart from shards of pottery in the low crumbling cliffs, but tourist development in the area has been barred because of its archeological significance. Consequently, there's just one **taverna**, the *Skandia* (June–Oct), behind the two-kilometre sand-and-pebble **beach** that stretches to either side of the headland – they have some rooms on the hillside above.

**Paleokástro**, the mountain to the west, is the site of ancient Kýthira, which was home to a sanctuary of Aphrodite, but again there's little to be seen today. Heading west from Paleópoli and crossing the river bridge onto the Kondoliánika road, an unpaved road off to the left leads up to a tiny, white-washed church. From there, a rougher track leads down to **Kaladhí**, a beautiful cliff-backed pebble beach with caves, and rocks jutting out to sea.

**AVLÉMONAS**, on a rocky shoreline 2km east of Paleópoli beach, is a small fishing port with an end-of-the-world feel as you approach from a distance. It becomes much more attractive once reached, and has a remarkable coordination of colour schemes – mainly white throughout the village. There is a small, unimpressive Venetian fortress, and two **tavernas**, *Korali* and *Sotiris*, both offering a wide selection of fresh, well-prepared and reasonably priced fish dishes. There are a number of **rooms**, including the apartments of *Popi Kastrisiou* (℡27360 33735; ❹), and various rooms at *Manti* (℡27360 33039, ❾www .manti.gr; ❺). The Petrohilos family has a number of rooms or studios, including those of *Evdokhia* (℡27360 34069; ❸) opposite the *Sotiris*.

## Andikýthira island

Thirteen kilometres to the south of Kýthira, the tiny, wind-blown 22-square-kilometre island of **ANDIKÝTHIRA** (❾www.antikythira.gr) has, theoretically, a twice-weekly connection with Crete on the Kýthira–Kastélli–Kýthira run (❾www.anen.gr), but landings are often impossible due to adverse weather. Rocky and poor, and a site of political exile until 1964, the island only received electricity in 1984. Local attractions include good birdlife (a bird observatory has been built in the old school at Laziianá) and flora, but with only 45 residents divided among a scattering of settlements – mainly in **Potamós**, the harbour, and **Sohória**, the village – people are rather thin on the ground. The only official accommodation is the set of **rooms** run by the local community (℡27360 33004, ✉info@antikythera.gr; ❷) at Potamós, which also has a couple of **tavernas**, but you'd be wise to bring plenty of supplies with you. In Sohória the only provisions available are basic foodstuffs at the village shop. Recent excavation work above Xeropótamos has revealed the site of ancient **Aigila**, a 75-acre fortress city of the Hellenistic period. At the harbour below are the remains of one of ancient Greece's best-preserved warship slipways, a *neosoikos*, carved out of the rock.

The island has one remarkable claim to fame, the **Antikythera Mechanism**, an ancient bronze clockwork "calendar computer" discovered in 1902 in a nearby shipwreck and dated to around 87 BC. It is thought to have been used for calculating the motion and positions of the earth, moon and five other planets, and is the earliest known mechanism with a differential gear by about 1600 years. It is now kept in the National Archeological Museum, Athens.

# Travel details

## Buses

### Corfu:
Corfu Town to: Athens (3 daily; 9–10hr); Thessaloníki (2 daily; 8–9hr).

### Kefaloniá:
Argostóli to: Athens (4 daily; 7–8hr); Pátra (1 daily; 4–5hr).
Póros to: Athens (1 daily; 6–7hr).
Sámi to: Athens (2 daily; 6–7hr).

**Lefkádha:**
Lefkádha Town to: Athens (1 daily; 5hr 30min); Pátra (2 weekly; 3hr); Préveza (4 daily; 30min); Thessaloníki (2 weekly; 10–11hr).

**Zákynthos:**
Zákynthos Town to: Athens (5–6 daily; 5hr 30min); Pátra (4 daily; 3hr); Thessaloníki (3 weekly; 12–13hr).

## Ferries

The following listings are based on summer schedules, which are often reduced drastically in winter; any services that stop altogether are marked as being summer only. Tourist craft and *kaḯkia* are not included below.

**Corfu:**
Corfu Town to: Eríkoussa/Mathráki/Othoní (3 weekly; 2–4hr); Igoumenítsa (every 10–45min; 1hr 15min); Pátra (6–10 daily; 6–9hr).
Lefkími to: Igoumenítsa (6 daily; 40min).

**Itháki:**
Fríkes to: Fiskárdho (Kefaloniá; 1 daily; 1hr); Vassilikí (Lefkádha; 1 daily; 1hr 30min).
Pisaetós to: Sámi (Kefaloniá; 2–3 daily; 45min).
Vathý to: Astakós (1 daily; 2hr 30min); Pátra (2 daily; 3hr 30min); Sámi (Kefaloniá; 1–2 daily; 1hr).

**Kefaloniá:**
Argostóli to: Kyllíni (1 daily; 2hr 15min); Lixoúri (every 30min; 20min).
Fiskárdho to: Fríkes (Itháki; 1 daily; 1hr); Vassilikí (Lefkádha; 2–3 daily; 1–2hr).
Pessádha to: Áyios Nikólaos (Zákynthos; 2 daily May–Sept; 1hr 30min).
Póros to: Kyllíni (3–5 daily; 1hr 15min).
Sámi to: Astakós (1 daily; 2hr 30min); Kérkyra Town (1–2 weekly; 5hr); Pátra (1–2 daily; 3hr 30min); Pisaetós (Itháki; 2–3 daily; 40min); Vathý (Itháki; 1–2 daily; 1hr).

**Kýthira and Andikýthira:**
Andikýthira to: Dhiakófti, Kýthira (2–3 weekly; 2hr 30min).
Dhiakófti to: Andikýthira (2–3 weekly in season; 2hr 30min); Kalamáta (1 weekly in season; 5hr 30min); Kastélli (1–6 weekly in season; 2hr 15min; 5hr via Andikýthira); Neápoli, (2–3 daily mid-season,

3–4 daily late July–Aug; 1hr); Pireás (2 weekly in season; 5hr); Yíthio (1–5 weekly in season; 2hr 30min).

**Lefkádha:**
Nydhrí to: Meganíssi (7 daily; 20min).
Vassilikí to: Fiskárdho (Kefaloniá; 2–3 daily; 1hr); Fríkes (Itháki; 1 daily; 2hr).

**Paxí:**
Gáïos to: Igoumenítsa (1–2 daily; 1hr).

**Zákynthos:**
Zákynthos Town to: Kyllíni (5–7 daily; 1hr 30min).
Áyios Nikólaos to: Pessádha (Kefaloniá; 2 daily May–Sept; 1hr 30min).

## International Ferries

Kérkyra Town is a main stop on many of the ferry routes to Italy from Pátra and a stopover can be added for free with many companies. The frequency and journey time to the various Italian ports is: Ancona (1–2 daily; 14hr); Bari (2–3 daily; 11hr); Brindisi (3–5 daily; 4–9hr); and Venice (2–3 weekly; 25hr).

## Hydrofoils

Corfu Town to: Gáïos (Paxí; 1–3 daily; 50min).
Gáïos to: Corfu Town (1–3 daily; 50min).

## Flights

All domestic flights listed below are on Olympic, Aegean or the Airsea Lines seaplane service. For international flights see "Basics" p.31.
Corfu to: Athens (4–6 daily; 1hr); Ioánnina (5 weekly; 40min); Kefaloniá (8 weekly; 1hr 15min–2hr 20min); Lefkádha (6 weekly; 45min–1hr 15min); Pátra (7 weekly; 1hr 10min–1hr 45min); Paxí (1–3 daily; 20min); Préveza (3 weekly; 25min); Zákynthos (3 weekly; 2hr).
Kefaloniá to: Athens (2 daily; 1hr); Corfu (8 weekly; 1hr–1hr 15min); Ioánnina (1 weekly; 5hr); Pátra (5 weekly; 40min); Paxí (5 weekly; 2hr 55min); Préveza (3 weekly; 25min); Zákynthos (3 weekly; 25min).
Kýthira to: Athens (1 daily; 50min).
Zákynthos to: Athens (4 daily; 55min); Corfu (3 weekly; 1hr 55min); Kefaloniá (3 weekly; 25min); Préveza (3 weekly; 1hr 15min).

# Contexts

# Contexts

# History

T he history of the Greek Islands is, broadly, the history of Greece, and it
is that history which follows. It is worth remembering, however, that the
last of the islands were only integrated into the Greek nation after World
War II and that the Greek state itself has been in existence for less than
two hundred years. In the context of well over five thousand years of civilization on the islands, and of constant trade between them and the wider world,
it is not surprising that individual islands have their own unique histories, not
always conforming to the overall pattern. What is consistent is that the position
of the Greek islands at the crossroads of Europe, Asia and Africa has long
presented them with unique opportunities and dangers, and made them a prize
much fought over. In the areas of politics, philosophy, literature, science and art,
Greece has influenced Western society more than any other nation in history;
and islanders have played a full part in that.

# Prehistoric Greece: to 2100 BC

Evidence of human habitation in Greece goes back half a million years, as
demonstrated by the discovery in 1976 of the skeleton of a **Neanderthal**
youth embedded in a stalagmite in the **Petralóna Cave**, 50km east of the
northern city of Thessaloníki, along with the earliest known site of a man-
made fire in Europe.

Only very much later, about 40,000 years ago, did **Homo sapiens** make his
first appearance in Greece after migrating out of Africa. At several sites in
**Epirus** in northwest Greece (including some on what are now the Ionian
islands, then attached to the mainland), *Homo sapiens* used tools and weapons of
bone, wood and stone to gather wild plants and hunt. Even between 20,000 and
16,000 years ago, when the Ice Age was at its peak, **Stone Age man** continued
to make a home in Greece, though only in around 10,000 BC did a considerably warmer climate set in and the glaciers retreat, raising sea levels and finally
separating many of the islands from the mainland.

## The Neolithic period

**Agricultural communities** first appeared in northern Greece around **6500 BC**.
Whether agriculture developed indigenously or was introduced by migrants
from Asia Minor is much debated: what is certain, however, is its revolutionary effect.

An assured supply of food enabled the Stone Age inhabitants of Greece to settle
in fixed spots, building mud-brick houses on stone foundations. Though still
reliant on stone implements, this new farming culture marked a significant break
with the past, so a "new stone age" or **Neolithic period** is said to have begun
in Greece from 6500 BC. As the strong kind of flint needed for weapons and
tools was rare in Greece, the mainlanders imported obsidian, the hard black glassy
stone formed by rapidly cooling volcanic lava, found on the island of **Mílos**
(ancient Melos) in the southern Cyclades. The earliest **seaborne trade** known
anywhere in the world, this clearly involved a mastery of building and handling
boats, skills that were to define the Greek islanders throughout their history.

## Cycladic culture and the beginnings of the Greek Bronze Age

Around **3000 BC** a new people settled in the **Cyclades**, probably from Asia Minor, bringing with them the latest metallurgical techniques. While continuing the old trade in obsidian, they also developed a **trade in tin** and were making prodigious voyages westwards as far as Spain by 2500 BC. The mining of **gold and silver** in the Cyclades may have dated from this period, too. Long before Crete or the Greek mainland, these new islanders became specialists in **jewellery-making**, **metalwork** and **stone-cutting**. From the abundant marble of the Cyclades, they sculpted statuettes, mostly of female figures. Slender, spare and geometric, these **Cycladic sculptures** are startlingly modern in appearance, and were exported widely, to Crete and mainland Greece. Usually described as idols, the statuettes were probably used in worship, as well as in burials – where they were perhaps intended as spirit guides. Indeed during the Early Bronze Age the Eastern Mediterranean witnessed a proliferation in the manufacture and trade of **ritual objects**, probably because ritual itself was increasingly elaborate as societies grew wealthier, more complex and more hierarchical.

In about 3000 BC, the introduction of bronze technology to the mainland, also from the Cyclades, marked the start of the **Bronze Age** in Greece. By **2500 BC**, thanks to a well-established network of long-distance trade, the widespread use of bronze had transformed farming and fighting throughout the Eastern Mediterranean and the Middle East. Because **tin** (which when alloyed with copper creates bronze) came from so far afield – in the east it could be obtained only in isolated pockets of the Caucasus, Persia and Afghanistan, while in the west sources were confined to Cornwall, Brittany, northwest Spain and northern Italy – the Aegean became an important trade route. Hence the burst of development that now took place along the eastern coast of **central Greece** and the **Peloponnese**, and on the **Aegean islands** which linked the Greek mainland to Asia Minor and the Middle East.

It is uncertain what **language** was spoken at this time on the mainland and the islands, but one thing is clear: it was not yet Greek. Indeed, when **Greek-speaking people** did arrive on the mainland in about 2100 BC, their destructive impact paralysed its development for five hundred years, while the large and secure island of **Crete** – which they did not invade or settle – flourished and dominated the Aegean.

## The coming of the Greeks

The destruction of numerous mainland sites in about **2100 BC**, followed by the appearance of a new style of pottery, has suggested to archeologists the violent arrival of a **new people**. They domesticated the horse, introduced the potter's wheel and possessed considerable metallurgical skills. These newcomers replaced the old religion centred on female fertility figures with **hilltop shrines**, thought to have been dedicated to the worship of male sky gods like Zeus. And with them came a new language, an early form of **Greek**, though they were obliged to adopt existing native words for such things as olives, figs, vines, wheat and the sea, suggesting that these new migrants or invaders may have come from distant inland steppes where they had been pastoral highlanders, not farmers, fishermen or sailors.

The shock of domination was followed by five centuries of adjustment and intermingling. The population increased, new settlements grew up, and there were advances in metallurgy. Yet in comparison with the Cyclades and Crete, which the invaders had never reached, the Greek mainland seems to have remained backward. Only around **1600 BC**, and then under the influence of Crete, did progress on the mainland quicken – until within little over a hundred years **Crete** itself was conquered by the Greek-speaking mainlanders.

# Minoan and Mycenaean civilizations: 2100–1100 BC

The history of the Aegean during the second millennium BC can be seen as a struggle between two cultures, the **Mycenaean culture** of the Greek mainland and the **Minoan culture** of Crete. Situated halfway between mainland Greece and Egypt, Crete exploited the Bronze Age boom in trade, to become the dominant power in the Aegean by the start of the second millennium BC. Its distinctive civilization, called Minoan, and beneficial economic influence were felt throughout the islands and also on the mainland. The subsequent Greek-speaking mainland invaders were "Minoanized", gradually developing a culture known as Mycenaean (after Mycenae, a principal mainland Bronze Age site) that owed a lot to Crete.

## Minoan Crete

Living on a large and fertile island with good natural harbours, the people of **Crete** raised sufficient crops and livestock on the coastal plains and highland pastures to export surplus quantities of oil and wool. Among their most impressive tools, literally at the cutting edge of new technology, was a four-foot-long bronze saw that readily converted the forest-clad mountains into an ample source of **timber for ships**. Some timber was probably also exported, most likely to treeless Egypt, while metalwork, jewellery and pottery of superb Cretan craftsmanship were shipped to the mainland and beyond. **Kamares ware**, as Cretan pottery of this period is known, was especially valued; it has been found all along the Cretans' 1400-mile-long maritime trade route to the East – on the Aegean islands of Rhodes and Sámos, on the coast of Asia Minor at Miletus, and in Syria and Egypt. There were imports too, of course: timber from Kefaloniá, for example, was used in the construction of Knossos.

On Crete itself, Minoan power was concentrated on three vast **palace complexes** – at **Knossos**, **Phaestos** and **Malia**, all in the centre of the island. First built around 2000 BC, their similarity of plan and lack of defences suggest that some form of confederacy had replaced any regional rivalries on the island, while Minoan sea power induced a sense of security against foreign invasion. Crete's maritime supremacy was consolidated by a network of **colonies**, or close allies throughout the islands – most famously **Thíra** (Santoríni), but also Kýthira, Mílos, Náxos, Páros, Mikonós, Delos, Rhodes and others. On Crete, prosperity was not confined to the palace centres; the numerous remains of villas of the Minoan gentry, and of well-constructed villages, show that the wealth generated by the palaces was redistributed among the island's population. Following an **earthquake** around 1700 BC, the palaces at Knossos and Phaestos were rebuilt, and a more modest palace constructed at Zákros on the east coast. This activity coincided with an apparent centralization of power at Knossos,

## The Trojan War

For the Greeks, the story of the **Trojan War** was the central event in their early history, and in their minds Homer's **Iliad** was not just a poem of heroic deeds sung at noble courts, but the epic of their first great national adventure.

Excavations in the late nineteenth century by Heinrich Schliemann (see p.633) uncovered many Troys of several periods, but the layer known as **Troy VIIa** clearly suffered violent destruction in about 1220 BC. The Mycenaeans are the likeliest perpetrators, though the abduction of a Greek beauty called **Helen** would not have been the only reason they launched a thousand ships against the Trojans. Mycenaean prosperity greatly depended on trade with the Eastern Mediterranean, where increasingly unsettled conditions made it imperative that the Mycenaeans secure their lines of **trade and supply**. Troy commanded a strategic position overlooking the Hellespont, the narrow waterway (today called the Dardanelles) dividing Europe and Asia and linking the Aegean to the Black Sea, where it controlled important trade routes. Trade was especially important to island peoples, which is why so many were involved in the expedition: Ithaca, Rhodes, Kós, Symí, Évvia, Kálymnos and Crete all sent ships to Troy.

The capture of Troy was the last great success of the Mycenaeans, and perhaps for that reason it was long remembered in poetry and song. It inspired later generations of Greeks to dream of overseas expansion, culminating in the fourth century BC when Alexander the Great carried a copy of *The Iliad* as he marched across Asia, founding Greek cities as he went, and stood with his army on the banks of the Indus River.

---

whose ruler installed a vassal at Phaestos and seems to have united the entire island into a single kingdom, giving rise to a **Minoan golden age**.

## Mycenaean dominance

Suddenly, however, around **1500 BC**, the mainland Mycenaeans gained control of the palace of Knossos and were soon in full possession of Crete. How this happened is unknown, but it probably marked the culmination of a growing rivalry between the Mycenaeans and the Minoans for control of the Aegean trade, which perhaps coincided with a **volcanic explosion** on the island of Thíra (Santoríni) and its consequent **tsunami**.

**Greek** now became the language of administration at Knossos and the other former Minoan palaces, as well as on the mainland – indeed this is the earliest moment that Greek language can definitely be identified, as the palace records on Crete are from now on written in a script known as **Linear B**, which when deciphered in 1952 was shown to be a form of Greek. Having wrested control of the Aegean trade from the Minoans, the **Mycenaeans** were dominant for another three hundred years. At the end of that period in about 1220 BC, they famously laid siege to, and destroyed, yet another rival, the city of **Troy**: those events form the basis of Homer's great poetic narrative, **The Iliad**.

Yet within a generation the Mycenaean world was overwhelmed by a vast **migration** of northerners from somewhere beyond the Black Sea. Probably victims of a catastrophic change in climate that brought drought and famine to their homelands, these **Sea Peoples**, as the ancients called them, swept down through Asia Minor and the Middle East and also crossed the Mediterranean to Libya and Egypt, disrupting trade routes and destroying empires as they went. With the palace-based Bronze Age economies destroyed along with the trade that sustained them (especially on the islands), the humbler village-based economies that replaced them lacked the wealth and the technological means to make a mark in the world. Greece was plunged into a Dark Age, and knowledge of the Minoan and Mycenaean civilizations slipped into dim memory.

# The Dark Age and the rise of the city-state: 1150–720 BC

The poverty and isolation that characterized Greece for the next five hundred years did have one lasting effect, **emigration**. Greeks spread to the Dodecanese islands, to Cilicia along the south coast of **Asia Minor**, and to **Cyprus**, which became Greek-speaking. Later, around 1000 BC, they also settled in large numbers along the western coast of Asia Minor. Even in the Dark Age, though, there were a few glimmers of light: **Athens**, for example, escaped the destruction that accompanied the fall of Mycenaean civilization and maintained trading links abroad. It became the route through which the **Iron Age** was introduced to mainland Greece with the importation of iron weapons, implements and technological know-how around 1100 BC.

A new cultural beginning was also made in the form of pottery painted in the **Geometric style**, a highly intricate and controlled design that would lie at the heart of later Greek architecture, sculpture and painting. But it was the **Phoenicians**, sailing from Sidon and Tyre in present-day Lebanon, who really re-established trading links between the Middle East and the Aegean world in the eighth century BC, and Greeks followed swiftly in their wake.

## Homer: The Iliad and The Odyssey

**The Iliad** and **The Odyssey**, the oldest and greatest works in Greek literature, were the brilliant summation of five centuries of poetic tradition, first developed by nameless bards whose recitations were accompanied by music. Completed by 725 BC, they are far older than the *Pentateuch*, the first five books of the Old Testament, which achieved their finished form only around 400 BC. The admiration of the whole Greek world for the Homeric epics was unique, and their influence upon the subsequent development of Greek literature, art and culture in general cannot be overstated. Few works, and probably none not used in worship, have had such a hold on a nation for so long.

*The Iliad* is the story of a few days' action in the tenth and final year of the Trojan War, which in its tales of heroic exploits recalls the golden age of the Mycenaeans. *The Odyssey* begins after the war and follows the adventures of Odysseus, who takes ten years to return to his island home of Ithaca on the western side of Greece, his voyages showing the new Greek interest in the area around the Black Sea and in Italy and Sicily to the west

Ithaca is usually taken to be Itháki, in the Ionian islands, though that's a subject of much debate among scholars. An even older chestnut is the question of authorship: did the blind poet **Homer** write *The Iliad* and *The Odyssey*? The best answer came from Mark Twain who said, "*The Iliad* and *The Odyssey* were written by the blind poet Homer or by another blind poet of the same name". In truth, virtually nothing is known of Homer beyond the tradition that he was blind and was born into the eighth-century BC world of the Asian Greeks, probably on the island of Híos or at Smyrna on the mainland opposite.

With wealth flowing in again, Greek civilization developed with remarkable rapidity; no other people achieved so much over the next few centuries. The institution most responsible for this extraordinary achievement, the **city-state** or **polis**, came into being at a time of rapidly growing populations, greater competition for land and resources, increasing productivity and wealth, expanding trade and more complex relationships with neighbouring states. The birthplace of **democracy** and of equality before the law, the city-state became the Greek ideal, and by the early seventh century BC it had spread throughout Greece itself and wherever Greeks established colonies overseas, with important centres growing up throughout the islands.

Trade also acted as a cultural stimulus. Contact with other peoples made the Greeks aware of what they shared among themselves, and led to the development of a **national sentiment**, notably expressed and fostered by the **panhellenic sanctuaries** that arose during the eighth century BC, of **Hera** and **Zeus** at **Olympia**, where the first **Olympic Games** were held in 776 BC, and of **Apollo** and **Artemis** on **Delos**, as well as the **oracles** of **Zeus** at **Dodona** and of **Apollo** at **Delphi**.

From the Phoenicians the Greeks obtained the basics of the **alphabet**, which they adapted to their own tongue and developed into a sophisticated tool for recording laws, composing literature and chronicling events. **Greek art**, under Eastern influence, saw the Geometric style gradually give way to depicting animals, mythical and real. Finally around 750 BC, for the first time in four hundred years, **human figures** were introduced to vase decorations, most strikingly in group scenes with a story to tell.

# Expansion and renaissance: 720–491 BC

The revival of seafaring and commerce early in the first millennium BC contributed to the rise of the city-state around 750 BC, which in turn had two dramatic results: the **colonization** of the Mediterranean and beyond, and radical **social and political change** at home.

The Greeks began by founding **colonies** in the Western Mediterranean. Those in **Sicily** and **southern Italy** became known as **Greater Greece**, while a century later, around 650 BC, further colonies were established round the shores of the **Black Sea**. By the fifth century BC Greeks seemed to sit upon the shores of the entire world, in Plato's words like "frogs around a pond". The islands were vital staging points en route to the new colonies, and thrived on the trade they brought.

One impetus for colonization was competition between the Greeks and the Phoenicians over trade routes; but there was also rivalry between the Greek city-states themselves. **Chalkis**, **Eretria** and **Corinth** were the major colonizers in the West, while the **Ionian Greeks**, prevented from expanding into the interior of Asia Minor by Phrygia and Lydia, were the chief colonizers around the Black Sea. When the Spartans needed more land, they conquered neighbouring Messenia in 710 BC, but generally land shortage drove Greeks overseas. Thus colonists were sent from Thera (Thíra) to found Cyrene in North Africa, and were forbidden to return on pain of death. Whatever the reason for their foundation, however, most colonies kept up close relations with their mother cities.

Meanwhile, at home in the city-states, political tensions were building between the **aristocratic rulers** and the **people**. A large class of farmers, merchants and the like were excluded from political life but forced to pay heavy taxes. The pressure led to numerous reforms and a gradual move towards **democracy**. Ironically, the transition was often hastened by **tyrants**. Despite the name – which simply means they seized power by force – many tyrants were in fact champions of the people, creating work, redistributing wealth and patronizing the arts. **Peisistratos**, tyrant of Athens during the sixth century BC, is perhaps the archetype. Successful and well-liked by his people, his populist rule ensured Athenian prosperity by gaining control of the route into the Black Sea. He also ordered that Homer's works be set down in their definitive form and performed regularly, and encouraged the theatrical festivals of Dionysus where Greek drama would be born.

City-states also flourished on islands throughout the Aegean, and they too had their tyrants and their artists. On **Lésvos**, for example, the poet **Sappho**, part of a long tradition of poetry on the island, was writing around the turn of the sixth century BC; some claim that her contemporary Aesop (of Fables fame) was also from Lésvos. Not long after their time, the island, along with other nearby territories, was captured by **Polycrates**, tyrant of **Sámos**, who built up his island's navy to establish himself as a regional power, at various times in alliance with the Egyptian pharaoh, the king of Persia and with Lygdamis, tyrant of **Náxos**. **Lygdamis**, in turn, was a close ally of Peisistratos.

# Athens and the Golden Age: 490–431 BC

**Democracy** itself was a very long way from universal. The population of **Athens** and surrounding Attica amounted to not more than 400,000 people, of whom about 80,000 were slaves, 160,000 resident foreigners and another 160,000 free-born Athenians. Out of this last category came the **citizens**, those who could vote and be elected to office, and their number amounted to no more than 45,000 adult men.

Yet if the powers of democracy were in the hands of the few, the energy, boldness and creative spirit that it released raised Athens to greatness. Throughout the **fifth century BC** the political, intellectual and artistic activity of the Greek world was centred on the city. In particular Athens was the patron of **drama**, both tragedy and comedy. Athenian tragedy always addressed the great issues of life and death and the relationship of man to the gods. And the Athenians themselves seemed to be conscious of living out a high drama as they fought battles, argued policy, raised temples and wrote plays that have decided the course and sensibility of Western civilization.

## The Persian Wars

The wars between Greece and Persia began with a revolt against Persian rule by Ionian Greeks in Asia Minor. Athens and Eretria gave them support, burning the city of Sardis in 498 BC. Provoked by their insolence **Darius**, the Persian king, launched a punitive expedition. The **Persians'** unexpected repulse at **Marathon** in 490 BC persuaded Darius to hurl his full military might against Greece, to ensure its subjection once and for all to the Persian Empire.

## The Olympian gods

A high proportion of the ancient sites still seen in Greece today were built as **shrines and temples to the gods**. They include spectacular sites such as Delphi and the Acropolis in Athens, but also many other sanctuaries, great and small, throughout the islands – everywhere, in fact, because the gods themselves were everywhere.

There were many lesser and local gods like the Nymphs and Pan, but the great gods known to all were the **twelve** who lived on **Mount Olympus**. Ten were already recognized by Homer in the eighth century BC: **Zeus**, the lord of the heavens and supreme power on Olympus; **Hera**, his wife and sister, and goddess of fertility; **Athena**, the goddess of wisdom, patron of crafts and fearless warrior; **Apollo**, the god of music, of prophecy and the arts; his sister **Artemis**, the virgin huntress and goddess of childbirth; **Poseidon**, the god of the sea and the forces of nature; the beautiful **Aphrodite**, goddess of love and desire; **Hermes**, the messenger who leads the souls of the dead to the underworld, but also the protector of the home and the market; **Hephaestus**, the lame god of craftsmen and for a while the husband of Aphrodite; and **Ares**, the god of war, who in cuckolding Hephaestus was subdued by the goddess of love. In the fifth century BC these were joined by two deities with a certain mystical quality of rebirth: **Demeter**, the goddess of crops and female fertility; and **Dionysus**, the god of wine and intoxication.

Though limited in number, the Olympian deities could be made to play infinite roles in local cult calendars by the addition of epithets; thus Zeus became "Zeus of the city" or "Zeus of mountaintops", as well as "kindly" or "fulfilling" as place and occasion required. The gods had human form, and were born and had sexual relations among themselves and humankind, but they never ate human food nor did they age or die. But whereas the gods of most nations claim to have created the world, the Olympians never did so. All they did was to conquer it and then enjoy its fruits, not so unlike mankind itself.

After Darius died in 486 BC, **Xerxes** took over. In 483 BC, he began preparations that lasted two years and were on a fabulous scale. Bridges of boats were built across the Hellespont for Persia's vast imperial army to parade into Europe, and a canal was cut through the peninsular finger now occupied by the Mount Athos monasteries, so that the Persian fleet could avoid storms while rounding the headlands of the Halkidhikí. Though the Greek historian **Herodotus** claimed that Xerxes' army held one million eight hundred thousand soldiers, his figure is probably a tenfold exaggeration. Even so, it was a massive force, an army of 46 nations, combined with a fleet of eight hundred triremes carrying almost as many sailors as there were soldiers in the army.

Despite their numerical superiority, the might of Asia was routed at sea off **Salamis** in 480 BC (see p.87). A significant part of the Greek fleet came from the islands: above all from Égina, then a major rival of Athens, but with ships from Náxos, Lefkádha, Styra on Évvia, Kýthnos, Kéa, Mílos, Sífnos and Sérifos (there were also ships from Rhodes and others in the Persian fleet). The following year the Persians were also defeated on land, first at **Plataea** and then within a few days near **Miletus**. Fearing a renewed uprising in Ionia, Xerxes left his army under the command of Mardonius and came to Sardis to take charge of his reserves. The Ionians had indeed sent to Greece for help, and now a Greek fleet sailed for **Mycale**, off Sámos, where the battle was won when Xerxes' subject Ionians went over to their fellow Hellenes. Xerxes could do no more than return to Susa, his capital deep in Persia, leaving the entire Aegean free.

Despite occasional reversals, this sudden shift in the balance of power between East and West endured for the next 1500 years. Within 150 years, Alexander the Great achieved in Asia what Xerxes had failed to achieve in Europe, and the Persian Empire succumbed to a Greek conqueror.

## The Rise of the Athenian Empire: 478–431 BC

The first consequence of the Greek victory against the Persians was not, as might have been expected, the aggrandisement of **Sparta**, the pre-eminent Greek military power, whose soldiers had obediently sacrificed themselves at Thermopylae and won the final mainland battle at Plataea. Instead, many Greek city-states voluntarily placed themselves under the leadership of Athens.

This Aegean confederation was named the **Delian League**, after the island of **Delos** where the allies kept their treasury; it included cities on virtually every island in the Aegean, plus many on the eastern coast Greece and western coast of Asia Minor. Its first task was to protect the Greeks of Asia Minor against a vengeful Xerxes. This was the opposite of the policy proposed by Sparta and its Peloponnesian allies, which called for the abandonment of Greek homes across the Aegean and the resettlement of Asian Greeks in northern Greece.

That typified the Spartan attitude throughout the Persian crisis, in which Sparta had shown no initiative and acted only at the last minute. Its policy was provincial, protecting its position in the Peloponnese rather than pursuing the wider interests of Greece. Thus over the coming decades Sparta lost prestige to Athens, which Themistocles had established as a maritime power and whose imperial potential was realized under Pericles.

This was the **Athenian golden age**, and in so far as Athens was also "the school of Hellas", as its leader **Pericles** said, it was a golden age for all Greece. The fifty

### Themistocles

The greatest Athenian statesman, and architect of the victory over Persia, was **Themistocles**. Following the Ionian revolt he understood that a clash between Persia and Greece was inevitable, and he had the genius to recognize that Athens' security and potential lay in its command of the sea. He began his life's mission of promoting his naval policy as archon in 493–492 BC, by developing **Piraeus** (Pireás) as the harbour of Athens. Though his pretext was the hostility of the island of Égina, his eyes were always on the more distant but far greater Persian danger.

When the Persians marched into Attica in the late summer of 480 BC, the oracle at Delphi told the Athenians to trust in their wooden wall. Many took that to mean the wooden wall around the citadel of the Athenian Acropolis, but Themistocles argued that it referred to the **Athenian fleet**. Determined to fight at sea, Themistocles warned his Peloponnesian allies against retreating to the isthmus where they too had built a wall, threatening that if they did the entire citizenry of Athens would sail to new homes in southern Italy, leaving the rest of Greece to its fate. On the eve of the Battle of Salamis, as the Persians stormed the Acropolis, slaughtering its defenders and burning down its temples, the taunt came back from the Peloponnesians that Athens had no city anyway. Themistocles replied that so long as the Athenians had 200 ships they had a city and a country.

The Greek victory at Salamis cut the Persians' maritime lines of supply and contributed to their defeat at Plataea the following year. It gave Athens and its allies command of the sea, ensuring their eventual victory throughout the Aegean. For his pains the Athenians later drove Themistocles into exile.

▲ Stone bust of Pericles, strategos of Athens

years following Salamis and Plataea witnessed an extraordinary flowering in architecture, sculpture, literature and philosophy; men recognized the historical importance of their experience and gave it realization through the creative impulse. Just as **Herodotus**, the "father of history", made the contest between Europe and Asia the theme of his great work, so **Aeschylus**, who fought at Marathon, made Xerxes the tragic subject of *The Persians* and thereby brought the art of drama to life. Indeed in the intoxicating Athenian atmosphere the warriors who turned back the Persian tide seemed to have fought in the same cause as Homer's heroes at Troy. In thanksgiving and celebration the temples upon the Acropolis that the Persians had destroyed were rebuilt, the city ennobling itself as it ennobled the houses of its gods – most notably with the building of the **Parthenon**.

Yet Athens was still just one among numerous city-states, each ready to come together during a common danger but reasserting its sovereignty as the foreign threat receded. This was illustrated by the ten-year struggle from 461 BC onwards between Athens (and her island allies in the Delian League) and various **Peloponnesian states**, itself a warning of a yet greater war to come between Athens and Sparta. Perhaps 451 BC marks the fatal moment when Athens passed up the opportunity to create an institution more generous, and more inclusive, than the city-state. Instead Pericles supported the parochial and populist demand that **Athenian citizenship** should not be extended to its allies, thereby stoking up the flames of envy and foregoing the chance of creating a genuine and enduring Greek confederacy.

## Pericles and his times

In 461 BC, **Pericles** (ca.495 BC–429 BC) was first elected to Athens' most important elected position, of *strategos* (general). The ten *strategoi* proposed the legislation that was then voted on in the Assembly. Pericles was so brilliant at winning over audiences in a society where the people were sovereign that in practice he governed the state for around thirty years; with only two exceptions, he was annually re-elected until his death in 429 BC.

Among his early triumphs – in the face of conservative opposition – was making **peace with Persia** in 449 BC, the better to turn his attention to **Sparta**. Pericles believed that Athenian power was not only Greece's best defence against Persia but also the best hope for the unification of Greece under enlightened rule. The visible expression of this cultural excellence could be seen atop the Acropolis, where Pericles was directly responsible for the construction of the Propylaea and the Parthenon, but it was true too in sculpture, painting, drama, poetry, history, teaching and philosophy, where Athenian influence is felt to this day. Politically, as both Pericles and his enemies understood, the advance of democracy in Greece depended on the success of that Athenian imperialism which grew out of the Delian League.

But whatever the excellence of Athens, whatever the ideals of its power, the jealousies of the Peloponnesians were excited all the more, and it is a testimony to Pericles that he was able to avoid war with Sparta for as long as he did. Thucydides, the historian of the Peloponnesian War, greatly admired Pericles for his integrity and also for the restraint he exercised over Athenian democracy.

# The decline of the city-state: 431–338 BC

The **Peloponnesian War** that began in **431 BC** was really a continuation of earlier conflicts between Athens and its principal commercial rivals, Corinth and Aegina (though technically a member of the Delian League, ancient Aegina – Égina – was also a jealous rival of Athens) and their various allies in the Peloponnese. Sparta had earlier stood aside, but by 432 BC when Corinth again agitated for war, the **Spartans** had become fearful of growing Athenian power.

The Athenian Empire was built on trade, and the city was a great sea power, with 300 triremes. The members of Sparta's **Peloponnesian League**, meanwhile, had powerful armies but no significant navy (though from time to time various islands, particularly in the Dodecanese, would ally themselves with Sparta). Just as Themistocles had sought to fight the Persians by sea, so Pericles followed the same strategy against Sparta and its allies, avoiding major battles against superior land forces. Athens and Piraeus were protected by their walls, but the Peloponnesians and their allies were allowed to invade Attica with impunity nearly every year, and Thrace saw constant warfare. On the other hand the Peloponnesians lacked the seapower to carry the fighting into Asia Minor and the Aegean islands or to interfere with Athens' trade, while the Athenians used their maritime superiority to launch attacks against the coasts of the Peloponnese, the Ionian islands and the mouth of the Gulf of Corinth, hoping to detach members from the Peloponnesian League. So long as Athens remained in command of the sea, it had every reason to expect that it could wear down its enemies' resolve.

**Pericles' death** in 429 BC was an early blow to the Athenian cause. Although **Kleon**, his successor, is widely blamed for Athens' eventual defeat, after Pericles the city was in fact always divided into a peace party and a military one, unable

## Thucydides: the first systematic historian

The writing of history began among the Greeks, first with **Herodotus**, then with Thucydides. Whereas Herodotus gives the feeling that he prefers telling a good story, that he still inhabits Homer's world of epic poetry, with **Thucydides** the paramount concern is to analyze events. In that sense Thucydides is the first modern historian; wherever possible he seeks out primary sources, and his concern is always with objectivity, detail and chronology. Not that there is anything dry about his writing; its vividness and insight make reading him as powerful an experience as watching a Greek drama.

Thucydides began writing his history at the outset of the **Peloponnesian War**, intending to give an account of its whole duration. For reasons unknown, however, he abruptly stopped writing in the twentieth year, though he is thought to have survived the war by a few years, living until about 400 BC. Born into a wealthy, conservative Athenian family around 455 BC, he was a democrat and an admirer of Pericles; his reconstruction of Pericles' speeches presents the most eloquent expression of the Athenian cause. But when Thucydides was exiled from his city seven years into the war, this was the making of him as a historian. As he put it, "Associating with both sides, with the Peloponnesians quite as much as with the Athenians, because of my exile, I was thus enabled to watch quietly the course of events".

Thucydides was himself a military man, who understood war at first hand. Hence his concern for method in his research and analysis in his writing, for he intended his book to be useful to future generals and statesmen. For these reasons we have a better understanding of the Peloponnesian War than of any ancient conflict until Julius Caesar wrote his own first-hand accounts of his campaigns.

to pursue a consistent policy. The final straw came in 415 BC, when a bold operation designed to win Sicily to the Athenian cause turned into a catastrophic debacle, thanks at least partly to political interference. Though not entirely defeated, Athens was never to be a major power again.

## City-state rivalries

The Peloponnesian War left **Sparta** the supreme power in Greece, but those whom the Spartans had "liberated" swiftly realized that they had simply acquired a new and inferior master, one that entirely lacked the style, the ability and the intelligence of Athens. Meanwhile Athens had lost its empire but not its trade, so its mercantile rivals faced no less competition than before. During the first decade of the fourth century, Athens managed to restore much of its naval power in the Aegean.

Adding to the intrigues between Persia, Athens and Sparta were a bewildering and unstable variety of alliances involving other Greek states. The most important of these was **Thebes**, which had been an ally of Sparta during the Peloponnesian War but came round to the Athenian side, and then for a spectacular moment under its brilliant general **Epaminondas** became the greatest power in Greece, in the process dealing Sparta a blow from which it never recovered. Theban supremacy did not survive the death of Epaminondas, however, and Greece subsequently found itself free for the first time in centuries from the dictates of Persia or any overpowerful Greek city-state. Exhausted and impoverished by almost continuous war, it was an opportunity for Greece to peacefully unite. But the political and moral significance of the city-state had by now eroded, and with the **rise of Macedonia** came the concept of an all-embracing kingship.

# The Macedonian Empire and Hellenistic Greece: 348–146 BC

Despite its large size and population, **Macedonia** played little role in early Greek affairs. Many in Greece did not consider the Macedonians to be properly Greek, not in speech, culture or political system. They did not live in city-states, which Aristotle said was the mark of a civilized human being, but as a tribal people, led by a king, were closer to the barbarians (such attitudes still rankle today, and inform some of the bitter debate over the name and status of FYROM, the Former Yugoslav Republic of Macedonia).

Towards the middle of the fourth century, however, the power of Macedonia grew, as **Philip II** strengthened royal authority by building up the army on the basis of personal loyalty to himself, not to tribe or locality. Philip was also determined to Hellenize his country. Borrowing from Greek ways and institutions, he founded the city of **Pella** as his capital and lured teachers, artists and intellectuals to his court, among them **Aristotle** and **Euripides**. An admirer of Athens, Philip sought an alliance that would make them joint-masters of the Greek world. But the Athenians opposed him, and he took matters into his own hands.

In **338 BC** Philip defeated the Theban and Athenian forces at **Chaeronia**, and effectively brought the whole of Greece including virtually all the islands (though not Crete) under one rule for the first time. His success was built on one of the most formidable fighting units the world has ever seen, the **Macedonian phalanx**. Armed with the *sarissa*, an eighteen-foot pike tapering from butt to tip, its infantrymen were trained to move across a battlefield with all the discipline of a parade ground drill. Instead of relying on a headlong charge, its effectiveness lay in manipulating the enemy line – its purpose always to open a gap through which the cavalry could make its decisive strike.

## Alexander's conquests

After Chaeronia, Philip summoned the Greek states to Corinth, and announced his plans for a panhellenic conquest of the Persian Empire. But Philip was murdered two years later and to his son **Alexander** fell his father's plans for an **Asian campaign**.

In the East too there was an assassination, and in 335 BC the Persian throne passed to **Darius III**, namesake of the first and doomed to be the last king of his line. Using essentially his father's tactics, Alexander led his army through a series of astonishing victories, usually against greater numbers, until he reached the heart of the Persian Empire. Alexander crossed the Hellespont in May of **334 BC**, with thirty thousand foot soldiers and five thousand horse. By autumn all the Aegean coast of **Asia Minor** was his; twelve months later he stood on the banks of the Orontes River in **Syria**; in the winter of 332 BC **Egypt** hailed him as pharaoh; and by the spring of 330 BC the great Persian cities of **Babylon**, **Susa**, **Persepolis** and **Pasargadae** had fallen to him in rapid succession until, at **Ecbatana**, he found Darius in the dust, murdered by his own supporters. Alexander wrapped the corpse in his Macedonian cloak, and assumed the lordship of Asia.

## Hellenistic Greece

No sooner had **Alexander** died at Babylon in 323 BC, aged 33, than Athens led an alliance of Greeks in a **war of liberation** against Macedonian rule. But the

The Golden Age of Athens under Pericles, and the city-state rivalry after the Pelopon-nesian War, saw the **birth of Western philosophy** under the towering figures of Socrates, Plato and Aristotle.

### Socrates (c.470–399 BC)

The son of an Athenian stonemason, **Socrates** followed his father's trade for a while, and fought bravely for Athens in the Peloponnesian War. He practised **philosophy** in his own peculiar style, promoting no position of his own, but ceaselessly asserting the supremacy of reason. Often this was done in the streets of Athens, button-holing some self-regarding Athenian of the older generation, asking him questions, picking his answers to pieces, until he came up with a definition that held water or, more likely, the spluttering victim was reduced to confess his own ignorance before crowds of Socrates' mirthful young supporters.

By this "**Socratic method**" he asked for definitions of familiar concepts such as piety and justice; his technique was to expose the ignorance that hid behind people's use of such terms, while acknowledging his own similar ignorance. Indeed when the Delphic oracle proclaimed that no man was wiser than Socrates, he explained this by saying wisdom lies in knowing how little one really knows. Because he valued this question-and-answer process over settling on fixed conclusions, Socrates never wrote anything down. Yet his influence was pivotal; before his time philosophical inquiry concerned itself with speculations on how the natural world was formed and how it operates; afterwards it looked to the analysis of concepts and to ethics.

Socrates' method could irritate, especially when he questioned conventional morality, and his friendships with people associated with oligarchy did not put him in good stead with a democratic Athens that had just lost an empire and a war. Probably many factors directed the city's anger, fear and frustration at Socrates, and Athenians wanted to see the back of him. Having tried him for impiety and corrupting the young, and sentenced him to death, they gave him the option of naming another penalty, probably expecting him to choose exile. Instead Socrates answered that if he was to get what he deserved, he should be maintained for life at public expense. At this the **death penalty** was confirmed, but even then it was not to be imposed for two months, with the tacit understanding that Socrates would escape. Instead Socrates argued that it was wrong for a citizen to disobey even an unjust law, and in the company of his friends he drank the cup of hemlock. "Such was the end", wrote Plato, describing the scene in *Phaedo*, "of our friend; of whom I may truly say, that of all the men of his time whom I have known, he was the wisest and justest and best."

### Plato (c.427–347 BC)

As a young man, **Plato** painted, composed music and wrote a tragedy, as well as being a student of Socrates. He intended a career in politics, where his connections would have ensured success; his father could claim descent from the last king of Athens, his mother from Solon, and the family had been close allies of Pericles. But Socrates' death made Plato decide that he could not serve a government that had committed such a crime, and instead his mission became to exalt the memory of his teacher. In Plato's writings, many of them dialogues, Socrates is frequently the leading participant, while at the Academy in Athens, which Plato founded, the Socratic question-and-answer method was the means of instruction.

Macedonians had built up a formidable navy which inflicted heavy losses on the Athenian fleet. Unable to lift the Macedonian blockade of Piraeus, Athens surren-dered and a pro-Macedonian government was installed. The episode marked the end of the city as a sea power and left it permanently weakened.

Plato's philosophy is elusive; he never sets out a system of doctrines, nor does he tell us which of his ideas are most basic, nor rank them in hierarchical order, nor show how they interrelate. Nevertheless, certain themes recur. He believed that men possess **immortal souls** separate from their mortal bodies. Knowledge, he believed, was the recollection of what our souls already know; we do not gain knowledge from experience, rather by using our reasoning capacity to draw more closely to the realm of our souls. The true objects of knowledge are not the transient, material things of this world, which are only reflections of a higher essence that Plato called **Forms** or **Ideas**. Forms are objects of pure thinking, cut off from our experience; but Forms also motivate us to grasp them, so that the reasoning part of us is drawn to Forms as a kind of mystic communion.

Plato's notion of a mystic union with a higher essence would play an important role in later religious thought. But more immediately his teachings at the Academy concerned themselves with logic, mathematics, astronomy and above all political science, for its purpose was to train a new ruling class. Prominent families sent him their sons to learn the arts of government. Plato, an aristocrat born into a calamitous age marked by Athens' imperial defeat, responded by teaching that the best form of government was a constitutional monarchy, at its head a philosopher-king with that higher knowledge of Justice and the Good drawn from the realm of Forms. Though it was a utopian vision, Plato's political philosophy helped prepare the intellectual ground for the acceptance of an absolutist solution to the increasing uncertainties of fourth-century BC Greece.

### Aristotle (c.384–322 BC)

**Aristotle** grew up in Pella, the capital of an increasingly powerful Macedonia, where his father had been appointed doctor to King Amyntas II; it is therefore not unlikely that Amyntas's son, the future Philip II, and Aristotle were boyhood friends. However, aged seventeen, Aristotle was sent to Plato's Academy at Athens to continue his education, and he remained there, first as a student, then as a teacher, a faithful follower of Plato's ideas. His independent philosophy matured later, during the years he spent, again at Pella, as tutor to **Alexander the Great**, and later still, after 335 BC, when he founded his own school, the Lyceum, in Athens.

Aristotle came to reject Plato's dualism. He did not believe that the soul was of a substance separate from the body, rather that it was an aspect of the body. Instead of Plato's inward-looking view, Aristotle sought to explain the physical world and human society from the viewpoint of an outside observer. Essentially a scientist and a realist, he was bent on discovering the true rather than establishing the good, and he believed sense perception was the only means of human knowledge. His vast output covered many fields of knowledge – logic, metaphysics, ethics, politics, rhetoric, art, poetry, physiology, anatomy, biology, zoology, physics, astronomy and psychology. Everything could be measured, analyzed and described, and he was the first to classify organisms into genera and species. He is probably the only person ever to assimilate the whole body of existing knowledge on all subjects and bring it within a single focus.

The exactitude of Aristotle's writings does not make them easy reading, and Plato has always enjoyed a wider appeal owing to his literary skill. All the same, Aristotle's influence on Western intellectual and scientific tradition has been enormous.

Greece was now irrevocably part of a new dominion, one that entirely altered the scale and orientation of the Greek world. Alexander's strategic vision had been to see the Mediterranean and the East as two halves of a greater whole. Opened to Greek settlement and enterprise, and united by Greek learning, language and culture, if not always by a single power, this **Hellenistic Empire** enormously increased international trade, created unprecedented prosperity, and established an **ecumene**, the notion of one world, no longer divided by the walls of city-states but a universal concept shared by all civilized peoples.

Asked on his deathbed to whom he bequeathed his empire, Alexander replied "To the strongest". Forty years of warfare between his leading generals gave rise to three dynasties: the **Antigonid** in Macedonia, which ruled over mainland Greece, the Ionian islands and most of those in the western Aegean; the **Seleucid** which ultimately centred on Syria and Asia Minor, including most of the Dodecanese and eastern Aegean islands; and the **Ptolemaic** in Egypt, ruled from Alexandria, founded by Alexander himself, which in wealth and population, not to mention literature and science, soon outshone anything in Greece. **Rhodes** in particular was caught up in the battles between the dynasties, enduring a long and ultimately unsuccessful siege in 305 BC – the Colossus of Rhodes was constructed to commemorate the event and the island became one of the leading powers of the succeeding age.

## The emergence of Rome

Meanwhile, in the Western Mediterranean, **Rome** was a rising power. **Philip V** of Macedonia had agreed a treaty of mutual assistance against Rome with Hannibal. After Hannibal's defeat, Rome's legions marched eastwards, and routed Philip's army at **Cynoscephalae** in Thessaly in 197 BC.

Rome was initially well disposed towards Greece, which they regarded as the originator of much of their culture, and granted autonomy to the existing city-states. However, after a number of uprisings, the country was divided into **Roman provinces** from 146 BC. For good measure Corinth was razed, and its inhabitants sold off, to deter any future Greek resistance.

# Roman Greece: 146 BC–330 AD

During the first century BC Rome was riven by civil wars, many of whose climactic battlefields were in Greece: in 49 BC **Julius Caesar** defeated his rival Pompey at **Pharsalus** in Thessaly; in 42 BC Caesar's assassins were beaten by **Mark Antony** and **Octavian** at **Philippi** in Macedonia; and in 31 BC **Antony** and his Ptolemaic ally **Cleopatra** were routed by **Octavian** in a sea battle off **Actium**, just north of Lefkádha in western Greece. The latter effectively marked the birth of the **Roman Empire** – an empire that in its eastern half continued to speak Greek.

By the first century AD Greece had become a **tourist destination** for well-to-do Romans (and a relatively comfortable place of exile for troublemakers). They went to Athens and Rhodes to study literature and philosophy, and toured the country to see the temples with their paintings and sculpture. They also visited the by now thoroughly professional **Olympic Games**. When the emperor **Nero** came to Greece in AD 67, he entered the Games as a contestant; the judges prudently declared him the victor in every competition, even the chariot race, in which he was thrown and failed to finish.

Roman rule saw much **new building** in **Athens** and elsewhere, notably by the emperor Hadrian. The centre of the Athenian Agora, which had long ceased to serve the purposes of a democracy, was filled with an odeion, a covered theatre seating a thousand people, the gift of Augustus's general Agrippa.

Hadrian built his public library nearby; he loved Athens and stayed there in 125 and 129 AD, completing the vast **Temple of Olympian Zeus** begun nearly six hundred years before by Peisistratos. **Herodes Atticus**, also a generous patron of the arts in Athens, built the odeion that bears his name at the foot of the Acropolis in the 160s.

Greece had an early taste of **Christian teaching** when **Saint Paul** came to preach in 49–52 AD. Brought before the Court of the Areopagus in Athens, a powerful body that exercised authority over religious affairs, he was asked to defend his talk of the death and resurrection of his foreign god, and dismissed as a crank. Paul then spent eighteen months in **Corinth**; he made some converts, but as his subsequent Epistles to the Corinthians show, their idea of Christianity often amounted to celebrating their salvation with carousing and fornication. His journeys also took him to Crete, and to other islands. In the last decades of the century, **Saint John the Divine**, who was proselytizing at Ephesus, was exiled by the Romans to Pátmos, where in a cave still shown to visitors today he is said to have written *Revelation*, the apocalyptic last book of the Bible.

Although the books of the New Testament were composed in Greek, their authors came from the Greek East, and Christianity seems to have made little headway among the inhabitants of Greece itself. Throughout all the **Roman persecutions** of the third and early fourth centuries, in which hundreds of thousands died in Egypt, the Middle East and Asia Minor, there are few recorded martyrs in Greece – probably, it is thought, because there were few Greek Christians.

# Byzantine and Medieval Greece: 330–1460 AD

The **Byzantine Empire** was founded in May 330 when the **emperor Constantine** declared Nova Roma (as he called the city of Byzantium – modern Istanbul) the new capital of the Roman Empire. Founded on the banks of the Bosphorus by Greek colonists in the seventh century BC, Byzantium occupied the one point from where the entire trade between the Black Sea and the Mediterranean could be controlled. **Constantinople**, the city of Constantine, as it became popularly known, was perfectly positioned for the supreme strategic task confronting the empire: the defence of the Danube and the Euphrates frontiers. Moreover, the new capital stood astride the flow of goods and culture from the East, that part of the empire richest in economic resources, most densely populated and rife with intellectual and religious activity.

## The Christian empire

Constantine's other act with decisive consequences was to **legalize** and patronize the **Christian church**. Here again Constantinople was important, for while Rome's pagan traditions could not yet be disturbed, the new capital was consciously conceived as a Christian city. Within the century Christianity was established as the religion of state, with its liturgies (still in use in the Greek Orthodox Church), the Creed and the New Testament all in Greek.

In 391 the emperor **Theodosius I** issued an edict banning all expressions of **paganism** throughout the empire. In Greece the mysteries at Eleusis ceased to be celebrated the following year, and in 395 the Olympic Games were

## Islam and the iconoclastic controversy

The advent of **Islam** in the mid-seventh century had its effect on Greece. The loss to the Arabs of the Christian provinces of Syria in 636 and Egypt in 642 was followed by an attack by an Arab fleet in 677 on Constantinople itself. In 717–718 a combined Arab naval and land force beleaguered the city again, while in 823 the Arabs occupied Crete, holding it for over a hundred years.

The proximity and pressure of Islam helped fuel the great **iconoclastic controversy**, which ignited passions and pervaded daily life throughout the Byzantine Empire for over a century. In 730 the emperor Leo III, who was born on the Syrian frontier and earned the epithet "Saracen-minded", proscribed images in the Orthodox Church, claiming they amounted to idolatry. His strongest support came from the farmer-soldiers of Asia Minor, that is those closest to the lands recently conquered by the Muslims, while his opponents, the iconodules, who favoured icons, were found in the monasteries and in Greece. Indeed, it was the empress Irene, an Athenian, who briefly restored the images in 780, though they were again proscribed by imperial decree from 815 to 843, with the effect that almost no representational Byzantine art survives in Greece from before the ninth century.

suppressed, their athletic nudity an offence to Christianity. Around this time too the Delphic oracle fell silent. The conversion of pagan buildings to Christian use began in the fifth century. Under an imperial law of 435 the Parthenon and the Erectheion on the Acropolis, the mausoleum of Galerius (the Rotunda) in Thessaloníki and other temples elsewhere became churches. Even this did not eradicate pagan teaching: philosophy and law continued to be taught at the Academy in Athens, founded by Plato in 385 BC, until prohibited by the emperor Justinian in 529.

In 395 the Roman Empire split into **Western and Eastern empires**, and in 476 **Rome fell** to the barbarians. As the Dark Ages settled on Western Europe, Byzantium inherited the sole mantle of the empire. Latin remained its official language, though after the reign of Justinian (527–565) the emperors joined the people in speaking and writing Greek.

**Thessaloníki**, the second city of the Byzantine Empire, was relatively close to Constantinople, yet even so the journey by land or sea took five or six days. The rest of Greece grew decidedly provincial, and conditions worsened sharply in the late sixth century when the country was devastated by **plague**. In Athens after 580 life almost came to an end, as the remaining inhabitants withdrew to the Acropolis, while at Corinth the population removed itself entirely to the island of Égina. The islands, especially those of the eastern Aegean closer to Byzantium, perhaps suffered less, though as central authority broke down so the threat of **piracy** grew. Remnants of very **early Christian churches**, from the sixth and seventh centuries onward, are scattered widely across the islands.

## The Crusades

In 1071 the **Byzantine army** was destroyed at **Manzikert**, a fortress town on the eastern frontier, by the **Seljuk Turks** who went on to occupy almost all Asia Minor. After the Byzantine emperor turned to the West for help, the Roman Catholic Pope replied by launching the **First Crusade** in 1095. Together, the Crusaders and the Byzantines won a series of victories over the Seljuks in Asia Minor, but the Byzantines, wary of possible Crusader designs on the empire itself, were content to see their Latin allies from the West advance alone on Jerusalem, which they captured in 1099.

The worst fears of the Byzantines were borne out in 1204 when the **Fourth Crusade** attacked and sacked **Constantinople** itself. Greece and its islands were shared out and endlessly changed hands between Franks, Venetians and many others in a bewildering patchwork of feudal holdings; for the maritime empires of Venice and Genoa, the islands held special appeal. Amid this endless infighting in the West, a new Turkish dynasty, the **Ottomans**, emerged in the late thirteenth century. By 1400 they had conquered all of mainland Byzantine Greece except Thessaloníki and the Peloponnese. In 1452 they invaded the Peloponnese as a diversion to the main attack on **Constantinople**, which fell on May 23, 1453. In 1456 the Ottomans captured **Athens** from the Venetians and turned the Parthenon church into a mosque, and in 1460 they conquered the **Peloponnese**. **Trebizond** fell the following year, and the Byzantine Empire was no more.

The fates of the islands were more varied. **Crete** enjoyed a spectacular cultural renaissance after the fall of Constantinople as a stream of refugees arrived from the east. Though increasingly embattled, it held out as a Venetian-ruled outpost for over two hundred years, before Iráklion was finally surrendered in 1669. In the **Dodecanese**, meanwhile, Rhodes and Kós had been built up as formidable fortresses during the Crusades, home to the **Knights Hospitallers of St John**. The Knights held out until 1522 before Süleyman the Magnificent finally drove them out; the trigger for the last Venetian islands in the Aegean, **Évvia** and **Égina**, to succumb not much later. In the west, closer to Venice, Corfu and the other Ionian islands were occasionally fought over, but never submitted for long – they remained in Venetian hands through most of the Turkish occupation, passing to France in the eighteenth century when Napoleon conquered Venice.

# Greece under Turkish occupation: 1460–1821

Although the Greeks refer to the Turkish occupation as *sklavía* – "slavery" – in practice, in exchange for submitting to Muslim rule and paying tribute, the Greeks were free to pursue their religion and were left very much in charge of their own religious and civil affairs. The essence of the Turkish administration was **taxation**; collection was often farmed out to the leaders of the Greek communities, and some local magistrates profited sufficiently to exercise a dominant role not only within their own region but also in the Ottoman Empire at large. On the mainland and larger islands, the Ottomans controlled the towns and the plains but left the mountains almost entirely to the Greeks. The fate of smaller islands depended largely on their resources; where there were none, they saw little interference.

The other important institution within Greece was the **Orthodox Church**. Greeks preferred to give their lands to the monasteries than have them occupied by the Turks, while the Muslims found it easier to allow the Church to act in a judicial capacity than to invent a new administration. Though often corrupt and venal, the Church did at least preserve the traditional faith and keep alive the written form of the Greek language, and it became the focus of Greek nationalism.

## Ottoman conquests and the eclipse of Venice

In 1570 Ottoman troops landed on **Cyprus**. Nicosia was swiftly captured, and 30,000 of its inhabitants slaughtered. Turkish brutality in Cyprus horrified Europe, and the **Holy League** was formed under the aegis of the Pope. Spain and Genoa joined Venice in assembling a fleet led by Don John of Austria, the bastard son of the Spanish king, its lofty aim not only to retake the island but in the spirit of a crusade to recapture all Christian lands taken by the Ottomans. In the event, it was utterly ineffectual; no serious attempt was made even to launch an expedition to relieve Cyprus. Yet out of it something new arose – the first stirrings of **Philhellenism**, a desire to liberate the people whose ancient culture stood at the heart of Renaissance thought.

There was, too, the encouragement of a naval victory, when in 1571 Don John's fleet surprised and overwhelmingly defeated the much larger Ottoman fleet, at its winter quarters at **Lepanto** on the Gulf of Corinth in western Greece. Two hundred and sixty-six Ottoman vessels were sunk or captured, fifty thousand sailors died, and fifteen thousand Christian galley slaves were freed. Throughout Europe the news of Lepanto was received with extraordinary rejoicing; this was the first battle in which Europe had triumphed against the Ottomans, and its symbolic importance was profound. Militarily and politically, however, the Ottomans remained dominant. The fall of **Crete**, in 1669, marked the end of the last bastion of Byzantine culture.

## Greek nationalist stirrings

During the eighteenth century the islanders of **Ýdhra** (Hydra), **Spétses** and **Psará** built up a Greek merchant fleet that traded throughout the Mediterranean, where thriving colonies of Greeks were established in many ports. The fleets were to form the basis of the Greek naval forces in the struggle for Independence, and these islands produced many of the movement's early leaders. Greek merchant families were also established in the sultan's provinces of **Moldavia** and **Wallachia**, the area of present-day Romania. The rulers of these provinces were exclusively Greeks, chosen by the sultan from wealthy **Phanariot families**, that is residents of the Phanar, the quarter along the Golden Horn in Constantinople and site of the Greek Orthodox Patriarchate which itself enjoyed considerable privileges and was an integral part of the administration of the Ottoman Empire.

These wealthier and more educated Greeks enjoyed greater than ever opportunities for advancement within the Ottoman system, while the Greek peasantry, unlike the empire's Muslim inhabitants, did not have to bear the burden of military service. Nevertheless the Greeks had their grievances against the Ottoman government, notably the arbitrary, unjust and oppressive system of taxation. But the Greek peasantry were primarily opposed to their Muslim neighbours – as much as one fifth of the population – and Ottoman overlords on religious grounds. Muslim leaders had long preached hatred of the infidel, a view reciprocated by the priests and bishops of the Orthodox Church.

# The War of Independence: 1821–32

The **ideology** behind the **War of Independence** came from the Greeks of the diaspora, particularly those merchant colonies in France, Italy, Austria and

Russia who had absorbed new European ideas of nationalism and revolution. Around 1814, assorted such Greeks formed a secret society, the **Filikí Etaría** (Friendly Society). Their sophisticated political concepts went uncomprehended by the peasantry, who assumed the point of an uprising was to exterminate their religious adversaries. And so when war finally broke out in **spring 1821**, almost the entire settled **Muslim population of Greece** – farmers, merchants and officials – was **slaughtered** within weeks by roaming bands of Greek peasants armed with swords, guns, scythes and clubs. They were often led by Orthodox priests, and some of the earliest Greek revolutionary flags portrayed a cross over a severed Turkish head.

## The war

While the Greeks fought to rid themselves of the Ottomans, their further aims differed widely. Assuming their role was to lead, landowners sought to reinforce their traditional privileges; the peasantry saw the struggle as a means towards land redistribution; and westernized Greeks were fighting for a modern nation-state. Remarkably, by the end of **1823** the Greeks appeared to have won their independence. Twice the sultan had sent armies into Greece; twice they had met with defeat. Greek guerrilla leaders, above all **Theodoros Kolokotronis** from the Peloponnese, had gained significant military victories early in the rebellion, which was joined by a thousand or so **European Philhellenes**, almost half of them German, though the most important was the English poet, **Lord Byron**.

But the situation was reversed in 1825, when the Peloponnese was invaded by formidable Egyptian forces loyal to the sultan. Thus far, aid for the Greek struggle had come neither from Orthodox Russia, nor from the Western powers of France and Britain, both wearied by the Napoleonic Wars and suspicious of a potentially anarchic new state. But the death of Lord Byron from a fever while training Greek forces at **Mesolóngi** in 1824 galvanized European public opinion in the **cause of Greece**. When Mesolóngi fell to the Ottomans in 1826, Britain, France and Russia finally agreed to seek autonomy for certain

▲ Panagiotis Zografos's vision of the 1821 Battle of Langada and Compoti, the War of Independence

parts of Greece, and sent a combined fleet to put pressure on the sultan's army in the Peloponnese and the Turkish-Egyptian fleet harboured in Navaríno Bay. Events took over, and an "accidental" naval battle at **Navaríno** in October 1827 resulted in the destruction of almost the entire Ottoman fleet. The following spring, Russia itself declared war on the Ottomans, and Sultan Mahmud II was forced to accept the existence of an autonomous Greece.

At a series of conferences from 1830 to 1832, **Greek independence** was confirmed by the Western powers, and borders were drawn in 1832. These included just 800,000 of the six million Greeks living within the Ottoman Empire, and territories that were largely the poorest of the classical and Byzantine lands: **Attica**, the **Peloponnese** and the islands of the **Argo-Saronic**, the **Sporades** and the **Cyclades**. The rich agricultural belt of **Thessaly**, **Epirus** in the west and **Macedonia** in the north remained in Ottoman hands, as did the Dodecanese and Crete. Meanwhile after the Napoleonic Wars the **Ionian islands** had passed to British control.

# The emerging state: 1832–1939

Modern Greece began as a **republic**, with its first capital on the island of Égina. **Ioannis Kapodistrias**, the first president, a native of Corfu, concentrated his efforts on building a viable central authority. Almost inevitably he was assassinated – by two chieftains from the ever-disruptive Mani region at Greece's southern tip – and perhaps equally inevitably the "Great Powers" – Britain, France and Germany – stepped in. They created a **monarchy**, setting a Bavarian prince, Otto (Otho), on the throne with a new capital at Athens. By 1834, Greece also had its own national, state-controlled **Orthodox Church**, independent from the Patriarchate in Constantinople; however, at the same time, two-thirds of the monasteries and convents were closed down and their assets used to fund secular public education.

Despite the granting of a constitution in 1844, **King Otto** proved autocratic and insensitive, filling official posts with fellow Germans and ignoring all claims by the landless peasantry for redistribution of the old estates. When he was forced from the country by a popular revolt in 1862, the Europeans produced a new prince, this time from Denmark. The accession of **George I** (1863–1913) was marked by Britain's decision to hand over the **Ionian islands** to Greece. During his reign, Greece's first roads and railways were built, its borders were extended, and land reform began in the Peloponnese.

## The Great Idea and expansionist wars

From the start, Greek foreign policy was motivated by the **Megáli Idhéa** (Great Idea) of redeeming ethnically Greek populations outside the country and incorporating the old territories of Byzantium into the new kingdom. There was encouragement all around, as Ottoman control was suddenly under pressure across the Balkans. The year 1875 saw revolts by Serbs and Montenegrins, followed by attacks by Russia on Anatolia and Bulgaria. These culminated in the creation of an independent Serbia-Montenegro and autonomous Bulgaria at the 1878 Treaty of Berlin, which also sanctioned a British takeover of the administration of **Cyprus**.

In 1881, revolts broke out among the Greeks of **Crete**, **Thessaly** and **Epirus**, aided by guerrillas from Greece. Britain forced the Ottoman Empire to cede

Thessaly and Arta to Greece, but Crete remained Ottoman. When Cretan Greeks set up an independent government in 1897, declaring *énosis* (union) with Greece, the Ottomans responded by invading the mainland and came within days of reaching Athens. The Great Powers came to the rescue by warning off the Turks and placing Crete under an international protectorate. Only in 1913 did **Crete** unite with Greece.

It was from Crete, nonetheless, that the most distinguished modern Greek statesman emerged: **Eleftherios Venizelos**, having led a civilian campaign for his island's liberation, was elected as Greek prime minister in 1910. Two years later he organized an alliance of Balkan powers to fight the **Balkan Wars** (1912–13), campaigns that saw the Ottomans virtually driven from Europe, and the Bulgarian competition bested in the culmination of a bitter, four-decade campaign for the hearts and minds of the **Macedonian** population. With Greek borders extended to include the **northeast Aegean islands, northern Thessaly, central Epirus** and parts of **Macedonia** (though not the Dodecanese, which had been seized by Italy in 1912), the Megáli Idhéa was approaching reality. Venizelos also shrewdly manipulated domestic public opinion to revise the constitution and introduce liberal social reforms.

Division, however, appeared with the outbreak of **World War I**. Although Venizelos urged Greek entry on the Allied side, hoping to liberate Greeks in Thrace and Asia Minor, the new king, **Constantine I**, who was married to the German Kaiser's sister, imposed neutrality. Eventually Venizelos set up a revolutionary government in Thessaloníki, polarizing the country into a state of **civil war** along Venezelist–Royalist lines. In 1917 Greek troops entered the war to join the French, British and Serbians in the Macedonian campaign against Bulgaria and Germany. Upon the capitulation of Bulgaria and the Ottoman Empire, the Greeks occupied **Thrace**, and Venizelos presented demands at Versailles for predominantly Greek **Smyrna** (modern Izmir), on the Asia Minor coast, to become part of the Greek state.

## The Catastrophe and its aftermath

The demand for Smyrna triggered one of the most disastrous episodes in modern Greek history, the so-called **Katastrofí** (Catastrophe). Venizelos was authorized to move forces into Smyrna in 1919, but a new Turkish nationalist movement was taking power under Mustafa Kemal, or **Atatürk**. After monarchist factions took over when Venizelos lost elections in 1920, the Allies withdrew support for the venture. Nevertheless the monarchists ordered Greek forces to advance upon Ankara, seeking to bring Atatürk to terms. The Greeks' **Anatolian campaign** ignominiously collapsed in summer 1922 when Turkish troops forced the Greeks back to the coast. As the Greek army hurriedly evacuated from **Smyrna**, the Turks moved in and **massacred** much of the **Armenian and Greek** population before burning most of the city to the ground.

For the Turks, this was the successful conclusion of what they call their War of Independence. World War I had already cost the Ottoman sultan his empire, and in 1922 the sultan himself was deposed. The borders of modern Turkey, as they remain today, were established by the **1923 Treaty of Lausanne**, which also provided for the **exchange of religious minorities** in each country – in effect, the first large-scale regulated ethnic cleansing. Turkey was to accept 390,000 Muslims resident on Greek soil. Greece, mobilized almost continuously for the last decade and with a population of under five million, was faced with the resettlement of over **1,300,000 Christian refugees** from Asia Minor. Many of these had already read the writing on the wall after 1918 and arrived of their own accord; significant numbers were settled across Macedonia, western Thrace, Epirus and in Athens, as well as on Límnos, Lésvos, Híos, Sámos, Evvía and Crete.

The Katastrofí had intense and far-reaching consequences. The bulk of the agricultural estates of **Thessaly** were finally redistributed, both to Greek tenants and refugee farmers, and huge shanty towns grew into new quarters around **Athens**, **Pireás** and **Thessaloníki**, spurring the country's then almost non-existent industry. Politically, reaction was even swifter. By September 1922, a group of Venizelist army officers "invited" King Constantine to abdicate and executed six of his ministers held most responsible for the debacle. Democracy was nominally restored with the proclamation of a **republic**, but for much of the next decade changes in government were brought about by factions within the armed forces. Meanwhile, among the urban refugee population, unions were being formed and the **Greek Communist Party (KKE)** was established.

## The End of Venizelos and the rise of Metaxas

Elections in 1928 **returned Venizelos to power**, but his freedom to manoeuvre was restricted by the Great Crash of the following year. Late 1932 saw a local crash and Venizelos forced from office. His supporters tried forcibly to reinstate him in March 1933, but their coup was put down and Venizelos fled to Paris, where he died three years later.

A 1935 plebiscite restored the king, **George II**, to the throne, and the next year he appointed **General John Metaxas** as prime minister. Metaxas had opposed the Anatolian campaign, but had little support in parliament, and when KKE-organized strikes broke out, the king dissolved parliament without setting a date for new elections. This blatantly unconstitutional move opened the way for five years of ruthless and at times absurd **dictatorship**. Metaxas proceeded to set up a state based on the fascist models of the era. Left-wing and trade-union opponents were imprisoned or forced into exile, a state youth movement and secret police were set up and rigid censorship, extending even to passages of Thucydides, was imposed. But it was at least a Greek dictatorship, and while Metaxas was sympathetic to fascist organizational methods and economics, he utterly opposed German or Italian domination.

# World War II and the Civil War: 1939–1950

When World War II broke out, the most immediate threat to Greece was **Italy**, which had invaded Albania in April. Even so, Metaxas hoped Greece could remain neutral, and when the Italians torpedoed the Greek cruiser *Elli* in Tinos harbour on August 15, 1940, they failed to provoke a response. **Mussolini**, however, was determined to have a war with Greece, and after accusing the Greeks of violating the Albanian frontier, he delivered an ultimatum on October 28, 1940, to which Metaxas famously if apocryphally answered "**ohi**" (no). Galvanized by the crisis, the Greeks not only drove the invading Italians out of Greece but managed to gain control over the long-coveted and predominantly Greek-populated area of northern Epirus in southern Albania. ("Ohi Day" is still celebrated as a national holiday.)

Mussolini's failure, however, only provoked Hitler into sending his own troops into Greece, while the British rushed an expeditionary force across the Mediterranean from Egypt where they were already hard-pressed by the Germans. Within days of the **German invasion**, on April 6, 1941, the German army was pouring into central Greece. Outmanoeuvred by the enemy's highly mechanized forces and at the mercy of the Luftwaffe, resistance was soon broken. When the Germans occupied Crete in May, King George and his ministers fled to Egypt and set up a government-in-exile. Metaxas himself had died before the German invasion.

The joint Italian-German-Bulgarian Axis **occupation of Greece** was among the most bitter experiences of the European war. Nearly half a million Greek civilians starved to death over the winter of 1941–42, as all food was requisitioned to feed the occupying armies. In addition, entire villages throughout the mainland, but especially on Crete, were burned at the least hint of resistance and nearly 130,000 civilians were slaughtered up to autumn 1944. In their northern sector, which included Thássos and Samothráki, the Bulgarians demolished ancient sites and churches to support any future bid to annex "Slavic" Macedonia. Meantime, the Germans supervised, during the summer of 1944 the **deportation** to extermination camps of almost the entire **Jewish population** of Greece.

No sooner had the Axis powers occupied Greece than a spontaneous resistance movement sprang up in the mountains. The National Popular Liberation Army, known by its initials **ELAS**, founded in September 1941, quickly grew to become the most effective resistance organization, working in tandem with **EAM**, the National Liberation Front. Communists formed

## Greek Jewry and World War II

Following the German invasion of Greece, Jews who lived in the Italian zone of occupation were initially no worse off than their fellow Greeks. But after Italy capitulated to the Allies in September 1943 and German troops took over from the Italian troops, the Jewish communities in Rhodes and Kos in the Dodecanese, as well as in Crete, Corfu, Vólos, Évvia and Zákynthos, were exposed to the full force of Nazi **racial doctrine**. The Germans applied their "final solution" in Greece during the spring and summer of 1944 with the deportation of virtually the entire Jewish population, about 80,000 in all, to extermination camps in Poland.

**Greek Christians** often went to extraordinary lengths to protect their persecuted countrymen. Thus when the Germans demanded the names of the Jews of Zákynthos prior to a roundup, Archbishop Khrysostomos and Mayor Loukas Karrer presented them with a roster of just two names – their own – and secretly oversaw the smuggling of all the island's 275 Jews to remote farms. Their audacious behaviour paid off, as every Zakynthian Jew survived the war. In Athens, the police chief and the archbishop arranged for false identity cards and baptismal certificates to be issued. Elsewhere, others were warned in good time of what fate the Germans had in store for them, and often took to the hills to join the partisans.

Too few survivors returned to Greece from the death camps for most islands or provincial towns to experience a revival, so most preferred to move to Athens – home to about 3000 of today's 5000 **Greek Jews** – or emigrate to Israel rather than live with ghosts. Thessaloníki now holds fewer than a thousand Sephardim, while Lárissa retains about three hundred, many in the clothing trade. Small Romaniot communities of a hundred or less also continue to exist in Halkídha, Ioánnina, Corfu, Tríkala and Vólos. The Kos, Haniá and Rhodes congregations were effectively wiped out, and today only about thirty Jews – many from the mainland – live in Rhodes Town, where the Platía ton Evréon Martáron (Square of the Jewish Martyrs) commemorates over 2000 Jews of Kos and Rhodes deported and murdered by the Germans.

the leadership of both organizations, but opposition to the occupation and disenchantment with the pre-war political order ensured they won the support of many non-communists. By 1943 ELAS/EAM controlled most areas of the country, working with the British Special Operations Executive (SOE) against the occupiers.

But the Allies were already eyeing the shape of postwar Europe, and British prime minister **Winston Churchill** was determined that Greece should not fall into the communist sphere. Ignoring advice from British agents in Greece that ELAS/EAM were the only effective resistance group, and that the king and his government-in-exile had little support within the country, Churchill ordered that only right-wing groups like **EDES**, the National Republican Greek Army, should receive British money, intelligence and arms. In August 1943 a resistance delegation asked the Greek king, George, in Cairo, for a postwar coalition government in which EAM would hold the ministries of the interior, justice and war, and requested that the king himself not return to Greece without popular consent expressed through a plebiscite. Backed by Churchill, King George flatly rejected their demands.

## Liberation and Civil War

As the Germans began to withdraw from Greece in September 1944, most of the ELAS/EAM leadership agreed to join a British-sponsored interim government headed by the liberal anti-communist politician **George Papandreou**, and to place its forces under that government's control, which effectively meant under command of the British troops who landed in Greece that October. But many partisans felt they were losing their chance to impose a communist government and refused to lay down their arms. On December 3, 1944 the police fired on an EAM demonstration in Athens, killing at least sixteen. The following day, vicious **street fighting** broke out between members of the Greek Communist Party (KKE) and British troops which lasted throughout the month, until eleven thousand people were killed and large parts of Athens destroyed. In other large towns, ELAS rounded up its most influential and wealthy opponents and marched them out to rural areas in conditions that guaranteed their deaths.

After Papandreou resigned and the king agreed not to return without a plebiscite, a **ceasefire** was signed on February 12, 1945, and a new British-backed government agreed to institute democratic reforms. Many of these were not implemented, however. The army, police and civil service remained in right-wing hands, and while collaborators were often allowed to retain their positions, left-wing sympathizers, many of them merely Venizelist Republicans and not communists, were excluded. A KKE boycott of elections in March 1946 handed victory to the parties of the right, and a **rigged plebiscite** followed that brought the king back to Greece. Right-wing gangs now roamed the towns and countryside with impunity, and by the summer of 1946 eighty thousand leftists who had been associated with ELAS had taken to the mountains.

By 1947 guerrilla activity had again reached the scale of a **full civil war**, with ELAS reorganized into the Democratic Army of Greece (DSE). In the interim, King George had died and been succeeded by his brother Paul, while the Americans had taken over the British role and began implementing the Cold-War **Truman Doctrine**, in which massive economic and military aid was given to an amenable Greek government. In the mountains American military advisors trained the initially woeful Greek army for campaigns against the DSE, while the cities saw mass arrests, court-martials and imprisonments. From their stronghold on the slopes of Mount Grámmos on the border of Greece and

Albania, the partisans waged a losing guerrilla struggle. At the start of 1948 Stalin withdrew Soviet support, and in the autumn of 1949, after Tito closed the Yugoslav border, denying the partisans the last means of outside supplies, the remnants of the DSE retreated into Albania and the KKE admitted defeat by proclaiming a supposedly temporary suspension of the civil war. Also in 1948, the **Dodecanese** islands finally became an official part of the Greek state.

# Reconstruction and dictatorship: 1950–74

After a decade of war that had shattered much of Greece's infrastructure (it is said that not one bridge was left standing by 1948), and had killed twelve percent of the 1940 population, it was a demoralized, shattered country that emerged into the Western political orbit of the 1950s. Greece was **American-dominated**, enlisted into the **Korean War** in 1950 and **NATO** the following year. The US embassy – still giving the orders – foisted an electoral system upon the Greeks that ensured victory for the Right for the next twelve years. Overt leftist activity was banned (though a "cover" party for communists was soon founded), and many of those who were not herded into political "re-education" camps or dispatched by firing squads, legal or vigilante, went into exile throughout Eastern Europe, to return only after 1974. The 1950s also saw the wholesale **depopulation of remote villages** and the virtual emptying of many of the smaller islands as migrants sought work in Australia, America and Western Europe, or the larger Greek cities.

## Constantine Karamanlis and Cyprus

The American-backed right-wing **Greek Rally** party, led by **General Papagos**, won the first decisive post-civil-war elections in 1952. After the general's death, the party's leadership was taken over – and to an extent liberalized – by **Constantine Karamanlis**. Under his rule, stability of a kind was established and some economic advances registered, particularly after the revival of Greece's traditional German markets.

The main ongoing crisis in foreign policy was **Cyprus**, where Greek Cypriots demanding *énosis* (union) with Greece waged a long terrorist campaign against the British. Turkey adamantly opposed *énosis* and said that if Britain left Cyprus it should revert to Turkish rule. A 1959 compromise granted independence to the island and protection for its Turkish Cypriot minority but ruled out any union with Greece.

By 1961, unemployment, the Cyprus issue and the presence of US nuclear bases on Greek soil were changing the political climate, and when Karamanlis was again elected there was strong suspicion of intimidation and fraud carried out by right-wing elements and the army. After eighteen months of strikes and protest demonstrations, Karamanlis resigned and went into voluntary exile in Paris.

## George Papandreou and the Colonels

New elections in 1964 gave the **Centre Union Party**, headed by **George Papandreou**, an outright majority and a mandate for social and economic reform. The new government was the first to be controlled from outside the right since 1935 and, in his first act as prime minister, Papandreou sought to heal the wounds of the civil war by **releasing political prisoners** and allowing exiles to return. When King Paul died in March and his son came to the throne as **Constantine II**, it seemed a new era had begun.

But soon **Cyprus** again took centre stage. Fighting between Turkish and Greek Cypriots broke out in 1963, and only the intervention of the United States in 1964 dissuaded Turkey from invading the island. In the mood of military confrontation between Greece and Turkey – both NATO members – Papandreou questioned Greece's role in the Western alliance, to the alarm of the Americans and the Greek right. When he moved to purge the army of disloyal officers, the army, with the support of the king, resisted.

Amid growing tension, elections were set for May 1967. It was a foregone conclusion that George Papandreou's Centre Union Party would win but **King Constantine**, disturbed by the party's leftward shift, was said to have briefed senior generals for a coup. True or not, the king, like almost everyone else in Greece, was caught by surprise when a group of unknown **colonels** staged their own **coup** on April 21, 1967. In December the king staged a counter-coup against the colonels, and when it failed he went into exile.

The junta announced itself as the **Revival of Greek Orthodoxy** against corrupting Western influences, not least long hair and miniskirts, which hardly helped tourism. Political activity was banned, independent trade unions were forbidden to recruit or meet, the press was heavily censored and thousands of communists and others on the left were arrested, imprisoned and often tortured. Among these were George Papandreou and his son Andreas, the composer Mikis Theodorakis and Amalia Fleming, the widow of the discoverer of penicillin, Alexander Fleming. Thousands were maimed physically and psychologically in the junta's torture chambers. Culturally, the colonels put an end to popular music and inflicted ludicrous censorship on literature and the theatre, including a ban on the production of classical tragedies. In 1973, chief colonel **Papadopoulos** abolished the monarchy and declared Greece a republic with himself as president.

## Restoration of democracy

The colonels lasted for seven years. Whatever initial support they may have had among Greeks, after the first two years they were opposed by the vast majority, including a great many on the right. Opposition was voiced from the start by exiled Greeks in London, the US and Western Europe, but only in 1973 did demonstrations break out openly in Greece – the colonels' secret police had done too thorough a job of infiltrating domestic resistance groups and terrifying everyone else into docility. After students occupied the **Athens Polytechnic** on **November 17**, the ruling clique sent armoured vehicles to storm the gates. A still-undetermined number of students (estimates range from 34 to 300) were killed. Martial law was tightened and Colonel Papadopoulos was replaced by the even more noxious and reactionary **General Ioannides**, head of the secret police. The end came within a year when the dictatorship embarked on a disastrous adventure in **Cyprus**. By attempting to topple the Makarios government, the junta provoked a **Turkish invasion** and occupation of forty percent of Cypriot territory. The army finally mutinied and **Constantine Karamanlis** was invited to return from Paris to resume office.

Karamanlis swiftly negotiated a ceasefire in Cyprus, and in November 1974 he and his **Néa Dhimokratía** (New Democracy) party were rewarded by a sizeable majority in elections. The chief opposition was the new Panhellenic Socialist Movement (**PASOK**), led by **Andreas Papandreou**, son of George.

# Europe and a new Greece: 1974 to the present

To Karamanlis's enduring credit, his New Democracy party oversaw an effective return to **democratic stability**, even legalizing the KKE (the Greek Communist Party) for the first time. Karamanlis also held a **referendum on the monarchy**, in which seventy percent of Greeks rejected the return of Constantine II. So a largely symbolic presidency was instituted instead, occupied by Karamanlis from 1980 to 1985, and again from 1990 to 1995. In 1981, Greece joined the **European Community**.

"Change" and "Out with the Right" were the slogans of the election campaign that swept the socialist party, **PASOK**, and its leader Andreas Papandreou to power on October 18, 1981. The new era started with a bang as long-overdue **social reforms** were enacted. Peasant women were granted pensions for the first time; wages were indexed to the cost of living; civil marriage was introduced; family and property law was reformed in favour of wives and mothers; and equal rights legislation was passed. By the time PASOK was returned to power in 1985, it was apparent the promised economic bonanza was not happening: hit by low productivity, lack of investment (not helped by anti-capitalist rhetoric from the government) and world recession, unemployment rose, inflation hit 25 percent and the national debt soared.

In the event it was the European Community, once Papandreou's *bête noire*, which rescued him, with a huge loan on condition that an austerity programme was maintained. Forced to drop many of his populist policies, the increasingly autocratic Papandreou turned on his former left-wing allies. Combined with the collapse of Soviet rule in Eastern Europe, his own very public affair with an Olympic Airways hostess half his age and a raft of economic scandals, PASOK's hold on power was not surprisingly weakened. Since 1989, when New Democracy was elected once more, the two parties have exchanged power in an increasingly stable political system, helped enormously by the growth and funding brought by European Union membership.

Nonetheless, the 1990s were not easy, with an economy still riven by unrest and division and huge foreign policy headaches caused by the break-up of the former Yugoslavia and the ensuing wars on Greece's borders. Some problems were largely self-inflicted: when one breakaway republic named itself **Macedonia**, the threatened Greeks fought tooth and nail against anyone recognizing the breakaway state, let alone its use of the name Macedonia. Ultimately, they failed miserably and were eventually forced to recognize FYROM – the Former Yugoslav Republic of Macedonia – with just minor concessions. Meanwhile, alone among NATO members, Greece was conspicuous for its open support of **Serbia**, ostentatiously supplying trucks to Belgrade via Bulgaria.

By the end of the Nineties, the economy was stabilizing, with inflation consistently in single figures, and in 1997 national morale was further boosted with the award of the 2004 Olympic Games to Athens. Abroad, a dramatic and unexpected change in Greece's always distrustful **relations with Turkey** came when a severe **earthquake** struck northern Athens on September 7, 1999, killing scores and rendering almost 100,000 homeless. Coming less than a month after a devastating earthquake in northwest Turkey, it spurred a thaw between the two historical rivals. Greeks donated massive amounts of blood and foodstuffs to the Turkish victims, and were the earliest foreign rescue teams to reach Turkey; in turn they saw Turkish disaster-relief squads among the first on

Greece may continue to occupy the EU's economic cellar with Portugal, but it's still infinitely wealthier (and more stable) than many of its neighbours, This has acted as a magnet for a permanent underclass of **immigrants**. Since 1990 they have arrived in numbers estimated at 800,000 to well over a million, a huge burden for a not especially rich country of just over ten million citizens. These days your waiter, hotel desk clerk or cleaning lady is most likely to be Albanian, Bulgarian or Romanian. There are also significant communities of Pakistanis, Egyptians, Poles, Bangladeshis, Syrians, Filipinos, Ukrainians, Russians, Equatorial Africans, Kurds and Georgians, not to mention ethnic Greeks from the Caucasus – a striking change in what had hitherto been a homogeneous and parochial culture.

The Greek response has been decidedly mixed. **Albanians**, who make up roughly half the influx, are almost universally detested, and blamed for all manner of social ills. For the first time, crime – especially burglaries – is a significant issue. The newcomers have also prompted the first significant anti-immigration measures in a country whose population is more used to being on the other side of such laws. A member of the Schengen visa scheme, Greece sees itself, as in past ages, as the first line of defence against the barbarian hordes from the East. The Aegean islands regularly receive boatloads of people from every country in Asia.

In June 2001, as an attempt to cope, **legal residence** was offered to the estimated half-million illegals who could demonstrate two years' presence in Greece, and pay a hefty amount for retroactive social security contributions. This and a subsequent amnesty legalized about 300,000 residents. Not that the other illegals are likely to be deported en masse, as they do the difficult, dirty and dangerous work that Greeks now disdain, especially **farm labour**, **restaurant work** and **rubbish collection**. From an employer's point of view, they are cheap and they are net contributors to the social welfare system, especially to pensions where Greece, like much of Europe, is seeing its population shrinking and aging. Albanians in particular are also buoying up the banking system by their phenomenal saving habits and wiring of funds home.

the scene in Athens. Soon afterwards, foreign minister George Papandreou announced that Greece had dropped its historic opposition to EU financial aid to Turkey and that it would no longer oppose Turkish candidacy for the EU.

## The twenty-first century

In March 2004, New Democracy took control of government again – PASOK having been in power for nineteen of the previous twenty-three years – and was re-elected with a perilously small majority in snap elections of September 2007. For an outsider one of the most striking aspects of modern Greek democracy is the clan-based nature of its leadership: Prime Minister **Kostas Karamanlis** is the nephew of former president Constantine, while PASOK is led by **George Papandreou**, son of Andreas, grandson of George.

With the **2004 Olympic Games** considered a triumph – which, despite a last-minute rush to complete the facilities, huge cost overruns and serious doubts over the long-term legacy, they probably were – Greek confidence was briefly at an all-time high. Joining the euro may have raised prices and industrial relations remain problematic, but nearly a fifth of the world's merchant fleet is owned by Greek companies, while infrastructure improvement, thanks to the Olympics and EU funds, would seem to provide a secure foundation for future development. Gloom, however, has descended as the worldwide downturn has hit the country hard, and weeks of riots in December 2008, provoked by a police shooting, reflect frustration at severely limited prospects for young people.

# Archeology

U ntil the second half of the nineteenth century, archeology was a very hit-and-miss, treasure-hunting affair. The early students of antiquity went to Greece to draw and make plaster casts of the great masterpieces of Classical sculpture. A number soon found it more convenient or more profitable to remove objects wholesale, and might be better described as looters than scholars or archeologists.

## Early excavations — and pillaging

The **British Society of Dilettanti** was one of the earliest promoters of Greek culture, financing expeditions to draw and publish antiquities. Founded in the 1730s as a club for young aristocrats who had completed the Grand Tour and fancied themselves arbiters of taste, the society's main qualification for membership (according to most critics) was habitual drunkenness. Its leading spirit was **Sir Francis Dashwood**, a notorious rake who founded the infamous Hellfire Club. Nevertheless, the society was the first body organized to sponsor systematic research into Greek antiquities, though it was initially most interested in Italy. Greece, then a backwater of the Ottoman Empire, was not a regular part of the Grand Tour and only the most intrepid adventurers undertook so hazardous a trip.

In the 1740s, two young artists, **James Stuart** and **Nicholas Revett**, formed a plan to produce a scholarly record of ancient Greek buildings. With the support of the society they spent three years in Greece, principally in and around Athens, drawing and measuring the antiquities. The first volume of *The Antiquities of Athens* appeared in 1762. The publication of their exquisite illustrations and the 1764 publication of **Johann Winckelmann**'s *History of Art*, in which the **Parthenon** and its sculptures were exalted as the eternal standard by which beauty should be measured, gave an enormous fillip to the study (and popularity) of Greek sculpture and architecture; many European Neoclassical town and country houses date from this period.

The Dilettanti financed a number of further expeditions to study Greek antiquities, including one to Asia Minor in 1812. The expedition was to be based in Smyrna, but while waiting in Athens for a ship to Turkey, the party employed themselves in excavations at **Eleusis**, where they uncovered the **Temple of Demeter**. It was the first archeological excavation made on behalf of the society, and one of the first in Greece. After extensive explorations in Asia Minor, the participants returned via Attica, where they excavated the **Temple of Nemesis** at **Rhamnous** and examined the **Temple of Poseidon** at **Soúnio**.

Several other antiquarians of the age were less interested in discoveries for their own sake. A French count, **Choiseul-Gouffier**, removed part of the **Parthenon frieze** in 1787 and his example prompted **Lord Elgin** to detach much of the rest in 1801. These were essentially acts of looting – "Bonaparte has not got such things from all his thefts in Italy", boasted Elgin – and their legality was suspect even at the time.

Other discoveries of the period were more ambiguous. In 1811, a party of English and German travellers, including the architect **C.R. Cockerell**, uncovered the **Temple of Aphaea** on **Égina** and shipped away the pediments. They auctioned off the marbles for £6000 to Prince Ludwig of Bavaria, and, inspired by this success, returned to Greece for further finds. This time they struck it lucky with 23 slabs from the **Temple of Apollo Epikourios** at **Bassae**, for which the British Museum laid out a further £15,000. These were huge sums for the time and highly profitable exercises, but they were also pioneering archeology for the period. Besides, removing the finds was hardly surprising: Greece, after all, was not yet a state and had no public museum; antiquities discovered were sold by their finders – if they recognized their value.

## The new nation

The Greek War of Independence (1821–28) and the establishment of a modern Greek nation changed all this. As a result of the selection of Prince Otto of Bavaria as the first king of modern Greece in 1832, the **Germans**, whose education system stressed Classical learning, were in the forefront of archeological activity. One dominant Teutonic figure during the early years of the new state was **Ludwig Ross**, who in 1834 began supervising the excavation and restoration of the **Acropolis**. Dismantling the accretion of Byzantine, Frankish and Turkish fortifications, and reconstructing Classical originals, began the following year.

The Greeks themselves had begun to focus on their ancient past when the first stirrings of the independence movement were felt. In 1813 the **Philomuse Society** was formed, aiming to uncover and collect antiquities, publish books and assist students and foreign philhellenes. In 1829 an orphanage on the island of Égina became the first **Greek archeological museum**.

In 1837 the **Greek Archeological Society** was founded "for the discovery, recovery and restoration of antiquities in Greece". Its moving spirit was **Kyriakos Pittakis**, a remarkable figure who during the War of Independence had used his knowledge of ancient literature to discover the Klepsydra spring on the Acropolis – solving the problem of lack of water during the Turkish siege. In the first four years of its existence, the Archeological Society sponsored excavations in Athens at the **Theatre of Dionysos**, the **Tower of the Winds**, the **Propylaia** and the **Erechtheion**. Pittakis also played a major role in the attempt to convince Greeks of the importance of their heritage; antiquities were still being looted or burned for lime.

## The great Germans: Curtius and Schliemann

Although King Otto was deposed in 1862 in favour of a Danish prince, Germans remained in the forefront of Greek archeology in the 1870s. Two men dominated the scene: Heinrich Schliemann and Ernst Curtius.

**Curtius** was a traditional Classical scholar. He had come to Athens originally as tutor to King Otto's family and in 1874 returned to Greece to secure permission to excavate at **Olympia**. He set up a **German Archeological Institute** in Athens and negotiated the **Olympia Convention**, under the terms of which the Germans were to pay for and have total control of the dig; all finds were to remain in Greece, though the excavators could make copies and casts; and all finds were to be published simultaneously in Greek and German.

This was an enormously important agreement, which almost certainly prevented the treasures of Olympia and Mycenae following that of Troy to a German museum. But other Europeans were still in acquisitive mode: **French consuls**, for example, had been instructed to buy any "available" local antiquities in Greece and Asia Minor, and had picked up the Louvre's great treasures, the **Venus de Milo** and **Winged Victory of Samothrace**, in 1820 and 1863 respectively.

At **Olympia**, digging began in 1875 on a site buried beneath river mud, silt and sand. Only one corner of the **Temple of Zeus** was initially visible, but within months the excavators had turned up statues from the east pediment. Over forty magnificent sculptures, as well as terracottas, statue bases and a rich collection of bronzes, were uncovered, together with more than four hundred inscriptions. The laying bare of this huge complex was a triumph for official German archeology.

While Curtius was digging at Olympia, a man who represented everything that was anathema to orthodox Classical scholarship was standing archeology on its head. **Heinrich Schliemann**, the son of a drunken German pastor, left school at fourteen and spent the next five years as a grocer's assistant, before enlisting as cabin boy on a boat bound for Venezuela where he hoped to seek his fortune. The boat foundered in a storm, and he was left for dead after being washed up on the Dutch coast. Following recovery from this mishap he took a job as a book-keeper in Amsterdam, where he began to study languages. His phenomenal memory enabled him to master four by the age of 21. Following a six-week study of Russian, Schliemann was sent to St Petersburg as a trading agent and had amassed a fortune by the time he was 30. In 1851 he visited California, opened a bank during the Gold Rush and made another fortune.

His financial position secure for life, Schliemann was almost ready to tackle his life's ambition – the **search for Troy** and the vindication of his lifelong belief in the truth of Homer's tales of prehistoric cities and heroes. Although most of the archeological establishment, led by Curtius, was unremittingly hostile, Schliemann sunk his first trench at the hill called Hisarlık, in northwest Turkey, in 1870; excavation proper began in 1871. In his haste to find Homer's city of Priam and Hector, and to convince the world of his success, Schliemann dug a huge trench straight through the mound, destroying a mass of important evidence, but he was able nevertheless to identify nine cities, superimposed in layers. In May 1873 he discovered the so-called **Treasure of Priam**, a stash of gold and precious jewellery and vessels. It convinced many that the German had indeed found **Troy**, although others contended that Schliemann, desperate for academic recognition, assembled it from other sources.

Three years later Schliemann turned his attentions to **Mycenae**, again inspired by Homer, and once more following a hunch. Alone among contemporary scholars, he sought and found the legendary graves of Mycenaean kings inside the existing Cyclopean wall of the citadel rather than outside it, unearthing in the process the magnificent treasures that today form the basis of the **Bronze Age collection** in the National Archeological Museum in Athens.

He dug again at Troy in 1882, assisted by a young architect, **Wilhelm Dörpfeld**, who was destined to become one of the great archeologists of the following century. In 1884 Schliemann returned to Greece to excavate another famous prehistoric citadel, this time at **Tiryns**.

Almost single-handedly, and in the face of continuing academic obstruction, Schliemann had revolutionized archeology and pushed back the knowledge of Greek history and civilization a thousand years. Although some of his results have been shown to have been deliberately falsified in the sacrifice of truth to beauty, his achievement remains enormous.

The last two decades of the nineteenth century saw the discovery of other important Classical sites. Excavation began at **Epidaurus** in 1881 under the Greek archeologist **Panayotis Kavvadias**, who made it his life's work. Meanwhile at **Delphi**, the **French** began digging at the **sanctuary of Apollo**. Their excavations continued from 1892 to 1903, revealing the extensive site visible today; work on the site has continued sporadically ever since.

## Evans and Knossos

The early twentieth century saw the domination of Greek archeology by an Englishman, **Sir Arthur Evans**. An egotistical maverick like Schliemann, he too was independently wealthy, with a brilliantly successful career behind him when he started his great work and recovered another millennium for Greek history. Evans excavated what he called the "Palace of Minos" at **Knossós** on **Crete**, discovering one of the oldest and most sophisticated of Mediterranean societies, which he christened Minoan.

The son of a distinguished antiquarian and collector, Evans read history at Oxford, failed to get a fellowship and began to travel. His chief interest was in the Balkans, where he was special correspondent for the *Manchester Guardian* during the 1877 uprising in Bosnia. He took enormous risks in the war-torn country, filing brilliant dispatches and still finding time for exploration and excavation. In 1884, aged 33, Evans was appointed curator of the Ashmolean Museum in Oxford. He travelled whenever he could, and it was in 1893, while in Athens, that his attention was drawn to Crete. Evans, though very short-sighted, had almost microscopic close vision. In a vendor's stall he came upon some small drilled stones with tiny engravings in a hitherto unknown script; he was told they came from Crete. He had seen Schliemann's finds from Mycenae and had been fascinated by this prehistoric culture. Crete, the crossroads of the Mediterranean, seemed a good place to look for more.

Evans visited Crete in 1894 and headed for the legendary site of Knossos, which had earlier attracted the attention of Schliemann (who had been unable to agree a price with the Turkish owners of the land) and where a Cretan,

▲ Sir Arthur Evans at an exhibition of relics from Knossos

appropriately called Minos, had already done some impromptu digging, revealing massive walls and a storeroom filled with jars. Evans succeeded in buying the site and in March 1900 began excavations. Within a few days, evidence of a great complex building was revealed, along with artefacts that indicated an astonishing cultural sophistication. The huge team of diggers unearthed elegant courtyards and verandas, colourful wall-paintings, pottery, jewellery and sealstones – the wealth of a civilization which dominated the eastern Mediterranean 3500 years ago.

Evans continued to excavate at Knossos for the next thirty years, during which time he established, on the basis of changes in the pottery styles, the **system of dating** that remains in use today for classifying **Greek prehistory**: Early, Middle and Late Minoan (Mycenaean on the mainland). Like Schliemann, Evans attracted criticism and controversy for his methods – most notably his decision to speculatively reconstruct parts of the palace in reinforced concrete – and for many of his interpretations. Nevertheless, his discoveries and his dedication put him near the pinnacle of Greek archeology.

## Into the twentieth century: the foreign institutes

In 1924 Evans gave the **British School at Athens** the site of **Knossos** along with his on-site residence, the Villa Ariadne, and all other lands within his possession on Crete (it was only in 1952 that Knossos became the property of the Greek State). At the time the British School was one of several foreign archeological institutes in Greece; founded in 1886, it had been preceded by the **French School**, the **German Institute** and the **American School**.

Greek archeology owes much to the work and relative wealth of these foreign schools and others that would follow. They have been responsible for the excavation of many of the most famous sites in Greece: the **Heraion** on **Sámos** (German); the sacred island of **Delos** (French); sites on **Kós** (Italian) and in central **Crete** (Italian, American, British); **Corinth**, **Samothráki** and the **Athenian Agora** (American), to name but a few. Life as a resident foreigner in Greece at the beginning of the twentieth century was not for the weak-spirited – one unfortunate member of the American School was shot and killed by bandits while in the Peloponnese – but there were compensations in unlimited access to antiquities in an unspoilt countryside.

The years between the two World Wars saw an expansion of excavation and scholarship, most markedly concerning the prehistoric civilizations. Having been shown by Schliemann and Evans what to look for, a new generation of archeologists was uncovering numerous **prehistoric sites** on the mainland and Crete, and its members were spending proportionately more time studying and interpreting their finds. Digs in the 1920s and 1930s had much smaller labour forces (there were just 55 workmen under Wace at Mycenae, as compared with hundreds in the early days of Schliemann's or Evans's excavations) and they were supervised by higher numbers of trained archeologists. Though perhaps not as spectacular as their predecessors, these scholars would prove just as pioneering as they established the history and clarified the chronology of the newly discovered civilizations.

One of the giants of this generation was **Alan Wace** who, while director of the British School at Athens from 1913 to 1923, conducted excavations at **Mycenae** and established a chronological sequence from the nine great tholos tombs on the site. This led him to propose a new chronology for prehistoric Greece, which put him in direct conflict with Arthur Evans. Evans believed that the mainland citadels had been ruled by Cretan overlords, whereas Wace not only concluded that Mycenae had been a culture independent of that of Crete but that the Mycenaeans in the later period had actually been in control at Knossós. The domineering Evans viewed this thesis as heresy and, now a powerful member of the British School's managing committee, published attacks on Wace's claims which resulted in the abrupt halt of the British excavations at Mycenae in 1923 and the no less sudden termination of Wace's job. Evans went to his grave believing he was right, but when Wace returned to Mycenae in 1950 and unearthed tablets similar to those earlier found at Knossós bearing the same "Minoan" **Linear B script**, the weight of evidence began to shift. The last piece in the jigsaw was provided by British architect **Michael Ventris** who deciphered the Linear B tablets in 1952 demonstrating that Minoan characters had been used to write the earliest known form of the Greek language. This was conclusive evidence that the Mycenaean Greeks had conquered the Minoans in approximately 1450 BC, and finally vindicated Wace.

**Classical archeology** was not forgotten in the flush of excitement over the Mycenaeans and Minoans. The period between the wars saw the continuation of excavation at most established sites, and many new discoveries, among them the sanctuary of **Asklepios** and its elegant Roman buildings on **Kós**, excavated by the Italians from 1935 to 1943, and the Classical Greek city of **Olynthos**, in northern Greece, which was dug by the American School from 1928 to 1934. After the wholesale removal of houses and apartment blocks that had occupied the site, the American School also began excavations in the **Athenian Agora**, the ancient marketplace, in 1931, culminating in the complete restoration of the **Stoa of Attalos**.

## More recent excavations

Archeological work was greatly restricted during and after World War II, and in the shadow of the Greek civil war. A few monuments and museums were restored and reopened but it was not until 1948 that excavations were resumed with a Greek clearance of the **Sanctuary of Artemis** at **Brauron** in Attica. In 1952 the American School resumed its activities with a dig at the Neolithic and Bronze Age site of **Lerna** in the Peloponnese, and **Carl Blegen** cleared **Nestor's Palace** at **Pylos** in Messenia. Greek archeologists began work at the Macedonian site of **Pella**, the capital of ancient Macedonia, and at the **Nekromanteion of Ephyra** in Epirus.

These and many other excavations – including renewed work on the major sites – were relatively minor operations in comparison to earlier digs. This reflected a modified approach to archeology, which laid less stress on discoveries and more on **documentation**. Instead of digging large tracts of a site, archeologists concentrated on small sections, establishing chronologies through meticulous analysis of data. Which is not to say that there were no spectacular finds. At **Mycenae**, in 1951, a second circle of graves was unearthed; at Pireás, a burst sewer in 1959 revealed four superb Classical bronzes; and a dig at the **Kerameikos** cemetery site in Athens in 1966 found four thousand potsherds used as ballots for ostracism. Important work has also been undertaken on restorations – in particular the **theatres** at the Acropolis in **Athens**, at **Dodona** and **Epidaurus**, which are now used in summer festivals.

A number of postwar excavations were as exciting as any in the past. In 1961 the fourth great **Minoan palace** (following the unearthing of Knossos, Phaestos and Malia) was uncovered by torrential rains at the extreme eastern tip of the island of Crete at **Káto Zákros** and cleared by Cretan archeologist

**Nikolaos Platon**. Its harbour is now thought to have been the Minoans' main gateway port to and from southwest Asia and Africa, and many of the artefacts discovered in the palace storerooms – bronze ingots from Cyprus, elephants' tusks from Syria, stone vases from Egypt – seem to confirm this. Greek teams have found more Minoan palaces at **Arhánes** and **Galatás**, and possibly at **Haniá** in the west and **Petrás** and **Palékastro** in the east of the island. Challenging previous orthodoxy, many of the new generation of scholars believed that these were ceremonial buildings and not the seats of dynastic authority, as Evans proposed. American excavations at **Kommós**, in central Crete, have uncovered another gateway site with an important harbour, like Káto Zákros, of the Minoan and Mycenaean periods.

At **Akrotíri** on the island of **Thíra** (Santoríni), **Spyros Marinatos** revealed, in 1967, a Minoan-era site that had been buried by volcanic explosion sometime between 1650 and 1550 BC – scientists (using carbon dating evidence) and archeologists (relying on dating of discovered artefacts) are still deliberating its exact date. Its buildings were two or three storeys high, and superbly frescoed. Marinatos was later tragically killed while at work on the site when he fell off a wall, and is now buried there.

A decade later came an even more dramatic find at **Vergina** – ancient **Aegae** – in northern Greece, the early capital of the Macedonian kingdom, which later became its necropolis. Here, **Manolis Andronikos** found a series of royal tombs dating from the fourth century BC. Unusually, these had escaped plundering by ancient grave robbers and contained an astonishing hoard of exquisite gold treasures. Piecing together clues – the haste of the tomb's construction, an ivory effigy head, gilded leg armour – Andronikos showed this to have been the **tomb of Philip II**, father of Alexander the Great. Subsequent forensic examination of the body's remains supported historical accounts of Philip's limp and blindness.

At the beginning of this century the various foreign schools, recently joined by the Australian, Austrian, Belgian, Canadian, Danish, Dutch, Finnish, Georgian, Irish, Norwegian, Spanish, Swedish and Swiss, along with Greek universities and the 25 *ephorates*, or inspectorates, of Prehistoric and Classical Antiquities, are still at work in the field, although the emphasis today is as concerned with **conserving and protecting** what has been revealed as unearthing new finds. All too often newly discovered sites have been inadequately fenced off or protected, and a combination of the elements, greedy developers and malicious trespassers – sometimes all three – have caused much damage and deterioration.

# Wild Greece

For anyone who has first seen Greece at the height of summer with its brown parched hillsides and desert-like ambience, the richness of the wildlife – in particular the flora – may come as a surprise. As winter warms into spring, the countryside (and urban waste ground) transforms itself from green to a mosaic of coloured flowers, which attract a plethora of insect life, followed by birds.

Despite an often negative attitude to wildlife, Greece was probably the first place in the world where it was an object of study. **Theophrastos** (372–287 BC) from Lésvos was the first recorded botanist and a systematic collector of general information on plants, while his contemporary, **Aristotle**, studied the animal world. During the first century AD the distinguished physician **Dioscorides** compiled a herbal study that remained a standard work for over a thousand years.

## Some background

In early antiquity most of the larger Greek islands were thickly forested: pines and oaks in coastal regions, giving way to fir, black pine or cypress in the hills and mountains. But this **native woodland** contracted rapidly as human activities expanded. By Classical times, a pattern had been set of forest clearance, followed by agriculture, abandonment to scrub and then a resumption of cultivation or grazing. Huge quantities of timber were consumed in the production of charcoal, pottery and smelted metal, and for ships and construction work. Small patches of woodland have remained, but even these are under threat from arsonists and land developers.

Greek **farming** often lacks the rigid efficiency of northern European agriculture. Many peasant farmers still cultivate little patches of land, and even city-dwellers travel at weekends to collect food plants from the countryside. Wild greens under the generic term *hórta* are gathered to be cooked like spinach. The buds and young shoots of capers and the fruit of wild figs, carobs, plums, strawberry trees and sweet chestnuts are harvested. Emergent snails and mushrooms are collected after wet weather. The more resilient forms of wildlife can coexist with these uses, but for many Greeks only those species that have practical uses are regarded as having any value. Nowadays, heavier earth-moving machinery means a farmer can sweep away an ancient meadow full of orchids in an easy morning's work – often to produce a field that is used for forage for a year or two and then abandoned to coarse thistles. Increasingly, the pale scars of dirt tracks crisscross once intact hill- and mountainsides, allowing short-termist agricultural destruction of previously undisturbed upland habitats.

Since the 1970s, tourist developments have ribboned along **coastlines**, sweeping away agricultural plots and wildlife havens as they do so. These expanding resorts increase local employment, often attracting inland workers to the coast; the generation that would have been shepherds on remote hillsides now works in tourist bars and tavernas. Consequently, the pressure of domestic animal grazing, particularly in the larger islands, has been significantly reduced, allowing the regeneration of tree seedlings; Crete, for example, has more woodland now than it has for the last five centuries. But **forest fires** remain a threat everywhere. Fires since 1980 have destroyed much of the tree cover in Thássos, southern Rhodes, Kárpathos, Híos and Sámos; the trees may well regenerate eventually, but by then the complex shade-dependent ecology is lost.

# Plants

Whereas in temperate northern Europe plants flower from spring until autumn, the arid summers of Greece confine the main **flowering period** to the spring, a narrow climatic window when the days are bright, the temperatures not too high and the groundwater supply still adequate. **Spring** starts in the southeast, in Rhodes, in early March, and then travels progressively westwards and northwards. Rhodes, Kárpathos and eastern Crete are at their best in March, western Crete in early April, the eastern Aegean mid- to late April, and the Ionian islands in early May, though a cold dry winter can cause several weeks' delay. In the high mountains the floral spring arrives in the chronological summer, with the alpine zones of central and western Crete in full flower in June and July.

The delicate flowers of early spring - orchids, fritillaries, anemones, cyclamen, tulips and small bulbs - are replaced as the season progresses by more robust shrubs, tall perennials and abundant annuals, but many of these close down completely for the fierce **summer**. A few tough plants, like shrubby thyme and savory, continue to flower through the heat and act as magnets for butterflies.

Once the worst heat is over, and the first showers of **autumn** arrive, so does a second "spring", on a much smaller scale but no less welcome after the brown drabness of summer. Squills, autumn cyclamen, crocus and other small bulbs all come into bloom, while the seeds start to germinate for the following year's crop of annuals. By the new year, early-spring bulbs and orchids are flowering in the south.

## Shore

Plants on the **beach** grow in a difficult environment: fresh water is scarce, salt is in excess, and dehydrating winds are often very strong. Feathery **tamarisk** trees are adept at surviving this habitat, and consequently are often planted to provide shade. On hot days or nights you may see or feel them sweating away surplus saltwater from their foliage.

## Lower hillsides

**Arable fields** can be rich with colourful weeds, and small, unploughed **meadows** may be equally colourful, with slower-growing plants such as orchids in extraordinary quantities. The rocky earth makes cultivation on some hillsides difficult and impractical, so agriculture is often abandoned and areas regenerate to a rich mixture of shrubs and perennials - known as **garigue**. With time, a few good wet winters and in the absence of grazing, some shrubs will develop into small trees, intermixed with tough climbers - the much denser **maquis** vegetation. The colour yellow often predominates in early spring, followed by the blues, pinks and purples of bee-pollinated plants. An abundance of the pink and white of *Cistus* rockroses is usually indicative of an earlier fire, since they are primary recolonizers. A third vegetation type is **phrygana** - smaller, frequently aromatic or spiny shrubs, often with a narrow strip of bare ground between each hedgehog-like bush. Many aromatic herbs such as lavender, rosemary, savory, sage and thyme are native to these areas.

Nearly 140 species of **orchid** are believed to occur in the Greek islands; their complexity blurs species' boundaries and keeps botanists in a state of taxonomic flux. In particular, the *Ophrys* bee and spider orchids have adapted themselves, through subtleties of lip colour and false scents, to seduce small male wasps. These insects mistake the flowers for a potential mate, and unintentionally assist the plant's pollination. Though all species are officially protected, many are still picked.

## Mountains and gorges

The **limestone peaks** of islands such as Corfu, Kefaloniá, Crete, Rhodes, Sámos and Thássos hold rich collections of attractive **rock plants**, flowers whose nearest relatives may be from the Balkan Alps or the Turkish mountains. **Gorges** are another spectacular habitat, particularly rich in Crete. Their inaccessible cliffs act as refuges for plants that cannot survive the grazing, competition or more extreme climates of open areas. Many of Greece's endemic plants are confined to cliffs, gorges or mountains.

# Birds

**Migratory species** which have wintered in East Africa move north, through the eastern Mediterranean, from around **mid-March to mid-May**. Some stop in Greece to breed; others move on into the rest of Europe. The southern islands are the first landfall after a long sea-crossing, and smaller birds recuperate for a few days before moving on. Larger birds such as storks and ibis often fly very high, and binoculars are needed to spot them as they pass over. In autumn birds return, but usually in more scattered numbers.

**Larger raptors** occur in remoter areas, preferring mountain gorges and cliffs. Buzzards are the most abundant, and often mistaken by optimistic birdwatchers for the rarer, shyer eagles. Griffon vultures, however, are quite unmistakable, soaring on broad, straight-edged wings, whereas the lammergeier is a state-of-the-art flying machine with narrower, swept wings, seen over mountaintops by the lucky few; the remaining nine or ten pairs in Crete are now the Balkan's largest breeding population.

In areas of **wetland** that remain undrained and undisturbed, such as saltmarshes, coastal lagoons, estuaries and freshwater ponds, ospreys, egrets, ibis, spoonbills, storks, pelicans and many waders can be seen feeding. Flamingos sometimes occur, as lone individuals or small flocks, particularly in the eastern Aegean salt pans between December and May.

# Mammals

The islands' small **mammal** population ranges from rodents and shrews to hedgehogs and hares, and the dark-red Persian squirrel on Lésvos. Medium-sized mammals include badgers, foxes and the persecuted golden jackal, but the commonest is the ferret-like stone (or beech) marten, named for its habit of decorating stones with its droppings to mark territory.

Occasionally seen running wild in Crete's White Mountains, but more often as a zoo attraction, is an endemic ibex, known to hunters as the *agrími* or *krí-krí*. Formerly in danger of extinction, a colony of them was established on the offshore islet of Dhía, where they thrived, exterminating the rare local flora.

# Reptiles and amphibians

Reptiles flourish in the hot dry summers of Greece, the commonest being **lizards**. Most of these are small, agile and wary, rarely staying around for closer inspection. Nocturnal **geckos** are large-eyed, short-tailed lizards. Their spreading toes have claws and ingenious adhesive pads, allowing them to cross

## Flora and fauna field guides

In case of difficulty obtaining titles listed below from conventional booksellers, try Summerfield Books (℡01768/484909; ⓦwww.summerfieldbooks.com).

### Flowers

**Hellmut Baumann** *Greek Wild Flowers and Plant Lore in Ancient Greece*. Crammed with fascinating ethnobotany, plus good colour photographs.

**Marjorie Blamey and Christopher Grey-Wilson** *Mediterranean Wild Flowers*. Comprehensive field guide, with coloured drawings; recent and taxonomically reasonably up to date.

**Lance Chilton** *Plant Check-lists* Small booklets written by the co-author of this guide, including birds, reptiles and butterflies for a number of Greek islands and resorts. Available direct at ℡01485 532710, ⓦwww.marengowalks.com.

**Pierre Delforge** *Orchids of Europe, North Africa and the Middle East*. A comprehensive guide, with recent taxonomy.

**John Fielding & Nicholas Turland** *Flowers of Crete*. Large volume (reprinted 2008) with 1900 coloured photos of the Cretan flora, much of which is also widespread in Greece.

### Birds

**Richard Brooks** *Birding on the Greek Island of Lésvos*. Superb guide with colour photos which includes a list of birdwatching sites, with detailed maps, plus an annotated species-by-species bird list with much useful information. Revised 2002, yearly updates available. Contact the author directly at ⓔemail@richard-brooks.co.uk.

**Lars Jonsson** *Birds of Europe with North Africa and the Middle East*. The ornithologist's choice for the best coverage of Greek birds, with excellent descriptions and illustrations.

### Mammals

**Corbet & Ovenden** *Collins Guide to the Mammals of Europe*. The best field guide on its subject.

### Reptiles

**Arnold, Burton & Ovenden** *Collins Guide to the Reptiles and Amphibians of Britain and Europe*. A useful guide, though it excludes the Dodecanese and east Aegean islands.

### Insects

**Michael Chinery** *Collins Guide to the Insects of Britain and Western Europe*. Although Greece is outside the geographical scope of the guide, it will provide generic identifications for many insects seen.

**Lionel Higgins and Norman Riley** *A Field Guide to the Butterflies of Britain and Europe*. A thorough and detailed field guide that illustrates nearly all species seen in Greece.

house walls and ceilings in their search for insects, including mosquitoes. The rare **chameleon** is a swivel-eyed inhabitant of eastern Crete and some eastern Aegean islands such as Sámos, but hard to spot as its coloration and slow movement enable it to blend into the surroundings.

Once collected for the pet trade, **tortoises** can be found on some islands, though not Crete. Usually their noisy progress through hillside scrub vegetation is the first signal of their presence, as they spend their often long lives grazing the vegetation. Closely related **terrapins** are more streamlined, freshwater tortoises which love to bask on waterside mud by streams or ponds. Shy and nervous, omnivorous scavengers, usually only seen as they disappear under water, their numbers have recently declined steeply on many islands.

**Sea turtles** occur mostly in the Ionian Sea, but can be seen in the Aegean too. The least rare are the loggerhead turtles (*Caretta caretta*), which nest on Zákynthos and Kefalloniá, and occasionally in Crete. Their nesting grounds are disappearing under tourist resorts, although they are a protected endangered species (see box, p.586).

By contrast, **snakes** are abundant in Greece and many islands; most are shy and non-venomous. Several species, including the Ottoman viper, the nose-horned viper and the localized Cycladic lebetina viper, do have a poisonous bite, though they are not usually aggressive; they are adder-like and often have a very distinct, dark zigzag stripe down the back. Snakes are only likely to bite if a hand is put in the crevice of a wall or a rock-face where one of them is resting, or if they are molested. Unfortunately, the locals in some areas attempt to kill any snake they see, greatly increasing the probability of their being bitten. Leave them alone, and they will do the same for you – if bitten, see the advice on p.61. Most snakes are not only completely harmless to humans, but beneficial since they keep down populations of pests such as rats and mice.

**Frogs and toads** are the commonest and most obvious amphibians throughout much of Greece, particularly during the spring breeding season. Frogs prefer the wettest places, and the robust marsh frog revels in artificial water-storage ponds, whose concrete sides magnify their croaking impressively. Tree frogs are tiny emerald green jewels, with huge and strident voices at night, and can sometimes be found in quantity on the leaves of waterside oleanders.

# Insects

Greece teems with insects: some pester, like flies and mosquitoes, but most are harmless to humans. From spring through to autumn, the islands are full of **butterflies**. Swallowtail species are named for the drawn-out corners of the hind-wings, in shades of cream and yellow, with black and blue markings. The unrelated, robust brown-and-orange pasha is Europe's largest butterfly. Tiger moths, with their black-and-white forewings and startling bright orange hindwings, are the "butterflies" occurring in huge quantity in sheltered sites of islands such as Rhodes, Níssyros and Páros.

Other insects include the camouflaged **praying mantis**, holding their powerful forelegs in a position of supplication until another insect comes within reach. The females are notorious for eating the males during mating. Corfu is famous for its extraordinary **fireflies**, which flutter in quantities across meadows and marshes on May nights, speckling the darkness with bursts of cold light to attract partners; look carefully in nearby hedges, and you may spot the less flashy, more sedentary and more widespread glow-worm.

# Traditional music

Song, dance and instrumental music have been an essential part of Greek life from ancient times to the present, and it's difficult to exaggerate their significance. Music and dance form an integral part of weddings, betrothals, baptisms, elections, saints days, name-days (for those who share the name of the saint) observed at private homes or tavernas, Easter week and the pre-Lenten Carnival.

Many pieces, which vary from island to island, are specifically associated with **weddings**. Some are processional songs/tunes (*patinádhes*), sung/played while going to fetch the bride from her home, or as the wedding couple leave the church, plus there are specific dances associated with different stages of the wedding ritual. It was common in the past for the music and dancing that followed a wedding to last for up to three days – nowadays overnight into the next day is more common. Some songs are heard only at **pre-Lenten Carnival** (*Apókries* in Greek), accompanied by the wearing of animal skins or costumes and, in some places such as Skýros, by the shaking of large goat-bells roped together. Such rituals, widespread across Europe, date back to pre-Christian times. Music also accompanies informal, unpublicized **private gatherings** in homes, *kafenía* and tavernas with facilities for musicians and patrons.

Don't be shy about asking people where you can hear *tá paradhosiaká* (traditional music); a few words of Greek go a long way towards inclining locals to

## Questionable innovations

Despite music being so central to island culture, it's possible to travel through the Aegean and hear only the most **modern versions** of older songs and tunes, or more recent compositions, interpreted in a style scarcely resembling the *nisiótika* (island music) of even the 1970s. Many island-born session musicians live and work in Athens and only tour the islands in the summer, and their sound has been dramatically altered during recent decades by contact with Western pop (and a simultaneous rejection by many Greeks of local traditional music). This process began during the mid-1960s, a trend accelerated by the ethos of the 1967–74 junta. During this period many musicians were deprived of (or actively scorned) the oral-aural transmission of technique from older master players, though fortunately such attitudes have now changed, and since the millennium there is a perceptible backlash in some quarters against bad-taste interpretations. CD re-releases of archival studio material, and high-quality field recordings of the last of the old-time players, are proving immensely valuable to a new generation attempting to recapture traditional musicianship.

A good case in point is **Náxos**, which until the 1970s supported a beautiful, unique musical tradition featuring many fine violinists, some of whom played in the older style, but then went "modern". Although some superb recordings of this traditional music have been issued, you'll no longer hear this in Náxos's public places or on local radio stations. At live-music events such as *paniyíria* (saints'-day festivals), you may find the violin's natural tone radically altered by excessive reverb, while the *laoúto*, a plucked-string instrument, is often played with a pick-up, making it sound too much like an electric guitar – sometimes an electric or electric-bass guitar will indeed be substituted. The *bouzoúki*, more at home in Greek urban musical genres, will also often be heard in a band alongside the *laoúto*, as well as percussion – anything from the *toumbéleki* (lap-drum) to a modern rock/jazz drum set. Although this type of instrumentation is typical nowadays, there are exceptions (see p.645) which can be found through luck and knowing what to look for.

help foreign travellers. Learn the Greek names of the instruments you would like to hear, or find someone to translate for you. Once it's clear that you're a budding *meraklís* (untranslatable, but roughly, aficionado), people will be flattered by the respect paid to "real" music, and doors will open for you.

## Island styles

Island musical **traditions** are wonderfully **diverse**, so only a general overview will be attempted here. Each archipelago has its dances, songs and customs which vary between islands and even between towns on the same island. Different dances go by the same name (eg *syrtós*) from place to place, while different lyrics are set to many of the same melodies and vice versa. The same tune can be played so idiosyncratically between neighbouring island groups as to be barely recognizable to an outsider. Compared to Western styles, Aegean music is more circuitous than linear, as would be expected from its Byzantine origins and later Ottoman influences. Although transcriptions exist, and there are some who teach with written notes, most folk pieces are learned by ear.

**Traditional island folk songs** – *nisiótika* – feature melodies which, like much folk music the world over, rely heavily on the pentatonic scale. Lyrics, especially on smaller islands, touch on the perils of the sea, exile and (in a society where long separations and arranged marriages were the norm) thwarted love. In Crete, **rhyming couplets** called *mantinádhes* are sung in alternation with instrumental interludes; similar satirical couplets are found in the Dodecanese (such as *pismatiká* on Kálymnos), while on Náxos such couplets are called *kotsákia*, and the short repeating melody to which they are set is called a *kotsátos*. Singers improvise such rhymed couplets on the spot, thinking of new lines during the short instrumental breaks and coming in again when ready with new lines. These often tease the wedding couple, praise the in-laws, lament the loss of a community member or chide a politician. There are also "set" couplets, sometimes mixed in with newly improvised material.

The **Sporades** – linked in many cultural ways to the Magnesian peninsula opposite – never had a *nisiótika* tradition, according to Yiorgos Xintaris, owner/main soloist of a successful rebétika (urban underground music) ouzerí on Skópelos. The soundtrack of his mid-twenieth-century youth was not only rebétika but *laïká* (popular songs), operatic arias and tangos.

Alone of all modern Greek territory, the **Ionian islands** (except Lefkádha) were never occupied by the Ottomans, but instead by the Venetians, and thus have a predominantly Western musical tradition. The indigenous song-form is both Italianate in names (*kantádhes*, *ariétes*, *arékia*), instrumentation (guitar and mandolin – as in Captain Corelli's) and vocals (harmonized choir). Style and nomenclature differ subtly between the various islands: the equivalent of *ariétes* on Kefalloniá are known as *arékia* on Zákynthos. All of the Ionians, especially Corfu, have a tradition of formal musical instruction and excellence.

The **rizítika** of Crete, slow elegies for historic events and personages with a bare minimum of instrumentation, are confined to the foothill villages of the Lefká Óri (White Mountains); over six hundred bodies of lyrics have been collected, but it's claimed that there are only 34 distinct melodies. Also Cretan are *tragoúdhia tís strátas* or travelling songs, sung a capella in pre-motor-car days to ease the boredom of long journeys between villages.

Many songs (except for the slow table songs, or *epitrapézia*, of which Cretan *rizítika* are a type) are in **dance rhythm**, with a vital interaction between dancers and musicians/singers. Dancers and listeners may also join in the song (solo or as a chorus), or even initiate verses. It is customary for the lead dancer to tip the musicians, often requesting a particular tune and/or dance rhythm for his party to dance to. Fairly similar dances for couples are called *soústa* in Crete but *bállos* across the rest of the Aegean. The *pendozális* of Crete ("five-step", *zála* being Cretan dialect for step) is an easy, slow-starting dance for all abilities, though the *pidhiktós* "jumping" dance requires more acrobatic ability.

An excellent introduction to the subject is Yvonne Hunt's *Traditional Dance in Greek Culture* (Centre for Asia Minor Studies, Athens 1996), which also covers important festivals, customs and the social role of music and musicians. Its fine bibliography lists works of significant Greek musicological researchers, anthropologists and travellers. This book can be purchased (with some persistence) online or sometimes at the Folk Art Museum, Kydhathinéon 17, at the **Museum of Greek Popular Musical Instruments** at Dhioyénous 1–3 in the Pláka district of Athens. This museum, besides stocking a good selection of folk recordings, also displays instruments from every region of Greece; headphones allow you to listen to brief samples of music played on them.

## The instruments

The violin (**violí** in Greek) supposedly appeared in Greece during the seventeenth century, migrating from Western Europe (followed some decades later by the clarinet, featuring mainly in mainland Greek music). Although the violin is also played on the Greek mainland, it is the principal melody instrument of the Aegean islands, with the striking exceptions of Crete, Kárpathos, Kássos and Hálki in the southern Aegean, where two kinds of *lýra* prevail (see p.646). The violin bridge may be sanded in Greece to a less highly arched form than that used for Western classical music (this is also done in Western folk traditions). An alternate **tuning** known as "*álla Toúrka*", more widespread in the past, is still used by some musicians on certain islands (eg Sífnos, Kýthnos and Kós). From high to low, its string values are D, A, D, and G, with a fourth between the two higher-pitched strings instead of the typical all-fifths arrangement. The lowered high string is slacker and "sweeter", and the violin's tonality altered by the modified tuning.

▲ Nisiótika musicians at Tholária, Amorgós

Playing **styles** vary widely within island groups (or even between villages) but Greek violin technique differs radically from both classical and Western folk styles. Modes (related to both the Byzantine and Ottoman musical systems) are used rather than western scales, there's a range of ornamentation techniques, and, in some places, unmetered solos (called *taxímia*) based upon the mode of the melody and subject to modulation into other modes. Idiosyncratic violin styles are still found on Sífnos or Kýthnos in the Cyclades, and on Kálymnos or Kós in the Dodecanese, with a few of the finest old-style performers only fairly recently deceased (eg Andonis Xanthakis and Andonis Mougadhis Komis in Sífnos). Bowing patterns in these places can be swift and angular, resulting in a more "fiddle"-like sound than styles that rely on smoother, longer bow-strokes.

The **laoúto** is a member of a family of instruments generally referred to as long-necked lutes. It has a fat, gourd-like back like the oud (*oúti* in Greek, *al-ud* in Arabic) from which the *laoúto* (and lute) derives its name and basic form, but a long fretted neck (the oud has a short, unfretted one) and four sets of double metal strings (the oud has gut ones). The Greek *laoúto* is tuned in fifths (C, G, D, A from lowest to highest), but the G actually has the lowest pitch, since the C is anomalously tuned a fourth higher than the G. On Sífnos and Kýthnos the heavier of the lowest-pitched doublet is removed to accentuate the treble, and make the *laoúto*'s sound less "thunderous".

In most of the Aegean, the *laoúto* is played with the *violí* or *lýra* and sometimes also with the island bagpipe, the *tsamboúna* (see opposite). Typical duos are *violí/laoúto* in the Cyclades or *lýra/laoúto* in Crete and the Dodecanese. In north Aegean islands (such as Lésvos and Samothráki) the *laoúto* may be played with violin and *sandoúri* or even in large ensembles which include brass instruments and accordion. In the hands of a competent player, the *laoúto* doesn't merely "accompany" a *violí* or *lýra*, but forms part of a true duo by virtue of well-chosen rhythmic patterns and melodic phrases in chime-like tones that make the whole more dynamic. Conversely, good violin- or *lýra*-playing can be ruined by the modern, mechanical *laoúto* style, with frequent chord changes and abrupt attack. The larger, more deeply pitched Cretan *laoúto* will play melody as well as chords to accompany violin or *lýra* more often than in other island groups, as well as solo *taxímia*. In any duo with *violí* or *lýra* and *laoúto*, at least one of the musicians sings while the *laoúto* chords continue, the verses alternating with instrumental passages.

The **sandoúri** is a member of the zither family, resembling the hammered dulcimer and played with the *violí* (or *violí* plus *laoúto*) in many of the Dodecanese and also the northeast Aegean islands, where it may also appear in much larger ensembles. It entered these island groups from nearby Asia Minor, especially after 1923 when it was (re)introduced by refugees, especially on Lésvos. The *sandoúri* plays both chords and melody, as well as introductory *taxímia*. While at times only basic chords are played to complement the violin, it can fill in with arpeggios, scale runs or melodic tags, and occasionally serves as a solo instrument, especially on Lésvos.

The term **lýra** refers to a family of small, pear- or bottle-shaped instruments which are held upright on the player's thigh with strings facing forward and bowed with the palm facing away from the body. Greek-island types are pear-shaped and have three metal strings, with notes played by pressing the fingernails laterally against the strings. The **Dodecanesian lýra** has a loose bow which can touch all three gut strings (the middle one a drone) simultaneously, making double chords possible; the bow in some cases has little bells on it which provide rhythmic accompaniment. Its tonal range matches that of the *tsamboúna* played in the Dodecanese and can be played alone, with *laoúto*, with *tsamboúna*, or both of these together, often accompanying vocalists. The **Cretan lýra** is a relatively modern instrument, having supplanted the Dodecanesian type which was used on Crete before the 1930s. The contemporary *lýra* is larger and fatter, lacks a drone string and is tuned lower and in successive fifths, thus extending the melodic range by a fifth beyond that of the older instrument. The old belled bow was abandoned, both because it was too heavy for the quick and elaborate tunes now possible, but also because its rhythmic function was replaced by the *laoúto* (and in earlier years by a lute-family member, the *boúlgari*). A fingerboard was added to make fingering easier, as well as a longer, narrow neck, and a modern violin bow replaced the older, more convex bow. Yet despite all these violin-like innovations, the *lýra* retains a very different tonal quality; even a skilled violinist can never entirely imitate its sound.

The **tsamboúna** (in Crete, *askomandoúra*) is a Greek-island bagpipe made of goatskin, with no drone and two chanters made of calamus reed. The left chanter never varies, having five holes which allow an incomplete diatonic scale from 'do' to 'fa'. The right chanter is of three types, with anywhere from two to five holes depending on the locale. In the Dodecanese this bagpipe may be played alone, with another *tsamboúna*, or with a *laoúto* and *lýra*; many songs are accompanied by these various combinations. In the Cyclades (and formerly Híos) the *tsamboúna* is (or was) played with a **toumbáki** or two-headed drum, only one side of which is struck with two wooden (or bone) drumsticks. It is suspended to one side of the player's torso by a strap. The *tsamboúna* and *toumbáki* are quintessential shepherds' instruments, their skins taken from their flocks. Along with the *lýra*, they are the oldest of the instruments played on the islands, though rare now except in some of the places mentioned above. On Náxos the *tsamboúna-toumbáki* duo is still heard during the pre-Lenten Carnival.

Accordion, clarinet, guitar and *bouzoúki*, all **imported** from the Greek mainland or urban traditions, are sometimes played along with the more traditional instruments on the islands.

# Discography

If you're stopping over in Athens en route to the islands (where CDs are exorbitantly priced and patchily stocked), you'll find the best **record stores** for island music – Tzina (no. 57), Xylouris (no. 39) and Music Corner (no. 56) – within a few paces of each other on Odhós Panepistimíou, near the eponymous metro station. Branches of big chain outlet Metropolis at the airport (both arrivals and departures) are also likely hunting grounds. With the rate at which recordings get deleted, don't overlook used dealer Zaharias, with premises in the Pláka district at Iféstou 20 and in Thessaloníki too, at Dhimtríou Goúnari 17. But Thessaloníki is mainly home to Studio 52 at no. 46 of the same downtown street, and online at ⊛www.studio52.gr, where just about any CD that's still being pressed can be ordered. An exception to the dismal island pattern is Aerakis, Dhedhálou 37, Iráklio, Crete (⊛www.aerakis.net), your best stop for everything Cretan.

In the **discography** that follows, the sometimes odd spellings used have been devised to match the Studio 52 and Aerakis websites' likeliest search results. All of the following CDs are on Greek labels, easiest obtained in Greece, except for the Ziyia entries.

# Collections

**Avthentika Nisiotika tou Peninda** (Lyra CD 0168). Good Cretan and Dodecanesian material recorded during the 1950s, from the collection of the late Ted Petrides, musician and dance master.

**Ellines Akrites** (FM Records). FM's folk pressings are generally to be approached with caution, but Vol. 1 of this 12-CD series (FM 801, "Híos, Mytilíni, Sámos, Ikaría") ,Vol. 2 (FM 802, "Límnos, Samothráki, Ímvros, Ténedhos") and Vol. 9 ("Pátmos, Kálymnos, Léros, Kós, Astypálea") feature excellent local musicians (*violí/lýra*) and singers such as Stratis Rallis of Lésvos, as well as violinist Kyriakos Gouvendas of Thessaloníki and the late Gavriel Yiallizis of Kós.

**Kalimera Theia – Samothrakiki Skopi ke Tragoudia/Good Morning Auntie – Tunes and Songs of Samothraki** (Arheio Ellinikis Musikis-AEM 014). The local repertoire from this north Aegean island, as well as pieces from neighbouring islands and Asia Minor.

**Kasos: Skopi tis Lyras/Lyra Tunes** (Lyra 0113; may be deleted). A 1990s collection from the bleakest, but one of the more musical, of the Dodecanese.

**Tis Kritis ta Polytima** (MBI 7056). Double box-set showcasing the best Cretan talent since the 1980s by Lyra/MBI artists, all the more valuable given that many of the source discs are now out of circulation. Mostly big names whom you're likely to see in concert: Vasilis Skhoulas, Yiorgo Xylouris, Lizeta Kalimeri, Psarantonis. Avoid the inferior single-disc offering.

**Tis Lerou ta Tragoudhia/Songs of Leros** (Politistikós ké Morfotikós Sýllogos Néon Lérou/Instructive & Cultural Lerian Youth Society), double CD produced by Music Folklore Archive. Live field recordings from 1996–98 of Lerian musicians and singers; *violí, sandoúri, laoúto* and bagpipes in various combinations, plus unaccompanied singing.

**Lesvos Aiolis: Tragoudhia ke Hori tis Lesvou/Songs & Dances of Lesvos** (Panepistimiakés Ekdhóseis Krítis/University Press of Crete, double CD 9/10). Two decades (1974–96) of field recordings of this island's last traditional music, a labour of love supervised by musicologist Nikos Dhionysopoulos. Expensive, but the quality and uniqueness of the instrumental festival tunes and dances especially, and the illustrated booklet, merit the expense (typically around €30).

**Lesvos: Mousika Stavrodhromia sto Egeo/Musical Crossroads of the Aegean** (University of the Aegean) Pricey five-CD set with an accompanying fat, illustrated booklet. Everything from originally Asia Minor music to carols and wedding songs.

**Iy Protomastores, 1920–1955** (Ⓦwww.aerakis.net; 10-CD set). Some of the artists on this massive retrospective of early Cretan recordings are a bit arcane, but the following four standout discs justify the price tag: Disc 1, Baxevanis, on *lýra* with small orchestra; Disc 4, Stelios Fousalieris, last master of the *voúlgari*, knowledge of which died with him; Disc 5, Yiannis Demirtzoyiannis, guitarist and epic singer; and Disc 6, Yiorgis Kousourelis, melodic *laoúto*.

**Seryiani sta Nisia Mas, Vol. 1** (MBI 10371). An excellent retrospective of various *nisiótika* hits and artists, mostly from the 1950s. The highlight of Vol. 1 (2 doesn't exist) is Emilia Hatzidhaki's rendering of "Bratséra".

**Skopi tis Kalymnou/Kalymnian Folk Music** (Lýkio tón Ellinídhon

E2-276-97). Double CD with excellent notes and song translations. Traditional Kalymnian repertoire and native musicians featuring Mikes Tsounias on violin, his grandson playing unison violin on some pieces, plus *tsamboúna* accompaniment.

**Skopi kai Tragoudhia apo tin Apirantho tis Naxou** (Aperathítikos Sýllogos TC-CP957). 1983 recording from the famous Náxos mountain village of Apíranthos, featuring Yiannis Zevgolis (violin) with singer Koula Klironomou-Sidheri, Yiorgos Karapatis on *laoúto*, plus others on guitar and *tsamboúna*. Beautiful renditions of traditional Naxian music, with many wistful and nostalgic songs from a past era.

**Songs of …**(Society for the Dissemination of National Music, Greece). A thirty-disc-plus series of field recordings from the 1950s–70s, each covering traditional music of one region or type. Lyrics in English, all available in CD form, especially at the Museum of Greek Popular Instruments (address on p.645). The best island discs, besides *Amorgos, Kythnos and Sifnos* (SDNM105), are:

**Songs of Kassos and Karpathos** (SDNM 103) The Kárpathos side is unremittingly poignant (or monotonous, depending on your tastes), enlivened by passages on the *tsamboúna*. You'll still hear material like this at Ólymbos festivals. The Kássos side is more sweetly melodic, closer to Crete musically and geographically.

**Songs of Rhodes, Chalki and Symi** (SDNM 104) The pieces from Sými are the most accessible, while those from Rhodes and Hálki show Cretan influence. All material was recorded in the early 1970s; you're unlikely to hear similar pieces today, though Sými retains the instrumentation (*violí, sandoúri*) heard here.

🎵 **Songs of Mytilene and Chios** (SDNM 110), **Songs of Mytilene and Asia Minor**

(SDNM 125) The Mytilene (Lésvos) sides are the highlight of each of these discs. Sublime instrumental and vocal pieces, again from the mid-1970s. Most selections are from the south of the island, particularly Ayiássos, where a tradition of live festival music was – and still is – strong.

**Songs of Ikaria & Samos** (SDNM 128) Much older material, from the 1950s; even then it was obvious that indigenous styles were dying out, as there is extensive reliance on cover versions of songs common to all the east Aegean and Anatolian refugee communities, and the music – mostly choral with string accompaniment – is executed by the SDNM house band of the time, directed by Simon Karas. The Ikarian side is more distinctive, though marred by an irritating voice-over.

**Songs of the North and East Aegean** (SDNM CD7) Features music of Límnos, Thássos, Samothráki, Lésvos and Híos including local dances (*pyrgoúsikos, kehayiádhikos*) using local musicians recorded during the early 1970s.

🎵 **Thalassa Thymisou/Sea of Memories: Tragoudhia ke Skopi apo tis Inousses** (Navtikó Mousío Inoussón-En Khordais CD 1801/1802). The result of a "field trip" by the En Khordais traditional music school of Thessaloníki to Inoússes, a small islet northeast of Híos, to rescue vanishing material with the help of the islanders' long memories; the result's superb, a mix of live sessions in Inoussan tavernas and some studio recordings. Thorough, intelligent notes, but no lyrics translations.

**Tragoudhia ke Skopi tis Patmou/Songs and Melodies of Patmos** (Politistikón Ídhryma Dhodhekanísou 201). Live 1995 field recordings of well-edited pieces, as raw but compelling as you'd hear them at an old-time festival. Local singers and instrumentalists on *violí, tsamboúna* and *sandoúri*.

# Individual artists/groups

**Anna Karabesini & Efi Sarri** CD reissues from old LPs: *Yialo Yialo Piyeno* (Lyra 0102067), *Tis Thalassas* (Lyra 10777) and *Ena Glenti* (Lyra 10717). Two singing sisters from the island of Kós, who were for the Dodecanese what the **Konitopoulos family** (see next entry) was for the Cyclades; that they performed only for private gatherings added to their cachet.

**Irini Konitopoulou-Legaki** *Athanata Nisiotika 1* (Tzina-Astir 1020). A 1978 warhorse, beloved of bus drivers across the islands. *Anefala Thalassina* (Lyra 4693) from 1993 is far less commercial than the usual Konitopoulous-clan offerings and one of the finest recordings from Náxos, featuring Naxian *lautiéris* Dhimitris Fyroyenis and Yiannis Zevgolis, one of the last old-style violinists. Then aged 61, Irini sung her heart out in a richer, deeper voice than she was known for on club stages.

**Argyris Kounadis** *Kefalonitikes Arietes* (Philips 526 492-2). Sweet without being syrupy, this is one of the very few still in-print collections of traditional vocal music from Kefalloniá (indeed from any of the Ionians); largely songs composed by Kounadis.

**Nikos Oikonomidis** *Perasma stin Amorgo / Passage to Amorgos* (Keros Music CD 101). A native of Skhinoússa islet, violinist and *lautiéris* Oikonomidis plays and sings traditional pieces from nearby Amorgós on this 2001 recording, with guest appearances by Yiasemi Saragoudha, wife of the great oudist, and folklorist Domna Samiou. His 1991 *Perasma sta Kythira / Passage to Kythera* (Keros, 1982) collection from that lesser-known island is also worth a listen, as is *Anatolika tou Aigaiou / East of the Aegean* (Verso CD 101). Despite a persistent, annoying

electric bass, Oikonomidis's playing is so clean and spirited that it is difficult not to enjoy this recording. His latest (2006) outing, *Antikeri*, is all-acoustic, with Oikonomidis's own compositions and lyrics.

**Andonis Xylouris (Psarantonis)** *Palio Krasi In'iy Skepsi Mou* and *Idheon Antron* (both Lyra MBI). Psarantonis – shunned by other Cretan musicians as too "out there" – has an idiosyncratically spare and percussive *lýra* style, but here unusual instruments are well integrated into a densely textured whole. Daughter Niki, now a star in her own right, executes a gorgeous rendition of "Meraklídhiko Poulí" on *Idheon Antron*, and also proves a highlight of Psarantonis's 2008 latest, *Mountain Rebels* (Network/Raki 495123), especially on "Kimáte o Ílios sta Vouná" and "Neraïdhas Yié", with brothers Yiorgos and Lambis on *laoúto* and oud respectively.

**Nikos Xylouris** *O Arkhangelos tis Kritis*, 1958–1968 (MBI 10376); *Ta Khronia stin Kriti* (2CD, MBI 10677/78). The best two retrospectives of the sweet-voiced Cretan singer (Andonis's brother), in traditional mode, with copious notes; the first covers his initial decade of recordings before he became a noted *éntekhno* (art music) star, with self-accompaniment on the *lýra*.

**Ziyia** (now reformed as **Edessa**) Fine arrangements and singing, by a five-member American group who simply run rings around most native-Greek session musicians. Their first outing, *From the Mountains to the Islands* (AgaRhythm, 1992) has more island music than *Travels with Karaghiozis* (AgaRhythm, 1995), which does, however, include a lovely song from Kálymnos. Available through ⓦwww.edessamusic.com or ⓦwww.ziyia.com.

# Books

The best books in this selection are marked ✥; titles currently out of print are indicated as "o/p". All of our recommendations are available **online** for a reasonable price. Amazon is an obvious first stop; for out-of-print or secondhand books, consult sites such as ⓦwww.abebooks.com/co.uk or ⓦwww.bookfinder.com. A UK specialist Greek **bookshop** is Hellenic Bookservice (49–51 Fortess Rd, London NW5 1AD ☎020/7267 9499, ⓦwww .hellenicbookservice.com); in Canada, Kalamos Books (2020 Old Station Rd, Streetsville, Ontario L5M 2V1 ☎905/542-1877, ⓦwww.kalamosbooks.com) is excellent. Bookshops in the Greek islands with a significant foreign-language stock are few and far between, mostly restricted to Crete and Corfu; if you're stopping over in Athens, the airport and mid-town outlets of Eleftheroudakis and Papasotiriou are likelier – if expensive – hunting grounds. Two UK **publishers** with a consistent track record in Greek-related titles are Archaeopress (ⓦwww.archaeopress.com), for annotated re-editions of travel and archeology classics, and C. Hurst and Company (ⓦwww.hurstpub.co.uk) for social and historical studies.

## Travel, memoirs, impressions

**James Theodore Bent** *Aegean Islands: The Cyclades, or Life Among the Insular Greeks*. Originally published in 1881, re-released by Archaeopress, this remains an authoritative account of Greek island customs and folklore, gleaned from a long winter's travel in the archipelago.

**Charmian Clift** *Mermaid Singing* (o/p). Clift and family's experiences living on 1950s Kálymnos – among the first post-war expats to do so. Last reissued around the millennium, it's easily found; her *Peel Me a Lotus*, about a subsequent sojourn on Ýdhra, may also appeal, and is often co-bound with *Mermaid Singing*.

**Charles Cockerell** *Travels in Greece* (ⓦwww.anagnosis.gr). One of this Athens publishers' pocket-sized "Grecian Journeys" series, excerpting longer accounts by Grand Tourists. Cockerell arrived in 1810, stayed four years, engaged in archeological pillaging typical of the era, and had more adventures on islands and mainland than he bargained for.

**Gerald Durrell** *My Family and Other Animals*. Durrell's 1930s childhood on Corfu where he developed a passion for the island's fauna while elder brother Lawrence entertained Henry Miller and others.

**Lawrence Durrell** *Prospero's Cell* and *Reflections on a Marine Venus*. The former constitutes Durrell's Corfu memoirs, from his pre-World War II time there. *Marine Venus* recounts his 1945–47 colonial-administrator experiences of Rhodes and other Dodecanese islands: rich in period detail but purple in the prose, alcohol-fogged and faintly patronizing towards the "natives".

**Peter France** *A Place of Healing for the Soul: Patmos*. A former BBC film-maker, France settled on Pátmos with his Greek Orthodox wife, and slowly adopted her faith. More spiritual than travel journey – albeit marred by unsound theology – but island life is nicely observed, too.

✥ **Roger Jinkinson** *Tales from a Greek Island*. Twenty-eight unadorned tales, long and short, set

651

in and around Dhiafáni, Kárpathos (identified cryptically as "The Village"), by turns poignant, revisionist about World War II heroics or blackly funny. The We (The Villagers, among whom part-time resident Jinkinson counts himself) vs. Them (tourists) tone can grate, but he's been there and done it, with special insight into the mysterious craft of Aegean fishing.

**Elias Kulukundis** *The Feasts of Memory: Stories of a Greek Family*. A journey back through time and genealogy by a diaspora Greek two generations removed from Kássos, poorest of the Dodecanese. A 2003 re-release, with an extra chapter, of his 1967 classic *Journey to a Greek Island*.

**Edward Lear** *The Corfu Years* and *The Cretan Journal*. Highly entertaining journals from the 1840s and 1850s. The first volume's watercolours and sketches of Corfu, Paxí and elsewhere offer a rare glimpse of the Ionian archipelago during the mid-nineteenth century.

**William Lithgow** *Rare Adventures* (ⓦwww.anagnosis.gr). Another "Grecian Journey", this time by a Scotsman, among the first English-speakers to write about Greece, exactly two centuries before Cockerell; bad-tempered but entertaining, even sensational (the Hiots supposedly "rented" their wives to male guests).

**John Lucas** *92 Acharnon Street*. A British poet moves to Athens in the mid-Eighties to teach literature, and gets hooked – not on the glories of the ancients, but on modern Greece, specifically its poets, tavernas, politics and foibles; plenty on Égina, his preferred island retreat, as well.

**Willard Manus** *This Way to Paradise: Dancing on the Tables* (ⓦwww.lycabettus.com). American expat's memoir of nearly four decades in Líndhos, Rhodes,

beginning long before its submersion in mass tourism. Wonderful period detail, including bohemian excesses and cameos from S.J. Perelman, Germaine Greer and Martha Gellhorn.

**Henry Miller** *The Colossus of Maroussi*. Corfu, Crete, Athens and the soul of Greece in 1939, with Miller completely in his element; funny, sensual and transporting.

**James Pettifer** *The Greeks: The Land and People Since the War*. Useful, if patchily edited, introduction to contemporary Greece – and its recent past up to 2000. Pettifer charts, among other things, the nation's politics, family life, religion and tourism.

**Dilys Powell** *The Villa Ariadne*. 1950s account of the British in Crete, from Arthur Evans to Patrick Leigh Fermor, viewed through the prism of the villa at Knossós which hosted all of them. Brings early archeological work to life, but rather syrupy style.

**Terence Spencer** *Fair Greece, Sad Relic: Literary Philhellenism from Shakespeare to Byron* (o/p). How Classics-educated travellers and poets – culminating in Byron – fuelled European support for the 1821 Revolution, despite misgivings about the contemporary Greeks. Demonstrates just how old the Zorba stereotype is (the feckless, "merrie Greeke" was already described in the 1500s).

**Tom Stone** *The Summer of My Greek Taverna*. Enjoyable cautionary tale for those considering a new life in the Aegean sun. Moving to Pátmos in the early 1980s, a rather trusting Stone tries to mix friendship and business at a beach taverna, with predictable (for onlookers anyway) results. His subsequent *Zeus: A Journey Through Greece in the Footsteps of a God* combines travel to Zeus-pregnant sites with enquiry into the life-cycle of the Great Sky God – especially good on his long middle age, twilight and appropriation by Christianity.

**Richard Stoneman**, ed *A Literary Companion to Travel in Greece*. Ancient and medieval authors, plus Grand Tourists – an excellent selection.

**Patricia Storace** *Dinner with Persephone*. A New York poet, resident for a year in Athens (with forays to the provinces, including Corfu), puts the country's psyche on the couch. Storace has a sly humour and an interesting take on Greece's "imprisonment" in its imagined past.

**William Travis** *Bus Stop Symi* (o/p). Chronicles three years' residence there in the mid-Sixties; fairly insightful (if rather resented on the island itself for its inaccuracies),

though Travis erroneously prophesied that Sými would never see tourism.

**Peter Trudgill** *In Sfakiá: Passing Time in the Wilds of Crete* (**@**www .lycabettus.com). Or more correctly, passing time (since the 1970s) in and around Hóra Sfakíon, as it evolves from backwater status to Samariá Gorge turnstile. A slow starter, but with genuine insights on Sfakian culture by the linguist-academic author.

**Sarah Wheeler** *An Island Apart*, re-issued as *Évvia: Travels on an Undiscovered Island*. Entertaining chronicle of a five-month ramble through Évvia, juxtaposing meditations on culture and history with an open approach to nuns, goatherds or academics. The main quibble is her success in making the island seem more exotic than it really is.

# Photo books

**Yann Arthus-Bertrand; Janine Trotereau**, text *Greece from the Air*. Veteran aerial photographer makes it look alluring, including the most remote islands and ancient sites.

**Kostas Balafas** *Ta Nisia* (Potamos/Benaki Museum, Athens). Stunning B&W photos of numerous islands by one of Greece's greatest twentieth-century photographers: rural pursuits, religious ceremonies, architecture, portraits.

**Vassilis Colonas** *Italian Architecture in the Dodecanese Islands, 1912–1943* (Olkos Press, Athens). A long-neglected topic put in proper historical context through essays by Colonas, with stunning photos by Yiorgis Yerolymbos.

**Jelly Hadjidimitriou** *39 Coffee Houses and a Barber's Shop* (Crete University Press). Loving elegy to the traditional *kafenía* of Lésvos, some of

which have disappeared since documentation. Accompanied by excellent short essays which explain their social role and why/how they arose in the nineteenth century.

**Constantine Manos** *A Greek Portfolio*. The fruits of a gifted Greek-American photographer's three-year 1960s odyssey through a country on the cusp of modernization; the quality and insight you'd expect from a member of the Magnum co-operative, in elegiac black and white.

**Hugh Palmer; Mark Ottaway**, text *The Most Beautiful Villages of Greece*. Not exhaustive, but a good survey of the mainland and islands in 285 images.

**Clay Perry** *Vanishing Greece*. Well-captioned photos depict threatened landscapes and relict ways of life in rural Greece.

Suzanne Slesin et al *Greek Style*.
Stunning – if sometimes designer-
tweaked – island interiors, from villas

to simpler village houses, primarily
on Rhodes, Corfu, Sérifos and Ýdhra.

# Ancient history and politics

Timothy Boatswain and Colin
Nicolson *A Traveller's History of
Greece*. Well-written overview of
crucial Greek periods and personalities, from earliest times to 2003.

A.R. Burn *Pelican/Penguin
History of Greece*; Paul Cartledge

*Cambridge Illustrated History of Ancient
Greece*. The two best general
introductions to ancient Greece;
choose between brief paperback, or
large illustrated tome.

## Early Greece

M.I. Finley *The World of
Odysseus*. Reprint of a 1954
warhorse, pioneering in its investiga-
tion of the historicity (or not) of
Homeric events and society. Breezily
readable and stimulating.

Oswyn Murray *Early Greece*. The
story from the Mycenaeans and

Minoans through to the beginning of
the Classical period.

Robin Osborne *Greece in the
Making 1200–479 BC*. Well-
illustrated paperback on the rise of
the city-state.

## Minoans

Reynold Higgins *Minoan and
Mycenaean Art*. Solid introduction to
the subject with plenty of illustrations; easily found.

J. Alexander Macgillivray
*Minotaur: Sir Arthur Evans and
the Archaeology of the Minoan Myth*.

Excellent monograph by a Crete-
based archeologist showing how
Evans fitted the evidence at Knossós
to his own preconception of the
Minoans as peaceful, literate and
aesthetic second-millenium BC
Victorians.

## Classical era

Paul Cartledge *The Spartans:
The World of the Warrior-Heroes of
Ancient Greece*. Reassessment of this
much-maligned city-state, secretive
and a source of outsider speculation
even in its own time.

John Kenyon Davies *Democracy and
Classical Greece*. Established, accessible

account of the Classical period and
its political developments.

Simon Hornblower *The Greek
World 479–323 BC*. Erudite
survey of ancient Greece from
the end of the Persian Wars to
Alexander's death.

Roger Ling *Classical Greece*. Covers the "golden age" from the fifth to the first centuries BC, taking in the arts, military and political history, and surveying the archeology, of the period.

## Hellenistic era

Paul Cartledge *Alexander the Great: The Hunt for a New Past*. An evocative, meticulous and accessible biography, stinting on neither the man's brutality nor his achievements.

Robin Lane Fox *Alexander the Great*. Another absorbing study, mixing historical scholarship with imaginative psychological detail.

F.W. Walbank *The Hellenistic World*. Greece under the sway of the Macedonian and Roman empires.

# Ancient culture and religion

Walter Burkert *Greek Religion: Archaic and Classical*. Superb overview of deities and their attributes, the protocol of sacrifice and the symbolism of festivals. Especially good on relating Greek worship to its antecedents in the Middle East.

James Davidson *Courtesans and Fishcakes*. Absorbing book on the politics, class characteristics and

## The classics

Many of the classics make excellent companions for a trip around Greece; reading Homer's *Odyssey* when battling with the vagaries of island ferries puts your own plight in perspective. Most of these are published in a range of paperback editions; particularly outstanding translations are noted.

**Mary Beard and John Henderson** *The Classics: A Very Short Introduction*. Exactly as it promises: an excellent overview.

**Herodotus** *The Histories*. Revered as the father of narrative history – and anthropology – this fifth-century-BC Anatolian writer chronicled both the causes and campaigns of the Persian Wars, as well as the assorted tribes and nations inhabiting Asia Minor.

**Homer** *The Iliad* and *The Odyssey*. The first concerns itself, semi-factually, with the late Bronze Age war of the Achaeans against Troy in Asia Minor; the second recounts the hero Odysseus's long journey home, via seemingly every corner of the Mediterranean. The best prose translations are by Martin Hammond, and in verse Richmond Lattimore. For a stirring, if very loose verse *Iliad*, try also Christopher Logue's recent *War Music*.

**Ovid** *The Metamorphoses* (trans A.D. Melville). Collected by a first-century-AD Roman poet, this remains one of the most accessible renditions of the more piquant Greek myths, involving transformations as divine blessing or curse.

**Thucydides** *History of the Peloponnesian War*. Bleak month-by-month account of the conflict, by a cashiered Athenian officer whose affiliation and dim view of human nature didn't usually obscure his objectivity.

**Xenophon** *The History of My Times*. Thucydides' account of the Peloponnesian War stops in 411 BC; this eyewitness account continues events until 362 BC.

etiquette of consumption and consummation – with wine, women, boys and seafood – in Classical Athens.

**Mary Lefkowitz** *Greek Gods, Human Lives: What We Can Learn from Myths*. Rather than being frivolous, immoral or irrelevant, ancient religion and its myths, in their bleak indifference of the gods to human suffering, are shown to be more "grown up" than the later creeds of salvation and comfort.

# Ancient archeology and art

**William R. Biers** *Archeology of Greece: An Introduction*. A good survey originally published in 1987 but revised in 1996.

**John Boardman** *Greek Art*. An evergreen study in the *World of Art* series, first published in 1964. For more detailed treatment, there are three volumes entitled *Greek Sculpture*, subtitled in turn: *Archaic Period, Classical Period* and *The Late Classical Period*.

**Reynold Higgins** *Minoan and Mycenaean Art*. Concise, well-illustrated round-up of the culture of Mycenae, Crete and the Cyclades, again part of the *World of Art* series.

**Colin Renfrew** *The Cycladic Spirit*. Illustrated with the collection of Athens' Goulandris Cycladic Art Museum, and convincing on the meaning and purpose of these artefacts.

**R.R.R. Smith** *Hellenistic Sculpture*. Recent reappraisal of the art of Greece under Alexander and his successors.

## Byzantine and medieval Greece

**Nicholas Cheetham** *Medieval Greece* (o/p). A general survey of the period's infinite convolutions in Greece, with Frankish, Catalan, Venetian, Byzantine and Ottoman forces jockeying for power; two chapters on the small islands and Crete.

**John Julius Norwich** *Byzantium: The Early Centuries*; *Byzantium: the Apogee* and *Byzantium: The Decline*. Perhaps the main surprise for first-time travellers to Greece is its Byzantine monuments. This is an astonishingly detailed yet readable – often witty – trilogy of the empire that produced them. There's also an excellent, one-volume abridged version, *A Short History of Byzantium*.

**Steven Runciman** *The Fall of Constantinople, 1453*. Unsurpassed narrative of perhaps the key event of the Middle Ages, and its repercussions throughout Europe and the Islamic world.

**Cecil Torr** *Rhodes in Ancient Times* and *Rhodes in Modern Times*. These erudite 1887 classics by a Victorian gentleman scholar are out in affordable Archaeopress reprints with new introductions and supplementary material by Ilias Kollias and Gerald Brisch. The latter title is misleading – the Byzantine era to the Ottoman conquest is covered.

## Byzantine art and religion

**John Beckwith** *Early Christian and Byzantine Art.* Comprehensive illustrated study placing Byzantine art within a wider context.

**Steven Runciman** *Byzantine Style and Civilization* (o/p). Survey of the empire's art, culture and monuments; well worth tracking down.

**Archbishop Kallistos (Timothy Ware)** *The Orthodox Church.* Good introduction to what is still the established religion of Greece, by the UK's ranking Orthodox archbishop. Part One describes the history of Orthodoxy, Part Two its current beliefs.

# Modern Greek history

**David Brewer** *The Flame of Freedom: The Greek War of Independence 1821–1833* (o/p). The best narrative on revolutionary events (with some black-and-white illustrations), strong on the background of Ottoman Greece as well as the progress of the war.

**Richard Clogg** *A Concise History of Greece.* If you read only one history, this should be it: a remarkably clear account, from the decline of Byzantium to 2000, with numerous maps and feature captions to well-chosen artwork.

**John S. Koliopoulos and Thanos M. Veremis** *Greece: The Modern Sequel, from 1831 to the Present.* Thematic rather than chronological study (up to 2002) that illuminates corners rarely discussed by conventional histories, with some tart debunkings; especially good on

Macedonian issues, brigandage and the Communists.

**Michael Llewellyn Smith** *Ionian Vision: Greece in Asia Minor, 1919–22.* The best work on the disastrous Anatolian campaign, which led to the population exchanges between Greece and Turkey. Llewellyn Smith's account evinces considerable sympathy for the post-1920 royalist government pursuing an inherited, unwinnable war.

**C.M. Woodhouse** *Modern Greece: A Short History.* Woodhouse, long a Conservative MP, was a key liaison officer with the Greek Resistance during World War II. Writing from a more right-wing perspective than Clogg, his account – from the foundation of Constantinople to 1990 – is briefer and drier, but scrupulous with facts.

# World War II and the civil war

**Antony Beevor** *Crete: The Battle and the Resistance.* The historian best known for his Stalingrad and Berlin epics actually made his debut with this short 1992 study, which first aired the theory that Crete was allowed to fall by the British to conceal the fact that they'd

cracked the Germans' Enigma code, in order to win the more strategic campaign in North Africa.

**Winston Churchill** *The Second World War, Vol. 5: Closing the Ring.* Includes the Allied Aegean campaigns, with detailed coverage of battles on and around Rhodes, Léros, Sámos and Kós.

**Alan Clark** *The Fall of Crete* Racy and sensational military history by the late maverick English politician, if less thorough than Beevor's tome (and lacking maps). Detailed on the battles, and more critical of the command than you might expect from a former cabinet minister.

**David H. Close** *The Origins of the Greek Civil War*. Excellent, even-handed study that spotlights the social conditions in 1920s and 1930s Greece that made the country so ripe for conflict; draws on primary sources to overturn various received wisdoms.

**Lew Lind** *Flowers of Rethymnon* (Efstadhiadhis, Greece). Gripping personal account of his part in the Battle of Crete and subsequent escape by a (then) 19-year-old Australian soldier. Shining through the battle carnage and general grim horror is the unflinching bravery of Cretan villagers who repeatedly put themselves in mortal danger of

German reprisals by helping trapped servicemen like Lind escape to Egypt.

**Mark Mazower** *Inside Hitler's Greece: The Experience of Occupation 1941–44*. Eccentrically organized, but the scholarship is top-drawer and the photos alone justify purchase. Demonstrates how the utter demoralization of the country and incompetence of conventional politicians led to the rise of the ELAS resistance movement.

**Adrian Seligman** *War in the Islands* (o/p). Collected oral histories of a little-known Allied unit: a flotilla of *kaïkia* organized to raid the Axis-held Aegean islands. Boy's Own stuff, with service-jargon-laced prose, but lots of fine period photos and detail.

**C.M. Woodhouse** *The Struggle for Greece, 1941–49*. Well-illustrated, never-bettered account of the so-called "three rounds" of resistance and rebellion, and how Greece emerged without a communist government.

# Ethnography

**Juliet du Boulay** *Portrait of a Greek Mountain Village* (Denise Harvey, Límni, Évvia). Ambéli village on Évvia, during the 1960s: habits and customs of a bygone way of life in an absorbing narrative.

**Bruce Clark** *Twice a Stranger: How Mass Expulsion Forged Modern Greece and Turkey*. The build-up to and execution of the 1923 population exchanges, and how both countries are still digesting the experience eight-plus decades on. Compassionate and readable, especially the encounters with surviving elderly refugees.

**Richard Clogg** (ed.) *The Greek Minorities*. Collection of articles on all the various Greek ethnic and religious minorities, as of the mid-1990s – despite its vintage, still authoritative.

**Loring Danforth and Alexander Tsiaras** *The Death Rituals of Rural Greece*. Many visitors and foreign residents find Greek funeral customs – the wailing, the open-casket vigils, the disinterment of bones after five years – disturbing; this book helps make sense of it all.

**Adam Hopkins** *Crete: Its Past, Present and People* (o/p). Excellent general introduction to Cretan history and society with interesting detail on diverse topics like the Battle of Crete, daily life, mass tourism and herbology, though beginning to show its age (1977).

**Margaret E. Kenna** *Greek Island Life: Fieldwork on Anafi.* Vivid account of the trials and rewards of 1966–67 doctoral research, when pre-tourism island culture still survived, relying on her notebook entries and letters home.

**John Cuthbert Lawson** *Modern Greek Folklore and Ancient Greek Religion: A Study in Survivals.* Exactly as it says: a fascinating, thorough study still applicable a century-plus after first publication.

**Michael Llewellyn Smith** *The Great Island: A Study of Crete* (o/p). Long before he became a known scholar (and twice ambassador to Greece), Llewellyn Smith debuted

with this fine volume emphasizing folk traditions, including a lengthy analysis of Cretan song.

**Anthony J. Papalas** *Rebels and Radicals: Icaria 1600–2000.* The lowdown on that most peculiar of mid-Aegean islands, delving into its Ottoman past, American diaspora links, unexpected Communist affilia- tions and recent touristic development.

**David Sutton** *Memories Cast in Stone: The Relevance of the Past in Everyday Life.* A 1990s ethnology of Kálymnos, where tenacious "traditional" practices such as dynamite-throwing *paniyíria* and dowry-collecting confront the new, pan-EU realities.

**John L. Tomkinson** *Festive Greece: A Calendar of Tradition.* Copiously photographed gazetteer by date of all the still-observed rites of the Orthodox Church, with their pagan substrata erupting frequently and vividly at popular *paniyíria*.

# Fiction

## Greek writers in translation

**Apostolos Doxiadis** *Uncle Petros and Goldbach's Conjecture.* Uncle Petros is the disgraced family black sheep, living alone in outer Athens; his nephew discovers that Petros had staked everything to solve a theorem unsolved for centuries. Math-phobes take heart; it's more a meditation on how best to spend life, and what really constitutes success.

**Rhea Galanaki** *Eleni, or Nobody.* Fine novelization of the life of Eleni

Altamura, Greece's first, mid- nineteenth-century woman painter, who lived for years in Italy disguised as a man.

**Vangelis Hatziyannidis** Hatziyan- nidis's abiding obsessions – confinement, blackmail, abrupt disappearances – get an airing in his creepy debut novel *Four Walls*, set on an unspecified east Aegean isle, where a reclusive landowner takes in a fugitive woman who convinces him to revive his father's honey trade – with unexpected consequences. His next novel, *Stolen Time*, revisits the same themes as an impoverished young student gets a tidy fee from a mysterious tribunal for agreeing to spend two weeks in the Hotel from Hell.

**Panos Karnezis** Karnezis has become the most accessible, and feted, Greek writer since the millennium. Greece-born, he now lives in London, writing in English, but his concerns remain utterly Greek. *Little Infamies* is a short-story collection set in his native Peloponnese during the late 1950s and early 1960s; *The Maze* is a darker-shaded, more successful novel concerning the Asia Minor Catastrophe. Both rely on old-fashioned plot twists – or a *soupçon* of magical realism, depending on your point of view. His 2007 *The Birthday Party* is based on events in the life of Aristotle Onassis and daughter Christina.

**Nikos Kazantzakis** *Zorba the Greek*; *The Last Temptation of Christ*; *Christ Recrucified/The Greek Passion*; *Freedom and Death*; *Report to Greco*. Whether in intricate Greek or not-quite-adequate English, Kazantzakis can be hard going, yet the power of his writing shines through. *Zorba the Greek* is a dark, nihilistic work, worlds away from the two-dimensional film. By contrast, the movie version of *The Last Temptation of Christ* – specifically Jesus's vision, on the cross, of a normal life with Maria Magdalene – provoked riots among Orthodox fanatics in Athens in 1989. *Christ Recrucified* (*The Greek Passion*) resets the Easter drama against the backdrop of Christian/Muslim relations, while *Freedom and Death* chronicles the rebellions of nineteenth-century Crete. *Report to Greco* – perhaps the most accessible – is an autobiographical exploration of his Cretan-ness.

**Artemis Leontis** (ed) *Greece: A Traveller's Literary Companion*. A nice idea, brilliantly executed: various regions of the country (including many islands) as portrayed in (very) short fiction or essays by modern Greek writers.

**Stratis Myrivilis, translated by Peter Bien** *Life in the Tomb*. Harrowing and unorthodox war memoir, based on the author's 1917–18 experience on the Macedonian front. Completing a kind of trilogy are two later novels, set during the 1920s on Lésvos, Myrivilis's homeland: *The Mermaid Madonna* and *The Schoolmistress with the Golden Eyes*. The cheap-and-nasty, heavily abridged Efstathiadis paperback editions of these are worth avoiding in favour of the original 1950s full-length hardbacks, readily available online.

**Alexandros Papadiamantis** *The Murderess* (o/p). Landmark novel set on the island of Skiáthos at the beginning of the nineteenth century, in which an old woman, appalled by the fate that awaits them in adulthood, concludes that little girls are better off dead. The quasi-mythic tales of grim fate in *Tales from a Greek Island* evoke Hardy and Maupassant.

**Nick Papandreou** *Father Dancing* (UK)/*A Crowded Heart* (US). Autobiographical *roman à clef* by the late prime minister Andreas's younger son in which Papandreou Senior, not surprisingly, emerges as a gasbag and domestic tyrant.

**Dido Sotiriou** *Farewell Anatolia* (Kedros, Greece). A perennial favourite since publication in 1962, this chronicles the traumatic end of Greek life in Asia Minor, from World War I to the 1922 catastrophe, as narrated by a fictionalized version of Sotiriou's father. In the finale he escapes across the narrow strait of Mykale to Sámos, as many did during those turbulent years.

Stratis Tsirkas, translated by Kay Cicellis *Drifting Cities* (o/p). Set by turns in World War II Jerusalem, Cairo and Alexandria, this unflinchingly honest and humane epic of a Greek officer secretly working for the Leftist resistance got its author expelled from the Communist Party.

Vassilis Vassilikos *Z* (o/p). A novel based closely enough on events – the 1963 assassination of Grigoris Lambrakis in Thessaloníki – to be banned under the junta, and brilliantly filmed by Costa-Gavras in 1968.

## Greece in foreign fiction

🏃 Louis de Bernières *Captain Corelli's Mandolin*. Set on Kefaloniá during the World War II occupation and aftermath, this accomplished 1994 tragi-comedy quickly acquired cult, then bestseller status in the UK and US. But in Greece it provoked a scandal, once islanders, Greek Left intellectuals and surviving Italian partisans noticed its virulent disparaging of ELAS. It seems the novel was based on the experiences of Amos Pampaloni, an Italian artillery captain on Kefaloniá in 1942–44 who later joined ELAS, and who accused De Bernières (forced to eat humble pie in the UK press) of distorting the roles of both Italians and ELAS on the island. The Greek translation was abridged to avoid causing offence, and the 2001 movie, watered down to a feeble love story as a condition for filming on Kefaloniá, sank without trace.

Oriana Fallaci *A Man* (o/p). Gripping fictionalization of the author's junta-era involvement with Alekos Panagoulis, the army officer who attempted to assassinate Colonel Papadopoulos in 1968 – and who himself died in mysterious circumstances in 1975.

🏃 John Fowles *The Magus*. Fowles' biggest and best tale of mystery and manipulation – plus Greek island life – based on his stay on Spétses as a teacher during the 1950s. A period piece that repays revisiting.

Peter Green *The Laughter of Aphrodite*. Historical novel by a distinguished classicist, in the same vein as Marguerite Yourcenar's *The Memoirs of Hadrian*; this recreates Sappho of Mytilene and her milieu, and largely succeeds.

Victoria Hislop *The Island*. The former leper colony of Spinalonga forms the backdrop to this tale of a young woman discovering her Cretan roots. A potentially good story is marred by the cloying, derivative nature of its telling.

Steven Pressfield *The Virtues of War*. Alexander the Great tells his warrior's life to brother-in-law Itanes. And he does it well, for Pressfield informs his drama with impressive scholarship.

Mary Renault *The King Must Die*; *The Last of the Wine*; *The Mask of Apollo*. Mary Renault's imaginative reconstructions are more than the adolescent's reading they're often taken for, with impeccable research and tight writing. The trio above retell, respectively, the myth of Theseus, the life of a Socratic pupil, and that of a fourth-century BC actor. The career of Alexander the Great is covered in *Fire from Heaven*, *The Persian Boy* and *Funeral Games*, available separately or in one economical volume (all Penguin). *The Praise Singer*, set largely in Polykrates' ancient Samos, follows the fortunes of the poet Simeonides and friends.

Evelyn Waugh *Officers and Gentleman*. This second volume of Waugh's brilliant, acerbic wartime trilogy includes an account of the Battle of Crete and subsequent evacuation.

## Greece in cartoons

Arkas Arkas (@www.arkas.gr; nobody knows his real identity, as he declines all publicity and interviews) has been drawing for two decades, during which time he's established himself as one of Europe's leading cartoonists. His work has been collected in dozens of books, translated into almost every European language, in various parallel sagas: *The After Life*, *Kastrato and Loukretia* (a dysfunctional cat couple), *The Rooster*, *Show Business*, *Experimental Animals*, *Low Flights* (crow father-and-smartarse-son), plus various one-offs like the hilarious *You Bring out the Animal in Me*. By turns profound, poignant, mean-spirited, mystical, topical without being overtly political, and with a draughtsmanship and palette that puts most Anglo-Saxon cartooning to shame.

# Greek poetry

With two twentieth-century Nobel laureates – George Seferis and Odysseus Elytis – modern Greece has an intense and dynamic poetic tradition. All of the following translations are excellent.

## Anthologies

**Peter Bien, Peter Constantine, Edmund Keeley, Karen Van Dyck** (eds) *A Century of Greek Poetry, 1900–2000*. Well-produced bilingual volume, with some lesser-known surprises alongside the big names.

**Nanos Valaoritis and Thanasis Maskaleris, eds** *An Anthology of Modern Greek Poetry*. English-only text, but excellent biographical info on the poets and good renderings by two native Greek speakers.

## Individual poets

**C.P. Cavafy** *The Collected Poems*, translated by Evangelos Sachperoglou; *The Canon*, translated by Stratis Haviaras. Perhaps the most accessible modern Greek poet, resident for most of his life in Alexandria. These two newish (early 2008) versions include all 154 of his finished works, the Haviaras edition bilingual on facing pages. Each have their strengths but – like the earlier attempts of Keeley/Sherrard and Rae Dalwen – both often founder on Cavafy's ultimate untranslateability.

**Odysseus Elytis** *Collected Poems*; *The Axion Esti* (translated by George Savidis and Edmund Keeley) and *Eros, Eros, Eros: Selected and Last Poems* (translated by Olga Broumas) covers almost his entire oeuvre.

**Yannis Kondos** *Absurd Athlete*. One of the best of the new generation of poets, well translated in a bilingual edition by David Connolly.

**Yannis Ritsos, translated by Edmund Keeley** *Repetitions, Testimonies, Parentheses*. A fine volume of Greece's foremost Leftist poet, including work from 1946 to 1975.

**George Seferis** *Collected Poems, 1924–1955*. Virtually the complete works of the Nobel laureate, with Greek and English verses on facing pages; later editions are English-only.

# Food and wine

**Rosemary Barron** *Flavours of Greece*. The leading Greek cookbook – among many contenders – by a recognized authority; contains over 250 recipes.

**Andrew Dalby** *Siren Feasts: A History of Food and Gastronomy in Greece*. Demonstrates just how little Greek cuisine has changed in three millennia; also revealing on the introduction of common vegetables and herbs.

**Konstantinos Lazarakis** *The Wines of Greece*. An excellent, up-to-2005 overview of what's happening in Greece's eleven recognized wine-producing regions.

**Nikos Stavroulakis** *Cookbook of the Jews of Greece* (@www.lycabettus .com). Tasty if often fiddly recipes interspersed with their relation to the Jewish liturgical year, plus potted histories of the communities that devised them.

# Specific guides

See also the Wildlife guides detailed on p.641.

## Archeology

**A.R. and Mary Burn** *The Living Past of Greece: A Time Traveller's Tour of Historic and Prehistoric Places* (o/p). This wide-ranging guide covers sites from Minoan through to Byzantine and Frankish, with clear plans and lively text.

**Costis Davaras** *Guide to Cretan Antiquities* (Eptalofolos, Athens). A fascinating guide to the antiquities of Crete, by a distinguished archeologist. Cross-referenced in gazetteer form, it has authoritative articles on all major

sites up to the Ottoman era, as well as topics as diverse as Minoan toilet articles and the disappearance of Cretan forests. Widely available at Cretan museums.

**Paul Hetherington** *The Greek Islands: Guide to Byzantine and Medieval Buildings and Their Art*. A readable, well-illustrated and authoritative gazetteer to most island monuments of the period, though there are some peculiar omissions.

## Hiking

**Lance Chilton** Various walking pamphlets (@www.marengowalks.com). Small but thorough guides to the best walks at various island resorts (including on Crete, Corfu, Rhodes, Sámos and Kálymnos) by a co-author of this guide, accompanied by three-colour maps.

**Marc Dubin** *Trekking in Greece* (o/p). Though many sections are showing their 1988–92 research age, still useful for the smaller islands in

particular, from another Rough Guide author's pen.

**Loraine Wilson** *The High Mountains of Crete*. Nearly a hundred walks and treks, from easy to gruelling, by the doyenne of foreign trekking guides in Crete. Mostly in the White Mountains, but also Psilorítis and the Lassíthi range. Reliable directions, clear maps, enticing photos – but no index.

## Regional guides

Rough Guides publishes regional guides to the Ionian islands, the Dodecanese and East Aegean islands, Crete and Corfu. You may also want to get:

**Lycabettus Press Guides** (@www.lycabettus.com). Despite long intervals between revisions, these small-format guides to Kós, Pátmos, Póros and the travels of Saint Paul pay their way in interest and usefulness.

**Constantine E. Michaelides** *The Aegean Crucible: Tracing Vernacular Architecture in Post-Byzantine Centuries*. As with *Making of the Cretan Landscape,* it's difficult to pigeonhole this sprawling, interdisciplinary study by a Greek-American

architecture professor on how island settlements – especially the Cycladic *kástra*, Ýdhra, Santoríni, fortified monasteries – came to be as they are, drawing on history, geology, climatic influences, agriculture and popular religion. The text, erudite without being technical, is directly keyed to copious illustrations and maps.

**Oliver Rackham and Jennifer Moody** *The Making of the Cretan Landscape*. It's hard to classify this impressive academic-press tome written for the casual visitor. It takes in geology, natural history, agricultural practices, place names, architecture and demography, all arranged by topic.

## Sailing

**Rod Heikell** *Greek Waters Pilot*. Updated to 2007; the standard

reference for Greek yachters: depths, anchorages, other available facilities.

# Language

# Language

# Greek

So many Greeks have lived or worked abroad in North America, Australia, South Africa and Britain that you will find **English**-speakers in the tiniest island village. Add the thousands attending language schools or working in the tourist industry – English is the lingua franca of most resorts, with German second – and it's easy to see how so many visitors return home having learned only minimal restaurant vocabulary.

You can certainly get by this way, but it isn't very satisfying, and the willingness and ability to say even a few words will transform your status from that of dumb *touristas* to the more honourable one of *xénos/xéni*, which can mean foreigner, traveller and guest all combined.

## Learning basic Greek

**Greek** is not an easy language for English-speakers – UK translators' unions rate it as harder than German, slightly less complex than Russian – but it is a very beautiful one, and even a brief acquaintance will give you an idea of the debt owed to it by Western European languages. Greek **grammar** is predictably complicated; **nouns** are divided into three genders, all with different case endings in the singular and in the plural, and all adjectives and articles have to agree with these in gender, number and case. To simplify life for beginners, all adjectives are arbitrarily cited in the neuter form in the lists on the following pages. **Verbs** are even more complex; they're in two conjugations, in both active and passive voices, with passively constructed verbs often having transitive sense. As a novice, it's best to simply say what you want the way you know it, and dispense with the niceties.

## Teach-yourself-Greek courses

**Alison Kakoura and Karen Rich** *Talk Greek* (book and two CDs). Probably the best in-print product for beginners' essentials, and developing the confidence to try them.

**Anne Farmakides** *A Manual of Modern Greek, 1, for University Students*. If you have the discipline and motivation, this is among the best texts for learning proper, grammatical Greek.

**Hara Garoufalia et al** *Read & Speak Greek for Beginners* (book & CD). Unlike many quickie courses, this provides a good grammatical foundation.

**David Holton et al** *Greek: A Comprehensive Grammar of the Modern Language*. A bit technical, but covers almost every conceivable construction.

**Aristarhos Matsukas** *Teach Yourself Greek* (book and optional cassettes or CDs). Another complete course, touching on idiomatic expressions too.

**Evris Tsakirides** *Spoken Greek*. An excellent cartoon-format primer, with plenty of real-life situations (not just tourist quandaries), only dated a bit by references to the vanished drachma.

# Phrasebooks and dictionaries

**Rough Guide Greek Phrasebook**. Current, accurate and pocket-sized, with phrases that you'll actually need. The English–Greek section is transliterated, though the Greek–English part requires mastery of the Greek alphabet.

**The Pocket Oxford Greek Dictionary by J.T. Pring**. A bit bulky for travel, but generally considered the best Greek–English, English–Greek paperback dictionary.

**Collins Pocket Greek Dictionary** by Harry T. Hionides. Very nearly as complete as the Pocket Oxford and probably better value for money. The inexpensive *Collins Gem Greek Dictionary* (UK only) is palm-sized but identical in contents – the best day-pack choice.

**Oxford Greek–English, English–Greek Learner's Dictionary**, by D.N. Stavropoulos. For a prolonged stay, this pricey, hardbound, two–volume set is unbeatable for usage and vocabulary.

# Katharévoussa, dhimotikí and dialects

The intrinsic complexities of Greek have been aggravated by the fact that since the early 1800s there has been fierce competition between two versions of the language: **katharévoussa** and **dhimotikí**.

When Greece achieved independence in 1832, its people were mostly illiterate, and the spoken language – *dhimotikí*, "demotic" or "popular" Greek – had undergone enormous change since the Byzantine and Classical eras. The vocabulary had numerous loan-words from the languages of the various invaders and conquerors – especially Turks, Venetians and Slavs – and the grammar had been considerably streamlined since ancient times.

Funding and inspiration for the new Greek state, and some of its early leaders, came largely from the diaspora – Greeks who had been living in the sophisticated cities of central Europe, in Constantinople or in Russia. With their Enlightenment conception of Hellenism, based on Greece's past glory, they set about obliterating traces of foreign subjugation in every possible field. And where better to start than by purging the language of foreign accretions and reviving its Classical purity?

They accordingly created what was in effect a new language, *katharévoussa* (literally "cleansed" Greek). The complexities of Classical grammar and syntax were largely reinstated, and long-forgotten Classical words and phrases were reintroduced. *Katharévoussa* became the language of the schools and the prestigious professions, government, business, the law, newspapers and academia. Everyone aspiring to membership in the elite strove to master it, and to speak it – even though there was no consensus on how many words were pronounced.

The *katharévoussa/dhimotikí* debate remained contentious, even virulent, until the early 1980s. Most writers – from Solomos and Makriyiannis in the nineteenth century to Seferis, Kazantzakis and Ritsos in the twentieth – championed the demotic, or some approximation of it, in their literature, with advocacy of demoticism becoming increasingly linked to left-wing politics during the twentieth century. Meanwhile, right-wing governments forcibly (re)instated *katharévoussa* at every opportunity. Most recently, the **colonels' junta** (1967–74) reversed a decision of the previous government to use *dhimotikí* for instruction in schools, bringing back *katharévoussa*, even on sweet wrappers, as part of their ragbag of notions about racial purity and heroic ages.

*Dhimotikí* returned permanently after the fall of the colonels. Perhaps the final blow to the classicizers was the official 1981 decision to abolish breath marks (which in fact no longer signified anything) and the three different stress accents in favour of a **single acute accent** (though there are still plenty of pre-1981 road-signs in the older system). *Dhimotikí* is used in schools, on radio and TV, and in most newspapers. The only institutions which refuse to update themselves are the Church and the legal profession.

All this has reduced, but not eliminated, confusion. The Metaxas dictatorship of the 1930s, elaborating on attempts at the same by previous regimes, changed scores of village names from Slavic, Turkish or Albanian words to Greek ones – often reviving the name of the nearest ancient site. These official **place names** still hold sway on most road signs and maps – even though the local people may use the *dhimotikí* or non-Greek form. Thus you will see "Plomárion" or "Spétsai" written, while everyone actually says "Plomári" or "Spétses"; Pándhrossos on Sámos, and Platáni on Kós, are still preferably known to locals as Arvanítes and Kermedés respectively.

## Dialects and minority languages

Greece exhibits considerable linguistic diversity, both in its regional dialects and minority languages. Ancient **dialects** survive in many remote areas, some quite incomprehensible to outsiders. Examples include the dialect of Sfákia in Crete, and those of Náxos and Lésvos, which are influenced by immigration from Crete and Asia Minor respectively. The dialects of Sámos and adjacent Híos are completely different from one another, Híos being considered a more pure "Ionian" (and this thousands of years after the Ionians arrived from the mainland), while the rough "Samian" variant owes much to the diverse origins of its settlers. Arvanítika – a form of medieval Albanian – was until well into the twentieth century the first language of many villages of southern Évvia, northern Ándhros, and much of the Argo-Saronic area; it is still (just barely) spoken or at least understood amongst the oldest generation. Lately the clock has been turned back, so to speak, as Albanian immigrant communities have been established on almost every island of the Aegean. On Rhodes and Kós there is a dwindling Turkish-speaking population, probably less than six thousand.

# The Greek alphabet: transliteration and accentuation

Besides the usual difficulties of learning a new language, Greek has an entirely separate **alphabet**. Despite initial appearances, this is in practice fairly easily mastered – a skill that will help enormously in getting around independently. In addition, certain combinations of letters have unexpected results. This book's transliteration system should help you make intelligible noises, but remember that the correct **stress** (marked throughout the book with an acute accent or sometimes dieresis) is crucial. With the right sounds but the wrong stress people will either fail to understand you, or else understand something quite different from what you intended. There are numerous word-pairs with the same spelling and phonemes, distinguished only by their stress.

The **dieresis** is used in Greek over the second of two adjacent vowels to change the pronunciation that you would expect from the table below; often in this book it can function as the primary stress. In the word *kaïki* (caique), the use of a dieresis changes the pronunciation from "cake-key" to "ka-ee-key" and additionally the middle "i" carries the primary stress. In the word *païdhákia* (lamb chops), the dieresis again changes the sound of the first syllable from "pay" to "pah-ee", but in this case the primary stress is on the third syllable. It is also, uniquely among Greek accents, used on capital letters in signs and personal-name spellings in Greece, and we have followed this practice on our maps.

Set out below is the Greek alphabet, the system of transliteration used in this book and a brief aid to pronunciation.

| Greek | Transliteration | Pronounced |
|-------|-----------------|------------|
| A, α | a | a as in father |
| B, β | v | v as in vet |
| Γ, γ | y/g | y as in yes except before consonants or a, o or ou when it's a breathy g, approximately as in gap |
| Δ, δ | dh | th as in then |
| E, ε | e | e as in get |
| Z, ζ | z | z sound |
| H, η | i | i as in ski |
| Θ, θ | th | th as in theme |
| I, ι | i | i as in ski |
| K, κ | k | k sound |
| Λ, λ | l | l sound |
| M, μ | m | m sound |
| N, ν | n | n sound |
| Ξ, ξ | x | x sound, never z |
| O, o | o | o as in toad |
| Π, π | p | p sound |
| P, ρ | r | r sound |
| Σ, σ, ς | s | s sound, except z before m or g; single sigma has the same phonic value as double sigma |
| T, τ | t | t sound |
| Y, υ | y | y as in barely |
| Φ, φ | f | f sound |
| X, χ | h before vowels, kh before consonants | harsh h sound, like ch in loch |
| Ψ, ψ | ps | ps as in lips |
| Ω, ω | o | o as in toad, indistinguishable from o |

## Combinations and diphthongs

| | | |
|-------|-----------------|------------|
| AI, αι | e | e as in hey |
| AY, αυ | av/af | av or af depending on following consonant |
| EI, ει | i | long i, exactly like ι or η |
| EY, ευ | ev/ef | ev or ef, depending on following consonant |

| OI, οι | i | long i, exactly like ι or η |
| OY, ου | ou | ou as in tourist |
| ΓΓ, γγ | ng | ng as in angle; always medial |
| NΓ, νγ | g/ng | g as in goat at the start of a word, ng in the middle |
| MΠ, μπ | b/mb | b at start of a word, mb if medial |
| NΔ, νδ | d/nd | d at start of a word, nd if medial |
| TΣ, τσ | ts | ts as in hits |
| TZ, τζ | tz | dg as in judge; j as in jam in some dialects |

# Greek words and phrases

## Essentials

| | | | | |
|---|---|---|---|---|
| Yes | Né | | Here | Edhó |
| Certainly | Málista | | There | Ekí |
| No | Óhi | | This one | Aftó |
| Please | Parakaló | | That one | Ekíno |
| OK, agreed | Endáxi | | Good | Kaló |
| Thank you (very much) | Efharistó (polý) | | Bad | Kakó |
| | | | Big | Megálo |
| I (don't) understand | (Dhén) Katalavéno | | Small | Mikró |
| Do you speak English? | Miláte angliká? | | More | Perisótero |
| | | | Less | Ligótero |
| Sorry/excuse me | Signómi | | A little | Lígo |
| Today | Símera | | A lot | Polý |
| Tomorrow | Ávrio | | Cheap | Ftinó |
| Yesterday | Khthés | | Expensive | Akrivó |
| Now | Tóra | | Hot | Zestó |
| Later | Argótera | | Cold | Krýo |
| Open | Anikhtó | | With (together) | Mazí (mé) |
| Closed | Klistó | | Without | Horís |
| Day | Méra | | Quickly | Grígora |
| Night | Níkhta | | Slowly | Sigá |
| In the morning | Tó proï | | Mr/Mrs | Kýrios/Kyría |
| In the afternoon | Tó apóyevma | | Miss | Dhespinís |
| In the evening | Tó vrádhi | | | |

## Other needs

| | | | | |
|---|---|---|---|---|
| To eat/drink | Trógo/píno | | Bank | Trápeza |
| Bakery | Foúrnos | | Money | Leftá/Khrímata |
| Pharmacy | Farmakío | | Toilet | Toualéta |
| Post office | Tahydhromío | | Police | Astynomía |
| Stamps | Gramatósima | | Doctor | Yiatrós |
| Petrol station | Venzinádhiko | | Hospital | Nosokomío |

## Requests and questions

To ask a question, it's simplest, though hardly elegant, to start with *parakaló*, then name the thing you want in an interrogative tone.

| | | | |
|---|---|---|---|
| Where is the bakery? | Parakaló, o foúrnos? | When? | Póte? |
| Can you show me the road to …? | Parakaló, ó dhrómos yiá …? | Why? | Yiatí? |
| We'd like a room for two | Parakaló, éna dhomátio yiá dhýo átoma | At what time …? | Tí óra …? |
| | | What is/ Which is …? | Tí íne/Pió íne …? |
| May I have a kilo of oranges? | Parakaló, éna kiló portokália? | How much (does it cost)? | Póso káni? |
| Where? | Poú? | What time does it open? | Tí óra aníyi? |
| How? | Pós? | | |
| How many? | Póssi, pósses or póssa? | What time does it close? | Tí óra klíni? |
| How much? | Póso? | | |

## Talking to people

Greek makes the distinction between the informal (*essý*) and formal (*essís*) second person, like the French "tu" and "vous". Young people and country people often use *essý* even with total strangers, though it's best to address everyone formally until/unless they start using the familiar at you, to avoid offence. By far the most common greeting, on meeting and parting, is *yiá sou/ yiá sas* (literally "health to you"). Incidentally, as across most of the Mediterranean, the approaching party utters the first greeting, not those seated at sidewalk *kafenío* tables or doorsteps – thus the silent staring as you enter a village.

| | | | |
|---|---|---|---|
| Hello | Hérete | Speak slower, please | Parakaló, na milísate pió sigá |
| Good morning | Kalí méra | How do you say it in Greek? | Pós léyete avtó stá Elliniká? |
| Good evening | Kalí spéra | | |
| Good night | Kalí níkhta | | |
| Goodbye | Adío | I don't know | Dhén xéro |
| How are you? | Tí kánis/Tí kánete? | See you tomorrow | Thá sé dhó ávrio |
| I'm fine | Kalá íme | See you soon | Kalí andhámosi |
| And you? | Ké essís? | Let's go | Páme |
| What's your name? | Pós se léne? | Please help me | Parakaló, ná mé voithíste |
| My name is … | Mé léne … | | |

## Accommodation

| | | | |
|---|---|---|---|
| Hotel | Xenodhohío | with a shower | mé doús |
| Inn | Xenón(as) | hot water | Zestó neró |
| Youth hostel | Xenónas neótitos | cold water | Krýo neró |
| A room … | Éna dhomátio … | air conditioning | Klimatismós |
| for one/two/three people | yiá éna/dhýo/tría átoma | fan | Anamistíra |
| | | Can I see it? | Boró ná tó dhó? |
| for one/two/three nights | yiá mía/dhýo/trís vradhiés | Can we camp here? | Boroúme na váloume ti skiní edhó? |
| with a double bed | mé dhipló kreváti | Campsite | Kámping/Kataskínosi |

## Greek's Greek

There are numerous words and phrases which you will hear constantly, even if you don't have the chance to use them. These are a few of the most common.

| | |
|---|---|
| **Éla!** | Come (literally) but also Speak to me! You don't say! etc. |
| **Oríste!** | Literally, Indicate!; in effect, What can I do for you? |
| **Embrós!/Léyete!** | Standard phone responses |
| **Tí néa?** | What's new? |
| **Tí yínete?** | What's going on (here)? |
| **Étsi k'étsi** | So-so |
| **Ópa!** | Whoops! Watch it! |
| **Po-po-po!** | Expression of dismay or concern, like French "O là là!" |
| **Pedhí moú** | My boy/girl, sonny, friend, etc. |
| **Maláka(s)** | Literally "wanker", but often used (don't try it!) as an informal term of address. |
| **Sigá sigá** | Take your time, slow down |
| **Kaló taxídhi** | Bon voyage |

## On the move

| | | | |
|---|---|---|---|
| Aeroplane | Aeropláno | How many hours? | Pósses óres? |
| Bus, coach | Leoforío, púlman | Where are you going? | Poú pás? |
| Car | Aftokínito, amáxi | I'm going to … | Páo stó … |
| Motorbike, scooter | Mihanáki, papáki | I want to get off at … | Thélo ná katévo stó … |
| Taxi | Taxí | | |
| Ship | Plío/vapóri/karávi | The road to … | O dhrómos yiá … |
| High-speed boat, catamaran | Tahyplöö, katamarán | Near | Kondá |
| | | Far | Makriá |
| Hydrofoil | Dhelfíni | Left | Aristerá |
| Bicycle | Podhílato | Right | Dhexiá |
| Hitching | Otostóp | Straight ahead | Katefthía, ísia |
| On foot | Mé tá pódhia | A ticket to … | Éna isitírio yiá … |
| Trail | Monopáti | A ticket one-way/ return | Éna isitírio aplí/mé epistrofí |
| Bus station | Praktorío leoforíon, KTEL | Beach | Paralía |
| Bus stop | Stássi | Cave | Spiliá |
| Harbour | Limáni | Centre (of town) | Kéndro |
| What time does it leave? | Ti óra févyi? | Church | Eklissía |
| | | Sea | Thálassa |
| What time does it arrive? | Ti óra ftháni? | Village | Horió |
| How many kilometres? | Póssa hiliómetra? | | |

## Numbers

| | | | | |
|---|---|---|---|---|
| 1 | énas/éna/mía | 3 | trís/tría | 673 |
| 2 | dhýo | 4 | tésseris/tésseres/téssera | ▬ |

| | | | |
|---|---|---|---|
| 5 | pénde | 40 | saránda |
| 6 | éxi | 50 | penínda |
| 7 | eftá | 60 | exínda |
| 8 | okhtó | 70 | evdhomínda |
| 9 | ennéa (or, in slang, enyá) | 80 | ogdhónda |
| | | 90 | enenínda |
| 10 | dhéka | 100 | ekató |
| 11 | éndheka | 150 | ekatón penínda |
| 12 | dhódheka | 200 | dhiakóssies/dhiakóssia |
| 13 | dhekatrís | 500 | pendakóssies/ pendakóssia |
| 14 | dhekatésseres | | |
| 20 | íkossi | 1000 | hílies/hília |
| 21 | íkossi éna (all compounds written separately thus) | 2000 | dhlo hiliádhes |
| | | 1,000,000 | éna ekatomírio |
| | | first | próto |
| | | second | dhéftero |
| 30 | triánda | third | tríto |

## Days of the week and the time

| | | | |
|---|---|---|---|
| Sunday | Kyriakí | Twenty minutes to four | Tésseres pará íkossi |
| Monday | Dheftéra | | |
| Tuesday | Tríti | Five minutes past seven | Eftá ké pénde |
| Wednesday | Tetárti | | |
| Thursday | Pémpti | Half past eleven | Éndheka ké misí |
| Friday | Paraskeví | In half an hour | Sé misí óra |
| Saturday | Sávato | In a quarter-hour | S'éna tétarto |
| What time is it? | Tí óra íne? | In two hours | Sé dhlo óres |
| One/two/three o'clock | Mía íy óra/dhýo iy óra/ trís íy óra | | |

## Months and seasonal terms

**NB:** You may see *katharévoussa*, or hybrid, forms of the months written on schedules or street signs; these are the spoken demotic forms.

| | | | |
|---|---|---|---|
| January | Yennáris | August | Ávgoustos |
| February | Fleváris | September | Septémvris |
| March | Mártis | October | Októvrios |
| April | Aprílis | November | Noémvris |
| May | Maïos | December | Dhekémvris |
| June | Ioúnios | Summer schedule | Therinó dhromolóyio |
| July | Ioúlios | Winter schedule | Himerinó dhromolóyio |

# A food and drink glossary

## Basics

| | |
|---|---|
| Aláti | Salt |
| Avgá | Eggs |
| (Horís) ládhi | (Without) oil |
| Hortofágos | Vegetarian |
| Katálogos, menoú | Menu |
| Kréas | Meat |
| Lahaniká | Vegetables |
| O logariasmós | The bill |
| Méli | Honey |
| Neró | Water |
| Psári(a) | Fish |
| Psomí ... | Bread ... |
| Olikís | Wholemeal |
| Sikalísio | Rye |
| Kalambokísio | Corn |
| Eliópasta | Olive paté |
| Thalassiná | Seafood |
| Tyrí | Cheese |
| Yiaoúrti | Yoghurt |
| Záhari | Sugar |

## Cooking terms

| | |
|---|---|
| Akhnistó | Steamed |
| Frikasé | Stew, either lamb, goat or pork, made with celery |
| Iliókafto | Sun-dried |
| Kondosoúvli | Any spit-roasted beast, whole or in chunks |
| Kourkoúti | Egg-and-flour batter |
| Makaronádha | Any spaghetti/ pasta-based dish |
| Pastó | Fish marinated in salt |
| Petáli | Butterflied fish, eel, shrimp |
| Psitó | Roasted |
| Saganáki | Cheese-based red sauce with tomato/ paprika; also any fried cheese |
| Skáras | Grilled |
| Sti soúvla | Spit-roasted |
| Stó foúrno | Baked |
| Tiganitó | Pan-fried |
| Tís óras | Grilled/fried to order |
| Xydháta | Marinated in vinegar |
| Yakhní | Stewed in oil and tomato sauce |
| Yemistá | Stuffed (squid, vegetables, etc) |

## Soups and starters

| | |
|---|---|
| Avgolémono | Egg and lemon soup |
| Bouréki, bourekákia | Courgette/zucchini, potato and cheese pie |
| Dolmádhes, yaprákia, ôalantzí | Vine leaves stuffed with rice and mince; are vegetarian ones |
| Fasoládha | Bean soup |
| Fáva | Purée of yellow peas, served with onion and lemon |
| Féta psití | Baked feta cheese slabs with chili |
| Galotýri | Curdled creamy dip |
| Hortópitta | Turnover or pie stuffed with wild greens |
| Kápari | Pickled caper leaves |
| Kopanistí, khtypití | Pungent, fermented cheese purée |
| Krítamo | Rock samphire |
| Lahanodolmádhes | Stuffed cabbage leaves |
| Mavromátika | Black-eyed peas |
| Melitzanosaláta | Aubergine/eggplant dip |
| Piperiá florínes | Marinated sweet Macedonian red peppers |
| Plevrótous | Oyster mushrooms |
| Rengosaláta | Herring salad |
| Revythokeftédhes | Chickpea/garbanzo patties |
| Skordhaliá | Garlic dip |
| Soúpa | Soup |
| Taramosaláta | Cod roe paté |
| Tiganópsomo | Toasted oiled bread |
| Trahanádhes | Crushed wheat and milk soup, sweet or savoury |

| | |
|---|---|
| Tyrokafterí | Cheese dip with chili, different from *kopanistí* |
| Tzatzíki | Yoghurt and cucumber dip |
| Tzirosaláta | Cured mackerel dip |

## Vegetables

| | |
|---|---|
| Ambelofásola | Crimp-pod runner beans |
| Angináres | Artichokes |
| Angoúri | Cucumber |
| Ánitho | Dill |
| Bámies | Okra, ladies' fingers |
| Boúkovo | Macedonian chili flakes |
| Briám, tourloú | Ratatouille of courgettes, potatoes, onions, tomato |
| Dákos, koukouváyia paximádhi | Cretan-style tomato, greens and *myzíthra* salad on a base of dark (rusks) |
| Domátes | Tomatoes |
| Fakés | Lentils |
| Fasolákia | French (green) beans |
| Fasóles | Small white beans |
| Horiátiki (saláta) | Greek salad (with olives, feta, etc) |
| Hórta | Greens (usually wild), steamed |
| Kolokythákia | Courgette/zucchini |
| Koukiá | Broad fava beans |
| Maroúli | Lettuce |
| Melitzánes imám/ Imám baïldí | Aubergine/eggplant slices baked with onion, garlic and copious olive oil |
| Patátes | Potatoes |
| Piperiés | Peppers |
| Pligoúri, pinigoúri | Bulgur wheat |
| Radhíkia | Chicory – a common *hórta* |
| Rókka | Rocket, arugula |
| Rýzi/Piláfi | Rice (usually with *sáltsa*– sauce) |
| Saláta | Salad |

| | |
|---|---|
| Spanáki | Spinach |
| Stamnangáthi | Spiny chicory (western Crete) |
| Vlíta | Notchweed – another common *hórta* |
| Volví skordhaláta | Pickled, slightly bitter wild bulbs, especially in Crete |
| Yígandes | White haricot beans |

## Fish and seafood

Varieties recommended for taste, value, or dependable freshness are marked with a ★. This cites the most commonly offered fish species, with English translation, their preferred method of preparation, seasonal/local particularities, and other warnings. For more information, look no further than Alan Davidson's *Mediterranean Seafood*, the early 1990's reprint.

### Scaly fish

★**Atherína** (Sand smelt) Fried whole with flour and onions as *begotó*, a favourite ouzerí snack; east Aegean speciality

★**Ballás** (Large-eyed dentex) Reddish, medium-sized; grilled

**Bakaliáros** (Hake, also cod) Fried in slices, served with *skordhaliá*; fresh whole specimens rare, usually dried Icelandic

★**Barboúni** (Red mullet) Fried, sometimes grilled; famous smoky flavour, but fiddly to clean

★**Fangrí** (Common bream, red porgy) Grilled; white, firm flesh, big specimens feed four

★**Filipáki, rouzhéti** (Small mullet) Unmistakably blunt-faced creature, very delicate white flesh, flash-fried; caught on sandbanks from Kós to Rhodes

**Galéos** (Hound shark, dogfish) Fried in slices, served with *skordhaliá*; fatty

★**Gávros** (Anchovy) Fried whole, late summer, suprisingly mild-flavoured; east Aegean speciality

**Glóssa** (Sole) Lightly sautéed; mild flavour, springtime

**Gópa** (Bogue) Fried whole; very common country-wide

**Hánnos** (Comber) Fried or in soup; bony but flavourful

**Hiloú** (Brown Wrasse) Best in soup

*****Hióna** (Sharpsnout bream) Excellent grilled, smoky flavour; alias *psilomýtis* and *mytáki*

*****Kefalás** (Axillary bream) Grilled, late summer to autumn, often on Ikaría

*****Khristópsaro** (John Dory) Baked, or in soup; rich white flesh, small bones

**Koliós** (Chub mackerel) Baked in tomato sauce, also grilled or marinated; rich

*****Koutsomoúra** (Goatfish) Fried; same taste as *barboúni* but far cheaper

*****Lakérdha** (White-fleshed bonito) Marinated; expensive treat, meant as an ouzerí starter, not a mains

*****Lavráki** (Sea bass) Baked or grilled; gourmet fare, but usually farmed

**Lithríni** (Red bream, pandora) Large bones, but tasty grilled

**Loútsos, sfinoúra** (Barracuda) Baked or grilled; usually caught May; heavy, mackerel-like flesh

**Marídha** (Picarel) Fried whole; common snack-fish

**Mayátiko** (Amberjack) Bony, so can be best in soup; Dodecanese and Sámos; spring to early autumn, when it's at its best grilled or baked

*****Melanoúri** (Saddled bream) Grilled; springtime; good value

**Ménoula** (Blotched picarel) Larger than *marídha*; often fried, but also marinated on Kárpathos

*****Mourmoúra** (Striped bream) Grilled; not really a true bream, but quite tasty

**Palamídha** (Bonito) Grilled; autumn fish

*****Pandelís, sykiós** (Corvina) Grilled; east Aegean native; flavour similar to *lavráki*

**Pérka** (Painted comber) Fried in batter; often frozen and rubbery, not esteemed

**Peskandrítsa, spehandrítsa** in some dialects (Monkfish) Usually fried, to its detriment; grilled by those who know; autumn

**Rofós** (Dusky grouper) Unmistakably huge; cut into slices for grilling; texture like shark, but much tastier – like monkfish

*****Salouvárdhos** Similar to *pandelís*; small, sweet, white-fleshed fish

**Sálpa** (Salema) Explicitly not recommended; insipid, only for cat food

*****Sardhélles** (Sardines) Grilled, wonderful east Aegean speciality

**Sargós** (White bream) Grilled; good value

**Savrídhi** (Horse mackerel) Fried whole; ouzerí food

*****Sfyrídha, stýra** (White grouper) Better than *rofós*, less bony, though richly fatty

*****Skáros** (Parrotfish) Fried or (less good) grilled; rather bony but exquisitely flavoured white flesh; needs to be cooked uncleaned; available much of the year but especially Aug/Sept

*****Skathári** (Black bream) Grilled; the succulent king of the breams, most abundant in spring and around Sámos/Foúrni; males are dark black; females larger, grey and preferable

*****Skorpína** (Scorpion fish) Excellent for grills, as well as a classic *kakaviá* (bouillabaisse) ingredient; meaty white flesh, the equal of monkfish

**Skoumbrí** (Atlantic mackerel) Baked in sauce; *estiatório* staple

**Spáros** (Annular or two-banded bream) Grilled or in soup

*****Synagrídha** (Dentex) Baked in sauce; delicious

**Tónnos** (Tuna) Grilled or baked; light-fleshed variety much more satisfactory; autumn season

*****Tsipoúra** (Gilt-head bream) Grilled; gourmet fare when wild, but usually farmed

**Xifías** (Swordfish) Baked, grilled; main season Feb–June

**Yermanós** (Leatherback) Bony and tough-skinned, bland but pleasant white flesh; fried only. Found in southern Dodecanese, spring

*****Zargána** (Garfish, saury) Small ones fried, big ones baked in sauce; east Aegean, autumn

## Other seafood

**NB:** Species indicated with ★★ must be eaten alive to avoid poisoning. If they flinch when you drizzle lemon juice on them, they're alive.

Ahini (Sea urchin) Raw; only the briny orange roe eaten as *ahinosaláta*; scarce, expensive

*Astakós (Aegean lobster) Steamed, baked or flaked into pasta as *astakomakaraonádha*; gourmet fare; closed season Sept 1–Jan 1

*Foúskes (*Violet* in French, *uovo de mare* in Italian) Scooped fresh out of unprepossessing husk, these are lovely and far superior to *fouskóalo*, the same creatures marinated in own liquor; most common in south Dodecanese, Aug–Oct. Locals recommend that you eat no more than five at a time

*Gámberi (Large prawns) Grilled or steamed

Garidhákia (Miniature shrimps) Steamed whole, served in oil/lemon dressing; found on Rhodes, Hálki, Sými, Kastellórizo. Unmistakably sweet when fresh

*Garídhes (Shrimp, prawns) Preparation as for *garidhákia*, or stewed in sauce if big enough

*Hokhlí (Sea snails) Served steamed in the shell; discard membrane and extract flesh with a pin (provided)

*Hokhlióalo (Sea snails) Extracted from shells, blanched, salted, served in oil and vinegar

Kalamária, kalamarákia (Small squid) Lightly fried; overcooking toughens

Kalógnomes (Noah's-ark shell) Larger than *mýdhia*; steamed, served on Kálymnos

Karavídhes (Crayfish) Steamed or grilled; mostly carapace

**Kydhónia (Cockles, alias warty Venus) Raw or lightly steamed whilst alive; a delicacy despite the bizarre alternate name

Mýdhia (Mussels) Steamed, or *saganáki*

*(O)khtapódhi (Octopus) Grilled, stewed in wine; only tentacles used

**Petalídhes (Limpets) Served live; ouzerí snack in spring or autumn

**Pínna (Fan-shell flesh) Served raw; another ouzerí snack; *spiní(o)alo* when marinated

*Soupiés (Cuttlefish) Grilled, or stuffed and baked; also cut up and cooked with their ink in rice and greens

*Strídhia (Oysters) Raised in beds, also wild-gathered; served raw; round, not lady's-slipper shape as elsewhere

*Thrápsalo (Deep-water squid) Bigger and not as delicately flavoured as kalamari, thus cheaper but excellent for grilling

Vátos, platý, seláhi (Ray, skate) Wings fried in slices, or steamed and shredded to be served with *skordhaliá*, or as soup

**Yialisterés (Smooth Venus) Similar to *kydhónia*; typical seafood ouzerí fare

## Meat- and poultry-based dishes

| | |
|---|---|
| Apákia | Smoked Cretan pork loin |
| Arní | Lamb |
| Bekrí mezé | Pork chunks in red sauce |
| Biftéki | Hamburger |
| Brizóla | Pork or beef chop |
| Hirinó | Pork |
| Keftédhes | Meatballs |
| Kokorétsi | Liver/offal roulade, spit-roasted |
| Kopsídha | Shoulder chops, pork or lamb |
| Kókoras krasáto | Coq au vin |
| Kotópoulo | Chicken |
| Kounélli | Rabbit |
| Loukánika | Spicy course-ground sausages |
| Manári | Spring lamb |
| Moskhári | Veal |
| Moussakás | Aubergine/eggplant, potato and lamb-mince casserole with béchamel topping |
| Païdhákia | Rib chops, lamb or goat |
| Papoutsákia | Stuffed aubergine/egg plant "shoes" like *moussakás* without béchamel |
| Pastítsio | Macaroni "pie" baked with minced meat |
| Pastourmás | Cured, highly spiced meat; traditionally camel, nowadays beef |

| | |
|---|---|
| Patsás | Tripe soup |
| Provatína | Female mutton |
| Psaronéfri | Pork tenderloin medallions |
| Salingária | Garden snails |
| Soutzoukákia | Minced meat rissoles/ beef patties |
| Spetzofáï | Sausage and pepper red-sauce stew |
| Stifádho | Meat stew with tomato and boiling onions |
| Sykóti | Liver |
| Tiganiá | Pork chunks fried with onions |
| Tziyéro sarmás | Lamb's liver in cabbage leaves |
| Yiouvétsi kritharáki | Baked clay casserole of meat and (short) pasta |
| Zygoúri | 1-to-2-year-old lamb |

## Sweets and dessert

| | |
|---|---|
| Baklavás | Honey and nut pastry |
| Bergamóndo | Bergamot (class of spoon sweet) |
| Bougátsa | Salt or sweet cream pie served warm with sugar and cinnamon |
| Galaktoboúriko | Custard pie |
| Glykó koutalioú | Spoon sweet |
| Halvás | Sesame-based sweetmeat |
| Karydhópita | Walnut cake |
| Kréma | Custard |
| Loukoumádhes | Dough fritters in honey syrup and sesame seeds |
| Pagotó | Ice cream |
| Pastélli | Sesame and honey bar |
| Ravaní | Sponge cake, lightly syruped |
| Ryzógalo | Rice pudding |
| Simigdhalísios | Semolina-based *halvás* |

## Fruits

| | |
|---|---|
| Akhládhia | Big pears |
| Aktinídha | Kiwis |
| Fistíkia | Pistachio nuts |
| Fráoules | Strawberries |
| Himoniátiko | Autumn (cassava) melon |
| Karpoúzi | Watermelon |
| Kerásia | Cherries |
| Krystália | Miniature pears |
| Kydhóni | Quince |
| Lemónia | Lemons |
| Míla | Apples |
| Pepóni | Melon |
| Portokália | Oranges |
| Rodhákina | Peaches |
| Sýka | Figs |
| Stafýlia | Grapes |
| Yiarmádhes | Autumn peaches |

## Cheese

| | |
|---|---|
| Ayeladhinó | Cow's-milk cheese |
| Féta | Salty, creamy white cheese |
| (Kefalo) graviéra | (Extra-hard) Gruyère-type cheese |
| Katsikísio | Goat cheese |
| Kasséri | Medium-sharp cheese |
| Myzíthra | Sweet cream cheese |
| Próvio | Sheep cheese |

## Drinks

| | |
|---|---|
| Alisfakiá | Island sage tea |
| Áspro | white |
| Boukáli | Bottle |
| Býra | Beer |
| Gála | Milk |
| Galakakáo | Chocolate milk |
| Kafés | Coffee |
| Krasí | Wine |
| Kokkinélli/rozé | rosé |
| Kókkino | red |
| Limonádha | Lemonade |
| Metalikó neró | Mineral water |
| Portokaládha | Orangeade |
| Potíri | Glass |
| Stinyásas! | Cheers! |
| Tsáï | Tea |
| Tsáï vounoú | "Mountain" (mainland sage) tea |

# A glossary of words and terms

**Acropolis** Ancient, fortified hilltop.

**Agora** Market and meeting place of an ancient Greek city; also the "high street" of a modern village (*agorá* in modern Greek).

**Amphora** Tall, narrow-necked jar for oil or wine.

**Áno** Upper; common prefix of village names.

**Apse** Curved recess at the east end of a church nave.

**Archaic period** Late Iron Age period, from around 750 BC to the start of the Classical period in the fifth century BC.

**Arhondikó** A lordly stone mansion, often restored as boutique accommodation.

**Astykó** (Intra) city, municipal, local; adjective applied to phone calls and bus services.

**Ayíasma** A sacred spring, usually flowing out of church foundations.

**Áyios/Ayía/Áyii** (m/f/plural). Saint or holy. Common place-name prefix (abbreviated Ag or Ay), often spelled *Agios* or *Aghios*.

**Basilica** Colonnaded, "hall-" or "barn-" type church adapted from Roman models, most common in northern Greece.

**Bema** Rostrum for a church oratory.

**Bouleuterion** Auditorium for meetings of an ancient town's deliberative council.

**Capital** The flared top, often ornamented, of a column.

**Cavea** Seating curve of an ancient theatre.

**Cella** Sacred room of a temple, housing the cult image.

**Classical period** From the end of the Persian Wars in 480 BC until the unification of Greece under Philip II of Macedon (338 BC).

**Conch** Concave semi-dome surmounting a church apse, often frescoed.

**Corinthian** Decorative columns, festooned with acanthus florettes; any temple built in this order.

**Dhimarhío** Town hall.

**Dhomátia** Rooms for rent in purpose-built block, without staffed reception.

**Dorian** Northern civilization that displaced and succeeded the Mycenaeans and Minoans through most of Greece around 1100 BC.

**Doric** Minimalist, unadorned columns, dating from the Dorian period; any temple built in this order.

**Drum** Cylindrical or faceted vertical section, usually pierced by an even number of narrow windows, upholding a church cupola.

**Entablature** The horizontal linking structure atop the columns of an ancient temple; same as *architrave*.

**Eparhía** Subdivision of a modern province, analogous to a county.

**Exedra** Display niche for statuary.

**Exonarthex** The outer vestibule or entrance hall of a church, when a true narthex is present.

**Forum** Market and meeting place of a Roman-era city.

**Frieze** Band of sculptures around a temple. Doric friezes consist of various tableaux of figures (*metopes*) interspersed with grooved panels (*triglyphs*); Ionic ones have continuous bands of figures.

**Froúrio** Medieval citadel; nowadays, can mean a modern military headquarters.

**Garsoniéra/es** Studio villa/s, self-catering apartment/s.

**Geometric period** Post-Mycenaean Iron Age era named for its pottery style; starts in the early eleventh century BC with the arrival of Dorian peoples. By the eighth century BC, with development of representational styles, the Archaic period begins.

**Hamam** Domed "Turkish" bath, found on Rhodes and certain northeast Aegean islands.

**Hellenistic period** The last and most unified "Greek empire", created in the wake of Alexander the Great's Macedonian empire and finally collapsing with the fall of Corinth to the Romans in 146 BC.

**Heroön** Shrine or sanctuary-tomb, usually of a demigod or mortal; war memorials in modern Greece.

**Hóra** Main town of an island; literally it means "the place". A hóra is often known by the same name as the island.

**Ierón** The sanctuary between the altar screen and the apse of a church, reserved for priestly activities.

**Ikonostási** Wood or masonry screen between the nave of a church and the altar, supporting at least three icons.

**Ionic** Elaborate, decorative development of the older Doric order; Ionic temple columns are slimmer, with deeper "fluted" edges, spiral-shaped capitals and ornamental bases.

**Kafenío** Coffee house or café.

**Kaïki** (plural *kaïkia*) Caique, or medium-sized boat, traditionally wooden and used for transporting cargo and passengers; now refers mainly to island excursion boats.

**Kalderími** A cobbled mule-track or footpath.

**Kámbos** Fertile agricultural plain, usually near a river mouth.

**Kantína** Shack, caravan or even a disused bus on the beach, serving drinks and perhaps sandwiches or quick snacks.

**Kástro** Any fortified hill, but most often the oldest, highest, walled-in part of an island hóra, intended to protect civilians.

**Katholikón** Central church of a monastery.

**Káto** Lower; common prefix of village names.

**Kendrikí platía** Central square.

**Koúros** Nude Archaic statue of an idealized young man, usually portrayed with one foot slightly in front of the other.

**Megaron** Principal hall or throne room of a Mycenaean/Bronze Age palace.

**Meltémi** North wind that blows across the Aegean in summer, starting softly from near the mainland and hitting the Cyclades, the Dodecanese and Crete full on.

**Metope** see Frieze.

**Minoan** Crete's great Bronze Age civilization, which dominated the Aegean from about 2500 to 1400 BC.

**Moní** *Katharévoussa* term for a monastery or convent.

**Moreás** Medieval term for the Peloponnese; the peninsula's outline peninsula was likened to the leaf of a mulberry tree, *mouriá* in Greek.

**Mycenaean** Mainland civilization centred on Mycenae and the Argolid from about 1700 to 1100 BC.

**Naos** The inner sanctum of an ancient temple; also, the central area of an Orthodox Christian church.

**Narthex** Western vestibule of a church, reserved for catechumens and the unbaptized; typically frescoed with scenes of the Last Judgement.

**Neolithic** Earliest era of settlement in Greece; characterized by use of stone tools and weapons together with basic agriculture. Divided arbitrarily into Early (ca. 6000 BC), Middle (ca. 5000 BC) and Late (ca. 3000 BC).

**Néos, Néa, Néo** "New" – a common prefix to a town or village name.

**Nomós** Modern Greek province – there are more than fifty of them. Village bus services are organized according to their borders.

**Odeion** Small theatre, used for musical performances, minor dramatic productions or councils.

**Orchestra** Circular area in a theatre where the chorus would sing and dance.

**Palaestra** Gymnasium for athletics and wrestling practice.

**Paleós, Paleá, Paleó** "Old" – again a common prefix in town and village names.

**Panayía** Virgin Mary.

**Pandokrátor** Literally "The Almighty"; generally refers to the stern portrayal of Christ in Majesty frescoed or in mosaic in the dome of many Byzantine churches.

**Paniyíri** Festival or feast – the local celebration of a holy day.

**Paralía** Beach, or seafront promenade.

**Pediment** Triangular, sculpted gable below the roof of a temple.

**Pendentive** Triangular sections of vaulting with concave sides, positioned at a corner of a rectangular space to support a circular or polygonal dome; in churches, often adorned with frescoes of the four Evangelists.

**Períptero** Street kiosk.

**Peristereónes** Pigeon towers, in the Cyclades.

**Peristyle** Gallery of columns around a temple or other building.

**Pinakothíki** Picture gallery; from ancient Greek *pinakotheke*.

**Pithos** (plural *pithoi*) Large ceramic jar for storing oil, grain, etc. Very common in Minoan palaces and used in almost identical form in modern Greek homes.

**Platía** Square, plaza.

**Polygonal masonry** Wall-building technique of Classical and Hellenistic periods, using

**L**

**LANGUAGE** | A glossary of words and terms

681

unmortared, closely joined stones; often called "Lesvian polygonal" after the island where the method supposedly originated. The much-(ab)used term "Cyclopean" refers only to Bronze Age mainland sites such as Tiryns and Mycenae.

**Propylaion** Monumental columned gateway of an ancient building; often used in the plural, *propylaia*.

**Pýrgos** Tower or bastion; also tower-mansions found on Aegean islands like Léros, Náxos or Lésvos.

**Skála** The port of an inland island settlement, nowadays often larger and more important than its namesake, but always younger since built after the disappearance of piracy.

**Squinch** Small concavity across a corner of a column-less interior space, which supports a superstructure such as a dome.

**Stele** Upright stone slab or column, usually inscribed with an edict; also an ancient tombstone, with a relief scene.

**Stoa** Colonnaded walkway in Classical-to-Roman-era marketplaces.

**Távli** Backgammon; a favourite café pastime, especially among the young. There are two more difficult local variations (*févga* and *plakotó*) in addition to the standard international game (*pórtes*).

**Témblon** Wooden altar screen of an Orthodox church, usually ornately carved and painted and studded with icons; more or less interchangeable with *ikonostási*.

**Temenos** Sacred precinct of ancient temple, often used to refer to the sanctuary itself.

**Theatral area** Open area found in most of the Minoan palaces with seat-like steps around. Probably a type of theatre or ritual area.

**Tholos** Conical or beehive-shaped building, eg a Mycenaean tomb.

**Triglyph** see Frieze.

**Tympanum** The recessed space, flat or carved in relief, inside a pediment.

**Votsalotó** Mosaic of coloured pebbles, found in church or house courtyards of the Dodecanese and Spétses.

**Yperastykó** Long-distance – as in bus services.

## Acronyms

**Anek** Anónymi Navtiliakí Etería Krítis (Shipping Co of Crete, Ltd), which runs most ferries between Pireás and Crete, plus many to Italy.

**Eam** National Liberation Front, the political force behind ELAS.

**Elas** Popular Liberation Army, the main Resistance group during World War II and predecessor of the Communist army during the civil war.

**Elta** Postal service.

**Eot** Ellinikós Organismós Tourismoú, National Tourist Organization.

**Fyrom** Former Yugoslav Republic of Macedonia.

**Kke** Communist Party, unreconstructed.

**Ktel** National syndicate of bus companies; also refers to individual bus stations.

**Lane** Lasithiakí Anónymi Navtiliakí Etería (Lasithian Shipping Company Ltd), based in eastern Crete.

**Laos** Laïkós Orthódoxos Synayermós (Popular Orthodox Rally), far-right nationalist/militantly Christian/Euro-sceptic party.

**Nd** Néa Dhimokratía (New Democracy), Conservative party.

**Nel** Navtiliakí Etería Lésvou (Lesvian Shipping Co).

**Ote** Telecoms company.

**Pasok** (Quasi-) Socialist party (Pan-Hellenic Socialist Movement).

**Syriza** Synaspismós tís Rizospastikís Aristerás (Coalition of the Radical Left) – alternative, "Euro"-Socialist party.

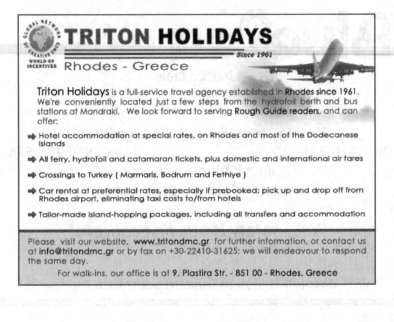

# Small print and
# Index

# A Rough Guide to Rough Guides

Published in 1982, the first Rough Guide – to Greece – was a student scheme that became a publishing phenomenon. Mark Ellingham, a recent graduate in English from Bristol University, had been travelling in Greece the previous summer and couldn't find the right guidebook. With a small group of friends he wrote his own guide, combining a highly contemporary, journalistic style with a thoroughly practical approach to travellers' needs.

The immediate success of the book spawned a series that rapidly covered dozens of destinations. And, in addition to impecunious backpackers, Rough Guides soon acquired a much broader and older readership that relished the guides' wit and inquisitiveness as much as their enthusiastic, critical approach and value-for-money ethos.

These days, Rough Guides include recommendations from shoestring to luxury and cover more than 200 destinations around the globe, including almost every country in the Americas and Europe, more than half of Africa and most of Asia and Australasia. Our ever-growing team of authors and photographers is spread all over the world, particularly in Europe, the USA and Australia.

In the early 1990s, Rough Guides branched out of travel, with the publication of Rough Guides to World Music, Classical Music and the Internet. All three have become benchmark titles in their fields, spearheading the publication of a wide range of books under the Rough Guide name.

Including the travel series, Rough Guides now number more than 350 titles, covering: phrasebooks, waterproof maps, music guides from Opera to Heavy Metal, reference works as diverse as Conspiracy Theories and Shakespeare, and popular culture books from iPods to Poker. Rough Guides also produce a series of more than 120 World Music CDs in partnership with World Music Network.

Visit www.roughguides.com to see our latest publications.

Rough Guide travel images are available for commercial licensing at www.roughguidespictures.com

# Rough Guide credits

**Text editors**: James Smart, Emma Gibbs,
Helena Smith
**Layout**: Ajay Verma
**Cartography**: Animesh Pathak
**Picture editor**: Emily Taylor
**Production**: Rebecca Short
**Proofreader**: Wendy Smith
**Cover design**: Chloë Roberts
**Photographer**: Chris Christoforou with Michelle
Grant, Geoff Garvey & Nick Edwards
**Editorial**: Ruth Blackmore, Andy Turner, Keith
Drew, Edward Aves, Alice Park, Lucy White, Jo
Kirby, Natasha Foges, Róisín Cameron, Emma
Traynor, Kathryn Lane, Christina Valhouli, Monica
Woods, Mani Ramaswamy, Harry Wilson, Lucy
Cowie, Helen Ochyra, Alison Roberts, Joe
Staines, Peter Buckley, Matthew Milton, Tracy
Hopkins, Ruth Tidball; **Delhi** Madhavi Singh,
Karen D'Souza, Lubna Shaheen
**Design & Pictures: London** Scott Stickland,
Dan May, Diana Jarvis, Mark Thomas, Nicole
Newman, Sarah Cummins; **Delhi** Umesh
Aggarwal, Jessica Subramanian, Ankur Guha,
Pradeep Thapliyal, Sachin Tanwar, Anita Singh,
Nikhil Agarwal

**Production**: Vicky Baldwin
**Cartography: London** Maxine Repath,
Ed Wright, Katie Lloyd-Jones; **Delhi** Rajesh
Chhibber, Ashutosh Bharti, Rajesh Mishra, Jasbir
Sandhu, Karobi Gogoi, Alakananda Bhattacharya,
Swati Handoo, Deshpal Dabas
**Online: London** George Atwell, Faye Hellon,
Jeanette Angell, Fergus Day, Justine Bright, Clare
Bryson, Aine Fearon, Adrian Low, Ezgi Celebi,
Amber Bloomfield; **Delhi** Amit Verma, Rahul Kumar,
Narender Kumar, Ravi Yadav, Debojit Borah,
Rakesh Kumar, Ganesh Sharma, Shisir Basumatari
**Marketing & Publicity: London** Liz Statham,
Niki Hanmer, Louise Maher, Jess Carter, Vanessa
Godden, Vivienne Watton, Anna Paynton, Rachel
Sprackett, Libby Jellie, Laura Vipond, Vanessa
McDonald; **New York** Katy Ball, Judi Powers,
Nancy Lambert; **Delhi** Ragini Govind
**Manager India**: Punita Singh
**Reference Director**: Andrew Lockett
**Operations Manager**: Helen Phillips
**PA to Publishing Director**: Nicola Henderson
**Publishing Director**: Martin Dunford
**Commercial Manager**: Gino Magnotta
**Managing Director**: John Duhigg

# Publishing information

This 7th edition published June 2009 by
**Rough Guides Ltd**,
80 Strand, London WC2R 0RL
14 Local Shopping Centre, Panchsheel Park,
New Delhi 110017, India
**Distributed by the Penguin Group**
Penguin Books Ltd,
80 Strand, London WC2R 0RL
Penguin Group (USA)
375 Hudson Street, NY 10014, USA
Penguin Group (Australia)
250 Camberwell Road, Camberwell,
Victoria 3124, Australia
Penguin Group (Canada)
195 Harry Walker Parkway N, Newmarket, ON,
L3Y 7B3 Canada
Penguin Group (NZ)
67 Apollo Drive, Mairangi Bay, Auckland 1310,
New Zealand
Cover concept by Peter Dyer.

Typeset in Bembo and Helvetica to an original
design by Henry Iles.
Printed in Singapore

© Lance Chilton, Marc Dubin, Nick Edwards,
Mark Ellingham, John Fisher, Geoff Garvey,
Natania Jansz/Rough Guides 2009

704pp includes index
A catalogue record for this book is available from
the British Library
ISBN: 978-1-85828-948-9

3   5   7   9   8   6   4   2

# Help us update

We've gone to a lot of effort to ensure that
the seventh edition of **The Rough Guide
to the Greek Islands** is accurate and up to
date. However, things change – places get
"discovered", opening hours are notoriously
fickle, restaurants and rooms raise prices or lower
standards. If you feel we've got it wrong or left
something out, we'd like to know, and if you can
remember the address, the price, the hours, the
phone number, so much the better.

Please send your comments with the subject
line "**Rough Guide Greek Islands Update**"
to ©mail@roughguides.com. We'll credit all
contributions and send a copy of the next edition
(or any other Rough Guide if you prefer) for the
very best emails.
Have your questions answered and tell others
about your trip at
Ⓦ community.roughguides.com

## Acknowledgements

**Lance Chilton** thanks wife Hilary, Mike and Fotini Akalestos in Parikía, Ioannis Karaoulanis in Ríva, Spyros Karelis in Batsí, Makis Korakis in Kamáres, Ioannis Kazantzakis in Gálissas, Andreas and Brigitte Mallis in Pollónia, Anna and Dimitri Sarris in Parikía, Julia Tzanidou-Zuberer of Porfyra Travel in Kýthira, Anna Vidou in Tínos, and Andy McCosh for yet more island info.

**Marc Dubin** thanks George Dhrosos of Madro Travel on Skópelos for local lore, Panayiotis and Aphrodite Sotiriou on Límnos, Theo and Melínda Kosmetos in Mólyvos, Markos Kostalas and Theo and Güher Spordhilis on Híos, Alexis and Dhionysia Zikas on Kós, David and Lisa on Tílos, Elina Scoutari on Pátmos, Rena Paradhisi on Lipsí, Kim Sjögren and his staff at Triton, Constance Rivemale, Patrick and Anne Camille at Pension Andreas and Spyros and Efi on Rhodes, Gerald Brisch for updates and bibliographic material, John Tomkinson for more reading matter, Denise Harvey in Límni, Roger Jinkinson on Kárpathos, Andonis and Themélina Andonoglou on Kálymnos, the management of the hotels Porphyris (Níssyros), Archipelagos (Foúrni), Australian (Astypálea), Crithoni's Paradise (Léros), Iapetos Village (Sými) and Irini (Tílos) for their support and Dudley der Partogh at Sunvil for travel facilities.

**Nick Edwards** would like to thank his Corfu connections, the super Zoupani, Kostas Vlachopoulos and Periklis Katsaros, for their usual immaculate help and hospitality; also to Maria of the Ionian Paradise on Lefkádha; on Kefalonia, Regina of Fiskárdho, Andronikos of Kiani Akti and Panayiotis of Hara in Argostoli; and finally to the Potamitis family and the ladies of Pension Limni on Zákynthos. Cheers to Vasso and family for the stopover in Agrinio and loving thanks for musical ditties throughout the whole Ionian jaunt to Maria E.

**John Fisher** would like to thank all those who helped in Athens, Crete and the Argo-Saronics, especially Rosy Agianozoglou and Kostas Antoniou on Angistri, Nikos and Christina Kimoulakis and Fotis Mylonas on Poros, Petros Tsamardinos on Spetses, Fotis Voulgarakis on Égina, Vangelis Androulamakis and Alex Stivanakis on Crete and Miranda Hounta and Kate Donnelly in Athens; not forgetting the team at Rough Guides and, as ever, A & the two Js for love, support and disrupting the research.

**Geoff Garvey** would like to thank Nikos Karellis, editor of Stigmes magazine, for help and advice regarding all matters Cretan. A special "efharisto pára polí" also goes to Manolis Sergentakis in Kastélli Kissámou, Irene Michaelaki in Haniá, Yiannis & Katerina Hatzidakis in Sitía, Heracles Papakakis in Spili, Lambros Papoutsakis in Thrónos, Yiorgos Margaritakis in Iráklion, Froso Bora in Réthymnon, and last but by no means least to Stelios Manousakas in Aryiroúpolis (long may his avocados flourish).

**Chris Christoforou** would like to say thank you to Emily Taylor for giving me the great opportunity to live this dream. To all the wonderful angels who helped me along the magical way on all the islands, to my family in Athens who are amazing! I would also like to say a very special thank you and farewell to two dear shiny souls, Hugh and Teo, who passed away at the time of this project, your love, light and joy were and are an inspiration, shine on bright ones! : )

## Readers' letters

Thanks to all the readers who have taken the time to write in with comments and suggestions (and apologies if we've inadvertently omitted or misspelt anyone's name):

Maggie Aldread, David Authers, Roman Balvanovic, Georgios Chaziris, Jake Cole, Vivienne Collis, James Finch, Peter Gaskell, Peter Gibbons, Chrissy & David Grimsey, Chris Hardy, Peter Hodgson, Rod Ingham, Chris Lawrence, Julian & Josette Lord, Alison McCormac, Andy McCosh, Amy Merrill, Ruth Miller & Martin Evans, Mike Keating, Peter Moore, Iain Muir, Darren Nicholls, Janet Nicolas, Senta Osti, Peter G. Overlaet, Steven Peeters, Elias Petroulias, John Purrington, Bernardine Raffety, Yizhar Regev, Ann Sacra, Carola Scupham, Roger & Irene Sharp, Arthur Spencer, Brenda Stanebury, Stein Thunberg, Terry Walsh, Dave and Rachel Ward, Valerie Warren, Steve Williams, Cameron Wyllie, Janice Wynton, Jola Ziaja-Donaldson.

ROUGH GUIDES

SMALL PRINT

# Index

Map entries are in colour.

INDEX

O

INDEX

INDEX

**I**

**INDEX**

**INDEX**

701

# Map symbols

maps are listed in the full index using coloured text

| | | | |
|---|---|---|---|
| – – – – | International boundary | 🕯 | Lighthouse |
| – – – | Chapter boundary | @ | Internet café |
| ▬▬▬ | Motorway | ⓘ | Information office |
| ═══ | Major paved road | ★ | Bus/taxi stop |
| ═══ | Minor paved road | Ⓣ | Tram stop |
| ──── | Unpaved road | ✈ | Airport |
| ▦▦▦ | Steps | Ⓗ | Helipad |
| ▬▬▬ | Pedestrianized street | 🅿 | Parking |
| - - - - | Path | ✡ | Synagogue |
| ──── | River | ⊠—⊠ | Gate |
| — — | Ferry route | ⊞ | Hospital |
| ▬▬▬ | Railway | ⊠ | Post office |
| ●----● | Cable car | ♦ | Point of interest |
| ──── | Wall | ⚶ | Viewpoint |
| ⋀⋀ | Mountain range | ⚠ | Campsite |
| ▲ | Peak | ◉ | Accommodation |
| 𝅘 | Waterfall | ✺ | Shipwreck |
| ◔ | Crater | ⚓ | Boat |
| ⫽⫽ | Steep slope | ⛪ | Mosque |
| 🗘 | Gorge | ⸸ | Monastery or convent |
| ◠ | Cave | ⸷ | Church (regional map) |
| ⚶ | Marshland | ⊞ | Church (town map) |
| 🇾 | Windmill | ⬭ | Stadium |
| 🔋 | Fuel station | ▬▬ | Building |
| ⋀⋁ | Spring/spa | ⊞⊞ | Cemetery |
| ∴ | Archeological site | ░░ | Park/forest |
| ♛ | Castle | ░░ | Beach |
| ♦ | Museum | | |